1001 | CLASSICAL
RECORDINGS
YOU MUST HEAR BEFORE YOU DIE

1001 | CLASSICAL RECORDINGS
YOU MUST HEAR BEFORE YOU DIE

GENERAL EDITOR MATTHEW RYE

PREFACE BY STEVEN ISSERLIS

A Quint**essence** Book

First published in Great Britain in 2007 by Cassell Illustrated
a division of Octopus Publishing Group Limited
2–4 Heron Quays, London E14 4JP
A Hachette Livre UK company

Reprinted in 2008 by Cassell Illustrated

A CIP catalogue record for this book is available from the British Library.

ISBN-13: 978-1-84403-579-3
QSS.K ALB

This book was designed and produced by
Quint**essence**
226 City Road
London EC1V 2TT

Senior Editor	Jodie Gaudet
Copy Editor	Katina Ellery
Editors	Jemima Dunne-Lord, Irene Lyford,
	Fiona Plowman, Frank Ritter
Editorial Assistant	Andrew Smith
Art Director	Akihiro Nakayama
Designer	Jon Wainwright
Picture Researcher	Sunita Sharma-Gibson
Editorial Director	Jane Laing
Publisher	Tristan de Lancey

Manufactured in Singapore by Pica Digital Pte Ltd.
Printed in China by SNP Leefung Printers Ltd.

Contents

Preface
By Steven Isserlis

I wonder how music was invented? Perhaps it happened like this: One day a particularly sensitive caveman, greeting his neighbor with the daily conversational "Ug," was suddenly distracted by the singing of birds over his head. Being unusually in touch with his inner cave-child, he decided that he preferred that sound to his own grunts and snorts, and would like to try it out—in the process creating the first musical sounds ever produced by a human being. His neighbor would probably have decided that he'd gone mad, and may have tried to help him recover his senses by knocking him gently on the head with a nearby rock. But once the music bug had entered the human race, I'm sure it spread fast. People *need* music. It can express our inner feelings even more powerfully than words—and in a universal language.

Today, music is everywhere, cascading around our lives. This has positive aspects, in that it can provide a colorful soundtrack to our day-to-day existence. In other ways, however, it is bad: its omnipresence dulls us. Great music should stir up emotions, thoughts, yearnings. If it is constantly in the background, the message gets lost, fading into a blur of aural wallpaper. Recordings, of course, are chiefly to blame for this loss of sensitivity. And yet—looking at the list chosen for this book, who could deny that they have brought more blessings than curses? It is all too easy to take for granted the ability to listen to all sorts of music, from Hildegard of Bingen to György Kurtág, at the flick of a switch; but it is in fact a miracle, and one for which we should be forever grateful. It is also a comparatively effortless way to get to know pieces of music. In the nineteenth century, almost the only way to become familiar with symphonies was to study them in piano-duet arrangements. Nowadays, when mastery of the piano is not exactly a social necessity, all we have to do is to press the *Play* button. But in fact, "effortless" is—or should be—the wrong word to use; a good listener will be almost as involved in the music as the performer. And an added advantage to recordings is that one can dance, sing, and conduct along with them—audience contributions that tend to be somewhat frowned upon in the concert hall (although they do happen!).

The sheer variety of music available to us now—even just within the "classical" genre—is bewildering. Where to start? Well, that's where this book might come in handy. Spanning some 900 years, the selection here has something—indeed many things—for everyone. If your taste is for austere choral music, dancing baroque concertos, windswept Romanticism, vibrant contemporary music—look no further. Or rather, start here, and then look *much* further—1,001 pieces may sound like a lot for a collection, but it is really just a beginning.

I'm glad that there are many surprises: Glière's Third Symphony, for instance, or Florent Schmitt's *Salomé*. I certainly don't know either of those—and I imagine that not many do, outside a small circle of enthusiasts. But there are also recommended recordings of practically the entire core repertoire of both the concert hall and the opera house. This book is therefore equally appropriate for those who are just entering the magical world of classical music, as for those who are already involved, but want to test new waters. And for the few who already know all the works and performances listed here, it will no doubt provide material for new and enjoyable diatribes. "Why that piece? And why in that performance?" Music constantly provokes arguments; friendships flourish and shrivel around it. Well, that's not surprising—after all, it is the most important thing in life . . .

Steven
Isserlis

London, 2007

Introduction
By Matthew Rye, General Editor

Music is everywhere in today's world and it sometimes seems as if the dedicated concert hall is almost the last place to find it. We can hear it when we don't want to, blaring out of bar doorways or leaking from iPod earphones; and when we do, from the radio in the kitchen, the living room CD player, or those same earphones on our own head. It all began with the launch of Edison's first commercially viable phonograph in 1888. Then came the "gramophone" and the transition from wax cylinders to flat discs; the arrival in the 1920s of electrical recording; the 78; the 33rpm "long-playing record" or LP; the cassette; the compact disc (CD) and the transition to digital recording in the early 1980s; the super audio compact disc (SACD); and most recently the MP3 file and its other online cousins. Music has in many ways been thoroughly democratized; the decision of when to hear a particular piece has been put in the listener's hands.

Although music of every kind has embraced the recorded media available and in more recent decades these media actually made certain types of music possible, classical music has benefited in a particular way. Most popular music is the preserve of performers as opposed to composers, and songs tend on the whole only to be recorded once, or at the most a handful of times in cover versions. Classical music, calling upon a vast repertoire stretching back to medieval times, can be and is performed by all and sundry. Given the talent (and money), anyone is theoretically free to give the world his or her own interpretation of a Beethoven piano sonata, a Brahms symphony, or even a Wagner music drama. It is this idea of a multiplicity of interpretations that gives the past century of classical recording its richness and diversity.

Is it possible to state categorically that one recorded performance is better than all the others? Of course not. For one thing, reception to performance is a personal thing—you only have to read press reviews of a concert or recording to realize that even those who are supposed to know everything about music might not always agree with each other. Opinions will always differ—that is in the nature of art. But in practical terms, what does the consumer do when faced with so many rival recordings of the same pieces all vying for shelf space, or, with the rise of online music sales, bandwidth? This book cuts to the chase and our distinguished expert writers—among them many of the leading music critics and academics from Britain, continental Europe, the United States, and Australia—recommend what they personally regard as the most satisfying interpretation in a given work's recorded history. And to take your listening even further, where space allows, they also list some alternatives—of the same piece or of related music not covered elsewhere; and many entries are enlivened by often trenchant quotations about the music, composer, or performers.

But more than simply recommending recordings, the writers use their expert knowledge to set each piece of music itself in context, describing its historical background and defining what makes it what it is. The book is so arranged that it also sets up a pantheon of the "1,001 pieces of classical music you must hear before you die." Indeed, a list of these works was the starting point and, like the choice of recordings, has been subject to its own criteria. The parameters have been fairly strictly set within the bounds of the Western classical tradition, both in Europe and as it has spread around the world, from Japan to Argentina, Australia to the United States. So there's little that would fall more naturally into jazz, world, or light music categories unless—like the limited number of operettas and musicals included—they have demonstrated a foothold in the "serious" concert hall or opera house.

What makes this book unique is in placing all 1,001 pieces of music in a chronology from the original *Carmina Burana*—a collection of songs and dances assembled by Bavarian monks in the 1100s—to the *Book of Hours*, coincidentally a work inspired by medieval illuminated manuscripts and composed in 2004 by Julian Anderson. If the exact sequence within a given year is known—as in the well-documented work lists of Mozart and Schubert—it has been adhered to. And where a work had a complicated compositional history full or revisions and rewrites—Bruckner is a prime example—the pragmatic route has been taken. Composers' collected works in a given genre, such as Mozart's piano sonatas, appear under the earliest date, while a single work written over several years—Wagner's *Ring* cycle is a famous example—is listed under the date of its completion.

This timeline approach has thrown up some intriguing examples of contemporaneity: We realize that Beethoven wrote the "Ode to Joy" of his "Choral" Symphony in the same year that Schubert contemplated mortality in his *Death and the Maiden Quartet*; that Wagner's *Ring* reached its concluding immolation in the same year that works as varied as Bizet's *Carmen* and Strauss's *Die Fledermaus* were written; and that, in 1928, the proto-Minimalism of Ravel's *Boléro* coincided with the complexity of Schoenberg's Variations for Orchestra and the tunefulness of Kurt Weill's *Threepenny Opera*.

In compiling the list, I have tried to set each piece against the admittedly subjective tests of "greatness" whether in the context of classical music as a whole, or within the output of a given composer. You may therefore find that works deemed merely "popular" are missing—see it as a distinction comparable to bestselling novels not necessarily being regarded as great "art." Similarly, shorter works have had to justify themselves more stringently: they've either been grouped together by genre—such as Chopin's *Nocturnes* or Poulenc's mélodies—or are there, as in the case of Rachmaninov's "Vocalise" or Johann Strauss's *Blue Danube* waltz, as the figurehead for a larger area of a composer's writing.

Purely on the grounds of transcendent greatness, the more than 1,001 pieces of Bach could conceivably have filled the book on their own; and mature Mozart could easily have taken up nearly half the pages. But in attempting to represent both the abundant genius and amazing range of classical music in a millennium of composition, I have made a point of including, alongside the established "greats," some lesser-known music that I feel is still worthy of the "must hear" imperative—and the burgeoning recording of rarities in recent decades from the smaller labels has thrown up some unmissable treats. Therefore the list is a personal one, although informed by opinion from different sources.

※

We live in turbulent times as far as the classical recording industry is concerned. In a technologically fast-changing world, some have already predicted the demise of the CD, with the emphasis turning to music on demand via the Internet. However, the classical music world is one where the CD might just survive longer than most. Sound quality is crucial to many music lovers and digital downloads, with their file compression and emphasis on relatively low-fidelity playback equipment, arguably can't yet match the quality of the best hi-fi setups playing a CD or SACD. The physical CD—and its latter-day offspring the surround-sound SACD—will always remain more collectible than an ephemeral computer file.

Many of the multinational companies that have been the industry's mainstay since the early days have to varying degrees abandoned wholesale recording of serious music, preferring the more lucrative world of classical crossover. Against the odds, however, many smaller independent companies appear to be thriving. This shift in emphasis from the big companies to the small means that the availability of many classic recordings from the vaults of the multinationals is capricious to say the least. While some, like Warner, have tried to mitigate things by making their whole back catalogs accessible as downloads, others seem to reissue and delete valuable recordings on a whim.

Given this flexible environment, we have endeavored to list only recordings that are currently available, even if that has meant choosing things that have been officially deleted by the companies, but that are still demonstrably for sale via major retailers at the time of writing. (Note that many Naxos Historical recordings are not legally for sale in the United States for copyright reasons.) We list the recording date for each disc, which should be of some assistance if the listed catalog number becomes completely unavailable, but the recording itself is later reissued. One useful source for deleted recordings is www.arkivmusik.com, which is offering digital downloads of thousands of otherwise unavailable discs in partnership with EMI, Universal (Decca, DG, Philips), and Sony BMG.

Finally, while this book is unashamedly devoted to recordings of classical music, it should never be forgotten that it's a music that was always intended to be heard in the flesh—in the concert hall, in the opera house, in the recital room, in the church. A CD, however well recorded and played, can never be a true substitute for the live experience, that unique sense of a relationship between the performer and audience. If one humbly hopes that this volume extolling the 1,001 greatest works of musical art does its bit to boost sales of CDs, there's also in it an aspiration that it will inspire in its reader the need to hear the music at firsthand.

{

This book would not be what it is without the dedicated work of the hand-picked contributors, and I have been humbled by the sheer amount of wisdom, authority, and enthusiasm they have brought to their writing in the face of a very specific brief and tight timescale, and also grateful for their generous flow of ideas and suggestions. I must give a special thank you to Katina Ellery and Sunita Sharma-Gibson, who put energy into copyediting and picture research respectively that went well beyond the call of duty; and finally to Jodie Gaudet and her editorial team at Quintessence for keeping the whole thing on the road.

Title Index

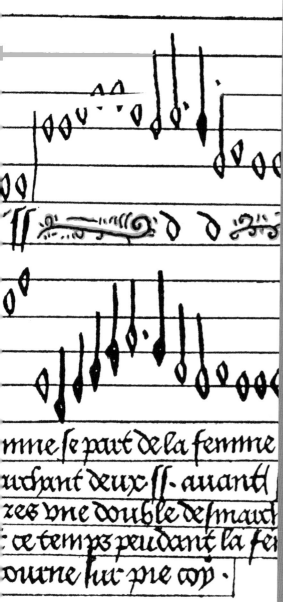

Music probably goes back to our earliest ancestors, but our practical knowledge begins about a thousand years ago when it began to be written down. Development was slow at first: single-line plainchant was elaborated into multi-voiced polyphony, at its peak during the Renaissance of the fifteenth and sixteenth centuries, when composers such as Josquin, Palestrina, and Victoria were at their height. The Baroque—a term borrowed from art history—emerged in the seventeenth century with Monteverdi, under whom the genre of opera became established, and the orchestra became the main instrumental medium.

Notation from the fifteenth-century illuminated manuscript *Danse de Cleves (Burgundian Basse Dance)*.

PRE-1700

Anonymous composers | Carmina burana (12ᵀᴴ CENTURY)

Genre | Vocal
Director | René Clemencic
Performers | Clemencic Consort
Year recorded | 1975
Label | Harmonia Mundi HMA 190336.38 (3 CDs)

CARMINA BURANA
CLEMENCIC CONSORT · INSTRUMENTS ANCIENS
RENÉ CLEMENCIC

harmonia mundi
FRANCE
190336.38

Although nowadays the title *Carmina burana* (Songs of Beuren) is most usually taken as that of Carl Orff's scenic oratorio (1936), in fact the title was given by Johann Andreas Schmeller to the original twelfth-century collection of Latin and early German songs when he completed his edition of this source in 1847. Orff, for his oratorio, made use of the lyrics from this very collection.

Discovered at a Benedictine monastery in southern Germany, the collection contains not only secular poems and songs but also festive plays in Latin. Its thousand or so lyrics encompass morality, satire, sex, and drinking; they reflect the flesh-and-blood life of the authors, who were perhaps Goliards (wandering clerics and scholars).

Some of the items have an early form of notation without staves called "neumes"—this was quite an archaic style of writing music even for the time the collection was being copied. CDs currently available are indebted largely to modern scholars' attempts to decode the notation with the help of roughly contemporary copies of some of the works found in clearer notation in sources from Limoges and Notre Dame.

René Clemencic's recording of this collection stands out not least because of his scholarly rigor—in fact, he was responsible for the first comprehensive musical edition of the collection published in 1979. The diversity in style that his performances employ (from the earthly power of "Bache, bene venies," the haunting chanting of "Homo, quo vigeas vide," and the gentle and strangely nostalgic lyricism of "Clauso chronos") not only matches the range of the subjects but seems to restore something of the authentic sonic landscape of these evocative songs from the misty past. **NM**

> *"In view of the lewd . . . nature of . . . the collection, it is miraculous that the manuscript survived at all."*
>
> Philip Pickett

Other Recommended Recordings

New London Consort • Philip Pickett
L'Oiseau-Lyre 443 143-2 (4 CDs)
Carmina burana "refined" rather than "authentic"

Ensemble Organum • Marcel Pérès
Harmonia Mundi HMA 1901323.24 (2 CDs)
Features the Passion Play from the Carmina burana collection decked out with the instrumental and vocal flamboyance of Pérès's exotic approach

Unicorn Ensemble
Naxos 8.554837
Another earthy rendition of Carmina burana. A bargain

The first page of the *Carmina burana* manuscript, unearthed in 1803. ➲

Regno.

regnabo

regnaui

ſum ſine regno

FS. AIT. Ætaſ ambulant paſſu fere pari. pro
diguſ non reddit uitium auari. uirtaſ temparancie
quadam ſingulari debet medium ad utrumqʒ uitiū
caute contemplari. Si legiſſe memoraſ ethicam ca
toniſ. in qua ſcriptum legitur: ambula cum boniſ.
cū ad dandi gloriam animum diſponiſ. inter cete
ra hec primum conſidera. quiſ ſit digniuſ doniſ. Dare
O fortuna uelud luna ſtatu uariabiliſ ſemp creſciſ aut decreſciſ uita de
teſtabiliſ nunc obdurat ꞇ tunc curat ludo mentiſ aciem et eſtatem poteſtate
diſſoluit ut glaciem. Soeſ inmaniſ ꞇ inaniſ rota tu uolubiliſ ⁊ tu maliſ
uana ſaluſ ſemp diſſolubiliſ obumbratam ꞇ uelatā in quoqʒ niteriſ nūc pium̄
roſū nudum feriſ turceleriſ. Soeſ ſalutiſ ꞇ uirtutiſ m nūc guaria ē affect ⁊
defectuſ ſemp iangaria hac i hora ſine mora cordiſ pulſū tangitur qᷝ ꝑ ſorte ſternit forte

Hildegard of Bingen | Antiphons (12ᵗʰ CENTURY)

Genre | Choral
Director | Benjamin Bagby
Performers | Sequentia
Year recorded | 1993
Label | Deutsche Harmonia Mundi 05472 77320 2

Born in 1098, Hildegard entered a combined Benedictine monastery and nunnery near Worms in the Rhineland at the age of fourteen and became abbess there in 1136. Seeking the freedom to reform practices within her order, she later moved, with a group of followers, to a new sanctuary at Rupertsberg, near Bingen. The new institution gradually gained recognition and Hildegard was officially aknowledged as the abbess in 1163.

Hildegard was particularly famous for the visions that she had experienced from her early years (although modern scholarship may attribute such a claim to her epileptic nature), and her output, both musical and literary, is said to have resulted from what she saw in her visions. Hildegard's musical compositions include seventy-seven vocal works (of which forty-three are antiphons); these are often collectively known as *Symphonia armonie celestium revelationum.* (An antiphon is a chant "sung against" a psalm in the Divine Office, often in the manner of a refrain between the verses of psalm.) Although Hildegard must have composed her antiphons with particular church feasts in mind, it is almost impossible now to allocate each piece to an exact occasion.

Among the several available recordings, Sequentia's is highly recommendable. The group, which specializes in medieval music, has released several CDs of Hildegard's legacy (four in addition to the one listed here). They interweave the beauty of refined yet natural voices with period instruments. This recording includes eight of Hildegard's antiphons, among which "O virga mediatrix" is supported by a harp while "Cum processit factura" is accompanied by two fiddles. The result is a superbly mystic atmosphere. **NM**

> "*I, a mere female and a fragile vessel, speak these things not from me but from the serene light.*"
>
> Hildegard of Bingen

Other Recommended Recordings

Anonymous 4
Harmonia Mundi HMU 907327
Includes three antiphons, performed in a refined way

Oxford Camerata • Jeremy Summerly
Naxos 8.550998
Contains three antiphons by Hildegard, two sung entirely by male voices

Schola der Benediktinerinnenabtei
Johannes Berchmans Göschl • Christiane Rath
Ars Musici 1202-2
Mediocre performances, but the performers are nuns at the present Benedictine Abbey of St. Hildegard

Guillaume de Machaut | Ballades (MID-14TH CENTURY)

Genre | Vocal
Director | David Munrow
Performers | Early Music Consort of London
Year recorded | 1973
Label | Virgin 5 61284 2 (2 CDs)

Guillaume de Machaut (c.1300–77) stands between two traditions: He was the last major figure to write single-line free melodies in the tradition of *trouvères* (troubadours), and one of the first to compose in the new polyphonic and rhythmic style of the so-called *Ars nova*.

In his youth, Machaut was in the service of Jean, King of Bohemia and Duke of Luxembourg, and followed the king's political adventures in various parts of Europe. Just before the king was killed at the Battle of Crécy in 1346, the composer became a canon at the Cathedral of Reims, where he spent the rest of his days.

Machaut's compositions clearly reflect the sacred and secular aspects of his life—he wrote a number of Latin works, together with pieces in the French language. Of his secular songs, the ballade was certainly his favorite type and he left forty-two of them. The poetic form of the ballade usually comprised three stanzas of eight lines, with the last two lines repeated in each verse as a refrain. Machaut set each stanza in the musical form: A (lines 1–3); A (lines 4–6); B (lines 7–8). With one exception, Machaut's ballades are all set polyphonically, demonstrating the composer's technical mastery.

David Munrow's recording includes seven ballades by Machaut. Munrow allocates the main voices to singers while the lower parts are taken by period instruments. The ballade "Dame se vous m'estés lointeinne" is performed by a bagpipe, since Machaut himself tells us that this instrument will bring out its "true nature." This recording is a lively, highly communicative reconstruction from which the listener can appreciate the interaction between one voice and another in the clearest way. This makes Munrow's contribution stand out even decades after his death. **NM**

> "*O flower of melodic masters . . . god of harmony, now that you have gone, who will replace you?*"

Franciscus Andrieu

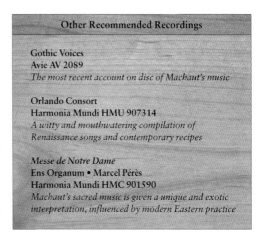

Other Recommended Recordings

Gothic Voices
Avie AV 2089
The most recent account on disc of Machaut's music

Orlando Consort
Harmonia Mundi HMU 907314
A witty and mouthwatering compilation of Renaissance songs and contemporary recipes

Messe de Notre Dame
Ens Organum • Marcel Pérès
Harmonia Mundi HMC 901590
Machaut's sacred music is given a unique and exotic interpretation, influenced by modern Eastern practice

Francesco Landini | Ballatas and Songs (LATE 14TH CENTURY)

Genre | Vocal
Performers | Anonymous 4: Susan Hellauer, Jacqueline Horner, Marsha Genensky, Johanna Maria Rose
Year recorded | 2000
Label | Harmonia mundi HMU 907269

Francesco Landini was born the son of a painter of the Florentine Giotto school, but his plan to follow in his father's footsteps was thwarted when he lost his eyesight as a result of contracting smallpox. However, he managed to establish himself as a skilled keyboard player, singer, and poet. His erudition encompassed philosophical, ethical, and astrological matters.

The detail of Landini's early life is unknown and certain episodes are dubious, such as a story that he was awarded the "Corona Laurea" by the King of Cyprus. However, there is more certainty about Landini's later life. In 1361, he became an organist at the monastery of Santa Trinità in Florence, and in 1365 was appointed head of the church of San Lorenzo, where he remained until his death in 1397.

Nowadays Landini tends to be remembered for a particular kind of musical cadence named after him—the Landini cadence—in which the top part goes down from the seventh degree to the sixth of the scale before moving to the tonic. Although this was not unique to Landini, he made it a hallmark of the fourteenth-century style.

Landini left 154 songs, including 140 ballatas and twelve madrigals. It was his ballatas that were particularly innovative. In the fourteenth century, the ballata had five sections: a refrain, two verses, a false refrain (which had the same poetic form and music as the refrain but different words), and a repeat of the original refrain.

This recording by Anonymous 4 conjures up the suave melodiousness of Landini's ballatas. Each item is beautifully projected by the singers' ethereal, floating voices, and even Landini's quirky rhythms soften to the bell-like chiming of their sound. Such a performance evokes a dream of the distant past. **NM**

> *"I regret seeing intelligent people forsaking my sweet and perfect sounds for the clamor of street songs."*
>
> Francesco Landini

Other Recommended Recordings

Ensemble Camerata Nova, Chominciamento di Gioia
Luigi Taglioni
Tactus 321201
Vivacious recording employing the accompaniment of various combinations of instruments

Alla Francesca
Opus 111 609206
Powerful and immediate performances

Gothic Voices, Andrew Lawrence-King
Christopher Page
Hyperion CDA 66286
A well-chosen compilation of Italian music

The only known portrait of Francesco Landini. ➔

Guillaume Dufay
Motets
(1420–c.1447)

Genre | Choral
Director | Paul Van Nevel
Performers | Huelgas Ensemble
Year recorded | 1999
Label | Harmonia Mundi HMC 901700

Antoine Busnoys
Motets
(LATE 15TH CENTURY)

Genre | Choral
Director | Andrew Kirkman
Performers | Binchois Consort
Year recorded | 2001
Label | Hyperion CDA 67319

Guillaume Dufay (1397–1474) started his career as a chorister at Cambrai Cathedral in 1409 and by 1420 was serving the Malatestas in Rimini, Italy. Then, it seems, he returned temporarily to France since he bids farewell to that country in his song "Adieu ces bon vins de Lannoys," which is dated 1426. He worked in Bologna, but political turmoil in 1428 made the composer flee to Rome where he stayed until 1433. During the 1430s, he was in the service of two patrons: Pope Eugenius IV and Duke Amadeus of Savoy. However, when Duke Amadeus became Pope Felix V, Dufay became aware of the potential jeopardy of his benefices from Burgundian towns and he left Savoy. By 1439 he had settled again in Cambrai, but after Felix V resigned and the Burgundian court reopened contact with the Savoy court, Dufay again found himself at the latter, where he stayed until 1458. He then returned to Cambrai, where he remained for the rest of his life.

Dufay left twenty-four motets, written between 1420 and (probably) 1447. Thirteen are "isorhythmic"—that is, in a rhythmic pattern not quite long enough for the melody to be repeated across two or three repetitions of that melody. Paul Van Nevel's recording gives us the complete collection of all thirteen. His interpretation was supported by rigorous musicological work—he took the trouble to prepare his own edition based upon all existing sources. His use of period instruments doubling the vocal parts is noteworthy, evoking the festive and pompous occasions for which the works would originally have been created. **NM**

Antoine Busnoys started his career in the French royal court in the Loire valley before he moved to Tours Cathedral. By 1465 he had found a position in the collegiate church of St. Martin, where he met Ockeghem. The two composers remained on friendly terms throughout their lives. Busnoys's next move was to the position of choirmaster at St. Hilaire le Grand, Poitiers. By 1467, the composer's name was listed as a *chantre* in the service of the future Charles the Bold of Burgundy. After Charles's death in 1477, Busnoys served his daughter Mary.

Busnoys sometimes set his own verses to music. In such cases, he often interwove a secret message in the text or made a little joke. For example, the text of "Anthoni usque limina," one of his few surviving motets, includes a pun on his name: "*Anthoni us*que limina . . . fiat in omni*bus noys*."

So far, there is no recording that features Busnoys's motets exclusively. This recording by the Binchois Consort includes two Marian motets by Busnoys: "Anima mea liquefacta est" and "Gaude celestis domina." The former is a three-voice work based upon a text taken from the Song of Solomon. Here the tenor sings the chant "Stirps Jesse" as cantus firmus, though the top part also paraphrases the chant prior as a kind of anticipation of the tenor part. The Binchois Consort sings the long melismas (vocal runs) found in this music with great poise and an unerring sense of direction. As its text would suggest, "Gaude celestis" is a joyful piece characterized by syncopated rhythms. It is sung with lightness and brilliance. **NM**

Jean de Ockeghem
Alma redemptoris mater
(LATE 15TH CENTURY)

Genre | Choral
Director | Edward Wickham
Performers | The Clerks' Group
Year recorded | 1994
Label | Gaudeamus GAU 139

It has recently been discovered that Ockeghem was born, perhaps around 1410, in Saint Ghislain, near Mons, in present-day Belgium—though his surname suggests a connection with Okegem, a town in East Flanders. In 1443 he was a singer at the church of Notre Dame, in Antwerp; by 1446 he had entered the service of the Duke of Bourbon in Moulins. Around 1452, he started working for the chapel of the French court where he remained until his death in 1497, serving three successive kings (Charles VII, Louis XI, and Charles VIII). Highly valued by the French monarchs, Ockeghem was given the lucrative and prestigious position of treasurer of the church of St. Martin of Tours.

Today only five sacred motets by Ockeghem survive, but this is the genre that the composer endeavored to redefine throughout his life, and *Alma redemptoris mater* is an interesting example. A four-voice setting of the Marian text, it has two clear-cut sections. Throughout the work, the alto part in long notes paraphrases the plainchant, while the soprano and bass parts quote the chant from time to time. The result is a spectacular display of allusion and transformation, as the liturgical melody rises above then sinks below the waves of vocal polyphony by turn.

The Clerks' Group has released several recordings of Ockeghem's music and established itself as a recognized specialist in this repertoire. With adroit control, the singers beautifully reveal the calm center at the heart of *Alma redemptoris mater*. The performance certainly casts new light on this relatively unknown masterpiece. **NM**

John Browne
Stabat mater
(COPIED *c.*1490–1502)

Genre | Choral
Director | Peter Phillips
Performers | Tallis Scholars
Year recorded | 2005
Label | Gimell 036

John Browne's *Stabat mater* is a jewel of polyphonic music of Tudor England. However, we know very little about the composer: He seems to have been associated with Oxford University, and a surviving document lists a John Brown as one of the chaplains in the service of John de Vere, Earl of Oxford. What is clear is that Browne's talent was recognized by his contemporaries, including members of the royal family—his *Stabat juxta Christi crucem* was used to celebrate the coming of age of Prince Arthur, who was about to start his independent life as the Prince of Wales.

Only thirteen works by Browne survive in their complete form, and ten of them (including *Stabat mater*) are found in the *Eton Choir Book*, the most important manuscript source of Tudor church music. *Stabat mater* is a setting of a Latin sequence that describes the agony of Mary as she stood by the cross where Jesus hung. In this setting, Browne portrays Mary's state in a generally restrained and introspective manner. However, phrases often conclude with surprising harmonic twists, perhaps reflecting the light and dark of that changing, redemptive moment. The whole scheme of the music succeeds in painting moments of the drama, which culminate in the scene of the crowd crying out "*crucifige*" (crucify him).

All these aspects of the *Stabat mater* are vividly presented in this recording. The approach of the Tallis Scholars is colorful without being too sentimental, and the nicely judged speed of the performance allows us not only to glimpse the drama but to reflect upon it. **NM**

Josquin des Prez | Missa Pange lingua (c.1514)

Genre | Choral
Director | Peter Phillips
Performer | Tallis Scholars
Year recorded | 1986
Label | Gimell CDGIM 009

Recent scholarship has challenged our previous understanding of the life and work of Josquin des Prez. We now know that there were several Josquins and that the one who worked in Milan between 1459 and 1472—who is sometimes confused with the great composer—was Josquin de Kessalia, another composer some ten years older than the composer of the *Missa Pange lingua*.

Josquin des Prez was born sometime between 1450 and 1455 and moved at an early age to Condé-sur-L'Escaut in northern France. In 1477, he was in the service of René of Anjou in Aix-en-Provence—the starting point of the composer's career. After working for the Milanese court in the 1480s and for the papal choir between 1489 and c.1495, Josquin was appointed as maestro di cappella by the Duke of Ferrara in 1503. He did not remain in the position long, returning the following year to Condé to become the provost of the church of Notre Dame.

Josquin's *Missa Pange lingua* seems to have been written around 1514. It is a Mass whose melodic material consists of variations on the Corpus Christi hymn "Pange lingua." This kind of variation technique is known as "paraphrase" and Josquin was a master of this art. The work was not included in the third collection of the composer's Masses published by the famous Venetian printer, Petrucci, in 1514. Even so it was popular enough to be contained in various contemporary manuscripts.

The Tallis Scholars's performance reveals the work's imitative texture with crystal clarity—elements of the hymn tune emerge and fade into the background in a kaleidoscopic manner. The listener's understanding is aided by their inclusion in the recording of the original hymn sung prior to the Mass. **NM**

"Josquin is the master of the notes . . . other composers must follow what the notes dictate."

Martin Luther

Other Recommended Recordings

Orlando Consort
Archiv 463 473-2
A subtle performance of Josquin's motets, the genre that best shows his development and innovations

A Sei Voci
Naïve, E 8809
Josquin's famous Missa L'homme armé is sung with solemnity

Hilliard Ensemble • Paul Hiller
Virgin 5623462
A compilation of Josquin's vocal music, including his masterpieces "Mille regretz" and "Elgrillo"

A possible portrait of Josquin, attributed to Leonardo da Vinci (1490). ➔

John Taverner | The Western Wynde Mass (1530s)

Genre | Choral
Director | Peter Phillips
Performers | Tallis Scholars
Year recorded | 2001
Label | Gimell CDGIM 027

Nicolas Gombert Motets (1530–1550s)

Genre | Choral
Director | Jonathan Brown
Performers | Henry's Eight
Recorded | 1996
Label | Hyperion CDH 55247

We do not know much about the life of John Taverner before he was documented as a member of the choir of the collegiate church at Tattershall, Lincolnshire, in 1524. In 1526, Taverner moved to Oxford to take up the post of principal instructor for the choir of Cardinal's College (now Christ Church). Following Cardinal Wolsey's political downfall, Taverner left Oxford and, by 1530, seems to have settled down in his native Lincolnshire. He worked for a time as a lay clerk at St. Botolph's, Boston, but retired when the church's finances were no longer able to pay him as a musician. He died as an alderman of the town.

The greater part of Taverner's sacred music was composed during his time at Tattershall and Oxford, the best known being the *Western Wynde Mass*, which employs a cantus firmus based upon the popular tune "Western wind, when will thou blow?" It is basically a series of contrapuntal elaborations around the melody, which is stated thirty-six times throughout the Mass. It is a tribute to Taverner's great skill and musical instincts that we never sense any monotony in these repetitions. Rather, the technique employed clearly impressed his contemporaries and two later composers, Christopher Tye and John Sheppard, also wrote Masses built upon this tune—though to less spectacular effect.

This recording neatly enables us to compare all three versions of the Mass, and to appreciate the structural clarity and tunefulness of Taverner's work, to which the later two composers paid homage in their compositions. The balanced voices of the Tallis Scholars successfully intensify the serenity of the piece. **NM**

Only in the last two decades has Gombert received anything like the attention he deserves. It is not as if he led an anonymous life: We know enough to surmise that he was a "troublesome priest"—or at least a cleric whose misdemeanors involving a choirboy had him banished to the high seas in the late 1530s. Plenty of music survives, including ten Mass settings and 160 motets.

Looking at the texture of the music itself may reveal the reason: It is ferociously hard to follow closely as either a singer or a listener. Waves of close counterpoint roll over each other like Pacific breakers, monumental, unstoppable. There is no room to catch your breath—it is almost reminiscent of the string writing of Xenakis, who was fed up with players leaving "gaps" between notes.

Specific word painting is spurned in favor of more long-term ambitions to capture the mood of what are often very dark texts—prophecies of doom outweigh songs of celebration in Gombert's output (the exception being Marian hymns such as the Magnificat and Salve Regina). Even his setting of the joyful Haec Dies ends in the minor, as different in temper as is imaginable from Byrd's anthem to the same text. The false relations that in English music pass at cadence points for expressive effect, multiply in Gombert into piles of suspended dissonance: In parts of the eight-voice Credo there is hardly a beat that is without some chromatic interposition to throw the tonal center of the work and the listener off balance. Thus clarity must be the performers' aim, far more easily in reach when sung with one voice per part, at least when the voices are of such reliable quality as Henry's Eight. **PQ**

Cristóbal de Morales
Motets (1545–47)

Genre | Choral
Director | Michael Noone
Performers | Ensemble Plus Ultra
Year recorded | 2004
Label | Glossa GCD 922001

Cristóbal de Morales was born in Seville around 1500 and, by the age of twenty-six, had been ordained priest and made maestro di cappella at Avila Cathedral. By about 1534, after several other appointments, he reached Rome and became a singer in the Papal choir. His music, almost exclusively sacred, became very well known, not least because he published 500 copies of a major collection that was performed throughout Europe and Latin America.

Music historians had assumed that Morales's inventive powers were waning when he returned to Spain and to Toledo Cathedral in 1545. But when Michael Noone was invited to study a damaged manuscript, made available for the first time in 2002, he discovered twenty pieces by Morales, of which the fourteen on this disc were then completely unknown. Noone's booklet notes include a fascinating account of transcribing the music from pages stuck together at the edges. Shining a flashlight through the parchment, he was able to see mirror images of notes and text, which he could then copy out.

The performance was recorded in the church of St. Jude-on-the-Hill in London, a gloriously spacious acoustic; it does not, though, veil the transparency of the thirteen unaccompanied voices and their shimmering sonority arising from pinpoint intonation. They are distinctive and rich, but with barely a trace of vibrato to cloud the texture. Most of the music is in four or five parts, but the final "Ave maris stella" grows magnificently in scale, in three parts, then four, and finally the spine-chilling density of six voices for the final verse. Hitherto unknown music from a master of the Spanish Renaissance—a disc to treasure. **GP**

Antonio de Cabezón
Diferencias (c.1560s)

Genre | Chamber
Conductor | Thomas Wimmer
Performers | Accentus Ensemble
Year recorded | 2001
Label | Naxos 8.554836

Keyboard music of sixteenth-century Spain reached its zenith with Antonio de Cabezón who, despite his blindness, became *músico de la cámara* to the Spanish court in 1538. He accompanied the future Philip II to London between 1554 and 1555 when the prince came to marry Mary Tudor.

Cabezón's music is largely preserved in two collections published in 1557 and 1578 respectively. The first, titled *Libro de cifra nueva*, includes thirty-seven compositions by Cabezón. The second, *Obras de música para tecla, arpa y vihuela*, published posthumously by his son Hernando, is devoted solely to Cabezón's work.

Diferencias are variations based upon themes derived from popular songs or dances. Usually, a set of *diferencias* is continuous, flowing without a break from one variation to another. In these examples, Cabezón deals with the original melody in two ways: either by placing it in the top part and adding elaborate ornamentations, or by giving it to one of the lower parts and treating it as a cantus firmus.

This recording presents a variety of Cabezón's music including four sets of his *diferencias*. The music is played by a mixed ensemble using different combinations of instruments from one piece to another, or even within one piece. This may not be as eccentric as it first seems. Cabezón's musical notation did not specify any particular instrument and, considering the variety of instruments available at the Spanish court, it could likely have been performed by a consort. This at least gives vivacity and color to the *diferencias*. The rapid stream of decorative notes is played with accuracy and suavity. **NM**

Thomas Tallis | Lamentations of Jeremiah (1565)

Genre | Choral
Performers | Hilliard Ensemble: David James, John Potter, Rogers Covey-Crump, Paul Hillier, Michael George
Year recorded | 1986
Label | ECM 833 308-2

Thomas Tallis
The Lamentations Of Jeremiah

The Hilliard Ensemble

ECM NEW SERIES

Early masterpieces by Tallis, such as the antiphon and Mass based on *Salve intemerata virgo*, show allegiance to the strong, smooth lines of the Italian school. For the next century, English music would lead the world in perfecting forms that had already bloomed elsewhere. Only after 1945 would England again produce composers of comparable stature and originality. Nothing in Victoria or Lobo matches the opening phrases of "In ieiunio et fletu" for harmonic surprise or the clear and remorseless expansion of their implications over a large-scale motet scheme, full of antiphonal, call-and-answer effects.

In a post-Reformation culture of accusation and expediency, Tallis retained his devotion to Roman Catholicism while writing music for and finding favor with four successive monarchs of very different religious persuasions. The delicacy of his political balance is also reflected in his music, from the open progressions of "If ye Love me" to the contrapuntal intricacies of "Loquebantur variis linguis."

Still, it is the Latin, Catholic work that lay closest to Tallis's art and heart—nowhere more explicit than in the *Lamentations of Jeremiah*. In a two-part scheme of unusual breadth, he anticipates the harmonic novelties of "In ieiunio," reserving his famous command of chromaticism for the long melismas over the Hebrew letters that announce each section.

There is no reason for choirs not to sing them, but the *Lamentations* speak of an age of chamber-scale confession and devotion, as do Byrd's Masses, and one voice per part is the disposition that does most justice to their horizontal and vertical glories: The members of the Hilliard Ensemble scale Tallis's architecture with uncanny precision. **PQ**

> *"The Hilliard Ensemble have Thomas Tallis's Lamentations in their blood. . . ."*
>
> David Fallows, *Gramophone*

Other Recommended Recordings

Salve intemerata, Mass, and Motet
Chapelle du Roi • Alistair Dixon
Signum SIGCD 001
Early Tallis, of medieval spareness and breadth

Gaude gloriosa, Loquebantur variis linguis, etc.
Cardinall's Musick • Andrew Carwood
Hyperion CDA 67548
The multi-part motets in electrifying performances

Spem in alium, Lamentations, Gaude gloriosa, etc.
Tallis Scholars • Peter Phillips
Gimell CDGIM 203
A reliable and wide-ranging collection

The Hilliard Ensemble specializes in both early and modern repertoire. ➔

Orlande de Lassus
Motets
(published 1555–1604*)*

Genre | Choral
Director | Andrew Carwood
Performers | The Cardinall's Musick
Year recorded | 1980
Label | Gaudeamus CDGAU 310

Giovanni Pierluigi
da Palestrina | Missa
Papae Marcelli *(published* 1567*)*

Genre | Choral
Conductor | Harry Christophers
Performers | The Sixteen
Year recorded | 1990
Label | Coro 16014

Outstanding talent can sometimes make a person's life difficult: According to legend, Orlande de Lassus was kidnapped three times as a boy because of the distinguished quality of his treble voice. His career as a professional musician began at the age of twelve when he left his native Mons to serve under Ferrante Gonzaga, with whom he went to various cities including Paris, Mantua, Palermo, and Milan. After his voice broke, Lassus worked in Naples for a time. He then transferred to the household of Cosimo I de' Medici in Rome, and in 1553 was appointed maestro di cappella of St. John Lateran. Between 1555 and 1556, he stayed in Antwerp where he organized the publication of two volumes of madrigals and motets. In the following year, Lassus entered the service of Duke Albrecht V of Bavaria and became internationally renowned.

Lassus left no fewer than 530 motets, which, taken together, represent the zenith of Renaissance polyphony. For these works, he preferred to choose texts that showed potential for dramatic presentation and a vivid and declamatory compositional style

This recording presents a fine introduction to the art of Lassus. It features mainly the *Missa Surge propera* and the motet "Surge propera amica mea," upon which the Mass is based, but it also includes several other motets from various periods of the composer's life. The group's performances emphasize the sensitivity and subtlety of Lassus's music, drawing us into his world with the aid of their suave and sensual vocal sound. **NM**

Born probably in Palestrina, a small town about twenty-five miles from Rome, Giovanni Pierluigi da Palestrina (1525/6–1594) spent most of his musical career in the papal capital. He was associated with several of the most authoritative and celebrated churches in this city: the Cappella Giulia at St. Peter's (where he started his professional career as a choir master in 1551 and spent his final years from 1571); the Sistine Chapel; St. John Lateran; and the Basilica of Santa Maria Maggiore (where he had originally trained as a boy soprano and returned as maestro in 1561).

The *Missa Papae Marcelli* was included in the composer's second book of Masses published in 1567. The story that this work persuaded the Council of Trent (held between 1545 and 1563) to reserve a place for polyphonic music in church services is rather far-fetched. However, its largely homophonic yet varied texture certainly achieved textual intelligibility, for which the church authorities had hoped. This work also offers evidence of the composer's supreme mastery of counterpoint. Its ordered treatment of dissonance, and the beautifully proportioned curves of its melodic lines, have provided a model for generations of composers who wished to master what has become known as the *stile antico* (old style) of counterpoint.

Harry Christophers's approach to this work is superb: extremely gentle and flexible phrasing, and a flowing and comfortable speed—these are everything that Palestrina must have intended. Moreover the voices of The Sixteen are blended so creamily that they sing as one. **NM**

Thomas Tallis
Spem in alium
(c.1569)

Genre | Choral
Conductor | David Hill
Performers | Choir of Winchester Cathedral
Year recorded | 1989
Label | Hyperion CDA 66400

Frequently feted as a Tudor Barnum and Bailey experience, *Spem in alium* had suitably theatrical origins: During his London visit in 1567, composer Alessandro Striggio caused a stir with a forty-part motet, *Ecce beatam lucem*. The hunt was then on for an Englishman to meet the challenge, and Tallis took it on. The first performance of *Spem in alium* probably took place at Nonsuch Palace, home of the Catholic Duke of Norfolk, on his release from prison in 1569. Tallis subsequently ensured the work's survival by making an English version, *Sing and Glorify*, which was duly sung at the investiture of Henry as Prince of Wales in 1610.

Numerological analysis of *Spem* suggests that Tallis may also have conceived it as an autobiographical monument in sound, much as Bach and Shostakovich wrote their names into their work. It is only at the fortieth long (measure) that the full ensemble of eight five-part choirs enters together, on the word "*Respice*"; the individual lines of counterpoint make little sense on their own, but they are woven together with a virtuosic delicacy that entirely belies the penitential humility of the text.

Grand and theatrical performances of *Spem* are not to be shunned: quite the contrary. Most modern performances assign one voice per part and inevitably suffer deficiencies in balance resulting from some voices being stronger than others. David Hill roots *Spem* in the English cathedral tradition by using boys' voices and adjusting the numbers and pacing accordingly to fill the warm halo of Winchester Cathedral's acoustic. **PQ**

Tomás Luis de Victoria
O magnum mysterium
(published 1572)

Genre | Choral
Director | Andrew Hope
Performers | Victoria Voices and Viols
Year recorded | 2001
Label | Gaudeamus GAU 338

Tomás Luis de Victoria (1548–1611) was born at or near Ávila, where he began his career as a choirboy. He was then sent to the Jesuit-run German college in Rome to further his education. He may have had an opportunity to study with Palestrina, who worked at the nearby Seminario Romano. In 1571, Victoria became the rector of the college and, in 1575, was appointed as its maestro di cappella. During most of his time in Rome, in addition to his regular salaries, Victoria was supported generously by Spanish benefices and he eventually returned to Spain, where he served the Empress Maria as a priest-organist in Madrid.

Victoria composed a substantial amount of sacred music, including forty-five motets, the most famous being "O magnum mysterium"—a four-voice Christmas motet first published in 1572. Twenty years later, he published a parody Mass based upon it. By comparison with Palestrina's setting of the same text, Victoria's motet employs freer polyphonic techniques and more dissonances and, as a result, seems musically more forward-looking.

On this recording, Andrew Hope presents the work in a semi-liturgical setting that is derived from late Renaissance practices. He makes use of both voices and string instruments; the viols play parts from the original composition suitable for their ranges, while the harp and theorbo fill out the harmonies and play the bass line. As well as successfully revealing the elaborate texture of the piece, this recording also emphasizes the work's mystic atmosphere. **NM**

Francisco Guerrero | Battle Mass (1582)

Genre | Choral
Director/Performers | James O'Donnell; Westminster
Cathedral Choir, His Majestys Sagbutts and Cornetts
Year recorded | 1998
Label | Hyperion CDA 67075

In 1599, the year of his death, Francisco Guerrero was described as "the most extraordinary of his time in the Art of Music." He spent virtually all his working life in Seville, though visits to Rome and Venice ensured that he was in touch with musical styles elsewhere. In turn, his own music was widely distributed, printed in Seville, Paris, Louvain, Venice, and Rome, and copies of it reached further throughout Europe and to Latin America.

Guerrero's *Missa de la batalla escoutez* uses some musical material from an immensely popular chanson by Janequin, "La bataille de Marignan," commonly known as "La guerre." But this was no more than a source of melodic inspiration. Guerrero developed none of the onomatopoeic fanfares, cannon-fire, or agonized cries of the wounded, but instead created a Mass setting of great melodic and contrapuntal beauty. Most of it is in five parts, but trio sections and a magnificent eight-part Agnus Dei provide striking variety. Some passages are doubled by instruments—cornetts, sackbuts, and *bajón* (a precursor of the bassoon). Justification for such colorful additions comes from Seville itself; the booklet notes include a photograph of a carved plaque on the lectern in the city's cathedral showing shawm, sackbut, and cornett players.

The sound quality of this all-male choir matches Guerrero's original forces, while the recording is very finely balanced, instruments coloring lines without intruding on the clarity of text. The disc includes hymns, a psalm setting, an antiphon performed on instruments alone, and a striking Trinity motet, "Duo seraphim," significantly for three choirs. It opens with solo boys' voices, then expands with voices and instruments to a thrilling climax. A superb example of the glories of the Spanish Renaissance. **GP**

> "*[Guerrero's] great legacy of liturgical music . . . its variety, its endless flow of beautiful melody . . .*"
>
> Bruno Turner, booklet note, 1999

Other Recommended Recordings

Westminster Cathedral Choir • James O'Donnell
Hyperion CDA 66910
By contrast with the Battle Mass, the Westminster voices are here unaccompanied

Chapelle du Roi • Alistair Dixon
Signum SIGCD 017
Nine voices creating a highly refined sound

La Colombina
Accent ACC 96114 D
Four solo voices in a sparkling program including witty secular ensaladas—"musical salads"

An engraving of Guerrero by the Spanish painter Francisco Pancheco. ➔

Claudio Monteverdi
Madrigals (1587–1651)

Genre | Vocal
Director | Stephen Stubbs
Performers | John Potter, Tragicomedia
Year recorded | 1993
Label | Teldec 4509 91971-2

William Byrd | My
Ladye Nevells Book (1591)

Genre | Instrumental
Performer | Christopher Hogwood
(harpsichords, organ, and virginal)
Years recorded | 1974–75
Label | Decca 476 1530 (3 CDs)

Throughout Claudio Monteverdi's career, the madrigal charted perfectly the changes in his musical style as they reflected the transition from the Renaissance to the Baroque. His initial style, which produced regularly accented, lighthearted, five-voice compositions, was eventually taken over by a more expressive form with daring dissonances and angular melodic inflexions. Gradually, the need to project the text more clearly made textures simpler; the top two voices became more prominent, and the lowest acted as a firm foundation for the harmony. This shift eventually produced madrigals with fewer voices, supported by an instrumental bass. Altogether nine collections of Monteverdi's madrigals were published—the first book was issued in 1587 and the ninth posthumously in 1651.

Monteverdi's madrigals were occasionally criticized by his more conservative contemporaries, but Monteverdi's brother defended the composer for the way he balanced the demands of words and music. The notion that "music is subservient to the text" became the composer's lifelong ideal, even though his actual tactics changed over time.

There are several good recordings of Monteverdi's madrigals. Among the numerous compilations, Stephen Stubb's recording excels not least because of the clever selection of the repertoire. The pieces are taken from the seventh and eighth books and his second *Scherzi musicali* collection (1632), which represent the best of the composer. Here, the singers' performances are effective and eloquent, and well supported by sensitive, unobtrusive instrumental accompaniments. **NM**

Considered to be the foremost composer of Renaissance England, William Byrd (c.1540–1623) spent his formative years as a choirboy at the Chapel Royal under Thomas Tallis. After working for Lincoln Cathedral for a time, Byrd returned to the Chapel Royal as Gentleman and organist, the latter position held jointly with Tallis. In 1575, Queen Elizabeth granted Tallis and Byrd a monopoly on music printing and they published a collection of Latin motets. After Tallis's death in 1585, Byrd alone produced two more motet collections and two anthologies of English songs.

Byrd's keyboard-music collection *My Ladye Nevells Booke*, however, survives only in a manuscript, dated 1591. The identity of "Lady Nevell" is subject to debate but she is probably Rachel, wife of Sir Edward Nevell, Member of Parliament for Windsor in 1588–89. The collection comprises two sections: The first contains pavans and galliards, and the second variations and fantasies. Each section begins with a ground dedicated to Lady Nevell.

Christopher Hogwood's recording is the definitive account of this collection—but not simply because it is one of the rare complete recordings. Hogwood's performances are carefully controlled and technically so secure that they give life to the varied styles found in the forty-two pieces. He uses four different instruments manufactured by modern makers but modeled upon the types available in Renaissance England—an English virginal; two harpsichords (Italian and Flemish); and a chamber organ. The differing timbres of these instruments help to add light and color to this magisterial procession of dances and character pieces. **NM**

William Byrd
Masses (c.1592–95)

Genre | Choral
Director | Andrew Carwood
Performers | The Cardinall's Musick
Year recorded | 1999
Label | Gaudeamus CDGAU 206

Although William Byrd remained a practicing Catholic throughout his life, his faith seems not to have hindered his career at the Chapel Royal during the reign of the Protestant Queen Elizabeth I. In 1593, however, when laws were tightened, Byrd moved from London to a small village in Essex, near the household of Sir John Petre, his powerful patron, who was himself a Catholic.

It was under these circumstances that the composer devoted the rest of his life to composing Catholic liturgical music. Between around 1592 and 1595, Byrd published his three settings of the Mass; one each for three, four, and five voices. All are free Masses; that is, they are not based upon plainsongs or other pre-existent works as models. Instead, the Masses employ the so-called "head-motif" technique, where each movement starts with one and the same musical material; the movements themselves are Kyrie, Gloria, Credo, Sanctus, and Agnus Dei. The Masses are comparatively small in scale and must have been intended for private worship. Byrd then pursued another grandiose endeavor: a setting of all the music sung in the Mass service throughout the year, not already included in the settings mentioned above. This was printed in two volumes known as *Graduale* in 1605 and 1607, notwithstanding the strong anti-Catholic climate after the Gunpowder Plot in 1605.

This recording is the fifth volume in the series of Byrd's sacred music by The Cardinall's Musick. It contains all three Masses. Each of the singers maintains a noticeable individuality that serves to recreate the intimate and secretive atmosphere of a private service. **NM**

Carlo Gesualdo
Madrigals (1594–1611)

Genre | Vocal
Director | Claudio Cavina
Performers | La Venexiana
Year recorded | 2000
Label | Glossa GCD 920934

Son of the Prince of Venosa and of the niece of Pope Pius IV, Carlo Gesualdo succeeded to the title upon his father's demise in 1586. In the same year, he married his cousin, Maria d'Avalos. However, fourteen years later, his marriage met its bloody end when Gesualdo killed his unfaithful wife and her lover. This double murder made inevitable his semi-secluded life, where he immersed himself in composition. In 1593, Gesualdo became engaged to the niece of the Duke of Ferrara and the following year saw him in this northern Italian city, the most advanced center of madrigal writing in the late sixteenth century.

The madrigal became the chief focus of Gesualdo's compositional skill and he published six collections during his lifetime. What makes his madrigals unique is their irregularity and complexity—sudden, almost irrational juxtapositions occur of florid short-value notes against static long-value ones. Such characteristics, together with the often erotic lyrics, seem to represent the passionate yet temperamental nature of the composer himself.

The strength of La Venexiana's performance of Gesualdo's *Quatro libro di madrigali* lies in the singers' acute understanding of the relation between text and harmony. They sing the repertoire at the original pitch, not in unnecessarily transposed keys like some other recordings, and they evoke the meaning of each word within the comfortable yet expressive range of the voices. They never flee from the clashes given by the composer and they clearly enjoy the moments of intensity. The group has also issued a disc of Gesualdo's *Fifth Madrigal Book*, which is also highly recommended. **NM**

John Dowland | Lute Songs (1597–1612)

Genre | Vocal
Performers | Charles Daniels (tenor),
David Miller (lute)
Year recorded | 1997
Label | EMI 7243 5 72266 2 2

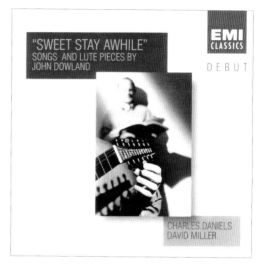

"SWEET STAY AWHILE"
SONGS AND LUTE PIECES BY
JOHN DOWLAND

EMI CLASSICS

DEBUT

CHARLES DANIELS
DAVID MILLER

The earliest concrete information about John Dowland (1563–1626) comes from a letter of 1584 in which he was mentioned as a "servant" to Henry Cobham, English Ambassador in Paris. In 1588, he was awarded a BMus degree from Oxford and around that time began to be acknowledged more widely as a musician. It seems he played for Queen Elizabeth in 1592, but in 1594, however, despite his growing reputation, his application for the vacant post of royal lutenist was rejected. The disappointment led to his subsequent European sojourn in Italy and Germany, after which, in 1598, he settled at the court of King Christian IV of Denmark. He left Denmark in 1606 and returned to his native country, where in 1612, he finally achieved his long-cherished desire—he was given a post by the English court, specially created for him.

It was Dowland who defined the English lute song as a genre through his four collections: the first, second, third books of songs (1597, 1600, 1603 respectively) and A Pilgrimes Solace (1612). His earlier songs are actually written for four vocal parts and lute (thus, they can be sung by a group of singers or, alternatively, performed by a single musician singing the top part while playing the lute.) His later songs, however, are intended more clearly for solo voice. Some of the later solo songs are supported by lute together with treble and bass viols.

Charles Daniels, accompanied by David Miller's excellent lute playing, displays a profound understanding in his vocal rendering of these Dowland songs. Technically his voice is first-rate, and his clear diction and coloring of the meaning of each word are a delight. He demonstrates that the English language has its own musical quality. **NM**

"John Dowland's abiding love of tears, grief, woe, anguish . . . and darkness has left a deep impression."

Anthony Rooley, *Early Music XI*, 1983

Other Recommended Recordings

Emma Kirkby, Anthony Rooley
Virgin 7243 5 62410 2 2 (2 CDs)
A balanced selection of Dowland's songs are performed with celestial clarity by Kirkby

John Potter, Stephen Stubbs, et al.
ECM 465 234-2
Potter's reflective approach is best presented in "In darkness let me dwell." Superb

Songs from the Labyrinth
Sting, Edin Karamazov
DG 072 2002
Raw, but passionate and tender accounts

The title page of Dowland's *First Booke of Songs or Ayres* (1597). ➔

Ptolomeus

Marinus

Aratus

Strabo

Hippaichus

Polibius

Geometria

Astronomia

Arithmetica

Musica

VIRESCIT VVLNERE VERITAS

THE
FIRST BOOKE OF
SONGS OR AYRES OF
foure parts, with Table-
ture for the Lute.

SO MADE, THAT ALL THE
parts together, or either of them
seuerally, may be sung to the Lute,
Orpherian, or Viol de gambo.

Composed by IOHN DOWLAND,
Lutenist and Bacheler of Musick
in both the Vniuersities.

Also an inuention by the said Author
for two to play vpon one Lute.

Newly corrected and amended.

Iohn Marsham. C.

Nec prosunt domino, quæ prosunt omnibus artes.

Imprinted at London by Humfrey Lownes
dwelling on Bredstreet-hill, at the signe
of the Starre. 1613.

MERCVRIVS

Giovanni Gabrieli | Sacrae symphoniae *(published 1597, 1615)*

Genre | Choral/Chamber
Conductor | Paul McCreesh
Performers | Gabrieli Consort and Players
Year recorded | 1995
Label | Archiv 449 180-2

ARCHIV PRODUKTION
GIOVANNI GABRIELI
MUSIC FOR SAN ROCCO
GABRIELI CONSORT & PLAYERS
PAUL McCREESH

Giovanni Gabrieli (*c*.1554/7–1612) established himself as a composer after training under Lassus at the court of Duke Albrecht V in Munich. After the death of the duke, Gabrieli returned to his native Venice and, in 1584, he found a temporary job as an organist at San Marco. In the following year, he secured his permanent position there and, at the same time, was elected as organist to the Scuola Grande di San Rocco, where he was involved in the sumptuous music making on many feast days.

Although Gabrieli began his career as a madrigal composer, his church duties in Venice meant that sacred music inevitably became his major focus. His works employ both vocal and instrumental forces, the latter for organ and ensemble. A large number of sacred compositions by Gabrieli appear in two printed collections titled *Sacrae symphoniae*. The first volume, published in 1597, reflects his work at San Marco, while the second, published posthumously in 1615, reveals the complexity and maturity of his music and seems more to mirror his activities at San Rocco.

Paul McCreesh's attempt to reconstruct the music for the feast day of San Rocco in 1608 was recorded at that very church. It features sixteen works by Gabrieli from various sources. The instrumental pieces are mostly taken from another posthumous collection, the *Canzoni e sonate* (1615), though five of the motets are from the second volume of *Sacrae symphoniae*. McCreesh succeeds in capturing the grandeur of the San Rocco tradition, and his attempts culminate in the astonishing splendor of the final thirty-three-voice Magnificat, the reconstruction here being based upon the better-known seventeen-voice Magnificat from the 1615 *Sacrae symphoniae*. **NM**

> " . . . *music, so good,*
> *so delectable, so rare, so*
> *admirable that it did even*
> *ravish and stupefy . . .* "

Thomas Coryat, *Coryat's Crudities*, 1611

Other Recommended Recordings

Timothy Roberts, His Majestys Sagbutts and Cornetts
Hyperion CDA 66908
Majestic performance of instrumental music from the Sacrae symphoniae *of 1597 and other sources*

Gabrieli Consort and Players • Paul McCreesh
Virgin 0777 7 59006 2 0
Revival of 1595 coronation of Venetian Doge using mainly the music of Andrea and Giovanni Gabrieli

Taverner Consort • Andrew Parrott
Virgin 7243 5 61934 2 0
Ravishing compilation of church music by G. Gabrieli and the following generation of Venetian composers

Paul McCreesh, director and founder of the Gabrieli Consort & Players. ➲

John Wilbye
Madrigals (1598–1609)

Genre | Vocal
Director | Anthony Rooley
Performers | Consort of Musicke
Year recorded | 1998
Label | Decca 458 093-2 (2 CDs)

Some time before 1598, John Wilbye became a servant at Hengrave Hall, near Bury St. Edmunds, Suffolk, of the Kytsons, a musical family who possessed many instruments and scores; this was the starting point of Wilbye's promising musical career. However, when he was granted a lease of some productive pastureland in 1613, his main interests shifted from music to farming.

Wilbye was a fine composer of the English madrigal, the genre England borrowed from Italy during the late 1580s and "anglicized" during the following decades. His first book of madrigals, published in 1598, contains several settings of poems in translation that were originally used by the Italian composer Luca Marenzio. Wilbye not only imitated the Italian's techniques, but also transformed them to suit English texts.

Respected and trusted by his fellow musicians, in 1600 Wilbye was involved in the publication of Dowland's second book of songs, and was, along with several other composers, chosen to contribute to *The Triumphs of Oriana* (1601), an anthology of madrigals in honor of Queen Elizabeth. Some pieces in Wilbye's second book of madrigals (1609) are quite forward-looking, making use of sequences and revealing his growing tonal awareness.

This recording is the most comprehensive available of Wilbye's output. Although it is a combined reissue of three separate recordings that feature Wilbye, Gibbons, and Morley respectively, it has by no means lost its authoritative value. The performance is superb in every respect from the stable vocal tone, the balance between voices, the diction, and the well-judged speeds. **NM**

Orlando Gibbons
Anthems (1600s)

Genre | Choral
Conductor | David Hill
Performers | Choir of Winchester Cathedral
Year recorded | 1989
Label | Hyperion CDH 55228

Diversity of accomplishment was key to Gibbons's renown both during his short life and to this day. "The Silver Swan" (secular madrigal); "Almighty and Everlasting God" (plain, full anthem); "O Clap Your Hands" (contrapuntal showpiece); "O Sing Unto the Lord" (verse anthem); "Lord Salisbury's Pavan" (keyboard fantasy): All are shaped by acute sensitivity to the demands of their different genres. Melodic continuity and smoothness of line are more important than the local applications of color that would predominate in the next generation. His music is most familiar to Christian worshippers through harmonizations published in *The English Hymnal*, notably the tune set to "O Lord Who at Thy Eucharist Didst Pray." Perhaps his skill as a keyboard player helped him to keep abreast of continental musical fashions; at any rate, what marks Gibbons from his contemporaries is a perfect balance between learned, sacred polyphony and radical, madrigalian harmonies. Glenn Gould sees this contemplative equilibrium as stemming from Gibbons's place between "the era of delicious anonymity . . . and the era of almost total, exploitative individuality of the Baroque."

The Clerkes of Oxenford made recordings of Gibbons's (and other Elizabethan) music that have scarcely been surpassed for the purity and delicacy of their singing. Until these are made available again, Hyperion's Winchester reissue will do nicely: It is distinguished by the inclusion of "O Sing Unto the Lord" and by Robin Blaze's poise in the "Record of John"—and marred only by the use of organ for the verse anthems instead of the unique, grainy sound of a viol consort for which Gibbons conceived them. **PQ**

Jan Pieterszoon Sweelinck
Organ Works (c.1600–21)

Genre | Instrumental
Instrument | Organ
Performer | Masaaki Suzuki
Year recorded | 2006
Label | BIS CD-1614

John Dowland | Lachrimae
or Seaven Teares (published 1604)

Genre | Chamber
Director | Peter Holman
Performers | Parley of Instruments
Year recorded | 1994
Label | Hyperion CDA 66637

Jan Pieterszoon Sweelinck was born near Amsterdam in 1562. By the age of eighteen, he was appointed as organist of the Oude Kerk in Amsterdam, a position held by his father until 1573, and later taken by Sweelinck's own son.

Not long before Sweelinck's appointment, Amsterdam had been officially converted to Calvinism. This had a huge impact on an organist's work since the reformed religion banned the use of the instrument during services. In fact Sweelinck's official status was that of a civil servant for the City of Amsterdam, and his duties required him to provide music for two daily sessions in the church: one before the morning service, the other after the service in the evening.

Sweelinck's organ music includes fantasies, toccatas, and sets of variations on secular and sacred themes. They are often technically demanding, characterized by elaborate contrapuntal writing. Although Sweelinck rarely left Amsterdam, he was aware of the new styles developed by various composers across Europe, including Cabezón and John Bull. Moreover, Sweelinck was an outstanding teacher: His pupils include Samuel Scheidt and Heinrich Scheidemann, who formed the so-called North German organ school and prepared the way for J. S. Bach.

In this recording of Sweelinck's organ music, Masaaki Suzuki, the director of Bach Collegium Japan, shows his secure technique as an organist. He uses a restored organ of a mid-seventeenth-century Dutch type found at Kobe Shinko Church in Japan. Its grave yet almost vocal timbre suits the program of toccatas and psalm variations. Suzuki's performance style is never ostentatious, and his reflective manner is in keeping with restrained Calvinism. **NM**

John Dowland, in his publication of 1604, presented seven pieces of consort music based upon the descending four notes of the *Lachrimae* theme, which he called *Lachrimae or Seaven teares figured in seven passionate pavans*. The publication contains altogether twenty-one pieces, most scored for solo lute and an ensemble of one treble, three tenors, and one bass instruments, either of viols or the violin family. The *Seaven Teares* forms a sequence of variations, each starting with the *Lachrimae* theme before developing other material that is then passed on from one piece to another. The generic title "pavan" refers to an early-sixteenth-century court dance, but here the reference is to the general style of that genre—these pieces are not appropriate for actual dancing.

Prior to the *Seaven Teares*, when Dowland published his second book of songs in 1600, he had already included a song version of the *Lachrimae* pavan with the text "Flow my tears." It is now thought that even earlier than this the composer had written a version for solo lute that might well have been the original form of the piece. In its various guises, the music achieved such a success that it appeared in about a hundred contemporary manuscripts and prints.

Peter Holman, a world expert in early modern English music, presents a complete recording of the 1604 publication. He has chosen violins because when Dowland was revising his works for this publication he was at the Danish court, where a violin consort was more readily available than viols. As a result, this performance of the *Seaven Teares* brings unexpected lightness and clarity to the texture, yet the poignancy of the music is intact. **NM**

Claudio Monteverdi | Orfeo (1607)

Genre | Opera
Conductor | John Eliot Gardiner
Performers | Monteverdi Choir, English Baroque Soloists
Year recorded | 1987
Label | Archiv 419 250-2 (2 CDs)

Born the son of an apothecary and surgeon in Cremona, northern Italy, Claudio Monteverdi was a prodigy, publishing collections of sacred and secular music as early as in his teens. By 1592 he had entered the service of the Gonzagas of Mantua, with whom he developed a long if checkered relationship.

The plot of *Orfeo* is based largely upon the Orpheus legend described by Ovid in his *Metamorphoses*. The work was performed first at the Gonzaga court during the carnival season, which was traditionally associated with extravagant musico-theatrical entertainments. This was just a few years after Florence, under the guise of restoring Greco-Roman tragedies, first produced musical dramas, that would later be called "operas." The early Florentine works included two settings of the same Orpheus story, both called *Euridice*, written by Peri and Caccini respectively—these acted as pale models for Monteverdi's extraordinary masterpiece. Although history has left us comparatively little information regarding the details of its premiere, *Orfeo* must have been a great success. The work was published twice during the composer's lifetime.

In fact, *Orfeo* stood between two traditions: Renaissance and Baroque. While its large and varied instrumentation and madrigalesque vocal ensembles indicate earlier practices, its organized tonality and emotive vocal writing pointed to the future. In this recording every aspect is in total control, but this in no way hampers its intensity and lyricism. Anthony Rolfe Johnson is a marvelous Orfeo, tackling brilliantly the super-demanding aria "Possente spirto." Anne Sofie von Otter as Messenger conveys to Orfeo and to the listener the death of Euridice with great poignancy. This is the definitive recording. **NM**

> *"In Orfeo we have . . . a masterpiece that is virtually the only example of a vanished art."*
>
> Romain Rolland

Other Recommended Recordings

London Baroque • Charles Medlam
Virgin 7243 4 82070 2 9 (2 CDs)
Nigel Rodgers's superlative techniques of coloratura make this an astonishing experience

New London Consort • Philip Pickett
L'Oiseau-Lyre 433 545-2 (2 CDs)
Refined performance emphasizes the Renaissance aspect of the work rather than that of the Baroque

Concerto Vocale • René Jacobs
Harmonia Mundi HMC 901553.54 (2 CDs)
Jacobs's experimental use of various instrumental timbres creates a festive mood

An anonymous portrait of Claudio Monteverdi as a young man. ➔

Girolamo Frescobaldi | Keyboard Works (*published* 1608–37)

Genre | Instrumental
Instruments | Harpsichord and organ
Performer | Sergio Vartolo
Year recorded | 2000
Label | Naxos 8.553547-48 (2 CDs)

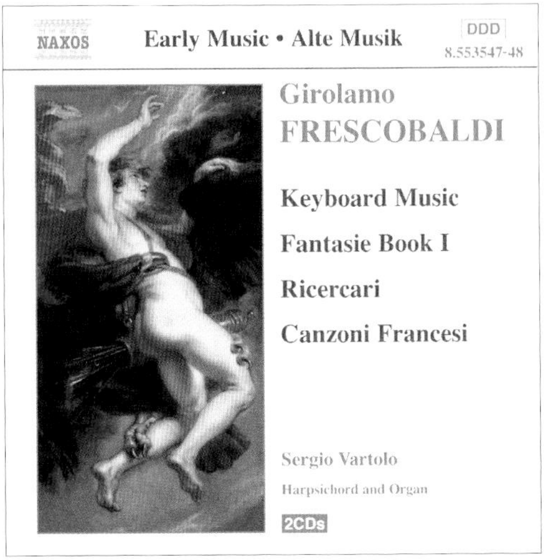

Born in Ferrara in 1583, Girolamo Frescobaldi studied there under Luzzasco Luzzaschi. By 1607 he had moved to Rome where he became a protégé of Cardinal Bentivoglio and secured the position of organist at Santa Maria in Trastevere. In the following year, after accompanying the cardinal on his travels to the Low Countries, the composer returned to Rome and was appointed as organist at St. Peter's. He remained in this prestigious post until his death, although he temporarily worked for Ferdinando II de'Medici between 1628 and 1634.

Most of Frescobaldi's keyboard music appeared in seven publications: two printed collections of toccatas and five books of other genres, such as canzones, ricercars, fantasies, and capriccios. His toccatas are characterized by the use of contrasting sections between which drastic tempo changes occur along with shifts of metrical accents. The connections between one section and another are loose, and the composer himself suggested that they might be performed separately. Canzones are usually decorative arrangements of song-melodies. The remaining genres were derived from the tradition of elaborate counterpoint. Some of Frescobaldi's works can be played on the organ as a prelude to church services.

An expert in Frescobaldi's music as both performer and scholar, Sergio Vartolo has issued complete recordings of the two volumes of the toccatas and the first volume of the capriccios. His Naxos recording features the ricercars and canzones performed on harpsichord. Vartolo's well-contemplated articulations not only reveal contrapuntal textures clearly but also seem to overcome the instrument's innate characteristics by evoking great fluency and color. **NM**

NAXOS   Early Music • Alte Musik   DDD
8.553547-48

Girolamo
FRESCOBALDI

Keyboard Music
Fantasie Book I
Ricercari
Canzoni Francesi

Sergio Vartolo
Harpsichord and Organ
2CDs

"The manner of playing must . . . be now slow, now rapid, and even suspended in the air . . ."

Girolamo Frescobaldi

A homage to Girolamo Frescobaldi dating from 1637. ➔

HIERONYMVS FRESCOBALDVS FERRARIENS ORGANISTA ECCLESIÆ D. PETRI IN VATICANO ÆT. SVÆ 86

In lode dell' Autore
Del Cau.e Pier fran.co Paoli da Pesaro

Tu cõ emulando il suon de l'ampie sfere
Per arricchir d'eterna gioia i cori
Spargesti i soauissimi tesori
De le tue dolci musiche miniere,
Qvali nutri nel cor voglie seuere
Contra i tuoi proprij armoniosi tenori,
Che accogli de le carte entro à gli horrori
A starsi mute hor le tue note altere?
Ah che pur quini à le più sagge menti
Dispiegan più che mai canori, e belli
Di tù, che le formasti, i pregi ardenti.
Tal de i Ciel nei volumi impressi anch'elle
Sembran mute caratteri lucenti,
E le glorie di Dio narran le stelle.

Claudio Monteverdi | Vespers (1610)

Genre | Choral
Conductor | Andrew Parrott
Performer | Taverner Consort, Choir & Players
Year recorded | 1984
Label | Virgin 7243 5 61662 2 6 (2 CDs)

Taverner Consort, Choir & Players · Andrew Parrott

MONTEVERDI Vespro della Beata Vergine 1610

veritas x2

Monteverdi's *Vespro della beata Vergine* was published together with his *Missa in illo tempore* in Venice in 1610. Dedicated to Pope Paul V, this publication was Monteverdi's first major collection of sacred music. It seems likely that he wrote the music over a fairly long period of time—it cannot have been written with San Marco in mind, since Monteverdi was not appointed as maestro di cappella at the basilica until 1613.

The 1610 publication as a whole shows Monteverdi's mastery of two opposing techniques: While the Mass, based upon materials from a motet by Nicolas Gombert, exemplifies the *stile antico*, the traditional way of writing polyphonic church music, the Vespers demonstrates the *stile moderno*, which incorporates instruments, solo items, and duets. The combination of these forces and textures in the Vespers creates a superb musical extravagance.

The Vespers has been a problematic work for modern scholars and performers. Monteverdi's setting not only includes the usual psalms, hymn, and Magnificat, but also some "Sacred Concertos" (Nigra sum, Pulchra es, Duo Seraphim, and Audi coelum), which seem not to have had a proper place in the Vespers service. Andrew Parrott, in this recording, argues that Monteverdi originally intended his composition for the Santa Barbara Church in Mantua. He reconstructs the liturgy as a whole by performing the items composed by Monteverdi, but he treats the Sacred Concertos as additions to the service. He inserts them after the psalms and before the following antiphons (brief chants that come either side of a psalm setting). Each item is performed with technical security, and this recording makes a strong case for the unity of this collection of Monteverdi's glorious compositions. **NM**

> *"Monteverdi's 1610 Vespers . . . looks back to the 16th century and forward to the 17th . . . "*
>
> Andrew Parrott and Hugh Keyte

Other Recommended Recordings

The Scholars Baroque Ensemble
Naxos 8.550662-63 (2 CDs)
The small-scale but well-balanced performances make this recording highly recommendable

Bach Collegium Japan • Masaaki Suzuki
BIS CD-1701/1702 (2 CDs)
A renowned Bach specialist, Suzuki excels also at the Vespers. This recording includes all the items in the 1610 publication

Gabrieli Consort & Players • Paul McCreesh
Archiv 477 6147 (2 CDs)
A generally fast but exciting performance

Thomas Weelkes | **Anthems** (1610s)

Genre | Choral
Conductor | David Hill
Performer | Choir of Winchester Cathedral
Year recorded | 1989
Label | Hyperion CDH 55259

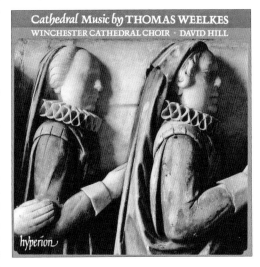

To call Thomas Weelkes the English Gesualdo might be stretching a point, but his is a strikingly individual voice in Tudor music, and one that perhaps could only arise from an unstable personality at the end of an unstable age. Based at the fastness of Chichester on the Sussex coast, he composed little consort music of the sort that tickled refined royal palates. The precinct of Chichester Cathedral, by contrast, seems to have been a sink of impiety to judge from the frequent punishments meted out to its inhabitants. Weelkes was one of the worst offenders: He died a drunkard, in debt, dismissed from his post.

At every turn, when comparing Weelkes with his contemporaries, his work stands out for eccentric intensity of invention and expression. This lends his many secular madrigals their color, and enables him to set long texts (such as *Thule, the Period of Cosmography*) with constantly varied contrapuntal and harmonic tricks. His anthems for the church tend to be more single-minded—typified by the hectoring exuberance of "Alleluia, I Heard a Voice" and "Gloria in excelsis Deo," and the alarmingly explicit lamentation of "Laboravi in gemitu meo" and "When David Heard." For Weelkes, false relations moved beyond their place in a tonal scheme to become an effect in their own right, not necessarily tied to word-painting: the collapse of any sense of key at the climax of "When David Heard" unravels the choral fabric into single threads: anachronistic comparisons with Mahler and Webern come to mind.

Cathedral choir recordings of Weelkes tend to shun the exaggeration of several madrigal recordings (nearly all of which are currently unavailable anyway); the Winchester choir is not too sober, but it is always accurately tuned and well turned. **PQ**

> " . . . *for in these humoures he will bothe curse & sweare most dreadfully, & so profane the service of God.*"
>
> **William Lawes**

Other Recommended Recordings

Gibbons, Weelkes & Tomkins: Madrigals and Fantasies
Deller Consort • Alfred Deller
Harmonia Mundi HMX 290219
Relaxed accounts of their unbuttoned moods

Vecchi: L'Amfiparnaso
I Fagiolini • Robert Hollingworth
DVD: Chandos CHDVD5029
Madrigal-comedy by eccentric Italian contemporary

Du Caurroy: Fantasies
Hesperion XX • Jordi Savall • Naïve Astree ES 9931
French contemporary on the cusp of the Renaissance and Baroque eras

Thomas Campion | Books of Ayres (1613–17)

Genre | Vocal
Performers | Steven Rickards (countertenor),
Dorothy Linell (lute)
Year recorded | 1996
Label | Naxos 8.553380

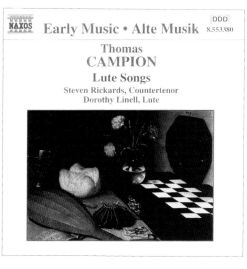

Early Music • Alte Musik

DDD
8.553380

Thomas
CAMPION
Lute Songs
Steven Rickards, Countertenor
Dorothy Linell, Lute

In 1605 Thomas Campion (1567–1620) received a medical degree from the University of Caen in France, after reading classics at Cambridge and law at Gray's Inn, London. However, although he practiced medicine, Campion established his fame through publishing Latin and English poems and five books of "ayres." His studies of poetry and music led to his publishing treatises on both subjects: *Observations in the Art of English Poesie* (1602) and *A New Way of Making Fowre Parts in Counter-point* (c.1614). He was also involved in masques and similar entertainments performed before the royal family at Whitehall.

For Campion, the ayre was an important genre. Through this apparently lightweight form, he revealed his talent by not only writing the music but also the texts. Altogether, Campion published 119 songs: twenty-one of them were included in Philip Rosseter's *First Book of Ayres* (1601) but the majority were printed in collections under Campion's own name. His first collection (of sacred and moral songs) appeared in 1613, the second collection (of light love songs) appeared shortly after, and the third and fourth (mainly of light-hearted songs) were both issued around 1617. Most of his ayres are composed for solo voice and accompanying lute (or viol), but some are given alternative versions with more voices. The charm of Campion's ayres lies in the natural flow of the melody and the liveliness of the rhythm.

This recording gives an especially good overview of this composer's style. Steven Rickards's pure voice presents Campion's musical microcosm through a variety of moods, ranging from the devotion of "Author of Light" to the delightful yarn "It Fell on a Sommers Daie." Linell's lute playing provides a subtle but telling support. **NM**

> *"In these English Ayres, I have chiefly aimed to couple my words and notes lovingly together."*
>
> Thomas Campion

Other Recommended Recordings

**Brian Asawa, David Tayler
RCA 09026 68818 2**
Brian Asawa's powerfully projected voice in songs mainly by Dowland and Campion

**Andreas Scholl, Andreas Martin
Harmonia Mundi HMC 90 1603**
English folk songs and lute songs, highlighting the beauty of Scholl's voice

**Michael Chance, Nigel North
Linn, CKD105**
A compilation of Campion's songs: Chance's clear diction is a definite advantage here

Campion's first two books of ayres, published c.1613–14. ➔

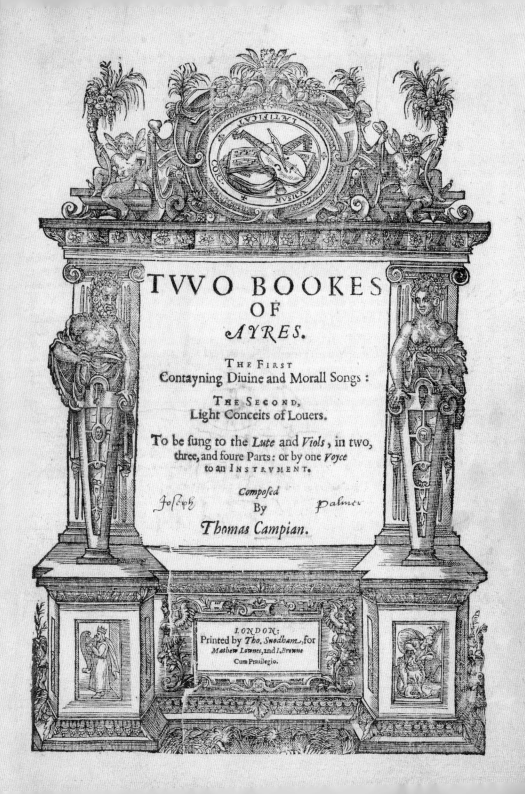

TVVO BOOKES
OF
AYRES.

THE FIRST
Contayning Diuine and Morall Songs :

THE SECOND,
Light Conceits of Louers.

To be sung to the *Lute* and *Viols*, in two,
three, and foure Parts: or by one *Voyce*
to an INSTRVMENT.

Ioseph   Composed   *palmer*
By
Thomas Campian.

LONDON:
Printed by *Tho. Snodham*, for
Mathew Lownes, and I. *Browne*
Cum Priuilegio.

Thomas Tomkins
Anthems (1620s)

Genre | Choral
Conductor | Christopher Robinson
Performers | Choir of St. George's Chapel
Year recorded | 1989
Label | Hyperion CDH 55066

Claudio Monteverdi
Combattimento (1624)

Genre | Music Theater
Conductor | Emmanuelle Haïm
Performers | Le Concert d'Astrée
Year recorded | 2006
Label | Virgin 0946 3 63350 2 5

The long life and work of Thomas Tomkins belong to the extended autumn of the English Renaissance. In the early 1600s, in the prime of his career, Tomkins was a member of the Chapel Royal circle that included his teacher William Byrd and Orlando Gibbons, writing anthems, madrigals, and consort music with a consistency that hardly rivals the industry of Tallis and Byrd or the brilliance of Gibbons, but speaks of diligence and rare craftmanship.

Tomkins is to his shorter-lived contemporary Weelkes what Springsteen is to Hendrix—a survivor of vicissitudes. When the two composers set the same text, as they often do, Tomkins is notable for his slow-burning restraint. "When David Heard" is the best-known anthem by both composers, two of many public demonstrations of grief over the premature death of Prince Henry in 1612. Where Weelkes goes all out for pathos, Tomkins builds to an extended passage of sighing imitation at "Would God I Had Died for Thee," which is surpassed in his work only by "Arise, O Lord, into Thy Resting Place" and "Almighty God, the Fountain of All Wisdom." The former shows a mastery of expressive timing that recalls Sibelius, especially during the expansive wind-down of "Turn Not Thy Face from Me." The Amen of the latter is studded with false relations with an extravagance that Tallis would have shunned.

The Choir of Trinity College, Cambridge, recorded a recital of Weelkes and Tomkins that is unrivalled for the quality of its selection and attention to sense and detail. Its absence from the catalogue is much to be lamented, but this recording from the Choir of St. George's Chapel, Windsor, edges past rivals on Naxos and Gimell. **PQ**

In 1613, after being sacked by the Gonzagas of Mantua in the previous year, Monteverdi was appointed as maestro di cappella at the Basilica San Marco in Venice. In addition to his church duties, the composer went on writing musico-dramatic works, which frequently featured at private gatherings, particularly during Carnival seasons.

Combattimento di Tancredi e Clorinda, based upon Torquato Tasso's poetic masterpiece, premiered in 1624 at the palace of Girolamo Mocenigo, in the presence of all the notable figures of Venice. The work was later published as part of his eighth book of madrigals (1638) and the preface to this publication clearly tells us that the work was intended to be performed in the "representative" (theatrical) manner, involving actions (the premiere even seems to have used some kind of imitation horses), with descriptions of those actions by "Testo" (a narrator). The instruments—four viole da braccio, a contrabasso da gamba, and a harpsichord—imitate the sound of battle in what Monteverdi calls the "agitated style"—part of this attempt to establish new ways of writing music.

The success (or otherwise) of the performance of *Combattimento* lies largely in the competence of the tenor who takes the role of Testo. The composer in the aforementioned publication clearly warns us that Testo must not make any throaty or trilling sounds and should deliver the words clearly "according to the passions of the oration." And in these respects, Rolando Villazón on this recording is unrivaled and brilliant. The instrumentalists are also excellent and Haïm shows her great dramatic sense in organizing the work as a whole. **NM**

John Jenkins
Fantasias (c.1630s)

Genre | Chamber
Performers | Fretwork,
Paul Nicholson (organ)
Year recorded | 1995
Label | Virgin 7243 5 45230 2 1

It is said that upon his father's death, John Jenkins was left a bandore, which seems to have prompted his career in music. Jenkins was among the musicians who participated in the masque *The Triumph of Peace* in London in 1634, and was once summoned by Charles I to perform on the lyra viol for his entertainment. In 1660, the restored monarch appointed him as a court theorbo player. However, owing probably to his then old age, he rarely attended the court and seems to have spent most of his time with various families including that of Roger North, a music critic.

The fantasia was a contrapuntal piece with no fixed form, which reached England during the sixteenth century. Most works of this type were written for solo keyboard or lute, but fantasias for instrumental ensembles became popular during Jenkins's lifetime. He left around a hundred fantasias, which are scored for from three to six parts. While the six-part fantasias show a clear indebtedness to those by preceding composers such as John Coprario and Alfonso Ferrabosco II, the three-voice medium was influenced by the newly developing Italian trio sonata.

Jenkins's fantasias, owing mainly to their contrapuntal nature and the heavy timbre created by a combination of organ and viols, may give an impression of a connoisseur's repertoire. However, the combination here of Fretwork and Paul Nicholson sweeps away such apprehension. They brilliantly project the eventful musical journey that each of Jenkins's fantasias unfolds, and the intricate textures of the music are presented in a relaxed manner. The Fantasia no. 6 in F major, based upon the folksong "All in a Garden Green," is performed with pastoral humor. **NM**

William Lawes
Consort Setts (1630s)

Genre | Chamber
Director | Lawrence Dreyfus
Performers | Phantasm
Year recorded | 1999
Label | Channel CCS 15698

William Lawes may have been overshadowed as a composer by his older, more prolific brother Henry, but, William was probably more talented. Sadly his career was cut short, when he was killed at the age of forty-three, fighting with the Royalist forces at the Battle of Chester.

William's talent was recognized early and he was sent to study under John Coprario in London. In 1635, he entered the service of Charles I, though it is likely that he had started working for the court earlier, since he had already been involved as a composer in various masques performed before the royal family, including *The Triumph of Peace* (1634).

Nowadays, William Lawes is known particularly for his consort setts in five and six parts. These are groups of ensemble music consisting of fantasies, pavans, almans, and more serious dances. Lawes's setts were mostly written in the later 1630s, and were intended for court entertainments. However, the frequent use of false relations, dissonances, and daring harmonies in this particular collection makes it the most original and forward-looking.

The Phantasm recording brings life to these five-part consort setts. Although the group plays the works without the aid of an organ continuo, there is nothing lacking here: The texture of fantasies is clear and the lyricism of the dances natural. Rapid passages, probably derived from Lawes's own techniques as a virtuoso viol-player, are executed with precision. Always noticeable is the group's energy, which sometimes almost reaches a frenzy. Yet the control is always there and the effects are beautiful. **NM**

Heinrich Schütz | Musikalische Exequien (1636)

Genre | Choral
Conductor/Performers | Harry Christophers, The Sixteen,
The Symphony of Harmony and Invention
Year recorded | 1998
Label | Coro COR 16036

Born in 1585, Heinrich Schütz was the founder of the great German musical tradition that culminated in Bach, born exactly a hundred years later. In 1609, he went to Venice to study with Giovanni Gabrieli, whose new Italian style is still evident in the *Musikalische Exequien* (German Requiem). This seventeenth-century German funeral service is far from unrelieved mourning. Prince Heinrich of Russ chose his own funeral text, an invitation for his long-time friend Schütz to revel in expansive and colorfully varied forces. Plainchant intonations introduce complex motet textures and modern Italianate "concerto-style" solo voices with continuo and double chorus. The Lutheran contributions are chorales, complex music not yet distilled into simple melodies for congregational singing.

Schütz described the opening part as a "Concerto in the form of a German burial Mass," a marriage of Gabrieli-style solos with German hymn-verses. Throughout this section, Christophers sustains a constant pulse, creating a wonderful sense of purpose and direction despite the constantly changing fragments of text and textures.

The second part is a motet on a grand scale, another Italian concept, using two four-part choirs, spatially separated—a thrilling sound as the voices call and answer each other, then combine in a rich, enveloping stereophony. Similarly divided choirs sing the final section, one taking the text of the farewell "Nunc dimittis" while the other, of sopranos and baritone only, represents angels welcoming the departed spirit into heaven.

Harry Christophers's few voices and colorful instruments—strings, cornetts, sackbutts and continuo—create a gloriously transparent sound, finely recorded in the resonant acoustic of a London church. **GP**

> *"Finally, dear readers, if my labor pleases you, may you use it to praise God the All-highest . . ."*
>
> Heinrich Schütz, preface to the *Psalms of David*

Other Recommended Recordings

Alsfelder Vokalsensemble, Himlische Cantorey
I Febiarmonici • Wolfgang Helbich
Naxos 8.555705
The huge reverberation of a German Cathedral cleverly tamed in a striking recording

La Chapelle Royale • Philippe Herreweghe
Harmonia Mundi HMC 901261
This recording has a bonus of six exquisite motets

Symphoniae Sacrae III
Cantus Cölln & Concerto Palatino • Konrad Junghänel
Harmonia Mundi HMC 901850.51 (2 CDs)
Schütz's final vocal and instrumental settings

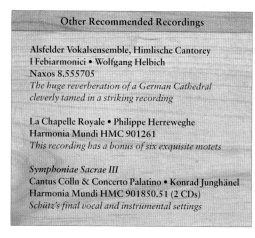

Heinrich Schütz, painted in Leipzig by Christoph Spetner, c. 1650–60. ❯

Gregorio Allegri
Miserere mei Deus
(*c.*1640s)

Genre | Choral
Conductor | Peter Phillips
Performers | Deborah Roberts (soprano), Tallis Scholars
Year recorded | 1994
Label | Gimell CDGIM 994

The story goes that when the fourteen-year-old Mozart visited Rome in 1770, he meticulously wrote out from memory Gregorio Allegri's *Miserere mei Deus*. A pupil of Giovanni Maria Nanino, Allegri was active as a singer-composer in the papal choir under Urban VIII, and was considered an important successor to Palestrina in his own time. Today, it is only his *Miserere* that is widely known.

Miserere is a setting of Psalm 1, but the version we hear now was edited by Ivor Atkins in the 1950s and has rather little to do with Allegri. His original setting comprises a simple chant for two choirs (five- and four-voice respectively), which sing alternately and then join together for the final section. During the eighteenth century, though, it became customary for ornamentation to be applied to the *Miserere* and other similar works. At the same time, singing the piece in a very high key also became customary, which gave an added frisson to the famous high soprano (or boy treble) solos that punctuate the work.

Among the extant recordings of this piece, the recording by the Tallis Scholars was in fact made in Santa Maria Maggiore in Rome, one of the churches associated with Palestrina. The DVD version of this recording (GIMDP 903) gives us a glimpse of the environment in which those Roman composers worked. As for this performance of *Miserere*, mention should be made of the almost transcendental perfection of Deborah Roberts's solo. Her well-projected, sweet timbre helps to restore for us those effects that fascinated the young Mozart. **NM**

Claudio Monteverdi
Il ritorno d'Ulisse in patria (1640)

Genre | Opera
Conductor/Performers | Nikolaus Harnoncourt;
Sven Olof Eliasson, Norma Lerer, Concentus Musicus Wien
Year recorded | 1971
Label | Teldec 2292 42496-2 (3 CDs)

Monteverdi's first attempt to write an opera for a commercial opera house, *Il ritorno d'Ulisse in patria* (*The Return of Ulysses to His Homeland*) was premiered at the Teatro Santi Giovanni e Paolo in 1640. The immediate success of the work led to its being performed at least ten times in Venice, revived at Bologna within a year of the premiere, and triumphantly returned to Venice in 1641.

The story is derived from Homer's *Odyssey*, but the opera centers on the anguish, nobility, and chastity of Penelope, as she waits for her husband Ulysses to return from the Trojan War. The opera's prologue emphasizes the quest for morality in an exchange between Human Frailty, Time, Fortune, and Cupid: Penelope's endurance will be rewarded at the end of the opera.

Despite the work's reputation during Monteverdi's lifetime, *Il ritorno* entered the modern operatic repertoire later than his other surviving operas and the number of extant recordings is fewer. Among them, Nikolaus Harnoncourt's version is highly recommendable because of its elegant presentation of the ancient drama. Norma Lerer (Penelope), supported by the noble sound of the harp, sings her opening aria "Di misera regina" beautifully and solemnly. The transformation of a shepherd boy into the goddess Minerva is represented not only by a spectacular explosion of vocal fireworks, but also by the change in accompanying instruments—from piffaro to organ. The final union between Ulysses (Sven Olof Eliasson) and Penelope is blissful. **NM**

Claudio Monteverdi
L'incoronazione di Poppea (1643)

Genre | Opera
Conductor/Performers | Richard Hickox; Arleen Auger, Della Jones, City of London Baroque Sinfonia
Year recorded | 1988
Label | Virgin 7243 5 61783 2 8 (3 CDs)

Monteverdi's last opera, *L'incoronazione di Poppea* (*The Coronation of Poppea*), premiered at the Teatro Santi Giovanni e Paolo, Venice, during the 1642–43 Carnival season. It deals with a controversial subject: the triumph of the illicit love between Emperor Nero and his mistress, Poppea. The reasons why such a theme was chosen have long been the subject of scholarly debate, but it seems that Republican Venice at its zenith dared to mock proud Rome with its history of autocratic emperors.

The opera unfolds the full range of human behavior: the sensuous exchanges between Nero and Poppea; the attempt on Poppea's life; the devastation of her husband, Ottone; his affair with Drusilla; amorous flirtations between male and female servants; the sexual and political ambition of the aging nurse; and the solemn suicide of Seneca. Monteverdi's mature musical skills powerfully portrayed all of these aspects of human life. The work met with great success, and the opera was revived in Naples in 1651.

There are many good recordings of this work, but Richard Hickox's version best sustains the level of dramatic intensity. Although the tempo in general is slow, his conducting manages to keep the music in full flow. Arleen Auger and Della Jones give a fully operatic performance here, not entirely in keeping with an early music aesthetic, but ravishing nonetheless. Their final duet "Pur ti miro"—which is not accepted by all scholars as being by Monteverdi—is both tender and compelling in this performance. **NM**

Giacomo Carissimi
Jephte (*c.1650*)

Genre | Oratorio
Director/Performers | Paul McCreesh; Janet Cowell, Angus Smith, John Mark Ainsley, Gabrieli Consort & Players
Year recorded | 1986
Label | Meridian CDE 84304

In 1629, Giacomo Carissimi was appointed maestro di cappella at the German College in Rome and remained the leading Italian composer of sacred vocal music until his death in 1674. He is noted as one of the first composers of oratorios, of which *Jephte* is his best-known work.

Based on the story told in the Old Testament, Judges 10:6–12:7, Jephte's daughter runs joyfully to greet him on his victorious return home from battle—but he has sworn to God that he will sacrifice the first living thing he encounters. The daughter, resigned to her fate, is granted two months to spend with her companions in the mountains, where she bewails her virginity. The narrative is carried on by a variety of voices from solo to four-part ensemble. The daughter's lament is a masterpiece of dramatic expression, all the more effective for its restraint, and subtly structured, with key phrases repeated and echoed by her companions. Only in the final chorus are sorrow and mourning allowed to flow unrestrained in one of the most poignant musical moments ever.

There have been several fine recordings, but none matches Janet Cowell's superb characterization of Jephte's daughter. Her voice is endearing, disarmingly young-sounding and natural, her companions echoing realistically among the mountains. Angus Smith's Jephte ranges from the controlled sincerity of his oath to the most bitter anguish at the tragic outcome. The music is accompanied by colorful continuo; the other two oratorios on the disc are splendid pieces as well. **GP**

Barbara Strozzi | Cantatas (1650s)

Genre | Vocal
Performers | Susanne Rydén (soprano),
Ensemble Musica Fiorita
Year recorded | 1998
Label | Harmonia Mundi HMC 905249

The adopted, possibly illegitimate, daughter of a Venetian intellectual and opera librettist, Barbara Strozzi (1619–77) established herself as an important singer-composer, particularly among members of the Accademia degli Unisoni, founded by her father in 1637. In their meetings, her singing often provided an incentive for their academic debates—though the reason some members became interested in her may not have been entirely cerebral.

A pupil of Venetian opera composer Francesco Cavalli, Barbara Strozzi published eight collections of vocal music. However, her work may have been necessitated by the fact that she herself became the mother of illegitimate children and her financial needs became even more problematic after her father's death in 1652. The works range from multi-voiced madrigals (op. 1) and solo arias (op. 6 and op. 8) to sacred music (op. 5), yet it is her solo cantatas that nowadays form the center of our interest in her music. These cantatas are usually based upon a complex of various vocal styles such as recitative, arioso, and aria, and are written mainly for soprano. Although she never attempted to write a full-scale opera, some of Strozzi's cantatas indicate her abilities as a dramatic composer.

As well as providing an outstanding example in the tradition of female composers, Barbara Strozzi has also become something of an icon of Baroque music. Quite a few sopranos attempt her work, but Susanne Rydén's recording stands out, thanks mainly to her acute approach to the text, which is essential to the aesthetics of the repertoire. Yet, at the same time, she is successful in showcasing the coloratura that Strozzi used abundantly; her voice is agile, substantial, and supple enough to give sensual nuance. **NM**

> "... with the expression of her sweet canary voice ... she impresses upon us the luminosity of a dawn."
>
> Anonymous member of the Unisoni

Other Recommended Recordings

Judith Nelson, William Christie
Harmonia Mundi HMX 2901114
Particularly effective is the flowing line and well-judged tempo for "Su'l Rodano severo"

Primo libro de madrigali
La Venexiana
Cantus 9612
Balanced, stylistically articulated performance

Arias, op. 8
Emanuela Galli, La Risonanza • Fabio Bunizzoni
GLOS GCD 921503
A nicely balanced performance by the ensemble

A possible portrait of Barbara Strozzi by Bernardo Strozzi (no relation). ➲

Francesco Cavalli
La Calisto (1651)

Genre | Opera
Director | René Jacobs
Performers | Maria Bayo, Marcello Lippi
Year recorded | 1994
Label | Harmonia Mundi HMC 901515.17

Francesco Cavalli (1602–76) had already made a name for himself as singer and organist before he wrote more than thirty operas, mostly for Venice. This followed the opening of the first public opera theater there in 1637, with the all-too-familiar constraints of public funding. Singers were paramount, with instrumental accompaniment reduced to continuo with a couple of violins, while choruses were of solo singers not involved in the current action. The written music was often very skimpy, with much detail added by improvisation or fragmentary scribblings in the score.

René Jacobs approaches all this boldly, rejecting purist "authentic" minimalism and adding freely to Cavalli's skeletal score. His twenty instrumentalists create a rich, luscious sound in sinfonias and dances. If the result is partially guesswork, it is nonetheless a soundly researched and magnificent experience of what might have been.

The plot is highly fanciful, gods and human beings tangled in love, jealousy, and mistaken identity. Giove disguises himself as the goddess Diana, replacing his bass voice with falsetto (an amazing feat by Marcello Lippi); Dominique Visse creates a hilariously childlike young satyr. At this stage in the development of opera, it was the comic scenes that were the more tuneful, while much of the more serious action is carried out in recitative. But Jacobs cleverly binds this together with a lively underlying pulse that moves the action on and slips seamlessly into the short ariosos that often end scenes.

The production, staged in 1993, retains its subtlety of pacing in the later studio recording. Despite being shorn of its visual elements, it is thoroughly entertaining. **GP**

Heinrich Schütz
The Christmas Story (c.1660)

Genre | Choral
Conductor | Paul McCreesh
Performers | Gabrieli Consort & Players
Years recorded | 1998–99
Label | Archiv 463 046-2

Heinrich Schütz's two visits to Venice were at crucial moments in Italian musical development. From 1608 to 1612 he studied with Giovanni Gabrieli, absorbing the new "concertato" style with solo voices and instruments over a strong harmonic framework. He returned in 1628, acknowledging the influence of Monteverdi's dramatic style, especially "speaking in music" through recitative.

The music for this wonderfully vivid account of the nativity was virtually lost for about 250 years as Schütz published only the Evangelist's recitative. Arnold Schering discovered the choruses and the descriptive intermedii (interludes) in 1908; the opening chorus has only its figured bass line, the rest needing editorial reconstruction.

The Christmas story is told by the Evangelist (Charles Daniels) in a syllabic melodic line supported by simple continuo harmony. There are moments of great subtlety—Herod's "exceeding wrath" at discovering he had been mocked by the wise men; the anguished Old Testament prophesy of "Rachel weeping for her children" after Herod ordered the slaughter of all the children in Bethlehem. But the most striking delights are the eight intermedii: the choir of angels glorifying God, accompanied by violins; the shepherds sprinting to the stable with recorders and dulzian; pompous high priests with trombones and reed organ; Herod's cynical instructions to the Wise Men.

In this recording, Paul McCreesh puts *The Christmas Story* (incorporating the Boys' Choir, magnificent organ, and superbly drilled congregation of Roskilde Cathedral in Denmark) within the context of Christmas Day Vespers for the Dresden Chapel, where Schütz was chapel master. **GP**

Dietrich Buxtehude
Organ Music (*c.*1668–1707)

Genre | Instrumental
Instrument | Organ
Performer | Julia Brown
Year recorded | 2005
Label | Naxos 8.557555

Heinrich Ignaz Franz Biber
Mystery Sonatas (*c.*1674)

Genre | Chamber
Performers | Andrew Manze,
Richard Egarr, Alison McGillivray
Year recorded | 2003
Label | Harmonia Mundi HMU 907321.22

The Danish composer Dietrich Buxtehude was born in 1637. After his appointment in 1668 as organist of the Marienkirche in Lübeck, his fame and influence spread throughout Europe. His afternoon concerts attracted audiences from far and wide, including the young Bach, who walked from Arnstadt to hear and study with him. Buxtehude cultivated the so-called *stylus phantasticus*, a free, improvisatory style of composing and playing, marrying it with disciplined, tautly worked-out counterpoint. The toccata that ends Julia Brown's program is a good example: a series of contrasting sections, some like improvisations, but with two quite strict fugues.

Chorale-based pieces served as musings on well-known hymn tunes, reminding congregations of their familiar texts. Forty-seven such works by Buxtehude are currently extant, six played on this disc. Two are extended chorale fantasias in several sections, each based on the chorale. Others are simple preludes, often with a fugal opening foreshadowing the melody presented as a contrasting solo and dripping with ornaments.

This disc is the fifth of a promised Naxos collection of Buxtehude's complete organ works. All are excellent, but this one stands out for the instrument used, built by Martin Pasi for St. Cecilia Cathedral, Omaha, in 2003. It features both modern equal-temperament and meantone, a compromise in which some keys are wonderfully sonorous, while others take on often quite lurid tone-colors—the Praeludium, BuxWV 148, shows this up with startling vividness. Superbly played, this is an ideal introduction to Buxtehude's organ music. **GP**

The 300th anniversary of Biber's death in 2004 produced a spate of fine recordings reaffirming just what an extraordinary violinist and composer he was. These fifteen sonatas are grouped in three sets of five, reflecting on the life, death, and resurrection of Christ. An introductory epistle explains that ". . . the Four Strings of my Lyre You will find retuned in fifteen ways in various Sonatas, Preludes, Allemandes, Courentes, Sarabandes, Airs, Ciaconas, Variations etc. together with bass continuo. . . . "

The retuning of Biber's "lyre"—his violin—refers to the process of "scordatura" or unorthodox tuning of the instrument's strings. The "Joyful Mysteries" explore some sharpening from normal pitch, imparting a brightness to the violin sound with several chords ringing out on open strings. The most intense of the "Sorrowful Mysteries," "The Agony in the Garden," has A flat and E flat fighting G and D to create an astonishingly choked, painful quality, while "The Resurrection," the first of the "Glorious Mysteries," rings out in G major tuning—with the two middle strings switched around to portray a cross between the violin's bridge and tail-piece. The notation requires the violinist simply to place the fingers as if in normal tuning, so the music looks quite incomprehensible to the eye: one distinguished performer has admitted to writing in thick blue pencil at the top of his score, "Have Faith!"

Andrew Manze and Richard Egarr bring profound understanding to their performance of these amazing pieces, varying continuo colors from harpsichord to organ—and adding cello to one sonata. An inspired bonus is a track demonstrating scordatura. **GP**

Henry Purcell | Anthems (1676–94)

Genre | Choral
Director/Performers | Robert King;
Choir of New College, Oxford, The King's Consort
Years recorded | 1992–93
Label | Hyperion CDA 66663

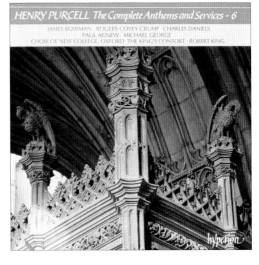

Charles II's restoration to the English monarchy in 1660 followed twenty years without church music; but the revival of earlier music was not to the King's taste—this "brisk & Airy Prince . . . was soon tyr'd with the Grave & solemn way, And Order'd the Composers of his Chappell to add symphonys &c. with Instruments to their Anthems." Purcell experienced this modern tradition when he joined the choir of the Chapel Royal, probably around 1667. He was appointed organist of Westminster Abbey in 1679, and in 1682 he also became an organist of the Chapel Royal.

Although he had a clear grasp of French music and the most modern Italian declamatory style, Purcell never visited continental Europe and his music has a strong English "accent"—startling dissonant clashes, unexpected harmonic progressions, and spiky rhythms.

Each disc in Hyperion's magnificent eleven-CD series reveals new delights, but this one includes first recordings of five major pieces, verse anthems—alternations of soloists and vocal ensembles on sacred texts—and devotional songs, often highly penitential in character. "Why Do the Heathen" opens with a string symphony, to be played by members of the King's twenty-four-piece string orchestra (the "four-and-twenty blackbirds" of the nursery rhyme). Its wistful harmony leads to a triple-time dance to set the King's feet tapping before a series of verses for various combinations of three singers. In remarkable contrast is the devotional song "Plung'd in the Confines of Despair," setting an almost self-indulgently doleful text with despairing chromatic continuo lines falling below solo voices as they enter in turn. This extraordinary music of immense variety, yet distinctively and gloriously from the pen of England's greatest composer. **GP**

"Confessedly the greatest Genius we ever had."

Thomas Tudway, friend and contemporary
of Henry Purcell

Other Recommended Recordings

Full Anthems & Organ Music, Music on the Death of Queen Mary • Oxford Camerata • Jeremy Summerly
Naxos 8.553129
Queen Mary's funeral music is intensely poignant

Music for Pleasure and Devotion
Taverner Consort, Choir & Players • Andrew Parrott
Virgin Veritas CDVB 5 62164 2 (2 CDs)
An ideal introductory selection

Evening Prayer
Chanticleer, Capriccio Stravagante • Joseph Jennings
Teldec 2564 60290-2
Includes the famous "Bell Anthem"

A nineteenth-century portrait of Henry Purcell after John Closterman. ❯

Henry Purcell
Chacony in G minor (c.1678)

Genre | Chamber
Director | Peter Holman
Performers | Parley of Instruments
Year recorded | 1987
Label | Hyperion CDH 55010

A *chaconne* uses the technique of variation to expand upon a short musical fragment. It is often on a ground bass, a fixed bass line repeated again and again below subtly altered melody, harmonic details, and rhythms. It began as a sixteenth-century Spanish dance, but its principle of varied repetition proved very popular during the Baroque era as a means of extending a piece of music.

No one was a greater master than Purcell at this art of subtle variation, his imagination seemingly fired by the self-imposed constraints. His chaconnes (or "chaconies") and grounds display an extraordinary level of invention. His most economical (from a "welcome song") is based initially on only two notes. Another has two recorders chasing each other through the same melody above a six-bar ground bass. Most well known is the heroine's "Lament" from *Dido and Aeneas*, the voice part phrased so independently of the repeated bass that the ear hardly notices the limitation at the music's core.

The familiar *Chacony in G minor* is set in eight-bar phrases, simple enough at the start although full of those momentary biting dissonances that set Purcell apart from his continental contemporaries. However, just as the bass line begins to seem immutable, it shifts up through each of the other three parts in turn and is later abandoned altogether for a strangely unbalanced fourteen measures—the predictable and the unexpected in perfect equilibrium.

Peter Holman makes a convincing case for using one violin, two violas, and cello with harpsichord, a rich, warm texture for this delightfully dance-like performance within a disc of Purcell's theater music. **GP**

Michel-Richard de Lalande
Grand Motets (1680–1700)

Genre | Choral
Conductor | William Christie
Performers | Les Arts Florissants
Year recorded | 1990
Label | Harmonia Mundi HMA 1951351

The overarching reputation of Lully in the first part of the French Baroque, and Rameau in the second, has meant that many fine reputations have been obscured. Charpentier has, over the last twenty years, come into his own in a host of fine recordings; his near contemporary Lalande is also at last much more than a name.

A first-rate keyboard player who was employed to teach royal princesses, Lalande came to dominate French sacred music in the early part of the eighteenth century. Although he composed music for instruments and the theater, he is best known for his seventy-seven grand motets. These large-scale vocal and choral works with orchestral accompaniment were composed for the Royal Chapel and Louis XIV who, in his later years, had a marked preference for Lalande's music and expressly ordered them to be preserved in court copies. The three representative works on this recording offer a generous conspectus of Lalande's genius. The last, *Confitebor tibi Domine* (1699) shows a richness in approach to harmony that comes close to Charpentier. The two earlier works are *Super flumina* (1687) and the 1684 setting of the Te Deum. This last is the very image of the court of Louis at prayer: alternately lyrical and magnificent, the inspiration in the work is near torrential.

Les Arts Florissants, with the musicians' marvelous feeling for ornamentation, bring a superb sense of ensemble to all their performances on this recording. The concerted voices have a burnished quality that suits the Te Deum setting in particular. As ever, their conductor William Christie has the knack of giving the music rhythmic swing without in any way trivializing it. **JS**

Henry Purcell
Fantasias (1680)

Genre | Chamber
Performers | Rose Consort
of Viols
Year recorded | 1995
Label | Naxos 8.553957

Despite his sadly brief life, from 1659 to 1695, Henry Purcell was the foremost English composer not only of his own time but arguably for the next two centuries. Although he incorporated into his music aspects of French and Italian style, he remained quintessentially English, above all in his piquant and adventurous harmony, nowhere more evident than in this extraordinary set of fifteen fantasias.

The fantasias are curiously retrospective in name and style, belonging to the past age of the Commonwealth with its ban on public performances. By the time Purcell wrote them in 1680, Charles II had introduced the latest French fashions, dances, violins, and lavish staged performances. The fantasias are for viols, use old-fashioned tempo instructions like "brisk" and "drag," and employ most subtle contrapuntal devices. On repeated listening, more and more becomes apparent—themes in imitation, upside-down, in longer or shorter notes, augmented and diminished. Three are in three parts, nine in four parts, and three more for five, six, and seven parts respectively. The last two use a fragment of a setting of the Latin *In nomine*, in long-held notes with such fluent counterpoint woven around that the flow sounds totally natural. The five-part fantasia is particularly bizarre, its tenor part on a single sustained note throughout—affording several non-string-playing musicians the pleasure of joining in the performance with polished professionals.

The Rose Consort of Viols does not let intellectual devices obscure the expressiveness and sense of sheer delight in *Fantasias*, and imitative entries are nicely pointed so that the counterpoint reveals itself to the listener. **GP**

John Blow
Venus and Adonis (c.1683)

Genre | Opera
Director | Philip Pickett
Performers | New London Consort
Year recorded | 1992
Label | Decca 473 713-2

John Blow was a child of the Restoration, one of the first choirboys in the Chapel Royal after England's return to monarchy. He was appointed organist of Westminster Abbey in 1668, made way for his pupil Purcell for sixteen years, then returned, and remained until his death in 1708.

Venus and Adonis is described as "A Masque for the entertainment of the King," but in fact it is an opera, the earliest English dramatic piece to be set wholly to music. The action could hardly be simpler: After a prologue, Venus encourages her lover, Adonis, to join in the hunt. While he is away, she and Cupid teach a group of little Cupids, including a hilarious spelling lesson. Finally Adonis returns, mortally wounded by a wild boar, and dies in Venus's arms.

Blow's genius is, in part at least, to imbue this flimsy plot with often profound and heartfelt music. The recitative is far from the perfunctory link between arias of later Baroque opera, but instead a subtle, flexible line slipping seamlessly in and out of lyrical arioso. Venus's plaint as she awaits Adonis's return is deeply moving, with daring dissonance between anguished voice and harmonic bass. The depth of feeling in the final chorus, "Mourn for Thy Servant," must have left its courtly audience deeply moved.

Excellent booklet notes explain some delightful ironies—for example, that Cupid, lecturing on marital fidelity, was sung by one of Charles II's many bastard offspring; that the spelling lesson imitates Blow's own duties teaching the royal choristers to read. Philip Pickett explains fully the rationale behind his choice and placing of instruments, contributing to a recorded sound of striking breadth and clarity. **GP**

Henry Purcell | Dido and Aeneas (1683 or 1689)

Genre | Opera
Conductor | Christopher Hogwood
Performers | Academy of Ancient Music and Chorus
Year recorded | 1992
Label | L'Oiseau-Lyre 475 7195

The 1689 libretto of *Dido and Aeneas* describes it as "An Opera Perform'd at Mr. Josias Priest's Boarding-School at Chelsey by young gentlewomen." The revelation, in 1992, that it was originally written for the court of Charles II six years earlier has had profound implications for its performance and staging. No longer is *Dido and Aeneas* a genteel enactment of a tragic Classical story by teenaged girls for an audience of parents and friends. Rather, it is a robust and passionate adult drama for professional voices, and these may well have been differently allocated: For instance, the role of Sorceress was probably intended for a bass, here a sneering, threatening David Thomas. Casting a male performer in a supposedly female part was a common contemporary convention.

Christopher Hogwood has restored several dances omitted from the first extant score with ingenious adaptations of neighboring pieces. His relatively large orchestral forces, twenty-five strings and generous continuo of archlute, guitars, theorbo, and harpsichords, would overstretch the capacity of most schools, but could well reflect the more generous resources of the court. He creates a fine sense of theatrical space and dramatic timing—and some terrifying sound effects.

Despite all the unanswered questions about its date and place of first performance, *Dido and Aeneas* is a deeply moving and powerful drama. Here, John Mark Ainsley is a fine Aeneas who, falsely summoned back home, drives Dido into a blind fury. Key to the whole opera is the casting of Dido herself—and no singer surpasses Catherine Bott's poignant acceptance of death in the famous "Lament," her heart broken at the loss of Aeneas, her deceived and unfaithful lover. **GP**

> *"Dido and Aeneas . . . is no exquisitely preserved art treasure; rather, it is a battered but noble torso."*
>
> Bruce Wood and Andrew Pinnock, on the evidence for redating *Dido and Aeneas*

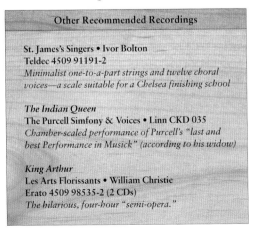

Other Recommended Recordings

St. James's Singers • Ivor Bolton
Teldec 4509 91191-2
Minimalist one-to-a-part strings and twelve choral voices—a scale suitable for a Chelsea finishing school

The Indian Queen
The Purcell Simfony & Voices • Linn CKD 035
Chamber-scaled performance of Purcell's "last and best Performance in Musick" (according to his widow)

King Arthur
Les Arts Florissants • William Christie
Erato 4509 98535-2 (2 CDs)
The hilarious, four-hour "semi-opera."

Dido and Aeneas as painted by Theodore van Thulden (1606–79). ➋

Jean-Baptiste Lully
Armide (1686)

Genre | Opera
Conductor | Philippe Herreweghe
Performers | Collegium Vocale
Year recorded | 1992
Label | Harmonia Mundi HMC 901456.57

Alessandro Scarlatti
Cantatas (1688–1720)

Genre | Vocal
Director | Robert King
Performers | The King's Consort
Year recorded | 1996
Label | Hyperion CDA 66875

An irony overshadows Lully's operatic career. Initially he had severe doubts about the viability of this Italian form winning favor among the French, but as soon as it became clear that opera would work in France, he tackled the genre with ruthless efficiency. By 1672 Lully had a monopoly over the composition and performance of opera, seen principally as the King's entertainment, in France.

Armide was the last of Lully's twelve full-scale operas, and one of the finest. In general, they follow a standard five-act structure with a prologue aimed at Louis XIV. His musical style can be on the bland side and he rarely approaches the harmonic richness of his much more talented contemporary, Charpentier, but there is a pervasive professionalism to his writing, and his melody is often enormously attractive. He could also provide music of color, notably in Isis, and excitement, as in Persée.

The subject matter of Lully's later operas abandoned Classical mythology for the Middle Ages and later. The plot of Armide is taken from Tasso's Gerusalemme liberata and tells the story of the fatal love of the eponymous sorceress. There is much opportunity for spectacular divertissement and the stage transformations beloved of French audiences, but unlike other of his operas, the closing scene does not see a triumph; instead the opera finishes with the destruction of Armide's palace.

Philippe Herreweghe's reading of the work (performed by the Collegium Vocale and Chapelle Royale Choir and Orchestra) is well paced and includes much fine solo work; he also shows considerable dramatic skill in dealing with the famous closing pages of the opera. **JS**

Alessandro Scarlatti (1660–1725) was extraordinarily prolific and widely performed in Italy during his lifetime. He wrote at least sixty-six operas and more than 600 chamber cantatas. They were intended for private performance, particularly in the Accademia dell'Arcadia, in Rome. The subject matter of the cantatas written for this sophisticated audience reflects the aims of the Accademia—to imitate in music and literature the simple rustic life and loves of Arcadian shepherds and nymphs. Despite their number, their conventional structure, and their almost constant subject matter, the cantatas reveal a fervid, seemingly inexhaustible imagination. Virtually every aria is distinctive, with memorable melodies and vivid descriptive responses to similes in the largely conventional and superficial texts. Many are for a single, high voice, accompanied only by continuo or strings. Often, strings enter only in the final ritornello, after the voice has finished, and other obbligato instruments are rare. Yet, for all their rarified emotion and subtly nuanced effects, they are very arresting, not least because of Scarlatti's fluency as a composer.

To date, barely a handful of this delightful repertoire is available on disc. Robert King's selection contrasts soprano and countertenor, and includes the now familiar "Su le sponde del Tebro," with Crispian Steele-Perkins's gloriously restrained natural trumpet matching the uncomplicated clarity of Deborah York's soprano. The disc includes the extended Christmas cantata "Oh di Betlemme altera povertà" for soprano, intended to delight the audience during a feast between the first Vespers of the Nativity and Midnight Mass on Christmas Eve. **GP**

Juan de Araujo
Dixit Dominus (c.1689)

Genre | Choral
Conductor | Jeffrey Skidmore
Performers | Ex Cathedra
Year recorded | 2004
Label | Hyperion SACDA 67524

On his disc entitled *Moon, Sun & All Things*, Jeffrey Skidmore presents some of the most staggering music to come from the Baroque era. He found it in Latin America, where, following the conquest, many Spanish composers went to work in churches and cathedrals, exporting the distinctive style of Iberia and fusing it with native culture, especially the vibrant rhythms of the Aztecs and Indians.

Juan de Araujo is arguably the greatest of the expatriate Europeans of the time. Born in 1646, he emigrated to Lima as a child and spent much of his working life at the cathedral in La Plata, Bolivia. His *Dixit Dominus* is for three solo voices and two full choirs doubled by strings, woodwind, and brass instruments. Evocative plainchant introduces the Psalm setting, which then bursts forth into wonderfully spacious dialogue between the three choirs.

The disc represents a Vespers service, with music by both Spanish and native Creole composers. Most exhilarating are the *villancicos*, described by contemporary commentators as "sacred entertainment for the masses." Here European melody and harmony and the wild, uninhibited rhythms of South America are combined in extraordinarily fanciful texts and music: one by de Salazar combines the nativity of Jesus with a bull fight; another, by Araujo again, exhorts the congregation to sing and dance—with every conceivable kind of exotic percussion to accompany them. The last track is pure magic, a mesmerically simple four-part setting of a Christian prayer, translated into the language of the Chiquitos Indians. Ex Cathedra performs it as a recessional, leaving one-by-one until the sound finally disappears. **GP**

Marc-Antoine Charpentier
Te Deum (1690s)

Genre | Choral
Conductor | William Christie
Performers | Les Arts Florissants
Year recorded | 1989
Label | Harmonia Mundi HMC 901298

Born in Paris in 1643, Charpentier was one of the greatest composers of the early French Baroque. For all his excellence, widely recognized at the time, he never held a court appointment under Louis XIV and was, for much of his career, overshadowed by the royal composer of choice, Jean-Baptiste Lully. Although he was prevented from composing full-scale operas during Lully's lifetime, he honed his dramatic skills with miniature musical dramas for the household of the noblewoman Madame de Guise. His experience bore operatic fruit after Lully's death with the remarkable *Tragédie lyrique*, *Médée*. Charpentier produced a vast amount of church music while working for a number of Jesuit foundations and in later life became master of music in the Sainte-Chapelle.

The Te Deum in D major (H146) with its infectious prelude is his most famous work. The sweep and imagination of the choral writing, including an almost Handelian concluding chorus, places it well beyond the scope of similar works by Lully. Interspersing the mostly celebratory choral writing are affecting and arresting solos, notably the reflective "Te ergo quaesumus" for soprano and the stirring "Judem crederis" for bass.

Of the many recordings available, none is completely satisfactory, but the best—for many reasons—is the one by William Christie and Les Arts Florissants. On the whole, this is a performance of enormous élan and vitality, much enhanced by the superb instrumental ensemble and committed, idiomatic solo singing. Christie's decision to preface the prelude with a timpani march by Philidor adds hugely to the sense of occasion. **JS**

Henry Purcell | The Fairy Queen (1692)

Genre | Opera
Conductor/Performers | Roger Norrington;
Schütz Choir of London, London Classical Players
Year recorded | 1999
Label | Virgin 7243 5 61955 2 3

Such is our reverence for Shakespeare today that it seems unthinkable that *A Midsummer Night's Dream* should be heavily adapted, with the introduction of new scenes set to music. The librettist is unknown, but Purcell composed extended interludes for each act, often with little or no relevance to Shakespeare's plot. Some of the interpolations derive from London society of the time; the drunken poet's scene cruelly satirizes the poet and playwright Thomas D'Urfey who was affected by a stammer. Elsewhere Purcell adds moving music to the night scene in Act 2, which includes an exquisite song and some delightfully delicate dance music as Oberon squeezes the magic juice on the eyes of the sleeping Titania. In contrast is the burlesque love-making of two foolish haymakers, Coridon, a tenor, and Mopsa, a bass in drag and a falsetto. London society's delight in the foreign and exotic is reflected in the setting of a Chinese garden of paradise in Act 5, with songs by a Chinese man and woman, and a dance by six monkeys. But the highlight of the whole semi-opera is "The Plaint," sung here by Lorraine Hunt, with dialoguing oboe over a haunting repeated ground-bass; it is a match for Purcell's most famous lament of all, at the end of *Dido and Aeneas*.

The forces in this recording are generous, aptly so as this was originally a lavish production. Purcell began composing the music in December 1691, but the performance was twice delayed, for the preparation of stage sets, costumes, and rehearsal, before its premiere in 1692. Roger Norrington's solo team of Hunt, Susan Bickley, Mark Padmore, and David Wilson-Johnson could hardly be bettered, and the recording sustains as much of the lively spirit of the original as is possible without the visual elements and spoken text. **GP**

> *"Shakespeare sublime in vain entic'd the Throng, Without the charm of Purcell's Syren Song."*
>
> From the eulogy on Purcell after his death in 1695

Other Recommended Recordings

The Scholars Baroque Ensemble
Naxos 8.550660/1 (2 CDs)
Small-scale forces but no less lively, at a bargain price

The Tempest
Aradia Baroque Ensemble • Kevin Mallon
Naxos 8.554262
Shakespeare play adapted and enhanced with music

Ayres for the Theatre
The Parley of Instruments • Peter Holman
Hyperion Helios CDH 55010
Instrumental suites from plays for which Purcell provided music, performed on period instruments

The Royal Opera famously staged *The Fairy Queen* in 1946. ➔

HENRY PURCELL

Sadler's Wells Ballet

Covent Garden Opera

THE FAIRY QUEEN.

AS PRESENTED AT THE
ROYAL OPERA HOUSE, COVENT GARDEN

A PHOTOGRAPHIC RECORD BY
EDWARD MANDINIAN
WITH ESSAYS BY
E. J. DENT, CONSTANT LAMBERT, & MICHAEL AYRTON

Henry Purcell | Come Ye Sons of Art, Away (1694)

Genre | Vocal
Conductor/Performers | Robert King;
Choir of New College, Oxford, The King's Consort
Year recorded | 1992
Label | Hyperion CDA 66598

There are twenty-four surviving odes and "welcome songs" by Purcell. Three honor the patron saint of music, St. Cecilia; nine are for welcoming ceremonies for royalty; six celebrate the birthday of Queen Mary, the popular consort of William III. The text of these odes was often banal and obsequious, and some are truly dreadful. Nahum Tate's celebration of the centenary of Trinity College Dublin includes: "After War's, Alarms repeated,/ And a Circling Age completed,/ Vig'rous Offspring thou dost raise;/ Such as to Juverna's praise;/ Shall Liffee make as proud a Name,/ as that of Isis or of Cam"—doggerel that Purcell's professionalism clothed in a charming echo duet for countertenors. However, Tate served Purcell well in this, his last birthday ode for Queen Mary, and the music is inspired and superbly crafted. The scoring is more expansive than normal with trumpets, oboes, and recorders with strings. Robert King argues the case for timpani, too, in the final chorus, an exhilarating climax to the ode.

Purcell's compositional technique provides some arresting moments: The opening song begins with countertenor singing a memorable theme that is then trumped by a glorious descant from sopranos when the choir enters. The countertenor duet "Sound the Trumpet" is justly familiar, the two voices alternating, then joining in joyous thirds above the bounding, rhythmic bass line—and concealing an in-joke: "list'ning shores" in the text is a pun on the Shores, trumpeters who notably did not "sound the trumpet" in this duet. "Bid the Virtues" is a wonderfully reflective duet, soprano imitated by oboe. For the opening and closing choruses, the Choir of New College, Oxford, surely matches anything the Chapel Royal choristers could have produced in the seventeenth century. **GP**

> *"Where the author's scanty words have fail'd, / Your happier grace, Purcell, have prevail'd."*
>
> Tom Brown, a contemporary poetaster

Other Recommended Recordings

Odes, including *Come, Ye Sons of Art*
Orchestra & Choir of the Age of Enlightenment
Gustav Leonhardt • Virgin 0777 7 59243 2 9
Polished performance with a mixed adult choir

Complete Odes and Welcome Songs, vol. 5
The King's Consort • Robert King
Hyperion CDA 66476
Smaller-scale pieces, recorded here for the first time

Odes for St. Cecilia's Day, Music for Queen Mary
Tavener Consort, Choir & Players • Andrew Parrott
Virgin 7243 5 61582 2 1 (2 CDs)
Chamber-scale performances, beautifully crafted

Antonio Caldara | Maddalena ai piedi di Cristo (c.1698)

Genre | Oratorio
Conductor | René Jacobs
Performers | Schola Cantorum Basiliensis Orchestra
Year recorded | 1996
Label | Harmonia Mundi HMC 905221.22 (2 CDs)

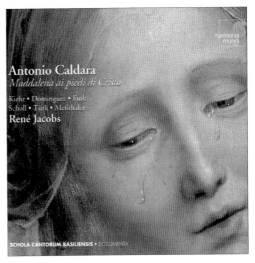

Antonio Caldara
Maddalena ai piedi di Cristo
Kiehr • Dominguez • Fink
Scholl • Türk • Melzhaler
René Jacobs

SCHOLA CANTORUM BASILIENSIS • DOCUMENTA

Though not exactly a household name, Antonio Caldara is a crucial figure in the history of music, noted chiefly as the first composer to set a substantial number of the so-called "reform" librettos of Apostolo Zeno and Pietro Metastasio. Caldara was also one of the most prolific composers of his generation, producing more than 3,000 works (mostly vocal), including forty-three oratorios. Serving first as maestro di cappella to the Duke of Mantua and later to Prince Ruspoli in Rome, he spent the last twenty years of his life at the Viennese court, where his output easily eclipsed that of his contemporaries.

Maddalena ai piedi di Cristo (*Magdalene at the Foot of the Cross*) is actually one of the earliest of Caldara's oratorios, written probably c.1698 when he was still working as a freelance musician in his native Venice. As the title suggests, the work deals with the penitent Mary Magdalene and portrays the mental turmoil of the sinner as she struggles between the forces of good and evil (represented allegorically by Amor Celeste and Amor Terreno), finally finding Christ's mercy when she decides to shun the path of pleasure and the "foolish vanity of the weaker sex," embracing the joys of celestial love.

The androgynous purity of Maria Cristina Kiehr's voice makes her the perfect choice for the role of Magdalene: her key arias are high points of the set. Andreas Scholl and Bernarda Fink are also strongly cast as Amor Celeste and Amor Terreno respectively, and the Schola Cantorum Basiliensis Orchestra under their conductor René Jacobs is bathed in the resonance of a generous acoustic. To hear this sensational recording for the first time is to submit to an experience as life-changing as that of the repentant Magdalene herself. **BM**

> *"Behind all of our efforts . . . lay the intention of producing the aura of sensual Venetian euphony."*
>
> René Jacobs

Other Recommended Recordings

La passione di Gesù Cristo signor nostro
Europa Galante • Fabio Biondi • Virgin 5 45325 2
Another of Caldara's forty-three oratorios

Handel: Dixit Dominus; Caldara: Missa dolorosa; Crucifixus • **Balthasar-Neumann Ensemble & Choir**
Thomas Hengelbrock
Deutsche Harmonia Mundi 82876 58792 2
A fine recording of Crucifixus & Missa dolorosa

Missa dolorosa; Stabat mater
Swiss-Italian Radio Chorus, Aura Musicale Ensemble
René Clemencic • Naxos 8.554715
More penitential music from Caldara's pen

The High Baroque was the era of Vivaldi, Handel, and J. S. Bach. Instrumental music was now as important as vocal genres had been in the Renaissance and was dominated by the suite and, above all, the concerto. Opera took further hold, especially in the many works of Handel, while religious music reached its peak in the cantatas, Mass, and Passions of Bach.

© Johann Sebastian Bach, *The Well-Tempered Clavier* manuscript (1742).

1700–1760

Arcangelo Corelli | Twelve Concerti Grossi, op. 6 (c.1700s)

Genre | Concerto
Performers | Brandenburg Consort
Director | Roy Goodman
Year recorded | 1992
Label | Hyperion CDD 22011 (2 CDs)

Corelli's influence lasted long after his death in 1713—Handel's set of twelve concerti grossi, for instance, also op. 6, are in imitation of and in homage to Corelli's. He lived and worked in Rome, as violinist, teacher, and composer—but exclusively of music for strings. Though "remarkable for the mildness of his temper and the modesty of his deportment," a contemporary witness of his playing wrote of "his countenance . . . distorted, his eyes . . . as red as fire, and his eyeballs [rolling] as if in an agony."

These twelve concertos are structurally backward-looking, in four or more movements rather than the later fast–slow–fast pattern of Vivaldi and Bach. They are also remarkably versatile, as the various recommended recordings show. As the three soloists always double orchestral strings, a trio alone can reproduce all the essential notes—melody and harmony. With a small orchestra, the effect is of differentiated dynamics and density rather than of virtuoso soloists pitted against the rest. Yet one contemporary gala performance reportedly sported more than eighty players, while a recording on the Tactus label adds recorders, trumpets, and oboes, in a fundamental reappraisal of these concertos.

The concertos include exuberant fast movements full of echo effects between small concertino and full ripieno, but also some breathtaking streams of unbroken harmony: in the opening of the "Christmas Concerto" no. 8, every cadence is foiled with a suspension, a harmonic twist or interruption until the very end.

Roy Goodman's Brandenburg Consort players, in a medium-scale performance, generate energetic allegros with spacious solo/tutti contrasts, and are finely poised in the endlessly spun slow harmonies. **GP**

> "The effect of the whole
> . . . [is] so majestic,
> solemn and sublime that
> they preclude all criticism."

Dr. Charles Burney on Corelli's concertos

Other Recommended Recordings

Ensemble 415
Chiara Banchini and Jesper Christensen
Harmonia Mundi HMX 2901406.07 (2 CDs)
Thirty-two strings, lavish continuo, in a gala-scale performance

Europa Galante
Fabio Biondi
Opus 111 OPS 30-147, OPS 30-155 (2 separate CDs)
Just ten strings, at the other end of the scale

Modo Antiquo • Federico Maria Sardelli
Tactus TC 650307-08 (2 CDs)
A real eye-opener with recorders, oboes, and trumpets

Arcangelo Corelli in a colorized image by John Smith after H. Howard. ➔

ARCANGELVS CORELLIVS.

Antonio Vivaldi | Gloria, RV 589 (1700s)

Genre | Choral
Conductor/Performers | Andrew Parrott; Emily van Evera,
Nancy Argenta, Margaret Cable, Taverner Consort
Year recorded | 1992
Label | Virgin 7 59326 2

Antonio Vivaldi's *Gloria* has been familiar to choral societies since its rediscovery in 1939. With the driving rhythms of its opening chorus, the lyrical charm of the "Laudamus te" duet, and the graceful oboe and soprano of "Domine Deus," it is among Vivaldi's most attractive and accessible sacred works.

The *Gloria* was written for the girls of the Pietà orphanage, yet the choruses are in four parts, the two lower ones sometimes specifically marked "tenore" and "basso." This raises the fascinating question of how they were actually performed. Some theorists have pointed out that mature teenage girls can develop exceptionally deep voices and, with Venetian pitch set higher than in most of the rest of Europe, it could all have been managed as written. An arguable alternative is to sing the "male" parts up an octave. Although this sometimes takes the rather unmelodic tenor part above the choral soprano line, the harmony emerges unscathed if it is doubled by instruments at the proper pitch, as the lower entries in "Cum Sancto Spiritu" show clearly. This is Andrew Parrott's solution. He also answers the inevitable question about why no contemporary commentators referred to this unique practice: they were hearing music new to them, with no score to hand, so assumed that it was notated purely for sopranos and altos.

The result is a refreshing lightness of texture, with excellent support from the Taverner Players. Parrott is well served by soloists: Emily van Evera and Nancy Argenta are well-matched in their "Laudamus te" duet; Margaret Cable's contralto is sustained and expressive, accompanied by a pensive cello, in "Domine Deus, Agnus Dei"; and a concerto-like soloist in the sprightly "Qui sedes." **GP**

> *"People come to Venice from all parts with the wish to refresh themselves with these angelic songs."*

Petr Andreevic Tolstoj, 1698

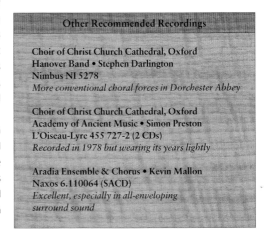

Other Recommended Recordings

Choir of Christ Church Cathedral, Oxford
Hanover Band • Stephen Darlington
Nimbus NI 5278
More conventional choral forces in Dorchester Abbey

Choir of Christ Church Cathedral, Oxford
Academy of Ancient Music • Simon Preston
L'Oiseau-Lyre 455 727-2 (2 CDs)
Recorded in 1978 but wearing its years lightly

Aradia Ensemble & Chorus • Kevin Mallon
Naxos 6.110064 (SACD)
Excellent, especially in all-enveloping surround sound

A caricature of Vivaldi by Pier Leone Ghezzi (1723). ➔

Il Svello noto compositor
di Musica insigne
L'opera a Cremonia del 1723

Johann Sebastian Bach
Preludes, Fantasias, Toccatas & Fugues (c.1705–48)

Genre | Instrumental
Instrument | Organ
Performer | Gerhard Weinberger
Year recorded | 2000
Label | CPO 999 754-2

Jean-Philippe Rameau
Pièces de clavecin (1706–47)

Genre | Instrumental
Instrument | Harpsichord
Performer | Christophe Rousset
Year recorded | 1989
Label | L'Oiseau-Lyre 425 886-2 (2 CDs)

Johann Sebastian Bach (1685–1750) was employed for most of his working life as a church musician and it is hardly surprising that his contribution to the organ repertoire is immensely significant. The bulk of it was composed during his time at Weimar, between 1708 and 1717, but he was still writing music for the organ until his final years. This impressive body of work divides neatly into two parts—works based on chorale tunes (chorale preludes and variations) and those that are musically independent (various combinations of preludes, fantasias, toccatas, and fugues). In the second category, his models were varied, drawing upon precedents in German, French, and Italian music, but the driving rhythms and concerto style of Vivaldi were very influential. Their dramatic, celebratory tone has made them prime candidates for later transcriptions for orchestra.

Many listeners will base their choices not only on the excellence of the particular performance but on the kind of instrument used. For the sweet-sounding organs of Bach's own time—various instruments around the Germanic lands—and for his always solid interpretations, Gerhard Weinberger is highly impressive in his cycle of the complete organ works on CPO. For a representative sample, try volume 8, played on the magnificently restored instrument in St. Martin's Church, Groningen, Holland, on which Weinberger concentrates on some of the toccatas (BWV 537, 538, 540, and 564) and fantasias (BWV 542, 537, 562, 563, and 570). **SP**

Although Rameau was primarily an organist, he left no music for the instrument. Instead, his keyboard music comprises three books for the solo harpsichord, some harpsichord pieces accompanied by violin (or flute) and viol, a couple of solos, and a handful of arrangements of music from the opera-ballet *Les Indes galantes*. Much of this music is notable for its rich combination of timbres, virtuoso effects, and innovative treatment of harmony.

Rameau's first collection of harpsichord music, published in 1706, looks backward to the seventeenth century, with a steady tread of familiar dances and a partly unmeasured, improvisatory prelude. But it also looks forward in its handling of instrumental color and technique. Rameau's later collections contain character pieces that include imitations of birds and theatrical entertainments as well as bold harmonic experiments, notably in "L'enharmonique" from the G minor Suite.

Christophe Rousset's recording of nearly all of Rameau's solo keyboard music is a magical combination of poise and virtuosity. Where the ornamentation in French Baroque harpsichord music can seem tiresome and overly artificial, in Rousset's interpretation it is not only integral but often adds a vital dimension to the overall articulation. Perhaps the most thrilling aspect of his playing, however, is his handling of rhythm—the inequalities, not actually written into the score but which are nevertheless crucial to the ebb and flow of the music, are superbly negotiated without any hint of artificiality. **JS**

Georg Philipp Telemann
Trumpet Concerto in D major (*c*.1708–14)

Genre | Concerto
Performer | Niklas Eklund (trumpet)
Conductor | Nils-Erik Sparf
Year recorded | 1995
Label | Naxos 8.553531

Antonio Vivaldi
Concerto for Two Trumpets (1711)

Genre | Concerto
Performers/Director | Mark Bennett,
Michael Harrison (trumpets); Trevor Pinnock
Year recorded | 1991
Label | DG 439 516-2

A prolific composer in all genres of music, Telemann wrote a large amount of diverse instrumental music, including about 125 concertos. This remarkable body of works showcases virtually a history of the concerto in Germany during the first half of the eighteenth century. Throughout this period the trumpet was a much-favored concert and ceremonial instrument, with virtuosic parts often intended for resplendent and lavish effect.

The Trumpet Concerto in D major, one of the finest in the instrument's repertoire, follows the four-movement form that Telemann favored for most of his concertos. A single trumpet also features in his famous *Tafelmusik* (1733). Although Telemann was considered one of the finest composers of his day by his contemporaries, his posthumous reputation has often suffered from criticism of his sheer fecundity: "in general, [Telemann] would have been greater had it not been so easy for him to write so unspeakably much. Polygraphs seldom produce masterpieces," wrote Hamburg professor Christoph Daniel Ebeling in 1770.

The recording by sweet-toned Baroque trumpet specialist Niklas Eklund appears on the first volume in Naxos's series "The Art of the Baroque Trumpet," which is a useful budget-price introduction to the golden age of the trumpet. It includes works for both trumpet and strings by Handel, Purcell, and Leopold Mozart, as well as those by the lesser-known Molter, Fasch, and Torelli, along with performances on period instruments. **DC**

Unique in Vivaldi's vast output of concertos, his spectacular C major Concerto for Two Trumpets, RV 537, remains one of his most famous, as shown by its inclusion alongside *The Four Seasons* in DG's *Mad About Vivaldi* collection. However, the composer did not pen a sequel, nor did he include a single trumpet in his multiple instrument concertos. This is slightly surprising, since the trumpet was a popular solo instrument in Italy.

At St. Petronio, Bologna, Giuseppe Torelli, Vivaldi's lesser-known compatriot, wrote more than thirty works for one to four solo trumpets, variously titled sinfonia, sonata, and concerto. His work played a major role in the development of the concerto, establishing the three-movement form, the solo versus ripieno duality, the thrusting triadic motifs, and the driving bass patterns that became the hallmarks of Vivaldi's style. It is likely, however, that Vivaldi felt that the trumpet's key limitations would restrict his adventurous ritornelli; in the double concerto he shows his characteristic ingenuity in solving the problem. This work also displays Vivaldi's predilection for self-borrowing—material for the short slow movement and the finale appeared originally in the Concerto for Strings, RV 110.

As members of major period-instrument orchestras in both the UK and abroad, trumpeters Mark Bennett and Michael Harrison are ideal performers for this work. *Mad About Vivaldi* is a fine introduction to the composer's most popular works. **DC**

Antonio Vivaldi | L'estro armonico (1711)

Genre | Concerto
Performers | Federico Guglielmo (violin),
Christopher Hogwood (harpsichord/director)
Year recorded | 2002
Label | Chandos CHAN 0689(2) (2 CDs)

Born in Venice in 1678, Antonio Vivaldi spent most of his working life there. He was ordained a priest, but was excused from saying Mass because of a chest condition. This did not inhibit his very active musical life as a violinist, composer, and teacher. He taught at the Pio Ospedale della Pietà, an orphanage for girls, many of whom learned music to a remarkably high standard. Vivaldi wrote more than 500 concertos, many of them for his talented pupils, and defined the formal structure that became the norm. Most of the concertos fall into three movements: fast–slow–fast, the first and last cast in ritornello form of an opening section for full orchestra, followed by alternating solo episodes and short "little returns" of parts of the opening material. Slow movements are often aria-like melodies of some passion.

The twelve concertos of L'estro armonico (roughly translating as The Musical Inspiration) became so influential because they were published in Amsterdam (1711) and were widely disseminated throughout Europe. Bach transcribed five of them for harpsichord and another for organ, learning his own craft from the exercise. The set is planned in four sub-sets— a concerto for four violins precedes another for two and then a solo concerto but, within this pattern, a major key is followed by minor until the end, where minor leads to up-beat major. The number of published part-books suggests that the concertos may be played one-to-a-part—at this stage, the energy, style, and structure of the music was enough to merit the term "concerto" without a soloist being pitted against a large orchestra. This is Christopher Hogwood's choice, creating vitality and glorious clarity in allegros, with warmly expressive slow movements. **GP**

> *"There is nothing more pleasing than . . . a pretty young nun . . . conducting the orchestra and beating time."*

Charles de Brosses, *Letters familières sur l'Italie*

Other Recommended Recordings

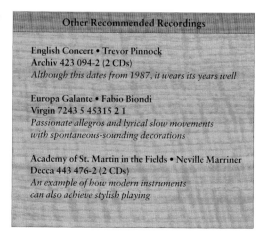

English Concert • Trevor Pinnock
Archiv 423 094-2 (2 CDs)
Although this dates from 1987, it wears its years well

Europa Galante • Fabio Biondi
Virgin 7243 5 45315 2 1
Passionate allegros and lyrical slow movements with spontaneous-sounding decorations

Academy of St. Martin in the Fields • Neville Marriner
Decca 443 476-2 (2 CDs)
An example of how modern instruments can also achieve stylish playing

Christopher Hogwood combines academic rigor with musical values. ➲

Antonio Vivaldi | Stabat mater (1712)

Genre | Vocal
Director | Robert King
Performers | Robin Blaze, The King's Consort
Year recorded | 1998
Label | Hyperion CDA 66799

The *Stabat mater* was one of Vivaldi's first sacred compositions, written for the patronal festival of the church of Santa Maria della Pace in Brescia, which he had visited first as a traveling violinist in 1711. So, unlike the sacred music for the girls of the Pietà in Venice, this was for male voice—castrato or falsetto. As its text is liturgical, it cannot be altered, except that a truncated version was used for Friday Vespers after Holy Week. This allowed Vivaldi to set only nine of the eighteen verses. It therefore achieves more consistency and expansiveness than works by, for example, Alessandro Scarlatti, who sets all eighteen verses in a fast-moving sequence of rather fragmented numbers. Vivaldi also repeated the music for the first three sections, adding more cohesion.

Despite his relative inexperience at writing in this genre, Vivaldi uses powerful musical rhetoric in response to details in the text. Some are quasi-visual: "pendebat" (hung) evokes an agonized falling chromatic figure. The second movement opens with sustained, unexpected harmonies, like an operatic scena, then illustrates Mary's sorrowing soul with passionate gasps from staccato strings. Similar descriptive patterns heighten the opening of the final three stanzas, "Eja mater."

Robin Blaze brings a strong but unexaggerated sense of sincerity to his singing. His voice recalls an Alfred Deller characteristic—a tiny upward swoop to the placing of notes that, discreetly used, is an attractive coloring of his tone. Robert King has thought deeply about the subtleties of phrasing and articulation and his strings add passion and technical finesse. The disc, the fifth of Hyperion's "Complete Vivaldi Sacred Music" series, includes five more gems for solo voices. **GP**

"[Tempi are] prescient of Haydn's Seven Last Words or Shostakovich's String Quartet no. 15."

Michael Talbot, program note

Other Recommended Recordings

Andreas Scholl, Ensemble 415 • Chiara Banchini
Harmonia Mundi HMC 901571
Scholl's clean, even vocal control and the clarity of his articulation make this a highly acclaimed option

James Bowman, Academy of Ancient Music
Christopher Hogwood
L'Oiseau-Lyre 414 329-2
Great artistry from Bowman in this recording

Marion Newman, Aradia Ensemble • Kevin Mallon
Naxos 8.557852
A striking display of how a female contralto contrasts tonally with the countertenors of other recordings

Santa Maria della Pace, where the *Stabat mater* was first heard. ➔

François Couperin
Twenty-seven Ordres (1713–30)

Genre | Instrumental
Instrument | Harpsichord
Performer | Scott Ross
Years recorded | 1980s
Label | STIL 0207 SAN 78 (12 CDs)

Johann Sebastian Bach
Orgelbüchlein (1715–c.1740)

Genre | Instrumental
Instrument | Joachim Wagner organ
Performer | Gerhard Weinberger
Year recorded | 1999
Label | CPO 999 652-2 (1), 999 653-2 (2)

François Couperin, born in Paris in 1668, was not a prolific composer by the standards of his time, but his legacy of two organ Masses, three Leçons de ténèbres, instrumental chamber music and, above all, his solo harpsichord music testify to a fastidiousness of detail.

Couperin's Ordres—a term that he used to denote groups of pieces in related keys, falling somewhere between a suite and an anthology—represent his most sustained achievement and must be regarded as among the harpsichordist's greatest challenges. Not only must he or she observe Couperin's detailed instructions, but also confront and interpret the enigmas, abstractions, and metaphors contained in so many of the pieces.

Only nine harpsichordists in more than half a century of commercial recording have completed Couperin's keyboard odyssey, and of these it is Scott Ross who most consistently reached the heart of Couperin's elusive musical idiom. Ross, who died in 1989, had an impeccable technique and an ability to accommodate Couperin's subtly colored images with playing that can be as majestic or as delicate as the subject requires. His feeling for noble statements allows the B minor "Passacaille" (Ordre no. 8), to unfold with supple grandeur, while in character pieces like "L'arlequine" (Ordre no. 23) he enlivens with irresistible charm the angular gestures implicit in Couperin's evocation of commedia dell'arte. Ross, in his scrupulous observance of Couperin's intricate ornaments, and in his realization both of grand design and transparent filigree, allows each and every one of these pieces to spring to life. **NA**

It is not known exactly when Bach composed each of the chorale preludes of the Orgelbüchlein (Little Organ Book), but most were probably written between 1713 and 1715, during Bach's tenure at Weimar. It is also highly likely that some works were written in the pre-Weimar period, but taken from stock, as it were, and revised to fit the new purpose. Bach's intention was that there should have been far more than forty-five pieces—the carefully pre-prepared index survives, showing that the Orgelbüchlein was planned to contain 164 chorale preludes. It seems likely that Bach set the project aside when he moved to Cöthen and his priorities shifted.

The chorale preludes of the Orgelbüchlein are essentially miniatures, each of which is a meditation on the spiritual significance of the Lutheran chorale tune at its heart. It functions also as a sort of instruction manual, both in organ playing and in compositional technique. Bach's resourcefulness is astounding: Each time he succeeds in finding the right form and figurations necessary for achieving an apposite mood, whether in the eloquent simplicity of the supplicatory "Ich ruf zu dir" or in the joyful New Year piece "In dir ist Freude," with its subtly insistent pedal motif.

Gerhard Weinberger's unhurried account, revealing rich inner detail, is played on the magnificent Joachim Wagner organ in the Nidaros Cathedral in Trondheim, Norway, and the Nicolaus Seeber organ at St. Johannes, Thuringen, and is spread over two discs. The second disc also includes the nine Chorale Partitas, BWV 767, the ten Chorale Partitas, BWV 770, and other works. **SP**

Antonio Vivaldi
Juditha triumphans (1716)

Genre | Oratorio
Conductor/Performers | Robert King;
Ann Murray, Susan Bickley, The King's Consort
Year recorded | 1997
Label | Hyperion CDA 67281/2 (2 CDs)

This is Vivaldi's only surviving oratorio and is a truly astonishing work. It was written for the girls' orphanage where Vivaldi taught, and would have been performed from behind screens in the galleries (visible to this day in the Venetian church of the Pietà). There is nothing hidden in the evocative music, however. The libretto by Giacomo Cassetti creates an imaginary stage on which the drama is acted out as characters enter, sit, are led from place to place, and fall asleep. But it is in the color of Vivaldi's instrumentation—a kaleidoscope of exotic sounds—that sets this unique drama apart. The girls of the Ospedale were gifted in every instrument, and Vivaldi made full use of their talents: this work features the chalumeau (an early relation of the clarinet with a husky, haunting quality); the short-toned mandolin with pizzicato strings, used to accompany an aria on the transience of life; oboe and organ in duet; and a pair of recorders to induce sleep. Strangest of all is a contemplative aria in which the voice is masked in the misty sound of violas d'amore and violins with lead mutes.

Since no men were permitted behind the screens of the Pietà, the cast is all female, although this is no more than a reflection of the preponderance of female voices in secular opera, where women would take on "trouser roles" if castrati were not available. Ann Murray is Judith, the leader of the Judeans, beautiful but ruthless, who decapitates her captor, Holofernes, with a sword. Maria Cristina Kiehr and Susan Bickley are both outstanding, while the nineteen-voice choir is alertly involved in the action—altogether a magnificent achievement. **GP**

George Frideric Handel
Water Music (1717)

Genre | Orchestral
Conductor | John Eliot Gardiner
Performers | English Baroque Soloists
Year recorded | 1991
Label | Philips 464 706-2

Handel was above all a theater composer, learning his craft first in his native Germany, then in Italy during an influential three years from 1706 until 1709. He moved to London, composing first around forty operas and then, when fashions and demands changed, some twenty-five oratorios. The story that the *Water Music* was a peace offering to King George I, whose employ Handel had left in Hanover, is probably untrue, but certainly the music that accompanied him up the River Thames and back in July 1717 was very well received. It was reportedly played by up to fifty musicians on a barge, a scale probably necessitated by the open-air acoustic and the noisy activity on the river for such an occasion.

Differences between Handel's manuscripts and early editions, suggest that the movements of the *Water Music* were not precisely ordered. They are normally collated into three Suites: one is in F major, incorporating French horns, and another in D major, a key suiting trumpets. The third, in G major, with quieter flutes and recorders, seems more appropriate for indoor performance.

The music of this Italian-trained German living in England is heavily influenced by France, with a Lully-inspired "ouverture" followed by a series of elegant airs and dances, several of them with French titles.

John Eliot Gardiner and the English Baroque Soloists field about ten fewer players than Handel's reported band, but they create a bold outdoor effect with brazen horns and sparkling trumpets. It is a fine, stirring sound, with pretty lively tempi—as research suggests they should be. A performance to delight a king. **GP**

Marin Marais | Pièces de viole, quatrième livre (1717)

Genre | Chamber
Performers | Christophe Coin, Christophe Rousset,
Vittorio Ghielmi, Pascal Monteilhet
Year recorded | 1996
Label | L'Oiseau-Lyre 458 144-2

Marin Marais was born in Paris in 1656. The son of a shoemaker, he became one of the most important musicians in the court of Louis XIV. He learned composition from Lully, the central musical figure in the court, and was much valued as a composer of opera—most famously *Alcyone* (1706)—and church music. But it was as a virtuoso on and composer for the bass viol that he is best remembered. As a student of the viol he eclipsed his teacher, the distinguished composer and performer Sainte-Colombe, in a matter of a few months. Unfortunately, the rising star of a younger viol virtuoso, Antoine Forqueray, and the failure of his opera *Semele* prompted Marais's early retirement some twenty years before his death in 1728.

Like his near contemporary, François Couperin, Marais was a consummate miniaturist and wrote nearly 600 pieces for the viol, many with alluringly descriptive designations, such as *Le labyrinthe* and *Allemande "la bizarre,"* and familiar dance types such as courante, sarabande, and gigue. Marais's highly expressive melodic style is tempered by a strong sense of rhythmic line, often spiced by a piquant approach to harmony.

Performing this highly colored music successfully requires not only a thorough knowledge of the exhaustive stylistic requirements of the mid-French Baroque, but a command of rhetoric, at times approaching the dramatic. Luckily, the soloist Christophe Coin possesses these qualities in abundance, as well as an unrivaled ability to negotiate the timbral complexities of Marais's chordal writing. His accompanying team, including Louis XIV's favored guitar, is also entirely in sympathy with Marais's richly allusive writing. **JS**

> "*. . . an incomparable Parisian viol player whose works are known all over Europe.*"
>
> Johann Gottfried Walther, 1732

Other Recommended Recordings

Alcyone—suites
Le Concert des Nations • Jordi Savall
Astrée Naïve ES 9945
A superb performance of instrumental music by Marais

Tous les matins du monde
Le Concert des Nations • Jordi Savall and soloists
Alia Vox AV 9821
Also contains music by François Couperin and Lully

Alcyone
Le Concert des Nations • Jordi Savall
Astrée Naïve ES 9908
Excerpts from Marais's five-act opera

The Viola da Gamba Player by Gerrit van Honthorst, c.1630. ➔

Johann Sebastian Bach
Violin Concertos
(1717–23)

Genre | Concerto
Performers | Simon Standage (violin),
Collegium Musicum 90
Year recorded | 1996
Label | Chandos CHAN 0594

Johann Sebastian Bach
Concerto for
Two Violins (1717–23)

Genre | Concerto
Performers | Hilary Hahn, Margaret Batjer
Director | Jeffrey Kahane
Year recorded | 2002
Label | DG 474 199-2

Although Bach's autograph scores of these concertos are lost, they are thought to have been written at Cöthen (1717–23), perhaps for the leader of the court orchestra, Joseph Spiess. In both works Bach adopted the three-movement formal layout, the basic alternating pattern of solo and tutti episodes, and the harmonic concept of Venetian and especially Vivaldian models. The A minor Concerto, BWV 1041, adheres more closely to Vivaldi than the other, yet the manner in which he treats the solo episodes transcends his contemporaries' technique. An unusual feature of the E major Concerto, BWV 1042, lies in its dance-like finale whose rondo scheme is of a kind seldom found elsewhere in Bach's music.

The well-trodden territory occupied by these concertos makes a choice difficult. A notable virtue of Simon Standage's recording lies in his chamber music approach, which allows us to listen to performances of unusual intimacy. This is highly effective in the slow movements, where his lightly bowed solo playing creates an atmosphere charged with poetic sentiment. Sometimes his intonation is just short of perfection but such moments never dilute his sensitive musicianship. A further strength of the playing lies in Standage's sense of just tempo, in which extremes in either direction are commendably absent. Perhaps occasionally we may feel the need for more robust vitality, but if there has been any sacrifice in this area it is always in the interests of lightly articulated and politely declaimed dialogue. **NA**

Bach's violin concertos are generally considered to date from the mainly happy period that he spent as Kapellmeister at Cöthen (1717–23). Earlier, at Weimar (1708–17), Bach had encountered and closely studied Italian concertos of the time, especially those of Vivaldi. In the present work though, the fugal and canonic devices, as well as the dialogue and imitative ideas of the solo parts, bear closer affinity with the Roman concerto grosso style of Corelli.

Performances of this—perhaps the best known and loved of all Bach's concertos—stand or fall by the treatment of the lyrically sustained Largo. In this sublimely poetic music, the song-like melody for the two violins lies above a gentle accompaniment and develops so engagingly that complexities in the writing are easily overlooked. It is in this movement, above all, that Hilary Hahn and her partner Margaret Batjer steal a march on most of their rivals. This is playing that, at every turn, reveals the intricacy and lyricism of Bach's writing. The sheer energy that Hahn brings to the third movement finale is hugely invigorating and it would be difficult to cite any other performance so fervently concentrated and committed as this one. What could so easily become an unseemly scramble maintains throughout a linear clarity and intellectual rigor that does the music full justice. Above all, perhaps, Hahn seems to have an intuitive feeling for gracefully contoured phrasing, and this conjunction of vigor and gentleness is outstandingly effective. **NA**

Johann Sebastian Bach
Orchestral Suites
(*c.*1717–*c.*1742)

Genre | Orchestral
Director/Performers | Ton Koopman;
Amsterdam Baroque Orchestra
Year recorded | 1988
Label | DHM RD77864 (2 CDs)

Bach's four orchestral suites adhere to a form developed in France by Lully during the seventeenth century. After Lully's death, his pupils and disciples cultivated and disseminated the French ouverture, with its appended suite of dances, while adding much of their own. The form was brought to its stylistic apogee by Bach, Handel, and Telemann. Although Bach's Orchestral Suites elude precise dating, it seems likely that most of the music belongs to his Leipzig years (post 1723). In its scoring for oboes, bassoon, and strings the Suite no. 1 in C major more closely resembles its French antecedents than the remaining three. Suite no. 2 in B minor is scored for flute and strings and is perhaps the latest in order of composition.

Ton Koopman and the Amsterdam Baroque Orchestra capture vividly the contrasting colors and textures of the music. Koopman is seldom lacking in demonstrative gestures, elegantly poised with some and ceremoniously grandiose with others; both ends of the spectrum have their place in these richly varied works. One of the greatest attractions, however, is the solo Baroque flute playing of Wilbert Hazelzet in the B minor Suite. Here is an artist of rare sensibility whose lovingly articulated phrasing and warm, rounded tone is an enduring delight. The resonant timpani and crackling trumpets in the D major Suites send blood coursing through the veins, while Koopman himself complements the playing at every turn with characteristically brilliant keyboard, if at times overly busy, continuo realizations. **NA**

Johann Sebastian Bach
Six Suites for Solo Cello (*c.*1720)

Genre | Instrumental
Instrument | 1711 Tecchler cello
Performer | Torleif Thedéen
Years recorded | 1995–96
Label | BIS CD-803/804 (2 CDs)

In his Suites for Solo Cello, Bach provided cellists with their ultimate raison d'être, their musical bible. It was the boy cellist Pablo Casals who, coming upon an old copy in a Barcelona shop in 1889 first acknowledged their greatness as complete works, to be played whole. "They had been considered academic works, mechanical, without warmth. How could anyone think of them as being cold, when a whole radiance of space and poetry pours forth from them!" he wrote. In his fantastical preludes and allemandes, swift courantes, rustic gigues, graceful minuets, and grave sarabandes, Bach explored all the myriad colors of the instrument and harmonic possibilities of his six chosen keys from the life-affirming second Suite in C major, to the introverted melancholy of the fifth in C minor, for which the player must tune the top string down a tone, to the crowning radiance of the final Suite in D major, written for a five-stringed cello and described by Rostropovich as "a symphony."

These six cello suites are works of great invention and beauty that can bear a number of interpretations. On the whole, recordings tend to fall into two categories: those performed with a modern cello, which treat the set as a powerful, virtuosic tour de force, and those performed with the Baroque set-up and bow, which focus on the qualities of the actual dances, and tend to be lighter and drier. The Swedish cellist Torlief Thedéen achieves an ideal balance in his performances, combining a vibrant tone with vivacious articulation. **HW**

Johann Sebastian Bach
Sonatas & Partitas for Solo Violin (1720)

Genre | Instrumental
Instrument | 1739 Pesarinius Baroque violin
Performer | Rachel Podger
Years recorded | 1998, 1999
Label | Channel CCS 12198/14498 (2 separate CDs)

Although Bach's sonatas and partitas are not unique—others had written for unaccompanied violin before—they are outstanding for their complexity, making them arguably the supreme achievement of the violin repertoire. Three four-movement sonatas all begin with a rhapsodic slow movement recalling the improvisatory "stylus phantasticus" of German organists. There follows a fugue, again ostensibly more apt for organ than for violin. Bach sustains the implication of quite complex counterpoint by multiple-stopping (on two or more strings) or by creating lines that produce their own harmony and imply two parts. They alternate with three partitas, suites of dances sometimes demanding up to four-part chords and including the familiar and highly virtuosic chaconne that ends the D minor Suite.

To manage all this on a single violin is remarkable. A violin of Bach's time, with flatter bridge and gut strings, proves a revelation. A short bow, flat rather than concave, encourages building phrases from brief motifs rather than extended, sustained melody. A bowing-arm raised less than nowadays contributes to the tonal scale being smaller, but once the ear has adjusted, the passion can be no less intense.

Rachel Podger is a fine technician and a most sensitive musician. Her intonation is superb throughout the complexities of line and richness of chords. The concerto-like opening movement of the third Partita is breathtaking, her sense of dance is delightfully light-footed, while contemplative movements like the very opening of Sonata I have an almost timeless quality. **GP**

"[One] never feels the same way on two given days; there is always more to discover."

Rachel Podger, on playing Bach

Other Recommended Recordings

Sigiswald Kuijken
DHM 05472 77527 2 (2 CDs)
*Resonant acoustic binds the lines together
into rich harmony*

Rudolf Gähler
Arte Nova 74321 67501 2 (2 CDs)
*Played with (almost certainly unauthentic) curved
bow, but revealing the implied counterpoint amazingly*

Yehudi Menuhin
Naxos 8.1109018, 8.110964
*The first-ever complete recording from 1934–36,
admirably transferred to CD*

Rachel Podger, one of today's most acclaimed early music violinists. ➲

George Frideric Handel
Keyboard Suites (1720, 1733)

Genre | Instrumental
Performer | Sophie Yates
Year recorded | 1998
Label | Chandos CHAN 0644, 0669, 0688
(3 separate CDs)

Johann Sebastian Bach
Brandenburg Concertos (1721)

Genre | Concerto
Performers | Hanover Band
Director | Anthony Halstead
Years recorded | 1991–92
Label | EMI 7243 5 86043 2 0 (2 CDs)

Handel assembled his first published set of suites to protect himself from "surrepticious [sic] and incorrect copies of them," probably pirated by an Amsterdam publisher. Significantly, he gave them a French title— "Suites de pièces pour le clavecin"—and most of their dance movements are in an elegant French style. Some of the preludes, too, have a specific French character, being notated in long-note chords intended to be expanded and decorated ad-lib by the performer—the opening suites of each set begin in this dramatic way.

Choosing a recording is as much a matter of selecting the instrument as the performer. Harpsichords vary greatly, by size, by country of origin, and by date as they grew in sonority and compass during the seventeenth and eighteenth centuries. Recording techniques are particularly telling: too close and their harsh transient sounds are emphasized; too far, and clarity of articulation gets lost in the ambient space.

Sophie Yates is well served by a modern copy of a quite early harpsichord, built in 1624 by a member of the Ruckers family in Antwerp. The instrument has a distinctive, slightly nasal tone that Yates sustains with great warmth where the occasion demands. Her performance is also excellent, achieving a greater range of expression than is shown by most other recordings. Her interpretation of the opening Adagio of the F sharp minor Suite is full of thoughtful rhetoric—and bitingly sharp E sharps in this relatively remote key—while she pulls off fast movements with great verve, but with such polished technique that they never sound unduly hurried. **GP**

The orchestral cornerstone of Bach's music is the collection of six concertos that he dedicated to the Margrave of Brandenburg in 1721. It is perhaps the most brilliantly diverse instrumental anthology ever assembled. No two concertos are scored for the same combination of instruments and the consequent range of color was almost without precedent. This rich variety, together with evolving issues of style and performance practice, has produced a wide conspectus of interpretation, and there are few remaining complete recordings that have not found their way onto CD.

Choosing an ideal recording of all six concertos is difficult, particularly in view of the widely disparate approach to instrumentation. Who would readily sacrifice the piano playing of Rudolf Serkin (Adolf Busch, 1936) or Kathleen Long (Boyd Neel, 1946) in the Fifth Concerto just because they were playing an instrument unknown to Bach? Yet nowadays a recording with period instruments is likely to afford more consistent and more evenly spread pleasure. Taking such considerations into account, this set has attractive credentials. Anthony Halstead is a talented musician who not only directs the performances but also plays the first horn part in Brandenburg Concerto no. 1, the solo harpsichord part in the Fifth Concerto, and the harpsichord continuo in all but the First Concerto. These are unflashy performances where an atmosphere of concentrated chamber music reigns. Tempi are effective, the ensemble is well-balanced, and each concerto is declaimed with the unhurried and articulately phrased syntax of elevated conversation. **NA**

Johann Sebastian Bach
Magnificat (1723)

Genre | Choral
Conductor | Philippe Herreweghe
Performers | Collegium Vocale Gent
Year recorded | 2002
Label | Harmonia Mundi HMC 901781.82

When Bach was installed as Kantor of Leipzig in 1723, after almost a year of wrangling, he hit the ground running. A stream of masterpieces ensued, with a hit-rate comparable only to the eighteen-year-old Schubert's *annus mirabilis* of songs and symphonies. They are crowned by the Magnificat he wrote for his first Christmas there. The twelve movements of the Latin text are spread over 600 measures: compare that with the 126 measures occupied by the opening Kyrie of the B minor Mass. There are only twelve or so minutes of choral singing, but they are some of the most demanding in his output, as though he wanted to show off the full capabilities of his freshly disciplined choir and instrumentalists. Combinations are whirled in festive bursts of color, with solos allowing brief respite from the pervasive choral exuberance—most memorably in the Italianate duo "Et Misericordia"— and no recitative to hold up the action.

Acceding to local tradition, Bach interpolated the Marian hymn with four "songs of praise" written for another orchestra and choir in antiphony. Several years later he removed these and altered the key from E flat to the more spectacular D. That is the version most widely known, but the interpolations deserve their turn in the sun, so Philippe Herreweghe's recording on this 2-CD set has even more to offer than its crack choir and ravishing solo contributions (especially soprano Carolyn Sampson). There's little sense of the strain that gives older recordings of the D major version their own excitement, but Herreweghe more than compensates with pacing that brings each twist of Bach's kaleidoscopic vision into focus. **PQ**

Johann Sebastian Bach
Great Cantatas (1723–29)

Genre | Choral
Conductor | Philippe Herreweghe
Performers | Collegium Vocale Gent
Year recorded | 2003
Label | Harmonia Mundi HMC 901843

Bach was involved in the composition, reworking, and performance of cantatas throughout almost all his musical life. Some have certainly been lost and the 200 or so surviving pieces seem a modest quantity beside the prodigious output of his contemporary, Telemann. Most of Bach's cantatas, however, are more substantial and of a transcendent beauty. Between 1723 and 1729, a period of creative fertility, Bach composed the main body of his surviving cantatas as part of his duties in providing music for the Lepzig Thomaskirche.

Extensive anthologies have been compiled by Karl Richter, Fritz Werner, Hans-Joachim Rotzsch, and Philippe Herreweghe, but it is Herreweghe's ongoing project that is, perhaps, the most consistently rewarding. He achieves a rapprochement between traditional values and those that are shaping historically based performances. His sixteen-voice choir is fresh-sounding and well rehearsed and his solo groups comparably accomplished, especially in more recent volumes. These virtues and others, too, are abundantly present in a recording of cantatas for Easter (BWV 12), and Trinity (BWV 38 and 75). While Herreweghe's emphasis is on the elegant shaping of phrases rather than on forceful textual declamation, these performances reveal rewarding insights to Bach's music. There are winning contributions from Carolyn Sampson in the soprano aria with oboe d'amore from BWV 75; Daniel Taylor whose alto aria in BWV 12 is complemented by Marcel Ponseele's sensitive oboe; and Mark Padmore whose tenor arias in BWV 38 and 75 are declaimed with eloquent restraint. **NA**

Johann Sebastian Bach | St. John Passion (1724)

Genre | Oratorio
Conductor | John Eliot Gardiner
Performers | Anthony Rolfe Johnson, Andreas Schmidt
Year recorded | 1986
Label | Archiv 469 769-2 (2 CDs)

There is a thesis to be written on what the changing fortunes of the *St. John* and *St. Matthew Passions* say about the temper of the times. The nineteenth century saw very few performances of the work, with audiences scarcely knowing what to make of it, while now the generous, epic scale of the *St. Matthew* compels modern audiences less than the arresting immediacy of its older cousin.

The opening of the *St. John* chorus cross-cuts between stabbing pleas for mercy and relentless counterpoint, continually intensified by a roiling bass line. This could be the soundtrack to a CNN story on the world's dispossessed: indeed, several opera directors have taken what they see as a natural step forward and given the Passion a full-blown staging. Characters are drawn with deft sketches: Peter denies Christ with shocking swiftness—even ease—and the impact is felt only afterward in the cruel tenor aria that ends Part 1, "Ach mein Sinn." The structure pivots not on an aria but on the confrontation between Christ and Pilate, as the governor ponders, "What is truth?" Only then does the pace begin to unwind in a series of increasingly frequent meditations that put the narrative on pause and culminate in the soprano's aria, "Zerfliesse, mein Herze."

A driven temperament and quite modern sensibility seem to be prerequisites for memorable recordings of the *St. John*, and, in this respect, John Eliot Gardiner is admirably fitted for the task. His 1986 recording set a gold standard for textural clarity and choral discipline that eluded many contemporary discs of early music, whatever their claims to "authenticity." Sometimes the lack of ornamentation appears quaintly traditional, but it reflects the bare, even savage energy that belongs to the work as much as the recording. **PQ**

"A perfect example of the gestural character of music."

Bertholt Brecht on the first recitative

Other Recommended Recordings

English Chamber Orchestra • Benjamin Britten
Decca 443 859-2 (2 CDs)
A one-off, in English, driven in every quarter,
with Peter Pears a searing Evangelist

Collegium Vocale Gent • Philippe Herreweghe
Harmonia Mundi HMC 901748.49 (2 CDs)
The 1725 version, with significant textual changes
and refined solo and choral singing

Bach Collegium Japan • Masaaki Suzuki
BIS CD-921/922 (2 CDs)
Uses Bach's final version of 1749,
more meditative and polished than most

The only surviving authentic portrait of J. S. Bach, by E. G. Haussmann. ➔

George Frideric Handel
Giulio Cesare (1724)

Genre | Opera
Conductor/Performers | Marc Minkowski; Magdalena
Kožená, Marijana Mijanovic, Anne Sofie von Otter
Year recorded | 2003
Label | Archiv 474 210-2 (3 CDs)

By 1720, Handel was impressively established on the London musical scene. *Giulio Cesare*, his fifth full-length opera for the Royal Academy, created a sensation at its premiere, partly because of the star quality of the castrato Senesino and the soprano Francesca Cuzzoni, partly because of the opera's sumptuous scoring and prodigious melodic invention.

The action takes place in Egypt under the joint rule of Cleopatra and her brother Ptolemy. The visit of the Roman commander Julius Caesar and his seduction by the wily Cleopatra generate a powerfully dramatic plot, while the emotional twists and turns are given vibrant expression by Handel at the height of his powers. The magnificence of Handel's scoring is exemplified in the double orchestra (including a stage band with muted strings, theorbo, harp, and concertante viola de gamba) deployed for Cleopatra's "V'adoro, pupille."

Archiv's recording features Magdalena Kožená as the seductive, despairing Cleopatra and Anne Sofie von Otter in the relatively subsidiary role of Sesto. Both are superb, while Marijana Mijanovic's Cesare and Charlotte Hellekant's Cornelia are also outstanding. Marc Minkowski's handling of the score is gloriously willful: veering from the thrillingly dramatic revenge arias to the poignantly moving tragic ones. Tempi tend toward extremes, while phrasing is sharply profiled. He allows his singers to ornament extravagantly da capo repeats. His reading is subjective, almost Romantic, but always within the Baroque style. The results are enthralling and at times—as in Kožená's aria "Piangerò"—heart-stopping. **BM**

Johann Sebastian Bach
Six English Suites (c.1725)

Genre | Instrumental
Instrument | Harpsichord
Performer | Christophe Rousset
Year recorded | 2003
Label | Ambroisie AMB 9942 (2 CDs)

"They are known by the name of the *English Suites* because the composer made them for an Englishman of rank. They have all great worth as works of art; but some single pieces among them, for example, the jigs of the fifth and sixth suite, are to be considered perfect masterpieces of original harmony and melody." Thus Bach's first biographer, Johann Nikolaus Forkel, summarized the English Suites in 1801. Bach probably never knew them by this title, preferring to call them "Suites avec prélude." Dates of composition are similarly ambiguous, but it was probably at Leipzig (c.1725) that Bach organized the suites into the collection we recognize today.

While Gustav Leonhardt's later EMI recording of the suites remains one of the finest in an ever-growing field, this more recent version by Christophe Rousset steals the show. His playing is endowed with bravura gestures, supported by a flawless technique. The extended prelude of the sixth suite, breathtaking in its formal diversity, is carried through with contagious exuberance. But it is in the first suite, the most stylistically French of the set, that Rousset draws furthest ahead of the competition. The profuse ornamentation of the courante is beautifully executed and the subtly expressive allemande is played with gently inflected elegance. The preludes to each suite are strikingly diverse in character and it is in these that Rousset is able to project his own musical credentials. All but the prelude of the first suite are of imposing dimensions, their inspiration deriving more from Italy than France. Rousset declaims their concerto-like qualities with flair and infectious enthusiasm. **NA**

George Frideric Handel
Rodelinda (1725)

Genre | Opera
Director/Performers | Alan Curtis; Simone Kermes,
Marijana Mijanovic, Steve Davislim, Il Complesso Barocco
Year recorded | 2005
Label | Archiv 477 5391 (3 CDs)

Handel's seventh full-length opera for the Royal Academy of Music, *Rodelinda*, was another stunning success. Set in seventh-century Lombardy, it tells the story of Queen Rodelinda, importuned by Grimoaldo, usurper of the Milanese throne that rightly belongs to her husband Bertarido. Lead roles were again taken by the castrato Senesino and soprano Francesca Cuzzoni.

The complex plot engages audiences over its three long acts with a succession of exhilarating and moving arias. Rodelinda's part runs the gamut of emotions, from lamentation to defiance, marital longing to unfettered joy. The arias of her husband Bertarido, on the other hand, include the celebrated "Dove sei?" in which he sings of his anguish at being separated from Rodelinda, and "Chi di voi," the opening of a prison scene unsurpassed for its pathos. In the final scene of Act 2, Handel seizes the opportunity of staging a confrontation of great menace and heartbreak. Grimoaldo, in a blustering aria, tells Rodelinda that her husband must die. Rodelinda and Bertarido, believing their fate to be sealed, pledge their undying love in one of Handel's most poignantly somber duets, "Io t'abbraccio."

Alan Curtis's excellent recording features a duet and a substitute aria composed for a revival, with the omitted aria included on a bonus track. The pacing is sharp, the phrasing clearly defined, and the casting strong. Simone Kermes plumbs the depths of Rodelinda's anguish and engages our sympathy and respect for the fortitude of the devoted heroine, while Marijana Mijanovic supplies an equally convincing Bertarido. **BM**

Antonio Vivaldi
The Four Seasons (1725)

Genre | Concerto
Performers | Concerto Italiano
Director | Rinaldo Alessandrini
Year recorded | 2002
Label | Opus 111 OP 30-363 (2 CDs)

The pictorial and programmatic elements in *The Four Seasons* have generated a phenomenal passion for the music. The concertos are the first four of a set of twelve—*Il cimento dell' armonia e dell' inventione* (*The trial of harmony and invention*). Their detailed programs are spelled out in the sonnets that accompany them, probably written by Vivaldi himself. The constantly changing imagery, successive solo episodes describing wildly contrasting scenes, make the movements structurally less cohesive than Vivaldi's usual ritornello form that, with more than 500 concertos, he established as the norm for the late Baroque.

Choosing a definitive recording is complicated by the tendency for every new performance to be more spectacular than the last and although it is fascinating to sample their extremes, certain criteria for the choice suggest themselves. It should be played on the instruments that Vivaldi intended rather than exploring all the alternatives; it should employ "period" instruments, reproducing as far as possible Vivaldi's sound; in order to maintain its sparkle, it should be played at or near the relatively high pitch that was used in Venice. Above all, while it should reflect the aural descriptions of Vivaldi's sonnets, it should retain musical integrity and cohesion.

Concerto Italiano shares the solos between four of the group's members. Their imagery is certainly vivid, but, more importantly, they sustain the rhythmic impulsion that is a vital element in any concerto allegro while managing to weave lovely lines in the more melodic slow movements. The quality of the sound is warm yet fresh and immediate. **GP**

Johann Sebastian Bach | Six Violin Sonatas (c.1725)

Genre | Chamber
Performers | Andrew Manze (violin), Richard Egarr
(harpsichord), Jaap ter Linden (viola da gamba)
Year recorded | 1999
Label | Harmonia Mundi HMU 907250.51 (2 CDs)

These six violin sonatas form a set—like the Brandenburg Concertos, keyboard partitas, cello suites—and are organized by major/minor modes in a mirror-pattern symmetry of intervals between the keys.

The sonatas are specifically not for conventional solo violin, bass line, and keyboard harmonic in-fill, but for obligatory harpsichord, playing fully written-out parts in both hands. Often, this produces a trio-sonata texture compressed onto two instruments, violin and harpsichord right hand above the bass with optional gamba. Elsewhere Bach is yet more inventive: Sonata no. 1 begins with four bars of harpsichord alone before the violin enters with an entirely independent line. The third movement of Sonata no. 2 has violin and harpsichord right-hand playing in canon throughout. No. 3 opens in a positively Classical style as violin floats freely over a full-textured keyboard, left-hand in octaves; the third movement has repeated harpsichord chords looking, on paper, thoroughly pianistic. Strangest of all is the third movement of Sonata no. 5, harpsichord accompanying in broken chords, violin accompanying in repeated double-stopping—and neither creating a melody. With the violin omitted altogether in the third movement of no. 6, this set stretches textures, forms, and the concept of the Baroque sonata to its limit.

Andrew Manze and Richard Egarr emphasize the "fantastic" nature of the music rather than its disciplined formality. No one creeps more discreetly into the first sonata than Manze. Elsewhere he's manically energetic and expressive. Egarr can coax sounds from a harpsichord like no one else, in particular drawing out a richly dense and creamy tone. **GP**

> *"The six harpsichord trios are among the finest works of my dear late father."*
>
> Carl Philipp Emanuel Bach

Andrew Manze is one of today's top Baroque violinists. ➡

Johann Sebastian Bach
Keyboard Partitas (1726–31)

Genre | Instrumental
Instrument | Harpsichord
Performer | Gustav Leonhardt
Year recorded | 1986
Label | Virgin 7243 5 61292 2 1 (2 CDs)

Johann Sebastian Bach
Motets (1726–35)

Genre | Choral
Conductor | John Eliot Gardiner
Performers | Monteverdi Choir
Year recorded | 1980
Label | Erato 2292 45979-2

Bach issued his harpsichord partitas at the rate of one a year, between 1726 and 1731, when he brought out the six together as his op. 1. The collection initiated his *Clavierübung* (keyboard practice) to which he added three further installments over the following decade. The partitas, whose title page declares they were "composed for music lovers, to delight their spirits," are highly sophisticated pieces, whose cosmopolitan language informs the music with warmth and charm. Bach wears his learning lightly and, notwithstanding the music's considerable technical difficulty, achieves an alchemy, irresistibly alluring to performer and listener alike, where French and Italian styles are integrated with features of Germany's own indigenous keyboard tradition.

The front-runner in a strong field of interpreters, Gustav Leonhardt brings distinctive gestures and profound insights to Bach's music, effortlessly reaching its heart. Leonhardt has recorded the partitas twice, but it is his later version that offers the greater pleasure—although, regrettably, he omits almost all repeats; with playing of this order, his decision to do so is our loss. There is a nobility about Leonhardt's interpretation that emerges as a result of his serving equally the interests of poetry and form. The architectural foundation of the prelude of the first Partita is revealed in all its strength while the limpid progress of the following allemande is eloquent and affecting. In movements on a grander scale, such as the allemande of the D major Partita or the sinfonia of the C minor—a melting pot of European styles—Leonhardt seems to have had a hotline to the composer's innermost thoughts. **NA**

Nobody knows quite how many motets Johann Sebastian Bach actually composed. His first biographer, Forkel, referred in 1802 to many single- and double-choir motets, and goes on to say that of the double-choir variety eight or ten were extant. Tantalizingly he names only the four that survive now—"Singet dem Herrn," "Der Geist hilft unser Schwachheit auf," "Fürchte dich nicht," and "Komm, Jesu, Komm!"—together with the five-part "Jesu meine Freude" and the four-part "Lobet denn Herrn," whose authorship has been subject to speculation. The six works we have are all superb examples, extremely testing for the singers and always thrilling to hear, with their constant changes of tempo, dynamic, texture, and mood.

With Bach a conductor often has important choices to make, and the six motets pose more questions than most. How many voices? Should there be any instrumental accompaniment? Should the chorus be of boys and men, as at Bach's own churches, or can it be an adult choir of mixed sexes? Should the double-choir pieces be sung with the choirs facing each other across a distance, or can they stand side by side?

John Eliot Gardiner in this shapely and sharp 1980 recording with the Monteverdi Choir and English Baroque Soloists plumps for mixed voices, although his altos are mostly male, and for a largish choir of between twenty and twenty-eight voices. He also scores more points by including other pieces he believes fall into the motet category, including the funeral motet "O Jesu Christ, meins Lebens Licht," BWV 118, and the fine "Sei Lob und Preis mit Ehren," BWV 231. **SP**

Johann Sebastian Bach
St. Matthew Passion (1727)

Genre | Choral
Conductor/Performers | Karl Richter;
Munich Bach Choir and Orchestra
Year recorded | 1958
Label | Archiv 439 338-2

The nineteenth century knew this as "The Great Passion": where the *St. John Passion* of three years earlier is terse, intimate, and violent, the *St. Matthew* is epic and meditative. Bach uses the two contrasting Gospel accounts of Christ's death to construct musical narratives of complementary reach and ingenuity. Bach and his librettist Picander follow Matthew in dwelling on the rich tapestry of human incident within the Passion story, using a huge ensemble in ever-changing combinations of color and force: two main choirs and two orchestras, with soloists from each choir stepping forward to place moments such as Peter's denial under fierce scrutiny. As well as the central roles of the Evangelist and Christus, a third choir of treble voices caps the monumental outer pillars of the first part. "There's nothing like it in all music," said Leonard Bernstein of the opening chorus, with its E minor song of lamentation swinging from choir to choir like a huge bell.

The finest recordings of "The Great Passion" preserve this monumental aspect whatever the size of their resources. Their choirs are fresh and keen, their soloists characterful yet willing to bend to Bach's rhetoric, their conductor adept at pacing the mix of reflection and narration. None have done it better than Karl Richter in his first recording. Likewise, Dietrich Fischer-Dieskau rarely recaptured the open-hearted ardor of his twenty-seven-year-old self in a selfless reading of the bass aria, "Mache dich." Irmgard Seefried's exquisite poise in the tiny final recitative, "Habt lebenslang," holds the purity of the whole achievement in a grain of sand. **PQ**

George Frideric Handel
Coronation Anthems (1727)

Genre | Choral
Conductor | Stephen Cleobury
Performers | King's College Choir
Year recorded | 2001
Label | EMI 7243 5 57140 2 2

It must have been through royal intervention that Handel was commissioned to provide these four anthems for the coronation of George II and Queen Caroline: Maurice Greene had been appointed organist and composer to the Chapel Royal only a few days earlier. The honor was not without its inherent problems. Handel had only two weeks to write the music, copy parts, and rehearse and, unsurprisingly, not everything went smoothly as the Archbishop of Canterbury noted in his diary entry for the day. The anthems had further airings, however, by being largely incorporated into two oratorios, *Esther* and *Deborah*. *Zadok the Priest* has been sung at every English coronation since 1727.

Three of the anthems are for full choir and orchestra, complete with trumpets and drums complementing oboes, bassoons, and strings. Handel paints words colorfully and sets scenes dramatically—the shattering choral opening of *Zadok* is preceded by a long build-up of broken upward chords and, most cleverly, a momentary harmonic side-step to delay the final impact. *My Heart is Inditing* was for the coronation of the Queen, a verse-anthem introduced by solo lines before their music is later taken over by full choir.

King's College Choir and the Academy of Ancient Music were recorded in King's College Chapel. The sound is immediate—from the perspective of the royal ears—yet wonderfully rounded. Only in the silence after final chords do you realize that there is a huge reverberation lingering in the background, to match that of the first performance in London's Westminster Abbey. **GP**

John Gay | The Beggar's Opera (1728)

Genre | Opera
Conductor/Performers | Jeremy Barlow; Sarah Walker, Charles Daniels, Bronwen Mills, The Broadside Band
Year recorded | 1991
Label | Hyperion CDA 66591/2 (2 CDs)

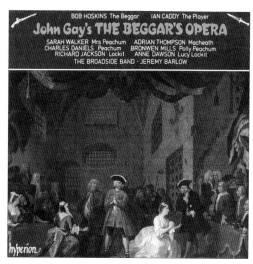

The Beggar's Opera proved to be the only lasting example of its kind—ballad opera. John Gay invented the genre: spoken comedy interspersed with brief songs, new words set to well-known tunes. When it burst upon the London social scene, audiences flocked to it, delighted by its satire of upper-class behavior, politicians, and Italian opera—there is a splendidly acrimonious duet between Polly Peachum and Lucy Lockit mocking the jealousy exhibited on stage between Handel's two principle sopranos. Inevitably some of the strictly topical references are not obvious to modern audiences, but much of the spoken humor remains hilariously funny. So, too, is Gay's versification for the songs, with pearls like "a zone is" providing a rhyme for "Adonis."

Although Gay selected the music to match his verses, he was a poet rather than a musician. So the Prussian composer Dr. John Pepusch provided the overture and accompaniment for the songs, for which his scoring is lost. Jeremy Barlow has reconstructed this, adding introductions and "playouts." Most songs are single verses, the second part repeated—still as memorable and singable as they were nearly 300 years ago.

Both performance and recording are superb. Sarah Walker is wonderful as Mrs. Peachum, freely adding chuckles and sighs to her script, while the cockney accents of the characters from London's criminal underworld are beautifully done. So, too, is the singing and the transparently scored accompaniment of strings, oboes, bassoon, and continuo.

The Beggar's Opera is a unique phenomenon, but still influential two centuries later when, in 1928, Brecht and Weill adapted it as *Die Dreigroschenoper*. **GP**

> ## "What think you of a Newgate pastoral among the thieves and whores there?"
>
> Jonathan Swift's initial suggestion, 1716

Other Recommended Recordings

Charles Dibdin: The Ephesian Matron, The Brickdust Man, The Grenadier • Opera Restor'd • Peter Holman
Hyperion CDA 66608
Three delightful English comic operas

John Frederick Lampe: Pyramus and Thisbe
Opera Restor'd • Peter Holman
Hyperion CDA 66759
A mock opera, from A Midsummer Night's Dream

Thomas Linley: Lyric Ode
Parley of Instruments • Peter Holman
Hyperion CDA 66613
A charming, fanciful Shakespearian ode

Hogarth's painting of the Newgate Prison scene in the first production. ➔

Johann Sebastian Bach
French Suites (1730)

Genre | Instrumental
Instrument | Harpsichord
Performer | Davitt Moroney
Year recorded | 1990
Label | Virgin 7243 5 61653 2 8

Like the English Suites, the French Suites remained unpublished in Bach's lifetime. It is very unlikely that he knew them by this title, although it was in use as early as 1762; but the truth is that neither these nor the English Suites possess characteristics that clearly or consistently keep faith with their implied national identity. Bach appears to have worked on the French Suites over a period of several years. Early drafts of some of the music are included in both the *Clavierbüchlein* (1722), which he compiled for his second wife, Anna Magdalena, and in another that he began shortly afterward. Bach seems to have completed his set of six suites in about 1730.

Davitt Moroney has immersed himself in the various preserved sources of the French Suites and has arrived at solutions that in some respects differ from those of other recordings of the work. In addition to the familiar suites, Moroney includes two further suites that frequently appear in manuscripts containing the French Suites. Extra movements, all of them little *galanteries*, are also included within the body of the standard six suites. Moroney's playing is relaxed, articulate, and also acutely aware of poetic content. Tempi are moderate and the music is declaimed with a conversational ease that imbues every phrase with significance. In some respects this playing is more liberally endowed with the conventions of the French harpsichord school than that of Gustav Leonhardt, yet it happily avoids anything in the nature of a stylistic straitjacket. Unlike in Leonhardt's version, all repeats are observed, and the performances in general are sympathetic and warmly expressive. **NA**

Georg Philipp Telemann
Paris Quartets (1730)

Genre | Chamber
Performers | Gustav Leonhardt, Barthold,
Sigiswald, and Wieland Kuijken
Year recorded | 1997
Label | Sony S3K 63115 (3 CDs)

You can have too much of a good thing, as is proved by Georg Philipp Telemann's posthumous reputation. In his day he was the first choice for the key music jobs in Germany (Bach only got the prestigious post of Kantor in Leipzig after Telemann withdrew). But in the years following his death, the sheer volume of his music proved off-putting. Today, we have a clearer notion of what a fine composer Telemann was and we are beginning to realize that his reputation in his lifetime was eminently justified.

Telemann's Paris Quartets are rightly seen as one of the pinnacles of his chamber music output. Published in Hamburg in 1730, they are the epitome of elegance and subtlety, with Telemann's acute ear for pleasing instrumental sonorities evident throughout. Unlike much chamber music of this period, which was written with the amateur in mind, these pieces were clearly aimed at professional musicians. Telemann's genius for contrapuntal writing is wonderfully demonstrated here, with the contrasting timbres of flute and violin used to great effect. This is not music that ranges over emotional extremes, but within its particular boundaries there is much contrast to be found, especially when played with such mastery by the extraordinarily talented Kuijken brothers and harpsichordist Gustav Leonhardt, one of the pioneering figures in the early music movement. They are particularly good at bringing out the different styles that Telemann alludes to in this delightful music: Italian and French and, more unusually, Polish national styles, with the composer producing a musical *entente cordiale* that is entirely convincing. **HS**

Georg Philipp Telemann
Tafelmusik (1733)

Genre | Orchestral
Director | Reinhard Goebel
Performers | Musica Antiqua Köln
Year recorded | 1988
Label | Archiv 427 619-2 (4 CDs)

A friend and near-contemporary of Bach, and godfather to his eldest son Carl Philipp Emanuel, Telemann has been declared the most prolific composer of all time—research suggests he left behind more than 3,000 works, though many have been lost. In such a huge output, some are better described as workmanlike rather than as the products of an imaginative genius but, in such a major project as the *Tafelmusik* (*Table music*), Telemann is at his best. The title is a generic description of music for entertainment rather than necessarily implying orchestral music to accompany eating. Telemann, however, had strong pedagogical leanings, and the chamber pieces in the three sections or "productions" are much more than mere incidental music.

The productions are highly organized. Each opens with an orchestral suite, a French overture followed by French-named dances. Next is a quartet, variously for flutes, oboes, and violins, the second of which comes with an alternative version, bassoon surprisingly replacing recorder. After a concerto is a trio sonata, then a solo sonata. Each production has an orchestral "conclusion." The myriad colors and the emphasis on wind instruments provide endless delight in this light-hearted and carefree music.

Reinhard Goebel and Musica Antiqua Köln have just the right exuberance for the *Tafelmusik*, uninhibited in fast movements, elegant and reflecting French *galanterie* in the dances, and warmly flexible in slow movements. The recording wears its age remarkably well and, as a complete collection of more than four hours of glorious music, it cannot be beaten. **GP**

Johann Sebastian Bach
Christmas Oratorio (1734–35)

Genre | Oratorio
Conductor | Gerhard Schmidt-Gaden
Performers | Collegium Aureum
Year recorded | 1973
Label | DHM GD 77046 (3 CDs)

The period from the mid-1730s onward was a time of consolidation for Bach in Leipzig. He had completed several cycles of cantatas, as well as numerous other sacred and secular works, and this set of six cantatas is a sign of his eye for posterity. Bach composed the recitatives and chorales afresh and stole arias and choruses from recent secular cantatas, fitting new words to old music with huge ingenuity. His mastery of every contemporary musical style is on display, from Italianate exuberance, to French pastoral serenity, to a Lutheran conclusion that keeps Christ's journey to the Cross in mind and ear with a reference to the *Passion Chorale*.

Successfully maintaining a narrative flow throughout this work is something that eluded older interpreters, who perhaps struggled with the music's diversity; nearly all the available recordings use period instruments and date from the last thirty-five years. This is one of the first. There is no question that Baroque wind instruments have been better made and played in the intervening period, or that the great conductors have cracked the whip with more incisive results. But what is the Christmas story without its rustic simplicity? Where would Christmas be without children, and where would Bach's music be without the all-male choir he wrote it for? All this and more makes Gerhard Schmidt-Gaden's pioneering recording with the impressive Collegium Aureum a continual source of pleasure, from the frisson of crackling timpani in the opening chorus to the easy, natural tempi throughout and the touching boy soloist in the second cantata's lullaby, "Schlafe, mein Liebster." **PQ**

George Frideric Handel | Ariodante (1735)

Genre | Opera
Conductor | Marc Minkowski
Performers | Anne Sofie von Otter, Lynne Dawson
Year recorded | 1997
Label | Archiv 457 271-2 (3 CDs)

Unjustly neglected until recent times, Handel's *Ariodante* has, since the mid-1990s, entered the repertoire of opera houses all over the world. The title role, written for the great castrato Giovanni Carestini, has an aria of heartbreaking poignancy, "Scherza infida," as well as a couple of show-stopping virtuoso numbers, "Con l'ali di costanza" and "Dopo notte."

Set in Edinburgh, the action tells the story of Prince Ariodante and his betrothed Ginevra, the daughter of the King of Scotland. Polinesso succeeds in persuading Ariodante—by means of an elaborate charade involving Ginevra's attendant, Dalinda—that he, too, is enjoying the princess's favors. Ariodante is assumed dead after being seen plunging from a cliff into the sea, while Ginevra is sentenced to death (as custom demands) for her alleged lack of chastity. Polinesso, however, is mortally wounded on the tournament field—fortunately not before confessing his deception—and Ariodante and Ginevra are happily reunited.

The suicidal despair of "Scherza infida," complete with mournful bassoon obbligato, in which Ariodante sings of his beloved's "infidelity," is rendered by Anne Sofie von Otter in a line that fragments under the emotional strain. She is abetted in this by Marc Minkowski, whose reading is similarly Romantic. Elsewhere he pushes tempi to the extremes and indulges in heavy accents and jerky rhythms not traditionally associated with the Baroque style. Lynne Dawson's Ginevra is more conventionally projected, while Verónica Cangemi's Dalinda is superbly sung. Ewa Podleś brings her formidable, gender-crossing alto to bear on the role of the villain Polinesso (originally intended to be sung by a woman). **BM**

> "*He who has not heard Carestini is not acquainted with the most perfect style of singing.*"

Johann Adolf Hasse

Other Recommended Recordings

Freiburg Baroque Orchestra • Nicholas McGegan
Harmonia Mundi HMU 907277
Excerpts from the opera, with the late, lamented Lorraine Hunt (Lieberson) in the title role

English Chamber Orchestra • Raymond Leppard
Philips Trio 00289 473 9552 (3 CDs)
Never cutting-edge stylistically, but a must for the singing of Janet Baker in the lead role

Handel Operatic Arias
Emma Bell, Scottish Chamber Orchestra • Richard Egarr
Linn CKD 252
Favorite arias by a rapidly rising star

Swedish mezzo-soprano Anne Sofie von Otter excels in Baroque roles. ➔

George Frideric Handel | Organ Concertos (1735–51)

Genre | Concerto

Performers/Director | Paul Nicholson (organ), Frances Kelly (harp), Brandenburg Consort; Roy Goodman

Year recorded | 1996

Label | Hyperion CDA 67291/2 (2 CDs)

Handel created an embryonic organ concerto as early as 1707 in his Roman oratorio *Il trionfo del Tempo e del Disinganno*, playing the short but exhilarating allegro movement himself. When he returned to oratorio from 1732, now in London, he again used the organ as a continuo instrument and, soon, as a concerto soloist. By 1735 it was the norm for him to play between the acts of these unstaged dramas. Several movements in the twelve concertos later published as op. 4 and op. 7 are only partly written out, as Handel would improvise during the solo episodes. The second set goes further. As blindness overtook him, he left out complete movements, filling the gaps with solo improvisation while the orchestra remained silent. The way in which modern performers approach these improvisational sections is therefore a crucial consideration in recommending a performance.

Some of the concertos have become very familiar. One is nicknamed "The Cuckoo and the Nightingale" because of the cuckoo call that pops out of the texture below a constant stream of high passagework in the second movement. The last concerto of op. 4 was originally intended for harp rather than organ, placed in the oratorio *Alexander's Feast* immediately after the text "Timotheus [. . .] with flying Fingers touch'd the Lyre: the trembling Notes ascend the Sky, and heav'nly Joys inspire." Several excellent recordings offer one or other of the two sets of six. Paul Nicholson and the Brandenburg Consort offer both, and very lively performances they are. Nicholson is fairly conservative in his realization of Handel's ad-lib passages but is always admirably stylish. The harp provides an attractive contrast, as well as being Handel's original intention, in no. 6 of op. 4. **GP**

> *"Handel . . . gratified the public by the performance of concertos on the organ."*
>
> Dr. Charles Burney

Other Recommended Recordings

Stephen Preston, English Concert
Trevor Pinnock
DG 469 438-2 (2 CDs)
A strong contender, from 1983

Jaroslav Tůma, Prague Virtuosi
Oldřich Vlček
Supraphon 11 1494 2 (3 CDs)
Rather bland, but recorded on a delightful 1739 organ

David Halls, Sonnerie • Monica Huggett
Avie AV 2055
One-to-a-part and a charming chamber organ

Jean-Philippe Rameau | Les Indes galantes (1735)

Genre | Opera-ballet
Conductor | William Christie
Performers | Les Arts Florissants
Year recorded | 1990
Label | Harmonia Mundi HMC 901367.69 (3 CDs)

RAMEAU
Les Indes galantes

LES ARTS FLORISSANTS
WILLIAM **CHRISTIE**

Although Rameau was entering his fifties when he turned to opera, he took to the genre with great confidence, establishing himself as the best of Lully's successors and one of the finest composers for the stage of the eighteenth century. The brilliant opera-ballet *Les Indes galantes* (best translated as *The Amorous Indies*), cast in the form of a prologue with four vocal ballets, was Rameau's third opera and (after much revision, including the removal of female disguise from the male hero) one of his most colorful. The settings for the opera, variously an Indian Ocean island, Incan Peru, Persia, and North America, reflected the taste for exotica beloved of Parisian audiences in the early eighteenth century.

The plots of the four main sections are equally fantastical, with Europeans sold into slavery being released by gracious foreign masters, an erupting South American volcano and a native-American "peace pipe" ceremony. For all the extravagance of the settings and plots, Rameau's characterization has real credibility and a near-Enlightenment appreciation for the noble savage. Above all, he brings both weight and near-tragic drama to the goings on in each of the four acts, which takes the usually frivolous opera-ballet genre to a new level.

William Christie and his dedicated forces give a splendid ensemble performance. The sizable and colorfully toned orchestra provides superb support and, where necessary, responds magnificently to the intensity of the drama, notably in the powerful conclusion to the scene in Peru with its dual volcanic eruptions. In sum, this is a remarkable tribute to the sophistication and insight that modern period-instrument performance can bring to the Baroque repertoire. **JS**

> *"He [Rameau] caused in dancing the same revolution as in music."*
>
> La Dixmerie

Other Recommended Recordings

Orchestral suites from Les Indes galantes
Orchestre de la Chapelle Royale • Philippe Herreweghe
Harmonia Mundi HMA 1901130
More characterful dances from this vibrant score

Naïs *(pastorale-héroïque),* Le temple de la gloire
Philharmonia Baroque • Nicholas McGegan
Harmonia Mundi HMU 90907121
Naïs was one of Rameau's most challenging scores

Platée
Les Musiciens du Louvre • Marc Minkowski
Erato 2292 45028-2 (2 CDs)
A wide-ranging opera, full of hilarious parody

Giovanni Battista Pergolesi | Stabat mater (1736)

Genre | Vocal
Conductor/Performers | Helmut Müller-Brühl;
Jörg Waschinski (soprano), Michael Chance (countertenor)
Year recorded | 2003
Label | Naxos 8.557447

PERGOLESI

Stabat Mater
Salve Regina

Jörg Waschinski,
Soprano
Michael Chance,
Counter-tenor
Cologne Chamber
Orchestra
Helmut Müller-Brühl
Deutschlandfunk

Pergolesi (1710–36) died of tuberculosis at the tragically early age of twenty-six, yet his impact on musical development in Europe was extraordinary. He studied and worked in Naples, the home of progressive opera, from around the age of fifteen. He is remembered particularly for his one-act intermezzo, *La serva padrona*, which led to quarrels between supporters of serious French opera and those of the new Italian comic opera.

The *Stabat mater* includes some forward-looking and bittersweet harmony, full of expressive chromaticism. The opening is especially striking with first violins then voices climbing up over successive dissonances. Elsewhere the music could come straight from the opera orchestra pit: the up-beat alto solo "Quae morebat" with off-beat rhythms and lilting pulse; similarly jaunty music for the duet "Inflammatus et accensus" toward the end, where the emphasis moves from Mary's contemplation to exhortation to all Christians to share her grief. Pergolesi was reproached for sections being "better suited to a comic opera than a song of mourning." Within the duets and arias, there is much vivid word- and mood-painting. Harsh string strokes suggest the piercing sword; a chromatic falling bass underlying extreme vocal leaps emphasizes Christ "dying, forsaken."

Jörg Waschinski's voice is a remarkable phenomenon, a true male soprano with a two-and-a-half octave range. He can as readily draw an ethereal vibrato-free line as express intense passion, while modern (high) pitch adds to the intensity of his tone. He is matched by Michael Chance's chillingly vibrato-free tone at the start. Helmut Müller-Brühl takes a prayerful and contemplative approach, often slower than other recordings. **GP**

> *"[He] who could remain . . . unmoved when hearing this does not deserve to be called a human being."*
>
> Johann Adam Hiller

Other Recommended Recordings

Emma Kirkby, James Bowman, Academy of Ancient Music • Christopher Hogwood
L'Oiseau-Lyre 425 692-2
Contrasting voices, generating a wide palette of colors

Gillian Fisher, Michael Chance, The King's Consort
Robert King
Hyperion CDA 66294
Chance again, sixteen years earlier

Dorothea Röschmann, David Daniels, Europa Galante
Fabio Biondi
Virgin 0946 3 63340 2 8
A vivid, lively, and theatrical contrast to the rest

Pergolesi in an anonymous eighteenth-century Italian portrait. ➲

Jean-Philippe Rameau | Castor et Pollux (1737, *rev.* 1754)

Genre | Opera
Conductor/Performers | William Christie; Howard Crook, Jérôme Corréas, Agnes Mellon, Les Arts Florissants
Year recorded | 1992
Label | Harmonia Mundi HMC 901435.37 (3 CDs)

One of the most important French composers of the Baroque era, Jean-Philippe Rameau claimed that his passion for opera began at the age of twelve. *Castor et Pollux*, the third of his operas, suffered at its premiere from adverse comparisons with his triumphant operatic debut, *Hippolyte et Aricie*, of four years earlier. It was not until a revival in 1754 that *Castor et Pollux* achieved the popularity that made it the longest lived of Rameau's operas in the repertoire before the Revolution.

This tale of brotherly love is complicated by the fact that Castor is the mortal twin of an immortal brother, Pollux. Heavenly intervention restores the dead Castor to life and, after lovelorn vicissitudes, the remarkable twins are placed by Jupiter in the Zodiac in a triumphant finale. Rameau provides music of both dignity and brilliance. The opening chorus, in which the Spartans mourn the dead Castor, has an epic grandeur and provided a model for such set pieces in later works. The sorrow of Télaïre, Castor's lover, is rendered with telling dignity in delicate instrumental coloring. By contrast, the celebrations of the end of the fifth act, which include a rather breathless short aria for an enthusiastic planet when all has been set right, have a touching charm.

William Christie's direction of this richly satisfying score is unfailingly idiomatic. He presents the original 1737 version of the score, and while this means that the dramatic benefits that the later revisions afforded are missed, one great gain is the presence of the brilliant, if somewhat irrelevant, prologue. The leading roles are delivered with commitment and conviction: Agnes Mellon is particularly affecting as the grieving Télaïre, while René Schirrer is a resonant Jupiter. **JS**

> "*We are gripped and moved by this tragic atmosphere.*"

Debussy, a great admirer of Rameau, on *Castor et Pollux*

Other Recommended Recordings

Hippolyte et Aricie
Les Arts Florissants • William Christie
Erato 0630 1551-2
The start of Rameau's extraordinary career

Anacréon
Les Musiciens du Louvre • Marc Minkowski
Archiv 449 211-2
A wonderfully concentrated dramatic ballet

Les Paladins
Les Talens Lyriques • Christoff Rousset
These excerpts from Rameau's last staged opera show show him at his most instrumentally imaginative

George Frideric Handel | Serse (1738)

Genre | Opera
Conductor/Performers | William Christie;
Anne Sofie von Otter, Lawrence Zazzo, Les Arts Florissants
Year recorded | 2003
Label | Virgin 07243 5 45711 2 1 (3 CDs)

Handel's last opera for the King's Theatre, first performed there in 1738 (and then not heard again until 1924), tells the story of the ancient Persian king Xerxes I and his expedition against Greece. Although the scenario is largely fictional, there are supposedly historical references: first, the attempt by Xerxes to build a bridge with boats over the Hellespont in order to unite Asia and Europe; second, the king's reverence for a plane tree. The latter was expressed in the aria "Ombra mai fù," which became universally known in a sentimentalized version entitled "Handel's Largo."

Serse contains elements of comedy, even satire, at the expense of the conventions of opera seria, a feature that lends itself to the kind of postmodernist staging that became popular in the 1980s and 1990s—most notably that by Nicholas Hytner for English National Opera. In addition to the title role—the absurdly self-important Serse—there is also a comic servant character called Elviro, sometimes seen as an anticipation of opera buffa servants such as Leporello. In fact, the opera moves fluently between farce and tragedy, and some of the most powerful music is found in the minor-key arias of Romilda, Arsamene, and Amastre.

William Christie's recording, made at the Théâtre des Champs-Elysées, Paris, in 2003, and easily the best available, stars the inimitable Anne Sofie von Otter in the title role. Her coloratura in the virtuoso aria "Se bramate" captures perfectly the character's absurdly tyrannical side, while Sandrine Piau contributes a touching Atalanta and Lawrence Zazzo an excellent Arsamene. Christie's lively pacing sweeps the drama on, but allows time for the lyrical beauties of the score to be savored too. **BM**

> *"My own judgment is that it is a capital opera notwithstanding 'tis called a ballad one."*

Earl of Shaftesbury

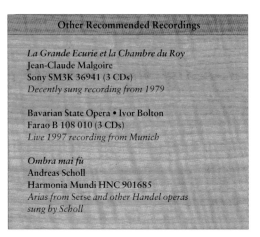

Other Recommended Recordings

La Grande Ecurie et la Chambre du Roy
Jean-Claude Malgoire
Sony SM3K 36941 (3 CDs)
Decently sung recording from 1979

Bavarian State Opera • Ivor Bolton
Farao B 108 010 (3 CDs)
Live 1997 recording from Munich

Ombra mai fù
Andreas Scholl
Harmonia Mundi HNC 901685
Arias from Serse *and other Handel operas sung by Scholl*

Johann Sebastian Bach | Harpsichord Concertos (*c.*1739)

Genre | Concerto
Performers | Trevor Pinnock (harpsichord/director),
The English Concert
Years recorded | 1979–84
Label | Archiv 463 725-2 (5 CDs)

Bach's thirteen concertos for one or more harpsichords with strings are products of his Leipzig years. It is probable that he produced them for performances by the Collegium Musicum of which he was director between 1729 and *c.*1744. The pieces are mostly arrangements of earlier concertos for violin(s) and were played on occasion at the Collegium Musicum concerts by Bach's sons, Wilhelm Friedemann and Carl Philipp Emanuel. Historically, Bach's harpsichord concertos are important in the later development of the keyboard concerto, though only one of them, the Concerto in C major (BWV 1061) seems to have been an original keyboard work for two harpsichords. Of this piece Bach's biographer Johann Nikolaus Forkel wrote that it seemed "as new as if it had been composed but yesterday. . . . The last allegro is a strictly regular and magnificent fugue."

No complete set of these concertos is uniformly satisfying but this is the most consistently rewarding. Trevor Pinnock, with his fellow soloists Kenneth Gilbert, Lars Ulrik Mortensen, and Nicholas Kraemer, gives a vibrant account of all thirteen concertos, though omits the fragmentary D minor movement (BWV 1059R), which is often reconstructed from music contained in Bach's BWV 35 Cantata. Pinnock's ability to settle upon a just tempo in Bach's music has always been a major feature of his performances and here he seldom lets us down. In the concertos for multiple harpsichords there is a pleasing conviviality and exchange of ideas between the soloists that enhance an already vivid presence. The English Concert blends stylish virtuosity with tasteful discretion to create performances that leave much of the competition far behind. **NA**

"The composer . . . created the form, thus blazing a trail for the pianoforte concerto of later generations."

Karl Geiringer

Other Recommended Recordings

Bob van Asperen, Gustav Leonhardt
Melante Amsterdam
Virgin 7243 5 61716 2 (4 CDs)
A close runner-up to the English Concert recording

Robert Hill, Cologne Chamber Orchestra
Helmut Müller-Brühl
Naxos 8.554604, 8.554605, 8.554606 (3 separate CDs)
Effective middle-of-the-road performances

Concertos BWV 1052–54
Lars Ulrik Mortensen, Concerto Copenhagen
CPO 999 989-2
Invigorating and informed Bach playing

Trevor Pinnock, acclaimed as both harpsichordist and director. ➔

George Frideric Handel
Concerti grossi, op. 6 (1739)

Genre | Concerto
Performers | Andrew Manze (violin/director), Academy of Ancient Music
Year recorded | 1997
Label | Harmonia Mundi HMX 2907228

Handel put together these twelve concertos astonishingly quickly, in just over a month. Most of the sixty-two movements were new, the few that were recycled illustrating the principle that a good piece is worth using again. There is evidence to suggest that he modeled his concertos on the earlier op. 6 of Corelli, who had influenced him greatly while he was in Italy. The textures are the same—two violins and cello as soloists, alternating with and echoing a larger band. Structurally they are in four or more movements rather than the "modern" three-movement form of Vivaldi. They are also thoroughly cosmopolitan: Movements include a French overture, dances with both French and Italian titles, and an English hornpipe. Some movements give the first solo violin a dominant role in Vivaldian fashion; some employ sound Teutonic fugal counterpoint.

The concertos are highly flexible. Like Corelli's, they are musically complete with just three strings and continuo—soloists play throughout, so orchestral parts can be omitted. They are most effective when the trio of soloists contrasts, in weight, tone, and spatial separation, with full orchestra. Andrew Manze has the solo group in the middle of the sound spectrum, but recorded distinctively forward of the rest. His interpretation is full of wit and imagination. He takes the Academy of Ancient Music to the limits—from manically energetic to subdued—and retains a sense of glorious spontaneity in the soloists' ornamentation. **GP**

Johann Sebastian Bach
The Well-Tempered Clavier (c.1740–42)

Genre | Instrumental
Performer | Gustav Leonhardt
Years recorded | 1968, 1973
Label | DHM GD 77011, GD 77012
(2 separate CDs)

Bach assembled the two books that make up his forty-eight preludes and fugues at different stages in his life. Only Book 1 carries the title *Das wohltemperirte clavier* (*The Well-Tempered Clavier*), and this dates from 1722. Book 2 was probably completed in the early 1740s. "Well-tempered" means well-tuned; various tunings existed in Bach's day and we do not know the precise nature of his tuning. It is an issue that he leaves open; by using the word "clavier" he leaves the choice of instrument open, too.

This "work of all works," as Schumann called it, has attracted pianists and harpsichordists in equal measure, as well as organists and clavichord players—each of these instruments brings out different qualities of the work. Among the recordings by pianists of the preludes and fugues, those by Edwin Fischer in the 1930s, Sviatoslav Richter, András Schiff, and Vladimir Ashkenazy are noteworthy. Harpsichord performances on disc did not exist before the early 1950s, when Wanda Landowska made her legendary recordings. In his recordings of Book 1 (1973) and Book 2 (1968), Gustav Leonhardt established stylistic criteria that have provided models for all later harpsichordists. Like Landowska, Leonhardt plays with authority, revealing the architectural coherence of each book. His rhythmic pulse is vibrant and his ability to sustain linear clarity in the interests of coherent argument highly effective. Only the sound quality of the instrument fails to ingratiate twenty-first-century sensibilities. **NA**

Domenico Scarlatti
Keyboard Sonatas
(1740s)

Genre | Instrumental
Instrument | Piano
Performer | Benjamin Frith
Year recorded | 1999
Label | Naxos 8.554792

Born in 1685, Domenico Scarlatti was the sixth child of Alessandro Scarlatti, the most influential composer in the development of Neapolitan opera. By 1721, Domenico had moved to the Spanish court in Lisbon, and later settled in Madrid, where he remained until his death in 1757. The young Maria Barbara, who later became queen, was Scarlatti's pupil and protector, and his astonishing 555 extant sonatas for keyboard were probably written largely for her. His relative isolation from the rest of Europe led him into a remarkably "modern" and idiosyncratic style. Every keyboard device imaginable appears within his vast output: flashing virtuosity, crossing of the hands, crashing dissonances, widely leaping lines, and heart-felt lyricism. In many of the sonatas there is a clear Spanish influence.

Scarlatti published thirty of the sonatas as *Essercizi* (exercises), though they are no more dry technical studies than are Chopin's *études*. Benjamin Frith plays sixteen of the sonatas on the modern descendant of the early piano of the Spanish court, distilling the essence of harpsichord techniques. He transports the spirit of the music to the new medium, with sparkling articulation, layered rather than gradual dynamic contrasts, and clean, unaccented ornaments. Naxos intends to record all of Scarlatti's sonatas, inviting different performers for each disc. Frith's contribution is Volume 5—a treasure-house of contrasting piano delights to convert the most die-hard "period-instrument" authenticist. **GP**

Johann Sebastian Bach
Goldberg Variations
(1741)

Genre | Instrumental
Instrument | 1985 Mietke/Kennedy
Performer | Pierre Hantaï
Year recorded | 2003
Label | Mirare MIR 9945

According to Bach's earliest biographer, Johann Nikolaus Forkel, the *Goldberg Variations* were composed for Count Keyserlingk, the Russian ambassador at Dresden who, Forkel tells us, requested Bach to write music "of a soothing and cheerful character" for his harpsichordist, Johann Gottlieb Goldberg, to play to him when he could not sleep at night. Even if we doubt the veracity of Forkel's account, it is to Goldberg that we owe the affectionate name by which the work—published in 1741 or 1742 under the title *Aria mit verschiedenen Veränderungen* (*Aria with Diverse Variations*)—has become universally known.

Although the *Goldbergs* are harpsichord pieces for which Bach stipulated the use of two manuals in eleven of the thirty variations, they have long been in the pianist's repertoire. Many such recordings exist, among which those by Glenn Gould, Rosalyn Tureck, James Friskin, and Miki Skuta are of particular interest. However, French harpsichordist Pierre Hantaï leads the field with a playing style that shows an elegant mix of learning, virtuosity, and entertainment. This rewarding conjunction of heart and mind ensures an absence of superficial gesture, while at the same time fostering a spontaneous but disciplined response to the music's poetry. More than in his earlier recording of the work, this later one reveals greater expressive freedom in which particular harmonic progressions are highlighted by hand-spreading, pauses, and brief rhythmic interruptions. **NA**

George Frideric Handel | Messiah (1742)

Genre | Oratorio
Conductor/Performers | René Jacobs; Clare College Choir, Freiburg Baroque Orchestra
Year recorded | 2006
Label | Harmonia Mundi HMC 801928.29 (2 CDs)

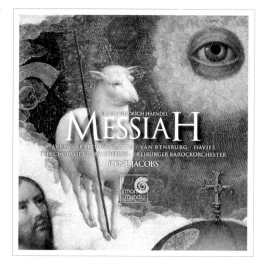

By the end of 1740, Handel, the most celebrated of a line of talented immigrants who had swelled the ranks of composers in England, was—if rumors were to be believed—considering leaving the country. The runaway success he had enjoyed in the theater had come up against the twin buffers of changing public taste and the rivalry of another opera company. It was the literary scholar Charles Jennens who contrived to woo Handel back to the oratorio.

What Jennens offered Handel was a somewhat revolutionary scheme: an ambitious oratorio in three parts, drawing on both Old and New Testaments (and the *Book of Common Prayer*), elaborating a grand narrative that would encompass all the major festivals of the Christian year. Although written with great speed, *Messiah* is a large-scale oratorio whose magnificence shows no sign of haste and which has, from the time of its composition, enjoyed the status of a national icon.

There are dozens of recordings of *Messiah*, ranging from the monumental Beecham performances, complete with cymbals and Heddle Nash or Jon Vickers, through Malcolm Sargent and the venerable Huddersfield Choral Society, to the leaner period-instrument versions of Trevor Pinnock, William Christie, Marc Minkowski, and others. René Jacobs's new reading is characteristically imaginative, however: dramatically conceived, sharply profiled, lithe, and muscular. Unexpected dynamic contrasts introduce a theatrical element into the "Hallelujah" chorus; a diminuendo heralds the final "Amen" chorus, itself phrased unconventionally. The approach to texture and rhythm is more varied than in traditional versions, with continuo interpolations, cadenzas, and other ornamentation. **BM**

> *"I hope he will lay out his whole Genius & Skill upon it, that it may excel all his former Compositions."*
>
> Charles Jennens

Other Recommended Recordings

Les Arts Florissants • William Christie
Harmonia Mundi HMC 901498.99 (2 CDs)
A fine period-instrument alternative

Les Musiciens du Louvre • Marc Minkowski
Archiv 471 341-2 (2 CDs)
Magdalena Kožená and John Mark Ainsley are among the strengths of this recommendable version

Royal Philharmonic Orchestra • Charles Mackerras
ASV CD DCS 230 (2 CDs)
Mozart's scoring presented by modern orchestra with large chorus (Huddersfield) under style-aware conductor

George Frideric Handel as painted by Thomas Hudson in c.1749. ➔

Carl Philipp Emanuel Bach
Keyboard Sonatas (1742–44)

Genre | Instrumental
Instrument | Harpsichord
Performer | Bob van Asperen
Years recorded | 1977–79
Label | Teldec 9031 77623-2 (3 CDs)

Born in 1714, Carl Philipp Emanuel Bach was the second son of Johann Sebastian Bach. He was already an accomplished keyboard player in his teens so it is not surprising to find that the composition and performance of harpsichord, clavichord, and organ music occupied him during his adult life. Some fifty harpsichord concertos have survived. Far more extensive, though, is his legacy of music for solo keyboard, of which the six Prussian Sonatas (1742–43), six Württemberg Sonatas (1744), the sonatas, rondos, and fantasies *für Kenner und Liebhaber* (for connoisseurs and amateurs); and the *Probe-stücke* are the most important.

Among the most valuable recordings of Emanuel Bach's keyboard music are those featuring the Prussian (Wq.48) and Württemberg Sonatas (Wq.50) played by Bob van Asperen. In these sonatas we are constantly reminded of the composer's belief that music should move the heart emotionally. This is not music that is always easily understood, but van Asperen captures the highly individual idiom of Emanuel's style with authority and technical finesse, embracing the "Empfindsamerstil" (sensitive style) aesthetic wholeheartedly and handling the interrupted rhythms, unexpected pauses, and short-winded dynamic markings with spontaneous aplomb. The music—above all in the Prussian Sonata—contains much by Bach that is experimental and, in the Württemberg set, his musical imagination seems to recognize no boundaries. Van Asperen takes it all in his stride, seeming to revel in the spirited outbursts so conspicuous in the third sonata of the set. **NA**

Johann Sebastian Bach
A Musical Offering (1747)

Genre | Chamber
Director | Reinhard Goebel
Performers | Musica Antiqua Köln
Year recorded | 1979
Label | DG 469 680-2

Toward the end of his life, Bach turned more and more to the purity of contrapuntal exploration. The high point was *The Art of Fugue*, left unfinished at his death. Before that, though, he wrote a collection of movements as a "musical offering" (*Musicalisches Opfer*) to King Frederick the Great of Prussia, based on a theme the king had given him on a visit in 1747 to the court at Potsdam. Bach saw this unpromising melodic idea as a challenge to his contrapuntal powers and set to creating a series of canons and ricercars (from the Italian *ricercare*, to seek or research—an old-fashioned term for a fugue) for ensembles of from one to four instruments. The most sizeable sections are the two ricercars, one in three voices, the other in six, and a four-movement trio sonata for flute, violin, and viola da gamba.

Bach was never a true innovator, instead taking the ideals and methods of the Baroque to their apogee. There is definitely a backward glance about *A Musical Offering*, composed at a time when the first stirrings of the Classical Enlightenment were in the air. The choice of ricercar is a case in point, though Bach did manage to make an appropriate acronym from it as his dedication: "*Regis Iussu Cantio Et Reliqua Canonica Arte Resoluta*" (the theme and the remainder resolved in the canonic art at the king's request).

Musica Antiqua Köln provides the kind of intimate chamber music experience for which it is renowned, with Wilbert Hazelzet's flute and Henk Bouman's harpsichord producing period-instrument performances that are immaculate yet sound fresh, even improvised. **MR**

George Frideric Handel
Judas Maccabaeus (1747)

Genre | Oratorio
Conductor/Performers | Robert King; Jamie MacDougall,
Emma Kirkby, Michael George, The King's Consort
Year recorded | 1992
Label | Hyperion CDA 66641/2 (2 CDs)

Despite the ruthlessness with which the Duke of Cumberland ("Butcher Cumberland" as he was known) put down the Jacobite Rebellion, the librettist Thomas Morell had no scruples about hailing him as a "Truly Wise, Valiant and Virtuous Commander" in the dedication of his word-book for Handel's *Judas Maccabaeus*.

In fact, the narrative is based on the first book of Maccabees, from the Apocrypha, telling the story of the Jewish resistance to the Syrian conquest of Judaea. Although there are no explicit references to the 1745 campaign in the work, martial valor and jingoistic heroism propel the text and the music alike. These qualities may have served the creators well in the years immediately after the quelling of the rebellion, but they have proved less popular with more modern audiences. That is a pity because, alongside the brazen heroics (epitomized by Judas Maccabaeus's exhilaratingly virtuoso "Sound an Alarm" and expertly negotiated here by Jamie MacDougall), is music of great charm and appeal. The Israelitish Woman (here stylishly sung by Emma Kirkby), for example, has both the genial "Come, Ever-smiling Liberty" and the no less attractive "So Shall the Lute and Harp Awake.""Father of Heaven," the serene alto aria that opens the third act—one of Handel's most inspired creations—is beautifully sung by James Bowman. Finally, at the heart of the work, are the many stunning choruses, which embrace the rousing splendor of "Fall'n Is the Foe" and the celebrated "See, the Conqu'ring Hero Comes!" as well as the pathos of "Ah! Wretched Israel." All are admirably delivered by the Choir of New College, Oxford. **BM**

Johann Sebastian Bach
Mass in B minor (*c*. 1749)

Genre | Choral
Conductor| John Eliot Gardiner
Performers | Monteverdi Choir, English Baroque Soloists
Year recorded | 1985
Label | Archiv 415 514-2 (2 CDs)

The first two movements of the B minor Mass (the Kyrie and Gloria) comprised one of the most sensational job applications in musical history: Bach sent them as an accompaniment to a request for a royal title from the Elector of Saxony in 1733. These two movements made up what was known as the Lutheran Mass. The other movements, Credo, Sanctus, Benedictus, and Agnus Dei, were a later compilation, mainly adapted from existing movements among his cantatas, produced by Bach toward the end of his life, and there is nothing to suggest that the work was performed as a whole during his lifetime.

The B minor Mass is today regarded as a pinnacle of the choral repertoire. The emotional and technical range is huge, from intense, learned counterpoint in the second Kyrie, through outbursts of cosmic joy at the start of the Gloria and the Sanctus, to the intimate and affecting Agnus Dei. With the possible exception of the *St. Matthew Passion,* there are few single works to rival the Mass as a conspectus of Bach's genius.

Performances from the early years of the recorded history of the Mass are likely to be too inflated and lumbering for modern tastes. A preference for speedier renditions, with smaller scale vocal and orchestral forces, has characterized many recordings since Nikolaus Harnoncourt's first on period instruments in 1968. John Eliot Gardiner's recording from 1985 proves to be a highly effective middle way, mingling solo and chorus. The sheer agility and unanimity of the Monteverdi Choir and the English Baroque Soloists produce an exhilarating response to Gardiner's persuasive handling of rhythm. **JS**

George Frideric Handel
Music for the Royal Fireworks (1749)

Genre | Orchestral
Conductor | Robert King
Performers | The King's Consort
Year recorded | 1989
Label | Hyperion CDA 66350

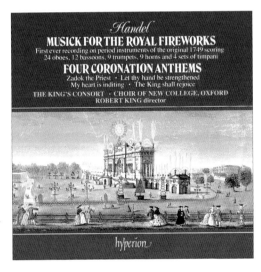

The fireworks in London's Green Park for the celebration of the Peace of Aix-la-Chapelle treaty in April 1749 were an unmitigated disaster. A contemporary account reports that "The rockets and whatever was thrown up into the air, succeeded mighty well; but the wheels, and all that was to compose the principal part, were pitiful and ill-conducted, with no changes of colored fires and shapes." The designer was so incensed that he drew his sword on the "comptroller of his Majesty's Fireworks," though he was fortunately disarmed and arrested before more harm could be done.

Handel's music fared better, though not before some acrimonious exchanges between the Duke of Montagu, on behalf of the king, and the composer. The subject was whether or not to have "violeens"—the king "hoped there would be no fidles." It is probable that only wind and percussion took part—fortunately, because it also rained. Still, the band was huge: nine each of trumpets and horns, twenty-four oboes, twelve bassoons, and three pairs of kettle drums together with side drums and a pair of extra-large "double drums," which Handel hired for the occasion from the Tower of London. A rehearsal in the Vauxhall Gardens produced an audience of more than 12,000, and one of London's earliest traffic jams.

Robert King with the King's Consort has assembled an equally grand ensemble. Given the unwieldy size of these forces (under their "foreman," oboist Paul Goodwin), Hyperion's recording is masterly. The blend of sound must surely be unique—weighty yet quite crisp in allegros and positively jaunty in the minuets. **GP**

> *"Such a stoppage on London Bridge, that no carriage could pass for three hours."*
>
> The Gentleman's Magazine, April 21, 1749

Other Recommended Recordings

English Concert
Trevor Pinnock
Archiv 423 149-2
From 1988, and wearing its years well

Scottish Chamber Orchestra
Alexander Gibson
ASV CDQS 6188
A lively account on modern instruments

London Philharmonic Orchestra
Hamilton Harty
Dutton CDLX 7016
Pure nostalgia—how it was heard back in 1935

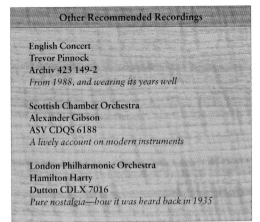

Duke of Richmond's fireworks over the Thames, held on May 13, 1749. ➲

Johann Sebastian Bach | The Art of Fugue (*c.*1750)

Genre | Instrumental
Instrument | Harpsichord
Performer | Davitt Moroney
Year recorded | 1985
Label | Harmonia Mundi HMX 2901169.70 (2 CDs)

Although it is now widely accepted that *The Art of Fugue* is best served by a keyboard performance, the fact remains that Bach did not specify an instrument or instruments for its performance. When he died, the engraving of what his son C. P. E. Bach described as "the most practical fugal work" was incomplete, leaving posterity with some unanswered questions. "The guiding thought of *The Art of Fugue,*" remarks the Bach scholar Christoph Wolff, "is the construction of a gigantic work of pedagogy in which the different possibilities of fugal composition are displayed in keyboard models. . . . Bach realized the dialectical principle inherent in the association of tradition and modernism and knew how to pass it on. Bach, in his old age, wrote music more advanced than ever before."

Recordings of *The Art of Fugue* vary widely both in instrumentation and in the choice and ordering of movements. While a preference is shown toward solo harpsichord, there are also recordings by organists, viol consorts, string quartets, and saxophone quartets. Mixed instrumental groups also feature and these mainly follow editions by Wolfgang Graeser (1924), Roger Vuataz (1937), and Hermann Scherchen (1965). Davitt Moroney's solo harpsichord recording is among the most satisfying of all the versions that adopt this approach. His clear reasoning is backed up by an elegant musical interpretation and a secure technique. His order of movements is influenced by up-to-date research and, while we may regret the omission of Bach's own reworkings for two harpsichords of the mirror fugues, Moroney still presents us with a powerful image of Bach's grand design. Though never underplaying either the didactic nature or the complexities of the music, Moroney seldom fails to underline its beauty. **NA**

" . . . pathos . . . gives this farewell the transcendental character of art conceived on the threshold of eternity."

Karl Geiringer

Other Recommended Recordings

Gustav Leonhardt (harpsichord)
Vanguard 08 2012 72 (2 CDs)
Only the recorded sound and the character of the instrument fail to match more recent versions

Hesperion XX • Jordi Savall
Astrée-Auvidis E 2001
Effective solutions are found by Savall's lucid, darkly colored ensemble

Juilliard Quartet
Sony S2K 45937 (2 CDs)
An ideal way of coming to grips with the structure and textures of Bach's contrapuntal masterpiece

George Frideric Handel | Theodora (1750)

Genre | Oratorio
Conductor/Performers | Paul McCreesh; Susan Gritton,
Robin Blaze, Paul Agnew, Gabrieli Consort and Players
Year recorded | 2000
Label | Archiv 469 061-2 (3 CDs)

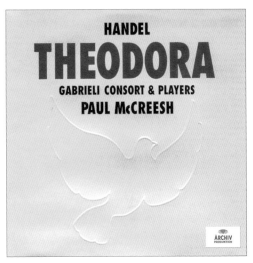

In the glorious Indian summer of his career, following hard on the heels of *Susanna* and *Solomon*, Handel wrote another dramatic oratorio, *Theodora*, that contains aria after aria of some of the most inspired music he ever penned. The heroine of this tale may be, to quote the eminent Handelian Winton Dean, "one of the most insufferable prigs in literature," but her aria "With Darkness, Deep" and the duet "To Thee, Thou Glorious Son" are profoundly moving.

Theodora, princess of Roman-occupied Antioch in the early fourth century, is a member of the persecuted Christian community. When Valens, the Roman president and governor, decrees that all must offer sacrifices to the heathen goddesses Venus and Flora, Theodora holds fast to her beliefs. Though prepared to face death, she is appalled to discover that her punishment is enforced prostitution. Eventually spared that fate, Theodora and Didymus, a Roman officer converted to Christianity by his love for her, are both condemned to die.

It was doubtless this downbeat ending, coupled with the refusal of Theodora to act like a conventional heroine, that turned Handel's audience against the oratorio. (The first performances in 1750 were poorly attended and Handel revived it only once, in 1755.) Powerful modern stagings, notably that by Peter Sellars, have shown the timelessness of the drama—chiefly the plea for toleration of personal beliefs. That and the supreme music written for the characters, wonderfully performed here by Susan Gritton, Robin Blaze, and Paul Agnew in the lead roles of Theodora, Didymus, and Septimius. Neal Davies is an aptly blustering Roman president and Susan Bickley a sympathetic Irene. **BM**

> *"As finished, beautiful and labour'd a composition, as ever Handel made. . . . The Town don't like it at all."*
>
> **Earl of Shaftesbury**

Other Recommended Recordings

Concentus Musicus Wien • Nikolaus Harnoncourt
Teldec 2292 46446-2 (2 CDs)
Roberta Alexander is a fine Theodora in this set

Philharmonia Baroque Orchestra • Nicholas McGegan
Harmonia Mundi HMU 907060.62 (3 CDs)
A frustrating set but with a moving Theodora from Lorraine Hunt

Handel Arias
Lorraine Hunt Lieberson, OAE • Harry Bicket
Avie AV 0030
The superb mezzo-soprano offers several arias from Theodora *in one of her last recordings*

William Boyce | Eight Symphonies, op. 2 (1760)

Genre | Orchestral
Conductor | Kevin Mallon
Performers | Aradia Ensemble
Year recorded | 2003
Label | Naxos 8.557278

 William
BOYCE
Eight Symphonies, Op. 2
Aradia Ensemble • Kevin Mallon

A successful organist and "Second Composer to the Chapel Royal," William Boyce (1711–79), a younger contemporary of Handel, has been rather overshadowed by that giant of the early eighteenth-century London scene. He had great respect for Handel, famously commending his musical borrowings as other people's "pebbles . . . turned . . . into diamonds." In turn, Dr. Charles Burney admired Boyce, who "neither pillaged nor servilely imitated [Handel]." Boyce's distinctive musical voice comes through clearly in the eight symphonies. All but one were collected together from overtures to odes and pastoral operas he had written from 1739 onward; the last was written for the Three Choirs Festival in Worcester, an annual event that Boyce conducted for at least twenty years. Pieces such as those composed by Boyce helped to satisfy an increasingly insatiable appetite for public concerts in London's pleasure-gardens and musical societies.

The symphonies have a sunny disposition. All but one are in major keys, with a preponderance of fast movements and lively dances—a smiling gavot (no. 4), a pert jigg, once heard, never forgotten (no. 7), a witty four-note repeated figure that lends a rustic air to the end of no. 1. While most are conventionally scored for strings, oboes, and continuo, there are some arresting colors. The middle movement of no. 3 has violins and violas with a haunting bassoon, all in unison over a simple bass; horns double violins in the Fourth Symphony; no. 5 opens with a martial flourish of trumpets and timpani.

Kevin Mallon founded the Aradia Ensemble, based in Toronto, Canada, and their foundation of eleven strings provides just the right scale for the symphonies. This recording is clean and refreshingly immediate. **GP**

> *"[These] are as characteristic of the eighteenth century as Handel's overtures and concerti grossi."*

Jack Westrup

Other Recommended Recordings

Complete trio sonatas
Members of Collegium Musicum 90 • Simon Standage
Chandos CHAN 0648(2) (2 CDs)
"Only Corelli's surpassed these pieces."—Charles Burney

Solomon – A Serenata
Bronwen Mills, Howard Crook, Parley of Instruments
Peter Holman • Hyperion CDA 66378
A recital of love between two characters: He and She

David's Lamentation over Saul and Jonathan
Hanover Band • Graham Lea-Cox
Gaudeamus CD GAU 208
World premiere recording and a real eye-opener

William Boyce in a late-eighteenth-century frontispiece. ➔

The Age of Enlightenment brought new thinking to all the arts in the eighteenth century. In music it marked the Classical period, when form, as in the Roman- and Greek-inspired architecture of the time, became as important as content, so it is unsurprising to find major genres such as the symphony and sonata being established as pinnacles of musical abstraction in the works of Haydn and Mozart, and later Beethoven.

1761–1800

Joseph Haydn | Symphonies nos. 6–8 (1761)

Genre | Orchestral
Conductor | Roy Goodman
Performers | Hanover Band
Year recorded | 1991
Label | Hyperion CDH 55112

A giant of the Classical era, Joseph Haydn (1732–1809) will be forever known as "father of the symphony" for his pioneering work on a form that he helped, more than any other composer, to establish as the pinnacle of orchestral art. He wrote more than a hundred symphonies, an incredible figure considering they are all substantial, often groundbreaking works. Many were written for the Austrian court of the Esterházys where Haydn worked for the bulk of his adult life, from 1761 until 1790. Although he wrote several operas, also for performance at the Esterházy court, Haydn's other great contributions to posterity are his numerous string quartets—a form that he invented almost single-handedly. After leaving the Esterházys, Haydn enjoyed a musical old age, reveling in his widespread fame and the affectionate epithet of "Papa" Haydn, and continuing to compose—his great oratorio *The Creation* is one of his last works. Much of Haydn's music is infused with a sparkling wit and humor, and it is perhaps for this more than anything that he is best loved today.

Haydn's early triptych of symphonies, "Le matin," "Le midi," and "Le soir" respectively, were written in his first year as court composer for the Esterházys in 1761. Taking Vivaldi's *The Four Seasons* as a model, the symphonies evoke different times of the day (morning, afternoon, and evening). Although not concertos, the works are dominated by soloistic elements. "Le matin" begins with a glorious sunrise, "Le midi" features a plaintive recitative for solo violin, and "Le soir" ends with a dramatic storm complete with thunder, lightning, and torrential rain.

Roy Goodman's Classical approach with this period-instrument band produces performances full of character, each symphony imbued with an individual color. **GR**

> *"As head of an orchestra I could experiment . . . improve, expand, cut, take risks."*
>
> Joseph Haydn

Other Recommended Recordings

Northern Chamber Orchestra • Nicholas Ward
Naxos 8.550722
Lively accounts in period style with modern instruments

Symphonies nos. 13–16
Hanover Band • Roy Goodman
Hyperion CDH 55114
Avant-garde symphonies from his early days at court

Symphonies nos. 1–104, etc.
Philharmonia Hungarica • Antál Dorati
Decca 448 531-2 (33 CDs)
Complete cycle from the 1970s, the only set to include every note of symphonic music Haydn wrote

Joseph Haydn in a portrait by Ludwig Guttenbrunn, *c.*1770. ➔

Christoph Willibald Gluck
Orfeo ed Euridice (1762)

Genre | Opera
Conductor/Performers | John Eliot Gardiner; Derek Lee Ragin, Sylvia McNair, Cyndia Sieden, Monteverdi Choir
Year recorded | 1991
Label | Philips 434 093-2

A turning point in operatic history, *Orfeo ed Euridice* premiered in Vienna on October 5, 1762. It was the first of three works later known as Gluck's "reform operas" (the others are *Alceste*, 1767, and *Paride ed Elena*, 1770). In them the Bavaria-born, Bohemia-raised Gluck (1714–1787) and his Italian librettist Ranieri de' Calzabigi explored a musico-dramatic vision, challenging Italian opera seria traditions.

"Beautiful simplicity" was Gluck's own phrase for what the pair had set out to accomplish. Commissioned for the Emperor's name day, *Orfeo* was daringly planned to go against the grain of the occasion. The retelling of the Orpheus myth is of unparalleled directness and concision, featuring an extraordinarily dominant alto-castrato hero. The integration of choral and dance episodes into the drama is without precedent in Italian opera; as is the musical plainness, which climaxes with emotional impact in the hero's folksong lament, "Che farò senza Euridice?"

A decade later Gluck expanded the opera for Paris, in the process diluting the immediacy of the original. The 1774 *Orphée et Eurydice*, in three acts, with a tenor hero and many beautiful new numbers, became Gluck's most popular opera. Posthumous adaptations included those with a female alto as Orpheus; in recent years the tendency has been to revive the work in its earliest, purest form.

Among several 1762 *Orfeo* recordings from the last two decades, Philip's on period instruments reigns supreme. The cast, led by countertenor Derek Lee Ragin, may have been improved upon, Gardiner's command of the music-drama has not. The set, studio-made in the wake of concert-hall performances, achieves the best of all worlds. **ML**

Leopold Mozart
Trumpet Concerto (1762)

Genre | Concerto
Performers/Conductor | Maurice André (trumpet), Berlin Philharmonic Orchestra; Herbert von Karajan
Year recorded | 1974
Label | EMI 7243 5 66961 2 9

Often mentioned only as father to a famous son, Leopold Mozart (1719–87) is nevertheless known as a composer and theorist. Born in Augsburg, Leopold studied philosophy and jurisprudence at the Benedictine University of Salzburg, but turned to music. He spent his entire career employed at the Kapelle of the Prince-Archbishop of Salzburg, as a violinist, advancing to court and chamber composer, and finally deputy Kapellmeister in 1763. Despite frequent absences taken for concert tours with his son, which may account for his slow advancement at court, Leopold's reputation was established by the publication in 1756 of *Versuch einer gründlichen Violinschule*. This treatise, translated widely and in many editions, became one of the most significant works of the time.

Although a large number of his compositions are lost (of thirty large serenades only one survives), many manuscripts exist, including symphonies, keyboard and chamber works, Masses, litanies, and offertories. Trumpeters are fortunate that this Trumpet Concerto in D major is one of the few concertos that survives. The two movements, scored for solo trumpet, two horns, strings, and harpsichord continuo, originally formed part of a more extensive Divertimento.

This well-loved recording, included in EMI's series "Great Recordings of the Century," features Maurice André, the first modern-age trumpeter well-known to the general musical public. Fêted for his performances of the Classical concertos, his real specialism lay in the taxing high range of the Baroque repertoire. Playing a modern valved instrument, he achieved a sound so sweet and lyrical that audiences scarcely recognized it as a trumpet. **DC**

Joseph Haydn
Cello Concertos (c.1762–c.1783)

Genre | Concerto
Performers | Christophe Coin, Academy of Ancient Music
Conductor | Christopher Hogwood
Year recorded | 1995
Label | L'Oiseau-Lyre 414 615-2

When Haydn arrived at Esterházy, he encountered an orchestra of talented musicians, bored by their current Kapellmeister. Haydn set about winning them over with a string of brilliant concertos, many of which have since disappeared. The Cello Concerto in C major was one such, only rediscovered in 1961 in the National Museum of Prague. A great discovery, indeed, as this is one of the finest cello concertos. The first movement with its martial, dotted rhythms belongs in the Baroque style, but the serene, sustained cantilena in the slow movement reveals Haydn the opera composer, and by the finale we are in the era of the Classical symphony. This athletic movement puts any cellist through their technical paces, but it is all in the service of music that fairly fizzes with excitement and high spirits. If Josef Weigl, for whom the first concerto was written, was a gifted cellist, then the dedicatee of the Concerto in D major, Anton Kraft, must have been even more so. Yet this is no empty showpiece, but a sunny, expansive work with tunes that get under the skin. The elegant, four-square first movement is interwoven with strands of melody, while the elegiac Adagio draws voluptuous lyricism from the soloist. The jolly rondo finale should go at speed despite the hurdles set for the soloist.

These works will withstand a number of interpretations, but the heavy bow and metal-strung power of the modern cello are apt to weigh them down, adding angles where there could be curves. Cellist Christophe Coin and the AAM produce wonderfully transparent textures and maintain a sense of flow. Coin's virtuosity is effortless, and, vitally, he persuades us this is music suffused with happiness. **HW**

Wolfgang Amadeus Mozart
Violin Sonatas (1763–88)

Genre | Chamber
Performers | Rachel Podger (violin),
Gary Cooper (fortepiano)
Year recorded | 2005
Label | Channel CCS SA 22805

One of only a handful of contenders for "greatest ever musical genius," Wolfgang Amadeus Mozart is an undisputed giant of the Classical age. His music has never been more popular, its Rococo charm, natural-sounding melodies and outward simplicity providing access to a vast inner depth of complex structure, intricate harmonies, startling originality and deep emotion. Born on January 27, 1756, Mozart was a child prodigy who became a prolific composer during his tragically short life, producing masterpieces in the fields of symphony, concerto, chamber music, and, perhaps above all, opera. His genius was never fully recognized in his lifetime; he was heavily in debt when he died on December 5, 1791, aged just thirty-five.

Mozart spent much of his youth touring Europe with his father Leopold, being shown off to courts as an extraordinarily precocious musician. He wrote some of his very first compositions at this time, violin sonatas that he performed at the keyboard with his father on the violin. The earliest of these dates from 1763, when he was just seven years old. Violin sonatas ran as a thread through Mozart's life; he notched up more than thirty. His last great example, K526 in A major from 1787, took the form to new heights of sophistication with a fully developed structure more akin to a grand concerto than a chamber work.

Rachel Podger on violin, and Gary Cooper on fortepiano, have recorded all Mozart's violin sonatas, which make up an outstanding set of discs. Each volume—this representative one features K7, K30, K303, K301, and K481—pairs early works with mature sonatas, in beautifully fresh, dynamic and insightful performances. **GR**

Giuseppe Tartini
Violin Sonata in G minor, "The Devil's Trill" (*c.*1765)

Genre | Chamber
Performers | Ida Haendel (violin),
Geoffrey Parsons (piano)
Year recorded | 1976
Label | Testament SBT 1258

Giuseppe Tartini (1692–1770) is legendary as a violinist, composer, and teacher of such excellent successors as Pietro Nardini. His most famous work has a distinct whiff of sulfur about it. The story is familiar: Tartini claimed to have dreamed of a visitation from the Devil who, on being handed his fiddle, played him an extraordinarily beautiful piece with an amazing trill. When he awoke, he wrote down the G minor Sonata, incorporating a truly devilish trill in the finale (the old edition of the sonata had a beautifully engraved picture of the Devil perching on the end of the sleeping Tartini's bed). However, Tartini admitted that his sonata was not as good as the music he had heard in the dream. Perhaps that was why, in the most popular edition of the piece, Fritz Kreisler rather expanded on Tartini's (and the Devil's) original final cadenza. The result has always been a favorite with fiddlers—even the purist Adolf Busch preferred it to the original. It is beautifully written for the violin and virtually everyone has recorded it.

No doubt, in these days of period authenticity, one should be choosing a historically informed recording; but with Eduard Melkus's rendering no longer available, there is no recommendable one—a much touted version is controversially played unaccompanied and the performance is both over the top and out of tune. In any case, as played by Ida Haendel (and others including David Oistrakh and Nathan Milstein), the Kreisler arrangement is a work of art. Haendel's gutsy, technically impeccable playing has been captured by an EMI team, and the Testament reissue is well refurbished. The Tartini is nicely complemented by pieces by Corelli, Nardini, and Vitali. **TP**

"An astonishing piece of eighteenth-century romanticism."

Boris Schwarz on "The Devil's Trill"

Other Recommended Recordings

Sonata in G minor, "Didone abbandonata"
Fabio Biondi (violin), Maurizio Naddeo (cello)
Naïve/Opus 111 OPS 59-9205
A sizzling performance on an all-Tartini disc

Violin Concertos in F major, in G major, & in C major
Felix Ayo, I Giovani Musici Italiani
Dynamic CDS 163
The veteran Spanish violinist is in superb form

Six Sonatas, op. 6
Enrico Casazza, Roberto Loreggian
Tactus TC 692001
Superbly played readings of these marvelous sonatas

Ida Haendel has been playing for more than seventy years. ➡

Christoph Willibald Gluck
Alceste (1767)

Genre | Opera
Performers | Teresa Ringholz (Alceste),
Justin Lavender (Adometo)
Year recorded | 1998
Label | Naxos 8.660066–68 (3 CDs)

The second so-called "Reform opera" on which Gluck and the librettist Ranieri de' Calzabigi collaborated for Vienna is among the eighteenth century's most radical undertakings: a rethinking of Italian opera seria. As first written, *Alceste* is the anti-opera seria par excellence. A stripped-down version of *Euripides* divested of Metastasian stagecraft and virtuoso vocal writing, it is a monumental construction based on slow-moving choral tableaux, pierced with simple instrumental effects, pinned to moods of sorrow and terror, climaxing in a chorus mourning the dead Alceste that is among the grandest opera scenes. Never before had a title character been so unrelentingly spotlit: the austere recitative and poignantly unadorned arias define Alceste's situation and emotional range.

For Paris nine years later *Alceste* was so drastically overhauled that the 1767 (in Calzabigi's Italian) and the 1776 (in du Roullet's French) should be seen as separate creations linked by shared musical and dramatic material. For modern revival the Paris *Alceste* is the choice—sensibly so, given its more "electric," varied handling, vividly demonstrated in the aria "Divinités du Styx!" that closes Act 1, Alceste's thrilling challenge to the underworld gods: a reworking and re-positioning of the Viennese Alceste's "Ombre, larve"—but here more vibrant with heroic defiance.

Yet it is the first Alceste that has received the most successful recording. Naxos has preserved Drottningholm festival's 1998 production, and specifically the intimacy, drive, and commitment that characterized it. Teresa Ringholz's lightish soprano depicts a tenderly rounded heroine. The whole possesses a Gluckian authenticity. **ML**

Andre-Ernest-Modeste
Grétry | Zémire et Azor (1771)

Genre | Opera
Performers | Mady Mesplé, Roland Bufkens, Jean-Claude Orliac
Year recorded | 1975
Label | EMI 7243 5 75290 2 0 (2 CDs)

Certain minor figures—"petits maîtres," the French call them—in the history of music inspire disproportionately strong affection. One such is Grétry (1741–1813), the Belgian-born composer whose dominance in Parisian popular opera made him crucially important in the development of *opéra comique* (the popular musico-dramatic form alternating speech and song).

Liège-born and Rome-trained, Grétry retained favor in the eras of Marie-Antoinette (one of his dedicatees), the Revolution, and Napoleon's rule. This was because he was a melodist: while in orchestral and harmonic terms his scores may seem primitive, a succession of memorably simple arias expertly fashioned for theatrical contexts ensured he achieved his goal of infusing sincerity and naturalness into French opera.

An early success, *Zémire et Azor* (from literary versions of *Beauty and the Beast*) was, and is still, his most-loved work. Mozart owned a score; Beecham reorchestrated it for a famous postwar revival. Its celebrated magic picture scene, in which the "beast" Azor conjures for Zémire, his captive, a vision of her family mourning her absence, retains a pure theatrical enchantment. This is only one moment of many highlighting Grétry's marriage of Italianate warmth and French delicacy. It comes across magically in this recording. The performance as a whole, with sung recitatives not by Grétry supplanting the spoken dialogue, may be far from "authentic," but the singing, notably of the soprano Mady Mesplé (Zémire) and the tenors Roland Bufkens (Azor) and Jean-Claude Orliac (Ali), is so elegant and stylish that flaws are easily forgiven. **ML**

Joseph Haydn
Keyboard Sonatas (c.1771–95)

Genre | Instrumental
Instrument | Piano
Performer | Alfred Brendel
Years recorded | 1979–85
Label | Philips 416 643-2 (4 CDs)

Haydn's inventiveness and innovation did not desert him when writing for the keyboard. Although he was composing for the relatively limited compass of the fortepiano or early examples of the pianoforte, his imagination was not restricted and the music responds well to the color and range of a concert grand. Haydn's keyboard sonatas are more whimsical than Mozart's examples in the genre, and enjoy a repartee that appealed to Beethoven. As in his other great music, Haydn takes his ideas on a twisting and turning journey that is often breathtaking and also wide-ranging in terms of character and emotion. Hoboken lists fifty-two piano sonatas in his catalog of Haydn's output (but Christa Landon's alternative numbering takes the list to sixty-two, although some she included exist only as fragments). The last four sonatas (Hoboken 49–52/Landon 59–62) are peerless examples of Haydn's genius: each is different, and each is a masterpiece. But earlier sonatas are equally magnificent; the C minor (Hoboken 20/Landon 33) includes a sublime slow movement, while the finale of the E minor (Hoboken 34/Landon 53) is a witty and capricious gem.

Alfred Brendel's devotion to Haydn is legendary. He has all the credentials to do Haydn full justice, bringing an analysis that discovers tangents and references to illuminate what he plays. His response digs deep into Haydn's capacity for profundity, and his sense of humor brings out Haydn's many musical jokes and puns. On this 4-CD set, Brendel gives glorious performances of eleven sonatas (including the last four and those cited), as well as other pieces, in recording quality that is consistently fine. **CA**

Luigi Boccherini
String Quintets (1772–1803)

Genre | Chamber
Performers | Vanbrugh Quartet
Richard Lester (cello),
Year recorded | 2001
Label | Hyperion CDA 67287

Luigi Boccherini (1743–1805) is arguably the greatest Italian composer of the Classical era—although he spent most of his working life in Spain. His distance from the Austro-German mainstream meant his music retained an individual voice, imbued with a refined *galant* grace. Often undervalued (he has been dismissed as "Haydn's wife"), there is a great deal to appreciate in Boccherini's uniquely expressive voice. His compositions include twenty-six symphonies, an opera, various sacred vocal pieces, and more than 300 quartets, quintets, and trios. A virtuoso cellist, Boccherini wrote eleven cello concertos, but his chief achievement is his string quintets featuring two cellos. After settling in Madrid in 1769, Boccherini had to provide, and perform in, chamber music for his employer Don Luis (brother of King Carlos III). The Don had a string quartet, which with Boccherini on cello, became a quintet; Boccherini composed over a hundred works for strings.

The Vanbrugh Quartet, with Richard Lester's additional cello, does full justice to Boccherini's music on this disc of three of his finest string quintets (op. 13 no. 5 in E major, op. 37 no. 19 in F minor, and op. 37 no. 13 in G minor). The E major Quintet includes the famous minuet (immortalized in the 1955 Ealing comedy *The Ladykillers*, staring Alec Guinness). Each Quintet is inventive in its own way, with regular switches between major and minor keys a characteristic device. The Vanbrugh's approach acknowledges period style, with well-sprung tempi and a fresh, clean sound. The performances are full of poise and evident enjoyment, making a compelling case for the oft overlooked Boccherini. **GR**

Joseph Haydn | Symphony no. 45, "Farewell" (1772)

Genre | Symphony
Conductor | Roy Goodman
Performers | The Hanover Band
Year recorded | 1990
Label | Hyperion CDH 55118

One of the most well-known of all Haydn's symphonies, the "Farewell" owes its fame to the circumstances surrounding its composition, and to its unique final movement—a musical joke with a serious message. Written a decade into Haydn's thirty-year service as Kapellmeister at the court of Austrian prince Nikolaus Esterházy, it gave voice to the increasingly frustrated court musicians when the prince's prolonged stay at his summer residence of Eszterháza was keeping them from their families. Deftly diffusing the potentially mutinous situation, Haydn composed a new symphony for the prince with a novel finale: a sedate minuet during which the musicians gradually snuff out their candles and walk from the stage one by one, leaving just a lonely pair of violins playing the final strains. Fortunately the prince got the message and took it in good humor, saying, "If they are all going, so too must we." Jokes apart, the "Farewell" Symphony would be fully deserving of a place in any musical hall of fame for the quality of the first three movements alone. A classic example of Haydn's *Sturm und Drang* writing (literally, "storm and stress"), the marvelously inventive and varied music is by turns dramatic and sublime.

Roy Goodman and the Hanover Band give a riveting performance, the period-instrument group playing with passion and impeccable style. The turbulent Allegro assai cracks along at an electrifying pace, imbued with terrific intensity. The delicate Adagio is beautifully poised, and the minuet has an invigorating swing. Goodman directs from the harpsichord, but picks up his violin for the final few bars of the work, after most of the orchestra has already stopped playing, to duet with the leader, Pavlo Beznosiuk, in an intimate and serene conclusion. **GR**

> *"I was cut off from the world . . . so I had to become original."*
>
> Joseph Haydn on his years at the Esterházy court

Other Recommended Recordings

"Sturm und Drang" *Symphonies nos. 26, 35, 38–52, 58, 59, & 65* • English Concert • Trevor Pinnock
DG 463 731-2 (6 CDs)
Outstanding—Haydn's most dramatic symphonies

Symphonies nos. 26, 35, 38, 39, 41–52, 58, 59, & 65
Orchestra of the Age of Enlightenment
Frans Brüggen • Philips 462 117-2 (5 CDs)
More relaxed approach on period instruments

Symphonies nos. 30, 55, & 63
Northern Chamber Orchestra • Nicholas Ward
Naxos 8.550757
Highly enjoyable disc in lively readings

A room at Eszterháza, the palace where the "Farewell" premiered. ➡

Wolfgang Amadeus Mozart | String Quintets (1773–91)

Genre | Chamber
Performers | Amadeus Quartet: Norbert Brainin, Siegmund Nissel, Peter Schidlof, Martin Lovett; Cecil Aronowitz
Years recorded | 1967–74
Label | DG 477 5346 (2 CDs)

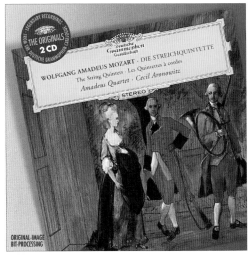

Far from seeing the string quintet as a string quartet with an extra part, Mozart conceived his six essays in the medium in a totally different way. The addition of a second viola and consequent enrichment of the middle register enabled him to "orchestrate" the music in a variety of ways: a high trio (two violins and viola) against a low one (two violas and cello); pairs of like instruments sharing the cello part as bass line; and duets of violin with viola or cello over a three-part accompaniment from the others are just some of the options he used.

Mozart's first work in the genre, K174 in B flat major, a charming piece that often gets overlooked, was inspired by quintets by his friend Michael Haydn. The C minor work K406 is a transcription of the Serenade for winds in that key, which was made in 1788, the year after his two greatest quintets: C major (K515) and G minor (K516). As Alfred Einstein has written, these monumental works are to Mozart's chamber music what the last two symphonies are to that genre. They are composed on a big scale, both first movements being the longest Mozart ever wrote. The last two quintets in D major (K593) and E flat major (K614) are Mozart's final chamber works and demonstrate a new sophistication of form and facture in his music.

While Mozart's string quintets, particularly K515 and K516, have always attracted ad-hoc groups of virtuoso players, for example the legendary line-ups including Jascha Heifetz, William Primrose, and Gregor Piatigorsky, they are best cared for by bona fide chamber musicians. Viola player Cecil Aronowitz became almost an honorary member of the Amadeus Quartet and their recording with him of the complete set of quintets is considered unbeatable. **CMS**

> *"The same wealth of feeling must needs be expressed [as in the G minor symphony] yet more economically . . ."*

Hans Keller in *The Mozart Companion*

Other Recommended Recordings

Amadeus Quartet with Cecil Aronowitz
DVD: EMI 5 99683 9
A moving visual memento (on DVD) of a great partnership

Griller Quartet with Max Gilbert
Dutton CDBP 9717
A virtuoso performance from 1948 of the G minor Quintet

Salomon Quartet with Simon Whistler
Hyperion CDD 22005 (2 CDs)
Four mature quintets brilliantly performed on original instruments

A portrait of Mozart from 1782, believed to show the best likeness. ➔

Wolfgang Amadeus Mozart | Piano Sonatas (1775–89)

Genre | Instrumental
Instrument | Piano
Performer | Mitsuko Uchida
Year recorded | 1991
Label | Philips 468 356-2 (5 CDs)

PHILIPS

The Piano Sonatas
Les Sonates pour piano · Die Klaviersonaten

Mitsuko Uchida

Mozart's keyboard sonatas were long underrated: fortunately leading soloists since the war, from Mieczyslaw Horszowski, Lili Kraus, Wilhelm Kempff, and Rudolf Serkin to Alfred Brendel, Alicia de Larrocha, Murray Perahia, Mitsuko Uchida, András Schiff, and Maria João Pires have corrected this imbalance. These works have suffered comparatively for not being, as Beethoven's sonatas were, continuously built up as a set—Mozart supplied his solo sonata catalog irregularly. The fact that piano-learners may tackle the simplest of them early on has been a motive for dismissiveness. The great Mozartean Arthur Schnabel said of the sonatas: too easy for children, too difficult for adults.

In fact the entire series of eighteen, which opens with six from early 1775, K279–84 (an earlier four are lost), and closes with the exhilarating K576 of 1789, contains no low points—the celebrated K545 "for beginners" is a masterpiece of technical wisdom that never stales. It is perhaps to the theme-and-variations finale of K284, in D major, large-scale in exploration of different tempi and expanding horizons, that the word "genius" first becomes applicable to Mozart. Thereafter, it is constantly required.

The most dramatic are the anguished A minor, K310 (from the time of Mozart's mother's death), and the darkly passionate C minor, K457; but the outwardly simple B flat major, K570, with its otherworldly central Adagio, does not reward attention less. For this reason, acquiring a complete cycle affords a special advantage—the evaluation of supposedly lesser and greater works side by side. Most of the recorded cycles of recent years have been of the highest quality; it is a love of Mitsuko Uchida's superfine, exquisitely color-sensitive, intellectually alert pianism that makes me return to hers more often than any other. **ML**

> *"What is slight is great if written in an easy style that flows naturally and is soundly composed."*
>
> Leopold Mozart

Other Recommended Recordings

Lili Kraus
Columbia Legends SM4K 87992 (4 CDs)
Classical clarity and a distinctive personality from this distinguished Hungarian pianist, a pupil of Schnabel

András Schiff
Decca 443 717-2 (5 CDs)
Light of touch, cool of approach, sometimes low-key, Schiff's readings possess special insight

Sonatas, K 310, K 311, K 533/494, Fantasia, K 397
Alfred Brendel
Philips 473 689-2
Veteran of Mozart, returning with mature authority

The Japanese pianist Mitsuko Uchida is renowned as a great Mozartian. ➔

Wolfgang Amadeus Mozart
Violin Concerto no. 5, "Turkish" (1775)

Genre | Concerto
Performers | Henryk Szeryng, New Philharmonia Orchestra
Conductor | Alexander Gibson
Year recorded | 1966
Label | Philips 464 810-2 (9 CDs)

After once hearing a performance of a violin concerto full of flashy virtuosic pyrotechnics, Mozart remarked to his father that although he enjoyed it, "I am no lover of difficulties." Mozart's violin concertos bear this out: there are no displays of brilliance for its own sake, although the apparent simplicity of the solo lines is deceptive. Mozart was a violinist (and a pianist), and performed his five violin concertos more than once. The earliest was composed in 1773, the other four were written within a few months in 1775, when the nineteen-year-old Mozart was living and working in his native Salzburg. The fifth is the most adventurous, featuring an unexpectedly wild episode in its final movement. Horns add a warm glow to the opening Allegro, where energetic tuttis contrast with solo passages. The central Adagio is simple but expressive and lyrical. The rondo finale is a graceful minuet that proceeds sedately until a surprise, dervish-like interruption in the Turkish style. Cheekily, the movement then resumes as if nothing untoward had occurred, ending as calmly as it began.

Henryk Szeryng's affectionate performance is delightful. His tone is sweet but never cloying, and the chamber-sized forces of the New Philharmonia under Alexander Gibson provide a sensitive accompaniment. The performance has a wonderfully relaxed feel, but remains alert with well-chosen tempi. Szeryng's execution of the "Turkish" episode is a highlight: an exciting and spirited sense of abandon, with no trace of coarseness. The bargain box includes the violin concertos with Szeryng, plus highly recommendable versions of the Sinfonia concertante for violin and viola, K364, and all the wind concertos. **GR**

"This concerto is unsurpassed for brilliance, tenderness, and wit."

Alfred Einstein

Other Recommended Recordings

Andrew Manze, English Concert
Harmonia Mundi HMU 907385
Concertos nos. 3–5 in vivid, "operatic" performances with a terrific sense of fun

Pamela Frank, Zürich Tonhalle Orchestra
David Zinman
Arte Nova 74321 72104 2 (2 CDs)
Fresh, modern interpretations of the violin concertos

Arthur Grumiaux, London Symphony Orchestra
Colin Davis
Philips 438 323-2 (2 CDs)
Stylish 1960s accounts of the violin concertos

Polish-born violinist Henryk Szeryng (1918–88), pictured in 1984. ➔

Wolfgang Amadeus Mozart
Piano Concerto no. 9, "Jeunehomme" (1777)

Genre | Concerto
Performers | Andreas Staier (fortepiano),
Concerto Köln
Year recorded | 1995
Label | Teldec 4509 98412-2

MOZART
PIANO CONCERTOS
NOS. 9 "JEUNEHOMME" & 17

ANDREAS STAIER
CONCERTO KÖLN

DAS ALTE WERK

The Piano Concerto no. 9 in E flat major, K271, could justifiably claim to be Mozart's first great masterpiece. Appropriately for a work that signifies a musical "coming of age," it was composed in the very month that Mozart turned twenty-one: January 1777. The concerto oozes confidence, as Mozart experiments with forms and styles. At its heart is a tragic Andantino in the style of an opera seria aria, muted violins setting an intimate, impassioned tone; none of Mozart's previous concerto movements had tapped into such a deep vein of emotion. The breathless rondo finale, by contrast, bubbles with the joie de vivre of opera buffa. But Mozart has a final trick up his sleeve: the energetic music abruptly comes to a halt, to be replaced by a completely unrelated minuet, whose elegant, cantabile theme is all the more magical for its total unexpectedness. Almost as suddenly, this episode is over, and the effervescent rondo theme resumes, bringing it to a rousing conclusion.

Played on a reproduction of Mozart's own fortepiano, Andreas Staier's performance with Concerto Köln bristles with excitement. Listening to the gutsy, ebullient playing of the period-instrument orchestra, one can imagine how Mozart first performed this daring work. The fortepiano is much lighter and more delicate in tone than a modern grand, making a revelatory difference to the texture; Staier conjures silky beauty and earthy percussiveness from it. There are many splendid recordings of this concerto with modern instruments, but Staier's deserves benchmark status for its sense of joy and evocation of live music as Mozart might have made it. **GR**

"His 'Eroica' . . . one of Mozart's monumental works that he never surpassed."

Alfred Einstein

Other Recommended Recordings

Alfred Brendel, Academy of St. Martin in the Fields
Neville Marriner
Philips 442 751-2 (2 CDs)
Exemplary musicianship from a great Mozart pianist

Howard Shelley, London Mozart Players
Chandos CHAN 9068
Shelley's elegant playing makes this a refreshing disc

Piano Concertos nos. 11 in F major, K413, 12 in
A major, K414 and 13 in C major, K415
Daniel Barenboim, Berlin Philharmonic Orchestra
Teldec 0630 13162-2
A delightful triptych of early concertos

Christoph Willibald Gluck
Iphigénie en Tauride (1779)

Genre | Opera
Conductor | John Eliot Gardiner
Performers | Diana Montague, Thomas Allen, John Aler
Year recorded | 1985
Label | Philips 476 171-2 (2 CDs)

Gluck's penultimate opera brought him his biggest triumph. The climax of his career was the controversial five-year period (1774–79) he spent producing large-scale operas for the Paris Opera, overhauling the *tragédie lyrique*—the French song-and-dance form trademarked by Lully and later Rameau, but moribund because of the Paris Opera's deteriorating standards. The new demands made by Gluck reinvigorated both the institution and medium.

Of the Paris works, each a masterpiece, it was *Iphigénie en Tauride* that won widest acclaim. By contrast with the earlier *Iphigénie en Aulide* (1774)—also descended from Euripides, but elaborately fashioned for a large cast—the *Tauride* opera is the tautest, most "modern" of *tragédies lyriques*, indeed of all Gluck's operas.

Control of means—flexible declamation, potently economical use of orchestral color, reshaping of traditional usages for striking new dramatic ends—is at a peak of concentrated effectiveness. As ever with this composer, the score contains large amounts of self-recycling—notably the heroine's sublime "O malheureuse Iphigénie!" adapted from his 1752 *La clemenza di Tito*—yet it is the consistency of the Classically plain musical language that helps make this one of opera's deepest experiences.

John Eliot Gardiner, his Lyon Opera Orchestra, and Monteverdi Choir, sound the work's depths with awesome completeness. Diana Montague's lyric mezzo-soprano may lack the dramatic-soprano grandeur required, but her beauty of tone offers continual compensation. Thomas Allen and John Aler in the roles of brother and friend have done nothing better on record. **ML**

"Some of the audience were seen to weep from beginning to end."

Mémoires secrets, May 21, 1779

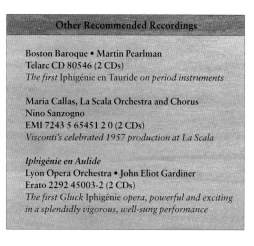

Other Recommended Recordings

Boston Baroque • Martin Pearlman
Telarc CD 80546 (2 CDs)
The first Iphigénie en Tauride *on period instruments*

Maria Callas, La Scala Orchestra and Chorus
Nino Sanzogno
EMI 7243 5 65451 2 0 (2 CDs)
Visconti's celebrated 1957 production at La Scala

Iphigénie en Aulide
Lyon Opera Orchestra • John Eliot Gardiner
Erato 2292 45003-2 (2 CDs)
The first Gluck Iphigénie *opera, powerful and exciting in a splendidly vigorous, well-sung performance*

Wolfgang Amadeus Mozart
Sinfonia concertante in E flat major (1780)

Genre | Concerto
Performers | Gidon Kremer, Kim Kashkashian
Conductor | Nikolaus Harnoncourt
Year recorded | 1984
Label | DG 453 043-2 (2 CDs)

Although Mozart wrote most of his violin concertos in his twentieth year, his Sinfonia concertante, although composed just four years later, must count as his only mature solistic work for string instruments. Strictly speaking, a sinfonia concertante is a different genre from a concerto, having several soloists, who characteristically have different thematic material from the orchestra. Mozart called just three of his compositions "sinfonie concertanti": a fragment for violin, viola, and cello with orchestra; a work for four winds that has not survived in its original form; and the present one.

Stylistically, it has characteristics from the Mannheim school of composition (an opening fanfare, a prolonged crescendo at the end of the first tutti, rich instrumental textures with divided violas) combined with elements from Salzburgian serenade music (like the alternative use of different instrumental colors), and operatic effusiveness. The violas of the time were smallish instruments with limited carrying power, and Mozart required the player to tune it half a step higher, to maximize its brilliance and allow it to compete on equal terms with the violin.

Nowadays this trick is not necessary, although the higher tuning does give the viola part a special coloration. Kim Kashkashian does not, but her golden, burnished tone is on a par with—and well contrasted to—Gidon Kremer's slender sound on the violin. Both soloists are given a solid Baroque frame by the Vienna Philharmonic under Nikolaus Harnoncourt. The three personalities strike sparks off each other, and their collaboration provides an endlessly fascinating performance. **CMS**

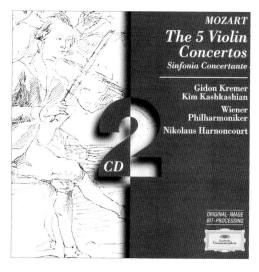

MOZART
The 5 Violin Concertos
Sinfonia Concertante

Gidon Kremer
Kim Kashkashian

Wiener Philharmoniker
Nikolaus Harnoncourt

ORIGINAL-IMAGE BIT-PROCESSING

"You don't realize just how well you play the violin."

Leopold Mozart to his son in 1777

Other Recommended Recordings

Igor Oistrakh, David Oistrakh
Moscow Philharmonic Orchestra • Kirill Kondrashin
Decca 476 7288 (2 CDs)
Big-boned Mozart from a unique father-and-son duo

Albert Sammons, Lionel Tertis
London Philharmonic Orchestra • Hamilton Harty
Naxos 8.110957
A virtuoso playing the higher tuning Mozart intended

Albert Spalding, William Primrose
Friends of Music Orchestra • Fritz Stiedry
Doremi DHR-7764
Spalding in the best company

Kim Kashkashian has been a frequent collaborator with Gidon Kremer. ➔

Wolfgang Amadeus Mozart | Idomeneo, re di Creta (1781)

Genre | Opera
Conductor | John Eliot Gardiner
Performers | Anthony Rolfe Johnson, Anne Sofie von Otter
Year recorded | 1990
Label | Archiv 431 674-2 (3 CDs)

Idomeneo, third of Mozart's four opera seria, is a remarkable example of fluctuating fortunes in musical history. One of eighteenth-century opera's masterpieces, it sums up everything its twenty-four-year-old composer was capable of when commissioned for the 1781 Munich Carnival season. Unfortunately its success there was without follow-up, apart from the 1786 private concert performance in Vienna for which Mozart considerably revised the score (notably Idamante's music, originally for soprano castrato and here reworked for tenor). Thereafter *Idomeneo* suffered total neglect: rarely performed and condemned as hopelessly antiquated. Rediscovery began in the twentieth century, but via heavy-handed rearrangements. The real revival was launched at Glyndebourne in 1951.

The libretto, an Italian refurbishing of an extant French text (1712) by Antoine Danchet, contains every dramatic situation that could be wanted to inspire the young Mozart: burgeoning young love, impending parental death, the difficulty of finding one's place in a hostile world. His response was white-hot. Infusing Gluck's *tragédie-lyrique* innovations (with which Mozart's 1778 Paris sojourn had given him close contact) with his own musical discoveries working with an orchestra in "progressive" Mannheim earlier that year, he created an incomparable dramatic frame in which grandeur is vivified and humanized by lyrical shine and dramatic passion.

No recording encompasses the work—not just its grandeur but its melodic abundance and color warmth—more fully than John Eliot Gardiner's. The choral singing is unbeatable; not so the slightly pale Ilia and Elettra, but Anthony Rolfe Johnson (in peak form) and Anne Sofie von Otter are superbly matched. **ML**

> *"It is only now, two centuries after its composition, that the work's greatness is beginning to be truly appreciated."*

David Cairns

Wolfgang Amadeus Mozart | "Haydn" Quartets (1782–5)

Genre | Chamber
Performers | Hagen Quartet: Lukas Hagen,
Rainer Schmidt, Veronika Hagen, Clemens Hagen
Years recorded | 1995–2001
Label | DG 477 6253 (7 CDs)

The title "Haydn" Quartets refers to six of Mozart's most confidently forward-looking string quartets, which, when considered together, encompass a wide range of manner and mood. It is entirely appropriate that they should be dedicated to Haydn, who had practically invented the string quartet medium and whose own considerable number had a profound influence on Mozart's writing. These newest quartets cost Mozart dear in terms of effort—we know this not only from his own comments but also from the numerous changes in the autograph scores—and what is remarkable is how highly contrasted they are, with each one occupying a world of its own. From the tense sonorities that open the aptly named "Dissonance" Quartet to the heady mood of the "Hunt" Quartet (which owes much to opera buffa in its energetic finale), what is striking about all these works is their degree of confidence and the way in which the first violin no longer hogs the limelight in terms of melodic interest. All four instruments get to shine and these are works that demand a quartet with four distinct personalities, as opposed to a perfectly honed, slick approach.

This they triumphantly find in the Hagen Quartet, which is never afraid to bring out the acerbities in the music. The players opt for tempi that exhilarate in the outer movements while finding time to relish the sheer beauty of slow movements, which have become the true heart of Mozart's quartets. The Andante of the A major, K464, is particularly irresistible in the Hagen's hands. There is drama aplenty, too, from this most accomplished group, as in the fizzing finales of the G major, K387, and E flat major, K428. Altogether, a set to cherish, and one that places these works in the context of the complete Mozart quartets. **HS**

". . . the fruits of a long and laborious toil . . ."

Wolfgang Amadeus Mozart,
writing in the dedication

Other Recommended Recordings

Alban Berg Quartet
Teldec 4509 95495-2 (4 CDs)
Readings that are both wise and revelatory, thanks to a lifetime spent in Mozart's company

Mosaïques Quartet
Auvidis Astrée E 8596 (3 CDs)
These seering period-instrument performances bring out the true novelty of Mozart's writing

Takács Quartet
Hungaroton HCD 12983/5 (3 CDs)
High-octane performances, which make much of the groundbreaking quality of the "Haydn" Quartets

Wolfgang Amadeus Mozart
Die Entführung aus dem Serail (1782)

Genre | Opera
Conductor/Performers | Karl Böhm; Arleen Augér,
Peter Schreier, Kurt Moll, Dresden Staatskapelle
Year recorded | 1973
Label | DG 429 868-2 (2 CDs)

Mozart moved to Vienna in March 1781. *Idomeneo*, premiered two months earlier in Munich, had engendered no new opportunities there, but in Vienna the dry spell was eventually broken by a commission for a *Singspiel* (a piece with songs and spoken dialogue) on the same "rescue from a harem" theme as that of Gluck's 1764 French-language *La rencontre imprévue*, which had enjoyed success. It came to him from the German-language company established by the Emperor Joseph II three years earlier to foster popular opera and counter the preference for Italian and French. The institution folded, yet its brief existence planted a seed that would bear important fruit.

The Emperor's often-quoted opinion on the opera— "Too beautiful for our ears, my dear Mozart, and monstrous many notes"—is probably apocryphal. Regularly recycled nevertheless, it embodies a perception about the central imbalance between libretto slightness and sheer musical exuberance. Marvels of sonority and melody in every bar heighten the delight, while undermining the dramatic continuity. Staging "Martern aller Arten," the showpiece Act 2 aria with its lengthy *concertante*-style instrumental introduction, is just one of several producer's nightmares.

Yet Mozart's dazzling "Turkish" orchestration, the combination of staggering vocal bravura and emotional depth in all the big musical numbers, and his portrait of the harem retainer Osmin, explain the work's perennial fascination and popularity. No recording gives a more flowing, balanced, and satisfying account than Böhm's, or features a vocally finer, less cliché-ridden Osmin than Moll's; Augér and Schreier, too, are at their best. **ML**

> *"In opera the [words] must altogether be the obedient servant of the music. . . . "*

Mozart in a letter to his father, October 13, 1781

Other Recommended Recordings

Erika Köth, Fritz Wunderlich, Bavarian State Opera
Orchestra and Chorus • Eugen Jochum
DG 459 424-2 (2 CDs)
Unmissable for Wunderlich's peerless Belmonte

Luba Orgonasova, Stanford Olsen,
English Baroque Soloists • John Eliot Gardiner
Archiv 477 559-3 (2 CDs)
Note-complete period-instrument performance

Gluck: La rencontre imprévue
Lyon Opera Orchestra • John Eliot Gardiner
Erato 2292 45516-2 (2 CDs)
High-caliber; not deep but continuously delightful

Karl Böhm was always associated with the music of his native Austria. ➡

Wolfgang Amadeus Mozart
Serenade in B flat major, "Gran partita" (c.1783)

Genre | Chamber
Conductor | Daniel Barenboim
Performers | English Chamber Orchestra
Year recorded | 1976
Label | EMI 7243 4 76918 2 9 (2 CDs)

Of Mozart's many serenades for wind instruments, the "Gran partita" shines as a special gem. Its uniquely rich scoring for pairs of oboes, clarinets, basset horns (mellow, lower-voiced cousins of the clarinet), bassoons, four horns, and a string bass, gives the piece a grand, symphonic feel. At more than fifty minutes, it is Mozart's longest chamber work. He completed the serenade shortly after moving to Vienna from Salzburg, and it shows a marked growth in maturity from the lightweight entertainment music he frequently had to turn out in his home town. The Adagio stands out as the work's emotional heart: divinely beautiful melody lines intertwine over a hypnotic, gently chugging accompaniment (it is this movement that composer Salieri describes in Peter Shaffer's play *Amadeus*).

Mozart had an affinity for the varied sonorities that could be conjured from wind instruments, and no group does the sound of this serenade more justice than the wind players of the ECO conducted by Daniel Barenboim. Unlike other recordings, you can appreciate the distinctive timbres of each individual instrument. The sound is excellent, creating a sense of space between the players and capturing the sumptuous tutti with a radiant bloom. The outer movements are lively, and the minuets trip with dance-like grace; the Adagio and Romanze are measured, imbued with Barenboim's innate sense of line. This superb account is reissued with concertos for flute and oboe and the delightful Sinfonia concertante for orchestra and solo wind quartet, K297b. **GR**

Wolfgang Amadeus Mozart
Mass in C minor "Great" (1783)

Genre | Choral
Conductor/Performers | John Eliot Gardiner; Sylvia McNair, Monteverdi Choir
Year recorded | 1988
Label | Philips 420 210-2

Mozart started work on the Mass in C minor shortly after his marriage, in August 1782, to the soprano Constanze Weber, who may have sung in its first performance. Fulfilling a vow made before his wedding to compose a Mass of thanksgiving for the union, the piece is on an ambitious scale. It is arguably Mozart's greatest choral work—although he never completed it, quite why is unclear. Mozart had written more than a dozen Masses during his service for the Prince-Archbishop of Salzburg, but in Vienna he discovered the music of Baroque masters Bach and Handel, and this had a profound effect on his own compositions. The C minor Mass is far grander, more ornate, and complex than his Salzburg Masses, incorporating the great Baroque fugal tradition; much of the choral writing is austere and somber. By contrast, many of the solos are modeled on operatic arias, with brilliant displays of coloratura for the soloists. These contrasts in style heighten the expressive power of the work.

John Eliot Gardiner's recording, with the period instruments of the English Baroque Soloists, makes a compelling case for the mixture of styles in the Mass, and features some beautiful solo singing. A highlight is the Sylvia McNair's ravishing "Et incarnates," sung with passion and ethereal devotion; the flute and oboe obligatos are sublime. The choir sings with clear, immaculate precision. The opening Kyrie chorus is suitably dark but buoyantly pointed, avoiding dirge-like leadenness; the Gloria is jubilant; and the Credo lively and vibrant. **GR**

Wolfgang Amadeus Mozart
Symphony no. 36, "Linz" (1783)

Genre | Orchestral
Conductor | Charles Mackerras
Performers | Prague Chamber Orchestra
Year recorded | 1986
Label | Telarc CD-80148

"On Tuesday, November 4, I am giving a concert in the theater here and, as I have not a single symphony with me, I am writing a new one at break-neck speed, which must be finished by that time. Well, I must close, because I really must set to work." So wrote Mozart to his father from Linz, the capital of Upper Austria, on October 30, 1783—just five days before the planned performance. Mozart's tone does not suggest that he was daunted by the task, and nothing about the finished piece indicates it was written in haste. Indeed, the work's slow introduction (the first time Mozart begins a symphony this way) gives the impression of carefully considered music, grand and serious in tone. The large-scale Allegro spiritoso that follows bristles with energy. The lilting Andante, in 6/8 time, unusually features trumpets and drums. The minuet and delicate trio are particularly dance-like, while the lively finale is a tour de force that takes the breath away.

Charles Mackerras directs a crisp and animated performance with an excellent band of Czech musicians. The string tone of the PCO is warm, and the woodwind playing full of character. The orchestra uses modern instruments, but the overall effect is in the period-practice mold. Mackerras divides first and second violins left and right, as Mozart would have done, the timpanist plays with wooden sticks, and there is a discreet harpsichord continuo line throughout. Speeds are carefully judged, the phrasing elegant. All repeats are observed, serving to give the symphony an even more substantial feel. **GR**

Joseph Haydn
Symphony no. 83, "La poule" (1785)

Genre | Orchestral
Conductor/Performers | Adam Fischer;
Austro-Hungarian Haydn Orchestra
Year recorded | 1992
Label | Nimbus NI 5419/20 (2 CDs)

In 1779 Haydn's employer, Prince Esterházy, allowed him to take on external commissions. One of the first Haydn accepted came from a masonic lodge in Paris for six symphonies, which inevitably became known as his "Paris" symphonies (nos. 82–87). An opportunity to taste life outside the Esterházy court, the commission also enabled Haydn to expand his artistic horizons. The lodge's orchestra was larger than Esterházy's (seventy players instead of twenty-five), and Paris musicians were famed for their brilliance—not only of their playing, but also their attire, in this case sky-blue dress coats and swords. Haydn was also writing for large audiences, rather than small court gatherings. The "Paris" symphonies were consequently conceived on a grand scale. The nickname for no. 83 in G minor, "La poule" ("The Hen"), refers to the second theme of the first movement, a chirpy violin tune with a "pecking" oboe motif that does indeed bring to mind a chicken.

Adam Fischer's recordings of all Haydn's symphonies, with a select band of musicians from Austria and Hungary, are very special. The venue for the fourteen-year project was the Esterházy Palace at Eisenstadt in Austria, which gives the recordings a unique selling-point. But the performances do not have to rely on this: they are full of music making of the highest order. No. 83 is a case in point: lively, muscular playing in the dramatic and turbulent passages contrasts with charmingly light and witty precision in the radiantly sunny sections. Influenced by period practice, this is a delightful, perfectly proportioned performance. **GR**

Wolfgang Amadeus Mozart | Piano Concerto no. 20 (1785)

Genre | Concerto
Performers | Clifford Curzon, English Chamber Orchestra
Conductor | Benjamin Britten
Year recorded | 1970
Label | Decca 468 491-2 (2 CDs)

Mozart's twenty-seven solo piano concertos constitute his richest achievement in instrumental music. Astonishingly, fifteen were produced between 1782 and 1786, his most successful years of Vienna concert-giving. In matters of thematic development, harmonic organization, soloist-orchestra integration, texture variation, and atmosphere, each achieves one astonishing advance upon another.

The musico-dramatic terms in which all were conceived proclaim ties with the adjacent operas in the Mozart catalogue. None more so than the Piano Concerto no. 20 in D minor (K466), the first of three from 1785: *Don Giovanni* was two years away, *Idomeneo* four in the past, yet the D minor storms and cataclysms of both operas are mirrored in the concerto's pre-Romantic turbulence.

In an opening full of *sotto voce* foreboding, tension builds, yet dramatic points are made as much by delicate suggestion—the piano's first entry with an enigmatically plain new theme—as by lightning flashes and tumultuous outbursts. The middle movement's simple B flat major lyricism provides contrast; so too the rondo's tensely upward-leaping first statement. The *coup de théâtre* is reserved for the coda. The key of D minor transforms itself into major, dark moods that give way to a merriment as unfathomable as it is unarguably, elatingly "right."

Decca's K466, fruit of the friendship between Clifford Curzon and Benjamin Britten, sustains an ideal balance between theater and pure music, drama, and repose. No recorded performance "stages" the closing transformation with greater naturalness, ease, or elegance, and few others in the Curzon discography capture his wondrous beauty of tone, its pianissimo possessed of (as critic Harold C. Schonberg said) "twenty degrees of shading." **ML**

> "The birth of the D minor is one of the great stages in its author's musical journey."

Cuthbert M. Girdlestone

Other Recommended Recordings

Alfred Brendel, Scottish Chamber Orchestra
Philips 462 622-2
"Late" Brendel Mozart, lean-toned and searching as ever, superbly supported by Charles Mackerras

Rudolf Serkin, Columbia Symphony Orchestra
Georg Szell
Sony SK 89029
Famously "Beethovenian" account of the score

Annie Fischer, Philharmonia Orchestra • Adrian Boult
EMI 0946 3 59979 5 8
Warm-hearted, large-scaled performance by a great, underrated Mozartean

Despite leaving a large discography, Clifford Curzon hated recording. ➲

Wolfgang Amadeus Mozart | Piano Concerto no. 21 (1785)

Genre | Concerto
Performers | Murray Perahia (piano/director),
English Chamber Orchestra
Year recorded | 1984
Label | Sony SK 92734

Mozart relished producing pairs of masterpieces, generically related yet distinct and contrasted in content. Only a month separates the 1785 completion date of the Piano Concerto no. 21 in C major (K467) from that of its predecessor in D minor; but while symphonic coherence, structural inventiveness, and use of the same orchestral forces unite them (horns, trumpets, and timpani), they could hardly be more different in dramatic impact.

So potent are the sensuous delights of K467, and so fresh, no matter how often one experiences them, that Mozart's originality in overall balancing of its shape and substance is in danger of being underemphasized. Its enormous popularity derives from the character of the F major middle movement, an Andante invitation to dream during which romantic melody pours out in an operatic manner unequalled elsewhere in his instrumental output, albeit foreshadowed by the D major Adagio of K216, the G major Violin Concerto. (The K467 Andante was used in the soundtrack of the 1967 film *Elvira Madigan*.)

Yet this middle movement is also a bold experiment in thematic and harmonic complexity disguised by the pervasiveness of the time-stopped atmosphere. And in the enclosing movements the same intellectual toughness achieves contrasting marvels of subterfuge and games of catch between orchestra and soloist. Indeed, the deceptive slightness of the C major thematic content creates a perfect frame for the Andante's expressive abundance.

From Perahia's 1980s complete cycle of concerto recordings—altogether an essential component of any Mozart collection—this perfectly poised K467 is a stand-out item: itself a miracle of balance between poetry and intellectual adventure, and a modern Mozart classic. **ML**

> "*K466 and K467 . . . [show] that the concerto could stand with equal dignity beside any other musical form.*"
>
> Charles Rosen

Other Recommended Recordings

Clifford Curzon
Bavarian Radio Symphony Orchestra • Rafael Kubelík
Audite 95.453
Radio recording from 1976—moments of pure magic

Maria João Pires
Chamber Orchestra of Europe • Claudio Abbado
DG 439 941-2
Bracingly enjoyable performance invigorated by its genuine all-round collaboration

Robert Casadesus, Cleveland Orchestra • Georg Szell
Sony SBK 67178
Casadesus's "objective" and coolly graceful approach

Wolfgang Amadeus Mozart | Piano Concerto no. 22 (1785)

Genre | Concerto
Performers | Malcolm Bilson, English Baroque Soloists
Conductor | John Eliot Gardiner
Year recorded | 1984
Label | Archiv 463 111-2 (9 CDs)

On December 16, 1785, Mozart completed a new concerto, and played it at a subscription concert twelve days later. Here, according to his father, "a rather unusual occurrence" took place: "he had to repeat the Andante."

At the close of an *annus mirabilis* for the Mozart piano concerto, this third one, the Piano Concerto no. 22 in E flat major (K482), was as distinct from its predecessors as they had been from each other. What all three share is immaculate craftsmanship, astonishingly inventive formal handling, keyboard mastery, and the indelible imprint of Mozart's theatrical imagination.

In K482, however, his concentration on contrasts of instrumental color, underlined by the addition of clarinets to the orchestra, proves even more sophisticated. At times it seems to be a wind divertimento inserted into a concerto that is itself a symphony. Exquisite woodwind shadings mark the moments of major-key consolation in the C minor Andante and of A flat major reverie at the center of the final Allegro; sensual pleasure is heightened.

Since work on *Le nozze di Figaro* had already begun, it is remarkable that the theater work most often evoked by K482, *Così fan tutte*, was still five years off. But in matters of key choice and relationship, and in the way an apparently sunny comedy passes through deep shadow, K482 and the 1790 opera demand recognition as blood relatives.

K482 notches a high point of the epoch-making Bilson-Gardiner Mozart concerto cycle on period instruments. It possesses marvelous tanginess of color; every participant, not just the fortepianist, shows extreme sensitivity to moments of color change. The effect is of an electrically charged whole rendered somehow all the more serene, expansive, and captivating in essential character. **ML**

" . . . the most notable characteristic of this concerto is a kind of luxuriant leisureliness."

Philip Radcliffe

Other Recommended Recordings

Robert Casadesus, Columbia Symphony Orchestra
Georg Szell
Sony SM3K 46519 (3 CDs)
Large-scale approach, controlled with infinite care

András Schiff, Camera Accademica of Salzburg
Mozarteum • Sándor Végh
Decca 425 855-2
Playful interpretation reading—Schiff's third-movement cadenza quotes from Così fan tutte

Christian Zacharias, Lausanne Chamber Orchestra
MDG 340 1182-2
A major Mozart pianist of the day at his most outgoing

Wolfgang Amadeus Mozart | Horn Concerto no. 4 (1786)

Genre | Concerto
Performers | Dennis Brain, Philharmonia Orchestra
Conductor | Herbert von Karajan
Year recorded | 1953
Label | EMI 7243 5 66950 2 3

Mozart reputedly expressed an early affinity with the horn, and his life-long friendship with the talented Viennese player Joseph Leutgeb later afforded him the opportunity to develop this interest fully. Born in Vienna in 1732 Leutgeb was, in 1763, appointed to the Esterházy Court Orchestra, commanding as high a salary as Haydn himself. Leaving within a month, however, he soon became first horn in the Prince-Archbishop's orchestra at Salzburg (Mozart's native city), where he stayed for fourteen years. Mozart's concertos date not from this Salzburg period, but from the 1780s after Leutgeb had returned to Vienna to run a cheese shop.

Scholarship has established that the traditional numbering of the horn concertos is incorrect; the present work, K495, is now known to be Mozart's third horn concerto, while the finale to his first (unfinished) concerto survives as the Concert Rondo, K371. Although the manuscript for K495 displays Mozart's humor in its use of four different colored inks, it is disappointingly incomplete; the first movement, part of the second, and two-thirds of the finale are missing. The standard performing edition is one published in Vienna in 1803 but this is by no means regarded as authoritative; the scholar John Humphries has produced a modern edition based on an early nineteenth-century copy known to have been owned by Aloys Fuchs.

Since its release, this legendary recording by Dennis Brain (in mono) has been regarded as the benchmark, despite other notable players. This is the first choice for any collection, but without hearing a period-instrument performance the listener misses Mozart's skill in turning the horn's limitations to musical advantage by pointing up the contrasting timbre of the stopped notes. **DC**

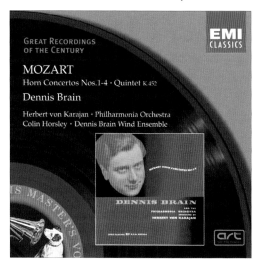

GREAT RECORDINGS
OF THE CENTURY

MOZART
Horn Concertos Nos.1-4 · Quintet K.452

Dennis Brain

Herbert von Karajan · Philharmonia Orchestra
Colin Horsley · Dennis Brain Wind Ensemble

"Mozart might have written the Horn Concertos for Brain to play."

Donald Mitchell

Other Recommended Recordings

Anthony Halstead,
Academy of Ancient Music • Christopher Hogwood
L'Oiseau-Lyre 443 216-2
Highly regarded period-instrument performance

Barry Tuckwell, English Chamber Orchestra
Decca 458 607-2
*Excellent value disc additionally offering
the Concert Rondo, K371, and fragments*

Radovan Vlatkovic,
English Chamber Orchestra • Jeffrey Tate
EMI 0777 7 64851 2 6
An outstanding horn player outside British tradition

Dennis Brain died at thirty-six, but left a formidable recording legacy. ➔

Wolfgang Amadeus Mozart | Piano Concerto no. 23 (1786)

Genre | Concerto
Performers | Wilhelm Kempff, Bamberg Symphony Orchestra
Conductor | Ferdinand Leitner
Year recorded | 1960
Label | DG 457 759-2

Mozart's mature piano concertos create worlds of their own; were any single one to be his essay in the medium, instead of supplying just one component of a vast musical monument, its sheer individuality would perhaps stand out more sharply. Piano Concerto no. 23 in A major (K488) proposes an unprecedented quantity of thematic material. The first movement alone pours out a prodigal abundance of memorable melodies, long-lined (unlike those at parallel points in the two previous piano concertos) and capable of endless developmental extension. With this chastely generous lyricism comes a sublime new delicacy of mood. Oboes, trumpets, and timpani having been removed, the orchestral intimacy gives prominence to clarinet colorations that look forward to two even more diaphanous A major works, the Clarinet Quintet, K581, and Concerto, K622. In this piano concerto the gentle character of the sound world is indivisible from its formal shape and dramatic purpose, yet with his outpouring of airily graceful melodies and sounds, Mozart disguises the taut coherence with which that indivisibility is accomplished.

Of the three piano concertos—K482, K488, and K491—composed alongside *Le nozze di Figaro*, the family resemblance is most apparent in the middle one: above all in its F sharp minor Adagio. In this same key, Barbarina opens the opera's fourth act, lamenting the loss of her pin. Simplicity of effect is the secret of mastery in both, yet in the concerto the expressive range is infinitely greater: few passages in Mozart achieve, indeed, such poignancy.

This work found in Wilhelm Kempff an ideal exponent. On form the most Apollonian of pianists, he irradiates this entire 1960 performance with the rarest kind of pianistic poetry: it proceeds on a current of pure inspiration. **ML**

> ## "Nowhere does Mozart sacrifice . . . power to attain this almost divine limpidity of expression."

Alec Hyatt King

Other Recommended Recordings

Clifford Curzon, Vienna Philharmonic Orchestra
Georg Szell
Decca 473 116-2 (4 CDs)
Suppressed during Curzon's lifetime, posthumously revealed in all its unrivalled tonal beauty

Clara Haskil, Vienna Symphony Orchestra
Paul Sacher
Philips 475 739-3 (7 CDs)
Magically simple and profound

Solomon, Philharmonia Orchestra • Herbert Menges
EMI 0946 3 53211 2 8
Wonderfully pertinent reminder of Solomon's poise

Wilhelm Kempff (1895–1991), pictured in 1964. ➤

Wolfgang Amadeus Mozart
The Marriage of Figaro
(1786)

Genre | Opera
Conductor/Performers | Charles Mackerras; Alastair Miles, Nuccia Focile
Year recorded | 1994
Label | Telarc CD-80388 (3 CDs)

"The Italian opera buffa has started [in Vienna] again," Mozart wrote to his father in 1783, "and is very popular. . . . Our poet now is a certain Abbate Da Ponte [who promises that soon] he will write a libretto for me." This was his first reference to the Veneto-born ex-priest and poet later to collaborate with him on opera's most perfect-ever union of notes and words. The partnership resulted in three works: *The Marriage of Figaro* (1786), *Don Giovanni* (1789), and *Così fan tutte* (1790). Together they form a triptych whose panels present contiguous aspects of human erotic love—each differently tinged with sadness and pain.

The Marriage of Figaro, the "domestic" comedy, unfolds a single *folle giornata* in one household. It was Mozart's idea that an opera should be made of Beaumarchais's notorious social satire, and while obstacles and cabals delayed its realization, the writing took (according to Da Ponte) only six weeks. Such speed testifies to Mozart's mastery of direction, likewise to the librettist's control of dramatic and verbal tone. Apart from two arias in Act 4 that are often cut, nothing is superfluous: *Figaro* is among the central, eternally self-renewing works of Western art.

It is conductor Charles Mackerras's feeling for this wholeness, his command of dramatic scale and style that make his Telarc recording "the one to have"—or at least to start with. Others may offer more striking individual contributions, although Mackerras's cast (Alastair Miles, Nuccia Focile, and Alessandro Corbelli) is without weakness. As a total experience I find his matchless. **ML**

Wolfgang Amadeus Mozart
Piano Concerto no. 24
(1786)

Genre | Concerto
Performer | Clifford Curzon
Conductor | Rafael Kubelík
Year recorded | 1970
Label | Audite 95.453

In the opinion of important Mozart scholars, the Piano Concerto no. 24 in C minor (K491) is his greatest concerto. The long-lined, soft-voiced opening string theme, is by no means the familiar genial invitation to pleasure, unlike that of the predecessor concerto, the A major, K488. Apparently announcing the departure of a spiritual journey, the phrase proves, however, strangely disturbing, even disorienting in its angular upward leaps, compensatory downward slithers, and pauses for breath. Oscillating string 16th notes herald new vistas; the piano's first entry, unaccompanied as it quietly ascends an octave, is the first "human" response to the orchestral portents. Throughout this and the following movements, Mozart sustains an atmosphere of solemnity, of which his insistence on concluding in the minor provides the summation. The whole bears overt traces of operatic kinship, while lacking the theatrical personality of its sibling concertos adjacent in the catalog. This affords a sharp contrast with the previous one in a minor key, no. 20, above all its ambiguous major-key opera-buffa ending. Instead, K491 throws a line to the otherworldliness of Mozart's final works.

Only a pianist capable of marrying infinite variety of tonal shading, effortless mastery of nuance, unblemished power of statement, and iron control of strong emotion will "make the journey." None does so more completely than Clifford Curzon. In addition, this Audite retrieval from the Bavarian Radio Symphony archives benefits inestimably from Rafael Kubelík's wise conducting. **ML**

Wolfgang Amadeus Mozart
Piano Quartet in E flat major (1786)

Genre | Chamber
Performers | Paul Lewis (piano),
Leopold String Trio
Year recorded | 2002
Label | Hyperion CDA 67373

Wolfgang Amadeus Mozart
Piano Concerto no. 25 (1786)

Genre | Concerto
Performer | Stephen Kovacevich
Conductor | Colin Davis
Year recorded | 1972
Label | Philips 476 5316

Mozart's two piano quartets are among his lesser played works. Mozart was originally commissioned by Franz Anton Hoffmeister, a composer and publisher, to write three. This was the era of amateur music-making, and there was a great demand for small-scale chamber music that was not too taxing. However, Mozart's first quartet (in G minor, K478) proved too technically and emotionally demanding, way beyond the scope of most amateurs. After it sold badly, Mozart was encouraged to take the money and run—he got the check and was politely requested to keep away from the piano quartet. But the medium intrigued him and he composed a second work, in E flat. It is no simpler than the earlier one, but Mozart's public belatedly caught up with him, and these works were acknowledged for the masterpieces that they are.

The Second Piano Quartet is a delight, and outwardly more genial than the first. The work is in many respects like a small-scale piano concerto and it demands keyboard playing that is both charismatic and democratic, as it blends with the strings. This it gets in spades in this recording from Paul Lewis and the Leopold Trio. The slow movement is particularly beautiful, large-scale in its thinking, but intimate in its sonorities, and is effortlessly and unaffectedly played by Lewis and his trio colleagues. It is a movement that benefits from a simplicity of approach and the players let it speak for itself. To end, a movement that combines grace and liveliness, and Lewis and the Leopolds extract every ounce of playfulness. **HS**

In the nineteenth century the Piano Concerto no. 25 in C major (K503) was the least loved of Mozart's piano concertos. Restored to the repertoire in the twentieth, it is now ranked among his most substantial compositions. The reason for its past rejection, though, is not hard to find. To the Romantics, who thrilled to the tragic C minor of its immediate 1786 predecessor, K491, or to the earlier K466's "demonic" D minor, there was something frigidly marmoreal about a concerto at once outwardly imposing in instrumentation and neutral in melodic material.

Parallels can be drawn with Mozart's last opera, *La clemenza di Tito*, once equally scorned and now reinstated in the repertoire. Both works open and close in ceremonial C major; both embody some of his most arresting adventures in Neo-Classicism and symphonic construction. This piano concerto's impact depends on a listener's awareness of its flawless placing of detail—such as the first movement's coloristic major-minor contrasts, or the finale's burst of lightly scored F major cantabile—and even more on an ability to comprehend that detail within the larger structure. It also depends on the performers: on the pianist's command of solo writing, and on the conductor's ability to hold the form while allowing each moment to speak. The combination of the young Stephen Kovacevich, Colin Davis, and the London Symphony Orchestra is thrilling when first encountered, and has increased in stature since. No recorded K503 is more impassioned or more completely convincing. **ML**

Wolfgang Amadeus Mozart
Symphony no. 38, "Prague"
(1786)

Joseph Haydn
Seven Last Words
(1787)

Genre | Orchestral
Conductor | Herbert von Karajan
Performers | Berlin Philharmonic Orchestra
Year recorded | 1977
Label | DG 429 668-2 (3 CDs)

Genre | Chamber
Performers | Rosamunde Quartet: Andreas Reiner,
Simon Fordham, Helmut Nicolai, Anja Lechner
Year recorded | 2000
Label | ECM 461 780-2

Mozart was appreciated in the Czech capital of Prague as nowhere else in his lifetime. Following the rapturous reception of *The Marriage of Figaro* in Prague, Mozart wrote to his father that "the one subject of conversation here is *Figaro*; nothing is played, sung, or whistled but *Figaro*." Mozart conducted a performance of the opera in Prague in 1787, as well as a new symphony written especially for the city. This is one of only three symphonies that Mozart begins with a slow introduction, a favorite device of Haydn. The Adagio here is on a grander scale than any other; the main Allegro is truly majestic, with a sense of drama that foreshadows *Don Giovanni* (commissioned by the Prague opera in 1786). This movement is one of the very few pieces for which Mozart left elaborate sketches, indicating just how complex the music is. The central Andante (there is no minuet) forms a profound core to the symphony, full of disquieting harmonic tensions and contrapuntal imitations, propelled by a gentle, but inexorable rhythmic drive. The final Presto is a brilliant, rousing conclusion.

Herbert von Karajan's well-honed performance with his Berlin players is big-band Mozart at its best. The Berlin Philharmonic sound is second to none, and although Karajan paints with a broad brush he is never too indulgent: the opening Adagio is gloriously magisterial, while the Allegro springs with a joyful lightness of touch. The Andante is intense and the Presto delightfully fleet. With no minuet to drag its feet in the usual Karajan manner, this recording can be unhesitatingly recommended. **GR**

In 1785 Haydn received a commission from the cathedral in Cádiz, southern Spain, for a piece based on the seven last words of Christ, to be played during the Good Friday service. His orchestral score consisted of seven adagio movements each prefaced by readings from the seven last words. The work begins with a solemn introduction, and ends with a fiery portrayal of the earthquake that followed Christ's death. Haydn found it "no easy task to compose seven adagios lasting ten minutes each, and to succeed one another without fatiguing the listeners." The result is a deeply moving work, which Haydn regarded as one of his greatest; he conducted it at his last public performance in 1803. Several years after its first performance Haydn added choral parts to the score in an attempt to re-model the work in the style of an oratorio, but it is the quartet arrangement that Haydn made in 1787 that does the piece most justice. The serenity of the music is best served by the more direct expression of a string quartet, uncomplicated by orchestral detail and the intimate scoring connects with the listener on a more personal, contemplative level.

The Rosamunde Quartet gives a historically informed account on modern instruments, which masterfully imbues each adagio movement with the sense of the text it follows. The players have a fresh, clean sound and use vibrato sparingly—resulting in a greater expressive impact when they do. The performance (without readings) has vitality and poise in equal measure and, above all, an emotional depth that leaves you transfixed. **GR**

Wolfgang Amadeus Mozart
Eine kleine Nachtmusik
(1787)

Genre | Orchestral
Conductor | Neville Marriner
Performers | Academy of St. Martin in the Fields
Year recorded | 1987
Label | Philips 464 022-2 (2 CDs)

One of Mozart's most famous works, the serenade *Eine kleine Nachtmusik* is an essay in simplicity, packed with well-known tunes that can be hummed by millions across the world. Scored for two violins, viola, cello, and double bass, it may have been intended for a chamber quintet rather than a full orchestral string section; such is its effortless grace that it works equally well performed on a small or larger scale. A model of perfectly concise writing, this is as well-rounded and complete a work as anything Mozart ever wrote (making it surprising that a further minuet and trio and sketches have recently been found).

It was composed in 1787, in the midst of Mozart's work on *Don Giovanni*, but little is known of the impetus for its appearance; the simplicity of the writing implies it was probably intended for amateurs. The title, literally "A Little Night Music," may more properly be styled "A Little Serenade": *Nachtmusik* is a direct German translation of the Italian for serenade, *serenata*.

There is no shortage of fine recordings of *Eine kleine Nachtmusik*, but Neville Marriner's with the peerless Academy of St. Martin in the Fields (ASMF) stands out. The orchestra plays with panache and dedication; the strings of the ASMF have never sounded so glorious. Marriner is a consummate Mozartean, and brings a wonderful sense of freshness to this overplayed score. The recording is full and reverberant, but captures an air of intimacy—essential for what is effectively a chamber work. The two-disc collection includes other splendid orchestral serenades. **GR**

Wolfgang Amadeus Mozart
Don Giovanni
(1787)

Genre | Opera
Conductor/Performers | Carlo Maria Giulini;
Eberhard Wächter, Joan Sutherland, Giuseppe Taddei
Year recorded | 1959
Label | EMI 7243 5 67873 2 2 (3 CDs)

Mozart's Prague commission for *Don Giovanni* resulted directly from the December 1786 triumph of *Figaro* there, seven months after its Vienna premiere. His and Da Ponte's choice of subject—Don Juan, the Spanish rake condemned to hell for refusing to give up his dissolute life habits—reinvigorated a theatrical tradition started by the sixteenth-century Spanish playwright Tirso de Molina.

The source material for this *Don Giovanni* was a recently written libretto by Giovanni Bertati, which Da Ponte amplified. Indeed, in this the second of the three Mozart–Da Ponte operatic comedies, the canvas is vastly enlarged: with its opening-scene murder and supernatural denouement, the content is by no means only "comic."

Widely considered opera's supreme achievement, *Don Giovanni* calls to mind Artur Schnabel's definition of masterpieces as being "greater than they can be performed." Near-insuperable staging problems result from the second act, from the excess of wonderful musical numbers in the version usually given, and the difficulty of keeping in balance the drama's awesome dark and brilliant light aspects.

On disc the *Don Giovanni* challenge has been met with surprisingly frequent success. No single set tells the whole story, of course, but EMI's from 1959, a "big house" interpretation combining beauty of vocal and instrumental sound, vitality of characterization, and that elusive overall command of balance, has become the standard by which all others are judged. **ML**

Wolfgang Amadeus Mozart
Piano Concerto no. 26, "Coronation" (1788)

Genre | Concerto
Performer | Robert Casadesus (piano)
Conductor | Georg Szell
Year recorded | 1962
Label | Sony SBK 67178

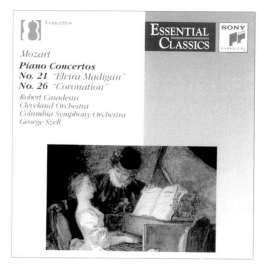

The completion of K503 in 1786 brought Mozart's period of abundant piano-concerto production to a close—he wrote only two more, the Piano Concerto no. 26 in D major (K537), the "Coronation," and the Piano Concerto no. 27 in B flat major (K595). His success as concert promoter-composer-soloist had also ended, thus the change of compositional emphasis after December 1786.

Intended for a Lent 1788 concert that appears not to have taken place, K537 gained its nickname because of a later event, Mozart's Frankfurt performance in October 1790 to coincide with Leopold II's coronation. The problem with the "Coronation" subtitle is that it offers a misleading foretaste of the work's character.

The "Coronation" is the most lightweight of all Mozart's mature orchestral compositions. In the nineteenth century this was the most frequently played of his piano concertos, so lightness was clearly the attraction. Today, however, the pendulum has swung a long way in the other direction, and the glittering charms of a work written to entertain are almost always underrated.

With orchestration of a translucence presaging the final Mozart concertos, it is a vehicle for solo virtuosity. In an interpretation that combines elegance of touch and a freely imaginative approach to melodic nuance, the experience can prove delightful. It does so here with Robert Casadesus, a master Mozartean, supported with perceptiveness and precision by master Mozartean, Georg Szell. The pianist's Gallic style, cool yet never cold, reaches a peak in one of the fastest finales on disc—perfectly appropriate, brilliantly controlled, and utterly dazzling. **ML**

> *"It is the closest to the early or proto-Romantic style of Hummel and Weber."*
>
> Charles Rosen

Other Recommended Recordings

Clifford Curzon, BBC Symphony Orchestra
Pierre Boulez
BBC Legends BBCL 40202
A beautifully poised "Coronation" with a supremely poetic Larghetto

Malcolm Bilson, English Baroque Soloists
John Eliot Gardiner • Archiv 431 211-2 (9 CDs)
Displaying all the advantages of period instruments

Mitsuko Uchida, English Chamber Orchestra
Jeffrey Tate • Philips 468 918-2
Uchida's coloristic sophistication and polished phrasing make this a major success

Robert Casadesus pictured in 1936 with his wife Gaby, also a pianist. ➲

Wolfgang Amadeus Mozart
Symphony no. 39
(1788)

Genre | Orchestral
Conductor | John Gardiner
Performers | English Baroque Soloists
Year recorded | 1990
Label | Philips 426 283-2

Mozart completed his final, and greatest, three symphonies in the summer of 1788—probably intended for a series of subscription concerts that seems not to have taken place. However, the myth that Mozart never heard them performed is almost certainly untrue. Each of the symphonies (nos. 39–41) has its own character; collectively they represent the pinnacle of the Classical symphony.

The key of E flat major in Mozart usually implies warmth and solidity, sometimes solemnity; all these characteristics are evident in Symphony no. 39. The Adagio introduction is stately, with dotted rhythms and gently cascading string figures. The main Allegro contrasts a questioning string theme with vigorous tuttis. It is likely that Beethoven was influenced by this movement when he wrote the Allegro con brio of his "Eroica" Symphony: both share the same key and the first-movement time signature of 3/4. The second movement begins serenely, but becomes agitated with dark, stormy episodes. The minuet is eminently danceable, while the spirited finale is full of delightful high jinks.

John Gardiner directs an unashamedly grandiose account with his smooth-toned period-instrument band. His approach, bordering on the Beethovenian, suits the symphony's varied, often ambiguous, moods—from the shimmering strings and grandiose trumpets and drums of the introduction, through the urgent playing of the turbulent Andante con moto, to the brilliance of the final Allegro. The sunny clarinet solo in the rustic trio is a particular joy. **GR**

Wolfgang Amadeus Mozart
Symphony no. 40
(1788)

Genre | Orchestral
Conductor | Trevor Pinnock
Performers | English Concert
Year recorded | 1994
Label | Archiv 471 666-2 (11 CDs)

There are few more striking beginnings in the symphonic repertoire than the hushed, pulsing intensity that opens Mozart's Symphony no. 40 in G minor. Mozart's circumstances in 1788 were increasingly grim: his financial situation was deteriorating, his popularity with the Viennese public fading, and his marriage to Constanze stormy. "Black thoughts . . . often come to me," he wrote in a begging letter to a friend, "thoughts that I push away with tremendous effort." It is tempting to see these "black thoughts" in this turbulent symphony, one of only two that he set in a minor key. But direct expressions of personal emotion are rare in Classical music. Donald Tovey points to the buoyant, opera buffa–like aspects of the score, suggesting that it is "difficult to see the depths of agony in the rhythms and idioms of comedy"—thus refuting Charles Rosen's view of it as full of "supreme expressions of suffering and terror." Such contrasting views highlight the enormous and continuing impact of this work.

Trevor Pinnock's chosen tempo for the opening Molto allegro is not too indulgent, nor too hurried, but perfectly measured. The playing is urgent, bristling with a subdued energy that erupts with full might in the fiery tutti passages. The Andante features beautiful string playing and immaculate phrasing, while the stormy menuetto still manages to retain a dance-like grace. The final Allegro assai is exhilarating without running away with itself; Pinnock maintains the serious mood while conjuring playing of astonishing energy. All repeats are observed. **GR**

Wolfgang Amadeus Mozart
Symphony no. 41, "Jupiter"
(1788)

Genre | Orchestral
Conductor | Leonard Bernstein
Performers | Vienna Philharmonic Orchestra
Year recorded | 1984
Label | DG 445 548-2

Wolfgang Amadeus Mozart
"Prussian" String Quartets
(1789–90)

Genre | Chamber
Performers | Petersen Quartet:
Muck, Weigle, Eschenburg, Süssmith
Year recorded | 1991
Label | Capriccio CAP 10434

The well-known "title" of Mozart's final symphony, "Jupiter," was not his own (it was most likely the nineteenth-century publisher Johann Baptist Cramer's), but it suits the work's Olympian character. This is evident immediately from the broad, commanding tutti strokes that open the work. The first movement unfolds with a wealth of thematic material that encompasses both militaristic swagger and graceful lyricism; one of the themes is an elaboration of an aria for bass, "Un bacio di mano," K541, that Mozart had written earlier. Muted violins give the Andante cantabile a subdued, unearthly melancholy, but the ensuing minuet restores the assertive mood. The final Allegro molto culminates in a breathtakingly brilliant fusion of no fewer than five separate melodies and motifs before hurtling to a triumphant conclusion in a blaze of trumpets and drums.

Leonard Bernstein's electrifying account, recorded at a concert at the Vienna Musikverein in 1984, manages to reconcile mellowness with a sparkling agility and consummate musical phrasing. Tempi are generally a shade or two slower than expected, especially from period-instruments, but are none the worse for it; rather, the heartfelt expressiveness allows the listener time to savor every nuance of Mozart's masterpiece. Bernstein takes all the repeats, with the result that the work stands as the grand monument that Mozart surely intended. The length is sustained by Bernstein's exhilarating interpretation, whipped up into a frenzy of excitement at the finale. The full-blooded VPO sound is sheer delight. **GR**

Mozart's three "Prussian" Quartets, in D major (K575), in B flat major (K589), and in F major (K590), date from shortly after a visit to Berlin and Potsdam early in 1789. The first, written shortly after his return to Vienna, is dedicated to "his Majesty, the King of Prussia"; borne more out of hopes for a court position rather than affection for the king. But Mozart made sure that the cello—the king's own instrument—featured prominently in all three works. He did the king proud, with such memorable passages as the cello opening theme in the slow movement of K589, and there are frequent instances of cello writing that make no concessions in terms of technique. In his earlier quartets, the first violin tends to take the melody, here equality is everywhere, and these works are all the stronger for it.

The Petersen Quartet is one of the most intelligent and compelling groups around today. These players have a wonderful sweep to their performances, their sound always generous yet spiced with intricate detail and delightful phrasing. They are particularly captivating in the finales of these quartets, which—especially in K590—are among the most carefree, spirited utterances ever penned by Mozart. But they also adopt just the right degree of tenderness in slow movements, and K575 is a particular charmer in their reading. Scherzos—and the three we have here are outstanding examples—are lithe and lively, that of K589 being a real high-kicking affair. If you wanted just one Mozart quartet disc, this would be a strong contender, particularly with performances as fine as these. **HS**

Wolfgang Amadeus Mozart
Clarinet Quintet (1789)

Genre | Chamber
Performers | Sabine Meyer (clarinet),
with members of Vienna String Sextet
Year recorded | 1988
Label | EMI 7243 5 67648 2 8

Mozart had a real love affair with the clarinet (unlike the flute, which he claimed not to like much), writing an exquisite concerto for it and this sublime Quintet in A major (K581). He also used it to great effect in a number of later symphonies and piano concertos. He had been inspired by the playing of two brothers, Anton and Johann Stadler, early exponents of an instrument that at the time was still in its infancy. Mozart first encountered Anton Stadler, for whom he wrote his Clarinet Quintet (and the concerto), when the latter played in one of his wind serenades at Vienna's National Theatre. Mozart exploits the clarinet's mellow quality to the full, blending it subtly with the strings and writing long aria-like melodies for it. It is in the mellow Larghetto second movement that Mozart uses the instrument's songful qualities to greatest effect, the strings initially providing a shimmering backdrop, the first violin then duetting delightfully with its wind colleague.

Nowhere are these qualities better brought out than in the delightful recording by the German clarinetist Sabine Meyer with members of the Vienna String Sextet. She has a melting tone through the entire range of the instrument, seemingly effortless breath control and unerring musicality. The delicacy with which they approach the finale's variations makes them as light as spun sugar. Above all, there is a tremendous sense of shared joy in music making, with each player in turn taking the limelight. The ending finds Mozart at his most insouciant, a mood that is superbly captured by the players here, enhanced by a recording that is so vivid it is as if the musicians are in the room with you. **HS**

Joseph Haydn
String Quartets, op. 64 (1790)

Genre | Chamber
Performers | The Lindsays
Year recorded | 1999
Label | ASV CDDCA 1083,
CDDCA 1084 (2 separate CDs)

Unlike some of the more outgoing Haydn quartets—such as opp. 20, 33, and 76—the op. 64 set is often overshadowed, for it is emotionally quieter, and gives up its secrets less readily. Like the earlier opp. 54 and 55 sets, these six were written for a quartet led by Johann Tost, the maverick lead second violinist of the famous Esterházy Orchestra, and certainly there is an overt tribute to his talent in the Fifth Quartet (aptly nicknamed "The Lark"), both in its soaring opening violin theme and the demanding moto perpetuo writing of the finale. This quartet may be the most famous of the set, but the others should not be overlooked.

The Sixth Quartet is on an equally elevated level, though far more introverted in its manner; The Lindsays, great champions of Haydn, have a complete empathy with the intensity of its first movement (based around a single theme, a device Haydn was fond of using for the formal unity and tautness of construction it gave) and the almost throwaway virtuosity of its finale. They are equally attuned to the quiet wit of the First Quartet and the sheer elegance of its slow movement. And the acidic wit of no. 2—a work that frequently seems to leave performers puzzled—makes perfect sense in their hands. It is a work that can seem unyielding, its composer far from the good-natured "Papa Haydn" figure of popular history, but the Lindsays make much of its harmonic individuality in the dark first movement and there is plenty of bounce in the menuet and fire in the *Sturm und Drang* finale. They are equally passionate advocates of the more straightforward nos. 3 and 4, and altogether this is an alluring set to cherish. **HS**

Wolfgang Amadeus Mozart
Così fan tutte (1790)

Genre | Opera
Conductor/Performers | Bernard Haitink;
Carol Vaness, Delores Ziegler, John Aler
Year recorded | 1986
Label | EMI 0777 7 47727 8 5 (3 CDs)

There is little background information available on the third of the Mozart–Da Ponte triptych of comedies. It is a sophisticated exercise in farce underpinned by Enlightenment philosophy, in which the cynical Don Alfonso wagers with two soldiers over the fidelity of their fiancées, encouraging them to disguise themselves and seduce the other's lover. The libretto is Da Ponte's masterpiece, a blend of music-friendliness, formal mastery, and beauty of diction marked by an enormous range of literary influences.

Così fan tutte may justly be called opera's greatest enigma. Many have noted a basic divergence in the seriousness with which Mozart and Da Ponte viewed the predicaments of the two young couples. The text treats them with elegant comic irony and despatch. The music, however, moves from delicious opera seria parody to some of the most impassioned emotional expression Mozart ever achieved. As a result the ending remains in perpetual doubt: will the lovers return to their original pairings? For such reasons, beneath its exquisitely euphonious, unruffled Mediterranean surface, this is arguably the cruellest and most disturbing opera ever written.

In parallel, no other Mozart opera benefits more from a wide variety of interpretative viewpoints. This Haitink recording makes an excellent starting point for *Così* exploration. Bearing the unifying stamp of one of the Glyndebourne Festival's most searching productions, it strikes an extraordinarily acute balance between comedy and seriousness, sun and shadow; in addition, the virtuoso Fiordiligi of Carol Vaness and brilliantly multi-faceted Alfonso of Claudio Desderi are outstanding. **ML**

Wolfgang Amadeus Mozart
Ave verum corpus (1791)

Genre | Choral
Conductor/Performers | Peter Marschik;
Vienna Boys' Choir, Chorus Viennensis
Year recorded | 1994
Label | Capriccio 10589

Beloved by choirs the world over, Mozart's exquisite motet "Ave verum corpus" for choir and orchestra was composed in June 1791—the last year of his life. It was written for Mozart's friend Anton Stoll, choirmaster at the spa town of Baden, where the composer's wife Constanze was taking the waters to assist her pregnancy-related illness. The motet was probably intended for performance on Corpus Christi Day: the text reflects on Christ's crucifixion, inspiring in Mozart a poignant setting that reconciles the personal and the universal—a theme that Mozart explored fully in his opera *The Magic Flute*. Considering Mozart's Salzburg background in church music, it is surprising that he wrote so few sacred works in adulthood; the Mass in C minor dates from nearly ten years earlier. Although only forty-six measures long, the "Ave verum" is one of the treasures of the choral repertory. The deceptive simplicity of the ethereal melody (closely related to that of an unfinished Adagio for cor anglais and strings, K580a) belies its immense difficulty for performers; Mozart's sole indication of expression is the solitary marking sotto voce.

The many first-class recordings of the work encapsulate its heavenly essence in their own ways, but the most successful is the simplest: that of the Vienna Boys' Choir and Chorus Viennensis conducted by Peter Marschik, with the Volksoper Orchestra. The uniquely sweet, angelic tones of the boys have an innocence of expression that perfectly suits the "Ave verum"; Mozart would certainly have had boys' voices in mind when he wrote it (a fact often strangely ignored by "authenticists"). Marschik directs an uncomplicated, direct, and beautiful reading. **GR**

Wolfgang Amadeus Mozart | The Magic Flute (1791)

Genre | Opera
Conductor/Performers | Colin Davis; Peter Schreier (Tamino), Margaret Price (Pamina), Kurt Moll (Sarastro)
Year recorded | 1984
Label | Philips 442 568-2 (2 CDs)

It used to be a given that Mozart's last years told of unrelieved personal suffering, and that as a result his final works breathe a spirit of detachment and resignation. Recent scholarship has forced re-evaluation, not least by showing that in spite of money difficulties and reduced opportunities, his prospects were far from wholly negative.

Likewise, it used to be suggested that he accepted the commission for *The Magic Flute*, or *Die Zauberflöte*, from Emanuel Schikaneder's Theater Auf der Wieden, home of popular Viennese *Singspiel*, in despair at the lack of openings higher up the scale. But this contradicts everything understood about Mozart's artistic outlook: he mourned the disappearance of Joseph II's German Theater (for which he wrote *Die Entführung aus dem Serail*), and he was an *appassionato* of popular theater.

Schikaneder's libretto—which sends a Prince, Princess, and Birdcatcher on a quest for knowledge, wisdom, and enlightenment, through magical realms of dark and light, fire and ice—was German, exotic, picaresque, and filled with spectacle; Mozart, a Mason since 1784, found additional stimulus in its Masonic imagery. It offered him the chance to exploit his every musico-dramatic skill; in doing so, and in thus ranging from folkish Singspiel ditties to elaborate opera seria–style arias, he transformed the genre and launched the German opera of the future.

This is an opera that never stales for children and adults, savants and groundlings alike. Of the many fine recordings available, it is this Philips's *Zauberflöte* that becomes the "opera for everybody." The singers are uniformly fine as are the actors, the orchestral playing is glorious, and conductor Colin Davis's mastery of mood, style, and meaning underpins every moment. **ML**

> *"A new genre [of German opera] . . . mixing playfulness and solemnity, the vernacular and the lofty."*
>
> David Cairns

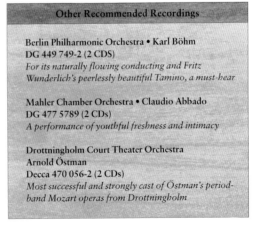

Other Recommended Recordings

Berlin Philharmonic Orchestra • Karl Böhm
DG 449 749-2 (2 CDS)
For its naturally flowing conducting and Fritz Wunderlich's peerlessly beautiful Tamino, a must-hear

Mahler Chamber Orchestra • Claudio Abbado
DG 477 5789 (2 CDs)
A performance of youthful freshness and intimacy

Drottningholm Court Theater Orchestra
Arnold Östman
Decca 470 056-2 (2 CDs)
Most successful and strongly cast of Östman's period-band Mozart operas from Drottningholm

Colin Davis is at home in the opera house pit as on the concert stage. ➔

Joseph Haydn | Symphony no. 94, "Surprise" (1791)

Genre | Orchestral
Conductor | Colin Davis
Performers | Amsterdam Concertgebouw
Year recorded | 1981
Label | Philips 442 614-2 (2 CDs)

Haydn's music has always been well loved for its unique humor, and there is no more obvious example of this than in the famous "Surprise" Symphony. Following the death of Prince Nikolaus Esterházy in 1790, Haydn left his rarified court life to settle in Vienna. Almost immediately he was invited to London by the violinist and impresario Johann Peter Salomon; Haydn's visit in 1791–92, and a subsequent return in 1794–95, resulted in the composition of twelve new symphonies, known as the "London" symphonies, nos. 93–104. Written to appeal to a broad, bourgeois public rather than a refined, insular court, the symphonies abound with simple, popular-style tunes, set into grandly constructed wholes. They were very well received, and remain among Haydn's most popular works; no. 94, the "Surprise," is probably the most famous.

The nickname refers to the unexpectedly loud chord that shatters the hitherto placid start of the second movement. A biography of Haydn asserted that he was annoyed by the English habit of snoozing through concerts after large dinners, and that the crashing "surprise" was calculated to cause a rude awakening. Another author claimed that Haydn was simply "interested in surprising the public with something new." Whatever the truth, it is a good joke that still sounds fresh today.

Colin Davis's interpretation of the "London" symphonies is a remarkable achievement, and his account of the "Surprise" one of the finest in the series. Davis clearly has a special affinity for this music, and every note is infused with an evident love and enjoyment, matched by the excellent Concertgebouw playing. **GR**

Wolfgang Amadeus Mozart La clemenza di Tito (1791)

Genre | Opera
Conductor | John Eliot Gardiner
Performer | Anthony Rolfe Johnson
Year recorded | 1990
Label | Archiv 431 806-2 (2 CDs)

As far as twenty-first-century audiences are concerned, Mozart's last opera is a checkered tale that ends happily: The work enjoyed several decades of popularity before vanishing for much of the last two centuries; since the 1960s it has been triumphantly reinstated.

Before then it was considered Mozart's single mature-opera failure. Received opinion at this time said Mozart was disheartened with his career, unhappy with this last-minute commission celebrating Leopold II's Prague coronation, and on automatic pilot for opera seria, a form already moribund. However, the genre was not dead but developing, and Mozart, as *Idomeneo* made clear, loved it. In *La clemenza di Tito* he modernized it further.

The 1734 *Pietro Metastasio* libretto, concerned with Emperor Titus's legendary clemency toward the Roman aristocrats plotting against him, had been set by at least forty composers; Mozart had it radically shortened. The "beautiful simplicity" that was Gluck's highest aim is manifest in a score marked by extraordinary tautness, concision, and economy. Perhaps these qualities were dictated by Mozart's need to work fast, likewise his delegation of the recitative-writing. But in his *Metastasio* overhaul, the compactness generates a music-drama that both sums up the past and looks far into the future.

This quality is undoubtedly the key to John Eliot Gardiner's electrifying performance (recorded live with the Monteverdi Choir and English Baroque Soloists) and the recording is so full of color, dramatic vitality, and superb singing, that any listener coming to *Tito* through it will find past neglect incomprehensible. **ML**

Wolfgang Amadeus Mozart
Piano Concerto no. 27 (1791)

Genre | Concerto
Performer | Clara Haskil (piano)
Conductor | Ferenc Fricsay
Year recorded | 1957
Label | DG 449 722-2

Mozart first performed his Piano Concerto no. 27 in B flat major (K595)—his last—at a Viennese concert in March 1791, two months after listing it in his works catalogue. It is characterized by exquisite gentleness of manner, complete avoidance of melodramatic gesture, unparalleled refinement of instrumental accompaniment, and an undercurrent of understated emotional intensity.

Such qualities relate K595 to its immediate concerto successor, the Clarinet Concerto, K622 (his final concerto). Perhaps because in the past the last months of his life tended to be understood in biographical terms only of failure, hardship, and illness, it became customary to view both concertos through a prism of autumnal poignancy, renunciation, and leave-taking. However, scholarship suggests that K595 may have been begun as early as 1788, so here hindsight was not entirely wise. Nevertheless, the musical moods are so peculiarly rarefied—even in the finale, with its 6/8 rhythms and similarity to a Mozart song, "Sehnsucht nach dem Frühlinge"—that the older view of the work cannot be dismissed. As with all the late Mozart concertos, surface beauty is deceptive: here the simplicity of lyrical manner disguises a sophisticated approach to harmonic movement.

No Mozart slow movement is barer, simpler, more hauntingly eloquent: ties of kinship with *The Magic Flute* are very evident. No pianist was more at home in the world of mature Mozart than Clara Haskil, and her gift of unadorned phrasing concealing a wealth of subtle nuance and profound musical insight was never more magically demonstrated than in this masterly performance. **ML**

Wolfgang Amadeus Mozart
Clarinet Concerto (1791)

Genre | Concerto
Performers | Charles Neidich (clarinet),
Orpheus Chamber Orchestra
Year recorded | 1987
Label | DG 469 362-2 (3 CDs)

Mozart's last concerto, composed in the autumn of 1791, is one of his most sublime works. Written for his friend, the virtuoso clarinetist Anton Stadler, it is supremely crafted to suit an instrument Mozart had always loved; he was arguably the first composer fully to appreciate its uniquely expressive capabilities. This concerto is often said to have a valedictory feel to it, completed just weeks before Mozart died, but evidence indicates that he was in good health and relishing his busy schedule (he had recently finished work on his final operas, *The Magic Flute* and *La clemenza di Tito*). The Allegro opens with a radiantly sunny theme that cannot fail to put a smile on the face of any listener. The principal melody of the intimate and tender Adagio is one of the most beautiful Mozart ever wrote, exploiting the clarinet's cantabile qualities with elegiac simplicity. The rondo finale is infectiously jubilant, and makes full use of the contrast between the brilliance of the clarinet's upper register and the rich soulfulness of its lower range.

This work was written for basset clarinet, an instrument with an extended low register, designed by Stadler. Although the autograph score is lost (the earliest surviving edition is an adaptation for standard clarinet), it has been possible to reconstruct the clarinet part as Mozart probably wrote it, based on his sketches. The basset clarinet version yields rich dividends, and it has a masterful exponent in Charles Neidich, accompanied by the wonderfully crisp and insightful playing of his colleagues in the democratically directed Orpheus Chamber Orchestra. The outer movements sparkle with lively tempi, and the Adagio is imbued with an especially magical poise. **GR**

Wolfgang Amadeus Mozart | Requiem (1791)

Genre | Choral
Conductor | Neville Marriner
Performers | Academy of St. Martin in the Fields & Chorus
Year recorded | 1990
Label | Philips 432 087-2

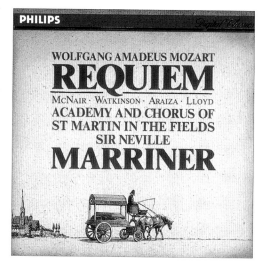

Mozart's final composition, left incomplete at his death on December 5, 1791, has been the subject of much romantic speculation over the years, owing to the unusual circumstances in which it was written. The truth, as we now know, is that the anonymous commission Mozart received for a Requiem Mass came from an unscrupulous count who intended to pass the work off as his own. Mozart eagerly took to the task, not only because he was being well paid: he had high hopes of being soon appointed Kapellmeister of Vienna's grand St. Stephen's Cathedral, and the commission would give him an opportunity to hone his rusty church-music skills. Although in good health when he began work on the score in October, Mozart soon became ill and was bed-ridden by late November. Inevitably, the dying Mozart came to see the work he was struggling to complete as a Requiem for his own death. Mozart completed most of the first half of the work, and left several sketches and instructions for the rest; it was eventually completed by his pupil Franz Xaver Süssmayer. It has been said that Mozart's reputation could rest on this great work alone. While that may be true, it is interesting to note that the Requiem represents a new stylistic direction, an innovative fusion of Baroque austerity with opaque harmonies and sublime melodic lines.

Neville Marriner's noble and committed 1990 account of the Requiem perfectly blends power and gravitas with stylistic finesse and lightness of touch. The dark-hued orchestral sonorities of the score are brought out superbly, and the chorus sings with immense passion. The solo quartet is superb. From horrific visions of terror to heartfelt grief and radiant beauty, this compelling performance delivers with utter conviction. **GR**

> "*. . . didn't I say to you before that I was writing this Requiem for myself . . .?*"

Mozart in his final illness

Other Recommended Recordings

Orchestre des Champs Elysées, Collegium Vocale Philippe Herreweghe
Harmonia Mundi HMC 901620
Dramatic and well-honed period-instrument account

Vienna Philharmonic Orchestra, Vienna State Opera Chorus • Georg Solti
Decca 433 288-2
Recorded on the bicentenary of Mozart's death

Michael Haydn: Requiem
The King's Consort • Robert King
Hyperion CDA 67510
A fascinating comparison with Mozart's Requiem

Marriner is forever linked with the Academy of St. Martin in the Fields. ➔

Domenico Cimarosa | Il matrimonio segreto (1792)

Genre | Opera
Performers | Graziella Sciutti (Carolina), Luigi Alva
(Paolino), Carlo Badioli (Geronimo), La Scala Orchestra
Year recorded | 1956
Label | EMi 7243 5 66513 2 6 (2 CDs)

Leopold II, the Habsburg emperor crowned in 1791, disliked Mozart's operas. By contrast, when Domenico Cimarosa (1749–1801)—a celebrated Neapolitan composer until recently maestro di capella in St. Petersburg— arrived in Vienna the same year, Leopold feted him with a Kapellmeister appointment and a Burgtheater operatic commission. The opera, *Il matrimonio segreto*, a treatment of the famous Colman-Garrick play *The Clandestine Marriage*, enjoyed a bigger success than any Mozart had had in Vienna: indeed, Leopold ordered a private performance repetition the evening of the 1792 premiere.

Two years in Vienna preceded Cimarosa's return to Naples—where in 1799–80 he was jailed for Republican sympathies, before dying in Venice a year later—and was the high point of a career of prolific composition (almost sixty-five operas, comic and serious, and much sacred and instrumental music). He was a sociable, warm-hearted person whose temperament is reflected in his work; it has been his misfortune to be much more greatly eclipsed by Mozart than Mozart was, briefly, by him.

Cimarosa's vivacity and easy, never careless tunefulness, and a gift of comic characterization in music, distinguish the ensemble writing in which *Il matrimonio segreto* is notably rich. Mozartean depths are missing, except in moments of poignant second-act recitative. But EMI's recording from the Piccola Scala, a by-product of Giorgio Strehler's legendary 1955 production, still gives bounteous delight. This uses a truncated score, so Daniel Barenboim's fine DG recording, with all musical numbers complete, is also needed. Even so it remains a treasure of gramophone history, with few equals in Italian comic style, vocal charm, and ensemble sparkle. **ML**

> "… [The style of] Cimarosa, with its glittering array of comic verve, of passion, strength, and gaiety."
>
> Stendhal

Domenico Cimarosa sated the Viennese appetite for Italian opera. ➔

Joseph Haydn | Symphony no. 101, "Clock" (1794)

Genre | Orchestral
Conductor | Eugen Jochum
Performers | London Philharmonic
Year recorded | 1973
Label | DG 474 364-2 (5 CDs)

After a successful year in London, Haydn left England in June 1792 to return to Vienna (en route meeting the young Beethoven in Bonn). Once home he began sketching more new symphonies for his next visit to London, which he embarked on in January 1794. Symphony no. 101, the "Clock," was first performed in March that year. It is one of Haydn's most confident, mature symphonies—the work of a great composer at the height of his powers. It opens with a dark-hued and sinuous Adagio. A silvery chromatic theme gingerly steps upward then winds back down before resolving into the energetic Presto. Haydn originally qualified the Presto marking with "ma non troppo" (not too much), but thought better of it, leaving performers to revel in the "very fast" music.

The symphony's nickname stems from the regular tick-tock motif underpinning the genial theme of the second movement, a rondo-like Andante with contrasting dramatic sections. The minuet is particularly opulent and richly scored, while the trio section features a simple solo flute melody over a rustic drone bass. The final Vivace is carefree but technically perfect, the largely monothematic elements culminating in a delicate fugato passage.

Eugen Jochum's set of the "London" symphonies is a joy, and there is no finer example than no. 101. Jochum conjures effervescent and lively playing from the London Philharmonic; the large scale of the ensemble is perfectly suited to the ebullience of Haydn's late symphonies. The outer movements are brisk and stylish, and the tempo of the Andante is judged to perfection, and its melody imbued with a delightful happy-go-lucky charm. **GR**

Joseph Haydn | Symphony no. 104, "London" (1795)

Genre | Orchestral
Conductor | Herbert von Karajan
Performers | Berlin Philharmonic
Year recorded | 1975
Label | EMI 7243 4 76889 2 8

Haydn's last symphony, no. 104, was first performed in London at an all-Haydn benefit evening on May 4, 1795. He also chose it for performance at his farewell concert three weeks later. The work erupts with a blaze of light, a majestic fanfare that morphs into a subdued, mysterious, and atmospheric adagio introduction in D minor. The Allegro begins gently, before the warm and sunny D major theme is taken up in rousing fashion. In the second movement Andante, sedate and graceful G major sections frame a colossal, minor-keyed, tutti episode: a late, refined example of *Sturm und Drang* drama.

A vigorous minuet encases a pastoral trio that foreshadows the country dance of Beethoven's Sixth Symphony. The sparkling finale is based around a folk tune of Croatian origin that Haydn probably recalled from his youth, although the same tune was also apparently cried out by London street peddlers at the time of his visits: "Hot cross buns!" and "Live cod!" It is possibly for this reason that this symphony was singled out for the sobriquet "London" from the eleven others Haydn wrote there.

The "London" was a favorite of Karajan's: he conducted it more than any other Haydn symphony. Perhaps he appreciated the work's forward-looking stance, for there are many similarities in its grand gestures and rustic charm with Beethoven. But it is first and foremost a last great flowering of the Classical tradition, and Karajan admirably treats it as such in his lovingly crafted 1975 recording with the magnificent Berlin Philharmonic. The performance is by turns muscular and powerful, delicate, and graceful—and the orchestral sound supremely beautiful. **GR**

Joseph Haydn
Trumpet Concerto (1796)

Genre | Concerto
Performers | Mark Bennett (trumpet),
Trevor Pinnock (harpsichord/director)
Year recorded | 1990
Label | Archiv 431 678-2

It is ironic that the most popular of all trumpet works, the Trumpet Concerto by Haydn, was written for a type of instrument that became largely obsolete thirty years after its invention. Haydn composed his great concerto for the Viennese court trumpeter Anton Weidinger, who had been experimenting in the 1790s with an "organisirte Trompete," an instrument with keys that could play chromatically. Haydn was Europe's leading composer, and Weidinger was fortunate in being able to demonstrate his new instrument with such a fine piece. Weidinger also commissioned composers such as Hummel, Süssmayer, and Leopold Kozeluch to write works for his keyed trumpet, which he performed throughout Europe. By the 1820s, however, the keyed action had been superseded by the vastly superior valve mechanism, and the keyed trumpet fell from favor.

Haydn wrote his Trumpet Concerto in 1796 following his second London sojourn and was his last purely orchestral work. It is scored for two flutes, two oboes, two bassoons, two horns, two orchestral trumpets, timpani, strings, and continuo—a typical orchestration for his late period. In the solo part Haydn recalls the brilliant sound of Baroque high-register trumpet writing and illustrates the technical improvements of the new instrument; in the second movement the trumpet is given a lyrical melodic line in its middle octave for the very first time.

This recording of Haydn's trumpet, oboe, and harpsichord concertos dates from golden age of the English Concert, featuring a young Mark Bennett as soloist alongside Trevor Pinnock. With exuberance and elegance Bennett shows the keyed trumpet in its best. **DC**

Luigi Cherubini
Médée (1797)

Genre | Opera
Conductor/Performers | Leonard
Bernstein; Maria Callas, Gino Penno
Year recorded | 1953
Label | EMI 7243 5 67909 2 6 (2 CDs)

Luigi Cherubini (1760–1842) is perhaps the most substantial composer never to have secured front-rank status in the operatic, orchestral, choral, and chamber categories in which he worked. Admirers—who in his lifetime included Beethoven and Schubert, thereafter Wagner and Brahms—reject that assessment. Technically he was a master: born in Florence, he was a key figure in Parisian music from 1789 to the end of his long life in 1842.

From 1795 he was first a teaching inspector at, and later director of, the Paris Conservatoire, where he was revered by students. He suffered estrangement from Napoleon, one reason why his operatic career, flourishing in the early 1790s, tailed off. In compensation he produced chamber and choral masterpieces: Berlioz praised the C minor Requiem for "sustained sublimity of style."

Cherubini's compositional personality, the epitome of turn-of-the-century Neo-Classicism, has been called severe, dry, even cold. But the driving power of *Médée*, a terrifying Classical tragedy, leaves no one unstirred. Its mixture of music and speech led to textual adaptation outside France: an Italian edition, much cut and using Franz Lachner's anachronistic recitatives, gained the opera its international repertoire toehold. This became most tenacious when the awesomely demanding title role figured among Maria Callas's supreme career achievements, as listeners to the EMI set—taken from a radio recording of her stupendous 1953 collaboration with another musical titan, Leonard Bernstein—will readily appreciate. But recent original-*Médée* revivals have rediscovered the work's own full, unrelentingly ferocious grandeur. **ML**

Joseph Haydn
String Quartets, op. 76 (1797)

Genre | Chamber
Performers | Angeles Quartet:
Lenski, Miller, Dembow, Erdody
Years recorded | 1994–99
Label | Philips 464 650-2 (21 CDs)

Haydn's op. 76 set is regarded as the pinnacle of his quartet achievement, demonstrating supreme confidence in his handling of the medium in six works that could not be more varied. They are more extrovert than the op. 64 quartets and written for public performance. They are more experimental than anything that comes before them: though still described as "menuetto," the third movements have become scherzos, ranging in mood from the pure drama of no. 1 to the stomping peasantries of nos. 2 and 4. Slow movements in this set are a particular delight, richly jewel-colored, often surprisingly simple. The theme of the slow movement of the "Emperor" (no. 3) gives rise to variations with seemingly unstoppable inventiveness.

Quartet no. 5 offers a ravishing slow movement, wonderfully played by the Angeles Quartet, one of the very few ensembles to have recorded all of Haydn's string quartets, and its commitment and stylistic understanding shines through. They are all great players, as you can hear in such movements as the opening of no. 4, which gets its "Sunrise" nickname from the sinuous rising line played by the first violin. They bring out Haydn's humor, too, in such places as the opera buffa-ish finale of no. 5. In the hands of the Angeles Quartet, this turns into a madcap caper, which is great fun. And that is the secret of this set—the group is alive to every subtle change in mood, whether it is the twists and turns of the finale of no. 2 or the mixture of major and minor in the fiery last movement of no. 1. This set will provide a lifetime of pleasurable listening. **HS**

Ludwig van Beethoven
Piano Sonata in C minor, op. 13, "Pathétique" (1798)

Genre | Instrumental
Instrument | Piano
Performer | Vladimir Ashkenazy
Year recorded | 1981
Label | Decca 452 952-2 (2 CDs)

You only need to hear the first chord of Beethoven's "Pathétique" Sonata to realize that he was alluding in his title to the spirit of Greek "pathos" rather than to a sense of the "pathetic." An arresting C minor chord launches the slow introduction, which returns twice, interrupting the bubbling Allegro. This is a foretaste of the heroic nature Beethoven (1770–1827) developed in his middle period, and it strengthens his association of C minor as a key representing struggle: a key to which he would return in the funeral march of the "Eroica" Symphony, the Fifth Symphony, and his last piano sonata (op. 111).

Appealing as this opening movement is, it is the song-like slow movement, with its warmly oscillating inner parts, that has attracted countless young piano students. Second in popularity only to the slow movement of the "Moonlight" Sonata, this Adagio has, in the words of one commentator, been "a prey to arrangers and derangers."

Vladimir Ashkenazy's introduction to the first movement features thunderously accented chords, creating a stark contrast with the more ruminative, melodic material. He approaches the Allegro with speed and brilliant articulation, creating a small explosion for the climax before the final return of the introduction. Rather than wallow in the slow movement, Ashkenazy adopts a fluent lyricism in its outer sections; and his third-movement rondo is unusually poised, but with a ringing clarity and capricious charm very apt for a movement that Beethoven is said to have played "with good humor." **EB**

Joseph Haydn
Mass in D minor, "Nelson" (1798)

Genre | Choral
Conductor | Trevor Pinnock
Performers | English Concert & Choir
Year recorded | 1987
Label | Archiv 423 097-2

Joseph Haydn
The Creation (1798)

Genre | Choral
Conductor | Thomas Henglebrock
Performers | Simone Kermes, Steve Davislim
Year recorded | 2002
Label | DHM 05472 77537 2

After the death of Prince Nikolaus Esterházy in 1790, the orchestra with which Haydn had worked for nearly thirty years was disbanded by the prince's unmusical son, Prince Paul Anton, and Haydn was relieved of his main courtly duties with a generous pension. Paul Anton retained Haydn's services for major occasions, such as the celebration of his name-day, which required a new Mass to be composed each year. The "Nelson" Mass was first performed on the prince's name-day in 1798. Neither of its titles was originally associated with the work, but Haydn later conferred the second of the two, *Missa in angustiis* (Mass for times of distress)—reflecting on the troubled backdrop of the Napoleonic wars. Haydn met Lord Nelson when the British admiral visited the Esterházys in 1800; the Mass was probably performed in his honor. It is the grandest of Haydn's settings, and his only in a minor key.

Only a period-instrument orchestra can do full justice to the pungent and vivid sonorities and textures of this distinctive score. In this superb recording, the piquant dissonances of the Kyrie are brought out by vibrant and urgent string playing, and brittle timpani rolls and piercing trumpet calls cut through with terrifying strength. Elsewhere the performance shines with joy and Classical grace. The choral singing is passionate and beautiful, with matching contributions from a splendid solo quartet: Felicity Lott (soprano), Carolyn Watkinson (contralto), Maldwyn Davies (tenor), and David Wilson-Johnson (baritone). The coupling is Haydn's triumphant *Te Deum*. **GR**

In writing his greatest oratorio Haydn was inspired by the large-scale performances he had heard in London of Handel's oratorios; but with *Die Schöpfung* (*The Creation*) he produced something uniquely his own. The strong narrative thread generated by the seven days of Creation as related in the book of Genesis, gave rise to masterly handling by Haydn who, in his mid-sixties, was at the height of his powers.

The text, which originated in English, is drawn from three sources: Genesis, the Psalms, and Milton's epic poem *Paradise Lost*. On his return to Vienna, Haydn entrusted the German translation to Baron Gottfried van Swieten and the work was published both in German and English. It is arranged in three parts; the first and second trace days one to six of the Creation, while the third part takes place on the day of rest in the Garden of Eden (the main characters here shifting from the three archangels to Adam and Eve). The chorus assists with utterances of praise and wonder.

Thomas Henglebrock's period-instrument recording with his Freiburg-based Balthasar-Neumann Ensemble and Choir keeps a tight grip of the unfolding narrative, with brisk speeds, deftly punctuated recitatives, and a spirited chorus. From the creeping "Representation of Chaos" at the opening to the first sunrise to the idyllic pastures of Eden, Haydn's detailed coloring is brilliantly realized. With an alert, agile chorus, and fine young vocal soloists, the result is a testament to the composer's optimism and youthfulness as he approached old age. **EB**

John Field
Piano Concertos (1799–1832)

Genre | Concerto
Performers | Benjamin Frith, Northern Sinfonia
Year recorded | 1996
Label | Naxos 8.553771

Dublin-born John Field was the son of a violinist, who became his first piano teacher. Progress was swift, with Field making his debut at the age of ten, after which he moved to London and was taken on by the leading teacher of the day, Muzio Clementi, who also had interests in both publishing and piano manufacture. After taking in Paris and Vienna, they visited Russia, where Field settled, marrying a French pupil. Settling there was an astute move as Russia lacked a piano tradition, most musical activities being taken up with the theater. He made his name as a pianist of great sensitivity, with a beautiful cantabile sound—in contrast with the taste for overt display that was the order of the day. As well as piano concertos, he wrote nocturnes, whose poetic nature was naturally attuned to his musical style. He was much in demand as a teacher, with pupils from Russia and abroad.

All seven of his piano concertos, the first of which he wrote at the age of seventeen, show a Mendelssohnian flair for melodies and a lightness in his orchestral writing that gives the pianist full rein. The Second Concerto (1811) was the most popular in his lifetime, and it is easy to understand why. Following a Classically conceived opening movement, Field's Poco adagio, with the piano accompanied by strings alone, is reminiscent of a nocturne, and the work culminates in a rondo that gives the soloist plenty of opportunities for virtuoso display. The Fourth Concerto (1814, rev. 1819), though slightly less well known, is every bit as enticing, particularly in a performance as sensitive and light-of-touch as that of Benjamin Frith and his Northern Sinfonia colleagues. **HS**

Joseph Haydn
String Quartets, op. 77 (1799)

Genre | Chamber
Performers | Mosaïques Quartet: Höbarth, Bischof, Mitterer, Coin
Year recorded | 1989
Label | Astrée E 8799

Haydn's last finished quartets (he began one more, but it exists only as a torso) were originally to have been another set of six. But the sixty-seven-year-old composer simply ran out of steam. What we do have, however, are two gems. They are more inward-looking than the irrepressible works of op. 76 (how could they not be?), but both are irresistibly genial. However, under that sunny exterior extraordinary structural experiments are going on. The first movement of no. 1, for instance, is exceptionally tautly written, being entirely constructed from a tiny motif. It abounds in dramatic key changes and explosive energy, aspects wonderfully brought out by the Mosaïques Quartet, its period instruments lending a leanness to the textures that means the listener can hear the inner workings of the pieces to a much greater extent than usual.

The members of the Mosaïques are ensemble musicians and soloists. It is this mixture that seems to be the secret of their success. Their equality is particularly effective in such places as the slow movement of no. 1, where Haydn sets melodic flights of fancy against a steady beat, or the punch and drive they find in the scherzo movement (still stubbornly called a menuetto despite its presto speed). The Second Quartet is perhaps less immediately appealing, but get to know it and it will steal your heart. The slow movement forms the heart of the piece. It is followed by a fun-loving scherzo (menuetto) and a swift, joyous final movement that glows with energy and twinkling good-naturedness. It is a fitting end to a genre that Haydn brought to great heights from the humblest of beginnings. **HS**

Ludwig van Beethoven
String Quartets, op. 18 (1800)

Genre | Chamber
Performers | Takács Quartet:
Dusinberre, Schranz, Walther, Fejér
Years recorded | 2002–03
Label | Decca 470 848-2 (2 CDs)

It is easy to forget, in the context of Beethoven's great quartets of his middle and late periods, that this first set is much more than a promising beginning. Beethoven took the quartets of Haydn—and to a lesser extent Mozart—and developed the form in dramatic new directions. He was thirty when he finished this set and had already completed a number of important works. And as if to set out his stall as the next great quartet composer, he dedicated them to the same patron as Haydn had his op. 77 quartets of 1799—Prince Lobkowitz. Beethoven's break the mold in many ways. Haydn always described his third movements as menuettos, even when it was quite clear they had become scherzos, Beethoven names them as such, sometimes he swaps them with slow movements. In mood and style, too, they range widely, from the soulful Adagio of no. 1 to the dramatic juxtapositions of texture in the second movement of no. 3, to its tarantella-like finale, comparable to the brilliance of that of no. 2. Beethoven delights in blurring boundaries, such as in the slow movement of no. 4, which is a scherzo in sonata form, or the scherzo of no. 6, with its dizzying offbeat accents.

Such innovation demands a quartet that is alive to the jagged drama of this period of Beethoven's music, and is supreme technically, but not so honed as to smooth over some of the craggier passages. The Takács Quartet reigns supreme among modern quartets in this music, which forms part of its complete Beethoven cycle. In these players' hands, the sense of a giant flexing his musical muscles is never in doubt. And on every hearing, something new seems to be revealed. **HS**

Ludwig van Beethoven
Symphony no. 1 (1800)

Genre | Orchestral
Conductor | George Szell
Performers | Cleveland Orchestra
Year recorded | 1964
Label | Sony SBK 89838

Beethoven wrote works in many genres before turning to the symphony, and his first effort in that field is sometimes regarded as relatively straitlaced when compared to his earlier compositions (and his later ones). Even so, it contains delights and surprises aplenty. The slow introduction famously begins on a chord that demands immediate resolution to a key that is not the tonic; the second movement belies its status as the slow movement by featuring a catchy rhythmic profile and a prominent part for timpani; the third is a driving, but elegant scherzo; and the theme of the finale begins with an ascending scale that is progressively (and humorously) assembled in the course of the brief slow introduction. The wind writing is more consistently prominent than in the symphonies of Haydn and Mozart. Finding a balance between the First's progressive tendencies and what appears to be a debt to its forebears is a considerable challenge.

George Szell developed the Cleveland Orchestra into the most immaculate and precise symphonic ensemble of the 1960s. Their recording of the First is a marvel of orchestral craft and polish that synthesizes both infectious energy and refined elegance against a background of deft control and aristocratic poise. Anyone who doubts the ability of carefully calibrated textures and balance to achieve a sense of fantasy should live with this recording. Szell's detailed, inventive account of the introduction to the last movement demonstrates the special quality of this recording as a whole—often such meticulous calculation makes a heavy-handed, dogmatic effect, but here it helps Beethoven's music to soar and sing. **DB**

Ludwig van Beethoven
Violin Sonata in F major, op. 24, "Spring" (1800)

Genre | Chamber
Performers | Adolf Busch (violin),
Rudolf Serkin (piano)
Year recorded | 1933
Label | APR 5541

Although Beethoven thought of his violin sonatas as pieces for piano first and violin second, violinists of the nineteenth century seized on a few of them, notably the "Spring" and the "Kreutzer," as vehicles for their virtuosity, usually working with accompanists who were kept in a subordinate position. The musicians who perform on this recording were largely instrumental in establishing the sonata recital as a vehicle for two equal participants. German violinist Adolf Busch (1891–1952) met Czech-born pianist Rudolf Serkin (1903–91) in Vienna in 1920 and for three decades they made up a formidable combination. From 1929 they played all their repertoire from memory.

The "Spring" was one of two sonatas from 1800, intended as a pair and published as op. 23 before the F major acquired a separate number. Its smiling first subject—introduced by the violin—contrasts with the dramatic second theme, which is especially important for the development. The Adagio has an eloquent main theme that flowers beautifully on the violin; toward the end there is a reference to the first movement. Beethoven throws in a concise, witty, off-beat scherzo before embarking on the powerful rondo that closes this lovely work.

It may seem strange to choose a recording that is more than seventy years old, but the simple fact is that this famous interpretation has never been surpassed. Both artists phrase like singers; their rhythmic control is uncanny; and their mutual understanding is telepathic. The little scherzo is the very soul of wit and timing. The recording, good for its age, is well balanced. APR's is the best of the modern transfers and also offers the Sonata in D, op. 12, no. 1, and the intense C minor work, op. 30, no. 2. **TP**

"From the first time we played together it was just like one."

Rudolf Serkin

Other Recommended Recordings

Henryk Szeryng, Ingrid Haebler
Philips Eloquence 469 152-2
A beautifully balanced, lyrical performance

Complete Sonatas
Augustin Dumay, Maria João Pires
DG 471 495-2
The most recommendable complete set, with a lovely "Spring"

Complete Sonatas
Itzhak Perlman, Vladimir Ashkenazy
Decca 421 453-2
These players are at their best in the "Spring" Sonata

Adolf Busch, one of the great chamber musicians of his time. ➲

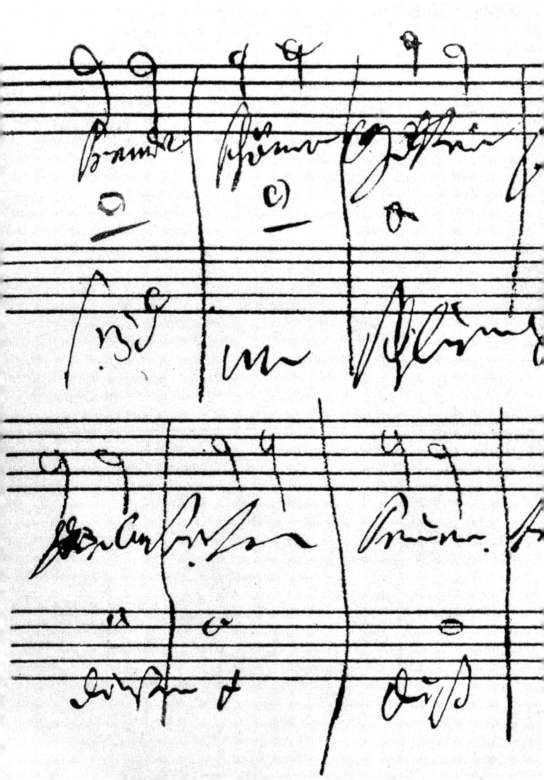

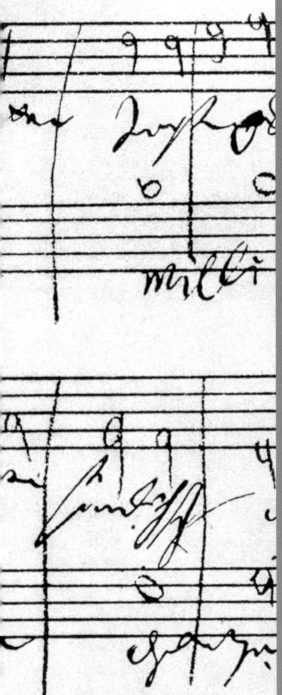

The early nineteenth century saw Classical purity swept away by the more impulsive ideas of the Romantics. Beethoven's revolutionary dynamism gave way to the true Romantic spirits: Mendelssohn, Chopin, Schumann, and Berlioz, who poured their inner beings into their music. Italy reinforced its position as the center of opera in the works of Rossini, Donizetti, and Bellini.

Ⓒ Ludwig van Beethoven's sketch for the "Ode to Joy" from his "Choral" Symphony.

1801–1850

Ludwig van Beethoven | Piano Sonata in C sharp minor, op. 27, no. 2, "Moonlight" (1801)

Genre | Instrumental
Instrument | Piano
Performer | Stephen Kovacevich
Year recorded | 1999
Label | EMI 7243 5 62700 2 2 (9 CDs)

The "Moonlight" label for this work was coined not by the composer but, five years after his death, by the German poet and music critic Ludwig Rellstab. However, Beethoven did describe the work (along with its partner, op. 27, no. 1) as "quasi una fantasia" (like a fantasy) and the rhapsodic approach this suggests is felt in its unorthodox form. It begins, unusually, with a slow movement, which connects to the next movement without a break. Beethoven calls for this calmly rippling first movement to be "played throughout with the utmost delicacy."

By 1801 Beethoven had begun to admit his oncoming deafness to the wider world; this and his dedication of the sonata to the young Italian countess Giulietta Guicciardi—a pupil around half his age—may account for the work's unusual and highly personal nature.

Stephen Kovacevich brings a hypnotic delicacy to the first movement, with a limpid accompaniment and serene, almost muted melody, which focuses the attention on the wider view rather than over-egging local turns of harmony and melody. The fluidity here enables him to trace a single continuous arc, describing an affective yet unsentimental impression: non-indulgent but highly moving.

Described by Liszt as "a flower between two abysses," the second movement is presented by Kovacevich as a fleeting, graceful dance. The relatively restrained speed here strengthens the effect of the bracing finale. Kovacevich makes the strongest possible impact here without actually crashing the piano. Tautly driven and fully powered, his gloves-off approach underlines the physicality of one of Beethoven's most stormy finales. **EB**

> "*Beethoven was always in love with someone, and, as a rule, to a violent degree.*"
>
> Franz Gerhard Wegeler, a friend of Beethoven

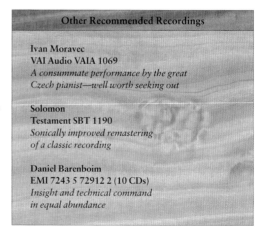

Other Recommended Recordings

Ivan Moravec
VAI Audio VAIA 1069
A consummate performance by the great Czech pianist—well worth seeking out

Solomon
Testament SBT 1190
Sonically improved remastering of a classic recording

Daniel Barenboim
EMI 7243 5 72912 2 (10 CDs)
Insight and technical command in equal abundance

Joseph Haydn
The Seasons (1801)

Genre | Oratorio
Conductor/Performers | Herbert von Karajan;
Gundula Janowitz, Werner Hollweg, Walter Berry
Year recorded | 1972
Label | EMI 0946 3 71482 2 8 (2 CDs)

Anxious to secure a swift follow-up to their enormously successful joint venture *The Creation*, librettist Baron Gottfried van Swieten approached Haydn in 1798 with ideas for a new oratorio. It was to tap even further into the popular vein that had made *The Creation* so appealing to the public, by adapting Englishman James Thomson's widely admired pastoral poem "The Seasons."

The subject may be less exalted than that of *The Creation*, but the work's depiction of the yearly cycle through the earthy scenes and occupations of the Austrian countryside contains some of Haydn's most inventive and delightful music, full of human warmth. Haydn was frequently exhausted while composing *The Seasons*, which turned out to be one of his last major works.

Each season is set as a series of landscapes, distinctively colored with its own melodic and harmonic character, and prefaced by a strikingly descriptive tone poem. The work was first performed in Vienna on April 24, 1801, and so immense was the clamoring throng that it had to be given twice more over the next few days.

Herbert von Karajan's large-scale reading highlights the anticipations of Beethoven, Schubert, and Weber in Haydn's late score but still remains faithful to its Classical roots. No other recording so successfully brings out the work's vivid drama and excitement while retaining a stylish poise and expressive depth. Many tempi are light and breezy while others, equally appropriately, are broad and expansive. The soloists are all excellent, a more consistent trio than many other versions, and the robust chorus makes a hugely impressive sound. **GR**

"*In this . . . masterpiece Haydn really spoke from the innermost part of his soul.*"

Sigismund van Neukomm, pupil of Haydn

Other Recommended Recordings

Academy of St. Martin in the Fields & Chorus
Neville Marriner
Philips 438 715-2 (2 CDs)
Well-characterized, chamber-sized performance

RIAS Chamber Choir, Freiburg Baroque Orchestra
René Jacobs
Harmonia Mundi 901829.30 (2 CDs)
Viscerally dramatic period instrument account

BBC Symphony Orchestra & Chorus • Colin Davis
Philips 464 034-2 (2 CDs)
Warm, affectionate and vibrant performance sung in English

Ludwig van Beethoven | Symphony no. 2 (1802)

Genre | Orchestral
Conductor | René Leibowitz
Performers | Royal Philharmonic Orchestra
Year recorded | 1961
Label | Scribendum SC 041 (5 CDs)

One of the great paradoxes of Beethoven's compositional career is the fact that he wrote his Second Symphony precisely when he was entertaining despairing and practically suicidal thoughts over the loss of his hearing. Despite that context, this remains one of his most optimistic and high-spirited works. Its extended slow introduction displays much of the adventurous and capricious quality that characterizes the three fast movements, while the second movement taps into a lyrical vein of serenity and beauty that makes it a perennial favorite. The Second Symphony, although not yet particularly innovative in its treatment of form, leaves behind any inhibitions that may have lingered in the First, and enters a new world of power and nervous energy—the climax in the coda of the first movement can be made to seem one of the most wrenching and jubilant in Beethoven's entire output.

The cycle of Beethoven symphonies recorded in 1961 by René Leibowitz and the Royal Philharmonic Orchestra appeared when the ranking Beethoven conductor in Britain was Otto Klemperer, whose influential performances resembled imposingly chiseled monuments of great weight and significance. By contrast, the brusque, fleet energy that Leibowitz favors seems to anticipate some of the flavor of more recent historically informed performances. No Beethoven symphony responds more successfully to such a perspective than the Second, and Leibowitz's wit and playfulness in both concept and detail make this recording an enthralling one. In particular, string flourishes in the fast movements seethe and swirl with daring and diablerie, the Larghetto teems with elfin apparitions, and the tumult at the end of the first movement sounds indescribably abandoned. **DB**

> *"Each one of its four sections is perfectly distinct and individual in its own proper character."*
>
> George Grove

Other Recommended Recordings

London Classical Players • Roger Norrington
Virgin 7243 5 6143 2 8 (5 CDs)
Norrington's breakthrough Beethoven still sounds fresh and challenging

NBC Symphony Orchestra • Arturo Toscanini
RCA 74321 55835 2 (2 CDs)
Molten lyricism and high intensity from 1949 to 1951

Zürich Tonhalle Orchestra • David Zinman
Arte Nova 74321 63645 2
Something completely different—an engaging experiment with articulation and ornamentation

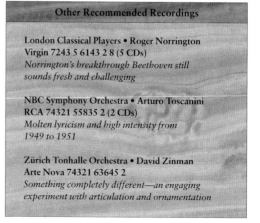

Ludwig van Beethoven | Piano Concerto no. 3 (1803)

Genre | Concerto
Performers | Mitsuko Uchida, Royal Concertgebouw
Conductor | Kurt Sanderling
Year recorded | 1994
Label | Philips 446 082-2

The origins of Beethoven's only minor-key concerto, the Piano Concerto no. 3 in C minor, date back as far as early 1796 when he noted down in one of his sketchbooks the idea of using the kettledrum at the cadenza. This strikingly novel idea later came to fruition in a slightly altered form, with the kettledrum creeping in at the close of the piano cadenza, underlining the dotted rhythm that pervades much of this movement in a ghostly reminiscence.

It is a work that surpasses his earlier two piano concertos in its deeply symphonic demeanor, with a military aspect in the dotted figures that punctuate the opening theme. The pianist's first entry emphasizes that quality, with an angular and pointed theme, only temporarily offset by a gentler mood. Beethoven offers up a big surprise in the slow movement, which switches from the dark drama of C minor to a seraphic E major—a key so foreign that even today it is still startling; for contemporary audiences it would have had the potency of an electric shock. Emotionally, too, the Largo is a world away from the vigor of the opening movement, drive replaced by tenderness, drama by warmth, with Beethoven taking a daring path in his key changes.

Mitsuko Uchida offers all the drama that this work needs. Her slow movement is effortlessly spun, pure, and completely without sentimentality, while her impish humor comes to the fore in the gruffly witty final rondo, which sparkles and dances. She enjoys a wonderful rapport with Kurt Sanderling, who coaxes marvelous playing from the Concertgebouw, with translucent chamber musical textures as soloists duet with the pianist. To describe their performance as "supremely intelligent" might imply a lack of emotion; but it possesses both, in spades. **HS**

"The Largo theme must sound like a holy, distant, and celestial Harmony."

Carl Czerny, *On the Proper Performance of all Beethoven's Works for the Piano*

Other Recommended Recordings

**Alfred Brendel, Vienna Philharmonic Orchestra
Simon Rattle • Philips 462 781-2 (3 CDs)**
*Brendel's wisdom, intelligence and dry humor
combine brilliantly with Rattle's freshness of approach*

**Martha Argerich, Mahler Chamber Orchestra
Claudio Abbado • DG 477 5026**
*For sheer energy and joie de vivre, you would
be hard pressed to find anything more electrifying*

**Yefim Bronfman, Zürich Tonhalle Orchestra
David Zinman • Arte Nova 82876 63010 2**
*A reading of great strength of purpose, with Zinman
once again showing his flair for Beethoven*

Ludwig van Beethoven
Symphony no. 3, "Eroica" (1803)

Genre | Orchestral
Conductor | John Eliot Gardiner
Performers | Orchestre Révolutionnaire et Romantique
Year recorded | 1993
Label | Archiv 439 900-2 (5 CDs)

The first of Beethoven's truly epochal orchestral works, the "Eroica" Symphony was originally entitled "Bonaparte" in honor of Napoleon, who in the early years of the new century gripped the imagination of much of Europe. When he named himself emperor, however, Beethoven altered his designation to "heroic symphony . . . composed to celebrate the memory of a great man."

The vast first movement plants seeds of drama, order, and discord that subsequently generate countless felicities and developments; the funeral march of the second movement allows for memories of grandeur and triumph as well as agonized grief. The rumbunctious scherzo, with its trio of horns in the central section, and the finale—a free set of variations on a theme Beethoven had used in earlier works—round out a composition that may be regarded as the musical nineteenth century's wake-up call.

John Eliot Gardiner's Beethoven symphony cycle creates perhaps the most satisfying Beethoven style for our time: sleek but powerful, played and recorded with great polish, performed on period instruments, with the sensibilities of the historical performance movement, but fully committed to the aesthetic significance and expressive force of these works. Although all the performances are front-runners, his "Eroica" is especially salutatory, since the prevailing performance tradition emphasizing the work's grand heroism has left a dearth of performances that make the piece sound sufficiently revolutionary. Gardiner triumphantly demonstrates that the "Eroica" requires a combination of fleetness and intensity in order to make its maximum impact. **DB**

" . . . a strong, a consummate individuality, to which nothing human is a stranger."

Richard Wagner

English conductor John Eliot Gardiner, photographed in 1990. ➔

Ludwig van Beethoven
Violin Sonata in A major, op. 47, "Kreutzer" (1803)

Genre | Chamber
Performers | Gidon Kremer (violin),
Martha Argerich (piano)
Year recorded | 1994
Label | DG 447 054-2

Beethoven was a pianist of brilliant technique and improvisatory flair and, although only of average competence on the violin, he knew his way around the instrument. His op. 47 Sonata, the more celebrated of two works in A major, should have come down to us as the "Bridgetower" Sonata, as Beethoven wrote it in 1803 for himself to play with the Afro-European virtuoso George Polgreen Bridgetower; but, typically, he cooled toward Bridgetower and dedicated the piece instead to the French violinist Rodolphe Kreutzer, who never played it.

This "sonata for piano and violin obbligato" was composed in a great hurry, and at the premiere in Vienna the composer played from a sketchy score of the first two movements, with Bridgetower reading the violin part over his shoulder. For the finale, Beethoven revived a gleeful tarantella originally meant for his first A major Sonata, op. 30, no. 1. It reminds us that the violin is the devil's instrument and makes a perfect fit, since (apart from the brooding introduction with its atmospheric violin double-stops) the heroic opening Presto and the central set of variations are equally virtuosic and extrovert in mood.

The "Kreutzer" needs a pianist who can really carry the battle to the violinist, and Martha Argerich not only has the necessary fire and virtuosity, but can turn it on in the studio. Gidon Kremer tends to divide opinion, yet his slight lack of warmth is not a drawback in this music and he has an excellent rapport with his partner. It is wonderful to hear two players who have no problems with the actual notes and can put all their effort into their joint interpretation. They are well recorded, too. **TP**

> *"A sonata written in a very concertante style, almost like a concerto."*
>
> Ludwig van Beethoven

Johann Nepomuk Hummel
Trumpet Concerto (1803)

Genre | Concerto
Performers/Conductor | Håkan Hardenberger,
Academy of St. Martin in the Fields; Neville Marriner
Year recorded | 1986
Label | Philips 420 203-2

Although his works are performed infrequently today, Hummel was a major figure in his lifetime (1778–1837), feted as both a composer and pianist. A child prodigy, he took piano lessons with Mozart and traveled extensively in Europe giving concerts. In 1803, Hummel was given the post of Konzertmeister to Prince Nikolaus Esterházy at Eisenstadt, but his most successful years were spent at Weimar. Unlike the impoverished Mozart, Hummel amassed quite a fortune from his various activities. In fact, such was his success that—together with Goethe—he became a tourist attraction; no visit to Weimar was complete without seeing Goethe or hearing Hummel play.

The Trumpet Concerto dates from Hummel's time in Eisenstadt, where it was performed on New Year's Day 1804. It was written for the Viennese trumpeter Anton Weidinger who had previously performed Haydn's Trumpet Concerto to great acclaim. Since the Haydn premiere, Weidinger had developed his keyed trumpet further, and while Haydn made use of the instrument's clarion (high) register Hummel, by contrast, concentrates on the lower register, fully demonstrating its new technical range. Grand in orchestration, scale, and form, Hummel's concerto suited the virtuoso Weidinger, who performed it frequently over the next few years.

This fine modern-instrument recording by the superb trumpeter Håkan Hardenberger includes both the Hummel and the Haydn concertos, together with those by Hertel and Stamitz. Those wishing to hear Hummel played on an original keyed trumpet should additionally seek out Reinhold Friedrich's recording. **DC**

> *"Great harmonic innovations ... arise from Hummel, Weber, Field, and Schubert."*
>
> **Charles Rosen**

Other Recommended Recordings

Maurice André, Berlin Philharmonic Orchestra
Herbert von Karajan
EMI 7243 5 66909 2 8
A classic recording

Reinhold Friedrich, Wiener Akademie
Martin Haselböck
Capriccio 10 598
Haydn and Hummel on period instruments

Wynton Marsalis, National Philharmonic Orchestra
Raymond Leppard
Sony CD 37846
Somewhat husky-toned bravura

Ludwig van Beethoven
Piano Sonata in F minor, op. 57, "Appassionata" (1805)

Genre | Instrumental
Instrument | Piano
Performer | Daniel Barenboim
Year recorded | 1966
Label | EMI 7243 5 72912 2 4 (10 CDs)

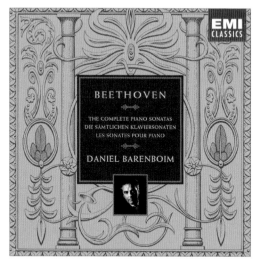

One of the few Beethoven piano sonatas to be colored throughout by a tragic tone, the "Appassionata" was apparently the composer's favorite sonata up until his "Hammerklavier" of 1818. It is a sonata of extremes—of form, emotional intensity, range, and volume (the last two enabled by the new, five-and-a-half octave French Erard piano that Beethoven received in 1803).

The stormy first movement is spiked with a foreboding four-note figure prefiguring the famous opening notes of the Fifth Symphony. An eerie, diminished-seventh chord ends the second movement and is violently seized upon at the opening of the demonic finale. According to the composer's friend Ferdinand Ries, the tempestuous rushing figure dominating the finale came to Beethoven during a walk in the woods. "The whole way," Ries reports, "he had been humming—or, at times howling—always up and down, though without singing specific notes."

Daniel Barenboim's view of the "Appassionata" is more probing than "impassioned." He reveals in the first movement a deeply troubled spirit with a remarkable combination of insight and imagination. The chords of the second movement's gentle chorale-like theme are impeccably balanced, and the following variations become deeper reflections along the inward-looking mood of the theme. In the whirlwind finale Barenboim may not match Stephen Kovacevich for sheer brutal energy, but there is a gradual uncoiling of tension toward the unleashing of the final stamping dance and its subsequent—here almost too exciting—Presto. The overall effect is both exhausting and breathtaking. **EB**

"He can really bring the knowledge of the structure . . . into one big shape."

Lang Lang on Barenboim's approach to Beethoven

Other Recommended Recordings

Stephen Kovacevich
EMI 7243 5 62700 2 2
*Bracing playing and consummate musicianship
from a Beethoven player of high repute*

Arthur Rubinstein
RCA 82876 761619 2
*Rubinstein's aristocratic recording from
1963 in remastered, hybrid CD/SACD format*

Melvyn Tan
Virgin 7243 5 62368 2 0 (5 CDs)
*An excitingly brittle finale, in particular, played on
a modern replica of a Viennese fortepiano from 1814*

Daniel Barenboim at the recording studio, November 15, 1942. ➔

Ludwig van Beethoven
Triple Concerto
(1805)

Genre | Concerto
Performers | David Oistrakh, Mstislav
Rostropovich, Sviatoslav Richter
Year recorded | 1969
Label | EMI 7243 5 66954 2 9

Ludwig van Beethoven
Piano Concerto no. 4
in G major (1806)

Genre | Concerto
Performers/Conductor | Emil Gilels,
Philharmonia Orchestra; Leopold Ludwig
Year recorded | 1957
Label | Testament SBT 1095

Beethoven's Triple Concerto was for a long time the ugly duckling among his concerto output, criticized for its long first movement and what can seem an ungainly finale. Certainly, it is a piece at odds with its time, when the Romantic ideal of pitting a soloist against near-insuperable odds (the orchestra) reigned supreme. But go back only a century or so and the multi-instrumental concerto, or concerto grosso, was a form that was not only in great vogue but also prompted many masterpieces along the way. Beethoven boldly updates this concept, producing a work that, in the right hands, is an utter delight. He deftly overcomes the challenges of giving each soloist enough of the limelight without making the work overly repetitive.

Any sense of shortcoming is banished in this recording, which brings together three fiery Russian soloists and the Berlin Philharmonic, with the legendary Herbert von Karajan at the helm. The soloists were frequent musical collaborators and it is this, as well as a shared heritage, that makes this performance so palpably exciting. After a first movement of considerable grandeur comes a brief Largo where David Oistrakh's wonderfully rich-toned violin soars above a chugging accompaniment, later handing over to the piano before reappearing, this time with cello too. There is a strong sense of shared joy in their trio playing and von Karajan ensures the most sensitive of accompaniments. In hands such as these, you are never in the slightest doubt that this is a great work, as it fizzes and dances to its dazzling end. **HS**

The solo piano opening of Beethoven's Piano Concerto no. 4 in G major is one of the most feared in the entire repertoire, not because of its difficulty, but because its very simplicity is so difficult to get right—and if it is not spot on, the entire magic of the concerto is compromised. One pianist who definitely did get it right was the great Russian artist Emil Gilels, captured in the studio with the underrated Leopold Ludwig and the Philharmonia Orchestra in fabulous form.

In this work, Beethoven took the concerto form by the scruff of the neck and shook it hard—the quiet solo entry would have been enough to have most of his audience looking askance at their neighbors (though Mozart did something almost as dramatic in his early E flat major Concerto, K271). And that is even before you get to the confrontational Andante con moto, where the piano gradually tames the orchestra and then, following a chordal sequence as chromatic as anything Liszt wrote, proceeds to hypnotize them with a cadenza featuring a sustained trill of searing intensity. It ends with one of Beethoven's most explosively ebullient dances, the piano twinkling above the orchestra, reacting to it, goading it, and then dancing off in yet another harmonic direction.

This is a work where the soloist is both highly integrated into the orchestral texture yet stands apart from it. Emil Gilels is master of every aspect of it, and his is a performance that continues to enchant, no matter how many times you hear it. **HS**

Ludwig van Beethoven
String Quartets, op. 59, "Razumovsky" (1806)

Genre | Chamber
Performers | The Lindsays: Cropper, Birks, Ireland, Gregor-Smith
Year recorded | 1984
Label | ASV CDDCS 207 (2 CDs)

Beethoven's three masterly "Razumovsky" Quartets get their name from Count Andrey Razumovsky, the Russian Ambassador in Vienna, who requested Beethoven to write him some quartets that included Russian melodies. Razumovsky was himself a keen player and frequently played second violin in quartets.

These works, the first quartets of Beethoven's so-called "middle period," are marked by an extreme economy of means and a further development (or deconstruction) of existing movements. The third quartet, for instance, is the first to begin with a slow introduction, a device that Beethoven returned to in his late quartets. It is hardly surprising that early audiences were more puzzled than wowed by these pieces. The first quartet is demanding in length alone, and the complex and sophisticated musical argument in the opening movement demands careful listening. The following scherzo, too, is complex in structure and vertiginous in its dramatic mood changes. Beethoven fulfilled the request for Russian folk tunes in the first two quartets, while the third makes up for their lack in the sheer energy of its outer movements. In all three works, slow movements provide serene centers of great beauty.

That mix of the frenetic and the still is brilliantly brought to life by the Lindsays, for whom the complete Beethoven quartets long formed a central part of their repertoire. Not only are they utterly inside this music, but the very rawness of some of their playing increases the visceral excitement of these interpretations. **HS**

Ludwig van Beethoven
Symphony no. 4 (1806)

Genre | Orchestral
Conductor/Performers | Frans Brüggen; Orchestra of the Eighteenth Century
Year recorded | 1990
Label | Philips 442 156-2 (5 CDs)

Beethoven's Fourth Symphony is an utterly remarkable work that is too little appreciated, sandwiched as it is between the more famous and powerful Third and Fifth. The slow introduction can be one of the most magically mysterious passages in all of Beethoven, and this mood foreshadows similar passages in the slow movement and at the end of the development section in the first movement proper. Several other spots in the first movement and the main theme of the striking scherzo, however, find Beethoven playfully displaying his penchant for disrupting the listener's rhythmic expectations, while the whirlwind finale is as entertaining for the listener as it is treacherously challenging for the performers. In the end, this symphony's character is too multivalent to be easily captured in performance or identified in a straightforward image—perhaps this quality is what gives it both its enduring fascination and its lesser degree of popularity.

Performances of the Fourth run the gamut from striving for a unified expressive profile to playing up the contrasts between introspection and high spirits; neither approach can make all the points worth making. This recording, however, offers a performance that is striking on first hearing and wears well on repeated listening. Although their perspective is generally forceful and lively, Brüggen and his orchestra make room for sweetness and depth when appropriate, while the tangy sonority of period instruments provides interesting character and ameliorates some of the brashness in their approach. **DB**

Ludwig van Beethoven | Violin Concerto (1806)

Genre | Concerto
Performers | Itzhak Perlman, Berlin Philharmonic Orchestra
Conductor | Daniel Barenboim
Year recorded | 1986
Label | EMI 0777 7 49567 2 7

Now considered the greatest of all violin concertos, Beethoven's op. 61 took a generation or more to establish itself in the concert hall. It was written in quite a short time for Franz Clement, concertmaster at the Theater an der Wien in Vienna; but so little time was available for rehearsal that at the premiere on December 23, 1806, Clement virtually sight-read it—and as an interlude between the first two movements, he treated the audience to tricks such as playing a piece with the violin held upside-down. No wonder the concerto made little impact.

The watershed in the work's acceptance was the performance by twelve-year-old Joseph Joachim at a Philharmonic concert in London on May 27, 1844, with Mendelssohn conducting. From then on, the Beethoven Concerto became the gold standard by which violinists were judged; and Joachim's successors, such as Fritz Kreisler, Adolf Busch, and Yehudi Menuhin, were renowned above all for playing it. The concerto demands a seamless legato and the ability to convey a deeply spiritual feeling in the first two movements. The finale, as so often with Beethoven, is a more genial affair.

Itzhak Perlman has the breadth of vision for the long opening movement and the athletic spring for the finale; but more importantly, he is one of the few players capable of reaching beneath the surface of the central Larghetto. His studio recording with Giulini has often been praised, but is somewhat undermined by the conductor's over-emphasis on legato. The live recording with Barenboim may not be quite so well recorded or so immaculately performed, but it is more meaningful. Perlman plays Kreisler's cadenzas and the apt couplings are the two Romances, recorded under studio conditions. **TP**

" . . . the most thoughtful concerto . . . which needs the violinist to be a great man as well as a great player."

Adrian Boult

Other Recommended Recordings

Thomas Zehetmair, Orchestra of the Eighteenth Century Frans Brüggen • Philips 462 123-2
A good period version, with Zehetmair casting off his usual mannerisms

Adolf Busch, New York Philharmonic-Symphony Orchestra • Fritz Busch • Music & Arts CD-1183
"Historic" sound, old-fashioned playing, imperishable musicianship

Yehudi Menuhin, Vienna Philharmonic Orchestra Constantin Silvestri • EMI 7243 5 74973 2 9
Probably the most glowing-sounding of Menuhin's myriad versions

---

Violinist Itzhak Perlman, pictured at a concert in 1986. ➔

Ludwig van Beethoven
Symphony no. 5 (1807)

Genre | Orchestral
Conductor | Carlos Kleiber
Performers | Vienna Philharmonic Orchestra
Year recorded | 1974
Label | DG 447 400-2

Beethoven's Fifth is undoubtedly the most famous and influential symphony ever written. Its distinctive power derives from the confluence of organic concentration and unity, rhythmic drive, and a sense of progression from tragedy to triumph. This latter dimension is spelled out on the tonal level by moving from dark C minor in the first movement to blazing C major in the finale (with many momentary glimpses of that eventual destination along the way), and experientially by means of a transition linking the eerie end of the scherzo to the beginning of the finale with a wandering but eventually inexorable crescendo. Every gesture and feature of this work has been pondered and emulated by later composers, and the experience that this symphony provides echoes in the Western psyche as though it were an expressive "big bang."

Carlos Kleiber's recording of the Fifth made a similar sort of impact on late twentieth-century performers and audiences. There had long been powerful and vivid performances of this iconic work, yet Kleiber's intense dynamism possesses a flexibility that made performances predicated merely on volume, monumentality, and drive seem blunt and unimaginative. From drastic, quick horn/wind crescendos early in the first movement to the evocative melodic tension and vulnerability in the second movement and the finale, this performance retains the brilliance and variety that both reinvigorated the tradition in which it appeared and encouraged the inspired attention to detail that was to animate the historical performance movement when it finally turned to Beethoven as a legitimate field for its endeavors. **DB**

" . . . conceived by a genius, it expresses the romantic nature of music . . . strongly."

E. T. A. Hoffmann

Other Recommended Recordings

Berlin Philharmonic Orchestra • Wilhelm Furtwängler
Music & Arts CD 954 (4 CDs)
Torrential sweep and triumphant energy, from 1937

Vienna Philharmonic Orchestra
Wilhelm Furtwängler
EMI 7243 5 86200 2 3
An account awesome in breadth, scale, inflection, and moral significance, from 1954

Vienna Philharmonic Orchestra • George Szell
Orfeo C 484 981 B
Szell the taskmaster goes for broke in his final Salzburg concert, recorded in 1969

Ludwig van Beethoven
Piano Trio in D major, op. 70, no. 1, "Ghost" (1808)

Genre | Chamber
Performers | Florestan Trio: Susan Tomes,
Anthony Marwood, Richard Lester
Year recorded | 2001
Label | Hyperion CDA 67327

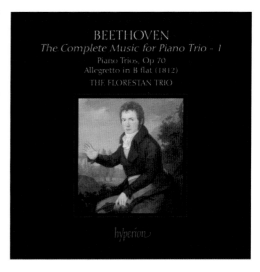

Beethoven himself did not name his Trio in D major the "Ghost." Like so many nicknames it was tagged on later for reasons that remain obscure. It may have been because of the eerie, spectral quality of the slow movement, or because ideas for a proposed opera on *Macbeth* were found on the same page as sketches for this movement. In the intervening centuries the "ghostly" Largo has acquired an almost mystical significance and, some might say, too heavy a symbolic weight, standing as it does between two zestful, rollicking movements. With its icy, falling scales and magnificently extended crescendos, the Largo is remarkable for the seemingly infinite vistas of its musical landscape, a foretaste of Schubert's "heavenly lengths." The two op. 70 trios were dedicated to Countess Marie Erdödy, an accomplished pianist with whom Beethoven stayed in Vienna in 1808.

Though amateurs the world over love to play this marvelous work, it is exceptionally difficult to realize, not least because the violin and cello parts are so often playing in unison, exposing the slightest difference in intonation, while the pianist is required, in the Largo, to sustain a veil of tremolo atmosphere quite alien to a percussive instrument. Then there is the issue of balancing the entire work with its light outer movements and long, profoundly introverted Largo: perhaps the trio led by Henryk Szeryng succeeded best in producing an entirely coherent, complete experience. But the Florestan Trio, steeped in Classical style, brings a welcome transparency, precision of articulation, range of dynamics and rhythmic buoyancy that illuminate the whole work anew. **HW**

> *"In his greatest works, [he] was 'possessed'—the mere human instrument . . . "*

Ernest Newman

Ludwig van Beethoven
Symphony no. 6, "Pastoral" (1808)

Genre | Orchestral
Conductor | Erich Kleiber
Performers | Amsterdam Concertgebouw Orchestra
Year recorded | 1953
Label | Decca 475 6080 (6 CDs)

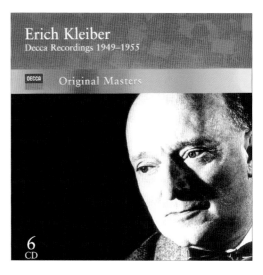

Written at the same time and premiered at the same concert as the Fifth Symphony, the Sixth has always seemed to complement Beethoven's usual power and vehemence with a mood more gracious and spacious. Each of the five movements bears a description that provides an expressive key to the music. And although the storm unleashes the awesome and violent tone at which Beethoven excels, the happiness, peacefulness, fun, and gratitude displayed in the remaining movements make this symphony a favorite for those who sometimes find Beethoven's style overly strenuous and intense. Memorable passages include stretches of static or hypnotically oscillating harmonies that underpin intertwining, kaleidoscopic textures in the first movement; birdcalls near the end of the second movement; and wind and thunderclaps in the storm.

Many performances of the "Pastoral" try to enforce a consistent mood, but Erich Kleiber's magnificent 1953 recording highlights the special quality of each movement, and this context of alert playing manages to turn the relaxed evocativeness realized in the second movement into something quite extraordinary. What graceful dynamic shading! How moving the sense that the players are listening and responding eloquently to one another! In the finale, it is impossible to describe adequately the sense of genuine, deeply felt, and spontaneous gratitude that seems to impel this performance. Kleiber's masterly fusion of melody, texture, dynamics, and phrasing endows this movement—and the symphony as a whole—with an unparalleled depth of sincerity. **DB**

> *"[I]t was not a single short spring day that inspired him to utter his cry of joy . . . "*
>
> Robert Schumann

Other Recommended Recordings

Bavarian State Orchestra • Carlos Kleiber
Orfeo C 600 031 B
Incomparably but unrelievedly bracing and urgent, from 1983

Berlin Philharmonic Orchestra • Eugen Jochum
DG 474 018-2 (5 CDs)
Quite leisurely in first movement, warmly involved thereafter, of 1954

Vienna Philharmonic Orchestra • Karl Böhm
DG 447 433-2
A memorably and consistently warm, gentle, and loving version

Erich Kleiber, celebrated interpreter of Beethoven and Mozart. ❯

Ludwig van Beethoven
Piano Concerto no. 5 in E flat major (1809)

Genre | Concerto
Performers/Conductor | Alfred Brendel, Vienna Philharmonic; Simon Rattle
Year recorded | 1998
Label | Philips 462 781-2 (3 CDs)

To Beethoven, key signatures had a symbolic significance of which we tend to be unaware today. Whereas C minor was a key of high drama and tragedy, E flat major had a heroic ring to it, as is found in the "Eroica" Symphony (no. 3), and this concerto—the only one of his five for piano and orchestra that he did not premiere himself, deafness having finally taken its toll. It was for this reason that Beethoven wrote his cadenzas into the score, clearly instructing performers not to insert their own. Here it is brought to the fore, with the solo piano introducing the work with an affirmative flourish. It is that sense of affirmation, and a strong whiff of the military, that provoked the popular but spurious title "Emperor" (war was raging between France and Austria at the time, though Beethoven's stance was anti- rather than pro-Napoleon).

This work has enjoyed an extensive and distinguished discography but it is hard to beat the combination of Alfred Brendel and Simon Rattle, whose Beethoven interpretations have caused such a stir for their combination of traditional orchestra and period-instrument rethinking. After a movement awesome in its power, brilliantly espoused by Brendel, Beethoven offers a complete contrast, rather as he did in his Third Concerto—the hymn-like piano theme seraphic and otherworldly, and to follow, the most self-confident, symphonic outpouring, the military flavor returning, with the piano rising dominant above the orchestra. It is not only Beethoven's cry of triumph, but that of Brendel and Rattle, too. **HS**

Fernando Sor
Guitar Works (c.1810–30s)

Genre | Instrumental
Instrument | Guitar
Performer | Adam Holzman
Year recorded | 1995
Label | Naxos 8.553450

Barcelona-born composer and guitarist Fernando Sor is remembered mainly for the music he wrote for guitar, although in his day he was also renowned for his ballets and vocal music. According to a London journal of 1820, "a new set of arietts from [Mr. Sor's] pen causes almost as much sensation as the publication of a new novel by the author of *Waverley*." Sor has been dubbed "the Beethoven of the guitar," although there is little similarity between the two composers other than their contemporaneous era—the refined, conservative style of much of Sor's output owes more to his Classical forebears Haydn and Mozart.

Sor's guitar works include many still-influential lessons and studies as well as an extensive body of concert pieces, enthusiastically adopted by modern masters of the instrument such as Andrés Segovia and Julian Bream, that fully deserves its continued reputation as among the most consistently great of its kind. Sor's once-celebrated vocal music shines through in his guitar writing, always effortlessly melodic despite frequently virtuosic technical demands; but there is also depth to the beauty, an underlying expressiveness and quiet emotion rarely present in similar repertoire by lesser contemporaries.

The most comprehensive survey of Sor's guitar music currently available is Naxos's superb ongoing complete edition. Adam Holzman's excellent recital of works from the early 1830s ranges from delightfully simple valses to a brilliant set of variations, and the sophisticated *Fantasie villageoise*, featuring mesmerizing harmonics. **GR**

Ludwig van Beethoven
Piano Sonata in E flat major, op. 81A, "Les adieux" (1810)

Genre | Instrumental
Instrument | Piano
Performer | Arthur Rubinstein
Year recorded | 1962
Label | RCA 82876 71619 2

Ludwig van Beethoven
Piano Trio in B flat major, op. 97, "Archduke" (1811)

Genre | Chamber
Performers | Beaux Arts Trio: Pressler, Greenhouse, Guilet
Year recorded | 1965
Label | Philips 464 683-2

On May 4, 1809, the Austrian Imperial family fled Vienna to escape the siege by Napoleon's French forces. Among them was Archduke Rudolph, the youngest brother of Emperor Franz and a pupil and patron of Beethoven, who two months earlier had established a consortium that guaranteed an annuity for the composer.

Beethoven composed this sonata to mark Rudolph's departure. The work takes its name from its first movement, "Das Lebewohl" ("The Farewell"), while the other two movements continue the cycle with "Abwesenheit" ("Absence") and "Das Wiedersehn" ("The Return") respectively. Beethoven was angry with his publisher for printing, against his wishes, a version with only French titles—not just because of his increasing nationalistic tendencies, but also since, as Beethoven wrote: "'Lebewohl' means something quite different from 'Les adieux.' The first is said in a warm manner to one person, the other to a whole assembly, to entire towns."

Arthur Rubinstein certainly creates an intimate warmth in this remastered recording from the early 1960s. Without ever over-sentimentalizing, he poetically captures the over-arching mood of each movement, bringing a rare, magical delicacy to the searching slow movement and an impressive textural clarity and unhindered exuberance to the joyful finale. There is an attractive depth to his fruity tone, too, and a youthful spirit that utterly masks the fact that Rubinstein was in his mid-seventies at the time this recording was made. **EB**

In his final large-scale piano trio, we find Beethoven at his most sublime, his most masterful, and, above all, his most playful. Yet, tragically, by the time of writing it, the composer was already deaf. Having heard an early rehearsal, his friend Louis Spohr wrote: "Little is left of his once celebrated virtuosity. In forte passages he hit the keys so hard that the strings rattled...."

Dedicated to the Archduke Rudolph of Austria, the trio was conceived on an unusually broad scale. The theme of the expansive, Olympian first movement is fully explored and exploited, while the witty scherzo bursts with high spirits, and jostles with a darkly chromatic underside. The serene, hymn-like slow movement has a memorably beautiful coda. The pianist leads the merry dance of the finale at speed with ever-more brilliant strings of scales.

There are many wonderful performances of this work: Some ensembles find a special depth in the slow movement, while others take flight in the glittering finale. But in the end, the Beaux Arts Trio's performance comes top for the young Menahem Pressler's extraordinary, crystalline piano playing. If other great recordings can be criticized for an occasional sense of the earth-bound, Pressler carries his ensemble along as if airborne, scattering pearls of sparkling humor as he goes. The eloquently assured Bernard Greenhouse and Daniel Guilet make the ideal companions for this fantastical journey. The tempi are fast but every detail is beautifully shaped and, more than forty years on, it sounds as fresh as the day it was made. **HW**

Carl Maria von Weber | Clarinet Concertos nos. 1 & 2 (1811)

Genre | Concerto
Performers | Antony Pay,
Orchestra of the Age of Enlightenment
Year recorded | 1987
Label | Virgin 7243 5 61585 2 8 (2 CDs)

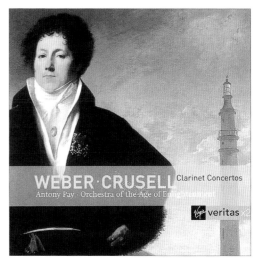

We were probably all told to "stop showing off" in childhood, and that may be what has left many grown-up music lovers with a deeply ingrained suspicion of music designed to show off a performer's skills. But virtuosity has been an essential part of music from Renaissance divisions to modern jazz solos, and it has always had a unique power to thrill an audience. The trick, for a composer, is to marry it with firm structures to accommodate all the flashy passage-work, and with some musical substance—good tunes in convincing sequences, interesting colors, and striking contrasts.

Weber, a piano virtuoso himself, understood this well, and he put it into practice in the two concertos he wrote in Munich for the principal clarinettist of the court orchestra, Heinrich Bärmann. Bärmann's virtuosity is given plenty of scope, but the first movements of the concertos are quite forceful in their different ways, and the finales are wonderfully inventive rondos. As for the central slow movements, both hint at Weber's flair for opera, the first with a solemn passage for the soloist with three horns, as if in the depths of the forest of Freischütz, the second with a stretch of eloquent recitative.

Although there are some fine versions on modern instruments of the concertos, and the slighter concertino, Antony Pay's recording with the period-instrument Orchestra of the Age of Enlightenment (now in a twin-pack with the concertos of Weber's clarinetist contemporary Crusell) matches them in technical prowess, musicianship, and collective spirit. And hearing Pay's instrument pushed to its limits—it is a copy of an 1800 clarinet not very different from Bärmann's own—intensifies the special frisson created by the best kind of musical showing-off. **AB**

> "In Bärmann's clarinet Weber found an instrument ... to match ... the brilliance of his own temperament."
>
> John Warrack

Other Recommended Recordings

Martin Fröst, Tapiola Sinfonietta • Jean-Jacques Kantorow • BIS SACD-1523 (hybrid SACD)
State-of-the-art recording and brilliant playing, but with occasional fussy phrasing and extreme tempi

Emma Johnson, English Chamber Orchestra Yan Pascal Tortelier, Gerard Schwarz ASV CD DCA 747
Neat, well-turned performances by soloist and orchestra

Walter Boeykens, Rotterdam Philharmonic Orchestra James Conlon Apex 8573 89246-2
Highly recommendable bargain alternative

Carl Maria von Weber wrote some of his finest music for the clarinet. ➔

Ludwig van Beethoven | Symphony no. 7 (1812)

Genre | Orchestral
Conductor | Carlos Kleiber
Performers | Vienna Philharmonic Orchestra
Year recorded | 1976
Label | DG 447 400-2

Even in Beethoven's output there is no more joyous and optimistic work than the Seventh Symphony. Apart from the second movement (Allegretto), which moves evocatively between poignant heartache and sweet consolation, this work is lithe, athletic, purposefully directed, and high-spirited. The moderately paced introduction establishes seriousness of intent by invoking a huge range in both dynamics and register; this spills into a powerful but infectiously rollicking Vivace. After the Allegretto (one of the most popular of Beethoven's symphonic movements during his lifetime) comes a forceful but playful scherzo alternating with a trio (appearing twice and almost a third time) that has sometimes been heard as a pilgrim's hymn; how markedly it is meant to contrast with the main tempo of the movement has always been a contentious issue. With the concluding Allegro con brio Beethoven plunges into one of the most invigorating maelstroms in all music—inspiring in the listener the sheer joy of being alive.

The last ninety seconds of Carlos Kleiber's Seventh constitute one of the most stimulating passages in all of recorded music. From a point of high excitement the music gradually sinks and softens to establish a pedal point that will generate further tension and anticipation. Meanwhile the violins are engaged in animated dialogue, an effect enhanced by deploying them antiphonally. As tension builds, the music reaches a theme that now is undercut by the pedal point, delaying the climax. When the wave finally crests, we glimpse behind the frantic activity a vast stillness that lends the music a transfiguring grandeur. The mastery and spirit of the performance as a whole are fully worthy of this cathartic moment. **DB**

> "... The apotheosis of the dance ... the loftiest deed of bodily motion incorporated in an ideal mould of tone."
>
> Richard Wagner

Other Recommended Recordings

New York Philharmonic • Arturo Toscanini
Naxos 8.110840
Marvelous ensemble, phrasing, line, and energy—a perpetual classic from 1936

Berlin Philharmonic Orchestra • Herbert von Karajan
DG 429 036-2 (5 CDs)
Canny synthesis of tradition and innovation, vintage 1962, yields an exciting performance

Dresden Staatskapelle • Colin Davis
Philips 475 6883 (6 CDs)
Weighty tempi given life by rich textures; humane, involved, powerful playing

Carlos Kleiber (1930–2004), son of Erich (see page 217). ➔

Ludwig van Beethoven
Symphony no. 8 (1812)

Genre | Orchestral
Conductor | Daniel Barenboim
Performers | Berlin Staatskapelle
Year recorded | 1999
Label | Warner 2564 61890-2 (6 CDs)

Beethoven is reported to have thought his Eighth Symphony "better" than the Seventh, which came into being at almost the same time. Perplexing as this point of view may seem to those who think of the Seventh as quintessential Beethoven, it deserves to be taken seriously. The Eighth is a provocative mixture of old and new—literally so in the middle two movements: In the third, Beethoven reverts to a minuet in olden style rather than the faster scherzo he customarily used, while in the second he pokes fun at the ticking of the newly invented metronome. The outer movements have moments of grace, playfulness, and wit but also feature a brusqueness that can be frightening. The finale has an unusual structure that remains puzzling and stimulating, while the central trio of the minuet features a particularly beautiful dialog between horns and clarinet over skittering cellos—proof that Beethoven's imagination for sonority had not left with his hearing. In short, despite its many beauties and its concise feeling, the Eighth is hard to pin down, while the Seventh is what it is.

Daniel Barenboim and the Berlin Staatskapelle hardly offer the last word in polish or detailed interpretation, but their Eighth is an absorbing experience. The violence in the first movement really takes off, the second movement trips along impersonally as though the metronome cannot stop, exaggerated phrasing in the minuet makes for some humorously ungainly lurches, and the alternation between nearly uncontrolled, hurtling desperation and stumpy, earthy punctuation from timpani and bassoons makes for a memorable, even draining account of the finale. **DB**

Carl Loewe
Ballads (1812–62)

Genre | Vocal
Performers | Dietrich Fischer-Dieskau (baritone), Jörg Demus (piano)
Years recorded | 1969, 1971, 1982
Label | DG 449 516-2 (2 CDs)

Listen to Carl Loewe's setting of Goethe's "Erlkönig," and you might be tempted for a moment to wonder just who was the finer songwriter, Schubert or Loewe. Two months older than his Austrian contemporary, Loewe outlived Schubert by forty years. From his boyhood in Halle to his mature years as professor at the Stettin Seminary, Loewe wrote operas, oratorios, piano sonatas, string quartets—and more than six hundred songs for voice and piano.

Loewe had a predilection for narrative poems, assimilating and extending the techniques of the eighteenth-century German ballad composers, and raising the art to something little short of cult popularity. The pastor and poet Johann Gottfried Herder was at the time busy translating Scottish and Nordic ballads, for which the appetite of the public was well nigh insatiable. It was he who provided the text for Loewe's early masterpieces such as "Edward" and "Herr Oluf." As Loewe's output increased, his virtuoso skill grew, in alternating scene and dialogue, dramatic and lyrical melody, strophic verse and sonata form—and touching everything with chillingly unpredictable harmonic twists and turns.

So why are Loewe's ballads still so infrequently performed today? They have all made it on to disc now, thanks to CPO's complete edition, but in the recital room today's singers and pianists seem daunted by Loewe's dramatic demands. Dietrich Fischer-Dieskau and Jörg Demus, in their highly intelligent performances, capture much of the ballads' compelling allure even on disc, recreating the epic narratives, the fairytale fantasies, and the meditative miniatures all with equal conviction. **HF**

Gioachino Rossini
Tancredi (1813)

Genre | Opera
Conductor/Performers | Alberto Zedda; Ewa Podles, Sumi Jo, Stanford Olsen
Year recorded | 1994
Label | Naxos 8.660037-38 (2 CDs)

Tancredi opened in Venice on February 6, 1813, and it did much to confirm Rossini's status as Italy's foremost composer of opera. Based on a play by Voltaire, it deals with internecine strife in eleventh-century Sicily; for the premiere, Rossini and his librettist departed from Voltaire's tragic conclusion, substituting a happy ending; a subsequent version restored the original plotline.

Argirio, ruler of the Syracusans, proposes to marry his daughter Amenaide to the family's enemy, Orbazzano, to form an alliance. Amenaide writes to her beloved in exile, Tancredi, who returns in disguise. Orbazzano intercepts the letter and accuses Amenaide of corresponding with Solamir, leader of the Saracen enemy. She is condemned to death but Tancredi agrees to be her champion; he wins the duel with Orbazzano then leads the Syracusans against the Saracens; the dying Solamir confirms that Amenaide was innocent, and all ends happily.

Tancredi displays a serious side to Rossini, hitherto a composer of effervescent comedies; the opera is full of beautiful melodies, spread through the formal structure of recitatives and encapsulated arias and duets. Conductor Alberto Zedda's budget version for Naxos is a bargain in every way; the principal protagonists are cast from strength—Ewa Podles's powerful, lyric mezzo-soprano is a perfect foil for soprano Sumi Jo's flights of coloratura, and Podles is no mean exponent of fioritura herself; tenor Stanford Olsen proves himself a thoroughly idiomatic Rossinian. Taken together, the cast's emotionally charged performances provide powerful advocacy for an opera that is rightfully regaining its place in the repertoire. **GK**

Gioachino Rossini
L'italiana in Algeri (1813)

Genre | Opera
Conductor/Performers | Jesús López-Cobos; Jennifer Larmore, Raúl Giménez
Year recorded | 1997
Label | Teldec 0630 17130-2 (2 CDs)

By the time he was twenty-one, Gioachino Rossini (1792–1868) had ten operas under his belt; his comic opera *La pietra del paragone* premiered at La Scala, Milan, in 1812; his first major serious opera, *Tancredi* followed in 1813, at La Fenice, Venice. Also in 1813 came *L'italiana in Algeri* (*The Italian Girl in Algiers*). Over the next sixteen years, Rossini transformed Italian opera from something genteel and agreeable into a barnstorming must-see theatrical experience characterized by structural rigor, elegant wit, knockabout humor, dazzling vocal pyrotechnics, and highly dramatic concerted crescendos.

L'italiana in Algeri is a madcap farce. Mustafà, Bey of Algiers, wants to marry his wife off to an Italian slave, Lindoro, and take an Italian wife for himself. Opportunity presents itself when Isabella is shipwrecked off the coast. Lindoro is Isabella's long-lost lover; they escape Mustafà's clutches under cover of an elaborate initiation ceremony into a fictitious order of "Pappataci," which they flatter the Bey into believing will smooth his path to Isabella's heart.

By now Rossini was versed in combining elements of opera buffa and opera seria, and his score sparkles on the one hand with the vocal idiocies of the Pappataci rituals, and on the other with passages of telling sentiment. Isabella is a toweringly resourceful character, and here Jennifer Larmore beats off all opposition with the sheer creamy beauty of her voice; she is ably supported by the quintessential Rossini tenor of Raúl Giménez, and John Del Carlo is a sonorous Mustafà. The sound balance is luxurious, López-Cobos leading a Lausanne Chamber Orchestra on superb form. **GK**

Louis Spohr
Nonet in F major (1813)

Genre | Chamber
Performers | Vienna Octet (founded by brothers Willi and Alfred Boskovsky)
Year recorded | 1952
Label | Testament SBT 1261

Spohr was immensely popular in his lifetime and all through the nineteenth century. Known at first as a virtuoso violinist, he settled into the solid life of a local Kapellmeister and composer at Kassel. The older generation of violinists—Albert Spalding, Adolf Busch, Erica Morini, Georg Kulenkampff, and Jascha Heifetz—played his violin concertos, or at least nos. 7, 8, and 9. But today he has mostly slipped below the surface, like an iceberg. Those who have discovered his oeuvre will find plenty of it in the CD catalogues, but will rarely hear it in concert. Yet he wrote an immense amount of tuneful, well-constructed music, including operas.

Those with a special yen for the harp or the clarinet will discover that Spohr composed for those instruments as well as for violin. Perhaps the best way into his world is via the chamber music for large groups, of which the Nonet is the best example. It has the usual four movements, with the scherzo second, and it bubbles with good humor throughout. As one would expect from Spohr, the first fiddle part is quite juicy, but it never takes over.

The old Vienna Octet—here losing a violin and gaining a flute and an oboe—had a special way with this kind of music. This, the premiere recording of the Nonet, was responsible for bringing the piece out of the shadows. Now carefully restored, it still sounds amazingly good. Those who need a newer version will find several good ones available, but no one has quite equalled the great Viennese violinist Willi Boskovsky in music that needs charm and humor. After more than half a century, this performance is still magical. **TP**

Ludwig van Beethoven
Fidelio (1814)

Genre | Opera
Conductor | Otto Klemperer
Performers | Christa Ludwig, Jon Vickers
Year recorded | 1962
Label | EMI 7243 5 67631 2 2 (2 CDs)

One of the lyric theater's core masterpieces, *Fidelio* is Beethoven's single opera: Despite a lifetime's searching he found only one subject that inspired him operatically. The three successive editions in which it exists—1805 original, 1806 first revision, 1814 final form—are an indication of his larger struggles with the medium.

Fidelio is also the ultimate realization of the European "rescue opera" fashion that grew in the wake of the French revolution. An actual incident during the Terror supplied the subject of *Léonore, ou l'amour conjugal*, Gaveaux's 1798 *opéra comique*; and it was this work's libretto by Bouilly on which the text for Beethoven's work was modelled. Since the original *Fidelio* was found too long and musically unwieldy, the text was overhauled in 1806, and again in 1814, when finally Beethoven—sacrificing much glorious music in the process—struck a feasible balance between plot, speech, and musical invention. In all versions, the influence of Beethoven's favorite opera, *The Magic Flute*, is palpable; likewise that of Cherubini, whom he revered for infusing Classical forms with new dramatic energy.

Two points of view dominate *Fidelio* criticism. The first praises a greatness achieved in spite of limited dramatic range and two-dimensional characterization; the second insists that through music of steadily enlarging spirituality Beethoven transcended every operatic convention to create a *sui generis* theatrical masterpiece. The towering Klemperer recording, by-product of his celebrated Covent Garden production, is a complete vindication of the second viewpoint. It is one of the mightiest acts of interpretative fidelity, indeed, in recording history. **ML**

Franz Schubert
Lieder (1814–28)

Genre | Vocal
Performers | Bryn Terfel (baritone),
Malcolm Martineau (piano)
Year recorded | 1994
Label | DG 445 294-2

At the end of his gargantuan project of recording every single song that Schubert wrote, Graham Johnson produced a recording of songs by Schubert's friends and contemporaries. Forty composers were included—most of them now totally forgotten. Schubert, on the other hand, survives the filter of every passing decade and every turning century. His name is synonymous with Lieder.

From the greatest poetry by Goethe (who, incidentally, stubbornly ignored Schubert's approaches), to the simplest folksong and the most raucous drinking ditty, Schubert's sensibility and musical soul metamorphosed the word into transcendent musical creation. And from the days when he was a teenager in love, composing song after song in the years of 1814–15, to the last wing-beats of inspiration in "Die Taubenpost," his very last song, Schubert's mind roamed freely where it would.

Schubert alchemized the emotional and spiritual experiences of his own short life through the words of countless poets and friends and in an ever-richer and more refined musical language. Schubert is notoriously difficult to pin down to any one compilation, any particular voice. For better and for worse, Elisabeth Schwarzkopf and Dietrich Fischer-Dieskau provided the templates of expectation for twentieth-century listeners. As the century came to a close, and the great Schubert anniversary year of 1997 approached, the Welsh baritone Bryn Terfel released a delectable cross-section of some of Schubert's greatest songs, sung with seriousness and flair, accompanied with great sensitivity, and revealing both authority and a vividly individual freshness of approach. **HF**

Ludwig van Beethoven
Cello Sonatas, op. 102 (1815)

Genre | Chamber
Performers | Miklós Perényi,
András Schiff
Years recorded | 2001–02
Label | ECM 472 401-2

Beethoven's five cello sonatas tell a fascinating story: Spanning, as they do, the length of Beethoven's creative life, they reveal the composer's experiments with the medium, his innovations, burgeoning ambition, and solutions to the problems of balance.

The first two sonatas, op. 5, dating from 1796, take on unconventional, compressed, two-movement forms and are driven by dramatic dynamism and displacement, particularly the Second in G minor, whose turbulent fury gives way in the rondo to a glorious flow of light.

The Sonata in A major, op. 69, is perhaps the most famous and best loved of the five. An expansive, sun-lit work, in which the partners are very much equals and mutually exchange melodies, it is notable for its deft, syncopated scherzo—a yearning, slow interlude that dissolves into the most ebullient of his finales.

The last two sonatas are arresting, terse, and highly original. Beethoven named the first in C major "a free sonata" because of its unusual structure—the work switches suddenly between ethereal lyricism and urgent march rhythms. The second, in D major, boasts a richly expressive adagio and an ingenious double fugue.

Two veteran Hungarian musicians, András Schiff and Miklós Perényi, have produced the most illuminating performances of these sonatas. While they communicate a sense of fresh surprise and irresistible delight in the music, they also bring the ease and naturalness of men who have been conversing through Beethoven's music all their lives. The balance is exquisite, the ensemble intimate, and the level of inspiration reaches heady heights. **HW**

Nicolò Paganini | Violin Concertos nos. 1–6 (*c.*1815–30)

Genre | Concerto
Performers/Conductor | Salvatore Accardo, London Philharmonic Orchestra; Charles Dutoit
Years recorded | 1974–76
Label | DG 463 754-2 (6 CDs)

Mentioning "Paganini concertos" a century ago would have drawn blank looks from violinists. Only one concerto was known: a piece called "La campanella" was played—but most people did not realize it was the finale of the Second Concerto. Even the well-known Concerto in D major was usually heard in a version by August Wilhelmj, cut down to one movement (Fritz Kreisler made a similar arrangement). This concerto, the longest, is known as the First although it was the second to be composed. The solo part was in D major but to make the effect more brilliant, Paganini tuned his violin up a semitone so that everything came out in E flat major. Today the entire concerto is usually played in D major. Paganini left no cadenza but there is an immensely difficult one by the French virtuoso Emile Sauret.

Violin playing and singing always advance hand in hand, and Paganini's style was of a piece with the bel canto operatic movement sweeping Italy—he was impressed by his younger colleague Rossini. Everything Paganini wrote was for his own use (he played little music by others). Since Yehudi Menuhin took up the D major Concerto in the 1930s, it has prospered and other concertos have been dusted off, notably the fine Second. The Fifth and Sixth needed orchestrating, a task that Federico Mompellio accomplished.

A recommendation for all six concertos is easy, since Salvatore Accardo's series from the mid-1970s has been packaged with his versions of the Caprices and other interesting music by Paganini. Accardo plays with marvellous virtuosity, but the effect is always musical. His tone has an Italianate warmth when required; at other times it has muscle or bite. He is well accompanied by the London Philharmonic, and clearly recorded. **TP**

> ## "Bit by bit, imperceptibly at first, he threw his magnetic chains into the audience."

Robert Schumann on Paganini

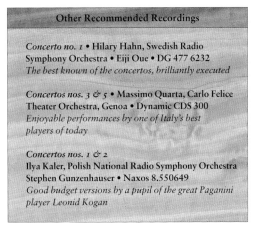

Other Recommended Recordings

Concerto no. 1 • Hilary Hahn, Swedish Radio Symphony Orchestra • Eiji Oue • DG 477 6232
The best known of the concertos, brilliantly executed

Concertos nos. 3 & 5 • Massimo Quarta, Carlo Felice Theater Orchestra, Genoa • Dynamic CDS 300
Enjoyable performances by one of Italy's best players of today

Concertos nos. 1 & 2
Ilya Kaler, Polish National Radio Symphony Orchestra
Stephen Gunzenhauser • Naxos 8.550649
Good budget versions by a pupil of the great Paganini player Leonid Kogan

Paganini's violin playing was the epitome of devilish virtuosity. ➔

Gioachino Rossini
The Barber of Seville (1816)

Genre | Opera
Conductor | Giuseppe Patanè
Performers | Cecilia Bartoli, Enrico Fissore
Year recorded | 1989
Label | Decca 425 520-2 (3 CDs)

Since its premiere in Rome in 1816, *The Barber of Seville* has enjoyed the distinction of never having been out of the international operatic repertoire; its ecstatic reception and constant revivals have established its claim to be the greatest comic opera in history.

The story is based on the Beaumarchais play that introduces characters also used by Mozart in *The Marriage of Figaro*. Rosina is the beautiful ward of Dr. Bartolo, who plans to marry her; Count Almaviva, in love with Rosina, enlists the services of the crafty barber Figaro to help him infiltrate Bartolo's house, first of all as a billeted soldier, then as a singing teacher. The comedy is driven by the attempts of the Almaviva party to achieve their aims by tricking members of the Bartolo household, who are determined to use similar means to win Rosina. The course of operatic true love naturally favors the young. . . .

Act 1 offers a succession of show-stopping numbers, including Figaro's headlong patter-song, "Largo al factotum" and Rosina's minxish aria "Una voce poco fa." There have been many fine recordings, but this Decca version provides the ultimate benchmark: In a venerable tradition, it is built around an idiomatic Italian cast of seasoned stage performers (only the Georgian bass Paata Burchuladze is imported). Cecilia Bartoli's performance is captivating for the clarity and bell-like resonance of her singing and her sense of fun; Enrico Fissore catches Bartolo's frustration, wounded dignity, and desperation perfectly. Crucially, conductor Giuseppe Patanè's measured tempi recognize that the latent energy of the music has no need of a heavy foot on the accelerator. **GK**

Franz Schubert
Symphony no. 5 (1816)

Genre | Orchestral
Conductor/Performers | Eugen Jochum;
Bavarian Radio Symphony Orchestra
Year recorded | 1957
Label | DG 477 5354

Of Schubert's first six symphonies—so-called "early" works—the Fifth has won particular popularity. It is not difficult to understand the acceptance of this B flat major symphony (although it must be stressed that its companions among these first six are each full of wonderful qualities and quite different from one another). The Fifth, though, is a delightfully graceful work of unassuming charm and capriciousness; at its heart is an extended slow movement that is a glorious outpouring of melody. It is a work for a slimmed-down symphony orchestra—there are no clarinets, trumpets or timpani—and would work just as well with a chamber ensemble. However, Schubert's modest scoring does not preclude color or variety of timbre.

This is an age preoccupied with authenticity regarding how Baroque, Classical, and early-Romantic music might have sounded in the days of the composers themselves; there is now more than a tendency to frown upon those "old-fashioned" and "traditional" interpretations that developed through the nineteenth and twentieth centuries. In February 1957, Eugen Jochum recorded an account of Schubert's Fifth Symphony that is moderately paced, beautifully articulate, and sensitively molded—and which remains a joy. The slow movement is engrossing and enjoys expressive shaping and beautiful playing from the Bavarian Radio Symphony Orchestra. A beguiling, perfectly judged account, in which the mono sound is airy and naturally balanced and allows Jochum's affection for the music, his rhythmic swing, and ear for inner detail, to live on. It is as instructive today as it is enjoyable. **SP**

Nicolò Paganini
Twenty-four Caprices (1817)

Genre | Instrumental
Instrument | Violin
Performers | Massimo Quarta
Year recorded | 2002
Label | Chandos CHAN 10276

Nicolò Paganini stands with Caruso and Toscanini as one of a handful of Italians who personify their particular branch of music. Paganini's mastery of the violin was so absolute that he was regarded, in his day, as the epitome of virtuosity, an example even to exponents of other instruments, such as Liszt. Yet he left few disciples and, with his death (and that of Alessandro Rolla), Italian instrumental music went into a century of decline. As a composer, he was rapidly forgotten and only in the late twentieth century was much of his music rediscovered.

An exception to the rule was his set of twenty-four Caprices, published in 1820 that set new standards for violin playing. The most famous is no. 24, a sequence of variations on a superb theme that has stimulated other composers, including Brahms and Rachmaninov; but all the pieces are worth hearing in their own right. Paganini was a child of his time and place, heavily influenced by the early ottocento opera composers and the bel canto style of singing, but within those parameters he was a resourceful, melodious composer.

Many fine violinists of recent decades have given us complete sets of the caprices: The chief merit of Massimo Quarta's recording is that, like Salvatore Accardo before him, he brings this quintessentially Italian music back to Italy. Playing with excellent technique and burnished tone, he characterizes each of the two dozen pieces with individuality but not idiosyncrasy. He is very well recorded, so that the overtones of the magnificent violin he is using—the 1716 "Maréchal Berthier" Stradivari once owned by Franz von Vécsey—have a convincing ring. **TP**

Franz Schubert | Violin
Sonata in A major (1817)

Genre | Chamber
Performers | Josef Suk (violin),
Jan Panenka (piano)
Year recorded | 1962
Label | Boston Skyline BSD 146

Schubert's early chamber music is easeful and pleasing, rather than profound, but this A major duo of 1817 finds him beginning to spread his wings. The previous year he wrote three shorter sonatas for violin and piano, so small-scale that their first publisher renamed them sonatinas. They were clearly designed for domestic performance; the A major, on the other hand, is more suitable for the public arena. In the four movements established by Beethoven, it reverses the usual order of the two inner movements, with the scherzo second.

The composer's nineteenth-century image as a jolly Biedermeier figure, scribbling songs on scraps of paper and always the life and soul of the party, has faded a little since his angrier, more tormented later works have become entrenched in the repertoire. But recent performers have tended to throw the baby out with the bathwater and play the earlier chamber music as if it were by the chronically ill, anguished Schubert of the D minor and G major Quartets, the C major Quintet, or the E flat major Trio.

Thank goodness for Josef Suk and Jan Panenka, who were a regular duo for many years. They realize all the sweetness of this music while not neglecting the dramatic moments. It is vital that the violinist should be able to convey Viennese warmth, and Suk, with his perfectly judged portamenti and glowing, Kreisler-like tone, is the ideal candidate. Panenka matches him phrase for phrase and the result is sheer delight. The Supraphon recording has been refurbished by an American audiophile label, along with the little D major Sonata and the Suk Trio's first recording of the B flat Trio. **TP**

Gioachino Rossini | La cenerentola (1817)

Genre | Opera
Conductor/Performers | Riccardo Chailly;
Cecilia Bartoli (Cenerentola), William Matteuzzi (Don Ramiro)
Year recorded | 1992
Label | Decca 436 902-2 (2 CDs)

La cenerentola (*Cinderella*) successfully premiered in Rome in 1817 and within a decade had traveled around the world, its popularity eclipsing that of *The Barber of Seville*.

The plot is based on Perrault's fairytale, *Cendrillon*; unlike the simple rags-to-riches story familiar from the pantomime tradition, the journey of transformation from scullery maid to princess is more complex for Rossini's Cinderella. Prince Ramiro's quest for a wife involves testing the available market by reversing roles with his valet, Dandini; Cinderella's path to the fateful ball is smoothed not by a fairy godmother but by a "philosopher," Alidoro (in beggar's disguise); Cinderella's father Don Magnifico has an enlarged role as court butler, would-be father-in-law for the Prince, and as his youngest daughter's cruel oppressor. A bracelet takes the place of the iconic glass slipper, probably to avoid the censors' certain disapproval of a shoeless female foot appearing on stage!

The opera's greatness lies in the richness of its musical palette, befitting a plot that ranges from the comic capers of its "buffo" patter-songs and ensembles, to moments of grand romance; in *Cenerentola* the music matches the characters' emotional growth.

Decca's recording (based on a staging in Bologna) stands head-and-shoulders above the opposition. It could hardly be otherwise in a cast led by Cecilia Bartoli, the world's reigning queen of coloratura: in trademark style, she delivers precisely articulated runs with bell-like clarity of tone; and from the high tessitura of her soprano range to the contralto depths, her voice travels with seamless ease. She is the brightest in a completely idiomatic star cast: under Riccardo Chailly's sprightly baton, this recording is pure delight from start to finish. **GK**

> "[Cecilia] Bartoli is one of those bearers of the sacred flame, who have the life of their art within them. . . ."

John Steane, critic

Other Recommended Recordings

Royal Opera House Chorus & Orchestra • Carlo Rizzi
Teldec 4509 94553-2 (2 CDs)
Excellent Covent Garden–based cast led by Jennifer Larmore

London Symphony Orchestra • Claudio Abbado
DG 459 448-2 (2 CDs)
Teresa Berganza leads an earlier generation of Italian buffo experts

Academy of St. Martin in the Fields
Neville Marriner
Decca 470-580-2 (2 CDs)
Philips recording with extra CD-ROM material

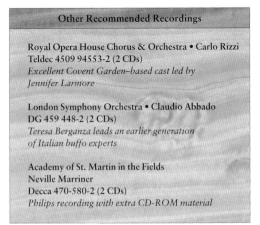

Cecilia Bartoli as Rossini's Cenerentola in 1992. ➲

Ludwig van Beethoven | Piano Sonata in B flat major, op. 106 "Hammerklavier" (1818)

Genre | Instrumental
Instrument | Piano
Performer | François-Frédéric Guy
Year recorded | 2005
Label | Naive V 5023

The "Hammerklavier" represents a peak not only within Beethoven's piano sonatas, but across piano literature in general. Its massive scale and its technical, intellectual, and interpretative demands present a titanic challenge to even the most richly endowed pianist.

The work's explosive expressive range is significant in the light of Beethoven's increasing financial difficulty at the time, his battle for custody of his nephew following his brother's death, and his now near-complete deafness. With his increasing withdrawal and self-absorption, Beethoven's thoughts and ideas became more radicalized. The aggressive fugue of the final movement is itself extreme, but the heartrending introspection of the third-movement Adagio unfolds over a vast expanse that traces an emotionally exhausting journey. With this sonata Beethoven opened up a new fascination with scale, soon to be mirrored by the *Diabelli Variations*, the choral Ninth Symphony, and the *Missa solemnis*; and he knew he was writing for the pianists of the future.

Young French pianist François-Frédéric Guy returned to this sonata for a second recording in 2005, and it is stunning for its sheer virtuosity and clarity. There is an irresistible propulsion to the first movement. After a lithe scherzo comes a truly arresting slow Adagio movement, deeply involving for its intimacy and sense of unfolding fantasy. If Guy here presents the essence of Romanticism, he manages the same in the celestial, almost Lisztian opening chord of the finale, before launching into its unforgiving, trill-laden three-part fugue with unerring power, concentration, and style. **EB**

beethoven françois-frédéric guy
PIANO SONATAS HAMMERKLAVIER, PATHÉTIQUE, Op. 49 No. 1

> *"To measure oneself against this sonata . . . is always a challenge . . . "*

François-Frédéric Guy on the "Hammerklavier"

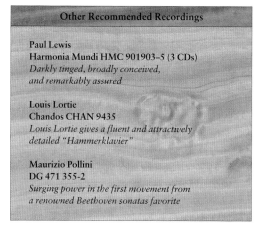

Other Recommended Recordings

Paul Lewis
Harmonia Mundi HMC 901903–5 (3 CDs)
Darkly tinged, broadly conceived, and remarkably assured

Louis Lortie
Chandos CHAN 9435
Louis Lortie gives a fluent and attractively detailed "Hammerklavier"

Maurizio Pollini
DG 471 355-2
Surging power in the first movement from a renowned Beethoven sonatas favorite

Beethoven's piano and violin on display at Bonn, Germany. ➡

Franz Schubert
Piano Quintet in A major, "Trout" (1819)

Genre | Chamber
Performers | Clifford Curzon (piano),
Members of the Vienna Octet
Year recorded | 1958
Label | Eloquence 467 417-2

Schubert's so-called "Trout" Quintet is one of the most urbane and popular works in the chamber music repertoire. It was apparently commissioned by the amateur cellist Sylvester Paumgartner, who had a particular affection for Schubert's song "Die Forelle" ("The Trout"). Paumgartner asked that Schubert's piece should have the same instrumentation as the quintet arrangement of Hummel's Septet (1816), which has a double bass instead of the more usual second cello or viola.

Full of high spirits, the first movement contrasts some quite brilliant passages with mysterious moments; but this secretiveness is never a threat to bonhomie. The slow movement is like a serenade, as if Schubert were in the coffee house, with the five musicians bringing convivial company; and there follows a spanking scherzo. The fourth movement is a set of variations on "Die Forelle," with a wide-ranging commentary on the song. The finale wraps up the work in buoyant and loquacious fashion.

Old-world charm informs the superb recording made by members of the Vienna Octet (musicians of the Vienna Philharmonic Orchestra) and Clifford Curzon. This unforced account has a ready wit and spontaneity to sustain it and the musicians display true chamber music give and take. There is a real sense of joy and unassuming craft that continues to make this recorded version a delight; and the sound itself—immediate, truthful, and well-balanced, and reproducing some fine foundation and rasping from the double bass—belies its years. **CA**

Frédéric Chopin
Mazurkas (1820–47)

Genre | Instrumental
Instrument | Piano
Performer | Garrick Ohlsson
Year recorded | 1999
Label | Arabesque Z 6730-2 (2 CDs)

The mazur was a staple dance of the Polish folk tradition long before Chopin got his hands on it; but it cast its spell early on the composer, who spent most of his life living outside his native Poland—his earliest surviving mazurka dates from 1820, when the composer was just nine. Over his lifetime, Chopin wrote more mazurkas than anything else and, what is extraordinary, is how varied they are. Chopin takes this simple triple-time dance, with its characteristic off-beat accents, away from its roots and into the most sophisticated salons of the day. Technically, some of them may be within the reach of the talented amateur, but interpretatively they are demanding in the extreme, and a great deal of pianistic sophistication is needed to get anywhere near a satisfactory result. Musically, they are highly stylized and often wildly experimental in their succession of keys, harmonies, and melody, and it is capturing that aspect, as well as the spirit of the dance, that is the secret of a great performance.

Arthur Rubinstein is much famed for his Chopin interpretations, but finer still is the American pianist Garrick Ohlsson, whose set of the mazurkas fully captures the range of Chopin's vision—be it in the wistful op. 24, no. 1 or op. 30, no. 1; or the strong narrative of the extended op. 33, no. 4, or the sheer delicacy of much of op. 63 and works such as op. 17, no. 4. Ohlsson is equally comfortable in those works where the mazurka's peasant origins come through strongly, never prettifying them unnecessarily or dampening their sheer joie de vivre. **HS**

Ludwig van Beethoven
Piano Sonata in E major, op. 109 (1820)

Genre | Instrumental
Instrument | Piano
Performer | Alfred Brendel
Year recorded | 1975
Label | Philips 438 374-2 (2 CDs)

After the massive scale of the "Hammerklavier" Sonata, op. 106, Beethoven's final trio of sonatas, opp. 109–11, aims at compactness, with each sonata running at roughly half the length of the "Hammerklavier."

In the E major Sonata, op. 109, as with its partners in the trilogy, there is a conscious shift in weight toward the last movement. Beethoven also surprises us at the beginning with an easy-going opening theme that trips along innocently before suddenly being hijacked by a more dramatic and expressive Adagio section. The first movement leads without a break into a vigorous Prestissimo, here in sonata form. The beguiling variation theme of the last movement begins as a hymn-like chorale, but transforms itself through varied treatments. The last variation broadens progressively as Beethoven doggedly sustains and thickens the "unstable" dominant with a build-up of trills, before the unadorned theme re-emerges, all the more expressive for its simplicity.

Alfred Brendel's recording from his second complete cycle of Beethoven's piano sonatas (this two-CD set comprises the last six sonatas) marries a concern for expression with a revealing transparency of texture. The *fantasia*-like adagio section of the first movement unfolds freely and the second movement bounds energetically without sounding brittle. In the all-important finale Brendel traces a seamless curve across the theme, its various incarnations (including a magisterial final variation), and its fragile, naked return at the end. **EB**

Carl Maria von Weber
Der Freischütz (1821)

Genre | Opera
Conductor/Performers | Nikolaus Harnoncourt; Endrik Wottrich
Year recorded | 1995
Label | Teldec 4509 97758-2 (2 CDs)

With its evocation of the dark, mysterious forest of German Romanticism, Weber's *Der Freischütz* is a truly iconic opera of the early nineteenth century. The world it evoked was already familiar from the elemental, supernatural themes of painters such as Caspar David Friedrich and Moritz von Schwind, but it struck a chord that resounded with German composers and audiences well after Weber's premature death in 1826.

The supernaturalism is at its most intense in the celebrated Wolf's Glen Scene, in which Caspar invokes the evil spirit Samiel to help cast the magic bullets that will put Max in his power. Weird apparitions and supernatural horror are depicted by stock musical elements but, with the help of Weber's masterly orchestration, these are invested with a demonic quality that chills the blood. At the same time, *Der Freischütz*, with its interspersed spoken dialogue, folk-song-inspired melodic style, and popular choruses, is rooted in the Singspiel tradition.

Nikolaus Harnoncourt returned to the autograph score and original dynamic markings in his search for the dramaturgical mainspring of this extraordinary work, and he brilliantly catches the brooding atmosphere of diabolism that so entranced audiences of the day. Endrik Wottrich and Matti Salminen are well cast as Max and Caspar respectively, while Luba Orgonasova's "Leise, leise" is a highlight of the performance. Admirable contributions too from both the Berlin Philharmonic and the equally excellent Berlin Radio Chorus. **BM**

Ludwig van Beethoven
Piano Sonata in A flat major, op. 110 (1821)

Genre | Instrumental
Instrument | Piano
Performer | Emil Gilels
Year recorded | 1985
Label | DG 457 900-2

BEETHOVEN
Klaviersonaten Nos. 27 · 28 · 30 & 31
Emil Gilels

GALLERIA

ORIGINAL-IMAGE
BIT-PROCESSING

Beethoven spent much of 1821 fighting illnesses so, although he completed the first of his intended triptych of piano sonatas (op. 109) by the autumn of 1820, the autograph score for op. 110 is dated more than a year later. "Now thank God," Beethoven writes in November 1821, "things are better and it appears that I am to be cheered up by the return of my health and may live again for my art."

This A flat major Sonata opens with an unmistakable melodic connection to the soulful, chorale-like theme from op. 109's last movement, but while in the former there is a sense of dark, inward journeying, in op. 110 the opening theme soon flowers into song-like expression. Also, like op. 109 (and op. 111), there is an economy of scale and an end-weighting that clearly reveals the last movement as the seat of gravity. After the eloquent first movement comes a gruff, march-like scherzo that quotes two popular songs of the time. This is followed by the most elevated of sentiments in the unusual final movement that opens with a startling recitative passage followed by a lonely arioso alternating with a fugue in a striking juxtaposition of heart-on-sleeve spontaneity and "academic" rigor.

Sadly Emil Gilels, one of the giants among twentieth-century pianists, died in 1985 before completing his cycle of Beethoven sonatas for Deutsche Grammophon. His op. 110 clearly shows off his wonderful cantabile tone and mastery in balancing chords. Even more finely voiced are the intertwining lines of the final-movement fugue, the inverted return of whose subject is a moment of breathtaking intimacy. From here Gilels generates an ever-reviving spirit before a triumphant end. **EB**

> *"Gilels had a very special sound of his own—a golden sound."*

Pianist Evgeny Kissin on Emil Gilels

Other Recommended Recordings

Solomon
Testament SBT 1192
Solomon's remastered recording from 1956 shows the poise and dexterity of a truly great artist

Alfred Brendel
Philips 438 374-2 (2 CDs)
A clearly conceived and luminously realized recording from a master of the Austro-German repertoire

Sviatoslav Richter
Philips 454 170-2
Stretches of greatness (despite a rather measured second movement) in a live recording from 1991

The Soviet pianist Emil Gilels pictured in 1965. ➔

Ludwig van Beethoven
Piano Sonata in C minor, op. 111 (1822)

Genre | Instrumental
Instrument | Piano
Performer | Maurizio Pollini
Year recorded | 1977
Label | DG 471 355-2

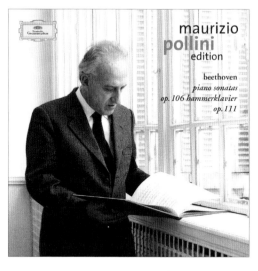

Beethoven's continual adapting of form in his piano sonatas led to the most unorthodox design in his last one, op. 111, which is cast in just two movements: an Allegro followed by a slow Adagio. There is no "finale"—the lack of which prompted Beethoven's French publisher to enquire whether a missing third movement had been left behind with the copyist. But the two movements depend upon and resolve one other, creating a balanced whole. The turmoil of the former is quelled by the lofty serenity of the latter. Together they present contrasts on many levels, leading one commentator to regard them respectively as the "material and spiritual worlds."

Though Beethoven himself reportedly confessed he had not had the time to write a third movement, a further appendage would seem redundant. As the organ professor Wendell Kretschmar suggests in Thomas Mann's *Doktor Faustus*: "A third movement? A new approach? A return after this parting—impossible!" Beethoven nevertheless continues his preoccupation with fugue with a deepening variation form, and with sustained trilling.

Maurizio Pollini's grasp of the elemental drama and thunderous spirit of the first movement is tireless: he introduces the cackling first angular fugue theme with due violence and his facility in elucidating the strands of counterpoint is a cause for quiet delight. The immediate stillness of the second-movement arietta theme is halting, and from the distant bass rumbling of the fourth variation through to the end there is a continuing sense of the ethereal. Three decades on, this recording remains a crowning interaction of conception and pianism. **EB**

"Yes, [op.] 111 is about a glorious death, isn't it?"

Conductor Kurt Sanderling, quoted by pianist Mitsuko Uchida

Other Recommended Recordings

Richard Goode
Nonesuch 7559 79211-2 (2 CDs)
Depth and not a little flair from a key modern interpreter of the Beethoven sonatas

Mitsuko Uchida
Philips 475 6935
Uchida's first recording of Beethoven piano sonatas sees a characteristic richness of passion and reflection

Mikhail Pletnev
DG 471 157-2
The hot-headed Russian in a typically spontaneous live performance from Carnegie Hall

Maurizio Pollini, photographed at La Scala, Milan, in 1987. ➔

Franz Schubert | Symphony no. 8, "Unfinished" (1822)

Genre | Orchestral
Conductor | Leonard Bernstein
Performers | Amsterdam Concertgebouw Orchestra
Year recorded | 1987
Label | DG 427 645-2

Schubert's "Unfinished" Symphony is an apt description of a popular and mysterious work. Schubert seems to have planned a four-movement symphony "in B minor," but completed only the first two. At this time, 1822, Schubert also began a Symphony "in E minor/major" that he did not finish. (This is now known as no. 7—confusingly, as sometimes this number is assigned to the "Unfinished," with the "Great C major" catalogued as no. 8.) Schubert then began the B minor work—sketching ideas for a scherzo and not, it seems, contemplating the last movement. Nevertheless, Schubert offered the first two movements to the Styrian Music Society as a thank-you for a diploma, although the symphony waited until 1865 to be performed. Maybe Schubert felt that the two movements complemented each other so perfectly that nothing more was needed; or, required to compose the time-honored scherzo and finale, he found himself unable to match the earlier movements' visionary intensity. They do indeed make a matchless pair, music that is highly personal in utterance and in its forward-looking manner—through power, foreboding, beauty, and enigma.

Leonard Bernstein made this recording in 1987, late in his career and at a time when his musical intervention divided opinion to polar extremes. Yet he found a direct approach with this two-movement work, with pacing and phrasing that gets to the heart of the music while investing contrast and accentuation to chart an emotional journey. To where is for us to speculate. In the first movement Bernstein judiciously balances impetus and reflection, and in the second he conjures a poetic refinement that is very affecting and transporting, played by the Concertgebouw Orchestra with expressive sensitivity. **CA**

> *"What do we need happiness for, since unhappiness is the only attraction left to us?"*
>
> Franz Schubert

Other Recommended Recordings

Academy of St. Martin in the Fields
Neville Marriner
Philips 470 886-2 (6 CDs)
An eminently straightforward account embracing Brian Newbould's four-movement "completion"

Cleveland Orchestra • George Szell
Sony SBK 48268
Meticulously prepared and symphonically taut

Chamber Orchestra of Europe • Claudio Abbado
DG 423 655-2
Using Schubert's autograph manuscript, Abbado sculpts a refined and resigned-to-fate version

Franz Schubert | Fantasy in C major, "Wanderer" (1822)

Genre | Instrumental
Instrument | Piano
Performer | Maurizio Pollini
Year recorded | 1973
Label | DG 447 451-2

Schubert approached composition as a songwriter. Of the four instrumental works based on themes from his songs—the "Trout" Piano Quintet, the "Wanderer" Fantasy for piano, the "Death and the Maiden" String Quartet and the C major Fantasy for violin and piano based on Schubert's setting of Rückert's "Sei mir gegrüsst"—the "Wanderer" was most revolutionary.

The "Wanderer" is cast in four movements, all tightly welded together. Schubert was fascinated by the challenge of unifying the movements of a traditional symphonic structure into a seamless and cohesive whole. In its structural and thematic organization, no less than its virtuoso and quasi-orchestral piano-writing, the "Wanderer" cast enormous influence over later composers, especially Liszt. The song fragment from "Der Wanderer" is the basis of Schubert's second movement, but its dactylic repeated-note rhythm (dum-da-da-dum) dominates the whole fantasy. Such is the scope of the writing, Alfred Brendel believes that the "Wanderer" relied—even more than Beethoven's mammoth "Hammerklavier" Sonata—on pianos of the future to come alive.

The recording by Italian Maurizio Pollini, made at the height of his powers, remains one of the finest things he has committed to disc. The sound is thin by modern standards, but perfectly satisfactory. While others bring more warmth and surface allure, Pollini strikes at the heart of the matter with playing of aristocratic poise and strength, full of dramatic contrasts and penetrating insights. He can be delicate and poetic, as in the filigree runs in the second movement, and also revels in steely virtuosity, especially in the finale. Overall, he strikes an ideal balance between visceral excitement and Classical restraint. **TLP**

> *"To wander is the Romantic condition; one yields to it . . . or is driven and plagued by finding no escape."*
>
> **Alfred Brendel**

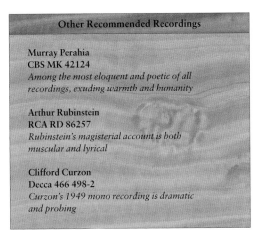

Other Recommended Recordings

Murray Perahia
CBS MK 42124
Among the most eloquent and poetic of all recordings, exuding warmth and humanity

Arthur Rubinstein
RCA RD 86257
Rubinstein's magisterial account is both muscular and lyrical

Clifford Curzon
Decca 466 498-2
Curzon's 1949 mono recording is dramatic and probing

Franz Schubert | Die schöne Müllerin (1823)

Genre | Vocal
Performers | Dietrich Fischer-Dieskau (baritone),
Jörg Demus (piano)
Year recorded | 1968
Label | DG 463 502-2

What are we to make of Schubert's *Fair Maid of the Mill*, and the lovelorn miller's apprentice? Is the composer's first song cycle a simple tale of unrequited love? Or is it a psycho-sexual exploration, riddled with referential nods and winks? What we know for certain is that Schubert, recently diagnosed with syphilis, wrote much of the music during a hospital stay, making his own careful selection from a cycle of poems published by Wilhelm Müller just three years earlier. The verse had started life as a sort of competitive parlor game: a domestic *Liederspiel*, in which all the parts were acted out, with Müller, as to the nomenclature born, playing the young miller himself.

Schubert noticed at once that these poems were a cut above the average party game. And his musical settings, fusing the exterior rhythms of mill-wheel and brooklet with the restless inner pulse of the infatuated heart, give singer and pianist a meticulously marked cardiogram. At the same time, the score offers almost infinite possibilities for interpretation and tone of voice, as the miller's moods are in constant flux with the current of the mill-stream.

Schubert originally conceived the cycle for tenor voice. But Dietrich Fischer-Dieskau's baritone seems to increase the sense of unease and foreboding as the emotional cycle turns and turns again. And in this comparatively recently exhumed recording, Jörg Demus nudges Fischer-Dieskau toward a stark, risk-taking performance, vibrant with a sense of discovery (and this despite the fact that Fischer-Dieskau first performed the cycle as early as 1949, and had already recorded it twice with Gerald Moore). In its verbal animation, its sprung rhythms, its ease of inflection and perfect pacing for a voice in its prime, this recording has a freshness that remains as evergreen as the cycle itself. **HF**

> *"The boy seems . . . attracted by rival forces—the female Müllerin, and the masculine brook which claims him."*

Graham Johnson

Other Recommended Recordings

Ian Bostridge, Dietrich Fischer-Dieskau,
Graham Johnson
Hyperion CDJ 33025
A meeting of master and apprentice, as Fischer-Dieskau recites the poems Schubert did not set

Werner Gura, Jan Schultsz
Harmonia Mundi HMC 901708
A beautifully enunciated and inflected tenor performance from 1999

Harry Sever, Nadanai Laohakunakorn
Tadpole Music TAD 0606
Offers surprising insights: boy soprano as miller's lad

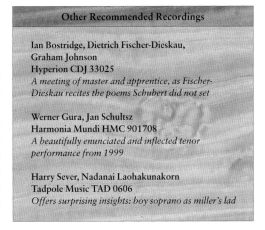

Dietrich Fischer-Dieskau, pictured in 1962. ➔

Ludwig van Beethoven | Missa solemnis (1823)

Genre | Choral
Conductor/Performers | Nikolaus Harnoncourt; Eva Mei,
Marjana Lipovšek, Anthony Rolfe Johnson, Robert Holl
Year recorded | 1992
Label | Teldec 9031 74884-2 (2 CDs)

Beethoven's *Missa solemnis* (Solemn Mass), which occupied him for nearly four years, stands today as one of the supreme masterpieces of the nineteenth century. The Mass was commissioned in 1819 for performance at an enthronement service for Archduke Rudolph the following year. It was not ready, however; Beethoven finally presented the finished score to the Archduke in March 1823. It was Beethoven's determination to compose a Mass setting that would serve as fully as possible the depth and splendor of the liturgical text that caused him such epic toil, and resulted in the work's monumental grandeur. The scale and scope is groundbreaking, but the work stems directly from the Viennese Mass tradition and owes much, in particular, to Haydn. Beethoven's own Mass in C, from 1807, directly expands on the grand style of Haydn's late Masses, but the *Missa solemnis* powerfully forges a new, expressive path, stretching the performers to their limits—and often seemingly beyond. It has been said that Beethoven did not know how to write for the voice, but the sense of struggle resulting from the notoriously fiendish chorus parts, especially the relentlessly high soprano line, is surely a calculated part of Beethoven's mission to achieve fidelity to the awe-inspiring text.

Nikolaus Harnoncourt's dynamic and spiritual account employs the mainly modern-instrument forces of the excellent Chamber Orchestra of Europe, but period trumpets, trombones and timpani provide important extra bite and urgency. With a stunning team of soloists and phenomenal choral singing, the performance is superbly articulated, and captures wonderfully the work's intense excitement and drama, as well as instilling an inspirational sense of devotion. **GR**

> *"From the heart—may it go to the heart!"*
>
> Ludwig van Beethoven

Other Recommended Recordings

Monteverdi Choir, English Baroque Soloists
John Eliot Gardiner
DG 429 779-2 (2 CDs)
Clear, unsentimental reading with period instruments

Leipzig Radio Chorus, Swedish Radio Choir,
Vienna Philharmonic Orchestra • James Levine
DG 435 770-2 (2 CDs)
Expansive account from the 1991 Salzburg Festival

Mass in C • Monteverdi Choir, Orchestre
Révolutionnaire et Romantique • John Eliot Gardiner
DG 435 391-2
Beethoven's often overlooked earlier Mass

Nikolaus Harnoncourt in Vienna's Musikverein in 2001. ➔

Ludwig van Beethoven
Diabelli Variations
(1823)

Genre | Instrumental
Instrument | Piano
Performer | Piotr Anderszewski
Year recorded | 2000
Label | Virgin 7243 5 45468 2 2

In 1819, Viennese music publisher Anton Diabelli circulated a banal waltz of his own invention, asking fifty composers to compose a variation each. This collaborative volume appeared in 1824 and included contributions from Schubert, Czerny, and an eleven-year-old Franz Liszt. Beethoven dismissed the project, but Diabelli's tune ignited his creativity and he set to work on his own set of variations, considered the finest ever composed. There were twenty-three at first, but in 1823 Beethoven interspersed a further ten, published as his op. 120.

Part of the power of Beethoven's Variations lies in the tension between Diabelli's trite theme and the imaginative scope of Beethoven's treatment. In its range of allusion, quotation, humor, parody, and transfiguration, it holds a unique place in Beethoven's output. Every facet of the theme is isolated for separate treatment, and the relationship between the variations and the subject is sometimes made blatant through exaggeration, or obscure through subtle transformation. Ranging from the comic to the spiritual, this hour-long journey requires utmost concentration from both pianist and listener.

In a crowded field of excellent recordings of the *Diabelli Variations*, Piotr Anderszewski's stands out for its penetrating focus and thoughtfulness, while also sparkling with life. He achieves a meditative stillness in variation 20, and is deeply imaginative in variation 22, with its humorous reference to Mozart's *Don Giovanni*. Few interpretations are so all-encompassing or satisfying. **TLP**

Juan Crisóstomo de Arriaga
String Quartets
(1824)

Genre | Chamber
Performers | Voces String Quartet
Year recorded | 1985
Label | Dabringhaus und Grimm
MDG 603 02362

Born in Bilbao on January 27, 1806, fifty years to the day after the birth of Wolfgang Amadeus Mozart, Basque composer Juan Crisóstomo Jacobo Antonio de Arriaga y Balzola came to share more than just his birthday with his Classical forebear. Arriaga's posthumously conferred epithet "the Spanish Mozart" refers less to any similarity in musical style than to marked biographical parallels: like Mozart, Arriaga was extraordinarily precocious, his talents evident from an early age; and, mirroring Mozart's tragically early end, Arriaga was ten days short of his twentieth birthday when he died. Given the astonishing maturity of his prolific output—which, over just eleven years, includes forays into every major genre—one can only imagine the great heights Arriaga might have scaled had he lived longer. As it is, we are left with much to enjoy: two operas, a symphony, a number of choral works, and several major chamber and piano pieces.

Little of his output has found its way onto CD, but there are several recordings of his three important string quartets from 1824, all masterpieces of the genre. The themes of the first, in D minor, contain clear echoes of Mozart's D minor Quartet, K421. Arriaga's development of the material, however, is boldly original—as are the Romantic harmonies, rhythmic invention, and depth of expression employed throughout the quartets, nudging at the boundaries of Classical refinement. The Voces String Quartet of Romania gives a spirited, elegant performance, making a compelling case for these unjustly neglected works. **GR**

Ludwig van Beethoven
Symphony no. 9, "Choral" (1824)

Genre | Orchestral/Choral
Conductor | Wilhelm Furtwängler
Performers | Bayreuth Festival
Year recorded | 1951
Label | EMI 7243 5 66901 2 7

From a mysterious, indefinite beginning to an unconventional finale, Beethoven's Ninth is arguably the richest and most provocative work in the canon. Its aesthetic ramifications stem in part from different interpretations of the finale, which begins by parading themes from earlier movements and then rejecting them in favor of a memorably simple melody that all can sing (in a symphony!). This led Wagner to see the development of music drama as a historic inevitability, an idea not countenanced by Brahms, who famously adapted Beethoven's tune for an exclusively instrumental context in his First Symphony. The Ninth's structure and meaning is still discussed not just because solutions are elusive, but because finding them continues to matter so long as the work's vision and Beethoven's perpetual relevance make the Ninth the heartbeat of Western musical culture.

The Ninth as performed by the Bayreuth Festival Chorus and Orchestra is irreplaceable for conveying the vastness of Beethoven's vision. Conductor Wilhelm Furtwängler's conception, developed with theorist Heinrich Schenker, combines elemental force with Dionysian spontaneity, causing tempi to fluctuate purposefully along the contours of expressive topography. From a cosmetic standpoint this performance is extremely messy, yet the indelible nature of the conception surmounts all blunders. Achieving an unparalleled ecstasy, Furtwängler's Ninth is to performances of the piece what the work itself is to the standard repertoire. **DB**

Franz Schubert
Octet in F major, D803 (1824)

Genre | Chamber
Performers | Nash Ensemble
Year recorded | 2003
Label | ASV Gold
GLD 4005

Schubert's Octet (composed for string quartet, double bass, clarinet, horn, and bassoon) is a six-movement work lasting about an hour. For all the domestic intent of the work, its sense of scale was determined by Schubert's wish to write a "grand symphony," which would come to fruition with the "Great" C major, Symphony no. 9. The Octet is a joyous and lyrical work, with song and dance prominent, and the whole is an uncomplicated feast of melody and color. The anticipatory slow introduction, which presents the instruments singly and in various combinations, leads to a bubbling Allegro; the slow movement gives an affecting melody to the clarinet and the ensuing scherzo is puckish in its rhythmic guile. For the fourth movement, Schubert borrows a trite but incessantly memorable ditty from his opera *Die Freunde von Salamanka* and subjects it to several ingenious variations. The penultimate movement is a sweet, but sad, minuet. The finale begins with an arresting and tense introduction; but rather than let storm clouds hover for too long, Schubert introduces a gaily tripping idea that has all the bounce of a balmy spring day and that sustains the finale to its ripe conclusion.

The Nash Ensemble's recording has a beguiling openness, transparency, and softness. The musicians display a sense of collective responsibility while revealing their individual stamp. Joyous buoyancy brings the faster music to life, inducing a smile in the listener—it is plain these musicians are enjoying themselves—and the slower pages have a gentle flow and subtle undulations. **CA**

Franz Schubert | String Quartet in D minor, D810, "Death and the Maiden" (1824)

Genre | Chamber
Performers | Emerson Quartet: Philip Setzer,
Lawrence Dutton, David Finckel, Eugene Drucker
Year recorded | 1987
Label | DG 477 045-2 (3 CDs)

This string quartet, probably the most popular of Schubert's works in this genre, once again looks to earlier material for inspiration; this time elements taken from Schubert's song "Der Tod und das Mädchen" ("Death and the Maiden") form the basis of the second movement's set of variations. This is one of Schubert's most dramatic and brooding works, in which the composer gives vent to his despair as he faces his own early-age mortality ("I feel as though I am the unhappiest, most miserable man on earth"). The music, however, is not unrelieved: Schubert's variegation of mood and material sustains the Classical construction. Overall, the work has something of the night about it, a fevered impulse that needs a taut and flexible involvement from the performers as well as staying power for the "dangerous" moto perpetuo that forms the finale.

The Emerson Quartet can, as an overall assessment of its playing style, be rather relentless and steel-capped in terms of tone color (and the other renditions in this 3-CD set, including the G major String Quartet and C major String Quintet, do not add up to an unqualified recommendation). In "Death and the Maiden," however, the four American musicians give a visceral and charged account that seems apt for this essentially tragic music and is gripping in its drive, intensity, and well-contrasted lyricism (both in terms of emotional oppositions and in changes of tempo). Closely recorded, such intimidation is valid, while the "Death and the Maiden" variations movement itself is effectively veiled in the presentation of its musical material. The finale, taken at a devilish presto, is remarkable for its incandescent fury and strength of purpose. **CA**

"What Schubert could only suggest in the song here finds exhaustive expression."

Alfred Einstein

Other Recommended Recordings

Takács Quartet
Hyperion CDA 67585
Schubert played with Classical propriety and textural lucidity

Kopelman Quartet
Wigmore Hall Live WHLive 0010
Accomplished and distinguished playing, consolatory rather than vehement

The Lindsays
ASV CDDCA 560
The Lindsays stress the music's sense of theater and impulsiveness

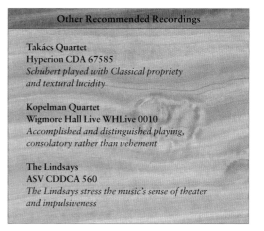

The Emerson Quartet is one of today's pre-eminent ensembles. ➔

Franz Schubert
Arpeggione Sonata (1824)

Genre | Chamber
Performers | Jean-Guihen Queyras (cello), Alexandre Tharaud (piano)
Year recorded | 2005
Label | Harmonia Mundi HMC 901930

The tender grace of Schubert's Arpeggione Sonata belies its technical difficulty to cellists, for whom it was never written. Schubert was persuaded to compose the sonata for the six-stringed arpeggione or "guitarre d'amour" in 1824, soon after the instrument's invention, by his friend Georg Staufer. Essentially it was a bass viol with guitar tuning, but it failed to inspire and this sonata is its only surviving monument. Since Schubert wrote no cello sonata it is a precious legacy, and one eminently suited to that instrument's range and timbre.

The work has little of the storm and tragedy of Schubert's string quartets, but an introspective, poignant elegance: opening with an expansive, exploratory first movement and closing with a gentle Rondo allegretto. The Adagio provides a brief, but achingly emotional heart to the work. Cellist Jean-Guihen Queyras comments on the sonata: "Its apparent carefree luminosity cannot conceal an anguish, which comes out into the open at the end of the second movement." If the shadows are revealed here, the final movement serves to heal and soothe, with its vigorous dance-like episodes and lilting lyricism.

The recording by these young French musicians provides a new benchmark performance of the work. Not only is Queyras's playing as focused, articulate, poetic, and supple as any of the great cellists, but both players bring a new level of finesse and subtlety to their ensemble. Moreover, they place the sonata in a fascinating Viennese context, programming it alongside Berg's Four Pieces and Webern's Three Little Pieces, and an arrangement of Schubert's own posthumous Sonatina for violin. **HW**

Ludwig van Beethoven
Late String Quartets (1825–26)

Genre | Chamber
Performers | Takács Quartet: Dusinberre, Schranz, Walther, Fejér
Years recorded | 2003–04
Label | Decca 470 849-2 (3 CDs)

Beethoven's "late" quartets consist of five works, opp. 127, 130–32, and 135—plus the *Grosse Fuge*, originally intended as the finale to op. 130, and as the name suggests, an epic, rigorous fugue of unparalleled intensity lasting a quarter of an hour. Not since Bach had such a strict form been used to such potent emotional ends.

So what is "late" Beethoven style? Firstly, it is more disjunct than previously, with abrupt juxtapositions that appear almost schizophrenic in their moods, such as the tiny Presto in op. 130—blink and you miss it. Other movements of heavenly lengths, such as the Adagio of op. 127, seem to stretch on endlessly. Secondly, time seems to stand still, with extremes of register making you more aware of the vertical structure than the forward motion of the music. And then there is the emotional aspect. It is easy to imagine that Beethoven's deafness had taken him so far inside his own world that he no longer needed to heed the reaction of the outside world. Beauty is there in spades, but as a side product rather than as a primary aim.

Truth, it seems, is more important, and one finds it in the most magical way in the Takács's performances of these pieces. There are unusually direct biographical references in this music too, such as op. 132, which contains at its center a "Hymn of Thanksgiving" to God, following Beethoven's recovery from an illness. Beethoven himself regarded op. 131 as his greatest quartet, and it is certainly a far cry in immensity of scale and dramatic power from the early quartets of Haydn. The Takács breathes new life into these pieces and the terse op. 135, always probing and perceptive in its interpretations. **HS**

Felix Mendelssohn
Octet (1825)

Genre | Chamber
Performers | Chamber Music Society of Lincoln Center
Year recorded | 2002
Label | Delos DE 3266

Mendelssohn's glorious octet for four violins, two violas, and two cellos is deservedly one of the composer's most celebrated chamber works—it is incredible that he wrote it when he was aged only sixteen. Growing up in a well-to-do family in Berlin, Mendelssohn was a child prodigy of a composer and was fortunate to be steeped in culture from the start, developing a passion for Shakespeare that led him to compose his overture to *A Midsummer Night's Dream* not long after the octet. His positive spirit, enquiring mind, and sheer zest for life all shine through the energetic and constantly engaging octet.

The work follows a traditional four-movement structure—opening Allegro, slow movement, scherzo, and finale—but beyond its formal outline, there is no obvious model. Octets were rare, and octets for strings virtually unprecedented—Schubert's, which Mendelssohn may have known, mixed strings and woodwind.

"This octet must be played by all the instruments in symphonic orchestra style," Mendelssohn declared. "*Pianos* and *fortes* must be strictly observed and more strongly emphasized than [one] is used to in pieces of this character." The verve of the music and the lightness and precision that the scherzo requires make it harder to bring off than one might suppose, but there are plenty of fine recordings.

The Chamber Music Society of Lincoln Center—eight individual players, many of them celebrated in their own right—give a particularly excellent account, led by violinist Cho-Liang Lin: as symphonic and strongly emphasized as Mendelssohn could have wished, it is well-polished yet brims over with joie de vivre. **JD**

Felix Mendelssohn | Songs
without Words (1825–45)

Genre | Instrumental
Instrument | Piano
Performer | András Schiff
Year recorded | 1986
Label | Decca 466 425-2 (2 CDs)

There had never been anything quite like Mendelssohn's forty-eight *Songs without Words* before, and there has been little in the same vein since. A series of short, self-contained piano pieces in which melody features as prominently as it would in Lieder, these pieces display a range of character, emotional shading, pianistic texture, and effortless imagination. They held a wide appeal for his devoted audience (from middle-class households to Queen Victoria herself) and while they are not too difficult for good amateurs to play, they remain challenging even for top professionals. Although certain pieces possess distinctive character, such as the "Gondola Songs" and the "Spinning Song," the "songs" are mainly abstract and stand perfectly well alone as pure music. They span almost the whole of Mendelssohn's compositional life.

Many of the *Songs without Words* are deceptively difficult: they call for lightness of touch, finesse of voicing, sensitivity of phrasing, and great musical poise, without which cynical modern audiences sometimes consider them over sentimental. Interestingly enough, Mendelssohn's aim in writing them was in part to restore dignity to contemporary piano repertoire, which was largely dominated by virtuoso showpieces.

A must-hear disc comes from the discerning Hungarian pianist András Schiff, who presents a personal choice of pieces in an order making emotional rather than chronological sense. His touch has all the requisite delicacy, songfulness, and fleetness of finger. He brings personality to even the most amiable of the pieces. The set also includes Schiff in Mendelssohn's piano concertos. **JD**

Franz Schubert
Piano Sonata in D major, D850 (1825)

Genre | Instrumental
Instrument | Piano
Performer | Mitsuko Uchida
Year recorded | 1999
Label | Philips 464 480-2

This is the most extrovert and ebullient of all Schubert's piano sonatas. It was composed during a tour of Upper Austria with friends in the summer of 1825, specifically in the spa town of Gastein. Schubert dedicated it to his friend Karl Maria von Bocklet, one of the outstanding pianists of the time, and it is plausible that the composer tailored the sonata's technical demands, especially the virtuoso character of the first movement, to Bocklet's talents.

The first movement, at an uncharacteristically fast tempo, is full of vivacious energy offset only by the slightly relaxed tempo for the "yodelling" second subject. The slow movement imitates horn calls and an obbligato violin, and contains some adventurous quasi-Wagnerian harmonies, while the scherzo continues the progression in this sonata from rhetorical urgency to contented relaxation. This is completed in the charming finale, with its apparently childlike "tick-tock" accompaniment. Schubert's decision to round off such a majestic work with a hushed coda that dissipates into nothing is entirely characteristic in its confounding of expectations.

Many seasoned Schubertians come unstuck with the challenges of this sonata, but Mitsuko Uchida takes everything in her stride. She conveys its physical excitement yet finds room for playfulness, and in the second and fourth movements shapes the song-like lyrical lines with exquisite expressiveness. No other pianist achieves quite the same delicacy and refinement in the passagework of the finale. **TLP**

Gioachino Rossini
Il viaggio a Reims (1825)

Genre | Opera
Conductor | Claudio Abbado
Performers | Sylvia McNair, Samuel Ramey
Year recorded | 1992
Label | Sony S2K 53336 (2 CDs)

The full title of the opera, translated, is *The Voyage to Reims* or *The Inn of The Golden Lily*—and everything about it is unusual to the point of wackiness. Rossini's last Italian opera—written after he settled in Paris in 1824—was an occasional piece: an offering for the coronation of King Charles X; and the event is the mainspring of the plot.

An international group of the great and good arrive at Madam Cortese's inn on their way to the coronation at Reims. Among the travelers is Corinna, a Roman poetess whose song neutralizes a number of jealous quarrels and whose beauty prompts male delegates to compete for her favors. When it is announced that no horses are available the group find themselves stranded, and decide to mount their own banquet and sing songs, to honor the new king.

Part of the opera's charm is that Rossini seems effortlessly relaxed and at ease in the music, which ranges from lyrical outpourings to ironic commentary, and the most sophisticated of parodies, as each character displays his or her own national traits. Among Rossini's most inspired moments are the unique "Concerted Piece for Fourteen Voices"—the extended ensemble that occurs on receipt of the bad news about the horses—and the finale of improvisations on the various national anthems.

Viaggio is a festival opera that requires an all-star cast: it gets it here. This is Abbado's second outing to Reims on CD—on balance this Sony version (which shares much of the cast with its 1984 DG rival) scores on sound, orchestral quality, and performances, having matured over time. **GK**

Franz Schubert
String Quartet in G major, D887 (1826)

Genre | Chamber
Performers | Busch Quartet: Paul Grümmer, Adolf Busch, Karl Doktor, Gösta Andreasson
Year recorded | 1938
Label | EMI 0946 3 61589 2 1

The last of Schubert's string quartets is the most "orchestral" in terms of sonic density and, in terms of structural ambition, is something of a symphony manqué. The work was written quickly, in around ten days, and the composer's white-heat inspiration is enshrined in music of emotion and suspense, with forward-looking harmonies and developmental force. Schubert's final quartet is a fascinating enigma: both masterly and individual but not easily giving its secrets away. The slow movement, which is both elegiac and consoling, offsets the tense impulse of the large-scale first movement. For the scurrying scherzo Schubert looks to his revered Beethoven for inspiration and then offers maximum contrast with the hymn-like trio. The finale returns to the conflicting avenues of the first movement, Viennese inflections countered by worldly-wise and haunted passions.

Potentially Schubert's farewell to the medium of the string quartet is a massive affair, one that invites spacious tempi and searching phrasing. Such viewpoints have come with renditions set down nearer to our own time. However, back in 1938, in Studio no. 3 at Abbey Road, London, the legendary Busch Quartet made a recording that crackles with energy. There is no lack of poise, shapeliness, and repose, but there is also a boundary-breaking quality that never suggests Schubert's writing as being disproportionately verbose. Taking forty minutes, the musicians seem to have found a balance between Schubert's innovative and emotional content. **CA**

Felix Mendelssohn
A Midsummer Night's Dream (1826, 1843)

Genre | Incidental Music
Conductor/Performers | Seiji Ozawa; Kathleen Battle, Frederica von Stade
Year recorded | 1992
Label | DG 439 897-2

Mendelssohn wrote his overture *A Midsummer Night's Dream* at the astonishing age of seventeen, after falling under the spell of Shakespeare's play. It is sheer magic, evoking enchantment from the moment its four iconic opening woodwind chords set matters in motion. The delight and inspiration of Mendelssohn's early response was rekindled in 1843, when King Friedrich Wilhelm IV of Prussia invited him to write incidental music for a stage production of the play in his palace. Mendelssohn was juggling a heavy schedule as music director in both Leipzig and Berlin, but produced a masterpiece all the same.

Besides redeploying themes from the overture, he created for it some of his most exquisite music, and, in the "Wedding March," some of his best known. The Scherzo epitomizes his lightness of touch and the Nocturne his lyricism, while his settings of Shakespeare's words are sensitive and apposite. The lovers' confusion in the forest is expressed in the turbulent intermezzo, and there is a spoof funeral march for the mechanicals' play-within-a-play, "Pyramus and Thisbe," besides a dance making the most of Bottom's theme with its donkey-bray.

For a complete performance of the incidental music it is especially rewarding to hear a version that places it in context by incorporating some Shakespeare. The Boston Symphony Orchestra has a secret weapon in narrator Judi Dench, on top of a warm and sparkling performance from the orchestra and some tremendous singing from the joint powerhouses Kathleen Battle and Frederica von Stade. **JD**

Franz Schubert | Piano Sonata in G major, D894 (1826)

Genre | Instrumental
Instrument | Piano
Performer | Arcadi Volodos
Year recorded | 2001
Label | Sony SK 89647

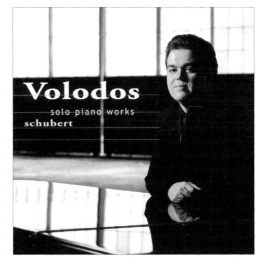

When Schubert composed the G major Piano Sonata, D894, in the autumn of 1826, it could be said that he was beginning to find his length. Like the "Great" C major Symphony (D944) and G major String Quartet (D887), which date from around the same time, the G major Sonata is an expansive work whose ideas need time and space to unfold. Especially in the first movement, it exudes the sort of mysterious serenity familiar from such songs as "Du bist die Ruh" or "Im Abendrot," which anticipates the contemplative intimacy of the B flat major Sonata, D960.

The opening Molto moderato e cantabile is one of Schubert's most beautifully lyrical conceptions (even the tempo marking is quintessentially Schubertian). With repeats this movement can last up to twenty minutes. The Andante has a homely charm and the minuet a stately rhythmic energy, while the rondo finale sparkles with rustic freshness. This sonata holds a special place in the affections of all Schubert-lovers.

The young Russian pianist Arcadi Volodos is best known for his coruscating virtuosity in Romantic showpieces, but he is also an incredibly refined and eloquent artist. The surface polish of his Schubert, with a tone so ravishing it seems to be wrapped in velvet, should not detract from his broader musical insights. Although some pianists (notably Brendel) bring more drama to this piece, Volodos maintains a subdued intensity that is powerful and deeply compelling. He shapes the long arching phrases like a great singer and expert accompanist rolled into one. When a more rigorous drive is required, as in the second and third movements, Volodos provides it, but always with a perfect sense of proportion. The recorded sound is ideal, too. A must for Schubert fans and converts. **TLP**

> *"Schubert is like Beethoven in heaven."*
>
> Edith Vogel

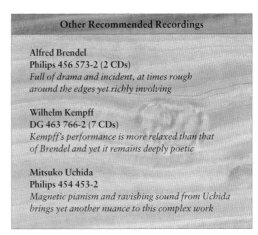

Other Recommended Recordings

Alfred Brendel
Philips 456 573-2 (2 CDs)
Full of drama and incident, at times rough around the edges yet richly involving

Wilhelm Kempff
DG 463 766-2 (7 CDs)
Kempff's performance is more relaxed than that of Brendel and yet it remains deeply poetic

Mitsuko Uchida
Philips 454 453-2
Magnetic pianism and ravishing sound from Uchida brings yet another nuance to this complex work

Franz Schubert | Piano Trio in B flat major (1827)

Genre | Chamber
Performers | Alfred Cortot (piano),
Jacques Thibaud (violin), Pablo Casals (cello)
Year recorded | 1926
Label | Naxos 8.110188

The first of Schubert's two full-blown piano trios (there are smaller works for the same forces) is an outgoing work full of melody and agreeable detail. The first movement opens with purposeful striding and eases the listener into the sweet lyricism of the second subject. The slow movement begins with a blissful melody allotted first to the cello; a song without words that is a haunting example of Schubert's gift for melody. The sparkling scherzo and the robustious, dancing finale complete an amiable work that may be at odds with Schubert's circumstances at the time (he was ill and death-haunted) but that has a temperate and confident demeanor.

Although recorded over eighty years ago, and with many subsequent rivals, the partnership of Jacques Thibaud, Pablo Casals, and Alfred Cortot remains a notable and vivid one. Here is a group of famous soloists interacting with each other in a considered and spontaneous account of Schubert's bountiful music; at this time, editing did not make recordings, so this is a "real" performance. Although repeats are in short supply, what particularly stands out is these musicians' refusal to indulge or bloat the music; integrity of purpose and flowing tempi are a significant part of this performance's success, together with a light touch, boldness, informality, and sparkle, and the musicians' own discerning individuality. Recordings such as this preserve playing styles now out of fashion; and this transfer allows the tones captured in 1926 (in Kingsway Hall, London) to reach the ear with fullness and clarity and without the over-processing that lesser "audio restorers" indulge in when trying to remove hiss and crackle. Here there is gentle "swish"—easily listened through—and the sonic result is as natural as the performance itself. **CA**

> ## *"A glance at Schubert's Trio and the troubles of human existence disappear; . . . all the world is bright again."*
>
> Robert Schumann

Other Recommended Recordings

Florestan Trio
Hyperion CDA 67273
Perhaps the finest modern version of this work

Jean-Philippe Collard, Augustin Dumay, Frédéric Lodéon
EMI 0946 3 65295 2 3 (2 CDs)
This trio of French musicians brings love and flexibility to disarm the listener

András Schiff, Yuuko Shiokawa, Miklós Perényi
Teldec 0630 13151-2 (2 CDs)
Joie de vivre and dynamism, and a keen response

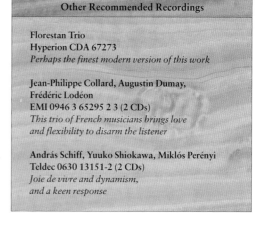

Franz Schubert
Impromptus (1827)

Genre | Instrumental
Instrument | Piano
Performer | Maria João Pires
Years recorded | 1996–97
Label | DG 457 550-2 (2 CDs)

Schubert's *Impromptus* may be popular fodder for amateur pianists—endangering them of degrading into cliché—but they contain a wealth of wonderful music. Immaculately proportioned and without ostentation, they are among the most eloquent manifestations of Schubert's natural lyricism and effortless purity of utterance.

The first set of four was not named "Impromptus" by Schubert, but the second was and was clearly indicated as a sequel. Each piece has a straightforward structure, developing a single thematic idea rather than exploring the more complex procedures of sonata form. The first set opens with an inventive exercise in monothematicism, before a brilliant showcase for right-hand scales, a sensuous nocturne in the remote key of G flat, and a more improvisatory final piece. Schumann thought the second set was a sonata in disguise, and there is a certain unity in the Hungarian flavor, as well as the tonality (F minor), of the first and last pieces. The second piece is a wistful minuet and trio, while the third is a set of variations on one of Schubert's best-loved tunes, from the incidental music he wrote for the play *Rosamunde*.

This is well-trodden ground, and most great Schubertians have recorded the *Impromptus*. One of the most richly expressive accounts is by Portuguese pianist Maria João Pires, who saturates this music with dramatic incident and radiant poetry. She projects melodic lines with a singing tone, yet never loses the essential quality of intimacy or private confession. This is not music designed for a concert hall, and Pires captures its essence. This is one of the greatest of all Schubert piano recordings. **TLP**

Franz Schubert
Winterreise (1827)

Genre | Vocal
Performers | Peter Schreier (tenor),
András Schiff (piano)
Year recorded | 1991
Label | Decca 475 268-2

The first performance of *Winterreise* (*Winter Journey*) was at the house of Schubert's friend Franz von Schober, on March 4, 1827. But this was only half the cycle as we know it. Soon afterwards Schubert found another twelve song texts by Wilhelm Müller and re-ordered their sequence, grouping Müller's darkest poems together at the end of the cycle and leading to the grinding hurdy-gurdy of that most desolate of all Schubert's Lieder, "Der Leiermann."

In 1827, Schubert himself sang the entire *Winterreise* to his friends, who were, Josef von Spaun wrote, "dumbfounded by the gloomy mood." Each century, each passing year catches its own reflection from the ever-shifting light of this long, existential winter journey of the soul. The lover's departure from his beloved's hometown sets up the rhythmic tread for those footprints in the snow. And the ice and the fire of his burning heart; the haunting presences of crows and will o' the wisps; the sense of cyclical movement to a non-existent destination—all this is recreated in a musical language that went further than Schubert had ever dared before.

It is a huge challenge for any singer and pianist to recreate the cycle's network of allusions, harmonic ambiguities, and sense of longing. Peter Schreier waited a long time to add *Winterreise* to his repertoire. After studying it with pianist Sviatoslav Richter, he made a live recording from their 1985 Dresden recital. And in 1991, Schreier presented a "definitive" recording of *Winterreise* with András Schiff as an extraordinarily perceptive accompanist. Minutely imagined, painstakingly yet instinctively recreated, this is a revelatory performance. **HF**

Franz Schubert | Piano Trio in E flat major, D929 (1827)

Genre | Chamber
Performers | Beaux Arts Trio: Menahem Pressler, Isidore Cohen, Bernard Greenhouse
Year recorded | 1985
Label | Philips 475 7571

The second of Schubert's two piano trios is a dramatic and searching work on its own terms, and seems even more so in comparison with its B flat major companion. In the E flat major work, Schubert is more expressing his inner self, his turmoil and contradictions. Abrupt, imploring and even tortured, the epic first movement is full of seismic mood changes occasionally leavened by glimpses of hope. As in the B flat major Trio, the cello has a plum of a tune to open the second movement, a rather forlorn melody (seemingly derived from a Swedish folksong but very much inhabited by Schubert's own muse) that is set to a slow march rhythm, the movement emotionally burdened. The scherzo, akin to a Viennese dance, is more insouciant—some light relief after much travail—and the finale begins with an element of humor; a foil, for the movement is substantial (even after the composer made cuts) and includes "Hungarian" elements and a reference back to the main melody of the slow movement.

If the Beaux Arts Trio, in the 1985 line-up of pianist Menahem Pressler, violinist Isidore Cohen and cellist Bernard Greenhouse, is rather too insistent and too inflected in the B flat major Trio, their style is suited admirably to Schubert's more intense E flat major work. These musicians make much of dramatic contrasts and bring a rough-hewn grandeur to the stormier and "heavier" episodes. They invest a human dimension into the music that reveals the composer expressing his circumstances, and his devotion to Beethoven. Finding a lighter touch, the musicians make the scherzo a delight and are unflinchingly trenchant with the finale. **CA**

Franz Schubert Fantasy in C, D934 (1827)

Genre | Chamber
Performers | Adolf Busch (violin), Rudolf Serkin (piano)
Year recorded | 1931
Label | APR 5543

Whereas most of Schubert's music for violin and piano was written with an eye to domestic performance—or half an eye in the case of the A major Sonata—the Fantasy in C and the *Rondo brillant* were intended for public display. In each case the impetus came from the young Bohemian violin virtuoso Josef Slavík, the most famous member of a musical family. Chopin compared his playing to that of Paganini; and Schubert, a competent violinist and violist, set him considerable difficulties in the fantasy, matching them with equal demands on the pianist.

Although it plays continuously, the fantasy is in four distinct sections, more or less making up a slow–fast–slow–fast sequence. The entire piece is permeated by the spirit of Schubert's 1822 Rückert song "Sei mir gegrüsst" and the third section is a series of variations on its melody. The problem for the performers is to make some very tricky writing for both instruments sound perfectly controlled, while digging below the often-glittering surface to reveal the heart of the piece.

Not often can one say that the first recording of a work has left all subsequent ones puffing in its wake. Adolf Busch and Rudolf Serkin had almost a father-son relationship, although there were only twelve years between them, and by the time these sessions took place they were playing all their repertoire by heart. They specialized in the Schubert Fantasy and it was one of the earliest pieces they chose to record. Without the benefit of editing, they give an almost perfect interpretation of wonderful intimacy at the start, buoyant rhythm in the faster sections, and beautiful "singing" in the variations. **TP**

Franz Schubert
Fantasy in F minor for piano duet, D940 (1828)

Genre | Instrumental
Instrument | Piano
Performers | Murray Perahia, Radu Lupu
Year recorded | 1984
Label | Sony 93015

While Schubert's piano sonatas are now part of the core repertoire for the instrument, his piano duets are more uneven in inspiration. There are many dances and marches that seem to have been churned out on the conveyor belt of Schubert's innate compositional facility, aimed solely for the domestic amateur market, and many are far more fun to play than to listen to. But Schubert also composed some of the masterpieces of the duet repertoire, and top of the pile is the F minor Fantasy composed in his final year, 1828.

Like the "Wanderer" Fantasy of 1822, the F minor Fantasy telescopes four movements into a single thematically unified structure, if anything more tightly bonded than the earlier work. The haunting opening theme returns as a sort of structural signpost, and brings the work to a close in a wonderfully fulfilling manner. A majestic Largo follows the first movement without a break, leading to a sprightly scherzo and trio before the opening theme returns to signal the finale, where it undergoes rigorous fugal treatment. The work ends with one of Schubert's most daring harmonic sequences.

When Murray Perahia and Radu Lupu, two of the finest musicians of their generation, came together to record Schubert (a composer with whom both have a special affinity), the results were predictably and uniquely treasurable. There is no clash of egos, just great music-making. The poetic purity is deeply moving, and their sound is impeccably balanced and shaded. Their mutual understanding enables the most finely judged sense of timing, especially at points of transition and phrase endings. Duet-playing does not come better than this. **TLP**

> "... what a glorious treasure [pianists] can find in Schubert's compositions."
>
> Franz Liszt

Other Recommended Recordings

Sviatoslav Richter, Benjamin Britten
Decca 466 822-2
A brisk and vivid performance from the 1965 Aldeburgh Festival

Maria João Pires, Ricardo Castro
DG 477 523-3 (2 CDs)
A profoundly moving account, gorgeously recorded

Christoph Eschenbach, Justus Frantz
EMI 0946 3 65326 2 2 (2 CDs)
A delightful rendition that is full of drama and color

Franz Schubert
Symphony no. 9, "Great" (1828)

Genre | Orchestral
Conductor | Adrian Boult
Performers | BBC Symphony Orchestra
Year recorded | 1969
Label | BBC Legends BBCL 4072-2

With the "Unfinished" Symphony, Schubert had broken through barriers to a heightened sense of expression, but with his C major Symphony (nicknamed "Great" to distinguish it from his Symphony no. 6, also in C major), he produced a work of power and weight, with each movement being cast to a similar (large) dimension and with a rhythmic unity that propels the music to inexorable climaxes. The march-like slow movement (Andante con moto) contains some of the most wondrous and emotionally explosive music Schubert ever composed. The finale is a tour de force of sustained momentum. Written in the last few months of his life, it only came to light posthumously in 1839, when Schumann found the score among a pile of manuscripts. Even then it took years for its greatness to be accepted (early performers are said to have laughed at the relentless demands of the finale).

Adrian Boult was a champion of Schubert's "Great." He recorded it in the 1930s and again in 1972—the latter being particularly celebrated. A few years earlier, he led this deeply compelling performance at "the Proms" (The Sir Henry Wood Promenade Concerts, presented by the BBC). Boult's conducting has an unimpeachable sense of line and the music's buoyancy and undulation is given with a superb spontaneity. Caught on the wing in decent (stereo) broadcast sound, the BBC Symphony Orchestra fills the cavernous Royal Albert Hall admirably and the occasional infelicitous detail is nothing compared with Boult's incomparable sweep through Schubert's majestic work. The opening horn call, which quells the audience's rustle, suggests something magical is about to unfold. It does. **CA**

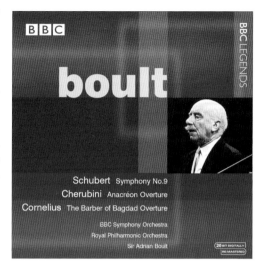

Schubert Symphony No.9
Cherubini Anacréon Overture
Cornelius The Barber of Bagdad Overture
BBC Symphony Orchestra
Royal Philharmonic Orchestra
Sir Adrian Boult

"It transports us into a world where we cannot recall ever having been before."

Robert Schumann

Other Recommended Recordings

Berlin Philharmonic Orchestra • Wilhelm Furtwängler
DG 447 439-2
Furtwängler digs deep into the music

Munich Philharmonic Orchestra • Sergiu Celibidache
EMI 7243 5 56527 2 0
Some will find Celibidache's conducting hopelessly plodding; others will appreciate his remarkable ear for color, sonic relationships and rapt expression

Bamberg Symphony Orchestra • Jonathan Nott
Tudor 7144
Flowing in conception, lithe and lucid in orchestral execution, Nott observes every repeat

Franz Schubert
String Quintet in C major
(1828)

Genre | Chamber
Performers | Hollywood Quartet,
Kurt Reher (cello)
Year recorded | 1951
Label | Testament SBT 1031

For many people, Schubert's String Quintet (two violins, viola, and two cellos) is a desert-island work. This is Schubert's last chamber music, composed in the year of his death, and it is easy, with hindsight, to read much into the music's machinations: easy to hear a life and death struggle being enacted in the first movement or to suggest that the intangible slow movement is Schubert's musical creation of a Utopia. Maybe, then, the finale, with its (Viennese) dance-like passages, harks back to happier times for the composer. Whatever lies behind the creation of the quintet, beyond its already considerable musical impulses—and different interpretations will create many suggestions as to extra-musical implications—it is an abundant and variegated work of fascinating possibilities.

Choosing the Hollywood Quartet and Kurt Reher's recording above the Amadeus Quartet's second recording with William Pleeth as the "extra" cellist is a difficult decision. Both groups are superb in this music and are distinguished foils for one another. While the Amadeus and Pleeth bring a naturalness and an identified approach to the Viennese elements of the music, the Hollywood and Reher (five musicians of diverse skills) have a little more gravitas. The group's honeyed tones and impeccable ensemble are other factors; above all, though, is the musicians' penetration into the music that never seems applied. This unsentimental approach, which nonetheless displays much feeling, strengthens the music immeasurably; and the sound (mono, of course) is full and immediate. **CA**

Franz Schubert
Schwanengesang
(1828)

Genre | Vocal
Performers | Dietrich Fischer-Dieskau
(baritone), Gerald Moore (piano)
Year recorded | 1972
Label | DG 463 503-2

The collective title of these swansongs was not Schubert's: his publisher assembled a group of the composer's last songs shortly after his death and, in a shrewd marketing move, created a cycle. Schubert may not have intended them to form a cycle at all. He set seven poems by Ludwig Rellstab and six by Heinrich Heine—plus one, the last song he wrote, by Johann Gabriel Seidl. The jury is out on the order in which the songs should be sung.

Each performance, though, is merely a variation on one of the most extraordinary spiritual and musical experiences in all Lieder. The settings of Rellstab move from the dark forebodings of lovers and warriors to the sun of spring and serenading, to ambivalent farewells. When it comes to the Heine group, Schubert stares into an abyss of darkness. We see, with him, the imagined picture of the beloved etched on a tear-drenched retina; the chill stillness of distant horizons and desolate seascapes; and finally the horrific encounter with a Doppelgänger.

These are songs that, in Dietrich Fischer-Dieskau's incomparable 1972 recording, reach the very heart of psychological and spiritual darkness. Fischer-Dieskau ends with that last, miraculous song that Schubert ever wrote, "Die Taubenpost"—the light wing-beat of a dove whose name is Longing—the perfect way to lift us out of an almost unbearable darkness, and the perfect word with which Schubert's soul should be assumed into the ether. No other performance in the catalogue has the same sustained intensity and searching insight. **HF**

Franz Schubert
Piano Sonata in C minor, D958 (1828)

Genre | Instrumental
Instrument | Piano
Performer | Radu Lupu
Year recorded | 1981
Label | Decca 417 785-2

In the summer of 1828 Schubert almost certainly suspected he did not have long left. His last six months were among the most productive of any major composer, both in quantity and quality. Among the most important works he wrote during this time were his last three piano sonatas, some of the most exalted in the instrument's literature.

The first of these sonatas, D958, is the most somber of the three, and also the most reminiscent of Beethoven. First there is the tonality, C minor—a Beethovenian key if ever there was one. Then there are similarities of certain melodic motifs—the opening, for example, recalls the latter's C minor Variations for piano—and the general mood of rhetorical heroism. But there is also a very personal kind of bleak nervousness, especially in the first movement and the third movement minuet. The finale is emotionally ambiguous: on the face of it a high-spirited tarantella, the music is laden with disturbing overtones.

The C minor is the least performed of Schubert's final three sonatas, but it has been well served on disc. Radu Lupu's great success comes in his acute and perceptive balance of Schubert's essential lyricism, his range of vocal color and nuance, with an undercurrent of darkness and despair. In Lupu's hands there is always more to the music than is immediately apparent on the surface. In the first movement he expertly controls Schubert's shifting moods while retaining a sense of structure, and in the finale he perfectly captures the essence of a manic dance spinning toward the abyss. **TLP**

Franz Schubert
Piano Sonata in A major, D959 (1828)

Genre | Instrumental
Instrument | Piano
Performer | Leif Ove Andsnes
Year recorded | 2001
Label | EMI 7243 5 57266 2 9

Schubert's A major Sonata was begun in the summer of 1828 and completed that September, just months before he died. Perhaps more than the other late sonatas, it captures the full range and scope of his artistry. As in the C minor Sonata, clear Beethovenian influences are evident, yet this work's drama, lyricism, poised reflection, and violent despair are juxtaposed with striking originality.

The first movement mixes trenchant thematic argument in the manner of Beethoven, with expansive lyrical sequences typical of Schubert, taking us through a series of haunting harmonic shifts. The finale has a clear Beethovenian model—the equivalent movement in the G major Piano Sonata, op. 31, no. 1. But most striking is the second movement, featuring extreme contrasts of meditative calm and forceful turbulence. Here Schubert produces something extraordinary: a moving other-worldly barcarolle is overrun by a manic eruption that deliberately shatters the music's coherence. Such despair is not what we expect of Schubert, yet in the final disintegration of his health it must be a true reflection of his state of mind.

The Norwegian pianist Leif Ove Andsnes has made a series of successful recordings coupling Schubert's piano sonatas with a selection of carefully chosen songs, sung by Ian Bostridge. Andsnes's performance of the A major Sonata is outstanding, and his clarity of tone, sensitive lyricism, and crisp articulation are a constant joy. In his hands the slow movement is achingly beautiful, and the frenzied outburst is especially shocking. **TLP**

Franz Schubert | Piano Sonata in B flat major, D960 (1828)

Genre | Instrumental
Instrument | Piano
Performer | Mitsuko Uchida
Year recorded | 1997
Label | Philips 456 572-2

For a long time Schubert's late piano sonatas were viewed with suspicion as being too long and introspective—especially the final Sonata in B flat major, D960. Now it is these very qualities—what Schumann called "heavenly length," and the delicate balance of emotional tension and sublime poetic contemplation—that make these pieces among the most revered of Schubert's piano works, indeed of all Romantic piano music.

The B flat Sonata is the most un-Beethovenian of the three. It recalls the expansive lyricism of the G major Sonata, D894, but transports it to a sublime level of contemplative ecstasy. The first movement (which with the exposition repeat lasts more than twenty minutes) has a deep solemnity, unfolding for the most part pianissimo, with points of climax that are short-lived. The slow movement is one of Schubert's miracles of intense expressive stillness, in the mould of the Adagio from the String Quintet of the same year. The third movement is a mercurial scherzo, forming a delightful interlude before the finale, with its Hungarian-tinged dance-tune that reveals—not for the first time in Schubert—a poignant emotional ambiguity. This was the last piece of instrumental music he composed.

Of the many fine recordings of this great sonata, Mitsuko Uchida's is special for its immaculate pianistic finish and its concentrated absorption. She certainly takes her time. But such is the intensity and deep poetry of her playing that the music never grinds to a halt. Uchida makes Schubert's long arching phrases more malleable than most pianists, yet in the slow movement especially she grips your attention and holds it tight for ten spellbinding minutes. This is profound music-making, and an overwhelming experience. **TLP**

"It sometimes seems to me as if I did not belong to this world at all."

Franz Schubert

Other Recommended Recordings

Wilhelm Kempff
DG 463 766-2 (7 CDs)
The zenith of Kempff's achievement in Schubert; here the master provides a deeply moving interpretation of this powerful work

Stephen Kovacevich
EMI 7243 62818 2 0
Kovacevich's powerful account has an unusually dramatic undercurrent of foreboding

Radu Lupu
Decca 440 295-2
Eloquent mastery from Lupu

Frédéric Chopin | Nocturnes (*c.*1829–47)

Genre | Instrumental
Instrument | Piano
Performer | Maria João Pires
Year recorded | 1996
Label | DG 447 092-2 (2 CDs)

Adopting a form first established by the Irish composer John Field, Frédéric Chopin composed nocturnes throughout much of his working life, hence the wide spread of opus numbers. Appropriately, given that the genre had also attained popularity as a vocal form, he often talked of the way that the pianist should "sing with the fingers," something that the outstanding Portuguese pianist Maria João Pires does marvelously well on this complete recording. She has always done things entirely her own way. She treats the music with great freedom, desynchronizing her hands to make poetic points, but never to the extent of self-indulgence, and the withdrawn quality she finds in these pieces is entrancingly realized, her tone sometimes withdrawn almost to the point of inaudibility.

Each switch of key seems to bring with it a miraculous change of color or hue. Pires is unafraid to linger to make a point but nothing is ever overstated and the resulting performances seem entirely unfettered by barlines, op. 9, no. 1 being just one outstanding example. In those nocturnes with dramatic shifts of mood—op. 15, nos. 1 and 2, or op. 62, no. 2—the contrast is dramatic but never sounds forced or self-conscious.

The overriding sensation is one of eavesdropping on a great pianist improvising for her own amusement rather than for her audience, and the effects are quite magical as you luxuriate in the warmth of sound and the apparent spontaneity of the music-making. Whether in the filigree tracery of op. 32, no. 2, the perfectly poised ending of op. 9, no. 2, or the dramatic recitative that breaks in during op. 32, no. 1, Pires draws you into a world where it is all too tempting to linger. **HS**

> "*One can never play Chopin beautifully enough. Realistic treatment . . . shatters his aerial architecture.*"

James Huneker, critic and Chopin authority

Other Recommended Recordings

Claudio Arrau
Philips 416 440-2 (2 CDs)
Deeply involving performances, complemented by Arrau's characteristic burnished tone

Arthur Rubinstein
RCA 09026 63026 2 (2 CDs)
Classic recordings that have deservedly entered the pantheon of great Chopin interpretations

Earl Wild
Ivory IC 70701 (2 CDs)
Earl Wild's unique pianism remains undimmed despite his advanced age when he made these recordings

Frédéric Chopin
Piano Concertos
(1829, 1830)

Genre | Concerto
Performers | Murray Perahia, Israel Philharmonic Orchestra
Conductor | Zubin Mehta
Year recorded | 1989
Label | Sony SMK 87323

The numbering of Chopin's two piano concertos is misleading, the "First" Concerto in E minor in fact being written the year after the "Second," F minor work, though it was the first to be published. Both these concertos were for a long time maligned for what were seen as overly piano-heavy textures, with the orchestra relegated to a backing role, the corps de ballet providing a decorative backdrop for the brilliant pirouetting of the soloist. However, that is to place them out of historical context. They come from a time when the soloist was the hero of the hour, and the more outlandishly virtuoso, the better. Chopin took a somewhat flawed model and elevated it to an altogether new level. True, these are not works where orchestral players get much opportunity to shine, but melodies flow from his pen with a seemingly unstoppable fecundity. They are works that demand a pianist who is unafraid of the limelight, yet does not overlook the opportunities to duet with orchestral players. Beauty of sound is a prerequisite, as is an agile virtuosity. The slow movements find Chopin at his most generously rhapsodic, the pianist diving off on sublime flights of fantasy while the orchestra offer a glowing curtain of sound.

Pianist Murray Perahia is the most persuasive of advocates, delighting in Chopin's invention: the third movement of no. 2 has a youthful ebullience; after all, Chopin was in his teens when he composed these pieces. And Zubin Mehta understands exactly what is needed—this is luxury casting, and the results are irresistible. **HS**

Frédéric Chopin
Waltzes
(1829–47)

Genre | Instrumental
Instrument | Piano
Performer | Arthur Rubinstein
Years recorded | 1960s
Label | RCA 82876 59422 2

As with so many other miniature forms, Chopin took the waltz and whirled it into a genre of startling variety and endless mastery. His works in the form certainly could not be danced to, with their copious rubato and musical complexity. Indeed, you might imagine that they are not the kind of pieces to be listened to in succession—too much three-in-a-bar, with the first beat emphasized, and a generally similar sentiment. That might well be the case in many lesser composers, but Chopin's waltzes are an exception to the rule. The variety to be found in them is startling, be it the open-hearted delight and almost militaristic precision of the aptly named *Grande valse brillante*, op. 18, the whimsicality of op. 34, no. 1, or the dancing lightness of op. 42. Any pianist approaching these pieces has to be alive to all these manifestations.

There is, consistently, a wonderful clarity to Arthur Rubinstein's playing, each waltz emerging as a perfectly chiselled masterpiece, and it is as if his right hand leads an entirely independent life from his left, though his rubato never feels over-applied. The tender sadness of the graceful op. 34, no. 2 is beautifully captured, while in the slower section of op. 64, no. 2 Rubinstein finds a yearning quality that is very moving. And he can dazzle like no other, in such whirling miniatures as op. 34, no. 3 or op. 70, no. 1. In fact, there is so much to enjoy in Rubinstein's performances that it is hard not to listen to them one after the other. Like the finest selection of chocolates, each seems more delectable than the last. **HS**

Felix Mendelssohn
String Quartets
nos. 1 & 2 (1829, 1827)

Genre | Chamber
Performers | Pacifica Quartet: Brandon Vamos,
Masumi Per Rostad, Simin Ganatra, Sibbi Bernhardsson
Year recorded | 2004
Label | Cedille CDR 90000 082 (3 CDs)

Mendelssohn's string quartets are perhaps the most underrated part of the composer's extensive output. Too often overshadowed among his chamber works by the ever-popular octet and the élan-filled piano trios, the seven quartets nevertheless have a great deal to offer and, in their entirety, form a fascinating journey through the emotional progress of their creator's too-short life.

The chronology of Mendelssohn's quartets has presented problems from the start—they were not written in the order in which they were published. Nos. 1 and 2 are, for our purposes, opp. 12 and 13, but there is an earlier work still, the posthumously published E flat major Quartet that the young composer wrote in 1823. The A minor Quartet, op. 13, officially no. 2, was composed in 1827 and the E flat major one, called no. 1, two years later in 1829.

In these expressive, fiery works, Mendelssohn makes his musical transition from gifted boy to man of many talents. Although the quartets' musical language is quintessentially Mendelssohnian, with all his habitual delicacy, extrovert passion, and intricacy of texture, Beethoven's presence is never far away, making itself felt in, to name just a few examples, the A minor Quartet's slow introduction, and in the use of "cyclic" (recurring) themes.

The Pacifica Quartet, a busy multi-national group from the United States, has made one of the finest recordings available of these beautiful quartets, within its complete set. Vivid and fresh, technically faultless, full of spirit and soul, it is irresistible playing. **JD**

Gioachino Rossini
Guillaume Tell
(1829)

Genre | Opera
Conductor/Performers | Lamberto Gardelli; Montserrat
Caballé, Nicolai Gedda, Mady Mesplé, Gabriel Bacquier
Year recorded | 1972
Label | EMI 0777 7 69951 2 0 (4 CDs)

Guillaume Tell (William Tell) was Rossini's last opera and, for many, his masterpiece. Its monumental scale reflected the composer's desire to furnish his new home city of Paris with a wholly French opera: visual spectacle, large-scale choruses and ensembles, ballets, passionate recitatives, and a grandly declamatory overall style are all here in abundance. Part of the fascination of Guillaume Tell lies in Rossini's creation of an opera that merges French style with his own trademark Italian compositional techniques.

Schiller's original story of medieval Switzerland's struggle for freedom from Austrian domination certainly provided Rossini with an epic historical canvas on which to hang the drama of William Tell's struggle against governor Gesler, and the vacillating Arnold's inconvenient love for Gesler's Habsburg sister, Princess Mathilde. The opera's nationalist elements suited the mood of the time in France, and also in Italy, where the Italian version has done more to retain the opera's rather tenuous hold on the repertoire.

French and Italian recorded versions of the opera make an excellent case for Tell—but French is preferred for authenticity. In 1972 EMI assembled a cast that established this as a vintage period of operatic recording. Gabriel Bacquier's Gallic gruffness reveals the uncompromising fighter in Tell; Montserrat Caballé brings intensity to the coloratura in the role of Mathilde; Nicolai Gedda adds his customary virile yet sensitive tone to the part of Arnold. Lamberto Gardelli's fine conducting makes this an exciting and wholly satisfying set. **GK**

Hector Berlioz | Symphonie fantastique (1830)

Genre | Orchestral
Conductor | Charles Münch
Performers | Boston Symphony Orchestra
Year recorded | 1954
Label | RCA 82876 67899 2

Not only did Hector Berlioz's *Symphonie fantastique* mark the definitive arrival of a new force in French music, but it effectively proved that, just three years after the death of Beethoven, a new, so-called Romantic era in music was on the move. If that sums up the idea of the tortured creator pouring all his emotions into his art then that is the case here: Berlioz even subtitled his Symphony "Episode in the Life of an Artist," and it is nothing short of a musical portrait of a man under the spell of the ideal woman. In his case this was the Shakespearean actress Harriet Smithson, a star of the Parisian stage in the late 1820s, whom he eventually married. His wooing included writing this symphony, which traces his pursuit as an opium-fueled flight of imagination: he dreams he kills his beloved, is guillotined for the murder, and sees her among a witches' sabbath sent to torment him.

Berlioz later revised his program to suggest the whole five-movement work was illustrative of an opium dream: "Rêveries—Passions," which introduces a musical *idée fixe* that follows the protagonist through the symphony; "Un bal," a sumptuous waltz; "Scène aux champs," an expansive pastoral evocation; "Marche aux supplice," where the hero meets his "end"; and "Songe d'une nuit de Sabbat," where Berlioz's orchestral mastery comes into its own, from tolling bells to demonic, screaming woodwind, and which provides one of the most exciting symphonic conclusions in all music.

Charles Münch's recording dates from the early days of stereo, but still sounds thrilling more than half a century later. Münch himself finds all the fire and fantasy in Berlioz's creation and his flexibility reminds us what a tremendous Berlioz conductor he was. **MR**

> ## "A young musician of morbid sensibility and fiery imagination poisons himself in a fit of amorous despair."

Berlioz's description of his original conception

Other Recommended Recordings

**London Classical Players
Roger Norrington
Virgin 0946 3 63286 2 1**
Fascinating rethinking on period instruments

**London Symphony Orchestra • Colin Davis
LSO Live LSO 0007**
The last of Davis's four recordings is not short of excitement

**ORTF Symphony Orchestra • Jean Martinon
EMI 7243 5 85124 2 (2 CDs)**
Coupled with Berlioz's peculiar sequel: Lélio,
ou Le retour à la vie

French conductor Charles Münch, an inspired conductor of Berlioz ➤

Gaetano Donizetti
Anna Bolena
(1830)

Genre | Opera
Conductor/Performers | Gianandrea
Gavazzeni; Maria Callas, Gianni Raimondi
Year recorded | 1957
Label | EMI 7243 5 66471 2 1 (2 CDs)

Anna Bolena made Donizetti's reputation north of the Alps in Paris and London. And it was this first of his three slices of Tudor history rewritten as opera that earned him his spurs at La Scala. For the first time the composer had a libretto worthy of his gifts, written by that prolific master Felice Romani; a drama of a wronged woman that seems to have moved Donizetti deeply and to have concentrated his mind musically as never before.

Anna's larghetto "Al dolce guidami" as she waits in the tower for her executioner is suffused with genuine feeling rather than Romantic sentiment, and the plaintive cor anglais accompaniment is masterly. Romani's libretto, based upon a pair of previous plays, provided Donizetti with new opportunities for exploring the psychology of his characters: Jane Seymour filled with remorse for her adultery with Henry, and the hapless Percy in love with Anna but determined to preserve her honor.

But the opera is Anna's and no singer has made the role more her own than Maria Callas. It was she who brought the work back into currency at La Scala in the 1950s and this radio broadcast of the work—a cut version but with a fine cast including the redoubtable Giulietta Simionato as Jane—finds Callas at her best. Her Anna is by turns tender, resigned, and a tigress. Listen to the venom with which she invests the line "Anna! ai giudici" when Enrico announces that she must defend her honor in court; or her singing of the final cabaletta "Coppia iniqua," in which coloratura runs and trills convey an anguish sliding into madness. **CC**

Felix Mendelssohn
The Hebrides, "Fingal's Cave" (1830)

Genre | Orchestral
Conductor | Claudio Abbado
Performers | London Symphony Orchestra
Year recorded | 1985
Label | DG 423 104-2

Mendelssohn's overture *The Hebrides* is, with good reason, one of his best-known works. It was among a number of pieces conceived during the composer's four-year travels through Europe; his trip to Scotland was particularly fruitful, also leading him to write his "Scottish" Symphony.

Inspired by the young composer's visit in 1829 to the mysterious grotto, Fingal's Cave, *The Hebrides* is as physically descriptive as music can be. There is no story, only atmosphere. Mendelssohn sketched out the first twenty-one measures almost at once and completed the overture the following year. It is not an overture to anything, but one of the first in a new generation of programmatic pieces suitable for starting a concert.

The first theme finds Mendelssohn evoking the swell and rock of the boat, while the second can be heard as a portrait of the open sea, clear air, and distant undulating hills. There is mystery, echoing horn calls, and moments of high drama—a delicious panoply in tune with the Romantic idealisation of Scotland. Mendelssohn's friend, the poet Carl Klingemann, who travelled with the composer, wrote: "A greener roar of waves surely never rushed into a stranger cavern—its many pillars made it look like the inside of an immense organ."

As the overture is a perennial favorite in concert programs, there is a huge list of recordings. The London Symphony Orchestra under Claudio Abbado gives a solid, satisfying account, capturing much of the sweep, grandeur and storms at sea that Mendelssohn expresses. **JD**

Frédéric Chopin
Études
(1830–37)

Genre | Instrumental
Instrument | Piano
Performer | Juána Zayas
Year recorded | 1982
Label | Music & Arts CD-891

With these groundbreaking works, published in two volumes of twelve each as op. 10 and op. 25, Chopin took the *étude*—or study—out of the practice room and onto the concert stage. He was by no means alone in writing highly demanding studies, but what elevated his above all others (at least until Liszt) was the way he combined technical challenges with musical ones, creating works as satisfying to listen to as they are to play. A pianist cannot approach them as they would, say, those by Czerny, Moscheles or Johann Cramer—each demands attention to every phrase repetition, every nuance, if these works are to dazzle and delight as they should.

Cuban-born Juána Zayas is a pianist *au fait* with every element of these complex pieces, and she shows a deep and apparently instinctive understanding in her interpretations. Whether it is in the effortless chromatic scales of op. 10, no. 2, the febrile nerviness of op. 25, no. 6 or the elegant voicings of op. 10, no. 7, in which she draws out a strong melodic line where many others simply bombard the listener with notes, she seems at one with these pieces. Technically, she is rock-solid, too, completely unfazed by such pianistic challenges as the dazzling op. 25, no. 8, the explosion of sound in op. 25, no. 11, or the tumult of op. 10, no. 12. And the more introverted pieces, such as op. 10, nos. 3 and 6, have a captivating narrative quality. Over the years, several of these *études* have acquired nicknames, but in these readings additional descriptions are superfluous: in her hands the music says it all. **HS**

Vincenzo Bellini
La sonnambula
(1831)

Genre | Opera
Conductor/Performers | Leonard Bernstein; Maria Callas, Cesare Valletti
Year recorded | 1955
Label | EMI 7243 5 67906 2 9 (2 CDs)

La sonnambula (*The Sleepwalker*) is a pastoral idyll set in a world untouched by the radical politics that would absorb the next generation of opera composers—a long Romantic breath before the clamor of the nineteenth century arrived on stage. Rodolfo, lord of the manor, sets his villagers at ease when an innocent Amina is accused of betraying her fiancé Elvino. It was just a case of sleepwalking. How ironic then that Bellini had originally intended to adapt Victor Hugo's deeply political play *Hernani*, only to be defeated by the Italian censors.

In the event, he and Felice Romani created a masterpiece, with Bellini clothing Romani's poetry in simple sweet-toned music that is always at the service of the text and the drama. Amina's opening aria is never the usual prima donna's vocal calling card, but a carefully worked portrait of a young heroine who is thoughtful about the future and excited by love. And the long-limbed melody that Bellini provides when his heroine is convinced that she has lost Elvino to her rival Lisa is one of the most affecting things he ever wrote.

Maria Callas was a supreme Amina and in this live recording she finds innocence, girlish delight, pathos, and a kind of resignation in the character. Listening to her interpretation you marvel at the technique, the accuracy of her coloratura, her nimbleness and the almost perfect legato. Never mind that, despite remastering, this is less than technically perfect: Callas is perfect, while a young Leonard Bernstein in the pit is on his best behavior. **CC**

Felix Mendelssohn | Piano Concerto no. 1 (1831)

Genre | Concerto
Performers/Conductor | Stephen Hough, City of
Birmingham Symphony Orchestra; Lawrence Foster
Year recorded | 1997
Label | Hyperion CDA 66969

By the tender age of twenty-two, Mendelssohn was already established as one of the greatest talents of his generation. He was spurred into writing his First Piano Concerto by that timeless inspiration, puppy-love. Delphine von Schauroth was a Munich aristocrat who could, by Mendelssohn's own admission, wrap the whole establishment around her little finger. Although she was a gifted musician and the concerto is dedicated to her, Mendelssohn had more pragmatic aims: he gave the work's first performance himself, during a tour in which he featured as composer, pianist, and conductor.

The concerto's three movements are performed without a break. The work displays Mendelssohn's ability to create music that is fresh, brilliant, and inspired while also allowing his soloist maximum opportunity to show off: the piano writing is often light and filigree and dashes forward at exuberant speed. But this is no empty virtuosity, something Mendelssohn detested: it is full of melodic wonders and unexpected little twists. The opening movement fizzes with drama, the slow movement is one of the composer's most lyrical, and the G major finale rounds matters off with exhilarating energy.

The British pianist Stephen Hough offers a particularly special account. He has a tremendous empathy for the fantasy, tenderness, and delicacy of Mendelssohn's world and plenty of imagination of his own to go with it; and there is well-balanced accompaniment from the CBSO under Lawrence Foster. The disc brings together for the first time all Mendelssohn's published works for piano and orchestra, including not only both of his piano concertos (if you like no. 1, you will love no. 2) but also three lesser-known works that are a joy to discover. **JD**

> ## *"[Mendelssohn is] the dearest pianist of all."*
>
> Clara Schumann

Other Recommended Recordings

András Schiff, Bavarian Radio Symphony Orchestra
Charles Dutoit
Decca 466 425-2
Schiff's clarity and feather-light touch is ideal

Lang Lang, Chicago Symphony Orchestra
Daniel Barenboim
DG 474 291-2
The Chinese virtuoso is a warmly Romantic advocate

Moura Lympany, Royal Philharmonic Orchestra
Malcolm Sargent
Ivory 70906
Recorded in the 1960s, with irrepressible wit and vigor

Stephen Hough has won seven Gramophone Awards to date. ➔

Vincenzo Bellini
Norma
(1831)

Genre | Opera
Conductor/Performers | Richard Bonynge; Joan Sutherland, Marilyn Horne
Year recorded | 1964
Label | Decca 470 413-2 (3 CDs)

Norma is the greatest of all bel canto operas, a near perfect fusion of words and music. And the character of the druid priestess Norma, torn between her duty to the Gauls and her love for the Roman proconsul Pollione, offers a coloratura soprano one of the greatest dramatic roles in the repertoire. Small wonder that this opera has rarely been off the stage despite its disastrous premiere at La Scala, where an anti-Bellini claque led the barracking.

But when Guiditta Pasta, the very first Norma, was presented with the score of "Casta diva," the priestess's supreme opening aria, she thought it ill-suited to her vocal gifts. Bellini had to promise to rewrite it if Pasta was still unhappy after a week of practicing. Like the generations who have followed, Pasta was won over. Perhaps because she came to understand that *Norma* is quintessentially a singer's opera; a work in which Bellini's simple lyrical music supports the voices, molding itself about their characterization and never the other way round.

Joan Sutherland recorded *Norma* twice, but it is in her first that the voice is at its most beautiful. There is a rapt intensity at the beginning of "Casta diva," and the cabaletta to the aria is never just an opportunity for vocal fireworks but all of a piece dramatically. In Marilyn Horne, Sutherland has the finest Adalgisa on disc and in their duet "Mira, o Norma," in which the younger priestess who also loves Pollione vows to give him up, the two voices blend like caramel and cream. John Alexander is a sturdy Pollione and Richard Bonynge the most considerate of conductors. **CC**

Gaetano Donizetti
L'elisir d'amore
(1832)

Genre | Opera
Conductor/Performers | Richard Bonynge; Joan Sutherland, Luciano Pavarotti
Year recorded | 1970
Label | Decca 414 461-2

Written in just six weeks, *L'elisir d'amore* (*The Elixir of Love*) is as perfect a comedy as any Donizetti composed before his last masterpiece *Don Pasquale*. And in one respect this earlier opera is perhaps superior, for beneath the giddy nonsense is a plot that beats with a moral muscle. When the curtain rises, well-heeled landowner Adina is a shrew in waiting; Nemorino, the country boy who loves her, a wimp; Sergeant Belcore a womanizing opportunist hoping to marry Adina's fortune; and Dulcamara—who sells Nemorino his elixir of love—a cynical exploiter of innocence. The older men will get their comeuppance while the lovers visibly mature. Love is indeed the potion that helps us find our better selves.

Donizetti interleaves a sequence of foot-tapping tunes with melodies that stop your heart. Dulcamara's patter song as he peddles his elixir is a torrent of words about nothing—pomposity skewered musically. The Act 1 duet for Adina and Nemorino positively aches with lost opportunities and "Una furtiva lagrima" is one of the tenderest arias the composer ever wrote. By now Donizetti was a master at psychologically plotting his characters.

To the eye, Joan Sutherland and Luciano Pavarotti were never the ideal Adina and Nemorino, but on disc they scarcely put a foot wrong. Pavarotti, in particular, was very much a genuine lyric tenor in 1970, and Sutherland displays real comic talent. Spiro Malas finds more in Dulcamara than usually meets the ear and Richard Bonynge presides with just the right blend of fizz and feeling. **CC**

Gioachino Rossini
Stabat mater
(1832, rev. 1841)

Genre | Choral
Conductor/Performers | Myung-Whun Chung; Luba Orgonasova, Cecilia Bartoli
Year recorded | 1995
Label | DG 449 178-2

When, in 1831, Rossini was invited by a wealthy patron to compose a *Stabat mater*, he was reluctant. Wary of producing a rival to the hugely popular setting by Pergolesi, he acquiesced on the understanding that the work would be for private use only. After setting the juiciest parts of the text, a thirteenth-century poem on the Virgin Mary's grief-stricken vigil at her son's cross, Rossini suffered an attack of lumbago. The remaining parts (nos. 2–4) were delegated to fellow Italian Giovanni Tadolini, and the completed score passed off as Rossini's. Years later, however, Rossini was appalled to discover that the manuscript had been sold to a publisher, potentially tarnishing his reputation. He was quick to retrieve the score and, removing Tadolini's contributions, set about finishing the piece. The final, all-Rossini, *Stabat mater* was first performed in Paris in January 1842, and triumphantly conducted in Bologna by Donizetti two months later.

Myung-Whun Chung's serenely beautiful recording with the glorious Vienna Philharmonic fully serves the solemnity and innate theatricality of Rossini's score but also conveys a special, inward-looking radiance. The team of operatic soloists is first-rate: strong, characterful voices that respond well to Chung's intimate vision. Cecilia Bartoli's heartfelt rendition of the cavatina "Fac, ut portem" is especially moving and the large-scale chorus sings with great intensity. From the darkly dramatic opening, through to the rousing "Amen" double fugue, this is a sensitive, dignified and powerful performance of great beauty. **GR**

Felix Mendelssohn
Symphony no. 4, "Italian" *(1833)*

Genre | Orchestral
Conductor | Guido Cantelli
Performers | Philharmonia Orchestra
Year recorded | 1951
Label | Testament SBT 1173

The young Felix Mendelssohn, undertaking culturally enriching European travels, spent a year in Italy beginning in 1830. The German-born former child prodigy was only twenty-four when he embarked on what would eventually be numbered as his Fourth Symphony. Like his Symphony no. 3, the "Scottish," it was directly inspired by his impressions of the country he was exploring. He declared that the "Italian" Symphony sprang from every aspect of Italy: its landscape, people, and culture.

The music is irresistibly exuberant, its opening and closing movements taking their rhythms from traditional Italian dances. Its slow movement is said to resemble a pilgrims' song and the minuet overflows with a generous warmth. Nevertheless, Mendelssohn was dissatisfied with the symphony and intended to redraft the finale, something he never got around to. This explains why it was not published until after his death, although it was premiered in Britain in 1833, by the London Philharmonic Society.

Unsurprisingly, the "Italian" Symphony has been recorded countless times. One of the most rewarding accounts is by the Italian conductor Guido Cantelli with the Philharmonia Orchestra. Cantelli died tragically in a plane crash in France five years later, at the age of just thirty-six. His joie de vivre here is second to none and it is easy to see why his career was championed by his fellow countryman, the conductor Arturo Toscanini. Cantelli's orchestra is polished to a gleam, but best of all is that the excitement and enthusiasm never fail from start to finish. **JD**

Hector Berlioz | Harold in Italy (1834)

Genre | Concerto
Performers/Conductor | Tabea Zimmermann (viola), London Symphony Orchestra; Colin Davis
Year recorded | 2003
Label | LSO Live LSO 0040

LSO Live

Berlioz
Harold en Italie
SIR COLIN DAVIS
Tabea Zimmermann
London Symphony Orchestra

After conducting a concert of his own music in April 1833, Berlioz was approached by an admiring Nicolò Paganini. The celebrated virtuoso asked him to write a piece to show off a Stradivari viola that he had recently purchased. Berlioz started working but, true to form, gave the orchestra a protagonist role. When Paganini saw the score of the first movement, he lost interest in the piece: "There are too many rests in here," he complained; "I must play all the time." Berlioz then wrote the rest of the composition according to his own taste, reducing the viola's role to that of a *primus inter pares* within the orchestra.

Harold in Italy was inspired by Lord Byron's *Childe Harold's Pilgrimage*, but, rather than illustrating particular passages from the poem, it adopts its notion of a traveler who observes life from the outside, commenting but not taking part in it. Thus, the viola plays various versions of its own theme during the four movements ("Harold in the Mountains," "Pilgrims' March," "Serenade," and "Orgy of the Brigands"). The finale, taking a leaf from Beethoven's Ninth, reviews the themes from previous movements, before the viola is swallowed up in an orchestral maelstrom.

Paganini, after eventually hearing a performance, was gallant enough to admit his mistake and presented the composer with a check for more than 20,000 francs (at the time more than twice a reasonable annual salary). *Harold* was further helped on its way by the piano transcription made in 1836 by Franz Liszt.

The great Berliozian, Colin Davis, has recorded *Harold* three times. He set down his last thoughts on the piece live in concert with the LSO, with Tabea Zimmermann an infinitely subtle soloist. **CMS**

> ## "[The performer must] stand looking urbane ... without distracting attention from events in the orchestra."
>
> William Primrose in *Walk on the North Side*

Other Recommended Recordings

William Primrose, Boston Symphony Orchestra
Serge Koussevitzky
Doremi DHR 7708
The premiere studio recording (1944), in gorgeous sound, with a star soloist

William Primrose, Royal Philharmonic Orchestra
Thomas Beecham
Sony SMK 91167
Primrose's remake, conducted by a master Berliozian

William Primrose, NBC Orchestra • Arturo Toscanini
Music and Arts CD 4614
A younger Primrose holds his own in front of Toscanini

Tabea Zimmermann, who plays new music in addition to Berlioz. ➔

Gaetano Donizetti | Lucia di Lammermoor (1835)

Genre | Opera
Conductor/Performers | Richard Bonynge;
Joan Sutherland, Luciano Pavarotti, Sherill Milnes
Year recorded | 1971
Label | Decca 410 193-2

Gustave Flaubert well understood how a whole generation was in thrall to Donizetti's "Scottish" opera. So when Emma Bovary meets Léon—the man who undoes her—at the theater in Rouen it is *Lucia di Lammermoor* that is playing there. A nineteenth-century sister or a daughter who disobeys her family and is driven mad after murdering her lover was both a warning to any woman tempted to rattle the chains of social convention and a thrilling example of Romantic disobedience.

Long after the high noon of European Romanticism had subsided in twentieth-century angst, *Lucia* maintained its place in the public's affections because it was such a good sing. Not just the celebrated sextet and the heroine's mad scene—with that haunting solo flute—that offered unparalleled opportunities for dizzying vocal exhibitionism, but arias such as Lucia's "Regnava nel silenzio" and Edgardo's last earthly words before he stabs himself, "Tu che a Dio spiegasti l'ali." It was Maria Callas who rescued the opera in the 1950s, finding a flesh-and-blood woman where once there had only been a canary, and then Joan Sutherland who found tragedy in the heart of a melodrama.

Sutherland's 1961 recording is closest in time and style to her celebrated debut in the role at Covent Garden in 1957, but ten years on in this later recording her diction has rediscovered its consonants and she finds new depths in the character. From the beginning this is a Lucia with a fragile grip on sanity. If Pavarotti is a rather wooden Edgardo, Sherill Milnes is a properly evil Enrico, obsessive from his opening scene. Richard Bonynge conducts the Royal Opera House forces in a magnificent piece of music theater, with respect but never reverence. **CC**

> "How can I say which opera is my favorite? A father has a preference for his crippled child, and I have so many."

Gaetano Donizetti

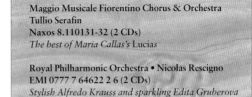

Other Recommended Recordings

Maggio Musicale Fiorentino Chorus & Orchestra
Tullio Serafin
Naxos 8.110131-32 (2 CDs)
The best of Maria Callas's Lucias

Royal Philharmonic Orchestra • Nicolas Rescigno
EMI 0777 7 64622 2 6 (2 CDs)
Stylish Alfredo Krauss and sparkling Edita Gruberova

Lyon National Opera Chorus & Orchestra
Evelino Pido
Virgin 7243 5 45528 2 3 (2 CDs)
Natalie Dessay is superb in Donizetti's darker French version, Lucie *not* Lucia

Lucia was Joan Sutherland's signature role, pictured here in 1966. ❯

Vincenzo Bellini | I puritani (1835)

Genre | Opera
Conductor/Performers | Richard Bonynge;
Joan Sutherland, Luciano Pavarotti, Nicolai Ghiaurov
Year recorded | 1973
Label | Decca 417 588-2 (3 CDs)

Like any Italian musician who looked to his laurels, Vincenzo Bellini crossed the Alps in search of success in the only city that mattered for an opera composer. And there in Paris he wrote *I puritani* (*The Puritans*), his last masterpiece before dying at the young age of thirty-three.

His contemporaries were hoping for another *Norma*, but Bellini surprised them with a work suffused with the sweet melancholy that had marked his earlier operas. Nevertheless, egged on by French tastes he continued to extend the format of the "numbers" opera, with separate arias and ensembles carefully separated by sung recitative. The beauty of *I puritani* is that one shades effortlessly and melodiously into another in this English Civil War story with its Roundhead heroine, Elvira, who loves a Royalist Arturo and goes mad when she misunderstands his relationship to Queen Henrietta Maria.

This is pre-eminently a singer's opera for an audience who, said the composer, had "little understanding of what real song was." And it was written for a quartet of the greatest singers of the age: Giulia Grisi, Giovanni Battista Rubini, Antonio Tamburini, and Luigi Lablache. There are rousing choruses; coloratura showstoppers such as Elvira's "Son vergin vezzosa"; perhaps the most beautiful cantabile that Bellini ever wrote, Arturo's "A te, o cara" when he comes to woo Elvira; and an exquisite mad scene.

Joan Sutherland, Luciano Pavarotti, Piero Cappuccilli, and Nicolai Ghiaurov make a formidable quartet, with Pavarotti revealing himself as a Bellini stylist in a role that makes enormous demands on the tenor, including a top C when he first appears and a top F in his finale. Sutherland is meltingly beautiful in the mad scene, and her coloratura sends shivers up and down your spine. **CC**

"The music drama must draw tears, inspire terror, make people die, through singing."

Vincenzo Bellini

Other Recommended Recordings

La Scala Chorus & Orchestra
Tullio Serafin
EMI 7243 5 56275 2 0 (2 CDs)
*A gripping Elvira from Maria Callas,
even if her voice is not in the best shape*

Palermo Teatro Massimo Chorus & Orchestra
Tullio Serafin
Bella Voce 7227
Sutherland in youthful voice in an early live recording

Philharmonia Orchestra • Riccardo Muti
EMI 0777 7 69663 2 8 (3 CDs)
Strictly for hard-line Montserrat Caballé fans

Robert Schumann | Études symphoniques (1835, *rev.* 1852)

Genre | Instrumental
Instrument | Piano
Performer | Murray Perahia
Year recorded | 1976
Label | Sony SMK 89716

The relatively prosaic title *Études symphoniques* gives a strong indication that Schumann had in mind something very different from his character-piece sequences such as *Papillons*, *Carnaval*, and *Davidsbündlertänze*. Each of these *études*, or studies, is designed to present a specific pianistic challenge, whether it is the fast staccato right-hand playing of no. 3, the march-like full-chordal writing of no. 4, or the thumb-only melody with interweaving accompaniment in no. 6. Yet, as with Chopin's Études, each becomes an accomplished musical work in its own right. This was the more public face of Schumann, at a rare moment without a story to tell or a secret to share.

The theme had been sent to Schumann in 1834 by Baron von Fricken, to whose daughter, Ernestine, he was still engaged at the time. He eventually used it as the basis of twelve *études*—variations, but not variations of the drawing-room confection type: these are boldly expressive, eschewing empty virtuosity. Unusually, Schumann discarded the theme for the rousing final *étude*, instead quoting the music of "Du stolzes England, freue dich" ("Proud England, rejoice!") from Heinrich Marshner's opera *Der Templer und die Jüdin* (*The Templar and the Jewess*), in a move designed to honor his British composer-friend William Sterndale Bennett, to whom the *Études* were dedicated.

Murray Perahia's recording shows his mastery of the technical challenges—the turbulent repeated inner chords of no. 2, the pin-sharp right-hand staccato of no. 3—but also a stylistic sensitivity, as in the French overture of no. 8 and the dreamily chromatic no. 9. He makes the widest possible contrast between the melancholic theme and the triumphal high spirits of the final variation. **EB**

> *"The subject ought always to be kept in view, but it ought to be shown through different colored glasses."*
>
> Robert Schumann, writing to Baron von Fricken

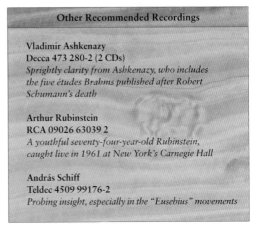

Other Recommended Recordings

Vladimir Ashkenazy
Decca 473 280-2 (2 CDs)
Sprightly clarity from Ashkenazy, who includes the five études Brahms published after Robert Schumann's death

Arthur Rubinstein
RCA 09026 63039 2
A youthful seventy-four-year-old Rubinstein, caught live in 1961 at New York's Carnegie Hall

András Schiff
Teldec 4509 99176-2
Probing insight, especially in the "Eusebius" movements

Robert Schumann | Carnaval (1835)

Genre | Instrumental
Instrument | Piano
Performer | Marc-André Hamelin
Year recorded | 1999
Label | Hyperion CDA 67120

In his earlier *Papillons* (1831), Schumann had dreamed up impressions of an imaginary masked ball, inspired by Jean Paul's novel *Flegeljahre* (*Years of Indiscretion*). Three years later the twenty-one pieces of *Carnaval* also depicted a ball, though its characters were more closely identified. The principal guest is Ernestine von Fricken, to whom Schumann was engaged (though he later married Clara Wieck). The letters of Ernestine's birth-town, Asch, are translated into their German note-names (giving A–E flat–C–B or A flat–C–B). These motifs drift discreetly across *Carnaval* and also form the basis of no. 10, entitled "ASCH–SCHA." In silent guise these motifs also appear—to be seen but not played—under the enigmatic title "Sphinxes."

Ernestine has her own portrait within these pieces, as do Schumann's alter egos, the poetic Eusebius and the passionate Florestan. Also at the ball are figures from the commedia dell'arte as well as Chopin and Paganini in musical portrait. At the end—in a march mischievously set in waltz-time—Schumann calls upon the "Davidsbünd" ("League of David"), his imaginary group of anti-conservative revolutionaries, to subvert the traditional "Grossvatertanz" waltz theme. The overall result is an imaginative haze of fleeting associations and wispish memories, all set against the formality of the costume ball.

Schumann's deft characterization is brilliantly realized by French-Canadian pianist Marc-André Hamelin. Building up a kaleidoscope of moods and characters, Hamelin shifts seamlessly between a mysterious "Pierrot" and playful "Arlequin," a delicate "Eusebius" and effulgent "Florestan." He makes no apology for his virtuosity in the breathlessly quick "dancing letters" of no. 10, or the shower of interlaced octaves in "Paganini." **EB**

> *"She is devoted to me, and remarkably musical— everything, in a word, that I might wish my wife to be."*

Schumann on the virtues of Ernestine von Fricken

Other Recommended Recordings

Mitsuko Uchida
Philips 442 777-2
Suitably capricious and technically sure, Uchida also gives voice to the usually muted "Sphinxes."

Arturo Benedetti Michelangeli
Testament SBT 2088
Breathtaking color and precision from a renowned keyboard perfectionist

Alfred Cortot
Pearl CD 9331
One of the great Schumann interpreters, recorded in 1928, and proving an unrivaled lyrical touch

Pianist Marc-André Hamelin is famous for his phenomenal technique. ➔

Robert Schumann
Piano Sonata no. 1 (1835)

Genre | Instrumental
Instrument | Piano
Performer | Evgeny Kissin
Year recorded | 2001
Label | RCA 09026 63885 2

Frédéric Chopin
Ballades (c.1835–43)

Genre | Instrumental
Instrument | Piano
Performer | Krystian Zimerman
Year recorded | 1988
Label | DG 423 090-2

In April 1834 Schumann co-founded the magazine *Neue Leipziger Zeitschrift für Musik* and in the same month met Ernestine von Fricken. But by the summer of 1835, while Fricken was in Asch, Schumann's continuing friendship with Clara Wieck, his piano teacher's daughter, began to blossom. By September he had dedicated his Piano Sonata no. 1 in F sharp minor to Clara, and the following January he broke off his engagement to Ernestine.

After the character-pieces of *Papillons* and *Carnaval*, the more "academic" sonata would seem an oddly restrained form at this emotionally unsettled time for Schumann, but Clara's presence is nevertheless deeply felt. The Sonata's first movement is based on a sketch for a fandango from 1832 that Schumann had even then based on a theme of Clara's. And the prominent rhythmic calling-fifths motif in the first movement also comes from an earlier piece by his new love. It is hard, too, not to hear the reverie of the second movement as a love-song to Clara. (Liszt referred to it as "a song of great passion, expressed with a fullness and calm.") The scherzo and finale movements were newly composed. The former is remarkable both for its mocking polonaise and for its caricatured recitative.

The two manifestiations of Schumann's personality—the introverted Eusebius and the fiery Florestan—are both present, and Evgeny Kissin is equally attentive to each. He spins a dream-like thread through the second movement, drawing an achingly beautiful vocal line (Eusebius). Yet his Florestan is unabashedly rampant. There is no sense here of just following the notes—there is a whimsical interpretative spirit that never seems quirky or overdone. **EB**

By the time Chopin adopted it, the ballade had become popular both as a poetic form and a type of vocal music. While this is in no way program music, unlike the ballades of Liszt, Chopin mixes together elements of lyricism and drama in each of these extended works. The First Ballade, which ushers in Chopin's more mature, less openly glittering style, begins with an arresting gesture before introducing two expansive, closely related themes, that are in turn alternated with stormier material. One formally groundbreaking aspect is the whirlwind coda, where he introduces apparently new themes, something that also occurs in the Second and Fourth Ballades.

If lyricism and tumult stand side by side in the First, this juxtaposition is still more dramatic in the Second Ballade. A lilting theme creates a mood of utter calm, but this is dashed away by a stormier section that seems to have come straight out of one of the darker *études*. Even though the calm section eventually wins out, its genial mood now seems deceptive. The Third, by contrast, is the gentlest of the four, and even an agitated central section ultimately gives way to a triumphant A flat major coda. The Fourth is generally acknowledged as the finest, developing the form to new heights. It opens with a wistful melody that, after a calmly rocking beginning, gradually whips up an almost Lisztian storm. Unlike the violent juxtapositions of the Second, here the drama is much more organic.

The distinguished Polish pianist Krystian Zimerman is completely at one with these pieces, applying not only an enormous range of color, but also finding beauty and drama in every bar. **HS**

Giacomo Meyerbeer
Les Huguenots (1836)

Genre | Opera
Conductor | Richard Bonynge
Performer | Joan Sutherland
Year recorded | 1969
Label | Decca 430 549-2 (4 CDs)

Meyerbeer's colleagues could never forgive him for being one of the richest men in Europe. Born in 1791 into a bankers' family, he could travel to the best teachers, observe the musical scene and take his time. Berlin-born, he spent his first professional years in Italy. His presence there probably prompted Rossini to emigrate to Paris, but Meyerbeer settled there too some years later (upon which Rossini retired). Together with the librettist Eugène Scribe, Meyerbeer defined the genre *grand opéra*.

Robert le diable (1831) became an icon of Romanticism, and the success of the historic pageant *Les Huguenots* was even bigger. Dissatisfied with the casts offered him, Meyerbeer held back *Le prophète* until 1849, when he could get the singers he wanted. After two incursions into the genre of the *opéra comique*, Meyerbeer's fourth and last grand opéra, *L'Africaine*, premiered posthumously.

Les Huguenots is set in August 1572 against conspirations culminating in the St. Bartholomew's Day massacre. Huguenot Raoul is in love with Catholic Valentine: their marriage will seal the peace between the conflicting factions. Because of a misunderstanding, Raoul repudiates her. By chance he overhears the preparations for the massacre, but Valentine retains him until it is too late to prevent it. Having converted to Protestantism, Valentine dies with Raoul at the hands of her own father.

Meyerbeer's score brims with delicious touches; he knew how to entertain his audiences. Richard Bonynge's recording is a real "night of the seven stars" (as successful performances of *Les Huguenots* used to be termed), with Joan Sutherland in one of her best roles. **CMS**

Felix Mendelssohn | String
Quartets, op. 44 (1837–38)

Genre | Chamber
Performers | Pacifica Quartet: Vamos, Per Rostad, Ganatra, Bernhardsson
Year recorded | 2004
Label | Cedille CDR 90000 082

After writing his op. 12 String Quartet in 1829, Mendelssohn did not try his hand at the medium again for eight years—partly because he was too busy. As conductor, pianist, and composer of large-scale orchestral and choral works, he was in international demand; in 1835 he was appointed director of the Leipzig Gewandhaus Orchestra and poured his energies into the job, transforming the orchestra into a musical powerhouse and championing works such as Schubert's Ninth Symphony.

As concertmaster, the violinist Ferdinand David was a welcome presence for Mendelssohn; he was a long-standing friend and musical partner. David used to hold chamber music evenings, attended by a handful of invited Leipzig cognoscenti, which spurred the composer into returning to the quartet medium. As with his earlier string quartets, the order in which his three op. 44 quartets were published did not reflect the order in which he wrote them; no. 1 was in fact the last.

The expertise of David and his colleagues gave Mendelssohn ample opportunity to make the most of this demanding medium's potential; and although they are not performed as often as they should be, these three quartets are forty-carat Mendelssohn, with their expert balance of Romantic idiom within Classical form, their virtuosity, high spirits, and effortlessly flowing melodies, and the scherzos that flicker magically in delicate half-lights.

Not as many recordings exist of the op. 44 quartets as one might expect, but as with the early opp. 12 and 13 works, the Pacifica Quartet brings us one of the loveliest possible performances, simply glowing with affection. **JD**

Robert Schumann | Davidsbündlertänze (1837)

Genre | Instrumental
Instrument | Piano
Performer | Andreas Haefliger
Year recorded | 1991
Label | Sony SK 48036

The Davidsbünd (League of David) was a fictitious group devised by Schumann to wreak havoc among the conservative Philistines. Posthumously co-opted into the band were Mozart and Beethoven, while its living members included Berlioz, Chopin, Schumann himself (in the guises of Florestan and Eusebius), and his close friend Clara Wieck. In his journal, the *Neue Zeitschrift für Musik*, a convenient mouthpiece for the group, Schumann expressed the desire "to attack as inartistic the immediate past, which is concerned merely with encouraging superficial virtuosity," and also "to help prepare and hasten the coming of a new poetic era."

Schumann began composing his *Davidsbündlertänze* (*Dances of the League of David*) in August 1837, less than a week after becoming engaged to Clara Wieck. Dedicated to her, "more emphatically than any of my other things," he described them to her as a *Polterabend*—a wedding-eve party—and noted they were "written in happiness." The jumping dotted-rhythm theme of the opening is borrowed from an earlier mazurka by Clara.

In the original edition, each of these eighteen pieces was ascribed to either Florestan or Eusebius, with some attributed to both; hence the mix of unbuttoned exuberance and rapt reflection.

Although these pieces are less suggestive and allusory than the masked-ball inspired *Papillons* and *Carnaval*, Andreas Haefliger delivers them with an unerring sense of poetic storytelling. This well-engineered recording captures both the richness and transparency of his playing, highlighting his continual spontaneity. And although the pieces are essentially unconnected, Haefliger ties them together with a broad sweep. **EB**

> *"If ever I was happy at the piano it was when I was composing these pieces."*
>
> Robert Schumann

Other Recommended Recordings

Alfred Cortot
Pearl CD 9331
Truly superlative playing, only mildly hindered by surface noise from this 1937 recording

Murray Perahia
Sony SMK 89714
A poised and thoughtful reading from a renowned interpreter of the Romantic repertoire

Leon McCawley
Avie AV 0029 (2 CDs)
McCawley's sharp characterization and elegance make this a distinguished release

Andreas Haefliger, a Swiss pianist and son of tenor Ernst Haefliger. ●

Hector Berlioz | Grande messe des morts (1837)

Genre | Choral
Conductor/Performers | André Previn; London Philharmonic Orchestra & Choir
Year recorded | 1980
Label | EMI 7243 5 69512 2 8 (2 CDs)

Berlioz is remembered for his love of the gargantuan and his *Grande messe des morts* (*Requiem Mass*) is certainly "grande." His setting of the Mass calls for a huge choir, a vast orchestra of more than 200 musicians, and was written for the cavernous spaces of Les Invalides in Paris. It nearly did not get performed, though. Berlioz had been commissioned to write a requiem for a commemoration in the summer of 1837 of the 1830 revolution, but for political reasons the event was canceled. The infuriated composer eventually persuaded the French government to feature it at the state funeral of General Damrémont, the French commander who had been killed in Algeria.

The performance went ahead at Les Invalides in December 1837 and as might be imagined, the occasion had its own moments of drama, which Berlioz recounts vividly in his famous *Memoirs*: "One of the choristers went into hysterics and the parish priest of the Invalides wept at the altar for a quarter of an hour after the ceremony." Yet although the work is "big," with the "Tuba mirum" employing four spatially separated brass bands and eight pairs of timpani, it is also paradoxically a work marked by intimacy, even asceticism: in the "Hostias," for example, Berlioz achieves a remarkably spine-chilling chordal effect with just three high flutes and eight low trombones.

It is quite a lot for a recording to try to capture, yet André Previn's 1980 account lacks nothing in impact and atmosphere, helped by the digital engineering. He captures the visceral excitement of Berlioz's big moments, but also shapes the sparer sections with unerring skill, reveling in the originality of the composer's orchestration. **MR**

Franz Liszt | Années de pèlerinage (1837–77)

Genre | Instrumental
Performers | First and second years: Alfred Brendel; Third year: Zoltán Kocsis
Year recorded | 1986
Label | Philips 462 312-2 (2 CDs)

Franz Liszt led one of the most flamboyant and colorful lives of any nineteenth-century musician. He became the supreme piano virtuoso of all time, a showman extraordinaire, an important composer, a sexually magnetic man whose three children were born to a beautiful countess who left her husband for him, a proud Hungarian patriot, a restless, questing spirit, and a leading piano teacher. These many dimensions made Liszt a mass of contradictions in which most observers nevertheless sensed a magnanimous personality that contained overwhelming magic and fascination.

Of all Liszt's collections of piano music, the one entitled *Années de pèlerinage* (*Years of Pilgrimage*) reveals the most variety in style—understandably so, since some of these pieces originated in the 1830s and the last was completed as late as 1877. The first volume portrays sites and scenery in Switzerland, while the second—set in Italy—focuses on works of art and literature (such as Petrarch's sonnets and Dante's *Inferno*). The third, which frequently anticipates the austere, harmonically experimental style of his last years, treats religious, heroic, and scenic topics; "Les jeux d'eau à la Villa d'Este" is a notable forerunner of Impressionism.

Some of these pieces have been much recorded, others far less frequently. Among (near-) complete versions, the Philips composite—with Alfred Brendel in questing, committed form in years 1 and 2 (but omitting the three-piece supplement to the second year, including the show-stopping "Tarantella") and Zoltán Kocsis forcefully relishing Liszt's phantasmagoric severity in the third year—has perhaps the most to offer. **DB**

Robert Schumann
Fantasy in C major (1838)

Genre | Instrumental
Instrument | Piano
Performer | Sviatoslav Richter
Year recorded | 1961
Label | EMI 7243 5 75233 2 5

Schumann's Fantasy begins with one of his most impassioned movements—a "deep lament" to his lover Clara Wieck, from whom he had been separated at the time of writing. But the overall work was intended as a fundraiser for a memorial statue of Beethoven to be erected in Bonn, the city of his birth. The three-movement Fantasy began life as a "Grand Sonata," subtitled "Friezes for Beethoven's Monument," whose movement titles—"Ruins," "Trophies," and "Palm Wreaths"—suggested the stages of Beethoven's career.

Beethoven's influence is also felt with the quotation from his song cycle "An die ferne Geliebte" ("To the Distant Beloved"). "Accept the songs I sang to you, beloved," go the words, and the quotation at the end of Schumann's first movement suggests a deep sense of longing.

The Fantasy's second movement is a march, which Clara heard as a victory march for returning warriors, with a more dainty episode suggesting "young maidens of the village all dressed in white, each with a wreath in her hand to crown the warriors."

The final movement is a breathtaking nocturnal romance—Schumann wrote over his sketch at one passage, "in blissful rapture." It is a mood that pervades the whole movement.

In his 1961 recording Richter conjures a wonderful fluidity in the first movement's swirling left-hand figuration, supporting Liszt's view of the movement as "pre-eminently dreamy . . . altogether the reverse of noisy and heavy." His luminous tone and unwillingness to sentimentalize result in a final nocturne that is truly sublime. **EB**

Robert Schumann
Kinderszenen (1838)

Genre | Instrumental
Instrument | Piano
Performer | Alex Slobodyanik
Year recorded | 1999
Label | EMI 7243 5 73500 2 0

Unlike the later *Album for the Young*, Schumann's *Kinderszenen* (*Scenes from Childhood*) were written not for children to play, but rather to capture elements of childhood. These thirteen pieces, he told his composer-friend Carl Reinecke, were "reflections of an adult for other adults." This said, their execution is within the reach of younger pianists.

The pieces were selected from thirty or so "curious little things" that Schumann had written in the early months of 1838. They offer glimpses of games ("Catch Me if You Can," "The Knight of the Hobby-Horse"), imagined scenes ("Of Strange Countries and People," "By the Fireside"), and child-like states ("The Entreating Child," "Reverie," "Child Falling Asleep"). By Schumann's admission to Clara, part of the inspiration may well have been "an echo of what you said to me once, 'that sometimes I seemed to you like a child.'"

This is not to deny the poetry of numbers such as the famously lyrical "Träumerei" ("Reverie"), or of the closing "The Poet Speaks," which we can take as Schumann's afterword to the sequence. Schumann exceled at these postludial reflections, which make the end of his later song cycles such as *Dichterliebe* (*A Poet's Love*) and *Frauenliebe und -leben* (*A Woman's Love and Life*) so devastating.

An uncanny innocence lies behind Alex Slobodyanik's recording for EMI, underpinned by a penetrating but lightly worn insight. Slobodyanik enjoys every curve of phrasing, and teases out each telling voice, without ever breaking his imaginative spell. He is suitably skittish in "Catch Me if You Can," while his "Träumerei" is daringly rhapsodic and increasingly somnolent. **EB**

Robert Schumann | Kreisleriana (1838)

Genre | Instrumental
Instrument | Piano
Performer | Evgeny Kissin
Year recorded | 2004
Label | RCA 82876 59412 2

Schumann
Kreisleriana
Fantasie
Op. 17

Evgeny Kissin

"There is a positively wild love contained in some of the movements, and your life and mine are found there, and some of your glances." Time and again Clara Wieck, whom Schumann later married, was the inspiration for his music. Yet even though he claimed "you and one of your ideas are the principal subject," he proceeded to dedicate these *Kreisleriana* to Chopin. The title relates to E. T. A. Hoffmann's character Johannes Kreisler, the eccentric, idealistic composer and conductor who, in Hoffmann's novel *Die Lebensansichten des Katers Murr* (*The Life and Opinions of the Tomcat Murr*), ends up sharing his biography with that of a would-be literary tomcat who has haplessly written his own life's story amid that of Hoffmann.

The sudden shifts between the two stories are reflected in the sharp mood-changes across and within Schumann's eight "fantasies." Unlike in the *Davidsbündlertänze*, Schumann did not ascribe any of these pieces to either of his contrasting alter egos, the impetuous Florestan and the dreamy Eusebius—but it is clear that Florestan inhabits the more passionate G minor movements, and Eusebius the more serene B flat major ones. So in *Kreisleriana*, as in Hoffmann's novel, two stories are sharply contrasted yet inextricably linked—a duality of which Hoffmann would surely have approved.

Some of Schumann's most intricate piano music is here, yet so are his greatest heights of storming passion and personal reflection. Evgeny Kissin, an undisputable lion of the keyboard, attacks the former with unrivaled vigor, powerfully conveying through his effortless technical command that the struggles are of the mind and not of the body. His wistful musings are equally effective, and all is bound together with an arresting Romantic sweep. **EB**

"Music is perhaps the only romantic art."

E. T. A. Hoffmann

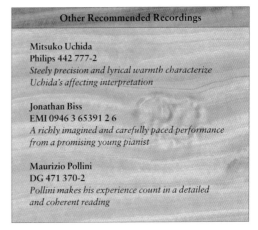

Other Recommended Recordings

Mitsuko Uchida
Philips 442 777-2
*Steely precision and lyrical warmth characterize
Uchida's affecting interpretation*

Jonathan Biss
EMI 0946 3 65391 2 6
*A richly imagined and carefully paced performance
from a promising young pianist*

Maurizio Pollini
DG 471 370-2
*Pollini makes his experience count in a detailed
and coherent reading*

Evgeny Kissin, famous for his dazzling pianism. ➲

Hector Berlioz | Roméo et Juliette (1839)

Genre | Choral
Conductor/Performers | Colin Davis;
Daniela Barcellona, Kenneth Tarver, Orlin Anastassov
Year recorded | 2000
Label | LSO Live LSO 0003 (2 CDs)

Of all Shakespeare's plays, *Romeo and Juliet* was the one destined to gel with the Romantic spirit of nineteenth-century composers. Berlioz first encountered the Bard's work in 1827, when he fell not only for the drama and poetry, but also for the leading lady, Harriet Smithson: the *Symphonie fantastique* was the immediate result. He saw her on the Paris stage as both Ophelia and Juliet, but his musical response to the latter role had to wait over a decade to come to fruition, when Paganini's payment of 20,000 francs for *Harold in Italy* gave him the freedom to work unencumbered.

The resulting work was neither an expected opera nor a symphonic poem but instead a "dramatic symphony" for soloists, choir, and orchestra that, rather than following the story's detailed narrative, encapsulates certain scenes from the drama: the strife between the rival families; the ball; the love scene; the tragic denouement; and so on. It nevertheless follows the general scope of a symphony, though one in seven parts with further subdivisions: the love music naturally forms the "slow movement," while the scherzo, one of the best-known stand-alone movements from the work, is a scintillating portrait of Queen Mab, the fairy of dreams from Mercutio's famous speech. More strangely, despite the vocal element, the only named character is Friar Lawrence (the bass); he, the tenor and mezzo soloists, along with the chorus, sing a specially written text by the French poet Émile Deschamps that comments on rather than partakes of the action.

In the wrong hands the hundred minutes of the symphony can sprawl, but Colin Davis is a master Berliozian, and his live London Symphony Orchestra recording is the most enthralling, combining tenderness with virtuosity. **MR**

> *"I shall marry Juliet and I shall write my biggest symphony on the play."*

Berlioz's purported remark in 1827

Other Recommended Recordings

Vienna Philharmonic Orchestra • Colin Davis
Philips 470 543-2 (2 CDs)
Davis's earlier account, coupled with overtures

Boston Symphony Orchestra • Charles Münch
RCA 74321 84587 2
A vintage account by another Berlioz master

Béatrice et Bénédict
London Symphony Orchestra • Colin Davis
LSO Live LSO 046
Another major result of Berlioz's Shakespearean obsession, his last opera from 1862

Hector Berlioz, the epitome of the Romantic composer. ➔

Frédéric Chopin | Preludes (1839)

Genre | Instrumental
Instrument | Piano
Performer | Grigory Sokolov
Year recorded | 1990
Label | Opus 111 OP 30336

These twenty-four preludes in all the major and minor keys reflect Chopin's fascination with Bach's great keyboard collection of forty-eight preludes and fugues, *The Well-Tempered Clavier*. Chopin completed the cycle during a disastrous stay in Majorca with the writer George Sand and her children, which was beset by bad weather and worse health. He uses the term "prelude" to indicate a small-scale, freestanding piece, rather than an introduction to a work, as had previously been the case. The small scale of the pieces, a third of them lasting under a minute, belies the considerable drama and discourse that can be found in every one of them. From the nervous agitato opening prelude, which gives way to a slow piece of utter desolation, Chopin seems to explore an entire world.

The great and elusive Russian pianist Grigory Sokolov gets absolutely to the heart of the music in his masterly live recording. Whether it is the gentle filigree of no. 3 (vivace), the tumult of no. 8, the wistful no. 11 (particularly treasurable in this reading), the extraordinarily demanding moto perpetuo right-hand writing of no. 16, the *étude*-like no. 18, or the gently nostalgic no. 23, Sokolov is mesmerizing in his imagination and pianistic prowess. Even the hackneyed no. 15, nicknamed "Raindrop," in his hands becomes a nocturne of the greatest tenderness, its dark middle section building to an impassioned climax. Never is there the slightest hint of saccharine, as there can be in some readings of the preludes. And with his rounded sound—which ranges from a mere whisper to the most brilliant, ringing climaxes—and an apparently invincible technique, Sokolov makes an undisputable case for the power of these tiny pieces when heard as a complete cycle. **HS**

> "When [Chopin] is simple there is no trace of vulgarity and when he is complicated he is still intelligible."

Leo Tolstoy

Other Recommended Recordings

Sviatoslav Richter
Praga PR 254 060
Strong, fearless readings that dazzle as much for their more intimate moments as for their virtuoso ones

Alfred Cortot
EMI 0946 3 61542 2 0
No one could spin a melodic line as effortlessly as Alfred Cortot

Evgeny Kissin
RCA 09026 63259 2
Kissin's range of dynamics, from an almost inaudible pianissimo to a thundering fortissimo, is mesmerizing

Felix Mendelssohn | Piano Trios nos. 1 & 2 (1839, 1845)

Genre | Chamber
Performers | Florestan Trio: Anthony Marwood (violin), Richard Lester (cello), Susan Tomes (piano)
Year recorded | 2003
Label | Hyperion CDA 67485

"Mendelssohn is the Mozart of the nineteenth century, the most illuminating of musicians, who sees more clearly than others through the contradictions of our era and is the first to reconcile them." Robert Schumann was describing Mendelssohn's Piano Trio no. 1 in D minor, op. 49 in these perceptive words, but the statement is no less true of no. 2 in C minor, op. 66: In both, Mendelssohn expresses the turbulence and yearning of German Romanticism through the Classical structures of Mozart and Beethoven. Rather than breaking new ground, Mendelssohn made existing musical forms entirely his own, transforming them with a personal voice replete with rich melodic lyricism. Six years separate the two trios and despite sharing a minor key ambience they each have their own character: no. 1 owes more to the Romantic Lied—its slow movement could have come from one of Mendelssohn's *Songs without Words*—while no. 2, composed after Schumann had taken up chamber music with a vengeance in 1842, is more motivically and instrumentally conceived.

> *"Felix Mendelssohn is the Mozart of the nineteenth century."*
>
> **Robert Schumann**

The Florestan Trio is probably the leading British chamber group of its type and its performance of Mendelssohn's trios is well nigh ideal. Pianist Susan Tomes, violinist Anthony Marwood, and cellist Richard Lester play with a seamless, apparently effortless sense of ensemble and excellent balance. They build up the intensity of the momentum into a thrilling, compulsive drive in the allegros; the scherzos are full of mystery; and the slow movements, virtually songs without words, have all the tenderness and simplicity one could hope for. And there is an almost palpable sense of triumph in the way they let the last movement of the C minor Trio blossom into its blazing chorale melody. **JD**

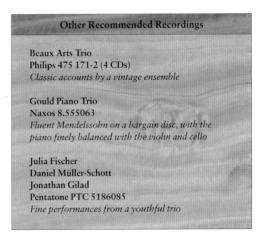

Other Recommended Recordings

Beaux Arts Trio
Philips 475 171-2 (4 CDs)
Classic accounts by a vintage ensemble

Gould Piano Trio
Naxos 8.555063
Fluent Mendelssohn on a bargain disc, with the piano finely balanced with the violin and cello

Julia Fischer
Daniel Müller-Schott
Jonathan Gilad
Pentatone PTC 5186085
Fine performances from a youthful trio

Frédéric Chopin
Piano Sonata no. 2 in B flat minor, "Funeral March" (1839)

Genre | Instrumental
Instrument | Piano
Performer | Sergei Rachmaninov
Year recorded | 1930
Label | RCA 09026 61265 2 (10 CDs)

The first of Chopin's great sonatas (the much earlier no. 1 may be seen as a cautious experiment compared to nos. 2 and 3) has become known by its third movement, which was in fact written slightly earlier, in 1837. Contemporary commentators were perplexed by the extreme differences between each of the movements, with Robert Schumann describing how Chopin had "bound together four of his wildest children." The very opening, with its dramatic rhetoric, seems to tell of some great tragedy. The figuration that follows is nervy, incessant, and fundamentally without melody—not at all the way that a conventional sonata movement would go. In the finest performances, the cumulative impact of this movement is one bordering on terror.

Rather than follow that with some kind of musical balm, Chopin instead offers a trembling, shaking scherzo that stomps its way up and down the keyboard. Technically, it is fiendish; musically, it is another apocalyptic movement. Even the famous funeral march brings little consolation, by turns somber, angry, and glorious, with an almost orchestral range of sonorities. Its trio section makes a silvery contrast, with a simple theme that gradually grows in warmth and conviction. But as the opening returns, we are left with tolling bells and the imperturbable spirit of death. How to top that? Chopin's solution is entirely original, with a wispy, ethereal, ghostly finale without any clear theme, just a feeling of billowing movement. In Rachmaninov's hands, terror, beauty, momentum, and emotional ambiguity combine in a way that has not been equaled since. **HS**

> *"I am writing a Sonata in B flat minor in which will be found that march you know."*
>
> **Chopin, in a letter to his friend Julian Fontana**

Other Recommended Recordings

Grigory Sokolov
Opus 111 OPS 30-289
A towering performance of the work, with overwhelming drama and emotion

Vladimir Horowitz
Sony S2K 52897 (2 CDs)
An edge-of-the-seat performance that almost explodes with personality

Mikhail Pletnev
Virgin 7243 5 61836 2 9
A reading of white heat and intensity captured in a recording of technical perfection

Pianist Sergei Rachmaninov in an early twentieth-century photograph. ●

Franz Liszt | Paraphrases & Transcriptions (1840s *onward*)

Genre | Instrumental
Instrument | Piano
Performer | Earl Wild
Year recorded | 1968
Label | Vanguard ATM-CD-1488 (2 CDs)

Essential to Liszt's career as a composer and pianist are his arrangements of other composers' music for his own use. It has long been unfashionable to approve of such appropriations, because with the existence of radio and recordings we are able to hear works in their original form. But in his day, these arrangements were of great importance for showcasing the music of others, filtered through Liszt's own keen musical sensibilities and overwhelming technical resources. Today we learn much about the way the nineteenth century perceived these pieces from examining and hearing Liszt's arrangements, and pianists still find expressive and technical challenges in mastering their sometimes ferocious difficulties.

It is impossible to describe briefly the range of works Liszt subjected to keyboard treatment—from Bach's organ works to Beethoven's symphonies; from songs by Chopin, Schubert, and Schumann to operas by Mozart, Verdi, and Wagner, the whole of music history as it then was understood falls under his purview. The distinction between works that are more or less faithful transcriptions and those that are creative paraphrases is frequently upheld but just as frequently denounced, since all of this body of music displays Lisztian features.

The recording that best portrays Liszt's unparalleled blend of virtuosity and creativity is Earl Wild's utterly tremendous account of *Réminiscences de Don Juan*, which interleaves treatments of three famous passages from Mozart's *Don Giovanni*. Wild's playing is almost impossibly brilliant but retains singing tone, demonstrates awareness of the vocal nature of the original, and invests every sparkling cascade of notes with musical, dramatic, and expressive meaning. **DB**

"The finest of [Liszt's] operatic fantasies juxtapose parts of the opera and bring out a new significance."

Charles Rosen

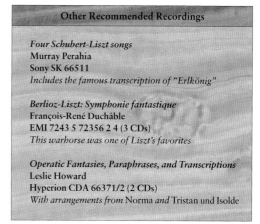

Other Recommended Recordings

Four Schubert-Liszt songs
Murray Perahia
Sony SK 66511
Includes the famous transcription of "Erlkönig"

Berlioz-Liszt: Symphonie fantastique
François-René Duchâble
EMI 7243 5 72356 2 4 (3 CDs)
This warhorse was one of Liszt's favorites

Operatic Fantasies, Paraphrases, and Transcriptions
Leslie Howard
Hyperion CDA 66371/2 (2 CDs)
With arrangements from Norma *and* Tristan und Isolde

Franz Liszt pictured by German photographer Edgar Hanfstaengl. ➔

Robert Schumann | Dichterliebe (1840)

Genre | Vocal
Performers | Dietrich Fischer-Dieskau (baritone),
Jörg Demus (piano)
Year recorded | 1965
Label | DG 477 5556 (3 CDs)

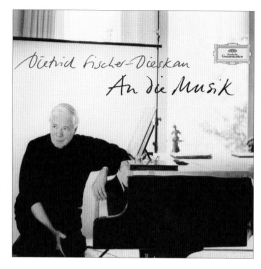

Here is Schumann's glorious month of May: the buds springing, the birds singing—and yearning and longing fills the heart of the Romantic poet. This is *Dichterliebe*, the song cycle Schumann wrote while awaiting legal permission to marry his beloved Clara. But all was not sweetness and light. Schumann was, after all, setting to music the work of poet Heinrich Heine—and there is a bitterness and irony within these verses that stings the heart. Did Schumann re-romanticize Heine's verse? Or did he comply in its often biting ambivalence of tone?

Each performer and each listener will have a different take on this "Poet's Love." But certainly one of the saddest, and greatest, songs ever written lies at the cycle's heart. "Ich hab' im Traum geweinet" recreates the numb grief of dream and its deceptions—and awakes in floods of tears. Schumann here composes as much silence as song.

It is finding the balance between dramatic projection and poetic introspection, between a sense of acute waking reality and dream—and maintaining the nervous energy generated by the tension between those states— that is the great challenge of this cycle.

Dietrich Fischer-Dieskau recorded *Dichterliebe* six times, gradually refining points of technique and interpretation, and ever deepening his insights. In 1965, he was working in a particularly fruitful partnership with Jörg Demus. The special quality of their shared responses was rediscovered when Deutsche Grammophon released the Complete Fischer-Dieskau Edition to celebrate the mastersinger's seventy-fifth birthday. Together, singer and accompanist play off Heine's poetry and Schumann's music in an ever-intriguing and engaging emotional drama of rapture, estrangement, acceptance, and endless renewal. **HF**

> *"Schumann drew a chord from the strings of Heine's heart . . . and in this way explored his own."*
>
> Wilhelm Killmayer

Other Recommended Recordings

Peter Schreier,
Christoph Eschenbach
Teldec 4509 97960-2
The definitive tenor Dichterliebe

Christoph Prégardien, Andreas Staier
Deutsche Harmonia Mundi 05472 77319 2
Tenor and fortepiano bring new insights to the fabric of this work

Christian Gerhaher, Gerold Huber
RCA 82876 58995-2
A young and ardent baritone performance of high intelligence

Robert Schumann | Frauenliebe und -leben (1840)

Genre | Vocal
Performers | Janet Baker (mezzo-soprano),
Geoffrey Parsons (piano)
Year recorded | 1968
Label | BBC Legends BBCL 4049-2

Schumann wrote *Frauenliebe und -leben* (*Women's Lives and Loves*) in just two days, less than a week after hearing that he could legally marry his beloved Clara Wieck without her father's permission. In his fevered state, Schumann turned to a cycle of poems that depicted a woman adoring her husband-to-be, and living only for him.

For us, there is an enigma at the heart of the cycle. Adalbert von Chamisso's poetry seems the embodiment of nineteenth-century patriarchal attitudes: wives should clearly be loyal, humble, even self-abnegating servants of their men. But Chamisso was a fervent supporter of female emancipation. So was the apparent subservience of this young woman all a matter of class? Is this, in fact, a triumphant upstairs-downstairs romance, celebrated by Schumann's musical setting?

It is, after all, quite some setting. Schumann's music gives exquisite voice to the hopes and fears of all lovers, regardless of gender, class, and epoch. And it is suffused with the sense of dangerous rapture—at times bursting out in ecstasy, at times held within a fragile inwardness—that is unique to Schumann's musical sensibility.

The constant shift between melody and speech inflection, the ever-changing pace and pulse of the vocal writing as the mood turns from shy wonder to joyful affirmation—much of this must be caught within the very first song. Janet Baker caresses each phrase in a wonderfully awe-filled and unbroken line of melody. And the light of love is always shadowed slightly by a cloud of vulnerable unknowing, which finally darkens into an anguished desolation. This live recording from Snape Maltings in Aldeburgh is the best of all Baker's recordings of this cycle, and still surpasses any other in the catalogue. **HF**

> *"Oh Clara, what bliss it is to write music to be sung!"*
>
> **Robert Schumann writing to his fiancée, Clara Wieck**

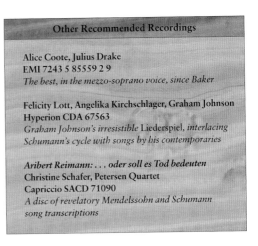

Other Recommended Recordings

Alice Coote, Julius Drake
EMI 7243 5 85559 2 9
The best, in the mezzo-soprano voice, since Baker

Felicity Lott, Angelika Kirchschlager, Graham Johnson
Hyperion CDA 67563
Graham Johnson's irresistible Liederspiel, interlacing Schumann's cycle with songs by his contemporaries

Aribert Reimann: . . . oder soll es Tod bedeuten
Christine Schafer, Petersen Quartet
Capriccio SACD 71090
A disc of revelatory Mendelssohn and Schumann song transcriptions

Robert Schumann | Liederkreis, op. 24 (1840)

Genre | Vocal
Performers | Ian Bostridge (tenor),
Julius Drake (piano)
Year recorded | 1997
Label | EMI 7243 5 56575 2 7

EMI CLASSICS

SCHUMANN
Liederkreis Op.24
Dichterliebe Op.48
& 7 Lieder

Ian Bostridge
Julius Drake

Schumann's op. 24 *Liederkreis* continues to be inexplicably overshadowed by his op. 39 Eichendorff cycle. But this first *Liederkreis*, or "circle of songs," written in the heady first flush of the year in which Schumann was to be married to Clara Wieck, is the real groundbreaker, the first quivering breath of a post-Romantic agony that was to sound its way through the century.

Schumann, who had met the poet Heinrich Heine in 1828, acknowledged that the wild fluctuations of mood, the disturbed dream world, and above all the ironic realism within Heine's poetry were likely to stimulate a "more artistic and more profound type of Lied, of which our predecessors could naturally have known nothing." Here are songs of lovesick insomnia, yearning pain, foreboding, and impassioned betrayal; of despair and new hope. In creating brief, flickering tableaux of experience, memory and allusion, the poet draws the reader in, only to distance him once again. Schumann plays a similar, though subtly different game: the erratic flexing of the vocal line against the piano writing is just one of the intriguing ways in which he challenges singer, pianist and listener to tease out the composer's responses to Heine.

This is a cycle of pounding and faltering pulses, of the palpitation of anger and the numbness of pain—and nothing recreates all of this as irresistibly as a youthful tenor voice. The young Ian Bostridge and his pianist Julius Drake engage ardently with the ever-shifting moods and tones of voice. In the song "Warte, warte, wilde Schiffmann," for instance, they reveal a virtuosity of imagination unsurpassed in the catalogue. The long-sighted grasp of the musical progress of this cycle, as shown by both musicians, becomes ever more apparent on repeated hearings. **HF**

"A collection on which I have worked long, and with heart and soul."

Robert Schumann

Other Recommended Recordings

Stephan Genz, Claar Ter Horst
Claves CD 50-9708
The very incarnation of tender, raw love, from a then twenty-five-year-old baritone

Peter Schreier, Norman Shetler
Berlin BC 2110-2
The earlier, 1974 Schreier recording, unsurpassed in its subtle sense of wonder

Brigitte Fassbaender, Irwin Gage
DG 415 519-2
The female take on Liederkreis *yields a fervent yet fragile intimacy*

Ian Bostridge is among today's leading Lieder singers. ➔

Robert Schumann | Liederkreis, op. 39 (1840)

Genre | Vocal
Performers | Wolfgang Holzmair (baritone),
Imogen Cooper (piano)
Year recorded | 1999
Label | Philips 464 991-2

In April 1840, Clara Wieck and Robert Schumann were making plans at last for their wedding. But pulsing through Schumann's heart and mind no less ardently than his love for Clara was a sequence of poems by Joseph von Eichendorff, which were to draw from the composer what he admitted was "my most Romantic music ever."

In making his choice of Eichendorff's poems, Schumann created a cycle that lacks both the stability of a theme and the coherence of narrative. This *Liederkreis* is a diorama of constantly shifting, arch-Romantic tableaux. From images of exile to sinister rides through the forest, and encounters with the Lorelei; from the bliss of solitude to strange, sinister nocturnes—what's to come is always unsure.

Eichendorff's landscapes are of the psyche: inner and outer worlds are indivisible. An old knight, sculpted from stone, sits high in his castle overlooking the Rhine. We look up at him in his eternity. He looks down at the fleeting present: a wedding scene on the river. The musicians play— but the bride is weeping. And Schumann's music binds past and present, viewer and viewed, together in a rich and strange moment. Only the most thoughtful and sentient of singers can hope to incarnate such songs convincingly.

Wolfgang Holzmair is the exemplar of this highly refined sensibility, and his partnership with the pianist Imogen Cooper goes to the very heart of Schumann. Their names would appear here more often had not Philips inexplicably deleted nearly all their fine Schubert and Schumann recordings from the catalogue. This outstanding performance remains, thank goodness, and is all the more revelatory by being placed in the context of settings of Eichendorff by composers such as Mendelssohn, Aribert Reimann, Hugo Wolf, Zemlinsky, and Korngold. **HF**

> *"Such music I have in me that I could sing the whole day through!"*

Robert Schumann

Other Recommended Recordings

Margaret Price, Graham Johnson
Hyperion CDH 55011
A performance high on awe and wonder, perfectly teamed with Schumann's Kerner Lieder

Soile Isokoski, Marita Viitasalo
Finlandia 0630 10924-2
Acute intelligence from these Finnish musicians, with a fine Frauenliebe und -leben *in tow*

Peter Pears, Benjamin Britten
BBC Legends BBCB 8006-2
Worth it for the piano playing alone: from Aldeburgh's Jubilee Hall in 1958

Austrian baritone Wolfgang Holzmair. ➲

Felix Mendelssohn
Variations sérieuses
(1841)

Genre | Instrumental
Instrument | Piano
Performer | Murray Perahia
Year recorded | 1982
Label | Sony MK 37838

Mendelssohn was an immensely accomplished pianist and counted such eminent concert artists as Clara Schumann among his close friends. In an era when virtuoso display often drew crowds to concerts more than pure music, Mendelssohn's piano music managed to put the pianist's technical accomplishment entirely at the service of musical ends.

The *Variations sérieuses* is one of Mendelssohn's most substantial piano works. The theme—its sighing nature and chorale-like elements as plangent and serious as the title suggests—has something in common with his friend Robert Schumann's *Études symphoniques*, written in 1835. The seventeen variations that follow grow increasingly virtuosic, but the overall mood remains somber—only one, no. 14, goes into the major. The contrapuntal writing shows how important an influence Bach was on Mendelssohn, but that does not stop the variations from culminating in a stunning coda full of high Romanticism.

Mendelssohn's piano writing is characterized by fleetness, lightness, and clarity that needs to be maintained even in the most powerful moments. Perhaps the pianist who captures this intent yet mercurial voice best of all is Murray Perahia, who recorded *Variations* in 1982 as part of an all-Mendelssohn recital. He achieves a near-perfect balance, essential in Mendelssohn's works, between Classical restraint and .Romantic sensibility, letting the composer's half-lights and tender-heartedness gleam through from behind the work's polished surface. **JD**

Robert Schumann
Symphony no. 1, "Spring" (1841)

Genre | Orchestral
Conductor/Performers | Leonard Bernstein; Vienna Philharmonic Orchestra
Year recorded | 1984
Label | DG 453 049-2 (2 CDs)

Schumann sketched his Symphony no. 1 in a mere four days in January 1841, and within a month the score was complete. At this time the composer was living in Leipzig; his wife Clara was pregnant with their first child, so it was a period of great anticipation. Schumann later confided that he was possessed by an intense "longing for spring" while he wrote the symphony, and said that he wanted this yearning quality to be conveyed in performance. That he created such a large work in such a brief timespan also reveals a great deal about the music's character.

The symphony begins with a stentorian call by the trumpets and horns—a "summons to awakening," in the composer's words. After an eventful slow introduction, the main allegro section of the first movement scampers away, its exuberance barely contained by myriad lyrical interludes. The symphony often seems to be pressing eagerly ahead, in fact. Even in the nocturnal calm of the slow movement, breathless subsidiary figures keep the adrenaline flowing. After a playfully syncopated scherzo, the finale presents a vision of pastoral bliss, with distant horn calls and a cadenza for the flute evoking birdsong. Then we're off again, as spring rushes into the blazing brilliance of summer.

Leonard Bernstein captures this atmosphere of teeming vitality in a performance so fresh it seems to burst from one's loudspeakers in a veritable riot of floral color. He is aided by the effulgent tone and technical aplomb of the Vienna Philharmonic, whose members manage to play beautifully even when the pace is breathless. **AFC**

Richard Wagner
Der fliegende Holländer
(1841, *rev.* 1860)

Genre | Opera
Conductor/Performers | Joseph Keilberth;
Hermann Uhde, Astrid Varnay, Ludwig Weber
Year recorded | 1955
Label | Testament SBT2 1384 (2 CDs)

Robert Schumann
Piano Quartet
(1842)

Genre | Chamber
Performers | Florestan Trio,
Thomas Riebl (viola)
Year recorded | 1999
Label | Hyperion CDA 67175

Having failed to take Paris by storm as he had hoped, the young Richard Wagner returned to Germany in 1842 where his grand opera *Rienzi* was performed, followed the next year by *Der fliegende Holländer*. The dark, demonic coloring of the latter actually found less favor with the first audiences than did the grand rhetoric and spectacular theatrical displays of *Rienzi*, though Wagner himself regarded *Holländer* as the first of his dramas to be written to a truly poetic text, and posterity has endorsed his view.

Based on the legend of the Flying Dutchman—the sea captain condemned to sail the seas for eternity as punishment for blasphemy—*Der fliegende Holländer* acquires, in Wagner's treatment, a characteristic twist: the tormented traveler can find redemption only in the form of the love of a faithful woman. Senta, who has long fantasized about the sea captain in a portrait in her father Daland's house, is that woman. She abandons the unpromising huntsman, Erik, to whom she was betrothed and leaps into the waves in a suicidal bid to prove her undying love for the Dutchman.

Hermann Uhde is one of the most convincing Dutchmen on disc, projecting the character's tormented and demonic qualities with a potent, darkly colored tone. Astrid Varnay is terrific in the delivery of Senta's ballad, singing through the dipthongs "Hui!" with eerie coloring, to chilling effect. Even if the sound is compromised by today's standards, Keilberth's finely controlled conducting maintains tension to powerfully expressive effect. **BM**

Schumann's beautiful Piano Quartet has long been overshadowed by the Quintet with which it shares its E flat major key. Perhaps that is because it gives up its secrets less readily than the self-confident Quintet. Its opening steals in softly, before erupting into a genial allegro, with the piano at the helm. The piano quartet is also a less common medium—it is easy enough to combine a pianist with a ready-made string quartet, but it is harder to find a viola player to work with a piano trio. Even Schumann's wife, Clara, was slow to take up the work, waiting seven years before performing it in public.

However, the rewards are rich, not least a slow movement that features one of the most sublime melodies ever to flow from Schumann's pen. It appears first on cello, simply accompanied by the piano. Its melting beauty is enhanced by the soulful playing of the Florestan Trio's Richard Lester. Then the violin (Anthony Marwood) soars in, duetting wonderfully with the cello. When the tune reappears at the other end of the movement the viola gets the theme, the violin weaving an ethereal line above it, before it is finally returned to its rightful owner, the cello. Nor are the other movements in any way less interesting, with an elfin scherzo and, to end, one of Schumann's most joyous finales. It demands a pianist with a real lightness of touch, and absolute unanimity on the part of the other players, something it triumphantly finds in this finely wrought recording by the Florestan Trio and the exceptionally fine violist Thomas Riebl. **HS**

Franz Berwald | Symphonies (1842–45)

Genre | Orchestral
Conductor | Sixten Ehrling
Performers | Malmö Symphony Orchestra
Year recorded | 1996
Label | BIS CD-795/796 (2 CDs)

Born in 1796, Berwald had little formal training, but followed in his father's footsteps as a violinist, earning a living in the court orchestra in Stockholm on and off from 1812 until 1828. Lack of compositional success in Sweden led him to move to Berlin, where he did not fare much better—a more lasting legacy was the orthopedic institute that he founded and ran from 1835 until 1841. That year he moved to Vienna, where he wrote the first of his surviving symphonies; three more followed after he had returned to Sweden, the second in 1842 and the last two in 1845. But recognition remained elusive, and he ran a glassworks to make a living while continuing to compose. It was only in the last decade of his life that his opera *Estrella di Soria* was well received; he achieved greater acknowledgement in the following years, before dying of pneumonia in 1868.

Berwald's problem was that he was ahead of his time in his attitude to harmony and form: passages in his Third Symphony, the *Sinfonie singulière*, could almost be by Carl Nielsen (who was an admirer). And Sweden did not have any tradition of purely orchestral music making at a professional level until after Berwald's death: only the *Sinfonie sérieuse* was performed during his lifetime. What the twentieth century discovered in his music was a true original, who had learned from Beethoven and Schubert in particular, but who showed individual melodic freshness, and an expert ear for orchestral textures.

Sixten Ehrling was a lifelong champion of Berwald, and these recordings, made with the Malmö Symphony Orchestra when he was seventy-eight, are at the same time loving, precise, and exciting, with all of Berwald's inventiveness coming up freshly painted. **MC**

> *"A stimulating, witty man, prone to bizarrerie, who lacked creative power and fantasy as a composer."*
>
> Eduard Hanslick

Swedish composer Franz Berwald in c.1860. ➔

Felix Mendelssohn | Symphony no. 3, "Scottish" (1842)

Genre | Orchestral
Conductor | Claudio Abbado
Performers | London Symphony Orchestra
Year recorded | 1989
Label | DG 427 810-2

Scotland, with its gloomy climate, mountain mists, and glorious scenery, was a focal point of inspiration to the Romantic movement. Together with its most famous literary exponent, Walter Scott, it spurred compositions from figures as diverse as Schubert, Bruch, and of course Mendelssohn.

Mendelssohn first visited Scotland in 1829 and it seems that from the start he intended to compose a symphony depicting his impressions. He sketched the opening the following year, declaring that he had found direct inspiration for the work's mysterious introduction while visiting Holyrood Palace:"The chapel beside it has now lost its roof, it is overgrown with grass and ivy, and at the broken altar Mary was crowned Queen of Scotland. Everything is ruined, decayed, and open to the sky. I believe I have found there today the beginning of my Scottish Symphony." The work nevertheless went unfinished until 1842 and was to be the last symphony Mendelssohn completed.

Mendelssohn intended that the four movements should be played without a break, and many of the themes are closely related to one another. The first and final movements focus on the dark, atmospheric, and warrior-like aspects of Scotland; the second movement, a lively scherzo, is full of charm and energy, characterized by the rhythmic "Scotch snap" of Scottish traditional songs and dances (even though Mendelssohn professed not to like folk music) and the slow movement, placed third, finds the composer at his most tender, indulging his gift for song-like melody.

Claudio Abbado conducts the London Symphony Orchestra in a classic account of this colorful work. They capture Mendelssohn's romantic warmth and enthusiasm beautifully and the nervous edge of the agitato in the first movement is especially spot-on. **JD**

> *"More than any other symphony, it forms a whole that is closely interrelated."*
>
> **Robert Schumann on the "Scottish" Symphony**

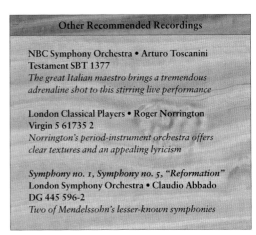

Other Recommended Recordings

NBC Symphony Orchestra • Arturo Toscanini
Testament SBT 1377
The great Italian maestro brings a tremendous adrenaline shot to this stirring live performance

London Classical Players • Roger Norrington
Virgin 5 61735 2
Norrington's period-instrument orchestra offers clear textures and an appealing lyricism

Symphony no. 1, Symphony no. 5, "Reformation"
London Symphony Orchestra • Claudio Abbado
DG 445 596-2
Two of Mendelssohn's lesser-known symphonies

Claudio Abbado conducting in Vienna in 1972. ➔

Robert Schumann
String Quartets (1842)

Genre | Chamber
Performers | Ysaÿe Quartet: Guillaume Sutre,
Luc-Marie Aguera, Miguel Da Silva, Yovan Markovitch
Year recorded | 2003
Label | Aeon AECD 0418

Schumann's three string quartets have been unjustly neglected for decades, not through any failing in quality but simply because people tend to regard Schumann first and foremost as a great song and piano composer —as indeed did his wife, Clara, who questioned whether he knew enough about the medium to dabble in it at all. But he did not let that stand in his way: after several years of harboring "quartettish thoughts," as he put it, his three quartets were written at white heat in June and July 1842. He dedicated them to Mendelssohn, whose own quartets he knew, as is very clear from such movements as the finale of the First Quartet, which, in its swashbuckling vigor and precipitate speed resembles a violent Mendelssohn scherzo.

This is wonderfully conveyed on a recording of the complete quartets by the Ysaÿe Quartet. However, the players are equally at home in the more introspective moments of this music, such as the inward Adagio of the First Quartet, not a piece to yield all its secrets at first listening. Even when Schumann spins the most serene melody, unease and darkness never seem to be far away. The Ysaÿe Quartet is also alive to the intricacies of this music, such as the rhythmically unsettled opening movement of the Third, where the musicians produce playing of tremendous subtlety and tenderness. Similarly, in the disconcerting rhythmic instability of the scherzo of the Second Quartet, they are fully responsive to the music's possibilities, contrasting it wonderfully with the lyrical opening movement. If any recording can really put these quartets firmly back on the musical map, it is this one. **HS**

Giuseppe Verdi
Nabucco (1842)

Genre | Opera
Conductor | Lamberto Gardelli
Performers | Tito Gobbi (Nabucco), Elena Suliotis (Abigaille)
Year recorded | 1966
Label | Decca 417 407-2 (2 CDs)

Giuseppe Verdi, the greatest Italian composer of the nineteenth century, was born of peasant stock in Le Roncole in 1813. His beginnings were not very promising: while his first opera, *Oberto, conte di San Bonifacio* (1839) met with only moderate success, his second one, *Un giorno di regno* (1840), was an outright failure. Private tragedy struck Verdi at the same time, with his wife and two children all dying within a short spell, and he swore never to compose again. The story has been often told of how La Scala's impresario thrusted the libretto of *Nabucco* into Verdi's pocket, and how the lines of the Hebrew Prisoners' Chorus ("Va pensiero sull'ali dorate") caught the composer's eye and then fired his imagination.

The biblical subject of the Hebrew captivity in Babylon under Nebuchadnezar (Nabucco)—who was struck with madness by God as punishment, and, restored to sanity, acknowledged God's might and let His people go— inspired Verdi to compose an opera that became a runaway success from its first performance. The aforementioned chorus regularly had to be encored, and eventually became an unofficial hymn for Italy. The opera's love interest between Nabucco's daughter and a young Hebrew, also loved by the intriguer Abigaille, provides additional tension in this typically Verdian conflict of power between church and state on one side and father and daughter on the other.

The classic recording features the great singing actor Tito Gobbi, slightly past his prime but almost painfully expressive, and the Callas sound-alike Elena Suliotis. It still packs a tremendous punch, with the Viennese forces sounding quite Italian under Lamberto Gardelli. **CMS**

Robert Schumann
Piano Quintet (1842)

Genre | Chamber
Performers | Martha Argerich (piano), Dora Schwarzberg,
Lucy Hall (violins), Nobuko Imai (viola), Mischa Maisky (cello)
Year recorded | 1994
Label | EMI 5 55484 2 (2 CDs)

The piano quintet was one of the great innovations of nineteenth-century chamber music, offering brilliant opportunities for the pianist in particular. In some hands it could virtually become a chamber-sized concerto. Schumann's Quintet is the earliest of note in the medium. He completed it in just over a fortnight, beginning on September 25, 1842, and finishing by October 12. The best performances convey that white-heat intensity at which the work was composed. Schumann was a manic depressive, alternating periods of extreme productivity with times when he sank into listless depression, and if any piece of Schumann could be said to exemplify the "up" side of his character, it is the marvelously life-affirming outpouring of the first movement of his Quintet.

Any performance involving the charismatic Argentinian pianist Martha Argerich is always bound to be a high-octane event, but doubly so when she is captured live, as here, in a concert from 1994. The joyous opening Allegro brillante contrasts dramatically with the march-like second movement that opens with a weary tread that in turn gives way to a quiet, serene melody, which gradually warms the emotional temperature until a more violent outburst once again drags the music down to the bleakest depths.

It takes musicians with a real mutual understanding, and trust in one another, to keep up with Schumann's mercurial mood-swings in this movement, but Argerich and her string players are superlative, as they are in the crazily driven scherzo and the energized, confident finale. The audience is raptly quiet throughout the performance, no doubt as mesmerized as anyone hearing this disc. **HS**

Mikhail Glinka
Ruslan and Lyudmila (1842)

Genre | Opera
Conductor/Performers | Valery Gergiev; Mikhail Kit,
Anna Netrebko, Vladimir Ognovenko, Larissa Diadkova
Year recorded | 1995
Label | Philips 446 746-2 (3 CDs)

Mikhail Glinka (1804–57) is regarded as the founder of the Russian "national" school. Such accolades are not always meaningful but in this case there are sound reasons for offering such a pedestal to the composer of the operas *A Life for the Tsar* and *Ruslan and Lyudmila*.

A Life for the Tsar (1836) moved the Russian music scene—hitherto notable only for liturgical music, folksong, and domination by external musical influences—onto an altogether higher plane: Glinka's orchestrations were new and freshly imaginative, and the music even made use of recurrent themes in ways that anticipated Wagner's "total art work" system of Leitmotivs (leading motives). The 1842 opera *Ruslan and Lyudmila* is based on a poem by Pushkin: the fairytale plot revolves around the attempts of Ruslan and other suitors to rescue his fiancée Lyudmila from the clutches of a dwarf with a long, magic beard. The score—something of a stylistic hodgepodge—incorporated many new musical ideas: lyrical phrasing of a distinctively Russian character; unusual harmonies reflecting the supernatural aspects of the story; the inclusion of Asian themes, contributing to an atmosphere of fantasy; and exotic choruses and dances, including waltzes.

This live recording of a performance at the Mariinsky Theater in St. Petersburg finds music director Valery Gergiev as briskly commanding as ever. He is well served by seasoned company stars: Galina Gorchakova, Larissa Diadkova, Gennadi Bezzubenkov, Vladimir Ognovenko and the rest make their fantastical characters real; and there is a chance to enjoy Anna Netrebko as a charming Lyudmila, recorded just as her international career took off. **GK**

Gaetano Donizetti | Don Pasquale (1843)

Genre | Opera
Conductor/Performers | Riccardo Muti;
Sesto Bruscantini, Mirella Freni, Leo Nucci, Gösta Winbergh
Year recorded | 1982
Label | EMI 0777 7 47068 2 7 (2 CDs)

By the 1840s Gaetano Donizetti had conquered Europe. Milan, Vienna, and London all clamored for new works, but it was in Paris that the composer really added a fortune to his fame. In September 1842 the manager of the Théâtre des Italiens in Paris begged Donizetti to write him an opera for a quartet of the most celebrated singers of the day, all of whom were under contract to the house. The result was *Don Pasquale*, one of the last of the opera buffa written in the first half of the nineteenth century and one of the greatest, too, with a diamond-bright score composed in little more than two weeks and a plot that ticks like clockwork. Donizetti wrote no greater comedy than the accelerating climax to Act 2 as the young widow Norina, disguised as a demure convent girl, becomes the wife from hell once she has been married off to Don Pasquale. And yet for all the fun as Norina dupes the decrepit Pasquale and wins the love of Ernesto, the nephew he had hoped to disinherit, there is a touch of melancholy in the work—a kind of shiver as the summer sun sets.

On Riccardo Muti's recording, Sesto Bruscantini's baritone Pasquale is sufficiently well differentiated from Leo Nucci's Malatesta—they are caramel and dark chocolate. Mirella Freni is a delectable Norina, wonderfully knowing, but innocent too and all done with an impeccable coloratura. But it is Gösta Winbergh as Ernesto who almost steals the recording—a light lyric tenor who is sweet and plaintive in his Act 1 aria as he thinks his hopes of winning Norina have been shipwrecked. Here and elsewhere Muti, quite as much as Winbergh, finds the dying fall that runs through Donizetti's last comic masterpiece. **CC**

> *"[Maestro Donizetti] will dash you off a long duet in an hour and, what's more, it will be beautiful."*

Giovanni Ruffini

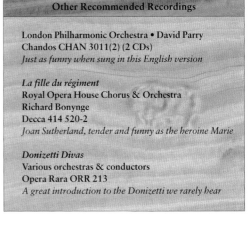

Other Recommended Recordings

London Philharmonic Orchestra • David Parry
Chandos CHAN 3011(2) (2 CDs)
Just as funny when sung in this English version

La fille du régiment
Royal Opera House Chorus & Orchestra
Richard Bonynge
Decca 414 520-2
Joan Sutherland, tender and funny as the heroine Marie

Donizetti Divas
Various orchestras & conductors
Opera Rara ORR 213
A great introduction to the Donizetti we rarely hear

Riccardo Muti, one of the key conductors of Italian opera. ➔

Felix Mendelssohn | Violin Concerto in E minor (1844)

Genre | Concerto
Performers/Conductor | Viktoria Mullova (violin),
Academy of St. Martin in the Fields; Neville Marriner
Year recorded | 1990
Label | Philips 432 077-2

Much of Mendelssohn's greatness lay in his ability to balance the imperatives of Classicism and Romanticism, and his mature Violin Concerto is a breathtaking example of his mastery. Its first stroke of genius is to do away with the usual opening orchestral tutti: after just one and a half measures of "accompaniment," the soloist glides in with one of the most insinuating melodies in the concerto repertoire. The concerto is also played without a break: the first two movements are linked by a little bassoon passage and there is a delightful bridge from the slow movement to the finale, which is in the composer's "fairy" style.

The concerto demands, but does not often get, absolute perfection of tone and technique from the soloist, along with the ability to touch the heart in just a few notes—nothing is overstated in this work. Viktoria Mullova, like her teacher Leonid Kogan, is able to play with the utmost virtuosity without ever making a point of doing so. This quality is especially important in the finale, which some players—notably Jascha Heifetz—rush off its feet. Mullova is fleet enough and light enough to catch the gossamer aspects of the music but also manages to pick out the more serious phrases. At every turn she is seconded by the seasoned, skillful conducting of Neville Marriner.

The disc also includes the youthful D minor Concerto, a nice bonus when it is so well played. Of course there are myriad excellent performances of the E minor work. Nathan Milstein always had a special feeling for it; and such players as Fritz Kreisler, Joseph Szigeti, Mischa Elman, and Yehudi Menuhin always seemed to get more out of the serious moments than their colleagues, while not quite competing in the finale. Mullova herself has made a second recording, without managing to trump this one. **TP**

> *"I feel ashamed of inaccuracies, of failing to achieve the musical levels I set myself."*
>
> **Viktoria Mullova**

Other Recommended Recordings

Yehudi Menuhin, Philharmonia Orchestra
Efrem Kurtz
EMI 7243 5 66958 2 5
A classic performance that still sounds amazingly fresh

Joseph Szigeti, London Philharmonic Orchestra
Thomas Beecham
Naxos 8.110948
A historic 1930s recording, superbly remastered

Nathan Milstein, Vienna Philharmonic Orchestra
Claudio Abbado
DG 419 067-2
Milstein's last version, showing undiminished mastery

Hector Berlioz | Le carnaval romain (1844)

Genre | Orchestral
Conductor | Colin Davis
Performers | Dresden Staatskapelle
Year recorded | 1999
Label | RCA 09026 68790 2

Arranged from parts of the initially unsuccessful opera *Benvenuto Cellini* (1834–37) and first performed in February 1844, Berlioz's overture *Le carnaval romain* (*The Roman Carnival*) is one of his most brilliant orchestral showpieces. Berlioz himself recognized its value, and often used it as a sort of calling card on his concert tours abroad. He wrote at a time when the orchestra was rapidly expanding both in size and in scope, and he exploited new possibilities to the full, becoming renowned for the often startling originality of his orchestration.

Deft, brilliant orchestration is certainly an important part of this overture. Indeed, in a work that begins with a reminiscence of the opera's haunting love scenes between Benvenuto and Teresa and continues with a vivid, swirling, meticulously scored and picturesque allegro, Berlioz is at his unrivaled, breathtaking best.

It is a relatively short piece, and so it inevitably comes coupled, sometimes with other overtures by Berlioz, quite often, as it happens, with the *Symphonie fantastique*, and sometimes with various other works. Two accounts in what is a fairly crowded market seem outstanding in curiously contrasting ways. Mariss Jansons and the Concertgebouw Orchestra, on an EMI disc that pairs the piece with the *Symphonie fantastique*, is as always admirably clear-sighted, never sensational for the sake of it, and may prove too sober for some. But Colin Davis's brilliant performance with the Dresden Staatskapelle on RCA—this is one of those discs where *Le carnaval romain* sits alongside Berlioz's other overtures—hits exactly the right spot. Davis has long been a champion of Berlioz's music, and his flair and understanding are both unmistakable. **SP**

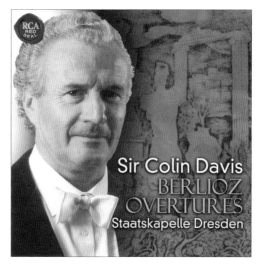

> *"Unhappy composers! Learn to conduct yourselves . . . for conductors are the most dangerous of interpreters."*

Hector Berlioz, *Memoirs*

Other Recommended Recordings

Royal Concertgebouw Orchestra • Mariss Jansons
EMI 7243 5 85041 2 5
Cool, maybe a bit reserved for some tastes, but clarity rules

London Symphony Orchestra • André Previn
EMI 7243 5 73338 2 5 (2 CDs)
Previn and the London Symphony Orchestra in the heyday of their partnership

Royal Philharmonic Orchestra • Thomas Beecham
Sony SMK 89807
An important reminder of the charismatic expertise in this music—then unfashionable—of Thomas Beecham

Frédéric Chopin | Piano Sonata no. 3 in B minor (1844)

Genre | Instrumental
Instrument | Piano
Performer | Dinu Lipatti
Year recorded | 1947
Label | EMI 7243 5 67567 2 4 (2 CDs)

Chopin may have been more renowned for his miniatures than his larger-scale works but the Third Sonata is among the greatest piano works of the nineteenth century, combining drama and extreme virtuosity with a deep vein of soulful lyricism, and as such it is hugely challenging. Many pianists fall into the trap of becoming overly self-conscious in conveying the work's rhetoric.

Not in the case of the great Romanian pianist Dinu Lipatti, however, who simply gets on and plays it—to staggering effect. The fact that this recording was made back in 1947 is of no import—the music making is as vivid as if he had gone into the studio last week. These days Lipatti is often remembered above all as a great poet of the piano, someone who could turn a percussive instrument into the most lyrical medium imaginable. It is a rare gift. But even rarer was his ability to combine that poetry with an awesome and apparently effortless technique. All the more tragic, then, that he died of leukemia at the age of thirty-three—even younger than Chopin himself.

Lipatti manages the pacing of this tricky work perfectly, and the results are unfailingly spontaneous-sounding. The scherzo second movement trickles like quicksilver, miraculously light and even. The slow movement, an outpouring of glorious melody, gleams under Lipatti's fingers, and he has a remarkable way of pointing out subtleties in the music that you have never heard before. His finale is all coiled power but he also allows himself the odd moment of jaunty phrasing to leven the seriousness. You always feel with Lipatti that he lets the music speak for itself—it is brilliant but also utterly disciplined. The result is a performance that moves and astounds and reveals something fresh every time you return to it. **HS**

> *"Why must you have so much talent and I so little? Is this justice on earth?"*
>
> Clara Haskil, herself a great pianist, writes jokingly in a letter to Dinu Lipatti

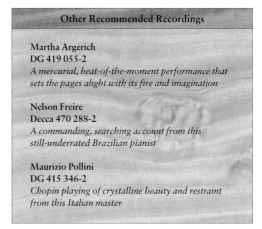

Other Recommended Recordings

Martha Argerich
DG 419 055-2
A mercurial, heat-of-the-moment performance that sets the pages alight with its fire and imagination

Nelson Freire
Decca 470 288-2
A commanding, searching account from this still-underrated Brazilian pianist

Maurizio Pollini
DG 415 346-2
Chopin playing of crystalline beauty and restraint from this Italian master

Dinu Lipatti's recorded piano performances are cherished today. ➤

Robert Schumann
Piano Concerto (1845)

Genre | Concerto
Performers | Sviatoslav Richter,
Warsaw National Philharmonic Orchestra
Year recorded | 1958
Label | DG 447 440-2

"I know that I cannot compose a concerto for virtuosos," Robert Schumann wrote to Clara Wieck, a virtuoso pianist and his wife-to-be. "I have to find a different way." That was in 1839. It ended up taking some six years for him to find that way. The first step came in 1841 with a Piano Concerto (known as *Fantasy*) for piano and orchestra, but Schumann shelved the score, and did not return to it until 1845. Picking it up again, though, he made quick progress. Within two months he had revised the *Fantasy* and added two contrasting yet complementary movements: a svelte, graceful intermezzo and a rollicking rondo finale.

Schumann's "different way" was an overt eschewal of the virtuoso flash normally associated with the genre. Or, to put it another way, there is far more poetry than prose in it. Not that the concerto is easy to play (it is not) but its challenges have more to do with the pianist's musicianship than his or her technical chops. The orchestration is delicate, almost like chamber music at times, as the pianist and individual orchestra members engage in a profound, sometimes playful, often passionate conversation.

Sviatoslav Richter captures the essential intimacy of Schumann's concerto without neglecting its grander gestures. His reading of the first movement is among the most volatile on disc, in fact, making the most of the music's sudden mood shifts. He plays the intermezzo with tender sincerity, and in passages of the otherwise zesty finale, he uncovers an ethereal delicacy that has eluded other pianists. Witold Rowicki and his Polish orchestra provide rhythmically secure support and the unusually characterful woodwind playing is a special delight. **AFC**

Richard Wagner
Tannhäuser (1845, *rev.* 1861)

Genre | Opera
Conductor | Daniel Barenboim
Performers | Peter Seiffert, Waltraud Meier
Year recorded | 2001
Label | Teldec 8573 88064-2 (3 CDs)

In its essentials, *Tannhäuser* is concerned with the rival claims of sensual and spiritual love—the former personified by the love goddess Venus, the latter by Elisabeth, the niece of the Landgrave. At the famous song contest (based on a real historical event), Tannhäuser shocks the assembled company by hymning the praises of Venus and only narrowly escapes summary execution. Filled with remorse, on account of his betrayal of Elisabeth, he joins a pilgrimage to Rome. The Pope refuses to absolve him, but Elisabeth struggles successfully with Venus for his soul, albeit at the cost of her life.

There is much memorable music in *Tannhäuser*, not only the well-known "Pilgrims' Chorus" and Wolfram's "Hymn to the Evening Star," but also two beautiful numbers for Elisabeth: her joyous greeting to the Hall of Song in the Wartburg and her third-act prayer.

The work exists in two versions: Dresden, as Wagner originally wrote it, and Paris, as he revised it for performance in the French capital in 1861. The latter version features some voluptuous music for Venus, written in the mature style Wagner had arrived at after composing *Tristan und Isolde*.

Barenboim cleaves primarily to the Dresden version, but with a Parisian interpolation in the Venusberg scene. Peter Seiffert, in the title role, succeeds in conveying the character's bravado and tortured conscience, while Waltraud Meier, one of the finest Wagner singers of her time, captures marvelously the complexity of Venus. René Pape is a splendid Landgrave, while Jane Eaglen is a no-nonsense Elisabeth. **BM**

Felix Mendelssohn
Elijah (1846)

Genre | Oratorio
Conductor/Performers | Paul Daniel;
Bryn Terfel, Renée Fleming, Patricia Bardon
Year recorded | 1996
Label | Decca 455 688-2 (2CDs)

Toward the end of his comparatively short but musically frenetic life, Mendelssohn received a commission from the Birmingham Festival Committee for a new work for its 1846 event. The score that resulted—*Elijah*—would come to be regarded in some quarters as his greatest. Composing initially to a German libretto, Mendelssohn engaged William Bartholomew to provide the English translation. Mendelssohn rehearsed the work in London, before conveying the performers to Birmingham by special train for the premiere, which boasted 271 singers and 125 instrumentalists.

The oratorio tells the story of the fiery prophet Elijah who holds to the worship of the ancient Hebrew deity, Yahweh—the one true God—in the face of King Ahab's promulgation of the heathen cult of Baal. Its success stems from Mendelssohn's ability to cover a wide emotional compass for soloists and chorus: fire and brimstone, tenderness and compassion, the earthly and the divine.

This recording is indispensable because of the Welsh baritone Bryn Terfel's total command of the title role. Without being over-operatic, from the opening declamation, "As God the Lord of Israel liveth," Terfel sets the pulses racing with an edge-of-the-seat dramatic characterization. Renée Fleming, Patricia Bardon, and John Mark Ainsley provide no mean competition to the veteran accounts—the sumptuous Decca sound, the youthful-sounding Edinburgh chorus's clean attack, and Paul Daniel's conducting of a period-instrument orchestra offer sufficient advantage in musical detail and emotional energy to make this set unbeatable. **GK**

Robert Schumann
Symphony no. 2 (1846)

Genre | Orchestral
Conductor | David Zinman
Performers | Zürich Tonhalle Orchestra
Year recorded | 2003
Label | Arte Nova 72372 10792 5

Schumann began writing his Symphony no. 2 in 1845 while convalescing from one of his many nervous breakdowns. Perhaps composing helped him to escape his mental anguish, for he later wrote that by the time he had reached the finale he had begun to feel more like his usual self, and that when the symphony was finished he felt "much better." This journey from darkness to light comes through in the music, and accounts for its emotional power.

The opening is dominated by trumpet calls, a sound that Schumann said had haunted him during his illness. And, indeed, the entire first movement is restless in character, its rhythms tense and obsessively repetitive. What is most remarkable, though, is the deep vein of lyricism that runs through it, binding the breathless phrases into cogent, articulate paragraphs. The scherzo is a kind of perpetual-motion machine—a flurry of frantic scales and arpeggios that puts the string sections of even the greatest orchestras through their paces. It is the slow movement, however, that is the symphony's molten core, its melody reaching in aching arcs accompanied by a relentless heartbeat-like throbbing. The finale is not without its obsessive qualities or troubled moments, yet it is suffused with joy, too—and in the radiant coda we feel the struggle has been won.

David Zinman's recording casts off the heavy Brahmsian cloak that hangs over most modern performances, revealing the full power of Schumann's most personal symphonic work. Tempi are uncommonly urgent (based on Schumann's own metronome markings) and combined with the sinewy sound and daring virtuosity of the Zürich orchestra generate enormous excitement. **AFC**

Robert Schumann | Piano Trios (1847–51)

Genre | Chamber
Performer | Beaux Arts Trio: Menahem Pressler (piano),
Isidore Cohen (violin), Bernard Greenhouse (cello)
Year recorded | 1971
Label | Philips 456 323-2 (2 CDs)

Schumann had hailed his friend Mendelssohn's Trio in D minor as "the master trio of the age," and chose the key for his own first trio some years later. It shares the extreme turbulence of Mendelssohn's trio, and plunges headlong into a surging seven-bar melody. This First Trio (1847) belonged to a time of "gloomy moods" for the composer, though it is no slough of despond, but a dynamic, searing journey of discovery. Schumann and his wife Clara had been studying counterpoint intensely at this time, and the results can be heard in the intricate, imitative part-writing.

The bold, major key opening of the Second Trio (also 1847) "makes a friendlier and more immediate impression" according to Schumann. Gorgeous song-like melody in the slow movement cascades down, while the piano part rises in steps below, a typical example of Schumann's gift for structural and harmonic tension. In this movement the listener apparently eavesdrops on an intimate conversation between the players: Schumann, the master of Lieder, had a gift for transforming melody into human expression.

His last trio (1851) has all but fallen out of the repertoire, its subtleties dismissed as compositional weaknesses. It is certainly exposing for players, particularly in its dream-like slow movement, where the strings lose themselves in improvisatory musing. "It is original," wrote Clara, "and increasingly passionate, especially the scherzo, which carries one along with it into the wildest depths."

The Beaux Arts Trio, at the peak of its form, reveals just how large a canvas Schumann was painting on in these chamber works: big-boned performances, yes, but with the emotional directness, and the requisite fluidity for this most mercurial of composers; the double CD set contains other important chamber works, too. **HW**

> *"I believe music to be the ideal language of the soul."*
>
> Robert Schumann

Other Recommended Recordings

Florestan Trio
Hyperion CDA 67063, 67175
A lighter, subtler approach, refined and richly imagined

Piano Trio no. 1
Henryk Szeryng, Pierre Fournier, Arthur Rubinstein
RCA 09026 63076-2
A classic account of the First Trio by three legends

Schumann: Violin Sonatas 1–3
Isabelle Faust (violin) Silke Avenhaus (piano)
CPO 999 597-2
Written in the same period as the last piano trio, these febrile, heartfelt works receive ideal performances

Robert Schumann, painted by an unknown artist. ➲

Giuseppe Verdi | Macbeth (1847, *rev.* 1865)

Genre | Opera
Conductor/Performers | Claudio Abbado;
Piero Cappuccilli, Shirley Verrett, La Scala Chorus & Orchestra
Year recorded | 1976
Label | DG 449 732-2 (2 CDs)

Verdi, who had long been familiar with Shakespeare's works (in an Italian prose translation), chose a Shakespearean drama for his tenth opera. From the beginning he saw it as something different from the usual melodrama of the time. The score contains more indications regarding vocal color than any other of his works. Verdi complained that a certain soprano's voice was "too beautiful" to do justice to the part of Lady Macbeth, who in his opinion "should not sing at all," and he famously kept rehearsing the duet between the two protagonists until shortly before curtain time, to get the inflections he was looking for (he regarded this duet as one of the opera's two main pillars, along with the somnambulism scene, which he also rehearsed for months on end).

Eighteen years after the first performances in Florence, Verdi refurbished the piece for the Paris Opéra. Apart from adding the obligatory ballet, he revised some numbers and rewrote others completely. This is the version usually heard today. While the new numbers are undoubtedly more refined than the ones they replaced, for that very reason they stand out from the rest, especially Lady Macbeth's "La luce langue," which Verdi substituted for a particularly brash *cabaletta*. There is thus a point in returning to the composer's first thoughts, as the BBC has shown with a 1979 recording of the 1847 *Macbeth* now available on CD.

However, most conductors opt for the revised score, cutting as a rule the ballet and sometimes adding Macbeth's death scene from the first version. This latter practice goes against Verdi's express wishes, but makes good theater, as can be heard in Abbado's recording, made in the studio after a successful run at La Scala, Milan, and thus having the best of both worlds. **CMS**

> "... *to say that I do not know, understand and feel Shachespeare [sic] – no, by God, no!*"
>
> Giuseppe Verdi

Other Recommended Recordings

Macbeth (1847 version)
BBC Concert Orchestra • John Matheson
Opera Rara ORCV 301 (2 CDs)
A convincing case for Verdi's original thoughts

Macbeth
Berlin Deutsche Oper Chorus • Giuseppe Sinopoli
DVD: Arthaus 100 141
An expressionistic reading of the 1865 text

Giovanna d'Arco
London Symphony Orchestra • James Levine
EMI 0777 7 63226 2 9 (2 CDs)
Verdi's first brush with great drama, strongly cast

Shirley Verrett in her dressing room at the New York Met, 1973. ❯

Charles-Valentin Alkan
Grande sonate "Les quatres âges" (1848)

Genre | Instrumental
Instrument | Piano
Performer | Marc-André Hamelin
Year recorded | 1994
Label | Hyperion CDA 20794

Charles-Valentin Alkan (1814–89) is one of the most peculiar and underrated composers to have emerged from mid-nineteenth-century Paris. A child prodigy, he made his pianistic debut at twelve; through his twenties he taught and performed in Paris, counting Chopin, Liszt, and Victor Hugo among his friends. He was, however, a character of extremes, and his Jewish background and faith were problematic amid prejudiced Parisian society; moreover, he disliked performing and became increasingly reclusive.

Most of Alkan's works are for piano. He sets challenges so excessive that only a few pianists can bring them off with total success. The *Grande sonate* "Les quatres âges" displays him at his most original. It traces the four ages of man, starting with a riotous scherzo ("20 ans"). The work's heart is the second movement, "30 ans, Quasi-Faust," with themes representing Faust, the Devil and Faust's beloved Marguerite. "40 ans, un ménage heureux" shows tranquil domesticity, but the last movement, "50 ans, Prométhée enchaîné" evokes fearsome existential torment; the end is anything but triumphant. And such was the fate of the work: publicity surrounding its publication suffered in the climate following the 1848 revolution. It went unreviewed and probably unperformed for more than a century.

The Québecois virtuoso Marc-André Hamelin is widely acclaimed as the ideal Alkan interpreter. His immensely intelligent playing maintains tremendous clarity and sensitive coloration even at the music's densest moments, while the technical heights are simply phenomenal. **JD**

Johann Strauss the Elder
Radetzky March (1848)

Genre | Orchestral
Conductor/Performers | Willi Boskovsky;
Vienna Philharmonic Orchestra
Year recorded | 1979
Label | Decca 468 489-2

Johann Strauss the Elder was the founder of a musical dynasty which included his sons Johann Jr., Josef, and Eduard. While pursuing an apprenticeship as a bookbinder, he took private lessons in violin and viola; music took over his life—he worked his way up through various orchestras before founding his own band in 1825, feeding its repertoire with his own work. Strauss and his music, which cut across social divisions, became the toast of Vienna and international success followed. Though his son Johann Jr. admired his father's music, there was open rivalry; Strauss the Elder's appointment by Emperor Ferdinand I as "Director of Music for the Royal Court Balls" did not prevent his reputation eventually being eclipsed by that of his son.

Strauss the Elder's best-known works are the waltz, *Echoes of the Rhein Lorelei*, and the *Radetzky March*, composed in honor of an Austrian Field Marshal. At the march's first performance, the army officers who heard it clapped along to the music's strong beat; audiences everywhere still find such participation irresistible, especially at the Vienna Philharmonic's annual New Year's Day Concert in the Vienna Musikverein.

Among the most memorable of these on disc is the 1979 event, presided over by Willi Boskovsky (1909–91), concertmaster of the Vienna Philharmonic from 1939 to 1971. Boskovsky's name is indelibly associated with Viennese music; here, his program includes Strauss the Elder's *Lorelei Waltz*, and Johann Jr.'s *Wine, Women, and Song*, the *Pizzicato Polka*, and the *Blue Danube*. **GK**

Franz Liszt
Hungarian Rhapsodies
(1848–53 & 1882–85)

Genre | Instrumental
Instrument | Piano
Performer | Georges Cziffra
Years recorded | 1972–75
Label | EMI 7243 5 75374 2 1 (2 CDs)

A neat combination of national exoticism (for their folk and folk-like borrowings), musical rhapsodizing—in keeping with the improvising gypsy bands—and fiendish technical display, Liszt's nineteen *Hungarian Rhapsodies* are a high-point of the composer's vast piano repertoire. Nos. 2, 6, and 12 remain the most popular, along with the demonic whirlwind of the "Rákóczy" March (no. 15).

The rhapsodies stem from earlier collections by Liszt (published as *Hungarian Melodies* and *Hungarian Rhapsodies*), in which the composer—having lived in Western Europe for thirty years—sought to celebrate the music of his homeland. The fact that the gypsy music he heard and borrowed was nearer to art music than true folk, or "peasant," music only mildy detracts from the sincere sentiment behind his homage. When the confection is on a lavish and audaciously ornamented scale such as this, one can hardly quibble over authenticity.

Given the virtuosity demanded by the cascades of octaves, rapid hand-crossings, multiple voices, and almost overbearing decoration, it is no surprise that Liszt became a performing legend in his own time, rumored like his violinist counterpart Paganini to have sold his soul to the devil, and stirring up hysteria among audiences.

Hungarian-born Georges Cziffra demonstrates unfailing power and precision in this collection of the complete rhapsodies. With an instinctive sensitivity to melodic coloring and a natural improvisatory feel, Cziffra proves he has few serious rivals in this repertoire. **EB**

Richard Wagner
Lohengrin
(1848)

Genre | Opera
Conductor/Performers | Claudio Abbado;
Siegfried Jerusalem, Cheryl Studer
Years recorded | 1991–92
Label | DG 437 808-2 (3 CDs)

The last of the great German Romantic operas Wagner wrote before his *Ring* cycle, *Lohengrin* occupies a special place in the canon. It has an abundance of melody, ravishingly scored harmonies and self-contained numbers that are popular outside the opera house. It is also the only work of Wagner's to end in unmitigated tragedy, the reason being that Lohengrin was conceived not only as a divine savior but as a metaphysical phenomenon whose contact with human nature could only end in disaster.

The story features the knight of the Grail, who mysteriously appears to champion a damsel in distress, Elsa by name. Elsa cannot refrain from asking the one thing her champion warned her not to ask: who is he and where does he come from? Lohengrin is forced, as a result, to return to Monsalvat, never to see Elsa again. To portray Elsa, nevertheless, as an over-inquisitive woman is to miss the point. Rather the question she asks is the key question: Elsa was seen by Wagner as the woman of the future.

Claudio Abbado conjures the mystical realm of the Grail and always shows great sensitivity for the work's lyricism, integrating the spheres of private intimacy and public clamor. Siegfried Jerusalem, in the title role, is similarly able to switch from mystical introspection (his narration really sounds like an evocation of a distant world rather than a mere set-piece) to forthright expressions of loyalty, love, or anger. Cheryl Studer's tender, passionate Elsa is as intelligently sung as any on record, while Waltraud Meier's blood-chilling Ortrud makes a formidable enemy. **BM**

Robert Schumann
Concertstück for Four Horns (1849)

Genre | Concerto
Performers/Conductor | American Horn Quartet; Dariusz Wiśniewski
Year recorded | 2003
Label | Naxos 8.557747

The horn is arguably the quintessential instrument of the Romantic era. Its ringing yet mellow tone evokes images of rolling hills, rustling woodlands, and the thrill of the hunt. Schumann taps into all of these qualities in his *Concertstück for Four Horns*, composed in Dresden in 1849. His interest in writing a major work for horns may have been sparked by an encounter with the music of Richard Wagner (another Dresden resident) as Wagner was among the first to make effective use of the valve-horn—a recently improved version of the instrument that allowed for far greater agility and opened up exciting new avenues of expressive possibility.

The virtuoso requirements of the solo parts remain daunting even today. At the end of the first movement, for example, the lead horn is required to leap fearlessly into the stratosphere. But beyond the visceral excitement created, the solo writing is ingenious, offering plenty of textural variety. At times the quartet plays as a unit, as in the exhilarating opening fanfare, yet just as often the players engage in a finely detailed contrapuntal dialogue. Schumann also expanded the instrument's lyrical capabilities, and the central "Romanze" movement is among his most hauntingly original creations.

The members of the American Horn Quartet play Schumann's *Concertstück* for all its worth yet manage not to blow away the orchestra sitting behind them—and a good thing, too, since the Sinfonia Varsovia matches the soloists in both spit and polish. **AFC**

Robert Schumann
Fantasiestücke, op. 73 (1849)

Genre | Chamber
Performers | Steven Isserlis (cello), Christoph Eschenbach (piano)
Year recorded | 1996
Label | RCA 09026 68800 2

Schumann originally wrote his three *Fantasiestücke* (Fantasy Pieces) for the clarinet, but was happy for them to be performed on the cello, viola, or violin. Voiced by the clarinet, these rhapsodic, spirited narratives are limpid and lyrical; the cello adds heft and depth.

The three pieces have no titles but their marked tempi and expression tell us much about the nervous, excitable, emotional world they depict. The first, "Zart und mit Ausdruck" (delicately, with expression), opens with a wonderfully elegant, expansive melody that gives way to more insistent, chromatic questioning phrases.

The second movement, "Lebhaft, leicht" (briskly, lightly), begins with gracious arabesques, until mischievous rising triplets hint at a playful game. It is here that a cellist needs exceptionally controlled, subtle bowing and a deft, well-nigh effortless turn of phrase.

The third part, "Rasch und mit feuer" (impetuous, with fire), bursts into existence in a storm of sixteenth notes, which explode into martial clarion calls. Tension builds in the rippling middle section in the minor, rich in harmonic sequences, before a return to the explosive opening theme.

These miniatures are so rich harmonically and in their quicksilver changes of mood that something new can be found on whichever instrument they are played. Great musicians, too, are needed to unpick the subtleties of Schumann's piano writing, and Steven Isserlis and Christoph Eschenbach rise most successfully to the combined challenge in an account of spontaneous poetry. **HW**

Otto Nicolai
The Merry Wives of Windsor (1849)

Genre | Opera
Conductor/Performers | Robert Heger;
Gottlob Frick, Fritz Wunderlich, Edith Mathis
Year recorded | 1963
Label | EMI 0777 7 69348 2 2 (2 CDs)

Despite—or perhaps because of—the solid German musical education Otto Nicolai received as a boy, he never became the prodigy his demanding father hoped for. He did sing the part of Jesus in Bach's *St. Matthew Passion*, but it was a visit to the Sistine Chapel that awakened his interest in Italian music and he traveled to various Italian cities in the hope of a contract to write an opera. He was at first unsuccessful, but by 1841 he had written four Italian operas and when he finally came to write the German masterpiece for which he is remembered, *Die lustigen Weiber von Windsor*—based on the Shakespeare play—the Italian influence remained strong.

The Italianate qualities are most evident in Nicolai's penchant for vocal decoration and in the nature of much of his melodic material. However, his handling of the comic situations is masterly and it is precisely the integration of Italian and German aspects that makes the opera the unique and attractive work it is.

The veteran conductor Robert Heger was nearly eighty when this recording was made, and although tempi are sometimes on the leisurely side, the comic timing is superbly judged and Heger allows his cast to project their characters as realistically as they would on the stage. Gottlob Frick's Falstaff is not inappropriately outsized, and is richly characterized. Fritz Wunderlich is wonderfully lyrical as Fenton, and Edith Mathis (as Anna) is the best of the female cast members—the merry wives themselves are not, it has to be said, the strongest aspect of the set. **BM**

Robert Schumann
Symphony no. 3, "Rhenish" (1850)

Genre | Orchestral
Conductor | Daniel Barenboim
Performer | Berlin Staatskapelle
Year recorded | 2003
Label | Teldec 2564 61179-2

Schumann once wrote: "Anything that happens in the world affects me . . . and finds an outlet in my music." In September 1850, he moved from Dresden to Düsseldorf, a bustling town on the River Rhine, and the change of scene indeed proved inspirational. Within three months he had composed his Cello Concerto and the grandest of his four symphonies. He titled the symphony "Rhenish," and its five movements give musical expression to some of the sights and sounds of his new homeland.

The spirit of the mighty Rhine courses through the entire score. In the opening movement, the melody surges forth in long-breathed phrases that carry the listener along on the musical equivalent of a whitewater adventure. Schumann called the second movement a scherzo, though it is more like a genial dance of lapping waves. The swell is gentler and more graceful in the intermezzo-like third movement—perhaps accompanying a romantic stroll by the shore. Next, we are transported downriver to Cologne and into its famous cathedral, whose Gothic splendor is evoked in darkly solemn music. The rhythmically bustling yet lyrical finale returns us to open air and warm sunshine.

Daniel Barenboim's Teldec recording stands out for its dynamism and flexibility; he knows just when to push ahead and when to linger over a detail, and his interpretation overflows with beguiling ideas. The Berlin Staatskapelle digs into the score with great gusto, conveying the feeling of a supercharged live performance—and it is aided by the immediacy of the recorded sound. **AFC**

Robert Schumann | Cello Concerto in A minor (1850)

Genre | Concerto
Performers/Conductor | Steven Isserlis (cello),
Deutsche Kammerphilharmonie; Christoph Eschenbach
Year recorded | 1996
Label | RCA 09026 68800 2

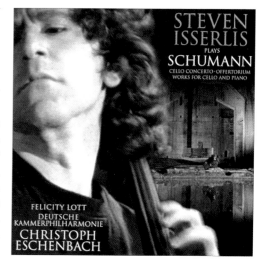

Schumann penned his Cello Concerto in 1850, in a rush of inspiration on his arrival in Düsseldorf, where he took up the post of music director. It was a short period of stability before the onset of his final illness, and, tragically, he never heard the piece performed. The cellist for whom it was written found the last movement too difficult and complained of a lack of long melodies. After Schumann's death it languished, until the Spanish cellist Pablo Casals breathed passionate life into it in the 1900s. Even then critics belittled it as a botched work by a failing composer and cuts were often made in the last movement. They were deaf, said Casals, to "one of the greatest works one can hear; from beginning to end the music is sublime."

Schumann never intended it to be a heroic concerto, originally titling it *Konzertstück*, as his more intimate arrangement for cello and string quartet acknowledges. Instead he gives voice to wave upon wave of the most personal, poetic Romantic expression. The two sides of Schumann's nature, famously identified by him as Eusebius (thoughtful, philosophical) and Florestan (impetuous, extrovert), are clearly struggling with each other in the first movement, the cello crying out against the orchestra's fierce triplets. The second movement achieves a still pathos of radiant beauty, its falling fifth interval evoking his beloved wife Clara, while the tempestuous final movement catches fire in a display of dazzling, playful virtuosity.

In our time, it is Steven Isserlis who has most closely identified with Schumann's musical temperament: he brings an exquisitely supple and sensitive approach to the music's sinuous line. He has eliminated the portentous rhetorical emptiness that has for long dogged performances and gives the music wings. **HW**

> *"This work takes us deeper into the inner life of its creator than virtually any other concerto."*
>
> Steven Isserlis

Other Recommended Recordings

Mstislav Rostropovich, London Symphony Orchestra
Benjamin Britten • BBC Legends BBCL 4110-2
Rostropovich's fire balanced by Britten's refinement

Pablo Casals, Prades Festival Orchestra
Eugene Ormandy • Sony SMK 58993
A flawed recording from 1953, but an important testament to the heroic reading of this work by one its most significant interpreters

Christophe Coin, Orchestre des Champs-Elysées
Philippe Herreweghe
Harmonia Mundi HMC 901598
A fascinating, lively period-instrument performance

Steven Isserlis is a devoted advocate of Schumann's late music. ➔

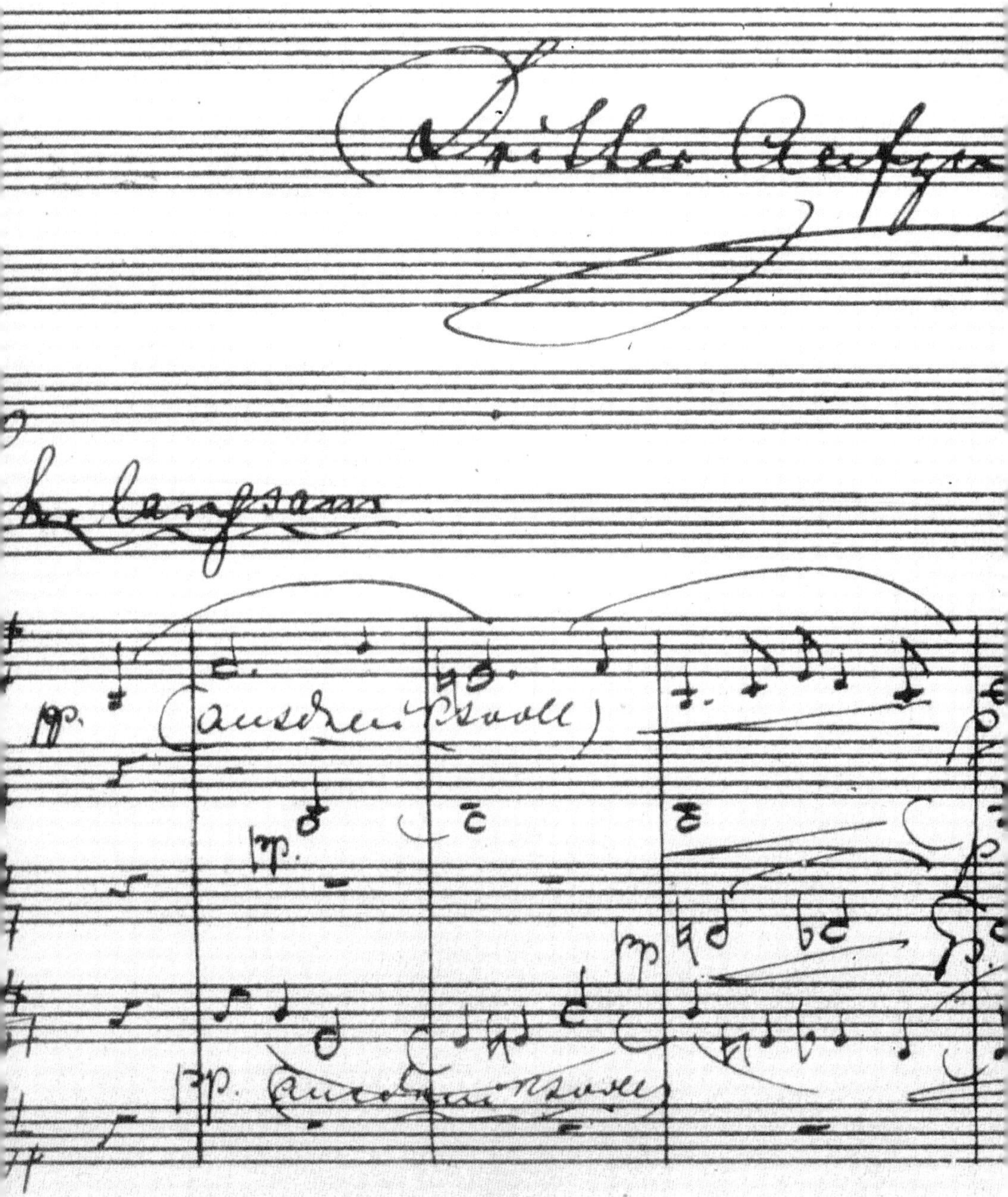
Dritter Aufzug
langsam
pp. (ausdrucksvoll)
pp
pp. (ausdrucksvoll)

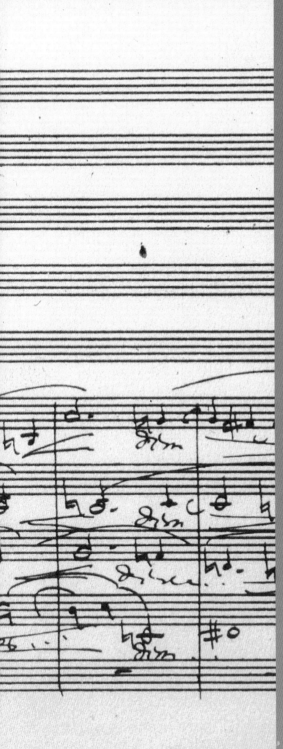

Austro-German music polarized in the second half of the nineteenth century between the advocates of Brahms and the followers of Wagner, between music as pure music and music as the conduit of drama. Wagner's great music dramas epitomize this period of High Romanticism. Nationalist schools of writing developed in places such as Bohemia (Dvorak, Smetana), Russia (Borodin, Mussorgsky) and Norway (Grieg), while in Italy the operatic tradition reached its peak in the works of Verdi.

1851–1900

Franz Liszt | Transcendental Studies (1851)

Genre | Instrumental
Instrument | Piano
Performer | Claudio Arrau
Years recorded | 1974–76
Label | Philips 456 339-2 (2 CDs)

Franz Liszt was the greatest and most influential piano virtuoso of the nineteenth century, renowned for what struck audiences as superhuman technical wizardry and showmanship in such rousing crowd-pleasers as the *Second Hungarian Rhapsody* and the *Grand galop chromatique*. Fame and success in this arena was nevertheless something of a double-edged sword, and from early in his career Liszt aspired to apply this virtuosity in works that had more serious artistic aspirations. The twelve *Études d'exécution transcendante* (Transcendental Studies as we know them today) are the third versions of pieces that had originated in 1826, when Liszt was fifteen. All but two bear poetic titles, and in order to do them justice Liszt does not confine himself to exploring a single technical difficulty in any individual étude. The challenge of these works is thus less didactic and pianistic than expressive, although the desired expression cannot be obtained without phenomenal and all-embracing technical mastery that can do equal justice to the filigree of "Feux follets," the leaps in "Mazeppa," the tremolos of "Chasse-neige," and heavy chordal writing in "Wilde Jagd."

These études are staples of the repertoire for virtuoso pianists, but Claudio Arrau's playing of them is in a class apart. Arrau, a student of Liszt's pupil Martin Krause, employed a technique that produced uncommonly rich tone, and his conviction that Liszt was an important composer assured that he sought out expressive meanings in these études. Made after he had turned seventy, Arrau's recording conveys a remarkable combination of depth and brilliance—both his stunningly athletic "Mazeppa" and reflectively paced "Feux follets" show his ability to find evocative music amid a welter of notes. **DB**

> *"In the* Transcendental *Studies . . . Liszt touched heights of virtuosity unknown before his time."*
>
> Claudio Arrau

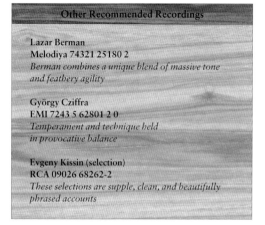

Other Recommended Recordings

Lazar Berman
Melodiya 74321 25180 2
Berman combines a unique blend of massive tone and feathery agility

György Cziffra
EMI 7243 5 62801 2 0
Temperament and technique held in provocative balance

Evgeny Kissin (selection)
RCA 09026 68262-2
These selections are supple, clean, and beautifully phrased accounts

Claudio Arrau, whose teacher was himself taught by Liszt. ➔

A Kurt Boxhorn cordialmente
Claudio Arrau
Buenos Aires 1946.

Giuseppe Verdi
Rigoletto (1851)

Genre | Opera
Conductor/Performers | Carlo Maria Giulini; Piero Cappuccilli, Plácido Domingo
Year recorded | 1979
Label | DG 457 753-2 (2 CDs)

During most of his career Verdi had problems with censorship, but they were seldom so great as in the case of *Rigoletto*, based on Victor Hugo's drama *Le roi s'amuse*. The censor in Austrian-occupied Venice objected to showing on stage a dissolute king of France seducing his hunchback court jester's daughter, who later sacrifices her life to save him from a murderer hired by her father, and whose corpse is dragged about the stage on a sack before being recognized by the latter. It took a great deal of negotiating before a consensus was reached, which implied among other things that the French king became an anonymous Duke of Mantua.

Verdi considered the character of the jester Rigoletto to be of Shakespearean depth, a cruel, mocking demon who is also a loving father. Also Shakespearean is the juxtaposition of comic or grotesque elements, like the first scene with the courtiers, or the hired killer's black humor. In this opera, Verdi took precious little consideration of the operatic world's conventions. There is just one traditionally built aria, the plot advancing rather in a chain of duets. With *Rigoletto*, he closed the door on his so-called "galley years," during which he had churned out numerous operas in close succession. From then on, he would pick and choose his subjects at his own leisure, and take his time to find the appropriate color (*tinta*, as he called it) for each of them.

Rigoletto's own dark *tinta* is magisterially realized by Carlo Maria Giulini in his Viennese recording, with Piero Cappuccilli inimitably spinning out Rigoletto's long melodies, Ileana Cotrubaş an appropriately frail Gilda, and Plácido Domingo in seductively golden voice as the Duke. **CMS**

Robert Schumann
Symphony no. 4 (1851)

Genre | Orchestral
Conductor | Wolfgang Sawallisch
Performers | Dresden Staatskapelle
Year recorded | 1972
Label | EMI 7243 5 67771 2 5

Schumann is celebrated first and foremost as a master miniaturist—the composer of sets of brilliant and beautiful piano pieces and songs. Yet he also rethought the large-scale structures, exploring novel ways to organize his extraordinary musical ideas while retaining the basic shape of Classical forms. Nowhere was he more inventive with form than in his Symphony no. 4 in D minor.

Among the symphony's most notable innovations is the way the movements are connected so that they flow together virtually without pause. Indeed, the shimmering, mysterious transition between the scherzo and finale is a stunning *coup de théâtre* and indicative of the symphony's overall dramatic character. There are also important thematic connections. The first movement's expectantly tense introduction reappears in the second movement "Romanze," for example, its expressive effect changed significantly by its new context. Soon thereafter, the Romanze's central segment returns as the trio section of the third movement scherzo. And so on. Many nineteenth-century composers experimented with melodically integrated structures but few succeeded as Schumann does with such intricate interleaving.

Wolfgang Sawallisch's recording of the Fourth Symphony is the crowning achievement of his renowned 1972 cycle. The outer movements are thrillingly propulsive yet the conductor never forgets the music's essential lyricism. And, throughout, phrases are bound together into large arcs that clarify the music's narrative structure. Best of all, perhaps, Sawallisch draws playing of exceptional transparency from the Dresden Staatskapelle. **AFC**

Johannes Brahms
Lieder (1851–96)

Genre | Vocal
Performer | Dietrich Fischer-Dieskau (baritone), with various accompanists
Years recorded | 1964–73
Label | EMI 0777 7 64820 2 6 (6 CDs)

The nineteenth century was a supremely literary age, and Brahms, as an avid reader, responded to lyric poetry from all periods throughout his life: his 213 songs span more than forty years of his composing career.

Schumann was Brahms's great friend and champion; but the songs of Schubert were his greater inspiration. Unlike Schubert, however, Brahms seldom set "great" poetry. Remembering, perhaps, Goethe's cold-shouldering of Schubert's offerings, Brahms was convinced that great poetry could not be elevated further by musical setting. Rather, he favored the work of minor poets and the huge body of European folksong so widely read and published in his day. Brahms, above all his contemporaries and predecessors—and uniquely before Bartók—achieved that fusion of what Walt Whitman was to call "heart-song and art-song," in which the directness of folk music was transmuted into the sophistication of high art.

Dietrich Fischer-Dieskau's complete recordings reveal with the highest intelligence and perception the ways in which Brahms metamorphosed into song many techniques from both his instrumental music and from folksong itself, expanding tonality in a way that was to influence Schoenberg. Fischer-Dieskau's several accompanists—Gerald Moore, Wolfgang Sawallisch, Daniel Barenboim, and Sviatoslav Richter—set the songs into fascinatingly shifting perspectives. These performances also capture that Brahmsian ambivalence between revealing and concealing his own emotional responses—something that may have contributed to the uneasy response to his songs felt by the likes of Tchaikovsky, Wolf, and Britten. **HF**

Giuseppe Verdi
Il trovatore (1853)

Genre | Opera
Conductor/Performers | Zubin Mehta; Plácido Domingo, Leontyne Price
Year recorded | 1969
Label | RCA 74321 39504 2 (2 CDs)

Verdi, who liked to keep abreast of the latest plays as potential operatic subjects, was much taken by Antonio García Gutiérrez's *El trovador*, which he put forward for production in Rome. The typically convoluted plot involves a gypsy, Azucena, who wants to take revenge on Count Luna, who had her mother burned at the stake as a witch; she abducts one of the Count's sons in order to burn him as well, but kills her own child by mistake, after which she brings up the abducted boy. Both of Luna's children grow up to be rivals in love and politics, and in the last scene the new Count unwittingly orders his brother's execution. The opera ends with three of the main characters dead, and the fourth one wishing he were likewise.

In spite (or because) of this truculent plot, *Il trovatore* became Verdi's biggest success to date. There are lighter moments like the gypsies' "Anvil Chorus," and vocal heavy guns like the tenor's "Di quella pira," with its traditional (if unwritten) high Cs. However, the predominant mood is nocturnal (most of the action takes place at night), with large parts of the score marked *piano* or *pianissimo*. Taking a step back from *Rigoletto*, Verdi again writes arias in the traditional form (cantabile and cabaletta), with the notable exception of Azucena—like Rigoletto an ambivalent character—who has the most original music in the score.

Zubin Mehta conducted the first absolutely uncut *Trovatore*. Sparks fly with Plácido Domingo (as Manrico) and Sherrill Milnes (as Luna) in their first complete opera recording. Leontyne Price sings seductively as the object of their desire, and Fiorenza Cossotto is in best voice as the crazied gypsy. **CMS**

Giuseppe Verdi | La traviata (1853)

Genre | Opera
Conductor/Performers | Riccardo Muti; Renata Scotto,
Alfredo Kraus, Renato Bruson, Philharmonia Orchestra
Year recorded | 1982
Label | EMI 0777 7 47538 8 3 (2 CDs)

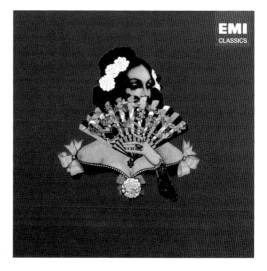

Alphonsine Du Plessis, the real-life *dame aux camélias* who inspired the play of the same name by Alexandre Dumas, died in 1847. When Verdi set her story to music, he was thus tackling a contemporary subject, and he intended to have the opera performed in modern dress. The Venetian censorship changed all that; the story of a couple (she being a former courtesan) living in sin might have made more than one member of the audience uncomfortable.

Violetta, the "woman gone astray" of the title, nobly renounces Alfredo Germont, the one true love of her life, when his father tells her that their relationship has brought shame upon his family. After a final reconciliation, she succumbs to that most Romantic of illnesses, tuberculosis. For the first performance, early eighteenth-century period costume had to be used; distance in time made the whole thing more palatable. However, the opera was a complete flop and only caught on at a later revival.

Verdi, who was at the time himself "living in sin" with the singer Giuseppina Strepponi, later to become his second wife, felt an obvious identification with his subject. He wrote for Violetta some of his most heartfelt music, making her one of opera's most complex characters. She must live through a wide range of emotions, from the self-deluding, forced joy of the first act through the abnegation of the second, to the desperation and brief hope of the final one.

Maria Callas was perhaps the most complete Violetta of recorded history, but was unfortunately let down by indifferent recording quality or less than average partners, and her performances were also cruelly cut. Riccardo Muti's complete recording has a superb protagonist in Renata Scotto, with those great stylists Alfredo Kraus and Renato Bruson as the Germonts. **CMS**

> "La traviata ... is the same
> as the one performed last
> year .... Then it was a fiasco;
> now it has created a furore."

Giuseppe Verdi, May 26, 1856

Other Recommended Recordings

Lisbon São Carlos Theater Chorus & Orchestra
Franco Ghione
EMI 7243 5 56330 2 6 (2 CDs)
Callas's celebrated "Lisbon Traviata"

Bavarian State Opera Chorus & Orchestra
Carlos Kleiber
DG 459 039-2 (2 CDs)
Despite a stellar cast, here the orchestra stands out

National Philharmonic Orchestra
Richard Bonynge
Decca 430 491-2 (2 CDs)
Old-style vocal happening with Sutherland and Pavarotti

Italian soprano Renata Scotto, pictured on stage in 1979.

Franz Liszt | Piano Sonata in B minor (1853)

Genre | Instrumental
Instrument | Piano
Performer | Sviatoslav Richter
Year recorded | 1965
Label | Palexa CD-0537

This sonata is Liszt's most ambitious piano work, written in Weimar after he had given up his career as a touring virtuoso. In it, Liszt cultivates a technique known as thematic transformation, in which several musical themes are stated at the beginning of the work and then subsequently appear in a variety of guises, with parameters such as tempo, register, mode, dynamic level, and articulation all subject to modification and manipulation. No one can definitively establish a program for this sonata, but its "subject" seems especially elevated, ranging from diabolical vehemence to beatific tranquillity. This sonata is also famous for superimposing single-movement sonata form onto a multimovement sonata structure. Liszt's original conception included a grand ending, but he rejected this in favor of a return of the quiet music from the sonata's central section, thereby achieving a masterstroke of poetic understatement.

Liszt's avoidance of a bombastic ending provides the key to Sviatoslav Richter's best recording of the sonata, made at a live performance in Carnegie Hall in 1965—unfortunately in less than ideal sound that nevertheless brilliantly conveys the scope of the pianist's dynamic range. Richter plays with remarkably febrile energy in places and molds the vast score into an astonishingly supple, dramatic, and palpably organic entity. But it is his way with the quiet passages of the middle section and the coda that makes this disc one of the most beautiful and unforgettable recordings ever made. The vast vistas of profound serenity that unfold here find their equal only in late Beethoven. **DB**

Robert Schumann | Scenen aus Goethes Faust (1853)

Genre | Vocal
Conductor/Performers | Benjamin Britten; Dietrich Fischer-Dieskau, Elizabeth Harwood
Year recorded | 1972
Label | Decca 476 1548 (2 CDs)

Goethe's *Faust* has inspired many musical settings. Yet while most composers have focused on the play's dramatic elements, Schumann responded more strongly to its poetic and philosophical qualities. He was the first to set the mystical final scene, for example. The work clearly meant a lot to him, too. He began composing it in 1844, following an arduous journey to Russia, and worked at it on and off for nearly a decade. The third and final section of the piece was finished first and performed in 1849 as part of the celebrations marking the centenary of Goethe's birth. Schumann continued adding scenes after that, gradually filling in the first and second parts. Alas, he never heard the work in its entirety. It was first presented in its final form in 1862, six years after his death.

Schumann was not an instinctive dramatist, and his music lacks the theatrical element one finds in, say, Berlioz's *La damnation de Faust*. Instead, the glory of Schumann's *Faust Scenes* lies in their songlike qualities. As in the best of his Lieder, he reveals the characters' inner lives, fleshing out their thoughts and emotions. Even though we are given only selected scenes from Goethe's play, Gretchen and Faust, in particular, appear as more full, rounded characters than in many other nineteenth-century musical adaptations.

It took a master songwriter like Benjamin Britten to uncover the inspired lyricism and profundity of Schumann's neglected masterpiece—and his recording is still the most satisfying on all counts. Dietrich Fischer-Dieskau is an ideal Faust: intelligent, arrogant, and hypersensitive, and his colleagues are equally invested in their roles. **AFC**

Hector Berlioz
La damnation de Faust (1854)

Genre | Choral
Conductor/Performers | Colin Davis; Giuseppe Sabbatini, Enkelejda Shkosa
Year recorded | 2000
Label | LSO Live LSO 0008 CD (2 CDs)

Although frequently staged as such, Berlioz's *The damnation of Faust* is not an opera but a concert piece. Berlioz actually called it a "dramatic legend." Its origins are found in the *Huit scènes de Faust*, which Berlioz composed in 1829, using Gerard de Nerval's French translation of Goethe's play, but withdrew soon afterward, aware of certain technical inadequacies. He returned to the subject in the 1840s, however, integrating his earlier material into the much larger-scale design we know today. A journalist, Almire Gandonierre, was commissioned to write the new portions of text, but could not keep up with Berlioz's pace. Berlioz therefore finished that job himself.

When the unpublished score was first performed in 1846, *Faust* failed dismally. Ever the fighter, Berlioz successfully performed sections of the work when he toured Russia and Germany the following year, and by 1854 felt able to revise and publish it. Even so, during his lifetime this vividly dramatic and beautiful piece was performed complete only rarely, and only in Germany and Austria rather than in France. It is ironic, then, that following Berlioz's death *La damnation de Faust* became in France the work by which he was best known at the end of the nineteenth century.

Colin Davis is the supreme Berlioz interpreter, and it is his bargain version on LSO Live that tops the list here. Recorded at public concerts at the Barbican in London in 2000, it has a thrilling, involving immediacy, focusing on the agonizing dilemma presented to Faust. The playing of the London Symphony Orchestra is refined and responsive, and the cast is first-rate. **SP**

Franz Liszt
Les préludes (1854)

Genre | Orchestral
Conductor | Herbert von Karajan
Performers | Berlin Philharmonic Orchestra
Year recorded | 1967
Label | DG 447 415-2

Upon settling in Weimar as a conductor in 1848, Liszt began a period in which he strove to be taken seriously as a composer of orchestral music, and toward this end he developed a new genre that he called the symphonic poem. He eventually wrote twelve such works and they constitute a remarkable body of work that greatly influenced other composers from Wagner to Richard Strauss and beyond. They all bear poetic titles, and indeed the compositional technique known as thematic transformation, which permeates these works, is particularly well suited to elucidating the narrative and programmatic dimension of Liszt's inspiration.

Les préludes is the most frequently performed of Liszt's symphonic poems. It may not be the boldest or most original of the group, but it achieves perhaps the best combination of memorable themes and cogent structure. The music in Liszt's piece originated earlier, but was eventually remade to correspond to a poem by French poet Alphonse de Lamartine, the four main sections of which consider love, destiny, war, and the countryside. Liszt rearranges this order but otherwise follows the mood and structure of the poem faithfully in his own work.

A considerable performance tradition has grown up around *Les préludes* as a result of its popularity with orchestras. Karajan recorded this score after he had absorbed the flamboyance preferred in earlier generations into a more monumental, abstract framework. The resulting performance is spectacular—brilliantly and fervently played, overflowing with character in all corners of the score, and coherent and cumulative in its overall structure. **DB**

Johannes Brahms | Piano Trio no. 1 (1854, *rev.* 1891)

Genre | Chamber
Performers | Beaux Arts Trio: Menahem Pressler (piano),
Isidore Cohen (violin), Bernard Greenhouse (cello)
Year recorded | 1993
Label | Philips 416 838-2

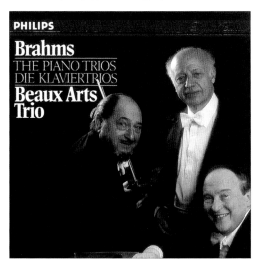

The B major Trio was the first major work Brahms completed after Schumann's madness and attempted suicide, but as originally composed in 1854, it contained miscalculations of structure and content, which irked Brahms as he grew older. In 1891 he issued a radically recomposed version of op. 8, transforming it from a flawed half-masterpiece to a full masterpiece. The original version had a series of half-quotations and allusions that seem to have referred to Brahms's own emotions, caught between veneration for his afflicted patron, Schumann, and growing love for Schumann's wife Clara. These were most patent in the first movement and finale, which in 1891 he rethought. The scherzo and slow movement needed less revision, but the overall result is more properly thought of as Brahms's "last" piano trio rather than his "first."

The first movement begins with the same magnificent first subject tune as in 1854 (one of the most majestic melodic inspirations of Brahms's early years) but thereafter nothing is the same: it is as if Brahms is releasing the dramatic and structural potential in the movement that his twenty-year-old self had merely fumbled at, and the result is magnificently dramatic. The finale is much altered, too, though its harried, feverish B minor main subject performs the role Brahms first allotted to it, creating a movement that is a kind of wild, ghost-ridden ride, inspired by the more spine-chilling side of Romanticism.

The Beaux Arts Trio recorded all the Brahms trios in the LP era and this second recording is all the more satisfying for the experience and authority the artists bring to the music. Their playing catches the special ardent glow of the melodic invention, and their phrasing and projection of line and rhythm is passionately committed. **MM**

"I was strangely affected by the old-new trio . . . I played on in a transport of delight."

Elisabet von Herzogenberg

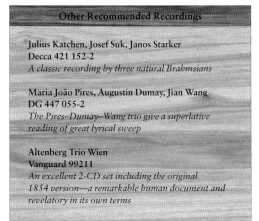

Other Recommended Recordings

Julius Katchen, Josef Suk, Janos Starker
Decca 421 152-2
A classic recording by three natural Brahmsians

Maria João Pires, Augustin Dumay, Jian Wang
DG 447 055-2
The Pires–Dumay–Wang trio give a superlative reading of great lyrical sweep

Altenberg Trio Wien
Vanguard 99211
An excellent 2-CD set including the original 1854 version—a remarkable human document and revelatory in its own terms

The Beaux Arts Trio in its longest-lasting lineup. ➜

Franz Liszt | Piano Concertos nos. 1 & 2 (1856, 1861)

Genre | Concerto
Performer/Conductor | Sviatoslav Richter (piano); Kirill Kondrashin
Year recorded | 1961
Label | Philips 446 200-2

Liszt invented the solo piano recital, but he also wrote music that would permit him to feature his talents against the backdrop of orchestral accompaniment, and his two concertos are the most substantial works of this type. Both were many years in the making but achieved final form when Liszt had developed his technique of thematic transformation, and both begin with a theme or motif that is subjected to countless permutations. Despite this similarity, the opening themes reveal the differences between the two works—whereas the first begins with grandiose gestures in the orchestra that are answered by a brilliant cadenza from the soloist, the second begins sweetly and the pianist's first contributions are garlands of figuration around a restatement of this tender theme. Although both go on to incorporate sections that correspond to separate movements—the most famous of which may be the "scherzo" of the first, which puts the triangle to work—they demonstrate Liszt's tendency to roll several movements into one continuous sequence.

Sviatoslav Richter's classic recording was made around the time of his first London performances of them, and wonderful though the BBC Legends recordings of those live accounts are, the commercial Philips recording adds another dimension. In the studio, the piano is more forwardly balanced, yet surprisingly mellow in tone and conveys more nuance in delicate passages while offering cataclysmic excitement in climactic moments. Kirill Kondrashin summons epic sweep from the London Symphony Orchestra, while Richter makes even brilliant playing sound expressive, thoughtful, and poetic. **DB**

Hector Berlioz | Les nuits d'été (1856)

Genre | Vocal
Conductor/Performers | John Barbirolli; Janet Baker, New Philharmonia Orchestra
Year recorded | 1969
Label | EMI 7243 5 62789 2 9

Berlioz's settings of six poems by Théophile Gautier originally appeared in 1841 in a version for voice and piano; only later did he come to orchestrate them, adding a range of expression that has secured these songs a firm place in the vocal—and orchestral—repertoire.

The songs are bound together by the theme of love. Nos. 1 and 6 project youthful optimism: the first, "Villanelle," listing the simple pleasures available to lovers in spring, and the closing "L'île inconnue" evoking a seafaring voyage to the "unknown island," on whose shores can be found undying love. But in between these the colorings are darker. The gorgeous, reverie-like "Le spectre de la rose" ("The Ghost of the Rose") is the song of a spirit-rose cherishing her fate as her wearer's buttonhole at a ball, though it leads to her death. The darkest song, "Sur les lagunes" ("On the Lagoons") is a doleful lament for a dead lover, while the luminous "Absence" yearns for a distant one. "Au cimetière" ("At the Cemetery") recalls the musical strains of a dove overlooking a tombstone, "a tune of morbid sweetness/both charming and deathly."

Janet Baker's 1969 recording with John Barbirolli and the New Philharmonia Orchestra remains a classic. There is an unmistakeable dramatic core to Baker's voice, though fluency and transparency never escape her. The climaxes are lovingly prepared and powerfully driven, while her twilit quality in "Absence" and "Au cimetière" contrasts with the sorrowful depths of "Sur les lagunes." Barbirolli's accompaniments are supple, carefully balanced, and evocative, facilitating an effortless natural cohesion between voice and orchestra. **EB**

César Franck | Six Pièces, opp. 16–21 (1856–64)

Genre | Instrumental
Instrument | 1885 Cavaillé-Coll organ
Performer | Marie-Claire Alain
Year recorded | 1995
Label | Erato 0630 12706-2 (2 CDs)

The Belgian-born composer César Franck (1822–90) settled in Paris, becoming organist of St. Clotilde in 1858. His improvisations attracted a wide audience, among them an admiring Franz Liszt, but during his lifetime (including a distinguished period as professor of organ at the Paris Conservatoire) his compositions at first commanded little attention or respect; latterly he was recognized as a pioneering genius whose music paved the way for Debussy, Ravel, and a host of later French composers.

Franck built a corpus of organ music that is central to the repertoire for the instrument. The most important pieces are the final works—the *Trois chorals*—and the group of *Six Pièces*, opp. 16–21, comprising the "Fantaisie" in C major, the "Grande pièce symphonique," the "Prélude, fugue et variation," a "Pastorale," a "Prière," and "Final." These pieces exploited the tonal palette of the new organs that were being built by the most famous French organ builder of all time—Aristide Cavaillé-Coll. As Marie-Claire Alain herself remarks, "Franck laid the foundations for a new style of French organ music that broke free from contemporary fashions and treated the organ as an orchestral instrument in a series of vast tonal frescoes."

Alain, doyenne of contemporary French organists, re-recorded the repertoire digitally in 1995, on the 1885 Cavaillé-Coll organ of St. Étienne de Caen. This is a reference recording in every way, from the technical command of the playing, the performing style and the tone-colors of the organ, to the booklet notes, written by Alain herself. This collection also includes the *Trois chorals* (1890) and the *Trois Pièces* (1878). **GK**

Giuseppe Verdi | Simon Boccanegra (1857, *rev.* 1881)

Genre | Opera
Conductor/Performers | Claudio Abbado; Piero Cappuccilli, La Scala Chorus
Year recorded | 1977
Label | DG 449 752-2 (2 CDs)

Verdi's fifth opera for Venice, *Simon Boccanegra*, derives—like *Il trovatore*—from a drama by Antonio García Gutiérrez. The plot is similarly complicated: the corsair Simon is elected Doge in fourteenth-century Genoa, only to die poisoned by Paolo, a former ally; the other plot line involves Amelia, Simon's long-lost illegitimate child by the daughter of his political enemy, the patrician Jacopo Fiesco, and her love for Gabriele Adorno, who is also Simon's adversary.

The opera was not a success; as Verdi wrote, it was "a fiasco . . . almost as great as that of *La traviata*." Critics found the music too complicated, and unremittingly dark. Not for the last time, the accusation of "Wagnerism" was hurled at Verdi, and after a couple of revivals the opera disappeared from sight. It was only more than twenty years later that Verdi agreed to revise it.

Apart from a new prelude and some retouches big and small, a completely new scene was conceived, which became the heart of the work. In it, the Doge Boccanegra pleads with Genoa's Senate for peace with Venice, arguing that both cities are part of one and the same country. This speech is set to the most eloquent music Verdi ever wrote for the baritone voice. This, the recognition duet with Amelia, and the last scene make *Simon Boccanegra* into one of Verdi's greatest baritone roles. Piero Cappuccilli's second recording of it, made after performances at La Scala, Milan, has attained classic status. A superb cast makes musical theater of the highest order, and the only possible reason for complaint is that Giorgio Strehler's beautiful production was not filmed. **CMS**

Jacques Offenbach
Orpheus in the Underworld (1858, *rev.* 1874)

Genre | Operetta
Conductor/Performers | Marc Minkowski;
Natalie Dessay, Yann Beuron, Jean-Paul Fouchécourt
Year recorded | 1997
Label | EMI 7243 5 56725 2 0 (2 CDs)

Orphée aux enfers can be said to mark the birth of French satirical operetta and the arrival of the master of the form, Jacques Offenbach. This was also the work that gave the world the best-known tune for the can-can, the "galop infernal" from Act 2. In later life Offenbach expanded his original two acts into four, turning an elegant valise into a grandiloquent cabin trunk.

Orphée aux enfers began as a burlesque that mocked the pretensions of the sacred Comédie-Francaise with party guests robed in togas. It was a daring target in the culturally conservative Second Empire. In its expanded two-act form the operetta also teases that other Neo-Classical monument, Gluck's *Orphée et Eurydice*, which sent opera off in a new direction at the end of the eighteenth century. Offenbach's Eurydice is bored to tears with Orpheus and already looking to fresh pastures and a new shepherd, Pluto in sheep's clothing. It is only Public Opinion that insists on Orpheus demanding the restoration of his conjugal rights from the Olympian Gods, who are busy complaining about the catering and the entertainment. It ends badly with Jupiter, disguised as a fly, deciding to have his own wicked way with Eurydice.

Two acts or four is the choice. Marc Minkowski makes a compelling case for the original two-act 1858 version, and his fine cast just about clinches it. Natalie Dessay is such a nagging wife that it is difficult not to feel sorry for Yann Beuron's sweet-natured Orpheus. Jean-Paul Fouchécourt is a wonderfully oleaginous Pluto in Act 1. The energy is infectious and it is an exact reading of the score right down to the quotations from Gluck's masterpiece. **CC**

> *"It is a great deal more difficult to write piquant, melodious tunes."*

Jacques Offenbach

Other Recommended Recordings

Capitol Toulouse Orchestra
Michel Plasson
EMI 0777 7 49647 2 2
A fine recording of the 1874 four-act version

Le Papillon (complete ballet)
National Philharmonic Orchestra • Richard Bonynge
Decca 476 7220
A delicious account of Offenbach's only ballet

Offenbach Overtures
London Philharmonic Orchestra • Jean Martinon
Decca 476 2757
A classic recording from the mono era

Richard Wagner
Wesendonck Lieder (1858)

Genre | Vocal
Conductor/Performers | Reginald Goodall;
Janet Baker (mezzo-soprano), BBC Symphony Orchestra
Year recorded | 1971
Label | BBC Legends BBCL 4086-2 (2 CDs)

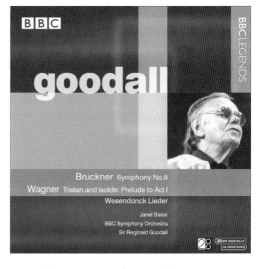

The precise nature of the relationship between Wagner and Mathilde Wesendonck—or rather whether it was consummated—remains one of the most titillating questions facing Wagner scholarship. In general, the evidence suggests that Mathilde acted as his muse and confidante for a short period in the 1850s, but that they did not overstep the bounds of propriety. Mathilde was in any case far more than a mere sex object: she published a sizable body of poetry and drama and unprecedentedly Wagner set five of her poems while working on his own *Tristan und Isolde* in late 1857 and early 1858.

There are in fact close links between the two works, in both philosophical and musical content. The songs are imbued with the ethos of *Tristan*, and two of them ("Im Treibhaus" and "Träume") were actually designated "Studies for Tristan and Isolde." In "Der Engel" the poet envisions an angel coming down to relieve the suffering of the human soul by transporting it to heaven. The "wheel of time" in "Stehe still!" is a reference to the Schopenhauerian/ Buddhist concept of life as an endless round of striving, the only escape lying in denial of the will, and consequent release from the cycle of suffering.

Janet Baker's recording with Reginald Goodall is taken from a memorable live performance at the Royal Festival Hall in London in 1971. Notable in Baker's singing are her habitual radiance of voice and her ability to inhabit the world of the text with rich, subtle coloring of the words. Goodall was one of the great Wagner conductors of his or any time, and his unfailing sensitivity to texture is evident in every bar. **BM**

> *"As long as I breathe,*
> *I shall strive, and that*
> *I owe to you."*

Mathilde Wesendonck to Wagner

Other Recommended Recordings

Waltraud Meier, Paris Orchestra • Daniel Barenboim
Warner 2564 60439-2
Coupled with Mahler's Kindertotenlieder *by the great mezzo-soprano Waltraud Meier*

Cheryl Studer, Dresden Staatskapelle
Giuseppe Sinopoli
DG 439 865-2
Coupled with Strauss's Four Last Songs

Jard van Nes, Northern Sinfonia
Richard Hickox
Chandos CHAN 9354
An exquisitely scored version by Hans Werner Henze

Hector Berlioz
Les troyens (1858)

Genre | Opera
Conductor/Performers | Colin Davis; Ben Heppner, Michelle DeYoung, Petra Lang
Year recorded | 2000
Label | LSO Live LSO 0010 (4 CDs)

Berlioz never saw a complete performance of his 1858 Virgil-inspired opera *The Trojans*. For five years or so after its completion, he tried to secure a performance at the Paris Opera, with which he had always had a tricky relationship, but to no avail. The best he could manage was a staging of the final three acts at the Théâtre Lyrique in 1863, but even that was, after just one performance, subjected to progressive cutting.

Problems with potential publishers meant that the full score was printed only in the late 1880s, and then thanks only to legal action on the part of Berlioz's executors. It was regarded as a behemoth, a work whose scale made it impractical, though there were productions in Germany in the 1890s. In France shortened versions were staged from 1921, but essentially two events in Britain enabled the work to gain its rightful place in the repertoire. Rafael Kubelík conducted a production at the Royal Opera House, Covent Garden, in 1957, and Colin Davis tackled the work at the same theater in 1969, also recording it as part of his Berlioz cycle. That year also saw the issuing of a definitive score, since when the work's reputation has gone from strength to strength.

Davis's mold-breaking 1969 recording is still available, but his second version, made with the London Symphony Orchestra, is now first choice. The cast, including Ben Heppner as Enée, Michelle DeYoung as Didon, and Petra Lang as Cassandre, is stellar, and the fact that the recording is taken from live performances—four of them, in all—means that there is the vital extra measure of tension and excitement in the air. **SP**

Johannes Brahms
Piano Concerto no. 1 (1859)

Genre | Concerto
Performer/Conductor | Nelson Freire; Riccardo Chailly
Year recorded | 2006
Label | Decca 475 7637 (2 CDs)

Brahms's titanic First Piano Concerto went through a real "is it a bird, is it a plane?" phase; originally conceived as a sonata for two pianos, he then orchestrated the first movement, thinking he would turn it into a symphony, before finally arriving at the idea of a piano concerto. That protracted struggle is clearly audible in the music—from the very opening measures it is filled with brooding and darkness. It certainly broke the mold of what people thought a concerto should be about—a work of brilliance rather than profundity, where the soloist was uppermost. Many contemporaries thought it was too serious for its own good, and its exceptional length—some forty-five minutes in most performances—proved an endurance test for the audience at the premiere.

The work has given rise to a wide range of interpretations, from ones that go hell-for-leather in the outer movements to those that spend so long luxuriating in the beauty of the slow movement that they almost draw to a halt. Nelson Freire's reading under the direction of Riccardo Chailly strikes a perfect balance, and the Leipzig Gewandhaus Orchestra lends an almost chamber-music-like clarity to this great score. The first movement is driven but never rushed, with Freire making much of his intimate dialogues with the orchestra. In the finale, there is an almost Mendelssohnian vivacity to this initially gruff dance of victory. And in the slow movement—thought by some commentators to be a homage to his great friend Schumann, who was seriously ill at the time—Freire and Chailly achieve solemnity and beauty without ever becoming ponderous. This is a mighty achievement. **HS**

Charles Gounod
Faust (1859)

Genre | Opera
Conductor/Performers | Fausto Cleva;
Jussi Björling, Cesare Siepi, Dorothy Kirsten
Year recorded | 1950
Label | Naxos 8.111083-85 (3 CDs)

Faust, the fourth of Gounod's twelve operas, had the nineteenth century on both sides of the Atlantic at its feet. A gentleman who seduces a young and innocent girl and does not quite get his comeuppance was very much to contemporary taste, while Marguerite's soul ascending to heaven at the end of the opera watched by a penitent Faust was redemption without the slog of theology or the duty of attending church. In concentrating on the relationship between Faust and Marguerite, Gounod and his librettists Jules Barbier and Michel Carré knew exactly what their audience wanted. As for Méphistophélès, he is less diabolic than a cynical Parisian *flaneur*. Then there was the sheer tunefulness of the opera, a hit for every kind of musical taste, from the "Soldiers' Chorus" to Faust's sweet-toothed "Salut! demeure chaste et pure," with Marguerite's "Jewel Song" as a particularly tasty titbit for canary fanciers.

Long after most of Europe had turned its back on Gounod's opera, the Metropolitan Opera House in New York kept it in the repertoire. So this recording of a live broadcast from the old Met in 1950 has a special kind of authority. It is wonderfully sung, too. Jussi Björling is a thrilling Faust, the top of the voice burnished with gold. And if Dorothy Kirsten is down-to-earth and not so dreamy as Marguerite, then that is all to the good. Cesare Siepi, a Met veteran, is everything you want from a Méphistophélès, dark-toned and knowing. The recording is remarkable for its age, though naturally in mono, and in the pit, the appropriately named Fausto Cleva lets Gounod's score work its magic. This is a properly dramatic reading of an operatic warhorse that sometimes sounds like a thoroughbred. **CC**

Giuseppe Verdi
Un ballo in maschera (1859)

Genre | Opera
Conductor/Performers | Herbert von
Karajan; Plácido Domingo, Leo Nucci
Year recorded | 1989
Label | DG 477 5641 (2 CDs)

Good opera plots seem always to have been at a premium. The historic murder of King Gustavus III of Sweden at a masked ball was taken up by quite a few composers, the most famous ones before Verdi being Daniel Auber (*Gustave III ou Le bal masqué*, 1833) and Saverio Mercadante (*Il reggente*, 1843). Italian censorship was still to be reckoned with, and the murder of a king on a theater stage could not be tolerated. Just as Mercadante had changed the setting to sixteenth-century Scotland, Verdi's Gustavo III had to be turned into Riccardo di Warwick, the English governor of Boston (for some reason these exotic settings were more acceptable than 1792 Sweden).

Otherwise, the libretto follows Eugène Scribe's for Auber quite closely. Riccardo loves Amelia, wife of his secretary Renato, and is reciprocated, although Amelia has never been unfaithful to her husband. Riccardo himself is torn between love and his duty as a friend and a sovereign. Renato, having discovered the affair, instead of revealing a conspiration he has just unveiled, ends up joining it, and it is he who kills Riccardo, who dies absolving everybody.

Just as the libretto was closely modeled on Scribe's, the music follows patterns of French grand opera. The orchestral palette is much more refined than was customary in Italy at the time, and strophic arias abound; of course, soaring melody is not forfeited either.

The most glorious realization of the score's many felicities is surely that of the Vienna Philharmonic under Herbert von Karajan in his last opera recording, strongly cast with Plácido Domingo as the vacillating hero, Gustavo (this version restores the Swedish setting). **CMS**

Richard Wagner | Tristan und Isolde (1859)

Genre | Opera
Conductor/Performers | Wilhelm Furtwängler; Ludwig
Suthaus, Kirsten Flagstad, Dietrich Fischer-Dieskau
Year recorded | 1952
Label | EMI 7243 5 85873 2 6 (4 CDs)

A four-hour orgy of passion, albeit unconsummated, *Tristan und Isolde* is one of the landmarks of Western civilization. Far more than merely a love story, it deals with fundamental questions of human identity and existence. It is also one of the most revolutionary works in musical history, its first chord challenging conventional analysis and its so-called "emancipation of the dissonance" anticipating Schoenberg's abandonment of tonality by half a century.

Tristan, sent by King Mark to Ireland to fetch the Princess Isolde as his queen, himself falls in love with her. Their illicit liaison is interrupted, and Tristan is taken to his castle in France mortally injured. Mark arrives to bless his union with Isolde, but too late. Tristan dies and Isolde, prostrating herself over his body, expires also. On one level the opera is a dramatization of events from Wagner's own life, with himself as Tristan, his muse and lover Mathilde Wesendonck as Isolde and her husband Otto as King Mark. But the work is not merely the ultimate glorification of love: it is also an idealization of love—an evocation of bliss unattainable in this world. The intensity of the lovers' yearning is raised to fever pitch; for unbridled sensuality, philosophical profundity, and full-blooded lyricism there is nothing in the repertoire to match it.

Wilhelm Furtwängler's recording acquired classic status from its first appearance, both because it was the first complete performance on record and on account of its supreme artistic quality. Its chief virtues are Furtwängler's conducting, which combines spontaneity and structural strength, and the Isolde of Kirsten Flagstad. Though other recordings have improved on this one in certain aspects, its iconic status is fully deserved. **BM**

> *"As I have never in my life tasted the true joy of love, I will raise a monument to this loveliest of all dreams."*
>
> Richard Wagner

Other Recommended Recordings

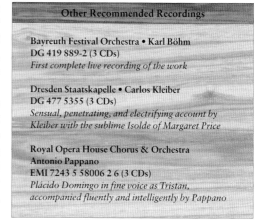

Bayreuth Festival Orchestra • Karl Böhm
DG 419 889-2 (3 CDs)
First complete live recording of the work

Dresden Staatskapelle • Carlos Kleiber
DG 477 5355 (3 CDs)
Sensual, penetrating, and electrifying account by Kleiber with the sublime Isolde of Margaret Price

Royal Opera House Chorus & Orchestra
Antonio Pappano
EMI 7243 5 58006 2 6 (3 CDs)
Plácido Domingo in fine voice as Tristan, accompanied fluently and intelligently by Pappano

Kirsten Flagstad, the greatest Isolde of her day. ➋

To George T. Keating
in remembrance of "Isolde"
and yours sincerely
Kirsten Flagstad
Dec. 1944

Johannes Brahms
String Sextets nos. 1 & 2
(1860, 1865)

Genre | Chamber
Performers | Menuhin, Masters,
Aronowitz, Wallfisch, Gendron, Simpson
Years recorded | 1963–64
Label | EMI 7243 5 74957 2 1

Brahms has been saddled with rather a serious reputation, but there was a side to his personality that was almost as sunny as Schubert's. It can be heard in his two orchestral serenades and also in the pair of serenade-like sextets that he wrote in response to his admiration for a similar work by Spohr. The Second Sextet, a particularly mellifluous piece, which even incorporates a waltz theme in its first movement, appears to reflect his remorse at the way he treated his girlfriend Agathe von Siebold, of Göttingen—the notes AGADH (in German notation) appear just after the waltz theme.

The two finest performances of the sextets belong to the Sony label: a mono version of the B flat from the 1952 Prades Festival with Pablo Casals as first cellist—unforgettable in the one really serious movement, the slow variations—and a glowing Marlboro Festival account of the G major led by Pina Carmirelli, unavailable at present. But most people would surely want to be able to buy both sextets on one disc; and the splendid Menuhin interpretations have already stood the test of time, being sympathetically played and pleasantly recorded.

Yehudi Menuhin was inclined to hog the limelight in his chamber music performances, but on these two occasions he took a much more democratic approach—and with such strong personalities as Robert Masters, Cecil Aronowitz, Ernst Wallfisch, Maurice Gendron, and Derek Simpson as his colleagues, there is no suggestion of the sextets being made into one-star vehicles. **TP**

Pyotr Ilyich Tchaikovsky
Songs
(1860–93)

Genre | Vocal
Performers | Ljuba Kazarnovskaya
(soprano), Ljuba Orfenova (piano)
Years recorded | 1997–99
Label | Naxos 8.554357, 8.554358, 8.555371

Tchaikovsky's 104 songs are still among the least known of all his works, inevitably overshadowed by both his operas and his symphonies. But they were remarkably successful in his own lifetime. Tchaikovsky arrived at very much the right place at the right time as far as Russian song was concerned. Although by the late nineteenth century there was no great Russian song tradition compared with that in France, Germany, or Italy, Mussorgsky, Balakirev, and Borodin had already laid down the foundations of a national school of song writing. Tchaikovsky also took German and Italian song and toyed with it.

Tchaikovsky differed from Mussorgsky in focusing not on individual character studies, but rather on the inner desires of emotionally vulnerable humankind. In choosing his texts, intensity of feeling mattered more to him than literary prowess: few of his songs set the work of truly great Russian poets. In fact, some of his most compelling settings are of folk poetry, and ditties for children.

Because so many of Tchaikovsky's songs remain little known, a complete set of his work in this genre really is a must. At bargain price, and with the indisputable advantage of a native Russian singer, the three Naxos volumes, with accompanying texts in both Russian and English, are exceptionally well programmed. Ljuba Kazarnovskaya's soprano is wide-ranging enough in both register, timbre and character to justify performance by a single voice; and her accompanist, Ljuba Orfenova, is vividly supportive. **HF**

Johannes Brahms
Piano Quartets nos. 1 & 3
(1861, 1874)

Edvard Grieg
Songs
(1861–1905)

Genre | Chamber
Performers | Marc-André Hamelin (piano), Leopold String Trio
Year recorded | 2005
Label | Hyperion CDA 67471/2 (2 CDs)

Genre | Vocal
Performers | Monica Groop (mezzo-soprano), Love Derwinger (piano)
Year recorded | 1993
Label | BIS CD-637

The genesis of Brahms's First Piano Quartet in G minor spans from the turbulent years of the mid-1850s to the more considered Classical stance of Brahms's late twenties. It combines a troubled Romantic vocabulary with a poised, almost symphonic mastery of musical architecture. Yet the finale, with its unbridled gypsy music, displays all the young Brahms's taste for vigorous horseplay. The whole quartet seems continually to strive beyond its chosen medium, toward an orchestral sense of color, scope of expression, and range of development. Marc-André Hamelin and the Leopold String Trio's breakneck tempo in the finale is breathtaking, but this is altogether an absolutely outstanding performance throughout, alive to every nuance of the subtle and complex work.

The origins of Brahms's Third Piano Quartet also go back to the mid-1850s. While he was racked by love for Clara Schumann and as her husband lay incarcerated in a mental institution, Brahms began but could not finish a piano quartet in C sharp minor, and put it away in a drawer. Nearly twenty years later he took up the work afresh and radically revised it in C minor, composing two new movements and destroying the original form.

The same musicians provide one of the most lyrical readings this work has ever had on disc, catching to perfection its youthful ardor recollected in comparative (but only comparative) tranquillity. The rapt playing of the slow movement is especially moving, but their virtuosity in the demonic scherzo is magnificent. **MM**

Grieg's songs were quite simply the best music he ever wrote. He was a natural miniaturist and the song was for him the miniature par excellence. Two outstandingly powerful sources of inspiration were to focus his talent: his love for the soprano Nina Hagerup, as cousin, fiancée, and finally wife; and the golden age of Norwegian lyrical poetry burgeoning around him as he lived and worked.

From native poets such as Henrik Ibsen, Björnstjerne Bjørnson, Aasmund Olavsson Vinje, and Arne Garborg, Grieg could also turn to the poetry of great Danes like Christian Winther and Hans Christian Andersen, who provided inspiration for some of his finest songs.

The inner music of the regional accents lively in every Norwegian fjord, the Landsmål dialect, and the physical energy of the *halling* and *springar* dances all animate Grieg's songwriting and give it the distinctive rhythmic vitality and melodic and harmonic palette that make it instantly recognizable.

The Finnish mezzo-soprano Monica Groop has taken on the responsibility of recording the complete songs, with different accompanists. This first volume, of seven projected discs, was a revelation when it first appeared in 1993. Groop's anthology is significant for its inclusion of some of the early German-language songs, as well as settings of Ibsen, such as the great "A Swan," and, above all, Grieg's vocal masterwork, the mystical and erotic *Haugtussa* cycle about a visionary herd-girl and her relationship with the landscape of southwest Norway. **HF**

Gabriel Fauré | Mélodies (1861–1921)

Genre | Vocal
Performers | Elly Ameling (soprano), Gérard Souzay
(baritone), Dalton Baldwin (piano)
Years recorded | 1970–74
Label | EMI 0777 7 64079 2 0 or Brilliant 92792 (4 CDs)

Fauré wrote his first song, "Le papillon et la fleur," as a
teenaged schoolboy; his teacher, Saint-Saëns, scribbled
a tongue-in-cheek cartoon on the manuscript. This
charming song marked the beginning of an enchantment
with the *mélodie* (French art song) that would last all
Fauré's life. With his exceptional gift for melody, his music's
intimate connection with the subtlety and flow of the
French language and his perfectionism in condensing his
musical ideas, the genre seemed virtually made for him.
Across sixty-odd years, Fauré's songs progressed from
nineteenth-century tonal perspective and Art Nouveau
decorative beauty toward impressionistic symbolism and,
ultimately, the independent path of a twentieth-century
musical visionary.

Fauré set some of the finest poets of his day, starting
with Victor Hugo and progressing through Théophile
Gautier, Leconte de Lisle, Charles Baudelaire, and Paul
Verlaine—the last a particularly happy meeting of artistic
minds. Fauré chose Verlaine's poetry for his most famous,
groundbreaking, and arguably most beautiful song cycle,
La bonne chanson (1892–94). Later, he set poems by the
Belgian symbolist Charles van Lerberghe in two mysterious
and fascinating cycles, *La chanson d'Eve* (1906–10) and *Le
jardin clos* (1914). His final cycle of four songs, the eloquent
and powerful *L'horizon chimérique*, used poems by Jean de
la Ville de Mirmont, tragically killed in World War I.

Soprano Elly Ameling and baritone Gérard Souzay,
sensitively accompanied by Dalton Baldwin, present here
Fauré's complete *mélodies*, including the cycles. Ameling
is a perfect Fauréan soprano, light-toned, precise, tender,
and subtle, while Souzay displays a deep empathy with
Fauré's refinement, elegance, and veiled sensuality. **JD**

FAURÉ
Mélodies
Gérard Souzay • Elly Ameling
Dalton Baldwin

"I adore this collection."

Marcel Proust on Faure's *La bonne chanson*

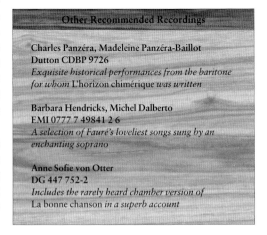

Other Recommended Recordings

**Charles Panzéra, Madeleine Panzéra-Baillot
Dutton CDBP 9726**
*Exquisite historical performances from the baritone
for whom* L'horizon chimérique *was written*

**Barbara Hendricks, Michel Dalberto
EMI 0777 7 49841 2 6**
*A selection of Fauré's loveliest songs sung by an
enchanting soprano*

**Anne Sofie von Otter
DG 447 752-2**
Includes the rarely heard chamber version of
La bonne chanson *in a superb account*

Elly Ameling, the Dutch soprano pictured in 1977. ❯

Franz Liszt
A Faust Symphony
(1861)

Genre | Orchestral
Conductor/Performers | Iván Fischer;
Budapest Festival Orchestra
Year recorded | 1996
Label | Philips 454 460-2

Liszt encouraged the Faustian enterprises of both Berlioz and Wagner, and after settling in Weimar, Goethe's home for many years, Liszt wrote this *Faust Symphony* of his own. Liszt regarded himself as a conflation of Faust and Mephistopheles, cynical yet a genuine seeker. The symphony, Liszt's orchestral masterpiece, is more than an hour in duration. It consists of three movements, which are character portraits of the questing, ardent Faust, the gentle, idealized Gretchen, and the sardonic Mephistopheles, respectively. The themes of each are transformed across the expanse of the work, which additionally incorporates depictions of dramatic events from Goethe's treatment of the legend.

A *Faust Symphony* was performed very infrequently in the nineteenth century and the first half of the twentieth. Its current level of popularity therefore comes at a cost: orchestras do not really have this music in their blood, and it requires skills that are not always those at which modern conductors and orchestras excel to bring it to life. Iván Fischer's recording with the Budapest Festival Orchestra is by far the most convincing realization of the score yet to appear. The challenge of this music is to strike a satisfying balance between vivid characterization and inexorable momentum, and Fischer is nearly the only one to demonstrate that the former quality can feed and enhance the latter. This recording includes the original instrumental conclusion as well as the later (and now standard) choral apotheosis with tenor soloist. **DB**

Henry Vieuxtemps
Violin Concerto no. 5
(1861)

Genre | Concerto
Performer | Jascha Heifetz
Conductor | Malcolm Sargent
Year recorded | 1961
Label | RCA 82876 71622 2

In the same way as the Dutch had a great era of painters, Belgium had a glittering line of violinists, lasting in an unbroken line from Charles de Bériot (1802–70) down to Arthur Grumiaux in the decades after World War I. The second in this royal line was Henry Vieuxtemps (1820–81), who actually had lessons from Bériot in Paris and like him wrote concertos for his instrument. Those by Vieuxtemps have proved to have more staying power, especially the Fourth and Fifth; and this is not so surprising when you consider that he studied composition with Antonín Rejcha.

The tuneful Fifth Concerto is a strange work formally, with a long, dramatic first movement full of virtuosic writing for the violin, a lovely but quite short slow movement and an even shorter finale lasting not much more than a minute. The great Russian-born violinist Jascha Heifetz recorded it twice, both times with Sargent conducting, and his later version has been given the most wonderful facelift in RCA's Living Stereo series. To hear Heifetz's celestial phrasing in the central Adagio is something special; and the couplings on the disc, Bruch's most popular works, are also superbly played.

It must be admitted that, as so often, Heifetz makes little cuts in the tuttis; but they are less injurious here than in other works. It is also worth looking out for his historic version of the better balanced Fourth Concerto from the 1930s, with Barbirolli. For a good modern recording, that by the brilliant Alexander Markov, coupled with the Second and Fourth Concertos, takes a lot of beating. **TP**

Giuseppe Verdi
La forza del destino
(1862, *rev*. 1869)

Genre | Opera
Conductor/Performers | Riccardo Muti;
Mirella Freni, Plácido Domingo
Year recorded | 1986
Label | EMI 0777 7 47485 8 2 (3 CDs)

After *Un ballo in maschera*, Verdi seemed "to have forgotten about music," as his wife put it, until an invitation from the tenor Enrico Tamberlik to write an opera for the Imperial Theater in St. Petersburg tempted him back to work. He chose *La fuerza del sino* by the Spanish playwright the Duke of Rivas. It is a madly romantic plot about Alvaro, scion of the last Incas, in love with Leonora, daughter of the haughty marquis of Calatrava. They are surprised when about to elope, and Alvaro accidentally kills the marquis. They are separated, and Leonora goes to live as a hermit near a monastery. After many adventures, Alvaro becomes a monk and ends up in the same monastery, where he is tracked down by Leonora's brother Carlo. They fight a duel, Carlo is fatally wounded and dies after stabbing Leonora. Alvaro hurls himself from a cliff, cursing himself and the whole human race.

After less than wholly successful premieres in Russia and Spain, Verdi revived the score of *La forza del destino* for the first La Scala performances, substituting a (slightly) more conciliatory ending, in which the dying Leonora exhorts Alvaro to resignation and prayer. He also omitted a big scene for Alvaro with chorus. Among other changes, he substituted the well-loved overture for the previous short prelude. In this form, the opera slowly won over audiences all over the world, although in Italy it is supposed to have the "jinx." Nevertheless, the recording from La Scala lets sparks fly, with Plácido Domingo and Giorgio Zancanaro in golden voice. **CMS**

Henryk Wieniawski
Violin Concerto no. 2
(1862)

Genre | Concerto
Performer | Gil Shaham
Conductor | Lawrence Foster
Year recorded | 1991
Label | DG 431 815-2

The untimely death of Henryk Wieniawski (1835–1880) was much deplored at the time, as this great Polish violinist was popular with both the public and his colleagues. With hindsight, it can be seen that his passing also deprived the world of a valuable teacher. Raised from an early age in the Franco-Belgian school of violin playing, Wieniawski apparently played with immense refinement but brought much of his Polish heritage to his fiery musicianship; and we can tell a great deal about him from studying his brilliant compositions. Of his two violin concertos, the first is a little long but the second, in D minor, is better balanced in its proportions and unfailingly tuneful.

At present, a few classic recordings are unavailable but even if they were still around, the version by Gil Shaham would give them a run for their money. He is a marvelous violinist with a beautiful tone—essential in this work—and although there is nothing of the show-off in his stage demeanor, he can match any of his rivals technically and compete with an orchestra in full flight. He is most eloquent in the central "Romance" of the concerto, which follows the first movement without a break. He also has the skill for the virtuoso finale in gypsy style, putting plenty of character into it without ever straining his technique. In a work that relies on sound for much of its effect, it is also good to have a modern digital recording. The main coupling is the youthful First Concerto, which Shaham plays brilliantly; but the disc also includes Wieniawski's haunting *Légende* and Sarasate's exciting *Zigeunerweisen*. **TP**

Johannes Brahms
Piano Quintet in F minor (1862, *rev.* 1864)

Genre | Chamber
Performers | Arthur Rubinstein (piano), Guarnieri Quartet:
Arnold Steinhardt, John Dalley, Michael Tree, Peter Wiley
Year recorded | 1966
Label | RCA 09026 63067 2

The Piano Quintet is a pinnacle of Brahms's chamber music output. A "bigger brother" to the piano trios and quartets he had already written, it brings his attempt to unify the dynamic tonal language of Beethoven with a Schubertian lyrical melodic impulse to its most intense expression so far. The result is a work full of tension and shadowed by minor-key conflict, magnificent in utterance but often somber or thunderous in its moods.

The first movement is both concentrated and redolent of *Sturm und Drang*, ending in a mood that suggests grim determination to outlast sorrow and attain tranquillity. Some of that tranquil mood persists into the slow movement, a calm ternary structure in A flat major. The dynamic percussive third movement is one of Brahms's greatest scherzos, disclosing a kinship to Beethoven's Fifth Symphony in its demonic, obsessive rhythmic figures. The finale opens with a slow introduction: numb, ghostly string figures grope their way toward the light, before the main movement arrives with a sturdy cello tune of Classical cut and Haydn-like aplomb. The second subject, though, is more Romantic, with a kind of fevered lyric pathos. It is this darker strain that eventually prevails, and the tragic mood is confirmed in the final headlong rush of the presto coda.

Arthur Rubinstein's performance with the Guarnieri Quartet was the product of a long-held desire to record the piece, and has an electric sense of occasion. The mixture of dramatic and lyrical elements is held in a majestic equilibrium that few performers achieve, and the slow movement produces some of the most intensely expressive Brahms playing on disc. **MM**

> "*... a masterpiece of chamber music ... not seen since Schubert's death.*"

Joseph Joachim

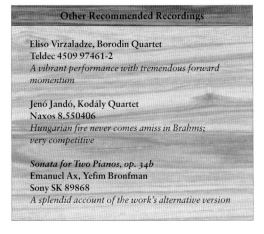

Other Recommended Recordings

Eliso Virzaladze, Borodin Quartet
Teldec 4509 97461-2
A vibrant performance with tremendous forward momentum

Jenó Jandó, Kodály Quartet
Naxos 8.550406
Hungarian fire never comes amiss in Brahms; very competitive

Sonata for Two Pianos, op. 34b
Emanuel Ax, Yefim Bronfman
Sony SK 89868
A splendid account of the work's alternative version

Camille Saint-Saëns
Introduction and Rondo capriccioso (1863)

Genre | Concerto
Performers | Itzhak Perlman (violin), Paris Orchestra
Conductor | Jean Martinon
Year recorded | 1974
Label | EMI 0724 5 62599 2 8

Not very much of Saint-Saëns's music is played regularly now, but this brilliant, excellently written piece for violin and orchestra has held its own in the recording catalogue. It is difficult to hear such pieces in the concert hall today, simply because they fit awkwardly into the usual scheme of things. In the nineteenth century, when concert programs contained more works, it was useful for a soloist to have an exciting piece to play in the second half, having delivered a major concerto before the interval.

Saint-Saëns had a great admiration for the Spanish virtuoso Pablo de Sarasate and wrote most of his violin music for this delightful but perhaps rather shallow artist. Like many Spanish musicians, Sarasate had put the final polish on his technique in Paris; and so he knew the French style well. Most of the great violinists have recorded the *Introduction and Rondo capriccioso*, but Itzhak Perlman's version continues to hold its own against all comers. It helps that he is partnered by a top French orchestra, under a sympathetic French conductor and composer.

Perlman himself has made a further recording of the piece, with the New York Philharmonic under his friend Zubin Mehta, but this is a case of lightning not striking twice. The earlier version is better balanced, more pleasantly recorded, and more buoyant and spontaneous. At the time, Perlman was probably the finest violinist in the world, with an excellent command of differing styles. His tone is consistently beautiful here and never too heavy. This famous recording has been issued in a multitude of couplings, but is usually found with other French pieces taped at the same sessions and equally well done. **TP**

> "*It is possible to be as much of a musician as Saint-Saëns; it is impossible to be more of one!*"

Franz Liszt

Other Recommended Recordings

Jascha Heifetz, RCA Victor Symphony Orchestra
William Steinberg
RCA 09026 61753 2
The old master gives a bewitching display of how to play the violin

Kyung-Wha Chung, Royal Philharmonic Orchestra
Charles Dutoit • Decca 425 021-2
Chung is typically individual in this performance

Shlomo Mintz, Israel Philharmonic • Zubin Mehta
DG 457 896-2
Not authentically French in style but still authentically exciting

Gioachino Rossini
Petite messe solennelle
(1863, *rev.* 1867)

Genre | Choral
Conductor | Robert King
Performers | The King's Consort
Year recorded | 2005
Label | Hyperion CDA 67570

Having written thirty-six operas in the space of nineteen years, Rossini retired from composing in 1829, at the age of only thirty-seven. The 1830s and 1840s were not a happy time, however—he was dogged by illness and a problematic lovelife—but in 1855 Rossini settled in Paris and returned, almost literally, to life. He began composing again, a series of songs and chamber miniatures, which he christened his "sins of old age," and embarked on his "final sin," a work that would be his memorial: the *Petite messe solennelle*. At nearly an hour and a half, the Mass is hardly "petite" in length. Rather, the epithet refers to its humble nature; the work is scored for just twelve singers accompanied by two pianos and harmonium.

It is a heartfelt religious work that also displays Rossini's great gift for the theatrical: dark and solemn, dramatic and lively—and full of glorious melodies. The Mass was never intended for the church; the first performance was to a select audience in a Paris town house salon in 1864. Rossini later orchestrated the piece (reckoning that if he did not, someone else would), but the work's intimate atmosphere is inevitably compromised in the larger-scale version.

The *Petite messe* has had a checkered recording history, its unique qualities often proving strangely elusive to performers. Robert King presents the Mass as it was first performed with nineteenth-century keyboards. Somber, gentle, vibrant, and joyful, this well-sung performance (with impeccable French pronunciation) marvelously captures the essence of this very special work. **GR**

Georges Bizet
The Pearl Fishers
(1863)

Genre | Opera
Conductor/Performers | Georges Prêtre; Ileana Cotrubaş, Alain Vanzo, Roger Soyer
Year recorded | 1978
Label | EMI 0946 3 67702 2 2 (2 CDs)

Georges Bizet (1838–75) was twenty-four when he composed *Les pêcheurs de perles* (*The Pearl Fishers*) at speed during the summer of 1863. Probably his sixth opera—but only the second to be staged—it is set in ancient Ceylon and pursues the theme of a priestess torn between earthly love and sacred duty.

The fishermen Zurga (baritone) and Nadir (tenor) fall in love with the same girl (Leïla) but vow to renounce her for the sake of their friendship. Leïla's return as a grown-up priestess of Brahma brings all the characters into emotional and spiritual conflict. Leïla and Nadir, discovered rekindling their love, are condemned by Zurga, now king of the fishermen. His nick-of-time realization that Leïla once saved his life allows him to spare theirs.

Bizet had an acute ear for the exotic in his music; in *The Pearl Fishers*—with its religious ceremonial and dancing—this is given full rein. Bizet's outstanding melodic gifts, vividly on display in the famous Act 1 duet, "Au fond du temple saint," have ensured that the opera is never far from the central repertoire.

Bizet's operas were plagued by theater producers and publishers who wanted to "improve" them, so corrupt editions abound: this recording restores the 1863 original. What makes it outstanding among competing recordings is the Leïla of Ileana Cotrubaş, a profoundly musical Romanian soprano with an affectingly plangent voice and power in reserve. Here, she is well supported by the male cast, with brisk conducting from Georges Prêtre. **GK**

Anton Bruckner
Masses nos. 1–3
(1864–68)

Genre | Choral
Conductor | Matthew Best
Performers | Corydon Singers & Orchestra
Years recorded | 1985–93
Label | Hyperion CDS 44071/3 (3 CDs)

Jacques Offenbach
La belle Hélène
(1864)

Genre | Operetta
Conductor/Performers | Marc Minkowski;
Felicity Lott, Yann Beuron, Michel Sénéchal
Year recorded | 2000
Label | Virgin 7243 5 45477 2 0 (2 CDs)

Bruckner's symphonies will always divide audiences. For some, they are sublime "cathedrals in sound"; for others, like Brahms, they are more like "symphonic boa-constrictors." But even if you side with Brahms, do not give up on Bruckner, for the church music is a different world. Bruckner was one of the supreme masters of choral writing, and each of his three great Masses has passages that fasten in the memory. Only that overused word "visionary" will really do for music like the luminous, Palestrina-inspired Sanctus from no. 2 or the intensely expressive, imploring harmonies of the Kyrie of no. 3—composed, Bruckner said, in an effort to pull himself out of a crippling depression. Clearly these works are the expression of a profound, and sometimes surprisingly lively faith, yet the music can also suggest how severely that faith was tested.

The performances of Matthew Best and his Corydon Singers are a wonderful corrective to traditional views of Bruckner. In place of ripe Germanic heaviness, there is a different kind of richness in the sound and expressive tone. Best is fully conscious of Bruckner's Romantic leanings: he makes no attempt to tone down the Wagnerian element in the gorgeous Benedictus from Mass no. 3. But he is also aware of how much Bruckner's style is rooted in the past: in the Masses of Schubert, Beethoven, Haydn, and Mozart and in the sublime counterpoint of Bach and Palestrina. A fine singer himself, Best has a way of getting the best out of his well-drilled choir, while the orchestra responds as though Bruckner had been in its blood for generations. **SJ**

In another age, *La belle Hélène* provoked a scandal, or at the very least was thought to be wickedly risqué. Now fun and games on the eve of the Trojan War when Hélène falls for Pâris and the Olympian Gods take a seaside holiday are simply charmingly funny. Nothing dates so fast as satire. Yet Henri Meilhac and Ludovic Halévy's libretto can still mock the follies of our political elders, and there is something nicely naughty about carving a boulevard comedy out of Homer's epic.

What keeps *Hélène* both belle and fresh is Offenbach's score. By the 1860s, he had found the *opéra-comique* three-act structure that he would work with for the rest of his career as well as a leading lady, Hortense Schneider, who for almost two decades was the pinup of Second Empire Paris and a tourist attraction in her own right. The composer had also found his own musical style. The melody for Hélène's aria "Amours divins!" is suffused with boudoir sorrow. And a sly dig at Wagner never went amiss in Paris. So there's more than a hint of *Tannhäuser*, which had caused such a catcalling scandal at the Paris Opera just three years earlier, in the vulgar fanfare that introduces Ménélas's word-spinning competition.

Felicity Lott is everything you could hope for in a Hélène—silver-voiced, full of fun, and witty. Pâris is handsomely sung by Yann Beuron and the veteran Michel Sénéchal as Ménélas is magnificently self-regarding. Best of all, Marc Minkowski coaxes a freshly idiomatic reading of Offenbach's score from Les Musiciens du Louvre. **CC**

Edvard Grieg
Lyric Pieces
(1864–1901)

Genre | Instrumental
Instrument | Piano
Performer | Emil Gilels
Year recorded | 1974
Label | DG 449 721-2

Grieg's musical studies began with the piano at home in Bergen: fortuitously, his mother was a piano teacher, said to be the best in town. The young Edvard made rapid progress and, later, some of his finest music would center on the instrument. Besides high quality in his piano works, there is also a remarkable quantity. The *Lyric Pieces* alone comprise sixty-six pieces in ten volumes; unsurprisingly, most recordings present judicious selections.

Taken *en masse*, though, the *Lyric Pieces* form an extraordinary kaleidoscope of an intensely personal artistic world: impressions sometimes rich in Norwegian character, at other times inspired by nature (Grieg described the op. 43 set of six pieces as "spring songs"). Often thought of as the most domestic, contented and sentimental of late nineteenth-century nationalistic composers, Grieg undoubtedly had a dark side, experiencing difficulties in his marriage, the death of his only daughter in early childhood, and long periods in which he felt unable to compose—and this, too, finds expression in the *Lyric Pieces'* inexhaustible array of emotional shades.

The great Russian pianist Emil Gilels recorded his disc of twenty selected *Lyric Pieces* in 1974, but it remains unsurpassed in terms of critical acclaim and personal enjoyment alike. Gilels produces a wonderfully singing and velvety tone, empathizing with everything from high spirits and tender introspection to the slight malevolence of the dazzling "Puck" and the subtle, elegiac "Remembrances," which closes the disc. Pure poetry. **JD**

Johannes Brahms
Cello Sonatas nos. 1 & 2
(1865, 1886)

Genre | Chamber
Performers | Steven Isserlis (cello),
Stephen Hough (piano)
Year recorded | 2005
Label | Hyperion CDA 67529

"A landscape torn by mists and clouds, in which I can see the ruins of old churches . . . that is Brahms." Grieg's is an apt description of Brahms's First Cello Sonata, a work that resonates with echoes of the musical past, with its quotation from Bach, and its Classically styled minuet and trio. The first movement seems to emerge from out of the Hamburg fogs, driven by a somber urgency. When it breaks into the sunshine of E major, there is a moment of consolation, as the movement winds down into glowing sunset. The sonata originally ended after its delicate minuet and chromatic, sinuous trio. Brahms only added the fast fugue movement, based on Contrapunctus nos. 16 and 17 from Bach's *Art of Fugue,* in 1865.

The Second Sonata, written twenty years later, has a grand, four-movement design and a symphonic sweep. A first movement full of bold statements and heroic ardor—the cello declaiming over a thunder of tremolo notes— gives way to a heartbreakingly tender slow movement. The dynamic, syncopated storm of a scherzo, marked passionate, hurls itself headlong at the listener, interrupted only by another heavenly outpouring of melody in its trio section. The carefree last movement can seem strangely inconsequential, and it is the performance of this movement that separates the great from the good.

Steven Isserlis and Stephen Hough rescue both sonatas from a tradition of portentous seriousness: where others are reverent, they are by turns explosive and ecstatic, fueled by an extraordinary energy and excitement. **HW**

Bedřich Smetana
The Bartered Bride
(1866, *rev.* 1870)

Genre | Opera
Conductor/Performers | Zdeněk Košler; Gabriela Beňačková, Petr Dvorsky
Year recorded | 1981
Label | Supraphon SU 3707-2 632

Richard Wagner
Die Meistersinger von Nürnberg (1867)

Genre | Opera
Conductor/Performers | Rafael Kubelík; Thomas Stewart, Gundula Janowitz
Year recorded | 1967
Label | Arts 430202 (4 CDs)

The Bartered Bride was the second of the operas that Bedřich Smetana wrote for the Prague Provisional Theater, the precursor of the famous National Theater. Although a near failure at its first outing in 1866, it rapidly became his most popular opera and the work that set the agenda for comic opera among the Czechs for the next generation. A major reason for the work's later popular success was a sequence of revisions that added sung recitative and the three famous dances: the "Polka," the "Furiant," and the "Skočná" (the ballet of the comedians).

While Smetana resisted the quotation of folk song in the opera, his highly effective use of popular dance rhythms, the superbly infectious overture, and the direct appeal of the lyrical writing in arias, ensembles, and choruses have come to define what is thought of as the Czech national style. The plot, involving mistaken identity, a deal of comic deception, and young love has a happy outcome, but as in most successful operatic comedies, the prospect of its tipping into tragedy adds urgency and depth to the drama and results in some very affecting exchanges between the two main characters, Mařenka and Jeník.

Zdeněk Košler's handsomely recorded performance has a marvelous sense of pace, balancing the elements of slapstick with the more soulful writing for the pair of lovers. The other great advantage of this performance is the presence of two of the finest Slovak singers of the 1980s in radiant voice, Gabriela Beňačková as Mařenka and Petr Dvorsky as Jeník. **JS**

Die Meistersinger von Nürnberg was one of the two operas—*Tristan und Isolde* was the other—for which Wagner broke off work on his great tetralogy *Der Ring des Nibelungen*. He had the idea in the summer of 1845 but only elaborated it in November 1861. At this time, Wagner was describing it to his publisher as a "thoroughly light and popular" opera, though the work that eventually emerged was anything but modest in scale—in sheer length alone (over four hours) it dwarfs most operas in the repertoire.

The opera tells the story of the knight Walther von Stolzing, who wins the competition of the mastersingers by composing and singing the finest song of all, winning the hand of his beloved Eva in the process. On one level, *Die Meistersinger* is a glorious affirmation of humanity and the value of art. The work may also be regarded, however, as the artistic component in Wagner's ideological crusade of the 1860s: a crusade to revive the "German spirit" and purge it of "alien" elements.

The performance under Kubelík with the Bavarian Radio Symphony Chorus and Orchestra, recorded in Munich in 1967, was not released until 1992 by Myto, but it is generally regarded as one of the finest recordings of the work. The late Thomas Stewart takes the part of the wise cobbler/poet Hans Sachs, while Gundula Janowitz is a radiant Eva, and Sándor Kónya an ardent, fresh-voiced Walther. Thomas Hemsley and Franz Crass add distinction to the cast as Beckmesser and Pogner respectively. Kubelík's direction is warmly eloquent and humane. **BM**

Johann Strauss II | The Blue Danube (1867)

Genre | Orchestral
Conductor/Performers | Nikolaus Harnoncourt;
Vienna Philharmonic Orchestra
Year recorded | 2003
Label | DG 474 250-2 (2 CDs)

The River Danube is not blue, of course, but Johann Strauss the Younger's romanticized view of the great European waterway—in truth, the famous waltz offers more of a cultural statement than a geography lesson—has nonetheless made its way around the globe to become one of the most recognized melodies of all time.

Following Austria's humiliating defeat by Prussia at the battle of Königgratz in 1866, Strauss hatched an idea for a morale-boosting musical homage to his country. The following year, the Vienna Mens' Choral Association approached Strauss for a new work; his response was to complete the project he had been thinking of, as a sung waltz; premiered in February 1867, *An der schönen blauen Donau* emerged in its familiar orchestral form—complete with introduction and coda—at the Vienna Volksgarten a month later. The rest is history.

Although studio recordings are enjoyable enough, the way to experience the full emotional interplay of the music within the Austrian psyche is to hear it in the context of a Vienna Philharmonic New Year's Day concert. Among many distinguished recordings by Willi Boskovsky, Herbert von Karajan, Lorin Maazel, Carlos Kleiber, and Riccardo Muti, Nikolaus Harnoncourt's 2003 concert stands out: under his baton you can hear unprecedented amounts of internal detail in *The Blue Danube* and throughout the mixed program of marches, polkas, and waltzes. For the first time the concert includes Brahms's Hungarian Dance no. 5, and Berlioz's orchestration of Weber's *Invitation to the Dance*. Whether in the headlong up-tempo numbers or the languid waltzes, Harnoncourt achieves something really special—the whole event captured in sumptuous sound by Deutsche Grammophon. **GK**

> "The Blue Danube—
> *unfortunately not
> by Johannes Brahms."*
>
> Johannes Brahms

Other Recommended Recordings

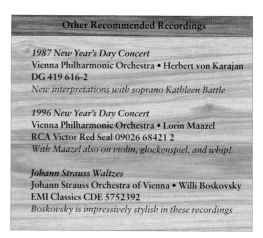

1987 New Year's Day Concert
**Vienna Philharmonic Orchestra • Herbert von Karajan
DG 419 616-2**
New interpretations with soprano Kathleen Battle

1996 New Year's Day Concert
**Vienna Philharmonic Orchestra • Lorin Maazel
RCA Victor Red Seal 09026 68421 2**
With Maazel also on violin, glockenspiel, and whip!

Johann Strauss Waltzes
**Johann Strauss Orchestra of Vienna • Willi Boskovsky
EMI Classics CDE 5752392**
Boskovsky is impressively stylish in these recordings

A 1925 engraving commemorating the centenary of Strauss's birth. ➔

"An der schönen blauen Donau"   1825 · Johann Strauß · 1925   "Frühlingsstimmen"

Wo Strauß den ersten Walzer schrieb

GUST. PEITH · 1925

Modest Mussorgsky | A Night on the Bare Mountain (1867)

Genre | Orchestral
Conductor | Valery Gergiev
Performers | Vienna Philharmonic Orchestra
Year recorded | 2001
Label | Philips 468 526-2

PHILIPS

VALERY GERGIEV
WIENER PHILHARMONIKER
MOUSSORGSKY
PICTURES AT AN EXHIBITION
NIGHT ON THE BARE MOUNTAIN

Mussorgsky, plagued by alcoholism and obliged to support himself with a lowly civil service job, left various compositions either incomplete or unfinalized after his death. *A Night on the Bare Mountain*, while not strictly falling into either of these categories, is nonetheless ambiguous in other ways. Originally entitled *St. John's Night on Bald Mountain*, the work was supposedly inspired by an imaginary scenario of witchcraft and devil-worship; the strident, vertiginous nature of the piece is perfectly evocative of its subject, although in careless hands it inevitably lends itself to overcooking.

Mussorgsky completed the original version in 1867 and was apparently entirely satisfied with it, yet the piece remained unpublished and unperformed until after his death. Even then, his contemporary Rimsky-Korsakov had decided to produce a revised version and to remove the reference to St. John from the title; it was in this form that the piece was first performed and how it has usually been heard since.

Valery Gergiev's ability to interpret the music of his homeland is unsurpassed, with this recording being a near-perfect example of his insight. He draws an intensely dramatic, almost aggressive performance from the Vienna Philharmonic, yet at the same time there is a crystalline lucidity that ensures no detail is lost; the latter fault can arise all too easily given the work's dynamic contrasts, helter-skelter rhythms and the blood-and-thunder approach of the orchestration. As is so often the case, this disc presents this relatively short piece as a makeweight for *Pictures at an Exhibition*, which is equally effective under Gergiev, but as both are widely performed works it is well worth investigating this disc for the former alone. **RT**

> *"It seems easy enough to correct Mussorgsky's defects, but . . . the result is no longer Mussorgsky."*
>
> Anatol Lyadov

Other Recommended Recordings

Berlin Philharmonic Orchestra • Claudio Abbado
DG 471 627-2
Various orchestral and choral works by Mussorgsky, including the original version of Bare Mountain

Strasbourg Philharmonic Orchestra • Alain Lombard
Warner 2564 62265-2
An understated but apprehensible Rimsky-Korsakov Bare Mountain *presented with other Russian works*

BBC Philharmonic • Matthias Bamert
Chandos CHAN 9445
This orchestration by Leopold Stokowski tends to attract polarized opinions

A portrait of Mussorgsky painted by Ilya Efimovic Repin in 1881. ➔

Репинъ 1881.

Giuseppe Verdi | Don Carlos (1867, *rev.* 1884, 1886)

Genre | Opera
Conductor/Performers | Claudio Abbado;
Katia Ricciarelli, Plácido Domingo, Ruggero Raimondi
Years recorded | 1983–84
Label | DG 415 316-2 (4 CDs)

In the nineteenth century, all composers worth their salt wanted to make their mark at the Paris Opera. Verdi, who in 1855 had written his first grand opera for Paris, *Les vêpres siciliennes*, was approached again by the Opera a decade later. He chose Schiller's pseudohistorical drama, with which he was well enough acquainted to insist that certain scenes must on no account be left out.

Princess Elisabeth of France is betrothed to the Spanish crown prince Carlos, but must agree to marry his father, Philippe II, instead. In an effort to forget his frustrated love, Carlos joins his friend Rodrigo's plans to free Flanders from Spanish oppression. When Princess Eboli, out of spite, reveals Carlos's love for the Queen, Rodrigo sacrifices his life to save him. Carlos is surprised by the King while taking leave of Elisabeth, but before the Inquisitors can arrest him, he is taken away by a mysterious monk, in whom Philippe recognizes his father, Emperor Charles V.

Verdi's monumental opera was never heard in its entirety; late in the rehearsal schedule he was forced to cut forty minutes, lest the audience miss the last trains to the *banlieues*. Also, the star baritone playing Rodrigo refused to lie "dead" on stage during the Act 4 finale, so that had to go (Verdi would reuse some of the music in the Requiem). When revising the work for the 1884 performance, Verdi left out the introductory act and rewrote much of the rest. In 1886, a third version was given, reinstating the first act. This is the version recorded by Claudio Abbado with La Scala Chorus and Orchestra; Abbado adds some of the music cut in Paris as an appendix. In spite of imperfect French, this is the best representation of Verdi's last thoughts on Don Carlos. **CMS**

"It is severe and terrible, like the savage monarch who built it."

Verdi while visiting Philip II's residence
at El Escorial, near Madrid

Other Recommended Recordings

BBC Concert Orchestra • John Matheson
Opera Rara ORCV 305 (4 CDs)
The uncut 1867 Paris Don Carlos *as Verdi himself never heard it, by a (mostly) French-speaking cast*

Berlin Philharmonic Orchestra • Herbert von Karajan
EMI 0777 769304 2 8 (3 CDs)
A widescreen interpretation of the 1881 four-act version (in Italian) with José Carreras in his prime

Metropolitan Opera Chorus & Orchestra
James Levine
DVD: DG 073 4085 (2 DVDs)
A lavish Met production (1886 version, in Italian)

Johannes Brahms | Ein deutsches Requiem (1868)

Genre | Choral
Conductor | Claudio Abbado
Performers | Swedish Radio Choir, Eric Ericson Chamber Choir
Year recorded | 1992
Label | DG 437 517-2

Brahms's "German Requiem" was his biggest work and the one that finally won him international fame. Setting not the Latin Mass but a cunning selection of texts from the Lutheran Bible that offers comfort to the bereaved rather than immortality for the departed, it draws upon the traditions of German sacred music back through J. S. Bach to Schütz, and it set off the trend toward "personalized" Requiems from liturgical and nonliturgical sources. Despite the majesty of its grand fugues and baleful funeral march, it is essentially an intimate work, above all in the sublimated waltz-music of the fourth movement and the piercing soprano solo of the fifth. This solo was added after the Requiem had premiered and strengthens the likelihood that Brahms was prompted to compose the work by the death of his mother, to whom he had been very close, although there are obvious references to the deceased Robert Schumann as well.

The paradoxical quality of intimacy on a grand scale lies at the heart of much of Brahms's music. His knowledge of scripture was profound: the texts' language is theistic, but at no point explicitly Christian, and he rejected an invitation to remedy this supposed omission. If anything this has broadened the Requiem's appeal and given it a universality matched by few sacred choral works of its size.

Claudio Abbado's Berlin performance, recorded at a live concert, is one of the warmest and most lustrous the work has ever had. His choice of tempi is perfectly judged, and the Berlin Philharmonic is backed by the rich, dark-voiced singing of two fine Swedish choirs. The vocal soloists, Cheryl Studer and Andreas Schmidt, are ringingly authoritative and altogether there is a quality of vision to this issue that the piece often misses. **MM**

"I confess I would gladly omit 'German' and simply put 'Human' in its place."

Brahms to Karl Reinthaler, the work's first conductor

Other Recommended Recordings

Schütz Choir of London, London Classical Players
Roger Norrington • EMI 7243 7 54658 2
Norrington's performance with period instruments is lean and muscular without sacrificing tenderness

Monteverdi Choir, Orchestre Révolutionnaire et Romantique • John Eliot Gardiner
Philips 432 140-2
A warmer and more spacious period account than Norrington's, although the soloists are less impressive

St. Hedwig's Cathedral Choir, Berlin Philharmonic
Rudolf Kempe • EMI 7243 7 64705 2
This 1955 recording in mono burns with intensity

Max Bruch | Violin Concerto no. 1 (1868)

Genre | Concerto
Performers | Jascha Heifetz, New Symphony Orchestra
Conductor | Malcolm Sargent
Year recorded | 1962
Label | RCA 82876 71622 2

Max Bruch (1838–1920) is known to the music-loving public for just one work, but it is superlative. The G minor Violin Concerto cost him immense effort—he claimed that between 1864 and 1868 he rewrote it at least half a dozen times, and one version actually premiered in the spring of 1866. Bruch then sent it to the great violinist Joseph Joachim: he made detailed suggestions, some of which were duly adopted. Ferdinand David also gave advice. Joachim played it a number of times, David took it up and the work was an immediate success. Unwisely, Bruch sold it outright to a publisher—it would have given him a handsome pension at the end of his long life, when he was in poverty.

The finished concerto is clearly modeled on Mendelssohn's E minor Concerto but has its own distinct personality—once you know other works by Bruch, the individuality of his orchestration becomes obvious. All three movements, which are played continuously, are in sonata form, the opening movement acting as a prelude to the beautiful slow movement. The finale is clearly influenced by Joachim in its Hungarian style.

No one comes near to Jascha Heifetz in his delivery of the brilliant solo part or in the silky elegance of his playing in the slow movement. The great Russian violinist is often rightly characterized as a not particularly profound artist, but in late Romantic music such as this he is supreme. His famous recording has recently been carefully restored from the original master tape, and the disc will give superb results on conventional or surround-sound equipment. As the couplings—Bruch's popular *Scottish Fantasy* and Vieuxtemps's Fifth Concerto—are also excellent, this is one of the best violin discs around. **TP**

> *"It is really easy for Bruch to write beautifully, it is in fact instinctive for him."*

Donald Francis Tovey, musicologist

Other Recommended Recordings

Violin Concerto no. 2, Scottish Fantasy
Itzhak Perlman, New Philharmonia • Jésus López-Cobos
EMI 7243 5 62589 2 1
Bruch's other two masterpieces for violin

Symphonies nos. 1–3
Leipzig Gewandhaus Orchestra • Kurt Masur
Philips 462 164-2
Mellow readings of these symphonies

Octet for Strings
Ensemble Ulf Hoelscher
CPO 999 451-2
A melodious late chamber work, beautifully played

German composer and conductor Max Bruch. ➔

Camille Saint-Saëns
Piano Concerto no. 2 (1868)

Genre | Concerto
Performer | Stephen Hough
Conductor | Sakari Oramo
Year recorded | 2000
Label | Hyperion CDA 67331/2 (2 CDs)

Saint-Saëns put the French concerto well and truly on the map, at a time when the Germans ruled the musical world. While most of his fellow countrymen were concentrating their efforts on the opera house, he reigned over the concert hall, reverting to Classical forms such as symphonies and sonatas, and producing no fewer than ten concertos, five of them for piano. The Second Piano Concerto is the most frequently performed today, and it is not difficult to hear why: it features a plethora of memorable melodies and a whole gamut of emotion from the dark opening movement to the gleeful finale.

The work opens with a rhetorical passage played by soloist alone. It is very reminiscent of a Bach organ prelude, which makes sense when you remember that Saint-Saëns was the greatest organist of his time and legendary for his ability to improvise at the keyboard. What is truly remarkable about this piece—and it could only be by a French composer—is the way drama and wit, charm and fire sit so comfortably side by side. The pianist is very much centerstage, but there is nothing dull about the orchestral writing, which is unfailingly atmospheric.

It demands a pianist of considerable skill but also one who is not afraid to charm the listener. Stephen Hough is the strongest possible advocate on both counts, with the City of Birmingham Symphony Orchestra minutely responsive to his every move under its youthful conductor Sakari Oramo. It is part of a complete recording of Saint-Saëns's works for piano and orchestra (not just concertos but shorter pieces, too), and all the artists clearly adore this unashamedly charming music. **HS**

Edvard Grieg
Piano Concerto (1868)

Genre | Concerto
Performer | Stephen Kovacevich
Conductor | Colin Davis
Year recorded | 1971
Label | Philips 464 702-2

This is one of the most popular concertos ever written, its Romantic sweep, catchy melodies, and rhythmic *joie de vivre* making it irresistible to pianists and audiences alike. It has even made an indelible entry into British popular culture in a sketch by the comedians Morecambe and Wise, with conductor André Previn gamely entering in on the joke. It was also a great favorite of the late comic (and accomplished pianist) Dudley Moore, though his rendition is hardly in the "must hear" category. The opening descending chordal cascade on the piano is one of the most famous passages in all classical music, and there is a sense throughout of a young composer (Grieg was only twenty-five when he wrote it) flexing his musical muscles.

The concerto is also a great example of a composer bringing together classical and folk music traditions, with most of the melodies either based on actual folk tunes or folk-inspired. The stomping finale is dominated by the dance rhythms of the *halling*, a Norwegian dance of which Grieg was particularly fond, whirling its way to a brilliantly lit conclusion. He completed the work in 1868, later showing it to the ultimate virtuoso of the day, Liszt, who sight-read it effortlessly and made various compositional suggestions, some of which Grieg took on board.

An excellent transfer brings the long-admired recording by Stephen Kovacevich and Colin Davis vividly back to life. Kovacevich is an unassuming virtuoso, though there is plenty of fire in his fingers. And in his hands, the meltingly tender slow movement has plenty of expression but not a hint of self-indulgence. This is young man's music, and this is a gloriously eternally youthful performance. **HS**

Henri Duparc
Mélodies (1868–84)

Genre | Vocal
Performers | Sarah Walker,
Thomas Allen, Roger Vignoles (piano)
Year recorded | 1988
Label | Hyperion CDA 66323

Before he reached the age of forty, Henri Duparc, one of César Franck's most promising students, abandoned composition forever as a mysterious, largely psychological condition made his life ever more painful. In time he went blind. At the time he ceased composing, Duparc's artistic legacy was just thirteen songs written between 1868 and 1884. Nearly everything else he had written was either suppressed or destroyed. Yet the handful of *mélodies* he bequeathed us is of surpassing beauty, and they are perhaps some of the greatest of all French art songs.

Duparc, like so many French composers of his generation, was deeply affected by Wagner's music. His mature songs, "Elégie" and "Extase" for example, are infected with the febrile chromaticism that Wagner had explored in *Tristan und Isolde*. But it is his choice of poets to set to music quite as much as the music he wraps about the words that distinguishes Duparc's songs: Théophile Gautier, Jean Lahor, Armand Sully-Prudhomme, and Charles Baudelaire. When Baudelaire published "L'invitation au voyage," he hoped that some composer of genius would set it to music for the woman he loved. Duparc, just twenty-two years old, did just that, dedicating the song to his wife, an Irish girl from County Cork.

Sarah Walker and Thomas Allen sing their way deep into the unique atmosphere of these songs. In their own manner, both embrace Duparc's emotional intensity and relish how well the words and music fit together. Roger Vignoles is a magisterial partner for both singers. The postlude to "Au pays où se fait la guerre," with a seemingly unresolved cadence, touches the tenderest nerve. **CC**

Arrigo Boito
Mefistofele (1868, *rev.* 1875, 1876)

Genre | Opera
Conductor | Oliviero de Fabritiis
Performer | Luciano Pavarotti
Year recorded | 1982
Label | Decca 475 6666 (3 CDs)

Arrigo Boito, born in 1842, is best remembered as the librettist of Verdi's late masterpieces *Otello* and *Falstaff*, as well as of other operas (such as Ponchielli's *La Gioconda*) written under the anagram "Tobia Gorrio." His historical importance has to be as a renewer of the operatic libretto, which he enriched with hitherto unused meters, turning it into a work of art in its own right. Since his student years, he had planned to write operas on the subjects of Goethe's Faust and the Roman emperor Nero (the latter remained unfinished at his death in 1918). The first performance of *Mefistofele* lasted six hours and ended in a scandal. Boito went back to his literary activities and it was almost a decade later that he revised his opera, after a successful performance of the "Prologue in Heaven" on its own. Unfortunately, he tore up the parts he cut or replaced, so that the first version is lost to us (only the libretto survives).

Uniquely among composers who tackled this subject, Boito ambitiously sought to encompass both parts of Goethe's epic parable of man's quest for knowledge. (The text follows Goethe quite closely.) Thus the love story with Gretchen (Margherita) occupies just the first two acts, being followed by Faust's infatuation with Helen of Troy and his death, after which he is taken to Heaven, leaving the Devil to gnash his teeth. The prologue and epilogue include bold spatial effects and angelic choirs, and the title role is a gift for a singing actor.

Oliviero de Fabritiis's last recording before his death, made with Luciano Pavarotti (Faust) and the National Philharmonic Orchestra, realizes Boito's huge canvas impressively, aided by Decca's technical crew. **CMS**

Ambroise Thomas
Hamlet (1868)

Genre | Opera
Conductor/Performers | Antonio de Almeida;
Thomas Hampson, June Anderson, Samuel Ramey
Year recorded | 1993
Label | EMI 0777 7 54820 2 7 (3 CDs)

Ambroise Thomas's *Hamlet* offers an excellent example of how an opera's fortunes can change over time. Thomas (1811–96) was a talented pianist who won the coveted Prix de Rome for composition while studying at the Paris Conservatoire; he returned to the institution as a professor, taking over as director from 1871 until his death. Conservative minded, he opposed Wagnerian innovations in music, and as an opera composer found himself influenced by more successful exponents such as Gounod.

Gounod's *Faust* prompted Thomas to write his own Goethe opera, *Mignon*, based on the author's *Wilhelm Meisters Lehrjahre*. Tapping into artistic Europe's enthusiasm for Shakespeare, Thomas followed Gounod's *Roméo et Juliette* with his own *Hamlet*. His librettists, Jules Barbier and Michel Carré, who had worked on *Mignon* and *Faust*, adapted the plot for French tastes, cutting the list of characters in half, adding inauthentic incidents, and contriving a happy ending in which Hamlet survives to become king. But interest in the opera stuttered: the end was changed, and full performances became rarities.

Thomas might have been a patchy talent, but *Hamlet* contains a wealth of excellent music. No other recording provides more persuasive advocacy: Thomas Hampson shines as Hamlet; as Ophélie, June Anderson's evident love for French language and music, and her dazzling coloratura technique, serve her well, especially in the extended Mad Scene. Antonio de Almeida draws sparkling playing from the London Philharmonic. An appendix provides listeners with the so-called "Covent Garden" unhappy ending and the rather undistinguished ballet music. **GK**

> "I recommend listeners . . .
> not just to dismiss [Thomas]
> as an operatic lightweight."

Lionel Salter, journalist and broadcaster

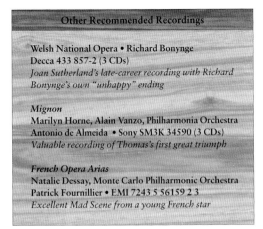

Other Recommended Recordings

Welsh National Opera • Richard Bonynge
Decca 433 857-2 (3 CDs)
Joan Sutherland's late-career recording with Richard Bonynge's own "unhappy" ending

Mignon
Marilyn Horne, Alain Vanzo, Philharmonia Orchestra
Antonio de Almeida • Sony SM3K 34590 (3 CDs)
Valuable recording of Thomas's first great triumph

French Opera Arias
Natalie Dessay, Monte Carlo Philharmonic Orchestra
Patrick Fournillier • EMI 7243 5 56159 2 3
Excellent Mad Scene from a young French star

Modest Mussorgsky

Boris Godunov (1869, *rev.* 1871–2, *reorch. Rimsky-Korsakov* 1896, 1908)

Genre | Opera
Conductor/Performers | Mark Ermler; Yevgeni
Nesterenko, Vladimir Atlantov, Elena Obraztsova
Year recorded | 1982
Label | Regis RRC 3006 (3 CDs)

Mussorgsky's only completed opera, *Boris Godunov*, was not, in the event, good enough, at least in the eyes of the Russian Imperial Theaters Committee, who famously rejected it for performance when the composer submitted it in 1871. Various reasons have been cited, all of which point to the work's unorthodox nature. It initially lacked anything approaching conventional (and usually romantic) roles for a lead soprano and tenor (the title role goes to a bass); its score was innovative in the way it brought a new naturalism to word-setting and focus on the words; and its narrative, based on Puskhin's historical drama focusing on Godunov's brief period as Tsar during the early seventeenth century, seemed fractured and lacking in cohesion. It fell to the composer's friends to organize the performance of three excerpted scenes in 1873, which was sufficiently successful to warrant a full performance a year later. The audiences on both occasions responded appreciatively, but the critical response to the full version was dismissive. This resulted in the first of the cuts, revisions, and variant editions that were to be visited upon the opera over the next eighty years.

This recording of the 1890s' version, mainly re-orchestrated by Rimsky-Korsakov, is both formidable and a bargain. (Many listeners would no doubt have paid rather more to cover the inclusion of the libretto.) It was recorded in the Bolshoi Theater in 1982, with the resident choir and orchestra, an all-Russian cast of soloists, and an expert conductor. The performances are outstanding and the work as a whole is delivered with unparalleled clarity and a superb sense of pace and timing. **RT**

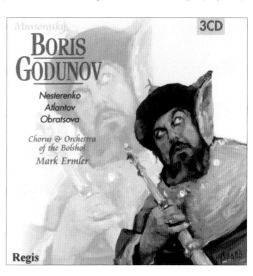

"His music is a . . . fathomless treasury of skill, inspiration, and discoveries."

Yevgeni Nesterenko, bass

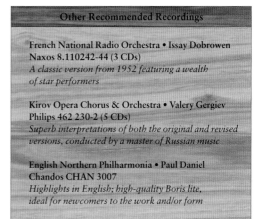

Other Recommended Recordings

French National Radio Orchestra • Issay Dobrowen
Naxos 8.110242-44 (3 CDs)
A classic version from 1952 featuring a wealth of star performers

Kirov Opera Chorus & Orchestra • Valery Gergiev
Philips 462 230-2 (5 CDs)
Superb interpretations of both the original and revised versions, conducted by a master of Russian music

English Northern Philharmonia • Paul Daniel
Chandos CHAN 3007
Highlights in English; high-quality Boris lite, ideal for newcomers to the work and/or form

Johannes Brahms | Hungarian Dances (1869, 1880)

Genre | Chamber
Performers | Walter Klien (piano),
Alfred Brendel (piano)
Year recorded | 1956
Label | Regis CDSX 3612 (5 CDs)

Brahms was, of course, not the first composer to be inspired by the vitality and exotic rhythms and colors of Hungarian popular music. Liszt—in most respects hardly a kindred spirit—had already composed the majority of his *Hungarian Rhapsodies* by the time Brahms began, in the 1850s, to arrange a selection of dance tunes that could be heard played by fiddlers in the cafés of Budapest.

These arrangements were originally for solo piano, but when ten dances were eventually published in 1869, they were adapted for piano duet, appealing to the domestic market. They made Brahms a small fortune. The solo piano versions of these ten dances—extravagant in their virtuoso demands—were finalized and published in 1872. Buoyed by the commercial success of the first set of dances, the publisher Simrock persuaded Brahms to prepare another set, which was issued in 1880.

The first ten *Hungarian Dances* draw extensively on popular *csárdás* and other stylized Hungarian dance tunes. Like Liszt's use of Hungarian material (but unlike the work of Bartók and Kodály), the sources emanate from middle-class entertainment music rather than genuine peasant folk music. Although Brahms made clear he was arranging preexisting melodies, unfortunately he did not acknowledge his sources, which led to accusations of plagiarism. Nevertheless, these are very much Brahms's compositions, just as the *Hungarian Rhapsodies* are Liszt's.

There is still no more infectious recording of the *Hungarian Dances* than the account from Walter Klien and Alfred Brendel, made back in the early stereo days. The recorded sound may betray its age, but Klien was a superb Brahmsian, and he and the young Brendel revel in the music's colorful tapestry and gypsy swagger. **TLP**

"Brahms—what a pianist! One of ten thumbs!"

Philip Hale, *Boston Herald*

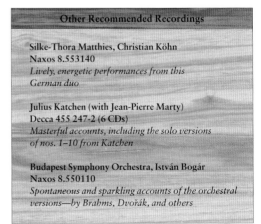

Other Recommended Recordings

Silke-Thora Matthies, Christian Köhn
Naxos 8.553140
Lively, energetic performances from this German duo

Julius Katchen (with Jean-Pierre Marty)
Decca 455 247-2 (6 CDs)
Masterful accounts, including the solo versions of nos. 1–10 from Katchen

Budapest Symphony Orchestra, István Bogár
Naxos 8.550110
Spontaneous and sparkling accounts of the orchestral versions—by Brahms, Dvořák, and others

Johannes Brahms lived off the proceeds of his *Hungarian Dances*. ❯

Mily Alekseyevich Balakirev
Islamey
(1869, *rev.* 1902)

Genre | Instrumental
Instrument | Piano
Performer | Boris Berezovsky
Year recorded | 1994
Label | Teldec 4509 96516-2

Balakirev was the leader of the group of five Russian Romantic composers who were known as "the mighty handful," sometimes referred to as "the five." United by their nationalism and their desire to produce distinctively Russian art music, partly through the use of Russian folk song and subject matter, they were a key part of a rich flowering of Russian culture in the late nineteenth century.

Balakirev's best-known work is the piano piece *Islamey*, an eight-minute "oriental fantasy" renowned for its supercharged virtuosity. Although he was a skilled pianist, some passages in *Islamey* were beyond him. Balakirev composed *Islamey* unusually quickly in 1869, after a trip to the Caucasus. There he was introduced to many folk tunes of the region, and one in particular—a dizzying tune called "Islamey" that he heard on an instrument something like a violin—inspired him to arrange it for piano. It became the opening theme of the piece; the lyrical central theme is a beautiful love song still known among Crimean Tatars. Throughout, such melodic richness is furnished with the sort of Lisztian virtuosity that has always been a compelling challenge to virtuosi.

Among the most formidably equipped of modern pianists, Boris Berezovsky relishes the work's technical demands and gives a performance of breathtaking fluency and aplomb. While others make you aware of the necessary physical exertion, Berezovsky never remotely sounds under strain and he strikes the perfect balance of awesome control and electrifying abandon. **TLP**

Pyotr Ilyich Tchaikovsky
Romeo and Juliet Fantasy Overture (1869, *rev.* 1870, 1880)

Genre | Orchestral
Conductor | Claudio Abbado
Performers | Chicago Symphony Orchestra
Year recorded | 1988
Label | Sony MK 44911

A relatively late starter as a composer, Tchaikovsky seemed destined for a career as a reluctant civil servant. In 1862, his life changed when he enrolled as one of the first pupils at the new St. Petersburg Conservatoire. He also had one foot in the camp of the Russian nationalists headed by the influential Mily Balakirev. There were a few Western composers of whom the nationalist circle approved, and no doubt it was with their idol Berlioz in mind that in 1869 Balakirev set Tchaikovsky on course for his first mature masterpiece, *Romeo and Juliet*. Balakirev drew up a program from Shakespeare's tragedy that contrasted the solemnity of the star-crossed lovers' chief helper Friar Laurence with swashbuckling music for the conflict of Montagues and Capulets, and of course the famous love theme that was supposedly inspired by an unrequited school romance. The standard version we hear is the first of Tchaikovsky's two revisions, replacing a rather bland theme for the Friar with a more exciting theme closer in character to Russian orthodox church music.

Italian conductors have often shown a special affinity with Tchaikovsky's most passionate utterances, and Claudio Abbado's Chicago performance is the more vivid of his two versions currently in the catalogue. An experienced man of the theater, he holds in perfect balance the brooding introduction, the focused energy of the fight music, and above all the bel canto tenderness of the great love theme, which Tchaikovsky turned into an operatic duet later in his career; it certainly sings here. **DN**

Léo Delibes
Coppélia
(1870)

Genre | Ballet
Conductor | Richard Bonynge
Performers | Suisse Romande Orchestra
Year recorded | 1969
Label | Decca 444 836-2 (2 CDs)

If *Coppélia* is the last Romantic ballet, then it is also the harbinger of the great full-length Russian ballets from the end of the nineteenth century. And no wonder, for Delibes was a pupil of Adolphe Adam, whose *Giselle* is the greatest of Romantic ballets, while the symphonic score and the heightened dramatic style of *Coppélia* undoubtedly anticipate Tchaikovsky. Both composers also turned to E. T. A. Hoffmann for scenarios. *The Nutcracker* was based on the German Romantic writer's story *The Nutcracker and the Mouse King*, while Dr. Copelius and his doll daughter Coppélia first appeared in *The Sandman*.

Delibes removed most of the ghostly shadows from his version of Hoffmann's story. His doctor is no cousin of Frankenstein, hoping to create life itself as he animates his doll daughter. It is the thwarted love affair between Swanilda and Franz that leads the dance when everything finally comes good after both of them have mistaken the doll for a real woman. Only in the third act finale when all are reconciled, the lovers and Dr. Copelius and perhaps his mechanical daughter too, does the invention seem to flag.

Richard Bonynge almost convinces you that Delibes's end is as good as his beginning. While each number is delineated there is an admirable feel for the architecture of this music, too. The Suisse Romande Orchestra is on top form on what was originally an analog recording. The sound is bright and forward: the strings produce a lush, rich tone and the winds are particularly good. For a recording of this vintage, everything is remarkably fresh. **CC**

Richard Wagner
Siegfried Idyll
(1870)

Genre | Orchestral
Conductor | Richard Hickox
Performers | Northern Sinfonia
Year recorded | 1994
Label | Chandos CHAN 9354

On Christmas Day 1870, Wagner's wife Cosima woke to the strains of the *Siegfried Idyll*, written for her birthday (actually the previous day but habitually celebrated on the 25th) and now performed on the staircase so that the music could waft into her room.

When it had finished, Wagner, who had been conducting, entered Cosima's bedroom with the five children and put into her hands the score of the "Symphonic Birthday Greeting." The entire household was said to be in tears. After breakfast, the orchestra performed the piece twice more, interspersed by other works.

The work both reflected and set the seal on the couple's newfound domestic bliss. After years of uncertainty and misery, they were at last happily, and legally, united at Tribschen on Lake Lucerne. The *Idyll* was at the same time a retrospective celebration of the birth of their son Siegfried (on June 6, 1869) and of the composition of the third act of *Siegfried*, also the previous year. In spite of its intimacy, the *Siegfried Idyll* was not intended for a small chamber ensemble: the size of the band for the first performance (probably fifteen players rather than the oft-cited thirteen) was dictated more by the width of the staircase at Tribschen than by aesthetic considerations.

Richard Hickox's recording with the Northern Sinfonia catches the rapt serenity of the lullaby music incorporated into the *Idyll*. The strings sing, the horns glow, and the sense is of enchantment, of a gift of love from a composer to his adored spouse. **BM**

Giuseppe Verdi | Aida (1871)

Genre | Opera
Conductor/Performers | Riccardo Muti;
Montserrat Caballé, Plácido Domingo, Fiorenza Cossotto
Year recorded | 1974
Label | EMI 7243 5 67617 2 8 (3 CDs)

Among the opening festivities for the Suez Canal was the inauguration of an opera house in Cairo. Verdi had been approached to write an opera for the occasion. It was based on a scenario by the Egyptologist Auguste Mariette, later versified by Antonio Ghislanzoni.

The Egyptian general Radames, loved by Princess Amneris, is himself in love with the slave Aida, who is in reality the daughter of the Ethiopian King, Amonasro. The latter is captured in battle and, concealing his identity, manages to obtain through Aida an important military secret from Radames. For this the general is sentenced to death by immurement; he refuses Amneris's offers to have him pardoned. Aida creeps into the tomb to die with him.

Not planning to attend the Cairo premiere, Verdi scored the opera beforehand at home instead of during rehearsals as was his wont. He took care to obtain "local color" by having long faux-antique trumpets especially made for the Triumphal March. The premiere was a huge success and earned Verdi the title of Commander of the Ottoman Order. With its extended dance sequences and mass scenes, *Aida* can be seen as continuing in the grand opera tradition, or *opera-ballo*, as it was known in Italy. It also belongs in the trend of operas with exotic locations stemming from Giacomo Meyerbeer's *L'Africaine* (1865) and Carlos Gomes's *Il Guarany* (1870), which would be continued in Léo Delibes's *Lakmé* (1883) and Giacomo Puccini's *Madama Butterfly* (1904). Muti's first opera recording boasts Montserrat Caballé, technically and emotionally in command of her role. Fiorenza Cossotto as her rival is equally good, and Plácido Domingo is supremely musical as Radames. Piero Cappuccilli and Nicolai Ghiaurov complete an all-star cast. **CMS**

> *"At least they have not accused me of Wagnerism, as the Italian press so graciously did . . ."*

Verdi, commenting on *Aida* reviews from Paris

Other Recommended Recordings

Vienna Philharmonic Orchestra • Herbert von Karajan
Decca 460 978-2 (3 CDs)
Idiomatic cast (Renata Tebaldi, Carlo Bergonzi, Giulietta Simionato) in a John Culshaw recording

Rome Opera House Chorus & Orchestra • Jonel Perlea
Naxos 8.111042-44 (3 CDs)
A classic 1950s cast, with meltingly beautiful singing from Zinka Milanov and Jussi Björling

Metropolitan Opera Chorus & Orchestra
James Levine
DVD: DG 073 001-9
A production with Plácido Domingo and Aprile Millo

Montserrat Caballé as Aida in Muti's 1974 production. ➔

Pyotr Ilyich Tchaikovsky
String Quartet no. 1 (1871)

Genre | Chamber
Performers | Jerusalem Quartet:
Pavlovsky, Bresler, Grosz, Zlotnikov
Year recorded | 2000
Label | EMI 7243 5 74349 2 8

Camille Saint-Saëns
Cello Concerto no. 1 (1872)

Genre | Concerto
Performer | Mstislav Rostropovich
Conductor | Carlo Maria Guilini
Year recorded | 1977
Label | EMI 7243 5 67594 2 8

Although Tchaikovsky is most celebrated for his orchestral scores, his chamber and instrumental music deserve far greater attention. In 1871, he determined to write a string quartet to be performed at a fundraising concert of his own music, the proceeds of which would help him to continue with his composing (he was a modestly paid teacher at the Moscow Conservatoire at the time). The result was an immensely attractive four-movement work that is expertly crafted, tuneful, and with much that is gracious and impetuous. The quartet's second movement is the Andante cantabile, a heartfelt folk song-related melody that has become world-famous as a separate piece, in many arrangements. The novelist Tolstoy was reportedly moved to tears by it; understandably so, for the music seems to sing its way into our soul and consciousness with a directness that is deeply moving. Yet the other movements of Tchaikovsky's First Quartet are no less enticing: the opening one begins with a phrase of ear-catching lyricism and the quartet as a whole is written with a clarity that seems to pay homage to Tchaikovsky's beloved Mozart. With no lack of intensity, but with no shortage of playfulness, the scherzo and finale are also brimful of rhythmic ingenuity and memorable invention.

The Jerusalem Quartet, one of the finest of the younger generation of string quartets, gives a capricious and detailed account of this lovely work, one that is pointed, elegant, and vital. In the Andante cantabile, the musicians' simplicity allows the glorious melody full rein without becoming overly sentimental. This well-engineered recording is on EMI's budget-price "Debut" label. **CA**

Saint-Saëns's Cello Concerto no. 1 is one of the first concertos cellists learn, and what an outlet for teenage passionate angst! This is a truly Romantic work, blazing with powerful rhetorical statements, heart-on-sleeve melodies, charming interludes, melancholy strains, and displays of (achievable) technical wizardry.

The concerto was written when the prolific thirty-seven-year-old Saint-Saëns was beginning to win recognition, along with Gounod, as a leading composer. Its premiere in the Paris Conservatoire, where long-dead composers were usually performed, was an indication of his status in French musical life. It was an immediate hit, and went on to become one of Pablo Casals's favorites.

Few concertos better show off the instrument's capacity to sing and to growl, and for this it is loved by all cellists. Although divided into three movements, it is constructed to sweep through without break and feels like an organic whole. Sandwiched between two dynamic movements is an old-fashioned minuet of arresting grace and simplicity. The score reveals a craftsman at work who could conjure a coherent concerto from the soloist's one, furious, descending scale and clothe it in dazzling orchestration. As Saint-Saëns himself wrote, "For me, art is form. Expression and passion seduce only the amateur."

Great virtuosi of the past played the concerto with a smoldering but contained fire. Rostropovich, who chose it for his orchestral debut, brings an irresistible youthful impetuosity and wild poetry to this recording with Giulini and the London Philharmonic Orchestra. His technique is effortless, and his spontaneity always stylish. **HW**

Anton Bruckner
Symphony no. 3 (1873–89)

Genre | Orchestral
Conductor/Performers | Bernard Haitink;
Amsterdam Concertgebouw Orchestra
Year recorded | 1963
Label | Philips 470 534-2 (2 CDs)

Bruckner's Third has the dubious distinction of being his most revised symphony. One can understand why he was so desperate to get it right. The symphony was dedicated to his idol Wagner, who praised its regal opening trumpet theme, and it represents a big step forward into uncharted symphonic territory, developing the Beethovenian idea of the journey from darkness to light in a breathtakingly original new way. However, it was all too new for the Viennese audience at the 1877 premiere and the performance was a fiasco, severely undermining Bruckner's confidence in the score. The final 1889 score is attractively short, but the cuts play havoc with structural sense, and some of Bruckner's later rewrites sound oddly out of character. The 1877 version is more consistent and the blazingly triumphant ending seems to come at exactly the right time, rather than as something of a surprise.

The appearance of Bernard Haitink's 1963 recording marked a big step forward in our understanding of this symphony—and of its composer in general. Haitink shows that the best way to approach the seeming problems in the Third is to take Bruckner's markings at face value, rather than trying to find ingenious new solutions. But he also shows a fine feeling for the unique atmosphere of this symphony: dark and mysterious as it is, it is often strangely calm, as though charting its way patiently through a huge labyrinth. Haitink also has a rare grasp of the shape and flow of Bruckner's long melodic lines. The famous passage in the finale where a carefree polka intertwines with a funereal hymn tune is especially well done. And how well the recording sounds too—over four decades later! **SJ**

Johannes Brahms
String Quartets (1873, 1875)

Genre | Chamber
Performers | Amadeus Quartet:
Brainin, Nissel, Schidlof, Lovett
Years recorded | 1959–60
Label | DG 457 707-2

Brahms was seen by many of his German contemporaries as the successor to Beethoven and this weight of expectation paralyzed him in two areas of musical invention, the symphony and the string quartet. He may have been exaggerating when he said he had destroyed his first twenty quartets but that number was probably not too far from the truth. Not until 1873 did he dare to publish the two quartets that made up his op. 51; and only one more followed, two years later, just before he completed his First Symphony. So what we have from him in the string quartet medium are the large-scale, almost heroic C minor, op. 51 no. 1, the bucolic, carefree B flat major, op. 67, with the A minor, op. 51 no. 2 falling somewhere between them in temperament.

To find one ensemble that fits all of these moods must involve a certain amount of compromise, but in the case of the classic Amadeus recordings, very little is necessary. This great British ensemble, three of whose members were Austrian refugees, knew Brahms's chamber music inside out and excelled in it. The recordings have been painstakingly refurbished for DG's "The Originals" series.

The players find the necessary "size" for the first and last movements of the C minor Quartet, but also know how to relax for the lovely Romanze that forms its slow movement, and the delicate scherzo. They have the full measure of the A minor, in some ways the hardest of the three to characterize, and they set out with a spring in their step in the outdoor B flat major. Its third movement highlights the viola, beautifully played by Peter Schidlof who also shines in the variation finale. **TP**

Edouard Lalo
Symphonie espagnole (1874)

Genre | Concerto
Performers | Vadim Repin, London Symphony Orchestra
Conductor | Kent Nagano
Year recorded | 1998
Label | Erato 3984 27314-2

Edouard Lalo's *Symphonie espagnole* has become his signature work. The brilliant *Le roi d'Ys Overture* and the lyrical Cello Concerto are also still played, but neither has the pungency of this big, colorful violin concerto. He called it a *symphonie* for good reason, because he had lavished attention on the orchestral sections of what is really a five-movement concert suite. But the real focus is the violin as hero, and the piece has remained in the repertoire partly as a virtuoso's proof of his or her instrumental credentials.

The symphony was inspired by the legendary Spanish virtuoso Pablo Sarasate and first performed by him in 1875. The Parisian Lalo was of Spanish descent and when Sarasate made his home there, the two became friends. Spain's exotic rhythms and sensuous harmonies had been seducing French composers for decades—Bizet, Chabrier, and Massenet all fell under its spell. Lalo's scoring might be described as professional rather than original, but there is sufficient dynamism and variety for a truly great violinist to create a compelling event. It begins with a bravura Allegro, the soloist displaying the darkest colors of the instrument, swings into a seguidilla rhythm accompanied by guitar-like pizzicato in the strings, and comes to rest on a slow intermezzo. The yearning Andante provides the perfect prelude to the effferverscent Rondo finale, glittering with technical fireworks and insouciant sleights of hand.

Lalo's *Symphonie* belongs to an all-but-lost tradition of violinistic exuberance. Vadim Repin, an impressive jazz improviser as well as fully-fledged virtuoso, has the ease, sangfroid, and old-fashioned charm to pull off this showpiece with panache. **HW**

Georges Bizet
Carmen (1874)

Genre | Opera
Conductor/Performers | Claudio Abbado; Teresa Berganza, Plácido Domingo, Sherrill Milnes, Ileana Cotrubaş
Year recorded | 1977
Label | DG 419 636-2 (3 CDs)

When *Carmen* was unveiled to the Paris Opéra-Comique public on March 3, 1875, the heroine's overt sexuality, the depiction of the female chorus smoking and fighting, and Carmen's violent death on stage provoked a furore. It took a couple of years for *Carmen* to establish itself as one of the greatest of all operas. Its success is based on a compelling story (after Mérimée's novel) of the ensnarement of a young soldier by a free-spirited gypsy girl, set to music of lyricism, rhythmic vigor, and vivid orchestral color.

As Don José, Plácido Domingo is characteristically passionate, his burnished tone an ideal foil for Teresa Berganza, a fiery Spanish mezzo-soprano whose inflections and temperament provide the perfect expression of Carmen's free-spirited sensuality. Sherrill Milnes's Toreador tempts Carmen away from José's country-boy soldier more by sheer nobility than testosterone-driven bombast; Ileana Cotrubaş's plangent impersonation of Micaëla—the faithful village girl Don José left behind—is the most affecting on record; and the supporting cast, all seasoned stage performers, offer further strength in depth.

But the factor that makes this recording stand out, in a very crowded market, is that it followed Piero Faggioni's 1977 production at the Edinburgh Festival: the dramatic relationships formed on the stage of the King's Theatre carry over into the recording, which is suffused with theatricality. Conductor Claudio Abbado's coiled-spring conducting, and the responsiveness of the sumptuous-sounding London Symphony Orchestra, makes this a recording as remarkable for its edge-of-the-seat drama as for the sheer beauty of the singing. **GK**

Johann Strauss II
Die Fledermaus (1874)

Genre | Operetta
Conductor/Performers | Willi Boskovsky; Nicolai Gedda,
Anneliese Rothenberger, Renate Holm, Brigitte Fassbaender
Year recorded | 1971
Label | EMI 7243 5 66223 2 6 (2 CDs)

Die Fledermaus (*The Bat*) is not only the most successful of the stage works by Vienna's Waltz King, Johann Strauss II (1825–99): it can unquestionably be claimed as the best operetta ever written. Operetta is entertainment music in operatic form: Strauss's genius was to take Jacques Offenbach's model and infuse it with waltz music, creating a highly delightful Viennese operetta style.

After a subdued opening run in Vienna (1874), *Die Fledermaus* traveled to Berlin, and enjoyed runaway success. In it, Dr. Falke arranges to entertain Orlovsky's guests with a trick played on his friend Eisenstein, by way of revenge for an earlier humiliation; Eisenstein, enjoying a final fling before spending five days in jail, is hoodwinked into attempting to seduce his own wife. The music is an unending stream of effervescent melodies, with comic dialogue and a star role in the shape of the drunken jailer.

In the face of stiff competition from Karajan's mono recording of 1955, conductor Willi Boskovsky's 1971 stereo version with the Vienna Symphony Orchestra beats all comers, not least because of the modern sound. The dialogue (supervised by opera director Otto Schenk, who plays Frosch) is delightfully polished. Nicolai Gedda's captivating Eisenstein is common to both sets; though she is not Elisabeth Schwarzkopf, Anneliese Rothenberger gives an appealingly idiomatic and relaxed performance as Rosalinde. Adolf Dallapozza's ardent Alfred makes Karajan's Helmut Krebs seem insipid, and Boskovsky also boasts the world's best Orlovsky—Brigitte Fassbaender. The aristocratic and normally reserved Dietrich Fischer-Dieskau twinkles as Falke, and sings superbly. **GK**

Giuseppe Verdi
Requiem (1874)

Genre | Choral
Conductor/Performers | Carlo Maria Giulini; Nicolai Gedda,
Elisabeth Schwarzkopf, Christa Ludwig, Nicolai Ghiaurov
Year recorded | 1963
Label | EMI 7243 5 67563 2 8 (2 CDs)

When Gioachino Rossini died in 1868, Verdi initiated a project to write a composite Requiem Mass in which every section was the work of a leading Italian composer, he himself contributing the final "Libera me." The *Messa per Rossini* was never performed and indeed only came to light in 1988. The poet Alessandro Manzoni died in 1873, and Verdi, who held him in great admiration and respect, set out to write a complete Requiem Mass in his memory. He went back to the unused "Libera me," and also remembered an especially beautiful passage from *Don Carlos* that he had been forced to cut before the first performance (this became the "Lachrymosa").

The German conductor Hans von Bülow rather offensively called the *Requiem* "Verdi's latest opera, though in ecclesiastical robes." He later apologized but he had a point—with the exception of the fugal passages in the first and last sections, the musical language is not very different from that of Verdi's recent operatic works. Be that as it may, the *Requiem* does contain some of Verdi's best music. The a cappella "Te decet hymnus" and the gossamer "Sanctus" are touchstones for a choir's technique, much more so than the more obviously effective "Dies irae." The four soloists have their "arias" and ensembles, requiring surely operatic voices, but even more an intelligent team of singers must exercise restraint and listen to each other. This was the case in the recording produced by Walter Legge in 1963, with conductor Carlo Maria Giulini and the Philharmonia Orchestra and Chorus, in which moments of breathtaking beauty are set off against the visceral excitement of Giulini's apocalyptic vision. **CMS**

Anton Bruckner
Symphony no. 4, "Romantic" (1874–88)

Genre | Orchestral
Conductor | Günter Wand
Performers | Berlin Philharmonic Orchestra
Year recorded | 1997
Label | RCA 09026 68839 2

Bruckner's Fourth has long been one of his best-loved symphonies. To an extent it lives up to its title, "Romantic." The magical opening horn-call, sounding through quiet shimmering strings; the dreamlike slow processional of the second movement; the elemental gallop across the skies in the scherzo; the finale's final awe-inspiring crescendo— it is music with an extraordinary power to suggest landscapes in particular, sometimes portrayed with down-to-earth affection, sometimes with a kind of transfiguring radiance like that of the great German painter Caspar David Friedrich. Yet there is a side to Bruckner that belongs to another, much earlier age—an age of all-embracing faith, viewed not with romantic nostalgia, but with a kind of patient devotion—that makes him stand out from his time. Indeed Günter Wand compared Bruckner to an "erratic block": a great slab of ancient stone deposited in a landscape with whose geology it has no connection.

Few conductors in our time understood Bruckner so profoundly as Wand, as this live recording shows. He conveys Bruckner's symphonic architecture as something supple and alive, not coldly monumental. Arguably, Bruckner never got the finale's shape quite right, but Wand finds more organic cohesion than most, without trying to smooth over clearly deliberate cracks in the structure. At the same time, it is a nobly beautiful performance, alternating between Schubertian pastoral lyricism and moments when Bruckner speaks with the grandeur of a latter-day Bach. It is also sumptuously recorded, with no intrusive audience noise. As an introduction to Bruckner's symphonies this could hardly be bettered. **SJ**

Günter Wand
Bruckner
Symphony No.4
Berliner Philharmoniker

Recorded Live

"I could write the way other people want, but I dare not."

Anton Bruckner

Other Recommended Recordings

Vienna Philharmonic Orchestra • Karl Böhm
Decca 446 374-2
A richly textured, warmly expressive performance

Royal Concertgebouw Orchestra
Nikolaus Harnoncourt
Warner 2564 60129-2
A crisp, refreshing, relatively light-footed version, but not short on power or grandeur

Linz Bruckner Orchestra • Dennis Russell Davies
Arte Nova 82876 60488 2
A compelling account of Bruckner's first version of the Fourth, fascinating to compare

Modest Mussorgsky
Pictures at an Exhibition (1874, *orch. Maurice Ravel* 1922)

Genre | Orchestral
Conductor | Mariss Jansons
Performers | Oslo Philharmonic Orchestra
Year recorded | 1988
Label | EMI 0946 3 50824 2 5 (2 CDs)

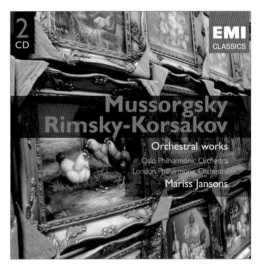

Although the friendship between Modest Mussorgsky and the artist Victor Hartmann had been brief, the painter's death at the age of thirty-nine greatly distressed the composer. On attending a memorial exhibition of Hartmann's work soon afterward, he decided to preserve his impressions of what he saw in a piano cycle that would offer musical representations of ten of the artist's drawings, many of them separated by "promenades" as if the viewer is moving from picture to picture. The work was subsequently orchestrated by several composers, most successfully by Maurice Ravel, whose version is by far the most widely performed.

Mussorgsky's musical thinking was innovative almost to the point of waywardness. He consciously avoided the influence of both earlier traditions and his contemporaries, preferring to construct his own musical models. The elegant segments of *Pictures*—portraying everything from fairytale characters to the concluding "Great Gate of Kiev"—conveys this approach very effectively. It also has an interesting subtext, in that it celebrates the artist's achievements in life rather than fretting over his death.

Pictures is a popular work and prone to overstatement, but Mariss Jansons is particularly skilled at retrieving its subtleties. This recording expertly defines the work as not only being representative of a series of pictures but also of the complex and contradictory emotional states that characterize grief. Neither bombastic nor tentative, he summons a wonderfully unified sound from the Oslo Philharmonic in a performance that is shot through with conviction but never once lapses into clumsiness. **RT**

> ## "[He] typifies the genius of Russia: a gigantic untrained child, strong and playful."
> **Havelock Ellis**

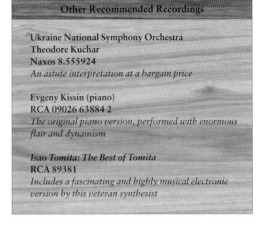

Other Recommended Recordings

Ukraine National Symphony Orchestra
Theodore Kuchar
Naxos 8.555924
An astute interpretation at a bargain price

Evgeny Kissin (piano)
RCA 09026 63884 2
The original piano version, performed with enormous flair and dynamism

Isao Tomita: The Best of Tomita
RCA 89381
Includes a fascinating and highly musical electronic version by this veteran synthesist

Richard Wagner | Der Ring des Nibelungen (1874)

Genre | Opera
Conductor | Daniel Barenboim
Performers | John Tomlinson, Anne Evans, Siegfried Jerusalem
Years recorded | 1993–94
Label | Warner 2564 62091-2 (14 CDs)

One of the most stupendous works ever conceived, Wagner's *Ring* cycle continues to present the supreme challenge to performers and audiences alike. Requiring four evenings and at least fourteen hours to perform, the *Ring* can only be ideally presented in the festival conditions originally intended by the composer.

Alberich trades love for gold and fashions a ring that is stolen by Wotan, subsequently hoarded by Fafner, won by Siegfried and finally returned to the Rhine on the destruction of the world. The meaning of this complex, contradictory work cannot easily be formulated: successive generations continue to find in it insights that may not have been clearly perceived by the composer himself. At the heart of the work, however, lies the conflict between love and power: humankind's progress toward self-knowledge and compassionate understanding of others is constantly threatened by the desire for political control and by the compromises we are forced to negotiate in our daily lives. On the surface a fairytale about gods, giants, dwarves, and dragons, the *Ring* is an allegory of the conflicts that arise when civilization and power politics obtrude on the innocent world of nature.

There are many fine recordings of the cycle, some featuring outstanding singers, others cogently conducted. The Teldec set is derived from the Bayreuth production of 1988–92, directed by Harry Kupfer. Daniel Barenboim displays astute musical and theatrical intelligence, while there are many excellent vocal contributions, notably from John Tomlinson, a magnificently rich, involving Wotan (inseparable from his prowling stage persona in Kupfer's production), Anne Evans as a perceptive Brünnhilde, and Siegfried Jerusalem as an eloquent Siegfried. **BM**

> *"[T]he Ring bores one in places yet [it] is . . . of the greatest importance, . . . an epoch-making work of art."*
>
> Pyotr Ilyich Tchaikovsky

Other Recommended Recordings

Vienna Philharmonic Orchestra • Georg Solti
Decca 455 555-2 (14 CDs)
The earliest available complete recording

Bayreuth Festival Orchestra • Joseph Keilberth
Testament SBT2 1390, SBT4 1391, SBT4 1392, SBT4 1393 (14 CDs)
Magnificently sung and conducted

Sadler's Wells Opera Orchestra • Reginald Goodall
Chandos CHAN 3054, CHAN 3058, CHAN 3045, CHAN 3060 (16 CDs)
English-language version, conducted by the incomparable Goodall with the singers he trained

Hugo Wolf | Lieder (1875–97)

Genre | Vocal
Performers | Hugo Wolf Society,
Alexander Kipnis (bass), and various singers
Years recorded | 1931–38
Label | EMI 7243 5 66640 2 9 (6 CDs)

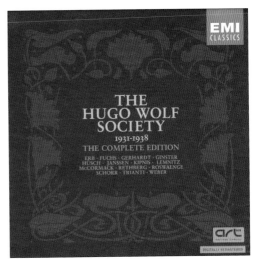

Hugo Wolf (1860–1903) was characterized by an idealistic, wildly enthusiastic, bitterly sarcastic, highly partisan personality. He studied at the Vienna Conservatoire from 1875 until 1877, thereafter making his way slowly as a composer, largely suspending those activities during a stint as a music critic (1883–86). His desire to excel in large forms was fostered by the advice of Wagner, Brahms, and Liszt, but he gradually discerned that his gifts lay primarily in the realm of song, where his insight into poetry allowed him to produce Lieder that are like distilled fire, demanding the utmost concentration and commitment from performers and listeners alike. Although the four large sets of songs featured elsewhere in these pages contain a high proportion of his best work, he wrote many other fine songs throughout his career, which ended in 1897, the year he was first institutionalized for madness brought on by the development of syphilis, contracted in 1878.

The Hugo Wolf Society, founded in the 1930s to record a representative overview of Wolf's Lieder, released six volumes of songs between 1932 and 1938; for subsequent reissues additional material originally intended for inclusion has been appended. Many of the most famous Lieder singers of the day participated in this project, and the recordings continue to be of seminal importance, showing just what has been gained—and lost—in performing Wolf's songs over the years. A particular highlight: bass Alexander Kipnis offers harrowing accounts of Wolf's last three songs (to texts by Michelangelo) and eloquent versions of several Eichendorff settings (including a magical "Verschwiegene Liebe") and "Wie glänzt der helle Mond"—originally intended for soprano but here sung with taste, delicacy, and potent character. **DB**

> "To place [Wolf], as some of us to do, above Schubert is not to disparage that wonderful genius."
>
> Ernest Newman

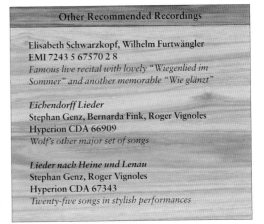

Other Recommended Recordings

Elisabeth Schwarzkopf, Wilhelm Furtwängler
EMI 7243 5 67570 2 8
Famous live recital with lovely "Wiegenlied im Sommer" and another memorable "Wie glänzt"

Eichendorff Lieder
Stephan Genz, Bernarda Fink, Roger Vignoles
Hyperion CDA 66909
Wolf's other major set of songs

Lieder nach Heine und Lenau
Stephan Genz, Roger Vignoles
Hyperion CDA 67343
Twenty-five songs in stylish performances

Edvard Grieg | Peer Gynt (1875)

Genre | Incidental music
Conductor | Ole Kristian Ruud
Performers | Håkan Hagegård, Marita Solberg
Year recorded | 2003
Label | BIS SACD-1441/42 (2 SACDs)

It is one of those paradoxes of musical history that Grieg got so little joy out of writing the music for which—the Piano Concerto apart—he is best remembered: *Peer Gynt*. He eagerly took up Henrik Ibsen's offer to write a score to accompany a staging of his dramatic poem, seduced not least by the money. But he found the work drudgery, felt uninspired by the unmusical nature of the subject, and he stayed away from the premiere in February 1876. Yet the play and his music were acclaimed and became inextricably linked as productions followed all over Europe. Acknowledging the success of his music, Grieg compiled two four-movement concert suites of highlights, including such famous numbers as "Morning Mood" (portraying dawn over the Moroccan desert) and "In the Hall of the Mountain King," but it was to his eternal dismay that he never saw the complete score published in his lifetime. In fact, that had to wait until the early 1980s, since when a number of recordings have offered various solutions to presenting it in concert form—and for all the popularity of the two suites it more than pays to hear the work in as full a form as possible.

The most successful presentation is also the fullest. Ole Kristian Ruud's recording with the Bergen Philharmonic (Grieg's hometown orchestra) and cast of singers and actors stretches to nearly two hours (the full play can last five), with a generous element of dialogue in between and as part of the musical numbers. But whatever one's knowledge (or lack) of Norwegian, it makes for a vivid dramatic experience, from "In the Hall of the Mountain King" complete with hollering trolls to the intensely moving death scene of Peer's mother Åse over the familiar string lament. **MR**

> *"It reeks so of cow dung, super-Norwegianism, and I'm-all-right-Jackness!"*

Grieg on his music for "In the Hall of the Mountain King"

Other Recommended Recordings

San Francisco Symphony • Herbert Blomstedt
Decca 476 7260
A one-disc alternative, but still with some spoken sections

Estonian National Symphony Orchestra • Paavo Järvi
Virgin 7243 5 45722 2 7
No dialogue, but an excellent performance

Peer Gynt Suites nos. 1 & 2
City of Birmingham Symphony Orchestra
Sakari Oramo
Warner 8573 82917-2
A refreshingly dramatic account of the Suites

German actor Theodor Loos as Peer Gynt. ➔

Pyotr Ilyich Tchaikovsky | Piano Concerto no. 1 (1875)

Genre | Concerto
Performers | Martha Argerich, Berlin Philharmonic
Conductor | Claudio Abbado
Year recorded | 1994
Label | DG 449 816-2

Tchaikovsky's First Piano Concerto has one of the most famous of all concerto openings—a glorious sweeping theme, passionate and noble, accompanied by thunderous chords on the piano. Yet this striking and memorable tune is not only presented in the "wrong" key but uniquely it does not recur for the rest of the work. It seems like a giant structural blooper, although this theme is more significant for what follows than is obvious to the casual listener. Tchaikovsky's decision not to repeat the "big tune" is surprising, although such apparent flouting of convention is perhaps part of the enduring charm and appeal of the work. The second movement is an innovative fusion of lyrical slow movement and scherzo (perhaps the model for Rachmaninov in his second and third concertos), while the finale is a fearsome tour de force.

Despite its ensuing popularity, the concerto had a difficult birth. As soon as Tchaikovsky had completed a first draft of the piece at the end of 1874, he took it to Nikolai Rubinstein—a famous pianist and director of the Moscow Conservatoire—asking for advice on the piano-writing. Rubinstein castigated the work. Not only was the piano-writing hackneyed and clumsy, but the music was trite, vulgar, and derivative. Tchaikovsky was devastated, but went ahead and published it anyway. Fortunately, other pianists were far more positive.

This concerto calls for a particular sort of soloist; it can easily sound labored. Martha Argerich achieves the perfect balance of heroic grandeur, chamberlike intimacy, and physical excitement. Of her various recordings of the concerto, perhaps the most successful is the Berlin performance with Claudio Abbado, which captures live her white-hot playing in all its unfettered glory. **TLP**

> "You deserve the gratitude of all pianists."

Hans von Bülow, letter to Tchaikovsky, 1875

Other Recommended Recordings

Vladimir Horowitz, New York Philharmonic Orchestra
George Szell
Palexa CD-0511
For visceral excitement, Horowitz takes some beating

Emil Gilels, New York Philharmonic Orchestra
Zubin Mehta
Sony SBK 46339
Gilels's epic interpretation is superbly controlled

Arcadi Volodos, Berlin Philharmonic Orchestra
Seiji Ozawa
Sony SH 93067
Volodos gives a reading full of color and contrasts

Martha Argerich performing at London's Barbican Centre in 1999. ➔

Anton Bruckner
Symphony no. 5 (1875–78)

Genre | Orchestral
Conductor | Günter Wand
Performers | NDR Symphony Orchestra
Year recorded | 1989
Label | RCA RD 60361

If any of Bruckner's symphonies deserves to be called a "cathedral in sound," it is the Fifth. It has a uniquely chaste, sometimes austere sound world, especially the strangely desolate oboe melody that opens the slow movement above skeletal pizzicato strings—if we are in a cathedral then this is surely a song from the crypt. Elsewhere the alternation of huge slabs of sound with still, spacious pianissimos suggests something primordial: a rough-hewn but tremendously impressive ancient monument. And the thematic coming-together at the end of the huge fugal finale is one of the most stirring conclusions in all Bruckner. Yet there are also moments where we glimpse a quirky, fantastical humor, in the weirdly disjointed dance music of the scherzo, and not least in the clarinet's perky dismissal of earlier themes at the beginning of the finale. This is a symphony full of riddles, which always reveals some new facet each time one returns to it.

Given such a huge structure—around an hour and a quarter—and Bruckner's typical determination not to be hurried, this symphony can become ponderous in performance. And when it loses its underlying momentum, the sudden breaks and changes in direction can be mystifying for the newcomer. Günter Wand however achieves a near miracle in keeping the music moving like a great river, however slow or full of eddies the current, without ever driving it too hard. And he has a better sense than most of how rooted in rural Austrian dance music Bruckner's language is. At the end though the sense of grand summation—without pomposity or inflation—is overwhelming. **SJ**

Gabriel Fauré
Nocturnes (c. 1875–1921)

Genre | Instrumental
Instrument | Piano
Performer | Jean-Philippe Collard
Year recorded | 1973
Label | EMI 7243 5 85174 2 2 (2 CDs)

Fauré's thirteen nocturnes are among the most perfect and poetic of all his numerous works for solo piano. They span almost his entire compositional career, the first—a brooding piece in E flat minor—dating from the period of his ill-fated relationship with Marianne Viardot, and the last—a searing, concentrated work of devastating power—from the period surrounding the death of his friend and teacher, Camille Saint-Saëns. In between is ranged a garland of glorious pieces that include moments of near-Lisztian virtuoso display, such as in nos. 2 and 5; Art Nouveau–style intricacy and sensuality in nos. 3 and 4; and the rich, mysterious worlds of nos. 6 and 7, which show Fauré at the peak of his mature, imaginative powers.

The later works track Fauré's style into its most exploratory phase, the onset of which—like Beethoven's—followed his tragic descent into deafness. His musical language became increasingly sparse, concentrated, and harmonically unpredictable. Gone are the teasing, decorative, intertwining figurations of the early nocturnes and in their place are distilled, refined evocations of anguish such as no. 11 and the unparalleled no. 13.

A number of extremely fine recordings exists of individual nocturnes and, indeed, the whole lot. Choosing one above the others is not easy, but my gut reaction brings me back to the set through which I was fortunate enough to learn the nocturnes: that by the French pianist Jean-Philippe Collard, who evokes a sense of deep, direct identification with these multifaceted pieces. His boxed set also includes the equally wonderful preludes, the Ballade and *Thème et variations*. **JD**

Johannes Brahms
Symphony no. 1 (1876)

Genre | Orchestral
Conductor | George Szell
Performers | Cleveland Orchestra
Year recorded | 1966
Label | Sony SBK 46534

Brahms's First Symphony was awaited with anticipation and some skepticism: knowing this, he was slow to give it to the music world. A version of the first movement was in existence by 1862, and Brahms probably first saw it as a whole design in 1868, for that year he sent Clara Schumann a birthday greeting inscribed with the "Alpine horn" theme we encounter in the symphony's finale. Even after the 1876 premiere he rewrote the second movement.

So there are personal allusions built into the symphony (the tense, fateful slow introduction, from which the first movement derives its material, makes use of the falling-rising shape that Schumann and Brahms both used as a motif for Clara Schumann). There is also a conscious drive to emulate, and escape, the example of Beethoven, whose Fifth Symphony is clearly evoked by the main key of C minor and the lithe, harried, scherzo-like motion of the ensuing Allegro. The inner movements (a gentle, romanza-like andante and a placidly tuneful intermezzo in place of Beethoven's customary powerful adagio and scherzo) show Brahms as much more naturally a Romantic contemplative, a follower of Schumann. But the last movement reengages with the Beethovenian archetype, with a stormy introduction out of which a great choric tune emerges (emulating the finale of Beethoven's Ninth). It seems to be Nature, rather than man, that triumphs here.

Szell's recordings of the Brahms symphonies are among his finest achievements and his First is best of all, thrusting and purposeful in the outer movements but very warm in the inner ones. He shapes the approach to the final climax with a superb sense of inevitability. **MM**

Alexander Borodin
Symphony no. 2 (1876)

Genre | Orchestral
Conductor | Jean Martinon
Performers | London Symphony Orchestra
Year recorded | 1961
Label | Decca 467 482-2

Cursed with a reputation as a "light classic," Borodin's Second Symphony is actually one of the most brilliant and original, as well as seductively tuneful things in the Russian symphonic repertoire. The stark unison opening is unlike anything in music before, and it caused some critical fulminating when it first appeared. "Who begins a symphony with a pause?" one famous critic grumbled—subtext: what else would you expect from those barbarous Russians? To anyone who is not terminally prejudiced however, the way Borodin develops this impressive idea can still be exhilarating in its freedom, freshness, and breathtaking confidence. Borodin used to be put down as an amateur or part-time composer (his "real" job was as a research chemist), but amateurs will sometimes take risks professionals would shrink from; and there is a sense in parts of this symphony that what one is hearing is pure, unprocessed spirit—particularly in the bracingly uninhibited dance-finale.

Jean Martinon's recording is four decades old, and one should not expect platinum refinement, but the edge in the sound suits the music well. More to the point, this is a sensationally successful performance. No recording since has quite matched its sense of unbridled enjoyment—this has to be the most joyous minor key symphony ever written. At the same time, Martinon has an exceptional feeling for the flair of Borodin's overall design. The surprise transition from the first movement to the scherzo sounds particularly audacious, but the slow movement has a touching beauty that throws the vodka-fueled exuberance of the scherzo and finale into sharp relief. **SJ**

Gabriel Fauré | Violin Sonata no. 1 (1876)

Genre | Chamber
Performers | Jacques Thibaud (violin),
Alfred Cortot (piano)
Year recorded | 1927
Label | Classica D'Oro 2020

Fauré's Violin Sonata no. 1 in A major was the young composer's first published chamber work and its success helped to establish him as a compositional force to be reckoned with. Fauré had been a pupil of Camille Saint-Saëns, who remained his champion for the rest of his life; in 1872, through Saint-Saëns, he met the great opera singer Pauline Viardot and her family, which included as live-in guest the Russian novelist Ivan Turgenev. For four years Fauré remained close to this gifted and artistically well-connected family while he courted Viardot's youngest daughter, Marianne. In a letter to her in 1877, during their brief engagement which she subsequently broke off, Fauré mentions "'our' sonata," undoubtedly this one. Its outpourings of ardor and melodic ecstasy cannot help but suggest a passionate spirit in a ferment of hope.

The A major Sonata's freshness and élan have always placed it among the composer's best-loved instrumental works. It is in four movements, sometimes evoking the tumultuous Romanticism of Schumann, Mendelssohn, and, of course, Saint-Saëns; but the lightness of touch, the subtle harmonic side-steps, the scherzo's skittering humor and the soaring, songlike lines of the violin writing are very much Fauré's personal language.

The recording by the legendary French violin and piano duo Jacques Thibaud and Alfred Cortot is eighty years old but remains a unique document from musicians who knew the composer personally—indeed, Fauré used to accompany Thibaud himself on occasion. Despite a few wrong notes, this performance is lively, subtle, and wonderfully balanced, and as "authentic" in its aesthetic idiom as you can get. It is also well worth hearing the same team in Fauré's beautiful miniature, the *Berceuse*. **JD**

> "*He offered a homage to Beauty in which there was not only faith, but a discreet yet irresistible passion.*"

Fauré's former pupil Georges Auric pays tribute

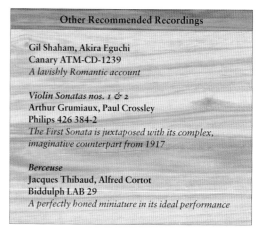

Other Recommended Recordings

Gil Shaham, Akira Eguchi
Canary ATM-CD-1239
A lavishly Romantic account

Violin Sonatas nos. 1 & 2
Arthur Grumiaux, Paul Crossley
Philips 426 384-2
The First Sonata is juxtaposed with its complex, imaginative counterpart from 1917

Berceuse
Jacques Thibaud, Alfred Cortot
Biddulph LAB 29
A perfectly honed miniature in its ideal performance

Jacques Thibaud, a regular collaborator with Cortot and Casals. ➲

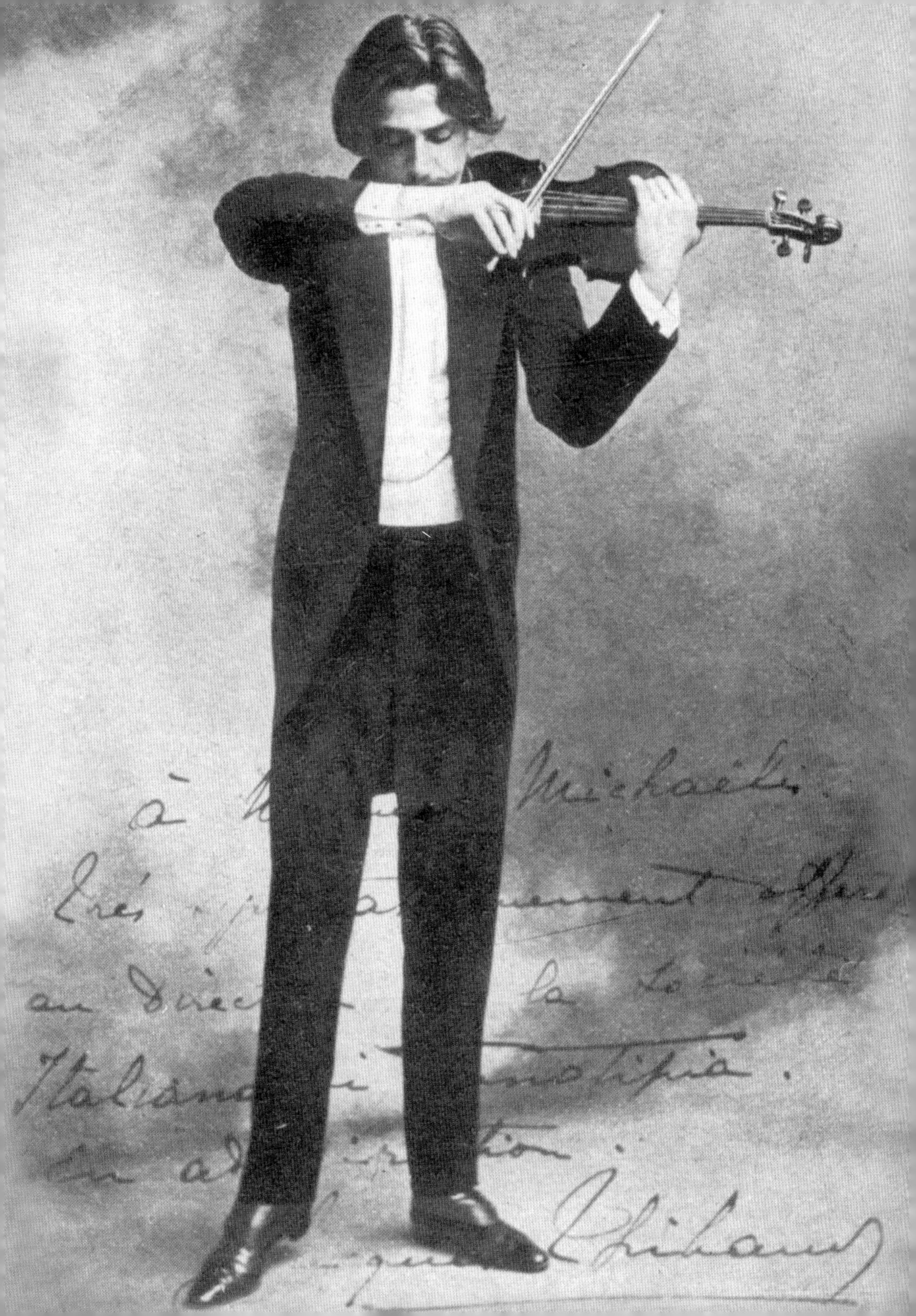

Amilcare Ponchielli
La Gioconda
(1876)

Genre | Opera
Conductor/Performers | Marcello Viotti;
Violetta Urmana, Plácido Domingo
Year recorded | 2002
Label | EMI 7243 5 57451 2 5 (3 CDs)

Poor Ponchielli: he was sandwiched between a pair of Italian musical giants, nineteen years younger than Verdi but old enough to have taught Puccini. To make things worse, he wrote only one opera that traveled, although *La Gioconda* has never really won the hearts and minds of English-speaking audiences, who pretend to hear too much Verdi and not enough verismo in this score. Somehow the setting is Verdi's Venice, and the intrigue with the banished Enzo Grimaldi creeping back to reclaim the wife of another nobleman is Verdian too. Yet the singer La Giaconda, who sacrifices all for love, is pure Puccini.

The secret of success is in the casting, for whatever Ponchielli's limitations as a composer he was undoubtedly a craftsman with an instinct for how to lay out his voices. *La Gioconda* is driven by a sequence of carefully conceived arias and duets—thrilling with the right voices.

Recorded when he was sixty-one, Domingo's Enzo is little short of miraculous. His aria "Cielo e mar" tells you why he was the finest tenor of the late twentieth century. A stream of pure unforced tone and well-nigh perfect legato, and that elegant finish to a phrase that sorts singers from stars. Violetta Urmana is his equal as La Gioconda: a smoky bottom to the voice reminds us that she began her career as a mezzo. In "Suicidio," her big Act 4 aria, she is as dramatic as Maria Callas and yet sings it with that absolute attention to musical detail that made Montserrat Caballé so exciting in this role. In the pit, Marcello Viotti almost makes you believe that musical craftsmanship can be art. **CC**

Bedřich Smetana
String Quartet no. 1, "From my Life" (1876)

Genre | Chamber
Performers | The Lindsays:
Cropper, Birks, Ireland, Gregor-Smith
Year recorded | 1991
Label | ASV CDDCA 777

Smetana saw that his duty as a composer was to provide his country with the foundations of an operatic repertoire, in such works as *The Bartered Bride* and the festival opera *Libuše*, and to celebrate its history and natural beauty in the six symphonic poems of *Má vlast* (*My Fatherland*). This was very much the public Smetana; he reserved his more personal utterances for chamber music. When a beloved daughter died tragically young in 1855, Smetana responded with the moving Piano Trio in G minor. When he went rapidly and irreversibly deaf as a result of syphilis (ending his career as a conductor), he commemorated the event with his First String Quartet, a dramatization of his biography, entitled "From my Life."

Each of the movements is inspired by some aspect of Smetana's life: the first begins with a premonition of the tragic fate awaiting him, but outlines the romantic and creative yearnings of his youth; the second, a rollicking polka, commemorates his love of dance; the third is a reminiscence of his love for his first wife and the finale projects his joy at energetic creation, but is cut short by the piercing note that marked the start of his deafness. Even though it was his first string quartet, Smetana shows enormous assurance in handling the idiom.

There are numerous fine recordings of this work, but none has quite the visceral intensity of The Lindsays's. The performers respond to the emotional extremes and deliver the extraordinary finale with a depth of understanding and dramatic skill that remains unmatched. **JS**

Pyotr Ilyich Tchaikovsky
Rococo Variations
(1876)

Genre | Concerto
Performers | Steven Isserlis (cello),
Chamber Orchestra of Europe
Year recorded | 1989
Label | Virgin 7243 5 61490 2 1 (2 CDs)

Pyotr Ilyich Tchaikovsky
The Seasons
(1876)

Genre | Instrumental
Instrument | Piano
Performer | Mikhail Pletnev
Year recorded | 1994
Label | Virgin 7243 4 82055 2 0 (2 CDs)

For Tchaikovsky, Mozart was the "Christ among composers," and he loved the "antique style" of the previous century, which set him apart from more radical contemporaries. His orchestral suites explore this style, with gorgeous melodies infused with the spirit of the dance. The same transparency of scoring and his feel for stringed instruments illuminate his *Variations on a Rococo Theme*, which, as a virtuoso showpiece, regularly brings the house down. It was written for the virtuoso Wilhelm Fitzenhagen, whose slightly shorter version is in common usage.

The Variations are based on a delicate theme, full of eighteenth-century proportion while remaining rich in harmonic potential, which Tchaikovsky proceeds to turn upside down, as well as forcing the cellist into the stratosphere. As Eric Blom commented, the instrument's "almost freakishly wide range is exploited here . . . with the greatest vivacity and brilliance."

The *Rococo Variations* is one of the great tests for a cellist: it needs to be thrown off with nonchalant grace. There must be room for intense poetry, arch humor, and dizzying speed. In concert, it can defeat the greatest virtuosi; even studio recordings rarely result in perfection. Steven Isserlis's performance shines because he brings out the seriousness and beauty in Tchaikovsky's melodies as well as dazzling us with his throwaway virtuosity. He also bucks the trend by recording the work in its original, longer version, enlarging the scale of the piece and turning it into one of Tchaikovsky's most perfect creations. **HW**

Tchaikovsky had a fairly low opinion of his own piano music. While it is true—at least for his numerous miniatures—that he often wrote for the piano as light relief from more serious and weighty projects, the modest scope of much of this music does not disguise many beautiful pieces. Among the finest are the twelve found in the collection known as *The Seasons*, composed between December 1875 and November 1876 in response to a commission from the music journal *Nouvelliste* for a piano piece for each of its monthly issues for 1876. The collection is sometimes referred to more literally as "The Months."

Each piece portrays a mood appropriate to the month, and each is in a simple ternary design. Tchaikovsky's melodic facility and sense for unexpected turns of phrase and harmonic spice means that even though he wrote these pieces quickly, they have a beguiling charm. The ghost of Schumann is never far away, and the best of the "months"—January's "At the Fireside," June's "Barcarolle," and October's "Autumn song"—are among the most delightful of all Romantic character pieces.

Although Mikhail Pletnev can sometimes over-indulge in interpretative point making, he is at his best in Tchaikovsky. There is no better recording of *The Seasons* than his strongly colored, boldly virile account. He makes something special of every piece and reveals a greater range and depth to this music than any other interpreter. This recording is generously coupled with more of Pletnev's Tchaikovsky, as both pianist and conductor. **TLP**

Pyotr Ilyich Tchaikovsky | Swan Lake (1876)

Genre | Ballet
Conductor | Wolfgang Sawallisch
Performers | Philadelphia Orchestra
Year recorded | 1992
Label | EMI 7243 5 85541 2 0 (2 CDs)

The idea for *Swan Lake* came from a family entertainment that Tchaikovsky devised for his nieces on the Ukrainian country estate of Kamenka, with wooden toy swans. The tale of Odette, transformed into a swan by the evil magician Von Rothbart, and her tragic love for the easily deceived Prince Siegfried did not take fuller shape until 1875, four years after that amateur staging, prompted this time by the Bolshoi Ballet's stage manager and one of its leading dancers. Standards at the 1877 premiere were none too high, given poor choreography, shabby sets and costumes, and downright bad orchestral playing. Tchaikovsky's first full-length ballet score eventually triumphed in a new production choreographed by Marius Petipa two years after the composer's death. In this version, Odette and her faithless Prince break the spell and are reunited in eternity, an ending many productions prefer to this day—though Matthew Bourne's smash-hit success with his company Adventures in Motion Pictures, focusing on an all-male swan ensemble, is a special case apart. The drama allowed Tchaikovsky plenty of scope for symphonic writing, a new dimension in ballet, in the lakeside scenes, but his ingenuity also rose to a dazzling range of melodic invention in the acts set at Prince Siegfried's birthday party and the ball where he must choose a bride.

Many listeners' introduction to the music of *Swan Lake* will have been through the traditional Suite, but there have been many complete recordings to show the depth and breadth of Tchaikovsky's full score. Wolfgang Sawallisch and the Philadelphia Orchestra give an aristocratic overview in spaciously recorded sound, and even include the "supplementary" Pas de deux in Act 3, mostly orchestrated by Vissarion Shebalin. **DN**

"I have wanted to try my hand at this kind of music for a long time."

Pyotr Ilyich Tchaikovsky

Other Recommended Recordings

New London Orchestra • David Lloyd Jones
Telarc CD-16451 (2 CDs)
Not quite complete, the "soundtrack" to Matthew Bourne's production has plenty of panache

Russian State Symphony Orchestra • Dmitri Yablonsky
Naxos 5.110005 (2 CDs)
Authentic Russian soul at budget price

Swan Lake Suite
Berlin Philharmonic • Mstislav Rostropovich
DG 449 726-2
Full-blooded account of the Suite, with a hair-raising account of the finale for good measure

Alexandra Danilova in a Ballet Russes production of *Swan Lake*. ➔

Johannes Brahms
Symphony no. 2 (1877)

Genre | Orchestral
Conductor/Performers | Adrian Boult;
London Philharmonic Orchestra
Year recorded | 1971
Label | Disky HR 705412

Having settled accounts with Beethoven in his First Symphony, in the D major Second Brahms could be much more himself and embrace a symphonic ideal that was less dramatic and more lyrical. In fact no. 2 has traditionally been considered the most genial of Brahms's four; in his own time, it was sometimes dubbed his "Pastoral" or even his "Viennese" Symphony. The first of those epithets is doubtless correct: the contemplation of nature is patently one of the work's themes. Romantic nature-symbolism (in horn calls, trilling birdlike flutes or clarinets, and so on) suffuses the score in a very rich harmonic context.

Yet it is also sometimes a dark one. Brahms himself admitted the work has melancholic undertones. If the first movement, with its expansive melodies, is like a vast waltz, it is one that occasionally strays into shadow, symbolized most of all by the mournful tones of the trombones, which contribute a dissonant canon to the development. These darker resonances are more consistently felt in the slow movement, whose knotty polyphony eventually provokes a tragic climax. The mood lightens in the second half: the ensuing intermezzo is light and deft, elegant rustic melody alternating with excitable fast dance-music. And the finale is the most sustained evocation of festive rejoicing in his orchestral output, its tremendous dynamism and Neo-Baroque figuration issuing in a joyous, full-hearted coda.

This is the finest member of Adrian Boult's late cycle of the four Brahms symphonies. His matchless understanding of the work combines with warmth and eloquence to provide an instinctual interpretation and plenty of power at the big moments. The LPO plays as if inspired. **MM**

Camille Saint-Saëns
Samson et Dalila (1877)

Genre | Opera
Conductor/Performers | Myung-Whun
Chung; Waltraud Meier, Plácido Domingo
Year recorded | 1993
Label | EMI 0777 7 54470 2 6 (2 CDs)

How odd that Saint-Saëns, who was so profligately successful in almost every other field of composition, should have written just one opera that has remained a crowd-pleaser. Even so, it was thirteen years after Samson et Dalila was first heard in Weimar that French audiences had their first taste of Saint-Saëns's grand seductress, and not in Paris but Rouen. Parisian opera managers were wary of biblical subjects and perhaps they misunderstood the symphonic nature of the score as well as the style of a work that sits halfway between Meyerbeer's grand five-act form and the lyric delights of Massenet to come.

Not that Saint-Saëns ever turns his back on a lyrical opportunity. Dalila's Act 2 aria "Mon coeur s'ouvre à ta voix" makes strong men weak at the knees. No wonder it was played in every café and on every street corner after the opera finally arrived in Paris. Samson et Dalila owes much to the oratorio tradition that the composer admired and the choral writing throughout is magnificent, with the Hebrews taking their cue from Bach and the Philistines belonging to Handel.

Plácido Domingo is a pensive rather than an impetuous Samson, yet always driven by his heart rather than his head. Waltraud Meier may not be the most liquid-toned Dalila on record, but her heroine is no sloe-eyed Hollywood vamp. This is a woman whose character deepens through each of the three arias. However, it is Myung-Whun Chung who makes this so satisfying an interpretation: he never lingers for the sake of single effects and coaxes a warm honeyed sound from the Bastille Opéra orchestra; the chorus is in glorious voice throughout. **CC**

Johannes Brahms
Violin Concerto (1878)

Genre | Concerto
Performer | Itzhak Perlman
Conductor | Daniel Barenboim
Year recorded | 1992
Label | EMI 7243 5 62598 2 9

Johannes Brahms often made heavy weather out of composing his largest works, yet the wear and tear was worth it. His Violin Concerto in D major marked the apogee of his collaboration with the Hungarian violinist Joseph Joachim. The concerto emerged a year after the Second Symphony, in the same key. Brahms originally planned four movements but substituted a "poor adagio" for the middle ones.

Joachim profoundly influenced the concerto, not least through his own earlier *Concerto in the Hungarian Style*. He found the Hungarian finale difficult to play and persuaded Brahms to qualify the Allegro giocoso marking with *ma non troppo vivace*. Fortunately most subsequent interpreters have opted for Brahms's faster tempo. The concerto made its way with difficulty: Joseph Hellmesberger said it was written "against the violin" and Pablo de Sarasate objected to standing around in the Adagio while the oboe had the best tune. But pupils of Joachim, such as Marie Soldat and Leonora Jackson, helped to establish it.

Hearing Itzhak Perlman play it, one finds it hard to understand how the concerto could ever have been so misunderstood. The Israeli-born violinist has the technique to command its every mood: expansiveness, loftiness, and lyricism in the first two movements, fireworks in the finale. His studio recording with Carlo Maria Giulini is fine but the live performance with Daniel Barenboim has the edge in spontaneity. He plays Joachim's cadenza. The Perlman Edition disc is well filled with the superb "FAE" Scherzo and four *Hungarian Dances* arranged by Joachim. **TP**

Pablo de Sarasate
Zigeunerweisen (1878)

Genre | Concerto
Performer | Jascha Heifetz
Conductor | William Steinberg
Year recorded | 1951
Label | RCA 09026 61753 2

One of the most colorful violinists of the late nineteenth century was Pablo de Sarasate (1844–1908), who hailed from Pamplona in Spain. He first learned the violin from his father, was playing in public at eight, and at ten was given a Stradivari by Queen Isabella. At twelve he went off to Paris to study at the Conservatoire with Delphin Alard, but took a first prize within a year—although he stayed on until he was fifteen to get a second prize in harmony. He had a long career of almost half a century, being particularly successful from the mid-1870s onward.

Sarasate's playing was light and mercurial. Many works by other composers testify to his prowess, but he was creative himself in the lighter vein of violin music. His *Spanish Dances* are underrated today but his most famous piece, *Zigeunerweisen* (*Gypsy Strains*), is still hugely popular. Curiously, it reflects not the Spanish gypsies of flamenco but the fiddlers of the Central European cafés. Some of the tunes were written by others but Sarasate makes them his own, as we can hear from the recording of the finale that he made in 1904.

Jascha Heifetz is in a class of one in this kind of music and both of his recordings are lessons in violin playing. The 1937 version with John Barbirolli still gives much pleasure but the 1951 remake with William Steinberg is the one to have. If modern stereo sound is a must, there are excellent alternatives by Itzhak Perlman and Gil Shaham, but Heifetz's hair-trigger virtuosity brings an extra dimension. He came from a background in which this kind of music was understood, even if he was more Eastern than Central European. **TP**

Antonín Dvořák | Slavonic Dances (1878, 1886)

Genre | Orchestral
Conductor | Nikolaus Harnoncourt
Performers | Chamber Orchestra of Europe
Year recorded | 2001
Label | Teldec 8573 81038-2

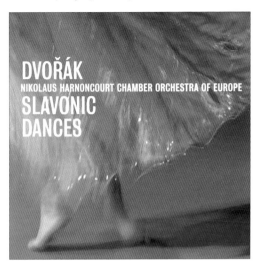

The spectacular success on publication in 1878 of Dvořák's first set of *Slavonic Dances* transformed his reputation from that of a promising provincial to one of international significance. Originally written for piano duet, the dances are based on popular Czech (namely the polka and furiant) and Slavonic dance rhythms. What made them one of the publishing hits of the day is Dvořák's combination of ear-catching melody with what Smetana described as an almost Beethovenian command of motivic development. In their orchestral guise, they are among the most popular short items and encores in concert.

Unsurprisingly, given the huge popularity of the first set, Dvořák's Berlin publisher Simrock was keen to have a second collection of dances. Dvořák, busy with commissions for England, including the Seventh Symphony, was disinclined to write what he considered such "small" pieces. However, negotiations over the fee for the Seventh Symphony resulted in Simrock securing the promise of a second set of dances; for his part, as he began to work, Dvořák warmed hugely to the task. If anything, the later dances have an even greater abundance of melody than the early set; they also have greater depth and in the case of the fifth a magically introspective quality.

Nikolaus Harnoncourt's track record in Dvořák interpretation has been impressive, with some landmark performances of the later symphonies. His recording of the *Slavonic Dances*, however, could easily be considered his finest reading of the composer to date. While he shows remarkable care in balancing instrumental lines and dynamics, this attention to detail never gets in the way of rhythmic spontaneity; throughout there is so much to delight in these remarkable interpretations. **JS**

> "... *Their orchestration was so successful that I can say it sounds like the devil.*"

Dvořák on the orchestral version of the second set of *Slavonic Dances*

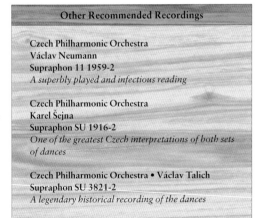

Other Recommended Recordings

Czech Philharmonic Orchestra
Václav Neumann
Supraphon 11 1959-2
A superbly played and infectious reading

Czech Philharmonic Orchestra
Karel Šejna
Supraphon SU 1916-2
One of the greatest Czech interpretations of both sets of dances

Czech Philharmonic Orchestra • Václav Talich
Supraphon SU 3821-2
A legendary historical recording of the dances

Dvořák (center) with friends Ferdinand Lachner and Hanus Wihan. ➲

Arthur Sullivan | H. M. S. Pinafore (1878)

Genre | Operetta
Conductor/Performers | Charles Mackerras; Richard Suart,
Thomas Allen, Rebecca Evans, Welsh National Opera
Year recorded | 1994
Label | Telarc CD-80374

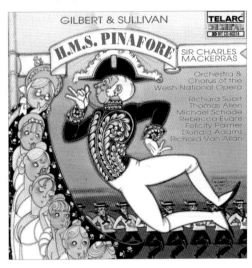

On St. Cecilia's Day, November 22, 1900, Arthur Sullivan died at the age of fifty-eight. There was a symmetry in the death, two months later, of Queen Victoria: the Queen had been an enthusiastic patron, and in the many forms and styles of his serious music—from hymns, anthems, songs, and cantatas to symphonies and chamber works—Sullivan was every inch a Victorian musician. A Chapel Royal chorister, at fourteen Sullivan became the first Mendelssohn Scholar at the Royal Academy of Music, and at sixteen began a four-year course at the Leipzig Conservatoire, where Mendelssohn had been the first director, and Schumann had also taught. The Leipzig experience confirmed Sullivan's immense gifts and launched him as a composer.

But Sullivan was elevated to the ranks of the musical immortals for establishing—with his librettist partner William Schwenck Gilbert—a new genre of English comic operetta: the pair enjoyed runaway success with such endlessly popular operettas as *H. M. S. Pinafore*, *The Pirates of Penzance*, *Iolanthe*, and *The Mikado*.

H. M. S. Pinafore premiered at London's Opera Comique in 1878; its run of 571 consecutive performances signaled that Gilbert and Sullivan had hit on a winning formula that would serve them well for a further decade and ten more operas. In this case, Gilbert's habitual "topsy-turvy" plot device sees Captain Corcoran's daughter Josephine narrowly thwarting the matrimonial designs of elderly Sea Lord, Sir Joseph Porter, to wed her truelove Able Seaman Ralph Rackstraw—actually a highborn who turns out to have been switched at birth with the lowborn Corcoran.

Charles Mackerras's single-CD recording is unsurpassed in sound, interpretation and the musical excellence of a truly outstanding cast. **GK**

> *"Stick close to your desks / and never go to sea / and you all may be Rulers of the Queen's Navee!"*

Sir Joseph Porter, KCB, *H. M. S. Pinafore*

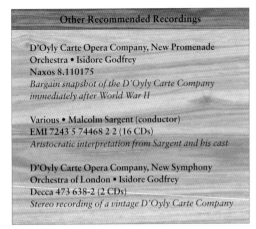

Other Recommended Recordings

**D'Oyly Carte Opera Company, New Promenade
Orchestra • Isidore Godfrey**
Naxos 8.110175
*Bargain snapshot of the D'Oyly Carte Company
immediately after World War II*

Various • Malcolm Sargent (conductor)
EMI 7243 5 74468 2 2 (16 CDs)
Aristocratic interpretation from Sargent and his cast

**D'Oyly Carte Opera Company, New Symphony
Orchestra of London • Isidore Godfrey**
Decca 473 638-2 (2 CDs)
Stereo recording of a vintage D'Oyly Carte Company

Pyotr Ilyich Tchaikovsky | Eugene Onegin (1878)

Genre | Opera
Conductor/Performers | Semyon Bychkov; Dmitri
Hvorostovsky, Nuccia Focile, Neil Shicoff, Paris Orchestra
Year recorded | 1992
Label | Philips 438 235-2 (2 CDs)

In Alexander Pushkin's verse-novel *Eugene Onegin*, a Russian classic, the impressionable teenage heroine Tatyana writes a passionate love letter to the world-weary fop Eugene Onegin. He rejects her advances, with disastrous consequences. Tchaikovsky was so absorbed by the scene of Tatyana's letter, which was the startingpoint for his most intimate opera in 1877, that he determined not to play Onegin to a young woman who had written to him, Antonina Milyukova. The subsequent marriage quickly went wrong, but the operatic *Eugene Onegin* was a success at its first performance at the St. Petersburg Conservatoire in 1879, while its more lavish reincarnation at the Imperial Theaters in 1885 helped in confirming Tchaikovsky's status as Russia's leading composer.

Tchaikovsky's selective treatment of the novel allows him to focus each act of the opera on one of the three principal characters. The first act belongs to Tatyana, with the impassioned "Letter Scene" as its centerpiece; the second shifts the center of attention to Vladimir Lensky, Onegin's poet friend whom he kills in a senseless duel; and the third finally shows Onegin in torment as he falls in love with Tatyana, now a high-society wife, too late.

By no means every recording has reflected the youthful ardor of the three principal characters, but one that comes close to several Russian ideals—none of them in the current catalogue—features baritone Dmitri Hvorostovsky early in his career as a suave Onegin. Nuccia Focile is a lighter, more girlish Tatyana than usual, and Neil Shicoff captures Lensky's passion, and later his remorse, with considerable poetry. The pleasures are compounded by a spirited Russian chorus and powerful conducting from Semyon Bychkov. **DN**

> "What a wealth of poetry there is in Onegin."

Pyotr Ilyich Tchaikovsky

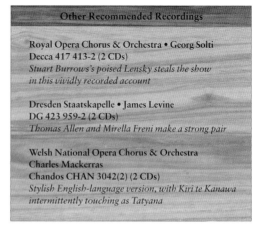

Other Recommended Recordings

Royal Opera Chorus & Orchestra • Georg Solti
Decca 417 413-2 (2 CDs)
Stuart Burrows's poised Lensky steals the show in this vividly recorded account

Dresden Staatskapelle • James Levine
DG 423 959-2 (2 CDs)
Thomas Allen and Mirella Freni make a strong pair

Welsh National Opera Chorus & Orchestra
Charles Mackerras
Chandos CHAN 3042(2) (2 CDs)
Stylish English-language version, with Kiri te Kanawa intermittently touching as Tatyana

Pyotr Ilyich Tchaikovsky | Symphony no. 4 (1878)

Genre | Orchestral
Conductor | Yevgeny Mravinsky
Performers | Leningrad Philharmonic Orchestra
Year recorded | 1960
Label | DG 477 5911 (2 CDs)

Tchaikovsky composed the Fourth Symphony at a turbulent time in his life. When he began it he was shortly to embark on an ill-advised marriage with a former conservatoire student, Antonina Milyukova; but another woman also entered the picture to provide financial support, the wealthy patroness Nadezhda von Meck. It was to her that Tchaikovsky disclosed the "precise program" of his most autobiographical symphony to date. The opening fanfare of the doom-laden first movement was "Fate, that inexorable force which prevents our aspirations to happiness from reaching their goal, which jealously ensures that our well-being and peace are not complete and unclouded, which hangs over our heads like the sword of Damocles, which with steadfast persistence poisons our souls. It is invincible, you will never master it."

Although Fate returns to harass the movement's limping waltzes and to interrupt the folk revels of the finale, there is solace in the "memories of the past" that relieve the melancholy musings of the slow movement and in what Tchaikovsky calls "whimsical arabesques" made by pizzicato strings in a dazzlingly inventive scherzo. His pupil Sergey Taneyev found fault with the overall shape of a long movement followed by three shorter ones, but Tchaikovsky defended his own originality.

Russia's greatest conductor, Yevgeny Mravinsky, made his most famous recordings of Tchaikovsky's last three symphonies within several months toward the end of 1960. The Fourth makes a formidable gateway, never tearing at the heart strings too indiscriminately but always expressive in its keen articulation. The brilliant scherzo is beautifully detailed, and Mravinsky keeps the finale's slightly manic revels in tight focus. **DN**

"The best of all that I have written."

Pyotr Ilyich Tchaikovsky

Other Recommended Recordings

Royal Philharmonic Orchestra • Daniele Gatti
Harmonia Mundi HMU 907393
A tautly dramatic performance that sheds fresh light on an often-recorded work

Colorado Symphony Orchestra • Marin Alsop
Naxos 8555714
Alsop draws world-class playing from the Colorado Symphony Orchestra

Budapest Festival Orchestra • Iván Fischer
Channel CCS 21704
Intense, febrile performance from Iván Fischer and his excellent Budapest orchestra

Mravinsky conducted the Leningrad Philharmonic for 50 years. ➔

Pyotr Ilyich Tchaikovsky | Violin Concerto (1878)

Genre | Concerto
Performers | David Oistrakh, Moscow Philharmonic Orchestra
Conductor | Gennadi Rozhdestvensky
Year recorded | 1968
Label | Melodiya 10 00740

Tchaikovsky had difficulties with all his concertos to start with, but the Violin Concerto and First Piano Concerto became two of his most popular works. It was while recuperating early in 1878 at Clarens, by Lake Geneva, that he wrote the Violin Concerto, spurred on by playing through Lalo's *Symphonie espagnole* with a young violinist friend, Josef Kotek. He had just gone through the agonizing crisis of his ill-judged marriage and the tensions of that episode fed into the dramatic opening movement.

The first problem concerned the slow movement: Tchaikovsky rejected his lovely original and later published it as one of three pieces with piano accompaniment (the version of this "Méditation" orchestrated by Glazunov has often been recorded). His replacement, the "Canzonetta," fitted better into the overall scheme. He thought of giving the dedication to Kotek, who had helped with the violinistic side, but instead chose Leopold Auer: he initially rejected the concerto, so it was finally premiered by its new dedicatee, Adolph Brodsky, in 1881 in Vienna—where the distinguished critic Eduard Hanslick savaged it.

Certainly the concerto declines slightly in quality with each successive movement, but a great performer can make it work. And there is none greater than David Oistrakh. He generally has several versions in the catalogue, all of them fine, but the live 1968 recording is the most thrilling. Oistrakh lifts the whole work onto a higher plane with his artistry and makes the rather trumpery finale sound first-rate. Unlike earlier Russian violinists who used Auer's interventionist edition, he takes the concerto at face value and gives it everything he has. The sound quality is a little fierce, in the way of Russian recordings of that vintage, but very impressive. **TP**

> *"David Oistrakh is a perfect violinist from every point of view."*
>
> George Enescu

Other Recommended Recordings

Leonid Kogan, Paris Conservatoire Orchestra
Constantin Silvestri
EMI 7243 5 74757 2 3
A towering performance by another Russian master

Bronislaw Huberman, Berlin Staatskapelle
William Steinberg
Naxos 8.110903
A legendary Polish player, in dazzling form in 1928

Julia Fischer, Russian National Orchestra
Yakov Kreizberg
PentaTone 5186 095
An all-Tchaikovsky program in state-of-the-art sound

Johannes Brahms | Violin Sonatas (1879–88)

Genre | Chamber
Performers | Josef Suk (violin),
Julius Katchen (piano)
Year recorded | 1967
Label | Decca 466 393-2

Brahms wrote only three violin sonatas but they are all of the highest quality, owing to a ruthless process of elimination. It is thought that he discarded at least five—having even privately performed one of them, in A minor, dating from 1853—before he finally let his friend Joseph Joachim have the Sonata in G major, op. 78, in 1879. It was written that summer in Pörtschach, southern Austria, and the ease of its melodic outpourings owed much to the experience of writing a concerto for Joachim. The almost equally lyrical Sonata in A major, op. 100, followed in 1886 during a golden summer in Thun, Switzerland, which also gave rise to sketches for the Sonata in D minor, op. 108, as well as the Second Cello Sonata and Third Piano Trio. Finished two years later, the D minor Sonata is a bigger work, both in its gestures and in having four movements rather than three.

The Brahms sonatas make an excellent program and such famous duos as Adolf Busch and Rudolf Serkin, or Zino Francescatti and Robert Casadesus, played them all in one evening. The pairing of Josef Suk and Julius Katchen did not have time to develop a comparable reputation because the pianist died from cancer in 1969 aged just forty-two. They did, however, produce one pearl of a record and it is still untouchable in its achievement. Katchen, a celebrated Brahms specialist, had already recorded two of the sonatas with Ruggiero Ricci, but in Suk he found a truer match. The Czech violinist, who has now retired from the concert stage, had an effortless technique that combined with his warm sound made him an ideal Brahms player. The recordings, engineered by the legendary Kenneth Wilkinson in the expansive Kingsway Hall acoustic, still sound wonderful. **TP**

> *"Here he comes as near perfection as human limitations permit."*

Daniel Gregory Mason on Brahms's 1879–90 chamber music

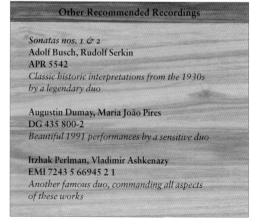

Other Recommended Recordings

Sonatas nos. 1 & 2
Adolf Busch, Rudolf Serkin
APR 5542
*Classic historic interpretations from the 1930s
by a legendary duo*

Augustin Dumay, Maria João Pires
DG 435 800-2
Beautiful 1991 performances by a sensitive duo

Itzhak Perlman, Vladimir Ashkenazy
EMI 7243 5 66945 2 1
*Another famous duo, commanding all aspects
of these works*

Bedřich Smetana | Má vlast (1879)

Genre | Orchestral
Conductor | Rafael Kubelík
Performers | Czech Philharmonic Orchestra
Year recorded | 1990
Label | Supraphon 11 1208-2

Having celebrated the history and mythology of his Czech homeland in the operas *The Brandenburgers in Bohemia*, *Dalibor*, and *Libuše*, Smetana turned his hand to commemorating it orchestrally. Between 1872 and 1879, he wrote the six symphonic poems of *Má vlast* (*My Fatherland*), a musical touchstone for the Czech nation. In these works, Smetana dealt with the nation's past and the beauties of its countryside. The cycle as a whole was much enhanced by a sense of personal struggle since while working on the first piece he went completely deaf.

The opening of the cycle, "Vyšehrad," named after the rocky fastness that stands above the river Vltava in Prague, is one of Smetana's finest inspirations, an image of ancient glory snuffed out by tragic defeat. The celebrated picture of the course of the river Vltava from source to its magnificent entry into Prague comes second. Before Smetana makes a return to nature in "From Bohemia's Woods and Fields," he gives the legend of "Šárka," (an Amazon maiden who tragically falls in love with a warrior sent to bring her to justice) distinctly operatic treatment. The two remaining symphonic poems are linked by a hymn of the Hussites, the religious reformers of the late middle ages often used as a national symbol by the Czechs: "Tábor" tells of their struggles and "Blaník," the hill in which the Hussite warriors slumber awaiting the hour of the nation's greatest need, begins with their defeat, but swells to a triumphant and bracing conclusion.

There are many classic performances of the cycle, but none has quite the incandescent force of Rafael Kubelík's, recorded at the Prague Spring Festival just months after the "Velvet Revolution" of 1989. The thrill of Czech freedom attained at last informs this powerful performance. **JS**

> *"On the basis of this melody the resurrection of the Czech nation, its future happiness and glory, unfold."*

Smetana on the concluding poem of *Má vlast*

Other Recommended Recordings

Czech Philharmonic Orchestra • Charles Mackerras
Supraphon SU 3465-2 031
Sumptuous recording of a brilliantly paced performance by one of the great interpreters of Czech music

Czech Philharmonic Orchestra • Václav Talich
Supraphon SU 3826-2
A classic interpretation from 1954 by the greatest Czech conductor of the twentieth century

Royal Liverpool Philharmonic Orchestra • Libor Pešek
Virgin 7243 5 61739 2 7
An affectionate reading by one of the most penetrating of recent Czech conductors

Gabriel Fauré | Piano Quartets 1 & 2 (1879)

Genre | Chamber
Performers | Augustin Dumay (viola), Bruno Pasquier
(violin), Jean-Philippe Collard (piano), Frédéric Lodéon (cello)
Years recorded | 1975–78
Label | EMI 7243 5 85282 2 0

The Piano Quartet no. 1 in C minor was Fauré's first substantial chamber work after his First Violin Sonata and finds him following in the footsteps of the exquisite piano quartets by Schumann—one of his musical idols—and Brahms, who was not popular in France yet whose music seems to have left some traces on the youthful Fauré. Like the sonata, it is a work full of passion and élan, as well as a lavish melodic lyricism that finds its apogees in the dark and soulful slow movement and the second subject of the driving finale, where it appears, oddly enough, to foreshadow one of the great love themes from Puccini's *Madama Butterfly*. The scherzo is delicate and fleeting, while the opening movement's main theme suggests the modal patterns that so often color and add variety to the composer's musical language.

"Fauré is delightful!"

Pyotr Ilyich Tchaikovsky, 1899

The Second Piano Quartet in G minor dates from just seven years later but shows Fauré in more sophisticated mode, as well as a generally more turbulent state of mind. The driving pace lets up infrequently, except for the slow movement, an episode of extraordinary, reflective beauty with personal significance for Fauré. He explained that he had evoked memories of "a peal of bells we used to hear of an evening, drifting over to Montgauzy.... Their sound gives rise to a vague reverie which, like all vague reveries, is not translatable into words...."

The recording by the all-French team of pianist Jean-Philippe Collard, violinist Augustin Dumay, violist Bruno Pasquier, and cellist Frédéric Lodéon offers particularly strong interpretations, making the most of these works' fabulous energy. Although many fine accounts of both quartets exist, this is the one that I personally return to time and again for its immediacy and ardor. **JD**

Other Recommended Recordings

Piano Quartet no. 1
Robert Casadesus, Joseph Calvet, Léon Pascal, Paul Mas
Biddulph LAB 116
Perfectly idiomatic account, recorded in 1935

Piano Quartet no. 2
Marguerite Long, Jacques Thibaud, Maurice Vieux,
Pierre Fournier
Biddulph LHW 035
Anguished account recorded in Paris in World War II

Pascal Roge, members of Ysaÿe Quartet
Decca 475 187-2
Great finesse from a matchless contemporary team

Modest Mussorgsky
Khovanshchina (1880)

Genre | Opera
Conductor/Performers | Claudio Abbado;
Marjana Lipovšek, Paata Burchuladze
Year recorded | 1990
Label | DG 429 758-2 (3 CDs)

The personal and the political are mutually reflected in this dense, mostly dark opera. The historically derived theme focuses on the tumultuous events surrounding the changes in Russian society at the end of the seventeenth century. Under the leadership of Peter the Great, Russia's hermetic isolation was gradually being displaced by a more outward-looking mindset that brought with it the decline of the feudal system and religious reform. All these elements are represented in the opera, the central plot of which concerns the downfall and assassination of Prince Khovansky, who is the embodiment of the old regime. Religious conservatism is represented by the Old Believers, a traditionalist sect; unable to accept change, they ritually immolate themselves, taking several of the other characters with them.

At the time of his death, Mussorgsky had yet to finish the closing scenes of the second and fifth acts and had only orchestrated two scenes. The completion of these tasks fell to Rimsky-Korsakov, although Shostakovich produced an alternative orchestration in 1958.

It is a testament to Mussorgsky's musical and theatrical imagination that his ideas have not simply survived these and other interventions but have emerged from them with such substance. Claudio Abbado reaches into every corner of the score to bring these ideas to the fore in a gripping performance that includes a gloriously robust contribution from the chorus and fine characterizations from the soloists. Sonically, this disc is also highly commendable, expertly balancing the excitement of a live recording with judicious engineering and production. **RT**

Gabriel Fauré
Élégie (1880)

Genre | Chamber
Performers | Steven Isserlis (cello),
Pascal Devoyon (piano)
Year recorded | 1988
Label | RCA 09026 68049 2

Fauré's *Élégie* is his best-known work for solo cello and the most substantial he produced for many years. It was originally intended to be the slow movement of a sonata, but Fauré never completed the rest and eventually published the piece on its own three years later.

The *Élégie* shows a considerable influence from Fauré's teacher, Saint-Saëns, in its simple ternary structure, heartfelt melody, and substantial piano part. The version with orchestral accompaniment is Fauré's own arrangement, but followed the piano original fifteen years later.

Fauré wrote the piece in 1880, when he was thirty-five years old. Some traumatic incidents had influenced him strongly in the 1870s: first, the Franco-Prussian War, in which he had served in an infantry regiment; later a romantic disappointment and broken engagement. These incidents exacerbated his already considerable tendency toward introversion and depression, even though he was also a great charmer and ladies' man. A series of works composed in the years following 1877 reflect this moodiness to some degree, perhaps the *Élégie* most of all. It is the last of Fauré's works to display such a strong element of heart-on-sleeve Romanticism.

Steven Isserlis's recording of Fauré's complete music for solo cello is a must-have CD. He and his admirable pianist, Pascal Devoyon, approach the music with immense empathy and fidelity. The *Élégie* emerges in a poised, deeply felt account, Isserlis's beautifully modulated playing ranging from restraint and elegance at the opening to an impassioned outpouring on the return of the main theme. Devoyon matches him quality for quality. **JD**

Hans Rott
Symphony in E major (1880)

Genre | Orchestral
Conductor/Performers | Dennis Russell Davies; Vienna Radio Symphony Orchestra
Year recorded | 2002
Label | CPO 999 854-2

In October 1880, the twenty-two-year-old Hans Rott was a highly promising former student of Bruckner's at the Vienna Conservatoire with, it seemed, an illustrious career ahead of him. On a train journey to Mühlhausen that month to take up a post as choirmaster, however, the first signs of Rott's mental deterioration were graphically evident. A fellow passenger, attempting to light a cigar, was confronted by Rott brandishing a revolver and claiming that Brahms, no less, had filled the train with dynamite. Rott's decline was precipitous: having been committed to an asylum, he was dead within three years.

Bruckner continued to promote his work, however, as did his fellow pupil Mahler. And indeed it is Rott's influence on Mahler that makes this symphony the fascinating document it is. Not only are there pre-echoes of Mahler symphonies yet to be written in all four movements, but the scherzo and introduction to the finale contain quite specific ideas subsequently used by Mahler.

Shortly after the world premiere of the work, in Cincinnati in 1989, a creditable recording was made by student forces from that city. While a certain rough-edged quality is not inappropriate in that the work itself exemplifies youthful exuberance and gaucheness, there is no doubt that Rott is better served by a professional recording such as the excellent one by the Vienna Radio Symphony Orchestra under Dennis Russell Davies. Had he lived, Rott would doubtless have honed his talent. As it is, we may appreciate the echoes of Bruckner and Brahms and the astonishing anticipations of Mahler as the unpredictable flights of genius they surely are. **BM**

Jacques Offenbach
The Tales of Hoffmann (1880)

Genre | Opera
Conductor/Performers | Richard Bonynge; Joan Sutherland, Plácido Domingo
Year recorded | 1972
Label | Decca 417 363-2 (2 CDs)

The Tales of Hoffmann contains three musical tales bound together by the same simple moral—that blind love only makes you blinder. The story follows the lover and poet, Hoffmann, in his new love for the diva Stella; his old love for Olympia, a mechanical doll; for the Venetian courtesan Giulietta; and for Antonia, who dies of a surfeit of singing. A prologue and an epilogue urge Hoffmann to see his loves as Art not Life.

Jacques Offenbach was writing *Les contes d'Hoffmann* to a libretto that drew on the life and art of the German Romantic writer E. T. A. Hoffmann right up until his death in 1880, by which time it was still unfinished. This flawed masterpiece exists in a number of versions, which have provided a happy hunting ground for musicologists hoping to second guess the composer's true intentions. For over a century, stage directors and conductors have imagined what Offenbach might have wanted had he lived to revise *Hoffmann*.

Not everyone who knows the work in the theater will agree with Richard Bonynge's decision to end with the Antonia rather than the Venetian act, but his recording makes it seem the right dramatic choice—Hoffmann may yet be redeemed by art. Joan Sutherland in all three of the soprano roles, and as Stella in the epilogue, gives a truly stellar performance. Plácido Domingo is, quite simply, the finest Hoffmann of his generation and in Gabriel Bacquier we have an authentic villain for each act. Bacquier and Bonynge even make the magician Dapertutto's aria "Scintille diamant" seem properly Offenbachian even if it was written by another hand. **CC**

Pyotr Ilyich Tchaikovsky | Serenade for Strings (1880)

Genre | Orchestral
Conductor | Daniele Gatti
Performers | Royal Philharmonic Orchestra
Year recorded | 2005
Label | Harmonia Mundi HMU 907394

Tchaikovsky composed what is perhaps his sunniest work back to back with the *1812 Overture*, declaring that while he composed the overture to order, with no special feeling of love, the Serenade for Strings was "a heartfelt piece and so, I dare to think . . . not lacking in real qualities." He was right. The serenade gives the lie to the stereotypical image of Tchaikovsky as a poet of doom and despair, offering only the slightest hint of melancholy in the later stages of its third movement, the "Elegy."

A descending figure begins and ends the work, at the very last minute drawing attention to its similarity with the second of the Russian folk songs Tchaikovsky engages for his lively finale. The main body of the first movement is a dancing inspiration, constructed along Mozartian lines as a simple sonatina, and capped in its irresistible lilt only by what is perhaps Tchaikovsky's most elegant waltz, encored at the first performance in 1881. This time the figure ascends, a device echoed in the slow movement; both are splendid examples of how much Tchaikovsky was able to extract, melodically speaking, from portions of a simple scale.

The serenade can sound very different according to whether the full strings of a symphony orchestra are engaged, making it sound lush and Romantic, or simply chamber-sized forces, which can be nimbler (Tchaikovsky initially wavered over whether to write a symphony or a string quintet). Daniele Gatti shows the flipside of Tchaikovsky's temperament on a disc that begins with the Sixth ("Pathétique") Symphony. He manages to coax the best of both worlds out of the Royal Philharmonic Orchestra strings, bold and majestic in the opening sequence but also extremely flexible in more intimate moments. **DN**

> ## "I composed the Serenade from inner conviction."
>
> Pyotr Ilyich Tchaikovsky

Other Recommended Recordings

New Stockholm Chamber Orchestra • Paavo Berglund
BIS CD-243
Best of the smaller-scale versions, supple and bright

Academy of St. Martin in the Fields • Neville Marriner
Decca 470 262-2
Long a speciality of Marriner and the Academy, the serenade sparkles in their hands

Souvenir de Florence
Norwegian Chamber Orchestra • Iona Brown
Chandos CHAN 9708
If you love the serenade, you'll love this arrangement of a string sextet

Italian conductor Daniele Gatti is a leading exponent of Russian music. ➔

Camille Saint-Saëns
Violin Concerto no. 3 (1880)

Genre | Concerto
Performer | Jean-Jacques Kantorow
Conductor | Kees Bakels
Year recorded | 2004
Label | BIS CD-1470

Saint-Saëns was such a facile composer that he could achieve virtually anything he put his mind to. He wrote a number of concertos, all of them effective, although just two for piano, one for violin, and one for cello hold their places in the repertoire. The third and last of his violin concertos, in B minor, is the favored one for that instrument: it is tuneful, well constructed, and gives the soloist plenty of display material without being merely showy. The first movement is quite strong, the central slow movement is lovely without exactly being deep, and unusually the finale is the longest of the three.

Like most of the composer's violin music, the concerto was written for the Spanish fiddler Pablo de Sarasate, a master of the Gallic style, who had considerable success with it. Some famous interpreters, such as Zino Francescatti, are not well represented in the catalogue; but even if they were, the version by Jean-Jacques Kantorow would be fully competitive. This highly skilled yet extremely musical player, comes of Russian stock but was born and trained in France.

In the past fifteen years Kantorow has turned to conducting, but fortunately he has not given up the violin. He has a close connection with the Tapiola Sinfonietta in Espoo, Finland, and he conducts some of this program, sensibly ceding the baton to Kees Bakels in the concerto. Kantorow is forceful where necessary in the first movement and keeps the finale spinning along nicely; but what makes this interpretation special is his disarming simplicity in the slow movement. The shorter pieces on this all-Saint-Saëns disc are nicely done and the recordings are superb. **TP**

Bedřich Smetana
From the Homeland (1880)

Genre | Chamber
Performers | Josef Suk (violin),
Jan Panenka (piano)
Year recorded | 1963
Label | Supraphon SU 3777-2

The father of Czech nationalist music, Bedřich Smetana, wrote very little chamber music—and most of it has a strong autobiographical content. An exception is the pair of lyrical pieces that he wrote for violin and his own instrument, the piano. The title *Z domoviny* (*From the Homeland*) might suggest a sort of chamber counterpart to Smetana's great cycle of symphonic poems *Má vlast*, but in fact these are gentle pieces, reflecting the peace that the tormented composer, racked by physical and mental illness, found in the countryside around Jabkenice in central Bohemia.

The spur for writing the two duos came from a publisher, who tried to impose a German title, leading Smetana to reject the contract. He dedicated the pieces to his patron Prince Alexander of Thun and Taxis, who responded with a garnet-encrusted ivory snuffbox. The duos alternate expressive, Romantic slow music with faster sections in Slavonic rhythms: the shorter A major is in ternary form, while the G minor is more complicated. For years they were published in a terrible edition, which means that historic performances by Váša Příhoda and others are a little suspect, for all their charms.

The famous recording by Josef Suk and Jan Panenka was the first to be generally available in a decent edition, and it still sounds fine. Suk, scion of a Czech musical dynasty, plays with colorful tone and expression, while Panenka takes care of the important piano part. The more rhythmic sections come naturally to these terrific musicians. If an all-Smetana disc is preferred, go for the Guarneri Trio on Supraphon. **TP**

Pyotr Ilyich Tchaikovsky
1812 Overture (1880)

Genre | Orchestral
Conductor/Performers | Antonio Pappano; Accademia di Santa Cecilia
Year recorded | 2006
Label | EMI 0946 3 70065 2 8

In 1882, there was much pomp and ceremony in Moscow: a grand Exhibition of Industry and the Arts coincided with the opening of the new Cathedral of Christ the Savior. Tchaikovsky, then at the height of his reputation, was persuaded to compose an overture, which, like the cathedral, was to commemorate the momentous events of 1812 in which Napoleon and the French army, having reached as far as Moscow, had been drummed out of Russia in a war of attrition. He was doubtful about the value of ceremonial music. "What," he asked his patroness, Nadezhda von Meck, "can you write on the occasion of the opening of an exhibition except banalities and generally noisy passages?"

In fact, he proved he was able to do much more than that in the *1812 Overture*, however dismissive he may have been of its worth. It begins with a moving string arrangement—optionally adaptable for choir—of the Orthodox chant "Save, o Lord, thy people," and offsets the conflict of battle with some very beautiful lyrical music adapted from an early opera, *The Voyevoda*. In an unashamedly noisy victory parade, the "Marseillaise" is routed by the Orthodox chant and the hymn "God save the Tsar." Optional cannon and bells turn this into a fully fledged spectacular that can still be effective in the concert hall and allows the opportunities for sonic display on disc.

Antonio Pappano's performance with Italian forces strengthens the purely musical values of the piece, lingering lovingly over the lyric respite and drafting in the choir to sing, in addition to the opening chant, a Russian folk song and "God save the Tsar." The special effects do not overwhelm the orchestra in the final triumph. **DN**

Charles-Marie Widor
Symphony no. 5 (1880)

Genre | Instrumental
Instrument | Organ of Notre Dame, Paris
Performer | Olivier Latry
Year recorded | 1986
Label | BNL 112617

Charles-Marie Widor (1844–1937) was born in Lyon; his grandfather was an organ builder, his father an organist, and his mother was related to the Montgolfier family (of hot-air balloon fame). After studying in Brussels with Lemmens, in 1870 Widor took up the much sought after post of organist of the prestigious St. Sulpice church in Paris, remaining there until 1933; he succeeded Franck as organ professor at the Paris Conservatoire, later assuming the chair of composition. He wrote a treatise on orchestration and profoundly influenced generations of organists and composers.

Widor composed in numerous genres, but is credited with inventing a new form: the organ "symphony"—freely structured multimovement works designed to exploit the orchestral sounds of Cavaillé-Coll's revolutionary new organs. Listeners usually turn first to the Fifth Symphony in F minor, op. 42, no. 1, with its Toccata—one of the most famous pieces in the entire organ repertoire, and now a wedding favorite. The Toccata concludes a five-movement symphony that begins with an extended set of variations; three contrasting sections follow, each demonstrating Widor's harmonic and melodic gifts, as well as his mastery of contrapuntal techniques derived from J. S. Bach.

Olivier Latry succeeded Pierre Cochereau as organist of Notre Dame de Paris, and is the leading French virtuoso organist of his generation. His recording of Widor's Fifth Symphony offers breathtaking dexterity and the chance to hear the blazing intensity of the Notre Dame instrument—a unique sound, essential to a proper appreciation of Cavaillé-Coll's achievements, and Widor's musical vision. **GK**

Alexander Borodin
String Quartet no. 2 (1881)

Genre | Chamber
Performers | Borodin Quartet: Dubinsky,
Aleksandrov, Shebalin, Berlinsky
Year recorded | 1962
Label | BBC Legends BBCL 4063-2

When it came to pouring out long, exquisitely singable melodies, Alexander Borodin was one of the most gifted of the nineteenth-century Russian nationalists. His Second String Quartet almost overflows with glorious themes, but there is so much more to this work than a medley of good tunes. Ideas flow from and into each other so naturally that it is easy to miss the subtle craftsmanship by which it is all achieved. At the same time Borodin's handling of the quartet medium has a distinctly personal mastery: who else could have conceived the lovely summer-night textures toward the close of the slow movement? Throughout, the balance between fastidious elegance and joyous spontaneity is near miraculous. No wonder this remains one of the most popular of all string quartets.

Soviet Russia's greatest chamber ensemble, the Borodin Quartet, recorded this work several times, but this live version from the 1962 Edinburgh Festival has something special. Borodin wrote this work as an expression of love for his wife, and this performance captures the seriousness of Borodin's devotion as well as tenderness and sensuous delight. The players also convey a rare sense of this work as a journey, eventually building to an exultant conclusion. The sense of the finale's folk-dance theme emerging from smoky darkness is especially subtle; by comparison so many other performers either underplay this passage or strive too hard to make something "profound" out of it. The mono recorded sound may not be of demonstration quality by modern standards, but everything that matters comes across clearly and tellingly. **SJ**

Johannes Brahms
Piano Concerto no. 2 (1881)

Genre | Concerto
Performers/Conductor | Leon Fleisher,
Cleveland Orchestra; George Szell
Year recorded | 1962
Label | Sony MH2K 63225 (2 CDs)

Brahms took the musical world by storm with his ultra-serious, ultra-symphonic First Piano Concerto. There was then a gap of more than twenty years before he produced his even more epic Second Piano Concerto. If the First left audiences perplexed with its symphonic outlook, the Second was equally mold-breaking. The biggest concerto ever written up to that time in terms of sheer length, this piece takes the symphony analogy still further by adding a scherzo movement. It is a masterstroke on Brahms's part: placed between the epic first movement and the luscious Andante, which opens with one of the most glorious solo cello melodies in all orchestral music, the scherzo functions as a palate cleanser in between substantial courses. It also demonstrates Brahms's quiet wit, a facet of his character that is all too often overlooked.

Brahms hardly spares the soloist, with handfuls of notes that need to be propulsive and light as well as dramatic. In the hands of Leon Fleisher and George Szell, the scherzo is a miraculous sparkling whirl. But they do not short-change the listener on the more grandiose aspects of this score either. The first movement—such a quiet opening for something so epic, with its solo horn answered by a quiet piano phrase—has all the nobility you could wish for yet it never drags its feet. This is not a concerto where the soloist and orchestra fight to the death for preeminence; rather, it is a dialogue between two godlike figures, and Leon Fleisher and George Szell understand this perfectly. And finally, an Allegretto grazioso, almost Haydn-esque in its lightness of tread and mood, sets the seal on one of the greatest concertos in the piano repertoire. **HS**

Richard Wagner
Parsifal (1881)

Genre | Opera
Performers | Plácido Domingo,
Waltraud Meier, Franz-Josef Selig
Year recorded | 2005
Label | DG 477 6006 (4 CDs)

"*Parsifal* is one of the loveliest monuments of sound ever raised to the serene glory of music," according to Debussy. And the score is indeed an evocation of the most unearthly sublimity. But the work is more than that: As the culmination of Wagner's life work, *Parsifal* is also the most refined expression of the moral and aesthetic issues with which he had been grappling in his last years. Compassion, fellow-suffering, and withdrawing from the temptations and tribulations of the world the better to realize one's own spiritual potential: all these ideas are developed.

Parsifal was the only one of Wagner's works to be written with the actual sound of the Bayreuth Festspielhaus in mind. Indeed, Wagner intended the work as a consecration of that festival stage and for many years it was not allowed to be performed anywhere else. No doubt because of the quasi-religious aura surrounding the work, it has often been associated with Good Friday, the sacred day alluded to in the text. Recent productions, however, have sought to confront that hallowed tradition and to reinterpret the features less appealing to a modern audience—celibacy, misogyny, racial supremacy—in a more positive light.

Christian Thielemann's live recording features Plácido Domingo, belying his years with an ardent yet suitably introspective account of the title role, with Waltraud Meier as Kundry, excellent in a part she has made her own over the years. What makes it even more special is Thielemann's ability to integrate the strength and solemnity of traditional interpretations with the more modern, streamlined tempi pioneered by Boulez—a *Parsifal* both timeless and for today. **BM**

Anton Bruckner
Symphony no. 6 (1881)

Genre | Orchestral
Conductor/Performers | Bernard Haitink;
Amsterdam Concertgebouw Orchestra
Year recorded | 1970
Label | Philips 473 301-2

For some strange reason, Bruckner's Sixth remains the Cinderella of the symphonies. It has so many features that ought to make it popular: comparatively short, it is full of striking and appealing ideas, and the ending of the slow movement is one of the most touching things Bruckner ever wrote. The first movement, too, has a bracing rhythmic drive that should win over those who find Bruckner too spacious or inclined to go off at seeming tangents. Perhaps it is the enigmatic ending—more ambiguous, less radiantly affirmative than in most of Bruckner's other mature symphonies—that keeps it from being a concert favorite. Written at a crisis point in Bruckner's life and career, it may indicate that his all-important faith was wavering. This is not the Bruckner of popular legend, but the more one knows the Sixth, the more rewarding it becomes.

Bernard Haitink thought long and hard about this symphony before recording it, and it shows. While he keeps up a relatively lively pace in the first movement and finale, he is always careful to give the ideas time to breathe, so the music never sounds hurried. In the finale in particular, he shows special understanding of the dark mysteries that open out between the seemingly confident brassy fortissimos. The sound of the Amsterdam Concertgebouw Orchestra—beautifully captured by the recording—is unforgettable in those sonorous tuttis, and still more in the gorgeous string writing at the close of the slow movement; but Haitink also has a way of letting light and air into the texture that prevents heaviness and keeps the music moving. **SJ**

Pyotr Ilyich Tchaikovsky
Piano Trio in A minor
(1882)

Genre | Chamber
Performers | Kempf Trio: Freddy Kempf,
Pierre Bensaid, Alexander Chaushian
Year recorded | 2002
Label | BIS CD-1302

In writing his only piano trio "in memory of a great artist"—pianist and director of the St. Petersburg Conservatoire Nicolai Rubinstein—Tchaikovsky created a Russian tradition: Rachmaninov would go on to write his Trio élégiaque in D minor for Tchaikovsky, and Arensky and Shostakovich both wrote memorial piano trios. Tchaikovsky's is an epic work of magnificence and melancholy lasting nearly an hour. He had had doubts about the genre, but decided against an orchestral tribute and a solo piano piece, and instead drew on the instrumental combination to paint a portrait of his friend, full of richness and exuberance.

The structure is unusual, beginning with an "elegiac piece" that is followed by eleven variations based on a Russian folk song, a reminiscence of a happy trip to the country made by Rubinstein. The piece ends with the triumphant, thunderous final variation and a mournful funeral march. The work has suffered criticism for its length: the variations certainly require huge energy and flexibility from their performers, ranging as they do from graceful waltz to tinkling musical box, vivacious mazurka, and academic fugue, and from witty scherzo to keening lament.

There are many passionate performances of this piano trio by some very famous musicians, but none can match the superlative quality of the young Kempf Trio. In these players' hands, this long, labor-intensive work pours forth in a spontaneous stream of melody—radiant, effortless, and straight from the heart. **HW**

Pablo de Sarasate
Concert Fantasy
on *Carmen* (c.1883)

Genre | Concerto
Performer | Itzhak Perlman (violin)
Conductor | Lawrence Foster
Year recorded | 1971
Label | EMI 7243 5 74765 2 2

The combination of chic French style, catchy melodies, and Spanish rhythms in Bizet's *Carmen* meant that for the great Spanish violin virtuoso Pablo de Sarasate, who was schooled in Paris, it was a natural to exploit. Sarasate wrote fantasies on themes from a number of operas: his *Faust* concoction sometimes gets a hearing today, but the *Carmen* one is the sole survivor in the mainstream repertoire. In fact, if you judge by length alone, it is his major contribution to violinists of the modern era.

Bizet's themes, which are virtually of jukebox popularity, cannot take all the credit for the work's success. Sarasate knows the nature and capability of the violin so well that he transfers the spirit as well as the letter of the tunes to the new medium, really making the violin sing in the legato sections; and if the result is still something of a ragbag, well, that is in the nature of the operatic fantasy as a genre.

Part of the success of Itzhak Perlman's interpretation is due to his sense of humor, which results in some delightful timing of the various effects. He has all the technique needed to make the difficulties sound as if they do not exist, his intonation is stunning, and his tone is consistently alive. He has made two excellent recordings, the more recent in digital sound with Zubin Mehta conducting, but perhaps the earlier one with Lawrence Foster just has the edge in ebullience. Very well recorded for its time, it has been issued over the years in various compilations, and this Spanish album will be the best buy for anyone interested in Sarasate, as it includes more of his pieces. **TP**

Johannes Brahms
Symphony no. 3
(1883)

Genre | Orchestral
Conductor/Performers | Mariss Jansons;
Oslo Philharmonic Orchestra
Year recorded | 1999
Label | Simax PSC 1204

Emmanuel Chabrier
España
(1883)

Genre | Orchestral
Conductor | Paul Paray
Performers | Detroit Symphony Orchestra
Year recorded | 1960
Label | Mercury 434 303-2

Hans Richter, the first conductor of Brahms's Third Symphony, called it his "Eroica." But it is his shortest, and the development sections in its three sonata-form movements are notably brief. The expositions and recapitulations, however, are expansive and generously supplied with memorable ideas, while internal and cross-movement unity is secured both by the use of a "motto" figure and its associated theme, and by the significant development in the finale of elements from the slow movement. The motto, boldly stated at the very outset, is a version of the Brahmsian figure F-A-F, said to stand for the composer's personal motto "frei aber froh" (free but happy).

In the transitions of the first movement there are references to Wagner's *Tannhäuser*, and the movement's development seems to be powered by a hectic and passionate waltz-tempo. The gentle slow movement is sublimated village-band music, and the ensuing intermezzo is a classic expression of Brahmsian bittersweet regret. Shadowy and mysterious at first, the finale bursts out into an ardent and dramatic allegro, crowned at the climax by the choleric transformation of a theme from the slow movement. An autumnal epilogue ends the work in a mood of hard-won serenity and experience.

Mariss Jansons draws coruscating playing from the Oslo Philharmonic in a superbly dramatic account with remarkably fine shading of the dynamic contrasts. Brahms's orchestral writing really glows, and all four movements are paced with power and purposefulness. **MM**

España is without doubt Emmanuel Chabrier's best-known piece. Yet it would be foolish to call it typical, for Chabrier was something of a chameleon of a composer. On the one hand, he was a deeply committed Wagnerian, moved to tears by *Tristan und Isolde* when he first saw that opera in 1880, and inspired to write the opera *Gwendoline* with the spirit of Wagner very much looking over his shoulder. On the other hand, when finding an opera house willing to stage *Gwendoline* turned out to be a little difficult, he calmly turned away from the piece, setting to work instead on the operetta *Le roi malgré lui*, instantly transporting himself to an entirely different musical world and adjusting his musical language accordingly. *España*, the product of a family trip to Spain lasting from July to December 1882, shows a third side of this musical personality. Wagnerian it is definitely not, though neither is it a work of Offenbachian frivolity. Instead it does just what its title claims it to do. It evokes, using authentic Spanish ideas and mannerisms, the exuberant spirit of a nation.

Since every first-rate orchestra and conductor likes to impress with readings of showy music, the catalogue abounds with sizzling performances. Paul Paray's 1960 account with the Detroit Symphony Orchestra is, however, outstanding. It really sparkles but also captures something of the laid-back nature characteristic of the work's subject. It comes with a fine selection of the best of Chabrier's orchestral music, including the Overture to *Gwendoline* and the catchy *Joyeuse marche*. **SP**

Anton Bruckner | Symphony no. 7 (1883)

Genre | Orchestral
Conductor | Karl Böhm
Performers | Vienna Philharmonic Orchestra
Year recorded | 1977
Label | DG 419 858-2

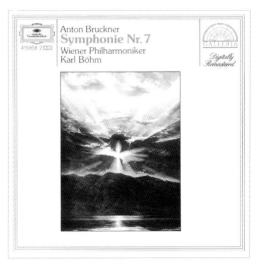

If recording and concert statistics are anything to go by, Bruckner's Seventh is now his most popular symphony. It is easy to see why. The opening, with a noble long melody rising in two great waves, is one of the most beautiful in the orchestral repertoire. Bruckner claimed that this idea came to him in a dream, with the assurance that it would bring him success—as the old saying goes, if it isn't true, it ought to be. The Adagio, a threnody for Bruckner's beloved "Meister," Richard Wagner, is possibly the most perfect of all his slow movements, with the elemental dance scherzo that follows the perfect foil. The Seventh is the most generously melodic of the symphonies, and despite the characteristically brassy fortissimo conclusion, the prevailing feeling is of one of warm serenity—clouded sometimes, but always returning.

The tendency of modern conductors to emphasize the architectural in Bruckner, sometimes at the expense of the more human elements, is nowhere more damaging than in the Seventh Symphony. So Karl Böhm's balance of clear-sighted formal understanding with a more fluid, supple approach to phrasing is close to ideal. Again, unlike many modern interpreters, Böhm grasps the need to keep the first movement flowing forward, though without driving anything too hard. Thus the Adagio can expand without the fatal feeling of one huge slow movement following another. Especially effective is the way the Adagio's blazingly triumphant, cymbal-topped climax fades into the contained grief of the coda—did Wagner the man deserve an elegy like this? And how richly textured the playing of the Vienna Philharmonic sounds in this music. The Viennese may have given Bruckner a rough time when he was alive, but they make up for it here. **SJ**

> *"One single cymbal clash by Bruckner is worth all the four symphonies of Brahms."*
>
> Hugo Wolf

Other Recommended Recordings

Berlin Philharmonic • Herbert von Karajan
EMI 7243 5 66095 2 5
Karajan's least grandiose, most purely beautiful recording of this symphony

NDR Symphony Orchestra • Günter Wand
RCA 09026 61398 2
Only a bad edit in the Adagio prevents this nobly beautiful performance getting top place

Royal Scottish National Orchestra • Georg Tintner
Naxos 8.554269
A finely shaped performance, especially convincing in the Adagio

Léo Delibes | Lakmé (1883)

Genre | Opera
Conductor/Performers | Michel Plasson; Natalie Dessay,
Gregory Kunde, Delphine Haidan, José van Dam
Year recorded | 1997
Label | EMI 7243 5 56569 2 6 (2 CDs)

Léo Delibes was born and educated into the opera. His maternal grandfather was a singer, and as a boy he sang at the premiere of Meyerbeer's *Le prophète*. Then as a young man he was appointed the accompanist for the Théâtre Lyrique, where he became chorus master in the 1860s, working on Gounod's *Faust* (for which he arranged the vocal score), Bizet's *Les pêcheurs des perles,* and Berlioz's *Les Troyens à Carthage.*

First performed at the Opéra Comique in April 1883, *Lakmé* was the fruit of all that Delibes had learned writing more than thirty works for the theater, both operas and ballets such as *Coppélia* and *Sylvia*. Based upon a novel by Pierre Loti, *Lakmé* slaked a fin de siècle thirst for all things Asian as Gérald, a young British officer in India, falls for the exotic daughter of a Brahmin priest who has sworn to revenge himself on the British for forbidding the practice of his religion. Colonialism, however, takes a backseat as Lakmé returns Gérald's love. Naturally, it all ends badly deep in a properly operatic forest.

The French soprano Natalie Dessay is consistently superb in this recording: the tone is sweetly silver and her formidable technique is always at the service of the role. So the coloratura fireworks in the celebrated "Bell Song" are part of her story, not an excuse for vocal exhibitionism. Here is a young woman sliding over the edge into love. Dessay is well matched by Gregory Kunde's Gérald, who is much more than an imperial stuffed shirt who "goes native," while José van Dam makes you care more than usual about the villain of the piece, the priest Nilakantha. Michel Plasson clearly loves this score, reminding us in every scene that Delibes was capable of genuine drama as well as the purely theatrical. **CC**

> ## "Muted passion is at the heart."
>
> **Léo Delibes**

Other Recommended Recordings

Monte Carlo Opera • Richard Bonynge
Decca 460 741-2 (2 CDs)
Joan Sutherland is an exquisite Lakmé in a
bargain-priced recording

Opéra Comique Chorus & Orchestra • Alain Lombard
EMI 7243 5 67745 2 0 (2 CDs)
Mady Mesplé sings a sumptuously seductive Lakmé

Highlights
Opéra Comique Chorus & Orchestra • George Sébastien
Decca 475 6158
With Mado Robin, one of the finest of twentieth-
century French coloratura sopranos

Jules Massenet | Manon (1884)

Genre | Opera
Conductor/Performers | Antonio Pappano;
Angela Gheorghiu (Manon), Roberto Alagna (Des Grieux)
Year recorded | 1999
Label | EMI 7243 5 57005 2 0 (3 CDs)

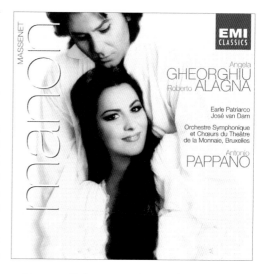

Born in 1842, Massenet was a successful composer of the Parisian fin de siècle, although by no means all his operas were unqualified triumphs. By the turn of the century, his major successes seemed to be behind him, when Raoul Gunsbourg, impresario of the Monte Carlo Opera, commissioned a string of operas that premiered there between 1902 and Massenet's death in 1912.

Manon, Massenet's fifth opera, was a success from the beginning; the story is taken from a novel by the eighteenth-century writer Antoine-François Prévost. On her way to entering a convent, the fifteen-year-old Manon meets and elopes with the young nobleman Des Grieux. He wants to marry her, but his father has him abducted to prevent the wedding. Manon goes off with the wealthy Guillot, but still yearns for Des Grieux. Upon learning that he will take holy orders, she goes to his cloister and seduces him into following her again. Accused by Guillot of cheating at cards, the lovers are arrested, and Manon is sentenced to deportation. On her way to Le Havre, she dies in Des Grieux's arms.

Manon was written for the Opéra-Comique, which meant that it had to include spoken parts (completely sung compositions were reserved for the Opéra by an age-old royal privilege). Massenet got around this convention by scoring a number of scenes as *mélodrames* (speech accompanied by music). The rococo atmosphere is well caught, one of Manon's showstopping arias being a gavotte. There are many duets, including the cloister scene with its religious eroticism so dear to the composer. The Belgian company under Pappano's detailed conducting sets the frame for ardent performances by Angela Gheorghiu and Roberto Alagna. **CMS**

> "*I would give the whole of Bach's* Brandenburg Concertos *for Massenet's* Manon."

Thomas Beecham

Other Recommended Recordings

Opéra Comique Chorus & Orchestra • Pierre Monteux
Testament SBT 3203 (3 CDs)
Victoria de los Angeles as Manon in a classic recording

Le roi de Lahore
La Fenice • Marcello Viotti
DVD: Dynamic DV 33487
Massenet's first big success, a Meyerbeerian grand opera in an appropriately B-movie-style production

Thaïs
Bordeaux Aquitaine National Orchestra • Yves Abel
Decca 466 766-2 (2 CDs)
A heady mixture of sex and religion

Alagna and Gheorghiu were opera's golden couple in the 1990s. ➔

César Franck
Prélude, choral et fugue (1884)

Genre | Instrumental
Instrument | Piano
Performer | Stephen Hough
Year recorded | 1996
Label | Hyperion CDA 66918

Composed in 1884, César Franck's *Prélude, choral et fugue* is one of the most important of all French Romantic piano works. As with Liszt—whom Franck met in 1842 and who took a great interest in the younger man's work—Franck's youthful determination to show off his keyboard virtuosity gave way to mature works of visionary beauty and at times an ecstatic and rarefied intensity.

The *Prélude, choral et fugue* bears the stamp of Liszt's influence in various ways. As well as aspects of its musical style and its assured handling of the piano's range of sonority, Franck was clearly indebted to the older composer's model of cyclic form. The work's two main themes—a falling chromatic line reminiscent of Bach's cantata *Weinen, Klagen, Sorgen, Zagen* and a motif in fourths related to the bell motif in Wagner's *Parsifal*—appear in all three movements, set in different contexts, developed, and ultimately combined in a manner that gives a wonderful sense of arrival and fulfillment.

There have been many fine recordings of the *Prélude, choral et fugue*, including those from Alfred Cortot, Murray Perahia, Sergio Fiorentino, Ivan Moravec, and Arthur Rubinstein. But perhaps the finest of all modern recordings is by the British pianist Stephen Hough, who combines a hypersensitive ear for texture and voicing with acute musical insight and astonishing dexterity. He creates the most ravishing pianissimos, while also reveling in the organlike regal splendor of Franck's climaxes. Few pianists mold Franck's musical phrases quite so seamlessly, and in Hough's hands the final homecoming at the end of the fugue is spectacular. **TLP**

Johannes Brahms
Symphony no. 4 (1885)

Genre | Orchestral
Conductor/Performers | Carlos Kleiber;
Vienna Philharmonic Orchestra
Year recorded | 1980
Label | DG 457 706-2

This is the most impressive result of Brahms's lifelong struggle to revivify the strict musical architecture of the Baroque and infuse it with the passion of the Romantic era in which he lived. The remarkable finale revives the ancient form of passacaglia, founded on a bass from the final chorus of Bach's Cantata no. 150. Brahms's inspired marriage of the contemporary and the archaic is reflected throughout the symphony, in which epic tragedy and melodic lyricism find their most powerful expression in the composer's entire output.

The troubled first movement already contains the seeds of the finale. The beauty of its opening subject, its deliberate motion, vibrantly ambiguous harmony, and most of all its intricate architecture all foreshadow elements to be developed in all four movements, coming to fruition in the last. The gorgeous slow movement continually plays off the austere coloring of the ancient, ecclesiastical Phrygian mode against the ardent warmth of a fully developed E major. The third movement disperses these somber shadows with an intoxicating physical energy and rhythmic urge. The passacaglia-finale submits the Bach-derived theme to thirty variations and a coda: the individual variations group themselves into large paragraphs to give a semblance of sonata shape. The sense of a continuous, irresistible flow of ideas is undoubtedly the most important aspect of the movement.

Carlos Kleiber's performance is justly renowned; this is a gripping interpretation, incandescent in its passion yet displaying scrupulous attention to detail, and attaining the irresistible thrust of a force of nature in the tragic finale. **MM**

Antonín Dvořák
Symphony no. 7 (1885)

Genre | Orchestral
Conductor/Performers | István Kertész;
London Symphony Orchestra
Year recorded | 1966
Label | Decca 430 046-2 (6 CDs)

Dvořák's spectacular rise to international fame in the late 1870s was soon followed by a range of commissions from across Europe. Vital to his burgeoning career was his success with British audiences in the 1880s. They took, in particular, to his *Stabat mater*, and Elgar was enthusiastic about his Sixth Symphony. Requests from the major choral festivals of Birmingham and Leeds prompted cantata, oratorio, and a Requiem Mass, but perhaps the most significant commission came from the venerable Philharmonic Society of London for a symphony.

The resulting Seventh Symphony is widely regarded as his greatest symphonic work. Dvořák himself was very conscious of high expectations, not just from London audiences, but from his friend and colleague Brahms, and subjected the work to rigorous revision before it reached a final form. The first movement has an intensity and urgency unmatched in his output and the slow movement is one of his most profound, with a magical solo for the French horn. The scherzo, based on the cross rhythms of the furiant, returns to the intensity of the first movement, while the finale brings the whole to a triumphant close. If there are affinities with Brahms, Dvořák's individuality is never in doubt in this compelling score.

The most successful performances of the work strike a balance between symphonic line and expressive gesture. István Kertész's vintage recording from the 1960s has stood the test of time. The London Symphony Orchestra is on excellent form throughout and the strength of purpose conductor and players generate throughout secures a near ideal reading. **JS**

César Franck
Symphonic Variations (1885)

Genre | Concerto
Performers | Clifford Curzon,
London Philharmonic Orchestra
Year recorded | 1955
Label | Decca 433 628-2

Like the *Prélude, choral et fugue*, the Symphonic Variations is a product of the late blossoming of Franck's genius. The title signifies that Franck wanted to create a work where an unbroken musical argument unfolds without the usual virtuoso rhetoric associated with the Romantic piano concerto. In one of his most subtle musical structures, Franck creates a cyclic form that combines elements of the dramatic recall of themes (as originated by Beethoven) with the procedure of thematic transformation familiar from Schubert's "Wanderer" Fantasy.

The work begins with defiant orchestral statements being offset by mollifying replies from the soloist. This introduction hints at and finally gives way to the main theme, which goes on to spawn a series of organically evolving variations (which often merge seamlessly). The piano and orchestra are now blended together in a more unified way, nowhere more so than in the delightfully ethereal sixth variation, where the soloist's delicate sixteenth note patterns dart around the hauntingly eloquent stillness of the strings. The work ends jubilantly, the earlier stern melancholy evaporating in a sparkling finale.

Clifford Curzon's 1955 recording has yet to be surpassed for charm and poetic freshness. Others have the benefit of modern sound, but in Curzon's hands the work's journey from darkness to light is majestically accomplished, and Boult's support is superbly judged. Curzon's playing seems to be both spontaneously poetic—with phrasing that has rhythmic freedom yet is never slack—and tautly focused. This is one of the highlights of this great British pianist's recorded legacy. **TLP**

Gustav Mahler | Lieder eines fahrenden Gesellen (1885)

Genre | Vocal

Performers/Conductor | Dietrich Fischer-Dieskau (baritone),
Philharmonia Orchestra; Wilhelm Furtwängler

Year recorded | 1952

Label | EMI 7243 5 67557 2 7

Gustav Mahler (1860–1911) was born in Bohemia near the Austrian border, studied at the Vienna Conservatoire between 1875 and 1878, and wrote his first important composition, the cantata *Das klagende Lied* (*Song of Lament*) in 1880, around the time he began his career as a conductor. He soon became recognized as one of the leading conductors of his day, eventually holding important posts in Budapest, Hamburg, Vienna, and New York. His compositional activities were thus largely restricted to summer holidays, but even so he managed to create a substantial body of work focusing on the genres of song and symphony, and various hybrids between the two. This music originally met with incomprehension and divided opinion, but it has subsequently (in accordance with Mahler's prophecy, "My time will come") touched a particularly emotional nerve in Western culture.

Lieder eines fahrenden Gesellen (*Songs of a Wayfaring Lad*) is the first of Mahler's works to embody his characteristic juxtaposition of happiness and despair (it was conceived in the wake of an unhappy love affair, and Mahler himself wrote the text). The musical character of the four songs ranges from simple, folklike tunes to chromatic harmonies and devastatingly hollow textures, especially apparent in the orchestral version prepared for the first performance in 1896, over a decade after the original piano-accompanied version was completed.

The young Fischer-Dieskau's voice was an uncommonly beautiful one—focused but capable of remarkable expressive range. In his first recording of these songs he was partnered by the great Wilhelm Furtwängler, who very capably evokes the world-weariness and rich ambivalence of feeling that make this work so memorable. **DB**

> *"When my sweetheart has her wedding, / has her merry wedding, / I have my day of mourning."*

First lines of Mahler's text

Other Recommended Recordings

Thomas Hampson, Vienna Philharmonic Orchestra
Leonard Bernstein
DG 431 682-2
Beautifully sung, conducted with great tenderness

Anna Reynolds, English Chamber Orchestra
Benjamin Britten
BBC BBCB 8004-2
Britten's conducting is expressive without being fussy

Dietrich Fischer-Dieskau, Daniel Barenboim
EMI 7243 4 76780 2 8 (2 CDs)
Rhapsodic performance of original piano-accompanied version; includes fourteen earlier songs

Johann Strauss II | Der Zigeunerbaron (1885)

Genre | Operetta
Conductor/Performers | Otto Ackermann;
Elisabeth Schwarzkopf, Nicolai Gedda, Hermann Prey
Year recorded | 1958
Label | EMI 5 67535 2 (2 CDs)

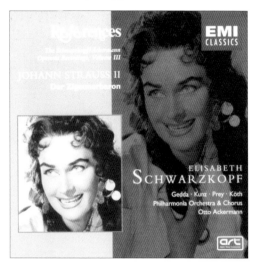

Strauss's *Der Zigeunerbaron* (*The Gypsy Baron*) opened in Vienna on October 24, 1885. It has clocked up a tally of revivals surpassed only by *Die Fledermaus* and although—like *Fledermaus*—it mixes elements of parody with that infectious Viennese sparkle that defines the style, *Zigeunerbaron* is unusual. It carries some historical baggage: first, it represents a stage in Strauss's ambition to write a full-blown opera; second, it deals with politics and prejudice; and third, since the show was as well received in Budapest as it was in Vienna, *Zigeunerbaron* has been credited with helping ease the tensions inherent in the conjoined monarchies of the Austro-Hungarian empire.

Der Zigeunerbaron is set in mid-eighteenth-century Hungary. Barinkay returns to his estate from exile; the local pig farmer, Tsupán, wants him to marry his daughter Arsena, but she loves another and in any case declares that she only wants a "baron." Local gypsies proclaim Barinkay as their long-last master, predicting he will find treasure and a wife. He styles himself their "Gypsy Baron," and through various plot convolutions the prediction comes true—the wife being Sáffi, daughter of the gypsy seer Czipra, and in reality a Turkish princess. War service rewards Barinkay with a real baronetcy: all happily marry their chosen partners.

The operetta offers a heady mix of Viennese waltz songs and Hungarian gypsy music: the parts of Barinkay and Sáffi are star vehicles, with Tsupán, Arsena, and Czipra offering scope for suitably fruity characterizations—opportunities grasped with relish, in this mono recording, respectively by Nicolai Gedda, Elisabeth Schwarzkopf, Erich Kunz, Erika Köth, and Gertrud Burgsthaler-Schuster. This is one of the series of 1950s operetta recordings produced for EMI by Walter Legge—they remain timeless classics. **GK**

> *"Another vintage champagne recording of Viennese operetta."*
>
> **Gramophone**

Other Recommended Recordings

A Night in Venice; Wiener Blut
Philharmonia Orchestra • Otto Ackermann
EMI 7243 5 67532 2 8 (2 CDs)
Walter Legge's seasoned operetta team in a double-bill

Wiener Blut
Philharmonia Hungarica • Willi Boskovsky
EMI 7243 5 66176 2 9
Vienna Blood, strongly cast, in spacious modern sound

Kálmán: Die Czárdásfürstin
Slovak Radio Symphony Orchestra • Richard Bonynge
Naxos 8.660105-06
Sparkling account of The Gypsy Princess

Pyotr Ilyich Tchaikovsky | Manfred Symphony (1885)

Genre | Orchestral
Conductor | Vladimir Jurowski
Performers | London Philharmonic Orchestra
Year recorded | 2004
Label | LPO 0009

The subject of Lord Byron's tormented hero Manfred, wandering the Alps in a desperate bid to forget an incestuous relationship, clearly appealed to Tchaikovsky, who by the time he came to take up the suggestion of senior composer Mily Balakirev in 1884 was himself leading a nomadic existence. Having taken a holiday from symphonic form in the shape of three lively orchestral suites, Tchaikovsky now felt ready to return to the fray.

The first movement is one of his finest achievements: Manfred's restless soul and the vision of his beloved Astarte inspired a vivid drama that fluctuates between torment and nostalgia. In the scherzo, the Fairy of the Alps appears to Manfred in a rainbow—cue for some of Tchaikovsky's most refined orchestration, in homage to Berlioz, and one of his loveliest melodies. The simple rustic life that begins the third movement soon becomes powerfully clouded with darker memories; and it is only in the finale, launched by an orgy in an underground cavern peopled by demons, that Tchaikovsky loosens his grip and ends by giving Manfred a romantic apotheosis—something that Byron, in his nihilistic poem, would never have countenanced. Some interpreters take matters into their own hands by cutting the end and reprising the first-movement coda instead, but this is not a solution Tchaikovsky sanctioned.

So doom-laden is the *Manfred Symphony* that many conductors are tempted to go for dramatic overkill. Vladimir Jurowski keeps his head and argues for the first movement's purely symphonic merits, shaping the phrases with implicit power and unleashing the fullest force only in the terrifying conclusion. The finale's subterranean antics are brilliantly etched, and even Manfred's redemption sounds less overwrought than usual. **DN**

"I myself think it's my best symphonic work."

Pyotr Ilyich Tchaikovsky

Other Recommended Recordings

Russian State Symphony Orchestra • Yevgeny Svetlanov
Warner 5101 12448-2
A Manfred of brute force from Svetlanov's powerful orchestra

Bournemouth Symphony Orchestra
Constantin Silvestri
BBC Legends BBCL 4007
Classic poise from Silvestri, an early champion of this underrated work

Russian National Orchestra • Mikhail Pletnev
DG 477 053-2 (3 CDs)
Pletnev brings a rare refinement to the score

Vladimir Jurowski, music director of the LPO and of Glyndebourne. ➔

Richard Strauss
Lieder (1885–1933)

Genre | Vocal
Performers | Christine Brewer (soprano), Roger Vignoles (piano)
Year recorded | 2004
Label | Hyperion CDA 67488

The more than 200 songs Strauss wrote during his productive life gave fresh impetus to the art of late-Romantic German Lieder. In the wake of the masterworks of Schubert, Schumann, and Brahms, audiences grew larger and more public. Strauss continued where Mahler left off, writing songs either conceived as orchestral Lieder, or else expansively written for piano and subsequently orchestrated.

Strauss's marriage in 1894 to the soprano Pauline de Ahna was also a marriage to the female voice: His op. 27, which contains some of his most exuberantly tender writing, was composed as a wedding present. After the premiere of Strauss's opera *Salome* in 1905, there was a thirteen-year break from song. And then came two strikingly original works: the 1918 *Kramerspiegel*, settings of eight satirical poems about music publishers; and, ten years later, the forward-looking *Gesänge des Orients*.

It is difficult to nominate a single representative disc of Strauss's *Lieder*, but given his lifelong love affair with the soprano voice, female performers must take priority. Many of the most irresistible recitals match a small selection of well-known songs with the *Vier letzte Lieder*, or with an orchestral work. So, for the broadest and most vivid cross-section of individual songs, perfectly matched to the performer's voice, go for Christine Brewer in the first volume of Hyperion's series of the complete Strauss songs. She includes both the ecstatic, quintessentially Straussian masterpieces such as "Zueignung"; and also the settings of Hans Bethge's translations of Persian and Chinese poetry in the *Gesänge des Orients*—all accompanied with consummate artistry by Roger Vignoles. **HF**

Arthur Sullivan
The Mikado (1885)

Genre | Operetta
Conductor/Performers | Charles Mackerras; Donald Adams, Richard Suart
Year recorded | 1991
Label | Telarc CD-80284

The Mikado was Gilbert and Sullivan's eighth collaboration. Neither could agree on a suitable new project, until—so the story goes—an ornamental sword fell off the wall in Gilbert's house, inspiring the librettist to translate the mid-1880s fashion for all things Japanese into a work that satirized English life and politics. *The Mikado* remains the duo's most performed, translated, and adapted operetta.

The Mikado's son Nanki-Poo flees to Titipu incognito to escape the amorous attentions of the elderly Katisha. He falls in love with Yum-Yum, ward of the town's dysfunctional executioner, Ko-Ko, who plans to marry her himself. As the Mikado expects beheadings from executioners, Ko-Ko will allow Nanki-Poo to marry Yum-Yum if he will later submit to decapitation; he agrees, and disappears. The Mikado arrives and is regaled with gruesome details of the "execution," until it transpires that compassing the death of the heir is a capital crime. Nanki-Poo makes his resurrection conditional on Ko-Ko relieving him of Katisha. The Mikado is placated and all rejoice.

Sullivan excelled himself in this score, incorporating the traditional English glee as well as music with Japanese inflections. The history of the D'Oyly Carte Opera Company in the twentieth century is charted in an extensive catalogue of recordings. Leading the field is Charles Mackerras, the versatile Australian conductor who is a Savoyard to the tip of his baton. Here he leads a faultless cast of seasoned performers: as the Mikado, Donald Adams provides a link to the great D'Oyly Carte days, while Richard Suart dons the mantle of Martyn Green and John Reed, as the patter-song virtuoso of our generation. **GK**

César Franck | Violin Sonata in A major (1886)

Genre | Chamber
Performers | Kaja Danczowska (violin), Krystian Zimerman (piano)
Year recorded | 1980
Label | DG 477 5903

César Franck's chamber music is unevenly distributed at the beginning and end of his career: a series of piano trios in 1839–42 and three late masterpieces in 1879–89, of which the A major Violin Sonata is the most popular. Franck had been considering a violin sonata for more than a quarter of a century before he wrote it in 1886; and he might never have produced it, had he not become intoxicated with the playing of his fellow Belgian Eugène Ysaÿe. In its size, elasticity, and structural strength, the sonata is a picture in sound of Ysaÿe's playing.

The work harks back to Baroque practice in its slow-fast-slow-fast outline, but the form within each movement is consistent with the style Franck had worked out in other mature pieces. Themes, especially the violin's first motif, recur throughout to create a cyclic impression, with no feeling of déjà vu as each movement appears. The writing for both instruments demands virtuosity, and Franck the contrapuntalist provides a canonic finale. The sonata is justly regarded as one of the peaks of Franco-Belgian music and the late Romantic era.

The performance by Kaja Danczowska and Krystian Zimerman is part of one of the best violin and piano discs ever made. It seems extraordinary that DG did not follow it with others by these fine Polish artists. They have the full measure of the beautiful work and capture the mood of each movement perfectly. They are given a splendid recording—carefully balanced and just resonant enough—that has recently been refurbished. The Szymanowski pieces that complete the program are also superbly played and make excellent companions for the Franck. **TP**

Camille Saint-Saëns Carnival of the Animals (1886)

Genre | Chamber
Performers | Martha Argerich, Nelson Friere, Mischa Maisky
Year recorded | 1985
Label | Philips 446 557-2 (2 CDs)

It is odd to think that Saint-Saëns's most popular work became widely known only after his death. He wrote it while on holiday in Austria in 1886, and, although it had a few private performances, he never allowed it to be published while he was alive. Liszt was one of the few people to have heard it, and he doubtless appreciated all the jokes in the score—the very jokes that made Saint-Saëns fearful for his reputation as a serious composer if the music ever got out into the public arena. He need not have worried—it has led many listeners to his other music, and given a more rounded view of his personality.

Saint-Saëns described the piece as a zoological fantasy, and in its fourteen short movements he portrays tortoises with a slowed-down version of the can-can from Offenbach's *Orpheus in the Underworld*; the elephant with a quote from Berlioz's "Danse des sylphes" as a double bass solo; and fossils with his own *Danse macabre* as well as some Rossini. However, humor is not its only virtue: The watery textures of "Aquarium," and the fluttering flute in "Aviary" are genuinely inspired pieces of program music, and the beautiful melody of "The Swan" has graced many cello recitals and ballet performances. It was the only part of the score that Saint-Saëns published during his lifetime.

Although it is often heard with full orchestra, the original chamber version allows the humor more edge, and the delicacy more focus. That is especially true in the version led by Martha Argerich, where every part is played by an international star—from Brazilian pianist Nelson Friere to celebrated Russian cellist Mischa Maisky—and every line is full of character. **MC**

Camille Saint-Saëns | Symphony no. 3, "Organ" (1886)

Genre | Orchestral
Conductor/Performers | Charles Munch;
Berj Zamkochian (organ), Boston Symphony Orchestra
Year recorded | 1959
Label | RCA 82876 61387 2

This is the only symphony that Camille Saint-Saëns wrote in his maturity, though he had begun exploring the form in his teens and had written various fragments and one complete work before the officially numbered First Symphony in 1853—the Second followed in 1859. So it was as a much more experienced fifty-year-old that he approached the commission for a symphony from the Philharmonic Society in London. He dedicated the work to the memory of his friend Franz Liszt, who died in 1886, and conducted the premiere in London himself, to enormous acclaim. Despite its eventual success, he had not been so sure of the work's likely reception when composing. "It will be terrifying," he told the Philharmonic Society. "Will it be a treat, though, for those who hear it?"

It is commonly nicknamed the "Organ" Symphony, because of the prominent role that instrument plays in two of its four movements: the Adagio, where it provides a soft bed of sound for a luscious string melody that rises to an ecstatic climax; and the finale, where it is unleashed with full force amid fanfares of brass before the main fugal part of the movement gets under way. It also plays a major part in the triumphant ending, ensuring that its sound is ringing in the audience's ears as they launch into the enthusiastic applause that the work inevitably inspires. Along the way there is also a part for piano duet—perhaps a reminder that Saint-Saëns was writing this symphony at the same time as *The Carnival of the Animals*.

Charles Munch's recording has rarely been out of the catalogue, and rightly so: not only is the sound quality stunning (even more so in this SACD surround sound remastering), but he grades and paces the music so that its progress is both inevitable and exciting. **MC**

> *"There goes the French Beethoven."*
>
> Charles Gounod (after hearing the "Organ" Symphony)

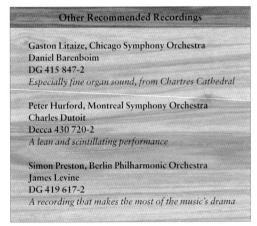

Other Recommended Recordings

Gaston Litaize, Chicago Symphony Orchestra
Daniel Barenboim
DG 415 847-2
Especially fine organ sound, from Chartres Cathedral

Peter Hurford, Montreal Symphony Orchestra
Charles Dutoit
Decca 430 720-2
A lean and scintillating performance

Simon Preston, Berlin Philharmonic Orchestra
James Levine
DG 419 617-2
A recording that makes the most of the music's drama

A nineteenth-century photograph of Camille Saint-Saëns. ❯

John Stainer | The Crucifixion (1887)

Genre | Choral
Conductor/Performers | Barry Rose; David Hughes, John Lawrenson, Gavin Williams, Choir of Guildford Cathedral
Year recorded | 1969
Label | EMI 7243 5 75779 2 2

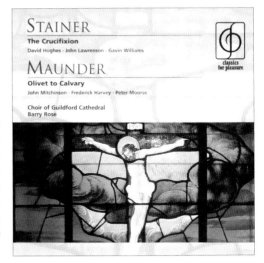

Viewed by some as an irreplaceable staple of the Passiontide church repertoire, and by others as the epitome of Victorian sentimentality, Stainer's *The Crucifixion* has undeniably stood the test of time—few comparable works of its period have achieved such a status. Stainer held the distinguished positions of organist of St. Paul's Cathedral and professor of music at Oxford University, but produced considerable quantities of music for parish choirs of average ability. The idea behind *The Crucifixion*, in fact, was to offer such choirs something more easily performed than the Passions of Bach, on which it was modeled.

A "meditation" rather than an oratorio—its full description is "Meditation on the Sacred Passion of the Holy Redeemer"—*The Crucifixion* deploys the minimal resources of tenor and bass soloists, choir and organ, available to the most modest churches, encouraging the congregation to join in the hymns (newly composed by Stainer, unlike in his Bach model). In terms of its unadventurous harmonic style, mildly spiced with chromaticism, the work looks back also to Mendelssohn.

The great virtue of the classic 1969 recording is the singing of the Guildford Cathedral choristers under Barry Rose, one of the finest choir trainers of his or any age. It may be saccharine and affected for some tastes, but it catches the spirit of the piece with unerring accuracy. Gavin Williams uses the Guildford organ to brilliant pictorial effect and the sound is better than ever in this digital remastering. David Hughes and John Lawrenson are the exemplary soloists. For those responsive to Victorian art in all its emotional vibrancy and heart-on-sleeve sincerity, Stainer's *The Crucifixion* is indispensable, and this unsurpassed recording captures its essence to perfection. **BM**

> *"Such music enters in the hearts of the people and lives there."*
>
> Herman Klein

Other Recommended Recordings

Choir of Clare College, Cambridge • Timothy Brown
Naxos 8.557624
Excellent choral singing, similarly recorded in Guildford Cathedral

Choir of St. John's College, Cambridge • George Guest
Decca 436 146-2
Richard Lewis and Owen Brannigan are the operatic soloists

Leith Hill Festival Singers • Brian Kay
Chandos CHAN 9551
Former King's Singer Brian Kay directs amateur forces with reinforcement of the BBC Singers

Reynaldo Hahn | Mélodies (1887–1947)

Genre | Vocal
Performers | Felicity Lott, Susan Bickley, Ian Bostridge,
Stephen Varcoe, Graham Johnson, London Schubert Choir
Year recorded | 1996
Label | Hyperion CDA 67141/2 (2 CDs)

Reynaldo Hahn was born in Caracas, Venezuela, but moved to Paris with his family at the age of three. There he studied at the Conservatoire under Massenet, and began to compose songs, the genre for which he is today best known. One of his first efforts, "Si mes vers avaient des ailes" ("If my verses had wings"), composed while he was still a student, brought him early fame and extraordinarily remains his best-known song, alongside "L'heure exquise," the fifth in another accomplished student work, the Verlaine cycle *Chansons grises*.

Hahn was himself something of a musical all-rounder. He sang with a light baritone and habitually accompanied himself in recital. He also conducted and wrote music criticism; and, besides all the songs, there is a large number of stage works, of which the most celebrated is the operetta *Ciboulette*, as well as a body of orchestral, chamber, and piano pieces. Yet it is still for those *mélodies* that he remains best known, and the best choice on CD is Hyperion's two-disc set.

First and foremost, this collection reveals Hahn as something more than the purveyor of superficial charm we assume him to be. Second, it includes besides the usual suspects the complete *Douze rondels* and the *Études latines*—both of which also involve the London Schubert Choir—a few numbers from the operettas *Ciboullete, Une revue,* and *O mon bel inconnu*, and some less well-known songs. Third, the illustrious team of Felicity Lott, Susan Bickley, Ian Bostridge, and Stephen Varcoe relish the belle époque elegance of it all. And fourth, they are beautifully accompanied by that master of program planning, of booklet-note writing and playing, and of all things song—Graham Johnson. **SP**

"A talented gossip who had a gift for grinding out operettas and . . . tastefully performed ballads . . ."

Hans Heinz Stuckenschmidt on Hahn

Other Recommended Recordings

La belle époque
Susan Graham, Roger Vignoles • Sony SK 60168
Broad selection, a gorgeously glowing voice, sensitively accompanied.

Chansons grises and other songs
Martyn Hill, Graham Johnson • Hyperion CDH 55040
Hill is the most stylish and poised of singers, the lightish weight of his voice perfect for these songs

Reynaldo Hahn conducts, sings, and accompanies
Reynaldo Hahn
Pearl GEMMCD 0003
Straight from the horse's mouth . . .

Alexander Borodin | Prince Igor (1887)

Genre | Opera
Conductor/Performers | Valery Gergiev; Gegam Grigorian, Galina Gorchakova, Olga Borodina, Kirov Chorus
Year recorded | 1992
Label | Philips 442 537-2

By his own admission a part-time composer, Borodin spent eighteen years working on his only opera, *Prince Igor*, and even then it was still unfinished at his death in 1887. What he left was fragmentary and often confusing, but the composer Alexander Glazunov—who had a phenomenal memory—reconstructed what he recollected from sessions with Borodin at the piano, and with further orchestration and editorial work from Nikolai Rimsky-Korsakov, a complete score was assembled. Glazunov may have exaggerated the authenticity of his contribution, but in any case the result is a vibrant, colorful, often very beautiful score. It could be argued that *Prince Igor* is more like a series of more or less magnificent historical tableaux than a genuine opera: It certainly is not strong on dramatic pace, but there is plenty to delight the ear, including the originals of the famous "Polovtsian Dances."

Even Rimsky-Korsakov's commanding edition—a labor of love if ever there was one—poses problems, and conductors have often opted for "creative" solutions. Act 3, for instance, can seem rather weak after the aural feast and splendid theatrical spectacle of the Polovtsian second act. Valery Gergiev gets around this by the bold step of reversing the first two acts, and he also restores material rejected by Rimsky-Korsakov. That alone makes it interesting enough, but it is Gergiev's energy and drive, along with a solo cast that not only shines individually but works superbly as a team, that makes this the frontrunner on CD. Not all the singing is perfectly refined, but it radiates conviction, especially Galina Gorchakova (Igor's wife Yaroslavna) and the excellent Olga Borodina (Kontchakovna, daughter of Igor's Polovtsian captor). The atmospheric live recording completes the experience. **SJ**

> *"How much pleading I had to spend on dear old Borodin to get him to work on [Prince Igor]!"*
>
> Nicolai Rimsky-Korsakov

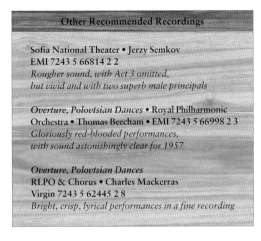

Other Recommended Recordings

Sofia National Theater • Jerzy Semkov
EMI 7243 5 66814 2 2
Rougher sound, with Act 3 omitted,
but vivid and with two superb male principals

Overture, Polovtsian Dances • Royal Philharmonic
Orchestra • Thomas Beecham • EMI 7243 5 66998 2 3
Gloriously red-blooded performances,
with sound astonishingly clear for 1957

Overture, Polovtsian Dances
RLPO & Chorus • Charles Mackerras
Virgin 7243 5 62445 2 8
Bright, crisp, lyrical performances in a fine recording

Nijinsky dressed as Prince Igor for a Ballets Russes version in 1912. ➔

Nicolai Rimsky-Korsakov
Capriccio espagnol (1887)

Genre | Orchestral
Conductor | Kurt Masur
Performers | New York Philharmonic
Year recorded | 1999
Label | Warner 2564 60374-2

Raised on folk music in his native town of Tikhvin in Russia, Nicolai Rimsky-Korsakov put his interest in the subject aside in favor of a passionate enthusiasm for the navy, which he joined as a cadet in 1856. Subsequently switching to a land-bound career as a musical academic, he was appointed professor of composition at the conservatoire in St. Petersburg. His technical knowledge was patchy, but he compensated by cramming subjects such as harmony and counterpoint while presumably simultaneously passing this knowledge on to his pupils.

The *Capriccio espagnol* was conceived as a Spanish counterpart to the composer's successful *Fantasia on Two Russian Themes* for violin and orchestra. In the *Capriccio*, however, the violin is reined in considerably, with the solo element confined to a brief but arresting passage of a few measures' length. The work fizzes with exuberant energy, its vivid Spanish thematic material enhanced by the composer's exceptional abilities as an orchestrator.

The *Capriccio* remains one of Rimsky-Korsakov's most popular works, but its virtuosic, all-or-nothing style combines the excitement of a firework display with the treachery of a minefield. Kurt Masur steers the New York Philharmonic through both aspects of this five-movement suite with enormous panache, never allowing the furious density of the piece to descend into the directionless muddle that can all too easily result. It is perhaps worth adding that the rehearsals for its 1887 premiere were routinely interrupted by spontaneous outbursts of applause—not from invited listeners, but from the members of the orchestra. **RT**

Jules Massenet
Werther (1887)

Genre | Opera
Conductor/Performers | Elie Cohen;
Georges Thill, Ninon Vallin
Year recorded | 1931
Label | Naxos 8.110061-62 (2 CDs)

Werther was composed between 1885 and 1887, but was turned down by the Opéra Comique as too gloomy. It was only after *Manon* successfully premiered in Vienna in 1890 that a chance of performing it there presented itself. The premiere took place (in German translation) in 1892. Interestingly, German-speaking audiences took much more to Massenet's adaptation of Goethe's early novel than they had to Gounod's treatment of *Faust*.

Werther meets and falls in love with Charlotte, who has sworn to her dying mother that she will marry Albert. Werther flees the town, but writes periodically to Charlotte, who invites him to come back for Christmas. After a stormy meeting with Charlotte, Werther shoots himself and dies in her arms after she admits to always having loved him.

The orchestra in *Werther* has a predominantly dark color and carries much of the musical argument, with an intricate web of leading motifs. Set pieces—like the "Lied d'Ossian" and the "Désolation" solo, which may have been added at the suggestion of the first interpreter of the title role—are embedded in a continuous flow. The role of Werther requires both delicacy and power for the big outbursts (the first Werther, Ernest van Dyck, was a Wagnerian stalwart), while Charlotte strides the soprano and mezzo-soprano registers and has been effectively sung by both.

The very first complete recording, amazingly the only one completely in French in the discography, still has claims to being the finest. Georges Thill has the necessary heroic ring, and Ninon Vallin's soprano Charlotte contrasts well with Germaine Féraldy as the cheerful Sophie. **CMS**

Johannes Brahms
Double Concerto (1887)

Genre | Concerto
Performers | Gil Shaham, Jian Wang
Conductor | Claudio Abbado
Year recorded | 2002
Label | DG 469 529-2

The Double Concerto, Brahms's last orchestral work, began life as sketches for a Fifth Symphony. It evolved into a concerto with a direct message to his old, estranged friend, the violinist Joseph Joachim. (Joachim had been a hugely important artistic colleague until Brahms took his wife's side in the couple's bitter divorce.) It was a gift, too, to the cellist Robert Hausmann, who had just successfully premiered Brahms's Second Cello Sonata. These two instrumentalists had provided the inspiration for much of Brahms's chamber music, and this concerto needs to be understood as a chamber dialogue within an almost Classical sinfonia concertante. The two instruments play intimately and harmoniously together in the main, with occasional conflicts. Emerging from the orchestra, the cello's opening soliloquy is echoed by the silver-tongued violin. The two set out on an adventure that takes them into a luxurious slow movement, with a melody stretching out like a cat in the sun, and culminates in a delightfully wicked dance, peppered with mercurial exchanges and mood swings.

Many great artists have tackled this concerto, but in their recent recording Jian Wang, Gil Shaham, and Claudio Abbado have produced the most melting, natural, tonally beautiful performance yet heard. Never has the work been so lovingly interpreted, particularly by Abbado, who unleashes the full power of the Berlin Philharmonic only at the biggest climaxes and creates a dark, velvet backdrop for the soloists. Shaham and Wang are a rare match, sharing a glowing sound and a sustained, lyrical view of the work. In the finale, they bring just the right devilish glint to the dance. **HW**

Anton Bruckner
Symphony no. 8 (1887–90)

Genre | Orchestral
Conductor | Günter Wand
Performers | Berlin Philharmonic Orchestra
Year recorded | 2001
Label | RCA 74321 82866 2

Bruckner's mighty Eighth Symphony is one of the greatest "darkness to light" journeys in symphonic music since Beethoven's Fifth. But where the Beethoven ends in almost frenzied affirmation, there can be something strangely calming about the brassy splendor of Bruckner's ending. In a truly understanding performance the coming together of the symphony's four main themes feels inevitable, as though this really is—in both musical and spiritual senses—the "answer" the symphony has been searching for since its restlessly probing beginning. The final affirmation is all the more impressive because the symphony goes through some very dark territory along the way: in the anguished longing and desolation of the Adagio, and particularly in the grim vision of death as the ultimate terror in the coda of the first movement, where the music's heartbeat ebbs into nothingness.

The great Bruckner conductor Günter Wand struggled long and hard to perfect his interpretation of this symphony in the recording studio. Three versions are currently available, each one with solid strengths. But this recording, made as the conductor was approaching his ninetieth birthday, has not only the ripe understanding of old age; it is also full of vitality and natural, unexaggerated, expressive warmth. Wand allows Bruckner to take his time when required, but the momentum never flags, and the final climax arrives with the inevitability of a huge ocean liner docking in harbor. The whole thing is beautifully recorded, and beautifully played—even in these days of obsessive perfectionism, it is hard to believe that this was a live recording. **SJ**

Richard Strauss | Violin Sonata (1887)

Genre | Chamber
Performers | Vadim Repin (violin),
Boris Berezovsky (piano)
Year recorded | 2000
Label | Erato 8573 85769-2

Richard Strauss's instrumental music comes from the beginning and the end of his life, whereas the true chamber music is all early. This is a shame, since he showed clearly that he had a real feeling for the genre. Some of us would gladly exchange one or two of the operas for a mature string quartet or quintet and perhaps a piano quintet. Of what we do have, the Piano Quartet of 1883–84 has its supporters, and some players have managed to make a good effect with the Cello Sonata—but the Violin Sonata is the clear winner.

It has a quite distinctive sound, which makes one regret all the more that the Violin Concerto of a few years earlier—equally individual in places—was neither revised nor followed with a second such work. The two outer movements of the sonata show how much Strauss had learned in the meantime: There is none of the short-windedness that makes the first movement of the concerto so disappointing; but the glory of the sonata is the central slow "Improvisation," which rewards a violinist with a well-controlled legato.

Two wonderful Russian violinists—Jascha Heifetz and Leonid Kogan—made something of a speciality of the sonata but persisted in recording it with accompanists rather than partners. Vadim Repin—the finest of today's Russian fiddlers—is in the same mold, although he is more like Kogan than Heifetz. Repin has established a superb duo with Boris Berezovsky and together they explore every facet of this beautiful sonata, while always keeping in mind that it is a youthful piece. Their performance is a genuine partnership, even if the ultimate impression it leaves is of Repin's fine sustaining of the musical line in the slow movement. **TP**

> *"They have grafted the high drama of Strauss's later music onto the contours of this early score."*
>
> Allan Kozinn

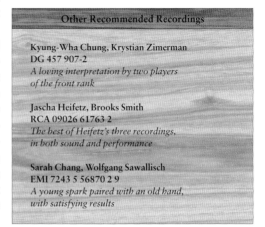

Other Recommended Recordings

Kyung-Wha Chung, Krystian Zimerman
DG 457 907-2
A loving interpretation by two players of the front rank

Jascha Heifetz, Brooks Smith
RCA 09026 61763 2
The best of Heifetz's three recordings, in both sound and performance

Sarah Chang, Wolfgang Sawallisch
EMI 7243 5 56870 2 9
A young spark paired with an old hand, with satisfying results

Vadim Repin, among the most distinguished Russian violinists. ➔

Giuseppe Verdi | Otello (1887)

Genre | Opera
Conductor/Performers | Carlos Kleiber; Plácido Domingo, Piero Cappuccilli, Mirella Freni, La Scala Chorus and Orchestra
Year recorded | 1976
Label | Music and Arts CD-1043(2) (2 CDs)

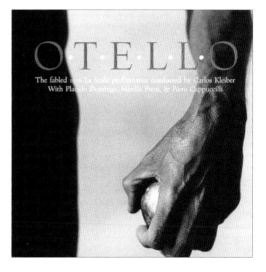

The fabled 1976 La Scala performance conducted by Carlos Kleiber With Plácido Domingo, Mirella Freni, & Piero Cappuccilli

After toying for years with plans for a *King Lear* that would never be written, Verdi turned his attention in 1879 to Shakespeare's *Othello*. Arrigo Boito contributed an exquisitely sophisticated libretto that is a work of art in its own right. Verdi took his time, working on the revised versions of *Simon Boccanegra* (again with Boito) and *Don Carlos* in the meantime.

The premiere of *Otello* took place exactly forty years after that of Verdi's first Shakespearean opera, *Macbeth*. A new Verdi opera was bound to be successful, but contemporary audiences were baffled, too, with George Bernard Shaw even insinuating that Verdi's new "harmonic elegances and orchestral sonorities" were there to compensate for the lack of tunes like "La donna è mobile." For the first Paris performances in 1894, Verdi added the obligatory ballet in the third act and rewrote (shortening it) part of the final concertato of the same act; neither change is usually adopted nowadays.

Otello is the earliest Verdi opera for which we have creators' records; both the first Otello (Francesco Tamagno) and the first Iago (Victor Maurel) left recordings of their solos. In particular, Tamagno, who had a stentorean voice, has cast a very long shadow over his successors, most of whom have been found wanting in sheer vocal heft when compared to him. However, a loud voice is neither indispensable nor enough on its own to do justice to the complex role. In the last quarter of the twentieth century, the greatest Otello has been without doubt Plácido Domingo, who first sang the role in 1975. Of his many recordings in audio and video, the one taken off the stage at La Scala benefits from Mirella Freni's angelic singing and the incandescent conducting of Carlos Kleiber. **CMS**

> "*The truth is that . . . *
> Othello *is a play written*
> *by Shakespeare in the*
> *style of Italian opera.*"

George Bernard Shaw in *Shaw's Music*, Vol. 3

Other Recommended Recordings

**NBC Symphony Orchestra • Arturo Toscanini
Guild GHCD 2275/77 (3 CDs)**
Toscanini leads a white-hot performance and can also be heard rehearsing it

**Metropolitan Opera Chorus and Orchestra
Ettore Panizza • Naxos 8.111018-19 (2 CDs)**
Classic pairing of the great Otello of the 1930s, Giovanni Martinelli, with Lawrence Tibbett as Iago

**La Scala Chorus and Orchestra • Riccardo Muti
DVD: TDK DVOPOTEL**
Graham Vick's psychologically astute production; Muti plays the Paris version of the concertato

Plácido Domingo, the greatest Otello of recent times. ➔

César Franck
Symphony in D minor (1888)

Genre | Orchestral
Conductor | Willem van Otterloo
Performers | Amsterdam Concertgebouw
Year recorded | 1964
Label | Philips 442 296-2

When Franck's Symphony in D minor was first performed in Paris in February 1889, the general reaction was puzzlement or even outrage. Franck was still best known as an organist; and while Saint-Saëns had included a prominent organ part in his Third Symphony (1886), the profoundly spiritual, incense-laden atmosphere of the Franck is far more potent. The central Allegretto movement sounds like a religious procession, for example, though there are scherzo-like elements blended in as well—a structural innovation that surely baffled some listeners. It was not until well after the composer's death that the symphony's unique character began to be appreciated.

For modern audiences, Franck's work may bring to mind the symphonies of Anton Bruckner: both composers used recurring themes to create a sense of unity and closure and both were influenced by the harmonies of Liszt and Wagner. What sets Franck's symphony apart, however, is its subtle play of light and shade, and careful balance between symphonic weight and Gallic grace.

Finding this balance in performance is no easy task. Pierre Monteux's high-voltage Chicago account is rightly famous, but Willem van Otterloo's recording is perhaps finer still. Otterloo's direction is clearheaded and thoughtful—a necessity in music with so many tempo changes—yet feels spontaneous, as if this were one of Franck's legendary organ improvisations. Amsterdam's Concertgebouw Orchestra is a major asset here, not only for the intensity and character of its playing, but for its shine. The sound is like a grand Gothic cathedral lit by thousands of candles. **AFC**

Gustav Mahler
Symphony no. 1 (1888)

Genre | Orchestral
Conductor/Performers | Rafael Kubelík;
Bavarian Radio Symphony Orchestra
Year recorded | 1967
Label | DG 449 735-2

Beginning with a famous seven-octave spread of the pitch A, sustained by string harmonics at a pianissimo dynamic level as the atmosphere for a passage designated "like a sound of nature," Mahler's First Symphony introduced a new aesthetic to symphonic writing. In this world, sonority is an inextricable part of the substance of the music, so that when at the beginning of the third movement the tune we know as "Frère Jacques" (only here in minor mode) is introduced by a solo double bass playing high in its register, we are to recognize the ungainliness of the result as a kind of parody. The juxtaposition of simple melodic materials, advanced harmonies, colorful orchestration, and a formal procedure that continues to attract attempts at explanation—all this combines to produce music that seemingly begs to be understood, even to be a context in which the listener can discover his or her own story.

Mahler's First was first performed as a five-movement symphonic poem in 1889 and was later given the title *Titan* (invoking the novel by Jean Paul), but after 1893 Mahler discarded both the second movement (called "Blumine") and the program, leaving the incorporation of joyful and dreamy passages from his *Songs of a Wayfarer*, the grotesque pastiche of vulgar and serene elements in the third movement, and the progression from cataclysmic despair to triumph in the finale as the most overt hints to meaning in this absorbing, still puzzling, but thrilling work.

Rafael Kubelík's second recording of this score is an evergreen, offering abundant energy and optimism in the first two movements, uncommonly vivid parody in the third, and an invigorating final triumph. **DB**

Nicolai Rimsky-Korsakov
Sheherazade (1888)

Genre | Orchestral
Conductor | Valery Gergiev
Performers | Kirov Orchestra
Year recorded | 2001
Label | Philips 470 618-2

Occasionally assumed to be an opera, *Sheherazade* is in fact something of a Rimsky-Korsakov speciality, an orchestral suite. The meaning of the term has changed over the centuries, but its most literal interpretation as a sequence of smaller units that "follow" in a specified order is well-suited to the narrative nature of this piece. It is one of three popular orchestral works that the composer wrote during a productive two-year period (1887–88), after which his efforts were chiefly devoted to opera. Based on four episodes from the *1001 Arabian Nights*, the music is suitably evocative of places oriental and showcases the composer's imaginative and fluent skills as an orchestrator, with the sections elegantly linked by passages for solo violin as the persona of the princess Sheherazade herself.

Like all Rimsky-Korsakov's works from this period, this is a much-loved composition that requires close attention from conductor and orchestra. The composer himself remarked that by this stage in his career his orchestration had "attained a considerable degree of virtuosity and warm sonority without Wagnerian influence"—a perfectly accurate analysis that still seems rather dry in comparison with the reality of this definitive orchestral showpiece. It is perhaps more helpful to think of the composer's impressive talent for evoking a festival in old Baghdad or the ebb and flow of the sea while maintaining the piece's inherent musicality. This is, of course, meat and drink to Valery Gergiev, whose passion for and informed understanding of the music of his homeland is, as ever, transmitted to and through the orchestra on this impressive Super Audio CD. **RT**

Hugo Wolf
Mörike Lieder (1888)

Genre | Vocal
Performers | Joan Rodgers,
Stephan Genz, Roger Vignoles
Years recorded | 1999–2000
Label | Hyperion CDA 67311/2 (2 CDs)

The fever of inspiration that Wolf experienced in 1888 left him bewildered; as the songs poured out of him he hardly knew to what to attribute them. "A divine song, I tell you!" he wrote to a friend about one; not quite a month later, "Today I have created my masterpiece"; the next day, a retraction, stating that yet another new song "is a million times better" than yesterday's masterpiece. By the end of November, he had completed the fifty-three songs on poems by Eduard Mörike that were to be published as a collection the next year. The variety of this collection is as bewildering as the quality—in the words of the pianist Graham Johnson, it contains songs that are "long and short, serious and comic, sacred and profane, simple and complex." Given these many varieties, it is not safe to generalize, but many commentators and listeners have noted that Wolf's Mörike songs tend to be more lyrical than those in any other of his collections. Consequently, they also tend to be the Wolf songs that most attract singers who do not sing much Wolf, and to attract much attention from those who do.

Given the resulting embarrassment of riches, the recording to hear is the only complete one of these songs, since only by hearing them all can one appreciate the magnitude of Wolf's justifiable claim that "of the ninety-two songs [written in 1888] not one is a failure." These performances are rarely the very best to be found, but they are communicative and thoroughly considered accounts that avoid the temptation of excessive and reverent calculation. The simulation of natural utterance in Wolf performance is not a virtue to be taken for granted. **DB**

Pyotr Ilyich Tchaikovsky | Symphony no. 5 (1888)

Genre | Orchestral
Conductor | Antonio Pappano
Performers | Accademia di Santa Cecilia Orchestra
Year recorded | 2006
Label | EMI 0946 3 53258 2 9 (2 CDs)

Returning to abstract symphonic form in 1888 after a gap of more than a decade, Tchaikovsky was determined to show he could write a symphony along Western Classical lines. His guide in this was the conservative Hamburg teacher Theodor Ave-Lallement, to whom the Fifth Symphony is dedicated. Outwardly the work is more evenly proportioned in its four movements than its predecessor, the Fourth Symphony, and features only timpani among the percussion. There is still, however, a program. The all-powerful figure of Fate that dominated the Fourth and returned to blight the folk merriment of its finale has now become Providence, subject to change. It lays down its brooding gauntlet at the start of the first movement before giving way to an allegro that Tchaikovsky described as "murmurs, doubts, laments, reproaches against . . . XXX" (presumably a reference to his homosexuality). Still threatening, "providence" twice bursts across the scene of the composer's finest slow movement before the *Pathètique* Symphony, the great Andante cantabile, and briefly stalks a gracious waltz. In the finale, its character has changed to one of noble defiance, and after a vigorous battle, it emerges noisily as the victor in a triumphant final parade.

Very much the centerpiece and the finest performance in Antonio Pappano's set of Tchaikovsky's last three symphonies, his Fifth is finely molded and beautifully shaped. While the first movement moves swiftly and effectively to its lyric climaxes, a spacious Andante cantabile, beginning with intense pianissimos from lower strings and a misty horn solo, reminds us how close Tchaikovsky comes to the world of Italian opera. The waltz is supremely elegant and the finale nobly blazes. **DN**

> *"My symphony is finished, and I certainly haven't made a hash of it."*
>
> **Pyotr Ilyich Tchaikovsky**

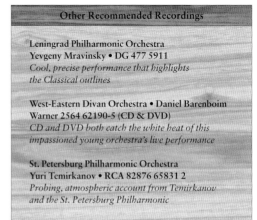

Other Recommended Recordings

Leningrad Philharmonic Orchestra
Yevgeny Mravinsky • DG 477 5911
Cool, precise performance that highlights the Classical outlines

West-Eastern Divan Orchestra • Daniel Barenboim
Warner 2564 62190-5 (CD & DVD)
CD and DVD both catch the white heat of this impassioned young orchestra's live performance

St. Petersburg Philharmonic Orchestra
Yuri Temirkanov • RCA 82876 65831 2
Probing, atmospheric account from Temirkanov and the St. Petersburg Philharmonic

Antonio Pappano, music director of the Santa Cecilia Orchestra. ➔

Nicolai Rimsky-Korsakov
Russian Easter Festival Overture (1888)

Genre | Orchestral
Conductor/Performers | Leonard Slatkin; St. Louis Symphony Orchestra
Year recorded | 1981
Label | Telarc CD-80072

There is a certain poignancy to this piece in that it was the last of the three major orchestral compositions (the others being *Capriccio Espagnol* and *Sheherazade*) that Rimsky-Korsakov had completed by early 1888, after which he focused on opera. Most of the overture's melodic components are taken from a collection of Russian Orthodox canticles, an approach that anticipated the "Holy minimalism" of Pärt and Tavener by nearly a century, but this is not simply a devotional work. The composer also conveys, as intended, the "legendary and heathen" celebratory origins of Easter. Unlike many overtures, the piece opens quietly, but then builds to a dramatic climax of strident brass and percussion. Throughout, the various traditional liturgical melodies intertwine with a serpentine beauty, interspersed with attractive violin cadenzas.

The key to a successful performance of this piece is to leave the audience sharing the composer's understanding of both the atavistic and religious forces at work within the music and the occasion it celebrates. Leonard Slatkin adopts fairly broad strokes in achieving this, but he and the St. Louis Symphony are so much in their element here that it hardly seems to matter, and the most significant contrasts (such as the emergence of the contemplative "Christ is Risen" theme) are expertly preserved, as is the multilayered effect of Rimsky-Korsakov's orchestration. This disc captures a performance delivered with exactly the right kind of conviction and deserves a place in any representative collection. **RT**

Erik Satie
Gymnopédies & Gnossiennes (1888, 1889–97)

Genre | Instrumental
Instrument | Piano
Performer | Aldo Ciccolini
Year recorded | 1983
Label | EMI 7243 5 67260 2 4

The creation of Erik Satie's famous *Gymnopédies* may have been prompted by some lines in a poem by J. P. Contamine de Latour, *Les antiques* (*The Ancients*). The poet was Satie's companion and presumed lover. Insecure and volatile, Satie endured extremes of critical opinion during his life. Dismissed from his original studies and branded a failure, he recommenced his musical education at the age of thirty-nine with far greater success. Debussy first admired then rejected him, Ravel supported him, and Cocteau idolized him. In 1911 his innovations began to be recognized, but this came too late to offset a lifetime of neglect exacerbated by alcoholism, and he died in 1925.

The *Gymnopédies* are best described as music imagined to accompany the gymnastic dances of ancient Greece. Written as gentle, lilting, melodic waltzes, they subvert the traditional sophistication of Classical pianism while also anticipating the subtracted approach of Scelsi and Glass, in which the most basic changes of pitch, chord structure, and dynamics become almost precipitously significant. The *Gnossiennes* (the term is of Satie's invention) essentially expand and develop these ideas.

All too often these pieces are treated and performed as little novelties, more suited to holistic therapy than to the concert platform. They are also all massively overrecorded, but Aldo Ciccolini's performance stands out from the rest of the pack. He makes his mark by recognizing the unassuming but ingenious musicality that Satie wrought in the pieces. **RT**

Alexander Scriabin
Preludes
(1888–1914)

Genre | Instrumental
Instrument | Piano
Performer | Evgeny Zarafiants
Year recorded | 1996
Label | Naxos 8.553997 (1), 8.554145 (2)

Although he wrote numerous large-scale works, Scriabin was by nature a miniaturist. And perhaps the most miniature of all his conceptions are the preludes for piano: some ninety pieces spread across twenty-two collections, composed during a span of twenty-six years.

Scriabin's preludes descend from the equally compact examples of Chopin, and anticipate the "fleeting visions" of Prokofiev. As one writer memorably put it: "Like a musical Fabergé, Scriabin is capable of creating a glittering world in a tiny space." In pieces contained in sometimes less than a page of music, Scriabin conjures a kaleidoscopic range of evocative imagery or states of mind, often exquisite, occasionally energetic and violently disturbing, ranging from dream-like to nightmarish. From the evaporating sonorities of the magical first prelude, op. 2, no. 2, to the desolate neurosis of the Five Preludes, op. 74, these works chart the long curve of Scriabin's stylistic development.

Evgeny Zarafiants is highly individual yet completely attuned to Scriabin's sound-world, capturing the febrile intensity, the manic vision, the complex textures, and the highly colored radiance of the lyrical writing. He is especially successful in the later preludes, where his dark-hued, probing accounts strike at the heart of this music. While other pianists, notably Vladimir Horowitz and Sviatoslav Richter, have made miraculous recordings of some of these pieces, there is no finer account of the complete preludes than this from Zarafiants, who is superbly recorded and available at budget price. **TLP**

Antonín Dvořák
Symphony no. 8
(1889)

Genre | Orchestral
Conductor | Colin Davis
Performers | London Symphony Orchestra
Year recorded | 1999
Label | LSO Live LSO 002

Dvořák's Eighth Symphony was decidedly a new departure for the composer. While his Sixth and Seventh had looked toward Viennese Classicism, the Eighth is marked by freewheeling formal experiment (particularly in the first and last movements) and almost superabundant lyricism. Dvořák wrote the work during the autumn of 1889, much of it at his country retreat of Vysoká in South Bohemia.

While much of the symphony has a sunny, pastoral quality, there are surprising depths lurking in many places. The very opening of the work is marked by a dark-hued, soulful melody that veers between minor and major modes before the texture opens out with an airy melody for the flute. The slow movement has a great emotional range: Beginning with a stately, almost vocal, melody, it seems at times the very image of contented rural life; at others it verges on extraordinary metaphysical violence. The scherzo and finale are much more openhearted.

Given its near-universal popularity, it is no surprise to find the Eighth very well represented in the catalogue. Colin Davis's 1999 performance is outstanding from a number of points of view. The recording was made at a concert and the sensation of live music making is overwhelming. Davis does not miss a single interpretative trick: the first movement unfolds with persuasive symphonic logic and his control of the dramatic mood swings of the slow movement are captured with a real sense of drama; nor does he overdo the tempo contrasts in the finale. All in all, this is a performance to treasure. **JS**

Hugo Wolf
Goethe Lieder (1889)

Genre | Vocal
Performers | Dietrich Fischer-Dieskau (baritone), Sviatoslav Richter (piano)
Year recorded | 1977
Label | Orfeo C 543 001 B

Wolf's settings of Mörike and Eichendorff helped to make these poets better known among musicians, but his decision to take on the poetry of Goethe, which had been extensively set by earlier composers, demonstrated his confidence in his powers. To be sure, he did go out of his way to find Goethe poems that spoke to him but that had not been set much (especially by Schubert)—consequently, of the fifty-one songs in this collection, a third are selections from Goethe's *Westöstlicher Divan*, which most composers would not have glanced at twice for musical treatment. But by beginning his collection with settings of the "Harfenspieler" and "Mignon" poems from Wilhelm Meisters Lehrjahre, and by ending with "Ganymed," "Prometheus," and "Grenzen der Menschheit," Wolf squarely faced the challenges of doing justice to highly demanding poetry and of inviting comparison with his great predecessors. Also among the Goethe songs, well-known jewels such as "Blumengruss" and "Anakreons Grab" appear with others that appealed to Wolf's sarcastic sense of humor. Throughout, despite the uneven appeal of the texts, Wolf's craft commands the greatest admiration.

Singers sometimes say that Wolf's songs are wonderful to contemplate in private but hard to put over to an audience. When Dietrich Fischer-Dieskau and Sviatoslav Richter then hold a Munich audience spellbound in a demanding program of eighteen Goethe songs, the reason lies not solely with the typical acuity, authority, and vocal gifts of the baritone but also with the pianist's ability to allow the singer to ride a wave of musical continuity too infrequently achieved by Wolf accompanists. **DB**

Pyotr Ilyich Tchaikovsky
The Sleeping Beauty (1889)

Genre | Ballet
Conductor | André Previn
Performers | London Symphony Orchestra
Year recorded | 1974
Label | EMI 7243 5 85788 2 9 (2 CDs)

The idea for *The Sleeping Beauty* came from the cultivated director of Russia's imperial theaters, Ivan Vsevolozhsky. He wanted to set it in the France of Louis XIV—the period familiar to the tale's author, Charles Perrault—with musical styles to match, if possible. Tchaikovsky was delighted to oblige, and his most generous ballet score teems with invention. He introduced Baroque spice to the palace of King Florestan and Mozartian grace to the court of Prince Desire, where fashions have moved on by a hundred years. There are piquant contrasts in the Prologue's *pas de six* for the fairies bringing blessings to the cradle of the infant Aurora, and in the humorous dances for other fairy tale characters celebrating her wedding to Prince Desire in the ballet's gorgeous last act. But it is above all in the conflict of good—as represented by the bittersweet music of the Lilac Fairy—and evil—embodied in the wicked fairy Carabosse—that Tchaikovsky excels himself. He was disappointed by the Tsar's lukewarm response to the lavish staging at the beginning of 1890, but the ballet has endured and is frequently seen in the ingenious choreography by Marius Petipa, to which the composer was so careful to tailor his score.

André Previn gives a spacious, handsomely recorded account of the full score, a fine specimen of his heyday with the London Symphony Orchestra, though it is a pity that in the interests of accommodating the ballet on two CDs the splendid romp for Hop-O-My-Thumb, noted by Shostakovich, has been omitted. Still, Previn has the edge over the rather glacial Mikhail Pletnev version, much admired by others. **DN**

Richard Strauss
Don Juan (1889)

Genre | Orchestral
Conductor | Herbert von Karajan
Performers | Berlin Philharmonic
Year recorded | 1972
Label | DG 447 441-2

Don Juan was the tone poem that first revealed Richard Strauss to the world as a composer of genius. When the twenty-five-year-old (son of the principal horn player at the Court Opera in Munich) began work on it in 1888, he had only just come out from under the shadow of his conservative Munich upbringing and was newly in thrall to the first, and as far as we know only, true love of his life—Pauline de Ahna, the major general's daughter whom he married six years later. Strauss's monogamous existence was far removed from the thousand-fold affairs of Don Juan, the insatiable nobleman of Spanish legend, and yet the composer could project his musical imagination sufficiently to provide all the cut and thrust as well as the amorous repose of the great lover.

Strauss took his cue not from Mozart's treatment in *Don Giovanni* but from a verse-drama by Nikolaus Lenau, in which the hero's life is cut short by a rapier thrust. This accounts for the bleak and abrupt ending, briefly foreshadowed, in an otherwise brilliant work. Don Juan's escapades and two of his loves are warmly delineated, the second with one of the most melting oboe solos in the orchestral repertoire; but the real coup of the work comes with the noble horn theme that makes its mark two-thirds of the way through an action-packed narrative.

This theme, and its overwhelming return at the tone poem's high noon, is where the superhero of Herbert von Karajan's *Don Juan* really comes into his own. Other Juans may lead a more purposeful existence—notably that of George Szell—but none is more masterful, or more ardent in the string department, than Karajan's. **DN**

Richard Strauss
Tod und Verklärung (1889)

Genre | Orchestral
Conductor | Herbert von Karajan
Performers | Berlin Philharmonic
Year recorded | 1972
Label | DG 447 422-2

The young Richard Strauss had no experience of what it was like to be on the brink of death when he composed his most somber tone poem in 1889; yet, sixty years later as he lay dying, he was able to confirm—perhaps with tongue characteristically in cheek—that he had got it exactly right. The narrative of *Tod und Verklärung* (*Death and Transfiguration*) focuses on a man who, from his sickbed, revisits scenes of his childhood and vigorous youth with the utmost clarity (and typical Straussian energy), but senses that there is still more to life. The theme that illustrates this, the so-called "ideology" motif, unfolds its full glory for the first time only as the protagonist is close to death, but the massive effort required leads to another bout of the terrible suffering that punctuates the first two-thirds of the work. Only in a long and glowing epilogue growing out of the mysterious strokes of the tam-tam—the "transfiguration"—is the "ideology" theme allowed to coast along at length, building toward a great climax before floating away into infinity. Strauss was to quote it once more, at the words "is this perhaps death?" in the fourth of his *Four Last Songs* from the end of his life.

Whether the final extended rhapsody of *Tod und Verklärung* sounds genuinely spiritual or simply banal depends very much on the dedication of the performance. Herbert von Karajan is one of the few conductors to light his transfiguration from within, thanks partly to the special glow of the Berlin Philharmonic. There is immense power, too, in the lower brass playing during the earlier death-throes of the tone poem and magnificent horn playing in the remembered episodes of fiery youth. **DN**

Ernest Chausson | Poème de l'amour et de la mer (1890)

Genre | Vocal
Performers | Susan Graham, BBC Symphony Orchestra
Conductor | Yan Pascal Tortelier
Year recorded | 2004
Label | Warner 2564 61938-2

Like all French composers of his generation, Ernest Chausson was subject to the twin influences of César Franck and Richard Wagner. The former he encountered when he attended (in an unofficial capacity) his classes at the Paris Conservatoire—he was officially studying under Massenet. The works of the latter he experienced at Munich and Bayreuth between 1879 and 1883. Essentially a miniaturist rather than an epic artist, however, Chausson worked hard to develop a characteristic style based on Classical principles but with a rich tonal palette and gentle chromaticism in tune with the spirit of the times.

The setting of Maurice Bouchor's text in the *Poème de l'amour et de la mer* demonstrates Chausson's poetic sensibility to perfection. The narrative of the verse is simple. A young man sees and falls in love with a girl on the beach. Returning the following year, he finds that she has forgotten him. But behind that simple outline lies a complex web of emotions: youthful passion, surging optimism, gnawing doubt, and bitter anguish. And there are several passages of highly individual word setting, including the frozen horror at the words "*l'oubli*," as the narrator realizes that he has been forgotten.

It would be difficult to imagine an interpreter more faithful to the *Poème*'s subtle blending of ardent passion and refined sensibility than the mezzo-soprano Susan Graham. The sensuality she projects through text and tone is almost miraculous, and the pain of rejection in the poem's third part is heart-stopping in its immediacy. Yan Pascal Tortelier meanwhile captures the piercing, throbbing anguish and the surging of sea and emotions. The disc also contains Ravel's *Shéhérazade* and Debussy's *Le livre de Baudelaire* in an orchestration by John Adams. **BM**

> *"Crushingly monotonous developments . . . not a theme can be grasped."*
>
> Contemporary critic in *Le Figaro*

Other Recommended Recordings

Jessye Norman, Monte Carlo Philharmonic Orchestra
Armin Jordan
Warner 0927 48992-2
Jessye Norman brings her sumptuous soprano to the solo part

Janet Baker, London Symphony Orchestra
Evgeny Svetlanov
BBC Legends BBCL 40772
Archive BBC recording by Baker and Svetlanov

Linda Finnie, Ulster Orchestra • Yan Pascal Tortelier
Chandos CHAN 8952
Fauré's Pelléas et Mélisande *is the attractive coupling*

Ernest Chausson at home with one of his five children. ➔

Hugo Wolf | Spanisches Liederbuch (1890)

Genre | Vocal
Performers | Elisabeth Schwarzkopf (soprano),
Dietrich Fischer-Dieskau (baritone), Gerald Moore (piano)
Years recorded | 1966–67
Label | DG 457 726-2 (2 CDs)

Although some of his Mörike songs have religious and spiritual themes (not surprisingly, since Mörike was himself a Lutheran pastor who felt his spirit stifled by that occupation), it comes as something of a surprise to encounter the first ten songs in Wolf's *Spanisches Liederbuch* (*Spanish Songbook*). Some of these sacred songs are lovely and peaceful, but others have an undercurrent of anxiety, while the penitential songs present some of the most anguished music Wolf ever wrote. The two songs portraying mystical dialogues between the suffering Christ and a distraught believer are high points in Wolf's output. The larger section of the songbook (taken from a selection of Spanish poems from the sixteenth and seventeenth centuries) consists of thirty-four secular songs, and here the expressive palette is again considerable, ranging from passionate eroticism ("Bedeckt mich mit Blumen" or the concluding "Geh', Geliebter, geh' jetzt!") to kittenish insouciance ("In dem Schatten meiner Locken"). The Spanishness of this music is sometimes evident in dance rhythms and implied castanets or guitars, but just as often it is extra harmonic intensity that seems to produce local color.

For a quarter of a century from the early 1950s, Schwarzkopf and Fischer-Dieskau were regarded as the world's leading Wolf singers, and their regular accompanist (on records, at any rate) for a large stretch of that time was Gerald Moore. This team's recording of the *Spanish Songbook* offers a fine example of their highly wrought and strongly characterized Wolf style; if Schwarzkopf makes a vocally effortful impression at times, one nevertheless feels gratitude to her for taking the songs and the act of bringing them alive so seriously. **DB**

"Wolf's most colorful and overtly passionate songbook."

Richard Wigmore

Other Recommended Recordings

Anne Sophie von Otter, Olaf Bär
Geoffrey Parsons (piano)
EMI 7243 5 55325 2 7 (2 CDs)
The only other complete set—a worthy rival to DG

Jan DeGaetani, Gilbert Kalish (piano)
Nonesuch 79263
Sixteen Spanish songs in meticulous performances

Songs (orchestrated by Wolf) • Mitsuko Shirai
Berlin Radio Symphony Orchestra
David Shallon • Capriccio 10 335
Fifteen songs (mostly Mörike and Goethe settings) sounding beguiling in orchestral garb

Soprano Elisabeth Schwarzkopf (1915–2006) was unrivalled in Wolf. ➔

Gabriel Fauré
Requiem (1890, *rev.* 1893)

Genre | Choral
Conductor/Performers | Matthew Best;
Corydon Singers
Year recorded | 1987
Label | Hyperion CDA 66292

Arguably his best-known and best-loved work, Fauré's *Requiem* was written while he was choirmaster at the Madeleine church in Paris. It marked a radical departure from existing works in this genre and demonstrated the degree to which Fauré was an independent thinker among his contemporaries. Influenced by the purity of plainchant, and evoking gentle consolation rather than hellfire and damnation, the work has been called "a lullaby of death."

To Fauré himself, the work's essence was humanistic rather than religious and it continues to speak its compassionate message to a wide range of listeners. First performed at the Madeleine for the funeral of a well-known architect, when Fauré explained to the priest that the music was his own work, he met with the response: "Monsieur Fauré, we don't need such novelties. The Madeleine's repertoire is quite rich enough already."

The work's original version featured only five movements and somber scoring with no violins. Fauré reworked the *Requiem* for slightly expanded forces in 1893, and later still for full orchestra; it is worth noting that he preferred a woman soloist in the "Pie Jesu" since its breath control demands are so stringent. As for the baritone, the last thing Fauré wanted was an operatic interpretation.

Although the work has been recorded hundreds of times, truly satisfactory accounts are surprisingly thin on the ground. The account of the intimate 1893 version, conducted by Matthew Best, is closest to the ideal, however—the tempi are beautifully judged, the pure-toned soloists Mary Seers and Michael George are just right, and the atmosphere is rapt and compelling. **JD**

Pietro Mascagni
Cavalleria rusticana (1890)

Genre | Opera
Conductor/Performers | Tullio Serafin;
Maria Callas, Giuseppe di Stefano
Year recorded | 1953
Label | EMI 7243 5 56287 2 5 (2 CDs)

Mascagni managed to escape the family baker's business for a life in music. Success as a composer having eluded him, he entered a competition for one-act operas organized by the publisher Sonzogno and wrote *Cavalleria rusticana* (*Rustic Chivalry*). The work was an instant hit with audiences around the world, but Mascagni spent the rest of his life trying to write another success.

Cavalleria rusticana is generally credited with being the first properly verismo opera, a style that turns its back on Romanticism. No tales here of medieval monarchs or Renaissance princes gripped in the vice of grand passions. Verismo aims at realism—everyday stories of lower-class life that are usually brutal and often sordid. But the southern Mediterranean setting and the curdled love affair between Santuzza and Turiddu perhaps owe as much to the success of Bizet's *Carmen* as to any desire to drag opera into the modern age. And it is Mascagni's lyricism and dramatic instincts that make the work a minor masterpiece. The celebrated Intermezzo is both a breath of musical air and a chilling lull before the storm breaks and Turiddu is knifed by Alfio.

Maria Callas was in her very best voice when she recorded her Santuzza, soaring out over the La Scala chorus in the Easter Hymn, and painfully vulnerable in "Voi lo sapete, o mamma." Giuseppe di Stefano is a splendidly caddish Turiddu and Rolando Panerai is one of the best Alfio's on record. But best of all is Tullio Serafin's absolute control in the pit. This may not be the most beautiful account of Mascagni's score, but it is undoubtedly the most dramatic. **CC**

Pyotr Ilyich Tchaikovsky
The Queen of Spades (1890)

Genre | Opera
Conductor/Performers | Valery Gergiev;
Gegam Grigorian, Irina Arkhipova
Year recorded | 1992
Label | Philips 438 141-2 (3 CDs)

Alexander Pushkin's short story, on which Tchaikovsky's opera is based, is one of the most concise and perfect in any language. It tells of a morose outsider, Hermann, obsessed by the secret of three cards that will bring him success in gambling. In order to get at the owner of the recipe, a decrepit Countess, he woos her ward Lisa. But it is only after Hermann has frightened the Countess to death that her ghost appears with the secret—the three, the seven, and the ace played in succession. Just when victory appears to be within Hermann's grasp, the card he expects to be his ace turns out to be the Queen of Spades, winking at him with the face of the Countess. He goes insane.

The kind of grand opera expected by Russia's Imperial Theater in 1890 imposed different demands. In Tchaikovsky's *Queen of Spades*, Hermann really does fall in love with Lisa, who commits suicide when he deserts her for the gambling table—and instead of going mad, he kills himself. On the way to the denouement, there are grandiose choruses and a Mozartian diversion at a high-society ball. But the one scene in which Tchaikovsky comes closest to Pushkin, set in the Countess's bedchamber, truly makes the flesh creep with vivid music theater of the highest order.

Valery Gergiev captures the hushed intensity of Tchaikovsky's most harrowing moments better than anyone. In Gegam Grigorian, he has a heroic-lyric tenor equal to the role's exhausting challenges, while luxury Kirov casting includes the veteran Russian mezzo-soprano Irina Arkhipova as the Countess and her natural successor, Olga Borodina, in the small part of Pauline. **DN**

Claude Debussy
Fêtes galantes (1891, 1904)

Genre | Vocal
Performers | Gérard Souzay (baritone),
Dalton Baldwin (piano)
Year recorded | 1961
Label | DG 463 664-2

It is said that in later life Debussy could be seen in music shops surreptitiously rifling through the published songs of Gabriel Fauré. But he had little to fear from his greatest rival as a songwriter. Since his earliest days he had written *mélodies* in his own style and, by the time he came to set the first three of Paul Verlaine's poems as *Fêtes galantes 1*, he had shuffled off the influence of Gounod and Berlioz, who between them had invented a new tradition of French song to rival that German Lieder. When he returned to Verlaine in 1904, he skirted round the Wagnerism that held so many of his Parisian contemporaries in thrall.

Both books of *Fêtes galantes* were inspired by incidents in Debussy's own life. The first was composed for Marie Vasnier, a married woman and a gifted coloratura soprano, who is said to have made Debussy a serious songwriter. The second set, composed some thirteen years later, was for Emma Bardac, who had been Fauré's mistress. The pastoral world of the seventeenth-century painter Watteau, ironically reinterpreted for a modern age from which nymphs and shepherds had long vanished, is Verlaine's chief theme in these six poems.

Gérard Souzay is both playful and serious in *Fêtes galantes*. In "Colloque sentimentale" there is a sudden glimpse of the depths of feeling beneath the surface of this sentimental dialogue between the ghosts of two lovers wandering through a wintry park. In "Claire de lune" from the earlier trio, the apparent happiness of the lovers walking in the moonlight is subtly undermined by Dalton Baldwin's faint air of ironic detachment. Few performers bring such authority to this music. **CC**

Jean Sibelius | Songs (1891–1917)

Genre | Vocal
Performers | Karita Mattila (soprano),
Ilmo Ranta (piano)
Year recorded | 1995
Label | Ondine ODE 856-2

Think Schubert, and you think song. Think Sibelius, and the mind's ear hears symphonies. Yet the works of both composers in both genres throw revelatory light on their innermost sensibilities—and on their complete output. Sibelius began to write songs ten years before he composed his first symphony: Indeed, his setting of Johan Ludvig Runeberf's "Serenade" was his first published composition. And he returned, obliquely, to song in the last year of his life, when he wrote a transcription for strings and harp of one of his op. 60 Shakespeare settings, "Come away, Death".

Sibelius's mother tongue was Swedish, the language in which, in his lifetime, the educated classes were raised. He embraced Finnish as soon as he began to learn it at the age of eight, and championed the language throughout his life as the incarnation of Finnish identity at a time of war and occupation. Only six of his songs, however, are in Finnish—and their molding of the language's vowel-rich sonority is uniquely beautiful. It was Swedish poetry that was to be the driving force behind Sibelius's appropriation and expansion of the *Romans*, the Nordic equivalent of the German *Lied* and the French *mélodie*.

Karita Mattila includes four of Sibelius's Finnish settings in her generous program of twenty-four songs, from the earliest Finnish setting, "To evening," to the exquisitely self-echoing "Echo-Nymph," and from the Runeberg masterpieces such as "Black Roses" to the rarely performed song cycle, *Flower Songs*, composed as late as 1917. With Ilmo Ranta's observant piano playing, Mattila's luminous soprano uniquely recreates the sensuous intimacy of these songs and, with an openhearted sense of wonder, the ecstasy at the heart of Sibelius's nature mysticism. **HF**

> "The songs are among the best kept secrets of the repertoire, and an enormous treasure."
>
> Robert Layton

Other Recommended Recordings

Anne Sofie von Otter, Bengt Forsberg
BIS CD-457
The perfect complement to Mattila's anthology

Luonnotar, Orchestral Songs
Soile Isokoski, Helsinki Philharmonic Orchestra
Leif Segerstam • Ondine ODE 1080-5
The relatively few orchestrated songs and a superb performance of the soprano tone-poem Luonnotar

Favorite Finnish Songs • Karita Mattila, Ilmo Ranta
Ondine ODE 892-2
Revelatory and beautiful songs by Sibelius's contemporaries: Kuula, Merikanto, and Kilpinen

Karita Mattila won the first Cardiff Singer of the World in 1983. ➲

Johannes Brahms
Clarinet Quintet (1891)

Genre | Chamber
Performers | Thea King (clarinet),
Gabrieli Quartet
Year recorded | 1983
Label | Hyperion CDA 66107

Brahms's Clarinet Quintet—the last really expansive piece that he wrote—explores at leisure a prevailing atmosphere of elegy and nostalgia. The intense beauty of its main ideas combines with an underlying sense of profound melancholy to produce a mood of autumnal resignation; within the lyric warmth, elements of dark fantasy hint at a wintry bleakness.

Though the first movement is a sonata design, there is no violent opposition between the gentle, unassertive first and second subjects. The magnificent Adagio is less at peace with itself, however. At its center arises a desolately beautiful series of florid clarinet arabesques that spiral and swoop over a rustling, wind-stirred string texture. Apparently a wild, spontaneous improvisation, this passage sublimates the free, fantastic Hungarian gypsy style that had fascinated Brahms all his adult life.

The brief third movement is gentle, ambling, serenade-like music, with a fleeter central section. The finale opens with a lyrical, slightly depressive theme, which is then developed in a series of five variations, the mood still predominantly gentle and nostalgic. The last variation is an impassioned waltz in 3/8 time; the opening theme of the entire quintet now reappears, mingled with fragments of the waltz, in a suddenly hesitant and somber coda.

Thea King and the Gabrieli Quartet give a highly compelling account of this deeply elegiac work, one that seems utterly spontaneous. The turbulent middle-section of the slow movement has never sounded wilder nor more desolate. The ebb and flow of expressive tension throughout the piece seems utterly natural. **MM**

Ruggero Leoncavallo
Pagliacci (1892)

Genre | Opera
Conductor/Performers | Nello Santi;
Montserrat Caballé, Plácido Domingo
Year recorded | 1998
Label | RCA 74321 50168 2

It is Tonio in the prologue who gives us a succinct definition of verismo, the style that gripped the generation of Italian composers who followed Verdi: We are about to see a drama taken from real life, the crippled clown leers at us. And blood will be spilled on stage and curdled in the audience by the time "la commedia è finita" and a jealous husband has stabbed his faithless wife and her lover.

Like Byron, Ruggero Leoncavallo went to bed and woke up famous. Within two years of its Italian premiere, *Pagliacci* had been translated into every European language, including Serbo-Croat, and Canio had become the "must-have" role for any Italian tenor worth his top Cs. It was the Metropolitan Opera in New York in 1893 that first yoked *Pagliacci* to *Cavalleria Rusticana*, seeing the emotional and artistic links between these two operatic warhorses. Indeed it was Mascagni's opera that had made Leoncavallo—who had been laboring over a huge slice of Italian Wagnerism—understand what audiences really wanted. In the event *Pagliacci* is perhaps a more interesting work musically, relying less on the old "numbers" opera formula and borrowing the Wagnerian leitmotif to great effect.

Sherill Milnes is an admirably hateful Tonio, positively smacking his lips in the prologue. When he tries to kiss Nedda, you wrinkle you nose with disgust. As Nedda, Montserrat Caballé is both innocent and knowing, and how sweetly she envies the birds' freedom in her aria "Stridono lassù." Domingo make Canio his own; his "Vesti la giubba" just about banishes the echoes of two generations of heroic Italian tenors before him. **CC**

Alexander Scriabin
Piano Sonatas (1892–1913)

Genre | Instrumental
Instrument | Piano
Performer | Marc-André Hamelin
Year recorded | 1995
Label | Hyperion CDA 67131/2 (2 CDs)

Scriabin's piano sonatas, like his preludes, span his creative life. The earliest of his published sonatas, no. 1 in F minor, op. 6, was written in 1892 when he was twenty; the last, the Tenth Sonata, op. 70, was completed in 1913, two years before his untimely death, and it is the culmination of a series of five deeply original single-movement sonatas (nos. 6–10) that Scriabin wrote in a white heat of inspiration. These late sonatas convey Scriabin's feverish imagination, encompassing a gamut of expressive worlds from the nightmarish terror of the Sixth Sonata, through the voluptuous ecstasy of the Seventh, the inward stillness of the Eighth's luminous trills, and the mysterious and menacing "Black Mass" Ninth Sonata, to the supreme formal balance of the trill-laden Tenth Sonata.

Before these revolutionary Expressionist works come the glorious two-movement Second Sonata (titled Sonata-Fantasy), the ravishing Third Sonata, in a conventional four-movement layout, and the Fourth and Fifth Sonatas, which take giant steps toward the feverish worlds associated with Scriabin's *Poem of Ecstasy*.

Many pianists have excelled in individual sonatas, but few have set down complete cycles that are uniformly successful. Perhaps the most consistent comes from the Canadian Marc-André Hamelin, who delivers the early sonatas with refined elegance but really comes into his own in the later sonatas. With his ability to clarify complex textures without ever sounding under technical strain, he is utterly at home with Scriabin's manic sound-world, capturing the rarefied and ethereal as well as the violently insistent and terrifying. **TLP**

Jean Sibelius
En saga (1892, *revised* 1902)

Genre | Orchestral
Conductor | Herbert von Karajan
Performers | Berlin Philharmonic Orchestra
Year recorded | 1976
Label | EMI 7243 4 76847 2 2

En saga was the first in Sibelius's sequence of apparently "nationalistic" symphonic poems that he allowed to reach publication. Even so the tighter version submitted to the printer was not prepared for ten years, the trigger being a Berlin performance arranged by Busoni, a personal friend as well as a composer and pianist of distinction. Like *Kullervo*, which the mature Sibelius sought to suppress altogether, *En saga*, as initially conceived, is indebted to Bruckner and Liszt and prone to abrupt transitions, subsequently smoothed away. While there is no specific folkloric inspiration, the piece contains in embryo just about every Sibelius thumbprint: It opens with an evocative gleam of Northern light from which emerges an epic, aspiring main theme typical of the young composer.

This 1976 recording is as fascinating for its myth-breaking flaws as its undoubted triumphs. For Herbert von Karajan, at least, the real action begins with the tempo change to allegro. Never prone to fussing over detail, Karajan's smoothed-over manner makes *En saga*'s initial stages curiously unmagical, before an abrupt acceleration into the main body of the piece raises the stakes. The orchestra is taken by surprise—even the august Berliners are not quite together. And yet the rest of the performance is articulate and thrusting, with huge, thrilling climaxes and a uniquely affecting last post from the clarinet.

This big-boned rendition comes in a first-rate survey of popular Sibelius in which only the somnolent *Karelia Suite* may disappoint. At his best Karajan combines unparalleled mastery of orchestral sonority with the natural sense of pulse, motion, and line essential in Sibelius. **DG**

Sergei Rachmaninov | Twenty-four Preludes (1892–1910)

Genre | Instrumental
Instrument | Piano
Performer | Vladimir Ashkenazy
Years recorded | 1974–75
Label | Decca 467 685-2

When Rachmaninov composed his Prelude in C sharp minor in 1892, at the age of nineteen, he would have been dismayed to learn that it would remain his most famous piece throughout his lifetime. The second of a set of five *Morceaux de fantaisie*, this prelude is a piece of striking originality, if not subtlety, evoking sonorous Russian bells—a sound world that was to remain a constant source of inspiration to the composer. Yet Rachmaninov came to resent repeatedly being asked to perform it. When the Ten Preludes, op. 23, were issued in 1903, Rachmaninov declared no intention of completing a "cycle" of twenty-four pieces encompassing all the major and minor keys, yet his alternation of major and minor modes enabled him to round off the series with the Thirteen Preludes, op. 32, composed in just nineteen days in 1910.

The op. 23 Preludes were composed during a period of creative resurgence stimulated by the success of the composer's Second Piano Concerto, and like that work they ooze thematic richness and lyricism. The op. 32 Preludes are less lush, more sinewy, and explore a broader scope than the familiar archlike structure—build-up, climax, aftermath—of many of the earlier preludes. These later preludes are more subtle and demanding, and they reveal Rachmaninov at the height of his creative powers.

Vladimir Ashkenazy's complete recording of the preludes is one of the crowning jewels of his vast discography. He brings special insights to every piece, with exquisite balance and voicing allied to the sort of technical bravura for which he was renowned in his younger days. Ashkenazy blends his characteristic full-throated sound with a soulful lyricism tinged with Russian melancholy in music making of rare directness and purity. **TLP**

"A six-and-a-half foot scowl."

Stravinsky on Rachmaninov

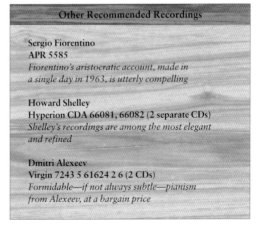

Other Recommended Recordings

Sergio Fiorentino
APR 5585
Fiorentino's aristocratic account, made in a single day in 1963, is utterly compelling

Howard Shelley
Hyperion CDA 66081, 66082 (2 separate CDs)
Shelley's recordings are among the most elegant and refined

Dmitri Alexeev
Virgin 7243 5 61624 2 6 (2 CDs)
Formidable—if not always subtle—pianism from Alexeev, at a bargain price

Vladimir Ashkenazy is at his best in Russian repertoire. ➔

Pyotr Ilyich Tchaikovsky | The Nutcracker (1892)

Genre | Ballet
Conductor | Valery Gergiev
Performers | Kirov Orchestra
Year recorded | 1998
Label | Philips 462 114-2

Who could be content with just the eight-movement *Nutcracker* Suite when the complete ballet is one of Tchaikovsky's most perfect inspirations? The plot might seem slender, a very selective adaptation of German fantasist E. T. A. Hoffmann's *The Nutcracker and the Mouse King* in which heroine Clara, given the Christmas gift of a nutcracker, finds herself in the middle of a midnight battle between malevolent mice and the Nutcracker's toy army. Victorious and transformed into a handsome prince, the Nutcracker rewards his rescuer by taking her through a forest of dancing snowflakes to the kingdom of sweets—cue for a divertissement containing many of the ballet's best-known numbers. So familiar are offerings such as the "Chinese Dance" and the "Dance of the Mirlitons" that we tend to overlook the piquancy of their delicious scoring.

The full score will come as a surprise to those who only know the suite: It rises to unexpected heights of dramatic expression as the magic begins in Act 1, where Tchaikovsky's imaginative use of rising scales is counterbalanced by the falling scales of the powerful pas de deux in Act 2. Originally presented in 1892 as part of a double-bill also featuring the one-act opera *Iolanta*, The *Nutcracker* was staged with what Tchaikovsky thought excessive lavishness; it continues to enchant adults and children alike every Christmas.

Valery Gergiev manages to present the entire ballet score on a single CD, which might suggest a rushed job. But his approach simply emphasizes the consistent genius of the score, allowing no slack between the melodic plums and driving the narrative portions of the ballet (Tchaikovsky's most original contribution to the art form) effortlessly toward a series of powerful climaxes. **DN**

> *"Everything is clear in The Nutcracker, and children are like that."*

George Balanchine

Other Recommended Recordings

London Symphony Orchestra • André Previn
EMI 0777 7 67586 2 6 (2 CDs)
Lavishly upholstered and sumptuously recorded account, now available at bargain price

Amsterdam Concertgebouw Orchestra • Antál Dorati
Philips 442 562-2 (2 CDs)
Dorati captures the sweep and glitter of the full score

Suite
Vienna Philharmonic Orchestra • Herbert von Karajan
Decca 466 379-2
Sweet-toothed account of the eight-movement Suite

A scene from Mark Morris Dance Group's staging of *The Nutcracker*. ➲

Johannes Brahms | Klavierstücke, opp. 116–19 (1892–93)

Genre | Instrumental
Instrument | Piano
Performer | Julius Katchen
Year recorded | 1962
Label | Decca 455 247-2 (6 CDs)

The delectable late works of Brahms show his complete mastery of miniature forms, in telling contrast to the epic utterances of the sonatas and variation sets of his earlier career. These *Klavierstücke* (simply, "piano pieces") consist of fantasies, intermezzos, romanzes, ballades, and rhapsodies. They are intensely personal pieces—their emotion contained rather than worn on the sleeve, but their inner agitation frequently boils up onto the surface. There is no sense of resignation or tranquility in these products of Brahms's Indian summer; indeed, even at this stage he is still experimenting with form, rhythm, ever more ambiguous harmonies, and pieces beginning in one key and ending in another.

The composer described the three Intermezzos of op. 117 as "lullabies of my pain," and the keys of the second and third, B flat minor and C sharp minor, are appropriately dark. In places, the agitation is more on the surface, such as in the third piece of op. 116, the final number of op. 119, or op. 118, nos. 1 and 3. But even apparently calmer pieces, such as op. 117, no. 1 and op. 118, no. 5, turn out to be nothing of the sort.

The complexity of these works requires a great Brahms pianist—a description that fits the eminent American Julius Katchen to perfection. One of the outstanding figures of the mid-twentieth century, he showed his empathy with the composer's music in a complete recording of the solo works. His readings of the late pieces gleam with a generous tone and a rich understanding, whether in the desolate last number of op. 118, with its ambiguous harmonies and bare textures; in op. 119, no. 2, with its cross-rhythms and its throwaway ending; or in the acerbic virtuosity of op. 116, no. 1. **HS**

> *"Like a gray pearl. Do you know them? They look as if they were veiled."*

Clara Schumann to Brahms on the B minor Intermezzo from op. 119

Other Recommended Recordings

Stephen Kovacevich
Philips 442 589-2 (2 CDs)
Kovacevich perfectly combines probing interpretations with a pleasing unfussiness

Radu Lupu
Decca 417 599-2
Lupu turns these intimate pieces into pure poetry, with a kaleidoscopic range of colors and voicings

Lars Vogt
EMI 7243 5 57543 2 5
Playing of great thoughtfulness and intelligence from one of the finest Brahms interpreters of modern times

Julius Katchen (1926–69) is best remembered for his peerless Brahms. ➜

Jean Sibelius
Kullervo (1892)

Genre | Choral
Conductor/Performers | Robert Spano; Nathan Gunn,
Charlotte Hellekant, Atlanta Symphony Orchestra
Year recorded | 2006
Label | Telarc CD-80665

Sibelius's breakthrough work was one he subsequently disowned, yet for early audiences its impact was profound. There had been nothing like this five-movement choral pseudo-symphony in Finnish music and little comparable in Western culture as a whole. Setting Finnish language texts drawn from the *Kalevala*, the national epic gathered together in the nineteenth century, *Kullervo* signaled with peculiar potency the possibility of artistic and political renewal for a people traditionally dominated by Swedes and latterly semiautonomous subjects of the Tsar.

Revived in full only after the composer's death, *Kullervo* was first taped commercially as recently as 1970. It has since made an astonishing comeback. Where earlier concerts and recordings relied on the importation of Finnish personnel this is no longer *de rigueur* and, once again, as in 1892, the score may even be considered an audience pleaser. This recording is not the most grandiose, rather it demonstrates the different approaches possible in a work that has no continuous performing tradition.

While Sibelius may have been embarrassed by the Romantic gaucheries of his younger self, Spano suspends disbelief. The central scena, "Kullervo and His Sister," contains the work's most extraordinary music, revealing a nascent operatic potential sadly unrealized by the composer. Spano's Atlanta Symphony and Men's Chorus are outstanding. The chorus, one of America's best, may lack the specificity of timbre and emphasis characteristic of Finnish groups but it acquits itself with distinction; the soloists are equally fine. This is buoyant, likable music-making captured in state-of-the-art sonics. **DG**

Claude Debussy
String Quartet (1893)

Genre | Chamber
Performers | Juilliard Quartet: Robert Mann,
Joel Smirnoff, Samuel Rhodes, Joel Krosnik
Year recorded | 1989
Label | Sony SK 52554

Although Debussy published this as his "Premier Quatuor," it was the only one he wrote. He had intended to compose another to please his friend Ernest Chausson, who had not taken to the work, but the two men fell out, and Debussy abandoned the idea. Chausson was not alone in finding it unpalatable: one critic described it as "a new manifestation of the prevalent lack of form," and it was certainly groundbreaking. Written only just before *Prélude à l'après-midi d'un faune*, and on a smaller scale, it makes the same radical re-evaluation of the ensemble, treating it as four separate individuals rather than a homogeneous unit. But the sheer beauty and variety of sounds that Debussy conjures from the ensemble make this one of the most joyous pieces in the quartet repertoire.

One of the nods to convention is that the quartet is in four movements. The opening movement, "Animé et très décidé" (animated and very decisive)—begins with a bold gesture that keeps returning (and does so throughout the piece) as the music seems to crosscut between various ideas and tonalities. The scherzo makes striking use of pizzicato and repeated figures, and the slow movement begins simply but finds its way to an impassioned climax. Despite Debussy's problems with the composition of the last movement, there is no sign of flagging, as the musical quick-changes succeed each other with dizzying speed.

Coping with the sheer sonic demands of the piece is a must for any quartet, and the Juilliard has it all: brilliant fireworks, sensitive blending of lines, acute sense of balance, and a suggestion that the piece is coming off the page as if it were written yesterday. **MC**

Engelbert Humperdinck
Hänsel und Gretel (1893)

Genre | Opera
Conductor/Performers | Donald Runnicles;
Jennifer Larmore, Ruth Ziesak, Hildegard Behrens
Year recorded | 1994
Label | Teldec 4509 94549-2 (2CDs)

After studying in Cologne and Munich, Engelbert Humperdinck won a composition prize that enabled him to travel to Italy in 1879. Here he came under the spell of Wagner, who was working on *Parsifal*, while convalescing in the Mediterranean. Humperdinck was embraced as a protégé by Wagner and after Wagner's death, he tried, with partial success, to assert his independence.

His fairy tale opera *Hänsel und Gretel* began as a setting of four nursery rhymes written by his sister, but ended up as one of the most popular operas ever composed, as indispensable to Christmas as Santa Claus. The first performance, conducted by Richard Strauss, took place in Weimar on December 23, 1893 and performances have been regularly given ever since. The story, taken from the fairy tales of the Grimm Brothers, deals with a boy and a girl who stumble upon a house made of gingerbread while out picking strawberries in the wood. The house's owner, a witch, is thwarted in her plan to add the children to her sweets collection only by their ingenuity. Beneath the surface lie issues such as poverty, deprivation, punishment by evil stepmothers, and German nationalism. Yet Humperdinck's ravishing score ensures that the work remains a Christmas-wrapped, marzipan-coated treat.

Nowhere is the loving care for such textural detail more evident than in Donald Runnicles's superbly conducted recording with the Bavarian Radio Symphony Orchestra. Ruth Ziesak's convincingly girlish Gretel and Jennifer Larmore's more mature Hänsel are both beautifully sung, while Hanna Schwarz wickedly camps up the cracked voice of the Witch. **BM**

Erik Satie
Vexations (1893)

Genre | Instrumental
Instrument | Piano
Performer | Steffen Schleiermacher
Year recorded | 2002
Label | MDG 613 1066-2

This article could easily have been nothing but a string of quotations about *Vexations*, for this is a piece more talked about than listened to, which is a shame. The score fits on one side of a single sheet of paper. There are no measure lines, only the instruction "very slow." A theme in the bass covers eleven tones of the twelve on a piano. It is repeated with two-part harmony above. The bass line is heard again, and then repeated once more with the previous harmony inverted. The score is headed "Pages mystiques" with a note "to the performer: to play this motif 840 times in succession, it would be advisable to prepare oneself beforehand, in the deepest silence, by serious immobilities." To do this takes twenty hours or more, as occasional performances have proved since 1963, when John Cage put on the first "complete" performance in New York (only Andy Warhol listened to all of it). The lack of key and preponderance of tritones make it surprisingly hard to play and satisfyingly hard to remember: certain progressions live in a state of suspended animation that recalls passages from *Tristan und Isolde* or *Parsifal* once their lubricious intent has been wiped from the page. In 1893 Satie had just broken up what appears to be his only love affair and formed a one-man church.

Is *Vexations* prayer music, "furniture" music, or an elaborate joke? Avant-garde pianist Steffen Schleiermacher takes an original, Satiean approach, letting the *Vexations* fade up and down again between other early piano works by the composer, as though they were always there in the background. Once heard, never quite forgotten, and never fully remembered. **PQ**

Antonín Dvořák
String Quartet in F major, "American" (1893)

Genre | Chamber
Performers | Pražák Quartet: Václav Remes,
Vlastimil Holek, Josef Klusoň, Michal Kaňka
Year recorded | 1998
Label | Praga PRD 250110

Dvořák's first year as director of New York's National Conservatory of Music was busy and exhausting. Composing was reduced to a minimum with the cantata, *The American Flag*, in the autumn of 1892 and the "New World" Symphony written in early 1893. When Dvořák took a holiday in the Czech-speaking town of Spillville, Iowa, he was able to compose. Two chamber works virtually poured out of him, the E flat major String Quintet and the most popular of his string quartets, the "American."

Sketched in a few hours over three days, the "American" is one of Dvořák's most spontaneously attractive works. The opening, with its gentle susurration for the upper strings and aspiring pentatonic melody for the viola breathes the contentment Dvořák felt in Spillville. The slow movement is one of his most intense, replete with bittersweet melody. Energy levels are high in the scherzo and finale, the latter characterized by a catchy ostinato rhythmic accompaniment. If his last two quartets, in A flat and G major, are more profound, he never quite recaptured the unaffected melodiousness of the "American."

As befits its status as one of the world's most popular chamber works, there are many excellent recordings. None, however, quite equals this one. This is a superbly prepared performance in which there is a wealth of ear-catching detail. The start of the first movement immediately captivates and the powerfully engaged reading of the slow one could hardly be more effective. Some quartets treat the last two movements in a slightly cavalier fashion; the Pražák Quartet gives them readings that balance humor with seriousness of intent. **JS**

"How beautifully the sun shines."

A comment by Dvořák written over the last bar of his manuscript of the "American" Quartet

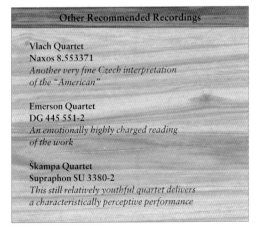

Other Recommended Recordings

Vlach Quartet
Naxos 8.553371
Another very fine Czech interpretation of the "American"

Emerson Quartet
DG 445 551-2
An emotionally highly charged reading of the work

Škampa Quartet
Supraphon SU 3380-2
This still relatively youthful quartet delivers a characteristically perceptive performance

The Pražák Quartet follows in a distinguished line of Czech ensembles. ➲

Giacomo Puccini | Manon Lescaut (1893)

Genre | Opera
Conductor/Performers | Giuseppe Sinopoli;
Mirella Freni, Plácido Domingo, Renato Bruson, Kurt Rydl
Year recorded | 1984
Label | DG 413 893-2

It was third time lucky for Puccini (1858–1924). After *Le villi* and *Edgar* had both drowned at the box office, *Manon Lescaut* announced the arrival of a worthy successor to Verdi. But Puccini's success was hard won. Altogether four writers tried to turn Abbé Prévost's novel into a libretto while Puccini's publisher ignored the project after the huge success of Massenet's version of the same story.

Puccini himself seems to have been full of doubts, too, even cutting Manon's celebrated aria "Sola, perduta, abbandonata" from the last act. Yet, with the right singers and a conductor who lets the score breathe, *Manon Lescaut* rarely fails in the theater. However, once the houselights come up we have perhaps been listening to a composer in search of a voice and a style. Act 1 is that familiar thing in Puccini's mature operas: hectic business intercut with lyrical repose. Act 2 collides the eighteenth century, all minuets and Sèvres porcelain figures, with red-blooded *verismo* passion, while Act 3 is built around a magnificently controlled ensemble as Manon and the convicted women are about to be deported to Louisiana. The final act overpays a debt to Wagner, being composed in a symphonic style that Puccini would keep at arm's length in the future.

Mirella Freni is a tender and a touching Manon, more victim than temptress, and Plácido Domingo finds real depths in Des Grieux—there is genuine despair in his "Ah, Manon, mi tradisce il tuo folle pensier" when Manon lingers over her jewels instead of escaping. Renato Bruson's Lescaut is a fine foil to the lovers—cynical and knowing. And what vocal luxury to cast Brigitte Fassbaender as the madrigal singer. Giuseppe Sinopoli coaxes glorious sounds from the Philharmonia Orchestra. **CC**

> ## "Puccini's . . . is the song of our paganism, of our artistic sensualism. It caresses us, and becomes part of us."

Review in *Corriere della Sera* of the first night

Other Recommended Recordings

La Scala Chorus & Orchestra • Tullio Serafin
EMI 7243 5 56301 2 4 (2 CDs)
A mono recording, but Callas takes no prisoners as Manon in the final act

New Philharmonia Orchestra • Bruno Bartoletti
EMI 0777 7 64852 2 5 (2 CDs)
Montserrat Caballé as a meltingly beautiful Manon

BRT Philharmonic Orchestra • Alexander Rahbari
Naxos 8.660019-20 (2 CDs)
A genuine budget bargain with a fresh-voiced Des Grieux from Kaludi Kaludov

Mirella Freni and Plácido Domingo in 1983. ➔

Pyotr Ilyich Tchaikovsky
Symphony no. 6, "Pathétique" (1893)

Genre | Orchestral
Conductor | Valery Gergiev
Performers | Kirov Orchestra
Year recorded | 1995
Label | Philips 456 580-2

This is Tchaikovsky's most powerful symphony of suffering, as his brother Modest's subtitle of "Pathétique" indicates. Not that he was in anything like a mood of suicidal despair when he wrote it in the summer of 1893: although he claimed to have "frequently wept copiously" during its composition, he was in full creative flow and declared, "how glorious it is to realize that my time is not yet over and that I can still work." His sudden death later that year, only days after he had conducted the first performance, fueled rumors that, like Mozart, he had composed a requiem for himself. Aspects of the work certainly suggest that: the Russian orthodox Mass for the dead is quoted in the development of the first movement, and the finale is a tragic Adagio lamentoso in which the light is extinguished.

Yet all of human life is here. There is love, in what is virtually an aria without words in the first movement, indebted to the example of the "Flower Song" from Bizet's *Carmen*, Tchaikovsky's favorite opera. There is wistfulness in the shape of a bittersweet waltz, while the scherzo combines brilliant fantasy and a rambunctious march.

One of several recent performances that capture every facet of this amazing symphonic edifice is Valery Gergiev's first recording with his Kirov Orchestra, preferable in every respect to his second with the Vienna Philharmonic Orchestra. On home ground, Gergiev goes straight to the heart of darkness in which the "Pathétique" symphony begins and ends, with somber colors from the depths of the magnificent Kirov, and in the central portions of the outer movements he pushes the expressivity of the music to powerful extremes. **DN**

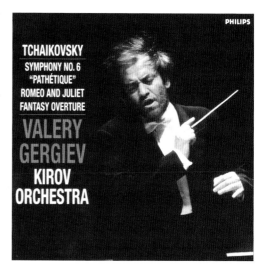

PHILIPS

TCHAIKOVSKY
SYMPHONY NO. 6
"PATHÉTIQUE"
ROMEO AND JULIET
FANTASY OVERTURE
VALERY
GERGIEV
KIROV
ORCHESTRA

"By far the most sincere of all my pieces."

Pyotr Ilyich Tchaikovsky

Other Recommended Recordings

Royal Philharmonic Orchestra • Daniele Gatti
DG 477 5911
Gatti draws world-class playing from the RPO

Swedish Radio Symphony Orchestra • Mikko Franck
Ondine ODE 1002-2
Idiosyncratic young Finn Mikko Franck favors the slow burn in a frequently overwhelming performance

Leningrad Philharmonic Orchestra
Yevgeny Mravinsky
DG 477 5911
The classic "Pathétique," measured and focused but never cold or neutral

Valery Gergiev, music director of the Mariinsky (Kirov) in St. Petersburg. ➔

Giuseppe Verdi
Falstaff (1893)

Genre | Opera
Conductor/Performers | Herbert von Karajan; Tito Gobbi, Elisabeth Schwarzkopf
Year recorded | 1956
Label | EMI 7243 5 67162 2 3 (2 CDs)

Ever since the failure of *Un giorno di regno* in 1840, Verdi had wanted to try his hand again at an opera buffa, but never found a libretto that would completely convince him. Meanwhile, he included some unforgettable comic scenes within his operas, such as the first scene of *Rigoletto*, or the second finale in *Un ballo in maschera*. With *La forza del destino*'s Melitone, he created a comic character of a completely new kind. Verdi was finally tempted by Boito's brilliant libretto, which combines the plot of Shakespeare's *The Merry Wives of Windsor* with Falstaff-related scenes from *Henry IV*. After some weak protest about his no longer being able to tackle a whole opera at his advanced age, he finally allowed himself to be convinced by the ever-faithful Boito and set to work on what would be their final collaboration.

The score of *Falstaff* is a miracle of subtle instrumental effects reflecting Boito's text, which itself even manages to add to Shakespeare's wit. To give just one example, Boito takes Falstaff's speech about the benefits of drinking wine (*Henry IV*, Part 2, Act 4, Scene 3) and builds into it a running pun on the words *brillo* ("drunk"), *grillo* ("cricket"), and *trillo* ("trill"), which is the cue for Verdi to compose a riotous crescendo on one continuous trill. Verdi wrote to a friend that he was enjoying himself and would often laugh out loud while composing.

Falstaff is an opera that needs, and amply repays, repeated listening to get to know its secrets. In Karajan's recording with the Philharmonia Orchestra, the hand-picked singers strike sparks off each other, making the most of what is effectively an ensemble showpiece. **CMS**

Jean Sibelius
Karelia Suite (1893)

Genre | Orchestral
Conductor/Performers | Neeme Järvi; Gothenburg Symphony Orchestra
Year recorded | 1992
Label | DG 447 760-2

The mature Sibelius tended to disparage his Romantic, nationalist side but, with Finland under Russian rule, the 1890s saw the composition of some of his most communicative works. These sprang from virtually virgin soil without the stimulus of a native tradition of advanced musical activity. The *Karelia Suite* was extracted from music performed in November 1893 at the innocuous-sounding "Festivity and Lottery in aid of education in the province of Viipuri." There were originally eight tableaux portraying episodes in *Karelian* history and, as usual, the self-critical composer had his doubts. When the full score was rediscovered in the 1930s he sought to destroy it, sparing only the overture, the elements familiar from the suite and the first number, "A Karelian Home—News of War."

The larger work has since been reclaimed from rediscovered orchestral parts but the *Karelia Suite* as we know it is in three concise movements. Two memorable marches, entitled "Intermezzo" and "Alla marcia," frame a melancholy "Ballade" whose cor anglais tune was originally taken by a baritone. The *Karelia Suite* was one of the scores that established Sibelius at home and abroad.

Neeme Järvi's no-nonsense reading benefits from lively tempi and a refusal to overinflate. He captures the open-air, celebratory mood of the outer movements and, more than most, keeps the "Ballade" on the move. The recording is finely engineered and comes either on this single disc, taking in soprano Soile Isokoski's first account of the unclassifiable song-cum-symphonic poem *Luonnotar*, or in a generous three-disc conspectus of Sibelius's tone poems into which this has been subsumed. **DG**

Antonín Dvořák
Symphony no. 9 (1893)

Genre | Orchestral
Conductor | Nikolaus Harnoncourt
Performers | Royal Concertgebouw
Year recorded | 2000
Label | Teldec 3984 25254-2

Anton Stepanovich Arensky
Piano Trio no. 1 (1894)

Genre | Chamber
Performers | Renaud Capuçon,
Gautier Capuçon, Polina Leschenko
Year recorded | 2003
Label | EMI 7243 5 62970 2 9 (3 CDs)

In the early 1890s, Dvořák was the Austrian Empire's most admired composer after Brahms. So it was hardly surprising that when a director for the New York National Conservatory of Music was needed, his name should spring to mind. Dvořák's two sojourns in the United States between 1892 and 1895 propelled him to becoming one of the superstars of Romantic music, with masterpieces such as the "New World" Symphony, the Cello Concerto, and the "American" String Quartet consistently among the most popular works in their respective genres.

Dvořák rarely felt at ease in New York, but he adapted well to its compositional requirements. He tailored his style to his American audiences with a greater simplicity of outline, dynamic rhythmic propulsion, and, above all, melody of a beguiling and memorable cut. This symphony, subtitled "From the New World," is a compendium of these qualities and was a hit on its first outing; it rapidly became his most popular orchestral work. Although its themes are all original, many are shaded by the pentatonic features that Dvořák noted in the music of American spirituals.

With more than 100 recordings of the "New World," there are many recommendable performances, among them István Kertész on Decca and Karel Ančerl on Supraphon. But the one that stands out is Nikolaus Harnoncourt and the Royal Concertgebouw. The orchestra is on unbeatable form, and Harnoncourt's respect for the letter of Dvořák's score is everywhere to be heard in the careful gradation of tempi and the instrumental balance. Time and again, he reveals unexpected details and sonorities, particularly in the famous slow movement. **JS**

Anton Stepanovich Arensky (1861–1906) was taught by Rimsky-Korsakov, but in this wonderful trio the strongest parallels are with Tchaikovsky and his Piano Trio. Both have an elegiac quality; in the case of Arensky's it laments the death of his friend, Karl Davidov, who had been the director of the St. Petersburg Conservatoire and a fine cello player—the instrument enjoys a prominent role, above all in the third movement. Like the Tchaikovsky trio, it has an almost symphonic scope, with particularly demanding piano writing; it is hardly surprising that it has attracted big virtuoso players throughout its recorded history.

The young French brothers Renaud and Gautier Capuçon together with pianist Polina Leschenko, caught live at the Lugano Festival, make spirited and eloquent advocates for this enticing work. Following the emotional tumult of the substantial first movement comes a charming, skittish waltz, a form of which Arensky was particularly fond. While the piano dashes up and down its entire register, the violin and cello have an elegant discourse, all tinkling crystal and murmured niceties, with a contrasting secondary galumphing theme introduced by the piano. In the third movement, explicitly titled "Elegia," cellist Gautier Capuçon is a most eloquent advocate. However, this grave mood is leavened by moments of pure sunlight, with the violin soaring above the texture. The compact finale then bursts in dramatically, but once again, Arensky cannot help but introduce quieter passages of utter charm. These young players give it their absolute all, and the audience is so rapt you would never imagine it was there, until the tumultuous applause bursts in at the end. **HS**

Claude Debussy | Prélude à L'après-midi d'un faune (1894)

Genre | Orchestral
Conductor | Leopold Stokowski
Performers | Symphony orchestra
Year recorded | 1957
Label | EMI 7243 5 67313 2 5

Until the first performance of *L'après-midi* (as it is familiarly known), Debussy was only a moderately successful composer. He had won the prestigious Prix de Rome, and his String Quartet and the cantata *La damoiselle élue* were beginning to make his name familiar to the concert-going public. But *L'après-midi* was his first great success, with its seductive orchestral palette, and free-flowing but tightly controlled form. The contemporary critic who described it as ". . . a curious fantasie, full of unprecise harmonies and fleeting phrases . . ." was missing the point.

Debussy's own note about the piece says it all: "The music of this prelude is a very free illustration of Mallarmé's beautiful poem. By no means does it claim to be a synthesis of it. Rather there is a succession of scenes through which pass the desires and dreams of the faun in the heat of the afternoon. Then, tired of pursuing the timorous flight of nymphs and naiads, he succumbs to intoxicating sleep, in which he can finally realize his dreams of possession in universal Nature." The languid opening with the unaccompanied flute is one of the most famous passages in all music, and the gently pulsing accompaniment at the climax conjures up the shimmer of heat haze over an idealized landscape.

Stokowski was always the ideal conductor for *L'après-midi*, with his acute sense of orchestral color, and this recording, made with a hand-picked orchestra, is distinguished by beautifully expressive wind playing, especially the flute of Julius Baker. What makes this recording totally beguiling is Stokowski's flexibility of pulse: the music flows unhindered by the tyranny of measure lines, until the chime of antique cymbals brings the piece to a close. **MC**

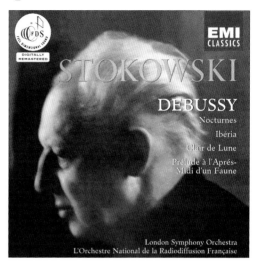

"Modern music was awakened by L'après-midi d'un faune."

Pierre Boulez

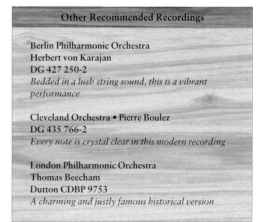

Other Recommended Recordings

Berlin Philharmonic Orchestra
Herbert von Karajan
DG 427 250-2
Bedded in a lush string sound, this is a vibrant performance

Cleveland Orchestra • Pierre Boulez
DG 435 766-2
Every note is crystal clear in this modern recording

London Philharmonic Orchestra
Thomas Beecham
Dutton CDBP 9753
A charming and justly famous historical version

Claude Debussy photographed with a bass clarinet in 1894. ➔

Gustav Mahler | Symphony no. 2, "Resurrection" (1894)

Genre | Orchestral
Conductor/Performers | Otto Klemperer; Elisabeth Schwarzkopf, Hilde Rössl-Majdan, Philharmonia Orchestra
Years recorded | 1961–62
Label | EMI 7243 5 67255 2 2

Mahler's Second Symphony is one of his most inspiring works: accessible, intense, filled with drama and poignant beauty, its variety always seems firmly linked to a profound progression from death to hope. Mahler conceived its first movement in 1888; originally intended as the first movement of a symphony, it was soon changed to a tone poem called *Todtenfeier* (*Funeral Rite*), which is still sometimes performed on its own. Eventually the symphonic ideal won through, however, and four more movements were added—a gentle *Ländler* (an Austrian/German folk dance), then two movements with connections to *Des Knaben Wunderhorn* (*The Youth's Magic Horn*, a folk poetry collection that inspired Mahler to two dozen songs between 1887 and 1901). The third movement, exclusively for orchestra, is based on Mahler's song "Des Antonius von Padua Fischpredigt" ("St. Antony of Padua's Sermon to the Fish"), while the fourth is a song for contralto, "Urlicht" ("Primeval Light"). Mahler could not decide how to conclude the symphony until he attended the funeral service of conductor Hans von Bülow in 1894, which included a boys' choir singing a chorale employing Klopstock's text "Rise again, yes rise again you will, my dust, after brief repose!" Mahler appropriated these words, added more of his own, and the massive finale took shape.

Otto Klemperer's powerful, perceptive EMI studio recording of the "Resurrection" Symphony with the Philharmonia Chorus and Orchestra remains indispensable because it offers stimulating, knotty counterpoint to more traditional views of the work. Some cherish individual moments of loveliness more than Klemperer, but his combination of characterization, energy, understanding, and structure grips the listener from beginning to end. **DB**

> "Mixing orchestral and vocal genres was fundamental to [Mahler's] conception of the symphony."
>
> Edward E. Reilly

Other Recommended Recordings

City of Birmingham Symphony Orchestra
Simon Rattle
EMI 0946 3 45794 2 1
Extremely perceptive even if calculatedly inflected

London Symphony Orchestra • Gilbert Kaplan
Conifer 75605 51277 2 (2 CDs)
Committed performance; package includes facsimile of score, Mahler's piano rolls, and much else

Todtenfeier
Chicago Symphony Orchestra • Pierre Boulez
DG 289 457 649-2
An account of the original version of the first movement

Otto Klemperer was renowned for his slow-burn performances. ➔

Johannes Brahms | Clarinet Sonatas (1894)

Genre | Chamber
Performers | Gervase de Peyer (clarinet),
Daniel Barenboim (piano)
Year recorded | 1968
Label | EMI 0946 3 55674 2 7

In his two clarinet sonatas, Brahms had virtually no Classical models to follow and single-handedly established a new genre. No. 1 in F minor has something of the turbulent passion that key always evoked in Brahms. No. 2 in E flat major is a fantasia-like conception in three movements, none of them really slow. Within these broad confines the works display a range of color and emotion, a propensity for mercurial shifts of texture and harmony. Brahms also made alternative versions for viola and piano.

The First Sonata's opening Allegro appassionato conveys an impression of gravity and tensile strength without compromising the predominantly lyrical nature typified by the yearning, wide-spanned melody that follows the brief piano introduction. The slow movement is a still, tranced nocturnal song, touched into motion by the clarinet's melancholy, rhapsodic turning figures and the slow descending arpeggios in the piano. The intermezzo is in the manner of an Austrian *Ländler*; its peasant vigor expands to a bracing and sometimes canny rondo.

The Allegro amabile with which the Second Sonata begins is Brahms's most unassuming sonata form. The central movement is a large and unexpectedly powerful scherzo. The finale's broad, glowing theme has a Classical poise, rhythmic solidity, intriguing asymmetry, and opulent harmony, all of which offer enormous potential for the five valedictory variations Brahms produces on it.

In spite of its age, Gervase de Peyer and Daniel Barenboim's recording still sounds full and rich, and that is what these performances are, too—perhaps the most intensely beautiful these much-recorded works have received. Playing of utter perfection from two masters of their instruments. **MM**

"The two clarinet sonatas . . . are but the soliloquies of his lonely hours—dreamy recollections . . . "

Richard Specht

Other Recommended Recordings

Gervase de Peyer, Gwyneth Prior
Chandos CHAN 8563
De Peyer again in more modern sound;
not quite as good as with Barenboim

Hans Christian Braein, Håvard Gimse
Simax PSC 1259
A very recent and spellbinding account

Lars Anders Tomter (viola), Leif Ove Andsnes
Virgin 7 59309-2
Many people prefer these sonatas with viola,
and this is an outstanding account with great range
of instrumental color

Richard Strauss | Till Eulenspiegels lustige Streiche (1895)

Genre | Orchestral
Conductor | Claudio Abbado
Performers | Berlin Philharmonic Orchestra
Year recorded | 1992
Label | Sony SK 52565

BERLINER
PHILHARMONIKER
CLAUDIO ABBADO

Richard Strauss

Don Juan
Burleske for Piano
and Orchestra
Till Eulenspiegels
lustige Streiche
Der Rosenkavalier

NEW YEAR'S EVE
CONCERT 1992
Martha Argerich
Kathleen Battle
Renée Fleming
Frederica von Stade
Andreas Schmidt
LIVE RECORDING

Humor in German music had been in conspicuously short supply until Richard Strauss composed his fourth orchestral tone poem, *Till Eulenspiegel's Merry Pranks*, in 1895. There had been a few precedents, not least Beethoven's Eighth Symphony and Strauss's own *Burleske* for piano and orchestra, but nobody expected anything as brilliant as this from the composer of dark and stormy program music such as *Death and Transfiguration*. Strauss would have seen something in common between his own rebellion against a conservative Munich upbringing and medieval wag Till's conflict with a group of German townsfolk, drafted as the plot of an opera in late 1894.

It was as well that Strauss settled instead on a short and incident-packed rondo, a musical form that stitches repetitions of its main subject matter with contrasting episodes. After a dreamy once-upon-a-time scene-setting, the eternal mischief-maker's character is deftly sketched in one of the orchestral repertoire's greatest horn solos, with a nose-thumbing transformation of the opening idea on shrill D clarinet. In between its reprises, Till causes havoc of various sorts, falls in love, and mocks a group of pedants until he is caught and hung; but his irrepressible spirit lives on.

When the fearsome critic Eduard Hanslick announced that "many charming, witty ideas spring up in the work, but not a single one that does not have its neck broken by the speed with which the next one lands on its head," he did not mean it as a compliment. Yet that is the intention conveyed by the most razor-sharp performances, and Abbado's, recorded in Berlin at a memorable all-Strauss New Year's Eve concert in 1992, never drops a stitch as it moves rapidly and eloquently between escapades. **DN**

> *"Analysis impossible for me. All wit spent in notes."*
>
> Richard Strauss in a telegram to the conductor
> of the first performance, Franz Wüllner

Other Recommended Recordings

Vienna Philharmonic Orchestra • Wilhelm Furtwängler
EMI 7243 5 62790 2 5
Surprising lightness of touch and a gift for comedy from the usually serious Furtwängler

Dresden Staatskapelle • Rudolf Kempe
EMI 7243 5 74756 2 4
A real charmer of a wag in the warm characterization of Rudolf Kempe

Cleveland Orchestra • George Szell
Sony 36721
Another lightning-speed journey through Till's merry pranks from Szell and the Clevelanders

Antonín Dvořák | Cello Concerto in B minor (1895)

Genre | Concerto
Performers | Pierre Fournier, Berlin Philharmonic Orchestra
Conductor | George Szell
Year recorded | 1961
Label | DG 423 881-2

Dvořák's famous B minor Cello Concerto is, in fact, his second for the instrument. As a young man in 1865, he had written one in A major for a fellow performer in the Prague Provisional Theater orchestra, which remained in piano score. Needless to say, the later concerto, written toward the end of Dvořák's second stay in America, far surpasses the earlier work and is widely regarded as the finest concerto for the instrument, despite his doubts as to the cello's suitability in combination with orchestra.

For all its outgoing qualities, this concerto is one of Dvořák's most personal works. He spoke volubly to friends back in Bohemia about the thrill that the great second melody of the first movement gave him, and there is a close connection between the slow movement, the finale, and the affection he had for his sister-in-law, Josefína. Just before beginning the Adagio, he heard that she was ill and so incorporated a quotation from her favorite song as the central part of the movement. On his return to Bohemia, Josefína died and Dvořák recast the end of the finale to include a meditation on this theme as a memorial to her. Even without these powerful motives, this work is rich in sentiment and characteristically full of memorable melody.

Performances of this concerto in the last forty or so years have tended to inflate the tempo differences in the first movement resulting in substantially longer performing times than Dvořák intended; quite often the central section of the movement slows to near andante. Pierre Fournier's classic performance maintains a strong sense of line throughout with little slackening of tempo as well as being superbly played with rich, singing tone. Even after more than forty years it remains a top recommendation. **JS**

> *"I want to show you one episode which I reflected on very greatly . . . . Every time when I play it I tremble."*

Dvořák on the horn melody from the first movement

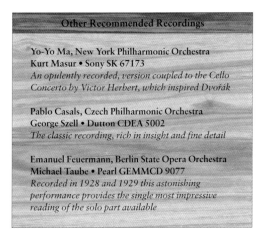

Other Recommended Recordings

Yo-Yo Ma, New York Philharmonic Orchestra
Kurt Masur • Sony SK 67173
An opulently recorded, version coupled to the Cello Concerto by Victor Herbert, which inspired Dvořák

Pablo Casals, Czech Philharmonic Orchestra
George Szell • Dutton CDEA 5002
The classic recording, rich in insight and fine detail

Emanuel Feuermann, Berlin State Opera Orchestra
Michael Taube • Pearl GEMMCD 9077
Recorded in 1928 and 1929 this astonishing performance provides the single most impressive reading of the solo part available

French cellist Pierre Fournier photographed in 1977. ➔

Serge Rachmaninov | Symphony no. 1 (1895)

Genre | Orchestral
Conductor | Mariss Jansons
Performers | St. Petersburg Philharmonic Orchestra
Year recorded | 1998
Label | EMI 7243 5 85459 2 0

Rachmaninov
Symphony No.1
The Isle of the Dead

St Petersburg Philharmonic Orchestra
Mariss Jansons

EMI
CLASSICS

For years, Rachmaninov's First was a non-symphony. After its catastrophic premiere in 1897 and subsequent savaging by the critics the score completely disappeared. Rachmaninov then plunged into a sterile depression from which he was only rescued by hypnotherapy. (Moral is never give your first symphony the opus number 13.) Nothing more was heard of the music until 1945, two years after the composer's death, when a two-piano arrangement and a set of orchestral parts were discovered in Russia. Fully reconstructed, the symphony was heard again, this time to tremendous acclaim. It was now clear that this was a precociously brilliant work, broadly indebted to Tchaikovsky, but full of originality, zest, and—especially in the remarkable ending—a searing passion that marks it out even in the Russian repertoire. It turned out that the symphony had a personal significance for Rachmaninov. Here, he poured out his feelings about a painful youthful love affair, heading the score with an ominous quotation from Tolstoy's *Anna Karenina*. No wonder its rejection was such a bitter blow.

The last thing this symphony needs is a conductor with critical reservations or inhibitions. Fortunately Mariss Jansons is able to bring tremendous force of feeling and conviction at every stage of the work's progress. But he is also able to keep a cool head when it comes to balancing structures: music that could so easily seem episodic is shown to have cogent dramatic purpose—you can almost hear the steady approach of Nemesis in the finale. And Jansons can be delicate as well as purposeful, especially in the fleet-footed scherzo. Refined as it is, the orchestral playing also has an indefinable Russian graininess that suits the music to perfection. **SJ**

> *"My dreams of a brilliant career lay shattered."*

Rachmaninov after the premiere of the First Symphony

Other Recommended Recordings

Russian National Orchestra • Mikhail Pletnev
DG 463 075-2
Refinement, poetry, and strong feeling for Rachmaninov's soaring melodic lines

Russian State Symphony Orchestra • Valeri Polyansky
Chandos CHAN 9822
Less visceral, but just as exciting as Jansons, beautifully recorded

Concertgebouw Orchestra • Vladimir Ashkenazy
Decca 448 116-2
Volatile, and stunningly played, there are some great moments here

Gustave Charpentier | Louise (1896)

Genre | Opera
Conductor/Performers | Sylvain Cambreling; Felicity Lott,
Jérôme Pruett, Belgian National Opera Chorus & Orchestra
Year recorded | 2000
Label | Erato 8573 82298-2 (3 CDs)

As a composer Gustave Charpentier, a student of Massenet, was a one-work wonder. It took him seven years to write the first of just two operas and from 1913 until his death in 1956, he played at being an artist but composed nothing of any worth.

In theory everything about his one success is wrong. *Louise* takes its cue from the gritty social realism championed by Émile Zola, with its working-class heroine yearning for more than a life of duty with her worthy but blinkered parents. Naturally Louise runs away with her lover, Julien. But where do they run to? To a never-never Paris where artists and models rub shoulders in bohemian Montmartre—a location that was throbbing with that other fin de siècle style, symbolism. The music is equally eclectic, with echoes of Berlioz and Wagner, and Gounod and Massenet.

Yet on stage *Louise* can be much more than just the sum of its disparate parts. Charpentier writes fine dramatic music for his public scenes, particularly when Louise is crowned muse of Montmarte in Act 3. And in "Depuis le jour," his gifts as a melodist shine bright as he gives his heroine one of the most enduring arias in all late nineteenth-century French opera.

Felicity Lott is impeccably French as the eponymous heroine and every word is crystal clear. If she lacks a sense of abandon in the Bohemian act, she invests "Depuis le jour" with a touching blend of pathos and longing with just a hint of lazy desire. Here is a young woman whose nose is pressed up against the window-pane of a world she longs to join. Jérôme Pruett is an ardent Julien, beefier than usual, and Sylvain Cambreling spins an appropriately Gallic line about the piece. **CC**

> *"Let your temperament speak for you. Find yourself a pretty young girl. Allow your heart to say what it will."*

Massenet's advice to his student Charpentier

Other Recommended Recordings

Metropolitan Opera Chorus & Orchestra • Thomas Beecham
Naxos 8.110102-04 (3 CDs)
Beecham coaxes a winning performance from Grace Moore, more movie star than prima donna

Paris Raugel Chorus & Orchestra • Eugène Bigot
Nimbus NI 7829
Generous excerpts from Ninon Vallin and George Thill, two of the greatest of pre-war French singers

New Philharmonia Orchestra • Georges Prêtre
Sony S3K 46429
Expensive rarity, with a young Domingo and Cotrubas

Umberto Giordano | Andrea Chénier (1896)

Genre | Opera
Conductor/Performers | Lovro von Matačić; Franco Corelli, Renata Tebaldi, Ettore Bastianini
Year recorded | 1960
Label | Orfeo C 682 062 I (2 CDs)

Andrea Chénier is as good as any of the *verismo* operas that high-minded audiences have scorned for over a century now. It is theatrically surefooted and as recent imaginative productions in Europe have shown, a good deal more interesting dramaturgically than its critics have allowed. And why should one be surprised? It was Luigi Illica, Puccini's long suffering collaborator, who carved a libretto out of a half-true slice of French Revolutionary history.

In reality the poet Chénier, a victim of the Terror, recited lines from Racine's play *Andromaque* en route to the guillotine in 1794. In Illica and Giordano's version, it is an opportunity for a great duet with the aristocratic Maddalena di Coigny, "Vicino a te." At last, the gulf between the privileged and the dispossessed that was carefully staged in Act 1, when the radical servant Gérard at the head of a band of angry peasants disrupted the Contessa di Coigny's elegant pastoral entertainment, has been bridged by love, of course, not revolution.

Characterization is not Giordano's strongest suit, but he knows how to shape the drama and never disappoints an audience in search of an aria to applaud. Chénier's Act 1 "Improvviso" and Maddalena's much excerpted "La mamma morta" are elegant examples of this composer's lyrical gifts. And he weaves local color into his score most effectively, with revolutionary songs such as "Ça ira" and the "Camargnole."

Corelli and Tebaldi are superb in this live recording from Vienna. Such is the intensity of their performances, and that of Ettore Bastianini as Gérard, the nominal villain of the piece, that any doubts about the work are swept aside as Lovro von Matačić carries all before him. This is *verismo* at its most compelling, properly full-blooded. **CC**

> *"Oh my pen! Poison, gall and horror, God of my life, Through you alone I carry on my struggle."*
>
> André Chénier, born 1762, executed 1794

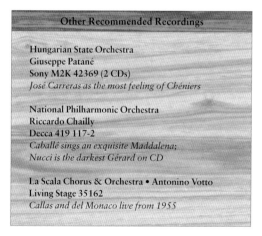

Other Recommended Recordings

Hungarian State Orchestra
Giuseppe Patané
Sony M2K 42369 (2 CDs)
José Carreras as the most feeling of Chéniers

National Philharmonic Orchestra
Riccardo Chailly
Decca 419 117-2
*Caballé sings an exquisite Maddalena;
Nucci is the darkest Gérard on CD*

La Scala Chorus & Orchestra • Antonino Votto
Living Stage 35162
Callas and del Monaco live from 1955

Italian tenor Franco Corelli, photographed around 1965. ➔

Anton Bruckner
Symphony no. 9
(1896, unfinished)

Genre | Orchestral
Conductor | Günter Wand
Performers | NDR Symphony Orchestra
Year recorded | 1988
Label | RCA 74321 84590 2

Bruckner intended his last symphony as a summation of his life's work, culminating in an orchestral hymn of praise to the "dear God" who had sustained him through grievous trials. But at his death, the finale was found to survive only in fragmentary form, with the crucial concluding pages missing (probably stolen). Fortunately the three completed movements make a satisfying, strangely moving final testament. There may be no radiant alleluias to counter the troubled searching of the first and third movements or the demonic fury of the scherzo—and the climax of the final Adagio is the most despairing thing in all Bruckner. But the Adagio's ending, glancing back at themes from some of Bruckner's most important works, is as touching a leave-taking as one could wish.

Günter Wand's 1988 version, recorded in the wonderfully atmospheric Lübeck Cathedral, is one of the most convincing accounts of this magnificent torso of all time. After the heart-easing beauty of the closing pages, you may even conclude that it is a good thing the finale remains only as a fragment. Wand does not hurry the journey as a whole (the acoustic would not let him), but there is a sustained underlying current that carries everything, even when—as in the first movement—the structure can seem full of gaping fissures. The range of mood and character—from the hallucinatory sensuality of the scherzo's central trio to the ethereal string chorale of the Adagio—is immense, yet it is all contained in one colossal vision. **SJ**

Ernest Chausson
Poème
(1896)

Genre | Concerto
Performer/Conductor | Philippe Graffin
(violin); Vernon Handley
Year recorded | 2006
Label | Avie AV 2091

Ernest Chausson's best-known work, the *Poème* for violin and orchestra, was written in spring of 1896. If its sound world evokes those of Wagner's *Tristan und Isolde*, Debussy's *Prélude à L'après-midi d'un faune*, and Franck's Violin Sonata, it is perhaps more closely associated still with a work by Chausson's friend the Belgian violinist Ysaÿe, the *Poème élégiaque*.

Also behind the inspiration of the *Poème* was a short story by Turgenev, *The Song of Love Triumphant*, which was a product of the emotional attachment of Turgenev to the singer Pauline Viardot, and possibly by an episode in the life of Fauré. Since Fauré was a friend of Chausson, it is interesting to speculate whether the latter was aware of the inspiration and if so, to what extent it colored the work. Episodes in Turgenev's story—not least a fatal stabbing—can, with a little imagination, be heard in the *Poème*.

What is unarguable is that the work is characterized by an almost oppressively erotic atmosphere. Cast in an unconventional single-movement form, it features irregular phrase lengths and highly charged harmonies that all speak of unrequited passion. Violinist Philippe Graffin's account, conducted by Vernon Handley, perfectly captures that sense of unbridled sensuality, but along with it the underlying melancholy that has endowed the piece with such undying popularity. Graffin never allows his performance to descend into mere technical display, while also demonstrating the mastery of the violin that Ysaÿe surely brought to it, too. **BM**

Jean Sibelius
Lemminkäinen Suite

(1896, *rev.* 1897–1939)

Genre | Orchestral
Conductor | Osmo Vänskä
Performers | Lahti Symphony Orchestra
Year recorded | 1999
Label | BIS CD-1015

Sibelius's *Lemminkäinen Suite* (also known by its subtitle, *Four Legends from the Kalevala*) had one of the most complicated geneses in all his music. It was completed in its original form in 1896 and premiered in Helsinki, but by the time of a repeat performance the following year Sibelius had made revisions, while all four movements were subjected to further reworking in 1900 and in 1939.

As with so much of his music, the suite found its inspiration in the Finnish national epic, the *Kalevala*, this time the adventures of the hero Lemminkäinen. First comes "Lemminkäinen and the Maidens of the Island," which charts his seductions and pursuit of the beautiful Kyllikki. Then comes the famous "Swan of Tuonela," an atmospheric portrayal of the majestic bird that guards the hell of Finnish mythology. In "Lemminkäinen in Tuonela," the hero is slain by a rival and magically brought back to life by his mother; and "Lemminkäinen's Homeward Journey" portrays the hero's battles as he returns home. Sibelius's music took on a more Wagnerian patina than the obviously Finnish *Kullervo* and *En saga*, but the merging of symphonic methods and atmosphere also shows how he brought the Lisztian tone poem to new heights.

Osmo Vänskä's consummate account of the score—drama and atmosphere losing nothing from his direct reading of Sibelius's performance indications—also has the advantage of coming packaged with the original versions of the outer movements and a couple of alternative excerpts from interim revisions. **MR**

Giacomo Puccini
La bohème

(1896)

Genre | Opera
Conductor/Performers | Thomas Schippers; Mirella Freni, Nicolai Gedda
Years recorded | 1962–63
Label | EMI 0777 7 6 96575 2 7 (2 CDs)

Puccini's *La bohème* is one of the most perfect of all operas. Each of its four short acts has its own pace and timbre; the characters are fully rounded; the score is bound together with a handful of easily remembered musical themes; and it can make a stone weep! Time never hangs heavy on your hands, or eyelids, even in the least successful productions.

Yet his Bohemians cost the composer dearly. Puccini was prey to massive doubts as he composed and he continued to demand rewrites from his collaborators, Giuseppe Giacosa and Luigi Illica. At one point it was decided that they would divide Act 2 into two parts thus separating the Bohemians' fun and games from their emotional opposite, the feelings that collide on the tenement stairs with Mimì and Rodolfo in "Che gelida Manina . . . Mi chiamano Mimì . . . O soave fanciulla." In the end, aesthetic common sense prevailed and while at the first performance, conducted by a twenty-nine-year-old Toscanini, the audience rather sat on their hands; within a year Mimì and Musetta, Rodolfo and Marcello had the world at their feet. The appeal of four young men "playing" as artists and students, drinking, falling in love, and gently thumbing a nose at authority has never diminished.

Mirella Freni's Mimì remains the most satisfying on CD, tender, vulnerable, but with a will of her own; and Nicolai Gedda is the most lyrical of Rodolfos. There may have been naughtier Musettas than Mariella Adani and angrier Marcellos, but it is the quality of the ensemble that counts in this recording quite as much as individual voices. **CC**

Gustav Mahler | Symphony no. 3 (1896)

Genre | Orchestral
Conductor/Performers | Jascha Horenstein; Norma
Proctor, Ambrosian Singers, Wandsworth School Boys' Choir
Year recorded | 1970
Label | Unicorn-Kanchana UKCD 2006/07 (2 CDs)

MAHLER
SYMPHONY No3
LONDON SYMPHONY ORCHESTRA
CONDUCTED BY
JASCHA HORENSTEIN

SOUVENIR SERIES

The Third Symphony is Gustav Mahler's longest. The massive opening movement (ultimately titled by Mahler "Pan awakes . . . Summer marches in") begins with a section reminiscent of the Beethoven-inspired tune from the finale of Brahms's First Symphony, and goes on to incorporate music of the most diverse styles and aims. The rousing march sequence seemed to many listeners of the time to throw open the floodgates to the vulgar and quotidian, but it then gives way to a tender, grazioso second movement ("What the Flowers in the Meadow Tell me") and a scherzo-like third movement (based on Mahler's *Wunderhorn* song "Ablösung in Sommer" ["Summer's Replacement"], here titled "What the Animals in the Forest Tell me"), with beautiful episodes featuring an offstage post horn.

The mysterious fourth movement ("What Man Tells me") introduces an alto solo declaiming a text by Nietzsche, and the fifth is a setting of the *Wunderhorn* text "Es sungen drei Engel" ("Three Angels were Singing") for children's chorus and alto solo ("What the Angels Tell me"), but the exalted, beatific final slow movement ("What Love Tells me") reverts to purely orchestral music and sets the seal on one of Mahler's grandest visions.

The Mahler renaissance of the 1960s was fueled in large part by the new vigor imparted by the conductor Leonard Bernstein, but in Britain especially, the interpretations of Jascha Horenstein were considered the touchstone. This recording shows Horenstein's Mahler at its best—such unforced, lyrically based naturalness seems inarguable. At every point the character of the performance fits both the immediate moment and the overall structure, an amazing achievement in so complex a work. **DB**

> *"[Mahler] raised his eyes from the joy and pain in his own heart to the harmony and disharmony of nature."*
>
> Bruno Walter

Other Recommended Recordings

New York Philharmonic • Leonard Bernstein
Sony SM2K 61831 (2 CDs)
Grand, extroverted, electric—Lenny at his most joyously communicative

Vienna Philharmonic Orchestra • Claudio Abbado
DG 410 715-2 (2 CDs)
A brilliantly prepared synthesis of poetry and energy

Thirteen songs from Des Knaben Wunderhorn
Anne Sofie von Otter, Thomas Quasthoff, Berlin Philharmonic Orchestra • Claudio Abbado
DG 459 646-2
Keenly characterized and beautiful performances

Jascha Horenstein helped the postwar rediscovery of Mahler's music. ➲

Camille Saint-Saëns
Piano Concerto no. 5 "Egyptian" (1896)

Genre | Concerto
Performer | Stephen Hough
Conductor | Sakari Oramo
Year recorded | 2000
Label | Hyperion CDA 67331/2 (2 CDs)

The last of Saint-Saëns's concertos, written nearly forty years after his first, shows his love for the exotic, and for the warmer climates to which he traveled to escape the cold, damp Parisian winters. Every note of his "Egyptian" Concerto reflects less the fact that is was finished in Cairo in 1896 than a general Mediterranean warmth. The most directly "oriental" movement is the middle one, though he was by no means the only French composer interested in the exotic (but surely he was the only one of his time not to be influenced by Wagner). In this movement, we find not only a melody based on a Nubian love song that he had heard being sung by Nile boatmen, but also the nighttime sounds of crickets and frogs. There are touches, too, of Javanese gamelan (which had taken Paris by storm in 1889), and also hints of Spain.

Like all of Saint-Saëns's concertos, this is a work that demands considerable panache and technical virtuosity from the soloist, which it receives in spades from Stephen Hough, with Sakari Oramo coaxing some wonderful solo playing from the City of Birmingham Symphony Orchestra. Hough is particularly fine in the subtle way that he approaches the work's exotic elements, which in lesser hands can seem trite. As with all the other pieces in their cycle, all the players appear totally in tune with Saint-Saëns's idiom, and the effect is one of great charm. The concerto ends with one of the composer's most delightful inventions, depicting a sea-crossing, and giving the soloist yet more opportunity for ebullient display. **HS**

Richard Strauss
Also sprach Zarathustra (1896)

Genre | Orchestral
Conductor | Bernard Haitink
Performers | Amsterdam Concertgebouw Orchestra
Year recorded | 1973
Label | Philips 442 281-2 (2 CDs)

Friederich Nietzsche's philosophical poem *Thus Spake Zarathustra* had an enormous impact on late nineteenth-century thinking, with its creed of the *Übermensch* (sometimes translated as "superman") who passes through stages of religious and scientific development before emerging into the light. Composers including Mahler and Delius were interested in translating the flavor of its vibrant images and sensuousness into musical terms. The same is true of Richard Strauss's tone poem of 1896.

Its main musical idea, Strauss wrote, was "the alternation between the two remotest keys." The key of C major represents nature and gives us one of the most famous of openings, the sunrise trumpet-call to attention so memorably used by Stanley Kubrick in his film *2001: A Space Odyssey*. Man appears in the key of B (both minor and major), and the opposition continues with much lush orchestral writing and tumult until the breakthrough of the transformation into the *Übermensch*. Strauss's Bavarian humor peers through as the "superman" takes his first steps to a Viennese waltz. The aftermath rises to orgiastic ecstasy, at the height of which the midnight bell sounds and the music subsides into a nocturne of great tenderness.

Any interpretation needs to balance the need for orchestral excitement with a respect for *Zarathustra's* atmosphere. This performance with the Concertgebouw has a special incandescence. The difficult orchestral balances are well-maintained and the recording certainly maintains a bewitching luminosity. **DN**

Hugo Wolf
Italienisches Liederbuch
(1896)

Genre | Vocal
Performers | Felicity Lott (soprano),
Peter Schreier (tenor), Graham Johnson (piano)
Years recorded | 1993–94
Label | Hyperion CDA 66760

If Wolf (1860–1903) is thought of primarily as a miniaturist, his *Italian Songbook* is the reason. These forty-six songs (a first book of twenty-two from 1890–91 followed by a second book of twenty-four from 1896), based on Paul Heyse's translations of Italian folk poems, contain his most jewel-like writing—each note and inflection is of crucial importance, yet the conversational text setting also encourages a light and spontaneous tone. The woman's songs are teasing, pouty, and temperamental by turns, while the male contribution is usually ardent and frequently spins out delicious conceits in his love songs. All of them are delectable, and none are of such a scope as to be obvious highlights. Suffice it to say that from the opening "Auch kleine Dinge" (which addresses the miniaturist aesthetic the songs embody) to the concluding "Ich hab in Penna" (in which the girl lightheartedly recites a list of how many lovers she has in each town in the region, culminating in a flashy piano postlude), this set demonstrates Wolf's mastery at its most accessible.

No performance of a single one of these songs can realize all its felicities; multiply that fact by nearly four dozen songs and it will be seen that no recording can be consistently preferred. In light of this, choice falls on the Lott–Schreier–Johnson account for several reasons: it is available; the performances are pungently sung and characterized; it is the only recording that uses Wolf's original keys; and Johnson's detailed booklet notes are a gold mine of information and stimulation. **DB**

Richard Strauss
Don Quixote
(1897)

Genre | Orchestral
Conductor/Performers | Herbert von Karajan; Mstislav
Rostropovich (cello), Berlin Philharmonic Orchestra
Year recorded | 1975
Label | EMI 7243 5 66965 2 5

There have been a fair few musical tributes to Miguel Cervantes's "knight of the sorrowful countenance," that chivalry-crazed gentleman who rode around early seventeenth-century Spain righting wrongs. None has made so idiosyncratic or elaborate an impact as Richard Strauss's "fantastic variations on a theme of knightly character," conceived in 1897 as a comic pendant to the tone poem that was to take shape as *Ein Heldenleben* (*A Hero's Life*). *Don Quixote* has become feted for its more graphic details, such as the bleating brass portraying the sheep Quixote mistakes for two mighty armies, or the wind machine that accompanies what he believes to be a flight through the air on a wooden horse. Strauss, who once claimed he could represent a spoon in music, stretches his descriptive power to the limits.

Yet all the fun and games conceal the work's phenomenal musical organization. Strauss takes a whole set of themes and submits them to a sequence of ever more ingenious variations. There is a generous role for solo cello, which Strauss conceived for the orchestral principal, but which is often taken by a distinguished virtuoso.

Mstislav Rostropovich's aristocratic knight eloquently dominates those portions of the score in which he comes to the fore, but does not overshadow the sumptuous glories of the Berlin Philharmonic Orchestra in such beauties as the vision sequence of Variation 3. Karajan emphasizes the idealism of the score without underplaying the moments of broad comedy. **DN**

Paul Dukas | The Sorcerer's Apprentice (1897)

Genre | Orchestral
Conductor | James Levine
Performers | Berlin Philharmonic Orchestra
Year recorded | 1987
Label | DG 419 617-2

Dukas (1865–1935) was a relatively late developer as a composer: he was twenty-six in 1891 when he wrote the overture *Polyeucte*, his first major piece. And his last, apart from a few trifles, was the ballet—or *poème dansée*, as he called it—*La Péri*, which appeared in 1912. Almost all the music he wrote outside this twenty-one year period was not up to his exacting standards, and he destroyed it, though not before giving a sight of some of it to musical friends. So he is mainly remembered as a teacher, whose pupils included Messiaen, Rodrigo, and Duruflé, and as the composer of one symphony, one monumental piano sonata, and one opera: *Ariane et Barbe-bleue*. And of course, one of the most popular orchestral pieces in the repertoire: *L'apprenti sorcier* (*The Sorcerer's Apprentice*).

This is a short-tone poem, subtitled symphonic scherzo, with a story from a ballad by Goethe. In the story the apprentice takes advantage of his master's absence to carry out his water-carrying chores by putting a spell on a broom to do all the hard work. But he does not know how to stop the broom, and splitting it in two just means double the trouble. Flood disaster is averted only by the return of the sorcerer, who sends the apprentice packing. Although Paul Dukas's piece had been popular since its first performance, it became familiar to millions after 1940, when Mickey Mouse played the apprentice in the Disney film *Fantasia*.

In this recording, the glittering orchestration is superbly caught by the virtuoso playing of the Berlin Philharmonic, and James Levine makes sure that every nuance counts in the inexorable build-up of the piece. At the same time, *The Sorcerer's Apprentice* comes across as a real scherzo, up-tempo and light on its feet. **MC**

> *"The idea generates the form, the contrary is inconceivable."*

Paul Dukas

Other Recommended Recordings

Symphony in C
BBC Philharmonic • Yan Pascal Tortelier
Chandos CHAN 9225
A work in the French tradition, with Beethoven in the background

Piano Sonata
Marc-André Hamelin • Hyperion CDA 67513
Virtuoso account of one of the great piano sonatas

La Péri
Suisse Romande Orchestra • Armin Jordan
Warner 0927 48725-2
Jordan makes the most of this colorful ballet score

Paul Dukas, whose reputation rests on *The Sorcerer's Apprentice.* ➔

Richard Strauss | Ein Heldenleben (1898)

Genre | Orchestral
Conductor | Rudolf Kempe
Performers | Dresden Staatskapelle
Year recorded | 1972
Label | EMI 7243 5 67892 2 7

Strauss was only thirty-four years old when he set out to encapsulate his experience of life so far in his eighth tone poem *Ein Heldenleben*. And this was to be depicted as no ordinary life, but, as the title translates, "A Hero's Life." He begins with a proud, virile portrait of his protagonist and goes on to describe his exploits with his adversaries (his critics); his finding of a companion (the composer's voluble and volatile wife Pauline is depicted by a solo violin); his battles (with the critics again); his works of peace (Strauss here quotes from some of his earlier symphonic poems); and finally his withdrawal from the world and feeling of accomplishment. But the work is less an exercise in megalomania—and let alone a musical counterpart to Kaiser Wilhelm's German militarism as some have seen it— than a more generic portrait of the artist, using Strauss's own experiences as reference points. Strauss himself told the French writer Romain Rolland, "I am not a hero; I haven't got the necessary strength."

No collection of Strauss recordings would be complete without the artistry of Rudolf Kempe, who committed the composer's major orchestral works to disc in the early 1970s for EMI. His conducting probes deeply into the music but does not distort and here in *Ein Heldenleben*— a work that can easily sound bombastic and vulgar if not treated sympathetically—he uncovers the music's humanity, the warmth and wit of Pauline (thanks to the suave playing here of solo violinist Peter Mirring), and the sublime sense of fulfillment in its closing pages. Kempe's orchestra is the Dresden Staatskapelle—which was Strauss's own orchestra in his time—and in this recording, Kempe exploits the sheen of its strings and its transparency of texture to the full. **MR**

> "*Any man who can construct a work that hangs together so well is not far from being a genius.*"
>
> Claude Debussy

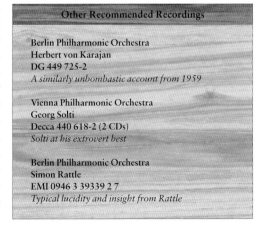

Other Recommended Recordings

Berlin Philharmonic Orchestra
Herbert von Karajan
DG 449 725-2
A similarly unbombastic account from 1959

Vienna Philharmonic Orchestra
Georg Solti
Decca 440 618-2 (2 CDs)
Solti at his extrovert best

Berlin Philharmonic Orchestra
Simon Rattle
EMI 0946 3 39339 2 7
Typical lucidity and insight from Rattle

Rudolf Kempe was the Strauss conductor *par excellence.* ➲

Edward Elgar | Sea Pictures (1899)

Genre | Vocal
Performers | Janet Baker, London Symphony Orchestra
Conductor | John Barbirolli
Year recorded | 1965
Label | EMI 7243 5 62887 2 0

It is interesting to note that Elgar's *Sea Pictures* and *Enigma Variations* were both given their first performances in 1899 and that four of the five settings of the former were composed in the month following the premiere of the orchestral work. Whereas *Enigma* is subtle and secretive, and very personal, *Sea Pictures* is outgoing and descriptive: music that is vivid, atmospheric, dramatic, and with more than a whiff of nationalism and Victorian pomp but with no shortage of heartfelt intimacy. It was first heard at the Norwich Festival, with rising star Clara Butt as soloist and with Elgar conducting; each of the five settings is melodically eloquent, not least "Where Corals Lie" (words by Richard Garnett), which has become very popular on its own terms due to its haunting yearning quality and a refrain that is infinitely touching—Elgar delving deep into human consciousness. The final setting, "The Swimmer" (Adam Lindsay Gordon), is an exciting and expanded counterpart to it, which might be envisaged as welcoming the proud fleet home.

Recorded in 1965 and long partnered on disc by Jacqueline du Pré's famous recording of Elgar's Cello Concerto, Janet Baker's account of *Sea Pictures* is a genuinely classic recording, one of those that has total identity with the music. Baker's enunciation makes every syllable tell and her vocal coloring and shading bring the words alive in the most vibrant way: she moves the listener, and presents "Where Corals Lie" as ineffably beautiful. John Barbirolli conjures wonderful colors from the London Symphony Orchestra and never shies away from showing generous emotions. What is especially compelling is that singer, conductor, and orchestral musicians are as one in their approach. **CA**

> "There is music in the air . . . all around us, the world is full of it and you simply take as much as you require."
>
> Edward Elgar

Other Recommended Recordings

Sarah Connolly, Bournemouth Symphony Orchestra
Simon Wright • Naxos 8.557710
A budget-price introduction to one of Elgar's undeclared masterpieces, The Music Makers

Bernadette Greevy, London Philharmonic Orchestra
Vernon Handley • EMI 7243 5 75306 2 0
At times sentimental and unevenly colored, but underpinned by Handley's discerning conducting

Larisa Avdeyeva, U.S.S.R. State Symphony Orchestra
Evgeny Svetlanov • Scribendum SC 032
Sea Pictures *sung in Russian, with an expressive soloist and plenty of fervor and impulse*

Janet Baker in the year of her *Sea Pictures* recording. ➲

Edward Elgar
Enigma Variations (1899)

Genre | Orchestral
Conductor | John Barbirolli
Performers | Philharmonia Orchestra
Year recorded | 1962
Label | EMI 7243 5 66322 2 6

It was Elgar's *Enigma Variations* that made his name as a composer, at the not-too-tender age of forty-two. Today *Enigma* is widely seen as the first real musical masterpiece to emerge in Britain since the death of Henry Purcell two centuries earlier. Elgar dedicated the Variations "to my friends pictured within," and they form an irresistible sequence of character studies, culminating in the composer's rousing, assured self-portrait—as though he were telling those friends, "See what you have made of me." But Elgar also confessed that the music contained a "dark saying," adding that the theme itself expressed his enduring sense of the "loneliness of the artist." So like many of Elgar's finest works, *Enigma* reveals two very different personae: the robust, brimming confidence of the self-made English gentleman and the restless, melancholic introspection of the outsider. That Elgar was truly both is one of the aspects of his music that makes him fascinating.

That is not the whole story: *Enigma* is also about warmth of feeling, tunefulness, and lively humor, and even—an unfashionable word today—nobility. Of the many recordings of the work, none comes closer to capturing all these sides of its musical personality than Barbirolli's 1962 version. From the first phrase of the famous theme there is an almost confidential immediacy that compels you to sit up and take notice. In the famous "Nimrod," or the cello melody of Variation 12, the open-heartedness is deeply touching, but still is not quite heart-on-sleeve. Elsewhere the sense of fun, of splendor, or exhilarating, swaggering vulgarity is just as captivating. This is a very rich *Enigma*, but never stodgy or overripe. **SJ**

Alexander Glazunov
The Seasons (1899)

Genre | Ballet
Conductor | Evgeny Svetlanov
Performers | Philharmonia Orchestra
Year recorded | 1978
Label | EMI 7243 5 69361 2 6 (2 CDs)

It is probably true to say that Alexander Glazunov (1865–1936) was born just a little too late. He was a musical conservative who found himself somewhat out on a limb as twentieth-century musical developments took hold. Essentially a melodist and a believer in traditional values, he learned his trade studying with Rimsky-Korsakov. Like most Russian composers of his time he used indigenous folk tunes or approximations of them while being generally more cosmopolitan than nationalistic (he died in France) and thus closer to Tchaikovsky in musical outlook than to Mussorgsky. Glazunov composed his ballet *The Seasons* in 1899. It is a work full of delightful invention, with attractive melodies, engaging modulations, and a powerful sense of atmosphere with much that is gentle and charming. The tableau depicting autumn, which includes some of the score's most beautiful music, is sometimes played separately; but the whole work is a pleasure.

Evgeny Svetlanov was a doughty champion of Russian music and left us a huge recorded legacy of this repertoire. In making this recording of *The Seasons* in London, he set down a symphonic reading, with tempi designed to reveal all the facets of Glazunov's superb orchestration and allow the slower and refined sections of the score time to breath and sparkle while mining to the full the Philharmonia's ability for softness, sheen, and sensitivity. In Moscow (Svetlanov's base), the orchestral timbres might have been edgier and earthier, and so more authentic; but Glazunov's refined sensibility is especially well served here in a loving and polished performance that ravishes the ear and touches the heart. **CA**

Arnold Schoenberg
Verklärte Nacht (1899)

Genre | Chamber
Performers | Hollywood Quartet,
Alvin Dinkin, Kurt Reher
Year recorded | 1950
Label | Testament SBT 1031

Schoenberg's first masterpiece was composed in three weeks, and is a powerful synthesis: a string sextet that is in effect a symphonic poem, after the poem *Verklärte Nacht* (*Transfigured Night*) by Richard Dehmel. A man and a woman wander among the trees on a cold moonlit night. She confesses she is pregnant by another man whom she took as a lover as she had believed that having a child would bring meaning, if not happiness, to her life. He assures her that the love they have found together will unite them and make the child their own.

Never before had Schoenberg written anything so passionate. The five-section layout of Dehmel's poem gives the basic form of the sextet, and every phrase is most sensitively illustrated in the music, from the dragging steps at the opening, to the radiant evocation of the "transfigured night" at the close. Yet on another level the music makes so much sense that one hardly feels the program to be a vital element in its structural logic.

The firm D major of the opening of the fourth section (the man's reply) is especially striking, and creates the work's main structural division, initiating a "second movement" that complements the first. Yet there are places where *Verklärte Nacht* seems to burst the bounds of Schoenberg's chosen string-sextet medium: he later arranged it for string orchestra, and in this form it has become his most-performed and recorded work.

Despite its age, this performance recorded with Schoenberg's blessing by the expanded Hollywood Quartet remains supreme. The playing is flawless and white-hot in intensity; the sound is still acceptable. **MM**

Louis Vierne
Organ Symphonies (1899–1930)

Genre | Instrumental
Instrument | Organ
Performer | Jeremy Filsell
Year recorded | 2004
Label | Signum SIGCD 063

Louis Vierne (1870–1937) was the gifted organist of Notre Dame in Paris for nearly forty years; he was beset from birth with blindness (partially restored in childhood) and with a string of personal tragedies. He died while giving a recital at Notre Dame, with his pupil Maurice Duruflé at his side.

Vierne's complex personality found vivid expression in his six organ symphonies; composed in a rising scale of minor keys, their orchestral character elaborates a few main themes symphonically; the two post–World War I symphonies (nos. 5 and 6) reflect contemporary trends by pushing the bounds of conventional tonality.

Most organists intent on recording these darkly glittering works head for the Gothic Abbaye de St. Ouen in Rouen. The attraction is to play the music on the last masterpiece of the iconic and innovatory French organ builder, Aristide Cavaillé-Coll, inaugurated in 1890 by Vierne's teacher Charles-Marie Widor.

Concert organists habitually cherry-pick from the many thrilling movements in Vierne's symphonies; for the serious listener the complete works brings additional rewards. Here, Jeremy Filsell concentrates on wringing every last drop of sonority from the St. Ouen organ in deeply felt, idiomatic performances. His booklet notes on Vierne's life, and the music, are enhanced by his insights into the recording process and the organ's idiosyncrasies. It takes a great recording to wrest one away from the benchmark for the Vierne symphonies set by David Sanger; but, for the opportunity to hear the music on the kind of organ Vierne would have known and heard in his head when composing the symphonies, Filsell takes the crown. **GK**

Jean Sibelius | Symphony no. 1 (1899)

Genre | Orchestral
Conductor | Leonard Bernstein
Performers | Vienna Philharmonic Orchestra
Year recorded | 1990
Label | DG 474 936-2 (3 CDs)

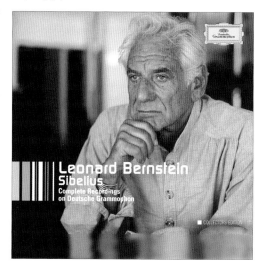

Sibelius's E minor Symphony, the first of his works to which the composer was prepared to grant full symphonic status, was the product of a conscious effort to market his locally resonant, primitivist music to the wider world. Tchaikovsky seems to have been one model, given his ability to produce abstract works from rhapsodic material (the "Pathétique" was performed in Helsinki in 1894 and 1897), Borodin was another.

The First Symphony was the highlight of the very first concert given by Leonard Bernstein outside the United States (in Montreal) and it also featured prominently in his final season. It is a piece he came to conduct in a deeply subjective, rather old-fashioned way, making frequent resort to massive sonorities and molding every phrase deliberately, as if to emphasize its debt to the Russian masters. Where the youthful maestro had tended to thrust aside potential opposition, lacing his scores with so much manic energy that it was impossible to resist, the older Bernstein makes this one sound yet more uniquely his own by stamping his outsize personality on every bar. Edited from live performances, it is an interpretation that operates at a higher voltage than almost any Sibelius on disc. While one might not always wish to hear the finale's sweeping big tune so heavily underlined, the playing is phenomenal and it is impossible to imagine greater intensity and commitment than the Viennese offer their favorite guest conductor.

More recently, the consensus has been to distance the symphony from the Slav tradition, deploying swifter tempi to remind us that this is also young man's music. Bernstein, however, believed in flamboyant revivification rather than some kind of reconstructed historical accuracy. **DG**

> ## "[The work seeks] to compel through the magnetic force of the conductor's identification with the music."
>
> James Hepokoski in DG booklet notes

Other Recommended Recordings

London Symphony Orchestra • Anthony Collins
Beulah 14PD8 (4 CDs)
A brisk, no-nonsense 1950s classic from the first symphony cycle to achieve international distribution

Berlin Philharmonic Orchestra • Herbert von Karajan
EMI 0946 3 72478 2 2
The conventional Romantic view, less extreme than Bernstein's, but still epic

Lahti Symphony Orchestra • Osmo Vänskä
BIS CD-861
Adhering to Sibelius's metronome markings, this is a lithe and transparent reading

Jean Sibelius, photographed in 1949. ➔

Giacomo Puccini | Tosca (1899)

Genre | Opera
Conductor/Performers | Victor de Sabata; Maria Callas, Giuseppe di Stefano, Tito Gobbi, La Scala Chorus & Orchestra
Year recorded | 1953
Label | EMI 7243 5 62893 2 1 (2 CDs)

Once dismissed as a "shabby little shocker," *Tosca* can be as dramatic and as intense as anything that Puccini ever wrote with the right cast and conductor. Though the composer possibly should have heeded the advice of his publisher Ricordi, who had reservations about the singer Tosca's final duet with her doomed lover, the painter Cavaradossi, which warms up music from Puccini's earlier opera *Edgar*. Nevertheless, Acts 1 and 2 display the composer's complete mastery of musical theater.

Puccini went to enormous pains to get the detail right in *Tosca*. He even made a special trip to Rome so that he could listen to the sound of Rome's church bells as heard from the top of the Castel Sant'Angelo from which Tosca leaps to her death. The details of the church setting in Act 1, where Tosca meets Cavaradossi and the police chief Scarpia blasphemously sings of his lust for the singer while the choir sing a Te Deum, were scrupulously checked with a friendly priest. But only the composer knew where the sinister sadism of the middle act came from, with Scarpia torturing Cavaradossi while toying with Tosca.

No singer has made Floria Tosca more hers than Maria Callas, and her first recording, produced by the estimable Walter Legge, remains the standard against which all others must be judged. Callas's Tosca is by turns a tigress and a deeply vulnerable woman. Tito Gobbi's Scarpia is the most stylish if not the darkest on record, while Giuseppe di Stefano is an ardent Cavaradossi whose fine singing makes liberals of us all as he aids Angelotti, the escaped political prisoner, and defies Scarpia's torturers. But in the end all that matters with this recording is Callas's incomparable interpretation, which quite simply transforms a popular melodrama into great art. **CC**

> ## "Art is a kind of illness."
>
> Giacomo Puccini

Other Recommended Recordings

Vienna Philharmonic Orchestra • Herbert von Karajan
Decca 466 384-2 (2 CDs)
Leontyne Price is a sumptuous Tosca in a magnificently sounding recording

Philharmonia Orchestra • Giuseppe Sinopoli
DG 431 775-2 (2 CDs)
Mirella Freni is a tender Tosca, Plácido Domingo a heroic Cavaradossi

Rome Opera Chorus & Orchestra • Oliviero Fabritiis
Naxos 8.110096-97 (2 CDs)
Recorded in 1938, Gigli produces an unusually rounded characterization of Cavaradossi

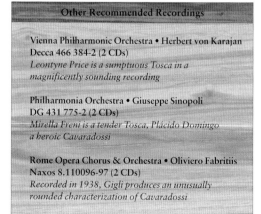

Tosca was perhaps Maria Callas's most famous role. ➔

Antonín Dvořák
Rusalka (1900)

Genre | Opera
Performers | Milada Subrtová,
Ivo Zidek, Eduard Haken
Year recorded | 1961
Label | Supraphon SU 0013-2

Dvořák was occupied with operatic projects during much of his composing career. This is unsurprising, given that nearly all the composers of the Czech national revival saw it as their duty to provide repertoire for their new theater. He wrote eleven operas, more than any other later nineteenth-century Czech composer, but *Rusalka* is the only one widely known outside the Czech lands. This is a pity given the abundant beauties to be found in the grand operas *Vanda*, *Dimitrij*, and *Armida*, and the comedies, *The Cunning Peasant*, *The Jacobin*, and *The Devil and Kate*. Nevertheless, *Rusalka* was Dvořák's operatic masterpiece.

In later life, Dvořák was drawn increasingly toward stories from Czech folklore, and although the roots of the story include Andersen's *The Little Mermaid*, the characters in *Rusalka* and the atmosphere of the opera all derive from Bohemian folk myth. This tale of a forest spirit who becomes human in order to know love, suffers rejection, and a terrifying fate hovering between life and death for eternity drew from Dvořák music of breathtaking lyrical beauty epitomized by his most famous single operatic number, the "Song to the Moon" from the first act. Equally lovely melody characterize nearly all of *Rusalka*'s arias.

Zdeněk Chalabala's performance conducting the Prague National Theater Chorus and Orchestra, ranks as one of the greatest recordings of any Czech opera. Milada Subrtová is a superbly passionate Rusalka, Ivo Zidek a convincingly ardent Prince, and Eduard Haken delivers his classic version of the Water Goblin. Above all, however, it is Chalabala's flexible approach to the opera's dramatic ebb and flow that makes this recording so unforgettable. **JS**

Edward Elgar
The Dream of Gerontius (1900)

Genre | Choral
Conductor/Performers | Adrian Boult;
Nicolai Gedda, Helen Watts, Robert Lloyd
Year recorded | 1976
Label | EMI 7243 5 66540 2 0 (2 CDs)

Elgar's *The Dream of Gerontius* has become such an institution that it is possible to overlook its daring and originality. Here is a work that attempts nothing less than a depiction of the soul's journey after death, climaxing in a searing split-second encounter with God. The work's explicit Roman Catholicism provoked a good deal of paranoid twittering when it first appeared (there were protests when *Gerontius* was scheduled for performance in Worcester Cathedral), while others were disturbed by Elgar's clear debt to Wagner's intoxicating mysticism. As so often, the guardians of public morality missed the point. *Gerontius* not only speaks to people of all religions, it can also offer something to those without belief in a supreme being or afterlife. The protagonist is no saint, but what Yeats called a "foolish, passionate man," facing the terror and grief of death with a range of feelings. And the Angel's final lullaby can touch the most resistant hearts—"Farewell, but not for ever."

In a work regarded as quintessentially English, it is good to be reminded that Elgar's continental roots also went deep—it is said he had an Italian tenor sound in mind for *Gerontius*. Nicolai Gedda certainly brings an un-Anglo Saxon intensity to the central role, making the dying man believable. Helen Watts's Angel is nobly tender, and free from Victorian sanctity. Robert Lloyd's Priest makes the soul's departure at the end of Part 1 a hair-raisingly powerful turning point. But it is Boult who, as unhistrionic as ever, brings the sense of coordinating vision. Dignity and grave beauty—they are not fashionable concepts today. Listen to this then and hear what today is missing. **SJ**

Gustav Mahler
Symphony no. 4 (1900)

Genre | Orchestral
Conductor | Michael Gielen
Performer | Christine Whittlesey
Year recorded | 1988
Label | Hänssler CD 93.130 (13 CDs)

Composed a few years after Mahler's Third Symphony, and the first to be composed after he became director of the Vienna Court Opera in 1897, the Fourth is one of his shortest, most touching, and cheerful. It stems from the music that was composed earliest: the last movement, a *Wunderhorn* song, "Das himmlische Leben" ("Heavenly Life"), written in 1892 for soprano and imagining a child's view of heaven. The rest of the symphony followed in 1899–1900; a few months before he died, Mahler was at pains to point out that the first three (purely orchestral) movements contain decisive thematic connections with, and foreshadowings of, the final song, which dies away in transfigured quietness in a key different from the one in which it began. The first movement sets the tone for the feeling of innocent, untroubled wonder that pervades the work by introducing sleigh bells and chirping flutes as a background for delicate, ardent melodic themes. The dancelike, vaguely sinister second movement features a solo violin tuned a whole step high to give it a strident, rustic character. The slow third movement is the longest; despite considerable intensity and passion, the feeling that we are experiencing life through a child's eyes remains.

Mahler had a formative influence on the Second Viennese School (Schoenberg, Berg, and Webern), and Michael Gielen's Fourth with soprano Christine Whittlesey makes the Webern connection clear by honing the transparency of the textures to an unusual degree. At the same time, the phrasing is natural and unaffected, and the glory of the performance is the restrained dreamscape created in the second movement. **DB**

Jean Sibelius
Finlandia (1900)

Genre | Orchestral
Conductor | Herbert von Karajan
Performer | Berlin Philharmonic Orchestra
Year recorded | 1984
Label | DG 413 755-2

With the possible exception of *Valse triste*, *Finlandia* was the most widely known of all Sibelius's compositions throughout his career and it is perhaps not surprising that he should have developed a love-hate relationship with a piece so bound up with the life of its time. At the end of the nineteenth century, with Finland's right to self-government and freedom of speech severely restricted by Tsar Nicholas II, he wrote a series of coded, quasi-political pieces. One series of events arranged in November 1899, ostensibly to raise money for the Press Pension Fund, climaxed in a gala performance at the Swedish Theater that included tableaux depicting events in Finnish history. Sibelius wrote the music and it was the finale, then entitled "Finland Awakes," that took the nation and later the world by storm. The title, *Finlandia*, was the suggestion of Axel Carpelan, Sibelius's most loyal and obsessive admirer. It is difficult not to hear its progress in terms of a people's emerging national consciousness. The famous, albeit derivative, central melody has been widely adopted as a hymn tune and frequently arranged for other forces. Sibelius himself transcribed *Finlandia* for piano, and permitted choral permutations, authorizing the Finnish-language mixed-voice choir "Finlandia Hymn" in the 1940s.

It is the familiar orchestral score that Karajan champions here, having recorded it on as many as four previous occasions. This session, in early digital sound, finds the Berliners on top form, their music making maximally tense and stirring, despite (or maybe because of) what was by now a stormy relationship with their maestro. The main item in this program is a powerful *Tapiola*. **DG**

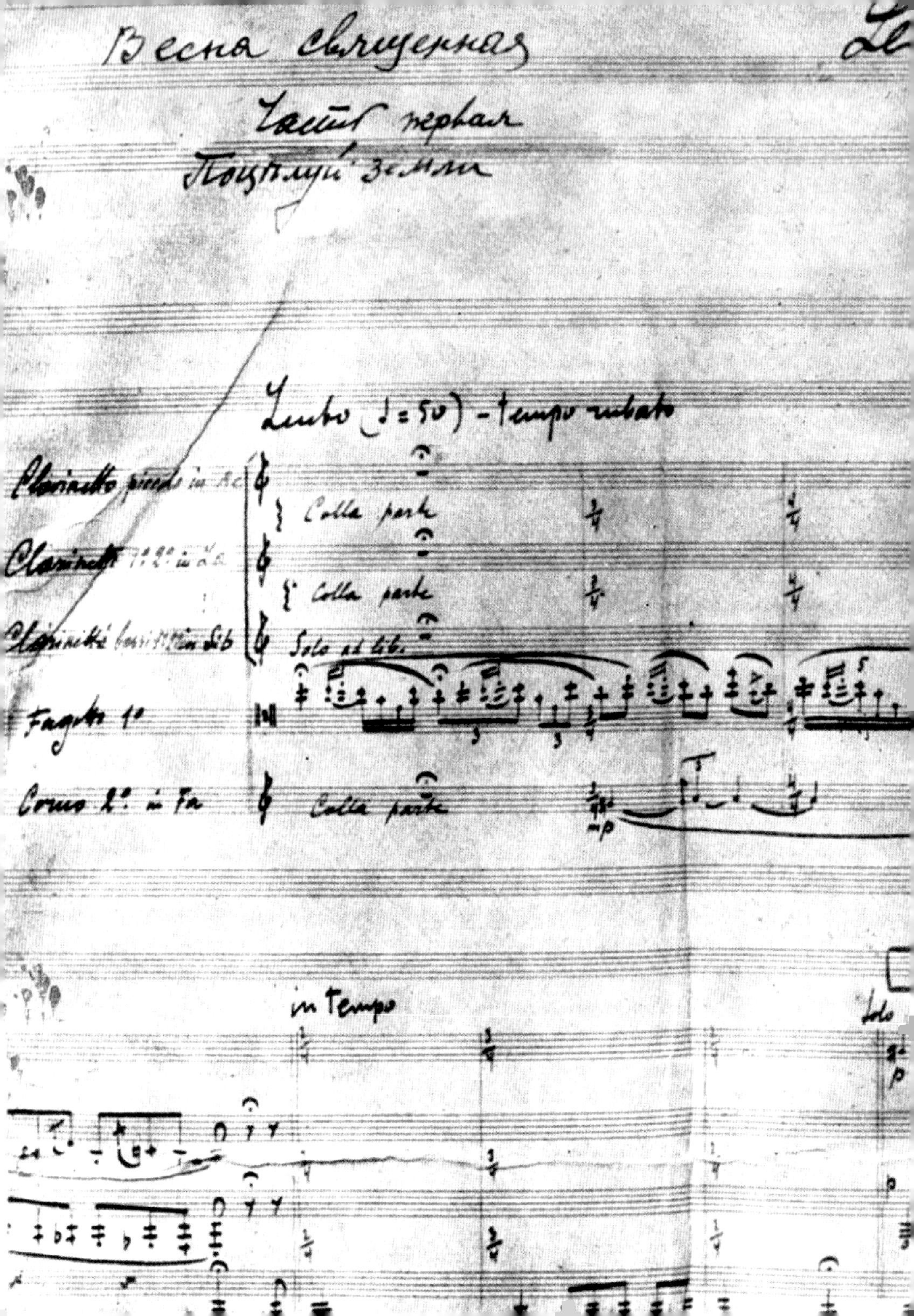

Весна священная

Часть первая
Поцелуй земли

Lento (♩ = 50) – tempo rubato

Clarinetto piccolo in Re	Colla parte
Clarinetto 1° in La	Colla parte
Clarinetto basso in Sib	Solo ad lib.
Fagotto 1°	
Corno 2° in Fa	Colla parte

in tempo

The Romantic ideal was extended by figures like Mahler, Strauss, Elgar, and Sibelius, but new revolutions were afoot. Schoenberg took Wagnerian chromaticism to its extreme and abandoned tonality altogether, inventing a new method of twelve-note composition; Stravinsky, meanwhile, cast Romanticism aside with the rhythmic violence of *The Rite of Spring*. The decades framed by the two world wars saw Expressionism giving way to objectivity and Neo-Classicism, and styles such as jazz and folksong made their mark.

1901–1950

Igor Stravinsky, manuscript of the opening of *The Rite of Spring* (1913).

Sergei Rachmaninov | Piano Concerto no. 2 (1901)

Genre | Concerto
Performers/Conductor | Sviatoslav Richter (piano), Warsaw
Philharmonic Orchestra; Stanislaw Wislocki
Year recorded | 1959
Label | DG 447 420-2

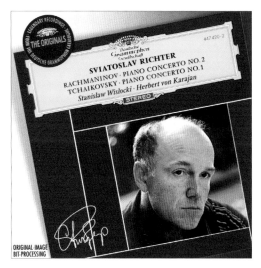

There is no more famous concerto opening than the chords that begin Rachmaninov's Second Piano Concerto. The composer seems to be emerging from dark uncertainty to the blazing confidence of the long, sumptuous melody that follows. Indeed, Rachmaninov had composed nothing of note for three years since the disastrous premiere of his First Symphony. Suffering from depression, he sought the advice of hypnotist Dr. Nikolai Dahl, who encouraged Rachmaninov that he would be able to write a new concerto finer than anything he had yet composed. This Second Piano Concerto is dedicated to Dahl. It achieved universal fame through its use in the film *Brief Encounter* (1945).

In fact Rachmaninov composed the first movement last. Curiously, given his newfound creativity, he based the second movement's piano figuration on an earlier work, but the famous clarinet theme that soars above it was new. Even for so melodically effusive a composer, the Second Piano Concerto's wealth of great tunes is extraordinary. Although far from easy, it is not so technically demanding as the Third Concerto, composed eight years later, and its accessibility to pianists and popularity with audiences make it one of the most performed of all concertos.

The reputation of Russian pianist Sviatoslav Richter grew to almost mythical status before he was allowed to travel to the West in 1960, fueled by his 1959 recording of Rachmaninov's Second Concerto in Warsaw. Richter's sovereign keyboard command, powerful all-Russian tone and inimitable way of shaping and coloring melodic lines, avoiding any sentimentality, give this recording a timeless quality, even if the unusually expansive tempo for the opening remains controversial. **TLP**

> *"If you do not want to leap to your feet cheering . . . you are probably not cut out for Rachmaninov's world."*
>
> Bill Parker

Other Recommended Recordings

**Vladimir Ashkenazy, London Symphony Orchestra
André Previn • Decca 444 839-2 (2 CDs)**
*Russian to the core, this is the finest of Ashkenazy's
recordings of this work*

**Leif Ove Andsnes, Berlin Philharmonic Orchestra
Antonio Pappano • EMI 7243 4 74813 2 1**
*Andsnes may hold emotion at arm's length but his
playing has an impeccable poise*

**Krystian Zimerman, Boston Symphony Orchestra
Seiji Ozawa • DG 459 643-2**
*Crystalline and acutely perceptive playing from
Zimerman*

Rachmaninov overcame depression with his Second Piano Concerto. ➔

Sergei Rachmaninov
Cello Sonata (1901)

Genre | Chamber
Performers | Truls Mørk (cello),
Jean-Yves Thibaudet (piano)
Year recorded | 1994
Label | Virgin 7243 5 45119 2 9

Rachmaninov's beautiful Cello Sonata opens, uniquely, with three languid questions: the cello asks them, the piano answers uncertainly, and then they join in posing them and resolving them together. This introduction, played as it should be as if the two instrumentalists had all the time in the world, gives us a deft portrait of their relationship. The piano is the dominant partner, but supports, cushions, and cherishes its star tenor, the cello. This is Rachmaninov, after all, one of the greatest pianists who ever lived, and the piano part has all the magnitude, color and drama of a concerto. The cello part is, however, a vital driving force in this turbulent Romantic work, especially in the gruff urgency of the Allegro scherzando and the bold, rollicking finale with its very Russian hymn of triumph. The hypnotic slow movement, which shifts mesmerically between the major and minor, is one of Rachmaninov's most inspired vocalises: here the song composer and master of the piano prelude combine to produce a miniature masterpiece, so imbued with love that the famous theme from the Second Piano Concerto pales in comparison.

Truls Mørk makes this sonata "speak" to the listener in a uniquely persuasive way; he brings an unbearable sincerity and poignancy to the melodies and shapes and drives the musical argument, but he also luxuriates in the gorgeous harmonies alongside Jean-Yves Thibaudet's spectacular, passionate reading of the piano part. Perhaps, in the end, it is the simplicity of their approach, combined with truly unassailable technique, that enables them to reach the heart of this enchanting work. **HW**

Roger Quilter
Songs (1901–39)

Genre | Vocal
Performers | Lisa Milne (soprano), Anthony Rolfe Johnson
(tenor), Graham Johnson (piano), Duke Quartet
Year recorded | 1997
Label | Naxos 8.557116

Roger Quilter was an Edwardian gentleman of private means and uncertain health, educated principally in Frankfurt (alongside Percy Grainger and others), and never in the vanguard even of Britain's notoriously conservative musical life. He wrote music for a children's play, *Where the Rainbow Ends*, which ran in the West End every Christmas for many years, a light opera, several times revised under different titles, and a few orchestral pieces. However, he's chiefly remembered for his songs, many of them taken up by leading singers of the day, but also crooned or bawled in countless genteel drawing rooms.

Why should we bother with these songs now, though, in a modern era when "home entertainment" has such a different meaning? Simply because Quilter had a rare gift for capturing the essential qualities of a poem in a perfectly formed melodic line and a subtly sympathetic accompaniment. Once you have heard his settings of, for example, Tennyson's "Now sleeps the crimson petal," or Shelley's "Love's Philosophy," or Waller's "Go, lovely rose," the words will seem forever enshrined in the music.

This disc contains these favorite solo songs and many more. But it scores through the variety of forces available, which enables it to include the *Three Pastoral Songs* with violin, cello and piano, and the Herrick cycle *To Julia* with string quartet and piano. Lisa Milne is in fine, fresh voice, Anthony Rolfe Johnson brings vocal finesse to his contributions, and both show great care for words as well as line, while Graham Johnson is his usual supportive and imaginative self. All do full justice to Quilter the modest but, in his own field, peerless miniaturist. **AB**

Francesco Cilea
Adriana Lecouvreur (1902)

Genre | Opera
Conductor/Performers | Mario Rossi;
Magda Olivero, Giulietta Simionato, Franco Corelli
Year recorded | 1959
Label | Opera d'Oro 1410 (2 CDs)

A paid-up member of the *verismo* generation that succeeded Verdi, Cilea never quite made the final cut. *L'arlesiana* (1897) was given a helping hand by Caruso, yet the opera soon faded from view. And *Adriana Lecouvreur* has never had much of a shelf life outside Italy and New York. This is a cause for regret, and not just among addicts of oversugared early twentieth-century Italian operatic confections. For while the plot of *Adriana Lecouvreur* has as many loose ends as an old sweater, thanks to Cilea condensing his score during first rehearsals, here is a composer with a genuine gift for melody.

Musically, and dramatically, everything is organized around the heroine, a French tragedian—the real Adrienne Lecouvreur starred at the Comédie in the early eighteenth century—who has fallen in love with Maurizio, the disguised pretender to the Polish throne who, in the way of these plots, is desired by the jealous Princesse Bouillon. It all ends badly with Adriana sniffing a poisoned bunch of violets. En route, Cilea writes elegant pastiches of eighteenth-century music and a pair of stunning arias for his heroine: "Io son l'umile ancella" and "Poveri fiori."

In old age the composer's own choice for Adriana was Magda Olivero and in this live performance she does not so much sing the role as live it from her first fluttering entrance until the poisoned violets bring down the curtain on her short life. Only Callas is capable of such intensity. As Cilea intended, the rest of the cast huddles together in a kind of half-light. Giulietta Simionato is suitably vicious as the jealous Princess, the voice curdling nicely, and Franco Corelli is a heroic Maurizio. **CC**

Gustav Mahler
Rückert Lieder (1902)

Genre | Vocal
Conductor | John Barbirolli
Performers | Janet Baker, New Philharmonia Orchestra
Year recorded | 1967
Label | EMI 7243 5 66996 2 5

Mahler turned to the poetry of Friedrich Rückert in 1902, and the set of five songs in this collection (along with the further five Rückert songs in *Kindertotenlieder*) contains some of his most intimate music. The poetic themes concentrate on the beauty of nature, the freedom of imagination, and the way in which one's real essence transcends and eludes outward achievements and reality. This set includes "Liebst du um Schönheit" ("If you Love for Beauty"), a love song for Mahler's fiancée Alma Schindler; the dramatic "Um Mitternacht" ("At Midnight"); "Blicke mir nicht in die Lieder" ("Please Don't Look at my Songs"); and "Ich atmet' einen linden Duft" ("I Breathed a Gentle Fragrance"). If the prevailing tone is one of loveliness, the most substantial masterpiece of the set, "Ich bin der Welt abhanden gekommen" ("I Have Lost Touch with the World"), takes this feeling to a new level—such peaceful, contented, inspiring inwardness is a language that Mahler alone seems to have mastered.

The recording of these songs by Janet Baker and John Barbirolli is one of the great classics of the Mahler discography. This singer is unusual in her combination of depth of commitment to the texts and beautiful singing. Baker's ability to encompass the exaltation, awe, and introspection demanded by these songs prompts wonder and gratitude. Barbirolli was one of Britain's great Mahler champions in the 1950s and 1960s, and despite his long record of successes this may be his greatest achievement. Vividly but naturally characterized, intense and deeply felt, but unfailingly lyrical and transparent, this performance embodies the best he had to offer. **DB**

Gustav Mahler | Symphony no. 5 (1902)

Genre | Orchestral
Conductor | Claudio Abbado
Performer | Berlin Philharmonic Orchestra
Year recorded | 1993
Label | DG 437 789-2

In February 1901, Mahler experienced a severe hemorrhoidal hemorrhage. The new lease on life he gained by surviving this crisis prompted him to embark on a self-proclaimed new style of greater contrapuntal complexity when he began the Fifth Symphony that summer. Mahler did not abandon his intriguing synthesis of song and symphony—he quotes his *Wunderhorn* song "Lob des hohen Verstandes" ("In Praise of Wisdom") at the beginning of the Fifth's finale, and the famous adagietto revisits the music of his Rückert song "Ich bin der Welt abhanden gekommen." But the Fifth and its two successors form a trilogy of purely orchestral works in which the textural richness and diversity add new dimensions to Mahler's already powerful expressive voice.

The Fifth is in three parts, in which two pairs of thematically related movements flank a massive central scherzo. The opening movement is a doleful funeral march; the second gives vent to grief but glimpses ultimate triumph near the end. The Adagietto is now recognized as a love-offering to his beloved Alma (whom Mahler met in November 1901) and thus has come to be played in a gentler, more flowing manner than was long the case. The finale features exaggeratedly contrapuntal busy-ness that culminates in a full-blown breakthrough of the triumph foreshadowed at the end of the second movement.

The Fifth has become one of the great orchestral showpieces in recent decades, sometimes to the detriment of the work's expressive possibilities. Claudio Abbado and the Berlin Philharmonic play with as much flash and panache as anyone, but manage to offer an enriched and imaginative view that consistently brings stimulating rewards. **DB**

> *". . . [the Fifth] opens up a most promising view of the future of art, both for Mahler and for us."*
>
> Max Kalbeck (1905)

Other Recommended Recordings

New Philharmonia Orchestra • John Barbirolli
EMI 7243 5 66910 2 5
A much-loved recording; trenchant characterization, weighty tempi

Bavarian Radio Symphony Orchestra • Rafael Kubelík
Audite 95.465
A live performance with much character and excitement

Frankfurt Radio Symphony Orchestra • Eliahu Inbal
Denon CO 1088
A stimulating, questing performance out of the mainstream; the Adagietto lasts beyond eleven minutes

Gustav Mahler entered a new phase of life with his Fifth Symphony. ➔

Claude Debussy
Pelléas et Mélisande (1902)

Genre | Opera
Conductor/Performers | Roger Désormière;
Jacques Jansen, Irène Joachim, Henri Etcheverry
Year recorded | 1941
Label | EMI 0946 3 45782 2 6 (3 CDs)

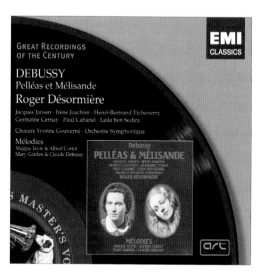

It is difficult to imagine the revolution that Debussy's only completed opera wrought on the Paris musical world when it was first performed at the Opéra Comique in 1902. With one work he swept away a tradition that had emphasized the "grand" in grand opera, and instead he went big, as it were, on subtlety. The subject matter of Maurice Maeterlinck's symbolist drama *Pelléas et Mélisande* almost cries out for it in its dream-world setting where the mysterious Mélisande raises the passions of Golaud, his half-brother Pelléas, and even the old king Arkel. Everything seems to be couched in half-lights—the music is elusive but at the same time gripping in its sense of atmosphere and suggestiveness.

Perhaps the most revolutionary aspect of Debussy's score is his word-setting: gone are the big arias and extended vocal lines common to most other operas of the time and in their place is a syllabic, parlando style that at once brings a psychological truth and sense of mystery to the drama. Debussy tends to save his big dramatic statements for the interludes that divide the scenes of this five-act work, though these were substantially expanded at the last minute to accommodate longer-than-expected scene changes in the first production.

Roger Désormière's recording, the first complete account on disc, benefited from the assistance of the soprano who created the role of Mélisande, Mary Garden, in its preparation, while the Pelléas and Mélisande themselves were young singers, which comes across in the freshness of their characterization. Despite the mono sound, this is a classic, not to be missed. **MR**

> *"In opera . . . the voice should blossom into full song only when this is called for."*

Claude Debussy

Other Recommended Recordings

Vienna Philharmonic Orchestra • Claudio Abbado
DG 435 344-2 (3 CDs)
The best modern stereo account, full of illuminating detail

Berlin Philharmonic Orchestra • Herbert von Karajan
EMI 7243 5 67057 2 2 (3 CDs)
Karajan emphasizes Wagner's influence on Debussy's Tristanesque drama

Concert Suite
Berlin Philharmonic Orchestra • Claudio Abbado
DG 471 332-2
Erich Leinsdorf's intriguing suite from the opera

Carl Nielsen
Symphony no. 2, "The Four Temperaments" (1902)

Genre | Orchestral
Conductor | Jukka-Pekka Saraste
Performers | Finnish Radio Symphony Orchestra
Year recorded | 2001
Label | Warner 2564 60431-2

Nielsen
Symphonies No.1
& No.2 'The Four Temperaments'

Finnish Radio Symphony Orchestra
Jukka-Pekka Saraste

elatus

One of the happiest memoirs of any composer's early years is Nielsen's *My Childhood on Fyn*, which was published two years after his sixtieth birthday and reveals how his upbringing on a small rural island shaped his attitude to life and art. Coming from a poor family—his father was a house painter and village musician—he progressed from singing to the violin, piano, and then the trombone, joining a military band in Odense when he was fourteen. Four years later, he entered the Copenhagen Conservatoire, where his main study was the violin, and for sixteen years he played in the Royal Chapel Orchestra. When he left, he was already seen as Denmark's first modern composer, and his six symphonies and three concertos in particular are firmly embedded in the international repertoire.

Nielsen took the idea for the Second Symphony from a painting that he had seen in a country inn in Zealand. It was divided into four parts, each symbolizing one of the four temperaments—choleric, sanguine, melancholic and phlegmatic. Even though he had laughed at the crudity of the art, Nielsen found himself constantly thinking of it, and "realized that these shoddy pictures still contained a kind of core or idea and even a musical undercurrent." It is the first of his orchestral works where he completely inhabits his own sound world, and the premiere was a great success.

Jukka-Pekka Saraste's excellent performance accurately characterizes the contrast between the moods of the four movements, from the violent anger of the opening, through romantic optimism, pensive sadness, to devil-may-care confidence, with a real sense of style from the Finnish Radio Symphony Orchestra. **MC**

> *"His ability to mix colors . . . neglects no opportunity to exercise the listening ear."*
>
> Leopold Rosenfeld, after the premiere

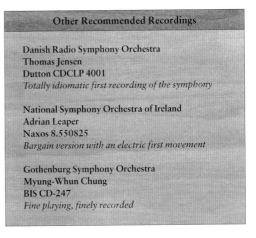

Other Recommended Recordings

Danish Radio Symphony Orchestra
Thomas Jensen
Dutton CDCLP 4001
Totally idiomatic first recording of the symphony

National Symphony Orchestra of Ireland
Adrian Leaper
Naxos 8.550825
Bargain version with an electric first movement

Gothenburg Symphony Orchestra
Myung-Whun Chung
BIS CD-247
Fine playing, finely recorded

Hubert Parry | I Was Glad (1902)

Genre | Choral
Conductor/Performers | Philip Ledger; Choir of King's
College, Cambridge, Cambridge University Musical Society
Year recorded | 1977
Label | EMI 7243 5 85148 2 7

Charles Hubert Hastings Parry (1848–1918) was born in a year of European revolution and died just as the "war to end all wars" drew to a close. His positions as director of the Royal College of Music (from 1895 until his death) and professor of music at Oxford (1900–08), and his composition of England's popular "alternative" anthem *Jerusalem*, marked him down as an Establishment figure; but critical reappraisal and some splendid recordings of his orchestral and chamber works have revealed Parry—in philosophical and musicological terms—to be a far more complex character than his image suggests.

I Was Glad was commissioned by Westminster Abbey's organist, Frederick Bridge, for Edward VII's coronation in 1902; the music was played during the royal procession up the nave, with interpolated cries of "Vivat!" from scholars of Westminster School. Parry later added an orchestral introduction and more brass, and the anthem became an indispensable part of British coronations.

This atmospheric, digitally remastered 1977 recording, made in the famously reverberant Chapel of King's College, Cambridge, is imbued with regal brilliance. The young voices of the large chorus give accuracy and weight to the choral writing, the King's boys floating above with their characteristically ethereal yet sharply focused sound in the semichoruses. The Band of the Royal Military School of Music edges this performance in front of all others with the kind of blazing brass contribution that sets the spine tingling from start to finish. The current reissue—To Their Majesties—couples the anthem with similarly thrilling and sympathetic performances of Elgar's *The Spirit of England* and *Coronation Ode*, in which the soprano Felicity Lott will melt your heart. **GK**

> *"Amid all the outpourings of modern English music, the work of Parry remains supreme."*

Vaughan Williams

Other Recommended Recordings

I Was Glad, Blest Pair of Sirens, Jerusalem
Choir of Winchester Cathedral, Waynflete Singers
David Hill • Decca 470 378-2
Stately performance of I Was Glad

Symphonies nos. 1–5, Symphonic Variations
London Philharmonic • Matthias Bamert
Chandos CHAN 9120-22 (3 CDs)
Pioneering symphonies are inspired by Schumann

Job
Guildford Choral Society, Royal Philharmonic Orchestra
Hilary Davan Wetton • Hyperion CDA 67025
Job *broke free from British nineteenth-century oratorio*

King Edward VII, pictured at the time of his coronation in 1902. ➔

Jean Sibelius
Symphony no. 2 (1902)

Genre | Orchestral
Conductor | Thomas Beecham
Performers | BBC Symphony Orchestra
Year recorded | 1954
Label | BBC Legends BBCL 4154-2

Eugen d'Albert
Tiefland (1903)

Genre | Opera
Conductor/Performers | Bertrand de
Billy; Lisa Gasteen, Johan Botha
Year recorded | 2003
Label | Oehms OC 312 (2 CDs)

Interpreted by many of Sibelius's contemporaries as a "liberation" symphony, a national call to arms, Sibelius's Second has also won critical praise for its Beethovenian blend of formal compression and oratorical power. In purely biographical terms, it transmutes into gold a personal crisis, arising from the death of a daughter and the suicide of a sister-in-law, during which the composer temporarily abandoned his family and fled to Italy. The score's ultimate, musical affirmation is hard-won but unequivocal and perhaps this is why, in today's more cynical world, it appears to be giving way to the Fifth as the Sibelius symphony most often played. Certainly, few contemporary performers have the measure of its blazing rhetoric as completely as Thomas Beecham in this live relay from London's Royal Festival Hall on the occasion of the composer's eighty-ninth birthday.

Some readers—a small minority no doubt—will think of Beecham as the archetypal English dilettante and blink incredulously at the easy ride he has had from critics. And yet, working away from his hand-picked, softer-grained Royal Philharmonic Orchestra, he turns in a reading of astonishing fervor, combining a degree of Romantic freedom with an impregnable sense of where the music is going. The occasional rough edge as he harries his players with an early downbeat is part and parcel of a unique, altogether thrilling experience. Only three factors might conceivably grate: the raw tone of the BBC Symphony Orchestra at full throttle, the incongruous towpath shouts with which Beecham rallies his players as if still at rehearsal, and the mono sound. **DG**

Eugen d'Albert was one of the more unusual figures in German music. He was born in Glasgow in 1864 of an English mother and an Italian father with a French name, and his German-ness was in some respects a wish fulfillment, though he died (six wives later) a Swiss citizen—in Riga, Latvia, in 1932. He first shot to fame as a virtuoso pianist, with Liszt among his mentors, but his legacy is largely as a composer of operas—twenty-two in all. And not typical Germanic operas at that. *Tiefland* (*The Lowlands*) is the only real example of a German-language opera in the Italian *verismo* mold of *Cavalleria rusticana*. So, an Italian form, Teutonic libretto (with generous nods to Wagner's sound world) and, for good measure, a Spanish setting.

Tiefland plays out a typical *verismo* drama of conflicting passions and rivalries on the slopes of the Pyrenees. Landowner Sebastiano arranges the marriage between one of his shepherds, Pedro, and his own mistress, Marta, ostensibly to put an end to village gossip about him; but his secret determination to maintain his lustful hold over her brings his own downfall.

After a shaky start, *Tiefland* became one of the most popular of German operas. The work later fell somewhat out of fashion, though if it has gained ground again on stage it has never received a truly big-name recording. But of the handful that have been made, the live Viennese concert performance conducted by Bertrand de Billy has the strongest cast—with Lisa Gasteen's sympathetic Marta and an eager Pedro from Johan Botha—and makes the most of d'Albert's bountiful orchestral fabric. **MR**

Maurice Ravel
String Quartet (1903)

Genre | Chamber
Performers | Cleveland Quartet:
Weilerstein, Salaff, Arad, Katz
Year recorded | 1985
Label | Telarc CD-80111

Maurice Ravel was born in Ciboure, a fishing village in the Basque region of southwestern France, in 1875. A few months later, the family moved to Paris. The young Ravel thrived in the culturally sophisticated atmosphere of the French capital. He studied at the Conservatoire with Fauré, and tried desperately to win the prestigious Prix de Rome. His repeated failure to be awarded first prize caused a scandal that brought him to the attention of the music-loving public. It was during these tumultuous years that Ravel's admiration for the music of Debussy reached its acme, and in 1902 he began work on a string quartet, using Debussy's Quartet as his model.

Ravel's debt to Debussy can be discerned in the extraordinary fluidity of the quartet's texture. Yet it is clear, too, that Ravel is not merely a slavish imitator. His astonishing harmonic mastery is reflected by the dramatic fluctuations in the music's emotional temperature, and in terms of sheer melodic appeal it could be argued that Ravel's quartet actually surpasses Debussy's. The initial Allegro moderato begins with a theme that unfolds as a gracious arch; the scherzo that follows suggests the snappy tunefulness of a folk dance; and the slow movement is a rich rhapsody of romantic expressivity. Only in the restless finale does Ravel seem more concerned with motivic development than melodic generosity.

This beautifully engineered Telarc CD is a precious memento of the Cleveland Quartet in its heyday. The ensemble's lustrous sound ravishes the ears, certainly, though it is the affectionate warmth of the interpretation that makes the performance so affecting. **AFC**

John Ireland
Songs (1903–38)

Genre | Vocal
Performers | Lisa Milne, John Mark Ainsley,
Christopher Maltman, Graham Johnson
Years recorded | 1997–98
Label | Hyperion CDA 97261/2 (2 CDs)

It has to be admitted that John Ireland is out of fashion. His subtle blend of the Romantic tradition and the delicate coloring of Impressionism can all too easily seem passé amid the sensations of the twenty-first century. But what gives his best music lasting value is its perfect workmanship, especially in his writing for his own instrument, the piano, and its individual sense of harmony and melody. Many of his pieces also have a strong sense of place: Chelsea, for example, where he lived for many years while teaching at the Royal College of Music; the Channel Islands of Jersey and Guernsey with their dramatic seascapes; or the haunting prehistoric sites of the English West Country.

Ireland was equally responsive to literature. His songs, which he wrote in the first four decades of the twentieth century, catch the moods of a wide range of poets, including Housman, Hardy, and Masefield. His early, uncharacteristically bluff setting of the latter's *Sea Fever* is well known, and it crops up fairly regularly on recital discs, as do a handful of other songs. But you will need Hyperion's generous (though not complete) two-disc survey to explore his song output in all its variety, with the indispensable Graham Johnson bringing the best out of Lisa Milne, John Mark Ainsley and Christopher Maltman.

The booklet quotes the opinion of the critic William Mann that in the history of English music Ireland's songs are "perhaps the most important between Purcell and Britten." Well, maybe: just thinking about the other possible candidates reveals what a galaxy of gifted song composers there was in the first half of the twentieth century. But among them, Ireland's star shines brightly. **AB**

Hugo Alfvén | Swedish Rhapsodies (1903–31)

Genre | Orchestral
Conductor | Petri Sakari
Performers | Iceland Symphony Orchestra
Year recorded | 1993
Label | Chandos CHAN 9313

What Grieg is to the Norwegians, Nielsen is to the Danes, and Sibelius to the Finns, so Hugo Alfvén is to the Swedes. He was the first Swedish composer since Franz Berwald in the first half of the nineteenth century to make an impact both at home and abroad, and emerged as one of Sweden's most distinguished symphonists, a worthy rival to his near-contemporary Wilhelm Stenhammar. He was a prolific composer, with five symphonies and a voluminous body of choral music to his name.

But he is probably best remembered outside his homeland for his three *Swedish Rhapsodies*, in which he combined folk music with a painterly encapsulation of time and place (he had originally wanted to be a painter before turning to music). The first, subtitled "Midsummer Vigil" and composed in 1903, is lighter in mood than much of his music, though it brings a fresh slant on the folk-inspired idioms of Grieg. The second, "Uppsala Rhapsody," from four years later, is a Swedish equivalent to Brahms's *Academic Festival Overture* with which it shares an ebullient use of student songs. The most original of the three, though, is the last, which dates from much later in the composer's career: the "Dalecarlian Rhapsody" from 1931 is a sophisticated portrait of Nordic gloom and melancholy.

The Iceland Symphony Orchestra under its Finnish conductor Petri Sakari brings Alfvén's music to life with more style and passion than any rival recording. As well as vibrant performances of the three *Rhapsodies*—the folk elements come across with particular rhythmic panache— their disc also includes the powerfully descriptive *Legend of the Skerries* and a highly affecting *Elegy*. And the warm, spacious sound is up to Chandos's best standards. **MR**

> *"There awoke within me a longing to attempt a depiction in music of this melancholy scene of nature."*

Hugo Alfvén on the birth of *Swedish Rhapsody no. 3*

Other Recommended Recordings

Symphony no. 2, The Prodigal Son
National Symphony Orchestra of Ireland • Niklas Willén
Naxos 8.555072
Alfvén's breakthrough symphony

Symphony no. 3, Swedish Rhapsody no. 3, Prodigal Son
Stockholm Philharmonic Orchestra • Neeme Järvi
BIS CD-455
Fine instalment in Järvi's cycle of the symphonies

Symphony no. 4, Legend of the Skerries
Stockholm Philharmonic Orchestra • Neeme Järvi
BIS CD-505
Arguably the most distinctive of the five symphonies

Hugo Alfvén painted by Robert Thegerström in 1900. ➔

Maurice Ravel | Shéhérazade (1903)

Genre | Vocal
Performers | Régine Crespin, Suisse Romande Orchestra
Conductor | Ernest Ansermet
Year recorded | 1963
Label | Decca 460 973-2

Ravel was never happier musically than when he was traveling, to Spain for choice, in search of a Boléro or the memory of a dead Infanta. Igor Stravinsky famously described him as a "Swiss watchmaker," probably alluding to the composer's concern for musical detail—Ravel is certainly a supreme orchestrator. In *Shéhérazade*, shimmering with orchestral detail, it is the exotic world of the East that is invoked in the three songs for soloist and orchestra. The singer's hushed cries of "Asie" in the first song is our invitation to a voyage far beyond the everyday, "a wonderful world of fairy tales."

This was the second work that Ravel christened *Shéhérazade*. Earlier he had written an overture with the same name, which having caused something of a scandal was promptly forgotten. Now he chose three poems by Tristan Klingsor, a fellow member of the Apaches, a group of young artists, writers and musicians who met in Paris every Saturday. "Asie," which Ravel originally intended should be heard last, is the first and longest movement. After "La flûte enchantée," which gives the composer ample opportunity to write for his beloved flute, comes "L'indifférent," carrying the emotional weight of the piece, a painful but delicately nuanced yearning for the exotic woman who catches the poet's eye but passes by indifferent to him.

No one has inhabited these songs quite like Régine Crespin and this recording was one of the landmarks of early stereo recording, with the voice resting on the orchestra as if reclining on the softest of pillows. Ansermet relishes Ravel's orchestral detail and Crespin makes the exotic East unbearably poignant in the closing pages of "L'indifférent." **CC**

> *"Music, I feel, must be emotional first and intellectual second."*
>
> Maurice Ravel

Other Recommended Recordings

Anne Sofie von Otter, Cleveland Orchestra
Pierre Boulez
DG 471 614-2
A seductive performance

Susan Graham, BBC Symphony Orchestra
Yan Pascal Tortelier
Warner 2564 61938-2
No one better conveys the melancholy of "L'indifférent"

Victoria de Los Angeles, Paris Conservatoire Concerts
Society Orchestra • Georges Prêtre
EMI 0946 3 45824 2 1
De Los Angeles brings a hushed intensity to this work

Ernest Ansermet, pictured in London in 1959. ➔

Richard Strauss | Symphonia domestica (1903)

Genre | Orchestral
Conductor | Neeme Järvi
Performers | Royal Scottish National Orchestra
Year recorded | 1987
Label | Chandos CHAN 10206X

On the face of it, the premise for Strauss's penultimate tone poem might not seem too promising: the composer's family life together with his wife Pauline and young son Franz, complete with bath time for baby, lovemaking for the parents, and a huge family quarrel. Certainly the 1904 American premiere, with Strauss conducting in New York's Carnegie Hall, gave rise to a certain amount of sensationalism. Yet for all its more outlandish gestures, the *Symphonia domestica* is a marvelous piece of musical construction, deriving all of its symphonic thought from the group of themes Strauss gives to himself, his wife, and his son "Bubi" (depicted by the plaintive tones of the oboe d'amore, an instrument not much heard in the orchestra since the time of Bach).

The scherzo depicting the child at play has a translucency and naive charm that set it alongside another half-naive work written not long before, Mahler's Fourth Symphony, while the Adagio makes an impressive job of building Strauss's depiction of himself at inspired work before the notorious bedroom scene builds to ecstatic heights in a way that is indebted to the example of Wagner's *Tannhäuser*. There is an impressionistic dream sequence, the quarrel is a superbly organized double fugue, and the happy end has real joy in it, as observed by Strauss's friend, the French writer Romain Rolland.

Such a special work needs a very personal affection from the conductor, and Neeme Järvi's performance from his heyday with the Scottish National Orchestra sounds like a labor of love. The more transparent portions of the score are delicately handled, while the riotous finale with its whooping horns goes, for once, at the outrageous fast pace Strauss demands. **DN**

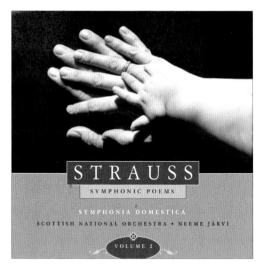

S T R A U S S
SYMPHONIC POEMS
SYMPHONIA DOMESTICA
SCOTTISH NATIONAL ORCHESTRA • NEEME JÄRVI
VOLUME 2

"Papa and Momma and Baby Celebrated in Huge Conglomeration of Orchestral Music."

New York newspaper review of the premiere

Neeme Järvi heads a dynasty of Estonian conductors. ➔

Alexander Zemlinsky | Die Seejungfrau (1903)

Genre | Orchestral
Conductor | Thomas Dausgaard
Performers | Danish National Radio Symphony Orchestra
Year recorded | 1997
Label | Chandos CHAN 9601

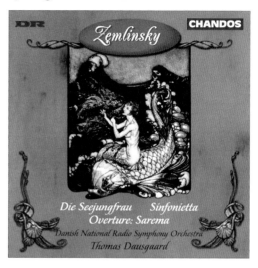

Alexander Zemlinsky started composing his three-movement symphonic poem *Die Seejungfrau* (*The Mermaid*) at a time of emotional upheaval—Alma Schindler, the great love of his life, was about to be married to Mahler. Confiding in his close friend Schoenberg, he suggested that *Die Seejungfrau* was "a preliminary study for my Symphony of Death" and, after completing the score, he wrote, "I feel distraught, cheerless and completely discouraged." Musically, Zemlinsky's decision to embark on a substantial piece for large orchestra was inspired by Strauss's *Ein Heldenleben*, but Zemlinsky's subject, Hans Christian Andersen's touching tale of a mermaid's unfulfilled love, is far more appealing than Strauss's egotistical program. Schoenberg was also tackling a large score, his *Pelleas und Melisande*, and the two works received their premieres at the same concert on January 25, 1905.

In fact, the works were scheduled by a Viennese musical society specially formed by Zemlinsky and Schoenberg for the promotion of contemporary music. *Die Seejungfrau* was well received, with the critics praising Zemlinsky's rich harmonies, passionate climaxes, and diaphanous orchestration, but the composer himself appeared to lose interest in the work and few further performances were given in his lifetime. Zemlinsky later gave the manuscript of the first movement to his friend Marie Pappenheim and it was not until the 1980s that researchers realized that this completed the two-movement score found in the composer's posthumous papers.

Among the several recommendable recordings of Zemlinsky's attractive score, the version by Thomas Dausgaard stands out for its languorous, languishing phrases and finely nuanced rubato. **DC**

> *"A seismographic capacity to respond to all the temptations with which he allowed himself to be inundated."*
>
> Theodor Adorno, on Zemlinsky

Other Recommended Recordings

Berlin Radio Symphony Orchestra
Riccardo Chailly
Decca 444 969-2
A former benchmark recording

SWF Baden-Baden Symphony Orchestra
Zoltan Pesko
Wergo WER 6209-2
Includes the excellent Sinfonische Gesänge, op. 20

Czech Philharmonic Orchestra
Antony Beaumont
Chandos CHAN 10138
Fine orchestral playing, but uninteresting coupling

Alexander Zemlinsky was a linchpin of Viennese musical life. ➔

Arnold Schoenberg
Pelleas und Melisande (1903)

Genre | Orchestral
Conductor/Performers | Herbert von
Karajan; Berlin Philharmonic Orchestra
Year recorded | 1974
Label | DG 457 721-2

Alexander Glazunov | Violin
Concerto in A minor (1904)

Genre | Concerto
Performer | Nathan Milstein
Conductor | William Steinberg
Year recorded | 1957
Label | EMI 5 58035 0

Maeterlinck's drama *Pelleas und Melisande* is a love triangle reduced to its essence and played out in a misty world of enigmatic legend. Golaud, the king's son, finds the beautiful waif Melisande wandering in the forest and takes her back to his castle by the sea, where her silence and unresponsiveness torment and obsess him. She falls in love with his younger brother Pelleas, arousing Golaud's murderous jealousy; he kills Pelleas, and Melisande dies of grief. Richard Strauss suggested that Schoenberg should write an opera on it, but Schoenberg boldly decided to use the play as the basis of a symphonic poem, which grew into his most "ultra-Romantic" orchestral utterance, on a par with Strauss's own symphonic poems.

Its single huge movement subsumes the characteristics of a four-movement symphony, plus introduction and epilogue. The smoldering, crepuscular atmosphere of the piece is highly individual, and its range of texture is astonishing. The instrumental invention includes some hitherto unprecedented effects, such as the sinister glissandos in the trombones, depicting the scene between Golaud and Pelleas in the castle vaults. The implicit one-movement symphony is articulated by the three main characters, characterized not by Wagnerian leitmotifs but by individual themes, all of which undergo development and variation in the course of the work, creating a soaring and tragic love-music in the work's second half.

Karajan's astonishing reading has an opulence and passion that surpasses all others. His shaping of the various sections is utterly convincing and the performance grows in power throughout—an overwhelming experience. **MM**

In the days when soloists played two or even three pieces in the same orchestral concert, Glazunov's A minor Violin Concerto rode high. But with a duration of twenty minutes or less, this delightful concerto does less well in today's stereotyped concert programs. Fortunately violinists are still lining up to record it. It is one of those blessed works that get better as they go along: Having enjoyed the first two marvelously concise movements, one still has the jaunty finale, with its memorable trumpet tune, to come.

Born in 1904, the year the concerto was completed, Nathan Milstein had claims to be the composer's favorite soloist in this work. He was still a boy when he first played it under Glazunov's direction in 1915, and he last performed it with the composer in 1925, just before leaving Russia for the West. Milstein recorded the concerto three times, twice with the same conductor, Steinberg, and it is his middle version that has the best combination of performance and sound quality. Milstein has the poise, tonal finish, and rhythmic flair to make the most of the piece and his interpretation is virtually definitive.

Of course, Jascha Heifetz has his supporters in this work. He too plays with admirable balance and tone, although the total effect may be too sweet for some tastes. Among a good crop of modern recordings, the one by Frank Peter Zimmermann is the best all round, presenting a more classical view of the piece, although those who like Maxim Vengerov's rather stagy style will enjoy his heart-on-sleeve interpretation. Violin fanciers may also like to look for an old Russian recording featuring David Oistrakh with the great conductor Kirill Kondrashin. **TP**

Leoš Janáček
Jenůfa (1904)

Genre | Opera
Conductor/Performer | Charles Mackerras; Elisabeth Söderström
Year recorded | 1982
Label | Decca 475 8227 (2 CDs)

Jenůfa was Janáček's third opera and first of the succession of operatic masterpieces that has secured his reputation as one of the twentieth century's most significant opera composers. Although *Jenůfa* was premiered in the Moravian capital, Brno, in 1904, it was not performed in Prague until 1916. The great success of the Prague premiere proved a major boost to Janáček's self-confidence as a composer and helped initiate his hugely productive final twelve years.

Jenůfa's uncomfortable subject matter involves illegitimacy, jealous love, betrayal and infanticide in a Moravian village, but the force of Janáček's music turns it from shocking melodrama into one of the most moving operas in the Czech repertoire. The two central female roles, Jenůfa and her guardian the Kostelnička, are magnificently drawn. The musical tensions—notably at the start of the opera as Jenůfa waits anxiously for news of Števa, her unborn baby's father, and at the end of the second act—are acute, but the end, in which Jenůfa accepts the love of the faithful Laca, is among the most cathartic in twentieth-century opera. Although written over ten years, the closing stages of the opera's composition acquired great emotional force as they coincided with the death of Janáček's beloved daughter Olga.

Charles Mackerras's 1982 version set new standards for recordings of Janáček operas. This was the first recording to return to the composer's pre-Prague score in which none of the jagged edges have been smoothed over. Beyond textual considerations, this superb ensemble performance has an intensity which remains unrivaled even after twenty years. **JS**

Anatoly Lyadov
Fairytales (1904–09)

Genre | Orchestral
Conductor | Vassily Sinaisky
Performers | BBC Philharmonic
Year recorded | 2000
Label | Chandos CHAN 9911

Anatoly Lyadov (1855–1914), with Taneyev, was one of the links between the nineteenth-century world of Tchaikovsky and the later generations of Stravinsky and Prokofiev (who was a pupil). Russian composers had various reasons for not writing as much as they could have done—Mussorgsky's drunkenness and Borodin's work as a research chemist come to mind. Lyadov's excuse was sheer indolence. He was expelled from Rimsky-Korsakov's class at the St. Petersburg Conservatoire for not bothering to turn up for lessons and gave Stravinsky his big break with *The Firebird* when he dithered too long in accepting Diaghilev's commission for the ballet. His output is thus small, but refined: mostly orchestral and piano miniatures.

Like Rimsky, he had a predilection for exoticism and his orchestral masterpieces—the three musical fairytales he composed between 1904 and 1909—are, with Stravinsky's roughly contemporary *Firebird*, very much the pinnacle of that particularly Russian strand of musical colorism. The "Picture from a Russian Folktale" *Baba-Yaga* (1904) vividly depicts the ugly gnome who gets about in a pestle and mortar (and whose "Hut on Hen's Legs" also features in Mussorgsky's *Pictures at an Exhibition*); the "Fairytale Picture" *The Enchanted Lake* (1909) is an evocative impression that seems to combine elements of Debussy with Scriabin; and *Kikimora* (also 1909) conjures up another mischievous goblin.

Vassily Sinaisky's recordings of these three miniatures are wonderfully vivid and the colors of the composer's orchestration and the music's rhythmic impetus come across with real panache. **MR**

Ferruccio Busoni | Piano Concerto (1904)

Genre | Concerto
Performers/Conductor | Marc-André Hamelin, City of
Birmingham Symphony Orchestra & Men's Chorus; Mark Elder
Year recorded | 1999
Label | Hyperion CDA 67143

Imagine taking one of Brahms's hardly small-scale piano concertos, adding on a couple of movements and introducing a male-voice chorus. That is exactly what the Italian composer Ferruccio Busoni did in his epic Piano Concerto, which runs for some seventy-five minutes. If that sounds rather too much of a good thing, think of it in terms of a Brucknerian dialogue and you will get the picture. It may be the ultimate Romantic concerto in terms of duration, but it has a strong Neo-Classical strain in its content, and Busoni himself saw it as a symphony with piano obbligato.

The opening has a quiet grandeur to it, a broadly conceived melody on strings that builds into a great dramatic argument, in which the piano participates with strongly etched chords when it finally enters, some four minutes later. The second movement, "Pezzo giocoso," is a devilish dance that dazzles and seduces. The "Pezzo serioso" that follows, a substantial movement in three sections with introduction, is by turns bleak, heartrending, and consoling. The tarantella fourth movement, "All'Italiana," makes explicit Busoni's roots and is shot through with Mediterranean warmth and a Rossinian sense of mischief, culminating in a dramatic piano cadenza. With the "Cantico" comes a return to a mood of solemnity, and the chorus sets the seal on this extraordinary work with a mystic hymn by the Danish poet Adam Oehlenschläger.

Among contemporary pianists, Marc-André Hamelin—a super-virtuoso if ever there was one—is unrivaled in his understanding and for the way he seems utterly to have got into Busoni's mind-set. Mark Elder paces the work ideally, and coaxes exceptionally fine playing from his Birmingham forces. It is a glorious achievement with one of the pinnacles of the concerto repertoire. **HS**

> *"He pays his listener the compliment of assuming that he is discerning."*
>
> Ronald Stevenson, on Busoni

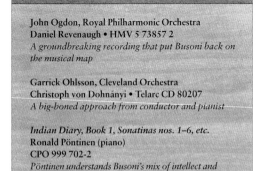

Other Recommended Recordings

John Ogdon, Royal Philharmonic Orchestra
Daniel Revenaugh • HMV 5 73857 2
A groundbreaking recording that put Busoni back on the musical map

Garrick Ohlsson, Cleveland Orchestra
Christoph von Dohnányi • Telarc CD 80207
A big-boned approach from conductor and pianist

Indian Diary, Book 1, Sonatinas nos. 1–6, etc.
Ronald Pöntinen (piano)
CPO 999 702-2
Pöntinen understands Busoni's mix of intellect and virtuosity, while his playing has subtlety and imagination

Ferruccio Busoni, pictured here in the 1890s, was lionized as a pianist. ➔

Gustav Mahler
Kindertotenlieder (1904)

Genre | Vocal
Conductor | Leonard Bernstein
Performers | Janet Baker, Israel Philharmonic Orchestra
Year recorded | 1974
Label | Sony SMK 61837 (2 CDs)

Three of Mahler's five songs set to poems from Rückert's *Kindertotenlieder* (*Songs on the Death of Children*) were written in 1901, and two more followed in 1904. Rückert's poems were a response to the death of two of his own children, but when Mahler composed these songs he was just beginning a family of his own, and the psychological reasons for his attraction to this theme have been a subject of much debate. The fact that his eldest daughter, Maria, died in the summer of 1907 before reaching five years of age ultimately exposed Mahler to the grief so eloquently portrayed in this music, composed originally with piano accompaniment but then inventively orchestrated. The relatively restrained and resigned nature of Mahler's setting undoubtedly stems from his understanding, derived from symbolism, that both life and death are stages in a process of eternal renewal.

In music as emotionally fraught as *Kindertotenlieder*, every listener will place the line separating a bland or aloof performance from an excessively sentimental one at a different spot. In at least this listener's experience, Janet Baker's live performance with Leonard Bernstein and the Israel Philharmonic maximizes the expressive potential of this music without becoming heavy-handed or mawkish; these two great musicians are both vivid communicators but also have grasped the dignity, tenderness, and restraint that gives *Kindertotenlieder* its special magic. After an opening phrase in which orchestra and soloist take a moment to reach interpretive rapprochement, the cathartic depths of this music come alive as in no other version. **DB**

Gustav Mahler
Symphony no. 6 (1904)

Genre | Orchestral
Conductor | Klaus Tennstedt
Performers | London Philharmonic Orchestra
Year recorded | 1983
Label | EMI 7243 5 72941 2 6 (11 CDs)

Completed in 1904, Mahler's Sixth Symphony is the severest of his works, both in the regularity of its structure and in its tragic mood. It begins by evoking a determined confrontation with fate, and although the first movement ends in apparent triumph, the extraordinary finale reverses this good fortune with three crushing hammerblows. An abbreviated kernel of this catastrophe can be found in the A major chord that turns to A minor, a motif heard just as the opening theme of the first movement reaches its conclusion and often thereafter. Mahler himself debated the correct order of the middle movements, but there are good reasons for preferring the original ordering in which the grim scherzo precedes the tender but despairing andante. The ultimate mood of this symphony is bleak and chilling in its depiction of an unsuccessful struggle against dark, impersonal, and ultimately triumphant forces; Mahler's wife Alma called it his most completely personal work.

Klaus Tennstedt's Mahler was imbued with a sense of life-or-death desperation that was particularly apt for the Sixth. His studio performance with the LPO is less than ideal in both playing and recording, but these potential shortcomings become virtues by enhancing the gritty, indomitable character of the performance. The first movement begins with an exemplary combination of weight and momentum, and ends with hallucinatory excitement. The finale is the other great glory of this performance: never has the introduction sounded more harrowingly doom-laden, and the battles of the protagonist are the more vivid because Tennstedt allows tension to ebb and flow rather than being incessantly driven. **DB**

Alexander Scriabin
Symphony no. 3 (1904)

Genre | Orchestral
Conductor | Mikhail Pletnev
Performers | Russian National Orchestra
Year recorded | 1998
Label | DG 459 681-2

The advance in Scriabin's writing for orchestra lagged behind that for the piano, in which, by the early twentieth century, he was fast becoming something of a modernist. But after a piano concerto (1896) and two interesting but not overly original symphonies (1900 and 1901), he achieved a personal landmark with his Third Symphony.

It is perhaps no coincidence that its composition followed Scriabin's discovery of the theosophical ideas of Madame Blavatsky, which, together with his reading of Nietzsche, led him to believe it was his destiny to take humankind on to a higher plane through his art. The symphony, which he subtitled "The Divine Poem," would be "the first proclamation of my new doctrine," he wrote. Although it is fairly traditional in its three-movement form and is written for large orchestra, he achieves a highly fluid sense of motion, of emotional ebb and flow, through the manipulation of contrasting motifs, and he treats his vast forces with as much delicacy as power.

The work is held together by an imposing motto theme, marked "divine, grandiose." But the movements each convey a different mood: a striving opening essay subtitled "Luttes" ("Struggles"), a central "Voluptés" ("Delights") colored by birdsong, and energy swathed in heavenly joy for the finale, "Jeu Divin."

The work has only recently come into fashion, with a fair number of new recordings over the past couple of decades. By far the most rounded is Mikhail Pletnev's: it is weightily Russian, but his handpicked orchestra also revels in the composer's array of timbres and finds a real transparency in the voluptuous central movement. **MR**

Charles Villiers Stanford
Songs of the Sea (1904)

Genre | Vocal
Conductor | Richard Hickox
Performers | Gerald Finley, BBC National Chorus of Wales
Year recorded | 2005
Label | Chandos CHSA 5043 (SACD)

Until recently, Charles Villiers Stanford has had to suffer that awful label of "precursor." He and Hubert Parry were seen as twin prophets of an English Renaissance that really got under way only with Elgar, and then Vaughan Williams and his folksong-hunting contemporaries. It is true that Stanford was an influential teacher, at the Royal College of Music in London, with pupils including Vaughan Williams and also Holst, Bridge, Bliss, and Howells. But a spate of recordings in recent years has revealed the quality of his own music, chiefly influenced by Brahms and Dvořák, but with touches of color from his native Ireland, and all produced at high speed with the utmost professionalism. The result has been quite a Stanford revival—though the Church of England could justifiably claim that his fine anthems and service music have never been forgotten.

Also never entirely forgotten, Stanford's *Songs of the Sea* are settings of poems by Henry Newbolt drawing on Britain's glorious naval past, but implicitly reflecting the tense international situation of his own time. Typical is the first song, inspired by the legend that the Elizabethan hero Francis Drake is not dead, but only sleeping "till the great Armada's come." There's some rip-roaring, tub-thumping stuff—the last song, "The Old Superb," has a refrain that will have you joining in by the end—but it is offset by more thoughtful numbers such as the lovely "Homeward Bound." Gerald Finley and Richard Hickox with BBC Welsh forces catch the various moods superbly, on a disc which also includes Newbolt's and Stanford's follow-up, *Songs of the Fleet*, and an earlier nautical piece, the choral ballad on Tennyson's *The Revenge*. **AB**

Giacomo Puccini | Madama Butterfly (1904)

Genre | Opera
Conductor/Performers | Herbert von Karajan;
Mirella Freni, Luciano Pavarotti, Christa Ludwig
Year recorded | 1974
Label | Decca 417 577-2 (2 CDs)

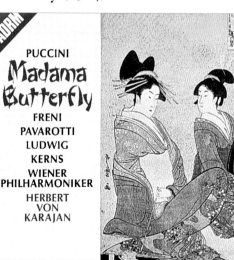

According to the impresario David Belasco, Puccini rushed backstage in tears after seeing a performance of the play *Madame Butterfly* in London in 1900, demanding to buy the operatic rights. Apparently the composer, who scarcely understood a word of English, had found another heroine who moved him to music. Another of his "little women" to be punished to death.

Yet the first performance of Puccini's *Butterfly* in February 1904 was a fiasco. Rosina Storchio, the first Cio Cio San, was having an affair with the conductor Arturo Toscanini and when her kimono blew open someone in audience shouted that she was pregnant. "And the child is Toscanini's," came the cry from another part of the house.

The press were equally unforgiving. Puccini called it a "lynching" and insisted that the work be withdrawn, returning his 20,000 lire fee to his publisher as he began to revise the work. Three acts were compressed into two; local color was cut from Act 1. Pinkerton became less of a lout and more a silver-tongued operatic hero when Puccini wrote a brand new Act 2 aria, "Addio fiorito asil," for the character. *Butterfly* was reborn as one of the most popular works in the repertoire.

The part of Cio Cio San makes enormous demands on a singer. Mirella Freni is magnificent, moving effortlessly from artless teenage girl to a mature woman. Others may have produced a richer, riper sound, but few singers have inhabited Cio Cio San so affectingly. Pavarotti is a sympathetic Pinkerton and in his vocal prime on this recording. Christa Ludwig is a peerless Suzuki, but it is Karajan's interpretation that gives this recording its edge over all comers to date. Tender, but never sentimental; dramatic but never theatrical. **CC**

> *"There is no comparison between my love for Mimì, Musetta, Manon and Tosca and that . . . for [Butterfly]"*
>
> Giacomo Puccini

Other Recommended Recordings

Rome Opera Chorus & Orchestra
Gianandrea Gavazzeni
Testament SBT 2168 (2 CDs)
Mono, but Victoria de los Angeles's Butterfly will break your heart

Accademia di Santa Cecilia Chorus & Orchestra
Alberto Erede
Decca 440 230-2 (2 CDs)
Renata Tebaldi is a sumptuously voiced Cio Cio San

Philharmonia Orchestra • Yves Abel
Chandos CHAN 3070(2) (2 CDs)
For those who prefer their Puccini in English

Giacomo Puccini photographed for an unidentified magazine, c. 1905.

Jean Sibelius | Violin Concerto (1905)

Genre | Concerto
Performers/Conductor | Viktoria Mullova (violin), Boston
Symphony Orchestra; Seiji Ozawa;
Year recorded | 1985
Label | Philips 464 741-2

In writing a concerto for his own instrument, Sibelius
was torn between the desire to provide a vehicle for the
virtuoso he himself might have been and his overriding
compositional drive for formal clarity and cohesion. It did
not help that he was spending far too much time in the
Helsinki drinking dens from which he had to be rescued
by his long-suffering wife, Aino. The miracle is that the
concerto, its final form achieved only after a long struggle,
has proved to be one of his greatest successes. The first
performance of the tauter revised version took place in
Berlin with Karel Halíř as soloist and Richard Strauss, no less,
conducting. Bristling with technical challenges of the kind
that players enjoy overcoming (and music critics affect
to despise) it is now firmly established as the twentieth
century's most recorded concerto.

That said, few executants of recent years have made it
so convincingly their own as Viktoria Mullova, whose heroic
objectivity, powerful technique and huge dynamic range
suit it down to the ground. In her first commercial release
following a headline-grabbing defection to the West
while on a tour of Finland in 1983, she gives the music a
steely toughness to unite its disparate elements, relating
the material more plainly to the later Sibelius than its
orthodox Romantic rhetoric might suggest. At the same
time, while she purges the relatively soft-core slow
movement of sentimental inflation, its glorious main
melody is in no way undersold. The clarity of Mullova's
articulation in the finale is just as phenomenal as her lyrical
playing, her bravura the more compelling when the violin
is forwardly balanced by the sound engineers to give it a
firm, realistic presence. It goes without saying that her
intonation is flawless. **DG**

> ## "[The finale is] evidently a polonaise for polar bears."

**Donald Francis Tovey, on Sibelius's Violin Concerto
in *Essays in Musical Analysis***

Other Recommended Recordings

**Ginette Neveu, Philharmonia Orchestra
Walter Susskind • Dutton CDBP 9733**
*Neveu's celebrated account is a wonderful souvenir
of an artist who died tragically young*

**Jascha Heifetz, Chicago Symphony Orchestra
Walter Hendl • RCA 82876 66372 2**
*Heifetz makes the concerto sound almost too easy but
his unique tone is well projected in this stereo remake*

**David Oistrakh, Moscow Philharmonic Orchestra/
Gennady Rozhdestvensky • Brilliant 92609 (10 CDs)**
*Oistrakh's dark-hued account under Rozhdestvensky
has the greatest emotional intensity of all his recordings*

Viktoria Mullova, one of today's most perceptive violinists. ➲

Maurice Ravel
Introduction and Allegro (1905)

Genre | Chamber
Performers | Osian Ellis (harp),
Melos Ensemble
Year recorded | 1962
Label | Decca 421 154-2

Ravel was not only a great composer but a master craftsman, too. The intricate detail and highly polished finish that is perceptible in all of his music suggests that he labored painstakingly over every measure. There is little doubt that Ravel did indeed work methodically, but it may also be true that his technical skill was innate and yet another facet of his genius. One of his most gemlike pieces backs up this assumption: The *Introduction and Allegro* was composed in a mere eight days.

It was, in fact, Ravel's first important commission and came from the instrument maker Erard as part of an effort to expand the repertoire for their double-action pedal harp. Ravel was eager to fulfill the commission, but he had also been invited for a long cruise on a luxury yacht, and was determined not to pass that up. One would never guess that the work was composed in haste: It is a perfectly proportioned concerto-in-miniature, complete with a cadenza. The small instrumental ensemble allows the harp to play complex, delicate music without being overwhelmed. All the musical material is developed from the themes presented in the first few seconds, yet the effect is not so much of clever motivic development as of an unending stream of melody.

Harpists adore this work, and it has been recorded frequently. It is far from straightforward, however, and requires rhythmic suppleness, restrained ardor, and a featherlight touch from all seven players. Osian Ellis and the Melos Ensemble provide all those qualities in spades, and Decca's recording captures their interpretation in warm, clear sound. **AFC**

Maurice Ravel
Miroirs (1905)

Genre | Instrumental
Instrument | Piano
Performer | Jean-Efflam Bavouzet
Year recorded | 2003
Label | MDG 604 1190-2

Because he was born some thirteen years after Debussy, it is commonly assumed that Ravel followed in the elder composer's footsteps. Ravel did learn a great deal from Debussy, but their musical relationship was, in fact, reciprocal. It was Ravel's *Jeux d'eau* (1901) that paved the way for much of Debussy's greatest contributions to the piano literature, for example. And with the five pieces of *Miroirs*, Ravel expanded the vocabulary even further.

As its title suggests, *Miroirs* is a series of images reflected through the composer's artistic personality. "Noctuelles" ("Night Moths") flits and flutters in a way that is at once indirect yet sharply focused. Ravel said "Oiseaux tristes" ("Sad Birds") was meant to evoke "birds lost in the torpor of a somber forest during the most torrid hours of a summer's day." And its restless harmonies do indeed create an uneasy, gorgeously oppressive atmosphere. The humid air is swept away by the bracingly cool breeze of "Une barque sur l'ocean" ("A Boat on the Ocean"), in which the sparkling, fluid piano writing Ravel explored in *Jeux d'eau* is made even more vividly pictorial and emotionally suggestive. "Alborada del gracioso" ("The Jester's Morning Song")—the most popular section of *Miroirs*—conjures Spain with strumming guitars, clicking castanets, and uninhibited melodic sensuality. The final piece, "La vallée des cloches" ("The Valley of the Bells") was reportedly inspired by the noontime ringing of Parisian church bells.

Jean-Efflam Bavouzet is a superb colorist. He paints "Noctuelles" in shades of pale, pearlescent white, and reveals the various textures of "Une barque sur l'ocean"— from liquid to foam to mist—in exquisite detail. **AFC**

Claude Debussy
La mer (1905)

Genre | Orchestral
Conductor | Pierre Boulez
Performers | Cleveland Orchestra
Year recorded | 1991
Label | DG 439 896-2

La mer is one of the most played French orchestral works of all time. But part of the inspiration behind it was distinctly un-French: a famous print by the Japanese artist Katsushika Hokusai—*The Great Wave off Kanagawa*—which Debussy used as the frontispiece in the first edition of the score. He began the work in 1903 in inland France, in Burgundy, with only his memories of the sea, describing them as "... worth more than a reality, which, charming as it may be, tends to weigh too heavily on the imagination."

The same year as he started *La mer*, he left his wife to live with Emma Bardac, and their child was born only a fortnight after its premiere. So the turbulence that is never far from the surface of the music is not only that of the wind and waves, but has an almost erotic tension. The first movement gradually increases in pace as it traces the course of "Dawn to Midday on the Sea"—Erik Satie naughtily said that he particularly liked the part at eleven-fifteen—and includes a magnificent passage for sixteen cellos. "Play of the Waves" is a glittering scherzo, and the final "Dialogue between the Wind and the Sea" paints a picture of the blues, grays and whites of scudding clouds and a restless sea.

Debussy hated being called an Impressionist, and if there is a counterpart to his music in visual art, it is much closer to pointillism: each muted trumpet note, each flurry in the flutes, each stroke of percussion, is like a tiny dot, all of which have to be exactly colored and in focus. And it is that precision, which Pierre Boulez conjures from one of America's premier orchestras, that makes this version of *La mer* so thrilling. **MC**

Gustav Mahler
Symphony no. 7 (1905)

Genre | Orchestral
Conductor | Michael Tilson Thomas
Performers | San Francisco Symphony
Year recorded | 2005
Label | SF Symphony 821936-0009-2

Written in 1904–05, Mahler's Seventh has long been his least understood work. It is in five movements. The second and fourth are called *Nachtmusik* (*Night music*); their largely comfortable yet haunting, evocative tone is at least tangentially related to the spooky playfulness of the scherzo placed between them. The first movement is another story, a large-scale sonata form movement bristling with harmonic, rhythmic, textural, and structural complexities. Its companion bookend, the finale, can be recognized to anticipate postmodernism, since the grand, triumphant C major spirit with which it begins is undercut by a bewildering jumble of musical styles ranging from rococo elegance to pretentious posturing, mixing in madcap capers and country dances along the way. This brilliantly orchestrated symphony remains endlessly fascinating.

Given its complex, internally contradictory nature, no definitive performance of Mahler's Seventh is possible—largely unsatisfying performances can achieve useful insights, and the best accounts cannot avoid missing points worth making. Michael Tilson Thomas's second recording, however, is unquestionably the most detailed and perceptive interpretation of the work ever recorded. In passage after passage, Tilson Thomas and the San Francisco Symphony bring the implications of the score to stimulating and convincing life. This is primarily true in the scherzo and the finale, where flexibility and unexpected juxtapositions demand resourceful and imaginative interpretation, but throughout one listens with the awe and delight one experiences upon witnessing a witty riposte to a perplexing conundrum. **DB**

Franz Lehár
The Merry Widow (1905)

Genre | Opera
Conductor/Performer | Lovro von Matačić; Elisabeth Schwarzkopf
Year recorded | 1962
Label | EMI 5 67370 2 (2 CDs)

The most successful operettas of Franz Lehár (1870–1948) seemed more Viennese than Vienna itself. It was the huge success of his waltz *Gold and Silver* (1902) that encouraged him to make a career in the theater. And two years later he wrote a masterpiece, one of the most perfect and the most popular of all operettas. Within weeks of its premiere at the Theater an der Wien in December 1905, all Vienna had clasped the widow to their bosoms, Europe followed their lead and a year later *Die lustige Witwe* had crossed the Atlantic where *Merry Widow* hats were all the rage.

The Merry Widow enjoys the best of both worlds—France and the Habsburg Balkans. It is set in Paris but the drama is played out in the Pontevedrian Embassy and Hannah Glawari's distinctly Habsburg home. Hannah, the richest woman in Pontevedro thanks to her late husband, must not be allowed to marry a foreigner and take her fortune out of the country. Count Danilo is the ambassador Baron Zeta's choice of husband for her but it takes three acts, a pair of parties and heavy flirting between Valencienne, the ambassador's wife and her admirer Camille before the widow is ready to become a wife. Only the stoniest of hearts could have remained unmoved by the celebrated ballad of "Vilja" or the sumptuous waltz that weaves its way through the third act.

Elizabeth Schwarzkopf was born to be Hannah Glawari and Walter Legge, her producer and husband, created a matchless showcase for her gifts in this classic recording. Eberhard Waechter is a stylish Danilo and Nicolai Gedda excels as Camille. Lovro von Matačić uncorks a bubbling performance from the Philharmonia Orchestra. **CC**

Frederick Delius
A Mass of Life (1905)

Genre | Choral
Conductor/Performers | Richard Hickox; Bournemouth SO and Chorus
Year recorded | 1996
Label | Chandos CHAN 9515(2) (2 CDs)

The designation of "English composer" has never sat very comfortably on Delius. Born in the north of England to an immigrant German family, he studied in Germany, lived a bohemian life in Paris for a few years, and then settled in rural France. So he is probably best viewed not as a compatriot of Elgar and Vaughan Williams but alongside Debussy, Richard Strauss, and Mahler. And it is Mahlerian comparisons that spring to mind for his magnum opus, *A Mass of Life*—or, since its texts from Friedrich Nietzsche's *Also sprach Zarathustra* are set in the original German, *Eine Messe des Lebens*. It is a huge piece lasting more than ninety minutes, scored for four soloists, double chorus and large orchestra —a visionary celebration of the richness of life and love enjoyed by those who can free themselves from the restrictions of organized religion, and the fear of death.

Richard Hickox's recording with the Bournemouth Symphony Orchestra and Chorus is the only stereo version in the current catalogue, but it is hard to imagine a rival that could outclass it. It is sung in German, with Peter Coleman-Wright sounding suitably Wagnerian at times in the central role of the prophet Zarathustra, leading an excellent solo quartet with Joan Rodgers, Jean Rigby, and Nigel Robson. The orchestra and choirs, including the Waynflete Singers, encompass the work's full range of expression, from calm amorous intimacy to earthshaking exultation. The value of the set is enhanced by the inclusion of the 1916 Requiem, which despite its liturgical title is an even more hard-line expression of Delius's atheism, ending with an unforgettable description of the eternal rotation of the seasons. **AB**

Jean Sibelius | Pelléas et Mélisande Suite (1905)

Genre | Orchestral
Conductor/Performers | Herbert von Karajan; Berlin Philharmonic Orchestra
Year recorded | 1982
Label | DG 410 026-2

Maurice Maeterlinck's *Pelléas et Mélisande* enjoyed a considerable vogue a hundred years ago. Fauré's incidental music was composed in 1897, Debussy's opera was unveiled in 1902, and Schoenberg had already embarked on his symphonic poem when Sibelius was himself commissioned to provide music for Swedish-language performances in Helsinki. Eschewing Debussy's poignant reticence, Sibelius concluded his score with a passionate depiction of "The death of Mélisande." A noted exponent of the role, Harriet Bosse (briefly Mrs. August Strindberg) recalled being "so moved that I cried at every performance." Similarly demonstrative is the opening scene, "At the Castle Gate," officially a depiction of the opening of the main gate at King Arkel's castle. For BBC, audiences its deployment as the signature tune for the long-running program, *The Sky at Night*, made explicit its wider resonances as a piece of nature painting.

The scene is drenched in saturated string tone by Herbert von Karajan and the Berlin Philharmonic, plainly relishing the cosmic grandeur of Sibelius's invention in their celebrated early digital recording. The conductor elicits a tremendous sunriselike climax here. And, with his special ear for sonority, he also makes much of the third number, "At the Seashore," an eerie, growling, nonmelodic piece evoking the surging undercurrents of the ocean. Less predictably perhaps, Karajan realizes the delicate poetry of the smaller miniatures, weaving them into a luminous art-nouveau backcloth of blues and grays. The results are unforgettable, a showcase for the superb polish and poise of an orchestra at its peak. **DG**

Richard Strauss Salome (1905)

Genre | Opera
Conductor/Performers | Giuseppe Sinopoli; Cheryl Studer, Bryn Terfel
Year recorded | 1990
Label | DG 431 810-2 (2 CDs)

The chapter dedicated to *Salome* and *Elektra* in Norman Del Mar's study of Richard Strauss is titled "The Stage Tone Poems." Indeed, both works are through-composed in one 100-minute continuous stretch, and their scores are closely knit tapestries of semantically charged motifs.

Strauss set Oscar Wilde's scandalous play in the German translation by Hedwig Lachmann, after cutting its verbosity by about one third. Just as the play had at first been forbidden, the opera met with great opposition from religious authorities; in New York in 1907, it survived just one performance, and it only reached Catholic Vienna in 1918. The story tells of the sexual awakening of the sixteen-year-old Salome, princess of Judaea, who is incestuously desired by her stepfather Herod, and, after being turned down by the ascetical Jochanaan (John the Baptist), seduces the former in order to have the latter decapitated and his head brought to her "on a silver platter." In the end, the sight of Salome fondling and kissing the severed head proves too much for Herod, who orders his stepdaughter to be crushed under the soldiers' shields.

Strong stuff indeed, and Strauss's music potentiates its effect with its luxuriant scoring, not least in the notorious "Dance of the Seven Veils." Earlier in the twentieth century it was usual for a dancer to take over at this point, but in later years there have been singers who, apart from "looking sixteen and having the voice of an Isolde" (Strauss's own description), have put on a mean strip show. As sound-only recordings go, Giuseppe Sinopoli gives an appropriately expressionistic traversal of the opulent score, with Cheryl Studer sounding both girlish and heroic. **CMS**

Carl Nielsen
Maskarade

(1906)

Genre | Opera
Conductor/Performers | Ulf Schirmer;
Aage Haugland, Gert-Henning Jensen
Year recorded | 1996
Label | Decca 475 214-2 (2 CDs)

As Smetana's *Bartered Bride* is to Czechs, and Erkel's *Bánk Bán* is to Hungarians, so is *Maskarade* to Danes—the opera that expresses the national sentiment, and which is rarely out of the repertoire. *Maskarade* is a comedy based on a play by Ludwig Holberg, a Norwegian who made his home in Copenhagen in the first half of the eighteenth century. Nielsen himself adapted the plot, but asked Vilhelm Andersen, a Holberg expert, to write the libretto.

The masquerade of the title is a masked ball, popular in Copenhagen in Holberg's time, as it allowed people of all classes to mix freely, and get away from the world of everyday respectability. At one of these balls, Leander meets and falls in love with Leonora, though, of course, neither is aware of the other's identity. But Leander's fusty old father, Jeronimus, has arranged a match for him with the daughter of another pillar of society, and forbids him to go to the following night's masquerade. So the stage is set for disguises, mistaken identities, and all the mechanisms of farce, before the final unmasking, when Leonora is discovered to be the bride intended for Leander all along.

This recording features the top Danish singers of the 1990s in sparkling form. Veteran Aage Haugland blusters effectively as Jeronimus, while Gert-Henning Jensen and Henriette Bonde-Hansen give real emotion to their duet in Act 2. And the assorted other characters all make the most of their witty turns as the plot unfolds, with Ulf Schirmer guiding the Danish National Symphony Orchestra around each improbable corner with impeccable ease. **MC**

Jean Sibelius
Pohjola's Daughter

(1906)

Genre | Orchestral
Conductor | Osmo Vänskä
Performers | Lahti Symphony Orchestra
Year recorded | 2000
Label | BIS CD-1225

On one level *Pohjola's Daughter* is a symphony in all but name. On another it is a symphonic poem that can be tied very closely to its storyline. The narrative is based on Canto 8 of the *Kalevala*, which describes an encounter between the ancient seer Väinämöinen and the beautiful daughter of the Northland (Pohjola). She sets him a series of impossible tasks, including the construction of a boat from a splinter of her spindle. Magic powers notwithstanding, Väinämöinen is forced to continue his journey alone.

Though plainly one of Sibelius's heroic-masculine utterances inspired by that Finnish national epic, *Pohjola's Daughter* also ranks among his more self-consciously European scores: Its wealth of orchestral color and programmatic detail owes something to Richard Strauss. Sibelius heard *Ein Heldenleben* under the baton of the composer during his Berlin visit in 1905 and at one point referred to his own piece as *L'aventure d'un héros*.

It was a Finn, Robert Kajanus (1856–1933), the most important early champion of Sibelius's music, who made the first recording of the work in England. And, in our own time, it is the tireless advocacy of Osmo Vänskä and his Lahti Symphony Orchestra that deserves pride of place. Their lean and vital reading brings a thrilling charge to the central episode, the strings digging in, the brass blazing. Their *Pohjola's Daughter* comes as part of a useful program of tone poems, familiar and unfamiliar, all texturally refreshed and well captured in a sound of sensational truthfulness and extended dynamic range. **DG**

Charles Ives
The Unanswered Question
(1906, *revised c.1935*)

Genre | Orchestral
Conductor/Performers | Michael Tilson Thomas; Chicago Symphony Orchestra
Year recorded | 1986
Label | Sony MK 42381

The Unanswered Question is a prophetic exploration of "stereophonic" orchestral sound, scored for solo trumpet (or cor anglais), a woodwind group, and a string orchestra. Each of these three entities is spatially separated from the others and sticks to its own material. The strings play a slow, soft, circular sequence of chords that endlessly repeats in its own time, with subtle variations. Upon this background the trumpet superimposes its "question," a repeated interrogatory six-note phrase. Ives said this represented "the Perennial Question of Existence," while the strings evoked "The Silences of the Druids—who Know, See and Hear Nothing." On every appearance except the last, the flutes (the "fighting answerers") respond with chromatic, polytonal heterophony, but while the trumpet remains unchanged, the woodwinds accelerate, become louder, more agitated and dissonant, until at last they fall silent and the question sounds one last time against the enigmatic tranquility of the strings.

Within its small, eerily beautiful compass, this work perfectly typifies both Ives's exploratory attitude to the stuff of music and his ability to conjure something rich and strange out of the simplest materials. He subtitled it "A Cosmic Landscape," and certainly its effect—though not untinged with humor—is one of metaphysical contemplation of the mystery of the universe.

Michael Tilson Thomas uniquely offers both the original and revised versions of the work, performed with ultra-refined playing and a real sense of inner stillness. **MM**

Arnold Schoenberg
Chamber Symphony
no. 1 (1906)

Genre | Chamber
Conductor/Performers | Simon Rattle; Birmingham Contemporary Music Group
Year recorded | 1993
Label | EMI 0946 3 71492 2 5 (2 CDs)

Schoenberg's First Chamber Symphony was a decisive reaction against the whole conception of the late-Romantic orchestral symphony. Not only does it require a mere fifteen players and collapse the traditional four movements into one, but its ebullient dynamism and new-minted vocabulary simultaneously point ahead toward new horizons and look back nostalgically to the world of the nineteenth century.

Schoenberg was thirty-one when he completed the work in July 1906, and in later years he always looked back to it as an expression of a hopeful time. It struck its first audiences as the last word in avant-garde experimentation; the idea of a symphony reduced to the dimensions of chamber music struck some contemporaries as bizarre. But nowadays it is easy to hear around the features that challenged those early listeners, and recognize the extrovert, optimistic nature of Schoenberg's invention, its debt to Schubert and Brahms, and its intoxicating sense of adventure. Of all Schoenberg's creations, this is the sunniest: pugnacious, humorous, and tender.

Simon Rattle's performance catches the youthful spirit of the work, and molds its transitions with great sensitivity, allowing the sheer richness of the harmony to make its full sensuous impact while illuminating the individual lines with admirable clarity. The Birmingham Contemporary Music Group is inspired to produce some of the most characterful playing and purest coloring heard on any recording of the work. **MM**

Josef Suk
Asrael Symphony (1906)

Genre | Orchestral
Conductor | Jiří Bělohlávek
Performers | Czech Philharmonic Orchestra
Year recorded | 1991
Label | Chandos CHAN 9640

Suk's *Asrael Symphony* is one of the greatest orchestral works in the twentieth-century Czech repertoire. A fine violinist, Suk went on to study composition with Dvořák, a creative relationship that became a personal one with his marriage to the composer's daughter, Otilie, in 1898. Although it owed a considerable debt to Dvořák's tuition, Suk's musical style after his earliest works was far from being slavish imitation of his teacher and displays a distinctively lyrical, often melancholic quality. While his works from the 1890s show that he was highly talented, there was little sign of real genius in his music until two personal tragedies struck: the unexpected death of his revered teacher and father-in-law, Dvořák, in 1904, followed a year later by that of his young wife. These twin bereavements transformed talent into genius, clearly manifest in the five-movement *Asrael Symphony*.

Taking its name from the biblical angel of death, the symphony is a movingly eloquent outpouring of grief; composed on a gigantic scale, it encompasses consolation in the fourth movement as well as relentless tragedy in the finale. Written relatively early in Suk's composing career, *Asrael* was the first of a sequence of remarkable, large-scale orchestral masterpieces including *A Summer's Tale* and *Ripening*.

Jiří Bělohlávek provides a richly textured reading of the symphony with the Czech Philharmonic on remarkable form. The depth of Bělohlávek's insight into the work is clear from his sensitive treatment of the numerous recurrent themes that give the symphony its epic qualities and, in the finale, deliver a strong sense of catharsis. **JS**

Frederick Delius
Brigg Fair (1907)

Genre | Orchestral
Conductor | Thomas Beecham
Performers | Royal Philharmonic Orchestra
Year recorded | 1956
Label | EMI 7243 5 67553 2 1

Many of Delius's orchestral pieces evoke landscapes, but they are more often the landscapes of France, or Florida, or Norway, than those of his native England. The best-known exception is *Brigg Fair*, which he subtitled "An English Rhapsody." It is based on a folksong that his friend Percy Grainger recorded on a wax cylinder in northern Lincolnshire, and later arranged for chorus. The tune is treated in a sequence of variations, clothed in different colors and moods over Delius's characteristic sliding harmonies. But there is also an introduction and interludes beautifully evoking the misty August morning on which the protagonist of the song sets out to meet his girl at Brigg Fair. In its later stages, though, the piece takes on a darker tone, with an intermittently tolling bell providing a reminder of mortality. So it is not just landscape, but also an expression of Delius's quintessential theme of love and loss.

Delius's favorite interpreter, Thomas Beecham, gave the first London performance of *Brigg Fair* in 1908, and made the last of his three recordings of it nearly half a century later, just into the stereo era. It is a wonderful example of his perfect judgment of tempo—for example in the almost imperceptible acceleration that keeps the first sequence of variations alive—and of the way he created the space for wind and string soloists to make their own expressive contributions. This *Brigg Fair* is the first track in a well-remastered compilation of Beecham's late-1950s Delius recordings, including also the Second Dance Rhapsody and many smaller pieces. You may have some of these in other versions—and the duplications inevitably pile up in a Delius discography, but this disc is special. **AB**

Gustav Mahler
Symphony no. 8 (1907)

Genre | Vocal/Orchestral
Conductor/Performers | Georg Solti;
Chicago Symphony Orchestra
Year recorded | 1971
Label | Decca 475 752-2

Sometimes called "Symphony of a Thousand" for the massive performance forces it requires, Mahler's Eighth is his most resolutely public work, one in which the musical language is less likely to cause puzzlement, discomfiture, or unseemly emotional response than most of its predecessors. The grand gestures of music on this scale come naturally to Mahler, and yet linking settings of the Latin hymn "Veni, creator spiritus" ("Come, creator spirit") (Part 1) and the closing scene of Part 2 of Goethe's *Faust* (Mahler's Part 2) in a work called "symphony" represents one of those idiosyncratic juxtapositions that only Mahler, with his all-inclusive vision of art, would be tempted to attempt. The premiere of the Eighth in Munich under the composer's direction less than a year before his death was perhaps his greatest outward triumph, and ever since then the work's vast scale and sense of elation have given it a special place in the symphonic and choral literature.

Georg Solti's classic Decca recording of Mahler's Eighth constitutes a "performance" that would be impossible to achieve under live conditions but that realizes numerous ideals toward which the work tends. First, the recorded balance permits the vocal soloists to make a decisive impact in the overall texture, and second, the studio conditions allow the performers to maintain the illusion that they are tireless and perpetually fresh despite the most strenuous demands of physical effort and endurance. Solti's incessant energy and drama are not to everyone's taste, but the exhilarating frisson his dynamism can produce, especially when coupled with such brilliant playing and magnificent recording, must be experienced to be believed. **DB**

Sergei Rachmaninov
Symphony no. 2 (1907)

Genre | Orchestral
Conductor/Performers | André Previn;
London Symphony Orchestra
Year recorded | 1973
Label | EMI 7243 5 66997 2 4

Rachmaninov's Second is perhaps the greatest post-Tchaikovskian symphony. It is certainly the longest. Full of glorious long-breathed tunes, sumptuously harmonized and orchestrated, it is also a compelling darkness-to-light journey, in which those expansive melodies take their place in a much larger, almost novel-like drama. The slow third movement is simply one of the finest late flowerings of Russian Romanticism. In completing this huge score, Rachmaninov at last exorcised the memory of the catastrophic failure of his First Symphony, and his exhilaration and newfound confidence positively explodes in the radiant finale. And yet for many years the Second Symphony was neglected, rarely performed in public or recorded in the West and anathematized in Stalin's Russia. When it was done at all, it was usually with major cuts—the kind of crass surgery that did nothing to enhance Rachmaninov's standing with critics as a serious symphonic architect.

Almost single-handedly, André Previn and the London Symphony Orchestra changed all that. Quite simply this recording marks a turning point in Rachmaninov's reputation. The truly remarkable thing is how immediate its freshness, luxurious warmth, and impassioned urgency still sound today, over three decades later. It is said that clarinettist Jack Brymer's first attempt at the glorious long slow movement theme in the studio was so fine that no retakes were considered necessary. But every solo is treasurable, while the sense of rich, rounded, taut ensemble Previn gets from the LSO is exceptional even from this vintage period in the orchestra's career. **SJ**

Nicolai Rimsky-Korsakov
The Golden Cockerel Suite (1907)

Genre | Orchestral
Conductor | Antal Dorati
Performer | London Symphony Orchestra
Year recorded | 1956
Label | Philips 475 6194 (SACD)

The Golden Cockerel was Rimsky-Korsakov's last opera. Based on a Pushkin story that was a thinly disguised satire on the corrupt court of the Russian Tsar Nicholas II and his incompetent military leaders, the opera fell foul of the censors; Rimsky's fight with officialdom affected his health and he died before witnessing the 1907 premiere.

At court, an Astrologer presents slothful King Dodon with a golden cockerel that will warn of imminent danger. The cockerel's crowing alerts the court to an invasion; the King promises to grant the astrologer his every wish. As Dodon suffers defeat in battle, the Queen of Shemakha appears and sings her winningly seductive "Hymn to the Sun"; a smitten Dodon proposes marriage, but the Astrologer claims the Queen in recompense for the magic cockerel. Dodon kills the Astrologer; the cockerel promptly pecks the king to death. The Astrologer reappears, confirming that the whole affair is a mere jest.

Rimsky's score gives full rein to his taste for highly coloristic orchestration and exotic themes. There is currently no widely available audio recording of the complete opera. The four movements of Rimsky's concert suite depict King Dodon in his palace, on the battlefield, with the Queen of Shemakha, and finally the marriage feast and Dodon's death.

In 1956, the Mercury Living Presence company shipped its mobile recording truck from the United States to Walthamstow Town Hall, London, for sessions with the LSO and its renowned conductor Antal Dorati. The engineers were hands-off: balance and dynamics were left entirely to the conductor, with unfailingly musical results. **GK**

"Rimsky-Korsakov—what a name! It suggests fierce whiskers stained with vodka!"

Musical Courier (New York, 1897)

Other Recommended Recordings

•
**Royal Philharmonic Orchestra • Thomas Beecham
Sony SMK 91171**
Beecham's care and affection for the music is abundantly evident

**Odense Symphony Orchestra • Edward Serov
Kontrapunkt 32247**
Part of Serov's highly regarded Rimsky series

**Various orchestras • Herbert von Karajan, Neeme Järvi, Lorin Maazel, Vladimir Ashkenazy, Igor Markevitch
DG 469 187-2 (2 CDs)**
Bargain compilation of quality performances, with Markevitch conducting The Golden Cockerel

An early portrait of Hungarian conductor Antal Dorati. ➲

Edward Elgar | Symphony no. 1 (1908)

Genre | Orchestral
Conductor | John Barbirolli
Performers | Philharmonia Orchestra
Year recorded | 1962
Label | EMI 7 64511 2

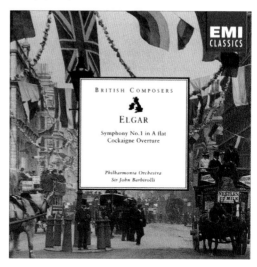

The premiere of Elgar's First Symphony in 1908 was one of the greatest triumphs in British music. It was widely hailed as "the first great English symphony," and in the following year there were nearly a hundred performances. As the composer's star began to sink in the 1920s, the symphony dropped out of fashion, but modern audiences have rediscovered it. Perhaps now, with Britain's imperial ambitions an increasingly distant memory, it is easier to hear the anxiety and aching sadness behind the apparent celebration of "glad, confident" Edwardian values. This richly complex symphony is one of the fullest portraits of Elgar with all his contradictions: nobly, grandly aspiring one moment, racked with doubt or painful longing the next.

Perhaps no other conductor had a grasp of Elgar's multifaceted nature than John Barbirolli. While he clearly understands the strength and subtlety of the symphony's architecture, his Elgar is unmistakably a creature of flesh and blood, and romantic to the core. The veneer of swaggering Anglo-Saxon self-mastery is precisely that—a mask concealing a vulnerable, fabulously imaginative, yet also possibly unstable character. In Barbirolli's hands even the "motto" theme that pervades the work—described by Elgar as expressing "massive hope"—is more than usually supple, and human in its expression. Then with one twist of the harmony the succeeding Allegro dispels all its seeming assurance. The range of poetry and feeling in what follows is remarkable, but Barbirolli makes each movement flow from one idea or poetic vista to the next as though it were a single huge melody. The recorded sound is exceptionally good for its time, and although it may not have the depth of some modern versions, the warmth and clarity still make it strongly recommendable. **SJ**

"God, how I love that music."

John Barbirolli on the First Symphony

Other Recommended Recordings

London Symphony Orchestra • Edward Elgar
EMI 5 67296 2
A composer's insight plus searing, at times almost breathless excitement

London Philharmonic Orchestra • Adrian Boult
Testament SBT 1229
All Boult's natural dignity and poise with a surprising touch of youthful fire

London Symphony Orchestra • Colin Davis
LSO Live LSO 0017
A very loving modern version, expansive but with mounting excitement at the close

Barbirolli's name was synonymous with Elgar's music in the 1960s. ➔

Maurice Ravel | Gaspard de la nuit (1908)

Genre | Instrumental
Instrument | Piano
Performer | Ivo Pogorelich
Year recorded | 1982
Label | DG 463 678-2

Composers do not always have the finest taste in poetry. Schubert set some very mediocre poems, for example, and were it not for Ravel's *Gaspard de la nuit*, surely Aloysius Bertrand's verses would have been long forgotten. Pianists remain grateful to Bertrand, however, for inspiring what Alfred Cortot described as "one of the most extraordinary examples of instrumental ingenuity ever produced."

Bertrand's poem conjures sinister nocturnal worlds, and Ravel clearly wanted his music to sound terrifying. It does just that—but only if it is played well, and to do so requires exceptional musical as well as technical resources. Indeed, *Gaspard* is terrifyingly difficult to play; every page holds terrors for even the most accomplished pianist.

The first movement portrays the water nymph Ondine attempting to lure a mortal man to her palace beneath the lake. As in *Jeux d'eau* and "Une barque sur l'océan" from *Miroirs*, Ravel creates an exquisitely textured world, one that hints of darkness and danger beneath its shimmering surface. "Le Gibet," the creepy second movement, depicts the swinging of a corpse hanging from the gallows with music of unsettling quiet and insistence. And what music is more chillingly macabre than "Scarbo"? Ravel's representation of the wicked dwarf is a virtuoso study in grotesquerie. Repeated notes evoke Scarbo's evil cackling; sudden, ominous silences and virtuoso, harmonically malevolent explosions suggest his supernatural powers.

Ivo Pogorelich's performance of "Scarbo" is hair-raising. The relentless rhythms of "Le Gibet" are lit with a ghostly pallor, and "Ondine" has never glimmered so alluringly nor suggested such peril. Coupled with an equally inspired Prokofiev Sixth Sonata, this recital shows Pogorelich at his most beguiling and persuasive. **AFC**

> "*I am pleased with the outcome of this recording. But what I had to do to make it happen!*"

Ivo Pogorelich

Other Recommended Recordings

Martha Argerich
DG 447 438-2
Argerich at her electrifying best in this critically acclaimed interpretation

Arturo Benedetti Michelangeli
BBC Legends BBCL 4064-2
Sublime technical mastery and sang-froid— a chilling, thrilling combination

Walter Gieseking
EMI 7243 5 74793 2 5
Some details are smudged but Gieseking's intense lyricism is compelling

Pogorelich's individuality makes him a highly-controversial musician. ➲

Isaac Albéniz
Iberia (1908)

Genre | Instrumental
Instrument | Piano
Performer | Alicia de Larrocha
Year recorded | 1986
Label | Decca 417 887-2 (2 CDs)

If any single work represents Spanish nationalism it is Albéniz's *Iberia*, not only the composer's greatest work, but the greatest piano work to come out of Spain. Comprising twelve extended pieces in four books, *Iberia* was not conceived as a cycle, yet the music reveals an inherent coherence of musical style and substance.

Albéniz, who was born in Catalonia in 1860, began composing *Iberia* in 1905 and completed it in 1908, a year before he died. Inspired by his discovery of the music of Debussy and Ravel, Albéniz transformed his earlier salon style, which produced charming but externalized "picture postcards" of Spain, into a far more complex musical language, creating a series of tone poems that embody the spiritual essence of the composer's homeland, from the nostalgic introspection of "Evocación" to the wonderfully exuberant flamenco spirit of "Eritaña." Harmonically, texturally, and pianistically, this is music of great ingenuity and intricacy. *Iberia* is one of those works that is harder to play than it sounds, with its extreme dynamic range, its cross-rhythms, and its elaborate piano-writing with much interweaving and crossing of hands as well as difficult leaps and treacherous chords. The music is deeply evocative, and contains a distinctive blend of Impressionist harmonies, Lisztian keyboard exploitation, and the pervasive influence of regional Spanish song and dance rhythms.

It is perhaps unsurprising that few pianists have done justice to the full set. The pianist most closely associated with *Iberia* is Alicia de Larrocha, who instills an authentic national flavor. **TLP**

Alexander Scriabin
The Poem of Ecstasy (1908)

Genre | Orchestral
Conductor | Valery Gergiev
Performers | Kirov Orchestra
Year recorded | 1999
Label | Philips 468 035-2

While working on his Third Symphony in 1904, Scriabin was already planning a fourth, a four-movement work entitled *Poème orgiaque*. What transpired was a single-movement piece, more tone poem than symphony, which attempted to express the ecstasy of the creative spirit. For Scriabin, the spiritual and physical were indistinguishable and his route to this state of ecstasy was expressed in music that is undeniably both erotic and priapic. He achieves this by alternating passages suggestive of "languid desire," often with woodwind and solo strings, with the upward striving of a trumpet theme he dubbed "victory."

After its premiere in New York in December 1908, *La poème de l'extase* soon became established as one of the key works of Russian Romanticism. But one should perhaps listen to it as merely a prelude to what would undoubtedly have been Scriabin's magnum opus (had he not died of blood poisoning in 1915): *Mysterium*, a week-long "happening" in the foothills of the Himalayas that he envisaged would involve all the senses and bring about the end of the world in a state of bliss. No wonder Rimsky-Korsakov, after hearing the composer play through his *Poem of Ecstasy* in Paris, felt the need to comment: "He's getting near the madhouse, don't you think?"

At twenty minutes in length, *The Poem of Ecstasy* is more often the filler than the main event on disc, as is the case with Valery Gergiev's exciting account with his Kirov Orchestra, the coupling for their recording of Stravinsky's *Rite of Spring*. The work may begin in dilatory languor, but Gergiev reveals how the energy of its rapturous trajectory is rooted in the harmonies. **MR**

Maurice Ravel
Rapsodie espagnole (1908)

Genre | Orchestral
Conductor/Performers | Charles Munch;
Boston Symphony Orchestra
Year recorded | 1956
Label | RCA 82876 66374 2

The *Rapsodie espagnole* is an orchestral tour de force, a tone poem so vividly scored as to seem both physically tactile and intoxicatingly aromatic. That it was Ravel's first major orchestral work only makes its brilliance more dazzling. He began work on it in late 1907, soon after completing another Spanish-themed piece, the one-act opera *L'heure espagnole*. Ravel, like many artists of his time, had a keen interest in the exotic—and thus Spain, with its flamenco dances and Moorish influences, held a strong allure. The seed for the *Rapsodie* was planted in 1895 with the *Habanera* for two pianos. Ravel was particularly proud of this piece—so much so that thirteen years later he felt it worthy to serve as the *Rapsodie*'s third movement. And it is a marvel: slinky and sensuous, it dances in small, melodically teasing phrases.

The *Rapsodie* begins, however, with a nocturnal prelude of moonlit silhouettes, soft caresses, and romantic exhalations. Next comes the "Malagueña," a strutting kind of waltz ornamented with arrogant trumpet calls and languorous piping from the English horn. Following the "Habanera," Ravel concludes his *Rapsodie* with the rhythmically dashing, vibrantly colorful "Feria."

With a fine orchestra and competent conductor, Ravel's *Rapsodie* can almost play itself. In a great performance—and one worthy of repeated listening—all the wondrous orchestral effects are not merely pretty brushstrokes but serve to define and enhance the music's character. Charles Munch and the Boston Symphony do just that in this classic recording. Every gesture and phrase, every dab of color, seems necessary, meaningful and thrillingly alive. **AFC**

Arnold Schoenberg
String Quartet no. 2 (1908)

Genre | Chamber
Performers | Anna Maria Pammer
(soprano), Aron Quartet
Year recorded | 2003
Label | Preiser PR 90572 (3 CDs)

The first performance of Schoenberg's Second Quartet caused a near-riot and established its composer as one of the most formidable personalities in early twentieth-century music. Arguably the most powerfully expressive of his five quartets, it was composed in the wake of discovering his wife was having an affair with the painter Richard Gerstl, and is rife with spiritual disquiet. Though still nominally in traditional tonality, its harmonic fluidity soon takes that to the edge of functionality—and eventually beyond. The first movement is deeply lyrical but also feverish; the second is a scrambling, stumbling scherzo in which the old Viennese street-song "O, du lieber Augustin" signals despair and alienation. The last two movements, though, bring a revolutionary enlargement of the genre. To the four string instruments Schoenberg adds a soprano, singing poems by Stefan George—"Litanei" ("Litany"), the work's slow movement, is a prayer for spiritual renewal, and in the finale, "Entrückung" ("Rapture"), beginning with the words "I feel air blowing from other planets," the music launches out beyond the gravitational pull of tonality to enact an ecstatic flight to union with the Divine. An amazing feat of imagination, this ascends to an overwhelming climax and sinks at last to rest and fulfillment. No work of Schoenberg's is more crucial to an understanding of the man and his expressive purpose.

The Aron Quartet's searing interpretation is part of a box of Schoenberg's complete music for string quartet. For textural and rhythmic clarity and expressive flexibility of phrasing and tempo, it rivals the Kolisch Quartet and is recorded in infinitely better sound. **MM**

Gustav Holst | Savitri (1908)

Genre | Opera
Conductor/Performers | Imogen Holst; Janet Baker,
Robert Tear, Thomas Hemsley, English Chamber Orchestra
Year recorded | 1965
Label | Decca 470 191-2

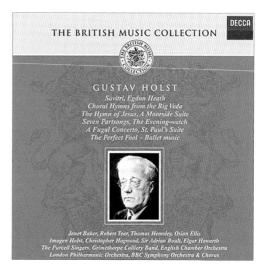

THE BRITISH MUSIC COLLECTION

DECCA

GUSTAV HOLST

Sāvitri, Egdon Heath
Choral Hymns from the Rig Veda
The Hymn of Jesus, A Moorside Suite
Seven Partsongs, The Evening-watch
A Fugal Concerto, St. Paul's Suite
The Perfect Fool – Ballet music

Janet Baker, Robert Tear, Thomas Hemsley, Osian Ellis
Imogen Holst, Christopher Hogwood, Sir Adrian Boult, Elgar Howarth
The Purcell Singers, Grimethorpe Colliery Band, English Chamber Orchestra
London Philharmonic Orchestra, BBC Symphony Orchestra & Chorus

Gustav Holst was born into a musical home in Cheltenham in 1874. His cosmopolitan roots—his forebears were of Swedish, German, and Russian stock who had emigrated from Riga, Latvia, in 1799—seem to have instilled in him an unusually internationalist range of cultural interests. While studying at the Royal College of Music at the end of the nineteenth century, he took courses in Sanskrit after becoming absorbed by the mysticism of the *Rig Veda* and the philosophy of the Bhagavad Gîtâ. He translated hymns from the *Rig Veda* to set to music and also wrote two operas based on Sanskrit literature, the Wagnerian tone of *Sita* contrasting with the chamber-scale world of *Savitri*, which was written for a mere three singers, off-stage choir, and a chamber orchestra. Despite its limited means, this thirty-minute opera had to wait eight years for its first performance, given in London in 1916.

The Mahabharata story of *Savitri* tells of a woman faced with Death coming to take away her husband, Satyavan. Death is so moved by the warmth with which he is greeted that he offers her any wish; she replies "Give me Life!" But when she goes on to say that her life can only exist with her husband, Death is defeated and goes away alone.

The economy of the opera's resources make it stand out from the gargantuism of the time (compare such contemporary works as Mahler's "Symphony of a Thousand" and Strauss's *Elektra*) and it has a rather frail mood that gives it an otherworldly aura. This is caught magically on the recording conducted by Holst's daughter Imogen in 1965, which is dominated (if that is the word in this delicate context) by the Savitri of Janet Baker. It is coupled with his *Rig Veda* hymns. **MR**

"There was a perfection about the work that he had never achieved before."

Imogen Holst in *Gustav Holst: A Biography*, 1969

Other Recommended Recordings

City of London Sinfonia • Richard Hickox
Hyperion Helios CDH 55042
Sensitive but less atmospheric than Imogen Holst

The Perfect Fool
London Philharmonic Orchestra • Adrian Boult
Decca Double Decca 444 549-2
The fizzing ballet suite from Holst's opera parodying Wagner

The Wandering Scholar
Northern Sinfonia • Richard Hickox
Chandos CHAN 9734
Lively account of Holst's Chaucer-esque comic opera

Imogen Holst championed her father's music as a conductor. ➔

Anton Webern | Passacaglia (1908)

Genre | Orchestral
Conductor | Herbert von Karajan
Performers | Berlin Philharmonic Orchestra
Year recorded | 1974
Label | DG 457 7602

ORIGINAL-IMAGE
BIT-PROCESSING

Born in 1883, Anton Webern studied theory and counterpoint at the Vienna Conservatoire, simultaneously pursuing research into the music of the fifteenth-century polyphonic composer Heinrich Isaac at the University of Vienna. Webern was composing prolifically from an early age, but his musical outlook changed radically in 1904 after he began intensive studies in composition with Arnold Schoenberg alongside his close friend Alban Berg.

Webern's *Passacaglia*, his first fully acknowledged opus, was one of the last compositions written directly under Schoenberg's tutelage. Performed for the first time in 1908, it is a dark and passionate work haunted by the death of the composer's mother. Its structural outline, an eight-note theme announced by pizzicato strings and subjected to twenty-three variations, owes much to the finale of Brahms's Fourth Symphony. At the same time, the highly charged musical language of Schoenberg's First Chamber Symphony, which stretches tonal harmony to its limits, is the most pervasive influence on this amazing score.

A technically challenging orchestral composition that manages to pack the intensity of a Mahler symphony into a mere ten minutes of music, *Passacaglia* has enjoyed a plethora of distinguished recordings over the years. The finest of all is undoubtedly the 1974 recording from Herbert von Karajan and the Berlin Philharmonic, which projects a tremendous sense of urgency and has a powerful dramatic impact. The rest of the disc—which features compelling performances of Schoenberg's Variations for Orchestra as well as the Three Pieces from the *Lyric Suite* and Three Orchestral Pieces op. 6 by Alban Berg—makes an ideal introduction to the music of the Second Viennese School. **EL**

> ## "Nothing appears accidental, nothing forced by a mania for originality."
>
> **Critic Elsa Bienenfeld on the *Passacaglia***

Other Recommended Recordings

Berlin Philharmonic Orchestra
Pierre Boulez
DG 447 099-2
A reading of clarity and musical insight

Dresden Staatskapelle
Giuseppe Sinopoli
Warner 0927 49832-2
Opulent account in gorgeous sound

Vienna Philharmonic Orchestra
Claudio Abbado
DG 431 7742
Mahlerian passion and intensity

Arnold Schoenberg | Erwartung (1908)

Genre | Opera
Conductor/Performers | Simon Rattle; Phyllis Bryn-Julson,
City of Birmingham Symphony Orchestra
Year recorded | 1993
Label | EMI 7243 5 55212 2 4

Schoenberg · Webern · Berg
EMI CLASSICS
Orchestral Works
City of Birmingham Symphony Orchestra
Simon Rattle

Erwartung (*Expectation*), Schoenberg's first stage work, has a strong claim to be considered the supreme example of Expressionism in music. The librettist, a young medical student from Pressburg (now called Bratislava), produced a dreamlike "interior monologue" rife with hysterical repression and delusion. Working at fantastic speed, Schoenberg composed the entire drama for voice and huge orchestra in just seventeen days. The result was thought "unperformable" and was not staged until 1924.

Schoenberg called the work an "anxiety-dream" (*Angsttraum*)—a slow-motion representation of a single second of maximum spiritual stress. The mise-en-scène is a moonlit forest. Through it a woman wanders, apprehensive, somnambulistic, seeking—yet fearing to find—her lover. She addresses her absent lover in a stream of consciousness made up of longing, jealousy, and exaltation, sense-impressions and memory-associations, the merging of past and present. Eventually she discovers his body—but has she, in fact, killed him herself?

Schoenberg secures an unprecedented range of sonorities: tone colors change with amazing fluency, as do the pace and the density of texture. The solo vocal line is demanding both in its intensity of expression and its variety—much of it in broken phrases, but also calling for a Valkyrie-like power and stamina at the big moments.

This is possibly Simon Rattle's greatest Schoenberg recording. Every detail in this score of a thousand luminous, tremulous details seems to have been considered, brought out to perfection, and placed in relation to the whole. Bryn-Julson negotiates the fiendish solo part with ease, revealing how natural a transcription of speech-rhythms it really is. **MM**

> *"The score is superbly orchestrated, almost everything sounds of its own accord."*
>
> Alexander Zemlinsky, conductor

Béla Bartók | String Quartets (1909–39)

Genre | Chamber
Performers | Takács Quartet: Edward Dusinberre,
Károly Schranz, Geraldine Walther, András Fejér
Year recorded | 1996
Label | Decca 455 297-2 (2 CDs)

Regarded as the greatest cycle of chamber works of the first half of the twentieth century, each of Bartók's six string quartets mirrors different phases in the composer's varied career. In the First (1909), Bartók takes his leave of the late-Romantic style, the combined influences of Beethoven's final period and Debussy liberating his imagination and national identity. The Second Quartet (1914–17) reveals a growing intensification of musical language generated to a certain extent by his experience of writing for the stage and by his discovery of Hungarian folk music. Both the compressed Third (1927) and the five-movement Fourth (1928) maintain structural rigor while expanding the tonal palette of the stringed instruments to incorporate such coloristic effects as glissando, snap pizzicato, and playing with the back of the bow and on the fingerboard. For the Fifth Quartet (1934) Bartók demonstrates a preoccupation with formal symmetry, while exploiting unusual and attractive Bulgarian folk rhythms in the central scherzo. The Sixth Quartet (1939), written on the eve of Bartók's departure from Hungary, is a work riddled with regret and bitterness—a reaction to the impending catastrophe that was about to engulf Europe.

Recordings of the quartets tend to divide along national lines. Those by Hungarians, such as the Végh, Hungarian, and Keller Quartets, emphasize the inherently lyrical qualities of Bartók's writing, while those from the Tokyo, Fine Arts, Juilliard, and Emerson Quartets project a more aggressive, dynamic approach. The Takács Quartet's interpretations on Decca seem to encapsulate the best of both worlds, intense and probing as well as rhythmically exhilarating. These are performances of great musical insight matched by almost flawless technical mastery. **EL**

"[Bartók's] six quartets tower over . . . contemporary chamber music like high mountain peaks."

Mátyás Seiber

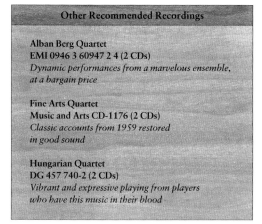

Other Recommended Recordings

Alban Berg Quartet
EMI 0946 3 60947 2 4 (2 CDs)
Dynamic performances from a marvelous ensemble,
at a bargain price

Fine Arts Quartet
Music and Arts CD-1176 (2 CDs)
Classic accounts from 1959 restored
in good sound

Hungarian Quartet
DG 457 740-2 (2 CDs)
Vibrant and expressive playing from players
who have this music in their blood

Bartók (right) with Rudolf Kolisch, who premiered the Sixth Quartet. ➔

Gustav Mahler | Das Lied von der Erde (1909)

Genre | Vocal
Conductor | Otto Klemperer
Performers | Christa Ludwig, Fritz Wunderlich
Years recorded | 1964–66
Label | EMI 7243 5 66944 2 2

Das Lied von der Erde fuses Mahler's joint interest in symphony and song in a work that many regard as the composer's crowning achievement. Based on poems from Hans Bethge's *Die chinesische Flöte, Das Lied* features three songs for tenor alternating with three longer ones for mezzo-soprano. The texts focus on the darkness of life and the consequent necessity of living for the moment, but also of the metaphysical attractions of withdrawal, sleep, rest, and death/renewal—hardly new thoughts for Mahler, but ideas made more relevant following profound personal upheavals in the summer of 1907. The music Mahler fashioned for conveying these meanings contains tinges of Orientalism but additionally evokes an unforgettable sense of vibrant yet static timelessness; the magical ending of the final song resolves to a chord containing a sixth along with the tonic triad, somehow endowing the universe with new life and meaning.

Three features place Otto Klemperer's EMI recording of *Das Lied von der Erde* in a special class. First, Fritz Wunderlich is magnificent. Few tenors sound anything other than stressed by this demanding music; consequently, his free, ringing tone and vivid emotional response are as welcome as they are unusual. Second, this is one of Christa Ludwig's greatest achievements—her technical command of the music is remarkable and her musicianship and expressive imagination cause the listener to cherish and ponder her every utterance. And third, the orchestral playing from the Philharmonia is of unforgettable eloquence. Never has the impression that the economically scored passages of this work resemble chamber music been more fully realized, and numerous wind solos are rendered so potently that it seems the music is about to become speech. **DB**

"That final chord is printed on the atmosphere."

Benjamin Britten

Other Recommended Recordings

Janet Baker, James King, Amsterdam Concertgebouw Orchestra, Bernard Haitink • Philips 454 014-2
Another favorite version featuring responsible and eloquent contributions from all concerned

Kathleen Ferrier, Julius Patzak, Vienna Philharmonic Bruno Walter • Decca 289 466 576-2
Walter's persistent advocacy for this work here encounters two especially distinctive soloists

Janet Baker, Richard Lewis, Cleveland Orchestra George Szell • Cleveland Orchestra TCO 93-75
Clear, direct, unfussy, flowing—a remarkably successful songlike approach

Christa Ludwig, one of the most admired mezzo-sopranos of her day. ➔

Gustav Mahler
Symphony no. 9 (1909)

Genre | Orchestral
Conductor | Claudio Abbado
Performers | Berlin Philharmonic Orchestra
Year recorded | 1999
Label | DG 471 624-2

Mahler did not live to hear his Ninth Symphony. Written in the summer of 1909 and completed the following year, it is generally conceded to deal with the idea of farewell. From beginning to end, it is loaded with references to music that evokes the leave-taking of death. It opens with what is undoubtedly the richest and most intricate movement Mahler ever attempted and offers powerful catharsis for issues of grief and despair. The second movement focuses on various kinds of dances, from the earthy to the manic and the tender, while the third hurtles savagely through attempts to be merry. The concluding Adagio alternates between earnest consolation and bleak loneliness, and ends with a gradual fading into nothingness that has no equal in music, despite the frequently noted parallels with Tchaikovsky's *Pathétique*.

Claudio Abbado has long been a committed and convincing Mahler champion, but in this Ninth he achieves true greatness. The first movement leaves nothing to be desired in warmth or poignant depth of feeling, while the second and third movements are vividly and irresistibly characterized, and the finale achieves an unusually soulful conclusion. Even the most controversial dimension of the performance brings rewards: The middle section of the Rondo-Burleske seems initially matter-of-fact, but when that material returns in the finale, its transfiguration retrospectively justifies the contrasting character of its first appearance. There are many fine Ninths, but this is the one that seems to invite and permit reflection on the work itself rather than on the way in which it is interpreted—and this work makes such reflection infinitely rewarding. **DB**

Sergei Rachmaninov
Piano Concerto no. 3 (1909)

Genre | Concerto
Performer/Conductor | Martha Argerich; Riccardo Chailly
Year recorded | 1982
Label | Philips 446 673-2

The largest and technically most difficult of Rachmaninov's four piano concertos, the Third Piano Concerto was written in 1909 for the composer's first concert tour of America. Although the work's critical acceptance was slow (it was initially viewed as little more than an excellent vehicle for Rachmaninov's stupendous pianism), it is now widely considered the finest of the composer's concertos.

The work begins with the simplest of thematic statements, containing a palpable sense of anticipation. The modest opening grows organically and goes on to unleash music of overwhelming power and energy. Rachmaninov composed two versions of the huge first-movement cadenza—the first a colossal chordal affair, the second a leaner, fleeter alternative. The glorious slow movement shows Rachmaninov at his most harmonically adventurous, while the dazzling finale culminates in one of his seemingly never-ending tunes that rides the crest of a very long wave, before the work ends in a blaze of glory.

Since Vladimir Horowitz's initial triumphs with this concerto in the 1920s, pianists have been drawn inexorably to it. The composer's own recording—unfortunately with the significant cuts he made in an unnecessary attempt to streamline the piece—is essential listening, although like Horowitz's finest recording (a live account from 1941) there are sonic limitations. Most modern pianists adopt slower tempi than those favored by the composer, but perhaps the finest recording comes from a live performance in 1982 by Martha Argerich, whose febrile spontaneity, compelling virtuosity, and soulful lyricism were thankfully captured for posterity. **TLP**

Richard Strauss
Elektra (1909)

Genre | Opera
Conductor/Performers| Georg Solti;
Birgit Nilsson, Tom Krause, Regina Resnik
Year recorded | 1967
Label | Decca 417 345-2 (2 CDs)

After *Salome*, Strauss looked for a subject in a lighter vein, but ended up with an even more morbid one. Like Wilde's play, it is practically a one-woman show, with a sexually frustrated protagonist on stage for most of the opera's one act. Sophocles's play was adapted and given a fashionably Freudian twist by Hugo von Hofmannsthal, who remained Strauss's collaborator for the rest of his life (he died in 1929).

The truculent story concerns the revenge sought by Elektra's brother Orest for the murder of their father by their mother and her lover. For most of the opera, Elektra awaits Orest's return from exile to accomplish his retribution by killing the pair—but when this eventually happens, she is much too deranged to join the celebrations. Left alone, she dances a wild, Salome-like dance of triumph before collapsing during the opera's last measures.

Elektra represents a peak in Strauss's achievement as an orchestrator; he employs heckelphone (bass oboe), basset horns, bass trumpet, and Wagner tubas, as well as dividing the string sections to achieve unique effects. The work places inordinate demands on the singer of the title role, and these have often been relieved by cuts, many of which have achieved almost official status. It was not until 1967 that a complete *Elektra* was recorded by Decca, with Birgit Nilsson the indefatigable protagonist. She is surrounded by a sterling cast, with Regina Resnik and Gerhard Stolze putting across the crazed Klytämnestra and Aegisth with frightening realism. Solti leads a performance of almost unbearable tension, every orchestral detail vividly caught by John Culshaw's recording team. **CMS**

Arnold Schoenberg
Klavierstücke (1909–31)

Genre | Instrumental
Instrument | Piano
Performer | Peter Hill
Year recorded | 1996
Label | Naxos 8.553870

Schoenberg was no pianist, yet he tended to use the instrument to make the first codification of his radical developments in musical language. The three *Klavierstücke* (*Piano Pieces*) op. 11 (1909) were the first works in which he decisively broke with traditional ideas of tonality; additionally, the third piece of the set abandons any kind of conventional symmetrical form but launches out into a flood of freely associating ideas. The tiny Six Little Pieces op. 19 (1911) are aphorisms, epigrams, snapshots of moments of intense feeling—most famously the numbed, bell-like final piece written after Mahler's funeral. The Five Piano Pieces op. 23 (1920–23) are a kind of musical laboratory—they record Schoenberg's first tentative steps toward his "method of composition with twelve tones related only to each other," ending with a twelve-note waltz. Bigger, richer in language and affect, the two op. 33 pieces (1929 and 1931) disclose renewed affinities with Romantic music without sacrificing any of their contemporary abrasiveness.

The bad old habits of playing these pieces cerebrally have long receded and contemporary accounts tap fully into the deep veins of emotion, fantasy, and elegy that they enshrine. No one does this better than Peter Hill. His tempi are generally on the slow side, but because of that the harmony speaks with unrivaled eloquence and humanity. He is never percussive, coaxing the sound from the keys even where the music is most dissonant; he shapes the lines always as melody, never mere gesture, and his sensitive pedaling makes sure the textures are never starved or dry. **MM**

George Butterworth | Songs (1909–12)

Genre | Vocal
Performers | Bryn Terfel (baritone),
Malcolm Martineau (piano)
Year recorded | 1995
Label | DG 445 946-2

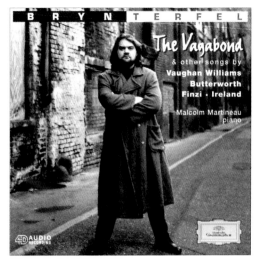

Although he lived for only thirty-one years, and wrote only two major song cycles, George Butterworth has come to represent the very epitome of English songwriting from the world of yesteryear, vanished forever since the two World Wars. Butterworth died in the trenches of the Somme in 1916, and his definitive settings of A. E. Housman continue to be all the more poignant for their oblique prophecy of the composer's own death as one of those soldiers who were "dear to friends, and food for powder."

Butterworth's upbringing was quintessentially English. The son of a general manager of Britain's North-Eastern Railway, he spent his boyhood in York, and was educated at Eton and Oxford before joining the Duke of Cornwall's Light Infantry and going off to war in September 1915.

That sense of English folksong that is subsumed into both *Six Songs from A Shropshire Lad* and his *Bredon Hill and Other Songs* came from his early years spent collecting (and performing) Morris dances in Oxfordshire and folksongs in Sussex, spurred on by his friendship with Cecil Sharp and Ralph Vaughan Williams.

Although several other composers were to set Housman's verse, it is Butterworth's instinct for what Gerard Manley Hopkins might have called "the roll, the rise, the carol, the creation" of the poet's work that has etched his settings so indelibly on the consciousness.

And perhaps it takes a Welshman, for whom English is his second language, to hear these songs afresh, purge them of cliché and preconception, and regenerate their impassioned appetite for life in the face of mortality. Bryn Terfel, beautifully accompanied by Malcolm Martineau, inhabits to the full every word, every sentiment of Butterworth's two cycles. **HF**

> "I think it was I who introduced [Butterworth] to folk song. This was his salvation . . ."

Ralph Vaughan Williams

Other Recommended Recordings

Christopher Maltman, Roger Vignoles
Hyperion CDA 67378
A quintessentially English baritone's take on the two great Butterworth cycles

Anthony Rolfe Johnson, Graham Johnson
Alan Bates • Hyperion CDA 66471/2 (2 CDs)
Housman's words both sung and read, in settings by Butterworth, Orr, Ireland, Moeran, and others

Robert Tear, City of Birmingham Symphony Orchestra
Vernon Handley • EMI 7243 5 75795 2 0 (9 CDs)
Butterworth's folksong settings in eloquent performances for tenor and orchestra

Bryn Terfel won the Cardiff Singer of the World song prize in 1989. ➔

Sergei Rachmaninov
The Isle of the Dead
(1909)

Genre | Orchestral
Conductor | Vladimir Jurowski
Performers | London Philharmonic
Year recorded | 2004
Label | LPO 0004

Few orchestral works are as luxuriously dark as Rachmaninov's symphonic poem *The Isle of the Dead*, written in response to the somber painting of the same name by the Swiss artist Arnold Böcklin, which shows a shrouded soul arriving by boat at a weird island cemetery. Rachmaninov actually saw a black-and-white reproduction, which may explain why his imagination was set free to create such a fantastically rich orchestral palette of sable-browns, blood-reds, deep greens, and inky blues. The music tells the story of the soul's arrival at its final destination, its desperate protestations, and ultimate acceptance. Yet, moving as *The Isle of the Dead* is, it is far from depressing—perhaps because there is also courage in Rachmaninov's musical confrontation with death.

There have been terrifyingly intense recordings of this work, but Jurowski's thoughtful, subtle approach scores highly on its own terms. He shows that there is no need for melodrama—that the ideas and the orchestral black magic are all the more effective if they are not hyped up. He also has an unusually strong sense of the work's overall shape. We go with the boat across the murky waters, follow the soul's last attempt to plead for life, then watch the boatman returning, his task accomplished. But there is also a sense of symphonic cogency, as Rachmaninov spins his most ingenious variations on the medieval requiem chant "Dies irae" (Day of Wrath), which haunted him to the end of his own life. The live recording captures faithfully the sense of an outstanding musical event. **SJ**

Arnold Schoenberg
Five Orchestral Pieces, op. 16 (1909)

Genre | Orchestral
Conductor/Performers | Simon Rattle;
City of Birmingham Symphony Orchestra
Year recorded | 1988
Label | EMI 7243 5 75880 2 7

By 1909, driven by creative forces stronger than his conscious will, Schoenberg was setting down music of previously unimagined dissonance and asymmetry. The Five Pieces are "inner visions" of emotional extremes—fear, hysteria, anguish—and the finest shades of fleeting, evanescent intuition.

We call such music "Expressionist" for its strong kinship with the equally radical contemporary work of Kandinsky and Kokoschka (with whom Schoenberg, himself a painter, collaborated—his canvases were shown in their exhibitions). Most painterly of these Pieces is no. 3: a still central point, based on a single chord, continually reinstrumented in a subtle, shifting kaleidoscope of color that also causes tiny shifts in the harmony.

The individual movements received their present titles in 1912, at the request of their publisher. Schoenberg noted in his diary that they would be called "1 Premonitions (everybody has those); 2 The Past (everyone has that, too); 3 Chord-colors (technical); 4 Peripeteia (general enough, I think); 5 The Obbligato (perhaps better the 'fully developed' or the 'endless') Recitative." Schoenberg revised the pieces several times—most recordings that claim to be of the "original version" use the score published in 1922, which was the third version. Rattle and the CBSO bring a particular focus and richness of sonority to these highly contrasted studies. The tonal nostalgia of no. 2 and the hypnotic, hallucinatory aura around the "starting" chord of no. 3 have never been better brought out. **MM**

Jean Sibelius
String Quartet
"Voces intimae" (1909)

Genre | Chamber
Performers | Emerson Quartet:
Drucker, Setzer, Dutton, Finckel
Year recorded | 2004
Label | DG 477 5960

Ralph Vaughan Williams
A Sea Symphony
(1909, *revised* 1923)

Genre | Vocal/Orchestral
Conductor | Vernon Handley
Performers | Joan Rodgers, William Shimell
Year recorded | 1988
Label | EMI 5 75308 2

As a student, Sibelius composed prodigious amounts of chamber music, including three complete string quartets, but there is only one such work from his maturity: the Quartet in D minor. Chronologically speaking, it falls between the Third and Fourth symphonies, a period during which Sibelius underwent a series of operations for throat cancer. It is a pivotal composition, breaking decisively with the expectations of contemporary listeners while turning its back on the various flamboyant musical modernisms espoused by Central European professionals. Sibelius penciled in the Latin title over three hushed, alien-sounding chords that mysteriously interrupt the flow of the central Adagio, in every sense the beating heart of this sometimes inscrutable five-movement structure.

Voces intimae remains comparatively rare on disc, so it is heartening to see an internationally acclaimed group taking up the cause—and the Emerson's emphatic projection brings a new dimension to the music. Very much part of the intended effect is Deutsche Grammophon's larger-than-life recording—exceptionally vivid if somewhat airless, the separation of the instruments achieved at the expense of tonal blend. This is objectified Sibelius for the twenty-first century—fierce, stoical, and determined. Not that these players are in any way reluctant to let rip in the second half of the finale, a wild toccata played here with devastating pace and unanimity. The apt couplings are Grieg's only complete mature quartet and Nielsen's brief threnody, "At the bier of a young artist." **DG**

Vaughan Williams's first symphonic essay started life as a series of choral settings of poems from *Leaves of Grass* by Walt Whitman. Like many talented young composers, he poured out original ideas but at first lacked the musical maturity to structure his arguments successfully; it took six years to be completed. The result is a marvelous, broad canvas of sea pictures, powerful in its sheer enormity of thought and variety of musical response to his chosen texts. It follows a typical four-movement symphonic design, opening with a brilliant fanfare that heralds a great outpouring of rich melody and orchestration. There are hints of Elgar here, but the overall tone clearly reveals a fine, individual, creative English voice.

The slow movement is a nocturnal reflection of the sea's "vast similitude" to the universe and the third an energetic scherzo testing the skills of both orchestra and chorus. In the finale the composer calls us to "steer for the deep waters only" with music of increasing calm. Vernon Handley's account of this vast work is splendid throughout. Joan Rodgers handles the soprano solos with a wonderful sheen; her clarity and control in the closing pages of the work bring added radiance to the glorious sustained textures of the chorus. William Shimell also brings energy and excitement to his performance. It is easy for the first movement to steal the center of gravity with its great surface excitement, but Handley's careful pacing gives due weight both to the warm sustained sounds of the second movement and the ultimate tranquility of the finale. **SW**

Ralph Vaughan Williams | On Wenlock Edge (1909)

Genre | Vocal
Performers | John Mark Ainsley (tenor),
Nash Ensemble
Year recorded | 1999
Label | Hyperion CDA 67168

Fresh from his studies with Ravel in Paris, Vaughan Williams set to work on poems from *A Shropshire Lad* by A. E. Housman. These popular, pessimistic poems explore themes of death and love in the context of a rural world now lost forever. Vaughan Williams chose six of these, beginning with "On Wenlock Edge." It is a fine poem, evoking Nature's raw power and its symbolic echo in the disquiet of the English yeoman who is narrating.

This song cycle marks an important stage in Vaughan Williams's development as a composer. He creates original melodies with a folklike quality, and the variety of textures he obtains from the accompanying piano and string quartet is truly impressive. A fine example is in the first song, when the tenor opens with a simple pentatonic tune that contrasts vividly with the wild and violent gestures flung between the accompanying instruments, suggesting the savage gale attacking the wood on Wenlock Edge in the English county of Shropshire. There is writing of real subtlety in "Bredon Hill," in which the distant echo of bell chimes is captured on delicate string and piano chords.

The opening movement is rendered with remarkable vividness by the string players of the Nash Ensemble. Their agitated trills and swirling patterns really bring the energetic force of nature alive, leaving the listener almost breathless. In stark contrast, they play their sustained wide chords of "Bredon Hill" with great delicacy and spaciousness. This committed playing provides an evocation of the Shropshire countryside around which John Mark Ainsley sings with impressive conviction. In the third song, "Is my Team Ploughing?" he indulges in the singers' histrionics, relishing the callousness of the soul still alive who has stolen his dead friend's sweetheart. **SW**

> *"I learned much from him. For example, that the heavy contrapuntal Teutonic manner was not necessary."*
>
> Ralph Vaughan Williams on his tutorials with Ravel

Other Recommended Recordings

Philip Langridge, Howard Shelley, Britten Quartet
EMI 7243 5 85155 2 7
Finely honed English spirit with some highly atmospheric singing and playing

Ian Partridge, Jennifer Partridge
Music Group of London • EMI 7243 5 65589 2 2
Sensitively and intelligently performed on this inexpensive release

Phantasy Quintet
Maggini Quartet, Garfield Jackson
Naxos 8.555300
Superb performance of this fine, yet underrated piece

A. E. Housman, whose poetry captivated English composers. ➔

Anton Webern
Six Orchestral Pieces, op. 6
(1909)

Genre | Orchestral
Conductor/Performers | Pierre Boulez;
Berlin Philharmonic Orchestra
Year recorded | 2000
Label | DG 447 099-2

Claude Debussy
Préludes, Books 1 & 2
(1910, 1913)

Genre | Instrumental
Instrument | Piano
Performer | Krystian Zimerman
Year recorded | 1991
Label | DG 435 773-2

Written at around the same time as Schoenberg completed his Five Orchestral Pieces, Webern's op. 6 establishes a striking contrast to the work of his teacher, in a style that is much more fragmented and concentrated in structure than that of Schoenberg's work.

There is little doubt that Webern's Six Pieces reflect upon the death of his mother in 1906, which was one of the most traumatic episodes in his life. The connection is made explicit in the fourth and most extended piece—a slow "Funeral March" that rises to a terrifying climax, the relentless procession of bells and gongs engulfing the rest of the orchestra at the very end. Surrounding this are movements that are much more epigrammatic and suggestive in mood—an uneasy premonition of death in the first, a hysterical and anguished outburst at the end of the second, a delicate vein of tenderness and nostalgia in the third, and finally the calm acceptance of the inevitable in the fifth and sixth pieces.

Few interpreters are better equipped to understand Webern's complex narrative than Pierre Boulez. The great French musician brings a textural clarity and logic to the composer's sometimes disjointed melodic lines, yet never sacrifices the expressive intensity of the music. With the Berlin Philharmonic responding brilliantly to every subtle nuance in the score, the performance evokes powerful resonances, the "Funeral March" in particular unleashing a torrent of anger and aggression that casts a disturbing shadow over the rest of the work. **EL**

Claude Debussy had reached the full powers of his musical maturity by the time he wrote his two books of Préludes for solo piano. He transformed this concise musical form, derived from Bach's Preludes and Fugues and Chopin's twenty-four visionary pieces, into overtly pictorial works.

Debussy's Préludes were inspired by a wide range of impressions, from the wonders of nature in "Ce qu'a vu le vent d'ouest" ("What the West Wind has Seen") to the poetry of Charles Baudelaire in "Les sons et les parfums tournent dans l'air du soir" ("Sounds and Perfumes Hang in the Evening Air"); from a postcard of the Alhambra in Granada, "La puerta del vino" ("The Door of Wine") and even the novels of Charles Dickens ("Hommage à S. Pickwick Esq. P.P.M.P.C"), to an American clown ("General Lavine—eccentric"). Shortly after completing them, Debussy wrote: "Composers alone have the privilege of capturing all the poetry of night and day, of earth and sky, of recreating their atmosphere and of setting their mighty pulsations within a rhythmic framework." Several of the pieces have achieved popularity on their own, including "La cathédrale engloutie" ("The Sunken Cathedral") and "La fille aux cheveux de lin" ("The Girl with the Flaxen Hair").

In this classic account, which won the Gramophone Record of the Year Award in 1994, the great Polish pianist Krystian Zimerman captures the full panoply of Debussy's intimacy, wit, brilliance, mystery, and unfailing originality, his matchless piano playing bringing every Prélude into vivid focus. **JD**

Engelbert Humperdinck
Königskinder
(1910)

Genre | Opera
Conductor/Performers | Heinz Walberg;
Adolf Dallapozza, Helen Donath
Year recorded | 1977
Label | EMI 7 69936 2 (3 CDs)

In Engelbert Humperdinck's fairytale opera, a humble goose-girl and a prince fall in love. Unrecognized by the townsfolk as their king and queen, they meet their end starving and penniless, victims of an uncaring society. The opera is a moving indictment of materialism, its fairytale elements—a wicked witch, a prince, a goose-girl, and a loaf of poisoned bread—deployed with passion and pathos. Left to freeze and starve to death, the royal children of the title share their last crust; unknown to them, it is poisoned.

Humperdinck was for a time a member of Wagner's circle and his works are charged with Wagnerian resonances, both musical and dramatic. As with his earlier fairytale opera *Hänsel und Gretel*, there is an element of sentimentality in *Königskinder* that some find off-putting; but understood as a protest against the harshness of the world of technology and "progress" coming into being at the turn of the century, it is a work that can be deeply touching in the theater. The opera was certainly very favorably received when it premiered, at the Metropolitan Opera, New York, in December 1910.

There is much fine music in this wonderfully lyrical opera and nowhere is it heard to better effect than in Heinz Wallberg's 1977 EMI account. Adolf Dallapozza and Helen Donath are the excellent prince and goose-girl. A key role is that of the enigmatic Minstrel, who also has some of the best music. Hermann Prey brings to it a mystery and throbbing poignancy not easily forgotten. **BM**

Gustav Mahler
Symphony no. 10
(1910)

Genre | Orchestral
Conductor | Simon Rattle
Performers | Berlin Philharmonic Orchestra
Year recorded | 1999
Label | EMI 5 56972 2

Composed hastily in the summer of 1910 and left incomplete upon the composer's untimely death the following May, Mahler's Tenth Symphony has only gradually come to be recognized as a crucial part of his output. For years the opening Adagio was regarded as the only movement sufficiently "completed" and substantial to be salvageable, but since 1964 Deryck Cooke's performing version of the composition draft has obtained increasing exposure in the concert hall, and it seems clear that our new century will witness ever-greater attention to this unusual but moving work.

The often choralelike serenity of the opening movement is shattered by a famously dissonant nine-note chord, but then regained with a magnificently spacious counterpart. The finale, beginning with a series of tragic drum strokes, reworks material from the first, third, and fourth movements, some of which was composed during Mahler's anguish at learning of his wife Alma's unfaithfulness. The tone of the work encompasses tenderness, anxiety, and rueful but profound tranquility.

Simon Rattle has long been a staunch advocate of the Tenth, and his second recording is the most satisfying yet made. This is due not so much to the interpretive decisions he proposes as for the general feeling of authority and confidence that pervades the performance. Energetic passages sound powerfully involved and, throughout, Rattle admirably characterizes striking moments while achieving convincing momentum. **DB**

Edward Elgar | Violin Concerto (1910)

Genre | Concerto
Performers | Albert Sammons, New Queen's Hall Orchestra
Conductor | Henry Wood
Year recorded | 1929
Label | Naxos 8.110951

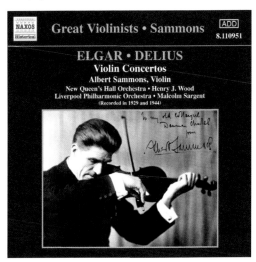

Elgar's Violin Concerto is one of a handful of works in which the whole range of this composer's complex and enigmatic personality stands revealed. It begins with bluff resolution and ends with a starburst of joyous hope—or so it seems. Elsewhere, however, one finds deep, introspective melancholy, exquisitely painful nostalgia, and—in the closing pages of the great slow movement—something very close to erotic tenderness, all tinged with intense regret. Somehow or other this stirringly personal document—almost a musical "confession"—also manages to be a superb showcase for the virtuoso violinist, as well as being one of the most impressively cogent symphonic concertos written after Brahms. The magical accompanied cadenza in the finale (with the strings at several points quietly strumming their instruments like guitars) is one of Elgar's most brilliant and poetic inspirations, and it has been enormously influential. No wonder this acutely self-doubting composer remained so proud of it.

Elgar's own 1932 recording with the sixteen-year-old Yehudi Menuhin is often held up as a classic, but Albert Sammons is surely more mature, subtler, with an emotional openness that makes it hard to believe one is listening to playing from more than seventy years ago. If this has not been widely appreciated for the glorious thing it is until now, that has more to do with the indifferent or downright poor quality of previous transfers. This splendid new Naxos version is therefore more of a restoration, with Sammons, in particular, sounding astonishingly clear and immediate. It really is not necessary to make significant allowances for the sound quality. In any case the performance sweeps the listener along with it so commandingly that any lingering perfectionist objections are soon silenced. **SJ**

"I have written out my soul in the concerto."

Edward Elgar

Other Recommended Recordings

Nigel Kennedy, City of Birmingham Symphony Orchestra • Simon Rattle • EMI 7243 5 56413 2 8
An exciting, emotionally demonstrative version, especially lovely in the slow movement

Yehudi Menuhin, London Symphony Orchestra Edward Elgar • EMI 7243 5 66994 2 7
Possibly Menuhin's greatest recording, and a superb partnership with the composer

Dong-Suk Kang, Polish National Symphony Orchestra Adrian Leaper • Naxos 8.550489
An unusually urgent performance, quicker than most but full of understanding

Albert Sammons on a tank in Trafalgar Square, London, c. 1916. ➔

Florent Schmitt
La tragédie de Salomé (1910)

Genre | Orchestral
Conductor | Marek Janowski
Performers | Radio France Philharmonic
Year recorded | 1988
Label | Warner 2564 62764-2

Composer, academic, and critic, Florent Schmitt (1870–1958) was an influential figure in French music in the early twentieth century. He was born in Lorraine, and the Germanic influence in that part of France seems to have given him a wider cultural outlook than that of many of his compatriots: He embraced the music of both Wagner and Strauss, yet followed the traditional training of most French musicians of the day.

Schmitt is chiefly remembered for his ballet score *La tragédie de Salomé*, which was composed originally for chamber ensemble in 1907 but refashioned into a symphonic poem for large orchestra three years later. Instead of turning to Oscar Wilde's notorious play (Strauss's opera was sweeping the world at the time), Schmitt based his scenario on a poem by Robert d'Humières that sets the Biblical story against the backdrop of Herod's palace by the Dead Sea. Schmitt's evocative music at once gives Debussy a run for his money in the opulence of his seascape and looks forward to Stravinsky's *Rite of Spring* in the rhythms and harmonies of the final "Dance of Fear." Stravinsky, indeed, acknowledged the influence of *Salomé* when writing his epoch-making ballet and was honored with the score's dedication.

In a limited field, Marek Janowski's French Radio recording stands out for the atmosphere it creates, from the languor of the opening scene-setting and in the later "Enchantment of the Sea," where wordless voices sing like sirens of fate. But it is also highly energized in Salome's various dances. The coupling is an equally vibrant account of Schmitt's ambitious 1906 setting of Psalm 47. **MR**

Fritz Kreisler | Liebesfreud
& Liebesleid (c.1910)

Genre | Chamber
Performers | Fritz Kreisler, Carl Lamson
Year recorded | 1926
Label | RCA 09026 61649 2 (11 CDs) or
Biddulph LAB 075

Electrical recording, bringing greater fidelity of sound via a microphone—as opposed to the old acoustic method —came along in 1925, just in time to catch the great Viennese violinist Fritz Kreisler (1875–1962) at his peak. The recordings he made (with his regular American accompanist Carl Lamson) for the Victor company over the next few years are easily his best for a combination of good sound and good playing. Kreisler belonged to a more leisured age and was particularly skillful at both writing and playing short pieces. We think of them as encores, but in his day they filled celebrity recital programs.

Perhaps Kreisler's most popular hits among his own compositions were the matching pair *Liebesfreud* (*Love's Joy*) and *Liebesleid* (*Love's Sorrow*). They were the first two items in a set he published as *Old Viennese Dance Tunes* (the other was *Schön Rosmarin*). In about 1910, soon after writing them, he ascribed the pieces to Lanner in a Berlin recital and was told off by a critic for playing his own *Caprice Viennois* next to work by the great Lanner. Thereafter he came clean, although it took another half century for him to acknowledge that many of his other "arrangements" of earlier composers were his own work .

Kreisler himself recorded each of the two pieces a number of times and although virtually every other violinist under the sun has had a go at them, there is no substitute for the composer's own winning amalgam of velvet tone, insinuating rubato, and Viennese charm. The RCA set is recommended to those who want to explore the legendary violinist's recordings in depth. For a single disc, the Biddulph will do nicely. **TP**

Franz Schreker
Der ferne Klang (1910)

Genre | Opera
Conductor/Performers | Michael Halász;
Elena Grigorescu, Thomas Harper
Year recorded | 1989
Label | Naxos 8.660074-75 (2 CDs)

In his day, Franz Schreker (1878–1934) was as famous as Richard Strauss—renowned as a teacher and a friend of Schoenberg, his operas at the cutting edge of modern music. But his Jewish roots ensured that he was a target of Nazism and he had to resign from his prestigious directorship of the Berlin Hochschule für Musik in 1932. Unable to emigrate, his life and career in ruins, he died a couple of years later. As one of the composers damned for writing "degenerate music," his work was largely forgotten and had to wait until the late twentieth century for rehabilitation. Now his opulent, late-Romantic operas are making headway, at least in the German-speaking world.

Schreker's first great operatic success was *Der ferne Klang* (*The Distant Sound*). Its bold mixture of Impressionism, Expressionism, Realism, and psychology had a profound influence on contemporary composers, most notably Berg, who prepared the opera's vocal score for publication. In typically autobiographical vein for Schreker, it as an opera about opera, or at least about a young composer in search of the "distant sound" that will make his own stage work complete and, at the same time, his search for Grete, the girl he initially abandoned to prostitution in his single-minded endeavor.

Only two commercial recordings have been made of this seminal work of twentieth-century opera, and the better of them is the one recorded after staged performances in Hagen, Germany. The cast, though not made up of well-known names, is excellent and the orchestra under Michael Halász sounds perfectly at home in Schreker's multifaceted writing. **MR**

Alexander Scriabin
Prometheus (1910)

Genre | Orchestral
Conductor/Performers | Claudio
Abbado; Berlin Philharmonic Orchestra
Year recorded | 1992
Label | Sony SK 53978

The myth of Prometheus was a predictable choice of subject for a composer as full of himself as Alexander Scriabin. The early twentieth-century Russian master undoubtedly saw a parallel between the Titan son's theft of fire to benefit mankind and what he felt was his own destiny to bring light to the world. And in this twenty-minute "Poem of Fire," completed in 1910, he brings real light in the shape of a part for a "color keyboard," designed to illuminate the auditorium in different hues to match the harmonic progress of the music.

That harmonic palette is one of the richest Scriabin devised, with a so-called "Prometheus chord" of piled-up fourths resolving itself at the end on to a blazing F sharp major chord, complete with organ and wordless chorus. There is also an important role for a solo pianist—not so much in a concerto sense as in that of a chamber musician combining with the filigree voices of Scriabin's richly detailed orchestration—though it is hardly reticent in its virtuosity. The composer himself was the piano soloist in the first performance in Moscow in 1911, with conductor Serge Koussevitzky, who would later become one of the major players in the American orchestral scene.

The lighting effects are of necessity missing on CD, but the combination of a pianist as fiery as Martha Argerich and a conductor as finely attuned to orchestral color as Claudio Abbado ensures a performance to stir the senses. Their live 1992 account, with the Berlin Philharmonic in full cry, features on a fascinating CD of a concert in which Scriabins's *Prometheus* sat among other works inspired by the myth by Beethoven, Liszt, and Nono. **MR**

Richard Strauss | Der Rosenkavalier (1910)

Genre | Opera
Conductor/Performers | Georg Solti;
Régine Crespin, Yvonne Minton, Manfred Jungwirth
Year recorded | 1968
Label | Decca 417 4932 (3 CDs)

The idea of writing a comedy along the lines of Beaumarchais's *Figaro* came from Hugo von Hofmannsthal, who liked to consider himself a Da Ponte to Strauss's Mozart. The composer was, of course, pleased with both the comparison and the subject matter, based on episodes from Louvet de Couvray's erotic novel *Les amours du Chevalier de Faublas*.

The Field Marshall's middle-aged wife has an affair with the much younger Count Octavian. Her uncouth relative, the dissolute Baron Ochs von Lerchenau, asks her to recommend a "Rose Knight" who, according to tradition, will bring a silver rose to his betrothed Sophie, daughter of the rich merchant Faninal, whom he is marrying for her father's money. Half foreseeing what will happen, she sends Octavian. He and Sophie fall in love at first sight. A trap is laid for Ochs: He is discovered during a rendezvous with the maid Mariandl, who is none other than Octavian in disguise. In one of the most heartbreaking moments in all opera, the Marschallin selflessly gives up her lover.

The opera was Strauss's biggest success to date. Although critics complained about the Vienna of Empress Maria Theresia being anachronistically characterized by an endless sequence of waltzes, the public loved the piece and special trains had to be scheduled to bring audiences to the performances in the Dresden Court Opera.

Many recordings of *Der Rosenkavalier* observe the cuts that became traditional in the theater, but not the one conducted by Solti, with the Vienna Philharmonic uniquely idiomatic in the waltzes and a number of elderly Viennese stars adorning the many comprimario roles. Régine Crespin brings welcome French chic to the proceedings, and Manfred Jungwirth makes his mark as Ochs. **CMS**

> *"Don't shoot! I'm Richard Strauss, I wrote Der Rosenkavalier!"*

Strauss to the GIs closing in on his house
at the end of the war

Other Recommended Recordings

Philharmonia Orchestra, Herbert von Karajan
EMI 7243 5 67609 2 9 (3 CDs)
Elisabeth Schwarzkopf was the Marschallin for a whole generation, and the Philharmonia make a good shot at being Viennese

Bavarian State Orchestra, Carlos Kleiber
DVD: DG 073 4072 (2 DVDs)
A most moving Marschallin from Gwyneth Jones

Vienna Philharmonic Orchestra, Robert Heger
Naxos 8.110191-92 (2 CDs)
Extended excerpts rather than a complete recording, but preserving some of Strauss's favorite interpreters

Georg Solti did little better than his Strauss recordings. ➔

Ralph Vaughan Williams
Fantasia on a Theme of Thomas Tallis (1910, *revised* 1919)

Genre | Orchestral
Conductor | John Barbirolli
Performers | Sinfonia of London, Allegri String Quartet
Year recorded | 1962
Label | EMI 7243 5 67264 2 0

With this piece Vaughan Williams created his first work of true mastery. It apparently confused the audience in Gloucester Cathedral who first heard it in 1910, but it has impressed countless concertgoers since. The Tallis theme of the title is a hymn tune that the composer had chosen when editing *The English Hymnal*. However it is not simply around Tallis's theme that ideas ebb and flow. With his freely modal language, Vaughan Williams takes something inherent in the rich polyphonic world of the great Tudor composer and draws on the pungent false relations and other striking harmonies of which the older composer was so fond. Whereas Tallis's church music was intended for an antiphonal choir, Vaughan Williams writes for the curious—yet highly effective—combination of full string orchestra, small string ensemble, and solo string quartet. He deploys these forces with real maturity of textural understanding, creating the luminous sounds that are the hallmark of all his string writing. The sense of spaciousness must have been especially remarkable in the glorious Norman cathedral—the best performances of this much-loved piece are found wherever the resonance off stone surfaces adds another dimension to the subtle scoring.

This glorious recording from London's Temple Church achieves just such an effect. The delicacy of the quietest moments creates an atmosphere of tentative beauty, and when the strings play at their most full-blooded they have a rapturous quality rarely matched on disc. There is some really subtle engineering at work here also, which introduces a true breadth of vision into the sound world, with the Allegri Quartet playing as if from afar. **SW**

> *"Its essential serenity [is] by no means untroubled by gusts of passion."*
>
> Michael Kennedy

Ralph Vaughan Williams was inspired by the British countryside.

Igor Stravinsky
The Firebird (1910)

Genre | Ballet
Conductor/Performers | Simon Rattle;
City of Birmingham Symphony Orchestra
Year recorded | 1987
Label | EMI 7243 5 85538 2 6 (2 CDs)

Stravinsky's masterpiece *The Firebird* marks the first full fruits of his long association with Diaghilev's Ballets Russes. With choreography by principal dancer Michel Fokine and sets by Léon Bakst, the ballet was an early example of the impresario's ability to bring together great talents and it was given a rapturous reception in Paris in 1910.

Stravinsky's parents disapproved of his career in music and encouragement came instead from Rimsky-Korsakov, whose spirit is strong in *The Firebird*, with its dazzling orchestral invention and exoticism. Nonetheless, the originality of Stravinsky's voice is clear throughout and the "Infernal Dance" in particular is rightly seen as being prophetic of *The Rite of Spring*. Stravinsky later made various suites, reducing the lavish orchestral requirements and with the extraordinary intertwined ostinatos of the magic carillon among the excisions. Aside from containing marvelous music, the full ballet is essential for understanding Stravinsky's musical antecedents and potential paths that might have led in different directions.

From the latent menace of the opening through to the ecstatic final chorale, Simon Rattle and the CBSO set a new standard with their recording of the complete ballet. It is not just that key scenes, such as "Dance of the Firebird" and "Infernal Dance," are perfectly paced and imbued with a kaleidoscopic range of color; it is that the more hushed moments of this performance really impress. The most stunning instance is in the "Complete Darkness," where the strings give the impression not so much of sound as of the air imperceptibly changing hue, before the light streams in for the joyful bell-like fanfares of the apotheosis. **CD**

Edward Elgar
Symphony no. 2 (1911)

Genre | Orchestral
Conductor | John Barbirolli
Performers | Hallé Orchestra
Year recorded | 1964
Label | EMI 0946 3 67918 2 1 (5 CDs)

Marginalized after its composer's death—"overlong and overblown" was one much-repeated verdict—Elgar's Second Symphony has been rediscovered in modern times. Elgar thought it one of his finest and most personal achievements, and was deeply hurt when its first audience seemed not to agree: "They all sat there like stuffed pigs."

Now most critics would probably agree with Elgar. The imaginative daring is exceptional, especially in the strange first-movement passage that Elgar compared to a "malign influence wandering in a garden in a summer evening," while the climax of the third movement, with its juggernaut brass and pounding mechanical percussion, is unsettlingly powerful. Did Elgar, in 1911, sense something of the carnage soon to come? At the symphony's heart is a noble, funereal slow movement rising to a high point, whose wild emotional intensity will startle anyone who still thinks of Elgar as a tightly corseted Edwardian worthy.

As so often with Barbirolli, it is the love of the music that shines from every phrase, carrying the ear through all the enigmatic twists and turns in the symphony's narrative. He gets the sweeping forward momentum of the opening music as well as Elgar in his own recording, but with firmer control and more rounded orchestral balance. While the performance is quite expansive, it never sounds loose, and the sustained build-up in the slow movement is extraordinarily compelling. "Intellectual" was not a term applied often to Barbirolli, yet few conductors have matched his sense of this huge work as a living, coherent, formal entity. It is rare to encounter a performance that succeeds on so many levels. **SJ**

Enrique Granados
Goyescas (1911)

Genre | Instrumental
Instrument | Piano
Performer | Alicia de Larrocha
Year recorded | 1976
Label | Decca 448 191-2 (2 CDs)

Granados was one of Spain's most important composers. Like Albéniz he was a proficient pianist and composed piano music renowned for its Spanish national character. *Goyescas* is Granados's masterpiece, and is—along with Albéniz's *Iberia*—one of the defining works of Spanish Romantic pianism. In composing *Goyescas*, Granados was inspired by the essence of Spain captured by the painter Francisco Goya. Its six pieces were first performed in 1911 and published in two sets either side of this date (a seventh piece—"El pelele: Escena goyesca"—was issued separately, but is usually considered part of *Goyescas*).

The music of *Goyescas* is highly colored, at times intoxicating in its harmony and keyboard sonority, with insistent melodic repetitions and highly individual rhythmic patterns. Unusually, Granados converted the suite into an opera, which was first staged at the Metropolitan Opera in New York in 1916 in the presence of the composer. Tragically, the British ship carrying Granados and his wife back to Europe via Liverpool was torpedoed in the English Channel by a German submarine. Both Granados and his wife drowned. Granados was forty-eight.

As with *Iberia*, *Goyescas* is associated primarily with Alicia de Larrocha, who has recorded it four times. Her 1976 Decca recording is the finest: uniquely idiomatic, exuding verve and spontaneity, from heel-clicking rhythmic vitality in "El fandango de candil" ("Candlelit Fandango"), to magical atmospheric delicacy in "Quejas ó la maja y el ruiseñor" ("Laments or The Maiden and the Nightingale"). She is in her element, and no one has recorded this repertoire with such authentic spirit and fervor. **TLP**

Maurice Ravel
Ma mère l'oye (1911)

Genre | Instrumental/Orchestral
Performers | Martha Argerich,
Mikhail Pletnev (piano duet)
Year recorded | 2003
Label | DG 748 817-2

Ravel wrote *Ma mère l'oye* (*Mother Goose*), a suite of five pieces for piano, four-hands, between 1908 and 1910 for the children of his friend Cipa Godebski. Godebski's daughter, Mimi, later recalled that she loved Ravel because he told her stories: "I would climb on his knee and he would begin, 'Once upon a time . . .' and it would be *Laideronnette* or *Beauty and the Beast* . . . ." Some of these stories became the inspiration for the piano duets themselves. In 1911, Ravel orchestrated the five pieces, and later that year greatly expanded the suite into a ballet score.

A mood of enchantment is maintained throughout the suite, although the five pieces are distinct in character. "Pavane de la Belle au bois dormant" ("Sleeping Beauty") is a melancholy lullaby; "Petit Poucet" vividly describes Tom Thumb's forlorn wandering after the birds have eaten the crumbs he left on the forest path; in "Laideronnette, Impératrice des pagodes," an Asian princess is serenaded by tiny figures made of jewels, crystal, and porcelain; "Les entretiens de la Belle et de la Bête" alternates Beauty's graceful, Satie-like waltz with the Beast's awkward grumbling; and the finale, "Le jardin féerique" depicts the tender awakening of Sleeping Beauty by the Prince.

Ravel's orchestration of *Ma mère l'oye* is ravishing, to be sure, but there's something about the pure spirit of the piano original that is equally if not more affecting—and especially in a performance as magical as this. Martha Argerich and Mikhail Pletnev bring all the colors and characters to life without a hint of affectation or artifice. The result is dazzling in its delicacy and will delight listeners of all ages. **AFC**

Béla Bartók | Bluebeard's Castle (1911)

Genre | Opera
Conductor/Performers | István Kertész; Walter Berry,
Christa Ludwig, London Symphony Orchestra
Year recorded | 1965
Label | Decca 466 377-2

Bartók's only opera was completed in 1911 but was not performed for the first time until seven years later. The libretto by his compatriot Béla Balázs was indirectly inspired by Maeterlinck's drama *Ariane et Barbe-Bleue*, which Paul Dukas had turned into an opera a few years earlier—although the storyline was changed so that the two central characters, Duke Bluebeard and his new wife Judith, remain on stage for the entire work.

The opera opens with a brief prologue before revealing the castle's Gothic hall. Bluebeard pleads with Judith to reconsider her decision to come and live with him, but she remains resolute, believing that she can bring love and warmth to the gloomy surroundings. Judith demands that Bluebeard fetch the keys to open the closed doors that she notices on her arrival. He reluctantly agrees and the first door is opened to reveal Bluebeard's torture chamber. Undaunted by this horrific vision, Judith becomes increasingly adamant that she should know the secrets that lie behind the other doors, even though all are likewise tarnished with blood. When the seventh and final door is opened Judith understands her fate. She follows Bluebeard's three former wives behind the closed door and darkness once again overwhelms the castle.

Inspired to a large extent by Debussy's opera *Pelléas et Mélisande*, Bartók composed a powerful psychodrama utilizing the forces of a late-Romantic symphony orchestra to compelling effect. Of the several fine recordings of this masterpiece, the mid-1960s team of Walter Berry and Christa Ludwig is most convincing in projecting the rising tension between the two protagonists, and the orchestral contribution from the London Symphony Orchestra under Kertész is spine-tingling. **EL**

"Spiritual loneliness is to be my destiny."

Béla Bartók

Other Recommended Recordings

**Stuttgart Radio Symphony Orchestra, Peter Eötvös
Hänssler 93.070**
Highly charged performance in excellent modern sound

**Chicago Symphony Orchestra, Pierre Boulez
DG 447 040-2**
Boulez brings wonderful transparency to Bartók's orchestration

**Opera North Orchestra, Richard Farnes
Chandos CHAN 3133**
Stunning recording makes a strong case for the opera to be sung in English

István Kertész tragically drowned while swimming in 1973. ➔

Jean Sibelius
Symphony no. 4 (1911)

Genre | Orchestral
Conductor/Performers | Herbert von Karajan; Berlin Philharmonic Orchestra
Year recorded | 1965
Label | DG 457 748-2 (2 CDs)

Sergey Taneyev
Piano Quintet (1911)

Genre | Chamber
Performers | Mikhail Pletnev, Vadim Repin, Ilya Gringolts, Nobuko Imai, Lynn Harrell
Year recorded | 2003
Label | DG 477 5419

Sibelius's singular style achieves its bleakest expression in the Fourth Symphony. Gone are the elements of nationalist rhetoric, melody, and color that won him acclaim. Personal problems and disenchantment with the world had led him into a black hole of introspection. The Fourth, so unlike anything written at the time, can, even today, bemuse those not attuned to the composer's idiom. Although Sibelius explicitly rejected attempts to associate the work with his experiences of the landscape at Mount Koli in east Finland, many listeners will find it conjuring images of the natural world in the dead of winter, bare branches gaunt against a threatening sky.

The public image of Herbert von Karajan as a maestro intent on manufacturing glossy accounts of standard repertoire might seem worlds away from such anti-cosmopolitan fare but in fact this was one of the few scores that shattered him emotionally—and there is no evidence that Sibelius regarded a concern with outward perfection as antithetical to the realization of inner meaning. At the time of Karajan's earlier mono LP, Sibelius wrote, "Especially in the Fourth Symphony, his great artistic line and the inner beauty of the interpretation have deeply impressed me." Inevitably, the present recording, made after a Helsinki concert in celebration of the composer's centenary, has been seen as too beautiful. Robert Layton, Sibelius's English-language biographer, at first likened it to "the Finnish landscape perceived through the windows of a limousine. . . . What I recognized later was great depth of feeling. That sense of something coming between the music and the listener had completely disappeared." **DG**

You may be wondering just who Taneyev was, and what a work written only two years before Stravinsky's *Rite of Spring* might sound like. Showing early promise, Sergey Taneyev became a composition pupil of Tchaikovsky at thirteen, and a professor of the Moscow Conservatoire (replacing Tchaikovsky himself) when he was twenty-two, becoming its director before he was thirty. He also taught Rachmaninov and Scriabin. All this teaching activity seems to have overshadowed his own music, which he composed slowly and painstakingly, taking as much care over its craft as its inspiration. If that makes him sound perhaps a tad worthy, that is far from the case.

The Piano Quintet has long been neglected in favor of his Piano Trio, and it has taken an outstanding recording by five of today's greatest players to put it back on the map. Mikhail Pletnev, as at home on the podium as on the piano stool, has long championed the orchestral works of Taneyev, whom he believes to be one of the greats in Russian music. Now he turns to the chamber music and makes his point triumphantly, in both the quintet and the trio with which it is coupled. By the time Taneyev composed the quintet, he'd long relinquished his duties at the Conservatoire. To judge from the demanding piano part, he must have been a pianist of considerable prowess. This is the grandest of all his chamber pieces, and if it is possible to detect hints of Tchaikovsky and Franck in its writing, the overall result is very much his own. The scherzo is particularly mesmerizing, with a wonderful lilting trio section. For anyone interested in lush, virtuoso chamber music, this is unmissable. **HS**

Sergei Rachmaninov
Études-tableaux (1911–17)

Genre | Instrumental
Instrument | Piano
Performer | John Ogdon
Year recorded | 1971
Label | Testament SBT 1295

Carl Nielsen
Symphony no. 3 (1911)

Genre | Orchestral
Conductor/Performers | Herbert
Blomstedt; San Francisco Symphony
Year recorded | 1989
Label | Decca 460 985-2 (2 CDs)

Rachmaninov spent most of his time working on large-scale projects, but small self-contained character-pieces usually brought out the best in him. The two sets of *Études-tableaux* (opp. 33 and 39) fuse technical and musical challenges with evocative poetic vision. Although these pieces tend to have a technical bias, exploring ideas rooted in particular piano figurations, they are primarily character-pieces, hence the "tableaux" (pictures) of the title. They are not actual pictures, in the Mussorgskian sense. Rachmaninov generally preferred to keep his sources of inspiration private; but while there are no bubbling streams, passing storms, or tweeting birds, Rachmaninov did disclose his extra-musical stimulations for five of the *études* to Italian composer Ottorino Respighi, who orchestrated them. The imaginative and narrative scope of these pieces is more suggestive than literal—though the music's emotional force has no less impact for that.

Many pianists give outstanding performances of individual *études-tableaux*, but only a handful have recorded both sets. The outstanding complete recording comes from British pianist John Ogdon. Recorded in 1971 (before Ogdon's illness, and not to be confused with his distressing 1988 revisit, which should never have been issued) this set finds Ogdon on prime form, and is a highlight of his recorded legacy. Ogdon distills the most complex and awkward piano writing with apparent nonchalance, yet plays with a fire-breathing drama and intensity that eludes more conservative pianists. True, not every detail emerges with pristine clarity, but he unfailingly captures the essence of every piece. **TLP**

Nielsen began work on this symphony in 1910 and completed it early the following year; it premiered in 1912 with his Violin Concerto. The symphony proved to be a turning point in his career, and a success with the public and the critics—one wrote that "It was at last the fully mature artistic personality that emerged here. . . . The first wholly and fully ripe apple from his tree." The same year as the premiere, Nielsen conducted it several times in Denmark, as well as at the Concertgebouw in Amsterdam. By that time he had added a title, *Sinfonia espansiva*, from the tempo indication for the first movement—allegro espansivo (lively and expansive). In a later program note, the composer described this movement as ". . . a gust of energy and life-affirmation blown out into the wide world."

This could stand as a motto for much of Nielsen's music, but what is most striking about this symphony is the slow movement, a gently moving pastoral, which reaches an ecstatic but restrained climax when two singers—a soprano and a baritone—join the orchestra from the distance in a long, intertwining, wordless melisma. Nielsen authorized the substitution of clarinet and trombone if singers weren't available—a version that is rarely heard.

The ideal performance of the *Sinfonia espansiva* has to be able to combine the mysticism of this Andante with the outgoing nature of the other movements, and this is what makes Herbert Blomstedt's version such a success. In the Andante, the soprano seems to be coming from another world, but the rumbustious approach to the outer movements and the poise of the third movement Allegretto have never been bettered. **MC**

Reinhold Glière | Symphony no. 3 "Ilya Muromets" (1911)

Genre | Orchestral
Conductor | Edward Downes
Performers | BBC Philharmonic
Year recorded | 1991
Label | Chandos CHAN 9041

Reinhold Glière (1875–1956), one of the great survivors among Russian composers, took the grand Romantic tradition well into the Soviet era. He was still writing music in the 1950s that would hardly have sounded out of place in the 1890s. But his brand of popularism awarded him with the chairmanship of the Union of Soviet Composers and the honor of People's Artists of the U.S.S.R. at a time when the more adventurous Prokofiev and Shostakovich had to watch their backs. His ballet scores from the Soviet period made some headway in the rest of the wider world, most notably *The Red Poppy* from 1927.

Back in the first decade of the century, though, when big-boned Romanticism was still fashionable, he began a massive symphony inspired as much by Wagner's *Siegfried* as by Rimsky-Korsakov and Scriabin. A vast programmatic structure, almost eighty minutes long, it narrates the story of a warrior hero from the dawn of Russian Christianity, Ilya of Murom. The music is appropriately epic, dynamic, and lush. Even if the long, birdsong-imbued slow movement is so obviously cribbed from Scriabin's *Divine Poem*, the symphony as a whole is full of memorable themes.

As was the case with Rachmaninov's Second Symphony, Glière's Third was long performed only in a heavily cut version—less than half its true length and rearranged by the inveterate Stokowski—but Edward Downes's Chandos recording was instrumental in restoring its full length and true reputation. The playing and recording are simply spectacular, with the sumptuous Andante emerging as languorously as the final "Heroic Deeds and Petrification" movement is dramatic. **MR**

Arnold Schoenberg Gurrelieder (1911)

Genre | Vocal/choral
Performers/Conductor | Sharon Sweet, Siegfried Jerusalem; Claudio Abbado
Year recorded | 1992
Label | DG 439 944-2

Completed in 1911, when the composer was just twenty-six years old, Schoenberg's enormous work is part song-cycle, part cantata, part post-Wagnerian operatic Liebestod. The text evokes the doomed love affair of the medieval Danish king Waldemar for the beautiful Tove, her murder, and his cursing of God, which causes him and his vassals to ride every night in a "Wild Hunt." Scored for gigantic orchestral and vocal forces at least the equal of Mahler's "Symphony of a Thousand," and requiring soloists for whom Wagnerian opera holds no terrors, it is one of the summits of musical late-Romanticism, but already—in its final section, with the satirical song for the king's Fool and the filigree "Wild Hunt of the Summer Wind" featuring a Speaker—begins to question the whole emotional and technical bases of its own richly post-Wagnerian language.

The work embraces such a diversity of styles and textures, and demands such a titanic vocal-operatic apparatus, that an "ideal performance" may be inherently unrealizable. Claudio Abbado's reading, recorded live at the Vienna Musikverein where the work received its 1913 premiere, has a boldness, sweep, and astonishing textural clarity, which may just give it the edge; despite the jarring vocalizations of Barbara Sukowa as Speaker (usually a male role) and the slightly lightweight Sharon Sweet as Tove. Otherwise this is a very strong cast, with Siegfried Jerusalem a truly Heldentenor Waldemar, and Philip Langridge a wonderfully vinegary Fool. Abbado directs the full forces in Part 3 with appropriately heaven-storming abandon. The recording is tremendously rich and spacious and conveys the electric sense of occasion necessary. **MM**

Igor Stravinsky
Petrushka (1911)

Genre | Ballet
Conductor | Leopold Stokowski
Performers | Philadelphia Orchestra
Year recorded | 1937
Label | Pearl GEMM CD 9031

Stravinsky's second ballet was supposed to be *The Rite of Spring*, but he interrupted work on his scenes of pagan Russia to write *Petrushka*. Though not as brutal, *Petrushka* is as radical a departure from the Rimsky-Korsakov–inspired sound world of *The Firebird* as *The Rite*, and its bright, clear-cut textures are as indicative of Stravinsky's later music. The hustle and bustle of a Shrovetide fair, evoked by a succession of mechanistic motifs, marks the emergence of his true compositional voice.

Originally conceived as a concert piece pitting piano against orchestra, Diaghilev encouraged Stravinsky to develop a ballet. Petrushka (the Russian equivalent of Pinnochio) is one of three puppets performing at the fair and owned by an old wizard. Away from the crowd, Petrushka is frustrated in love for the ballerina puppet, and indignant at being the wizard's captive. Searing trumpet calls and the sonorities of barrel organs and hurdy-gurdies characterize Petrushka. Stravinsky's great trick, though, is to contrast the automated, emotionless music of the people with the more fluid, expressive music of the puppets.

A recommendation of a pre-war performance usually requires a health warning about sound quality, but Leopold Stokowski's 1937 account is one of a handful of extraordinary early recordings that sounds as if it was made decades later. Moreover, this is a prime example of Stokowski at his effervescent best, with a stunning performance in which there is never the slightest doubt about where the music is going. Everything is clearly delineated, yet the orchestral soloists are given latitude in evoking the humor and bathos of the story. **CD**

Sergei Prokofiev
Piano Concerto no. 1 (1912)

Genre | Concerto
Performers/Conductor | Evgeny Kissin,
Berlin Philharmonic; Claudio Abbado
Year recorded | 1993
Label | DG 439 898-2

A precociously gifted pianist and composer, Prokofiev wrote reams while still a child; at the age of thirteen, he became one of the youngest students at the St. Petersburg Conservatoire. He graduated in 1914, by which time he was already well known on the Russian music scene, winning the coveted prize of a grand piano by playing his own First Concerto in a competition at which the other students played safe. Not everyone was delighted—one of his mentors at the Conservatoire, Alexander Glazunov, awarded the prize with the greatest reluctance. The concerto is a dazzling compendium of his many stylistic traits as a young man, and was dubbed "footballish" by critics intending to snub its audacity.

The grandiose opening is deceptive—the soloist immediately dismisses it with quick-fire repartee before settling on a playful tune that Prokofiev had composed much earlier. A more somber theme represents Prokofiev's love of dark fantasy, while the brief slow movement, which follows like everything in this compact work without a break, suggests the influence of the mystic composer Scriabin. More high jinks and a hard-hitting cadenza review most of the earlier material before the big tune of the introduction rockets skyward in a parody of bigger concertos like Tchaikovsky's First.

No example survives of Prokofiev's own performance, but one imagines that it would be something like Evgeny Kissin's bravura execution. Making light work of the concerto's virtuoso demands, he forges an ideal partnership with Abbado and the Berlin Philharmonic, breathtakingly deft and nimble. **DN**

Maurice Ravel | Daphnis et Chloé (1912)

Genre | Ballet
Conductor | Pierre Monteux
Performers | London Symphony Orchestra
Year recorded | 1959
Label | Decca 475 7525

Few works caused Ravel so much trouble as his ballet *Daphnis et Chloé*—but it was worth the effort. The commission came from the Russian impresario Sergei Diaghilev during his Ballet Russes's spectacular first season in Paris in 1909. Ravel was understandably thrilled and immediately set to work with the choreographer Mikhail Fokine. But Ravel was not comfortable with the overly erotic nature of Fokine's scenario—drawn from Greek mythology—and even after negotiating a compromise musical progress was painfully slow. Originally planned for the 1910 season, Daphnis did not premiere until 1912. It was a modest success as a ballet, though the score quickly became a classic. Ravel considered it his most important creation, describing it as "a great choreographic symphony" and "a vast musical fresco," noting that its tight thematic construction assured a "symphonic homogeneity."

The dramatic element is strong, too. Indeed, one of the glories of *Daphnis* is its wealth of incident. Ravel makes the orchestra laugh grotesquely one minute and soar gracefully the next. His evocation of sunrise (at the beginning of Part 3) is a masterpiece of tone-painting—woodwinds swirl mistlike as glimmering strings gradually illuminate the scene—and the wild abandon of the riotous bacchanal that concludes the ballet is one of the most thrilling moments in the entire literature.

Pierre Monteux brought a lifetime of experience to his celebrated recording, having conducted *Daphnis* at its premiere in 1912. He is aware of every detail and attends to these lovingly—yet what makes his interpretation unique is its symphonic coherence. Other performances may dazzle more in their virtuosity, but none convey the score's narrative sweep so effectively. **AFC**

> *"One of the most beautiful products in all of French music."*
>
> Igor Stravinsky

Pierre Monteux conducted the premieres of many key works. ➔

Sergei Rachmaninov
Vocalise and Other Songs (1912)

Genre | Vocal
Performers | Joan Rodgers, Maria Popescu,
Alexandre Naoumenko, Sergei Leiferkus, Howard Shelley
Years recorded | 1994–95
Label | Chandos CHAN 9477

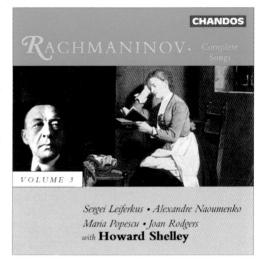

That Rachmaninov's "Vocalise" should have become his best-loved solo song is a little ironic. It is not that it does not deserve its popularity—the sinuous, slowly falling soprano line seems to sum up that mood of voluptuous melancholy one encounters so often in Rachmaninov. But it is also wordless and, listening to the other songs on this disc, one realizes how deeply Rachmaninov's vocal style was rooted in the Russian language and song tradition. No wonder he felt unable to write for the solo voice after his exile in 1917. "Vocalise" is presented here as it first appeared, as the culmination of the magnificent op. 34 cycle, where its wordless simplicity is even more touching—there are thoughts that lie too deep for words, it seems to say. The final op. 38 set shows Rachmaninov expanding his musical horizons towards Impressionism and beyond, but so often it is Rachmaninov's heart-tugging lyricism that really holds the ear.

This third and final volume in Chandos's revelatory Rachmaninov Complete Songs edition brings together four outstanding vocal talents. Having real Russian voices (Alexandre Naoumenko and Sergei Leiferkus) is always an advantage in music that wrings the essence from the sounds of words, and Leiferkus is particularly impressive. The English Joan Rodgers is fluent in Russian and has an empathy with its sounds and meanings that few outsiders can match. She even manages a touch of Slavic coloring in the "Vocalise," but here it is her musicality, refinement, and feeling that carry the day. Howard Shelley, himself a distinguished Rachmaninov player, is as accompanist about as close to ideal as one could wish. **SJ**

"Musicians should only have to reach for the words and a song would be ready."

Sergei Rachmaninov

Other Recommended Recordings

Joan Rodgers, Maria Popescu, Alexandre Naoumenko, Sergei Leiferkus, Howard Shelley
Chandos CHAN 9405
Vol. 1 of Chandos's complete song series performed with the same loving and perceptive dedication

Chandos CHAN 9451
Vol. 2 with a wide range of songs, from the comic to the powerful "I am not a prophet"

Russian State Symphony Cappella & Symphony Orchestra • Valeri Polyanski
Chandos CHAN 10311
Includes Six Choruses for Women's Voices, op. 15

Arnold Schoenberg
Pierrot lunaire (1912)

Genre | Vocal/Chamber
Performers | Jane Manning (reciter), Nash Ensemble
Conductor | Simon Rattle
Year recorded | 1977
Label | Chandos CHAN 6534

The actress Albertine Zehme commissioned Schoenberg to set a German translation of Albert Giraud's poetic cycle *Pierrot lunaire* (*Moonstruck Pierrot*), for her to declaim over instrumental accompaniment. His response was one of his most characteristic (and notorious) creations. Significantly for his op. 21, he selected "three times seven" of Giraud's rondels, disposing them for eight instruments and a solo voice in *Sprechstimme*. Despite its technical demands and weirdly ambiguous character, *Pierrot* has remained one of his best known and most frequently performed creations: an ironic epilogue to the ultraintense "Expressionist" works that Schoenberg had been composing.

In Giraud's verses, Pierrot, the white-faced, melancholy, moonstruck clown of Bergamo, moves in nightmarish realms, transforming into a morbid parody of the artist, helpless in the grip of the Expressionist vision. The first of Schoenberg's three parts is a series of character-portraits and nocturnes. Part 2 is invaded by images of guilt and retribution; but in Part 3 these ebb away again, despite some episodes of surreal sadism. Nostalgia enters verse and music, with a kind of homecoming at the end. Schoenberg described the work as "light, ironic, satirical," and his choice of ensemble (each number uses a different combination of instruments) evokes fleeting resemblances to a kind of surrealist cabaret act.

Jane Manning has very much made the work her own, and her partnership with Simon Rattle may be regarded as definitive. Her interpretation of the *Sprechstimme* stresses the wit and irony of Schoenberg's vision and the individual ensemble players are uniformly excellent. **MM**

Schoenberg
Pierrot Lunaire

Webern
Concerto, Op. 24

Jane Manning
Nash Ensemble
Simon Rattle

collect

". . . not the end of music, but the beginning of a new stage in listening."

Alfred Kerr, *Pan,* **1912**

Other Recommended Recordings

Christine Schäfer, Ensemble Intercontemporain
Pierre Boulez • DG 457 630-2
The sweet-toned soloist is more melodic than usual and Boulez produces unusual clarity

Jane Manning, Vesuvius Ensemble
Regis Forum FRC 9106
This 1967 recording by Manning with an unconducted ensemble has a wonderfully spontaneous feel

Mary Thomas, London Sinfonietta
David Atherton • Decca 425 626-2
A very theatrical version emphasizing the Expressionistic cruelty

Sergei Rachmaninov | Piano Sonata no. 2 (1913, *rev.* 1931)

Genre | Instrumental
Instrument | Piano
Performer | Yevgeny Sudbin
Year recorded | 2005
Label | BIS CD-1518

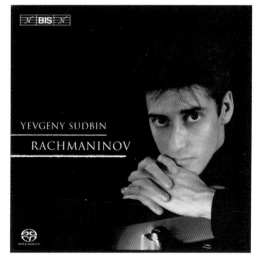

Rachmaninov's large-scale solo piano works are not as uniformly successful as his miniatures, the Preludes in particular, and he was frequently beset with creative doubt and crises of confidence. Nevertheless, the Second Piano Sonata—the most popular of Rachmaninov's big piano works—encapsulates the composer's mature style: It blends a propulsive dramatic sweep, soulful lyricism, virtuosity, intricate polyphony, and complex structural and thematic interrelationships between its three movements. It also begins to reveal the cooler emotional objectivity that marked Rachmaninov's later works. Like the Third Piano Concerto, written four years earlier, the basic thematic ideas are subtly modified and used to link the movements, and the work goes out in a virtuoso blaze of glory, which always appeals to pianists and audiences.

Despite its organic unity and pianistic credentials, Rachmaninov was not happy with the sonata. He was keen to shorten the work and thin out what he saw as its over-composed polyphony. But Rachmaninov was not the best at cutting his own work. The 1931 revised version is more terse and less dense, but many feel that the composer went too far and excised important material, even if they accept that the original version is rather prolix.

Horowitz was the first pianist to combine aspects of both versions, which he did with Rachmaninov's approval, and the young Russian pianist Yevgeny Sudbin follows the same path. Sudbin's performance is hugely exciting and imaginative, and full of pianistic color. Many pianists make the Second Sonata sound unwieldy and outsized, yet in Sudbin's hands it is perfectly proportioned. He makes the piano sing and he makes it roar; both Horowitz and Rachmaninov himself would have approved. **TLP**

> *"One of Rachmaninov's greatest piano works."*
>
> Yevgeny Sudbin

Other Recommended Recordings

Vladimir Horowitz
Sony SK 53472
Larger-than-life pianism from Horowitz, captured live at Carnegie Hall

Zoltán Kocsis
Philips 475 7779
The best recording of the original 1913 version; Kocsis delivers with flair and clarity

Simon Trpceski
EMI 7243 5 57943 2 1
A fine account of the revised 1931 version, with Trpceski on thrilling form

Wilhelm Stenhammar | Serenade (1913)

Genre | Orchestral
Conductor | Neeme Järvi
Performers | Gothenburg Symphony Orchestra
Year recorded | 1985
Label | BIS CD-310

Stenhammar's Serenade in F major forms a striking contrast to his Second Symphony. In the latter, the Romanticism is contained and disciplined within a strong, purposeful, Classical framework. In the serenade, however, the composer turns southward—to the lush, very late Romanticism of Richard Strauss and to memories of an Italian holiday in 1906–07. One can almost feel the Mediterranean sun working on his imagination, tempting him to loosen his stays and revel in the sheer impulsiveness of inspiration. A finely drawn melodic line will suddenly melt into shimmering Impressionism; an elegant quasi-Baroque minuet suddenly becomes bewitched and leads off in beguiling new directions. Yet there remains something distinctly Nordic about the sound world, as though Sibelius's magical evocations of Northern lights have never quite been forgotten.

"Like a spring dithyramb from Florence."

Stenhammar on the Serenade

The serenade originally had six movements, but then, without explanation, Stenhammar deleted the "Reverenza" second movement. Neeme Järvi thinks he made a mistake, and duly restores it here. Listeners with programming facilities on their CD players can easily choose whether to include it or not. Either way they are in for a treat. Järvi has a finely attuned feeling for Stenhammar's Impressionistic textures and for spontaneity as the essence of the musical argument. The dreamlike "Notturno" emerges as the quiet high point of the work, gently eclipsing memories even of the bacchanalian scherzo that precedes it. While Järvi is a little too free in his BIS recording of the Second Symphony, unbalancing some of the structures, here he feels absolutely at home and the energy, freshness, and lyrical charm all seem to come naturally to him. Even if you have never heard of Stenhammar, give this a try. **SJ**

Other Recommended Recordings

Royal Stockholm Philharmonic Orchestra
Andrew Davies
Warner 0927 43075-2
Exuberant, colorful, with rewarding attention to detail

Stockholm Philharmonic Orchestra, Rafael Kubelik
Swedish Society SCD 1115
A pioneering performance from 1964,
full of warmth and wonderfully shaped

Love Derwinger, Malmö Symphony Orchestra
Paavo Järvi • BIS CD-550
A strong, sympathetic performance of Stenhammar's
Piano Concerto no. 1, a brilliant and fresh early work

Claude Debussy
Jeux (1913)

Genre | Ballet
Conductor | Victor de Sabata
Performers | Accademia di Sta Cecilia
Year recorded | 1947
Label | Testament SBT 1108

This was one of Debussy's last three orchestral works, all of them ballets and the only one that he completed himself. It was his sole commission from the great Russian impresario Diaghilev, with choreography by Nijinsky, but its first performance was not an enormous success, and it was largely forgotten until the 1950s when its technical features made it a beacon for the European avant-garde, led by Pierre Boulez. Its failure was probably due to two factors. It was completely eclipsed by the scandalous premiere of Stravinsky's *Rite of Spring* a fortnight later—also choreographed by Nijinsky, and conducted by Pierre Monteux. And it was short, used only three dancers, and had a rather thin and silly plot, beginning in a garden at dusk, with a young man and a girl searching for a lost tennis ball. They start to play games, which become increasingly erotic, until another tennis ball lands at their feet, breaks the spell, and they run off into the night.

Perhaps the understated nature of the music, with its elusive melodies and textures, worked against it as well. It has one of Debussy's most mysterious openings, before the games begin, and shards of themes whirl around, receding into the background, or suddenly rearing up in the foreground, but never quite coming into focus until a delirious waltz toward the end.

If Victor de Sabata had never entered a recording studio again, this version—the first to be issued—would still put him among the greats. His sense of pacing in what can be a fragmentary score is absolutely unerring, and he balances and inflects the lines so that the music has a real beauty and sense of purpose. **MC**

Edward Elgar
Falstaff (1913)

Genre | Orchestral
Conductor | John Barbirolli
Performers | Hallé Orchestra
Year recorded | 1964
Label | EMI 5 66322 2

Elgar called his *Falstaff* a "symphonic study," which is a remarkably dry way of describing one of the great Shakespearean portraits in music. On one level, this can be appreciated as a highly original, colorful one-movement symphony, but it is the vividness with which Elgar brings Shakespeare's rogue to life that makes this work so enjoyable. There are moments of comedy, such as the drunken bassoon solo, and Elgar also makes an uncharacteristic but effective detour into Elizabethan pastiche. But there is also tenderness, sweet nostalgia as Falstaff remembers his childhood, and the ending—in which the fat knight's former companion, Prince Hall, cruelly rejects him—is surprisingly chilling. Writing something on the character of Falstaff was an endeavor that Elgar contemplated for years before finally undertaking it. Perhaps he saw something of himself in this seemingly hearty, inwardly deeply sensitive, melancholic man.

One or two other conductors may have made *Falstaff* more boisterous or more symphonically purposeful than John Barbirolli's version, but no one has ever brought out so many facets of its character, or made the brusque ending sound so unsettling. The impression is sometimes more of a tour around a gallery than of one commanding overview, but there is no impression of disunity—this is definitely a conducted tour. And throughout there is Barbirolli's wonderful melodic phrasing, which allows Elgar's often rhythmically repetitive lines to sing out with a spontaneous, supple warmth. It is a performance full of love as well as thorough understanding, redolent of a kind of Englishness that has all but vanished. **SJ**

Ivor Gurney
Songs (1913–22)

Genre | Vocal
Performers | Paul Agnew (tenor),
Julius Drake (piano)
Year recorded | 2000
Label | Hyperion CDA 67243

Of all English songwriters composing in the first decades of the twentieth century, Ivor Gurney is perhaps the connoisseur's choice. He was both composer and poet: his verse some of the most individually turned of all the war poets; his song outstandingly sensitive in its word-setting.

Born in 1890, Gurney determined to have a musical career after years as a cathedral chorister in Gloucester and he studied with Charles Villiers Stanford before setting off for war in 1915. His *Five Elizabethan Songs* were written between 1913 and 1914; thereafter his intense sense of yearning grows apace—the omnipresent rhyming echo of "sleep" and "weep" tolls its way through his later songs.

In 1917 Gurney was wounded, gassed and shell-shocked in the trenches. Back home, increasing bouts of mental instability led to his spending his last years in a mental hospital. Interest in Gurney has grown since the publication of his biography in 1978 and of his *Collected Letters* in 1991. Many songs—some of them incomplete and even incoherent—are being examined and added to the published canon. This collection of twenty-five of the very best of his published songs spans his entire creative life, from the early *Elizabethan Songs*, to those written in the feverishly creative years of 1919–22.

Paul Agnew captures uniquely the smoldering sensuousness within the yearning languor of Gurney's long legato lines; and Julius Drake's playing has the measure of the rhapsodic, and sometimes impetuously instinctive, nature of the composer's piano writing, animating afresh the fantasy within his settings of Walter de la Mare and Hilaire Belloc. **HF**

Sergei Rachmaninov
The Bells (1913)

Genre | Choral
Conductor/Performers | André Previn;
London Symphony Orchestra and Chorus
Year recorded | 1975
Label | EMI 0777 7 631142 5

There is nothing like Rachmaninov's *The Bells* in all Russian music—which is curious, because its theme has a potent national significance; for centuries the bell has been a compelling symbol of the soul of Russia. In this huge choral symphony, Rachmaninov portrays bells in four different characters: bright sleigh jingles, softly voluptuous wedding chimes, the terrifying clangor of the tocsin, and finally the death-knell. The music is unflaggingly glorious, swinging backward and forward between ecstasy and terror, melancholy and serenity, and always wonderfully orchestrated. The soprano solo at the heart of the second movement is one of the most rapturously beautiful things Rachmaninov ever composed.

While some Russian conductors have brought a special blistering energy and abandon to this music, the choral and solo singing has usually let their recordings down. André Previn's is probably the most roundly successful version ever to appear. It has plenty of drive where needed, balanced by contemplative beauty. Orchestra and chorus are exceptionally well disciplined without sounding inhibited—the last thing one wants in music like this. Balancing such diverse forces is a headache for the production team, but the EMI recording manages it very well. Previn also has two excellent soloists: Sheila Armstrong in particular has all the necessary security and refinement, plus an expressive intensity that at times sounds more Slavic than Anglo-Saxon. Most importantly, Previn conveys a sense of this work as a spiritual journey, culminating—as so often in Rachmaninov—in the all-important confrontation with mortality. **SJ**

Albert Roussel | Le festin d'araignée (1913)

Genre | Ballet
Conductor | Jean Martinon
Performers | ORTF National Orchestra
Year recorded | 1969
Label | Erato 2564 60577-2

ROUSSEL
SYMPHONIE N° 2 EN SI BÉMOL MAJEUR OP. 23
FESTIN DE L'ARAIGNÉE OP. 17

Orchestre National de l'ORTF Jean Martinon

Roussel was one of music's late developers. Born in Tourcoing in northern France in 1869, he was orphaned at seven and lived with other members of his family until going to naval college at the age of fifteen. But he always wanted to be a composer, and studied with Vincent d'Indy in Paris for nine years, a period culminating in his First Symphony. He became renowned as a teacher—his pupils included the Czech composer Martinů—and he was one of the composers commissioned for the fiftieth anniversary of the Boston Symphony Orchestra in 1930, for which he produced his Third Symphony.

Le festin d'araignée (*The Spider's Banquet*) was his first commission, and still one of his most-played pieces. The ballet begins in a garden, represented by a sensual flute melody, before groups of insects arrive—the ants with military precision to a side-drum beat, the more lumpen dung beetles, and the spider herself, who catches a butterfly in her web and dances in triumph. More prey follow—a mayfly and two mantises, but as the spider is about to feast, one of the mantises escapes and kills her. The ballet ends with the funeral of the mayfly and the return to the calm of the garden.

Strangely, Roussel chose to omit most of the spider's music when he made the suite of symphonic fragments, so the full range of the music comes only from the complete ballet. And the best version of that is conducted by Jean Martinon, himself a composer and pupil of Roussel, who knows the music intimately, and responds to its languor as well as its violence, and does not lose sight of the fact that it has to dance. With a French orchestra, the ORTF National Orchestra, he conjures up all the tangy sonorities that make up Roussel's world. **MC**

> *"I do not know why, but the garden theme of* The Spider's Banquet *clings in my mind. . . ."*
>
> Albert Roussel

Other Recommended Recordings

BBC Philharmonic, Yan-Pascal Tortelier
Chandos CHAN 9494
Another of Roussel's ballets, Bacchus et Ariane, in sumptuous sound

Via Nova Quartet
Warner 2564 61368-2 (2 CDs)
The String Quartet, one of Roussel's lesser-known masterpieces

Toke Lund Christiansen
Kontrapunkt 32218/9 (2 CDs)
Chamber works with flute: the latter an important thread running through Roussel's music

Albert Roussel forged a distinctive path in French music. ➔

Igor Stravinsky | The Rite of Spring (1913)

Genre | Ballet
Conductor | Igor Markevitch
Performers | Philharmonia Orchestra
Year recorded | 1959
Label | Testament SBT 1076

Igor Markevich
Stravinsky: Le Sacre du printemps
(1951 & 1959 recordings)
Philharmonia Orchestra

TESTAMENT

The Rite of Spring is one of those works, like Beethoven's *Eroica* or Wagner's *Tristan und Isolde*, that changed the notion of what a musical work could do. Culminating in a "Sacrificial Dance," in which a girl dances herself to death to propitiate the gods of Spring, this evocation of pagan Russia was Stravinsky's third great collaboration with Diaghilev's Ballets Russes, with choreography by Nijinsky. The opening night in May 1913 has entered into legend for the riot that broke out between detractors and advocates, leaving Diaghilev pleased and Stravinsky completely taken aback. Whatever the causes of the furor, *The Rite* soon forged a life independent of the theater, a development strongly encouraged by Stravinsky.

In its early years, reaction to *The Rite* focused upon the dissonant harmonies and sudden jumps between different types of music. Over time it came to be appreciated that the emancipation of rhythm as the principal driving force of the music was the true advance amid the searing power of this masterpiece. Perhaps the most remarkable thing about *The Rite* is that, despite endless imitations, it has lost none of it power.

Neither Igor Markevitch nor EMI intended to make this 1959 recording. Sessions were booked for a Klemperer recording, but he fell ill. Markevitch had already made a well-received mono recording of *The Rite* in 1951 (also on this disc) and, rather than cancel the orchestra and studio time, EMI engaged him at very short notice to re-record the work in stereo, resulting in a sleepless night contacting the extra musicians needed. The result is an electrifying performance with everyone clearly on their toes, but it is the beauty of the more reflective moments that separates this from more one-dimensional accounts. **CD**

> ## "[The Rite of Spring] haunts me like a beautiful nightmare."
>
> Claude Debussy

Other Recommended Recordings

Columbia Symphony Orchestra, Igor Stravinsky
Sony SS 89062 (SACD)
The best of the composer's own recordings is intense and rhythmically incisive

City of Birmingham Symphony Orchestra
Simon Rattle • EMI 0777 7 49636 2 6
Rattle takes the "Sacrificial Dance" slower than most, giving it a relentless power

Atlanta Symphony Orchestra • Yoel Levi
Telarc CD-80266
Recorded in stunning sound, every detail is audible yet nothing is lacking in excitement

Igor Markevitch in his twenties, when he was known as a composer. ➔

Ralph Vaughan Williams
A London Symphony (1913, *rev.* 1933)

Genre | Orchestral
Conductor | Adrian Boult
Performers | London Philharmonic Orchestra
Year recorded | 1952
Label | Decca 430 366-2

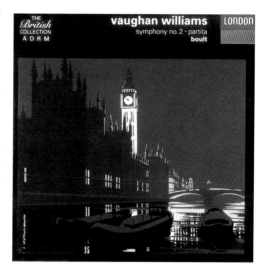

Following the success of *A Sea Symphony*, Vaughan Williams was encouraged by fellow composer George Butterworth to write a complete symphony that did not rely on a text. The composer's response was to evoke the essence of London without following a specific program. He was keen that the music should be "self-expressive, and stand or fall as 'absolute' music." Nevertheless, there is a musical image of grandeur and calm—perhaps this is the broad Thames, with the chimes of Big Ben carried on harp harmonics adding an authentic touch. Into this calm erupts a new idea in the allegro, a shattering chromatic theme that augurs something bleakly negative. Shortly after, a rousing march appears and lively development ensues. This continues in the slow movement, "Bloomsbury Square on a November Afternoon." Just as Haydn evoked street sellers in his "London Symphony," so Vaughan Williams uses the calls of a lavender seller and the sounds of passing hansom cabs to bring a human touch here. After the suggestions of mouth-organ music in the scherzo, the work closes with a cheerless epilogue, suggested to the composer by the closing words of H. G. Wells's novel *Tono-Bungay*, "The river passes, London passes, England passes."

Boult's is a highly dramatic reading, encouraging sweeping effects from the LPO. As the players surge up to the first allegro, they strike a note of terror that returns later with string sul ponticello shivers and savage brass interjections. Boult balances the aggression of the opening movement with moments of grandeur and beauty. No other recording equals the sublime expression of his slow movement and the epilogue. **SW**

"Have we not all about us forms of musical expression which can purify . . . ?"

Vaughan Williams, *Who Wants the English Composer?*

Other Recommended Recordings

Royal Liverpool Philharmonic Orchestra
Vernon Handley
EMI 7243 5 75309 2 7
Distinguished and warmly embracing playing

Queen's Hall Orchestra
Henry Wood
Dutton Lab CDBP 9707
Fascinating historical account with remarkably diverse speeds

London Symphony Orchestra, Richard Hickox
Chandos CHAN 9902
Ravishing account of the original 1913 version

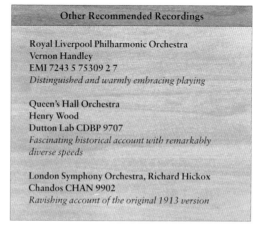

Adrian Boult is best remembered for his "stiff upper lip" persona. ➔

Ernő Dohnányi | Variations on a Nursery Song (1914)

Genre | Concerto
Performers | Howard Shelley (piano), BBC Philharmonic
Conductor | Matthias Bamert
Year recorded | 1998
Label | Chandos CHAN 9733

The Hungarian composer Ernő Dohnányi (also known by his Germanized name of Ernst von Dohnányi) was a slightly older contemporary of Kodály and Bartók, whose style remained rooted in the Austro-Germanic tradition of Brahms. His output is relatively small—not least because his life was divided between performing (he was one of the greatest pianists of all time), conducting, and teaching as well as composing—but contains substantial chamber works, symphonies, and concertos. He was a key figure in his country's musical life before World War II, but was forced to flee from accusations by the fledgling Communist regime of betraying his nation (he had left Hungary for Austria in 1944, following years of standing up for Jewish colleagues), and spent his later years in Florida.

Although Dohnányi's music maintains the seriousness of the Romantic tradition, his best-known work is a sheer piece of parody. *Variations on a Nursery Song* for piano and orchestra was written in 1914 and pokes fun at a whole array of musical targets through the most innocent of themes, known in French as "Ah, vous dirai-je, Maman" and in the English-speaking world as "Twinkle, Twinkle, Little Star." The work's portentous opening hardly prepares us for the piano's simple entry with the tune, nor for the virtuosity that soon takes over the solo part—Dohnányi enjoying exploiting his playing skills as much as his compositional expertise.

Howard Shelley has the technique and charismatic sparkle to bring Dohnányi's creation vividly to life and he is warmly supported by the exemplary playing of the BBC Philharmonic under Matthias Bamert, who also includes on this CD the Suite in F sharp minor and the humorous ballet score *The Veil of Pierrette*. **MR**

> "*For the enjoyment of humorous people and the annoyance of others.*"
>
> **Ernő Dohnányi on the Variations**

Other Recommended Recordings

Spectrum Concerts Berlin
Naxos 8.557173
Fine performance of the Serenade for String Trio, one of Dohnányi's most characterful chamber works

BBC Philharmonic, Matthias Bamert
Chandos CHAN 9455
The warmly Romantic Second Symphony and some action-packed miniatures, wonderfully played

Martin Roscoe, BBC Scottish Symphony Orchestra
Fedor Glushchenko • Hyperion CDA 66684
Piano Concertos nos. 1 & 2 demonstrate the full force of Dohnányi's virtuoso piano style

Ernö Dohnányi was a leading figure in Hungarian music. ➔

Manuel de Falla | Siete canciones populares Españolas (1914)

Genre | Vocal
Performers | Victoria de los Angeles (soprano),
Gonzalo Soriano (piano)
Year recorded | 1961–62
Label | EMI 7243 5 67590 2 2 (2 CDs)

Manuel de Falla was born in Cádiz in 1876, and was one of a group of composers who studied with Felipe Pedrell, the founder of Spanish musical nationalism. His distinctive personality emerged with his opera *La vida breve* (*Life is Short*), written in the early years of the twentieth century, but performed only in 1913, when the composer was living in Paris. With his fastidious approach to composition, coupled with a frail constitution, Falla wrote a relatively small amount, though he died in 1946 with an enormous project on the legend of Atlantis unfinished. The music from his ballets *El sombrero de tres picos* and *El amor brujo*—particularly the famous "Ritual Fire Dance"—is frequently heard in the concert hall.

Siete canciones populares Españolas (Seven Popular Spanish Songs) was an immediate success at the first performance in Madrid in 1915. Falla took the melodies that he'd known all his life and added piano parts that are far too individual and emotionally enhancing to be called mere accompaniments. It is a perfect set of songs, with a wide variety of pace and moods, from the rumbunctious dance rhythms of the seguidilla and jota, through the calm of a lullaby, to the agony and heartbreak of unrequited or betrayed love.

Victoria de los Angeles performed these songs as a central part of her repertoire throughout her career, and made at least four complete recordings of them. Without a doubt, it is the one with Gonzalo Soriano—another native Falla expert—that finds her in her absolute prime, living every word and note with complete authority and intensity, and in a partnership where the piano is her equal in defining the world for each song: fiery, cynical, tender, and sorrowful by turn. **MC**

> "... the songs of Andalusia in his blood, and a Moorish Nanny ... a combination [that fired] his music...."
>
> María Martinez Sierra

Other Recommended Recordings

Conchita Supervia, Frank Marshall
Pearl GEMMCD 9975
A classic version—
Spanish fire from 1930

Marilyn Horne, Martin Katz
Vaia VAIA 1207
A great American singer live at the
1979 Salzburg Festival

Gérard Souzay, Jacqueline Bonneau
Testament SBT 1311
The alternative baritone version,
characterfully sung

Spanish soprano Victoria de Los Angeles, pictured in the mid-1960s. ➔

To Mr Richard Bebb
with best wishes

Vichia de ....

1985

Max Reger
Variations and Fugue on a Theme of Mozart (1914)

Genre | Orchestral
Conductor | Leif Segerstam
Performers | Norrköping Symphony Orchestra
Year recorded | 1998
Label | BIS CD-771

One of the most important Austro-German late-Romantic composers, and a true successor to Brahms, Max Reger followed in the footsteps of his great predecessor by focusing his creative energies on producing large-scale, abstract orchestral, chamber, and instrumental music. In an era when Liszt and Wagner exercised such a powerful influence on musical developments, it is significant that Reger steadfastly avoided composing for the stage and only occasionally wrote works of a more programmatic nature. Although such an attitude might suggest a musical figure of a distinctly conservative frame of mind, Reger's penchant for writing dense contrapuntal textures and chromatic harmonies pushed the boundaries of conventional tonality to their very extreme—a tendency that makes him a crucial forerunner of Schoenberg.

The Mozart Variations remains Reger's most popular orchestral work. Following the tried and tested structure pioneered in Brahms's Haydn Variations and subsequently perfected in Reger's own monumental sets of Variations by Bach, Beethoven, and Hiller, the theme—taken from the opening movement of Mozart's Piano Sonata in A major, K331—is subjected to imaginative and unexpected transformations, alternating voluptuous textures with moods that are more sardonic and playful, and culminating in a magnificent and ingenious fugue.

Over the years there have been some fine recordings of this work, but this performance is the most persuasive, demonstrating a necessary capacity on the part of the conductor to draw textural clarity from music that in lesser hands can so easily sound bloated. **EL**

"I consider him a genius."

Arnold Schoenberg on Max Reger,
in a letter to Zemlinsky

Other Recommended Recordings
Bavarian Radio Symphony Orchestra, Colin Davis **Orfeo C090841A** *A beautiful account of Reger's Hiller Variations, his other great orchestral work*
Karl Leister (clarinet), Vogler Quartet **Nimbus NI 5644** *Warmly sensitive interpretations of the String Quartet in E flat major op. 109 and the Clarinet Quintet*
Marc-André Hamelin (piano) **Hyperion CDA 66996** *Stunning playing of the Bach Variations, Telemann Variations, and Five Humoresques*

Ralph Vaughan Williams
The Lark Ascending (1914, *rev.* 1920)

Genre | Orchestral
Conductor/Performers | Neville Marriner;
Iona Brown (violin), Academy of St. Martin in the Fields
Year recorded | 1972
Label | Decca 430 093-2

Written in the year that changed the twentieth century most profoundly, this single movement "Romance" for orchestra and solo violin takes its name from a poem by George Meredith. The music displays the composer at his most securely Edwardian, creating a distinctly English sound, yet it has Impressionist and hazy textures for all its emotional stability. To some extent this nationalist quality comes from his folksong-like melodic contours. Many of the central sections' woodwind solos have the quality of half-remembered native tunes, though none quotes one exactly. Interestingly, the piece was not actually performed until after the Great War and Vaughan Williams was never again to evoke a pastoral tone so free of trauma and anxiety. The imagery conveyed throughout the work is of a single bird seeking something unknown; the violin swoops around initially in free swirls of sound, rising and falling, sometimes playful, sometimes bold; and its dialogue with the rest of the orchestra drives the piece forward. The overall tone is of rhapsodically free expression but the work has symphonic, rondo-like qualities that bring direction and intelligent musical argument.

A sense of wonder pervades this performance, a world of beauty and nescience evoked from beginning to end. Neville Marriner has great control, both in the livelier details that emerge in the woodwind phrases and in the warmth that fills the outer sections of the piece. Iona Brown has a similar variety of characteristics in her lovely playing. At times her trills are capricious and knowing, yet as she soars upward into the infinite at the end her tone is pure and untainted. **SW**

> *"He rises and begins to round / He drops the silver chain of sound."*
>
> "The Lark Ascending," George Meredith

Other Recommended Recordings

Nigel Kennedy, City of Birmingham Symphony Orchestra • Simon Rattle
EMI 7243 5 56413 2 8
Serene and inspiring playing with Nigel Kennedy on fine form

Hugh Bean, New Philharmonic Orchestra
Adrian Boult
EMI 0777 7 64022 2 2
A finely judged performance, full of inner contentment

Tasmin Little, BBC Symphony Orchestra
Andrew Davis • Warner 0927 49584-2
Poetic reading enriched by Little's sweet tone

Zoltán Kodály
Duo for Violin and Cello
(1914)

Genre | Chamber
Performers | Renaud Capuçon (violin),
Gautier Capuçon (cello)
Year recorded | 2002
Label | Virgin 7243 5 45576 2 0

Zoltán Kodály is one of the most important Hungarian composers of the first half of the twentieth century. Educated at the Budapest Academy of Music, he reacted against the overtly Germanic orientation of the musical environment in his native country through the discovery of Hungarian folk music which, from 1905 onward, he began to collect. Further study with Charles-Marie Widor in Paris brought him into contact with the music of Debussy; the Frenchman's exploratory harmonic style and coloring exercised a profound impact upon his own work.

Kodály's early output focused almost exclusively on chamber and instrumental music. The Duo for Violin and Cello was conceived in the summer of 1914 while the composer was in Switzerland. Forced to flee the country at the outbreak of war, Kodály was detained by Austrian soldiers for several days before being allowed to return to Budapest, where he completed the work. To what extent these disturbing experiences impacted on the character of the duo is difficult to estimate, but there is little doubt that the anguished and sometimes aggressive quality of the writing proved extremely disconcerting to audiences.

Among the many fine recordings of this compelling masterpiece, the performance from the Capuçon brothers is particularly distinguished, demonstrating an excellent unanimity of ensemble throughout the three movements. Both players respond with verve and aural imagination to the challenges of Kodály's writing, and the rest of their recital is just as engaging. **EL**

Maurice Ravel
Piano Trio
(1914)

Genre | Chamber
Performers | Kalichstein-Laredo-
Robinson Trio
Year recorded | 1999
Label | Arabesque Z 6736-2

Many musicians and commentators have been so awed by the intricate, polished finish of Ravel's music that they assume there is not much else to it. They are wrong, of course. The Piano Trio, for example, is a work of expressive richness and profundity. Composed in 1914, it reflects the anxiety and volatility of the time with unflinching honesty.

The work begins with a lilting theme then careens between fervent exhortations and tender meditations. The second movement is called "Pantoum," after a Malayan poetic form that Ravel translates to music, using it to structure the restless opening melody. A sweet, lyrical tune provides contrast, though accompanied by some nervous movement in the background. The trio's grieving heart is the "Passacaille," a series of variations over a repeated bass line. Perhaps Ravel chose this rigorous form as a means of articulating emotions that might otherwise be too overwhelming to express. The finale attempts to sweep away the angst in a frenzy of virtuosity.

Pianist Joseph Kalichstein, violinist Jaime Laredo, and cellist Sharon Robinson give a performance that reveals just how searing Ravel's score can be. They dig into the second movement with a vengeance, sharpening the music's jagged edges, and burn through the finale with abandon. Lyrical passages are tenderly embraced and there is delicacy and subtlety throughout. In the "Passacaille," the players' unaffected eloquence and focused intensity yields the richest rewards; no other performance on disc is as wrenching or as noble. **AFC**

Béla Bartók
Romanian Folk Dances
(1915)

Genre | Instrumental
Instrument | Piano
Performer | Zoltán Kocsis
Year recorded | 1991
Label | Philips 464 676-2

Claude Debussy
Douze Études
(1915)

Genre | Instrumental
Instrument | Piano
Performer | Mitsuko Uchida
Year recorded | 1989
Label | Philips 464 698-2

Bartók's earliest works were strongly influenced by late-Romantic music, but his stylistic orientation changed dramatically through his friendship with fellow student Zoltán Kodály at the Royal Academy in Budapest. Most important of all was his decisive encounter, through Kodály, with the rich and relatively unexploited resources of Hungarian folk music. The two of them went on several field trips, collecting and annotating folk songs from their native land and neighboring countries.

Increasingly influenced by the unconventional melodic and rhythmic patterns of folk music, Bartók resolved to bring this material into the wider public domain through his own transcriptions, of which the *Romanian Folk Dances* are probably the best known. Originally conceived for solo piano, the six succinct and contrasting movements were subsequently arranged for small orchestra by the composer in 1917, and also exist in effective versions for violin and piano and string orchestra. Although the orchestral arrangement allows Bartók greater opportunity to exploit varied colors and textures, the piano original has a greater rawness and energy that particularly comes to the fore in the last two dances. These elements are delivered with marvelous rhythmic exhilaration and characterization in Zoltán Kocsis's stunning performance. The recital also includes two of Bartók's most substantial piano works from the 1920s, as well as the extraordinary Fourteen Bagatelles (1908), which demonstrate Bartók's modernist leanings at a very early stage in his career. **EL**

Debussy's *Twelve Études* for piano follow in the footsteps of the two sets of twelve by Chopin, transforming this demanding and very specific genre into something far greater than the sum of its technical parts. The *études* were directly inspired by Chopin, following Debussy's close encounter with the Polish pianist-composer's music when he accepted a commission from his publisher Durand in 1914 to make a new edition of some of his works. The set turned out to be his last work for the piano, for he was already suffering from the cancer that would kill him in 1918.

Debussy's *études* match Chopin's in technical difficulty, sophistication, and sheer virtuoso imagination. They also reveal Debussy's humor, notably when the first *étude* opens with a five-finger exercise that every beginner will recognize, which is transformed in spectacular fashion.

While each study has the ostensibly technical purpose of developing the ability to play in sixths, octaves, or repeated notes, for example, the music itself is perhaps the most forward-looking that Debussy produced for the piano. In many ways the *études* are studies in compositional techniques, from harmonic structure to the many coloristic properties of keyboard sonority.

Mitsuko Uchida's recording of the *études* is one of the most celebrated. She injects personality with a tigerish energy and grace, while her technical ability is staggering. Her tone quality ranges from jeweled glitter and precision to the subtlest softness, with precisely layered textures. No devotee of piano music should be without it. **JD**

Alban Berg | Three Orchestral Pieces, op. 6 (1915, *rev.* 1929)

Genre | Orchestral
Conductor/Performers | Claudio Abbado;
London Symphony Orchestra
Year recorded | 1971
Label | DG 449 714-2

Born in Vienna in 1885, Alban Berg played the piano as a boy and started to write songs without any formal composition training as a teenager. In 1904 Berg met Arnold Schoenberg, an encounter that had a profound impact upon his musical development. For the next six years, Berg studied composition with Schoenberg. His first acknowledged opus was the Piano Sonata composed in 1908, and at the end of his tutelage with Schoenberg, he completed a substantial String Quartet.

A painstakingly slow, methodical, and highly self-critical composer, Berg worked on his Three Orchestral Pieces over a period of two years from 1913, revising the work in 1929, the year before it received its first complete performance in Oldenburg. Conceived for a huge orchestra, the Three Pieces are exceedingly complex in terms of their structure and texture, yet retain a sound-world that is often close to Mahler. There are some extraordinarily evocative sonorities in the first piece (entitled "Prelude") in which almost disembodied notes in the percussion eventually give way to a more fully formed and intense melodic line. The second piece (entitled "Rounds") distorts the familiar musical topoi of the Viennese waltz and Austrian Ländler to chilling effect. Finally there is an overpowering "March" whose relentless ferocity seems to mirror the socio-political circumstances of the period and also foreshadows the disintegration of the Austro-Hungarian Empire.

Undoubtedly the most powerful and compelling performance of the Three Orchestral Pieces is the earlier of Claudio Abbado's two recordings, in which he conducts the London Symphony Orchestra. A seasoned Mahlerian, Abbado has an instinctive feeling for this style, projecting all its pent-up emotions with great urgency. **EL**

"The best music always results from ecstasies of logic."

Alban Berg

Other Recommended Recordings

Netherlands Radio Symphony Orchestra
Eri Klas
Naxos 8.554755
Convincing performance at a bargain price

Bavarian Radio Symphony Orchestra
Colin Davis
Philips Duo 470 531-2 (2 CDs)
Excellent orchestral playing

SWR Symphony Orchestra
Michael Gielen
Hänssler CD 93.029
Matches intellectual rigor with emotional commitment

Austrian composer Alban Berg in 1910, with his young nephew Erich. ➜

Manuel de Falla | Nights in the Gardens of Spain (1915)

Genre | Concerto
Performers | Alicia de Larrocha, London Philharmonic
Conductor | Rafael Frühbeck de Burgos
Year recorded | 1983
Label | Decca 410 289-2

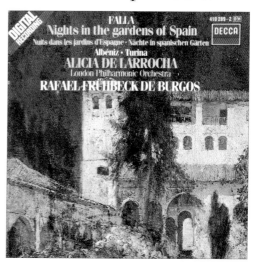

This is not only a piano concerto in all but name—the subtitle is "Symphonic impressions for piano and orchestra"—but the greatest Spanish piano concerto in existence. Falla's idea was originally for a set of solo piano nocturnes for the pianist Ricardo Viñes, who suggested that the concept might work better if an orchestra were included. The strange thing is that Falla, though a Spaniard through and through, had never seen the Generalife—the scented gardens at the Alhambra in Granada—when he started work on the piece in Paris in 1909. But he visited them when he returned to Spain at the outbreak of World War I, and that gave him the impetus to finish the work.

There is more than a touch of French Impressionism in the score, especially the orchestration, and even hints of a Russian influence: Stravinsky's *Firebird* sometimes opens her wings in the background. But the opening could not be anything but Spanish, as the orchestra sets the scene in the Generalife for one of the most magical piano entries in music. The faster second movement is a distant cousin of the Spanish Dance in *La vida breve*, leading directly into the festive finale in the Gardens of the Sierra de Córdoba. But this ends quietly, with the evanescence of a dream—has it really happened at all?

Alicia de Larrocha was the undisputed doyenne of the Spanish piano repertoire, and her performance brings a flexibility and richness that perfectly complements that of the work itself, striking a balance in the climaxes between power and overbearing brutality, and bringing the most delicate filigree to the work where it is called for. And Rafael Frühbeck de Burgos again proves himself to be an ideal conductor for his compatriot, conjuring a sultry palette of colors from his British players. **MC**

> "... the music of these nocturnes does not try to be descriptive, but rather simply expressive ..."
>
> Manuel de Falla

Other Recommended Recordings

Daniel Barenboim, Chicago Symphony Orchestra
Plácido Domingo • Teldec 0630-17145-2
*The great singer as an idiomatic conductor;
in superb sound*

Clifford Curzon, National Symphony Orchestra
Enrique Jordá
Dutton CDK 1202
*Aristocratic pianism in one of Curzon's earliest
recordings (1945)*

Martha Argerich, Paris Orchestra • Daniel Barenboim
Warner 0927 46720 2
Impulsive and fluid playing from a keyboard tigress

Manuel de Falla in a Parisian restaurant in the 1920s. ➔

Claude Debussy
Sonatas (1915–17)

Genre | Chamber
Performers | Nash Ensemble:
Crayford, Chase, Van Kampen
Year recorded | 1989
Label | Virgin 7243 5 61427 2 5

Manuel de Falla
El amor brujo (1915, *rev.* 1925)

Genre | Ballet
Conductor/Performers | Igor Markevitch;
Spanish Radio and TV Symphony Orchestra
Year recorded | 1966
Label | Eloquence 468 313-2

Debussy signed these works "*un musicien français*," a term both literal and heavy with symbolism. When he wrote the three chamber sonatas at the end of his life, it was in an attempt to establish his music as part of the true French tradition of Rameau and Couperin. While World War I raged in the north, the sick, despairing composer made a last attempt to express the quintessence of French genius "fantasy in sensitivity," against the "heroic theatrics" of the Germans, personified, of course, by Wagner.

He succeeded. These three fragile, beautiful, late flowers of chamber music seem to concentrate into less than an hour Debussy's dreamlike vision of pure music. He planned six pieces, but lived to complete only three. First is the sinuous, feline Cello Sonata, with its pizzicato high-jinks and eerie on-the-bridge chattering. Next comes the other-worldly Sonata for Flute, Viola, and Harp, a combination with the translucent texture of water, the viola lost in thought staring into the pool. There is a quiet desperation to its wistful, middle minuet movement and its palpitating, free-wheeling finale. The Violin Sonata, written when Debussy was dying, is a swan song of extraordinary fantasy and mastery. A riot of hot color, it needs to be played with complete abandon and absolute control.

No single recording has all three in their finest performances. The Nash Ensemble, however, gives overall the most spirited and beautifully realized readings. Marcia Crayford's Violin Sonata is deliciously sensuous, Roger Chase's viola playing idiomatic and poignant, while Christopher Van Kampen approaches the Cello Sonata with the relish of a gourmand. **HW**

El amor brujo was the first large-scale piece that Falla wrote after his return to Spain in 1914, following seven stimulating years in Paris. Perhaps it was a need to reimmerse himself in his heritage that led him to respond to a commission from the great Pastora Imperio, a dancer with gypsy roots, for a piece including both song and dance, based on stories told to her by her mother.

The original version for voice and eight instrumentalists was a failure at its first performance, but Falla removed the dialogue that held up the action, rescored it for full orchestra, and generally tightened the structure. In its final version, it has become one of Falla's most played works.

The title literally means "Enchanted Love," but it is always translated as "Love the Magician." The story is simple: A gypsy disposes of the unwanted attentions of the jealous ghost of her former lover by tricking him into making love to another woman. Falla's score packs a lot into twenty-five minutes, from the opening fanfares, through three songs bewailing the pain of love, a "Dance of Terror," and the more peaceful "Magic Circle," to the joyous peal of morning bells after the ghost is exorcised.

Given the work's strong gypsy background, it is not surprising that a Spanish orchestra produces the right sort of sound for the music, with edgy, vibrant strings, and brass and wind with a feeling of the hot Iberian landscape. Igor Markevitch, a composer as well as a conductor, has a visceral approach to the music, making the most of the famous "Ritual Fire Dance," and Ines Rivandeneyra, with her plangent, earthy tone and Latin temperament, is the ideal soloist. **MC**

Charles Ives
Concord Sonata (1915)

Genre | Instrumental
Instrument | Piano
Performer | Marc-André Hamelin
Year recorded | 1994
Label | Hyperion CDA 67469

Ives's majestic, passionate, and labyrinthine Second Piano Sonata, subtitled "Concord, Mass., 1840–1860," was inspired by the writings of five different authors—the "New England Transcendentalists" Emerson, Hawthorne, Thoreau, and the educationalist Bronson Alcott and his novelist daughter Louisa May Alcott—who lived in the Massachusetts town of Concord. Published in 1920 with an accompanying book of musico-philosophical commentary, *Essays before a Sonata*, the work is nevertheless an object lesson in music's ability to go beyond words, to project feelings and ideals where language is insufficient.

The four movements are a turbulent allegro ("Emerson") with many thematic elements that are developed throughout the work; a mercurial scherzo ("Hawthorne"), a peaceful domestic Andante ("The Alcotts"), and a wide-ranging, ecstatically meditative finale ("Thoreau"). Concord is harmonically kaleidoscopic, from extreme dissonance to peaceful consonance, rhythmically highly involved, requiring stamina as well as bravura technique. It is one of Ives's most significant works and one of his most continually surprising, and the richness of its thematic interconnections leads one to return to it repeatedly.

This is Marc-André Hamelin's second recording of a work to which he feels particularly close, and it is close to being the definitive interpretation. The range of keyboard color and exquisite soft tone he produces in passages that in other hands are merely percussive signal his depth of understanding, but his power, dexterity, and command of the most taxing passages display a virtuosity that it seems almost impertinent to praise. **MM**

Hans Pfitzner
Palestrina (1915)

Genre | Opera
Conductor/Performers | Rafael Kubelík; Nicolai Gedda, Dietrich Fischer-Dieskau
Year recorded | 1989
Label | DG 427 417-2 (3 CDs)

Identified later in life as an arch-conservative, Hans Pfitzner was regarded with some suspicion in his student days for the idiosyncratic nature of some of his harmonic experimentation. His first opera, *Der arme Heinrich*, displayed unmistakable Wagnerian tendencies, while his second, *Die Rose vom Liebesgarten*, similarly fused elements of *Parsifal* and Rosicrucian mysticism.

Pfitzner's masterpiece was unquestionably his fourth opera *Palestrina*, for which he wrote his own libretto. The trials and tribulations undergone by the central character, the renowned sixteenth-century Italian composer Palestrina, clearly represent the struggles faced by Pfitzner himself, endeavoring to safeguard, as he saw it, an endangered heritage. In a last-ditch attempt to preserve the polyphonic tradition, Palestrina composes his *Missa Papae Marcelli*, which, according to legend, won the historic argument at the Council of Trent in favor of polyphonic music. The conservative nature of the material often dictates old-fashioned stylistic features, as when Pfitzner quotes from Palestrina's Mass.

The title role in the classic recording by Rafael Kubelík is taken by Nicolai Gedda, who succeeds in bringing to it a sense of both ideological passion and resignation. Dietrich Fischer-Dieskau is no less impressive in the other lead role of Cardinal Borromeo, the man who persuades the Pope to decide the matter in question by the composition of an exemplary Mass, investing the part with menace and burning conviction. The vast roster of characters is strongly cast and deployed with skill by Kubelík, who brings both urgency and lyrical expansiveness to the score. **BM**

Franz Schreker | Die Gezeichneten (1915)

Genre | Opera
Conductor/Performers | Lothar Zagrosek;
Heinz Kruse, Elizabeth Connell, Monte Pederson
Years recorded | 1993–94
Label | Decca 444 442-2 (3 CDs)

Following the success of Schreker's first major opera, *Der ferne Klang*, each new work from his pen was greeted with great expectation—and *Die Gezeichneten* (*The Marked Ones*), completed in 1915, fulfilled all hopes. In 1911 fellow composer Alexander von Zemlinsky had asked Schreker to write an opera libretto about the tragedy of the ugly man, but Schreker was so taken with the theme that he decided to use it himself. Zemlinsky later used an adaptation of Oscar Wilde's *The Birthday of the Infanta* for his own opera on a similar idea, *Der Zwerg*.

Schreker created his own scenario, set in Renaissance Genoa. The main characters are three figures marked by fate (the "marked ones" of the title): Alviano, a nobleman who has created an artificial paradise island as a kind of reaction to his own ugliness (though he will not go there for fear of spoiling it); the dissolute pleasure-seeker Count Vitelozzo Tamare, who brings about their downfall; and Carlotta, a physically frail painter who is caught between both men. Despite the Italian milieu, the opera is pure Viennese in its exploration of complicated psychology. And the music—fervent, lush, hyperactive—is the epitome of the late-Romanticism so much in vogue then (think Strauss mixed with Puccini and then double it). The opera was a huge success when premiered in Frankfurt in 1918 and more than two dozen productions followed before Schreker's music was banned by the Nazis in 1933.

The work's latter-day revival was spearheaded by the early 1990s recording in Decca's enterprising "Entartete Musik" series exploring the works forgotten in the wake of the Nazis' cultural purges. It projects the work in all its lurid, passionate detail, reminding us in no small measure that Schreker was a self-confessed eroticist. **MR**

> "There was no sexual-pathological aberration [Schreker] would not have set to music."
>
> "Entartete Musik" exhibition, Düsseldorf, 1938

Other Recommended Recordings

Deutsches Symphony Orchestra Berlin • Kent Nagano
DVD: EuroArts 2055298
Nikolaus Lehnhoff's thought-provoking production of Die Gezeichneten *from the 2005 Salzburg Festival*

Hamburg Opera • Gerd Albrecht
Capriccio 60 010-2 (2 CDs)
A fine recording of Der Schatzgräber, *Schreker's most popular opera in his day*

Kiel Opera • Ulrich Windfuhr
CPO 999 958-2 (2 CDs)
Das Spielwerk und die Prinzessin *can be seen as a post-Freudian* Magic Flute *that ends with immolation*

Franz Schreker was a particularly influential figure in his day. ➔

Sergei Rachmaninov
All-Night Vigil (Vespers) (1915)

Genre | Choral
Conductor | Vladislav Chernushenko
Performers | St. Petersburg Capella
Year recorded | 1992
Label | Saison Russe 788050

For centuries the all-night vigil has been celebrated on the eve of the main feasts of the Orthodox Church, offering a chance for reflection in the beauty of the setting sun, and in the dawn of the new day. Rachmaninov's *All-Night Vigil* magically evokes the austerity and mystery of this ancient tradition. It was composed in 1915 against the background of World War I, at a time when the forty-one-year-old composer-pianist was touring Russia giving concerts in aid of the war effort. More elaborate and intense than his previous large-scale liturgical work for choir (the *Liturgy of St. John Chrysostom* of 1910), the *Vigil* uses authentic *znamenny* and Greek chants. Rachmaninov describes much of his setting as a "conscious counterfeit of the original" church music. Although the piece owes an obvious debt to Russia's rich heritage of religious music, Rachmaninov's inspiration was equally political, the work a potent affirmation of nationalism during the war. First performed in concert rather than church, the work was so well received it was repeated four times during the season.

No choir more finely captures the reflective and celebratory essence of this powerful music than the St. Petersburg Capella—a history-steeped group with its origins in the fifteenth century. The outstanding soprano section is capable of great beauty in the stratospheric chants in thirds, while the splendidly resonant basses —a special preserve of Russian choirs—underpin the velvety sonorities with effortlessly rich low Cs. The descending scale down to a low B flat at the end of "Nyne otpushchayeshi" is breathtaking. The singing has a unique intensity and amazing dynamic contrast. **GR**

Wilhelm Stenhammar
Symphony no. 2 (1915)

Genre | Orchestral
Conductor | Stig Westerberg
Performers | Stockholm Philharmonic
Year recorded | 1978
Label | Caprice CAP 21151

Although Sweden has produced no towering musical genius, Wilhelm Stenhammar comes close, and his Second Symphony is possibly the finest thing he ever created. Sibelius's shadow may fall across some passages, but the overall flavor is so fresh and distinctive, the writing so full of vitality and imagination, that it hardly matters. Stenhammar's sound-world is unmistakably Nordic: plenty of long-breathed, slightly melancholic melodies, alongside passages where a magical vista suddenly opens up. Nature is a constant presence, even if it is not always easy to explain how the music evokes it so vividly. But Stenhammar is no simple dreamy rhapsodist—the symphony has a strong formal backbone as well as cool, airy Northern poetry.

Stig Westerberg keeps both those elements in fine balance throughout this performance. The playing positively exhales conviction and love for the music, but there is also a strong sense of a shaping hand. The first movement builds majestically from its measured but purposeful beginning. The cortège-like slow movement also has sweeping grandeur and dignity as well as tender intimacy. But the lilting, dancing scherzo is a wonderful contrast, like a sudden gust of spring air, preparing the way very effectively for the monumental fugal finale—not the only time in the symphony that one can hear how much Stenhammar admired Bruckner. When this recording first appeared, it persuaded many critics and listeners outside Scandinavia (and one or two within) to think again about Stenhammar, and it still manages to convey something of that sense of excited rediscovery. Three decades on, the recording too still sounds remarkably good. **SJ**

Richard Strauss
Eine Alpensinfonie (1915)

Genre | Orchestral
Conductor | Antoni Wit
Performers | Weimar Staatskapelle
Year recorded | 2006
Label | Naxos 8.557811

Richard Strauss's last orchestral tone poem reflects his preoccupation with the beauties of the Bavarian Alps. Conceived in 1911 but not completed until 1915, the symphony binds twenty-one descriptive sections within a single symphonic movement, framed by a brooding picture of the mountain at night, and placing as its central climax the full panorama surveyed from the summit.

It is unusual among Strauss's orchestral works in that human character comes second to the wonders of nature. Nevertheless, the essential narrative follows the journey of a group of mountaineers who burst onto the scene shortly after a majestic sunrise, witness the pleasures of a brilliantly orchestrated waterfall as well as an Alpine meadow full of clanking cowbells, and undergo some "dangerous moments" on a glacier before reaching their goal. The way down is largely dominated by a colossal storm, atmospherically prepared, and once the sun has come out again, the climbing party calmly reflects on the day's events in one of Strauss's most ecstatic epilogues, the consummation of a work teeming with generous melody.

Antoni Wit coaxes a performance of great tenderness and transparency from the underrated Weimar orchestra, which boasts an especially full-throated proclamation of the summit's glories from a very fine horn section. The interpretation is much more expansive than Strauss's own recording made in 1941 with the Bavarian State Orchestra, but it is never self-indulgent; and in a work where the more thickly scored passages often run the danger of congestion, Wit is assisted immeasurably by the recording's airy concert-hall ambience. **DN**

Karol Szymanowski
Myths (1915)

Genre | Chamber
Performers | Lydia Mordkovitch (violin), Marina Gusak-Grin (piano)
Year recorded | 1989
Label | Chandos CHAN 8747

Szymanowski's genius, while in some ways elusive in character, is also very wide-ranging. Wagner was an early infatuation, but as his teenage years went by, Chopin, Scriabin, Strauss, and Reger all played a role in his developing style. Travels in Italy, Sicily, and North Africa gave him a rich appreciation of Classical and Arab culture, and meeting Debussy, Ravel, and Stravinsky in Paris shortly before World War I was a crucial musical experience.

Many of these influences crystallized as Szymanowski approached maturity as a composer. The *Myths* for violin and piano, composed in 1915 and published in 1921, is among the first works to display his now distinctive style. With the help of his friend Pawel Kochański, a talented violinist, Szymanowski felt that he had created a new style of violin writing. Each of the three movements also reflects Szymanowski's fascination with Classical mythology. The first, entitled "The Fountain of Arethusa," has an impressionistic fragility reminiscent of Debussy while exploring novel and personal tonal realms; "Narcissus," the second, at times seems almost to be looking forward to Messiaen; while the last, "Dryads and Pan," has both shimmering brilliance and depth.

All three movements make formidable technical demands on both performers, while still needing the greatest delicacy in performance. Although much of the focus has to be on instrumental color, performers also need to focus on the sense of dramatic development that underlies each. Lydia Mordkovich, with her dazzling array of tone, and Marina Gusak-Grin are ideal in this repertoire, delivering performances of great distinction. **JS**

Jean Sibelius | Symphony no. 5 (1915, *rev.* 1919)

Genre | Orchestral
Conductor | Osmo Vänskä
Performers | Lahti Symphony Orchestra
Year recorded | 1997
Label | BIS CD-863

Sibelius's Fifth Symphony had the longest gestation period of any of his works save the Eighth (substantially complete by 1933 but ultimately suppressed). As originally conceived, the Fifth had four rather than three movements and more obviously occupied the stylistic ground won by the Fourth. It was speculatively "modern" and wonderfully atmospheric, but not concentrated enough to convince the composer. The 1919 Fifth, his third version, is the one we know today. It has greater certainty and focus even if its reputation for triumphalism has perhaps been oversold. In 1917, Finland had come through a bloody civil war and Sibelius himself was back on the bottle. The cosmic grandeur is still there but must seem hard-won.

As the only conductor permitted to record (and latterly pair) both surviving manifestations of the piece, Osmo Vänskä has special claims. The sound, as throughout BIS's Sibelius series, is state-of-the-art, allowing the outer movements' quiet, misterioso sections to be reproduced at the threshold of audibility. The lean sonority of the Lahti orchestra ensures that we hear evolving processes and interactions that might otherwise be missed. Connoisseurs may appreciate that the slow movement's conventional-sounding surface stratum of variations sits on top of a slowly rotating chorale as if from another universe: Vänskä helps you hear that. And there are revelations aplenty in the finale. In 1915 the unforgettable theme for horns, described by Sibelius's friend, Axel Carpelan, as "that swan hymn beyond compare," lacked the plaintive song that forms its upper layer. Even the symphony's massive final chords were not yet separated into hammer blows. When these players perform the definitive work, it is as if they have secured a special entrée to its world. **DG**

> "*There is always this . . . ambivalence in Sibelius's music, as though the music sounds 'through the tears.'*"
>
> Osmo Vänskä, *The Cambridge Companion to Sibelius*

Other Recommended Recordings

London Symphony Orchestra • Robert Kajanus
Divine Art 27801
Brave, bracing, and rough, the pioneering 78 r.p.m. set
from the composer/conductor closest to Sibelius

New York Philharmonic Orchestra • Leonard Bernstein
SM4K 87329 (4 CDs)
A viscerally exciting, only sometimes gushing account
from early in Bernstein's New York tenure

Berlin Philharmonic Orchestra • Herbert von Karajan
DG 457 748-2 (2 CDs)
Usually considered the best of four recordings from
the master of transition and continuity

Ernest Bloch | Schelomo (1916)

Genre | Concerto
Performers/Conductor | Truls Mørk (cello), Radio France
Philharmonic Orchestra; Paavo Järvi
Year recorded | 2005
Label | Virgin 5 45664 2

Ernest Bloch may have started his working life selling Swiss tourist trinkets in his father's business, but he ended it as one of his country's most successful musical exports. Born in Geneva in 1880, he studied music across Europe, from Brussels and Paris to Frankfurt and Munich, but his composing was a part-time occupation until the premiere of his opera *Macbeth* at the Paris Opéra-Comique in 1910 brought him fame. He was invited to the United States in 1916 as conductor for Maud Allan's dance company and eventually settled there. He held various teaching posts at American music conservatories before retiring to Portland, Oregon, where he died in 1959.

One of Bloch's first big successes in America was his "Hebraic Rhapsody" *Schelomo* (*Solomon*), which premiered in New York in May 1917. This was the culmination of his so-called "Jewish Cycle," which included psalm settings and a large vocal symphony, *Israel*. *Schelomo* was originally conceived as a vocal setting of texts from Ecclesiastes, but a meeting with the cellist Alexander Barjansky persuaded him of the eloquence of a cello voice instead. This short rhapsody, roughly twenty minutes in length, is a kind of musical dialogue between the solo instrument, representing King Solomon, and the "Jewish people" of the orchestra. The music—dramatic, lush, and plaintive—uses the modes and outlines of Hebraic melody to great effect, without ever quoting from existing ideas.

The work has long been beloved of cellists, and this recent recording from Truls Mørk—passionate, wonderfully rhapsodic, and forcefully accompanied by Paavo Järvi and the French Radio orchestra—is perhaps the best to have come along since Emanuel Feuermann's pioneering account with Stokowski. **MR**

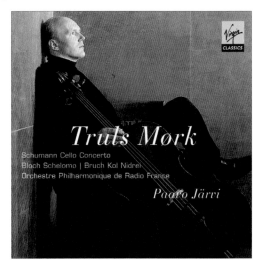

"*Why shouldn't I use . . . a voice vaster and deeper than any spoken language— [the] cello?*"

Ernest Bloch, discussing his setting of Ecclesiastes

Other Recommended Recordings

Emanuel Feuermann, Philadelphia Orchestra
Leopold Stokowski • Biddulph LAB 042
Classic account for those who can cope with restricted mono sound

Miriam Kramer, Simon Over
Naxos 8.554460
A well-played sampling of Bloch's chamber music, including Suite Hebraïque *and Violin Sonatas.*

Seattle Symphony & Chorale • Gerard Schwarz
Delos DE 3135
Bloch in patriotic and Neo-Classical vein, with America *and Concerto Grosso no.* 1

Karol Szymanowski
Symphony no. 3, "The Song of the Night" (1916)

Genre | Orchestral
Conductor/Performers | Jerzy Semkow; Wiesław Ochman,
Polish Radio National Symphony Orchestra & Chorus
Year recorded | 1982
Label | EMI 7243 5 85539 2 5 (2 CDs)

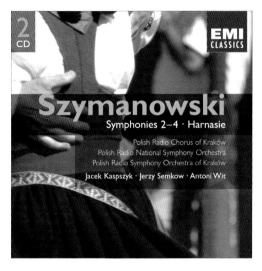

Szymanowski's first attempt at writing a symphony was not a happy experience. He withdrew it after the first performance in 1909 and only the two outer movements still exist today. A little over a year later, he completed his Second Symphony, which showed far greater command of texture, instrumentation, and relatively conventional structure. His Third Symphony, however, is anything but conventional. Effectively a symphonic poem, settings of the thirteenth-century Persian poet Mevlana Jalal al'Din Rumi, in Polish translation, frame a scherzando passage.

Szymanowski evokes the sensuous metaphysics of the poem with at times a near-atonal palette. Scriabin is occasionally brought to mind, but there is much of the mature Szymanowski in the aspiring melodic lines, notably those given to the solo violin, and the work clearly anticipates the Dionysian elements in the opera *King Roger*. The central scherzando section is more overtly focused on Szymanowski's fascination with the East; it is rich in fascinating timbral combinations and concludes with a hushed passage for the timpani. The final section returns to the manner of the first and rises to an ecstatic climax illuminated by more tonally oriented coloring before subsiding to a delicately shaded close.

Wiesław Ochman is simply superb in the solo role. The clarity of his diction is remarkable and his voice appears to soar effortlessly over the music of the vast accompanying ensemble. He is well supported by conductor Jerzy Semkow, who displays an acute understanding of the symphony's carefully structured climaxes, allowing them all to unfold with due impact. **JS**

". . . Your soul is the hero of this night . . ."

A line from the verse on which the Third Symphony is based

Other Recommended Recordings

BBC Philharmonic • Vassily Sinaisky
Chandos CHAN 9496
The early Concert Overture, showing clear indications of genius

Polish State Philharmonic Orchestra • Karol Stryja
Naxos 8 553683
Szymanowski's first attempt at writing a symphony

BBC Philharmonic Orchestra
Vasilij Sinaisky
Chandos CHAN 9478
Clear symphonic mastery of a slightly German cut, in Szymanowski's Second Symphony

Karol Szymanowski
Violin Concerto no. 1 (1916)

Genre | Concerto
Performers/Conductor | Thomas Zehetmair (violin),
City of Birmingham Symphony Orchestra; Simon Rattle
Year recorded | 1996
Label | EMI 7243 5 55607 2 8

Szymanowski's First Violin Concerto dates from 1916, a year after the *Three Myths* for violin and piano, the work that marked a new phase in his writing for the instrument. The composer's approach to the orchestra had also moved away from an adherence to German late-Romantic models, in which structural considerations dominated his approach, to one in which the exploration of ranges of color was the main goal. As with the *Myths*, the violinist Pawel Kochański played a major role in determining the nature of the solo writing and even contributed a cadenza.

It seems that an extravagantly symbolist poem, *May Night* by Tadeusz Miciński, was in part the inspiration for the work; certainly the fantastical nature of the verse with its images of animals and strange mix of Classical, Nordic, and Arabic reference appears to be evoked in the introduction to the soloist. Cast in a single movement, the concerto falls into subsections, each of considerable variety. Although the orchestra for the piece is large, and with a substantial percussion section, it is used with great delicacy throughout, supporting and reacting to the soloist, at times evoking the sound-world of Stravinsky's *Petrushka*. For much of the concerto, the solo line is sweetly rhapsodic, but at times it takes a more forceful role.

Thomas Zehetmair is a near ideal soloist. Not only does he float the cantilena lines of the solo part above the orchestra with exquisite tone, he leads with conviction in the more vigorous passages. Characteristically, Simon Rattle does much more than just accompany, crafting the various instrumental groupings to provide maximum interaction with the soloist. **JS**

"*A new, different music.*"

Szymanowski on his First Violin Concerto

Other Recommended Recordings

Lydia Mordkovitch, BBC Symphony Orchestra
Vassily Sinaisky • Chandos CHAN 9496
Coupled with the Second Violin Concerto, this
captures superbly the energies of the latter sections

Lydia Mordkovitch, Marina Gusak-Grin
Chandos CHAN 8747
Nocturne and Tarantella *display conventionally*
virtuoso writing for violin

Graf Mourja, Natalie Gous
Harmonia Mundi HMC 901767
The Violin Sonata in D minor, op. 9, an engaging
early work

Percy Grainger | In a Nutshell (1916)

Genre | Orchestral
Conductor | Simon Rattle
Performers | City of Birmingham Symphony Orchestra
Year recorded | 1996
Label | EMI 7243 5 56412 2 9

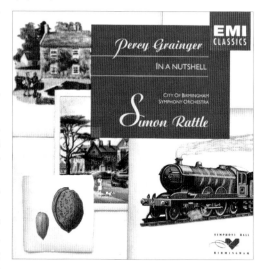

Percy Grainger (1882–1961) was one of music's one-offs. Despite his friendships with Grieg and Delius, his music never really owed allegiance to any particular school or tradition; and although he spent much of his life divided between Australia and America (he was born in Melbourne and died in White Plains, New York), it was northern Europe that provided his inspiration. Some dodgy, if not repugnant, views on Nordic racial supremacy, a self-proclaimed passion for rough sex, and an equally athletic way at the piano aside, Grainger is chiefly remembered for his work on rescuing folksongs from oblivion and for the distinctive controlled anarchy of his approach to music in general. His most famous piece, *Country Gardens*, is in fact an arrangement of an old morris dance tune, while earlier arrangements such as *Irish Tune from Country Derry* (popularly known as "Danny Boy") and the shanty *Shallow Brown* have powerful emotional impact.

With so many miniatures to his name (*The Warriors*, music for an "imaginary ballet," is, at just under twenty minutes, his longest single movement), it is difficult to choose a representative work, but the four-movement suite *In a Nutshell* probably lives up to its name in best encapsulating what Grainger was about. It forms the title work on a simply ravishing disc of Grainger's music recorded by Simon Rattle and the CBSO. Here is the essence of his quirky style—refreshingly bracing pieces such as the opening movement "Arrival Platform Humlet" (the sort of tune one might hum waiting for a train) and "The Gum-Sucker's March" (recalling his Australian roots). Also included is the perennially fresh *Country Gardens*, *The Warriors* and a pair of Grainger's percussion-rich arrangements of Ravel and Debussy. **MR**

> *"I hardly ever think of ought else but sex, race, athletics, speech, and art."*

Percy Grainger

Other Recommended Recordings

Monteverdi Choir, English Country Gardiner Orchestra • John Eliot Gardiner
Philips 475 213-2
A refreshing look at Grainger, familiar and unfamiliar

BBC Philharmonic • Richard Hickox
Chandos CHAN 9493
Another Nutshell *in a treat of a Grainger collection*

Danish National Radio Choir & Symphony Orchestra
Richard Hickox
Chandos CHAN 9721
An intriguing exploration of Grainger's interest in Danish and other Nordic music

Percy Grainger (right) checking a piano roll in New York, c. 1915. ➲

Ottorino Respighi | Roman Trilogy (1916–28)

Genre | Orchestral
Conductor | Lorin Maazel
Performers | Pittsburgh Symphony Orchestra
Year recorded | 1994
Label | Sony SK 66843

Rome has inspired countless painters, poets, novelists, and composers—Puccini's *Tosca* is set there—but surely the most affectionate musical homage is Respighi's trilogy of tone poems—*Fountains of Rome* (1916), *Pines of Rome* (1924), and *Roman Festivals* (1928). Respighi was actually born and bred in Bologna and did not take up residence in Rome until he was in his mid-thirties. Once there, though, he never left, and his love for the city—its history and atmosphere—is palpable on every page of these scores.

Pines of Rome, the most famous of the three, portrays four landmarks conspicuously adorned by stands of pine trees. At the Villa Borghese we hear the boisterous sounds of children playing; mysterious chanting echoes through the catacombs; a nightingale sings in the moonlight on the Janiculum hill; and along the Via Appia, we are gradually overwhelmed by (in the composer's words) "a fantastic vision of bygone glories." In the more delicate *Fountains of Rome*, Respighi's ravishing orchestration suggests water bubbling and sparkling in the sunlight. *Roman Festivals* is something else again, conjuring up bold, dramatic images: martyrs preparing to die in the arena, pilgrims marching toward Rome, a harvest festival in the vineyard, and the raucous celebration on the eve of Epiphany.

Lorin Maazel has proved himself a devoted advocate of Respighi's tone poems, and this Sony CD—his only traversal of the complete trilogy—is a blockbuster. The conductor's ear for detail never fails to dazzle and delight. And under his expert baton the Pittsburgh Symphony proves that it belongs in the top tier of American orchestras. Sony's engineers have worked a small miracle, too, resulting in a recording of stunning warmth, clarity, and wall-rattling power. **AFC**

"With the present constitution of the orchestra, it is impossible to achieve more."

Ottorino Respighi

Other Recommended Recordings

Chicago Symphony Orchestra
Fritz Reiner
RCA 82876 71614 2
An early stereo classic

Philadelphia Orchestra
Riccardo Muti
Brilliant 7565
Muti's incisive, dramatic account, played with gusto

Montreal Symphony Orchestra
Charles Dutoit
Decca 410 145-2
Respighi en français—graceful and piquant

Respighi forged a path for orchestral music in opera-obsessed Italy. ➡

Carl Nielsen
Symphony no. 4
"Inextinguishable" (1916)

Genre | Orchestral
Conductor | Jean Martinon
Performers | Chicago Symphony Orchestra
Year recorded | 1966
Label | RCA 82876 76237 2

Richard Strauss
Ariadne auf Naxos
(1916)

Genre | Opera
Conductor/Performer | Herbert von
Karajan; Elisabeth Schwarzkopf
Year recorded | 1954
Label | EMI 7243 5 67077 2 6 (2 CDs)

The Fourth Symphony is optimistic in outlook, like its predecessors, but it is a completely different type of optimism. The *Sinfonia espansiva* was an extrovert work, with, as the writer Max Brod said to Nielsen, ". . . a song of a happy, work-filled and yet Arcadian and innocent future for humanity." Such an innocent future had clearly become an impossibility when Nielsen began work on the *Inextinguishable* after the outbreak of World War I. But he still believed in a future for humankind, one that would be won through the indomitable will to live of the human spirit, though achieved only with a struggle.

That struggle reaches its height in the finale when a second timpani player enters after having been silent for more than twenty-five minutes. "I have an idea for a duel between two sets of timpani, it has to do with the war," said Nielsen, and it is the most striking point in the work. After a hesitant initial reception, the *Inextinguishable* was welcomed in Denmark as "a masterwork that towers up to the sky," and it was the work that Nielsen chose to bring to London in 1923; ". . . A strongly personal utterance . . . austere, even bleak music, such as will not appeal to the sensuous," in the view of one critic.

In his only recording of a Nielsen symphony, Jean Martinon goes for fast speeds and violent contrasts, and the whole performance has a reckless urgency. With the Chicago Symphony on top form, and a timpani battle that has rarely been as riveting or as well recorded, this is a classic version. **MC**

In gratitude for the help that the famous director Max Reinhardt had given Strauss and Hofmannsthal during rehearsals for *Der Rosenkavalier*, the poet conceived "a new kind of entertainment" for Reinhardt's Deutsches Theater in Berlin. Molière's play *Le bourgeois gentilhomme* would be given with Strauss's incidental music, followed by *Ariadne auf Naxos* as the opera Monsieur Jourdain puts on in the play. The work proved too much for Reinhardt's resources, however, and the premiere took place in Stuttgart.

The mixture of genres was not well received, and soon afterward a new version was conceived, replacing the play with a prologue. "The richest man in Vienna" is putting on an entertainment for his guests and, as things are running late, he dictates that both scheduled pieces, a comedy and a tragic opera, be performed simultaneously. The action begins with the comedians intruding into the plot, commenting upon it. Strauss took delight in portraying the haughty prima donna and pompous tenor, while reserving his most eloquent music for the idealistic young Composer, whom he pictured as a young Mozart-like genius. Zerbinetta, the comedian, is a coloratura role requiring a virtuoso technique.

Walter Legge handpicked both the singers and instrumentalists for a recording that belies its mono origins. Irmgard Seefried was Strauss's own favorite Composer, Rita Streich transcends her role's difficulties, and Elisabeth Schwarzkopf has a ball parodying the prima donna breed. **CMS**

Charles Ives
Symphony no. 4
(1916)

Genre | Orchestral
Conductor | Michael Tilson Thomas
Performers | Chicago Symphony Orchestra
Year recorded | 1991
Label | Sony SK 44939

Although Ives conceived the plan for his Fourth Symphony in about 1909, the work only premiered in 1965. It is Ives's most synoptic work, combining his modernism and his traditionalism, his most raucous sonic inventions, and his homeliest hymn-derived tunes.

After a questioning prelude, the second movement is the most extreme piece Ives ever wrote, a "comedy" crammed full of invention and incident, incredibly dense textures, riotous multitudinous polyrhythms, quarter-tone harmonies, and countless tunes. The third movement's calm fugue is an utter contrast, noble, serene, and comfortingly familiar. The finale starts very softly with the percussion alone, playing in a slow 4/4 pulse. This group continues independently throughout the movement, while in exquisite gradations of color and quiet dynamics the orchestra introduces other material around it, in different pulses. The symphony dissolves into a mirage of bell-sounds and drum-rhythms, its gaze fixed on Eternity.

Though Stokowski's original 1965 recording has incredible intensity, it is let down by constricted sound. No such drawback with Michael Tilson Thomas's blazing account (the first to use the Ives Society Critical Edition), which deals amazingly well with the layered and terraced dynamics of the "Comedy," a real palimpsest of a movement. He draw searingly eloquent playing and singing from his Chicago forces and, interestingly, the disc includes performances of some of the hymns Ives wove into the symphony's texture. **MM**

Gustav Holst
The Planets
(1917)

Genre | Orchestral
Conductor | Charles Dutoit
Performers | Montreal Symphony Orchestra
Year recorded | 1986
Label | Decca 417 553-2

Holst's The Planets is a marvel. It was the first British work of the twentieth century to take on board what the most advanced European composers of the time (Strauss, Debussy, Stravinsky, even Schoenberg) were up to and somehow reconcile their diverse influences with the accents of English folksong. Even more improbably, it was a success, right from its first performance. Audiences responded to its wealth of good tunes, its imaginative scoring for an opulently large orchestra, and the clearly defined character of each of its seven movements. But perhaps not everyone realized then, or realizes now, what the piece is really about—not (as dozens of LP and CD covers suggest) astronomy, but astrology. As some fascinating research by Raymond Head has established, Holst got the idea for the piece from a book by one "Alan Leo," which set out the astrological view of the influence of the planets on the human spirit. And the unusual but highly effective ordering of the seven movements is designed, Head suggests, to portray "the unfolding experience of human life from youth to old age."

A successful recording of The Planets needs an orchestra of the highest quality, a conductor who can create the right atmosphere for each movement and galvanize the musicians, and a sound picture of clarity, warmth, and depth. The one by the Montreal Symphony and Charles Dutoit, recorded nine years into their historic twenty-five-year partnership in the spacious church of St. Eustache, does full justice to Holst's astonishing vision. **AB**

Lili Boulanger | Psalm 130, "Du fond de l'abîme" (1917)

Genre | Choral
Conductor/Performers | Mark Stringer; Sonia de Beaufort, Martial Defontaine, Namur Symphonic Choir
Year recorded | 1998
Label | Timpani 1C1046

Psalm 130, "Du fond de l'abîme" is the most ambitious score of Lili Boulanger's short career. Completed in the autumn of 1917, just a few months before her death in March 1918 at the age of twenty-four, this psalm setting seems to encapsulate her fortitude. Far from reflecting her physical fragility, the sense here is of the profound inner strength that sustained a life lived in the shadow of terminal illness.

Following in the footsteps of her older sister, Nadia, Lili had entered the competition for France's most prestigious prize for composers, the Prix de Rome. Nadia had only managed a second prize, but in 1913 Lili became the first woman to win this coveted competition. That the jury's faith was not misplaced is confirmed by the remarkable sequence of works that Boulanger produced over the next five years, foremost among which are three psalm settings. Her harmonic language seems to bridge the gap between the Debussy of *Le martyre de Saint Sébastien* and the Messiaen of *Chants de terre et de ciel*. Influences can be heard, but Boulanger was rapidly assimilating the latest trends while making developments that foreshadow later Roussel and Honegger, not to mention Ernest Bloch, with whom there are remarkable parallels.

This was the first recording to do full justice to Boulanger's three psalm settings, especially the striving for light amid darkness of Psalm 130. Mark Stringer keeps a masterly grip on events, from the long brooding orchestral introduction and the numbed opening lament from the depths, to the latter's return at the end modified by more hopeful phrases from above. Both here and in the settings of Psalms 24 and 129, the performers clearly feel passionately about this extraordinary music, their fervent advocacy reflecting Boulanger's spirit. **CD**

> *"She was able to find the necessary elements for expressing her own very personal message . . ."*
> Nadia Boulanger

Other Recommended Recordings

Clairières dans le ciel
Jean-Paul Fouchecourt (tenor), Alain Jacquon (piano)
Timpani 1C1042
This song cycle shows Boulanger's enormous potential

Faust et Hélène
BBC Philharmonic • Yan Pascal Tortelier
Chandos CHAN 9745
A superb account of Boulanger's Prix de Rome cantata

In memoriam
Naoumoff, Charlier, Sabrié, Reinhardt
Marco Polo 8.223636
Marvelous vocal, chamber and instrumental pieces

Lili Boulanger, whose destiny for greatness was tragically cut short. ➔

Sergei Prokofiev
Violin Concerto no. 1 (1917)

Genre | Concerto
Performer/Conductor | David Oistrakh;
Lovro von Matačić
Year recorded | 1954
Label | EMI 7243 5 62889 2 8

Created at a momentous time, Prokofiev's First Violin Concerto only partially reflects the upheavals in Russia and the outside world. Its central scherzo has much of the spikiness with which this enfant terrible of Russian music laced most of his works in his youth; but the moderately paced movements that begin and end the concerto are relatively mild. It comes as no surprise that Prokofiev's next work was the "Classical" Symphony.

The concerto had to wait six years before Marcel Darrieux premiered it in Paris, and by then music had moved on, and the Parisian avant-garde were a trifle disappointed by it. The Moscow premiere that took place three days later went better; and as soon as Joseph Szigeti took the piece up its fortunes changed. Today, for all the poise, poetry, and equanimity in the outer movements, it seems considerably more forward-looking than the predominantly lyrical Second Concerto.

David Oistrakh brought an extra dimension to the concerto and became close to the composer, who was embarrassed to be reminded that when Oistrakh first played the scherzo to him, he delivered a humiliating public lecture to the young man. All that was long past when Oistrakh recorded the work in London, fiddling with heroic technique, massive control, firm rhythm, and kaleidoscopic tonal variety. If his Russian version with Kirill Kondrashin were available, it might be first choice, but this EMI version boasts superior sound and has been nicely revamped for CD issue. Those who need digital recording will find Frank Peter Zimmermann's performance (for EMI) a superb substitute. **TP**

Sergei Prokofiev
Symphony no. 1 (1917)

Genre | Orchestral
Conductor | Claudio Abbado
Performers | Chamber Orchestra of Europe
Year recorded | 1986
Label | DG 429 396-2

There is no trace in this bright and breezy masterpiece of the fraught circumstances under which it was composed. Shortly before beginning work on it, the composer had been dodging the street-fighting of the February 1917 Revolution in Petrograd (St. Petersburg). With little inkling of the upheavals still in store, he set off for the countryside, where he worked on the "Classical" Symphony without a piano to hand—a risk worth taking, he thought, for "a rather simple thing like this symphony." He knew that while conservatives would take him to task for his apparent audacity in applying the Classicism of Mozart or Haydn to a contemporary composition, the public would simply take pleasure in a work that was so cheerful "and will surely applaud it"—which they did at the first performance, conducted by the composer the following April.

While the Mozart touch is apparent in the light, airy scoring and the elegant bustle of the outer movements, there is an element of surprise to the way in which the themes step upward or downward into neighboring keys before returning home—a hallmark of Prokofiev's style. This is especially true of the second theme in the first movement and of the gavotte, which is a supreme example of Prokofiev's concision.

Large-scale orchestras often present the "Classical" Symphony as a curtain-raiser to more imposing events, but the most delectable performance on CD comes from a more compact ensemble—the Chamber Orchestra of Europe under the direction of Claudio Abbado. Here the rhythms are clear, the song-lines well defined, and the wit effortlessly projected. **DN**

Erik Satie
Parade (1917)

Genre | Ballet
Conductor | Antal Dorati
Performers | London Symphony Orchestra
Year recorded | 1965
Label | Mercury 434 335-2

Richard Strauss
Die Frau ohne Schatten (1917)

Genre | Opera
Conductor/Performers | Georg Solti;
Julia Varady, Plácido Domingo
Years recorded | 1989–91
Label | Decca 436 243-2 (3 CDs)

Stravinsky's ballet *The Rite of Spring* is remembered for the uproar that surrounded its 1913 premiere, but something not dissimilar greeted Satie's *Parade*, a fifteen-minute ballet about circus performers that was first staged in Paris four years later. Commissioned by Diaghilev, choreographed by Massine, designed by Picasso, conducted by Ansermet, and based on a scenario by Jean Cocteau, the work featured industrial "instruments" such as foghorns, typewriters, and a pistol. It seems as if no single work could contain such a blend of wayward creativity; the almost inevitable civil disturbance that followed saw Satie spending a week in jail. Perhaps unsurprisingly, the music is fairly unsubtle, for the most part, with a rapid-fire episodic structure that is, in all fairness, typical of music for dance. However, the piece is jocular and highly listenable, which in itself was regarded as somewhat vulgar by the critics of the day—so it merits inclusion here for its sheer cheek.

The capriciousness of Satie's music is not routinely associated with British orchestras, but Antal Dorati has no problem in persuading the LSO to accept the humor of the piece, while at the same time astutely realizing that the provocative comedy of such stuff is inherent and that to exaggerate it in performance is to miss the point altogether. This he duly avoids. In between all the gunshots and typewriter clatters, there are some splendidly euphonious string textures and snatches of sophisticated melody, even if these are set up only to be knocked down again. These, too, are expertly handled and are integrated with assured elegance into the fizzy atmosphere of the piece as a whole. **RT**

If *Der Rosenkavalier* had been a *Figaro* writ large, *Die Frau ohne Schatten*, with its story of trial and redemption, became a heavyweight *Magic Flute*. The opera is one of Strauss's longest and most complicated scores, including wind and thunder machines, glass harmonica, organ, tamtam, and five tuned gongs. The premiere of such an ambitious piece was unthinkable in wartime, and it could take place only in 1919.

The libretto is heavy with symbolism and concerns a half-divine woman who has married a mortal emperor; since she does not cast a shadow, she cannot conceive his child and this will cause her husband to turn into stone. The Empress and her nurse descend to Earth and cheat the shrewish wife of the dyer Barak of her shadow. Seeing Barak's unstinting love for his wife, the Empress in the end renounces the shadow and her sacrifice liberates both couples from their trials. Strauss's scoring differentiates subtly between the divine and human worlds, reflecting Hofmannsthal's complicated net of symbols.

The opera was well received at its Vienna premiere and was soon performed across the German-speaking world. The enormous demands it makes on the principal singers meant that few performances or recordings have been really complete. Solti's is, and it boasts a heterogeneous but convincing cast, with Plácido Domingo brilliant as the Emperor, in his only Strauss role to date. José van Dam sings a heartfelt and humane Barak (the only character in this opera who has a name), and the three main female roles are gloriously taken. The recording is a tour de force, revealing the huge score in all its amazing detail. **CMS**

Ottorino Respighi | Ancient Airs and Dances (1917–32)

Genre | Orchestral
Conductor | None
Performers | Orpheus Chamber Orchestra
Year recorded | 1991
Label | DG 437 533-2

As a student in Bologna, Respighi developed a keen interest in early music. This was back in the days when even the work of such an important master as Monteverdi was largely unknown, and little or no thought was given to authentic performance practice. In 1917, he adapted and orchestrated several of Chilesotti's transcriptions of sixteenth-century Italian lute music, with the aim of introducing modern audiences to these forgotten treasures. Respighi titled his suite *Ancient Airs and Dances*; a second suite followed in 1923, and a third in 1932.

Respighi's arrangements are exquisite, preserving the melodic charms of the originals while enriching their harmonies and "colorizing" their presentation with a wealth of orchestral detail. To twenty-first-century ears used to the more austere tone of period instruments in this repertoire, these *Ancient Airs and Dances* may sound slightly decadent. Even the most simply scored of the suites, the third (for strings only), has a velvety plushness that feels distinctly deluxe.

The conductorless Orpheus Chamber Orchestra's performance of the Third Suite is not the most luxurious available. What sets it apart is its intimate character, as if this were chamber music. And with string tone that is so delicate and sweet, and the ensemble's lithe and loving phrasing, its version is perhaps the most ravishing of all. In the more lavishly scored First Suite, it is the orchestra's collective grace that delights. The Second Suite is omitted here, but it is replaced by *The Birds*, an equally charming collection based on seventeenth- and eighteenth-century lute and harpsichord pieces. The CD also includes the *Trittico botticelliano*, a tender, lustrous score inspired by three well-known Botticelli paintings. **AFC**

"... the Romanticism of yesterday will again be the Romanticism of tomorrow."

From an artistic manifesto coauthored by Respighi

Other Recommended Recordings

Philharmonia Hungarica
Antál Dorati
Mercury 470 637-2
Dorati brings out the music's balletic character

Lausanne Chamber Orchestra
Jesús López-Cobos
Telarc CD-80309
Ultrarefined interpretations, sumptuously recorded

Boston Symphony Orchestra
Seiji Ozawa
DG 419 868-2
Grandeur and elegance in equal measure

George Enescu | Symphony no. 3 (1918)

Genre | Orchestral
Conductor | Gennady Rozhdestvensky
Performers | Leeds Festival Chorus, BBC Philharmonic
Year recorded | 1997
Label | Chandos CHAN 9633

Composer, violinist, teacher, pianist, conductor, cellist—
there was hardly an area of music in which George Enescu
(1881–1955) did not excel. Arguably the greatest musician
ever to have come out of Romania, he divided his career
between his homeland and Paris, where he taught, among
other great violinists in the making, Arthur Grumiaux
and Yehudi Menuhin. As a composer, he is probably best
remembered for his first *Romanian Rhapsody* of 1901, one
of those reputation-making works that the composer
comes to regret writing, so fully does it mask all his other
work in the public imagination. That body of work, though
only extending to thirty-three opus numbers, includes
many chamber pieces, a four-act opera on the story of
Oedipus, and three large-scale, Romantic symphonies (as
well as two late works left unfinished at his death).

The third of these, one of the last flowerings of the
central European symphonic tradition, was composed
during the latter stages of World War I, and some have
seen in its three-movement design a kind of "Purgatory–
Inferno–Paradise" program. There is certainly more than
a hint of militarism in the central scherzo, while the finale
proclaims hope in the future with the aid of a wordless
chorus. While the music's language is not as obviously
folk-imbued as, say, his *Romanian Rhapsodies*, its modalism
still proclaims its geographic origins, while its themes are
highly memorable.

The BBC Philharmonic has long since proved itself
to be one of the best orchestras there is for this kind of
late-Romantic sound-world and here, under Gennady
Rozhdestvensky's fluid direction, it brings out all the
richness of Enescu's elaborate orchestral writing. The
coupling is the ubiquitous Rhapsody. **MR**

> *"Perfection . . . does not interest me. What is important is to [make oneself and others] vibrate."*

George Enescu

Other Recommended Recordings

Symphony no. 1
BBC Philharmonic • Gennady Rozhdestvensky
Chandos CHAN 9507
The First, sumptuously played, and Suite no. 3

Symphony no. 2
BBC Philharmonic • Gennady Rozhedstvensky
Chandos CHAN 9537
The final installment with Romanian Rhapsody no. 2

Oedipe
Vienna State Opera Orchestra • Michael Gielen
Naxos 8.660163-64 (2 CDs)
A powerful opera live from the Vienna State Opera

Francis Poulenc | Mélodies (1918–60)

Genre | Vocal
Performers | Pierre Bernac, Gerard Souzay, Nicolai Gedda, Francis Poulenc, Dalton Baldwin
Years recorded | 1945–98
Label | EMI 7243 5 66849 2 8 (5 CDs)

It might seem that Francis Poulenc wrote songs as easily as breathing, but like the *mélodies* of his great predecessor Gabriel Fauré, whose heir he is, Poulenc's songs are hard-won, charting a sophisticated dialogue between words and music. They are by turns playful and serious and, as with so much of Poulenc's music, the door into the nightclub is never far from the chancel steps.

Poulenc's first songs, settings of six poems from Apollinaire's *Le bestiaire* written in 1918–19, revealed a sharp ear for contemporary French poetry. But it would be over a decade before he established his mature style as a *mélodiste*. On April 3, 1935, Poulenc and the baritone Pierre Bernac gave their first recital in a platform partnership that would continue for nearly a quarter of a century. They included the first performance of *Cinq poèmes de Paul Eluard*, which, with *Tel jour, telle nuit*, a sequence of lovesongs composed the following year, revealed Poulenc as a master songwriter. Poulenc weighs his words as carefully as Benjamin Britten across the Channel; voice and the piano often work independently of each other dynamically and the accompaniment never outdoes the singer.

Led by the composer himself and the eminent French baritone Pierre Bernac, this fine recording gathers together performances of all of Poulenc's *mélodies* by artists with a particular affinity with this music. It is perhaps invidious to pick out particular performances, but Gérard Souzay and Dalton Baldwin give a fine account of the *Cinq poèmes de Paul Eluard*, and there is a passionate intensity in Nicolai Gedda's *Tel jour, telle nuit*. For Poulenc at his most lighthearted, listen to Elly Ameling sing his last song cycle, *La courte paille*, which was written in 1960 for the French opera singer Denise Duval to sing to her young son. **CC**

> "*You know that I am as sincere in my faith . . . as I am in my Parisian sexuality.*"

Francis Poulenc

Other Recommended Recordings

Felicity Lott, Anthony Rolfe Johnson, Ann Murray, Graham Johnson
Hyperion CDA 66147
Always elegant and with perfect French, Felicity Lott has the lion's share of the mélodies

Michel Piquemal, Christine Lajarrige
Naxos 8.553642
An inexpensive introduction to Poulenc's songs

Norah Amsellem, Dalton Baldwin
Claves 2410
There is a special Frenchness to Amsellem's Poulenc on this recital disc

Francis Poulenc, pictured in 1930, could be urbane as well as frivolous. ➡

Leoš Janáček
Taras Bulba (1918)

Genre | Orchestral
Conductor/Performers | Rafael Kubelík;
Bavarian Radio Symphony Orchestra
Year recorded | 1970
Label | DG 439 437-2

Russian literature was a constant inspiration for Janáček. He visited Russia regularly and cofounded a Russian circle in Brno in 1898. Themes from Russian literature influenced his chamber music and opera, notably *Katya Kabanova* and *From the House of the Dead*, and in 1915 the orchestral rhapsody *Taras Bulba*. Janáček had first come across Gogol's short novel, heroic and brutal in equal measure, in 1905. His enthusiasm for *Taras Bulba*, prompted mainly by the inner strength of the Russian people in the face of foreign oppression as depicted in the novel, remained with him for ten years before he set pen to paper.

Each of the three movements of *Taras Bulba* is based on a cathartic episode from Gogol's account of the struggles of the eponymous Cossack chieftain against Polish invaders. The first movement deals with the elicit love— painted in long, yearning musical lines—and death of Taras's first son Andri, the next with the death of his second son Ostap. The finale sees the heroic end of Taras himself at the hands of the Poles. In a characteristically broad peroration, Janáček paints a picture of nobility and fierce independence triumphing—in the grandest orchestral coloring, reinforced by an organ—over pain and death.

Given the magnificence of the work's conclusion, most performances save their best shot for the closing pages of the finale. The most satisfying, however, engage with the volatility of the drama as it unfolds. In Rafael Kubelík's 1970 recording, he and the marvelously committed orchestra capture Janáček's frequently jagged instrumental lines as well as the work's abundant expansive passages; the end is suitably opulent, not overblown. **JS**

Giacomo Puccini
Gianni Schicchi (1918)

Genre | Opera
Conductor/Performers | Gabriele Santini;
Tito Gobbi, Victoria de los Angeles
Year recorded | 1959
Label | EMI 7243 5 62806 2 5

How sad that Puccini wrote only one comic opera—and then as the final part of a trilogy of one-acters, *Il trittico*, which premiered in New York in 1918. Was he intimidated by the near perfection of Verdi's *Falstaff*? He had no reason to be as *Gianni Schicchi* scarcely puts a foot wrong, combining a masterly musical exposition of character with impeccable comic timing. Indeed the scene in which Schicchi, impersonating the dead Buoso Donati, wills himself and not the wealthy merchant's greedy relatives the bulk of the deceased's fortune sometimes seems to be the last act of the great buffa tradition that had dominated Italian comic opera for nearly two hundred years.

Yet there is nothing at all mechanical or heartless about *Gianni Schicchi*. Puccini, never happier than when tugging at the heartstrings, gives half of the work over to Lauretta, Schicchi's daughter who is head over her Florentine heels in love with the dead man's nephew Rinuccio. "O mio babbino caro," in which Lauretta begs her father to make the marriage possible, is rightly a showstopper. That it is the daughter of the lowly born Schicchi who gets the big tune only underscores Puccini's point about how little the upper classes understand about true feelings.

No one else on record has inhabited Gianni Schicchi so completely as Tito Gobbi. He casts a wonderfully cool eye over the relatives squabbling around the deathbed and finds tenderness in his relationship with Lauretta. Victoria de los Angeles sings "O mio babbino caro" with a winning charm, the voice light and airy, in love with Carlo del Monte's stylish Rinuccio—and the fortune-hunting relatives are a glorious gallery of vocal grotesques. **CC**

Igor Stravinsky
The Soldier's Tale (1918)

Genre | Music Theater
Performers | David Timson, Benjamin
Soames, Jonathan Keeble, Nicholas Ward
Year recorded | 1995
Label | Naxos 8.553662

During World War I, the extravagances of Stravinsky's three early scores for the Ballets Russes became neither practicable nor tenable. It is a moot point whether he would have turned away from the oversized orchestra of *The Rite of Spring* regardless, but the war imposed a drastic scaling-back. By 1918, Stravinsky was based in Switzerland and, in partnership with the writer Charles-Ferdinand Ramuz, he conceived *The Soldier's Tale*. With two actors, a dancer and narrator bound by music from an idiosyncratic ensemble of seven instrumentalists who are also on stage, this became the prototype for twentieth-century music theater. The idea, never quite realized, was to tour Swiss villages by truck, giving performances.

A variant on the Faust story, *The Soldier's Tale* is also prophetic of *The Rake's Progress*, and the story is centered around a bargain being struck with the devil. Musically, it reflects Stravinsky's fascinations of the time, including a tango and a ragtime, and is notable for the music given to the instrument at the center of the drama—the violin.

The work is most often encountered in the suite that presents most of the music, dispensing with the dialogue. Nonetheless, *The Soldier's Tale* truly comes to life in the context of a theatrical presentation, as in this fine account led by the violin of Nicholas Ward. Stravinsky encouraged translating the text (none of which is sung) and adapting it to local needs, and the English version adroitly captures the spirit of the original. The music's wit and pathos is also keenly felt, the central sequence of dances especially characterful, and only the hardest of hearts could resist the Puckish drama of this morality tale. **CD**

Arnold Bax
Tintagel (1919)

Genre | Orchestral
Conductor | Vernon Handley
Performers | BBC Philharmonic
Year recorded | 2003
Label | Chandos CHAN 10122(5) (5 CDs)

A Londoner whose close identification with Ireland caused him to develop a parallel career as a poet under the pseudonym of "Dermot O'Byrne," Bax described himself as "a brazen Romantic," though he ended his career as Master of the Queen's Music. He was deeply affected by the events of the 1916 Easter Rebellion in Dublin (some of the executed leaders were personal friends), and much of his finest music was written in the years during and just after the Great War. His most colorful orchestral writing is to be found in his numerous tone poems inspired by nature and Celtic myth—as illustrated by *Tintagel*, his most famous work. Dedicated to his mistress Harriet Cohen (with whom he had just had an extended Cornish holiday), and taking its name from the ruined castle on the Cornish headland where, according to legend, King Arthur was born, it might be considered the English *La mer*. In its exalted, three-part span, *Tintagel* alternates some of the most vivid evocations of seascape in the British repertoire with passionate and stormy music that Bax ascribed to memories of the traditions "connected with King Arthur, King Mark, and Tristram and Iseult." (A "wailing chromatic motif" in this section develops into Wagner's "sick Tristan" motif from *Tristan und Isolde*.)

There are classic performances of *Tintagel* by Adrian Boult and John Barbirolli, but Vernon Handley's more recent version has an especial glow and conviction, coming from a lifelong champion of Bax's works. Wild and eloquent, this sounds like the performance of a lifetime, and he inspires the BBC Philharmonic to playing of utter conviction. **MM**

Manuel de Falla | The Three-Cornered Hat (1919)

Genre | Ballet
Conductor | Ernest Ansermet
Performers | Teresa Berganza, Suisse Romande Orchestra
Year recorded | 1961
Label | Decca 466 991-2

LEGENDARY Legends 1961 PERFORMANCES

Falla
El sombrero de tres picos
El amor brujo
ANSERMET

96kHz 24-bit Super DIGITAL Transfer

Like his earlier work *El amor brujo*, *The Three-Cornered Hat* has its roots in an earlier piece of music theater that Falla wrote for Spanish consumption—*El Corregidor y la molinara* (*The Magistrate and the Miller's Wife*). Based on the book *El sombrero de tres picos*, it is a brief, almost Chaucerian episode of Spanish country life, where the magistrate—whose symbol of office is the hat of the title—wants to have his way with the Miller's wife, but is outwitted and exposed. Falla's music was written for a small ensemble, and the piece was successfully performed in Madrid in 1917. It was there that Serge Diaghilev saw it and half-cajoled, half-bullied Falla into converting it into a full-length ballet for his Ballets Russes.

The work was given its premiere in London, conducted by Ernest Ansermet, with sets and costumes by Picasso, the Miller's Wife danced by Lydia Sokolova, and the Miller by Léonid Massine, who was also the choreographer. Massine had delved into traditional Spanish dancing, and, with Diaghilev, had insisted that Falla intensify the Spanish elements in the music—the final jota, the climactic dance, was completely new, and accompanied a scene where the disgraced magistrate was tossed in a blanket by the locals. The ballet was an immediate success with its colorful story and music, including lusty cries of "*Olé*" and a sultry mezzo-soprano voice.

Teresa Berganza's voice is one of the great attractions of this 1961 Decca recording, giving real class to the vocal passages. And there is always something special about performances by first interpreters—you can hear Ansermet relishing the memory of that 1919 premiere, with its astonishing gallery of star names, and recreating it anew for the stereo age. **MC**

> *"It was wonderful to think that quiet little man . . . gave birth to this explosion of melody and rhythm."*
>
> Lydia Sokolova

Other Recommended Recordings

Victoria de los Angeles, Philharmonia Orchestra
Rafael Frühbeck de Burgos
EMI 7243 5 67587 2 8 (2 CDs)
Another great singer, with fiery Spanish conducting

Jennifer Larmore, Chicago Symphony Orchestra
Daniel Barenboim
Teldec 0630 17145-2
Brightly played modern recording

Maria Oran, Spanish National Orchestra
Rafael Frühbeck de Burgos
Classic FM 75605 57035 2
Native recording with exciting singing

Spanish mezzo-soprano Teresa Berganza. ➔

Edward Elgar | Cello Concerto (1919)

Genre | Concerto
Performers | Jacqueline du Pré, London Symphony Orchestra
Conductor | John Barbirolli
Year recorded | 1965
Label | EMI 7243 5 62886 2 1

GREAT RECORDINGS
OF THE CENTURY

EMI
CLASSICS

ELGAR
Cello Concerto · Sea Pictures
Overture: 'Cockaigne'
Jacqueline du Pré · Janet Baker
Sir John Barbirolli

London Symphony Orchestra
Philharmonia Orchestra

ELGAR

CELLO CONCERTO
JACQUELINE DU PRÉ

SIR JOHN BARBIROLLI
LONDON SYMPHONY ORCHESTRA

SEA PICTURES
JANET BAKER

Few, if any, works in the cello repertoire have come to be so closely identified with the instrument as Elgar's Cello Concerto. When the soloist declares the somber opening chords, that plangent tenor voice captures the essence of the cello. British audiences also hear a valediction: Elgar's farewell to Edwardian England in the aftermath of World War I, and to his own life as a composer. If this very private work has become something of a national memorial, then it has also enshrined the memory of the British cellist who burned it into the public consciousness. Jacqueline du Pré released the work from its rather gentlemanly tradition with her bold, visionary, heart-on-the-sleeve performances. Her passionate abandon will forever be associated with the long rising E minor scale that explodes into the first movement's main theme. And the tragedy of her life, cut short by multiple sclerosis when she was only twenty-seven, has become inseparable from the tragic nobility of the concerto.

These layers of cultural consciousness could not have accrued around a lesser work; but this is one of Elgar's finest, most original creations. The terse first movement is followed by a breakneck, skittering scherzo, while the intense Adagio, with its heart-wrenching appeals, returns to haunt the rumbustious finale in a visionary coda.

Du Pré's 1965 recording with Barbirolli remains mesmerizing, despite her tendency to wring every last drop from each note. Such playing may not be fashionable, but du Pré was an artist of rare powers, who could engage directly with her audience at a profoundly emotional level. For an alternative and equally compelling approach, there is Yo-Yo Ma's, in which it is his restraint that proves unutterably moving. **HW**

> *"Elgar has become part of the national consciousness at those moments when he [retires into solitude.]"*
>
> Ralph Vaughan Williams

Other Recommended Recordings

**Yo-Yo Ma, London Symphony Orchestra
André Previn • Sony SMK 89712**
A uniquely grave and beautiful performance

**Torlief Thedéen, Malmö Symphony Orchestra
Lev Markiz • BIS CD-486**
*A profoundly thoughtful reading; no one has
brought such tenderness to the slow movement*

**Truls Mørk, City of Birmingham Symphony Orchestra
Simon Rattle
Virgin 7243 5 45356 2 8**
*A reading of freshness and sincerity from the
Norwegian virtuoso*

Jacqueline du Pré, pictured in 1969. ➲

Darius Milhaud
Le boeuf sur le toit

(1919)

Genre | Ballet
Conductor | Jean-Claude Casadesus
Performers | Lille National Orchestra
Year recorded | 2003
Label | Naxos 8.557287

Darius Milhaud (1892–1974) owes his fame to his extraordinary talent, of course—though his friendship with the poet and diplomat Paul Claudel was surely significant as well. As a young composer, Milhaud wrote music for several of Claudel's dramas, and when Claudel went to Brazil in 1916 to serve as the French ambassador, he brought Milhaud along as a cultural attaché. The infectious syncopations and sweet tunefulness of the popular music Milhaud heard in Brazil echoes throughout much of his subsequent work.

One of the earliest works to reflect Milhaud's South American experience is the ballet *Le boeuf sur le toit* (*The Bull on the Roof*). He later wrote: "Still haunted by my memories of Brazil, I assembled a few popular melodies, tangos, maxixes, sambas." These he transcribed and inserted into "a rondo-like form." At first, he thought his "fantasia" would be the perfect accompaniment for a Charlie Chaplin film. But Jean Cocteau convinced Milhaud his music would be better suited to a ballet. Cocteau created a surreal scenario, and presented it—along with pieces by Satie and Poulenc—in 1919. The performance caused a sensation.

To modern ears, Milhaud's music no longer sounds outré; it is merely good, clean, clever fun. Jean-Claude Casadesus captures the lively, lighthearted spirit of *Le boeuf sur le toit* to a tee. The rhythms dance and sway easily, and though the music's more lyrical moments are played with real tenderness, there is not a trace of sentimentality. **AFC**

Sergei Prokofiev
The Love for Three Oranges

(1919)

Genre | Opera
Conductor/Performers | Valery Gergiev;
Evgeny Akimov, Anna Netrebko
Years recorded | 1997–98
Label | Philips 462 913-2 (2 CDs)

A strange meeting of knockabout farce and fairytale, *The Love for Three Oranges* seems so modern, and yet it has its roots in the improvised drama of the eighteenth-century Venetian playwright Carlo Gozzi. Battling with various theatrical factions, a group of eccentrics proposes a drama with a difference, one in which they will interfere at key points: the story of a hypochondriacal prince who only learns to laugh again when a malevolent witch takes a tumble. She curses him with a love for three oranges, lodged in the house of a formidable giantess and guarded by a ferocious cook (sung in the opera by a bass in drag). The liberated oranges are unpeeled to reveal three princesses, two of whom die before water can reach them. After further tribulations, the prince is reunited with princess number three.

Prokofiev was the ideal composer to provide the score for this mixture of moonshine and broad comedy. His penchant for the supernatural was well served by the scenes featuring the witch, Fata Morgana, and her minions, while for the prince's various predicaments the orchestra sighs, dances, and laughs along with his sidekick Truffaldino.

Set to a Russian text, *Three Oranges* was first performed in French. It has been recorded in both languages, as well as in English, but it is the Kirov performance, sung by a true ensemble cast in the composer's native tongue and brilliantly paced by Valery Gergiev, which captures the best of Prokofiev's many sound worlds. **DN**

Maurice Ravel
Le tombeau de Couperin
(1919)

Genre | Orchestral
Conductor/Performers | Bernard Haitink; Amsterdam Concertgebouw Orchestra
Year recorded | 1977
Label | Philips 473 991-2

Joaquin Turina
Danzas fantásticas
(1920)

Genre | Orchestral
Conductor | Max Bragado Darman
Performers | Castile and León Symphony
Year recorded | 1994
Label | Naxos 8.555955

While waiting to enlist in the French army early in 1915, Ravel began sketching a suite for piano inspired by the composers of the French Baroque. His work was interrupted when duty finally called that April, and it was not until 1917, following his official discharge, that he was able to return to composition in earnest. This was an especially difficult time for Ravel. His beloved mother had just died, and he had lost many friends in the war. Thus, *Le tombeau de Couperin* became a kind of memorial; each of the suite's six movements was dedicated to a comrade who had fallen in battle. In 1919, he fastidiously crafted an orchestral version, opting to omit two movements: the fugue and final toccata.

Ravel was an extremely private man, and upon first hearing there is little if anything in *Le tombeau de Couperin* that suggests it is a memorial. The "Prélude" bubbles blissfully along, the snappy rhythms of the "Forlane" suggest cheerful insouciance, the "Menuet" is graceful and tender, and the "Rigaudon" is a joyful dance. Yet, listening more closely, a faint air of melancholy can be discerned. It is there in the gentle dissonances of the "Forlane," as well as in the suddenly ominous climax of the "Menuet."

Bernard Haitink explores the tension between the music's surface charm and its darker undercurrents in his Philips recording. Everything is right here. Tempi are gauged so they flow without sounding either lazy or breathless, and the Amsterdam Concertgebouw Orchestra has never sounded so suavely sophisticated. **AFC**

Together with Falla, Albéniz, and Granados, Turina made up the big four of Spanish music in the early twentieth century. He was born in Seville in 1882, and, although he did not live there after the age of twenty, it remained an important inspiration for his music. In many ways he was the most conventional of the four composers, writing in the traditional European forms, especially in the realm of chamber music. As well as being a composer, he was also active as a conductor, critic, and teacher: he was professor of composition at the Madrid Conservatoire, and a commissioner at the Ministry of Education. He died, after a long battle with cancer, in 1949.

The *Danzas fantásticas* is a set of three dances, based on the novel *La orgía* by José Más, and first performed in 1920 to great popular acclaim. It is one of those colorful pieces that has rarely been out of the catalogue in one version or another, though live performances are thinner on the ground. The first dance, "Exaltación," is a jota, whose rhythms and melodic contours recall Chabrier's *España*. "Ensueño" ("Dream") is a more lilting dance, and the closing "Orgía" evokes the sound of flamenco.

The bright colors of these dances find their match in the rhythmic, focused and vibrant playing of this Spanish orchestra and conductor—neither household names, but a terrific example of how horses for courses often produce an unexpected winner. They do not sentimentalize the central "Dream," and bring the "Orgy" to an exciting conclusion, with detailed recording to match. **MC**

Erich Wolfgang Korngold | Die tote Stadt (1920)

Genre | Opera
Conductor/Performers | Erich Leinsdorf; René Kollo (Paul),
Carol Neblett (Marietta), Munich Radio Orchestra
Year recorded | 1975
Label | RCA GD 87767 (2 CDs)

Erich Wolfgang Korngold, born in Brno in 1897, was said to be the greatest child prodigy composer since Mendelssohn. At age ten, growing up in Vienna, he played for Mahler, who declared him a genius; by the time he was thirteen, his works were being performed at the Vienna Hofoper. With his exceptional gift for crafting drama and atmosphere, he was in his element writing opera—which stood him in good stead when, as a refugee from the Nazi regime, he settled in Hollywood and composed film scores for Warner Brothers, including classics such as *The Adventures of Robin Hood* and *The Sea Hawk*.

Die tote Stadt (*The Dead City*) was the most successful of his five operas. It enjoyed huge acclaim throughout Europe during the interwar years, though later vanished from the repertoire until its gradual rehabilitation at the end of the twentieth century. Based on the Belgian author Georges Rodenbach's psychological masterpiece *Bruges-la-Morte*, its story concerns a widower, Paul, who cannot come to terms with the death of his wife, Marie, and grows convinced that she has been resurrected in the person of a vivid, life-loving dancer, Marietta. In this extraordinary opera, its music combining influences from Puccini, Mahler, Expressionism, and Viennese operetta, Korngold captured the zeitgeist of his troubled era, with its longing for a world that was vanishing into an irrevocable past.

Erich Leinsdorf's recording remains the finest available of this difficult, intense work. The roles of Paul and Marietta require the utmost in stamina, control, power and characterization; René Kollo and Carol Neblett excel at every turn. Hermann Prey, in the supporting role of Fritz, the Pierrot, gives a gorgeous account of the showstopping "Pierrot Tanzlied." **JD**

"He has so much talent that he could easily give us half—and still have enough left for himself."

Giacomo Puccini

Other Recommended Recordings

Das Wunder der Heliane
Berlin Radio Symphony Orchestra • John Mauceri
Decca 436 636-2 (3 CDs)
Korngold's most ambitious opera brilliantly realized

Die Kathrin
BBC Concert Orchestra • Martyn Brabbins
CPO 999602-2 (3 CDs)
His last opera in a fine BBC recording

Music from the films: The Sea Hawk, etc.
London Symphony Orchestra • André Previn
DG 471 347-2
Unsurpassed accounts of movie classics

Erich Leinsdorf spent most of his career in the United States. ➔

Maurice Ravel
La valse

(1920)

Genre | Orchestral
Conductor | Jean Martinon
Performers | Paris Orchestra
Year recorded | 1974
Label | EMI 7243 4 76960 2 2 (2 CDs)

Ravel was just one of many composers who admired the Strauss waltzes. As early as 1906, he had considered writing a homage to the Viennese master. By 1914, his concept had broadened; it would now be a symphonic poem entitled *Wien*. Ravel described the work in its final form as a "choreographic poem," and there were plans for Diaghilev to stage it as a ballet. The Russian impresario declared *La valse* a "masterpiece" but said it was "not a ballet." Regardless, *La valse* quickly became a favorite in the concert hall—though not necessarily for the right reasons.

Of course, it is possible to approach *La valse* as a sumptuous, swirling apotheosis of the beloved Viennese dance; but the music really tells a different story, beginning as it does with low rumblings and what sounds like an anxious heartbeat in the basses, progressing through a series of increasingly volatile episodes, and culminating in the violent destruction of the waltz's essential "1-2-3" rhythm. That Ravel manages to cloak such a darkly dramatic "story" so attractively is a testament to his genius.

Jean Martinon gets right to the heart of the work by transferring quite a lot of the dense orchestral detail from the background to the foreground. The result? Slippery, slithery woodwinds cling to the violins' elegant melodies, and the percussion almost takes on an ominously militaristic sound. Certainly, there are prettier performances out there, but none so gripping or so poignant. In a sense, Martinon's *La valse* is closer in spirit to Stravinsky's *Rite of Spring* than to Strauss's *Blue Danube*. **AFC**

Igor Stravinsky
Pulcinella

(1920)

Genre | Ballet
Conductor/Performers | Claudio Abbado; London Symphony Orchestra
Year recorded | 1978
Label | DG 453 085-2 (2 CDs)

With its witty presentation of eighteenth-century music viewed through the prism of a distinctly twentieth-century approach to rhythm and orchestration, *Pulcinella* is the archetypical Neo-Classical work. Leonide Massine's scenario also harks back to an earlier age, drawing upon characters from the *commedia dell'arte*.

The seeds for *Pulcinella* were sown by Diaghilev, who wanted an appropriate orchestration for some of Pergolesi's music. Initially reluctant, Stravinsky agreed to view the music, later recalling that "I looked, and I fell in love." He went much further than expected, recomposing the pieces by (or attributed to) Pergolesi and transforming them into an unmistakably twentieth-century work. Though Stravinsky noted that "the remarkable thing about *Pulcinella* is not how much but how little was added or changed," rhythms have a distinctly modern kick, while the orchestra resembles eighteenth-century models only for juxtapositions of double bass and trombone, the latter sliding in music hall style, to confound any sense of pastiche.

Humor and exuberance inform every measure of Claudio Abbado's classic account. The vocal numbers are utterly enrapturing, with all three soloists in prime form. Too often *Pulcinella* sounds labored, but there is a sense of grace and bounce here throughout, keeping the music flowing as befits a work intended for dancers. Abbado's great feat is to make everything sound so right that his guiding hand is invisible—Stravinsky would have approved. **CD**

Igor Stravinsky
Symphonies of Wind Instruments (1920, *rev.* 1947)

Genre | Chamber
Conductor/Performers | Pierre Boulez; Berlin Philharmonic Orchestra
Year recorded | 1996
Label | DG 457 616-2

Stravinsky described *The Symphonies of Wind Instruments* (written in response to the death of Debussy) as being "an austere ritual that is unfolded in terms of short litanies between different groups of homogeneous instruments," and, rather than allusions to Debussy, this memorial evokes some austere, archaic ceremony in his honor.

Lasting less than ten minutes, it feels nonetheless like a substantial piece, and its distinctive sound world and approach to form have had an influence on subsequent composers that far outstrips the modest proportions of the *Symphonies*. It was not an immediate success with the public—sitting awkwardly at its first performance amid pieces by Glazunov, Rachmaninov, and Scriabin, its stark writing is the antithesis of such lush Romanticism.

This recording draws its creative spark from the pairing of the Berlin Philharmonic, that most opulent of orchestras, and Pierre Boulez, the quintessential arch-modernist. The result is an ideal combination of superlative playing, with full tone color, and the glassy clarity that Stravinsky stressed was so essential in his music. Moreover, Boulez's ability to follow the gradations of tempo, so that the proportions of the whole are as set out in the score, is unsurpassed. So often performances of the *Symphonies* convey disjointedness, never seeing past the surface juxtapositions. Boulez, by contrast, imbues this sequence of refrains and episodes with a solemn sense of inevitability toward the final chorale, all the more powerful for the objectivity of his and Stravinsky's vision. **CD**

Federico Mompou
Cançons i danses (1921–79)

Genre | Instrumental
Instrument | Piano
Performer | Stephen Hough
Year recorded | 1996
Label | Hyperion CDA 66963

The piano pieces of the Catalan composer Federico Mompou represent a secluded corner of the piano repertoire, cut off from the mainstream, yet thoroughly enchanting. Mompou spent thirty years in Paris, where he was welcomed by the irreverent group of composers known collectively as Les Six. With Satie, the group's spiritual father figure, Mompou shares a striking fondness for simplicity, though without any hint of irony or self-knowing. Instead Mompou captured a naive sincerity and innocent wonder that was the trademark of his sixty-year composing career. He aimed for a "maximum expressiveness with minimum means," even to the point of abandoning key signatures and measure lines on occasion. Most of his output features piano miniatures and songs, though later in life he also turned to sacred choral works. Elegant, intimate, poetic, sometimes melancholic, Mompou's music, according to one biographer, reflects "a longing for the Forgotten Garden of Childhood."

The *Cançons i danses* (*Songs and Dances*), written over nearly six decades, are the most famous and immediately pleasing of his piano pieces, most of them based on Catalan themes. On his Mompou album, Stephen Hough includes six of these and a well-selected sprinkling of other pieces, among them six of the eleven *Préludes* and the more beguiling sounds of the *Cants màgics* and *Charmes*. Whether he is aiming at unassuming innocence or hypnotic charm, Hough's fondness for the music and his guardianship of its spirit shines through. **EB**

Béla Bartók
Violin Sonatas nos. 1 & 2

(1921, 1922)

Genre | Chamber
Performers | György Pauk (violin),
Jenö Jandó (piano)
Year recorded | 1993
Label | Naxos 8.550749

Bartók's two violin sonatas display an assimilation of his early influences, from native folk music, Debussy's modes and whole-tone scales, and Schoenberg's treatment of Serialism. "Mine is the realm of dissonance," wrote Bartók, but the particular Expressionism heard here is fired by the spirit of wild folk dance and very far from Vienna. The First Sonata erupts like a rhapsody, riven with violent interruptions, the two instruments embarking on a tormented journey with no shared material. This is a feature of both sonatas: the violin dominates, and the piano is only there to underline, clarify, or intensify with pungent comment. Bartók thus achieves a unique ensemble sound, never to be repeated. After the slow movement, a meditative tour de force, the music explodes into a primtivistic moto perpetuo dance.

The Second Sonata was written for Jelly Arányi, a violinist of "exceptional, almost tumultuous rapture," according to Milhaud. Terser and more tightly constructed than the First, it follows the Hungarian *verbunkös* style, a slow, "speaking" movement followed by a whirling dance over a coolly percussive piano part.

Hungarian violinist György Pauk has lived with these works all his life. There is an indefinable rightness to his performances of the sonatas: both follow the score to the letter, but the effect in the First Sonata is one of boundless freedom, flexibility, and improvisatory searching; in the Second, we are hit by the music's raw, dark power, unmediated by any apparent "interpretation." **HW**

Leos Janáček
Kátya Kabanová

(1921)

Genre | Opera
Conductor/Performer | Charles
Mackerras; Elisabeth Söderström
Year recorded | 1976
Label | Decca 475 7518 (2 CDs)

The major success achieved by the premiere of *Jenůfa* in Prague in 1916, combined with the fact that Janáček soon fell in love with a much younger woman, unleashed twelve years of astonishing creativity from the composer. *Kátya Kabanová* was the first of a sequence of four operas that are among the most significant and rewarding in the twentieth-century repertoire. Although the opera lasts barely an hour and a half, its emotional range is vast and delivered with a force and volatility that commands attention at every stage.

The story of a young woman driven to an illicit affair by the claustrophobia of provincial life in rural Russia, a weak, abusive husband, and a domineering and manipulative mother-in-law from hell drew from Janáček music of astonishing poignancy. Kátya herself, the woman at the center of the storm, is one of the great portrayals in the operatic canon: her fragility, dignity, and the tragedy of her breakdown and suicide are captured with unerring insight. Equally compelling is her antithesis, the unremittingly awful Kabanicha who presides over her destruction.

Charles Mackerras's mid-1970s recording was a classic in its day and remains the most satisfactory all-around performance of the work, notwithstanding some impressive competition. Elisabeth Söderström is magnificent in the title role and is well matched by Peter Dvorský as her decidedly flawed lover, Boris. There are no weak links in the cast and the Kabanicha of Naděžda Kniplová is a terrifying study in operatic evil. **JS**

Erwin Schulhoff
Suite for Chamber Orchestra (1921)

Genre | Orchestral
Conductor/Performers | Israel Yinon;
Brno Czech State Philharmonic
Year recorded | 1993
Label | Koch/Schwann 3-1437-2

The Czech-German composer Erwin Schulhoff (1894–1942) was one of the most experimental of composers working in the years between the two world wars. In the early 1920s, for example, he managed to absorb the contradictory aesthetics of both Viennese Expressionism and the German Dadaists. Jazz, too, was a major influence in various instrumental works and even in his magnum opus, the opera *Flames*, a typically individual treatment of the Don Juan story.

Schulhoff's opposition to German fascism led him to put his trust in Soviet Communism (he set the Communist manifesto to music in 1932 and his Sixth Symphony of 1941 was dedicated to the Red Army). Following the German occupation of Czechoslovakia in 1939, he attempted to emigrate to the U.S.S.R., but before he could do so, he was incarcerated as a political prisoner (and Jew) and died in a German camp in 1942. Like so many of his Central European contemporaries, he was blotted from cultural memory, and it was really only with his centenary in 1994 that this onetime figurehead of the European avant-garde began to be rediscovered.

His Suite for Chamber Orchestra is typical of his earlier, Dadaist work—instead of Bach's Baroque dance forms, Schulhoff uses jazz styles, including a "Ragtime," a "Tango," and a "Shimmy." This fresh, witty work has plenty of life in Israel Yinon's hands, and comes on a disc that also includes the rugged *Festival Prelude* and dance-filled First Symphony. **MR**

Charles Ives
Three Places in New England (1921)

Genre | Orchestral
Conductor/Performers | David Zinman;
Baltimore Symphony Orchestra
Year recorded | 1994
Label | Decca 476 1537

Not long after Debussy put the finishing touches to his three orchestral *Images*, Charles Ives began work on his *Three Places in New England*. Stylistically and aesthetically, these two composers seem to have little in common. Yet in this evocative triptych, Ives demonstrates Impressionist credentials worthy of comparison with the French master.

The first "place" is "The 'St. Gaudens' in Boston Common"—a bas-relief depicting a regiment of African-American soldiers who fought in the Civil War. This movement grew out of a "Black March" that Ives composed in 1911, but it is not a march in any traditional sense: the steady, square rhythm can be only be discerned when it emerges intermittently from a nostalgic cloud of sub-conscious melody. In "Putnam's Camp," Ives depicts a youth's daydream during an Independence Day picnic, the raucous, celebratory music capturing the essential, childlike giddiness of such an event. "The Housatonic at Stockbridge" holds a memory of a walk Ives took with his wife one summer. Ives later wrote that "the distant singing from the church across the river . . . the mist . . . the running water, the banks and elm trees were something that one would always remember." It is all there in the music—a magical movement and one of Ives's most moving creations.

Surely, the plainspoken poetry of David Zinman's performance would have pleased Ives tremendously. The players of the Baltimore Symphony sing, march, and dance through the music's complexities with abandon, and Decca's engineering is both clear and atmospheric. **AFC**

Edgard Varèse | Amériques (1921, *rev.*, 1927)

Genre | Orchestral
Conductor | Christoph von Dohnányi
Performers | Cleveland Orchestra
Year recorded | 1991
Label | Decca 443 172-2

Varèse arrived in New York from Paris at the end of 1915. Virtually all of his previous compositions have perished, so in *Amériques*, the first work he began in the United States, Varèse steps straight onto the stage of musical history as a fully formed personality, an invincibly lion-hearted radical, with one of the most stunning showpieces of the twentieth-century orchestral repertoire.

In the opening sections of the work, Varèse's European roots are nevertheless still evident: the ghosts of Debussy, the Stravinsky of *Rite of Spring* and *Petrushka*, and the Expressionist Schoenberg all make their appearance. But a new character is at once evident, building a new kind of structure by the abrupt juxtaposition of fierce blocks of sound, through extreme contrasts of timbre, liberating the sounds as sounds (the use of sirens in the orchestra is only the most sensational aspect of this), and releasing enormous rhythmic energy through an unprecedented, and often very subtle, use of the percussion. In the awesome, jazz-inspired trumpet riff at the work's center, and in the pounding pile-driver rhythms of its final climax, the Old World has been truly left behind.

Performances of *Amériques* have always been a rare event since Stokowski gave the premiere with the Philadelphia Orchestra in 1926, partly on account of the enormous orchestral demands of the score. Christoph von Dohnányi, with the gleaming apparatus of the Cleveland Orchestra on top-notch form, gives what has become the definitive reading of the work in its final 1927 form. The recording copes amazingly well with the huge dynamic range and the most note-filled textures, and Dohnányi perfectly projects the work's visceral rhythms as well as its pages of opalescent mystery. **MM**

> *"As a boy, the mere word 'America' meant all discoveries, all adventures. It meant the unknown . . ."*
>
> Edgard Varèse explains the title

Other Recommended Recordings

New York Philharmonic Orchestra • Pierre Boulez
Sony SK 45 844
A long-time champion of Varèse, Boulez turns in a typically authoritative performance

Utah Symphony Orchestra • Maurice Abravanel
Vanguard VSD 71156
The first recording, made shortly after Varèse's death, still packs a superb punch

Royal Concertgebouw Orchestra • Riccardo Chailly
Decca 460 208-2
Chailly's excellent version is the only recording of the original, and fascinatingly different, 1921 score

Edgard Varèse pioneered the use of electronics in music. ➔

Sergei Prokofiev | Piano Concerto no. 3 (1921)

Genre | Concerto
Performers | William Kapell, Dallas Symphony Orchestra
Conductor | Antal Doráti
Year recorded | 1949
Label | Naxos 8.110673

By 1921, Prokofiev the virtuoso pianist needed a new vehicle with orchestra to showcase his skills, especially as by this time he was more in demand as a performer in Western Europe, where he had recently settled. The Third Piano Concerto is a composite of themes dating back as early as 1911, but most of the work on it was done at the summer resort of St. Brevin-les-Pins on France's Atlantic coast. Prokofiev's neighbor and fellow countryman, the poet Konstantin Balmont, composed a sonnet in its honor, hymning its variety and saluting Prokofiev's youthful vitality. Certainly the most multifaceted of Prokofiev's five piano concertos, the Third quickly became one of his most popular concert works and has remained so ever since.

It begins wistfully with a clarinet theme redolent of mother Russia, but soon the fun and games begin. There is no slow movement, only a theme in the form of one of Prokofiev's favorite antique dance forms, the gavotte, subject to a set of vividly contrasted variations; and the composer eventually makes up for lost lyricism by placing a big Romantic melody at the heart of a racy finale. Prokofiev's friend, the composer Miaskovsky, amusingly described it as "a man with a fat belly and short arms and legs."

It all sounds scintillating, if a bit breathless, in the only concerto recording Prokofiev left behind. Surpassing him in sheer dexterity, though, is the brilliant American pianist William Kapell, who recorded the Third in 1949, four years before his untimely death in a plane crash at the age of thirty-one. The articulation is dazzling, and Kapell is unique in making even the most difficult passages in the finale sound effortless. **DN**

> *"Prokofiev! Music and youth blossom."*
>
> Konstantin Balmont, sonnet on the Third Piano Concerto

Other Recommended Recordings

Sergei Prokofiev, London Symphony Orchestra
Piero Coppola
Dutton CDBP 9706
Classic 1932 recording with the composer as soloist

Martha Argerich, Berlin Philharmonic Orchestra
Claudio Abbado
DG 447 438-2
Argerich is incandescent in a mercurial partnership

Evgeny Kissin, Berlin Philharmonic Orchestra
Claudio Abbado
DG 439 898-2
More scintillating teamwork

William Kapell, whose recordings have gained a cult following. ●

Edgard Varèse
Offrandes (1921)

Genre | Vocal
Conductor/Performers | Kent Nagano;
Phyllis Bryn-Julson (soprano), French National Orchestra
Year recorded | 1992
Label | Apex 2564-62087-2 (2 CDs)

The two songs Varèse called *Offrandes* (*Offerings*) are the first manifestation of his "modernist" persona. The instrumentation is already characteristic: a small orchestra of single wind, harp, and string quintet is counterbalanced by a huge array of percussion, requiring eight players. Varèse called it "a very small-scale work, a purely intimate piece." Yet it is also a bridge between the Old World and the New, and in that sense symbolizes the composer's own migration from war-torn France to a new life among the seemingly infinite possibilities of America.

Both poems are by friends, Latin-American literary modernists, and "Chanson de là-haut" is sung from a very specific place "on high"— the text is extracted from *Tour Eiffel* by the Chilean Vicente Huidobro. It evokes a view of Paris, seen from the top of the Eiffel Tower, and the expanding horizons to which the radio station recently installed there broadcast its messages. José Juan Tablada's "La croix du sud" is a sonnet whose form has deliquesced, under the pressure of its fantastic imagery, into a kind of surrealist rhapsody. Just as the text is more exuberantly and assertively free-associating than Huidobro's, so is Varèse's setting of it. Altogether the musical language of this second song is much more radical, its opening already poised on the borders of sheer noise.

Kent Nagano brings out superbly Varèse's sonic refinement, rhythmic subtlety, transparent percussion writing, and sculpted lyricism, and Phyllis Bryn-Julson's glorious voice is sensitive to every surreal textual nuance. For all its modernism, the work has never sounded more fragile, more exquisitely Debussian. **MM**

> *"Always before, music had seemed to slither off me . . . this time it penetrated."*

Varèse's wife Louise, listening to the first rehearsal

Other Recommended Recordings

Rachel Yakar, Ensemble InterContemporain
Pierre Boulez • Sony SK 45844
Piercing singing and crystalline ensemble

Ecuatorial
Radio France Choirs, Ensemble InterContemporain
Pierre Boulez • Sony SMK 68334
Staggering: a Mayan prayer for deliverance, set for wind, organ, and two electronic ondes martenots

Nocturnal
Phyllis Bryn-Julson, French National Orchestra
Kent Nagano • Erato 0630-14332-2
A surreal nightmare to a text by Anaïs Nin

Igor Stravinsky
Three Movements from "Petrushka" (1921)

Genre | Instrumental
Instrument | Piano
Performer | Evgeny Kissin
Year recorded | 2005
Label | RCA 82876 65389 2

When Stravinsky composed his ballet score *Petrushka* for Diaghilev in 1911, he ensured that the piano took a prominent role within the orchestra from start to finish; the score involved a reworking of some sketches he had made a little while before for a *Konzertstück* for piano and orchestra. The instrument virtually mirrors the role of Petrushka himself, the unfortunate fairground puppet with a soul. Ten years later, the composer arranged three of the most striking episodes from the ballet into a phenomenally challenging version for solo piano, on the request of his friend, the pianist Arthur Rubinstein. It was said that Rubinstein paid him a larger fee for the piano pieces than Diaghilev had for the whole ballet score.

The ballet is set in a Russian fair, full of colorful characters and incident, reflected imaginatively in Stravinsky's atmospheric music. The piano pieces endeavor to bring that glittering orchestral kaleidoscope to life on the piano keyboard alone, and the finest performances succeed in doing precisely this. Opening with the vivid "Danse russe," continuing with "Chez Petrushka," and ending with the fairground scene "La semaine grasse," the pieces are a glorious showcase for any performer.

Unfortunately, Rubinstein himself did not record the pieces, but numerous others have done so. Of recent accounts, one of the finest is that by the Russian pianist Evgeny Kissin, whose staggeringly impressive technique can encompass anything Stravinsky cares to throw at it. His immense power and tremendous clarity of touch help to make the most of the pieces' orchestral scale and multilayered textures. **JD**

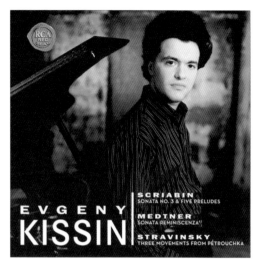

> "*Lesser artists borrow, great artists steal.*"
>
> Igor Stravinsky

Other Recommended Recordings

Denis Matsuev
RCA 82876 78861 2
A dazzling young virtuoso sails through the pieces

Petrushka (complete, arr. Rudy)
Mikhail Rudy
EMI 5 56731 2
Russian pianist expands the transcription magnificently

Serenade in A major
Leon Fleisher
Vanguard ATMCD 1796
This beautiful recital includes one of Stravinsky's best piano works, the lyrical Serenade

Arthur Bliss | A Colour Symphony (1922, *rev.* 1932)

Genre | Orchestral
Conductor/Performers | David Lloyd-Jones; English Northern Philharmonia
Year recorded | 1995
Label | Naxos 8.553460

Arthur Bliss began his career as an enfant terrible, writing naughtily experimental pieces that caused a stir in post–World War I London. He ended it embedded (despite his American descent) in the British musical Establishment: He was director of music at the BBC during World War II, knighted in 1950, and Master of the Queen's Music. He is hardly the only composer to have made that transition—think of William Walton, or even of the present Master of the Queen's Music, Peter Maxwell Davies—but in Bliss's case it began surprisingly early, when he was asked by Elgar to write an orchestral piece for the 1922 Three Choirs Festival. His response was *A Colour Symphony*, its four movements inspired by the associations of different colors in heraldry. The piece still has some of the brittle Stravinskian rhythms and sharp discords of Bliss's early music. But it is well behaved in terms of form, even ending in—of all academic things—a double fugue; and it is given plush, Elgarian orchestral treatment. Sadly Elgar himself, perhaps influenced by the inadequacies of the premiere in the reverberant acoustic of Gloucester Cathedral, disliked it. But the critics were impressed by Bliss's new seriousness and solidity. He was on his way.

These days the modernity of *A Colour Symphony* can all too easily seem a bit faded. But in Naxos's recording, sharply focused within a generous acoustic, it comes up fresh as new paint. The disc also includes Bliss's 1946 ballet score *Adam Zero*, an example of a genre that often brought out the best of the composer. It is one of several recent issues suggesting that it is worth taking a new look at Bliss. **AB**

Maurice Ravel | Sonata for Violin and Cello (1922)

Genre | Chamber Music
Performers | Renaud Capuçon (violin), Gautier Capuçon (cello)
Year recorded | 2001
Label | Virgin 7243 5 45492 2 9

Between Ravel and Claude Debussy, there was rivalry but also mutual admiration. Debussy died in 1918, soon after the death of Ravel's mother, and when the composer was also dealing with the emotional wounds he sustained in the war. In 1920, Ravel was invited to pay his musical respects by a publisher who was putting together a collection in Debussy's honor. He responded with a masterpiece: the Sonata for Violin and Cello, lavishing some two years' labor on the twenty-minute score.

The sonata is strikingly austere, particularly by comparison with the lushness of his earlier work. Ravel admitted that he had purposely "pushed thinness of texture to the extreme" and "renounced harmonic charm"—arguably to follow the aesthetic laid out in Debussy's late chamber works. The result still sounds very much like Ravel, though more conspicuously modern, with angular melodies, tense rhythms, and tart harmonies. This may not sound very appealing, but what is great about this sonata is that it encompasses such a variety of mood and tone. There is fragile tenderness in the opening movement, sardonic wit in the scherzo, profound deliberation in the slow movement, and earthy playfulness in the finale.

None of Ravel's music is easy to play, but the sonata is especially thorny. Interpretatively, too, there are significant challenges, as there is a tendency to overcompensate for the score's textural asceticism. Renaud and Gautier Capuçon play with an easy virtuosity, respecting the music's essential intimacy without compromising its unique character. The sonata has never sounded so appealing. **AFC**

William Walton
Façade (1922, *rev.* 1923–51)

Genre | Entertainment
Conductor/Performers | David Lloyd-Jones; Eleanor Bron, Richard Stilgoe
Year recorded | 2000
Label | Hyperion CDA 67239

Peter Warlock
The Curlew (1922)

Genre | Vocal
Performers | John Mark Ainsley (tenor), Nash Ensemble
Year recorded | 1997
Label | Hyperion CDA 66938

If you were looking for an example of the wildly experimental nature of the avant-garde in the Roaring Twenties, you could not do better than Walton's *Façade*. It consists of poems by Edith Sitwell, set for a reciter and a colorful instrumental sextet. Walton wrote the first version as a nineteen-year-old Oxford dropout who had been taken into the bosom of the aristocratic, eccentric Sitwell family. The first performance in 1922 was in their London drawing room, with Edith speaking through a megaphone from behind a curtain. The following year Walton revised and expanded the piece for a public performance, which caught the attention of the press and the "chattering classes": "Drivel They Paid to Hear," said one headline. Walton went on tinkering with the piece, adding numbers that placed music more in the foreground and dropping some with subservient accompaniments. It was only in 1951 that he published a definitive selection of twenty-one—with a collection of leftovers following as late as 1977. And meanwhile, some of the more tuneful movements had become well known in concert suites and as a ballet score, in Walton's joyous orchestrations.

In David Lloyd-Jones's recording, the poems are read with precise enunciation and rhythm, if sometimes questionable regional accents, in unusually good balance with the excellent Nash Ensemble. But the disc's special merit is that it brings together all thirty-four surviving numbers of *Façade*. You can still skip tracks to select the canonic twenty-one, but listening to the lot gives you an even better idea of the glorious inventiveness of poet and composer in the age of Bright Young Things. **AB**

When Delius heard *The Curlew*, Peter Warlock's setting of verse by W. B. Yeats, he told his protégé to turn to music without more ado. Warlock did—and, from more than a hundred songs written in his short lifetime, it is this unique and incomparably eloquent masterwork that defines Warlock as a songwriter and composer.

Born Philip Heseltine in 1894, the composer was largely self-taught, working toward composition through his writing and his musicological research and editing of sixteenth- and seventeenth-century music. He paid tribute to his great musical and emotional father figure in his book, *Frederick Delius*; and to Dowland and Campion in *The English Ayre*. As Peter Warlock, he began publishing his own musical compositions in 1919. The string writing of *The Curlew* can be heard as a wonderful distillation of Warlock's responses to the music of Henry Purcell and Matthew Locke, while his minutely sensitive understanding of verbal inflection is surely influenced by his study of composer-poets such as Campion and Dowland.

It is easy to attribute Warlock's death by gas poisoning in 1930 to a biographical checklist beginning with the loss of his father when he was two, to an openly split personality, and a fascination with the occult. But the numb desolation at the end of *The Curlew* speaks for itself. The cor anglais, which gives voice to the curlew, and the flute mimicking the peewit's call, also cry for the human heart. The sheer physical presence of this recording and the playing of the Nash Ensemble sets it apart. John Mark Ainsley's tenor responds with close and subtle imaginative sense to Warlock's own responses to Yeats. **HF**

Jacques Ibert | Escales (1922)

Genre | Orchestral
Conductor | Charles Dutoit
Performers | Montreal Symphony Orchestra
Year recorded | 1992
Label | Decca 440 332-2

Jacques Ibert (1890–1962) was a Frenchman through and through and yet widely traveled—the typical cosmopolitan Parisian. His journeying began when, in 1919, he entered the Paris Conservatoire's Concours de Rome ("a joke you don't make twice," he quipped) and won first prize, that dream of so many French composers from Berlioz onward. The award itself was a three-year period of study in the Italian capital, where the winner was expected to send back musical "envois" to Paris. But eager to see more of the world, Ibert managed to combine his trip with his honeymoon, which began with a cruise around the Mediterranean. This in turn neatly provided the theme for the most significant of his envois and the work that would make him famous, *Escales (Ports of Call)*. At first, he kept the geography secret, but was eventually persuaded to reveal the inspiration behind each of the three movements.

The first piece languidly introduces us to the Sicilian port of Palermo, breaking out into the rhythms of the tarantella; the second is entitled "Tunis-Nefta" and is based around an Arabic chant that Ibert had heard on a trip into the desert; the finale, "Valencia," is another one of those Iberian portraits that reinforce the idea that the best Spanish music was written by Frenchmen.

Charles Dutoit's Montreal Symphony Orchestra—once dubbed the best French orchestra in the world—brings out all the atmosphere in Ibert's Mediterranean travelogue: it is seductive in Palermo, mysterious in the Tunis desert, and vibrant in Valencia. The suite is accompanied on this disc by equally fine performances of some of Ibert's other most characteristic pieces: the Flute Concerto, the *Bacchanale* and the portrait of his home city, *Paris*. **MR**

> *"Of all our composers, Jacques Ibert is certainly the most authentically French."*
>
> Henri Dutilleux, 1945

Other Recommended Recordings

Lamoureux Concerts Orchestra • Yutaka Sado
Naxos 8.554222
Another colorful account, plus the Divertissement

Persée et Andromède
Strasbourg Philharmonic Orchestra
Jan Latham-Koenig
Avie AV 0008
A mini-opera that pokes fun at the myth of Perseus

Quatre chansons de Don Quichotte
José van Dam, Lyon Opera Orchestra • Kent Nagano
Virgin 0946 3 63310 2 7
Ibert's Don Quixote song cycle, on a large scale

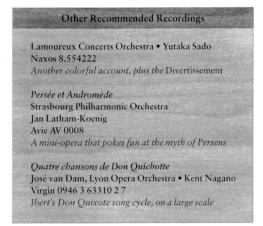

French composer Jacques Ibert, pictured in *c.* 1947. ➔

Carl Nielsen
Symphony no. 5 (1922)

Genre | Orchestral
Conductor | Leonard Bernstein
Performers | New York Philharmonic
Year recorded | 1962
Label | Sony SB3K 89974 (3 CDs)

The shadows of World War I still loomed over Nielsen as he began work on this symphony in 1920, and there is an element of conflict here as strong as in the Fourth Symphony, though again it is resolved in a positive way. Nielsen wrote most of the first movement in spring 1921 while staying with friends outside Copenhagen, but had to interrupt work to fulfill a commission. So the second movement was composed under pressure, and finished only days before the premiere in January 1922. Nielsen himself conducted, and the symphony was well received, and soon performed internationally.

"I've divided the Symphony into two large, broad sections," Nielsen said in a press interview. "The first begins slowly and peacefully, and the second one is more active." That is an understatement: there is drama aplenty here. True, the symphony does begin with a rocking viola figure and plaintive bassoons, but it is not long before clouds loom and a martial side drum makes a menacing appearance, leading to a sinister march. At the climax of the movement, the side drum is instructed to improvise, as if to stop the rest of the orchestra. Although it does not meet with success, the final clarinet solo is far from celebratory. The second movement is turbulent from the word go, and the tension keeps going, through two uneasy fugues, to a much delayed final resolution.

Of all Bernstein's Nielsen recordings, this is the finest, with electric playing in the battle of wills in the first movement, and an exceptionally heart-wrenching clarinet solo. The fugal passages all intensify the mood, and the joyous end is hard fought and justly earned. **MC**

Alban Berg
Wozzeck (1922)

Genre | Opera
Conductor/Performers | Claudio Abbado;
Franz Grundheber, Hildegard Behrens
Year recorded | 1987
Label | DG 423 587-2 (2 CDs)

Berg started work on his first opera, for which he composed his own libretto, after attending a performance of Georg Büchner's drama *Woyzeck* in Vienna in 1914. Progress on the opera was interrupted by the political turmoil of World War I and the score was only completed eight years later. *Wozzeck* eventually received its first and highly successful performance at the Berlin State Opera in December 1925 under the conductor Erich Kleiber.

The story, presented in fifteen short scenes—each one is a nicely self-contained musical structure—concerns the impoverished soldier Wozzeck, who experiences increasing mental disintegration, partly as a result of jealousy. This leads him eventually to kill Marie, the mother of his child, who has been seduced by another soldier, the Drum Major. As Wozzeck tries to earn his way and financially support the child, he is taunted by his employers, the bourgeois Captain and the megalomaniac Doctor. After stabbing Marie, Wozzeck returns to the scene of his crime and, in a deranged attempt to recover the murder weapon, drowns in the lake.

Ever since Dimitri Mitropoulos recorded a highly charged account of *Wozzeck* back in the early 1950s, the opera has enjoyed a sequence of distinguished recordings, though none is quite as compelling as the live Vienna performance conducted by Claudio Abbado. Both Wozzeck and Marie are powerfully characterized, and even if there are occasions where the orchestral balance is not quite as sophisticated as it might have been in the studio, theatrical immediacy provides more than ample compensation. **EL**

Béla Bartók
Dance Suite (1923)

Genre | Orchestral
Conductor | Iván Fischer
Performers | Budapest Festival Orchestra
Year recorded | 1996
Label | Philips 454 429-2

Bartók's *Dance Suite* was commissioned by the Budapest municipal authorities in celebration of the fiftieth anniversary of the union of three cities on the banks of the Danube that formed the Hungarian capital. First performed in November 1923, the *Dance Suite* is written in a much more accessible style than some of the composer's works of the time. Yet despite the greater simplification of its musical material, Bartók constructs the work with the same degree of intellectual rigor as in his string quartets and concertos. There are six interlinked dance movements of widely contrasting character and tempo, each drawing its melodic and rhythmic ideas from the different folk-music traditions that Bartók absorbed during his travels through Hungary, Romania, Bulgaria, and North Africa. A gentle lyrical passage, described by the composer as "such a faithful imitation of a certain kind of Hungarian folk melody that its derivation might puzzle even the most knowledgeable of musical folklorists," acts as a highly effective bridge passage between the movements. The final movement reviews and extends all the material heard earlier, and brings the work to an immensely satisfying conclusion.

The *Dance Suite* is one of the most frequently recorded of Bartók's orchestral compositions, but probably the most compelling of all is the mid-1990s version featuring the Budapest Festival Orchestra under Iván Fischer. Fischer is adept at projecting the vibrant driving rhythms of the faster movements, the Hungarian orchestra feeling entirely at home in the idiom. Equally impressive is the wonderfully luminous sound Fischer secures from his players in the mysterious clusters of the fourth movement. **EL**

Joseph Canteloube
Chants d'Auvergne (1923–54)

Genre | Vocal
Performer | Netania Davrath
Conductor | Pierre de la Roche
Year recorded | 1963
Label | Vanguard ATM CD 1189

For Joseph Canteloube (1879–1957), folk music was an essential element in composition. He came to this belief in part from his studies with Vincent d'Indy, and it was through d'Indy that he became actively involved in the preservation of French regional folksong. He arranged many of the songs he collected for choir or voice and piano to be performed and enjoyed at home or in concert. Canteloube also wrote operas, choral, orchestral, and chamber music, but is now remembered almost exclusively for his *Chants d'Auvergne* (*Songs of the Auvergne*), a ravishing collection harvested from the rural province in central France where he was born and bred.

These particular songs are more than simple transcriptions, however. They are lushly harmonized and orchestrated with an expert hand. The settings are rather like pastoral tone-paintings, and reflect Canteloube's desire to evoke the songs' natural context. There are five volumes of *Chants d'Auvergne*, with more than thirty songs in all, and there is not a dud in the bunch. The cycle is rarely performed or recorded complete, though; most singers opt for a selection. A few individual songs, like the rapturous "Baïlèro," are often heard in recital as encores.

The *Chants d'Auvergne* are not easy to sing and demand a well-trained voice. But Canteloube did not want them to be sung in an overtly operatic fashion; he preferred an earthier, more unaffected approach. And that is the great glory of Netania Davrath's classic recording. The Ukrainian-born soprano (1931–87) has a lovely, sweet tone, but there is a pleasing suggestion of sinew in it, and her artless interpretations convey a magical, rustic atmosphere. **AFC**

Leos Janáček | String Quartets nos. 1 & 2 (1923, 1928)

Genre | Chamber
Performers | Škampa Quartet: Pavel Fischer,
Jana Lukášová, Radím Sedmidubský, Peter Jarůšek
Year recorded | 2001
Label | Supraphon SU 3486-2

The tradition of mingling program and autobiographical reference in Czech chamber music has a venerable history; Janáček, for whom the abstract musical statement held little attraction, based all of his chamber music on preexisting material. In the case of his First Quartet, "The Kreutzer Sonata," his lifelong passion for Russian literature provided the background. The drama, passion, and even violence of Tolstoy's novella of the same name are vital to the energies that impel Janáček's extraordinary work.

It is unlikely that the creativity of Janáček's last twelve years would have had its extraordinary, highly personal character were it not for his love for Kamila Stösslová. They met in the summer of 1917 at Janáček's favorite spa retreat, Luhačovice, at a time of renaissance for the composer. Over the next eleven years, a flood of letters from Janáček to Kamila plot the course of this palpably one-sided infatuation.

His Second String Quartet, "Intimate Letters," is a kind of musical pendant to these missives. If it is less explicitly programmatic than the First Quartet, there is no doubting the ardor of the passions evoked. Janáček even originally planned to replace the string quartet's usual viola with the romantic viola d'amore. If anything, the technical demands in this quartet are more extreme than in his first. The mood swings are even more pronounced with melodic lines constantly verging on near-vocal rhetoric.

The Škampa Quartet is one the most exciting of the younger generation of Czech chamber ensembles. The players give a blistering account of Quartet no. 1 and the most convincing recording of no. 2. What differentiates their performances from the generality is their attention to expressive detail and the letter of score. **JS**

". . . I have started to write something nice. Our life will be in it."

Janáček to Kamila on his Second String Quartet

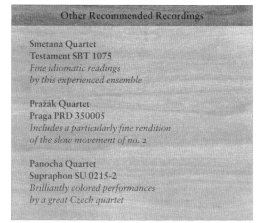

Other Recommended Recordings

Smetana Quartet
Testament SBT 1075
*Fine idiomatic readings
by this experienced ensemble*

Pražák Quartet
Praga PRD 350005
*Includes a particularly fine rendition
of the slow movement of no. 2*

Panocha Quartet
Supraphon SU 0215-2
*Brilliantly colored performances
by a great Czech quartet*

Arthur Honegger | Three Symphonic Movements (1923–33)

Genre | Orchestral
Conductor | Hermann Scherchen
Performers | Royal Philharmonic Orchestra
Year recorded | 1954
Label | Westminster Legacy 471 245-2

Born in Le Havre in 1892 to Swiss parents, Arthur Honegger entered the Paris Conservatoire in 1911, becoming a pupil of Gédalge and Widor, and also taking conducting lessons with d'Indy. After World War I, Honegger's name became indelibly associated with fellow composers Poulenc, Milhaud, Auric, Durey, and Tailleferre (collectively dubbed by the critic Henri Collet as "Les Six"). In reality, however, his aesthetic outlook was far removed from the frivolous and anti-Germanic attitudes of his colleagues.

During the early 1920s, Honegger developed a reputation for depicting aspects of urban life in music that emphasizes machinelike rhythms and brusque melodic patterns. This trend began with the ballet *Skating Rink*, but secured its widest dissemination with the first and most successful of his symphonic movements, *Pacific 231*, in which Honegger used large orchestral forces to convey the physical impact of an American steam locomotive speeding through the countryside. A similar attempt to portray the sensations of movement and speed in the sporting arena is projected in the second symphonic movement entitled *Rugby* (1928). But by the time he came to write his Third Symphonic Movement five years later, Honegger resisted the temptation to provide a referential subtitle—a reflection perhaps that the composer was no longer so infatuated with the notion of illustrative music.

Although *Pacific 231* remains one of Honegger's most frequently recorded works, the three symphonic movements have rarely featured together on the same disc. One notable exception is the powerfully driven mid-1950s mono recording featuring the great German conductor Hermann Scherchen, which still sounds remarkably good for its age. **EL**

> "... a sort of grand and varied chorale interwoven with counterpoint in the manner of J. S. Bach."

Honegger's description of *Pacific 231*

Other Recommended Recordings

New Zealand Symphony Orchestra • Takuo Yuasa
Naxos 8.555974
Decent playing at bargain price

La danse des morts
Orchestre de Picardie • Edmon Colomer
Calliope CAL 9526
Fascinating work setting a text by Paul Claudel

Complete Chamber Music
Dong-Suk Kang (violin), Pascale Devoyon (piano),
Raphael Wallfisch (cello), Ludwig Quartet
Timpani 1079 (4 CDs)
Unexpected musical riches in this excellent boxed set

Darius Milhaud | La création du monde (1923)

Genre | Ballet
Conductor | Leonard Bernstein
Performers | Columbia Chamber Orchestra
Year recorded | 1951
Label | Sony SMK 61697

It was in London in 1920 that Milhaud discovered jazz. Then, in 1922, he visited Harlem and fell in love. It was like nothing he had heard before. "Against the beat of the drums," he wrote, "the melodic lines crisscrossed in a breathless pattern of broken and twisted rhythms." He resolved to use these novel sounds in a chamber work, and the opportunity presented itself almost immediately upon his return to France, when he was asked to provide music for a ballet. The subject was the creation of the world based on African folklore, and he modeled his instrumental ensemble on those he had heard in New York.

Yet, for all its novelty, *La création du monde* (*The Creation of the World*) is firmly rooted in the European tradition. It begins with a prelude and fugue—and it is a proper, well-developed fugue, too, shimmying syncopations and all. The lyrical theme that follows seems drawn directly from the world of the *Rhapsody in Blue*, though Gershwin was still at work on his *Rhapsody* when *La création du monde* premiered in Paris in 1923. Notice, too, the brash Stravinsky-like quickstep that intrudes on the Gershwin-esque idyll, and the riotous passage near the end where all seventeen instruments seem to be going in different directions. The effect is very much like the one Milhaud himself described from his Harlem visit.

Like Milhaud, Leonard Bernstein straddled the worlds of classical music and jazz. Naturally, then, he had an innate feeling for the French composer's composite, cosmopolitan style. Bernstein first recorded *La création du monde* very early in his career with a group of crackerjack New York musicians. It is still the recording of choice—sassy and sophisticated, one can imagine Lenny smiling gleefully all the way through. You will smile, too. **AFC**

> "The Creation of the World *emerges . . . not as a flirtation but as a real love affair with jazz.*"

Leonard Bernstein

Other Recommended Recordings

Orchestre National de Lille
Jean-Claude Casadesus
Naxos 8.557287
Well-mannered and dapper, an idiomatically Gallic reading

Orchestre National de France
Leonard Bernstein
EMI 0946 3 45809 2 2
Bernstein's later version is less taut but still charismatic

Darius Milhaud
Pearl GEMM 124
Cool-headed and plainspoken—a historic document

Milhaud pictured in 1963 in California, where he had settled in 1940.

Leoš Janáček | The Cunning Little Vixen (1923)

Genre | Opera
Conductor/Performers | Charles Mackerras; Lucia Popp,
Eva Randová, Dalibor Jedlička
Year recorded | 1981
Label | Decca 417 129-2 (2 CDs)

Few operatic composers have ranged as widely in their subject matter as Leoš Janáček. After the very human drama of *Kátya Kabanová*, he found the inspiration for his next work in the unprecedented world of a newspaper strip cartoon, and one featuring animals as its main characters at that. The serial *Bystrouška* had been commissioned in 1920 from the journalist Rudolf Těsnohlídek to accompany a series of nineteenth-century line drawings for publication in a Brno paper. It tells how a vixen is captured and taken home by a forester, but after escaping, she evicts a badger from his sett and sets up home with a fox. The forester attempts, but never manages, to recapture her.

Janáček extended the story to turn it into a profound reflection on the whole cycle of nature: the forester shoots the vixen dead but then in a dream imagines the next generation acting just like the last. By giving his woodland animals human characteristics and also by counterpointing the impulses of the natural world with the trials and tribulations of the villagers—gamekeeper, priest, schoolteacher— Janáček produced a work of depth as much as entertainment.

Of all Janáček's mature operas this was one of the last to gain a life on stage outside Czechoslovakia, not receiving wide acceptance until the 1950s. It is now one of his most popular stage works—a rare piece of art that is as engaging to children as it is to adult sensibilities. Charles Mackerras's recording, as part of his acclaimed Decca cycle from the early 1980s, has never been surpassed in its exploration of one of Janáček's most inventive orchestral tapestries, with its fine Czech cast is led by Lucia Popp as the most vocally resourceful of vixens. **MR**

> "*Each [of my operas] gave me a long headache. But I just played with Bystrouška as if she were tame.*"
>
> Leoš Janáček, in his autobiography

Other Recommended Recordings

Osud (Fate)
Welsh National Opera Orchestra • Charles Mackerras
Chandos CHAN 3029
Janáček's autobiographical parable on creativity

The Makropulos Case
Vienna Philharmonic Orchestra • Charles Mackerras
Decca 430 372-2 (2 CDs)
Elisabeth Söderström is gripping as the immortal who wants her mortality back

From the House of the Dead
Vienna Philharmonic • Charles Mackerras
Decca 430 375-2 (2 CDs)
Janáček's Dostoyevsky-inspired prison drama

Costume designs by Josef Čapek for the Prague premiere of the *Vixen.* ●

Francis Poulenc
Les biches (1923, *rev.* 1939–40, 1947)

Genre | Ballet
Conductor | Georges Prêtre
Performers | Ambrosian Singers, Philharmonia Orchestra
Year recorded | 1981
Label | EMI 7243 5 62959 2 6

Arnold Schoenberg
Suite for Piano (1923)

Genre | Instrumental
Instrument | Piano
Performer | Peter Hill
Year recorded | 1996
Label | Naxos 8.553870

Just in case you were wondering, the title of *Les biches* means "the female deers." It was applied to this one-act ballet, adventurously commissioned from the then unknown composer by Diaghilev for his Ballets Russes, because Poulenc's models for the work were the painter Jean-Antoine Watteau's depictions of Louis XIV flirting with various women in his Parc aux biches at Versailles. In the three sung movements, Poulenc's texts were taken from popular seventeenth-century songs. The tunes have that sort of spirit, too.

The world premiere took place in Monte Carlo on January 6, 1924. The ballet was an instant success and has since remained Poulenc's most popular piece, thanks to its catchy, cheeky tunefulness, its feeling of irrepressible confidence, and its brilliant orchestration. Even so, Poulenc reorchestrated the work in 1939–40, at the same time fashioning a suite by excluding the overture and the three sung numbers. As Milhaud, an enthusiastic supporter, wrote at the time of its first performance, "it has no scenario, no theme. . . . We are in a complete fantasy world. . . . Melody pours out ceaselessly, insinuating, unfolding with a richness, elegance, charm and tenderness which are found in such abundance and generosity only in the works of Poulenc." But so is a touch of anti-Romantic humor in little patches that parody Wagner, Tchaikovsky, and the rest.

Oddly, recordings of the complete work are hard to find. But no account could capture more perfectly the duality of such tenderness and sparkling mischief as that made by a famous champion of the composer, Georges Prêtre, with the Philharmonia Orchestra in the early 1980s. **SP**

From 1912 on, Schoenberg was searching desperately for a guiding principle that would allow him to control the totally chromatic, apparently keyless harmonic forces he had let loose in his Expressionist scores such as *Erwartung*, and allow him to build large-scale, satisfyingly patterned structures again. He arrived at it during the years 1920–23: a method of composition in which a fixed series of the twelve semitones functions as the matrix of melody and harmony, its transpositions being analogous to changes of key.

The op. 25 Suite is the breakthrough work, all its six movements derived from a single twelve-note series; that Schoenberg should have cast it in the form of a Baroque keyboard suite, with a gavotte, a musette, a minuet, and a gigue among its movements, eloquently illustrates the "conservative" nature of his revolutionary tendencies. The crystaline formal clarity and the familiarity of the deliberately "old-fashioned" dance steps balance the high level of dissonance, the angular lines, the apparent nonfunctionality of the cadences. Some of it may seem fierce, but there is a genuine playfulness in much of the music, real elegance in the dance movements, and a dreamy nocturnal Impressionism in the fourth-movement intermezzo that place this work among Schoenberg's most attractive, as well as most important for his development.

The time is long past when pianists used to present the suite as a grim, unsmiling, modernist statement. Nowadays there is plenty of élan and elegance to be found in the recorded versions, but Peter Hill's witty and affectionate rendering is still, by some degrees, the warmest and the most humane. **MM**

Igor Stravinsky
Octet (1923)

Genre | Chamber
Conductor | Vladimir Ashkenazy
Performers | European Soloists Ensemble
Year recorded | 1994
Label | Decca 473 810-2 (2 CDs)

As with several of his other works, the initial inspiration for the Octet was, according to Stravinsky, a dream, in which he found himself "in a small room surrounded by a small number of instrumentalists who were playing some very agreeable music." Although he could not remember any of the music when he awoke, he recalled that he had counted eight musicians and that he then "saw that they were playing bassoons, trombones, trumpets, a flute and a clarinet." Although it is very much a tonal work and one of the first fruits of the composer's Neo-Classical years, the second movement's theme and variations includes a form of the idiosyncratic approach to Serialism that Stravinsky would explore more thoroughly in later years.

The spirit of the Octet, as caught delectably by Vladimir Ashkenazy's ensemble, is bright and breezy. The opening of the first movement, "Sinfonia," looks back to the more dreamy passages of *The Soldier's Tale* and forward to the pastoral writing in *The Rake's Progress*, before leaping into life with great jollity. The bassoons of the European Soloists Ensemble throw caution to the winds where needed (no pun intended) in driving along the periodic eruptions of the second movement, yet are full of easygoing charm for the opening of the finale. Too often the final chord is overplayed, performers wishing to emphasize the end of the work. While it might seem ridiculous to place great emphasis on this briefest of details, the full-voiced yet light touch given to the chord stands as testimony to the exceptionally fine musicianship on display here. In Ashkenazy's hands, there is no danger of the Octet seeming slight, but it is always hugely enjoyable. **CD**

Alexander Zemlinsky
Lyric Symphony (1923)

Genre | Vocal
Conductor/Performers | Christoph Eschenbach;
Christine Schäfer, Matthias Goerne, Paris Orchestra
Year recorded | 2006
Label | Capriccio CAP 71081

Zemlinsky wrote his opulent, ravishing orchestral masterpiece at the close of his most productive decade as a composer, and, in retrospect, it is clear that the *Lyric Symphony* marks the end of an era in terms of his compositional style; his ensuing work, the Third String Quartet of 1924, is pared down, with more economical, austere textures. Indeed, at the first performance of the *Lyric Symphony* during a new-music festival in Prague, some of the audience may well have considered Zemlinsky's richly perfumed score to be the product of a previous epoch.

Although Zemlinsky himself pointed out that his new symphony owed something to the example of Mahler's *Das Lied von der Erde*, the similarity is superficial; the *Lyric Symphony* is through-composed, with leitmotivic treatment of some of the themes, and Zemlinsky reinforced this operatic concept by calling for a heroic baritone and a "youthful dramatic soprano." The seven poems, taken from Rabindranath Tagore's *The Gardener*, are given alternately to soprano and baritone and form the outline of a love drama; there is no conventional narrative but each song reveals a telling moment of self-awareness. Like many of Zemlinsky's works, the *Lyric Symphony* is partly autobiographical, and Tagore's texts allow Zemlinsky moments of both heightened emotion and hushed stillness, where "moments become hours."

There have been several praiseworthy recordings of this fine work. Chief among them is Christoph Eschenbach's glorious version with the superb soloists Christine Schäfer and Matthias Goerne—a highly desirable disc. **DC**

Igor Stravinsky | Les noces (1923)

Genre | Ballet
Conductor/Performers | Robert Craft; Alison Wells,
Susan Bickley, Martyn Hill, Alan Ewing
Year recorded | 2001
Label | Naxos 8.557499

STRAVINSKY
Oedipus Rex
Les Noces
Edward Fox • Soloists • Simon Joly Chorale
Tristan Fry Percussion Ensemble • Philharmonia Orchestra
Robert Craft

Stravinsky's gift for exploring novel textures and dramatic situations extends in new directions with this remarkable work. The music was written between 1914 and 1917 but the orchestration assumed various guises until it reached its final form in 1923 for four pianos and percussion. This brilliantly brittle sound world offers varied accompaniment to the voices throughout, until the final page when the pianos alone evoke the wedding bells. The melodies have a genuine Russian flavor; they are mostly original yet cleverly evoke the uneven and unbalanced phrase structures and irregular meters of Russian folk tunes. Stravinsky's harmonies echo this, too, in a marked twentieth-century manner, with their angularity and varied colors. In the second movement, there is a suggestion of the parallel harmonies and more somber textures of Russian Orthodox church music.

Like *The Rite of Spring*, this piece embraces the mystery of life ending and life beginning. It follows four scenes of a peasant Russian wedding that run without a break. In the first, the betrothed woman is being prepared for the wedding rite by her friends, who dress her and braid her hair. There follows a scene with the bridegroom as he seeks his family's blessing. In the third, the bride departs and her parents sing of their distress at losing their daughter, and in the final scene the wedding feast is celebrated, followed by the parents' vigil outside the nuptial room.

The composer's biographer, Robert Craft, directs a performance of invigorating alacrity supported by marvelously exact and intelligent ensemble playing. The singers convey the earthy, peasant sense of these pieces, with all four soloists adding character and insight to Stravinsky's idiomatic sound world. **SW**

> *"It ranks high in the by no means crowded company of indisputable twentieth-century masterpieces."*
>
> Robert Craft, on *Les noces*

Other Recommended Recordings

English Bach Festival Chorus and Orchestra
Leonard Bernstein
DG 423 251-2
Exciting version brought to life with real gusto

New London Chamber Choir and Ensemble,
Voronezh State Institute Choir • James Wood
Hyperion CDA 66410
Fascinating recording with authentic Russian flavor

American Concert Choir, Columbia Percussion
Ensemble • Igor Stravinsky
Sony SMK 46291
An account of historical interest sung in English

Igor Stravinsky (seated) with his amanuensis Robert Craft in 1962. ➡

Eugène Ysaÿe | Six Solo Violin Sonatas, op. 27 (1923)

Genre | Instrumental
Instrument | Violin
Performer | Oscar Shumsky
Year recorded | 1982
Label | Nimbus NI 7715

Although excellent pieces were written for solo violin before those by Bach, every composer since Bach has had to move in his shadow when creating music for an unaccompanied stringed instrument. It was not the least achievement of the twentieth century that superb music was provided for solo violin, viola, or cello by Reger, Bartók, Kodály, Hindemith, Britten, and Stravinsky. To that select list can be added the name of Eugène Ysaÿe, the Belgian violinist who was also a resourceful, melodious composer.

Like Reger and Bartók, Ysaÿe made no attempt to hide the influence of Bach, even using the famous Prelude from the E major Partita in the first movement of his Second Sonata, "Obsession." The immediate spur for writing his solo sonatas was a solo Bach recital given by the Hungarian violinist Joseph Szigeti. At his summer home at Le Zoute in the summer of 1923, Ysaÿe sketched all six sonatas in one intense period of twenty-four hours and revised them in the following weeks, publishing them in 1924. The dedicatees were violinist friends: Szigeti, Jacques Thibaud, George Enescu, Fritz Kreisler, Mathieu Crickboom, and Manuel Quiroga.

Only in modern times have complete sets been recorded. One version stands out from the crowd, even though it is somewhat strangely recorded. Oscar Shumsky was underrated for much of his career but enjoyed a late flourish in his sixties. He plays the sonatas with superb tonal and rhythmic control and brings out the individual characters that Ysaÿe built into them—only the Spanish Quiroga is allowed a hint of nationalistic color but the pieces are portraits of their dedicatees to an extent. Shumsky includes an extra phrase that Ysaÿe asked Kreisler to add to the lovely Sarabande of the Fourth Sonata. **TP**

> *"Here was perhaps the last representative of the truly grand manner of violin playing."*
>
> Joseph Szigeti on Ysaÿe

Other Recommended Recordings

Frank Peter Zimmermann
EMI 7243 5 55255 2 9
This 1994 set is magnificently played and recorded

Takayoshi Wanami
Somm SOMMCD 012
A Japanese pupil of Szigeti performs with great understanding

Sonata no. 1
Efrem Zimbalist
Pearl GEM 0032
One of the few historical recordings by a great Russian player

Eugène Ysaÿe was one of the most unshowy of violin virtuosos. ➔

Béla Bartók
The Miraculous Mandarin
(1924)

Genre | Ballet
Conductor/Performers | Pierre Boulez;
Chicago Symphony Orchestra
Year recorded | 1994
Label | DG 447 747-2

Ferruccio Busoni
Doktor Faust
(1924)

Genre | Opera
Conductor/Performers | Kent Nagano;
Dietrich Henschel, Kim Begley
Year recorded | 1998
Label | Erato 3984 25501-2 (3 CDs)

The Miraculous Mandarin was Bartók's second ballet score, the first being *The Wooden Prince* (1917). The new ballet was subtitled "A Pantomime in One Act," and its scenario reflects the influence of silent cinema upon cultural developments after World War I, and exploits the tension between unrestrained innocence and a corrupt urban civilization.

The lurid narrative, graphically illustrated in the music itself, is set in the middle of a busy city. Three rogues and a prostitute occupy an upstairs room of a tenement block. The prostitute lures three men into the building and as she makes love to each of them, the rogues hope to divest her clients of all their money. First, there is a shabby old rake. He happens to be penniless so is quickly thrown down the stairs. The same fate awaits the second client, a poor, shy young man. Finally a Mandarin appears, but his strange appearance repels the prostitute. The rogues relieve him of his valuables but when he resists, they make three attempts to kill him. To their horror, the Mandarin survives suffocation and stabbing. He is then hung from the light fitting, but his body starts to glow with a greenish blue light—a section in the music represented by the eerie use of a wordless chorus. Finally he dies when the prostitute accepts his embrace, and his wounds begin to bleed.

Although Bartók fashioned a suite from the ballet for use in the concert hall, the shattering impact of the music is best experienced when the work is heard in its entirety, as in Pierre Boulez's brilliant and incisive recording with the Chicago Symphony Orchestra. **EL**

If in his day, Busoni was best known as a pianist and for the music he wrote for his own instrument, posterity probably judges his greatest achievement to have been his final opera, one of the most original adaptations of the perennially magnetic Faust legend. It occupied him for a number of years, from the early months of World War I to his death in 1924. Indeed, he left it incomplete, though his pupil Philip Jarnach put it into a performable state for its world premiere in 1925, while in more recent decades Busoni scholar Antony Beaumont has come up with an alternative completion, based on a more thorough investigation of the composer's sketches.

Not unlike Berg's *Wozzeck*, written at almost exactly the same time, *Doktor Faust*'s operatic structure is based around closed forms (Busoni had started by composing a Sarabande and a Cortège, which are sometimes heard in concert), though it is less a series of acts than one of scenes and interludes. He treats the story with an emphasis on Faust the seeker of truths and concludes with the idea that he must destroy both the Devil and God to make humanity free. Musically, its style is eclectic—at the same time looking back to Bach and forward to Hindemith.

One of only two recordings of the opera, Kent Nagano's complete account offers both Jarnach's and Beaumont's endings. The recording followed performances at the Lyon Opera and certainly has a theatrical feel, with Dietrich Henschel as a driven, single-minded Faust and Kim Begley a wily Mephistopheles. **MR**

Karol Szymanowski
King Roger
(1924)

Genre | Opera
Conductor/Performers | Simon Rattle;
Thomas Hampson, Elzbieta Szmytka
Year recorded | 1998
Label | EMI 7243 5 56823 2 1 (2 CDs)

To say that Karol Szymanowski was obsessed with the exotic would be an understatement. Although it never lost its Polish cultural roots, much of his middle-period music bathes itself in the warm light of the Mediterranean. His magnum opus, the opera *King Roger*, is set in twelfth-century Sicily, at a time when the island was a melting-pot of cultures: Byzantine, Norman, Islamic, ancient Greece—all made their presences felt then and cast a shadow over this most opulently fecund of music dramas.

The titular protagonist is the historical King Roger II, whose devotion to Christianity is threatened by the arrival of a mysterious shepherd with a paganist philosophy of beauty and pleasure. The shepherd's "seduction" of the king and his queen, Roxana, has sexual overtones as the voluptuous music makes clear, but on another level it is the old conflict between the Apollonian and Dionysian. The opera ends with Roger alone in a ruined Greek theater offering himself to the sun: Apollo has triumphed over Dionysus and the king has resisted temptation.

For a piece that lasts little more than eighty minutes, Szymanowski's score certainly crams a lot in, from the archaic Sanctus of its opening, through the most gorgeous tapestry of orchestral colors conjured up by any composer to the harmonic and melodic encapsulation of yearning.

Simon Rattle's complete EMI recording combines his unrivaled feeling for complex late-Romantic textures with singing, orchestral playing and sound that no earlier Polish recording can match. **MR**

Jean Sibelius
Symphony no. 7
(1924)

Genre | Orchestral
Conductor/Performers | Paavo Berglund;
London Philharmonic Orchestra
Year recorded | 2003
Label | London Philharmonic LPO 0005

A masterpiece so extraordinary that even the composer could not categorize it precisely, Sibelius's Seventh Symphony began life as a freestanding "Fantasia sinfonica," only to find a definitive place in the cycle of symphonies after its premiere. The single-movement structure came together over a seven-year period during which some accounts suggest that Sibelius was again reliant on alcohol. Whatever the case, his compositional mastery shows no wear and tear. The Seventh is perhaps only superficially heroic in spirit, the conventional worldly optimism of earlier works having been jettisoned in favor of a kind of stoical pantheism. Tune and accompaniment scarcely feature; the argument is punctuated by cryptic Beethovenian archetypes rather than the broad melodies of yesteryear.

Having edited Hansen's critical edition of the Seventh, Paavo Berglund must know the score better than anyone. His 2003 live recording from London is wonderfully granitic in conception, yet not without the odd awkward passage, which may or may not have something to do with a veteran's physical frailty. So powerful a reading will nevertheless be de rigueur for Sibelians who prefer their string polyphony gaunt and unsweetened. One word of warning though: Berglund at times quite forgets himself, singing along and shouting encouragement in best Beecham style, overlaying awesome climaxes with alarming vocalizations. But this late engagement with a much-loved work engenders a realization of overwhelming force. **DG**

George Gershwin | Rhapsody in Blue (1924)

Genre | Concerto
Performers | James Levine (piano and director),
Chicago Symphony Orchestra
Year recorded | 1990
Label | DG 431 625-2

There are not many individual pieces that can truly be said to have changed the course of musical history—but the *Rhapsody in Blue* is one. Its first performance ended a concert with the resounding title "An Experiment in Modern Music," presented by the dance band leader Paul Whiteman in New York in February 1924. Gershwin had written the piece in a hurry, leaving the scoring to arranger Ferde Grofé, and as pianist even improvised some of the solo passages: Whiteman's score had gaps followed by the instruction "Wait for nod." This did not, however, impede the work's success that afternoon—soon to be followed by its triumphal progress through the world's concert halls. Gershwin was rapidly elevated from the status of promising Broadway songwriter to that of international celebrity. More than that, his piece showed that it was possible to take material in a popular, jazz-derived idiom, subject it to classical methods of extension, variation, and development within a traditional structure, and produce a convincing result—not "crossover," but fusion. Jazz gained respectability, "serious" music a new dimension.

The history of editions and recordings of the *Rhapsody* is something of a mess. Grofé followed his original band scoring with another for theater orchestra, now almost forgotten, and a third for full orchestra, which became the norm. Printed editions have shortened some of the solo episodes, and various interpretive traditions of doubtful validity have become firmly entrenched. Among currently available recordings of the generally preferable original version, James Levine's is most successful in presenting the solo part with fantasy that does not tip over into idiosyncrasy, and the Chicago Symphony brings the band part to vivid life. **AB**

> *"I heard it as a sort of musical kaleidoscope of America . . . of our blues, our metropolitan madness."*

George Gershwin on *Rhapsody in Blue*

George Gershwin, pictured in *c.* 1936, a year before his death. ➲

Carl Nielsen
Symphony no. 6 (1925)

Genre | Orchestral
Conductor | Herbert Blomstedt
Performers | San Francisco Symphony
Year recorded | 1989
Label | Decca 460 988-2 (2 CDs)

Nielsen's last symphony, subtitled "Sinfonia semplice," is a strange piece. It has been dismissed as the work of a composer with failing powers, seen as a satirical response to the new stylistic currents sweeping through music, described as postmodern, and valiantly defended as an example of Nielsen's control of tonality at its most subtle. Nielsen was not in good health when he started composing this symphony in 1924—he had started to have heart attacks after completing his Fifth Symphony in 1922, and was diagnosed with angina. So the sometimes chaotic progress of the music may reflect an inner uncertainty. In a sixtieth birthday interview in 1925, he said: "If I could have my life again I would whip all artistic whims out of my head, and be apprenticed to a trade or do some other useful piece of work in which I could see a real result."

The first movement begins sunnily enough, but there are soon shadows, and a climactic discord like a howl of pain. There is disagreement between the wind and brass instruments in the following "Humoreske," with grotesque, angular lines, rackety percussion, and a beery trombone that cannot take any of it seriously. The controlled passion of the Adagio comes as a complete surprise, as does the finale, a theme with variations that moves rapidly through various styles, ending on a raspberry from the bassoons.

Herbert Blomstedt inspires the San Francisco Symphony to turn on a dime with all the virtuosity of quick-change artists, which is exactly what this symphony needs to project its bewildering kaleidoscope of events as a coherent whole. **MC**

Dmitri Shostakovich
Symphony no. 1 (1925)

Genre | Orchestral
Conductor | Eugene Ormandy
Performers | Philadelphia Orchestra
Year recorded | 1959
Label | Sony 82876 86844 2

Shostakovich's First Symphony is a student work and an astonishing one. Its success transformed his prospects overnight. The score contains ideas that appear time and again in subsequent works. Already there is a marked enthusiasm for the grotesque and the paradoxical, together with a good deal of Miaskovsky-like foreboding. During the finale, timpani announce what sounds like the prelude to an execution, though Shostakovich himself came to regard the side-drum crescendo that launches the movement as "a somewhat vulgar effect." Those facets of the piece, perhaps less evident in later years, include a certain Romantic dreaminess; a subtle treatment of time and meter, most obvious in the playful second movement; and an impressive overall refinement of approach.

In Eugene Ormandy's hands, it is these aspects that strike home with renewed impact. Taped in the presence of the composer in 1959, this is not a performance that views the work through the prism of Shostakovich's subsequent personal and political difficulties, and some may find it a little tame on that account. Ormandy was, however, a staunch Shostakovich champion who gave local premieres of many of the symphonies and recorded them. The deletions axe has not been kind to his recorded legacy, but here at least we can register the sheer professionalism of his "fabulous Philadelphians," especially the tonal richness of the strings. What makes the disc all the more indispensable is the coupling—Mstislav Rostropovich's legendary first recording, with the same forces, of Shostakovich's First Cello Concerto. The Symphony's reverberant sonics stand up well, too. **DG**

George Enescu
Violin Sonata no. 3 (1926)

Genre | Chamber
Performers | Peter Csaba (violin),
Arto Satukangas (piano)
Year recorded | 1992
Label | Ondine ODE 789-2

George Enescu was an outstandingly gifted violinist, conductor, and composer. Inspired by such influences as French Impressionism, Romanian folk music, and late German Romanticism, his music eluded classification and was therefore accused of stylistic ambiguity. In fact, Enescu could not have been more clear of his direction. Subtitled "in a popular Romanian character," it expresses a powerful, nostalgic longing for his native land using the vibrant playing style of the Moldavian fiddle. He borrowed no actual folk music but created his own exotic, improvisatory melismas and urgent dances. The opening movement, marked "malinconio," has a haunted, keening atmosphere that can only be compared to Bartók. The second has a hypnotic quality, the violin lamenting over a thin, glassy piano part, at times breaking into the husky open tones of the shepherd's flute. Alfred Cortot thought it evoked "the mysterious feeling of summer nights in Romania: below, the silent, endless deserted plain; above, constellations leading off into infinity." The Allegro explodes into frenzied dancing and violinistic pyrotechnics, both instruments breaking out of their conventional confines and entering an incandescent world of lavish fantasy.

George Enescu's works are sadly under-recorded, though this sonata was performed by his pupil Yehudi Menuhin, who called Enescu "the greatest musician I ever experienced." Of the few recent recordings, Transylvanian violinist Peter Csaba best captures the ferocious, untamed spirit of this work. He penetrates the sonata's enigmatic heart, and transforms his instrument into the wild, raucous folk fiddle in the helter-skelter Allegro. **HW**

Frank Martin
Mass for double choir (1926)

Genre | Choral
Conductor/Performers | James O'Donnell;
Westminster Cathedral Choir
Year recorded | 1997
Label | Hyperion CDA 67017

Frank Martin (1890–1974) was born in Geneva and studied there with Joseph Lauber from 1906 to 1914. He then took courses in Zürich, Rome, and Paris, returning to Geneva in 1926 as a pianist and harpsichordist, and teaching at the Institut Jacques-Dalcroze until 1937. In 1946 he moved to the Netherlands, becoming professor of composition at the not-too-distant Cologne Hochschule für Musik.

Martin served an unusually long musical apprenticeship before establishing his own distinctive voice. At first he professed the greatest enthusiasm for French music, but later became fascinated by Schoenberg's twelve-note composition. Although the Mass was one of Martin's earliest acknowledged works, there are features in the score that anticipate his mature style, not least a fondness for melodic material that oscillates between a few small intervals and the use of modal harmonies and pedal points. This setting also reflects his profound reverence for old masters such as Palestrina and Bach.

Although Martin worked on the Mass for five years, it was first performed as late as 1963, the manuscript having remained in his drawer for nearly forty years because he harbored doubts as to the relevance of sacred music in the twentieth century. Since its premiere, however, this Mass has come to be recognized as one of Martin's most inspired works. Among the most distinguished of recent recordings, the performance of the Westminster Cathedral Choir under James O'Donnell stands out for the sheer beauty of the singing, outstanding engineering, and an immensely impressive and imaginative coupling of the *Messa di Requiem* by the Italian Ildebrando Pizzetti. **EL**

Sergei Rachmaninov | Piano Concerto no. 4 (1926, *rev.* 1941)

Genre | Concerto
Performers/Conductor | Arturo Benedetti Michelangeli
(piano), Philharmonia Orchestra; Ettore Gracis
Year recorded | 1957
Label | EMI 7243 5 67258 2 9

For a long time Rachmaninov's Fourth was the ugly duckling of his piano concertos. It is not difficult to see why it is so different from his previous concertos: they were all composed well before the Great War, a catastrophe that shattered European cultural self-esteem and forced lyrically effusive Romanticism to be deemed not only unfashionable but garish and repellent. A whole generation of composers was affected, and many fell virtually silent after 1918, while others had to adopt a new, more objective, less openly self-expressive idiom. Having left Russia in 1917 and settled in America the following year, Rachmaninov knew full well his brand of emotional grandiloquence was outmoded, but he despaired: "I cannot cast out the old way of writing, and I cannot acquire the new," he wrote.

It is therefore not surprising that Rachmaninov's Fourth Piano Concerto seems riddled with paradoxes and insecurities. After a thrillingly original opening, the first movement ends abruptly, while the similarity of the theme of the second movement to the tune "Three Blind Mice" was a source of amusement to early American audiences. In the wrong hands, this difficult concerto can easily sound vacuous or emotionally artificial.

In the right hands, it is a masterpiece. And half a century on, there are no better hands in this concerto than those of Arturo Benedetti Michelangeli, who recorded it at the height of his powers. It remains a landmark of the gramophone, one of the great recordings of any concerto. Michelangeli's combination of aristocratic lyricism and combustible virtuoso grandeur has never been surpassed in this work. Had Rachmaninov lived to hear this recording, his creative doubts would surely have been dispelled. **TLP**

> *"I feel like a ghost wandering in a world grown alien."*
>
> Sergei Rachmaninov

Other Recommended Recordings

Stephen Hough, Dallas Symphony Orchestra
Andrew Litton
Hyperion CDA 67501/2 (2 CDs)
Hough's poised performance is deeply moving

Earl Wild, Royal Philharmonic Orchestra
Jascha Horenstein
Chandos CHAN 7114 (2 CDs)
Perhaps the most dazzling of all accounts

Sergei Rachmaninov, Philadelphia Orchestra
Eugene Ormandy
RCA 09026 61265 2 (10 CDs)
The composer's recording is of great historical interest

Karol Szymanowski | Mazurkas (1926–34)

Genre | Instrumental
Instrument | Piano
Performer | Marc-André Hamelin
Year recorded | 2002
Label | Hyperion CDA 67399

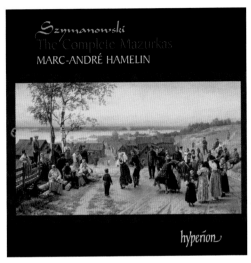

Karol Szymanowski's Twenty Mazurkas for solo piano, op. 50, form the only substantial set of such pieces to follow in the footsteps of those by his compatriot, Frédéric Chopin. As with Chopin's, a rich panoply of inventive pianistic writing offsets distinctive Polish folk idioms—drone basses, modally inflected harmonies, irresistible and often complicated rhythms, and more. Szymanowski was a fine pianist; though not a virtuoso, he always composed at the piano and counted the pianist Arthur Rubinstein among his friends. The instrument remained central to his work throughout his career.

Szymanowski was not interested in folk music for the sake of it. Rather, he used it as a means to an end: "Folklore is significant to me only as a fertilizing agent," he once commented. "My aim is the creation of a Polish style ... in which there is not one jot of folklore." And yet, far more than Chopin, he explored the differing traditions emanating from various parts of the country, notably the highland music of the Tatra mountains. The mazurkas were of course contemporaneous with folkloric explorations of composers ranging from Bartók in Hungary to Vaughan Williams in Britain—and so Szymanowski, whether or not he intended it, was a Polish part of a global trend.

Szymanowski's piano music, with its exotic, rich textures and demanding, subtle harmonic idioms, is inevitably a musical niche; it is also immensely challenging for performers. Among the handful of available accounts, Marc-André Hamelin's takes a great deal of beating, dealing with this elusive music's refinement, quirkiness, and delicious chromatic harmonies with immense sensitivity. The disc is completed by the composer's Two Mazurkas, op. 62, the *Valse romantique* and Four Polish Dances. **JD**

"My discovery of the essential beauty of Górale (Polish highlander) music ... is a very personal one."

Karol Szymanowski

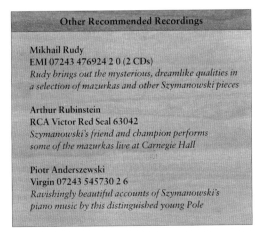

Other Recommended Recordings

Mikhail Rudy
EMI 07243 476924 2 0 (2 CDs)
Rudy brings out the mysterious, dreamlike qualities in a selection of mazurkas and other Szymanowski pieces

Arthur Rubinstein
RCA Victor Red Seal 63042
Szymanowski's friend and champion performs some of the mazurkas live at Carnegie Hall

Piotr Anderszewski
Virgin 07243 545730 2 6
Ravishingly beautiful accounts of Szymanowski's piano music by this distinguished young Pole

Karol Szymanowski | Stabat mater (1926)

Genre | Choral
Conductor/Performers | Simon Rattle; City of Birmingham Symphony Orchestra and Chorus
Year recorded | 1993
Label | EMI 7243 5 55121 2 3

Szymanowski's *Stabat mater* is not only one of the great choral works of the 1920s, it also draws together so many of the features that make Szymanowski such a fascinating composer. The spiraling complexity of his early phases, some of which was driven by an infatuation with the music of Strauss and Reger, has long gone, although there are still vestiges of the Impressionist coloring that makes his music from the 1910s so texturally fascinating. Most interesting of all is the presence of the ecstatic urgency that propels so much of his opera *King Roger*, completed just two years earlier. The atmosphere evoked for the paganisms of medieval Sicily, which much of that work celebrates, transfers surprisingly well to the Catholic poetry of the *Stabat mater*. Although there is an undertow of sensuality, it is Szymanowski's directness of address, in part impelled by his late fascination with Polish folksong, that to this day touches both performers and audiences.

Although the score was published with the original Latin of Jacopone da Todi's hymn, Szymanowski set the text of the *Stabat mater* in Polish translation and it is in this form that it is most effective. A number of fine performances are available, but Simon Rattle's rendition with the City of Birmingham Symphony Orchestra and Chorus in excellent form is memorable for a number of reasons. Rattle looks beneath the surface beauty of Szymanowski's writing to reveal, time and again, the depths to be found in his new simplicity, and he seems always aware of the gentle rhythmic ebb and flow that gives the work its hypnotic qualities. Coupled with this is an excellent team of soloists, in particular Elzbieta Szmytka and Florence Quivar. **JS**

> *"Something both peasant and ecclesiastical . . . naively devotional; a kind of prayer for souls."*
>
> Szymanowski's original intention for the *Stabat mater*

Other Recommended Recordings

Litany of the Virgin Mary
City of Birmingham Symphony Orchestra & Chorus
Simon Rattle • EMI 7243 5 55121 2 3
*Exquisite settings for women's chorus,
soprano solo, and orchestra*

Six Kurpian Songs
Russian State Symphonic Cappella • Valeri Polyansky
Chandos CHAN 9937
Neglected but lovely settings of peasant wedding poems

Songs of the infatuated muezzin
Riszard Minkiewicz, Polish State Philharmonic
Karol Stryja • Naxos 8.553688
A more sensuous Szymanowski as a vocal composer

Szymanowski at his country retreat in the Polish resort of Zakopane. ➔

Leoš Janáček
Sinfonietta (1926)

Genre | Orchestral
Conductor | Charles Mackerras
Performers | Vienna Philharmonic
Year recorded | 1980
Label | Decca 448 255-2 (2 CDs)

The end of the Austrian Empire in 1918 heralded the dawn of a new era for the freshly minted state of Czechoslovakia. Braced by love and newfound success, Janáček was determined to celebrate the nation and his countrymen. The second part of his opera *The Excursions of Mr. Brouček* (which focused on the triumphs of those icons of Czech national freedom, the late medieval religious reformers the Hussites), was a first sally in Janáček's campaign to glorify his nation. The Sinfonietta was intended as a celebration of the modern Czech "free man." It started life in 1926 as a fanfare for a gymnastics festival, but soon grew into the five-movement work that remains to this day Janáček's most popular orchestral composition.

Janáček gave broad hints of the pictorial content of the four movements that unfold after the terrific introductory fanfares. It is clear that his inspiration was stirred by the growing greatness of the Moravian capital, Brno, with descriptive titles mentioning the city's castle, the Queen's Monastery, the street leading to the castle, and the town hall. Although these four movements loosely outline the shape of a sinfonia, none of the movements follow a predictable pattern; instead they paint vivid sound pictures of the beloved city and reach a climax in the triumphant return of the opening fanfares.

Charles Mackerras's recording with the Vienna Philharmonic Orchestra on terrific form is superb for appreciating Janáček's bold approach to orchestral sonority. As ever, Mackerras is meticulous in his treatment of Janáček's score and structures the blazing conclusion with unerring dramatic skill. **JS**

Maurice Ravel
Chansons madécasses (1926)

Genre | Vocal
Performers | Janet Baker (mezzo-soprano), Melos Ensemble
Year recorded | 1966
Label | Decca 476 7091

When the date came for the premiere of his *Chansons madécasses* in Paris in June 1926, Ravel had only completed "Aoua!," the second of the three settings of poems by Evariste-Désiré de Parny, and a passionate denunciation of the maltreatment of black people by their white colonizers. At the time, France was militarily engaged in Morocco and when an encore was insisted upon, one member of the audience got up and left declaring that he refused to listen to such things while France was fighting in North Africa.

At a stroke Ravel had satisfied two impulses close to his heart: his radical politics and a taste for the exotic. In fact the *Chansons madécasses*, set for solo voice and a trio comprising flute, cello, and piano, are not quite as exotic as they might appear. The eighteenth-century writer De Parny borrowed Madagascan verse forms rather than, as he maintained, translated traditional verses by the island's people. Ravel responded with three miniature masterpieces that are among the greatest of his later works. On either side of the angry "Aoua!" are two sensual love songs. If "Aoua!" takes its cue from Schoenberg's song cycle *Pierrot lunaire*, then "Nahandove" and "Il est doux" seem to evoke the tropical paradise that Gauguin imagined in the South Seas.

Janet Baker, always a fine interpreter of the French repertoire, brings intelligence and passion to these songs. There is a special fury in "Aoua!" and a yearning in the other two songs that is so much a part of Baker's vocal character. This is a great artist at her peak. And the utterly dependable members of the Melos Ensemble are equal partners in what Ravel himself called "a sort of quartet." **CC**

Jean Sibelius
Tapiola (1926)

Genre | Orchestral
Conductor/Performers | Herbert von Karajan; Berlin Philharmonic Orchestra
Year recorded | 1984
Label | DG 413 755-2

Tapiola was a commissioned work, never intended to represent any kind of leave-taking, but as Sibelius proved unable to complete or, more precisely, unwilling to release, his Eighth Symphony, its reputation soared. Many would regard it as Sibelius's crowning compositional achievement—or even as his musical death wish. At the very least, it is to the northern forests what Debussy's *La mer* is to the sea, evoking an unpopulated natural world with severity and grandeur. The music has an almost cinematic quality as it shifts from one texture to another, seeming to focus on details of an imaginary landscape, yet all its material derives from the deceptively simple opening statement.

In September 1926, Sibelius sent a telegram to the publishing house Breitkopf & Härtel requesting *Tapiola*'s return. Fortunately he made no drastic changes ahead of the premiere to be conducted by Walter Damrosch in New York. More usefully, he supplied an explanation of the role of Tapio in Finnish mythology from which was prepared the quatrain adorning the score:

> *"Widespread they stand, the Northland's dusky forests,*
> *Ancient, mysterious, brooding savage dreams;*
> *Within them dwells the Forest's mighty God,*
> *And wood-sprites in the gloom weave magic secrets."*

Herbert von Karajan's fourth(!) recording of the piece has the Wagnerian weight and majesty one might expect from this source. "Never," suggests Sibelius scholar Robert Layton, "has it sounded more mysterious or its dreams more savage. . . . And the buildup to the storm has never struck such a chilling note of terror." **DG**

Maurice Ravel
Violin Sonata (1927)

Genre | Chamber
Performers | Arthur Grumiaux (violin), István Hajdu (piano)
Year recorded | 1962
Label | Eloquence 468 306-2

Ravel's Violin Sonata in G major was inspired by his burgeoning friendship with the violinist Hélène Jourdan-Morhange. He began work in 1923, yet within just a few months had abandoned hopes of completing it. "My depression is worse than ever," he wrote to a friend. When Ravel was not depressed and in a productive mode instead, what sometimes slowed him down was his perfectionism. His student Manuel Rosenthal remembers Ravel burning the finale he had originally intended for the sonata. By the time the work was finished in 1927, Jourdan-Morhange was crippled by rheumatism and unable to play it. George Enescu gave the premiere with the composer at the piano.

The sonata is Ravel at his mercurial best. The first movement begins with a lilting tune in the piano that suggests blithe innocence. Rapidly, though, the mood changes—growing skittish, fantastical, melancholy, and back again. Each transformation is managed seamlessly. "Blues" is the title of the second movement. Both instruments take turns imitating a banjo; the violin swoops and slides like a blues singer, yet with its wry wit and dramatic edge, the sound is unmistakeably Ravel. The finale is an exhilarating study in perpetual motion; the violin essentially sprints a four-minute mile while the piano hops nervously on the sidelines.

Arthur Grumiaux and István Hajdu masterfully negotiate the tricky transformations in the first movement, and their finale is among the most invigoratingly fizzy on disc. Best of all, though, is their dry, rhythmically taut account of the "Blues"—it is prickly yet still debonair, and Grumiaux wisely does not overdo the slides. **AFC**

Gustav Holst | Egdon Heath (1927)

Genre | Orchestral
Conductor | Andrew Davis
Performers | BBC Symphony Orchestra
Year recorded | 1993
Label | Apex 8573 89087-2

Holst
The Planets
Egdon Heath

apex

BBC Symphony Orchestra
Sir Andrew Davis

If you do not know *Egdon Heath* (and it is unlikely you will ever have heard it in a concert hall), you probably suspect it is yet another pleasant piece of English pastoral. After all, it is a thirteen-minute tone poem inspired by the description of a rural landscape in the first chapter of Thomas Hardy's novel *The Return of the Native*. But Hardy's Dorset heath is a bleak place, which he said was like human nature in being "slighted and enduring; and withal singularly colossal and mysterious in its swarthy monotony." Holst's piece is pretty bleak, too, drifting about in sparse textures, largely in five- and seven-beat measures, with the heath's inhabitants represented by wearily trudging bass-lines, short-lived expressive woodwind phrases, and a brief, ghostly morris dance. But it is those human figures that make the difference between the utter remoteness of "Neptune" at the end of *The Planets*, some ten years earlier, and the stoicism of *Egdon Heath*. The latter has, in the phrase with which Holst late in life summed up his ideal, a "tender austerity." And it is just as characteristic of the composer as the colorful *Planets*, or the ecstatically dancing *Hymn of Jesus*, or the hearty Suites for wind band, or the shining Hindu choral hymns. Indeed, Holst himself thought it was his best work.

A successful interpretation of *Egdon Heath* has to hold the balance between the landscape and the figures in it, allowing the expressive phrases to bloom while everything else remains impassive and implacable. Andrew Davis's account does just that, with the help of refined orchestral playing and a first-class recording. And the layout of this bargain disc places *Egdon Heath* straight after *The Planets*, highlighting both its similarity to "Neptune" and the crucial, human difference. **AB**

"It had needed no stretch of the imagination to create anew the colossal, mysterious atmosphere of the heath."

Imogen Holst

Other Recommended Recordings

Egdon Heath, The Perfect Fool, etc.
London Philharmonic Orchestra • Adrian Boult
Decca 470 191-2 (2 CDs)
Boult's 1961 classic as part of an invaluable collection

Egdon Heath, Beni Mora, Hammersmith, etc.
Royal Scottish National Orchestra • David Lloyd-Jones
Naxos 8.553696
An unusually expressive Egdon Heath

Hammersmith, Suites nos. 1 and 2, etc.
Royal Northern College of Music Wind Orchestra
Timothy Reynish • Chandos CHAN 9697
The original Hammersmith *with the breezy Suites*

Andrew Davis conducting the BBC Symphony Orchestra. ➔

Leoš Janáček
Glagolitic Mass (1927)

Genre | Choral
Performers/Conductor | Danish NRSO and Chorus; Charles Mackerras
Year recorded | 1994
Label | Chandos CHAN 9310

While Janáček composed most of the *Glagolitic Mass* in 1926, material for three of the movements goes back as early as 1907. Although nominally a Mass, it proved to be anything but conventional. Rather than using the traditional Latin text, Janáček chose to set it in Old Church Slavonic, hence the title, "Glagolitic." For him, the incense of his cathedral was the scent of woods at his favorite spa, Luhačovice; the church bells were the ones on a flock of sheep; and his candles, the stars lighting the tips of tall fir trees. This pantheistic vision of liturgy adds to the elemental qualities of this extraordinary work.

The word-setting is characteristically explosive, the musical treatment far from predictable. The news of the resurrection of Christ, for example, is delivered as a whisper rather than a roar of triumph. In fact, many of the mysteries present in the Credo movement are dealt within a broad orchestral meditation punctuated by destructive interventions from three sets of pedal timpani and the solo organ. It has, however, become a staple of the twentieth-century choral repertoire, though not in the form originally intended. Owing to rehearsal difficulties, revisions were made and Janáček's bold original vision somewhat tamed.

The Danish National Radio Symphony Orchestra and Chorus's excellent performance under Charles Mackerras uses Paul Wingfield's reconstruction of Janáček's original version of the score. The Intrada, usually heard at the end, is also played at the start. The succeeding Introduction is rhythmically more complex and the astonishing timpani interruptions in the Credo are restored. The effect in such a committed, expert performance is all but overwhelming. **JS**

Joseph Jongen
Symphonie concertante (1927)

Genre | Concerto
Performers/Conductor | Michael Murray, San Francisco Symphony; Edo de Waart
Year recorded | 1984
Label | Telarc CD-80096

Joseph Jongen (1873–1953) ranks as one of the most important composers in his native Belgium. He studied at the Conservatoire in his home city of Liège; winning the prestigious Prix de Rome for his cantata *Comala*, a scholarship enabled him to travel in Europe, and brought him into contact with Brahms, Richard Strauss, D'Indy, and Fauré. A stint as the professor of harmony in Liège was followed with a stay in England during World War I. He then took up a professorship at the Brussels Conservatoire and was director from 1925 to 1939.

Jongen's name is familiar to organists for his *Chant de May* and *Sonata eroïca*—challenging concert pieces. But his late masterpiece, the *Symphonie concertante*, op. 81, deserves to be better known: along with Saint-Saëns's "Organ" Symphony and Poulenc's Organ Concerto, it is one of the great showpieces for organ and symphony orchestra. Dedicated to his brother Léon, it was originally commissioned for the inauguration of the organ in Wanamaker's store in Philadelphia—a project aborted by the death of the proprietor. Jongen played the organ part at its premiere in Brussels in 1928.

The piece has four contrasting movements: a symphonic introduction in open sonata form, a highly rhythmic scherzo, a harmonically adventurous slow movement, and a coruscating toccata. This recording celebrated the inauguration of the Fratelli Ruffatti organ at San Francisco's Louise M. Davies Symphony Hall. The exuberant playing of Michael Murray is complemented by the robust yet sensuous accompaniment of the San Francisco Symphony under Edo de Waart. **GK**

Bohuslav Martinů
La revue de cuisine (1927)

Genre | Ballet
Conductor/Performers | Christopher Hogwood; Saint Paul Chamber Orchestra
Year recorded | 1991
Label | Decca 433 660-2

One of the many musical impulses that seized Bohuslav Martinů (1890–1959) as a near-impoverished composer in Paris in the 1920s was a fascination with jazz. He himself often not only practiced it with piano improvisations in cafés, but also incorporated aspects of the style into his compositions from the mid-1920s onward. There are times when it is hard to differentiate between his use of the style to energize otherwise classically orientated works and full-blown jazz compositions, such as the orchestral *Le jazz*.

La revue de cuisine was his third ballet score to be influenced by jazz, or more specifically Dixieland. The ballet was first performed in Prague in November 1927 to a peculiar mise-en-scène involving the love and vicissitudes of kitchen utensils. As a four-movement concert suite scored for a sextet comprising clarinet, bassoon, trumpet, violin, cello, and piano, the work was premiered in Paris in 1930 and has proved to be one of Martinů's most popular shorter works. Both the prologue and finale start with jaunty fanfares launching syncopated marchlike material. The two central dances are a steamy tango and a Charleston whose low-key opening belies its riotous conclusion.

Christopher Hogwood went back to Martinů's original score in preparing these exemplary performances. The instrumentalists of the Saint Paul Chamber Orchestra really identify with this repertoire, proving themselves idiomatically adept in the more overtly jazz-influenced passages: the Charleston especially moves with uninhibited verve and the clarity of the sympathetic recording imparts a marvelous sense of immediacy to the proceedings. **JS**

Igor Stravinsky
Oedipus rex (1927)

Genre | Opera
Conductor/Performers | Colin Davis; Ralph Richardson, Ronald Dowd
Years recorded | 1961–62
Label | EMI 07243 5 85011 2 4

Stravinsky's long-held interest in dramas of the ancient Mediterranean world was celebrated most vividly in this "opera-oratorio" based on Jean Cocteau's libretto, derived from the tragedy by Sophocles. The action is explained in the audience's vernacular by a speaker, while the sung material is in Latin. Stravinsky intended movement to be kept to a minimum and the singers to appear with no sense of depth on stage, in costumes that allow only heads and arm movement. He thus hoped to reduce any suggestion of spectacle and instead to focus on the inner world of the drama. The role of fate guiding all human destiny was a theme that he often returned to, but here he depicts its most terrifyingly human and bloody impact.

The music uses Classical forms (arias, duets, and choruses). Appropriately, the language of melody and harmony is also retrospective, with simple triads and scale-based melodies applied from a Modernist perspective. Rhythms are repetitive, as if to suggest the inevitable force of fate directing the drama. In two acts, the story tells how Oedipus tries to rid the city of Thebes of the plague but learns through the Sphinx's riddles that he killed his own father and has married his mother. Overcome with self-loathing, he blinds himself, stabbing his eyes with Queen Jocasta's golden brooch while she hangs herself.

This is a thrilling account from Colin Davis; vivid details emerge from the macabre score with glorious richness of color. The excellent soloists are supported by fabulous playing from the Royal Philharmonic Orchestra, especially in the biting wind writing, while Ralph Richardson's narrations are authoritative and impassioned. **SW**

Zoltán Kodály | Háry János Suite (1927)

Genre | Orchestral
Conductor | Iván Fischer
Performers | Budapest Festival Orchestra
Year recorded | 1998
Label | Philips 462 824-2

Kodály composed the singspiel *Háry János* during the mid-1920s, its first staged performance taking place at the Royal Hungarian Opera House in Budapest on October 16, 1926. The scenario based on János Garay's comic verse concerns the imaginary exploits of János Háry, a veteran soldier who served in the imperial Austrian army at the turn of the eighteenth century. Looking back over his life, Háry boasts about the heroic deeds that he was supposed to have accomplished in his youth, including rescuing the daughter of the Kaiser, being nominated a general, managing alone to win a battle against Napoleon, and conquering the heart of the Emperor's wife.

In the following year, six of the more extended numbers from *Háry János* were subsequently extracted from the full-scale stage work to form a highly effective orchestral score, which remains the composer's most popular work. Opening with a graphic representation of a giant sneeze (a sign that what follows should be taken with a pinch of salt), the rather meditative first movement is followed by the delightful "Viennese Musical Clock" and an intense "Love Song" that gives particular prominence to the cimbalom, an indigenous Hungarian instrument. After a fourth movement offering a humorous portrayal of Háry's apocryphal defeat of Napoleon, there is an extended intermezzo in the Hungarian style and finally a dazzling march entitled "Entrance of the Emperor and his Court."

Of the many recordings of this wonderfully imaginative score, Iván Fischer's interpretation with the Budapest Festival Orchestra deserves pride of place for its strong characterization of both the humorous and poetic aspects of the music and an instinctive empathy with the folk inflections of Kodály's musical language. **EL**

PHILIPS

KODÁLY
"HÁRY JÁNOS" SUITE
DANCES OF GALÁNTA
& MAROSSZÉK
CHILDREN'S CHORUSES

IVÁN
FISCHER
BUDAPEST
FESTIVAL ORCHESTRA

"He does not lie but simply tells fairy tales."

Kodály on the protagonist János Háry

Other Recommended Recordings

Psalmus hungaricus
Danish National Radio Symphony Chorus & Orchestra
Charles Mackerras • Chandos CHAN 9310
Kodály's finest choral work delivered with conviction

Peacock Variations
Budapest Philharmonic Orchestra • Arpad Joo
Arts Red Line 473792
Accomplished performance of Kodály's most extended orchestral work

Solo Cello Sonata
Pieter Wispelwey • Channel CCS 15398
One of the greatest solo cello pieces after Bach's Suites

Zoltán Kodály was a key figure in twentieth-century Hungarian music. ➔

Eugène Goossens | Oboe Concerto (1927)

Genre | Concerto
Performers/Conductor | Joel Marangella (oboe), West Australian Symphony Orchestra; Vernon Handley
Year recorded | 1996
Label | ABC 476 7632 (3 CDs)

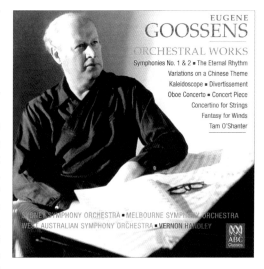

While Eugène Goossens's abilities as a conductor were obvious from an early age, he had a much harder time convincing his European and American audiences that he was also a composer of significance. Only in Australia, where he became a revered figure as the Sydney Symphony Orchestra's inaugural chief conductor from 1947 until a scandal involving the importation of occult pornography drove him from the country in 1956, was he acknowledged among the first rank of composers. Even then, his eclectic works tended only to be wheeled out for important occasions.

And yet when he avoided overarching ambition and instead wrote for his own family (his siblings included harpists Marie and Sidonie, and the world-class oboist Leon), the results could be impressive. The Oboe Concerto in particular, originally intended for Leon to play on an American tour in 1928, can rightfully take its place alongside similar works by Richard Strauss and Vaughan Williams. Filled with melody, surprisingly pastoral in feel, and with a warmth and charm not typical of much of Goossens's other music, its popularity was immediate and the passage of time has only increased its appeal.

While Goossens himself conducted it many times, he never recorded it. In his absence, however, the piece is well served by Goossens's Australian soul mates, the West Australian Symphony Orchestra with their stellar oboist Joel Marangella. In just twelve minutes of inspired lyricism, this loving reconstruction of Goossens's most perfectly crafted work sums up all that is good about a composer whose time for a more considered appreciation may yet lie ahead. The attractive three-CD set with all Goossens's other orchestral music can only help to make the case. **MB**

"My heart just loosens when I listen to Mr. Goossens."

Noël Coward, *Russian Blues*

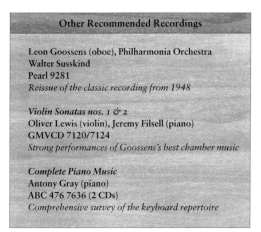

Other Recommended Recordings

Leon Goossens (oboe), Philharmonia Orchestra
Walter Susskind
Pearl 9281
Reissue of the classic recording from 1948

Violin Sonatas nos. 1 & 2
Oliver Lewis (violin), Jeremy Filsell (piano)
GMVCD 7120/7124
Strong performances of Goossens's best chamber music

Complete Piano Music
Antony Gray (piano)
ABC 476 7636 (2 CDs)
Comprehensive survey of the keyboard repertoire

Constant Lambert | The Rio Grande (1927)

Genre | Choral/Concerto
Conductor/Performers | David Lloyd-Jones;
Jack Gibbons, Sally Burgess, Chorus of Opera North
Year recorded | 1991
Label | Hyperion CDA 66565

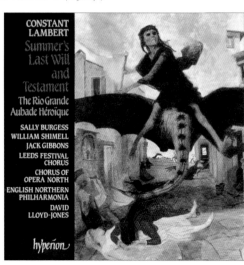

For not much more than a quarter of a century, Constant Lambert (1905–51) blazed multiple trails across London's musical life. He was an expert conductor and the founding musical director of the future Royal Ballet. He wrote entertainingly, not least in *Music, Ho!*, a survey of contemporary music that is still highly readable and thought-provoking. He published editions of eighteenth-century music. And he was a composer of remarkable gifts, perhaps never completely fulfilled.

His career certainly got off to a brilliant start. At the age of nineteen, he became the first British composer to write a ballet score for the Diaghilev company. And at twenty-two, he composed his most popular piece, *The Rio Grande*. It is a setting of an impressionistic poem by his friend Sacheverell Sitwell describing crowds dancing by a (fictitious) Brazilian river. The scoring is unique: solo piano, chorus with a solo alto, and orchestra of strings, brass, and percussion. And the musical language is unique, too. It combines brittle, jazzy syncopation—reflecting the huge impact American jazz bands and George Gershwin made on 1920s London—with lithe Latin-American dance rhythms and a vein of haunting nostalgia, in a lucid single-movement structure.

David Lloyd-Jones's recording suffers a little from its cavernous acoustic, but it boasts incisive singing, with the relatively small chorus numbers Lambert preferred, alert orchestral playing, and a dazzlingly idiomatic account of the piano part by Jack Gibbons. The main coupling is Lambert's later *Summer's Last Will and Testament*, a large-scale cantata on an Elizabethan text, which he clearly meant as his masterpiece. It was not: to his chagrin, he never surpassed *The Rio Grande*. **AB**

"The Rio Grande . . . sparkles and glitters one moment, then seduces us the next . . ."

Christopher Palmer

Other Recommended Recordings

The Rio Grande, Horoscope Suite, etc.
Kyla Greenbaum (piano), Philharmonia Orchestra
Constant Lambert • Pearl GEM 0069
Lambert's own recordings from 1949

Concerto for piano and nine players, etc.
Ian Brown (piano), Philip Langridge (tenor)
Nash Ensemble • Lionel Friend • Hyperion CDA 66754
A jazz-infused chamber concerto

Horoscope Suite
English Northern Philharmonia • David Lloyd-Jones
Hyperion CDH 55099
Atmospheric music from his most celebrated ballet

Edgard Varèse | Arcana (1927)

Genre | Orchestra
Conductor | Leonard Slatkin
Performers | Philharmonia Orchestra
Year recorded | 1996
Label | RCA 09026 68819 2

Holst The Planets
Leonard Slatkin
Philharmonia Orchestra
Varèse Arcana

Arcana, Varèse's greatest orchestral work, has had few true successors, although it is now eighty years old. Rhythmically compulsive, amazingly inventive, sometimes sardonically humorous, it explores the boundaries of the sonically acceptable in a series of thunderous climaxes, with a passion and strength that make it as exciting today as it was at its first performance. The work typifies Varèse's search for a music that "throws open the whole world of sound," in the spirit of the Renaissance Hermeticists seeking to expand human consciousness through the influence of the stars. Its opening measures present a complex of three ideas—a pounding, muscular figure shared between low bass instruments and timpani; a dissonant brass/woodwind fanfare; and a jagged flourish on high strings, clarinets, and xylophone. The music thus rushes to occupy space from the depths to the heights of the orchestra, a tendency observable throughout the work.

From these opening premises a multitude of other ideas evolve. The huge percussion body emerges frequently as a sonic entity on its own, self-sufficient in timbral and rhythmic structure. After a last climax of awesome, hieratic power, the music evanesces into silence on violin harmonics, Chinese blocks, and a tremolo cluster on low strings sul ponticello: a rapt gaze, so it seems, into the immensity of the night sky.

Leonard Slatkin's unexpectedly visceral performance is superbly recorded and is excellent not only for the vividness with which it delineates Varèse's kaleidoscopic sonic invention and dynamic dissonance, but also his powers as a musical architect. The work's masterly symphonic sweep and inexorable progression from one climactic event to the next are never in doubt. **MM**

> *"One star exists, higher than all the rest. This is the apocalyptic star."*

Paracelsus (Theophrastus Bombastus von Hohenheim): Varèse's epigraph on the title page of *Arcana*

Other Recommended Recordings

Chicago Symphony Orchestra • Jean Martinon
RCA 09026 63315 2
This intense 1966 performance remains one of the best the work has ever had

New York Philharmonic Orchestra • Pierre Boulez
Sony SK 45844
Every effervescent sonority is superbly delineated in Boulez's cooler approach

Royal Concertgebouw Orchestra • Riccardo Chailly
Decca 460 208-2 (2 CDs)
A well-nigh definitive account, part of Chailly's complete Varèse box set

George Gershwin | An American in Paris (1928)

Genre | Orchestral
Conductor | Arthur Fiedler
Performers | Boston Pops Orchestra
Year recorded | 1959
Label | RCA 74321 68019 2

An American in Paris is happy music. Gershwin wrote it as a follow-up to his Rhapsody in Blue and Piano Concerto, as his first piece for symphony orchestra alone (scored by himself, as was everything he did for the concert hall after the Rhapsody). And, since he began it during a visit to Paris, he chose to make it a loosely structured tone poem suggesting an American wandering round the city, being touched by homesickness, but concluding (to quote Gershwin's introduction to a broadcast) "Home is swell! But after all, this is Paris—so let's go!" France is represented by echoes of Debussy, Les Six, and Chabrier, and above all an array of genuine Paris taxi horns; America by a blues melody (trumpet with hat mute, saxophones added to the orchestra), and a rackety Charleston. The piece is episodic, certainly, but the transitions between episodes are smoothly worked, the tunes are terrific, and it is all great, life-enhancing fun.

There is a tradition of performing An American in Paris with the more lyrical bits taken really slowly and the jazz elements exaggerated: the wire-brush rhythms under the blues not equal sixteenth-notes but dotted in a "hot potato, hot potato" rhythm, the Charleston melody also swung, the bluesy minor thirds bent. But Gershwin would have known how to notate these details for classical musicians, and he chose not to. And that superb light-music conductor Arthur Fiedler shows that you can bring off the piece successfully at a brisk pace and pretty much straight. With gleefully responsive playing from his Boston musicians (and a recording sounding as if it could have been made yesterday), the result is an irresistible expression of—in this context, the phrase is inescapable—joie de vivre. **AB**

> *"It's not a Beethoven symphony, you know . . . It's a humorous piece, nothing solemn about it."*
>
> George Gershwin, reported in the *Cincinnati Post*

Other Recommended Recordings

New York Philharmonic • Leonard Bernstein
Sony 516234 2
Very different from the Fiedler, with far more relaxation of tempo and some jazzed-up rhythms

Chicago Symphony Orchestra • James Levine
DG 431 625-2
Jazzy in the Bernstein vein, with sleek orchestral sound

Victor Symphony Orchestra • Nathaniel Shilkret
Naxos 8.120664
The first recording, made a few weeks after the premiere, with the original taxi horns, and Gershwin allegedly playing the celesta part

Maurice Ravel | Boléro (1928)

Genre | Ballet
Conductor | Jos van Immerseel
Performers | Anima Eterna
Year recorded | 2005
Label | Zig-Zag Territoires ZZT 060901

Ravel's *Boléro*—one of the most popular pieces in the entire classical literature—owes its life to the dancer Ida Rubinstein and a twist of fate. In 1927, Rubinstein commissioned the composer to orchestrate six movements from Isaac Albéniz's *Iberia*, which she was planning to choreograph. By the time Ravel set to work, however, he discovered that another composer had already secured the exclusive rights, and was making his own arrangements for a different choreographer. Ravel was despondent. Then, one day, a friend found him at the piano, playing the melody for what would become *Boléro*. "Don't you think there's something insistent about this tune?" Ravel asked. "I'm going to try to repeat it a good number of times without any development while gradually building it up with my best orchestration."

Ravel was surprised and rather perplexed by *Boléro*'s phenomenal success. He took pains to explain that it was merely an "experiment," a piece of "orchestral tissue without music." And, in a sense, that is an accurate description. Over a reiterated rhythm in the snare drum, a long, looping melody repeats with more instruments added each time until the tune collapses under its own weight. Nevertheless, there is something about the tune's obsessive character and presentation that continues to inspire and stimulate audiences.

Ravel was very particular about how *Boléro* should be played, and even scolded Toscanini for choosing too fast a tempo. Jos van Immerseel intensively studied the composer's own recording, and his measured yet fluid account—featuring instruments of Ravel's day—is both the most transparent and colorful of the 200-odd versions out there. **AFC**

> *"I've written only one masterpiece—Boléro. Unfortunately, there's no music in it."*
>
> Maurice Ravel

Other Recommended Recordings

Amsterdam Concertgebouw Orchestra
Bernard Haitink
Philips 473 991-2
Tightly controlled and sharply etched—a virtuoso performance

Paris Orchestra • Jean Martinon
EMI 7243 4 76960 2 2
Martinon's light step reminds us Boléro *is a ballet*

Boston Symphony Orchestra
Seiji Ozawa
Eloquence 476 8500
A provocative mix of sensuousness and swagger

The Russian dancer Ida Rubinstein, pictured in *c.* 1936. ➔

Arnold Schoenberg
Variations for Orchestra (1928)

Genre | Orchestral
Conductor/Performers | Herbert von
Karajan; Berlin Philharmonic Orchestra
Year recorded | 1973–74
Label | DG 457 760-2

Premiered by the Berlin Philharmonic under Furtwängler in December 1928, Schoenberg's Variations for Orchestra was received with almost total incomprehension. The first piece for full orchestra that Schoenberg composed according to the twelve-note method he had been developing since World War I, the work enshrines a new, lean orchestral sound of extraordinary refinement and clarity—the orchestra treated essentially as a large group of interdependent soloists.

The theme, and its nine variations, are framed between a large-scale and more free-ranging introduction and finale, which themselves extend the variation process. The mysteriously atmospheric introduction gradually brings the theme to birth out of a kind of amniotic sea of sound, a tidal ebb and flow of ostinato patterns, accumulating the twelve chromatic pitches. The theme itself, lyrical and meditative, is stated by the cellos; the ensuing variations seldom stray unrecognizably far from its contours, phrase-lengths, pitches, and rhythms. Wit, Viennese waltz-rhythms, and extraordinarily wide-ranging orchestration counterpoint the serious business of organic growth.

Herbert von Karajan's 1973–74 recordings with the Berlin Philharmonic created a new benchmark in the understanding of the Second Viennese School. Bringing a romantic sumptuousness and long-limbed expressiveness to even the spikiest twelve-note writing, these were interpretations seemingly devoid of all technical difficulties and tensions, getting to the music's beating heart, and the Variations for Orchestra—the warmest, most elegant of all recorded performances—was the biggest triumph. **MM**

Igor Stravinsky
Apollo (1928)

Genre | Ballet
Conductor/Performers | Simon Rattle;
City of Birmingham Symphony Orchestra
Year recorded | 1988
Label | EMI 0777 7 49636 2 6

Although Stravinsky's music had undergone something of a stylistic transformation early in the 1920s, it seemed that his preferences in terms of instrumental sound were clear. As someone who wrote at the piano, and for whom rhythm was such a vital element in his compositional armory, a marked predilection for winds and percussion was clear, the strings no longer being the orchestra foundation. The appearance, then, of Apollo, scored for "the multi-sonorous euphony of strings," can be seen as just as radical a departure as any that Stravinsky made in his long career.

Beginning work shortly after the premiere of Oedipus rex in May 1927, the "white ballet" of Apollo is also based upon Greek mythology. He wanted his music to reflect "the beauty of line in classical dancing," and the marvelously lithe quality of Simon Rattle's recording suggests that he may have been familiar with Georges Balanchine's brilliant choreographic realization of this ideal of balletic perfection. The CBSO strings are on peak form, outclassing several bigger-name orchestras. The score's nods toward Lully and Tchaikovsky's Serenade are apparent, but Rattle resists the temptation to wallow in the singing beauty, concentrating instead on the dancelike quality of each episode. The three swelling chords that mark the birth of Apollo seem to glow from within, while Rattle captures the essence of each variation in the central "Pas d'action," where the three muses (Calliope, Polyhymnia, and Terpsichore) present their wares to Apollo. Rattle's masterly account of The Rite of Spring steals the headlines on this disc, but this performance of Apollo is an even greater achievement and is one of his best recordings. **CD**

Kurt Weill
Das Berliner Requiem (1928)

Genre | Choral
Conductor | Philippe Herreweghe
Performers | Chapelle Royale Chorus
Year recorded | 1992
Label | Harmonia Mundi HMC 901422

Kurt Weill (1900–50) was born in Dessau and secured a scholarship to study in Berlin with the eminent post-Wagnerian composer Engelbert Humperdinck. After returning to his native town, he was lured back to the German capital, becoming a postgraduate composition student of Ferruccio Busoni. Weill's precocious talent was recognized at an early age, his one-act opera *Der Protagonist* attaining considerable acclaim after its first performance in Dresden in 1925. During this period, Weill composed in a brittle and sometimes atonal style, but a chance encounter with the writer Bertolt Brecht in 1927 altered his musical development in many fundamental ways, not least in the often ironic appropriation of popular and commercial idioms that were utilized to challenge the established order in Weimar Republic Germany.

The collaboration between Brecht and Weill, which lasted from 1927 until 1933, resulted in several pioneering works, of which *Das Berliner Requiem* is one of the most significant. Commissioned by the Frankfurt Radio Station to mark the tenth anniversary of the end of World War I, the work is scored for two solo voices, male voice chorus and a spartan instrumental ensemble, and sets five provocative poems by Brecht that are highly critical of Germany's war effort and its devastating impact on the population at large.

Philippe Herreweghe brings exactly the right degree of cool objectivity to this work. The Chapelle Royale Chorus responds with incisive singing, while the "Two Reports of the Unknown Soldier," in which Weill emulates the Bach of the Passions, is incredibly moving. **EL**

Kurt Weill
Die Dreigroschenoper (1928)

Genre | Opera
Conductor/Performers | H. K. Gruber;
Max Raabe, Nina Hagen, Sona McDonald
Year recorded | 1999
Label | RCA 74321 66133 2

Die Dreigroschenoper (*The Threepenny Opera*) was the most commercially successful work that Weill and the playwright Bertolt Brecht created during their six-year collaboration. Running for more than 350 performances over its first two seasons, it was soon adapted for the sound cinema and translated into numerous languages. Many of its most popular numbers, in particular "The Ballad of Mac the Knife," have become perennial favorites.

A modern adaptation of John Gay's eighteenth-century *The Beggar's Opera*, *Die Dreigroschenoper* was conceived primarily to challenge post-Romantic conventions of opera. Principal roles were taken by singing actors from the spoken theater, cabaret, and operetta rather than by opera singers, and through-composed music drama was replaced by separate numbers. The orchestral accompaniment, pared down to an ensemble of twenty-three instruments exploiting saxophone, trumpet, percussion, banjo, and guitar, appropriates idioms more commonly associated with popular music. The whole work is deeply ironic, the provocative social criticism of Brecht's text underlined by the acidic qualities of Weill's haunting melodies.

Based on the new critical edition of the score, H. K. Gruber's recording is definitive. Not only does the cast respect Weill's original intentions that the work should be sung by musically gifted performers rather than bellowed by aggressive actors, but they also manage this without any hint of self-consciousness. The instrumental accompaniment from the Ensemble Modern fizzes with exhilaration and exuberance, making this a very special performance indeed. **EL**

Arnold Bax | Symphony no. 3 (1929)

Genre | Orchestral
Conductor | Vernon Handley
Performers | BBC Philharmonic
Year recorded | 2002
Label | Chandos CHAN 10122(5) (5 CDs)

After his copious output of symphonic poems around the time of World War I, Arnold Bax (1883–1953) embarked on a series of seven symphonies that occupied him intermittently throughout the 1920s and 1930s. He was not a natural symphonist—but Celtic lyricism and dance-rhythms, a Russian-derived sense of orchestral color, a highly personal chromatic harmony and (latterly) the influence of Sibelius made for a potent mix. Bax saw his first three symphonies (1922–29) as forming a self-consistent trilogy, the storm and stress of nos. 1 and 2 being resolved in the more balanced and ultimately serene no. 3. It is certainly one of his most consistently successful works in any form, with a genuine sense of organic growth. Like all the other symphonies, it is in three movements. The first of these is by turns brooding and frenetic, while the central slow movement has an intense, visionary quality mingled with a sense of dreamlike landscape. The ebullient third movement combines the functions of scherzo and finale and is crowned by a long, deeply lyrical slow epilogue that manages to close proceedings with a sense of profound inner peace that is very rare for this composer.

Vernon Handley has been a lifelong champion of Bax, and his performance of Symphony no. 3, part of his superb set of the complete symphonies on Chandos, surpasses his modern rivals and even the historic first recording by John Barbirolli and the Hallé Orchestra. Chandos's recording admirably captures the opalescent half-lights and instrumental subtleties of the slow movement, and the BBC Philharmonic plays the finale as if possessed. Other Bax symphonies you should definitely hear are nos. 1, 2, 5 and 7—all can be found in Handley's set performed to a similarly high standard. **MM**

> *"My wisdom became pregnant on lonely mountains; Upon barren stones she brought forth her young."*
>
> Nietzsche, written by Bax on his sketch-score

Other Recommended Recordings

Hallé Orchestra • John Barbirolli • EMI 7 63910 2
Recorded in 1944, issued on 78rpm (but never on LP), this first-ever recording of a Bax symphony is legendarily good, though in mono sound

Royal Scottish National Orchestra
David Lloyd-Jones • Naxos 8.553608
More relaxed than Handley in the first movement, this budget-price account is a distinguished competitor

London Philharmonic Orchestra • Bryden Thomson
Chandos CHAN 8454
A good account but at somewhat lower temperature than the others

Arnold Bax, whose symphonies are seeing something of a renaissance. ➔

William Walton | Viola Concerto (1929, *rev.* 1937, 1961)

Genre | Concerto
Performer | Frederick Riddle (viola)
Conductor | William Walton
Year recorded | 1937
Label | Pearl GEM 0171

Walton's concertos were all written with a famous soloist in mind. With the Viola Concerto, the conductor Thomas Beecham suggested that the young composer write a piece for Lionel Tertis, the man who put the viola on the map as a solo instrument. Initially, Tertis did not like the work, finding "the innovations of its musical language . . . too far-fetched." He did change his mind and performed it many times, and it is now a staple of the repertoire.

It has been observed that Walton took Prokofiev's First Violin Concerto as a blueprint for his own composition, as many details of structure and instrumentation (from the soloist's first tremolo-accompanied phrase onward) demonstrate. The piece, with its echoes of Stravinsky, Ravel, Hindemith, and Gershwin, stands firmly in the mainstream of 1920s modernism. Unfortunately, performances have grown progressively slower in the course of time, thus somewhat blunting its mordant wit.

Walton, a fine conductor of his own music, led many performances of this piece, including three recordings, and accepted input from his soloists. The player in the first recording, Frederick Riddle, contributed many suggestions regarding the phrasing and articulation of the solo part. Walton wished these to be included in the printed music, but this happened only with the critical edition published in 2002. Walton revised the orchestral score in 1961, reducing the woodwinds and adding a part for a harp. The first recording still has strong claims, in spite of its sound quality. Under the composer's guidance, Riddle, who learned the piece in days after Tertis became unavailable, catches its wistful atmosphere to perfection. **CMS**

Frank Bridge | Oration (1930)

Genre | Concerto
Performer | Alban Gerhardt (cello)
Conductor | Richard Hickox
Year recorded | 2003
Label | Chandos CHAN 10188

For years Frank Bridge (1879–1941) was remembered chiefly as the teacher and mentor of the young Benjamin Britten. But he is now becoming recognized as a major creative figure in his own right. His career followed an unusual course. A pupil of Stanford and a highly professional violist and conductor, he rapidly acquired what Anthony Payne has called "a masterly technique, and a flair for tailoring his music both to the taste of his audience and the capabilities of his performers." But in the last two decades of his life, under the influence of the new music of mainland Europe, his musical language became tougher and more radical, and a good deal less immediately pleasing—opening the way to subsequent long neglect.

An example of this late development, and probably Bridge's greatest orchestral masterpiece, is *Oration*, a "concerto elegiaco" for cello and orchestra. A long-delayed expression of his response as a pacifist to the horrors of World War I, it is a single half-hour movement in a large arch shape, with the cellist as the declamatory orator suggested by the title. It is chiefly in march rhythms, sometimes funereal and sometimes bitterly sardonic. But it ends—apparently as an afterthought, and if so an inspired one—with a calm, gentle lullaby.

Richard Hickox has made a major contribution to the current Bridge revival through his Chandos series with the BBC National Orchestra of Wales. *Oration* comes on Volume 4, alongside the choral *A Prayer* written while the War was still going on, and the late overture *Rebus*. Alban Gerhardt is an impressive and eloquent soloist, and the performance does full justice to this magnificent work. **AB**

Albert Roussel
Symphony no. 3 (1930)

Genre | Orchestral
Conductor | Charles Munch
Performers | Lamoureux Orchestra
Year recorded | 1965
Label | Elatus 0927 46730-2

Igor Stravinsky
Symphony of Psalms (1930)

Genre | Choral
Conductor | Karel Ančerl
Performers | Prague Philharmonic Choir
Year recorded | 1966
Label | Supraphon SU 3674-2

Albert Roussel was in good company when Serge Koussevitzky asked him to write a piece for the fiftieth anniversary of the Boston Symphony Orchestra: the other commissions included Honegger's First Symphony, Prokofiev's Fourth, Hindemith's *Concert Music for Strings and Brass*, and Stravinsky's *Symphony of Psalms*. Koussevitzky, who had championed Roussel before, thought highly of the work, as did the composer, who said after the premiere, "As far as I can tell after this concert, it is the best thing I have done." It is the most popular of Roussel's four symphonies, and its success encouraged a renewal of interest in symphonic writing in France.

The opening of the first movement is full of excitement, with pounding rhythms under a syncopated string melody. This energy is contrasted with more lyrical music in a structure that does not waste a note. The whole symphony is concise in expression—using a motto theme to bind the music together. The slow movement begins with a variant of this theme that has a slight American accent, as if Roussel had been listening to Copland. The scherzo is light and dancing, while the final movement recaptures the muscular drive of the opening, and ends with the motto theme triumphant. It is all over in twenty-five minutes.

Munch was one of the first conductors to take up the piece, and his recording is superbly paced. He has the advantage of a French orchestra with a French sound, before internationalization made such things vanish. The brass has a bright vibrato, the tone of the winds is narrowly focused, and the strings are not too sweet, even when playing expressive lines. Exactly right for the symphony. **MC**

In 1925, an abscess on Stravinsky's finger "miraculously healed," reinvigorating his religious convictions in the process. The *Symphony of Psalms* was Stravinsky's first large-scale expression of this renewed faith. Each of the symphony's three movements sets a psalm, sung in the Latin of the Vulgate version of the bible. The movements become progressively longer: the first is a cry of despair to God, the second counsels patience, and the third exquisitely presents Psalm 150's paean of praise.

As with *Oedipus Rex*, Stravinsky's choice of a dead language imbues the work both with a universality of intent and a detachment from understanding. The music is deliberately archaic in feel, with the composer omitting the upper strings and the soft tones of the clarinets. The gestures are often simple, though never simplistic.

Stravinsky's customary economy of means is apparent from the first entry of the chorus, which sticks cautiously to just two notes. Alongside more glossy ensembles, Ančerl's forces, the Czech Philharmonic Orchestra and the Prague Philharmonic Choir, can seem rather crude. The thin oboe sound, especially in the opening of the second movement, is unsettling, but is perfect for the asceticism of these contrapuntal lines, and is matched by the open-throated, but not harsh, singing. When the chorus becomes the assuager with the heartfelt "Alleluia" that opens the final movement, the effect is profoundly moving, yet there is also the sense of the latent force that becomes the kinetic energy of the central section. It is the kind of slow-burning performance, in which any skepticism is swept aside, that made Ančerl such an exceptional conductor. **CD**

Maurice Ravel | Piano Concerto for the Left Hand (1930)

Genre | Concerto
Performers/Conductor | Samson François (piano), Société du Conservatoire Orchestra; André Cluytens
Year recorded | 1959
Label | EMI 7243 5 66957 2 6

Ravel wrote his Concerto for the Left Hand for Paul Wittgenstein, an Austrian pianist who had lost his right arm fighting in World War I. Perhaps because of Ravel's own experiences in the conflict—he spent most of 1916 driving military transport vehicles, often working perilously close to the front lines—Wittgenstein's commission evoked a powerful response.

The concerto begins with deep rumblings in the basses and a whalelike song by the contrabassoon. Much of what follows is hard-edged or bitterly ironic, including militaristic marches and bluesy, mock-Oriental dances. Yet there are moments when these brittle emotions are pushed aside, revealing a yearning vulnerability that one encounters only rarely in Ravel's music. The expansive cadenza near the concerto's end is particularly poignant. Running up and down the keyboard in vast arpeggios, the pianist painstakingly plucks out a tender tune. The sense of struggle—one hand imitating two—is palpable and only enhances the elusive character of the music, which is at once contemplative and rhapsodic.

Samson François understands this fragile dichotomy, and his is not only the darkest interpretation on CD but also the most emotionally devastating. From the opening burst of explosive chords, there is a ferocity to his playing that hits you right in the pit of your stomach. But, then, François was known for his volatility—and though this did not always work to his favor, interpretively speaking, his raw yet thoughtful expressivity is precisely what is required here. Aided by the edgily brilliant tone of the Paris-based orchestra under André Cluytens, this is the perfect foil for Arturo Benedetti Michelangeli's ultrarefined recording of the G major Concerto. **AFC**

> *" . . . it is essential to give the impression of a texture no thinner than that of a part written for two hands."*

Maurice Ravel, on his Piano Concerto for the Left Hand

Other Recommended Recordings

Leon Fleisher, Baltimore Symphony Orchestra
Sergiu Comissiona
Vanguard 1614
Fleisher brings grandeur as well as urgency to Ravel's concerto

Krystian Zimerman, London Symphony Orchestra
Pierre Boulez • DG 449 213-2
A poetic account notable for its clarity and color

Louis Lortie, London Symphony Orchestra
Rafael Frühbeck de Burgos
Chandos CHAN 8773
Lortie's darkly meditative interpretation yields

Kaikhosru Shapurji Sorabji | Opus clavicembalisticum (1930)

Genre | Instrumental
Instrument | Piano
Performer | Geoffrey Douglas Madge
Year recorded | 1983
Label | BIS CD-1062/1064 (5 CDs)

Though born of a Parsi father and a Spanish-Sicilian mother (who christened him Leon Dudley), Kaikhosru Shapurji Sorabji (1892–1988) exhibited an eccentricity that was indubitably English, though his remarkable gifts in florid, continually unfolding piano writing may indeed owe something to his Parsi origins. Sorabji was a pugnacious critic who admired Busoni, Szymanowski, Medtner, and other ultravirtuosic composers. He took their techniques to a ne plus ultra of textural complexity in his piano works—often of immense length and difficulty—unlike anything else in the piano repertoire. His *Opus clavicembalisticum* (*Work for Keyboard*) mingles strict music forms (chorale prelude, passacaglia, theme and variations, double, triple, and quadruple fugues) with free movements of ever-exfoliating fioriture, like vertiginous figurational cadenzas. At four hours, it is not his longest piano work. However, the *Opus* exercises an almost hypnotic power that tends—like Wagner's *Ring* cycle—to restructure the listener's sense of time.

Mediocre pianists do not touch Sorabji; the music is infinitely too demanding in terms of technique, intelligence, culture, and understanding. That does not automatically make it *great* music, but certainly it is a repertoire of its own to which only great pianists have the key. Only two pianists have essayed the complete *Opus clavicembalisticum* since the composer premiered it in 1930. John Ogdon's 1988 South Bank performance was complemented by a studio-recorded CD release by Altarus. Geoffrey Douglas Madge's recording is of a live performance in Chicago. It is long admired by Sorabji purists as it is possibly the most faithful rendering the Brobdingnagian work has ever been given. **MM**

"... the harmony bites like nitric acid, the counterpoint grinds like the mills of God."

Sorabji, on his *Opus clavicembalisticum*

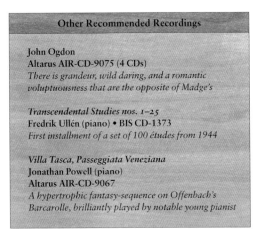

Other Recommended Recordings

John Ogdon
Altarus AIR-CD-9075 (4 CDs)
There is grandeur, wild daring, and a romantic voluptuousness that are the opposite of Madge's

Transcendental Studies nos. 1–25
Fredrik Ullén (piano) • BIS CD-1373
First installment of a set of 100 études from 1944

Villa Tasca, Passeggiata Veneziana
Jonathan Powell (piano)
Altarus AIR-CD-9067
A hypertrophic fantasy-sequence on Offenbach's Barcarolle, brilliantly played by notable young pianist

Ralph Vaughan Williams | Job (1930)

Genre | Ballet
Conductor | David Lloyd-Jones
Performers | English Northern Philharmonia
Year recorded | 1995
Label | Naxos 8.553955

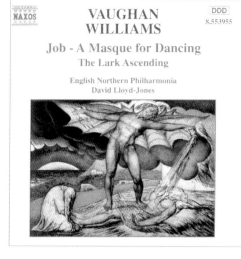

The lasting effect of his experiences in wartime France did not cause Vaughan Williams to abandon the richly lyrical pastoral style that had evolved over the previous fifteen years or so. Rather, it broadened his vocabulary significantly as he sought musical depictions that encompassed the darkest human emotions. Nowhere is this more evident than in *Job*, which Vaughan Williams described as a "masque for dancing." He wrote it in response to William Blake's twenty-one illustrations of the Book of Job. The ballet was intended for Diaghilev but was rejected for being "too English," perhaps referring to some of the composer's chosen dance forms such as the pavan and galliard.

The story tells how Job's faith in God is put to the test through the suffering he has to undergo at the hands of Satan. After an initial tableau introducing Job's comfortable family existence, Satan challenges God and is allowed to test Job. Following Satan's spiteful "Dance of Triumph," the seven sons and daughters of Job are killed. The protagonist then has a dream and sees plague, pestilence, famine, and battle in a vision before learning that his wealth is destroyed. He is then offered pretend sympathy in the "Dance of Job's Comforters" but eventually, God's blessing on Job assures the old man of happy final years as he has kept faith with his God.

David Lloyd-Jones leads the English Northern Philharmonia in a beautifully compelling performance. There is wonderful grace and lyricism in the gentler moments with the warmly rapturous quality of the full orchestra captured entirely convincingly by the fine engineering. The sudden tutti appearances of Satan are especially frightening as a sheer wall of sound bursts forth from the orchestra. **SW**

> *"It marks the emergence of English ballet, allowing it at a crucial moment to free itself from imitative influence."*
>
> Michael Kennedy

Other Recommended Recordings

London Philharmonic Orchestra
Vernon Handley
EMI 7243 5 75314 2 9
A distinguished account, gloriously alive and also very well recorded

BBC Symphony Orchestra • Andrew Davis
Warner 0927 444 394-2
Spacious live recording; the sixth scene's organ entry should make you jump out of your seat

London Symphony Orchestra • Adrian Boult
EMI 7243 5 73924 2 6
Compelling performance from the ballet's dedicatee

William Walton | Belshazzar's Feast (1931, *rev*. 1948, 1957)

Genre | Oratorio
Conductor/Performers | William Walton;
Denis Noble (baritone), Huddersfield Choral Society
Year recorded | 1943
Label | Pearl GEM 0171

In 1929, the young William Walton was commissioned by the BBC to write a new oratorio. He had already had much success with his poignant Viola Concerto, but the new work was to make a huge impact on the musical life of Great Britain. It took him two years to complete (having got stuck for seven months on setting the word "gold"), yet the score exudes all the fizzing imagination of a brilliant young composer. This is true of the vivid word-setting, the chromatically rich harmonic language and the dazzling orchestration. The words were drawn from biblical texts by Walton's friend Osbert Sitwell; the simple story begins with the lamentation of the Hebrews, captive in Babylon. The King, Belshazzar, orders a great feast to various idols—of Gold, Silver, Iron, and other materials—and demands that the sacred vessels from the Temple of Jerusalem be used. That evening, a mysterious hand appears and writes on the wall that Belshazzar has been judged. The King is slain that night and the oratorio ends with a chorus of great rejoicing from the Israelites.

The quality of this disc—transferred from gramophone 78s—is rather rough, with some distant placing of microphones and occasional lack of detail. Nevertheless this is a vintage performance, with the original, more percussive orchestration that Walton later revised, and well worth hearing. Walton himself conducts with remarkable vigor, drawing thrilling playing from the instrumentalists and very high quality of singing. The words communicate with great clarity and there is subtle gauging of sorrow and joy. Denis Noble is a superb soloist, also singing with real intelligibility and demonstrating convincingly the way that the composer intended the unaccompanied recitative to be sung. **SW**

> "*As you'll never hear the thing again, my boy, why not throw in a couple of brass bands?*"

Thomas Beecham, convinced the work would never succeed

Other Recommended Recordings

Bryn Terfel, BBC Singers, BBC Symphony Orchestra & Chorus • Andrew Davis
Warner 0927 44394-2
Glorious live recording from the Proms

Gwynne Howell, Bach Choir, Philharmonia Orchestra
David Willcocks
Chandos CHAN 8760
Lively rendition enhanced by Howell's warm tone

Bryn Terfel, Bournemouth Symphony Orchestra & Chorus • Andrew Litton
Decca 470 5082
Boisterous performance with a sense of grand spectacle

Igor Stravinsky | Violin Concerto (1931)

Genre | Concerto
Performers | Anne-Sophie Mutter, Philharmonia Orchestra
Conductor | Paul Sacher
Year recorded | 1988
Label | DG 477 5376

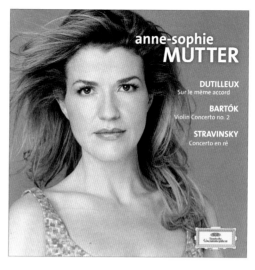

Igor Stravinsky was initially cautious over the idea of a violin concerto. The suggestion had come in 1930 from Willy Strecker of Schott, the music publisher that had just taken over the rights for some of Stravinsky's early music. Strecker was keen for the composer to write a piece for his friend, the violinist Samuel Dushkin, but Stravinsky initially demurred. After consulting Hindemith, though, he was reassured that, far from being a hindrance, his lack of firsthand knowledge of the instrument would be an asset "as it would make me avoid routine technique." This is borne out by the widespread chord that opens all four movements and was described as the "passport" to the Concerto. On being shown it in a restaurant by Stravinsky, it was Dushkin's turn to balk, telling the composer that the enormous stretch could not be played. On returning home, Dushkin found to his astonishment that the chord was indeed possible, and he telephoned Stravinsky at once.

Although nominally in the key of D major, the focus of the concertos by Beethoven, Brahms, and Tchaikovsky, the drama in Stravinsky's Concerto is not in a tussle between soloist and orchestra. The model of discourse here is closer to Bach, even if the musical idiom strains against harmonic niceties, and two "arias" replace the traditional slow movement. Dushkin was not a technical wizard, and the strength of Anne-Sophie Mutter's exceptional account is that she wears her virtuosity lightly. There is plenty of vim and vigor in the outer movements, but it is within the context of a genuine dialogue between soloist and various groupings within the orchestra. The lyricism of the second "Aria" is sublime rather than soupy, and the mischievous buoyancy of the final "Capriccio" is irresistible. **CD**

> ## "*I was not a complete novice in handling the violin.*"
> Igor Stravinsky

Other Recommended Recordings

Samuel Dushkin, Lamoureux Orchestra
Igor Stravinsky
Biddulph WHL 037
A valuable and absorbing performance

Lydia Mordkovitch, Suisse Romande Orchestra
Neeme Järvi
Chandos CHAN 6654(5) (5 CDs)
Vibrant and witty playing from Mordkovitch

Kyung-Wha Chung, London Symphony Orchestra
André Previn
Decca 425 0032
Chung and Previn have a spring in their step

Anne-Sophie Mutter has a special affinity with modern music. ➔

Maurice Ravel | Piano Concerto in G (1931)

Genre | Concerto
Performer | Arturo Benedetti Michelangeli
Conductor | Ettore Gracis
Year recorded | 1957
Label | EMI 7243 5 67258 2 9

GREAT RECORDINGS OF THE CENTURY

RAVEL
Piano Concerto in G
RACHMANINOV
Piano Concerto No. 4
Arturo Benedetti Michelangeli
Ettore Gracis
Philharmonia Orchestra

EMI CLASSICS

Even the greatest composers enjoy being self-deprecating at times, and Ravel was no exception. He admitted, for example, that he had seriously considered the idea of using the title "Divertissement" instead of "Concerto" for his Piano Concerto in G major. True, the concerto's outer movements are predominantly blithe and bubbly; note the use of the whip at the very beginning. But there is more than mere witty repartee here—there is mystery, tenderness, and drama. The Adagio assai, which sits at the concerto's heart, is not only the epitome of Gallic grace but also among the most sweetly melancholy and drop-dead gorgeous slow movements in the entire literature for piano and orchestra.

Ravel originally composed the concerto for his own use; he planned to perform it as part of a sweeping international tour in the late 1920s. Due to various interruptions and bouts of bad health, though, the score took far longer to complete than he had hoped. By the time it was ready, in 1931, his physical and mental health had deteriorated to the point where he no longer felt able to play it publicly. He conducted the orchestra at the premiere instead, with Marguerite Long at the piano.

Long later recorded the concerto under the composer's supervision. Her crisp, stylishly understated interpretation is invaluable, though Arturo Benedetti Michelangeli's legendary recording gets much closer to perfection. The Italian pianist's manner is relatively cool, but his technical control is simply astounding. In the first movement's cadenza, his trills flutter with exquisite evenness, and in the Adagio, his pearlescent tone reflects every curve and shadow of the elongated melodic line. Conductor Ettore Gracis elicits an equivalently sophisticated sound from London's Philharmonia Orchestra. **AFC**

"The music of a concerto should, in my opinion, be lighthearted and brilliant, and not aim at profundity."

Maurice Ravel

Other Recommended Recordings

Monique Haas, RTF National Orchestra • Paul Paray
DG 477 5353
A no-nonsense interpretation in the classic French style

Martha Argerich, London Symphony Orchestra
Claudio Abbado
DG 447 438-2
There is Latin fire in Argerich and Abbado's playful, passionate performance

Samson François, Paris Conservatoire Concerts
Society Orchestra • André Cluytens
EMI 7243 5 66957 2 6
François reveals subtle tensions in the music's core

Italian pianist Arturo Benedetti Michelangeli, pictured in 1959. ❯

Béla Bartók
Piano Concerto no. 2 (1931)

Genre | Concerto
Performers/Conductor | Maurizio Pollini (piano),
Chicago Symphony Orchestra; Claudio Abbado
Year recorded | 1977
Label | DG 477 6353

Edgard Varèse
Ionisation (1931)

Genre | Chamber
Conductor | Riccardo Chailly
Performers | Asko Ensemble
Year recorded | 1997
Label | Decca 460 208-2

Completed when Bartók was fifty, the Second Piano Concerto secured its first performance in Frankfurt am Main in early 1933 with the composer as soloist. Stylistically it occupies a fascinating position in the concerto repertoire. On the one hand, the formidable technical challenges of the solo piano part appear to match, and even exceed, the levels of virtuosity one might expect from a work by Liszt or one of his disciples. On the other, the musical material and orchestration suggest that the composer was responding in his own inimitable way to the contemporary zeitgeist of Neo-Classicism. This is particularly the case with the first movement, whose overall structure emulates that of the Baroque concerto grosso, the piano engaging in a kind of Bachian dialogue with an ensemble consisting exclusively of wind, brass, and percussion. The second movement presents a quite dramatic contrast in mood—an eerie chorale for strings framing a furtive Presto scherzo section, its twittering sounds reminiscent of the composer's famous piano piece *From the Diary of a Fly*. The sudden call to attention at the beginning of the finale comes as something of shock, all the more so as the musical argument becomes increasingly frantic and percussive.

Although the Second Piano Concerto has enjoyed the advocacy of pianists such as Sviatoslav Richter and John Ogdon, one of its most formidable exponents is Maurizio Pollini; his late 1970s recording with the Chicago Symphony Orchestra under Claudio Abbado projects the outer movements with energy and exhilaration yet conveys the aura of mystery for the central Adagio. **EL**

This tour de force for percussion alone is one of Varèse's most characteristic and influential utterances: one of those very rare pieces that have helped to change the way we perceive music itself. What distinguishes it from all previous examples of percussion music is the size and scope of the chosen ensemble (the thirteen players wield about forty instruments); the intricacy and complexity of its rhythms and colors; and the fact that the work is structurally as highly developed as Varèse's music for more orthodox instrumental lineups.

Throughout almost the entire piece we hear instruments of indeterminate pitch (plus two sirens, which Varèse uses to secure what he called "parabolas of sound"). Thus *Ionisation* seems to anticipate some of the effects of electronic music and renounces melody and harmony. Instead, rhythm and timbre are its patent concerns.

Two principal ideas—an opening penumbra of soft metallic sounds and the lonely wails of the sirens, then a kind of march-theme, associated with side-drum, bongos, and maracas—are developed throughout *Ionisation* with an evocativeness and a frequent violence that seem to suggest the poetry and alienation of a phantasmagorical modern city. In the final bars, the pitched instruments, together with the deepest gong, make their long-delayed appearance with an effect akin to revelation, bringing the work to an end in a solemn, bell-like tolling.

Riccardo Chailly's powerfully focused and superbly recorded reading brings out the fierce poetry and compulsive rhythmic dynamism of this extraordinary piece with unequaled clarity and focus. **MM**

Francis Poulenc | Concerto for Two Pianos (1932)

Genre | Concerto
Performers/Conductor | Katia and Marielle Labèque, Boston Symphony Orchestra; Seiji Ozawa
Year recorded | 1989
Label | Philips 426 284-2

Francis Poulenc Sextet (1932, *rev.* 1939)

Genre | Chamber
Performers | Nash Ensemble, Ian Brown (piano)
Year recorded | 1999
Label | Hyperion CDA 67255/6 (2 CDs)

Francis Poulenc's Concerto for Two Pianos, one of the composer's most enduringly popular pieces, was commissioned by the notable socialite and philanthropist Princess Edmond de Polignac, also known as Winnaretta Singer. It was given its premiere at the august-sounding International Society for Contemporary Music Festival in Venice on September 9, 1932, when Poulenc and his close friend, Jacques Février, played the solo parts, and the orchestra of La Scala, Milan, was conducted by Desire Defauw. By no stretch of the imagination can this twenty-minute essay be said to be a work of much profundity. Rather, the young composer seems free of care, willing and eager simply to impress and entertain (though in reality Poulenc was far from free of care—he suffered from bouts of severe depression). It makes its impact through the sheer brilliance of its writing, through a sense of innocent, effervescent joy in its own teeming inventiveness, and, not least, through good-natured parody—this is not satire—of everything from Romantic melodrama to music hall to Mozart (at the beginning of the central slow movement). Poulenc also relishes doing the unexpected, for instance at the end of the first movement, where he places an extended passage of atmospheric, almost nocturnal calm.

Such vivid music demands a large measure of flamboyance in performance, and it certainly gets that in the sizzling reading by sisters Katia and Marielle Labèque with the Boston Symphony Orchestra crisply conducted by Seiji Ozawa. A big sound they make, too, both here and in the fillers, other pieces for two pianos or piano duet by Poulenc, and Milhaud's ever-popular *Scaramouche*. **SP**

There are some listeners who just do not get Poulenc. It is not that the music is difficult to listen to. If anything, it can seem too easy, rattling along cheerfully or swooning sentimentally in an idiom seemingly borrowed from the Parisian music halls, sharpened by touches of Stravinsky. But there is enormous art in Poulenc's shaping of every phrase, and in the way he puts phrases and larger sections together to build up perfectly balanced mosaic structures. And his best pieces can end up saying something surprisingly profound about the human condition.

The best of Poulenc's chamber works is probably the Sextet for piano and wind quintet (flute, oboe, clarinet, horn, and bassoon). He certainly took enormous trouble over it: he missed its initial deadline of a 1931 concert, finished it only the following year, and revised it thoroughly at the end of the decade before finally giving it to his London publisher, Chester. Its textures are very detailed, with the piano expertly inlaid into the wind sonorities. And all three movements balance bubbling, quick music with episodes that are tender or even bleak—until the slow, solemn coda of the finale gives the whole work an unexpected breadth and depth.

The Nash Ensemble's performance of the Sextet comes at the start of its two-disc set of Poulenc's chamber music (complete bar a couple of larger ensemble pieces), and it immediately establishes the high quality of the enterprise. This is music making of great verve and subtle sensitivity, led from the piano by the superb Ian Brown. If you have been left cold by Poulenc up until now, this might just be the piece, and the performance, to win you over. **AB**

Richard Strauss
Arabella (1932)

Genre | Opera
Conductor/ Performers | Rudolf Kempe;
Lisa Della Casa, Hermann Uhde
Year recorded | 1953
Label | Testament SBT 21367 (2 CDs)

Looking for subjects for a new collaboration with Strauss after *Die ägyptische Helena* (1927), Hugo von Hofmannsthal concocted a scenario with elements from several older projects. The result was an intentionally improbable love story set in 1860s Vienna. Arabella is being courted by three counts but, hoping to find *der Richtige* ("Mr. Right"), keeps them at bay, even though the family's fortunes depend on her marrying a financially solid party. Mandryka, nephew of a friend of Arabella's father and incredibly rich, appears out of the blue and it is love at first sight. After a misunderstanding involving one of Arabella's former suitors is cleared, nothing stands in the way of a happy end in which Arabella's sister is also united with the man she secretly loves. Hofmannsthal died within days of delivering the draft libretto, and Strauss, out of respect for his memory, refrained from making any changes.

Arabella has similarities with *Der Rosenkavalier*—the Viennese setting, the prominent use of waltz tunes—which has hindered its acceptance. The opera's creators were conscious of this risk and took pains to minimize it. Another important element is the use of Balkan folk tunes to represent Mandryka and his courting of Arabella. The first performances were very successful. For Strauss's seventy-fifth birthday, a shortened production that ran the second and third acts together was presented in Munich.

Lisa Della Casa's portrait of Arabella is the most complete in the opera's history; of its several recorded incarnations, a souvenir from the Bavarian State Opera's 1953 visit to Covent Garden is further distinguished by Hermann Uhde's outstanding Mandryka. **CMS**

Igor Stravinsky
Duo Concertant (1932)

Genre | Chamber
Performers | Lydia Mordkovitch (violin),
Julian Milford (piano)
Year recorded | 1998
Label | Chandos CHAN 9756

After finishing his Violin Concerto in 1931, Stravinsky, always the most fastidious composer, felt that he wished to explore violin writing further, particularly in terms of chamber music. The acoustical contrasts of piano strings being struck by hammers and violin strings bowed or plucked fascinated him. He was also keen to write again for the fine violinist Samuel Dushkin—for whom the concerto had been written—and the result was the *Duo Concertant*. In this work, he aimed to recover qualities of lyricism, as defined by the bucolic poets of antiquity. This is shown especially clearly in the two *eclogues*, a Greek term denoting music of a pastoral nature; Stravinsky called them "Eglogues," and placed them at the heart of the work. There is such rhapsodic freedom of expression in this suite, however, that two of the other movements come from distinctly different musical worlds. Stravinsky opens with an impassioned "Cantilène"—juxtaposing two distinct thematic ideas—and the fourth movement, "Gigue," is a lively (if overlong) piece with the drive of an Italian tarantella. The final movement, "Dithyrambe," again recalls Ancient Greece: originally this was a poem to the god Dionysius. Here the language is beautifully introspective.

This recording has great freshness and intimacy. Lydia Mordkovitch's artistry has impassioned Russian spirit, with brooding intensity emerging in the darkest moments and conveying strong contrasts of character between the movements. Her fine pianist, Julian Milford, is equally subtle. His variety of tone emphasizes the delicate shades of nuance here, making the trickiest material sound fluid and utterly under control. **SW**

Arnold Schoenberg | Moses und Aron (1932; *unfinished*)

Genre | Opera
Conductor/Performers | Pierre Boulez; David Pittman-Jennings, Chris Merritt
Year recorded | 1996
Label | DG 449 174-2

Only Schoenberg, perhaps, could have wanted to write an opera about the incommunicability of the nature of God; and only he could succeed in turning it into a gripping existential drama, formally satisfying and emotionally draining. Founded on the biblical story of Moses leading the Israelites out of Egypt to the Promised Land, it is the longest and most ambitious work Schoenberg wrote according to the twelve-note method. Numerologically superstitious, Schoenberg called Moses's brother Aron, not Aaron, to avoid a title with thirteen letters.

Part philosophical debate, part biblical spectacle (the orgiastic dances around the golden calf are a high point of Schoenberg's orchestral wizardry), the opera dramatizes the struggle between appearance and reality in the conflict between the two main protagonists: Moses, whose part is throughout in unpitched *Sprechstimme* ("speech-song") to convey his painful inarticulacy, and his brother Aron, a supple, golden-voiced tenor, able to dazzle crowds, whom Moses must use to put his ideas across even though his eloquence cheapens the religious ideal.

No team attempts this daunting work without courage, artistry, and long preparation. Boulez is the only conductor to record it twice, and his radiant second account gets closer to the opera's heart. David Pittman-Jennings is an impressively tragic Moses, Chris Merritt a supple, vigorous Aron; Gabriele Fontana injects far more character than we normally hear in the small role of the Young Girl. The Royal Concertgebouw Orchestra plays as if possessed; the recorded sound is warm, bright, and fully equal to Schoenberg's vast coloristic gamut. **MM**

Dmitri Shostakovich | Lady Macbeth of Mtsensk (1932)

Genre | Opera
Conductor/Performer | Mstislav Rostropovich; Galina Vishnevskaya
Year recorded | 1978
Label | EMI 7243 5 67779 2 7 (2 CDs)

Even Shostakovich cannot have imagined the effect his opera *Lady Macbeth of Mtsensk* would have on his subsequent career. Early in 1936, Stalin came to see it at the Bolshoi; a couple of days later, an editorial in *Pravda* condemned the opera as "muddle instead of music" and Shostakovich's life would never be easy again.

It was indeed his most provocative work to date: a coruscating satire on nineteenth-century middle-class society, where the merchant's wife, Katerina Izmailova, is portrayed as the victim of a feeble husband, predatory father-in-law, and opportunist lover. Her murder of the first two eventually leads to her being shipped to Siberia, but on the way she commits suicide by leaping into a river. Based on Nikolai Leskov's novel of 1865, though recasting Katerina from cruel harridan to tragic antiheroine, the opera has obvious parallels with Ostrovsky's *The Storm*, the basis of Janáček's *Kátya Kabanová*. But Shostakovich's musical means are far more brazen than the Czech composer's: the sex scenes are as graphic as music will allow; all the men in the piece are portrayed musically as grotesques; and his treatment of authority figures, such as the chief of police and priest, is pure mockery.

He made an expurgated version—reentitled *Katerina Izmailova*—in the early 1960s, which at least won favor in the Soviet Union, but the 1932 original is well-established again and recognized as a masterpiece among twentieth-century operas. Rostropovich's recording greatly helped its revival, with his wife Galina Vishnevskaya giving an all-consuming portrayal of the title role along with Nicolai Gedda, Dimiter Petkov, and Werner Krenn. **MR**

Karol Szymanowski
Symphony no. 4 (1932)

Genre | Concerto
Performers/Conductor | Howard Shelley,
BBC Philharmonic; Vassily Sinaisky
Year recorded | 1995
Label | Chandos CHAN 9478

Szymanowski composed his Fourth Symphony in a matter of weeks in the spring of 1932, on his own admission in record time. Although billed as a symphony, it was effectively the fulfillment of a wish, made as early as 1912, to write a concerto for the piano. Nevertheless, the subtitle "Symphonie concertante" is remarkably suitable since the piano is often joined by other solo instruments, in particular the flute and violin.

The formal coherence that pervades the symphony is much enhanced by the clear tonal outlines that Szymanowski adopted. The melodic material is alternately athletic and lyrical, and at times has an unmistakably Neo-Classical cut. In the finale, which the composer described as "almost orgiastic," he identified the presence of two national dance types, the oberek and the mazurka.

The directness of its appeal and relative simplicity of the musical language accounted for huge public success at its premiere, in which Szymanowski himself played the solo part, and has ensured that it has remained one of his most popular works to this day. The same qualities, however, prompted those in Poland more inclined to the avant-garde, among them the thirty-year-old Witold Lutosławski, to take a more censorious view of the venerable composer's more approachable demeanor.

As one of Szymanowski's most frequently recorded works, the symphony is available in a number of recommendable performances. Howard Shelley's vigorous treatment of the solo part is captivating throughout. Just as important in a symphonic work is the handling of the orchestra, which Sinaisky manages in expert fashion. **JS**

Charles Tournemire
L'orgue mystique (1932)

Genre | Instrumental
Instrument | Organ
Performer | Georges Delvallée
Years recorded | 1995–99
Label | Accord 476 1059 (12 CDs)

As a body of music, L'orgue mystique—a cycle of fifty-one suites of organ music associated with the Roman Catholic Mass and covering the entire liturgical year—stands comparison with the complete organ works of J. S. Bach.

Charles Tournemire (1870–1939) was born in Bordeaux, securing his first organist's post there at the age of eleven; he later entered the Paris Conservatoire, studying with César Franck, whose lifelong disciple he became. Profoundly affected by Franck's death in 1890, Tournemire went on to take first prize in Widor's organ class, before beating off stiff opposition to become Franck's successor as titular organist of St. Clotilde, a post he retained for forty-one years until his death. Renowned as an improviser, Tournemire exerted a profound influence on European organist-composers of the twentieth century, including Duruflé, Messiaen, Peeters, Langlais, and Litaize.

Each "Office" is made up of five movements—Prelude for the Introit, Offertory, Elevation, and Communion; Tournemire might then conclude with a Fantasy, a Choral, a Rhapsody, or a Toccata. L'orgue mystique bears witness to an extraordinarily fertile musical imagination, the like of which France would not see again until Jehan Alain and Olivier Messiaen. Monumental to compose, and an Everest to record, L'orgue mystique found a champion in Georges Delvallée, the first organist to broadcast the cycle complete in francophone countries, and the first to commit it to disc. The recordings were made on Cavaillé-Coll organs such as St. Ouen de Rouen, St. Sernin de Toulouse, and St. Croix d'Orléans. Prodigal and incense-laden as it is, the music could hardly enjoy better advocacy. **GK**

Dmitri Shostakovich
Piano Concerto no. 1 (1933)

Genre | Concerto
Performers/Conductor | Martha
Argerich, Guy Touvron; Jörg Faerber
Year recorded | 1993
Label | DG 439 864-2

Kurt Weill | Die sieben
Todsünden (1933)

Genre | Vocal Ballet
Conductor | Herbert Kegel
Performer | Gisela May
Year recorded | 1966
Label | Berlin 0020692 BC

Shostakovich's First Piano Concerto—also known as his Concerto for Piano, Trumpet, and Strings—is considered to be the first notable example of the piano concerto to come out of Soviet Russia (Prokofiev's five are either pre-Revolution or date from his years in Paris). Shostakovich wrote it for himself to play, and a recording he made in 1958 is still available. The inclusion of a significant part for a solo trumpet was no doubt partly inspired by Alexander Schmidt, the much-admired principal trumpet of the Leningrad Philharmonic, and partly by the masterful piano and trumpet pairing in Stravinsky's *Petrushka*.

The first performance, given by Shostakovich, Schmidt, and the Leningrad Philharmonic strings, was praised by critics, who commented particularly on the lyricism of the score. Modern audiences are more struck by the work's dramatic extremes; the lyricism is combined with the slapstick of circus routines. In the finale, Shostakovich runs the gamut of humorous quotations from a Haydn piano sonata, a Beethoven rondo, and folksongs, alongside Prokofiev pastiche, culminating in what one commentator called "the Rossini-meets-Mickey-Mouse conclusion."

The performers on this recording, joined by the Württemberg Chamber Orchestra Heilbronn, must surely rank among the work's strongest advocates. Martha Argerich's consummate artistry allows her to shape and color every phrase, illuminating the work's lyricism, humor, and bravura. Touvron executes his first-movement arpeggios and brilliant fanfares in the finale with precision, while the expressive muted solo in the slow movement—fiendishly low in the trumpet's range—is suitably lyrical. **DC**

Within weeks of Hitler coming to power in Germany, Kurt Weill realized that he could no longer stay in his native country. He escaped by car over the border to France, hoping to be able to rebuild his career in Paris. One of the first commissions he accepted came from Les Ballets in 1933, a newly formed offshoot of the Ballets Russes directed by the choreographer George Balanchine. For this work, Weill temporarily resumed collaboration with Bertolt Brecht with whom he devised the scenario for a ballet with songs entitled *The Seven Deadly Sins of the Bourgeoisie*. The work was first performed to somewhat mixed acclaim in Paris in June 1933 and in the following month in London.

The ballet traces the story of Anna, a young girl sent out into the world to earn money in order to build her family a house in Mississippi. Anna is represented by two people: Anna I, the singer projecting the realistic and pragmatic aspects of her character, and Anna II, the dancer who remains an idealist, and whose moral doubts are eventually overcome by Anna I. Each scene is set in a different American city, with Anna II attempting to avoid the seven deadly sins before returning home with sufficient money to accomplish her initial objective.

Of the many recordings of this haunting score, the mid-1950s performance with the Leipzig Radio Symphony Orchestra featuring Lotte Lenya, singing the role of Anna I in the world premiere, has obvious historical interest. However, for a version that follows the Lenya tradition yet offers a better recording and a clearer delineation of the orchestral part, I would undoubtedly opt for Gisela May's compelling and charismatic interpretation. **EL**

Zoltán Kodály
Dances of Galánta (1933)

Genre | Orchestral
Conductor | Antál Dorati
Performers | Philharmonia Hungarica
Year recorded | 1973
Label | Decca 443 006-2 (2 CDs)

Kodály was commissioned to write the *Dances of Galánta* for the eightieth anniversary of the foundation of the Budapest Philharmonic Orchestra. Together with the *Háry János* suite, it remains one of the most popular of his orchestral compositions and, like the earlier and less well-known *Dances of Marosszék* (1929), reflects his lifelong desire to transfer the harmonic, rhythmic, and melodic elements of Hungarian folk music into the concert hall.

Scored for a modestly sized orchestra that is notable for the absence of lower brass, the *Dances of Galánta* was inspired by some of the gypsy orchestral music Kodály heard in his boyhood town of Galánta, between Vienna and Budapest. All the melodies that the composer used were in fact drawn from volumes of Hungarian dances that were first published in Vienna in about 1800.

The work is structured in the form of the traditional *verbunkos*—literally a Hungarian military recruiting dance in several sections that alternates slow and fast tempi. The haunting melody announced by the cellos at the opening acts as an effective bridge passage between several dances that feature brilliant quasi-improvisatory passages for the solo flute, oboe, and clarinet and become successively more animated toward the conclusion.

As one of Kodály's most distinguished composition pupils, the conductor Antál Dorati really has this music in his bones, and inspires the Philharmonia Hungarica to deliver a totally idiomatic performance that exudes plenty of seductive warmth and charm in the more lyrical sections of the score, but finds plenty of room for an extra dose of paprika in the work's final pages. **EL**

Karol Szymanowski
Violin Concerto no. 2 (1933)

Genre | Concerto
Performers/Conductor | Roman Lasocki, Polish State Philharmonic; Karol Stryja
Year recorded | 1989
Label | Naxos 8.553685

Completed four years before Szymanowski died, his Second Violin Concerto suggests no diminution in creative energy. Although it is quite different from his first with its Impressionist coloring, there is a connection with the earlier work in that he again collaborated with his lifelong violinist friend Paweł Kochański on the solo part, and once again Kochański provided the cadenza that lies at the heart of the work. Another strong point of similarity with the earlier concerto is that it is cast in a single movement in which two large spans frame the central cadenza.

As in many of the works of Szymanowski's last compositional phase, the melodic material of the concerto is touched by his enthusiasm for the native music of the Polish mountains surrounding his retreat at Zakopane. It includes a certain amount of modality—also a notable feature of Kochański's cadenza—and pedal writing, although this never amounts to explicit quotation. The first part of the concerto seems at times rather inward-looking, but this does not prevent Szymanowski, who at all times keeps a very tight grip on the motivic development, building a powerful and extrovert climax leading up to the soloist's cadenza. The folk accent is more pronounced at the start of the second main section, and the conclusion is rich in virtuoso opportunities for the solo violin.

Roman Lasocki and Karol Stryja show every sign of a deep understanding of Szymanowski's late musical language: neither is seduced into triviality in his treatment of the folk elements. Balance between soloist and orchestra is exemplary and a strong command of pace ensures that the two major climaxes have full force. **JS**

Edward Elgar | Symphony no. 3 (1934, *compl. Payne* 1997)

Genre | Orchestral
Conductor/Performers | Paul Daniel;
Bournemouth Symphony Orchestra
Year recorded | 1999
Label | Naxos 8.554719

Dmitri Shostakovich Cello Sonata (1934)

Genre | Chamber
Performers | Steven Isserlis (cello),
Olli Mustonen (piano)
Year recorded | 1996
Label | RCA 09026 68437 2

Received opinion can be a deadly legacy. For decades after Elgar's death in 1934, the same verdict was repeated over the sketches for his Third, and last, Symphony—the material was uninspired, repetitive, or it was mostly a reworking of old ideas, a tired old man vainly trying to recapture his former powers. Composer Anthony Payne was sure this was wrong, and the very least you can say for his extraordinary creative "elaboration" of Elgar's sketches is that it shows that Elgar's genius was on the ascent again. Partly inspired by his feelings for an intelligent and musical younger woman, Elgar had embarked on another major symphonic journey, taking in perhaps his most impressive and moving confrontation with death in the slow third movement. Payne's biggest problem was that Elgar left no clue as to the symphony's ending, but, during a sleepless night in an American hotel, the idea struck him to model it on Elgar's late miniature "The Wagon Passes" from the *Nursery Suite*. The result is a highly original conclusion.

There have been several fine versions of "Elgar-Payne," but Paul Daniel's is perhaps the most roundly convincing. The fast music has something of the impetuous "flying" quality that comes across in Elgar's own recordings, but in the gentler music there is an exquisite tenderness—the first movement's contrasting second melody is after all a "love theme." Best of all is the slow movement, for which the word "great" hardly seems inappropriate. But Daniel clearly sees the work as a whole—a single statement, even if it is the product of two minds. Listening to this performance, it is hard to believe that Elgar Three has not been in the repertoire for at least half a century. **SJ**

Shostakovich's Cello Sonata was written for his friend, the cellist Viktor Kubatsky, two years before the composer was officially censored for his opera *Lady Macbeth of Mtsensk*. The work begins conventionally enough, Classical in structure with spacious scoring and a long-limbed lyrical opening over lilting arpeggios. But the opening song is immediately disturbed by a peppering of notes that do not belong. Veering between the romantic minor and cheerful major, we begin to feel slightly queasy. The gloriously limpid second subject, which arches up heavenward and resolves on a major chord, seems to settle the question but is immediately undermined by the military rat-a-tat-tat that dominates the development. The starkly beautiful coda, which should be played with a dead sound, seems to set the seal on the truth of the work, and prefigures the dark, still tragedy of the Largo.

In between comes a savage scherzo, which tears away at a repeated figure before bumping into a comedy nursery tune and zooming into the stratosphere with high cello harmonics. The final movement is ironically comic, as Ian MacDonald has written: "a one-fingered rondo melody, idiotically pleased with itself, parades up and down between interludes of deranged academic exercises . . . ."

The work has a very particular taste: it is exquisitely written, but something at its heart has gone sour. It is not technically difficult, but it presents a puzzle that only the greatest artists can solve. Steven Isserlis and Olli Mustonen combine savage humor with romantic abandon in a reading that captures something of the diamond-bright hardness of Shostakovich's own performance. **HW**

Sergei Prokofiev
Lieutenant Kijé Suite (1934)

Genre | Orchestral
Conductor | Claudio Abbado
Performers | Chicago Symphony Orchestra
Year recorded | 1977
Label | DG 447 419-2

Lieutenant Kijé was Prokofiev's first commission to provide music for the new sound cinema in 1933. The success of the *Kijé* movie, composed at a time when he had one foot in the new Soviet Union and the other in Western Europe, where Paris was still his home, was one of the reasons why he eventually decided to return to Russia in 1936. Based on a satirical tale by Yuri Tynyanov, Alexander Faintsimmer's movie focuses, if that is the right word, on a soldier who has to be artificially created to avert Tsar Paul's displeasure. The nonexistent lieutenant is exiled to Siberia, brought back to St. Petersburg, promoted to colonel, married off in a hilarious wedding scene where a crown is held above his invisible head, and finally buried in an empty coffin.

Prokofiev's job was to provide simple illustrative music with a flavor of the early eighteenth century, the period in which the movie is set. Two of the movements, the "Romance" and the "Troika," are songs in the original, but for the suite Prokofiev provided orchestral alternatives as well as solos for baritone and orchestra, and it is in the instrumental form that the numbers, especially the celebrated "Sleigh Ride," have become best known. The wedding celebration is an especially jaunty inspiration, and the lively opening, with its military jingles, resurfaces in a slightly nightmarish mêlée before Kijé is buried to a traditional salute played on the cornet.

The more lurid the performance the better, and Claudio Abbado draws razor-sharp solos and riotous ensembles from the Chicago Symphony Orchestra. This is music that seems simple but is difficult to bring off successfully, and Abbado catches exactly the right tone. **DN**

> ## "*[Lieutenant Kijé] tells how a non-existent man becomes an existent one . . .*"

Dmitri Shostakovich

Other Recommended Recordings

St. Petersburg Philharmonic Orchestra
Yuri Temirkanov
RCA 82876 62319 2
Atmospheric account from Kijé's home city

Berlin Philharmonic Orchestra • Seiji Ozawa
DG 463 761-2 (7 CDs)
A chance to hear the Kijé vocal numbers in their original form, sung by Andreas Schmidt

West German Radio Orchestra Cologne
Mikhail Jurowski
CPO 65831
Boris Statsenko poetically delivers the two numbers

Sergei Rachmaninov
Rhapsody on a Theme of Paganini (1934)

Genre | Concerto
Performers | Stephen Hough, Dallas Symphony Orchestra
Conductor | Andrew Litton
Year recorded | 2003
Label | Hyperion CDA 67501/2 (2 CDs)

When Rachmaninov left Russia in 1917—moving to the United States in 1918—he stopped composing and concentrated on his career as a pianist. While his next work, the Fourth Piano Concerto (1926), met with a mixed reception, his final work for piano and orchestra—the *Rhapsody on a Theme of Paganini* of 1934—was an immediate and lasting success. Here, Rachmaninov avoided the outmoded emotionalism of his natural style by composing a work where he was able to step back from his usual manner and assume a variety of roles, from lyrical effusion to elegant wit.

Paganini's theme, from his Caprices for solo violin, op. 1, had already inspired Liszt and Brahms, and was later famously used by Andrew Lloyd Webber. Rachmaninov's twenty-four variations on it also interweave the plainchant of the *Dies irae*—a recurring motif in his music. Such is the thrilling inventiveness of this piece, it seems that Rachmaninov felt liberated by being able to compose in a range of styles, including his old-fashioned lyrical richness as illustrated by the famous eighteenth variation.

Stephen Hough's studio recording of the *Rhapsody* is a highlight of his set of otherwise live recordings of Rachmaninov's complete concertos. In his hands the music is lean and fast, yet never skittish. Hough's ravishing tone is seductive, and his vivid range of pianistic color gives this music an energizing sense of vitality and variety. Whether in darkly brooding sonorities (as in Variation 17), perfectly judged aching rubato (Variation 18), or sparkling rhythmic fizz (Variations 19 onward), Hough is both meticulously controlled and electrifyingly spontaneous. **TLP**

> *"Music is enough for a lifetime, but a lifetime is not enough for music."*

Sergei Rachmaninov

Other Recommended Recordings

Earl Wild, Royal Philharmonic Orchestra
Jascha Horenstein
Chandos CHAN 6605
Earl Wild's full-blooded performance oozes panache

Julius Katchen, London Philharmonic Orchestra
Adrian Boult
Decca 460 834-2
Katchen's account is big-boned and exhilarating

William Kapell, Dallas Symphony Orchestra
Antal Doráti
RCA 68992 2
A 1951 recording renowned for its demonic brilliance

Paul Hindemith | Mathis der Maler Symphony (1934)

Genre | Orchestral
Conductor | Claudio Abbado
Performers | Berlin Philharmonic Orchestra
Year recorded | 1995
Label | DG 447 389-2

In 1933 Hindemith (1895–1963) began work on an opera based around the life of the famous sixteenth-century painter Matthias Grünewald, who had, for a time, defied his religious patrons and taken cause with the peasants during the Thirty Years War. Grünewald's experiences exposed the dilemma as to whether an artist should place their creative output over and above their political conscience—a theme that had obvious contemporary relevance given Hitler's recent rise to power. Fully aware of the potentially controversial nature of this work, Hindemith nonetheless hoped to win over the new regime, and in preparation for a planned staging, first produced a symphony whose material is drawn from the opera.

Initially this strategy appeared to work because the symphony, whose three movements depict scenes from Grünewald's famous Isenheim altarpiece, was performed with some success in Berlin during March 1934, and elsewhere. However, his fortunes were to change drastically as a result of a Nazi-organized campaign of vilification against the composer. At a political rally in December 1934, Hindemith was publicly attacked by Joseph Goebbels. He became persona non grata in his native country, leaving Germany for Switzerland in 1938.

The warm, expressive tonal language of the *Mathis der Maler Symphony* marks a turning point in Hindemith's development away from the more abrasive style that he had pursued prior to the Nazi era. Highly accessible and direct in its expression, the work has enjoyed many fine recordings over the years from a host of world-famous conductors. Of the currently available versions, the Berlin Philharmonic under Claudio Abbado on DG offers particularly intense and opulent playing. **EL**

> *"There are only two things worth aiming for, good music and a clean conscience."*

Paul Hindemith

Other Recommended Recordings

Symphonic Dances, Ragtime (Well-Tempered),
Pittsburgh Symphony • BBC Philharmonic
Yan Pascal Tortelier • Chandos CHAN 9530
Includes two of Hindemith's finest orchestral works

Kammermusik nos. 1–7
Royal Concertgebouw Orchestra • Riccardo Chailly
Decca 473 722-2 (2 CDs)
Hindemith's iconoclastic music from the 1920s

Violin Concerto, Cello Concerto • André Gertler, Paul
Tortelier, Czech Phiharmonic Orchestra • Karel Ančerl
Supraphon SU 3690-2
Two of the composer's most expressive concertos

Paul Hindemith, a major figure in German music between the wars. ➔

Ralph Vaughan Williams | Symphony no. 4 (1934)

Genre | Orchestral
Conductor | Richard Hickox
Performers | London Symphony Orchestra
Year recorded | 2001
Label | Chandos CHAN 9984

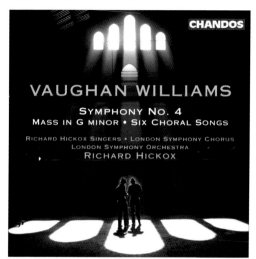

Although writers have exaggerated the impact of the unexpected musical language Vaughan Williams used for his Fourth Symphony of 1935, it certainly breaks out in a new direction compared with his other symphonies. In no previous work had the composer exposed so unremitting an outpouring of violent anger, and for the first time there is no hint of a program; each of the three previous symphonies had a subtitle affirming their extra-musical stimuli. Elements of this more brutal vocabulary were present in the music of Satan from *Job*, "a masque for dancing," which he had been working on from 1927 to 1930, though the ballet score also has extended periods of warm lyricism. Vaughan Williams had never before written so tightly knit a symphonic work; two small motifs heard at the start dominate the entire piece. This more obsessive language, as well as the structure of the symphony, owes something to the Fifth Symphony of Beethoven; in this sense Vaughan Williams is at his most Classical here.

The opening movement is in sonata form, contrasting the menacing, biting dissonances of the opening with disjointed and unsettled secondary themes. The morose Andante offers no relief from the F minor chromatic writing and the following third movement is a startling scherzo that dashes across the orchestra in energetic devilry. A lengthy pedal note links this up with the boisterous finale that whips up into a fugal epilogue, developing to extremes the two motifs that govern the whole work.

Richard Hickox brings the red heat of the composer's inspiration to the surface in his thrusting and, at times, frightening account. The LSO is on superb form, driving the intensity of the work forward with spine-tingling playing, and never allowing the tension to relent. **SW**

"I don't know whether I like it, but it's what I meant."

Vaughan Williams, on his Fourth Symphony

Other Recommended Recordings

London Philharmonic Orchestra • Bernard Haitink
EMI 7243 5 67221 1 5
Impassioned, energetic, and muscular version,
with a highly driven opening movement

NBC Symphony Orchestra • Leopold Stokowski
Cala CACD 0528
A vivid radio broadcast performance
(even if it is in mono) from 1943

Bournemouth Symphony Orchestra • Paul Daniel
Naxos 8.557276
Fine playing capturing the disturbing darkness
of the piece

Sergei Prokofiev | Romeo and Juliet (1935)

Genre | Ballet
Conductor | Valery Gergiev
Performers | Kirov Orchestra
Year recorded | 1990
Label | Philips 464 726-2 (2 CDs)

Kirov Orchestra,
St Petersburg
VALERY GERGIEV

By the time he came to compose his richest and most popular ballet score, Prokofiev had plenty of experience writing ballets for Sergei Diaghilev. But a full-length score for the Soviet stage, first discussed in 1934, was something altogether different. He knew it had to be relatively traditional, and the good news was that classic subjects were still permitted in Stalin's Russia. With the theater director Sergei Radlov, Prokofiev worked on a detailed scenario drawn from Shakespeare's drama of star-crossed lovers, composing everything rapidly during the Bolshoi Theater's summer retreat in Polenovo in 1935. Due to various complications, both political and artistic, *Romeo and Juliet* was not performed until 1938, in Czechoslovakia, but the 1940 Leningrad premiere was a triumph.

Prokofiev's score is a masterly summing-up of his multifaceted musical personality. There is violence and angularity in music for the Montagues and Capulets, moonstruck romanticism for Romeo and Juliet, and a host of deft characterizations for the other figures in the drama, from Romeo's friend Mercutio and Juliet's nurse to the dignified Friar Laurence. The ballet itself is perhaps best known now in Kenneth Macmillan's choreography, seen in a British television documentary where English schoolchildren collaborated with Royal Ballet dancers.

The score is most often heard in one or more of the three orchestral suites that Prokofiev extracted from the ballet, reordering and sometimes reorchestrating the original. But the full version has an overwhelming impact comparable to Wagnerian music drama. No one tells the whole story better than Valery Gergiev and the Kirov Orchestra, who have vindicated the music's ability to stand alone in full-length concert performance. **DN**

> *"His music lives for me, it is the very soul of the dance."*
>
> Galina Ulanova, creator of the role of Juliet

Other Recommended Recordings

London Symphony Orchestra • André Previn
EMI 7243 5 86254 2 4 (2 CDs)
Lush, expansive treatment of the lovers' music

Suites
Cincinnati Symphony Orchestra • Paavo Järvi
Telarc CD-80597
All three suites in focused performances

Highlights
Berlin Philharmonic Orchestra • Claudio Abbado
DG 453 439-2
Abbado makes his own glittering, generous selection combining the suites and the ballet

Alban Berg | Lulu (1935, *compl. Cehra* 1975)

Genre | Opera
Conductor/Performers | Pierre Boulez; Teresa Stratas,
Yvonne Minton, Franz Mazura, Kenneth Riegel
Year recorded | 1979
Label | DG 476 2524 (3 CDs)

Three years after the first performance of *Wozzeck* in 1925, Berg began work on his second opera, *Lulu*. The libretto—tracing the rise and fall of the dancer and femme fatale who seduces a string of men and attracts a lesbian admirer, Countess Geschwitz, but ultimately meets her demise at the hands of Jack the Ripper—was adapted by the composer from two of Frank Wedekind's plays, *Erdgeist* and *Die Büchse der Pandora*, a production of the latter having exercised a profound impact on the composer as long ago as 1905. A meticulous and slow worker, Berg made steady progress on the opera, and by 1935, the year of his death, had completed the first 360 measures of orchestration of Act 3, Scene 1, leaving the rest in short score.

The opera was first staged in an incomplete form in Zürich in 1937 and continued to be heard in this way for the next forty years, Berg's widow having refused any attempt to complete the orchestration after Schoenberg had turned down her invitation to undertake this task. After her death in 1976, however, the Austrian composer Friedrich Cerha orchestrated the third act and the complete score was first performed in Paris in 1979.

It was fortunate that DG's engineers were on hand to record this epoch-making premiere, for despite a few technical flaws that are an inevitable consequence of a live performance, Pierre Boulez draws impressive clarity and precision of texture from the Paris Opera Orchestra but still manages to preserve the Mahlerian glow of Berg's orchestration. The cast is also impressive; Teresa Stratas is an alluring and sensual Lulu, while Yvonne Minton delivers an impassioned and moving portrayal of Countess Geschwitz. Both are ably supported by Franz Mazura as Dr. Schön and Kenneth Riegel as Alwa. **EL**

> *"When I decided to write an opera, my only intentions were to give the theater what belongs to the theater."*
>
> Alban Berg

Other Recommended Recordings

English National Opera Orchestra • Paul Daniel
Chandos CHAN 3130 (3 CDs)
No-holds-barred performance sung in English

Lulu Suite, Lyric Suite, Fragments from Wozzeck
Alessandra Marc (soprano), Dresden Staatskapelle
Warner Elatus 0927 49009-2
Powerful performance of Berg's 1934 opera extracts

Chamber Concerto
Pinchas Zuckerman (violin), Daniel Barenboim
(piano), Ensemble InterContemporain • Pierre Boulez
DG 447 405-2
Definitive account of Berg's 1920s masterpiece

Pierre Boulez, who premiered the completed Lulu in 1979. ➔

William Walton | Symphony no. 1 (1935)

Genre | Orchestral
Conductor | André Previn
Performers | London Symphony Orchestra
Year recorded | 1966
Label | RCA 74321 92575 2 (2 CDs)

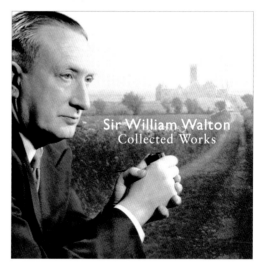

There was a lot hanging on Walton's First Symphony. After flirting with the avant-garde in *Façade*, he had moved progressively closer to the mainstream with the *Portsmouth Point* overture, the Viola Concerto, and the oratorio *Belshazzar's Feast*. A symphony was the obvious next step, not least as a challenge to Elgar and Vaughan Williams of the older generation. Walton began composing one in 1931, but in a rather desultory fashion, and he missed several deadlines. He eventually halted altogether in 1934 after finishing the first three movements, which he allowed to be performed on their own. They are a powerful, urgent opening Allegro, a spiky scherzo marked "with malice," and a "melancholy" slow movement with an intense climax. The following year he added a finale, part fugue and part processional. The first complete performance caused a sensation rare in British musical history.

Can you hear the join? The finale is thematically linked to the earlier movements, but it can all too easily sound as if it is at a lower voltage. One friend of the composer said, "The trouble was that Willie changed girlfriends between movements." And it is true that the affair that had initially fired the symphony—and that Walton later recalled as involving "jealousy and hatred all mixed up with love"—ended in 1933, to be supplanted by a more easygoing liaison. But it is one of the great merits of André Previn's classic 1966 account (now in a bargain twin-pack with all Walton's concertos) that he does not allow you to notice the join. After a first movement that maintains a scorching intensity throughout, a biting scherzo, and a passionate slow movement, there is a finale that never loosens its grip for a moment—not cop-out, but culmination. **AB**

> *"It is simply colossal, grand, original, and moving to the emotions to the most extreme degree."*
>
> John Ireland

Other Recommended Recordings

London Symphony Orchestra • Colin Davis
LSO Live LSO 0076
Superbly conducted and played: best buy with modern sound quality

English Northern Philharmonia • Paul Daniel
Naxos 8.553180
Recommendable bargain version despite the resonant acoustic

New Zealand Symphony Orchestra • William Walton
Bridge 9133 A/B (2 CDs)
Only recording currently available of the composer himself conducting the symphony, from a 1964 tour

William Walton, pictured in 1965. ➡

Alban Berg
Violin Concerto (1935)

Genre | Concerto
Performers/Conductor | Henryk Szeryng,
Bavarian Radio Symphony; Rafael Kubelík
Year recorded | 1968
Label | Eloquence 469 606-2

During the last year of his life, Berg interrupted work on the opera *Lulu* in order to fulfill a commission from the American virtuoso Louis Krasner to write a Violin Concerto. Initially his motive for undertaking this task was purely financial, since he was now suffering a considerable loss in performance revenues, particularly after the Nazis had come to power. But the sudden and unexpected death from poliomyelitis of Manon Gropius, the eighteen-year-old daughter of Alma Mahler-Werfel, acted as a further spur, inspiring him to complete the work in an uncharacteristically short period of time, and also to dedicate it to her memory. Unfortunately Berg was to die himself from a blood infection only a few months after he had finished the score. It was first performed as a tribute to Berg by Krasner in Barcelona, on April 19, 1936.

Whether or not Berg was aware that the Violin Concerto would be his own swan song, there is little doubt that the music inhabits a shifting world of turbulence, nostalgia, and resignation. The moods are intensified and to a certain extent resolved in the work's closing section by the introduction of a set of variations on the Bach chorale *Es ist genug* (*It is enough*), as well as the moving recall of a tender Carinthian folk tune initially heard at the end of the first movement.

Among the many recordings of this wonderful score, the version featuring Rafael Kubelík and the violin of Henryk Szeryng is exceptional. Although the recording does not allow for as much clarity from the orchestral part as some more recent releases, Szeryng's projection of the solo part is simply spellbinding. **EL**

George Gershwin
Porgy and Bess (1935)

Genre | Opera
Conductor/Performers | Simon Rattle;
Willard White, Cynthia Haymon
Year recorded | 1988
Label | EMI 7243 4 76832 2 0 (3 CDs)

Porgy and Bess is Gershwin's masterpiece, and a great American opera; despite attempts over the years to turn it into a musical, an opera it truly is. The text, skillfully adapted from DuBose Heyward's novel *Porgy*, is set continuously in through-composed, imaginatively orchestrated, musically coherent scenes. And the music rivals any other operatic score in its vivid delineation of character: the whole Catfish Row community on the South Carolina seaboard, and individuals such as the murderous Crown, his woman Bess, the cripple Porgy with whom she sets up an unlikely household, and the drug dealer Sportin' Life, who tempts her away to New York. The only reasons for questioning the work's operatic status are its idiom, full of jazz and blues and spirituals, and the fact that some of the main numbers are recognizably "Gershwin songs," to the extent that they have become "standards" for cabaret and jazz performers. But that is just snobbery, isn't it? Gershwin himself was not slow to point out that "nearly all of Verdi's operas contain what are known as 'song hits.'" Gershwin had enough confidence in his score to publish it before the first night. He then had to trim it for the Broadway production, with numerous cuts and some second thoughts.

John Mauceri's spirited Nashville recording presents this "original 1935 production version," and fascinating it is, too. But there is no evidence that Gershwin preferred the cut version, and for the historic 1986 Glyndebourne production and the subsequent recording Simon Rattle used the published score, uncut. His inspired conducting, with a starry cast and a lively chorus (all black, as the Gershwin estate insists), fully justifies the decision. **AB**

Sergei Prokofiev
Violin Concerto no. 2 (1935)

Genre | Concerto
Performer | Leonid Kogan
Conductor | Basil Cameron
Year recorded | 1955
Label | Testament SBT1224

Samuel Barber
Adagio for Strings (1936)

Genre | Orchestral
Conductor | Thomas Schippers
Performers | New York Philharmonic
Year recorded | 1965
Label | Sony SK 94739

Unquestionably Prokofiev's return to the Soviet Union in the 1930s coincided with a softening and universalizing of his style. But the idea put about by some writers that he temporized artistically with the regime will not wash. His reengagement with his native Russia took place over about three years, before he finally took the plunge; and his greatest score, *Romeo and Juliet*, was the first major fruit. Another from roughly the same time was the Second Violin Concerto, material for which had been maturing in his mind—and in sketches—for some time.

The kick needed to complete it came from French admirers of the violinist Robert Soetans, who wanted to commission a concerto for him. He duly gave the premiere in Madrid in December 1935, and other violinists took it up—notably Jascha Heifetz, who made the first recording. The piece is overwhelmingly lyrical, with a moderately paced opening movement, a memorable slow movement, and a brilliant finale with much good humor.

Those buying David Oistrakh's recommended First Concerto also get a humane account of the Second, but just as the D major belongs to Oistrakh, the G minor is "owned" by his colleague Leonid Kogan. No one else has penetrated so deeply into this lovely work, while at the same time playing with the most transcendent virtuosity. Kogan was one of the elect few who could make a simple legato line tug at the heart, by fiercely concentrating on spiritual values. His Russian recording of a few months later with Kirill Kondrashin is perhaps even better as a performance, but the sound on this British one has such depth and definition, it could almost be stereo. **TP**

Samuel Barber (1910–81) was born in West Chester, Pennsylvania. His aunt was the great American contralto Louise Homer, and before Barber became known as a composer, he, too, distinguished himself as a singer. Perhaps it is this combination of his lineage and performing experience that gave him a special understanding of the human voice. Indeed, even though Barber first made his mark in the realm of instrumental music, there is a singing quality in all his music, including the Adagio for Strings.

The Adagio was originally conceived as the slow movement for his String Quartet of 1936. Barber immediately recognized something extraordinary in the music, and described it to a friend as "a knockout." He was right. Arturo Toscanini added an arrangement of the Adagio to his repertoire, performing it first in New York as part of a radio broadcast that was heard across the entire United States; soon after, he took it on tour to England and South America. Everywhere it was played, the music struck a deep chord. Its intense, elegiac character and noble eloquence has made Barber's Adagio the natural accompaniment for moments of public mourning; it was heard at the funerals of Albert Einstein, John F. Kennedy, and Princess Grace of Monaco, among others.

The most heartfelt—yet still dignified—recorded account remains that of Barber's friend Thomas Schippers. This talented American maestro, who died in 1977 while still in his forties, was most at home in the opera house. Here he inspires the string players of the New York Philharmonic to sing from the depths of their souls. The CD also includes the original string quartet version. **AFC**

Carl Orff | Carmina burana (1936)

Genre | Choral
Conductor/Performers | André Previn; Sheila Armstrong
(soprano), Gerald English (tenor), Thomas Allen (baritone)
Year recorded | 1974
Label | EMI 7243 5 66951 2 2

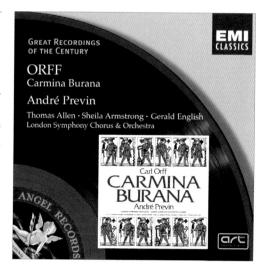

GREAT RECORDINGS
OF THE CENTURY

EMI
CLASSICS

ORFF
Carmina Burana

André Previn

Thomas Allen · Sheila Armstrong · Gerald English
London Symphony Chorus & Orchestra

Carl Orff (1895–1982) studied at the Munich Academy of Music just before World War I, but soon repudiated its conservative training through an early infatuation with the music of Debussy and Schoenberg. In the 1920s, he began to immerse himself in the works of Monteverdi and other seventeenth-century masters, and founded a school where he developed his pioneering educational ideas that tried to synthesize gesture, poetry, and music. These preoccupations, together with his growing fascination for aspects of Classical antiquity, shaped his musical development, and by the 1930s he had determined to focus on the sphere of music theater. Indeed, his best-known composition, *Carmina burana*, was originally conceived for the stage, though nowadays it is most frequently encountered in the concert hall.

The text for *Carmina burana* is drawn from the collection of sometimes bawdy twelfth-century Latin and German poems written by the monks of Benediktbeuern. Orff divides these into three sections dealing with nature, the tavern, and love, and the work is framed by an imposing opening and concluding chorus in praise of Fortune, the goddess of fate, that has frequently been misappropriated for the purposes of advertising.

The simple, direct musical language of *Carmina burana*, mixing Stravinskian rhythmic exuberance with passages of romantic warmth and opulence, exerted instant appeal at its first performance in Frankfurt. In an extremely competitive field, the mid-1970s recording featuring a stellar cast of soloists, the dynamic and incisive direction of André Previn, and the London Symphony Orchestra & Chorus is especially notable, projecting an unabashed enjoyment of the music. **EL**

"Everything I have written to date can be destroyed. With Carmina burana *my collected works begin."*

Carl Orff writing to his publishers, Schott

Other Recommended Recordings

Deutsche Oper Berlin Chorus & Orchestra
Eugen Jochum
DG 447 437-2
Performance officially endorsed by the composer

Pavel Kühn Choir, Prague Symphony Orchestra
Gaetano Delogu
Supraphon SU 3576-2
Eastern European exhilaration: a different perspective

Shin-Yu Kai Choir, Berlin Philharmonic Orchestra
Seiji Ozawa
Philips 464 725-2
Brilliant and dynamic account

Carl Orff, pictured composing in 1939. ➔

Sergei Prokofiev
Peter and the Wolf (1936)

Genre | Orchestral
Conductor | Claudio Abbado
Performer | Sting (narrator)
Year recorded | 1990
Label | DG 429 396-2

From one of the classics in twentieth-century ballet, *Romeo and Juliet*, Prokofiev next turned to a musical story for children, for narrator and orchestra, that itself would become a much-loved part of the repertoire—*Peter and the Wolf*. He supposedly put together the whole half-hour piece—creating the outline story, narration, and music—during two weeks in April 1936. Written for a children's theater company in Moscow, it was intended to be both entertainment and educational, to tell a story and to introduce children to the instruments of the orchestra. The young boy, Peter, is represented by the orchestral strings, the bird by a flute, the duck by an oboe, the cat by a clarinet, the grandfather by a bassoon, the wolf by the horns, and the huntsmen by the timpani. Each character also has its own musical theme, tailored to its instrument and presented and developed in the manner of Wagnerian leitmotifs. The story itself tells of how Peter, in defiance of his grandfather's instructions, sneaks out of his garden just as a wolf emerges from the forest; the wolf swallows the family duck before Peter manages—with the bird's help—to put a noose around its tail. Just in time the huntsmen arrive and to a grand, marchlike presentation of Peter's theme, everyone goes to the zoo with the captured wolf.

The story has been recorded by a wide range of well-known figures, from Ralph Richardson to Patrick Stewart, from David Bowie to Dame Edna Everage—and that is just the English-language versions. Accompanied by a delightfully fresh account of the score from the Chamber Orchestra of Europe under Claudio Abbado, the rock star Sting delivers a most lively rendering of the story. **MR**

Olivier Messiaen
Poèmes pour Mi (1936)

Genre | Vocal
Performers | Ingrid Kappelle (soprano),
Håkon Austbø (piano)
Year recorded | 2004
Label | Brilliant 7448 (2 CDs)

In a century dominated by cynicism and in which abstraction has at times become a sacred cow, the irrepressible optimism with which Olivier Messiaen expressed his religious convictions, allied to his faith in music's ability to portray, can only be described as remarkable. His colorful harmonic approach, rhythmic innovations, and rich melodic vein can be heard right from his earliest works. Messiaen's songs are probably the least well-known area of his output, yet, in many ways, they are the most remarkable. All three great cycles, *Poèmes pour Mi* (1936), *Chants de terre et de ciel* (1938), and *Harawi* (1945), were inspired by his passionate love for his first wife, Claire Delbos. The first, *Poèmes pour Mi* (Mi was Messiaen's pet name for Delbos), expresses the joy of the couple's marriage, placed, typically for the composer, within the context of his faith. Often surreal imagery is matched by music that largely ignores the niceties of a song recital.

The first performances of each cycle were given by Marcelle Bunlet, a reputed Wagnerian who was Messiaen's preferred vocalist (she can be heard in a live, poorly recorded account of *Harawi*). Ingrid Kappelle comes closest of modern singers to matching Messiaen's ideal. She has a full-bodied, powerful voice, while her ability to convey the quietest hush is extraordinary. Her ace, though, is Håkon Austbø. He has recorded all of Messiaen's solo piano music, an experience reflected throughout in terms of touch, color, and tempo. Although Kappelle's pronunciation is occasionally quirky, she is much more rounded than other singers and is never mundane. This set also has the bonus of some rarely heard pieces. **CD**

Sergei Rachmaninov
Symphony no. 3 (1936)

Genre | Orchestral
Conductor | Mariss Jansons
Performers | St. Petersburg Philharmonic
Year recorded | 1992
Label | EMI 7243 5 62810 2 8

Anton Webern
Variations, op. 27 (1936)

Genre | Instrumental
Instrument | Piano
Performer | Maurizio Pollini
Year recorded | 1976
Label | DG 447 431-2

After Rachmaninov left Russia in 1917, he virtually stopped composing for almost a decade. The revival began slowly with the Fourth Piano Concerto and the *Paganini Rhapsody*, followed in the mid-1930s by the Third Symphony. By this time Rachmaninov's distinctly Tchaikovskian late Romanticism had fallen out of fashion, and the symphony was dismissed by most "serious" critics. Now we can see it more clearly for the truly original work it is. Deeply nostalgic on one level (the slow movement's opening horn and harp solo is in Rachmaninov's most exquisite Russian pastoral vein), the symphony also shows how much Rachmaninov learned from his adopted U.S. home: from the brilliance of American orchestras, from Gershwin, and even from the subversive rhythmic energy of jazz. The great tunesmith is also fully reborn, especially in the first movement's long-breathed second theme. Yet the final impression is of a complex work, with secrets buried in the furtive middle section of the Adagio, and lingering anxiety behind the finale's apparently abandoned dancing.

Mariss Jansons balances the extrovert and reflective sides of Rachmaninov's temperament beautifully. He can be openhearted without being in the least schmaltzy, wild and controlled at the same time, and keep tight formal control without inhibiting the symphony's more fantastical flights. He has a way of shaping Rachmaninov's melodies so that they take flight, but also of presenting tiny phrases within the long arching lines so that they catch the ear, too. The St. Petersburg Philharmonic brings Russian edge and intensity, but also a brilliance and polish rare in Russian orchestras in the Soviet era. **SJ**

Unlike his teacher Schoenberg, Webern wrote very few piano pieces, the Variations remaining his only acknowledged mature work for the instrument. In some respects, the title may appear somewhat misleading since, on initial hearing, the Variations seem not to have been prefaced by some kind of identifiable theme. Webern once referred to the work as a sort of three-movement suite.

Further acquaintance confirms the degree to which variation principles remain germane to the music's structure. In the first movement, Webern exploits the expressive potential of two- or three-note phrases that are passed between the right and left hands in an unbroken sequence that seems to defy any notion of a regular rhythmic pulse. There is a brief and dynamic scherzo where a single melodic line, also divided between the hands, is occasionally punctuated by overlapping notes and chords. The final and longest movement seems closest to conventional variation form with clearly delineated sections ruminating on the idea presented at the outset.

The most convincing performance of Webern's Variations is arguably one that is absolutely faithful to the directions in the score. Maurizio Pollini, of course, follows this principle impeccably, but in the process manages to find much more. He gently caresses the answering phrases of the first movement with a Debussy-like tonal sensibility. The ensuing scherzo is delivered with considerable wit and rhythmic verve, while Pollini reserves his most intense and concentrated playing for the final movement. Altogether Pollini triumphantly negates the suggestion that Webern's Variations is calculated and forbidding. **EL**

Béla Bartók
Music for Strings, Percussion, and Celesta (1936)

Genre | Orchestral
Conductor | Fritz Reiner
Performers | Chicago Symphony Orchestra
Year recorded | 1958
Label | RCA 82876 61390 2

The *Music for Strings, Percussion, and Celesta* is the first of three commissions Bartók secured from the enlightened Swiss conductor and philanthropist Paul Sacher; the others are the Sonata for Two Pianos and Percussion (1937) and the Divertimento for String Orchestra (1939). Premiered with considerable success by the Basel Chamber Orchestra under Sacher in January 1937, it parallels such contemporary works as the Fifth String Quartet in effecting an ideal balance between a strongly defined emotional character and a rigorous control of structure and thematic ideas; the notes of the haunting fugue subject at the opening generate the material for the entire four-movement composition. This rigor can also be discerned in the very precise performance directions presented in the score and in the idiosyncratic seating disposition of the instruments, with the strings divided into two equal sections to the right and left of the conductor, and the tuned timpani, cymbals, side and bass drum, celesta, xylophone, piano, and harp in the center. Bartók uses these forces with incredible virtuosity and aural imagination throughout the work.

Few conductors manage to convey the same degree of interpretative subtlety in this work as Bartók's great compatriot Fritz Reiner. Just listen to the way in which Reiner shapes the opening fugue subject, managing to persuade the violas to project a sense of desolation as well as restlessness. Marvel also at the punch and power of the Chicago Symphony Orchestra strings in the ensuing movement, the emotional temperature reaching boiling point at several moments in the score. **EL**

> *"His being breathed light and brightness: his eyes burned with a noble fire."*

Paul Sacher on Bartók

Other Recommended Recordings

Berlin Radio Symphony Orchestra • Ferenc Fricsay
DG 447 443-2
Fricsay's fine account presents the music in a more lyrical manner

Chicago Symphony Orchestra • Georg Solti
Decca 475 7711
Typically feisty interpretation from the Hungarian maestro

Chicago Symphony Orchestra • Pierre Boulez
DG 447 747-2
Boulez's razor-sharp control of rhythm and texture is second to none

Fritz Reiner, who enjoyed a golden age with the Chicago Symphony. ➔

Dmitri Shostakovich | Symphony no. 4 (1936)

Genre | Orchestral
Conductor | Kirill Kondrashin
Performers | Moscow Philharmonic Orchestra
Year recorded | 1962
Label | Melodiya MEL CD 10 01065 (11 CDs)

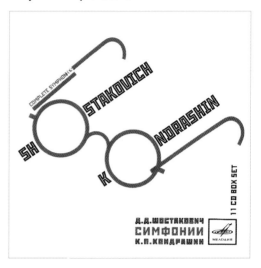

Shostakovich's Fourth Symphony occupies a unique place in his output, not least because it tells us what kind of composer he might have become without the weight of official "guidance." It was during its composition that Stalin famously attended a performance of *Lady Macbeth of Mtsensk*, prompting a savage attack on the opera in a *Pravda* editorial. The inference was clear: no longer were composers at liberty to take risks in their work.

While Shostakovich made no stylistic compromises with the work in hand, its planned first performance by the Leningrad Philharmonic did not take place. A two-piano reduction was published in 1946, but it was not until December 30, 1961 that Kirill Kondrashin conducted the reconstructed full score in Moscow. Shostakovich chose not to revise the Fourth, declaring that it was in many respects better than his recent symphonies, a reaction widely shared by musicians and commentators at the time and since. Its rehabilitation was very much Kondrashin's project and it is no surprise that his recording should have held its place at the top of the pile.

Coursing through the notes with the urgency and panache for which he was renowned, Kondrashin may not explore surreal byways with the Zenlike patience of a conductor like Gennady Rozhdestvensky, whose recordings are sadly unobtainable at present, but you certainly feel that he knows where the bodies are buried. Its three movements present Shostakovich at his most Mahlerian, seeking to embrace the world. And what a world it is. Is it Mahler, or the incipient Great Terror, that stalks the coda of the finale? At the very least, Shostakovich's Fourth succeeds in confronting us with a world seriously out of joint. **DG**

> *". . . the Fourth so prolific with ideas, with a tumultuous exuberance amounting at times to wildness . . ."*

Benjamin Britten in a Shostakovich birthday tribute

Other Recommended Recordings

Dresden Staatskapelle • Kirill Kondrashin
Profil 06023
Radio relay of the work's East German premiere

City of Birmingham Symphony Orchestra
Simon Rattle
EMI 7243 5 55476 2 0
Thrilling example of what a relatively objective, thoroughly "modern" approach can reveal

Kirov Orchestra • Valery Gergiev
Philips 470 842-2
Gergiev captures the savage, nightmarish ferocity of the piece, with a few of his personalized touches

Franz Schmidt | Das Buch mit sieben Siegeln (1937)

Genre | Oratorio
Conductor/Performers | Nikolaus Harnoncourt; Dorothea
Röschmann, Kurt Streit, Herbert Tachezi, Wiener Singverein
Year recorded | 2000
Label | Teldec 8573 81040-2 (2 CDs)

Franz Schmidt (1874–1939) was born in Pressburg, now
Bratislava, and was an instrumentalist and conductor
before he took up composition. In fact, he was a pianist
of such accomplishment that, when his hard up family
moved to Vienna in 1888, he was able to earn a living
playing for dance classes. At the Vienna Conservatoire,
he was briefly a pupil of Bruckner, and later taught
composition, piano, and cello there. Although he was
dogged by poor health, he also headed the Vienna
Conservatoire after it was renamed the Hochschule. He
then enjoyed a short retirement, before his death.

His musical style is a typical late-Romantic one—
Herbert von Karajan refused to conduct *Das Buch mit
sieben Siegeln* (*The Book of the Seven Seals*) on those
grounds: strange for an exponent of Richard Strauss.
Brahms is firmly in the background, and there are hints
of Liszt, Bruckner, and Reger. Schmidt was also a friend of
Schoenberg, but did not follow that particular Modernist
path. He was principally known as a symphonist during
his lifetime, and for his works that include left-hand piano,
written for the one-armed pianist Paul Wittgenstein. *Das
Buch mit sieben Siegeln* is an apocalyptic oratorio, based
on the Book of Revelation, and has always been in the
repertoire of Austrian choral societies.

Nikolaus Harnoncourt seems an unlikely conductor for
this work, but this recording, taken from live performances
with the Vienna Philharmonic Orchestra, captures the full
drama of the oratorio, with Kurt Streit bringing lyricism to
the taxing narrative part of St. John, and Herbert Tachezi
excelling in the organ part with its important solos. Above
all, Harnoncourt marshals his forces with the discipline
needed for the work to make its full impact. **MC**

> "[*Schmidt*] *was . . .
> composing a work that
> reflects what it is to live
> on the edge of a volcano.*"
>
> Nikolaus Harnoncourt

Other Recommended Recordings

Bavarian Radio Symphony Orchestra & Chorus
Franz Welser-Möst
EMI 72435 85782 2 5 (2 CDs)
Mid-price alternative, with Stig Fogh Andersen

Symphony no. 4
Vienna Philharmonic Orchestra • Zubin Mehta
Decca 440 615-2 (2 CDs)
Recording that returned Schmidt to the mainstream

Piano Quintet in G major
Jörg Demus, Barylli Quartet
Preiser 90598
A left-hand piano work, played with Viennese warmth

Benjamin Britten
Variations on a Theme of Frank Bridge (1937)

Genre | Orchestral
Conductor | Benjamin Britten
Performers | English Chamber Orchestra
Year recorded | 1966
Label | Decca 475 6051 (7 CDs)

The young Benjamin Britten (1913–76) was very fortunate to have composition lessons from an early age with the professional composer Frank Bridge, and Britten's fondness and respect for Bridge was lifelong. *Variations on a Theme of Frank Bridge* is one of the younger composer's earliest published works, a touching act of homage to his former teacher. It was commissioned at very short notice in May 1937 to be performed at the Salzburg Festival in August of that year. Britten sketched the work astonishingly quickly—in ten days—exploiting the resources of the strings with unprecedented invention and boldness.

The theme Britten chose was taken from Bridge's *Idyll no. 2* for string quartet, written in 1906. In all, it goes through ten transformations, exploring a great variety of string techniques and textures with many a nod to European musical manners alongside British ones; from his earliest published works, Britten was keen to demonstrate that his compositions were international, not just national, in outlook. So, for example, variation six is a witty Viennese waltz, teasingly playing with this occasionally saccharine form, no doubt to raise a smile in the Austrian audience. Before this, the composer writes an "Aria italiana," merrily invoking the spirit of Rossini, and then a French "Bourée classique." More seriously, the eighth variation is a profound funeral march showing a heartfelt appreciation of Mahler.

Britten's own recording is really first-rate. He captures the contrasts of character between the movements with judicious insight, making the lighthearted moments sparkle with knowing wit and drawing great richness of sound from the ECO strings in the darker moments. **SW**

"It remains one of the landmarks of string orchestral writing . . ."

Boyd Neel, who conducted the first performance

Other Recommended Recordings

Northern Sinfonia • Richard Hickox
ASV Resonance CD RSN 3042
Great, glowing acoustic adds sympathetic warmth to this emotionally all-embracing performance

English Chamber Orchestra • Steuart Bedford
Naxos 8.557200
Wonderfully recorded version coupled with the Prelude and Fugue for Eighteen-Part String Orchestra

BBC Symphony Orchestra • Andrew Davis
Apex 8573 89082-2
Well-judged rendition with sensitive responses from the players; such a wistful "Romance"

Benjamin Britten, pictured in the 1960s, owed much to Frank Bridge. ➔

Dmitri Shostakovich
Symphony no. 5 (1937)

Genre | Orchestral
Conductor/Performers | André Previn;
London Symphony Orchestra
Year recorded | 1965
Label | RCA 82876 55493 2

From its very first performances, given at the height of Stalin's Great Terror, Shostakovich's D minor Symphony has seldom failed to move an audience. Tagged "a Soviet artist's practical creative reply to just criticism," it is at once the most popular and the most mysterious of twentieth-century symphonies, its precise intentions hotly debated by commentators. Everyone agrees that the Fifth was a make-or-break work for the composer, the first piece in which he squares the circle, writing music of obvious integrity and frank emotional appeal, at the same time effectively remaking himself as composer laureate of a totalitarian regime. An astonishing achievement in context, but then Shostakovich had few options left after Stalin walked out of a performance of the composer's opera *Lady Macbeth of Mtsensk*. While the Fifth might still be read as the progress of an intellectual from a state of individualistic error to a nirvana of self-transcendent solidarity with the masses, that is not what it means to us today.

Many exponents come at the work with entrenched political extra-musical opinions which, consciously or not, they seek to dramatize through the notes. One recording that seems not to do so is this plainspoken account that helped establish André Previn's reputation as a "serious" musician. Some might find his music making a little soft-grained, yet the Largo is as intensely committed as any, its dark progress perfectly sustained at an exceptionally slow tempo. True, the LSO does not sound like a Soviet orchestra, and the finale bolts joyously for home as it usually did in pre-*Testimony* days, but this remains an extraordinary document of a very special musical partnership. **DG**

Richard Strauss
Daphne (1937)

Genre | Opera
Conductor/Performers | Karl Böhm;
Hilde Güden, Fritz Wunderlich, James King
Year recorded | 1964
Label | DG 445 322-2 (2 CDs)

Like *Salome* and *Elektra*, *Daphne* is a continuous stretch of music of almost two hours' length, with a vocally murderous title role, but the similarities end there. For all its symbolic opposition of Apollonian and Dionysiac principles, *Daphne* is a much lighter work, with few of the orchestral outbursts that characterize the older pieces.

Daphne, daughter of Mother Earth and the river god Peneios, is a nature child, who cannot identify with the shepherds' profane joys and stays away from their Midsummer feast. She feels vaguely attracted to a stranger (Apollo in disguise), provoking the jealousy of her childhood friend Leukippos, who defies Apollo and is killed by him. The god regrets having abused his power, and begs Jove to transform Daphne into a laurel tree, in order to have her always with him (a laurel crown being one of Apollo's attributes).

Strauss reflects the piece's bucolic atmosphere in his prominent use of woodwind instruments. The title role has been instrumentally conceived, having to compete with the woodwinds on equal terms, to unforgettable effect in the scene of Daphne's transformation, in which the human voice gradually metamorphoses into instrumental sound.

The score of *Daphne* carries a dedication to "my friend Dr. Karl Böhm", and it is precisely Böhm who conducts a recording that, in spite of small cuts, is uniquely authoritative. Taken live from the Theater an der Wien in Strauss's centenary year, it preserves the breathtakingly virtuosic Daphne of Hilde Güden and a classic pairing of Fritz Wunderlich in the lyric tenor role of Leukippos and James King as the heroic tenor Apollo. **CMS**

Dag Wirén
Serenade for Strings (1937)

Genre | Orchestral
Conductor | Richard Studt
Performers | Bournemouth Sinfonietta
Year recorded | 1994
Label | Naxos 8.553106

The music of Swedish composer Dag Wirén (1905–86) evolved from a fairly comfortable synthesis of Classical and Romantic influences to a much sparser style that did not so much amount to proto-minimalism as a kind of cold-shower severity. However, as was to be the case with the Polish composer Henryk Górecki many years later, Wirén's international popularity was largely derived from a single work, the Serenade for Strings, originally composed for the Stockholm Chamber Orchestra.

Unlike the case of Górecki's Third Symphony, however, Wirén's serenade was typical of his output, at least during the first, more conservative phase of his career. Having studied at the conservatoire in Stockholm under Ernst Ellberg until 1931, Wirén's early preference for tried and tested compositional techniques owed much to his teacher, but other influences included Bach, Mozart, Nielsen, Stravinsky, Honegger, Prokofiev, and, inevitably, Sibelius, whose ideas about orchestration have penetrated much of the music of Scandinavia.

The serenade is a tuneful, approachable piece, and has long since crossed over into light music (notably the final movement, a cheerily rustic march). The only way to give a proper account of such music is to enter completely into the spirit of the composition, treating its airy melodies and just-so cadences as if they were entirely new inventions to be performed with the kind of commitment normally reserved for grand symphonic themes. Richard Studt's recording does exactly that, which is the best possible recommendation, with the serenade and the other works on the disc providing the ideal context for each other. **RT**

Francis Poulenc
Organ Concerto (1938)

Genre | Concerto
Performer | Maurice Duruflé
Conductor | Georges Prêtre
Year recorded | 1961
Label | EMI 7243 5 62649 2 2

The instigator of Poulenc's Concerto in G minor for Organ, Strings and Timpani was the Princesse de Polignac (the sewing machine heiress Winnaretta Singer); she maintained a vigorous salon, notable for being furnished with a Cavaillé-Coll organ and two grand pianos. The organ concerto was originally offered to Jean Françaix, but he was too busy and the project fell to Poulenc.

Poulenc began work on the concerto in 1936, writing to Claude Rostand: "It gave me a lot of trouble . . . It isn't the pleasant Poulenc on his way to the cloister, a fifteenth-century Poulenc, if you will." Notwithstanding, the declamatory opening theme recalls a model from the early eighteenth century: Bach's G minor Organ Fantasia. Indeed, the concerto's seven continuous movements resemble an extended Baroque fantasy, encompassing contrasting tempi and moods—from the grandiose and profound, to the febrile and skittish. The work stands out in Poulenc's catalogue of compositions, and is without equal in the concerto repertoire for organ and orchestra.

The organist-composer Maurice Duruflé advised Poulenc on specifying the organ's registrations (tone colors) for the concerto. This 1961 EMI recording, made in the presence of the composer, is still regarded as definitive—one of the great recordings of the twentieth century. The rhythmic vigor of Duruflé's playing is matched by the pungency of St. Étienne-du-Mont's Cavaillé-Coll organ—a visceral sourness that in truth comes from moments when the organ is exposed as not perfectly in tune. However, this drawback may be safely ignored in the face of Duruflé's towering performance. **GK**

Béla Bartók | Violin Concerto no. 2 (1938)

Genre | Concerto
Performers/Conductor | Yehudi Menuhin (violin),
Minneapolis Symphony Orchestra; Antal Doráti
Year recorded | 1957
Label | Mercury 475 6255 (5 CDs)

Bartók's Second Violin Concerto was commissioned by the Hungarian violinist Zoltán Székely, who gave the first performance of the work with the Amsterdam Concertgebouw Orchestra under Willem Mengelberg in 1939. Given Bartók's vast experience in writing orchestral music, which included a First Violin Concerto completed some thirty years earlier, though never performed in his lifetime, it is somewhat astonishing to discover that he remained anxious as to whether he had managed to achieve a satisfactory balance between soloist and orchestra. Fortunately such fears proved groundless. The concerto is virtuosic in the best sense of the word, both musically and technically challenging for the interpreters. Like all great masterpieces, it is also very much a compositional tour de force, the finale ingeniously transforming and varying all the thematic material that is presented in the opening movement. Bartók later claimed that this intense preoccupation with variation form came about through his rigorous study of folk music.

Yehudi Menuhin not only enjoyed the privilege of performing the work in the presence of the composer, but also recorded it no fewer than six times. Of these recordings, the mid-1950s release with the Minneapolis Symphony Orchestra under Antál Dorati is arguably the most satisfying, not only brilliant in delivering the necessary pyrotechnics, but also probing beneath the work's surface. There it reveals a tremendous variety of moods that can move almost schizophrenically from the passionate and the brutal to the nostalgic and introspective, while also incorporating elements of bitterness, irony, playfulness, and humor along the way. **EL**

> ## "Bartók is a composer whose sincerity and skill are universally agreed to be beyond praise."
> Ralph Hill, reviewing the first British performance

Other Recommended Recordings

Gil Shaham, Chicago Symphony Orchestra
Pierre Boulez
DG 459 639-2
Coolly analytical approach from Shaham and Boulez

György Pauk, Polish National Radio Symphony
Orchestra • Antoni Wit
Naxos 8554321
A violinist who has this music in his blood

Laurent Korcia, City of Birmingham Symphony
Orchestra • Sakari Oramo
Naïve V4991
High-voltage performance from young French virtuoso

Yehudi Menuhin had a special affinity with Bartók's music. ➔

Herbert Howells | Hymnus paradisi (1938)

Genre | Choral
Conductor/Performers | Richard Hickox; Joan Rodgers,
Anthony Rolfe Johnson, BBC Symphony Orchestra & Chorus
Year recorded | 1998
Label | Chandos CHAN 9744

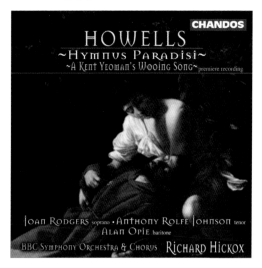

The English composer, organist, and teacher Herbert
Howells (1892–1983) wrote music of distinctive and
striking harmonic originality, although its sound world
is rooted in the music of Elgar and Vaughan Williams. He
was associated throughout his life with choral music, and
he left behind a large body of organ pieces and richly
chromatic settings of church canticles that are permanent
fixtures in the repertoires of cathedral choirs today.

In 1935 Howells was devastated by the death of his
nine-year-old son Michael; but grief was channeled into
musical inspiration, of which *Hymnus paradisi* is the
supreme example. As Andrew Green has noted, it "became
what he called a 'medical document,' helping him to work
through his grief . . . a deeply personal masterpiece which
transfigured that grief into a whole range of emotions—
hope, defiance, consolation, even ecstasy."

Although it was largely finished by 1938, Howells
suppressed the work until 1950. It uses words from
the Requiem Mass, Psalms 121 and 23 (among other
liturgical texts), and—asserting that it is "no churchy
work"—Howells attaches great musical importance
to the universal symbolism of "light." Showing many
characteristics of the music of Delius, *Hymnus paradisi*
is rhapsodic and transfiguring in the extreme. In an
outstanding, sumptuous recording from Chandos, Richard
Hickox, soloists Joan Rodgers and especially Anthony
Rolfe Johnson, capture this essence, while the well-drilled
BBC Symphony Chorus brings a sharper focus to the
choral writing. *Hymnus paradisi* is coupled with a unique
recording of a Howells rarity, *A Kent Yeoman's Wooing Song*,
with the persuasive, resonant baritone of Alan Opie adding
distinction to the music. **GK**

> *"I love music as a man can love a woman. . . . I have composed out of sheer love of trying to make nice sounds."*

Herbert Howells

Other Recommended Recordings

The St. Paul's Service, etc.
Christopher Dearnley, St. Paul's Cathedral Choir
John Scott • Hyperion Dyad CDD 22038 (2 CDs)
Collection of Howells's organ and liturgical music

Choral Works
Finzi Singers • Paul Spicer
Chandos CHAN 241-34 (2 CDs)
Includes Requiem, *which preceded* Hymnus paradisi

Orchestral Works
London Symphony Orchestra/Richard Hickox
Chandos CHAN 241-20 (2 CDs)
Bargain anthology of Howells's orchestral works

Bohuslav Martinů | Double Concerto (1938)

Genre | Concerto
Performers | Czech Philharmonic Orchestra
Conductor | Jiří Bělohlávek
Year recorded | 1990
Label | Chandos CHAN 8950

After Janáček, Martinů is the most significant Czech composer of the twentieth century. Hugely prolific, he wrote in all musical genres from opera to chamber and solo keyboard music, symphony, concerto, choral music, and song. While Debussy and Stravinsky were important influences on his compositional style, Martinů had forged a distinctive musical accent by the late 1920s characterized by driving motor rhythms and luminous instrumentation; as his style developed through the 1930s, his musical language became conspicuously tonal in orientation, though never descending into banality.

The Double Concerto for two string orchestras, piano, and timpani was commissioned by Paul Sacher for his Basel Chamber Orchestra. Composed in 1938, it was written under the shadow of the Nazi threat to Europe and more specifically to Martinů's homeland, Czechoslovakia. Unsurprisingly, it is a work of intensity that externalizes much of the torment Martinů felt regarding the onset of World War II. The composer's admiration for Bach and the Baroque concerto grosso is clear in the vital rhythmic qualities of the outer movements—both of which pursue a headlong course with frequent violent outbursts—and the near continuo-like use of the solo piano. These tensions are maintained in the austerely beautiful slow movement, with its extensive rhapsodic piano solo writing.

Jiří Bělohlávek has a superb command of the work's ebb and flow. While he maintains a firm hold of the rhythmic power of the first movement and finale, he also recognizes that an important feature of the work is the way in which Martinů builds his climaxes with suitably contrasting material, and his reading of the slow movement has radiance as well as intensity. **JS**

> *"The atmosphere of tragic events . . . is engraved on the pages of the score."*
>
> **Bohuslav Martinů**

Other Recommended Recordings

BBC Symphony Orchestra
Charles Mackerras
BBCR 15656 9135-2
An authoritative account by a noted interpreter of Martinů

Czech Philharmonic Orchestra • Karel Šejna
Supraphon SU 1924-2
A superbly expressive account by one of the Czech Philharmonic's greatest postwar conductors

Vienna Philharmonic Orchestra • Rafael Kubelík
Orfeo C 521991 B
A heartfelt reading by a fellow Czech exile

Roy Harris | Symphony no. 3 (1938)

Genre | Orchestral
Conductor | Leonard Bernstein
Performers | New York Philharmonic
Year recorded | 1961
Label | Sony SMK 60594

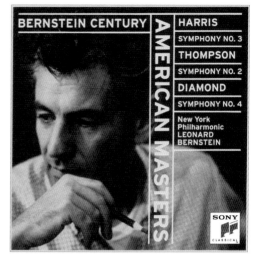

Roy Harris (1898–1979) claimed he was born on the plains of Oklahoma in a log cabin built by his father. Whether this is the truth or a self-made myth is irrelevant; what matters is that Harris viewed himself as an American Pioneer. Like many composers of his generation, he went to Paris to study with Nadia Boulanger. Unlike his fellow students, however, Harris openly rebelled against Boulanger's method of disciplined study. He wanted to do things his way or not at all. Did Harris have the talent to back up this iconoclastic attitude? Several influential musicians thought so. Among them was Serge Koussevitzky, conductor of the Boston Symphony, and the catalyst for a great many twentieth-century masterpieces. Koussevitzky commissioned what is arguably Harris's greatest work: the third of his fourteen symphonies. Premiered in Boston in 1939 and recorded immediately thereafter for RCA, the Third Symphony instantly put Harris in the front rank of American composers.

Cast in a single movement, the symphony is built in an expansive arch form. From the opening melody in the cellos—modal and hymnlike—Harris creates a powerful trajectory that moves through rugged emotional terrain with an impressive sense of inevitability. Passages of gritty grandeur flow into luminous pastoral interludes on the way to the work's shockingly dark and bitter conclusion—and the force of the coda is magnified by its suddenness and concision.

Leonard Bernstein, a protégé of Koussevitzky, was another ardent champion of Harris's symphony. Of the two recordings he made with the New York Philharmonic, the earlier one (now on Sony) is tauter and more sharply focused—though, really, both versions are very gutsy. **AFC**

> "I think that nobody has captured in music the essence of American life . . . so well as Roy Harris."

Serge Koussevitzky

Other Recommended Recordings

Symphonies nos. 3 & 4, "Folksong Symphony"
Colorado Symphony Orchestra & Chorus
Marin Alsop • Naxos 8.559227
A tuneful, charming piece of Americana

Symphonies nos. 8, "San Francisco" & 9, etc.
Albany Symphony Orchestra • David Alan Miller
Albany TROY 350
A pair of hugely underrated symphonies superbly performed in audiophile sound

Piano Quintet; String Quartet no. 3; Violin Sonata
Third Angle New Music Ensemble • Koch 7515
The Quintet is one of Harris's most affecting creations

Roy Harris was well known for his idiosyncratic teaching methods. ➔

Ralph Vaughan Williams | Serenade to Music (1938)

Genre | Vocal
Conductor | Henry Wood
Performers | Sixteen soloists, BBC Symphony Orchestra
Year recorded | 1938
Label | Dutton CDBP 9707

The *Serenade to Music* is a little piece of magic—fourteen minutes of perfection. Vaughan Williams wrote it in 1938 for Henry Wood, the founder of the celebrated Promenade Concerts at the Royal Albert Hall, who had asked him for a piece for a London concert celebrating his golden jubilee as a conductor. It was Wood's idea to have sixteen of the leading British singers of the day as soloists. But it was Vaughan Williams who chose the text from Shakespeare's *The Merchant of Venice*, a shared meditation on the moonlit night sky, the music of the spheres, and earthly music making. And it was his idea to set it with each of the sixteen given a solo moment precisely tailored to his or her voice—not to mention a rapturous solo violin part for Wood's regular leader, Paul Beard. Later, probably fearing the piece would never be performed again, Vaughan Williams authorized performances with four-part chorus, and even made a version for orchestra alone. But it is the original that has lasted, and continues to grace special occasions devoted to the art of singing or to music itself.

As for a recording, you cannot get anything more special than the one made ten days after the premiere by the same conductor and the same solo team, beautifully remastered on a disc of Wood's Vaughan Williams performances. There is a real thrill in hearing soaring Isobel Baillie, growling Norman Allin, straight-as-a-die Eva Turner, and the rest in the parts that Vaughan Williams wrote for them; and a wonderful feeling that everyone is united in homage to a conductor, and an art, they all love. At the premiere, Sergei Rachmaninov, who had played his Second Piano Concerto earlier in the concert, was moved to tears. It is not hard to hear why. **AB**

> "*Music is often described as 'glowing.' This Serenade shines, as strongly and clearly as the full moon.*"
>
> Michael Kennedy

Other Recommended Recordings

Soloists, English Chamber Orchestra • Matthew Best
Hyperion CDA 66420
Affectionate performance by sixteen of the best British singers of 1990

Soloists, London Philharmonic Orchestra • Adrian Boult
EMI 0777 7 64022 2 2
The cream of the 1969 crop, under a great champion of Vaughan Williams

Royal Liverpool Philharmonic Choir and Orchestra
Vernon Handley
EMI 7243 5 75313 2 0
The choral alternative, well sung and played

Henry Wood was the man behind London's Promenade Concerts. ➔

Silvestre Revueltas
Sensemayá
(1938)

Genre | Orchestral
Conductor | Esa-Pekka Salonen
Performers | Los Angeles Philharmonic
Year recorded | 1998
Label | Sony SK 60676

Silvestre Revueltas (1899–1940) was, with his contemporary Carlos Chávez, one of the first great Mexican composers. A child prodigy, he had already made a name for himself before going to study violin in Chicago, later leading an orchestra in Texas. He supported the Republicans in the Spanish Civil War, and returned to Mexico, where he composed *Homenaje a Federico García Lorca*, in memory of the poet killed in that conflict, as well as the film scores *Redes* and *La noche de los mayas*. He spent several periods in mental hospitals, and died of alcoholism at age forty.

Sensemayá—chant for the killing of a snake—is the work by which he is best remembered. Leopold Stokowski recorded it in 1947, a version that led a British recording guide of 1951 to describe it as "a hideously dull and noisy piece . . . fortunately short." Much has changed since then, and its earthy violence and repetitious intensity now seem ahead of their time, foreshadowing many of the concerns of the harder side of minimalism. Although Revueltas originally wrote it for voice and chamber orchestra in 1937, it is his version for full symphony orchestra (including fourteen percussion instruments) from the following year that has the greater impact, and is more often played.

And it is certainly impact that you get from Esa-Pekka Salonen and the Los Angeles Philharmonic, with the bite and color of the score leaping off the page in a fiercely etched performance, superbly caught in all its force by the engineers. This is the finest modern recording available of a succinct masterpiece. **MC**

Igor Stravinsky
Concerto in E flat, "Dumbarton Oaks" (1938)

Genre | Orchestral
Conductor/Performers | Pierre Boulez ;
Ensemble InterContemporain
Year recorded | 1981
Label | DG 447 405-2

"Dumbarton Oaks", as the Concerto in E flat is generally known, takes its name from the Washington, D.C. home of Mr. and Mrs. Woods Bliss, the venue in 1944 for the conference that prepared the blueprint for the United Nations. The American diplomat and his wife were generous patrons of the arts and they commissioned a work from Stravinsky to mark their thirtieth wedding anniversary.

Stravinsky himself drew attention to the fact that he was immersed in the Brandenburg Concertos while writing "Dumbarton Oaks," and, remarkable as it may seem now, the work provoked a stream of critical opprobrium for its supposed borrowing from Bach. Now recognized as a high watermark of Neo-Classicism, the work's genial nature masks some of Stravinsky's more complex metrical writing, ensuring that, rather than staid pastiche, this could only be a product of the twentieth century.

At first sight, Pierre Boulez, who as a young firebrand whistled in derision on first hearing Stravinsky's works from the 1930s, might seem an odd proponent of this archetype of Neo-Classicism. Yet the Ensemble InterContemporain is in typically fine form, and, in Boulez's hands, many points of resonance emerge between two composers often regarded, at least at this point in Stravinsky's career, as diametrically opposed: a Modernist versus a Neo-Classicist. It is a vivacious reading, full of charm and taking its strength from the fact that, if not evident of a zealous convert, Boulez's account is no unthinking acceptance of what Stravinsky was trying to achieve. **CD**

Anton Webern
String Quartet, op. 28 (1938)

Genre | Chamber
Performers | Artis Quartet: Schuhmayer, Meissl, Kefer, Müller
Year recorded | 2001
Label | Nimbus NI 5668

Webern completed his last instrumental work only two weeks after Hitler made his triumphant entry into Vienna and annexed Austria into the German Reich. Commissioned by the enlightened American patron Elizabeth Sprague Coolidge, the String Quartet was first performed in the United States by the Kolisch Quartet in September 1938. The composer, however, was unable to secure a performance of the work in his native land.

The quartet must be regarded as one of Webern's more austere and Classically orientated works. Of its three movements, the first is the most extended—a set of variations in moderate tempo inspired, according to the composer, by the slow movement of Beethoven's String Quartet in F major, op. 135. The following two movements have something of the character of a scherzo and include some intricate fugal and canonic writing. Webern's indebtedness to the great traditions of the past lies also in the intervallic patterns of the tone row upon which the work is based; these are strongly related to that of the incomplete fugue subject from Bach's *The Art of Fugue*.

The String Quartet is undoubtedly a difficult and complex work to appreciate on first hearing. It certainly benefits from being presented alongside the rest of Webern's slender output for string quartet, a practice adopted in the outstanding recording from the Artis Quartet. These Vienna-based players really have this music in their bones, and are able to project its latently expressive qualities with great immediacy. **EL**

Benjamin Britten
Les illuminations (1939)

Genre | Vocal
Performer | Peter Pears
Conductor | Benjamin Britten
Year recorded | 1963
Label | Decca 439 395-2

Britten had already revealed his mastery of the string-orchestra medium in his *Frank Bridge Variations* when he came to set nine prose-poems of Arthur Rimbaud for high voice and strings two years later in 1939. But just as fresh as his instrumental writing is that for the voice—indeed, this is the first mature work of his that matches great poetry to ideal word-setting. Britten is remembered as the best setter of English since Purcell, but he was just as sensitive to the needs of French. In fact, his first foray into French had been over a decade earlier, when his wrote his *Quatre chansons françaises* at the age of fifteen (a work premiered posthumously in 1980); and here he responds to the fantastical imagery of Rimbaud's writing with consummate imagination and originality. This exotic world must have struck chords with him as he contemplated emigration to the United States (the cycle was completed in Amityville, New York) and juggled various personal relationships.

Unlike most of his famous song cycles, this one was conceived not for Peter Pears, but for a soprano, Sophie Wyss, who gave the premiere in London in 1940. Yet the cycle has come to be associated with Pears as much as the *Serenade for Tenor, Horn, and Strings* or the great operatic roles such as Grimes and Vere, and the final song, "Being Beauteous," which Britten dedicated to him, can be heard as a passionate love song. Pears's own recording comes from the same sessions in 1963 as his remake of the Serenade, with Britten himself conducting. It is a prime example of the tenor's agility and sensitivity to words. **MR**

Benjamin Britten
Violin Concerto
(1939)

Genre | Concerto
Performer | Mark Lubotsky
Conductor | Benjamin Britten
Year recorded | 1970
Label | Decca 417 308-2

The predominance of stage and vocal music in Britten's output has tended to obscure the quality of his instrumental works—and their originality. The Violin Concerto, written in Canada early in the composer's North American sojourn, seems to be conventional in its language, though we should not overlook how Britten, as so often, makes good old major and minor sound fresh and new. But the form is certainly unusual. There is a tensely lyrical opening movement, a brilliant and very taxing central scherzo, a transitional cadenza, and as culmination a mostly slow Passacaglia, with an impassioned climax and an ambiguous midair ending. The concerto's first soloist, the Spanish violinist Antonio Brosa, thought that the piece was affected by the progress of the Spanish Civil War, although a more personal influence on it may have been the deepening of Britten's relationship with his partner, Peter Pears, around this time. As Britten wrote to his publisher, the work is "rather serious" in tone.

Serious does not necessarily equate to slow, however, and some recent recordings have stretched the slower tempos to the point where the lyrical music does not flow and the ending nearly comes to a standstill. But there is no danger of that with the composer himself in charge. In the Russian violinist Mark Lubotsky he found a willing and able ally, technically adroit and expressive without heaviness. With the coupling of the Piano Concerto, recorded the same year with Lubotsky's great compatriot Sviatoslav Richter as soloist, this is an essential Britten recording. **AB**

Joaquín Rodrigo
Concierto de Aranjuez
(1939)

Genre | Concerto
Performer | Carlos Bonell
Conductor | Steuart Bedford
Year recorded | 1989
Label | Regis RRC 1090

Blinded by diphtheria three years after his birth in 1901, Joaquín Rodrigo composed his entire output in Braille and by dictating the music to a copyist. He studied musicology in Paris, but his scholarship was withdrawn during the Spanish Civil War. As a result, he and his wife spent the late 1930s in poverty.

Rodrigo's earliest composition dates from 1923, but shortly before his return to Spain in 1939 he composed what remains the definitive Spanish guitar concerto, the *Concierto de Aranjuez*. First performed in Barcelona in 1940, the piece was immediately recognized as the work of one of Spain's greatest compositional talents. Receptive to many influences ranging from Scarlatti to Stravinsky and from the nationalism of Albéniz and Falla to traditional Moorish music, Rodrigo understood the principles of Postmodernist musical fusion more than half a century before its time. The three movements of the concerto balance two spirited Allegro sections around a central Adagio, with the distinctive opening chords of the *Concierto* being a favored doodle of every guitar student. Following the performances of the concerto, Rodrigo was greatly honored both at home and abroad.

Despite its inherent vigor, the *Concierto* is all too often reduced to tinkly mood music. In the case of this recording, however, both Carlos Bonell and Steuart Bedford are clearly inspired by the work's vitality and they extract vibrant, animated interpretations from guitar and the English Chamber Orchestra respectively. **RT**

Dmitri Shostakovich
Symphony no. 6
(1939)

Genre | Orchestral
Conductor | Yevgeny Mravinsky
Performers | Leningrad Philharmonic
Year recorded | 1965
Label | Scribendum SC 031 (4 CDs)

After the apparent transparency and structural cohesion of the Fifth Symphony, the Sixth, written between April and October 1939, keeps its negations on the surface, a lopsided triptych of apparently unrelated panels to reflect perhaps the contradictory spirit of the times. The opening movement is masterful, a Mahlerian evocation of benumbed stillness as potent as anything in that composer's output, but its successors are increasingly superficial and garish. This was an era in which the material rewards for approved activity were considerable; the Nazi-Soviet pact was signed during its composition. Some feel that the ideal performance must convey an air of corrosive menace and moral corruption for the work to succeed.

Small wonder that solutions come in all shapes and sizes. Shostakovich can be Beethovenian in his allocation of seemingly unworkable metronome marks and most conductors blunt his excesses. Yevgeny Mravinsky, the old-school disciplinarian with the most unimpeachable credentials in this repertoire, gives the first movement more momentum than the score suggests, yet potently conveys the near-paralysis at its heart. It helps that his orchestra has the correct timbral specificity that would have been in the composer's ear as he was writing. The blistering attack of the Leningrad strings is unmistakable, along with the unrefined winds. Mravinsky was the composer's favorite interpreter for many years; since his interpretations did stiffen in old age, this 1965 concert really is the one to seek out. **DG**

Michael Tippett
Concerto for Double String Orchestra (1939)

Genre | Orchestral
Conductor / Performers | Neville Marriner;
Academy of St. Martin in the Fields
Year recorded | 1971
Label | Decca 476 7960

Tippett's Concerto for Double String Orchestra was a true "breakthrough" work. It brought Tippett (1905–98) his first, modest taste of public success, and it was also the piece in which, in his early thirties and after a long self-imposed apprenticeship, he found his personal voice—or rather, given his restless creative drive, the first of several personal voices. The concerto is like nothing else that was being written at the time. It is resolutely in recognizable keys or modes, and bursting with melodies, some of them with a touch of English folksong. It has the three-movement outline of an eighteenth-century concerto, and the fast outer movements emulate the hallowed sonata forms of Beethoven. But the textures are of almost continuous counterpoint, made clearer, if also more complex, by the division of the string orchestra into two equal halves. And there is an extraordinary, dancing vitality, created through a combination of changing meters, syncopations, and cross-rhythms, and inspired equally by Bartók and Stravinsky, Elizabethan madrigals, and jazz.

The earlier of Neville Marriner's two recordings of the concerto has never been out of the catalogue for long, and it is currently available on a disc combining Tippett's string music with his delightful suite celebrating the birth of Prince Charles. It still sounds magnificently alive, with a shine to it that comes both from the engineering and from the quality of Marriner's handpicked players. If you are new to Tippett, this is just the piece, and just the performance, to get you on to his wavelength. **AB**

Sergei Prokofiev | Alexander Nevsky (1939)

Genre | Choral
Conductor/Performers | Neeme Järvi; Linda Finnie
(mezzo-soprano), Scottish National Orchestra & Chorus
Year recorded | 1987
Label | Chandos CHAN 8584

Prokofiev's first collaboration with the great Russian moviemaker Sergei Eisenstein was born out of necessity. Alexander Nevsky, the thirteenth-century prince whose forces defeated the invading Teutonic knights on a frozen lake, served as a good example to Stalin's Soviet Union. By 1938, both Eisenstein and Prokofiev still needed to ingratiate themselves with the regime, but the movie they created transcended its propagandist outlines.

Eisenstein was so struck by Prokofiev's precision in providing the necessary musical illustration to his succession of unforgettable images that in some instances he even encouraged him to write the music first. In 1939, the year after the movie's successful premiere, Prokofiev extracted a seven-movement cantata for concert use, altering the orchestration and providing an overwhelming sequence for the climactic battle on the ice. Around it, songs of stirring patriotism conflict with the threat and the consequences of enemy invasion. The cantata remains the most popular form in which *Alexander Nevsky* is heard today, though screenings with Prokofiev's original score played by a live orchestra are not uncommon.

The original soundtrack to the movie was one of the big disappointments of cinematic history, recorded on primitive equipment; but since then, there have been many demonstration-quality versions of the cantata. Neeme Järvi's wide-screen spectacular captures the icy intensity in the scenes of devastation and the glitter of the musical patriotism in equal measure. The cantata's heart and soul, the somber song of a girl looking for her rival suitors on the field of the dead, is delivered with authentic Russian-sounding richness by Linda Finnie, and the Scots chorus phrases the big melodies with plenty of heart. **DN**

> *"The music of Prokofiev shows in an amazing way the inward progress of events."*
>
> Sergei Eisenstein

Other Recommended Recordings

Vera Soukupová, Czech Philharmonic Orchestra & Chorus • Karel Ancerl • Supraphon SU 36962
Classic account of the cantata from Czech forces

Marina Domaschenko, Ernst Senff Choir, Berlin Radio Symphony Orchestra • Frank Strobel
Capriccio 71 014
First complete recording of the original film score

Ivan the Terrible
Liubov Sokolova, Nikolay Putilin, Kirov Chorus, Rotterdam Philharmonic Orchestra • Valery Gergiev
Philips 475 7778
Prokofiev's second and darker film score for Eisenstein

William Walton | Violin Concerto (1939, *rev.* 1943)

Genre | Concerto
Performers | Joshua Bell, Baltimore Symphony Orchestra
Conductor | David Zinman
Year recorded | 1996
Label | Decca 475 7710

There is an air of relaxation about Walton's late music that is surely linked to the home he made after World War II, with his young wife Susana, on the Italian island of Ischia. And there is a foretaste of that in his Violin Concerto, begun in 1938 in a villa overlooking the Mediterranean at Ravello—though in the company of an earlier love, Alice Wimbourne. The first movement begins and ends in a mood of luxurious tranquility summed up by the instruction *sognando*, "dreaming." The central scherzo "in Neapolitan style" has a trio called "canzonetta," or "little song." And the finale also has a strong element of lyricism, culminating (as Elgar's Violin Concerto does) in a rhapsodic accompanied cadenza. But this lyrical vein is especially appropriate because Walton was writing the concerto for Jascha Heifetz, a player of supreme sweetness and purity in long melodic lines. And as Heifetz was also a master of violin technique, Walton exploited that too in all three movements, in passages of dazzling virtuosity, matched by incisive orchestral writing. Heifetz himself recorded the concerto twice: in Cincinnati in 1941 (predating Walton's revision of the orchestration), and in London nine years later with the composer himself conducting. His accounts have a unique and winning blend of brilliance and charm.

But the opulence of Walton's scoring really demands a modern recording. Pick of the current bunch is the exceptionally well-balanced performance by Joshua Bell with the excellent Baltimore Symphony and David Zinman. Bell is a player of complete technical assurance, and his subtle gradations of dynamics and vibrato and imaginative use of portamento (gliding between notes) are perfectly in accordance with the essentially Romantic nature of Walton's gorgeous sunlit concerto. **AB**

> *"For sheer beauty of melody, brilliance of detail, and impassioned eloquence, it ranks among the greatest . . ."*
> Michael Kennedy

Other Recommended Recordings

Jascha Heifetz, Philharmonia Orchestra
William Walton
RCA 74321 92575 2 (2 CDs)
Authoritative and incomparably exciting

Nigel Kennedy, Royal Philharmonic Orchestra
André Previn
EMI 7243 5 62814 2 4
Kennedy at his brilliant best

Dong-Suk Kan, English Northern Philharmonia
Paul Daniel
Naxos 8.554325
A slender-toned but very persuasive soloist

Samuel Barber
Violin Concerto (1940)

Genre | Concerto
Performer | Joshua Bell
Conductor | David Zinman
Year recorded | 1996
Label | Decca 475 7710

Benjamin Britten
Sinfonia da requiem (1940)

Genre | Orchestral
Conductor | Benjamin Britten
Performers | New Philharmonia Orchestra
Year recorded | 1964
Label | Decca 425 100-2

Barber's Violin Concerto was an unqualified success when it premiered in Philadelphia in 1941, and it is easy to understand why. The first two movements, which together comprise the vast majority of the work, overflow with melody, giving the soloist the chance to play his or her heart out. The terse finale zips unexpectedly in the opposite direction; a rhythmic juggernaut full of frantic runs, hops, skips, and jumps, it is the kind of adrenaline-pumping showpiece that, if performed well, is virtually guaranteed to bring an audience to its feet. Yet, after the last of the virtuoso pyrotechnics have faded away, it is the intense songfulness of the concerto that remains with you, and that is its true heart. Barber would later describe the music as "lyric and simple"—a succinct summation.

What may be difficult to fathom is why it took so long for the star qualities of Barber's concerto to be appreciated (by performers, at least). Despite its successful premiere and some other notable performances, it was not until the 1980s or so that it finally took its rightful place in the repertoire. Perhaps it was that Barber's simple lyricism was thought to be too simple during the heyday of the avant-garde from the 1950s to the 1970s. Thankfully, the concerto has—not surprisingly—become Barber's second most popular work after the Adagio for Strings.

Of the many fine recordings of Barber's concerto now extant, Joshua Bell's stands out. His tone is elegantly sweet, his intonation impeccable, and best of all, he has an innate feeling for the vocal nature of the solo part. Bell dances nimbly through the finale, and even uncovers an undercurrent of lyricism in the jagged lines. **AFC**

Britten was usually good at commissions, but one major exception was the *Sinfonia da requiem*, written during his U.S. sojourn for the Japanese government's celebrations of the 2,600th anniversary of the Imperial dynasty. Although his initial proposal for a work expressing his "anti-war convictions" was apparently accepted, the Japanese authorities were hardly likely to smile on a pacifist work with titles from the Catholic Requiem Mass. Britten was allowed to keep the commission fee, but the Japanese performance was canceled and the premiere took place instead in New York, under John Barbirolli.

However, Britten's insistence on writing what he wanted to write resulted in one of his all-too-few orchestral masterpieces. The large orchestra is handled with Mahlerian confidence, and the three compact, linked movements are perfectly paced and balanced: the "Lacrymosa" sorrowing and obsessive, the "Dies Irae" a furious dance of death, and the "Requiem aeternam" assembling earlier fragments into a more sustained expression of consolation and healing.

Britten was an outstanding (if reluctant) conductor, and his 1964 account of the *Sinfonia da requiem* with the New Philharmonia traces its course from grief and protest to acceptance with unmatched passion and conviction. And it takes only the fierce opening drumbeats to silence any possible doubts about the age of the recording: it was very good to start with, and it has been expertly remastered. The only conceivable complaint is that the next track follows too quickly, when what is really needed is about a minute of stunned silence. **AB**

Dmitri Shostakovich
Piano Quintet (1940)

Genre | Chamber
Performers | Elisabeth Leonskaja (piano), Borodin Quartet
Year recorded | 1995
Label | Warner 2564 60813-2

Sergei Prokofiev
Piano Sonata no. 6 (1940)

Genre | Instrumental
Instrument | Piano
Performer | Ivo Pogorelich
Year recorded | 1982
Label | DG 463 678-2

The Piano Quintet dates from a period when Shostakovich began to develop a serious interest in writing chamber music. Having completed his First String Quartet in 1938, the year after the triumphant first performance of the Fifth Symphony had ensured his "rehabilitation" in Soviet musical life, he wanted to compose a work that he could perform on a regular basis with the Beethoven Quartet, the ensemble that in the coming years would become the most devoted exponent of his burgeoning output of string quartets. Conceived in five movements, the quintet opens in a defiantly Neo-Classical manner with a Prelude and Fugue that reveals the composer's admiration for Bach and Stravinsky. The brilliantly ironic scherzo offers necessary relief from the work's earlier tensions, though a feeling of intense loneliness affects the ensuing Intermezzo. As in many of Shostakovich's works of this period, the gentle playfulness of the finale does not entirely dispel an overwhelming feeling of regret.

Although recorded on a fairly regular basis by artists throughout the world, Russian interpreters seem best equipped to empathize with the music's equivocal character. Undoubtedly one of the finest accounts comes from pianist Elisabeth Leonskaja and the Borodin Quartet, whose musical journey opens with a magisterial Prelude that provides the sharpest possible contrast to the almost disembodied timbres in the opening paragraph of the Fugue. Such extreme mood swings are incisively drawn in the rest of the work, a suitably solemn scherzo followed by a heartrending Intermezzo and a finale that portrays laughter momentarily breaking through the tears. **EL**

This is the first of the three piano masterpieces commonly bracketed together as Prokofiev's "War" Sonatas. Although it was completed before Russia entered World War II, its first movement is certainly dissonant and embattled, with a development so abrasive that at one point Prokofiev indicates the cluster of notes should be played with the fist. Pianist Evgeny Kissin hears in its motto-theme, which returns with terrifying effect at the end of the sonata, a musical portrait of Stalin, and a suggestion of the purges through which Prokofiev lived before the war began. Whatever the truth, the anguish is heartfelt, its depths enshrined in the deeply nostalgic slow waltz of the third movement, powerfully swept aside in a keening central lament, and although the familiar Prokofiev style, barbed and playful, resurfaces in the scherzo, there is more of an edge to it than in any of his early works.

There is much to be said for hearing the magisterial range of the great Russian pianist Sviatoslav Richter, an early interpreter approved by the composer, but none of his recordings has the benefit of a full sonic range, so necessary to the powerful climaxes of the piece. Surely the most haunting performance comes from the charismatic Ivo Pogorelich, who manages to express depths in this tortured work that many other harder-hitting pianists fail to perceive. Although Pogorelich has a reputation for reticence, his playing of the outer movements is firm and focused. His obsession with sonority never comes at the expense of the sonata's substance, and he brings a polished, withdrawn, heartfelt nostalgia to the great slow movement that has never been surpassed. **DN**

Aram Khachaturian | Violin Concerto (1940)

Genre | Concerto
Performers | David Oistrakh (violin), Philharmonia Orchestra
Conductor | Aram Khachaturian
Year recorded | 1954
Label | EMI 0946 3 61571 2 2

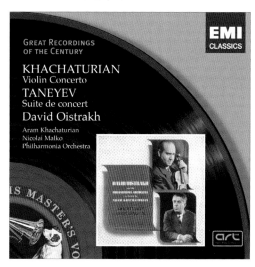

By coincidence Aram Khachaturian (1903–78), the best composer from Armenia so far, wrote his three concertos for the players who eventually teamed up to become the Oistrakh Trio. Although the Piano Concerto (for Lev Oborin) and the Cello Concerto (for Sviatoslav Knushevitzky) have their champions, only the Violin Concerto—written for David Oistrakh himself—has become part of the mainstream repertoire. It is a colorful score, exciting if not particularly profound in its outer movements. What makes a listener return to it is the lovely central slow movement, which gives a great violinist the chance to brood a little and show off his or her legato.

The privilege of hearing the original soloist, with the composer conducting, is too much to pass over, even if the recording is in mono. Late mono is often more impressive than early stereo; and this historic performance has now been carefully refurbished for EMI's "Great Recordings of the Century" series. David Oistrakh was a colossal violinist, stockily built with immense strength and stamina to support his fireproof technique and innate musicality. He loved this concerto and often played it, but felt the original cadenza was too long. When Khachaturian seemed to take his time to change it, Oistrakh wrote his own cadenza, which was published alongside the composer's. He plays his own version here.

Composers conducting their own music are liable to take tempi that are faster than the ideal, but Khachaturian was always effective both in concert and the studio. He performed the concerto with other Russian fiddlers, such as Leonid Kogan, and had a good understanding with Oistrakh. As further enticement, this disc couples the concerto with the *Suite de concert* by Sergei Taneyev. **TP**

> *"When in 1940 I conceived the Violin Concerto, my head was full of the sounds of Oistrakh's violin."*
>
> Aram Khachaturian

Other Recommended Recordings

Leonid Kogan, Boston Symphony Orchestra
Pierre Monteux
RCA 09026 63708 2
An ideal version for those who must have stereo

Piano Concerto
Lev Oborin, Czech Philharmonic Orchestra
Yevgeny Mravinsky • Praga PR 50017
Fabulous performance with the dedicatee as soloist

Ballet suites
Vienna Philharmonic Orchestra • Aram Khachaturian
Decca 460 315-2
A hi-fi spectacular in its day and it still sounds good

Aram Khachaturian with his wife Nina Makarova in c. 1940. ➡

Igor Stravinsky | Symphony in C (1940)

Genre | Orchestral
Conductor | Igor Stravinsky
Performers | CBC Symphony Orchestra
Year recorded | 1962
Label | Sony MK 42434

The Symphony in C was written against a background of upheaval and heartbreak. In less than a year, from 1938 to 1939, Stravinsky's eldest daughter, his wife, and his mother all died from tuberculosis (the composer himself was also diagnosed with the disease). The outbreak of war in Europe was the catalyst for a trip to the United States, which would develop into permanent residency. There is little sign of these terrible events in the symphony itself, which Stravinsky said was "composed during the most tragic year of my life." He explained that he "survived in the weeks following [my daughter's death] only by working on the symphony—which is *not* to say that the music exploits my grief"; that kind of direct correlation would have run counter to Stravinsky's entire creative philosophy.

Cast in four movements, with a clear motif as its basis, the work comes nearest of all Stravinsky's mature works entitled "symphony" to the conventional understanding of the genre, even though Stravinsky eschews the organic development usually associated with symphonic writing. The influence of Beethoven and Tchaikovsky can be felt, especially in the more emphatic outer movements, while the two middle movements foreshadow the pastoral innocence and urban decadence of *The Rake's Progress*.

Incisive and witty, Stravinsky's 1962 recording of the symphony is a compelling example of the composer at his best in the role of the conductor. His presence on the podium inspires the CBC Symphony Orchestra to play above itself, with charming woodwind in the second movement and a heart of fire in the final movement. You may hear more polished or better recorded accounts, but, for once, the impression here is of the music precisely as envisioned by Stravinsky himself. **CD**

"One may detect elegance but never affectation."

Sol Babitz, *Musical Quarterly*, January 1941

Other Recommended Recordings

Suisse Romande Orchestra • Neeme Järvi
Chandos CHAN 6654(5) (5 CDs)
Järvi brings a Beethovenian strength to the symphony

Royal Scottish National Orchestra
Alexander Gibson
Chandos CHAN 241-8 (2 CDs)
Gibson's reading is more Classical than Romantic in spirit

Finnish Radio Symphony Orchestra
Jukka-Pekka Saraste
Virgin 7243 5 62022 2 1 (2 CDs)
A fresh and breezy account

Igor Stravinsky at a recording session in London in 1958. ➔

Sergei Rachmaninov
Symphonic Dances (1940)

Genre | Orchestral
Conductor/Performers | Mariss Jansons;
St. Petersburg Philharmonic Orchestra
Year recorded | 1992
Label | EMI 7243 5 62810 2 8

Arthur Honegger
Symphony no. 2 (1941)

Genre | Orchestral
Conductor/Performers | Herbert von
Karajan; Berlin Philharmonic Orchestra
Year recorded | 1969
Label | DG 447 435-2

For some, Rachmaninov's *Symphonic Dances* is simply the greatest thing he ever wrote. Rachmaninov was haunted by death from his earliest youth, but in this, his last work, he produced some of his most stirring and voluptuous musical poetry. The three "Dances" (more like the three movements of a symphony) were originally subtitled "Noon," "Evening," and "Midnight," and subtle self-quotation suggests an autobiographical subplot, with Rachmaninov's beloved medieval funeral chant *Dies irae* (*Day of Wrath*) playing a significant part. But in contrast to the somber *Isle of the Dead*, the *Symphonic Dances* ends in blazing victory, with a transfiguration of the climactic "Alliluya" from Rachmaninov's great choral church work, *All-Night Vigil*. At the same time, Rachmaninov's writing for piano and alto saxophone has a unique, haunting flavor.

At best, a Russian orchestra can bring something sharply distinctive to its own great repertoire. The strings of the St. Petersburg Philharmonic in particular have a grainy intensity that suits Rachmaninov's long melodic lines perfectly. Jansons manages the difficult feat of making the *Symphonic Dances* sound like both vivid tone poems and gripping symphonic arguments—while not forgetting that they are also rooted in dance. The first movement drives like a proud, furious troika ride, after which the central waltz is both sinister and slyly seductive—a dance of death with a subtle erotic charge. Then the buildup to the triumphant ending is stunning—assisted by a very immediate recording. Even those who normally resist Rachmaninov's heart-on-sleeve lyricism may find this surprisingly persuasive. **SJ**

Like so many great string-orchestra works of the twentieth century, Honegger's Second Symphony owes its existence to the Swiss conductor and philanthropist Paul Sacher, who had pestered the composer over a number of years to write something for his Basel Chamber Orchestra. Honegger eventually got down to working on the score in 1938, but intervening events, in particular the Nazi occupation of Paris, impeded its progress. The symphony eventually received its first performance in Switzerland in 1942 and was later given in France to triumphant acclaim. As an acutely sensitive artist, Honegger was deeply affected by the turbulent political situation that was engulfing Europe at the time, and the symphony reflects something of this anguish from the outset of the first movement—a deeply somber slow introduction followed by a highly aggressive Allegro. The central Adagio mesto is no less gloomy, any feelings of hope that momentarily try to shine through the darkness remaining illusory. The stage is now set for a tempestuous finale that eventually battles through to a more optimistic conclusion, the unexpected introduction of solo trumpet intoning an affirmative chorale at the close.

The great French conductor Charles Munch became an enthusiastic exponent of the work, but he was not always served by the most incisive orchestral playing. For this quality, one need look no further than the brilliant 1969 recording from Herbert von Karajan and the Berlin Philharmonic Orchestra. Karajan seems completely fired up by the music, galvanizing his orchestra to play at a level of urgency that easily outstrips most rivals by a mile. **EL**

Olivier Messiaen | Quartet for the End of Time (1941)

Benjamin Britten String Quartets (1941–75)

Genre | Chamber
Performers | Jean Pasquier, André Vacellier, Etienne Pasquier, Olivier Messiaen
Year recorded | 1956
Label | Accord 461 744-2

Genre | Chamber
Performers | Belcea Quartet: Belcea-Fisher, Samuel, Chorzelski, Lederlin
Years recorded | 2003–04
Label | EMI 7243 5 57968 2 0 (2 CDs)

Written and first performed while a prisoner of war in Stalag VIIIA, the *Quatuor pour le fin du Temps* marks a watershed in Messiaen's musical development, especially rhythmically, but the circumstances in which it was created are undoubtedly key to its reception. The extraordinary premiere on a freezing January evening in 1941 has entered into musical legend (and, like all legends, includes some embellishments), with the half-starved musicians heard in rapt silence by their fellow prisoners. Inspired by the vivid imagery of the *Book of Revelation*, the *Quatuor* includes a fearsome depiction of the trumpets of the Apocalypse, two movements dedicated to the angel who announces that there will be no more Time, and a contemplative evocation of the eternal to open the work. Then there are the two "Louanges," one each for cello and violin: long paeans of praise with melodies soaring to celestial heights. The *Quatuor* is a remarkable statement of faith and hope in the most desolate circumstances.

The importance of this performance does not merely lie in the fact that Messiaen and Pasquier could draw on memories of the camp. It also stems from a different performance philosophy from other versions, with much greater fluidity. The composer does not, for instance, play the repetitive piano figures of the "Louanges" as a mechanistic, unflinching Modernist chugging, but allows a considerable ebb and flow. Remarkably, the same tempo flexibility applies to the formidable unison rhythms of "Danse de la fureur." The sheer beauty of Messiaen's playing is a joy to behold, with any rough edges being transcended by the sheer musicality of the whole. **CD**

The viola desk is traditionally reckoned to be the best place to absorb the subtleties of the string quartet medium. Britten was an enthusiastic violist and chamber-music player in his youth, and his teacher Frank Bridge was a former violist in a leading quartet as well as a composer of quartets. It is therefore unsurprising that several of his apprentice pieces, unpublished for many years, were for string quartet. But the three numbered quartets came later—and the last of them much later.

The First Quartet, written in California in 1941, is a work of great freshness, with a ravishing, slow, quiet opening, not simply an introduction but integrated into the first movement. The Second, written four years later, has an equally inviting start, but its weight falls on the last movement, an extended passacaglia or "Chacony"—a homage to the great composer of ground basses, Henry Purcell, to mark the 250th anniversary of his death. And then there is a gap of thirty years before the Third Quartet of 1975, written during what turned out to be Britten's last illness: he only lived to hear a private play-through by the Amadeus Quartet. The piece is a suite of five varied movements, with the weight again falling on the last, a moving "Recitative and Passacaglia" that draws on ideas from Britten's last and most personal opera, *Death in Venice*.

The talented Belcea Quartet plays these three canonical quartets, plus the Three Divertimenti from the 1930s, with fastidious attention to detail and an unrivaled range of tone colors, from unashamed roughness to intensely inward beauty. Britten himself would surely have admired such superbly accomplished playing. **AB**

Manuel Ponce
Concierto del sur (1941)

Genre | Concerto
Conductor/Performers | André Previn;
John Williams, London Symphony Orchestra
Year recorded | 1972
Label | Sony M2K 44791

Ponce (1882–1948) is often called the "father of modern Mexican music," though he was much less of a revolutionary than his younger compatriots Chávez and Revueltas. Reacting against the stultifying atmosphere of the Mexico National Conservatoire, he freelanced as a pianist and critic and sojourned in Italy, Germany, France, and Cuba before returning to Mexico and making his reputation as a composer. It was his collaboration with the great guitarist Andrés Segovia that led him to write works that established an international reputation. Starting with solo guitar pieces—including a suite in Baroque style that Segovia played as if by Bach's contemporary Silvius Leopold Weiss—he worked up to his only concerto for the instrument, *Concierto del sur* (*Concerto of the South*), dedicated to and popularized by Segovia. Though written in failing health, it has become his best-known work.

The scoring, for quite a small orchestra, deftly solves the perennial problems of instrumental balance inherent in a guitar concerto. "The south" in this case would seem to include Central and South America—as in the Mexican dance-rhythms deployed in the fiestalike finale—and also the south of Spain, in the Flamenco and Sevillana rhythms of the first movement and the Andalusian-Moorish inflections of the slow movement. Despite such folk allusions, however, the themes are entirely Ponce's own.

John Williams's recording, nominated for a Grammy Award for Best Classical Performer (Instrumental) in 1973, has all the character of Segovia's own but with more orchestral color and rhythmic drive. There are also good alternatives by Alfonso Moreno and Sharon Isbin. **MM**

Richard Strauss
Capriccio (1941)

Genre | Opera
Conductor/Performer | Wolfgang
Sawallisch; Elisabeth Schwarzkopf
Year recorded | 1959
Label | EMI 7243 5 67391 2 3 (2 CDs)

It was Stefan Zweig who called Strauss's attention to the 1788 libretto *Prima la musica, poi le parole*, written in Vienna by Giambattista Casti for Antonio Salieri, and started adapting it for him. In the end, after Zweig's forced emigration from Germany, Strauss wrote the text with help from conductor Clemens Krauss, among others.

The action takes place at the time of Gluck's reform of opera. The musician Flamand and the poet Olivier compete for the favors of countess Madeleine, their rivalry symbolizing the age-old argument about the supremacy of music over words (or the other way around), which makes up most of the dialogue in the piece. In the end, Madeleine is left awaiting the arrival of both her suitors; they expect her to tell them "the end of the opera," but of course we never learn what her choice will be.

Capriccio was intended to be a summation both of Strauss's work and of operatic history. The opera is brimful of quotations and allusions to aesthetic arguments about the nature of musical drama, and of definite works; for example, the sonnet written for Madeleine by Flamand (and set to music by Olivier) is by Ronsard. There are parodies of secco recitative and Italianate coloratura, and a buffo role for the impresario La Roche.

The affected artificiality of the story suits Elisabeth Schwarzkopf's studied artistry like a glove, and Madeleine was one of her best roles. She is surrounded by a handpicked cast (including Hans Hotter, who had sung at the opera's premiere), lovingly conducted by Wolfgang Sawallisch in one of the legendary recordings for EMI made by Schwarzkopf's husband, Walter Legge. **CMS**

Michael Tippett
A Child of Our Time (1941)

Genre | Choral
Conductor/Performers | Colin Davis;
Jessye Norman, Janet Baker
Year recorded | 1975
Label | Decca 475 717-2 (4 CDs)

It must have been a strange occasion, the premiere of Tippett's *A Child of Our Time* in a London West End theater on a Sunday afternoon in March 1944. With World War II still raging, here was a so-called oratorio with words and music by an atheist and pacifist, one who had even been to prison as a conscientious objector. It was based on the killing of a German diplomat by a young Polish Jewish refugee in Paris in 1938, and the savage Nazi reprisals of *Kristallnacht*. But it treated these events at a distance, drawing the Jungian conclusion that, to prevent such things recurring, each of us must come to terms with the shadow or evil side of our own personality, rather than projecting it onto an enemy. What helped to get across this difficult message must have been the extraordinary clarity and radiance of Tippett's music, with its echoes of eighteenth-century recitative, its lithe counterpoint, and its firm, satisfying cadences. And then there was his masterstroke: the inclusion, as the equivalent of the chorales in Bach's Passions, of negro spirituals, the songs of the victims of oppression half a world away. It is surely these simple, moving settings, as much as anything else in the work, that have ensured its continuing popularity.

Despite strong competition, the benchmark recording of *A Child of Our Time* remains the one conducted by Tippett's loyal, understanding advocate Colin Davis. It has a strong quartet of soloists, led by soprano Jessye Norman; the BBC Singers & Choral Society and Symphony Orchestra are excellent. Davis's performance seems full of compassion, and a burning conviction that the work is no 1940s period piece. The child is always of our time. **AB**

Alberto Ginastera
Estancia (1941)

Genre | Ballet
Conductor | Jan Wagner
Performers | Odense Symphony Orchestra
Year recorded | 2001
Label | Bridge 9130

Born in Buenos Aires of a Catalan father and an Italian mother, Alberto Ginastera (1916–83) was unquestionably the most significant figure in twentieth-century Argentine music. He combined deep interest in his country's authentic folk music with the pursuit of steadily more radical musical techniques to embody his personal vision.

The ballet *Estancia* is loosely based on the Argentine national epic *Martín Fierro* by José Hernández, which depicts in heroic and nostalgic terms the hard life of the nomadic gauchos in the desolate Argentinian plains. In the ballet, a city boy comes to the plains and has to master all the athletic skills of the gauchos before he can win the love of a beautiful ranch-girl. In the event, the complete score was not performed until 1952. But Ginastera's orchestral suite, the form of the work that is usually heard, premiered in Buenos Aires in 1943 and was instantly popular.

The malambo, an exuberant dance associated with the gauchos, had also come to be accepted as a national musical symbol. Its characteristic rhythmic structure (six measures of 6/8, divided in two groups of three) can be sensed in the suite's opening movement, and is present elsewhere, especially in the spectacular "Danza final," representing a dance tournament between the gauchos: an exhilarating explosion of kinetic energy, creating a toccata-like momentum of furious ostinato rhythms. This is not a work that calls for expressive subtlety but for a flood of adrenalin and physical energy, and Jan Wagner's excellently recorded performance (coupled with three other characteristic pieces from Ginastera's early years) provides that perfectly. **MM**

Dmitri Shostakovich | Symphony no. 7 "Leningrad" (1941)

Genre | Orchestral
Conductor | Leonard Bernstein
Performers | Chicago Symphony Orchestra
Year recorded | 1988
Label | DG 427 632-2 (2 CDs)

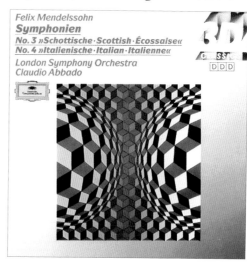

Felix Mendelssohn
Symphonien
No. 3 »Schottische · Scottish · Écossaise«
No. 4 »Italienische · Italian · Italienne«
London Symphony Orchestra
Claudio Abbado

The Seventh Symphony is a special case, however you look at it. While some commentators build a revisionist case on the basis of Shostakovich's reported assertion that "it's not about Leningrad under siege, it's about the Leningrad that Stalin destroyed and that Hitler merely finished off," even *Testimony* (the dodgy, Solomon Volkov-ghosted memoir) implies that the music was also intended as a morale booster for a country at war.

The symphony's reception history is instructive. Its most extraordinary realization was one given in the besieged city itself by a scratch orchestra, based on the remnants of the Leningrad Radio Orchestra, under Karl Eliasberg on August 9, 1941. Meanwhile, the score had been sent abroad on microfilm. Henry Wood conducted it in the United Kingdom on June 22, and the American premiere broadcast of July 19 was entrusted to Arturo Toscanini, the most vehemently anti-Fascist of the great conductors.

Were there perhaps extra-musical considerations behind Leonard Bernstein's revival of the piece at a time of renewed East-West tension in the early 1960s? When he revisited it in a rare series of concert dates with the Chicago orchestra, his interpretation had, not uncharacteristically, slowed but also deepened. This is the grandest rendering ever committed to disc and also the most electrifying. After the first movement's notorious central *Boléro*-like section, it is the quiet, almost dreamlike closing pages that impress most. Some have found the shadowy Mahlerian second movement too deliberate, but the third, with its hieratic wind chorales and impassioned string recitatives, is executed with matchless power and finesse. In the finale, the Chicago brass are tireless and the coda simply sensational. Fortunately the sonics are remarkable, too. **DG**

> *"I suppose that critics . . . will damn me for copying Ravel's* Boléro. *Well, let them. That is how I hear war."*

Shostakovich, as reported by Isaak Glikman

Other Recommended Recordings

St. Petersburg Philharmonic Orchestra
Vladimir Ashkenazy
Decca 448 814-2
An objective, unexaggerated recording

BBC National Orchestra of Wales
Mark Wigglesworth
BIS CD-873
Strongly individual music making from a young conductor

Royal Concertgebouw Orchestra • Mariss Jansons
RCO Live RCO 06002
A polished, anti-bombastic, even sleek conception

Shostakovich and his "Leningrad" Symphony made the cover of *Time*. ➦

TIME

THE WEEKLY NEWSMAGAZINE

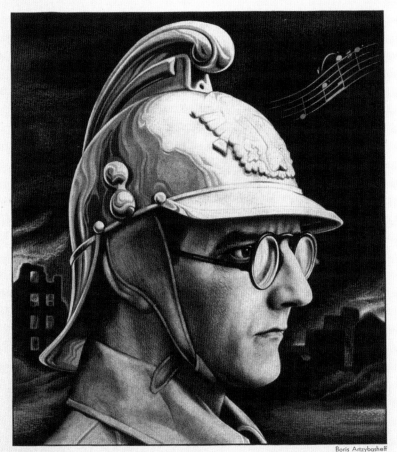

Boris Artzybasheff

FIREMAN SHOSTAKOVICH
Amid bombs bursting in Leningrad he heard the chords of victory.

(Music)

Maurice Duruflé | Prélude et fugue sur le nom d'Alain (1942)

Genre | Instrumental
Instrument | Organ
Performer | John Scott
Year recorded | 1989
Label | Hyperion CDA 66368

A prodigious keyboard player from an early age, Maurice Duruflé (1902–86) received his musical grounding—especially in Gregorian chant—as a chorister at Rouen Cathedral. After studying with Charles Tournemire, Duruflé found an ideal mentor and friend in Louis Vierne, the partially blind organist of Notre Dame Cathedral. During the 1920s, Duruflé's student career at the Paris Conservatoire was garlanded with prizes, and, in 1930, he secured his own position as titular organist of the church of Saint-Étienne du Mont in Paris. Duruflé was joined as co-titular by his former pupil, then wife, Marie-Madeleine, and together they served at St. Étienne till the end of their lives.

Duruflé's *Prelude and Fugue on the Name of Alain* is one of the greatest musical tributes made by one composer to another: in this case, the dedicatee was Jehan Alain, brother of the organist Marie-Claire. He was destined to become one of France's greatest composers, but was killed in action against the Germans in 1940. The prelude quotes the theme from Alain's organ work *Litanies*, and the fugue is a stunning piece of contrapuntal writing with a strong rhythmic pulse.

Duruflé's complete organ music fits neatly on one CD and all of it matches the quality of the *Alain* prelude and fugue. John Scott beats all comers hands down: on the organ of St. Paul's Cathedral, London, he contends with massive reverberation and a multidepartmental instrument to bring out as much Frenchness as possible, in a clearly articulated and balanced way. Scott achieves consummate phrasing, perfectly judged crescendos, and great atmosphere. His playing of all the Duruflé organ works is magisterial in its sheer elegance, discriminating taste, and devotion to the music. **GK**

> *"Teaching hones the critical spirit so much that you become unable to muster the courage to write."*
>
> Maurice Duruflé

Other Recommended Recordings

Maurice Duruflé
EMI 7243 5 74866 2 0 (5 CDs)
A fascinating opportunity to hear the composer's own interpretation

Marie-Madeleine Duruflé-Chevalier
Gothic G 49107
Spirited recording by Duruflé's most trusted interpreter—his wife

Vincent Warnier
Intrada INTRA 003
Vivid recent recording by the current organist of Duruflé's own church

Aaron Copland | Rodeo (1942)

Genre | Ballet
Conductor | Aaron Copland
Performers | London Symphony Orchestra
Year recorded | 1968
Label | Sony SM2K 89323 (2 CDs)

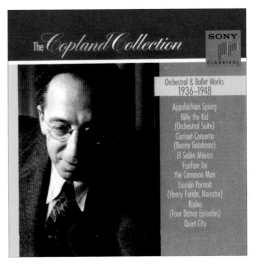

During the 1930s, Aaron Copland once famously said that he felt "an increasing dissatisfaction with the relations of the music-loving public and the living composer," and decided "to see if I couldn't say what I had to say in the simplest possible terms." Among the fruits of this populist approach were his three great ballet scores all based on American subjects.

Rodeo is the second of these, and the second on a cowboy subject. But, in contrast to the dramatic and ultimately tragic *Billy the Kid*, it is a comedy. The scenario, devised by Agnes de Mille for the United States–based Ballet Russe de Monte Carlo, is set on a Texas ranch around 1900. It is about a young cowgirl who fails to attract the head wrangler with her tomboyish exploits at the Saturday afternoon rodeo, but puts on a dress for the Saturday night party and gets her man.

The music—all but about five minutes' worth gathered into the familiar suite of *Four Dance Episodes*—uses several traditional folksongs and square-dance tunes. For the most part, *Rodeo* is extrovert and joyful, not least in the riotous "Hoe-Down" finale. But the "Corral Nocturne," in which Copland said he was striving for "a sense of the isolation felt by the heroine," strikes a deeper and more personal note.

Copland took up conducting quite late in his career, and although he never acquired a cast-iron technique, he became very good at getting his own music to sound just the way he wanted it—even with the British orchestras with which he made most of his recordings. The sound of his 1968 *Rodeo Dance Episodes* has held up well; the performance is exuberant, witty, incisive, and, not least, full of Copland's essential humanity. **AB**

> "This is the story of the Taming of the Shrew—cowboy style. It is not an epic. . . . It is a pastorale, a lyric joke."

Agnes de Mille, scenario for *Rodeo*

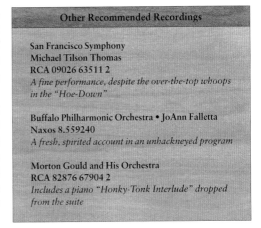

Other Recommended Recordings

San Francisco Symphony
Michael Tilson Thomas
RCA 09026 63511 2
A fine performance, despite the over-the-top whoops in the "Hoe-Down"

Buffalo Philharmonic Orchestra • JoAnn Falletta
Naxos 8.559240
A fresh, spirited account in an unhackneyed program

Morton Gould and His Orchestra
RCA 82876 67904 2
Includes a piano "Honky-Tonk Interlude" dropped from the suite

Gerald Finzi | Let Us Garlands Bring (1942)

Genre | Vocal
Performers | Janet Baker (mezzo-soprano),
Geoffrey Parsons (piano)
Year recorded | 1983
Label | BBC Legends BBCL 4117-2

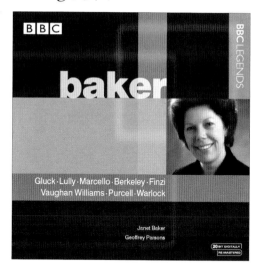

Finzi's settings of five songs from Shakespeare's plays were, for the most part, written in a time of war. Finzi (1901–56) was from an old Italian-Jewish family, and was a pacifist: the concentration and urgency of his writing during this period was surely a reflection of his view of the artist as holding the torch for civilization in barbaric times.

The songs, written over a period of thirteen years, were assembled as a seventieth birthday present for his mentor, Ralph Vaughan Williams. They were given their first performance, in the original version for baritone and piano, on his birthday, October 12, 1942, at a lunchtime concert in London's National Gallery (Finzi also presented Vaughan Williams with the largest apple from his orchard of rare fruit trees). There is also an arrangement by Finzi for string orchestra, and this premiered just six days later.

Finzi's vast library of English literature (now preserved in the Finzi Book Room of Reading University Library in Berkshire, England) was frequently rifled for his great settings of Traherne, Milton, Wordsworth, and Hardy. Constantly honing his own responses to English language and prosody, Finzi achieved in his Shakespeare settings a true refinement of his craft. Inflection crisscrosses with meter, in ever-supple, animated lines of melody.

Janet Baker, as a supreme interpreter of English song, reactivates and recreates Finzi's own impassioned yet sophisticated response to Shakespeare's words. In her performance of "Fear No More the Heat o' the Sun" from *Cymbeline*, the song at the emotional heart of the cycle, it seems as though Finzi's setting had existed forever, its melody implicit within Shakespeare's poetry. And this live recital, from the 1983 Cheltenham Festival, resonates with Baker's unique communication with her audience. **HF**

> *"Finzi's principle was that no words were too fine or too familiar to be inherently unsettable by a composer . . ."*
>
> Diana McVeagh

Other Recommended Recordings

English Orchestral Songs
Christopher Maltman, BBC Scottish Symphony
Orchestra • Martyn Brabbins • Hyperion CDA 67065
An eloquent performance for string orchestra and baritone

The Vagabond
Bryn Terfel, Malcolm Martineau • DG 445 946-2
Finzi's garlands entwine Ralph Vaughan Williams's
Songs of Travel *and songs by Butterworth and Ireland*

The Very Best of English Song
Various artists • EMI 7243 5 75926 2 8 (2 CDs)
Finzi's settings of Robert Bridges and Thomas Hardy in the wider context of English song

Gerald Finzi, whose songs are among the best in the English repertoire. ➡

Sergei Prokofiev | Piano Sonata no. 7 (1942)

Genre | Instrumental
Instrument | Piano
Performer | Maurizio Pollini
Year recorded | 1972
Label | DG 447 431-2

This is the shortest but in some ways the toughest of Prokofiev's three so-called "War Sonatas," his chronicle of suffering that reflects not just the horrors of the German invasion but also the insecurity of life in Stalin's Russia. The style of this sonata reflects the characteristic mixture of abrasiveness and lyricism that had marked out Prokofiev's piano music from the beginning, but with a new intensity that reflected the unquiet spirit of the times. The work begins with restless nervous energy followed by a vain attempt to escape into the world of dreams. The central slow movement virtually quotes a Schumann Lied, with a telling reference to the words "no one hears the pain in my song." If we were in any doubt of the pain, it rises in waves to be greeted by the tolling of funeral bells. The last movement is a justly celebrated fiendish dance in perpetual motion, its syncopated repeated figure making it sound like jazz; but menace held in check spills over into the devastating coda.

Maurizio Pollini is the finest interpreter of Prokofiev's most concise late sonata since the pianist who gave its first performance, Sviatoslav Richter. If anything, he makes the modernity of the work even more striking. The angular phrases of the opening movement are crisp and clear, initially putting us off our guard for the crouching tiger that lurks ready to pounce without warning. Pollini is the ideal quick-change artist, able to switch from nimble dancing to ferocious intensity without ever making the common performer's error of pounding the piano unmercifully to signal the change. He has the full measure of the slow movement's nostalgia, and gives us a coruscating finale, taken at a dangerously fast pace but brilliantly articulated from first note to last. **DN**

> *"Chaos and uncertainty reign. We see murderous forces unleashed."*
>
> Sviatoslav Richter

Other Recommended Recordings

Vladimir Horowitz
RCA GD 60377
A more virtuosic approach from the keyboard wizard, recorded in 1945

Barbara Nissman
Pierian 0007/9 (3 CDs)
Nissman gives the most full-blooded account of the finale as part of a complete cycle

Sonata no. 8
Sviatoslav Richter
DG 449 744-2
The third and most poignant of the "War Sonatas"

Arnold Schoenberg | Piano Concerto (1942)

Genre | Concerto
Performers/Conductor | Alfred Brendel (piano),
SWF Baden-Baden Symphony Orchestra; Michael Gielen
Year recorded | 1993
Label | Philips 446 683-2

Schoenberg composed his Piano Concerto in Los Angeles: he intended it for the jazz pianist Oscar Levant, and it is among the most approachable of all his mature twelve-note compositions, with plenty of tonal feeling to its invention. As in some of his early works, he ran the elements of four distinct movements into a continuous sequence, but it is easy enough to sense the familiar shape of lyrical first movement, disruptive scherzo, profound and searching slow movement, and ebullient finale.

In fact, it is a masterpiece of a thoroughly traditional kind, a conscious continuation of the genre to which Mozart, Beethoven, Schumann, and Brahms committed some of their finest music. And its harmonic and tonal idiom should present no problem to any listener who has assimilated the concertos of Bartók. The soloist opens the proceedings alone, with instruments gradually joining in as the piano states a graceful, lilting, very Viennese melody and starts to explore its implications. At the very end of the work, this tune returns, broadened into a resolute march. In between, the scherzo has something of the raw emotion and nightmarish orchestral sonorities of Schoenberg's earlier Expressionist works, while the deeply serious Adagio is among his most profound inspirations.

Alfred Brendel has very much made the concerto "his" work, and the recommended version is his third and best recording of it, evoking its varied moods with the wisdom of maturity while utterly in command of its difficulties. Brendel is unrivalled in his flexible shaping of Schoenberg's melodies, and at bringing out the first movement's lyricism and the finale's sense of joie de vivre achieved against odds. Michael Gielen, a highly experienced Schoenberg conductor, gives excellent support. **MM**

> *"Life was so easy*
> *Suddenly hatred broke out*
> *A grave situation was created*
> *But life goes on."*

Schoenberg, interpreting the Piano Concerto

Other Recommended Recordings

Mitsuko Uchida, Cleveland Orchestra
Pierre Boulez
Philips 468 033-2
A more visceral view of the concerto

Glenn Gould, CBC Symphony Orchestra
Jean-Marie Beaudet
CBC PSCD 2008
A fascinating live broadcast of 1953

Violin Concerto
Rolf Schulte, Philharmonia Orchestra • Robert Craft
Koch International 3-7493-2
Schoenberg's deeply expressive and passionate work

Richard Strauss
Horn Concerto no. 2
(1942)

Genre | Concerto
Performers | Dennis Brain (horn),
Philharmonia Orchestra
Year recorded | 1956
Label | EMI 7243 5 67783 2 0

Marooned in Nazi Germany and horrified by the destruction of the civilized world he had served with his music, Richard Strauss turned to the past. This Horn Concerto is testament to the solace he found in Mozart's music and the memories of his father Franz, first horn in the Munich Court Orchestra, who provided the inspiration for his First Horn Concerto written when Strauss was only nineteen. This concerto, like its predecessor, is in the horn-friendly key of E flat major, but strikes a more mellow tone. It heralds the "Indian Summer" of Strauss's life, which also included the Oboe Concerto and the *Duett-Concertino* for clarinet, bassoon, and orchestra. Here, the serene mood is more that of a second spring. The style is utterly distinctive with piquant harmonies and unexpected turns of phrase. After the opening fanfares, the soloist alternates between song and playfulness, relaxing into the lullaby-like second movement. The finale is Strauss's homage to his Mozartian model, in which the horn leads the orchestra a merry dance until the orchestral horns call it a day.

No one has ever brought out the mood of the concerto more beguilingly than the great Dennis Brain, who tragically died in a car crash a year after this recording. He slips from spot-on fanfaring to smooth singing with the greatest of ease, and there are plenty of well-balanced dialogues between the soloist and the characterful woodwind of the Philharmonia, deftly conducted by Wolfgang Sawallisch. The sound is remarkably clear and well-balanced for its age. **DN**

Benjamin Britten
Serenade for Tenor, Horn, and Strings (1943)

Genre | Vocal
Performers | Peter Pears (tenor), Dennis
Brain (horn), Boyd Neel Orchestra
Year recorded | 1944
Label | Decca 468 801-2

Britten's *Serenade for Tenor, Horn, and Strings* is an archetypal example of his work. It shows his setting of the English language at its most refined and it was one of the first works openly to exploit the tenor voice of his partner, Peter Pears. It stands out in the song-cycle medium through the inventiveness of its scoring. The horn is no coloristic adjunct to the cycle, but an equal to the voice. Relying on natural harmonics, the player frames the work with a prologue and an epilogue that conjure up the theme of the songs—night. Six of Britten's most masterly song settings are enclosed within, with poetry ranging from an anonymous fifteenth-century "Dirge" to Keats's sonnet "O Soft Embalmer of the Still Midnight," by way of Jonson and Tennyson. As in the earlier cycle *Les illuminations*, the onus of accompaniment falls to an orchestra of strings, and calls upon Britten's effortless skill in conjuring up atmosphere.

As well as being a gift for Pears, the work was written for the brilliant horn player Dennis Brain, who recorded it with Pears and Britten soon after the premiere. Although in some respects superseded by a later, 1960s account with Pears and Barry Tuckwell, this recording is more than just a historical document. Its mono sound is understandably restricted, though it does have unusually rich low frequencies for the day—the by-product of attempts to amplify the sound of German submarines. It captures Pears's voice at a fresher stage of his career than the 1963 Decca remake, while Brain is unrivaled in the fluency and tonal suavity of his playing. **MR**

Sergei Prokofiev
War and Peace

(1943, *rev.* 1952)

Genre | Opera
Conductor/Performers | Valery Gergiev;
Elena Prokina, Gegam Grigorian
Year recorded | 1991
Label | Philips 434 097-2 (3 CDs)

It is no easy task to turn one of the greatest and most wide-ranging novels ever written into an opera, but that is what Prokofiev began to do with Leo Tolstoy's *War and Peace* in 1941. There were parallels between the German invasion and Napoleon's foolhardy attack on Russia, and as Prokofiev's work proceeded, he was "advised" by Soviet committees to "beef up" the patriotism of his war sequences. The extra choruses occasionally detract from the serious critique of war's senseless destruction, but there is one gain: the last-minute aria provided for the Russian leader, General Kutuzov, set to one of the most stirring melodies in twentieth-century opera. The first, "peace" half of this epic opera centers around the impetuous young Natasha Rostova, the novel's heroine. Prokofiev's selection of events is telling and, like the novel, achieves tremendous cumulative impact.

Deciding how much of Prokofiev's lengthy narrative to include is a difficult decision for any opera company, but in 1991, the centenary year of the composer's birth, Valery Gergiev persuaded his Kirov Opera Chorus and Orchestra to present the opera very nearly complete. The result is a vivid theatrical experience, sometimes overwhelmed by stage noise (a DVD is also available). The company works well as a whole, but very much the star is Elena Prokina's palpitating Natasha. She is heartbreaking in the scene where her failed elopement with the seasoned roué Anatol Kuragin goes wrong and touching in her final reunion with the dying Prince she once betrayed. **DN**

Ralph Vaughan Williams
Symphony no. 5

(1943)

Genre | Orchestral
Conductor/Performers | André Previn;
London Symphony Orchestra
Year recorded | 1972
Label | RCA 82876 55708 2 (6 CDs)

The Fifth Symphony is generally viewed as Vaughan Williams's most successful creation in this genre. This is partly because his musical language by the 1940s was fully mature; the combination of folk-melodic idiom with his own, at times almost French, harmonic vocabulary is convincing. The grasp of true symphonic thought is shown in the recurring ideas that bind the work. The symphony's opening, disturbed, unstable horn call with string descants is transformed into a landscape of glorious calm. Vaughan Williams was working on this piece at the same time as his "morality," *The Pilgrim's Progress*, and a number of themes from that work appear in the symphony. He was never a man of strong faith, yet here his vision suggests religious feelings. Anyone who knows his much-loved hymn tune *Sine nomine* (sung to *For All the Saints*) will be struck by his use of the "Alleluia" from that as a recurring theme.

André Previn brings Vaughan Williams's vision to beautiful fruition in his fine recording. At times he exaggerates the written instructions (the string playing at the opening is surely quieter than piano and the last movement is paced more slowly than the metronome mark) but the effect is magical. The LSO strings handle the high, sustained melodies with remarkable sweetness and there is real tenderness and subtle control with moments of poignant rubato. Their gossamer threads of sound contrasting with the dark woodwind tones of the first movement are compelling and the symphony's final hymnlike cadences are played with nobility. **SW**

Béla Bartók
Concerto for Orchestra (1943, *rev.* 1945)

Genre | Orchestral
Conductor | Fritz Reiner
Performers | Chicago Symphony Orchestra
Year recorded | 1955
Label | RCA 82876 61390 2

Leaving his beloved Hungary for the United States in 1940, Bartók hoped to rebuild his career in his adopted country. Unfortunately, few of the opportunities that had been promised to him actually materialized, leaving him desperately homesick and impoverished, and in increasingly poor health. The intervention of two compatriots, the conductor Fritz Reiner and the violinist Joseph Szigeti, proved critical to a revival in his fortunes, for they managed to persuade Serge Koussevitzky to commission Bartók to write a major work for the Boston Symphony Orchestra. In response, Bartók composed his Concerto for Orchestra, which as its title suggests, was designed to display the extraordinary talents of Koussevitzky's players. But the work amounts to more than a virtuoso showpiece; its first and third movements have dark and unsettling moments that refer back to Bartók's opera *Bluebeard's Castle*, and the finale's life-asserting conclusion is not achieved without a sense of struggle.

With its highly accessible musical language and brilliant scoring, it is hardly surprising that the Concerto for Orchestra has maintained a stable place in the repertoire since its first performance in December 1944. A number of fine recordings of the work could easily qualify for classic status, none more so than the 1955 performance featuring Fritz Reiner and the Chicago Symphony Orchestra. Reiner may not always drive the music with the same degree of ferocity as Georg Solti or Antál Dorati, but he enjoys the benefit of superbly articulated orchestral playing on disc. Newly restored to the catalogue on SACD, the recording hardly betrays its age and sounds magnificent. **EL**

"Undoubtedly the finest orchestral piece to have been written in recent years."

Serge Koussevitzky

Other Recommended Recordings

Budapest Festival Orchestra
Iván Fischer
Philips 476 7255
An unusually lyrical account from the finest of all Hungarian orchestras

Philadelphia Orchestra
Christoph Eschenbach
Ondine ODE 10725
Brilliant playing captured in demonstration sound

Chicago Symphony Orchestra • Georg Solti
Decca 475 7711
Typically high-voltage interpretation

Paul Hindemith | Symphonic Metamorphosis after Themes by Carl Maria von Weber (1943)

Genre | Orchestral
Conductor | Herbert Blomstedt
Performers | San Francisco Symphony
Year recorded | 1987
Label | Decca 475 264-2 (3 CDs)

The somewhat verbose title Hindemith gave to this work suggests something of serious intent and convoluted structure. Yet nothing could be further from the truth: the *Symphonic Metamorphosis* proves to be a witty and brilliant orchestral showpiece that transforms some pretty innocuous thematic material by Weber into music that is typical of its composer. Three of its four movements betray the work's initial conception as a ballet planned with the great choreographer Leonid Massine. Although nothing came of the project, the Hungarian-style opening Allegro, a gently contemplative siciliano, and a rousing march certainly convey the spirit of the dance. The most spectacular movement of all is the *Turandot* scherzo, a set of highly inventive variations on a Chinese theme with an exuberant passage for solo percussion and a jazzy fugue.

First performed by the New York Philharmonic under Artur Rodzinski in January 1944, the *Symphonic Metamorphosis* has remained one of Hindemith's most popular and frequently recorded works. Among the most distinguished of its earlier recordings are the composer's own 1950s DG release with the Berlin Philharmonic and Sony's superb 1960s version with the Cleveland Orchestra under George Szell. Undoubtedly the finest release is this one with the incisive San Francisco Symphony under Herbert Blomstedt—it is a performance that combines necessary high spirits with wonderful textural clarity. Now reissued as part of a three-disc set, it affords a marvelous opportunity to hear the *Symphonic Metamorphosis* as well as outstanding performances of many of Hindemith's other major orchestral works. **EL**

"A loyal friend ... elegant in behavior and with a delightful fund of humor."

Igor Stravinsky on Hindemith

Other Recommended Recordings

Berlin Philharmonic Orchestra
Claudio Abbado
DG 447 389-2
An Abbado speciality delivered with tremendous energy

Cleveland Orchestra • Georg Szell
Sony SBK 53258
Szell in his element

Berlin Philharmonic Orchestra
Paul Hindemith
DG 474 7702 (3 CDs)
Authoritative 1950s account directed by the composer

Dmitri Shostakovich | Symphony no. 8 (1943)

Genre | Orchestral
Conductor | Yevgeny Mravinsky
Performers | Leningrad Philharmonic Orchestra
Year recorded | 1982
Label | Regis RRC 1250

Shostakovich composed his C minor Symphony at astonishing speed in the summer of 1943, dedicating it to the conductor Yevgeny Mravinsky, its earliest and possibly greatest interpreter. The authorities were not impressed—the piece was inescapably pessimistic and lacked the propaganda possibilities of its predecessor—but until singled out for attack at Stalin's henchman Andrei Zhdanov's notorious congress of 1948, it was not publicly reviled and Mravinsky was permitted to conduct it. Now the Eighth has come in from the cold and there is even a revisionist view of it. A score conventionally admired for its symphonic cogency, it has now begun to attract criticism for the baldness of its melodic content and perceived lack of ironic distancing. Attitudes can change but, even allowing that, the symphony is unlikely to return to the shadows. It is a sonic mausoleum—long, loud, and just the right length for compact disc—although obviously there is far more to it than that.

Mravinsky's 1982 version makes an obvious first choice, its close-up sound much better than might be expected from a Soviet-sourced tape. Indeed, the authentic timbres of the Leningrad Philharmonic have rarely been so well captured on disc, the woodwind tearing into their phrases, the string sound inimitable. Although the playing is not quite immaculate, the effect is more convincing than in many concert relays from this late in Mravinsky's career. There is no want of feeling, the first movement a suitably exhausting haul even at a tempo that disregards Shostakovich's metronome marks, and the structure is held together without difficulty. There is an authenticity of experience here, an overwhelming vehemence that does duty for a more conventionally "expressive" manner. **DG**

> *"A performance of extraordinary vehemence and power, vivid contrast and bitter intensity."*
>
> Michael Oliver writing in *Gramophone* magazine

Other Recommended Recordings

Leningrad Philharmonic Orchestra
Yevgeny Mravinsky
BBC Legends BBCL 4002 2
This 1960 Royal Festival Hall rendition kept the symphony's reputation alive in the United Kingdom

Berlin Symphony Orchestra • Kurt Sanderling
Berlin 0020642 BC
Perhaps the most deeply considered of them all

Amsterdam Concertgebouw Orchestra
Bernard Haitink
Decca 425 071-2
Haitink's strongly architectural reading

The Eighth was dedicated to its greatest interpreter, Mravinsky. ➔

Aaron Copland | Appalachian Spring (1944)

Genre | Ballet
Conductor | Aaron Copland
Performers | Boston Symphony Orchestra
Year recorded | 1959
Label | RCA 09026 61505 2

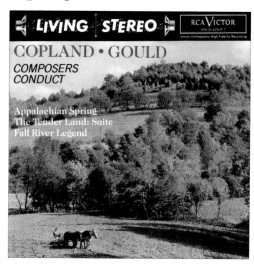

Appalachian Spring is the last panel in Copland's triptych of ballets on American themes. And it is a key work in his output, marking the point at which his ambition to write music accessible to the general public coincided most completely with his natural inclination toward formal clarity and cohesion. The piece was written for Martha Graham's modern dance company, and her scenario (in the last of many versions) centers on a celebration of spring in the Pennsylvania hills "by a man and a woman building a house with joy and love and prayer; by a revivalist and his followers in their shouts of exaltation; by a pioneering woman with her dreams of the Promised Land." Copland matches the atmosphere perfectly with a score containing not only square-dance rhythms and a sequence of variations on the Shaker hymn "The Gift to be Simple," but also episodes of reflection and prayer that have a magical intimacy and simplicity.

The piece was originally written for a luminous ensemble of no more than thirteen instruments—woodwind, piano, and strings—and lasted more than half an hour. But it soon became widely popular in Copland's brilliant reworking of it for full orchestra, as a continuous suite with about eight minutes taken out. Then, later, the composer both completed the orchestration of the full-length ballet and published the suite in the original thirteen-instrument scoring. You can make a good case for any of the four versions, and in the right recordings they are all well worth hearing. But the one that stands out is the first of Copland's own two accounts of the orchestral suite, made in Boston in 1959. It is a reading full of the freshness and tenderness that make *Appalachian Spring* such a special and lovable piece. **AB**

> *"The music is so knit and of a completeness that it takes you in very strong hands and leads you . . ."*
>
> Martha Graham

Other Recommended Recordings

Columbia Chamber Ensemble • Aaron Copland
Sony SM2K 89323 (2 CDs)
The composer conducts his original full-length thirteen-instrument ballet score

Harmonie Ensemble New York • Steven Richman
Bridge 9145
The thirteen-instrument suite, well played in a good modern recording

San Francisco Symphony • Michael Tilson Thomas
RCA 09026 63511 2
To complete the set, the full-length ballet resplendent on full orchestra

The Martha Graham Dance Company version of *Appalachian Spring*. ➲

Sergei Prokofiev
Cinderella (1944)

Genre | Ballet
Conductor/Performers | André Previn;
London Symphony Orchestra
Year recorded | 1977
Label | EMI 7243 4 76945 2 3 (2 CDs)

After the troubled birth pangs of *Romeo and Juliet*, Prokofiev's first full-length ballet for the Soviet stage, his second, *Cinderella*, was more straightforward and provided another leading role for Galina Ulanova, the ballerina who had created the role of Juliet. "Although the tale . . . exists in all countries," wrote Prokofiev, "I wanted to treat it as a real Russian fairytale, and Cinderella herself not only as a fairytale character, but as a real person who feels and suffers." He endowed her character with a brace of themes, all of which develop as the story progresses. She is surrounded by Prokofiev's penchant for the grotesque, in the shape of the Ugly Sisters, the courtiers at the ball, and twelve tap-dancing dwarves who leap out of the midnight clock. There is also gentler magic in the shape of the Fairy Godmother and the entertainment of seasonal fairies before Cinderella sets off for the ball. The heart and soul of the ballet is the pas de deux danced by Cinderella and her Prince, a fine example of Prokofiev's gift for melody.

The score, leaner in its textures and more elusive in character than *Romeo and Juliet*, needs a special helping hand when detached from the stage. Mikhail Pletnev's account with the Russian National Orchestra has been highly praised, but lacks the momentum necessary to connect the many individual numbers. Warmer and more glittering in its orchestral sound is Previn's recording with the LSO. Together they rise to the challenge of the big set pieces at the ball and provide sophisticated allure to the more contrived inspirations of the third act, where the Prince travels the world in search of the glass slipper's rightful owner. **DN**

Sergei Prokofiev
Symphony no. 5 (1944)

Genre | Orchestral
Conductor/Performers | Klaus Tennstedt;
Bavarian Radio Symphony Orchestra
Year recorded | 1977
Label | Profil PH 05003

In a radio broadcast of 1945, Prokofiev declared that he conceived the Fifth Symphony—composed the previous summer at white heat and his first symphonic work in sixteen years—as "a symphony of the greatness of the human spirit." Its premiere, conducted by the composer at the beginning of that year, coincided with the impending triumph of Russia's struggle against Germany, and many heard the work as a victory symphony. Yet, as in Shostakovich's symphonies, not everything is quite as it seems. The heroic breadth of the first movement, accumulating brassy weight as it lumbers to a colossal conclusion, is mocked by a dark and racy scherzo. The slow movement's private anguish and funeral processions seem to be relieved by a jolly gallop in the finale, but even that spins out of control in a coda that rips its most optimistic themes to shreds. Although the tragedy that dominates the symphony's successor, the powerful Sixth, is less apparent here, Prokofiev carefully ensures it has a place.

The Fifth is Prokofiev's most popular symphony after the succinct high spirits of no. 1, the "Classical." Its range of sonorities, capped by the dazzling conclusion, mark it out as a stunning showpiece. Whether it turns out to be anything more depends on the conductor. Klaus Tennstedt, more familiar for his intense interpretations of the Austro-German symphonic repertoire, extracts the utmost weight and vividness in this Bavarian Radio performance. Romantic breadth of line keeps the broader arguments of the first and third movements alive, while the spirited clarinet playing is typical of a more than usually lurid, sarcastic scherzo and a bracing finale. **DN**

Dmitri Shostakovich
Piano Trio no. 2 (1944)

Genre | Chamber
Performers | Vienna Piano Trio: Wolfgang Redik, Marcus Trefny, Stefan Mendl
Year recorded | 1998
Label | Nimbus NI 5572

"My whole development I owe to him. It will be unimaginably difficult for me to go on living without him." Shostakovich wrote these words on learning of the unexpected death in February 1944 of his close friend Ivan Sollertinsky. Working at the time on his Second Piano Trio, Shostakovich dedicated his latest composition to Sollertinsky's memory, following a precedent set some sixty years earlier by Tchaikovsky, whose Piano Trio paid homage to the recently deceased Nikolai Rubinstein. The mournful and despairing tone is announced in the opening, the disembodied cello harmonics matched by a numbingly somber melody on the violin. A sardonic and brutal scherzo is followed by a slow passacaglia movement based around a sequence of eight stiflingly percussive chords. These act as a prelude to the trio's final and longest movement, with its notable use of Jewish klezmer music, a reflection of the composer's horror at the atrocities that were being committed against the Jews in Nazi extermination camps during this period.

The players of the Vienna Piano Trio are outstanding advocates of this masterpiece. They respond with acute sensitivity to the music's mood swings, sometimes deceptively naive, but more often oppressive and threatening. They are particularly adept in tracing and sustaining the narrative of the extended finale, saving their most impassioned playing for the return of the opening material just before it sinks into utter desolation at the coda. Appropriately, the disc also features the youthful First Piano Trio and the Piano Trio by Alfred Schnittke, a work of equally searing power and emotional fervor. **EL**

Leonard Bernstein
On the Town (1944)

Genre | Musical
Conductor/Performers | Michael Tilson Thomas; Thomas Hampson, Kurt Ollman
Year recorded | 1992
Label | DG 476 7145

Roughly contemporary with *Oklahoma!* and *Carousel*, Bernstein's *On the Town* exemplified the musical's newfound interest in dance: with its mix of music, movement, and scenography, the genre had found its *Gesamtkunstwerk*. Bernstein collaborated with the then equally up-and-coming Betty Comden and Adolph Green on book and lyrics and the result is a piece of youthful exuberance, sassy in its musical score, unapologetically brash in its dramatic impact. Moreover, it is a young man's celebration of the excitement of city life. Indeed, its opening number—where we meet the three sailors—has become something of an anthem for the Big Apple: "New York, New York! It's a helluva town!" The plot mixes the touching and the absurd as the three make the most of their shore leave in pursuit of girls and fun. The music is a nonstop procession of memorable songs, from the helter-skelter taxi ride of "Come Up to My Place" to the yearning of Gabey's "Lonely Town," while the best of the score's dance numbers—first choreographed by Jerome Robbins—have become familiar in concert as Three Dance Episodes.

The musical is best known through the 1949 movie version starring Gene Kelly and Frank Sinatra. Bernstein directed an original cast recording in 1958 (with himself anagrammatically as "Randel Striboneen" playing the nightclub barker). Even that cannot beat the vibrancy of the only other version, Michael Tilson Thomas's account with the LSO and London Voices, taped live at London's Barbican. The cast is second to none, with charismatic performances from the leads as well as stars like Samuel Ramey, Cleo Laine, and Adolph Green. **MR**

Olivier Messiaen | Vingt regards sur l'Enfant-Jésus (1944)

Genre | Instrumental
Instrument | Piano
Performer | Yvonne Loriod
Year recorded | 1973
Label | Warner 2564 62162-2 (18 CDs)

Written in Paris between March and September 1944, *Vingt regards sur l'Enfant-Jésus* (*Twenty Glances on the Baby Jesus*) marks the end of a burst of creativity for which the extraordinary young pianist Yvonne Loriod was the catalyst and the German occupation the backdrop. The initial impetus was a request for fifteen minutes of music for Maurice Toesca's *Douze regards*, a set of picturesque vignettes on the Nativity. Messiaen substantially exceeded Toesca's requirements, not just by writing *Vingt regards*, but also in creating a work that goes beyond the Nativity and becomes a profound contemplation of Jesus's existence.

As pianistic endeavors go, Messiaen's cycle is among the most daunting. The fact that this overwhelming challenge is being tackled in ever-greater numbers diminishes neither its difficulty nor its allure. It requires not only a formidable technique, but also the temperament to jump from periods of the utmost calm to bursts of ferocious velocity while keeping a sense of the spiritual framework. Several themes, notably the theme of God, permeate it like Wagnerian leitmotifs. Each movement is furnished with an inscription, indicating the theological stimulus at every stage on the journey, from the calm opening to the jubilant final peroration in heaven.

Loriod not only gave the premiere of the *Vingt regards* in the febrile atmosphere of post-liberation Paris, but hundreds of subsequent performances. Despite occasionally poor editing, this classic recording captures the essence of her art, with a feverishly exciting dash through the daunting sixth regard, "Par Lui tout a été fait." Her technical command is matched by profound belief both in the music and its spiritual message, not to mention her love for the man who wrote it. **CD**

> *"I knew that they would be played by Yvonne Loriod ... because everything is possible to her."*
>
> Olivier Messiaen

Other Recommended Recordings

Steven Osborne
Hyperion CDA 67351/2 (2 CDs)
A wonderful all-round performance

Peter Hill
Regis RRC 2055 (2 CDs)
A performance that needs to be heard in its entirety

Louise Bessette
Atma ACD 2 2219/20 (2 CDs)
Bessette draws upon a seemingly orchestral palette of color

Yvonne Loriod, a phenomenal pianist, was Messiaen's greatest muse. ➡

Benjamin Britten | Peter Grimes (1945)

Genre | Opera
Conductor/Performers | Benjamin Britten; Peter Pears, Clare Watson, James Pease, Royal Opera House
Year recorded | 1958
Label | Decca 467 682-2 (2 CDs)

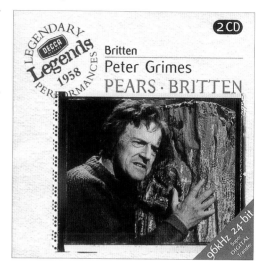

The first performance of *Peter Grimes* in 1945 ensured Britten's standing at the forefront of British composers, and brought him international recognition. A new operatic tradition was founded and Britten went on to make several more important contributions in this genre. The plot focuses on Grimes, a fisherman in the remote Borough who fails to fit in with his local community despite his best wishes. He hopes to marry the kindly schoolmistress Ellen Orford and set up a respectable business. Within the town he remains disliked; there are suspicions about the rough treatment he deals to his young boy apprentices and the occasions when he reveals his extraordinary, visionary, and poetic aspects are met with incomprehension and ridicule. Although Ellen and Captain Balstrode view him sympathetically, his inner turmoil and violent responses seal his fate and, following the death of a new apprentice, he is driven to madness and suicide by the hostile villagers.

The astonishing quality of Decca's remastering of Britten's classic recording cannot be exaggerated. There are so many moments of intelligently engineered dramatic situations that the opera comes magnificently to life. Characters enter and leave the stage completely convincingly; for example, as the savage chorus marches toward Grimes in his hut in Act 2, they move gradually away from our hearing and the introspective world of the four women left behind emerges with wonderful control.

Peter Pears is on superb form, shifting from joy and optimism to vile anger, and ultimately to madness in a persuasive performance. Other solo roles are also handled with complete conviction and the Royal Opera House Chorus and Orchestra work at the height of their powers under Britten's direction. **SW**

> *"Grimes is not a hero nor is he an operatic villain. . . . There are plenty of Grimeses around still I think!"*
>
> Peter Pears, in 1946

Other Recommended Recordings

Royal Opera House Chorus & Orchestra
Bernard Haitink
EMI 0777 7 54832 2 2 (2 CDs)
Very strong all-round, with Sarah Walker a glorious Mrs. Sedley

City of London Sinfonia • Richard Hickox
Chandos CHAN 9447/8 (2 CDs)
Dramatic performance with Philip Langridge in fine form

London Symphony Orchestra • Colin Davis
LSO Live LSO 0054 (2 CDs)
A less highly driven version, most atmospheric

Peter Pears (center front) as Peter Grimes in the opera's original staging. ➔

Béla Bartók | Piano Concerto no. 3 (1945)

Genre | Concerto
Performers | Géza Anda, Berlin Radio Symphony Orchestra
Conductor | Ferenc Fricsay
Year recorded | 1959
Label | DG 447 399-2

ORIGINAL IMAGE
BIT-PROCESSING

In the summer of 1945, Bartók began work on his Third Piano Concerto. Suffering from leukemia and depressed by his precarious financial situation, he still managed to complete the work before his death in September, the final bars having been orchestrated by his pupil Tibor Serly. Composed primarily for his wife, the pianist Ditta Pástory, the Piano Concerto is far less problematic in terms of its technical demands than its predecessors. Yet the musical language is also simpler in character with clearer tonal centers and a noticeable absence of the percussive keyboard writing that is associated with Bartók.

The simplicity of this work is deceptive. Although the mood of the opening material is calm and somewhat impressionistic in texture, and the finale has a rhythmically exuberant conclusion, Bartók never relaxes his customary subtle control of the structure, and there are occasional hints of more disturbing resonances beneath the surface. Nevertheless, for the most part the piece breathes an air of almost otherworldly serenity, nowhere more poignantly projected than in the central slow movement with its haunting juxtaposition of a radiant chorale with one of the composer's shimmering evocations of nocturnal music.

Bartók's Third Piano Concerto quickly established itself in the repertoire and there are many fine recordings, especially from Hungarian artists who have a particular empathy for its understated character. In terms of an innate understanding of the music and the wonderful interaction between soloist, conductor, and orchestra, Géza Anda's recording with Ferenc Fricsay conducting the Berlin Radio Symphony Orchestra is peerless, a partnership that underlines the music's sadness and nostalgia, while conveying a glimmer of hope in the finale. **EL**

> *"Bartók was the kind of man who wanted to make everything on earth better and more beautiful."*
>
> Zoltán Kodály

Other Recommended Recordings

Stephen Kovacevich, BBC Symphony Orchestra
Colin Davis
Universal 468 188-2
Fine and expressive playing from Kovacevich

Jénő Jandó, Budapest Symphony Orchestra
András Ligeti
Naxos. 8.550771
Fluent Hungarian performance at a bargain price

Hélène Grimaud, London Symphony Orchestra
Pierre Boulez
DG 477 5330
Grimaud and Boulez explore unexpected resonances

Hungarian-born pianist Géza Anda was renowned for his Bartók. ➲

Erich Wolfgang Korngold | Violin Concerto (1945)

Genre | Concerto
Performers/Conductor | Jascha Heifetz (violin), Los
Angeles Philharmonic Orchestra; Alfred Wallenstein
Year recorded | 1953
Label | RCA GD 61752

Why a work as lyrical and memorable as Korngold's Violin Concerto should have gone virtually unplayed for decades is a mystery. Or rather, it is one of those peculiar quirks of twentieth-century musical ideology that decreed the use of melody and harmony passé in the late 1940s, and likewise that any composer who wrote music for Hollywood movies could not possibly be any good. "This is a Hollywood concerto," sniffed one critic. Fortunately posterity has proved them wrong. Korngold had, in any case, become a "Hollywood composer" out of necessity—a former child prodigy, Korngold and his family were exiled upon the Nazi occupation of Austria in 1938. Hollywood effectively saved their lives.

In one sense, though, that critic was right: this really is a Hollywood concerto because it is full of music recycled from Korngold's movie scores. Although the composer was excited about the musical possibilities of film—he regarded his scores as "operas without singing"—when the movie vanished from the cinema, so did his music. Reusing the best material would rescue it from oblivion. The title melody from *Another Dawn*, a little-known movie starring Errol Flynn, was well worth saving: this exquisite theme opens the concerto. Also notable is the main theme of the final movement, a melody from *The Prince and the Pauper*, which forms the basis for a set of lively variations.

The 1953 recording by Jascha Heifetz, who gave Korngold's concerto its world premiere in 1947, is still a classic account. While some other violinists lay on the sugar, the work's bittersweet beauty is strong enough without that. Heifetz's incisive, questing sound and immense musical personality never falls into that trap. To many, he is the original and the best. **JD**

> *"Korngold loved life, he accepted life, and he gave back in music the wonder that he found in it."*
>
> **The Los Angeles Examiner, 1959**

Other Recommended Recordings

Gil Shaham, London Symphony Orchestra
André Previn
DG 439 886-2
A fabulous interpretation, overflowing with empathy

James Ehnes, Vancouver Symphony Orchestra
Bramwell Tovey
Onyx 4016
Young violinist gives a passionate performance

Cello Concerto, Much Ado About Nothing, etc.
Zuill Bailey, Bruckner Orchestra Linz • Caspar Richter
ASV CDDCA 1146
Colorful Korngold orchestral works played with gusto

The great Russian-born violinist Jascha Heifetz pictured in c. 1928. ❷

Béla Bartók | Viola Concerto (1945, *unfinished*)

Genre | Concerto
Performers | Kim Kashkashian (viola),
Netherland Radio Chamber Orchestra
Year recorded | 1999
Label | ECM 465 420-2

In 1945, during the last months of his life, Bartók worked on two compositions, both of which were destined to remain unfinished: the Third Piano Concerto (a birthday present for his wife) and the Viola Concerto, which had been commissioned earlier that year by the Scottish virtuoso William Primrose. At the time of his death on September 26, the Piano Concerto was almost finished, while the latter—which the composer had said to be quite finished in his mind—was found to be in an embryonic state. The Bartók estate commissioned his friend, fellow Hungarian Tibor Serly, to "prepare the piece for publication."

Primrose premiered the Viola Concerto in 1949 with Antál Dorati conducting, and it went on to become a staple of the instrument's repertoire, being taken up by all violists worth their salt. However, Serly has received a lot of criticism of his work, being accused of adding too much of his own to Bartók's sketches and of un-Bartókian orchestration. When Bartók's sketches surfaced, it was found that Serly had also beefed up the solo part to make it more virtuosic, changing many pitches in the process. Many violists have returned to the original version, as far as it is preserved in the manuscript. In 1995, Bartók's son Peter published an alternative realization of the sketches, which, however, has proved no less controversial and did not catch on. A more radical version by Hungarian violist Csaba Erdélyi (for copyright reasons published only in Australasia) is to my ears the most Bartókian of all.

Kim Kashkashian's recording of a lightly revised Serly version offers virtuoso playing of the highest order, with Peter Eötvös contributing fiery Hungarian flavor. **CMS**

Frank Martin | Petite symphonie concertante (1945)

Genre | Orchestral
Conductor | Thierry Fischer
Performers | Geneva Chamber Orchestra
Year recorded | 1996
Label | Dinemec DCCD 012

In 1944 the Swiss philanthropist and conductor Paul Sacher commissioned Frank Martin to write a composition for his Basel Chamber Orchestra. Although Sacher made no stipulations as to either the exact instrumentation or the form for the work, he floated the idea that Martin might think of writing something that matched the string orchestra with the instruments that would be employed in the basso continuo of a Baroque concerto grosso. Excited by this, Martin went one stage further and set himself the task of utilizing two string orchestras as well as piano, harp, and harpsichord, the two keyboard instruments featuring as soloists in the overall ensemble.

Ironically, soon after the premier in Zürich in 1946, Martin decided to rescore the work for full orchestra fearing that its unconventional orchestration would hinder wider dissemination. He was wrong, as the original *Petite symphonie concertante* is Martin's most famous piece. The work epitomizes all the finest musical characteristics of this underrated composer—a brilliant and refined ear for sonority, a tautly argued and clearly defined structure, as well as a capacity to transform distinctive and memorable material out of highly chromatic and angular musical lines.

Throughout his career, Swiss conductor Thierry Fischer has been a particularly enthusiastic exponent of Martin's work, and his recording of the *Petite symphonie concertante* with the Geneva Chamber Orchestra offers the most dynamic, expressive, and exciting account on CD. This disc also features the Concerto for Seven Wind Instruments, Timpani, Percussion, and Strings from 1949, another dazzling experiment in sonority. **EL**

Bohuslav Martinů
Symphony no. 4 (1945)

Genre | Orchestral
Conductor | Václav Neumann
Performers | Czech Philharmonic Orchestra
Year recorded | 1977
Label | Supraphon 11 1967-2

Dmitri Shostakovich
Symphony no. 9 (1945)

Genre | Orchestral
Conductor/Performers | Kirill Kondrashin;
Moscow Philharmonic Orchestra
Year recorded | 1965
Label | Melodiya MEL CD 10 01065 (11 CDs)

Martinů came relatively late in his career to symphonic compositions. His orchestral music from the 1930s inclined more to the concerto, but in 1938, he wrote the *Three ricercari* that, despite their rather Baroque-sounding title, looked forward to his symphonic style of work. Having escaped wartime Europe in 1941, Martinů and his wife Charlotte arrived in New York, a city that he found decidedly uncongenial where musical inspiration was concerned. However, he rapidly made a name for himself and in 1942, Koussevitzky commissioned a large orchestral work that became his first symphony. Four more followed in more or less annual succession, but the Sixth Symphony did not appear until 1951.

The Fourth Symphony, completed in mid-June 1945 at Cape Cod, is arguably the most captivating. Although it is written in a concerto-grosso style, Martinů adapted superbly to the requirements of symphonic writing. The Fourth has a persuasive coherence and sweeping impetus that engages the listener from its disarming, slightly quizzical opening. The scherzo and trio have an almost Beethovenian drive and the slow movement is one of Martinů's most beautiful inspirations. The finale begins in pensive mood and leads to the most extrovert conclusion of any of the composer's symphonies.

Václav Neumann was one of the Czech Philharmonic's most distinguished latter-day conductors, and his recording of the Martinů symphonies was one of his greatest achievements. With a steady grip on the organic qualities of the work, his performance of the Fourth Symphony remains one of the most rewarding. **JS**

The composition of a Ninth Symphony led to a great amount of soul searching for Shostakovich and, in the end, he unveiled neither the great war memorial expected of him nor some grandiloquent tribute to the Leader and Teacher. Instead he produced this modest "scherzo-symphony," a take on Prokofiev's "Classical" with a sourer edge. Shostakovich's Eighth is superficially recalled in the work's five-movement shape, only this time he is operating on a smaller scale. Should we see the result as an "anti-Ninth" put together against the background of daunting musical expectations, or admit the likelihood of a political subtext?

Whatever your point of view, Kirill Kondrashin's interpretation has little time for insouciant wit. Things quickly turn edgy and the finale is overtly sinister, making it difficult not to hear echoes of the tyranny from which the conductor ultimately defected. After Mravinsky's failure to undertake the premiere of the Thirteenth in 1962, Shostakovich seems to have regarded Kondrashin as his most stalwart interpreter, while Kondrashin said of Shostakovich, "Dmitri Dmitriyevich never interfered with my work. He always held in his hands a box of Russian cigarettes ('papirosi'), on which he noted down whatever he wanted to tell me afterwards. With great pride I remember him saying to me, 'Kirill Petrovich, you're a hard man to work with. Just as I write down some point, you're already making it to the musicians.'" Clearly then, Shostakovich cycles do not come any more authentic. Kondrashin finds in these scores an unrivaled degree of forward momentum and dramatic tension. Performed this way, the Ninth's sarcastic intent cannot fail to register. **DG**

Richard Strauss | Metamorphosen (1945)

Genre | Orchestral
Conductor | Herbert von Karajan
Performers | Berlin Philharmonic Orchestra
Year recorded | 1980
Label | DG 410 892-2

Early in the final year of World War II, the Vienna and Dresden opera houses were destroyed by allied bombing. For the seventy-eight-year-old Richard Strauss, who had lived on in Nazi Germany loathing the barbarous regime that governed his country, this was the last straw in the systematic devastation of a culture he adored. Although he had pointedly avoided giving any kind of expression to the terrible events he had witnessed, now at last he produced a response in the shape of a "study for twenty-three solo strings," *Metamorphosen*. The title refers to a term used by the great genius of German literature, Goethe, to describe his changing thought patterns, and a late poem by Goethe was found among the sketches for *Metamorphosen*.

As Strauss came to complete *Metamorphosen* in April 1945, he realized that one of his generous themes bore a marked resemblance to the funeral-march slow movement of Beethoven's Third Symphony, the "Eroica," and so he quoted it in the double basses at the end, with the words "In Memoriam" beneath it. Despite the somber tone with which it begins and ends, *Metamorphosen* is not all grief and lamentation; in a typically lush middle section, a fond remembrance of things past rises to ecstatic heights, only to be swept aside by a powerful reiteration of the solemn chords with which the work began.

Herbert von Karajan made three recordings of this remarkable memorial. The first, recorded in a devastated Vienna in 1948, has a special intensity, no doubt because it was closest in time to the events that prompted Strauss to write *Metamorphosen*. Yet Karajan's two Berlin recordings are distinguished by even more powerful delivery from the finest string section in the world. **DN**

"What goes on in the world, no one understands rightly."

Goethe poem quoted alongside *Metamorphosen*

Other Recommended Recordings

Dresden Staatskapelle • Rudolf Kempe
EMI 0946 3 45831 2 1
Another great Straussian in a more intimate performance than Karajan's

Zürich Tonhalle Orchestra • David Zinman
Arte Nova 74321 95999 2
Bargain performance from an excellent team in first-rate sound

Scottish National Orchestra • Neeme Järvi
Chandos CHAN 8732
The Scottish strings play with passion and warmth for the great Neeme Järvi

Richard Strauss wrote some of his most personal works in his old age. ➔

Benjamin Britten
The Young Person's Guide to the Orchestra (1945)

Genre | Orchestral
Conductor/Performers | Simon Rattle;
City of Birmingham Symphony Orchestra
Year recorded | 1995
Label | EMI 7243 5 55394 2 7

Was there ever a great composer who wrote with such sympathy and imagination for children as Benjamin Britten? The reasons for this lie deep within his complex personality; but the results are to be enjoyed by all of us. This favorite piece was written for a project that is impossible to imagine getting off the ground today, an instructional film called *The Instruments of the Orchestra*, distributed by the British Ministry of Education. The film had a commentary by Montagu Slater, the librettist of *Peter Grimes*, which was replaced in the published score by one written by Britten's collaborator Eric Crozier. But the score also has options for leaving out the narration.

Writing the piece at the end of the year of the 250th anniversary of Henry Purcell's death, Britten chose to construct it as, to quote his subtitle, "Variations and Fugue on a Theme of Purcell." The variations highlight each orchestral section in turn—never a soloist, except the lone harp. The fugue brings in the instruments in the same order, and toward the end it is counterpointed by the majestic return of the theme on the brass. It is a brilliant scheme, triumphantly executed, with each variation perfectly calculated to show off the featured instrument.

Simon Rattle's recording of the *Young Person's Guide* boasts immaculate instrumental playing and well-chosen tempi: the speed of the fugue is headlong, but never breakneck. It also has an exceptionally clear recording, with the magnificent Symphony Hall acting almost as an additional instrument. **AB**

Igor Stravinsky
Symphony in Three Movements (1945)

Genre | Orchestral
Conductor/Performers | Igor Stravinsky;
SWR Baden-Baden Symphony Orchestra
Year recorded | 1954
Label | Music & Arts CD-1184(2) (2 CDs)

Stravinsky came closer to providing an extra-musical program for the *Symphony in Three Movements*, composed between 1942 and 1945, than anywhere else in his output. In 1963, he linked each movement to specific images from World War II. The first movement was inspired by a documentary on scorched-earth tactics in China; newsreel footage of goose-stepping soldiers was behind the opening of the third movement; and the end was associated with "the rise of the Allies after the overturning of the German war machine." The final "rather too commercial" D flat sixth chord reflected his "extra exuberance in the Allied triumph." Lest too much be read into this, Stravinsky stated that "the symphony is not programmatic. Composers combine notes. That is all."

As forceful in spirit as the Symphony in C is charming, the *Symphony in Three Movements* has quasiconcertante parts for the piano then harp in the first two movements, bringing them together in the last. Like many of his mature works, the symphony places blocks of stylistically divergent music next to each other.

This recently released radio broadcast from 1954 was made when Stravinsky was approaching the peak of his abilities as a conductor, while the SWR Symphony Orchestra was forging a reputation as a highly professional advocate of contemporary music. Moreover, effects of the events that provided the backdrop to the composition of the symphony were still keenly felt. The resulting performance is without peer for its weight of purpose. **CD**

Heitor Villa-Lobos
Bachianas brasileiras no. 5 (1945)

Genre | Vocal
Performers | Jill Gomez (soprano)
Pleeth Cello Octet
Year recorded | 1987
Label | Hyperion CDA 66257

Aaron Copland
Symphony no. 3 (1946)

Genre | Orchestral
Conductor | Leonard Bernstein
Performers | New York Philharmonic
Year recorded | 1985
Label | DG 419 170-2

Heitor Villa-Lobos (1887–1959) was charismatic, prolific, and blessed with a musical intuition that allowed him a unique insight into the common ground that existed between the European Classical tradition and the music of his native Brazil. He spent the latter part of the 1920s in Paris, where he was inspired by Satie and Milhaud, encouraged by Rubinstein, and admired by Messiaen, yet rather than allowing his compositional style to become homogenized by these influences, he took them with him on his return to Brazil in 1930, where he received an official position in music education. During this period he composed the *Bachianas brasilieras* series, a group of compositions that knitted the counterpoint of Bach, whose music he also greatly admired, into the lively folk melodies of Brazil.

The fifth of the *Bachianas brasilieras* is both one of the most attractive and one of the most unusual of classical compositions. The original is scored for wordless soprano and a group of at least eight cellos. This massed ranking of a single instrument (occasionally referred to as a "choir") is more common in recent and contemporary music, but is nevertheless an adventure for both composer and listener.

This CD features an outstanding vocal contribution from Jill Gomez, whose versatility is coupled with a rare empathy with the piece. This disc also features the first composition in the series and a Bach arrangement by Villa-Lobos, making the homage complete. The recording is both lucid and expertly balanced—essential given the unusual instrumentation. **RT**

The Great American Symphony does not loom as large in the public imagination as does the Great American Novel. Nevertheless, in the middle decades of the twentieth century, that ever-elusive goal seemed to be in the minds of several composers. The result was the coming-of-age of the American symphony. Among the many fine works from this period, Copland's Third stands particularly tall.

Composed soon after the completion of Copland's brilliant trio of ballets—*Billy the Kid, Rodeo,* and *Appalachian Spring*—the symphony maintains the populist tone of those scores. Copland explained that it is "an end-of-war piece … intended to reflect the euphoric spirit of the time." It is an expansive work, too, in both length and character. The opening movement unfolds with a lyrical grandeur that evokes images of vast plains. Driving rhythms and emphatic motifs in the second movement suggest powerful machinery at work. Only in the outer sections of the third movement, where the melodies wander searchingly, does Copland suggest insecurity. But any uncertainties are answered by the finale, with its dramatic, decisive use of the *Fanfare for the Common Man*.

Leonard Bernstein, Copland's most persuasive advocate on the podium, recorded the Third Symphony in 1966 and 1985 and choosing between the versions is tough. The earlier account is admirably taut and aptly muscular, but the intensity of the later interpretation—recorded live in New York—gives it a special eloquence. The superior sound of the DG recording seals the deal. **AFC**

Benjamin Britten
The Rape of Lucretia (1946, *rev.* 1947)

Genre | Opera
Conductor/Performers | Benjamin Britten; Janet Baker,
Benjamin Luxon, Peter Pears, English Chamber Orchestra
Year recorded | 1970
Label | Decca 425 666-2 (2 CDs)

Following the huge success of *Peter Grimes,* Britten
was keen to continue writing operas. With *The Rape of
Lucretia* he surprised many by writing on a much smaller
scale, using six singers and a chamber ensemble only.
His librettist, Ronald Duncan, has been criticized both
for the "Christian frame of the Male and Female Chorus"
and the self-indulgent language, but his scenarios and
poetry inspired Britten to draw marvelous effects from his
chamber ensemble.

The story begins outside Rome, where three army
generals debate about women and their honor. The
Etruscan, Tarquinius, is full of lust for Lucretia, the virtuous
wife of the Roman general Collatinus. He rides for Rome
where he calls at her house and seeks a bed for the night;
in the middle of the night he rapes her. The following day,
Lucretia tells her husband and kills herself.

There is much to be commended in Britten's own
recording. Janet Baker suggests Lucretia's nobility and
honor with her strong interpretation and Collatinus is
given wonderful dignity by John Shirley-Quirk. Benjamin
Luxon's Tarquinius is horribly real, his baritone voice
colored with violent envy and lust. Heather Harper brings
deep empathy to the Female Chorus role and Peter Pears
has fine moments too; his *Sprechgesang* description of
Tarquinius approaching Lucretia's bedroom is horribly
eerie. Britten conjures some impressive playing from the
English Chamber Orchestra, both in the more virtuosic
passages, such as Tarquinius's ride to Rome, and the poetic
moments, notably the trio for alto flute, bass clarinet, and
muted horn that cradles the sleeping Lucretia. **SW**

> *"It is as an essay in evocative
> sonorities . . . that* Lucretia
> commands admiration.*"*
>
> Michael Kennedy

Other Recommended Recordings

City of London Sinfonia • Richard Hickox
Chandos CHAN 9254/5 (2 CDs)
Dramatically charged reading

Albert Herring
English Chamber Orchestra • Benjamin Britten
Decca 421 849-2 (2 CDs)
Lively rendition of Britten's comic chamber opera

Phaedra
Janet Baker, English Chamber Orchestra
Stuart Bedford
Decca 425 666-2 (2 CDs)
Baker on fine form again in this work written for her

Arthur Honegger
Symphony no. 3, "Symphonie liturgique" (1946)

Genre | Orchestral
Conductor | Mariss Jansons
Performers | Royal Concertgebouw Orchestra
Year recorded | 2006
Label | RCO Live RCO 06003

The cataclysmic events of World War II cast a dark shadow over Honegger's Third Symphony. Conceived and completed in the months after the victory of the Allies, its overriding mood remains equivocal and anything but triumphalist. The decision to preface each of its three movements with a title derived from the Catholic Mass for the Dead may well have been inspired by Britten's 1940 *Sinfonia da Requiem*, though the musical language remains entirely typical of its composer. In the opening movement, "Dies irae," Honegger depicts violence, savagery, and despair in stark contrast to the tender entreaties of the ensuing slow movement, "De profundis clamavi." In the finale, "Dona nobis pacem," these two emotional polarities are juxtaposed to startling effect. First there is another graphic representation of the war machine with a barbaric march rising to an apocalyptic climax. Then out of the ruins comes the faintest possibility of hope for the future, a flute and a solitary solo violin soaring above the gentle texture to conjure up an ineffably moving vision of peace.

Herbert von Karajan's 1969 recording with the Berlin Philharmonic on DG remains one of the most compelling versions of this symphony, but there is little doubt that the physical impact of Honegger's orchestration is better conveyed in more up-to-date sound. So I would opt for the relatively recent live performance from Mariss Jansons and the Royal Concertgebouw Orchestra recorded on their own label. Not only is the work played with stunning virtuosity, but Jansons has the full measure of its architecture and knows exactly how to pace its dramatic narrative to maximum effect. **EL**

"The reaction of modern man against barbarity, stupidity, suffering..."

Honegger describing his Third Symphony

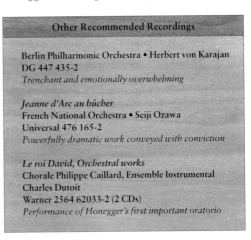

Other Recommended Recordings

Berlin Philharmonic Orchestra • Herbert von Karajan
DG 447 435-2
Trenchant and emotionally overwhelming

Jeanne d'Arc au bûcher
French National Orchestra • Seiji Ozawa
Universal 476 165-2
Powerfully dramatic work conveyed with conviction

Le roi David, Orchestral works
Chorale Philippe Caillard, Ensemble Instrumental
Charles Dutoit
Warner 2564 62033-2 (2 CDs)
Performance of Honegger's first important oratorio

Xavier Montsalvatge
Canciones negras (1946)

Genre | Vocal
Performers | Teresa Berganza (mezzo-soprano), Félix Lavilla (piano)
Year recorded | 1975
Label | DG 435 848-2 (2 CDs)

Sergei Prokofiev
Violin Sonata no. 1 (1946)

Genre | Chamber
Performers | David Oistrakh (violin), Sviatoslav Richter (piano)
Year recorded | 1972
Label | Orfeo C 489 981 B

Catalan Xavier Montsalvatge (1912–2002) was one of the most original and adventurous voices to emerge from Spain in the twentieth century. He was highly regarded in his lifetime as a major orchestral composer, and his eclectic style reflects a broad range of influences, encompassing folk music from his native Antilles, the nationalism of his Catalan predecessors, the Impressionism of Debussy, and the abrasiveness of Stravinsky. Inspired by the vogue in the 1930s and 1940s for African-American music (Negro spirituals were popularized in Barcelona at this time), Montsalvatge found a special affinity with West Indian, and specifically Cuban, rhythms. These particularly resonated with him because of the close historical ties between Cuba and Catalonia. In the 1940s Montsalvatge traveled around the Costa Brava collecting the exotic hybrid songs of Catalan emigrants who had returned home from Cuba after the War of Independence; many of these songs were published in his *Album de habaneras* (1948).

Later Montsalvatge partially abandoned tonality, writing a number of important works, but rarely recaptured the flare of his West Indian phase. The best-known works of this period are the *Cuarteto indiano for strings* (1952) and the *Canciones negras* (*Negro Songs*) of 1946: a vibrant collection that combines striking originality with popular appeal. Rhythmically and melodically infused with West Indian spice, the songs are also unmistakably Spanish. Montsalvatge later treated them to sumptuous orchestrations, but it is the original versions with piano that Spanish mezzo-soprano Teresa Berganza performs on her splendid "Canciones españolas" recital. **GR**

Just as the two violin concertos by Sergei Prokofiev are different in style and mood, so his two violin sonatas have individual personalities, though they were both written for David Oistrakh. Prokofiev began thinking of the F minor First Sonata in 1938, but the war came in 1939 without much progress being made. Meanwhile in 1943 he wrote his delightful Flute Sonata, of which Oistrakh helped to prepare a violin version, giving its first performance in 1944 with his regular sonata partner Lev Oborin. Two years later, Prokofiev finished the "First" Sonata, which the same players premiered on October 23, 1946.

The dark-hued opening movement is written in the composer's most uncompromising style and it is followed by a fierce, scherzo-like Allegro brusco. The slow movement is among Prokofiev's most haunting. The rondo finale sums up all the moods of the piece, including a reprise of a pianissimo passage from the first movement, which, Prokofiev told Oistrakh, ought to sound "like the wind in a cemetery." Oistrakh, who considered this sonata "the most remarkable event of my musical life," chose the two outer movements to play at Prokofiev's funeral.

Although the recording made with Oborin is no longer available, the live one from the 1972 Salzburg Festival is almost as good. He is partnered by Sviatoslav Richter and both artists are in good form, with Oistrakh, near the end of his life, showing no decline. This sonata is Oistrakh's piece and his tone and technique are ideally suited to it. What is important, however, is his intuitive understanding of the idiom. The recording is excellent and the acoustic of the Salzburg Mozarteum is kind to the violin. **TP**

Franz Waxman
Carmen Fantasy (1946)

Genre | Concerto
Performers/Conductor | Jascha Heifetz, RCA Victor Orchestra; Donald Voorhees
Year recorded | 1946
Label | RCA 09026 61752 2

The fantasy on themes from a popular opera was a thriving industry in the nineteenth century. In particular such potpourris were compiled for the flute and violin; and it was inevitable that the many hit tunes from Bizet's *Carmen* would be plundered. Two great violinists, Sarasate and Hubay, wrote *Carmen* fantasies, but today most fiddlers prefer one composed by Franz Waxman (1906–67). Classically trained in his native Germany and originally spelling his name Wachsmann, he played jazz piano and first became involved with the movie industry when he arranged and conducted the score (uncredited) for Marlene Dietrich's *The Blue Angel*. Arriving in the United States as a refugee, he became one of the leading Hollywood soundtrack composers of the 1940s and 1950s.

This piece was part of the music Waxman composed or arranged for the 1946 release *Humoresque*, in which John Garfield played a violinist and Joan Crawford committed suicide to the accompaniment of Wagner's *Liebestod*. Waxman received his sixth Oscar nomination for the score and Isaac Stern played for the soundtrack, and provided the violinist's hands for the close-ups. Jascha Heifetz was quick to seize on the *Carmen Fantasy* and his recording has never been bettered, though Leonid Kogan came close, and Michael Kugel has recorded it spectacularly on the viola. This music is Heifetz country, and when you hear him effortlessly surmounting the technical problems, yet maintaining perfect rhythmic poise, and producing an unfailingly beautiful tone, you can understand why he is described as *the* violinist of the twentieth century. Above all, he makes this piece sound fun. **TP**

Kurt Weill
Street Scene (1946)

Genre | Opera
Conductor/Performers | John Mauceri; Josephine Barstow, Samuel Ramey
Year recorded | 1990
Label | Decca 433 371-2 (2 CDs)

Forced to flee from Germany after the Nazis came to power in 1933, Kurt Weill eventually settled in America where he pursued a career primarily on Broadway. This move has caused many people to think of Weill as almost two different composers—the first an iconoclastic modernist who provided a biting critique of the Weimar Republic, the second a purveyor of entertainment music driven by commercial rather than artistic principles.

Inevitably these distinctions and divisions are too simplistic. In reality Weill never relinquished his interest in writing innovative theater music. Although his musical language may have softened considerably after his arrival in the United States, Weill retained a desire to portray the realities of modern life on stage and managed to write just as effectively for the voice in English as in German. Nowhere are these qualities more brilliantly illustrated than in *Street Scene*.

Described by Weill as an "American Opera," *Street Scene* presents a convincing attempt to reflect on the trials and tribulations of life in a poor apartment block in New York. The drama focuses in particular on the difficult marriage of Frank and Ann Maurrant, the latter embroiled in a torrid affair with Sankey the milk collector. Amid continuing threats of eviction from the authorities, the situation moves to a dramatic and desperate climax as Frank murders his wife and is subsequently arrested by the police.

John Mauceri's recording draws upon the vivid experience of the production mounted by Scottish Opera in the 1990s. It is distinguished by outstanding singing and sense of theatrical immediacy. **EL**

Ned Rorem | Songs (1946–99)

Genre | Vocal
Performers | Susan Graham (mezzo-soprano),
Malcolm Martineau (piano), Ensemble Oriol
Year recorded | 1999
Label | Erato 8573 80222-2

The art song—one voice and piano—has, for a long time, been rumored to be a dying genre, a victim of pop music or opera or simply of the ubiquity of the orchestra. And, a hundred-odd songs by Ives and a dozen by Copland notwithstanding, it has rarely been seen as an American specialty. But Ned Rorem (born in 1923) has stood firm for decades as the great American song composer, and since Britten's death surely the finest upholder of the tradition anywhere in the world. He is by no means exclusively a composer of songs, or even of vocal music in general: in fact, he won a Pulitzer Prize for an orchestral work, *Air Music*. But his greatest gift is for capturing the essence of a poem—English, French, or, especially, American—in a singable melodic line and an effective, sometimes virtuosic, piano part.

In one of his many collections of writings—he is a prolific author, not least of some famous, or notorious, *Diaries*—Rorem argues that music's national character stems from language, and therefore "in theory, the definitive interpreter of a country's songs should be a singer from that country." The American mezzo-soprano Susan Graham certainly proves a very persuasive advocate of Rorem's songs, responding unfailingly to the mood, the sense, and the sheer verbal music of each poem. But an equal reason for recommending her recital is that she has one of the most beautiful voices you are ever likely to hear. Add to that the brilliant piano playing of Malcolm Martineau, and a well-constructed and well-varied program—including four of the cycle of *Santa Fe Songs* with piano quartet—and you have a disc that makes the best possible case both for Rorem and for the contemporary American art song. **AB**

"My lifelong affair with songwriting stems from a love not of singing but of poetry."

Ned Rorem

Other Recommended Recordings

Songs • Carole Farley (soprano), Ned Rorem (piano)
Naxos 8.559084
Rorem himself accompanies a winning program

Six Songs for high voice, Ariel, etc.
Laura Aikin (soprano), Nicola Jürgensen (clarinet),
Gerhard Zank (cello), Donald Sulzen (piano)
Orfeo 620 041 A
Three cycles, two with an obbligato instrument

Symphonies nos. 1–3
Bournemouth Symphony Orchestra • José Serebrier
Naxos 8.559149
Rorem the orchestral composer, still essentially lyrical

Ned Rorem, pictured in the 1960s, is best known for his song-writing. ➲

Arnold Schoenberg | A Survivor from Warsaw (1947)

Genre | Choral
Conductor/Performers | Claudio Abbado; Gottfried Hornik (narrator), Male Chorus of the Vienna State Opera
Year recorded | 1989
Label | DG 431 774-2

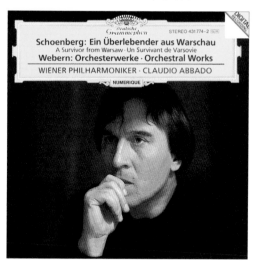

This brief and shattering work is Schoenberg's personal tribute to the Jews who died under the Nazi persecution, based on a story that he had heard from survivors of the 1944 Warsaw uprising. In this work, his unparalleled gift for the depiction in sound of extreme anguish, fear, nightmarish unreality, and emotional disorientation found a perfect subject. So, too, did his equal capacity for expressing passionate anger and heroic affirmation in the bleakest of circumstances. The combination raises the music to the highest power of genius.

The narrator (whose part is notated in *Sprechstimme*, with approximate pitches above and below a central line) tells of a group of prisoners wakened before dawn and beaten by their captors. The Nazi sergeant orders them to count their numbers out loud, so he knows how many are left to be herded into the gas chambers. But in the middle of the counting, they break into the ancient Hebrew song of triumph, "Shema Yisrael"—a last, "grandiose" assertion of their human dignity.

This music-drama is "protest music," growing out of an outrage committed against a specific racial group at a particular point in history (and out of a deep personal involvement—Schoenberg lost family members and pupils at the hands of the Nazis). This is one of the central tragic statements in twentieth-century music, and a classic affirmation of human values against insuperable odds.

Claudio Abbado directs a towering live performance notable for the vividness of the instrumental detail from the Vienna Philharmonic Orchestra; a fast tempo that keeps the narration moving; and a superbly harrowing speaker. The climax is simultaneously shocking and triumphant—a combination almost impossible to bring off. **MM**

> "Survivor from Warsaw made tremendous impression upon performers and audience."
>
> Kurt Frederick, in a telegram to Schoenberg

Other Recommended Recordings

John Shirley-Quirk, BBC Symphony Orchestra & Chorus • Pierre Boulez
Sony SMK 62022
A very vivid and dramatic reading

Simon Callow, London Voices, London Symphony Orchestra • Robert Craft
Koch International 3-7263-2
An excellent version by veteran Schoenberg conductor

Ode to Napoleon
Michael Grandage, Schoenberg Quartet
Sepp Grotenhuis • Chandos CHAN 9939
Schoenberg's wrathful wartime setting of Byron

Ralph Vaughan Williams | Symphony no. 6 (1947, *rev.* 1950)

Genre | Orchestral
Conductor | Adrian Boult
Performers | New Philharmonia Orchestra
Year recorded | 1968
Label | EMI 7243 5 73924 2 6 (6 CDs)

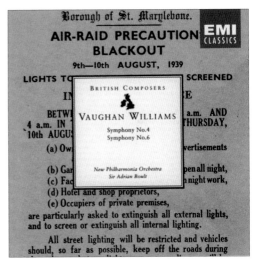

Following the serene conclusion of his Fifth Symphony, Vaughan Williams reveals a remarkable change of tone at the start of his next symphonic utterance. The language here is astonishingly violent in the opening outpouring of impassioned clashes of major against minor thirds. The slow movement, with its awful, insistent grotesque figure somehow suggests W. B. Yeats's horrible *The Second Coming*, which insinuates some foul aberration "slouching toward Bethlehem to be born." The insistent side drum that takes over the simple three-note figure upon which the movement obsesses recalls nightmares from Nielsen or Shostakovich; but the ideas carried here are clearly twisted versions of a composer's voice already well established. The scherzo has fun twisting ideas also. Once again there is a sense of loss of control—carefully judged, of course— and the most devilish intervals and chromatic shapes fly across the score. Vaughan Williams explores further this misshapen notion in the short negative epilogue, that suggests a devastating bleakness of conclusion.

Boult's interpretation gets into the guts of this piece with great intensity. The opening descent of ideas seems to pour with devastation through the orchestra and the brass punctuations bark out of the texture with nasty virulence. There is also highly effective pacing of the sounds as the second main theme—itself a devilishly misshapen tune—emerges from the preceding ideas. Only Boult could bring about the change of character of the theme into an E major Holst-like hymn at the conclusion of the movement with so unnoticeable a sleight of hand. The New Philharmonia Orchestra is on splendid form; its recounting of the fragile material is chilling and almost without hope. **SW**

> ## "Malcolm Sargent says it needs another tune."
>
> Vaughan Williams on his Sixth Symphony

Other Recommended Recordings

BBC Symphony Orchestra • Andrew Davis
Warner Apex 0927 49584-2
Spaciously recorded, gritty version full of power

Royal Liverpool Philharmonic Orchestra
Vernon Handley
EMI 7243 5 75312 2 1
A great wealth of sound captured on this highly sympathetic performance

London Symphony Orchestra • Richard Hickox
Chandos CHAN 10103
Hickox brings an appropriately veiled approach, especially to the final movement

Maurice Duruflé | Requiem (1947)

Genre | Choral
Conductor/Performers | George Guest; Robert King (treble), Christopher Keyte (baritone), Stephen Cleobury
Year recorded | 1974
Label | Decca 436 486-2 (2 CDs)

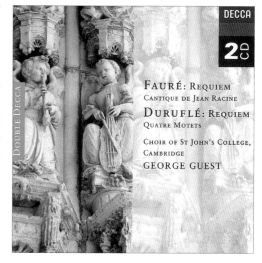

FAURÉ: REQUIEM
CANTIQUE DE JEAN RACINE
DURUFLÉ: REQUIEM
QUATRE MOTETS
CHOIR OF ST JOHN'S COLLEGE, CAMBRIDGE
GEORGE GUEST

Paradoxically, we must be grateful for the small compositional output of Maurice Duruflé. The virtuoso organist-composer felt unworthy to add works to the piano, string quartet, or song repertoire (for fear of invidious comparisons with Schumann, Fauré, or Schubert). So he stuck to organ, orchestral, and choral music, producing a few pieces united in their exquisite and fastidious perfection. Unlike his contemporary, Olivier Messiaen, who forged a new harmonic language of his own, Duruflé drew his inspiration from his teacher Paul Dukas, and from the legacy of Debussy, Ravel, and Fauré.

The Requiem dates from 1947 and is dedicated to Duruflé's father. It shares with Fauré's Requiem its choice of sung texts (save for most references to the Day of Judgment), and its overall mood of consolation. Duruflé's characteristically Debussian sense of lyrical flow is applied to the underlying Gregorian chants and their corresponding texts. The music exists in a version for orchestra (which can sound overblown) and for organ with cello obbligato. George Guest's recording of the organ version with the Choir of St. John's College, Cambridge, remains entirely unsurpassed in matching the feminine warmth of the boys' singing to the music's intimate mood of ethereal contemplation; Stephen Cleobury accompanies brilliantly on the organ.

The current re-release of the Requiem couples the music with Duruflé's *Prélude et Fugue sur le nom d'Alain* for organ and works by Fauré and Poulenc; the Duruflé Requiem itself is worth the cover price—the remaining repertoire, on which Guest (in his finest ever recordings) lavishes the same care and sensitive direction, makes the entire package irresistible. **GK**

> "*His work is an interior elevation that disposes the heart and spirit of others to the infinite encounter . . .*"
>
> Monsignor Jehan Revert, words at Duruflé's funeral

Other Recommended Recordings

Lamoureux Orchestra • Maurice Duruflé
Erato 3984 24235-2 (2 CDs)
The orchestral version, and other works performed by the composer and close colleagues

Desborough School Choir, New Philharmonia Orchestra • Andrew Davis
Sony SBK 67182
Lush recording of the orchestral version

Choir of Westminster Cathedral • James O'Donnell
Hyperion CDA 66757
Digital recording (organ version) with Westminster choir on bright, brilliant form

Samuel Barber | Knoxville: Summer of 1915 (1947)

Genre | Vocal
Conductor | David Zinman
Performers | Dawn Upshaw, Orchestra of St. Luke's
Year recorded | 1988
Label | Nonesuch 79187-2

DAWN UPSHAW KNOXVILLE: SUMMER OF 1915
Music of Barber, Menotti, Harbison and Stravinsky
ORCHESTRA OF ST. LUKE'S DAVID ZINMAN, *Conductor*

For Barber, the summer evening evoked in James Agee's bittersweet reminiscence, "Knoxville: Summer of 1915," stirred up memories of his own childhood. "Agee's poem was vivid and moved me deeply," the composer wrote, "and my musical response that summer of 1947 was immediate and intense. I think I must have composed *Knoxville* within a few days." Barber later referred to his work as a "lyrical rhapsody"—and the music certainly has the character of a rapt, nostalgic, and at times almost improvisatory meditation.

But *Knoxville* is not sentimental. The voice that sings of grown-ups sitting on their proches "rocking gently and talking gently" seems, at first, to be that of a child; gradually it becomes clear from the text that, really, this is the voice of an adult remembering what it was like to be a child. Near the end, for example, Agee writes, "who shall ever tell the sorrow of being on this earth, lying, on quilts, on the grass, in a summer evening"—an overtly mature view of childhood's fragility. Barber conveys this in melodious music that glows with ever-increasing melancholy.

Sopranos (Americans, in particular) have come to treasure *Knoxville* for its emotional directness. It is not easy to sing convincingly, the text must be articulated clearly yet without a hint of archness. It is not music for a diva; simplicity and sincerity are as essential as a pure and pretty tone. Dawn Upshaw has those qualities and then some. She relishes the rich alliteration of Agee's language as much as she does the lilting sweetness of Barber's melodies, and she captures *Knoxville*'s spirit to perfection. Conductor David Zinman follows Barber's markings scrupulously, resulting in an intimate interpretation that unfolds with the naturalness of a memory. **AFC**

> *"You can* smell *the South in it."*
>
> Leontyne Price, soprano

Other Recommended Recordings

Leontyne Price, New Philharmonic Orchestra
Thomas Schippers
RCA 09026 61983 2
Price's conversational style is imaginative and insightful

Karina Gauvin, Royal Scottish National Orchestra
Marin Alsop
Naxos 8.559134
The most achingly melancholic version available

Elenor Steber, Dumbarton Oaks Chamber Orchestra
William Strickland • Sony MPK 46727
Steber's takes an unabashed adult view
in Knoxville's *first recording*

Roberto Gerhard
The Duenna (1947)

Genre | Opera
Conductor/Performers | Antoni Ros-Marbà;
Claire Powell, Susannah Glanville
Year recorded | 1996
Label | Chandos CHAN 9520(2) (2 CDs)

Roberto Gerhard (1896–1970) was born near Barcelona of a German-Swiss father and an Alsatian mother. He had an international, multilingual outlook, but he was Catalan by birth and culture. Study with Granados and Pedrell led to several years in Vienna and Berlin as Schoenberg's pupil. In Barcelona he befriended Miró and Pablo Casals and was an energizer in the flourishing literary and artistic avant-garde of Catalonia; after the Spanish Civil War, Gerhard fled to France in 1939, and subsequently settled in England.

His early compositions related explicitly to aspects of Spanish and Catalan culture, and this tendency matured during the 1940s, culminating in the ballet *Don Quixote* and the opera *The Duenna*. The legacy of Schoenbergian Serialism engendered a radical approach to composition that, by the 1960s, placed Gerhard in the ranks of the avant-garde and brought wider international recognition. It was only after the death of Franco that his works were played again in Spain, and he was recognized as one of the most important twentieth-century Spanish composers.

The Duenna is a Spanish opera composed to an English comedy, by Sheridan, about the marriage market in eighteenth-century Seville. The most felicitous of its marriages is the wedding of English prosody to the Iberian musical vernacular. It is a masterpiece about the outraging of convention, the power of true love, and fortune favoring those resourceful enough to seize their chance.

Opera North's production with English Northern Philharmonia does this humane and effervescent piece full justice, with Susannah Glanville outstanding as the heroine and Claire Powell a sensuous as well as wily Duenna. **MM**

John Cage
Sonatas and Interludes (1948)

Genre | Instrumental
Instrument | Prepared piano
Performer | Nora Skuta
Year recorded | 2004
Label | Hevhetia HV 0011-2-131

Like so many innovations in music—from the symphony to the saxophone—the prepared piano, at least as John Cage used it, was a revolutionary idea inspired by a down-to-earth problem. In the late 1930s, Cage had been asked to compose some music to accompany a dance created by the choreographer Sybilla Fort. At the time he was fascinated by percussion instruments, but, aware that the space designated for the performance was too small for a percussion ensemble, he began experimenting with a piano, inserting various mutes of metal and rubber at various points between the strings to produce a cascade of harmonic and tonal variation, combining the sounds of gamelan with a variety of percussive effects, yet allowing the piano to be played conventionally.

Cage subsequently composed many works for the instrument, with this cycle of nineteen short pieces being the best and the best known. It has been recorded several times, but this SACD by Nora Skuta stands head and shoulders above others. Having met Cage and performed several of his pieces in 1992, she has refined her technique in exactly the way any virtuoso might grapple with the idiosyncrasies of a more conventional instrument. The resulting performance is unparalleled, and gives the piece a freshly minted aspect—no mean feat in itself, given that this seminal and quintessentially "modern" piece will soon reach its sixtieth birthday. Despite John Cage's reputation as a legendary eccentric of the American avant-garde, this work is highly listenable and, given the piece's resonant physicality, is also ideally suited to the spaciousness afforded by the multichannel SACD format. **RT**

Aaron Copland
Clarinet Concerto (1948)

Genre | Concerto
Performers/Conductor | Benny Goodman,
Columbia Symphony Strings; Aaron Copland
Year recorded | 1963
Label | Sony SM3K 46559 (3 CDs)

Copland had an on-and-off relationship with jazz. While he was studying in Europe, he seized on jazz idioms as a way of developing an identifiably American national style; and on his return to the United States, in the wake of Gershwin's *Rhapsody in Blue*, he wrote a piano concerto full of jazz colors, rhythms, and turns of phrase. But that was not much more than parody, and he soon decided to drop jazz. By then, though, it had already seeped under the surface of his music, to give his harmonies their distinctive bite and his rhythms their unique loose-limbed energy. And it resurfaced when he was asked to write a concerto for the famous band leader and clarinettist Benny Goodman. In fact, Goodman's commission was intended not so much to bring jazz into the concert hall as to gain himself classical respectability. As if to fall in with that, Copland scored the piece for strings with harp and piano, and began it with a melting slow waltz in the manner of Satie's *Gymnopédies*. But this leads via a long, increasingly brilliant cadenza to a quick finale full of jazz feeling, sometimes parodied again—there is a hilarious episode with "slap bass" accompaniment—but mostly as a source of light-footed rhythmic verve.

Goodman gave Copland a tough time over the piece, asking for rewrites of some tricky high passages in the finale (the original music is restored in Charles Neidich's recording), and delaying the premiere for a couple of years. But the second of the two recordings he made with the composer set a standard for the piece that has never been bettered, with a first movement full of tender feeling, and a finale of irresistible energy, brilliance, and joie de vivre. **AB**

Conlon Nancarrow
Player Piano Studies (1948–93)

Genre | Instrumental
Instrument | Player piano
Performer | Conlon Nancarrow
Year recorded | 1988
Label | Wergo WER 6907-2 (5 CDs)

Born in the United States, Conlon Nancarrow (1912–97) played jazz trumpet before studying music formally with Roger Sessions, Walter Piston, and Nicholas Slonimsky. Effectively exiled from his native land because of his membership in the Communist Party, he moved to Mexico in 1940 and became a Mexican citizen. His complex and demanding early works were rarely performed, but his increased isolation in his adopted homeland made this situation worse. Inspired by the writings of Henry Cowell, Nancarrow hit upon the idea of creating compositions by punching notes into the rolls used in mechanical player pianos. This allowed him to devise pieces that made the greatest possible use of the piano's range and sound, but that were physically impossible for a human pianist to play. The result was a series of roughly fifty studies for player piano. In their early stages, their processes anticipated electronic sequencing by many decades and resulted in a cascading musical language that displays influences ranging from jazz to Serialism but that ultimately is unique.

Compelling though they may be, when considered individually Nancarrow's works for player piano can seem like novelty items, but as is the case with the composers of the great symphonic and operatic cycles, it is only possible to get a proper handle on his extraordinary approach by taking it in a large dose. This five-disc set really is the best possible solution to this. Its 140-page booklet written by composers Charles Amirkhanian and James Tenney turn it into a one-stop portable Nancarrow workshop, who is quite correctly (if spookily) credited as the performer on the Ampico Reproducing Piano heard here. **RT**

Olivier Messiaen
Turangalîla Symphony (1948)

Genre | Orchestral
Conductor/Performers | Kent Nagano;
Pierre-Laurent Aimard, Dominique Kim
Year recorded | 2000
Label | Teldec 8573 82043-2

The central panel of Messiaen's "Tristan" triptych, his *Turangalîla symphonie*, is a ten-movement, exotic bundle of energy that is characterized by an irrepressible joie de vivre. This seventy-five-minute work for piano, ondes martenot (an early electronic instrument), and very large orchestra is a heady brew. Ideas fall over each other right from the opening rush of strings, with bold catchy tunes alongside abstruse number-crunching, and gamelan-inspired sonorities underpinning the orchestral textures.

The commission from Serge Koussevitzky was certainly enticing: "Choose as many instruments as you desire, write a work as long as you wish, and in the style you want." Messiaen's initial response was a conventional four-movement symphony. He then added three movements, also called "Turangalîla" (a Sanskrit word broadly combining aspects of "energy" and "love"). Still not happy, two further movements were written, a "Chant d'amour" and a "Développement de l'amour." Something else was still needed, resulting in the most famous movement: "Joie du sang des étoiles." This uninhibited *moto perpetuo* provides a foil at the heart of the piece for the sustained reverie of the slow movement, "Jardin du sommeil d'amour," and encapsulates the effervescent spirit of the *Turangalîla*.

The Berlin Philharmonic was a far from obvious choice of orchestra, but its lack of familiarity, combined with the edge that comes from a live recording, gives this performance a freshness that is too often lacking. Pierre-Laurent Aimard's approach to the piano part is electrifying, while Kent Nagano's pacing of the whole reflects an intimate knowledge of Messiaen's music. **CD**

Dmitri Shostakovich | From
Jewish Folk Poetry (1948)

Genre | Vocal
Performers | Tatiana Sharova,
Ludmila Kuznetsova, Alexei Martynov
Year recorded | 1996
Label | Chandos CHAN 9600

This is Shostakovich's first musical response to the renewed ideological clampdown imposed by Stalin's henchman Andrei Zhdanov in February 1948. Composition of its eleven numbers is paraded as a piece of heroic subversion. The song cycle could not be unveiled to the general public in the state-sponsored anti-Semitic atmosphere that climaxed in the accusation that Jewish doctors were conspiring to poison the Soviet hierarchy; Solomon Mikhoels, director of the Moscow State Jewish Theater, had been killed in suspicious circumstances in January. Yet Stalin's Russia granted recognition to the state of Israel and, in September, Golda Meir became Israel's first ambassador to the U.S.S.R. In the wake of the resolution against "formalism," Shostakovich's resort to national, folk-derived materials was in line with official policy. The songs' wider dissemination came in the post-Stalin era.

The work reveals the profound affinity between the composer's musical language and Russian-Jewish folksong, and a real empathy with the victims of persecution. He chooses texts whose negative sentiments may be passed off as applying to the past, but whose positive messages about an emancipated present ring hollow.

Surprisingly for an accessible score with a heavyweight reputation, there have been few satisfactory recordings. Given the unavailability of the definitive version, whose lineup included Nina Dorliak (Mrs. Sviatoslav Richter) and Shostakovich himself at the piano, Valery Polyansky offers authentic Slav voices, spacious tempi, and modern sonics and the Russian State Symphony Orchestra; the orchestrations are the composer's own. **DG**

Dmitri Shostakovich
Violin Concerto no. 1 (1948)

Genre | Concerto
Performer | Maxim Vengerov
Conductor | Mstislav Rostropovich
Year recorded | 1994
Label | Warner 0927 46742-2

Richard Strauss
Four Last Songs (1948)

Genre | Vocal
Performer/Conductor | Gundula
Janowitz (soprano); Herbert von Karajan
Year recorded | 1973
Label | DG 447 422-2

The Sibelius is the twentieth century's most recorded violin concerto, but Shostakovich's First is coming up on the rails. It is perhaps the clearest demonstration of the composer's place in the history of music that, with the arts in the U.S.S.R. under surveillance as never before and the monumental instrumental genres in which he specialized under particular attack, he should have completed such a work "for the drawer." His public production at the time was of patriotic choral music and movie scores to satisfy officials and earn a crust. It was not until October 1955 that a premiere was sanctioned. The work's performance history was for years bound up with David Oistrakh, who recorded it in 1956 just after giving the American premiere.

Today its challenges are being relished by a new generation. Maxim Vengerov's recording was made with the London Symphony Orchestra soon after a performance of a lifetime at London's Barbican Hall. On that occasion, the wunderkind from Novosibirsk broke a string at a crucial stage in the finale's dash to the finishing line. But the ovation was not entirely due to the soloist's ability to pick up the thread with scarcely a moment's pause. Vengerov's manners are less consistently refined than Oistrakh's, his impassioned climaxes even a shade forced. Yet he achieves a nobility and poise that are worlds away from the superficial accomplishment of most modern virtuosi. In heartfelt communion with his conductor, the score's brooding, silver-gray reveries are superbly realized. This unmistakably great playing has everything: dynamic variety, spot-on intonation, thrilling emotional power, and seamless continuity. **DG**

After a lifetime of songwriting, with many of the most distinguished songs written for the long-breathed talents of his soprano wife Pauline, the octogenarian Richard Strauss had to summon up all his most magical gifts to provide an effective curtain. He did so with the *Four Last Songs* for soprano and lush, late-Romantic orchestra. The song that is usually heard as the fitting epilogue to the sequence, "Im Abendrot" ("In the Sunset"), was the first to be composed, in May 1948. The poem by Joseph von Eichendorff describes a couple walking hand in hand. At the point at which they ask of the tranquil peace "is this perhaps death?" Strauss quotes on the horn the noblest theme from his early tone poem *Death and Transfiguration*.

Another mellow horn theme distinguishes one of the three Hermann Hesse settings, "September," which follows the radiant "Spring"; and there is a glorious violin solo whose soaring the voice imitates in "Beim Schlafengehen" ("Going to Sleep"). Strauss died just over a year after the completion of the *Four Last Songs*, on September 9, 1949; the first performance followed in May 1950 at London's Royal Albert Hall, with soprano Kirsten Flagstad and Wilhelm Furtwängler conducting.

The *Four Last Songs* demand a special glow, which many listeners' favorite choice, Elisabeth Schwarzkopf, cannot provide. Soprano Gundula Janowitz boasts the most luminous voice in the business, soaring and dealing effortlessly with the very long phrases even at the very slow tempi her conductor, Herbert von Karajan (with the Berlin Philharmonic), demands. Her Lieder-singer's intelligence also makes impressive sense of the texts. **DN**

Leonard Bernstein

Symphony no. 2, "The Age of Anxiety" (1949, *rev.* 1965)

Genre | Orchestral
Conductor | Dmitry Sitkovetsky
Performers | Marc-André Hamelin (piano), Ulster Orchestra
Year recorded | 2000
Label | Hyperion CDA 67170

Bernstein never wrote a straight-up-and-down abstract orchestral symphony. All three of his symphonies belong to what he once called "the work I have been writing all my life ... about the struggle that is born of the crisis of our century, a crisis of faith." The First, "Jeremiah," ends with a mezzo-soprano singing the Hebrew prophet's lamentation over the fall of the temple. The Third, "Kaddish," includes choirs singing Jewish liturgical texts, and a narrator (for which read Bernstein himself) carrying on a one-sided and increasingly anguished conversation with his God. And the Second Symphony is "The Age of Anxiety," without voices but with a solo piano (for which read Bernstein again—he played the part in early performances), and with a detailed program based on a long poem by W. H. Auden about the search for meaning and faith in empty lives. The "empty lives" bit, corresponding to a desultory late-night party, is predictably the most fun, a scherzo with a virtuosically jazzy piano part accompanied by celesta, harp, bass, and (a lot of) drums. The rest is more serious, eclectic in style but with an inner core of coherence and purpose.

Among several fine recordings of "The Age of Anxiety," this one stands out for the brilliance and sensitivity of Marc-André Hamelin's piano playing, the incisiveness and imagination of the Ulster Orchestra's contribution under its then principal conductor, and recording that combines body and clarity. (There is an interesting coupling, too, in William Bolcom's Piano Concerto, a gleefully interrogative response to the American Bicentennial.) If you do not know the piece, give it a try. It might not change your life, but it could convert you to the symphonic Bernstein. **AB**

"[When played] *as instructed ... it communicates a sense of overwhelming love.*"

Humphrey Burton

Other Recommended Recordings

Jeffrey Kahane, Bournemouth Symphony Orchestra
Andrew Litton • Virgin 7243 5 61612 2 1 (2 CDs)
An idiomatic performance in a bargain compilation

Michelle DeYoung, James Tocco, BBC Symphony
Orchestra • Leonard Slatkin
Chandos CHAN 9889
A good "Age of Anxiety," and outstanding "Jeremiah"

Symphony no. 3, "Kaddish"
Montserrat Caballé, Michael Wager, Vienna Jeunesse-
Chor, Vienna Boys' Choir, Israel Philharmonic
Orchestra • Leonard Bernstein • DG 457 757-2
Bernstein's second recording of the "Kaddish"

Gerald Finzi
Clarinet Concerto (1949)

Genre | Concerto
Performers | Robert Plane (clarinet), Northern Sinfonia
Conductor | Howard Griffiths
Year recorded | 1995
Label | Naxos 8.553566

If you are drawn to English music that reminds you of the English countryside, you will love the music of Gerald Finzi. It can sound a bit like Elgar, a bit like Vaughan Williams, occasionally a bit like Walton or Holst. But as you get to know it, it sounds like Finzi, too. There are clear textures, often with a melody and a counter-melody over a moving bass, a technique that he must have learned from Bach. The melodies have the rise and fall of a line of hills seen in the distance. And in the slower music there is a very personal vein of rapt outdoor meditation. Actually, it is odd that Finzi should have allied himself so firmly with the English pastoral tradition, since he was born in London to Italian Jewish parents. But he chose to live most of his life in the gentle country west and south of the capital; and the music really does sound like it.

Finzi wrote this concerto for clarinet and strings for the Three Choirs Festival in 1949. The composer completed it at unusual speed—he often spent decades agonizing over a work. Today, it stands as a characteristic and popular example of his art. You could criticize it for the way the strings supply most of what drama and tension there is, while the clarinet consistently provides the soft answer that "turneth away wrath." But it is one of the merits of this exceptional performance that Robert Plane's mellifluous playing is so perfectly suited to the clarinet's role as peacemaker, while the Northern Sinfonia strings add the necessary edge when it is required. Just listen to the start of the finale, when an angular string introduction ushers in a relaxed, graceful clarinet tune that will stick in your memory for a long time. **AB**

> "... *smoothly argued and best proportioned of Finzi's full-scale compositions.*"

Stephen Banfield

Other Recommended Recordings

Cello Concerto, Eclogue, Grand Fantasia and Toccata
Tim Hugh (cello), Peter Donohoe (piano), Northern Sinfonia • Howard Griffiths • Naxos 8.555766
Finzi's late, large-scale Cello Concerto

Dies natalis, Intimations of Immortality
John Mark Ainsley (tenor), Corydon Singers and Orchestra • Matthew Best • Hyperion CDA 66876
Rapturous settings of Traherne and Wordsworth

I Said to Love, Let us Garlands Bring, Before and After Summer • Roderick Williams (baritone), Ian Burnside (piano) • Naxos 8.557644
Three cycles by an outstanding British baritone

Gian-Carlo Menotti
The Consul (1949)

Genre | Opera
Conductor/Performers | Richard Hickox;
Susan Bullock, Spoleto Festival Orchestra
Year recorded | 1998
Label | Chandos CHAN 9706(2) (2 CDs)

Gian-Carlo Menotti (1911–2007) was born in Cadegliano on the shores of Lake Lugano, Italy, in 1911. He had already composed two operas when, at age thirteen, he entered the Conservatoire in Milan. In 1928, he transferred to the Curtis Institute in Philadelphia, where he met Samuel Barber; the two enjoyed a long partnership. Menotti's big break came in 1938, when his one-act opera *Amelia Goes to the Ball* was performed at New York's Metropolitan Opera. Within a decade, Menotti had established himself as the leading opera composer in the United States. His supernatural melodrama, *The Medium* (1945), for example, started in opera houses but ended up playing in a Broadway theater.

Menotti's success is easy to understand. The composer had a keen theatrical sense—he always wrote his own libretti and (after 1942) insisted on stage directing as well—and his music is imbued with an Italianate lyricism that echoes Mascagni and Puccini.

The Consul (which also ran on Broadway) is arguably the most powerful of all Menotti's operas. Composed in the shadow of World War II and reflecting the tensions of the Cold War, it portrays a woman's struggle to obtain a visa so she and her family can escape a brutal police state. Her efforts are thwarted by what Menotti has described as "the tyranny of bureaucracy," and the tale ends tragically.

This superb recording was made in Italy at the 1998 Spoleto Festival—an annual cultural event founded by Menotti in 1957—in a production directed by the composer himself. The singing is at once handsome and gutsy, and Richard Hickox sustains the score's tense atmosphere from the first note to the last. **AFC**

Sergei Prokofiev
Cello Sonata (1949)

Genre | Chamber
Performers | Mstislav Rostropovich
(cello), Sviatoslav Richter (piano)
Year recorded | 1951
Label | Russian Revelation RV 10102

There is a swaggering pomp to Prokofiev's bold-as-brass Cello Sonata in C major that does not ring quite true. Sure enough, after the opening's broad sweep a mischievous little tune bubbles up and we suspect the composer of making fools of us all. Indeed, the piece is a veritable circus of clownish tricks and flights of extravagant fancy with a completely over-the-top celebratory finale. But it is a miracle Prokofiev managed to pull off such a glorious work at all, since he had little to celebrate. It was written four years before his death, when, already suffering from ill health, he had been subject to Stalin's notorious "trials" and accused of writing "formalist" music, not suitable for the Soviet masses. This sonata is a caustic response to the authorities: I can do you a sugary comedy, if that is what is required, I can even stuff it with gorgeous, singable melodies—but I shall add a tincture of poison, so beware those who swallow it! There is a moment when he lets his guard down, a twilit interlude in the extrovert finale, where time stands still, and the instruments glimpse the abyss.

Prokofiev prefaced the manuscript with a quotation from Gorky—"Man, that has a proud sound"—a comment that could be taken literally or ironically, but the sonata cries out for the fullest, most resonant sound a cellist can muster. Mstislav Rostropovich, a close friend, and for whom the sonata was written, has a unique understanding of this work. He and Richter play it absolutely straight, in a powerful, spacious performance, given just after they premiered it in the presence of Prokoviev in 1951. There is an electric atmosphere, and a specific, historical dimension that makes it especially moving. **HW**

Astor Piazzolla
Tangos (*c.* 1950–92)

Genre | Chamber
Performers | Piazzolla, Console,
Malvicino, Suarez Paz, Ziegler
Year recorded | 1985
Label | Nonesuch 7559 79469-2

Malcolm Arnold
English Dances (1950, 1951)

Genre | Orchestral
Conductor/Performers | Andrew Penny;
Queensland Symphony Orchestra
Year recorded | 1995
Label | Naxos 8.553526

The explosion of interest in the tango, spearheaded by the Kronos Quartet in the 1980s, has ensured that Astor Piazzolla (1921–92) has become almost a household name. Performed by such illustrious artists as Daniel Barenboim, Yo-Yo Ma, and Gidon Kremer, Piazzolla is one of few best-selling crossover composers also highly rated by the classical music establishment.

A child prodigy on the bandoneón (the square-built button accordion used in the tango ensembles of Argentina, Uruguay, and Brazil), Piazzolla has become its most famous exponent, while in his teens he worked with Aníbal Troilo, a leading bandleader in Buenos Aires, and studied classical composition with Ginastera. During a period of study in Paris with Nadia Boulanger, Piazzolla was encouraged to compose tangos. His classical training gave him the technical means to experiment with the traditional form and instrumentation of the tango; he introduced such things as dissonance, fugue, and elements of jazz. Although it is this experimentation that gives Piazzolla's tangos the variety so admired today, Argentinian tango composers and bandleaders of the time deemed his works sacrilegious; it was only after acclaim abroad that he was accepted at home. He composed about 750 works including two film scores—*Tangos: the Exile of Gardel* (1985) and *Sur* (1987).

In his own ensemble, the Quinteto Nuevo Tango, Piazzolla experimented with the instrumentation of bandoneón, bass, guitar, violin, and piano. This collection, *Tango: Zero Hour*, was recorded in New York and has since been regarded as his definitive album. **DC**

Opinion about the music of Malcolm Arnold (1921–2006) is as divided after his death as it was during his lifetime. Some find him a major figure, an ironic symphonist whose use of deliberately banal material places him in a line of descent from Mahler and Shostakovich. It is tempting to wonder if they are not partly influenced by his biography—a tragic history of overwork, depression, and breakdown. Others find the banal stuff just that, the musical procedures simplistic, and the desolation of some of the later music mere emptiness. But such accusations could simply reflect a snobbish contempt for anything the average music lover might actually respond to.

What only the most snobbish can ignore is that, at his best, Arnold was a first-rate composer of light music—a genre that depends on directness of expression, polished orchestration, and inspired melodic invention. An excellent example is his *English Dances*, two sets of four each, written when his publisher asked for some equivalents to the Dvořák *Slavonic Dances*, similarly based on folksy, but original tunes. They have something of the postwar breeziness and optimism associated with the 1951 Festival of Britain, with which they more or less coincided, offset by a couple of numbers of touching plaintiveness.

Andrew Penny's Queensland recording, prepared with advice from the composer himself, presents the dances in clear, well-judged performances. The disc includes all the other, later sets of national and regional dances—Scottish, Cornish, Irish, and Welsh—graphically charting Arnold's headlong descent into obsession and despair. And so the arguments continue. **AB**

9

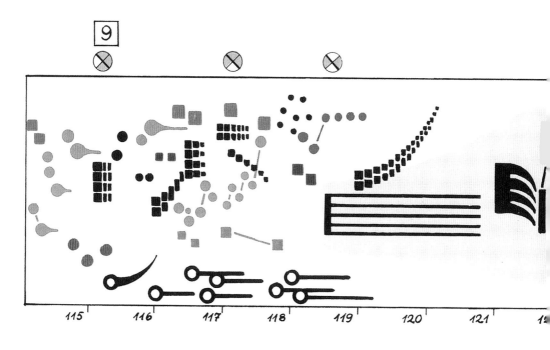

115   116   117   118   119   120   121   12

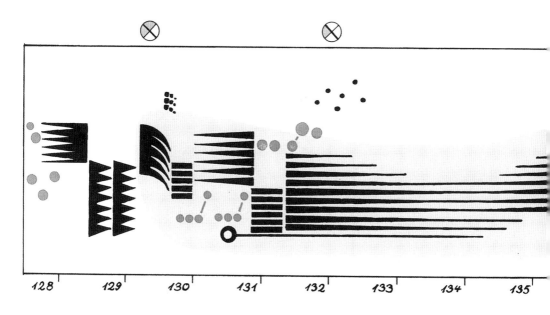

128   129   130   131   132   133   134   135

World War II cleared the air, allowing composers to explore new media and new forms: Modernists clustered around figureheads such as Stockhausen, Boulez, and Cage. In time there was the inevitable reaction, leading to a new reductionism in the Minimalist works of Reich and Glass. By century's end, it was no longer possible to detect a single trend other than one of polystylism: now anything goes…

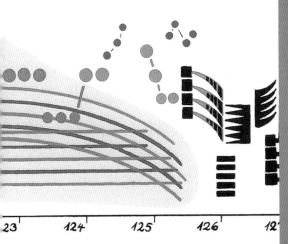

23   124   125   126   12

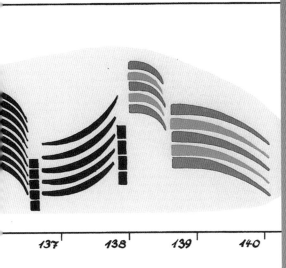

137   138   139   140

Θ György Sándor Ligeti, *Articulation*, score for the electronic composition (1958).

1951–PRESENT

Benjamin Britten
Billy Budd (1951, *rev.* 1960)

Genre | Opera
Conductor/Performers | Benjamin Britten; Peter Glossop,
Peter Pears, Michael Langdon, London Symphony Orchestra
Year recorded | 1968
Label | Decca 417 428-2 (3 CDs)

Commissioned to write an opera for the 1951 Festival of
Britain, Britten returned to a maritime world last addressed
in *Peter Grimes*. However, this time the composer
evokes the harsh, biting winds and damp, misty clouds
enveloping the dark world of HMS Indomitable. On board,
Captain Vere, a man of action and a hero to his crew,
shares his story from centuries ago. He was faced with an
absurd accusation of mutiny from the evil Master-at-arms,
John Claggart, about the popular, fine, and handsome
Billy Budd, a new recruit to the ship. In his disbelief at the
accusations, Budd stammers and expresses his fury with a
single blow to the head of Claggart and kills him. Vere is
vexed with an impossible decision between good and evil
and must decide Budd's fate.

For once, Britten's fascination with innocence suggests
a litigious meaning, but the opera's real concern is the
Captain's maturing to come to terms with the coexistence
of good and evil. Vere's final aria in which he acknowledges
"the far-shining sail that's not fate" remains one of Britten's
most satisfying operatic conclusions, a rare moment of
optimism in an otherwise grim and negative world.

Britten subsequently condensed its four acts into
two (also cutting a scene) and conducts this version with
consummate skill, drawing dramatic shapes from the LSO
and a hearty response from the all-male chorus. Pears
relishes the role of this authoritative figure, learned and
sensitive in dealing with his crew and commanding when
engaged in chasing a French frigate. Glossop is a hearty
Budd and Langdon's Claggart has a delicious dark-edged
tone that conveys the dreadful Iagolike character. **SW**

> "If wind and water could
> write music it would sound
> like Ben's."

Yehudi Menuhin

Other Recommended Recordings

London Symphony Orchestra • Richard Hickox
Chandos CHAN 9826 (3 CDs)
*Superbly dramatic reading with marvelous
performances all around*

Hallé Choir & Orchestra • Kent Nagano
Erato 3984 21631-2 (2 CDs)
*Brilliantly driven and dramatically urgent reading
of the original four-act version*

Royal Opera House Chorus & Orchestra
Benjamin Britten
VAIA 1034-3
Fascinating recording of the first performance

Dmitri Shostakovich
Twenty-four Preludes and Fugues (1951)

Genre | Instrumental
Instrument | Piano
Performer | Vladimir Ashkenazy
Years recorded | 1996–98
Label | Decca 466 066-2 (2 CDs)

Shostakovich conceived his earlier piano music in the context of his own performing career. The Preludes, op. 34, were written in haste in 1933, ushering in a period in which he wanted to devote more time to giving concerts, less to composing. The Twenty-four Preludes and Fugues, op. 87, though, constitute a more substantial project that was approached as much more of a musical challenge than the earlier cycle. The composer might never have considered writing them but for the inspiring Bach playing of the young Russian pianist Tatiana Nikolayeva. He worked on the cycle from October 10, 1950 to February 25, 1951, but the times were scarcely propitious. Following the 1948 Zhdanov crackdown, Shostakovich was more than ever expected to address contemporary life from the perspective of an idealized future, and portray social defects as positive forces serving to push society toward the goal of socialism. Instead Shostakovich came up with an intellectual challenge for connoisseurs, the nearest twentieth-century equivalent to Bach's *The Well-Tempered Clavier*. Was it also a declaration of artistic independence?

Notwithstanding the ardent championship of its dedicatee, Vladimir Ashkenazy is probably the most accomplished pianist to essay a recording of the whole set. (Many practitioners have preferred to pick and choose—which is what Shostakovich as pianist actually did himself.) Despite his fame, Ashkenazy had to fight hard for the realization of this project. In his hands, the music moves with greater fluidity and is sometimes more extrovert than one is used to, yet it symbolizes the composer's on-and-off confrontation with Soviet ideas about the role of art. **DG**

"Beyond question, this is Ashkenazy's finest piano recording in years."

Jed Distler on *classicstoday.com*

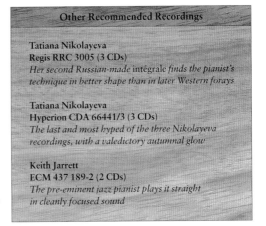

Other Recommended Recordings

Tatiana Nikolayeva
Regis RRC 3005 (3 CDs)
Her second Russian-made intégrale *finds the pianist's technique in better shape than in later Western forays*

Tatiana Nikolayeva
Hyperion CDA 66441/3 (3 CDs)
The last and most hyped of the three Nikolayeva recordings, with a valedictory autumnal glow

Keith Jarrett
ECM 437 189-2 (2 CDs)
The pre-eminent jazz pianist plays it straight in cleanly focused sound

Francis Poulenc
Stabat mater (1951)

Genre | Choral
Conductor/Performers | Richard Hickox;
Catherine Dubosc, City of London Sinfonia
Year recorded | 1999
Label | Virgin 0946 3 63294 2 0

The *Stabat mater*, which Poulenc composed at his country retreat in Noizay in 1950, was his first religious work with orchestra. It was written in memory of the painter Christian Berard, and, in the variety of mood-shadings shown in its twelve relatively brief movements, it imitates quite deliberately the grand motet form cultivated by Charpentier, Lully, and Lalande in seventeenth- and eighteenth-century France. When it was first given at the Strasbourg Festival on April 22, 1951, there must have been many expecting to hear a work in the vein of the reflective *Litanies à la Vierge Noire*, the piece written fifteen years earlier when, following the death of a close young composer friend, he had experienced a spiritual revelation at the shrine of the Black Virgin in Rocamadour, France. (Prior to this, he had been renowned for wittier, jazzier, spikier, and certainly more secular music.) But in fact, the *Stabat mater*, despite its purpose, and the religious integrity that lies behind it, is an outward-looking, very public work. Some have called it earthy, even vulgar, but that is merely to criticize it for engaging with the world. It is a work of suave nuance that takes much from Stravinsky.

The perfect recording must capture this teasing duality. Richard Hickox's account admirably fits the bill. Never one to display ebullience for its own sake, he exhibits the right balance between spirituality and theatricality. The Westminster Singers are excellent, and soprano Catherine Dubosc shows an appealing delicacy well suited to this music. The other works on the disc almost choose themselves—the exuberant *Gloria* of 1959 and those *Litanies à la Vierge Noire* of 1936. **SP**

Igor Stravinsky
The Rake's Progress (1951)

Genre | Opera
Conductor/Performers | Igor Stravinsky;
Alexander Young, Judith Raskin
Year recorded | 1964
Label | Sony SM2K 46299 (2 CDs)

Though Stravinsky had considerable experience in music theater pieces, he only wrote one true opera, *The Rake's Progress*. It took three years to complete and remains one of the most popular twentieth-century works in the operatic repertoire. The plot, cleverly formulated by W. H. Auden and Chester Kallmann, is based around scenes from William Hogarth's series of paintings entitled *A Rake's Progress*. This is relevant since the opera is the most Neo-Classical of Stravinsky's works, deriving many elements from others' music. There are touches of Gluck, Beethoven, Mozart's *Don Giovanni*, and even Bizet's *Carmen*.

The rake of the title is Tom Rakewell, a handsome young man who wants more from life than simply settling down with his love, Anne Truelove. Tom's alter ego, Nick Shadow, offers him a life elsewhere and leads him to the delights of Mother Goose's brothel in London. Constantly seeking new pleasures and freedoms, Tom is persuaded to marry Baba the Turk, a freak, bearded lady. He takes to gambling and ultimately loses not just his fortune, but also his mind, ending up in Bedlam. The Epilogue summarizes the tale's moral: "For idle hands and hearts and minds / The Devil finds a work to do."

This LP transfer to CD works very effectively. Stravinsky conducts his own work with relish; there are delightful moments of orchestral detail: brittle woodwind textures and vivid spiccato string figures emerge with fine clarity. The auction in Act 3 captures the composer's bubbling ideas wonderfully. Alexander Young is a fine Rakewell with Judith Raskin's all-forgiving Anne sweetly moving, and John Reardon an insinuating Nick Shadow. **SW**

Sergei Prokofiev
Symphony-Concerto (1951)

Genre | Concerto
Performer | Mstislav Rostropovich (cello)
Conductor | Seiji Ozawa
Year recorded | c.1986
Label | Warner 0927 46745-2

We owe this piece, Prokofiev's final large-scale work, to its dedicatee Mstislav Rostropovich. It is a glorious memorial to the inspiration the young cellist gave to an exhausted, oppressed artist at the end of his life. The work is based on the Cello Concerto, op. 58 (1933–38). When Prokofiev heard the student Rostropovich perform it in 1947, he was so excited by his talent that he went backstage to tell him that he was going to rewrite it. In fact, it was not until 1950 that he began what turned into a thorough recomposition, producing this vast "Symphony-Concerto." Rostropovich collaborated closely, and they became fast friends. First performed in 1952, it was withdrawn and revised again: sadly, Prokofiev died having never heard his final version.

Unlike his other late works, this ambitious Symphony-Concerto harks back to the younger, happier man: the work opens with an outpouring of song from the cello, while the huge middle scherzo combines the best of his polychromatic orchestration, and a cadenza of death-defying feats of virtuosity with one of the most heartfelt cantabile melodies. In the finale's theme and variations, there are playful parodies of Mahler, Rossini, and Britten, rising to a luminescent plateau before the soloist takes on the stormy might of the entire orchestra and escapes.

Though his early recordings have scandalously been deleted, Rostropovich still brings a unique spirit to this work: in this performance with the London Symphony Orchestra he was nearing sixty, and we feel the force of the cellist who knocked Prokofiev sideways. It is not just his visionary sense, his intelligence, or his special élan; it is the perfect marriage of music with musician. **HW**

Heitor Villa-Lobos
Guitar Concerto (1951)

Genre | Concerto
Performers | Narcisco Yepes,
London Symphony Orchestra
Year recorded | 1988
Label | DG 423 700-2

By the time Villa-Lobos had written the main body of his Guitar Concerto—also known, accurately enough, as the Concerto for Guitar and Small Orchestra—in 1951, he had accumulated what must have felt like several lifetimes' worth of experience, both musical and otherwise. Growing up after the collapse of Brazil's imperial regime, he seemed to personify his nation's headlong rush into modernity. His formal musical education was desultory, yet he mastered several instruments, played in commercial and opera-house orchestras, researched the traditional music of his country's interior, and played urban folk with street bands, before marrying a pianist and settling down to compose, and accept a government position in music education.

This concerto was commissioned by Andrés Segovia, who, in the 1920s, had asked Villa-Lobos for a guitar study, only to be presented with a dozen virtuoso pieces, all evoking Brazilian popular culture. These did not persuade Segovia to accept the concerto, described as a *Fantasia concertante*, as it stood; rather, he refused to play it, as it was insufficiently virtuosic. In 1956, Villa-Lobos inserted a cadenza between the otherwise continuous second and third movements and retitled the work concerto. Segovia settled for this and premiered the work in the same year.

Despite the fact that the orchestra features no more than six individual wind instruments plus a string section, this concerto is an extraordinarily expressive work. Brazilian popular music is once again a significant inspiration here, particularly in the dynamic first movement, while the composer's grasp of orchestral color and agile melodic sense is clearly evident across all three movements. **RT**

Sergei Prokofiev
Symphony no. 7 (1952)

Genre | Orchestral
Conductor | Valery Gergiev
Performers | London Symphony Orchestra
Year recorded | 2004
Label | Philips 475 7655 (4 CDs)

Prokofiev's last symphonic work has often been seen as puzzlingly lightweight after the epic adventure of the Fifth and the unequivocal tragedy of the Sixth. It is certainly true that the notorious show trials of 1948, in which Stalin's right-hand man Andrei Zhdanov brought Soviet composers to heel, meant that complex scores were out of the question in the years between then and Stalin's death on March 5, 1953 (the same day as Prokofiev's own untimely demise). Yet, though the Seventh Symphony started life in 1952 as music for children's radio, it is not quite as simple as it seems. The opening is dark and tragic, and, though its mood is alleviated by a soaring theme that could have come straight from the world of Prokofiev's ballet *Cinderella*, the fairytale tintinnabulations that make up the last of the opening movement's three ideas are enigmatic. They return to conclude the symphony in a mood of wistful resignation—though Prokofiev was persuaded to tack on a reprise of the finale's jolly gallop in order to win much-needed Stalin prize money. Whether the Seventh Symphony ends with that, or with the more poetic original, is up to the performers.

In his unforgettable Prokofiev cycle at the Barbican in May 2004, Valery Gergiev had the best of both worlds—he gave two performances of the Seventh, each ending in a different way. Thankfully the one that has made it to CD is the quiet close, and it is very much in tune with his pensive and profound interpretation. By no means everything in this Prokofiev cycle is as thoughtful, but this performance demonstrates why the London Symphony Orchestra took the unpredictable Gergiev to its heart. **DN**

Michael Tippett | The
Midsummer Marriage (1952)

Genre | Opera
Conductor | Colin Davis
Performers | Alberto Remedios, Joan Carlyle
Year recorded | 1970
Label | Lyrita SRCD 2217

"There is only one comic plot: The unexpected hindrances to an eventual marriage." So wrote Tippett in detailing the birth pangs of his first opera, *The Midsummer Marriage*. But the result was no ordinary comedy, rather a journey of self-discovery modeled on the trials of Mozart's *The Magic Flute*, whereby Mark and Jenifer must achieve self-knowledge before they marry. Jungian archetypes, Celtic, Greek, and Hindu mythologies all have their part in the process. It almost completely flummoxed audiences at its Covent Garden premiere in 1955, and is still a challenge to stage today, with its blend of multilayered symbolism and 1950s suburban commonality, ritual, and nature. But from the first, the lyricism and power of Tippett's music helped to mitigate the weirdness of the plot and the awkwardness of his own libretto (he wrote his own texts for all his operas). The four "Ritual Dances" symbolizing the battle of the sexes have achieved a life of their own, while other highlights include the rhythmically charged choruses and a heart-stopping monologue for the medium Madame Sosostris.

Colin Davis's account with the Royal Opera House Chorus and Orchestra, made after the works revival there in the late 1960s, is undoubtedly one of the great recordings of the opera. Davis has always been Tippett's finest interpreter and here captures all the music's vitality, lyrical beauty, and atmosphere. The cast is superb, with Alberto Remedios and Joan Carlyle's fresh-voiced Mark and Jenifer, a sonorous King Fisher from Raimund Herincx, and Helen Watts's cavernous Sosostris, and the recording itself has body and clarity. Rarely has a "difficult" opera been so triumphantly vindicated in musical terms. **MR**

Dmitri Shostakovich
Symphony no. 10 (1953)

Genre | Orchestral
Conductor | Herbert von Karajan
Performers | Berlin Philharmonic Orchestra
Year recorded | 1966
Label | DG 429 716-2

Michael Tippett
Fantasia concertante (1953)

Genre | Orchestral
Conductor | Andrew Davis
Performers | BBC Symphony Orchestra
Year recorded | 1993
Label | Warner 8573 89098-2

The Tenth Symphony was unleashed on the world by the Leningrad Philharmonic under Yevgeny Mravinsky months after Stalin's death. Shostakovich's first symphony since the 1948 campaign against "formalism," it seems to have a double purpose: to satisfy as a universal, abstract entity while encapsulating implicit messages concerning personal identity and integrity. The second movement, a short and violent scherzo, is often said to be "a musical portrait of Stalin." While Mravinsky may have interpreted the horn calls of the third movement as alluding to himself, and despite the reference to *Das Lied von der Erde*, we now know that they encode the name of Elmira, an ex-pupil with whom Shostakovich was temporarily obsessed. The other key element here is his own motivic signature, consisting of the notes D-E flat-C-B, or D-Es-C-H in German notation. After an introduction in which the patches of sunlight never quite break through the gloom, the mood of frustrated self-assertion is swept aside as the finale proceeds, his monogram reigning triumphant at the close.

Karajan may be an unexpected champion for such music (he expressed interest in the Eighth, too, though he never conducted it), but he projects the ferocious drive of the scherzo as successfully as he shapes the first movement's long-term buildup and decay. His orchestra can boast an unsurpassed first horn and it is only if you feel that the finale's rejoicing ought to be proletarian, boisterous stuff that this, the earlier of two Karajan recordings, might fail to satisfy. It helps that the Tenth is not one of the Shostakovich symphonies that seems to insist upon the distinctive timbre of Russian winds. **DG**

Michael Tippett was always interested in early music; and his *Fantasia concertante on a Theme of Corelli* is a fascinating exercise, not just in writing variations on an old theme, but in entering a different musical world. It was commissioned to mark the tercentenary of the Italian violinist-composer Arcangelo Corelli, and its scoring echoes and elaborates that of Corelli's famous op. 6 Concerti Grossi: a concertino group of two violins and cello, and not one but two string orchestras, placed left and right. Despite the title, it is based not on a single theme by Corelli, but on two consecutive passages, slow and fast, from his Concerto op. 6, no. 2. These are varied in turn in music of increasing floridity and freedom; there is a fugue incorporating parts of a Bach organ fugue on two more Corelli themes; and the piece reaches its furthest point from home in a richly textured pastorale that has less to do with the famous finale of Corelli's *Christmas Concerto* than with the ecstatic English pastoral tradition.

In praising the *Fantasia concertante* as Tippett's "perfect" work, his biographer Ian Kemp says that "not a note is out of place, not a moment misconceived or miscalculated." That is all very well, but there are an awful lot of notes, and they are impossible to fit in at Tippett's metronome markings, which are substantially miscalculated on the fast side. Most conductors ignore the markings, and simply allow the music to expand luxuriantly. But Andrew Davis makes the most of the BBC strings' technical prowess in a bold attempt to get somewhere near them. In the process, he rediscovers an element of the piece that is often lost; a dancing lightness that finds its own route to ecstasy. **AB**

Leonard Bernstein | Serenade (1954)

Genre | Concerto
Performers | Joshua Bell (violin), Philharmonia Orchestra
Conductor | David Zinman
Year recorded | 2000
Label | Sony SK 89358

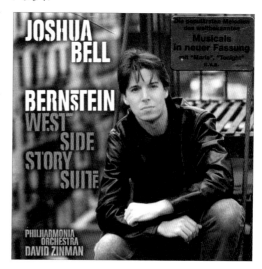

Serenade after Plato's "SYMPOSIUM" for Solo Violin, Strings, Harp, and Percussion, it is called on the title page of the score. Would it be played more often if it were simply "The Bernstein Violin Concerto"? Maybe so. But, although it is sometimes said that you can enjoy the music without knowing anything about the *Symposium*, the summary in the composer's program note does explain the construction of the work as an oddly proportioned suite. And now that biographers have told us so much about Bernstein's profligate personal life, it is fascinating to see how he was inspired by a series of speeches in praise of different kinds of love. In any case, whether you hear it as abstract or program music, the Serenade is one of his finest concert pieces. It is eclectic, of course, as Bernstein always is, with echoes of Copland, Bartók, and, especially, Stravinsky; hints of tunes to come in *Candide* and *West Side Story*; and some convincing big band jazz sounds for strings. But it contains some of the composer's most polished and coherent music: sparkling in the little scherzo called "Erixymathus;" deeply moving in the intense slow movement, "Agathon."

Though the Serenade is still something of a rarity in concert, and despite some recent deletions, there is a strong field of recordings to select from, including magnificent accounts by Joshua Bell and Anne-Sophie Mutter. Bell's performance (marooned on a disk otherwise devoted to arrangements of Bernstein theater music) just gets the palm because of its slightly clearer orchestral detail, and an extra ounce of inwardness in the more meditative music. Both players have the ability to make you think, in the slower music, that you have never heard anything more beautiful. And perhaps you haven't. **AB**

> *"A series of related statements in praise of love."*
>
> Leonard Bernstein

Other Recommended Recordings

Anne-Sophie Mutter, London Symphony Orchestra
André Previn
DG 474 500-2
Close rivals to Bell and Zinman in every respect

Gidon Kremer, Israel Philharmonic Orchestra
Leonard Bernstein
DG 469 829-2 (7 CDs)
The composer's own second recording

Philippe Quint, Bournemouth Symphony Orchestra
Marin Alsop
Naxos 8.559245
A highly recommendable bargain disc

Benjamin Britten | The Turn of the Screw (1954)

Genre | Opera
Conductor/Performers | Benjamin Britten; Peter Pears,
Jennifer Vyvyan, David Hemmings, English Opera Group
Year recorded | 1955
Label | Decca 425 672-2 (2 CDs)

britten the turn of the screw

In his darkest opera Britten tells the story of the ghost-inhabited world of Bly and explores issues of trust and the abuse of trust. At the center of the drama is the care of the unnamed Governess for her charge, "little Master Miles." She is at Bly at the behest of the boy's mysterious, absent, handsome uncle and as she settles into life at the claustrophobic house, she learns more and more about the worryingly close relationship between his valet, Peter Quint, and the boy. Increasingly, she sees it as her role to protect Miles from Quint, now beyond the grave. In so doing she becomes obsessed with the boy, twisting the events at the house toward their tragic end.

The Henry James novella on which Britten and his librettist, Myfanwy Piper, based the opera, leaves it unclear whether the two ghosts, Quint and Miss Jessel, are real or figments of the Governess' imagination. They exist in the opera and articulate their desire with the Yeats quote "The ceremony of innocence is drowned." Nevertheless, the ambiguity of whether Miles's final line "Peter Quint, you devil" is addressed to him or the Governess is retained.

A mono recording could be seen as a distinct disadvantage for an opera; here, however, it emphasizes the unpleasant claustrophobia of the piece, written, like *The Rape of Lucretia* and *Albert Herring*, for chamber ensemble. Jennifer Vyvyan is spot-on as the Governess, herself somehow innocent at the start of the piece as she travels to her new home and increasingly frenetic in tone as her view of the situation darkens. Peter Pears as Quint is superb. His first virtuosic calls are gloriously seductive and, at his most evil, he conjures up his character's evil intent. Hemmings is a perfect Miles; boyish, clever, and knowing just a little bit too much. **SW**

> *"Like squeezing toothpaste out of a tube that's nearly finished."*
>
> **Britten on the composition process of** *The Turn of the Screw*

Other Recommended Recordings

Aldeburgh Festival Ensemble • Steuart Bedford
Naxos 8.660109-10 (2 CDs)
Vivid and colorful instrumental playing accompanies this fine cast

Mahler Chamber Orchestra • Daniel Harding
Virgin 7243 5 45521 2 0 (2 CDs)
A fine reading, full of impressive characterization and recorded with great clarity

Royal Opera House Orchestra • Colin Davis
Philips 446 325-2 (2 CDs)
Colin Davis oversees an atmospheric and darkly frightening interpretation

Aram Khachaturian
Spartacus (1954)

Genre | Orchestral
Conductor/Performers | Aram
Khachaturian; Vienna Philharmonic
Year recorded | 1962
Label | Decca 460 315-2

The story of Spartacus, who led an uprising of slaves against the Romans in the first century BCE, has provided inspiration for many revolutionaries—including Karl Marx. No wonder, then, that Khachaturian presented his 1954 ballet *Spartacus* to the Soviet authorities as "a monumental fresco" depicting "the mighty avalanche" of the slaves' rebellion "on behalf of human rights." In reality, though, its ideological slant is of little importance. Khachaturian's real inspiration came from the opportunities the tale offered for blending adventure, romance, and spectacle. To borrow a slogan for Stanley Kubrick's 1960 film—"Spartacus has everything that makes entertainment great!"

In fact, Khachaturian's *Spartacus* is an epic of cinematic proportions. Its melodic opulence is made all the more glamorous by the lush exoticism of the harmonies—reflecting the composer's love for the folk music of his native Armenia—and the oversaturated, Technicolor brilliance of the orchestration. In its finest moments, such as the soaring, sinuous "Adagio for Spartacus and his wife Phrygia" (famous as the theme music for the BBC television series *The Onedin Line*), Khachaturian achieves a lyrical radiance that would have made Tchaikovsky proud.

The complete ballet has been recorded, and there are fine versions of the various suites drawn from the score, but none match the panache of the composer's performance of four excerpts (including the aforementioned "Adagio") with the Vienna Philharmonic. The CD also includes selections from Khachaturian's earlier ballet *Gayane* (1942), with its celebrated "Sabre Dance." The vintage Decca recording still sounds fabulous. **AFC**

Witold Lutosławski
Concerto for Orchestra (1954)

Genre | Orchestral
Conductor | Yan-Pascal Tortelier
Performers | BBC Philharmonic Orchestra
Year recorded | 1993
Label | Chandos CHAN 9421

It was his next big work, the *Funeral Music*, that Witold Lutosławski (1913–94) dedicated to the memory of Bartók, but the Concerto for Orchestra takes a vital step in this direction and several others. Lutosławski began it in 1950; in the same year, after a performance of his First Symphony, the Polish vice-minister of culture said that he ought to be thrown under a streetcar. Retrenchment and synthesis were needed.

The concerto's appeal is obvious, right from a tense, pounding opening that does not give away any expressive secrets. The whole Intrada movement could be colored by totalitarian violence or state-sanctioned folklorism, Bartókian modal energy, or a generalized, even Romantic rhetoric that suggests a young composer still finding his voice. The hushed, open-ended conclusion to the Intrada (shades of Stravinsky's Symphony in Three Movements) ushers in a spectral scherzo with more unapologetically good melodies. The second one prefigures the "Big Tune" of the finale, which like many later Lutosławski works, contains the concerto's main argument. It is spread over a passacaglia with eighteen variations, an explosive toccata, and culminating chorale; old forms, studded with bundles of novelty in harmony, orchestration, or phrase-lengths.

Any good recording has to match up to the showpiece challenge that makes it a favorite of touring orchestras. Really vivid engineering helps: Chandos offers a resonant ambience for the BBC Philharmonic. Yan-Pascal Tortelier's fairly brisk speeds and playful articulation score high on the thrillometer while never neglecting the interesting and contradictory directions in which the piece faces. **PQ**

Joaquin Rodrigo | Fantasia para un gentilhombre (1954)

Genre | Concerto
Performers/Conductor | Carlos Bonnell, Royal Philharmonic; Jacek Kasprzyk
Year recorded | 1994
Label | RPO 204450

With a life that spanned the twentieth century and a career that included the post of professor of music history at Madrid University, it is logical to think of Rodrigo as a composer with a profound sense of how musical styles evolve over time. Despite having been blind for most of his life and enduring a period of exile during the Spanish Civil War, his music is unfailingly optimistic and animated. His style, described as "neocasticismo," is an intriguing fusion of both traditional and modern Spanish music. After returning to Spain in 1939, he composed eleven concertos, a wide variety of vocal, choral, and instrumental pieces, and music for films and theater productions.

The Fantasia was commissioned by the virtuoso guitarist Andrés Segovia and dates from 1954. Segovia is not the "gentilhombre" ("gentleman") of the title; it is a reference to the seventeenth-century Spanish guitarist and composer Gaspar Sanz, whose compositions inspired this work—its four movements derive from a set of dances incorporated into a treatise on the guitar that Sanz published in 1674. The idea of retrieving catchy melodies from earlier music and giving them a modern going-over is not unlike that behind Peter Warlock's popular Capriol Suite; Rodrigo expertly stirs the dance melodies into a heady mixture of modern orchestration with gently subversive results.

Carlos Bonnell has recorded the Fantasia several times, but this version is particularly fine, with the orchestra providing a rich and detailed backdrop to Bonnell's forceful and precise performance. The latter, though, is anything but facile, as the tricky juggling of threes and sixes in the final movement attests. **RT**

Iannis Xenakis Metastaseis (1954)

Genre | Orchestral
Conductor/Performers | Konstantin Simonovic; French Radio National Orchestra
Year recorded | 1965
Label | Chant du Monde 278368

Iannis Xenakis (1922–2001) was born in Romania, but lived in Greece from the age of ten. Most of his compositions have Greek titles, but despite his identification with Greek culture and nationality, his contribution to twentieth-century music was very significant from an international perspective. Trained as an architect, he worked as an assistant to Le Corbusier from 1948 until 1959 while simultaneously pursuing a career as a composer. He received some tuition from Milhaud and Honegger, but was primarily self-taught. Xenakis was an outspoken critic of Serialism, regarding rigidity of the twelve-note system as not only unacceptably authoritarian, but also futile; as one of the pioneers of computer-based composition, he contended that the very notion of an octave divided into a sequence of semitones was arguably redundant. He also dismissed the proposition that music was similar to language, maintaining instead that musical structure was similar to "the categories of space and time."

Metastaseis (Transformation) demonstrates much of this thinking. His first published composition, it is written for a sixty-piece orchestra consisting mainly of strings. The work combines architectural and mathematical ideas to produce a composition that is a landmark in modern music. Despite its seemingly cerebral nature, the piece was inspired by recollections of an anti-Nazi demonstration in Athens. This recording is sonically impeccable and benefits from the obvious insight and commitment on the part of the performers. In addition, Mode's Xenakis Edition is an indispensable resource for anyone who wishes to investigate this intriguing composer's output further. **RT**

Alan Hovhaness
Symphony no. 2, "Mysterious Mountain" (1955)

Genre | Orchestral
Conductor | Fritz Reiner
Performers | Chicago Symphony Orchestra
Year recorded | 1958
Label | RCA 09026 61957 2

Alan Hovhaness (1911–2000) is a curious figure in American music. He published more than 450 works, including sixty-seven symphonies. For much of his career, his music was considered unfashionable, although now it seems he was ahead of his time. His fusion of Western counterpoint (especially Renaissance polyphony) and Eastern traditions (including folk music from his ancestral Armenia) anticipated the work of John Tavener, Arvo Pärt, and other "holy minimalist" composers.

This symphony was Hovhaness's first and perhaps greatest success. It was commissioned by Leopold Stokowski, who conducted the premiere in Houston in 1955. It begins with a warm-toned hymn, establishing an atmosphere at once mysterious and soothing. Ancient and exotic-sounding harmonic inflections, piping woodwind tunes, and gentle chimes ornament the mood. Contrast is provided by a masterful double fugue in two parts—the first broadly lyrical, the second bounding breathlessly forward. Calm returns in the finale, as a chantlike melody ebbs and flows, like the soaring arches of a cathedral.

Fritz Reiner recorded "Mysterious Mountain" for RCA in 1958. Though this is Hovhaness's most frequently recorded symphony, no version has surpassed Reiner's account. His pacing is sure. He maintains a serene flow in the outer movements, and pushes hard in the fast part of the double fugue, generating heart-pounding excitement. The Chicago Symphony's playing conveys a sense of commitment that helps draw one into Hovhaness's strange but wonderful world, and RCA's engineers captured every nuance of the orchestra's gloriously burnished tone. **AFC**

> *"Simplicity is difficult, not easy. Beauty is simple."*
> Alan Hovhaness

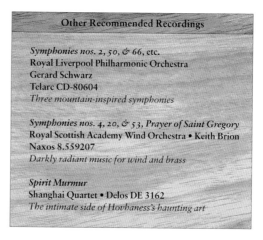

Other Recommended Recordings

Symphonies nos. 2, 50, & 66, etc.
Royal Liverpool Philharmonic Orchestra
Gerard Schwarz
Telarc CD-80604
Three mountain-inspired symphonies

Symphonies nos. 4, 20, & 53, Prayer of Saint Gregory
Royal Scottish Academy Wind Orchestra • Keith Brion
Naxos 8.559207
Darkly radiant music for wind and brass

Spirit Murmur
Shanghai Quartet • Delos DE 3162
The intimate side of Hovhaness's haunting art

Alan Hovhaness was something of an outsider in American music. ➔

Pierre Boulez | Le marteau sans maître (1955)

Genre | Vocal
Conductor | Pierre Boulez
Performers | Hilary Summers, Ensemble InterContemperain
Year recorded | 2001
Label | DG 477 5327

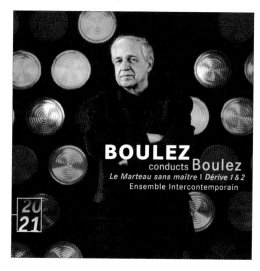

Pierre Boulez, born in 1925, is one of the giants of twentieth-century music, whose activities as a composer, conductor, and organizer have had a profound effect on the musical landscape in Europe in particular. His early works use a strict serial technique, but he soon found that he needed a more fluid and dramatic way of working, of which the most famous flowering is *Le marteau sans maître*. Later he introduced limited elements of choice in his works—in *Pli selon pli* and *Rituel*—and used electronics: these became a major part of his work at IRCAM—L'Institut de Recherche et Coordination Acoustique/Musique—in the 1970s and 1980s. His fastidious ear has also made him a successful conductor, particularly in works where the utmost clarity is important.

Le marteau sans maître is one of the few indisputable classics of the twentieth-century avant-garde, and a recognized success from its premiere. Using contralto and a mixed ensemble of alto flute, viola, guitar, vibraphone, marimba, and untuned percussion, Boulez avoids any suggestion of a bass line, and the kaleidoscope of sounds seems to float in midair in a very non-European way. This feeling is reinforced by the words: surrealist poems by René Char, rich in texture, but elusive in meaning.

Boulez has recorded the piece several times, but his latest version is the best. The complexities of the writing are now commonplace, especially to the virtuoso members of the Ensemble InterContemperain, and the wide leaps and awkward melismas of the vocal line are thrillingly negotiated by Hilary Summers. The crystal clear recording allows us to hear every detail of the score, and marvel again at its edgy, sometimes uncomfortable, always miraculous beauty. **MC**

"An admirable, well-ordered score . . . I frankly find it preferable to many things of his generation."

Igor Stravinsky

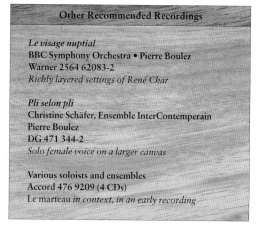

Other Recommended Recordings

Le visage nuptial
BBC Symphony Orchestra • Pierre Boulez
Warner 2564 62083-2
Richly layered settings of René Char

Pli selon pli
Christine Schäfer, Ensemble InterContemperain
Pierre Boulez
DG 471 344-2
Solo female voice on a larger canvas

Various soloists and ensembles
Accord 476 9209 (4 CDs)
Le marteau in context, in an early recording

Leonard Bernstein | Candide (1956, *rev.* 1971, 1988–89)

Genre | Operetta
Conductor/Performers | Leonard Bernstein; Jerry Hadley,
June Anderson, London Symphony Orchestra & Chorus
Year recorded | 1989
Label | DG 474 472-2 (2 CDs)

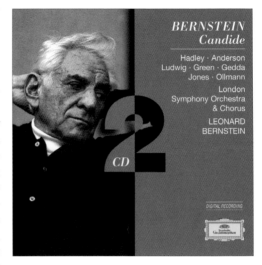

"All is for the best in the best of all possible worlds."
For many years, the philosophical proposition so
comprehensively ridiculed in Voltaire's 1759 satire *Candide*
hardly applied either to Bernstein's adaptation of the work
as something between a musical and an operetta. After
a protracted and acrimonious genesis, the show more or
less flopped on Broadway. And while some revivals were
more successful, this was achieved by blunting the satire,
reducing the scoring, shifting some numbers to different
scenes, and ditching others altogether. All this obscured
the extraordinary quality and variety of Bernstein's musical
invention, which thanks to the wide-ranging story line runs
through a series of gleeful parodies of different styles, from
chorale to waltz, and tango to twelve-note. Only toward
the end of Bernstein's life did a "final revised version" bring
the work back to full scoring and length, and in the process
restore its underlying seriousness of purpose.

It is this version that Bernstein conducted in concert
in London in 1989 (available on a DG DVD), and then
recorded in the studio. The CDs have only the musical
numbers, but the booklet prints John Wells's witty linking
narration within the libretto. A remarkable cast, ranging
from the stunningly operatic June Anderson, and old
opera hands Christa Ludwig and Nicolai Gedda, to the
personable Jerry Hadley and the conversational Adolph
Green, clearly has tremendous fun. So does Bernstein
himself, reveling in the sheer over-the-top quality of the
score—and not only when it is humorous. The finale,
"Make Our Garden Grow," has less to do with Voltaire's
resigned conclusion than with the need for an uplifting
Broadway finish. But you can know that perfectly well, and
still find tears in your eyes. **AB**

> ## *"A Valentine card to European music."*
> Leonard Bernstein

Other Recommended Recordings

Trouble in Tahiti
Picardy Orchestra • Pascal Verrot
Calliope CAL 9391
One-act television opera with an eclectic score

Mass
Rock band and orchestra • Leonard Bernstein
Sony SM2K 63089 (2 CDs)
Large-scale "theater-piece" subverting Catholic ritual

Dybbuk, Fancy Free
Nashville Symphony • Andrew Mogrelia
Naxos 8.559280
Two ballet scores, one dramatic, the other a jazzy romp

William Walton | Cello Concerto (1956, *rev.* 1975)

Genre | Concerto
Performers | Yo-Yo Ma (cello), London Symphony Orchestra
Conductor | André Previn
Year recorded | 1984
Label | Sony MK 39541

Elgar & Walton
Cello Concertos
Yo-Yo Ma
London Symphony Orchestra
André Previn

We have Gregor Piatigorksy to thank for Walton's languid Cello Concerto. The Ukrainian star cellist, exiled in the United States, apparently offered Walton $3,000 in 1955 ($30,000 today), to which the pragmatic composer responded: "I'm a composer. I'll write anything for anybody if he pays me!" Work proceeded apace, with Piatigorsky collaborating on the work, even requesting a different ending.

Walton confided to Piatigorsky that it was the favorite of his three string concertos: It certainly feels very personal and confounds all the usual rules of concerto writing. In the lovely, dreamlike first movement, as the soloist yawns and stretches, luxuriating in glistening, impressionistic orchestral textures, we might be listening to a tone poem rather than a concerto. Walton dabs iridescent flecks of wind color in a wash of strings, evoking nothing so strongly as the sun-drenched gardens of his Italian island home. By contrast, the capricious scherzo bursts into life, soloist and orchestra chasing each other at speed, with knuckle-breaking chords and whistling harmonics from the cello, until it comes to rest on a shimmering, slow melody high on the A string. The final lento returns to bask in the sun but emerges as a long "theme and improvisations," in the composer's words. After these rhapsodic explorations, the concerto's opening theme is heard again, and the work slips into a smoldering musical sunset.

Yo-Yo Ma is an ideal performer for this work, being a musician of such effortless elegance. He is not afraid to luxuriate in Walton's long-limbed melodies and subtle, searching cadenzas, but he can produce the virtuoso high-jinks with precision and panache. André Previn, too, who knew Walton well, handles the work with great gentleness, producing a visionary performance from the LSO. **HW**

"I'll write anything for anybody if he pays me . . . naturally I write much better if I'm paid in dollars!"
William Walton

Other Recommended Recordings

Gregor Piatigorsky, Boston Symphony Orchestra
Charles Münch
RCA 82876 66375 2
Focused virtuosity from the concerto's dedicatee

Raphael Wallfisch, London Philharmonic Orchestra
Bryden Thomson
Chandos CHAN 8959
A reading of elegance and fantasy

Daniel Müller-Schott, Oslo Philharmonic Orchestra
André Previn
Orfeo C 621 061 A
A young talent brings verve and dynamism

Yo-Yo Ma has one of the widest ranges of repertoire of any cellist. ➔

Malcolm Williamson
Piano Works (1956–84)

Genre | Instrumental
Instrument | Piano
Performer | Antony Gray
Year recorded | 1998
Label | ABC 472 902-2 (2 CDs)

As a young Australian composer-pianist making his name in London, Malcolm Williamson (1931–2003) led a charmed existence. At the age of twenty-six, his First Symphony was premiered by Adrian Boult. Later, Yehudi Menuhin commissioned a violin concerto, Sadler's Wells produced his operas, and back home Robert Helpmann choreographed *The Display* for the Australian Ballet. But, ironically, from the moment he was appointed Master of the Queen's Music in 1975, his popularity began to wane.

Only since his death has this composer undergone a reversal of fortunes. Chandos has released some of his more important orchestral work (he completed seven symphonies and seven concertos), while the sheer diversity of his smaller pieces, ranging from charming little educational trifles to hard-core serial extravaganzas, have finally begun to resurface.

Nowhere is the breadth of Williamson's stylistic interests more apparent than in his piano music. Written mainly for himself during the height of his solo performing career in the 1950s and 1960s, they range in style from the travelogue-style *Haifa Watercolors* and *The Bridge that Van Gogh Painted* to the masterly post-serial techniques of the Piano Sonata no. 2—one of four such sonatas that contain the essence of Williamson's lyrical musical personality.

Australian pianist Antony Gray's two-CD set of Williamson's complete works for piano is based on close consultation with the composer and they are played with utmost respect and fidelity to the scores. While the orchestral and choral works are better known, they encapsulate the essence of his latterly underrated art. **MB**

Francis Poulenc | Dialogues
des Carmélites (1956)

Genre | Opera
Conductor/Performers | Kent Nagano; Catherine Dubosc, Jean-Luc Viala, Rita Gorr
Year recorded | 1998
Label | Virgin 0946 3 58657 5 1

When the management of La Scala commissioned a ballet from Poulenc in 1953, he chose to write an opera. And with *Dialogues des Carmélites* he created a drama that digs deep into the roots of spiritual terror and yearns for grace: truly a work for the dark middle years of the twentieth century. The final scene, when the Carmelite nuns of Compiègne, joined at last by fearful Sister Blanche, go one by one to the guillotine singing "Salve regina," is without parallel. The rising minor thirds that have signaled terror and the Revolutionary Terror throughout the work are overcome by the confident beat of a traditional Catholic hymn.

Poulenc found his libretto in a play by Georges Bernanos, which was first a novel by a young German nun, who had been attracted to the story of the martyrdom of the Carmelite sisters at the time of the French Revolution, written by Mère Marie, the one survivor of the order. Bernanos was dying as he wrote his play and so was Poulenc's lover when Poulenc began to compose the most harrowing scene in the opera, the death of the old Prioress. "You will see it is terrifying. When I play it to you, you will weep and weep," the composer wrote to a friend. One can only guess at what this cost the composer.

Rita Gorr would move the stoniest heart as the dying Prioress. And there is anxiety in almost every phrase that Catherine Dubosc sings as Sister Blanche, with a properly French vocal style. That same anxiety is in that particular head tone from Jean-Luc Viala as the Chevalier, when he confronts his sister for the last time in the convent parlor. Overall an utterly committed performance from Kent Nagano and the Lyon Opéra Chorus and Orchestra. **CC**

Leonard Bernstein
West Side Story (1957)

Genre | Musical
Performers | Carol Lawrence, Larry Kert, Chita Rivera
Year recorded | 1957
Label | Sony SK 60724

In the fall of 1957, Leonard Bernstein was on top of the world: newly appointed as conductor of the New York Philharmonic and the composer of a ground-breaking Broadway hit. It had been eight years since the choreographer Jerome Robbins had had the idea of a musical transposing of the *Romeo and Juliet* story to present-day New York. He had quickly coopted Bernstein, and the playwright Arthur Laurents; the lyricist, the young Stephen Sondheim, came in later. But Robbins's role was crucial because the element of dance played such a dominant role in *West Side Story*, and it required a young, lively cast to do it justice. It also allowed Bernstein to characterize the rival Puerto Rican and American gangs with different dance rhythms: mambos and cha-cha-chas and a huapango on one side, up-to-date cool jazz and even rock 'n' roll on the other. But the score is not just colorful: it is full of soaring melodic invention yet tightly integrated, and the ending is genuinely tragic.

As for a recommendable recording, there is a clear-cut choice. The 1957 original Broadway cast album is slightly rough-and-ready in recording and execution, but it is crackling with youthful energy and conviction. Bernstein's own 1984 recording presents a fuller version of the score than could be squeezed onto a 1950s LP, and the playing and sound are exceptionally vivid. But it is fatally flawed by the casting of mature opera singers in the two main roles: José Carreras especially sounds all wrong (even, with his Spanish accent, in the wrong gang). You may disagree—in which case the Bernstein on DG is for you. But life is not so short that you do not have time to hear both! **AB**

Dmitri Shostakovich
Piano Concerto no. 2 (1957)

Genre | Concerto
Performer | Dmitri Shostakovich (piano)
Conductor | André Cluytens
Year recorded | 1958
Label | EMI 7243 5 62648 2 3

Shostakovich's concertos for his own instrument are among his most enjoyable, least demanding works, snappily Neo-Classical in manner, but with a not-quite-concealed vein of poetic feeling. Caustically dismissed as having "no artistic value" by the composer himself in a letter to his radical colleague, Edison Denisov, the Second Piano Concerto is so light and airy that it is tempting to read into the music the optimism and sense of freedom that followed Stalin's death. In point of fact these were sad times for Shostakovich: his first wife, Nina, had recently died and he was entangled in an unsuitable and short-lived second marriage. With its plentiful stock of first-rate melodic material, the concerto reflects rather Shostakovich's closeness to his son. It was Maxim who premiered the work in Moscow on May 10, 1957; Shostakovich recorded it in Paris, and Leonard Bernstein introduced it to the United States.

There are the usual three movements, but the central panel is particularly affecting, with a dreamy atmosphere tapping into a range of archetypes from Grieg to Rachmaninov. Some have dismissed it as pure kitsch, which belittles Shostakovich's skill, even if he appears here as the adaptable and popular composer of movie music rather than the granitic titan of Soviet symphonism.

In this classic mono recording, Shostakovich tends to press forward rather than indulging in sentiment. At the time of these Paris sessions, he was just starting to be troubled by an incapacitating illness later diagnosed as a type of polio. Thrilling, indisputably authentic, and a little scrappy would be a fair verdict. **DG**

Samuel Barber | Vanessa (1957, *rev.* 1964)

Genre | Opera
Conductor/Performers | Dimitri Mitropoulos; Eleanor
Steber, Rosalind Elias, Nicolai Gedda, Metropolitan Opera
Year recorded | 1958
Label | RCA 07863 57899 2 (2 CDs)

Barber was destined to be an opera composer. His aunt was a world-renowned contralto who sang alongside Caruso, Gigli, and other Golden Age greats. Barber himself was a fine baritone and possessed an intimate understanding of the human voice. He had a keen dramatic sense, too, as works such as *Knoxville* (1947) amply demonstrate. It is strange, then, that his first opera came relatively late in his career. Then again, *Vanessa* is a work of such lyrical beauty, dramatic confidence, and emotional maturity that perhaps he was wise to have waited.

For the libretto, Barber turned to his longtime companion Gian-Carlo Menotti. The story, adapted from one of Isak Dinesen's *Seven Gothic Tales*, tells of two beautiful women—Vanessa and her young niece Erika—and a tragic love triangle that takes shape when the son of Vanessa's former lover, Anatol, shows up unexpectedly at the door of their country manor. Premiered at the Metropolitan Opera to great acclaim, *Vanessa* was awarded a Pulitzer Prize in 1958 and became the first American opera to be produced at the prestigious Salzburg Festival.

Like the operas of Puccini and Richard Strauss, *Vanessa* is a conspicuously opulent score. And, as with *Tosca* or *Arabella*, the leading roles demand voices of strength and beauty, as well as singing actors who can dig beneath the plot's melodramatic surface to reveal its poignant human truths. Barber was lucky enough to find those qualities in the original cast, and RCA had the good sense to record the result for posterity. Eleanor Steber (who stepped into the title role a mere six weeks before the premiere), Rosalind Elias, and Nicolai Gedda sing with glowing intensity throughout, egged on by the incendiary conducting of Dimitri Mitropoulos. **AFC**

"At last, an American grand opera!"

Dimitri Mitropoulos

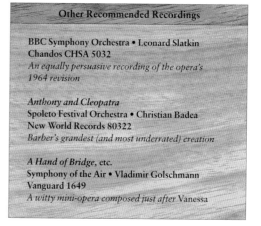

Other Recommended Recordings

BBC Symphony Orchestra • Leonard Slatkin
Chandos CHSA 5032
*An equally persuasive recording of the opera's
1964 revision*

Anthony and Cleopatra
Spoleto Festival Orchestra • Christian Badea
New World Records 80322
Barber's grandest (and most underrated) creation

A Hand of Bridge, etc.
Symphony of the Air • Vladimir Golschmann
Vanguard 1649
A witty mini-opera composed just after Vanessa

A scene from the premiere production of *Vanessa* at the New York Met. ➔

Karlheinz Stockhausen | Gruppen (1957)

Genre | Orchestral
Conductors | Arturo Tamayo, Peter Eötvös, Jacques Mercier
Performers | WDR Symphony Orchestra Cologne
Year recorded | 2004
Label | Budapest Music Center BMCCD 117

Stockhausen was twenty-seven when his wife, Doris, decided she wanted a holiday. Karlheinz was not so keen, so while she took their two young children to the beach, he stayed in an Alpine hamlet for six weeks and shaped the outline of *Gruppen*, inspired by the mountain range he could see from his rented room. He broke off for two years to explore his discovery that the infant science of electronic music offered a way of unifying harmony, rhythm, and timbre: the holy grail of total Serialism. The score was finished within the space of months in 1957 and signed off with a "Deo gratias" in the manner of Bach and Haydn. Musicians from Klemperer to Stravinsky quickly recognized a modern masterpiece.

Less than a decade separates *Gruppen* from Strauss's *Four Last Songs*. At least on the surface, Strauss's legato leave-taking to a lost age could not be more distant, but a surprising degree of continuity and tradition lies behind the young man's Straussian delight in orchestral virtuosity. A miniature violin concerto is shared between the leaders of three separate orchestras; this is one of the fifty-two *gruppen* ("groups") that constitute the whole. Several of them segue in quasi-military pomp to reach the work's famous climax, where the same chord is tossed between the brass groups of each orchestra at the point that any standard sonata-form movement reaches its climax.

Gruppen has yet to be recorded in the surround sound that would convey its spatial depth and impact in a domestic setting. Partial compensation is available on DVD in a Birmingham performance staged by Simon Rattle (Arthaus). The CD choice is clear: Peter Eötvös has known the composer and his music for decades; so has the Cologne orchestra, which gave the first performance. **PQ**

> *"An unavoidable monster."*
>
> Simon Rattle

Other Recommended Recordings

Biber: Missa Salisburgensis (1682)
Gabrieli Consort and Players • Paul McCreesh
DG 457 611-2
Six groups, fifty-three parts: a Baroque Mass

Carter: Symphony of Three Orchestras (1976)
New York Philharmonic Orchestra • Pierre Boulez
Sony SMK 68334
Less sonic than Gruppen, *more cinematic panorama*

Stockhausen: Carré (1960) (with *Gruppen*)
NDR Symphony Orchestra & Choir
Karlheinz Stockhausen, etc. • Stockhausen Verlag CD 5
More fluid and chilled than Gruppen

Stockhausen in the Cologne Radio electronic music studio in 1964. ➲

Igor Stravinsky
Agon (1957)

Genre | Ballet
Conductor | Hans Rosbaud
Performers | Southwest German Radio Orchestra
Year recorded | 1957
Label | Accord 476 886-2 (4 CDs)

A gap of ten years separates *Agon* from Stravinsky's preceding ballet, *Orpheus*, and, as Robert Craft has observed, admirers of Stravinsky's music for dance had feared that he would never compose for the genre again. By the mid-1950s, it was clear that Stravinsky was turning away from Neo-Classicism toward a new, serial-inspired approach, a development helped by the realization that his techniques were inherently proto-serial in any case.

Musically, *Agon* is a transitional work, but the methods used are ultimately irrelevant. The title is intended to mean a dance match or dance contest, and it is the vibrancy and joie de vivre of this music that is most striking. There is no plot to *Agon*. Rather the music provides the catalyst for a sequence of abstract dances for which the principal inspiration was neither Schoenberg nor Webern but a mid-seventeenth-century French dance manual (it included an engraving depicting two trumpeters performing the accompaniment to a "bransle simple" inspiring the instrumentation of the section of that name). The orchestra is one of Stravinsky's largest, though it is never heard in its entirety, and *Agon* is notable for the high proportion of up-tempo music, reflecting the composer's quicksilver mind.

This performance under the masterly direction of Hans Rosbaud was captured less than a year after the premiere and it is easy to see why he was so highly regarded. The Southwest German Radio Orchestra is far from cowed by this new score, with incisive playing and plenty of wit, while Rosbaud also manages to draw some remarkably supple playing from them in the quieter passages and allows the music some space to breathe. **CD**

"Agon, composed at seventy-five, is the music of a young man."

Robert Craft in *Stravinsky: Glimpses of a Life*

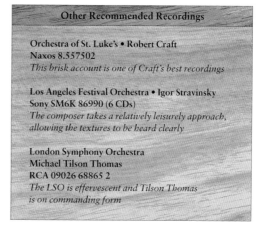

Other Recommended Recordings

Orchestra of St. Luke's • Robert Craft
Naxos 8.557502
This brisk account is one of Craft's best recordings

Los Angeles Festival Orchestra • Igor Stravinsky
Sony SM6K 86990 (6 CDs)
The composer takes a relatively leisurely approach, allowing the textures to be heard clearly

London Symphony Orchestra
Michael Tilson Thomas
RCA 09026 68865 2
The LSO is effervescent and Tilson Thomas is on commanding form

Dmitri Shostakovich
Symphony no. 11, "The Year 1905" (1957)

Genre | Orchestral
Conductor | Mstislav Rostropovich
Performers | London Symphony Orchestra
Year recorded | 2002
Label | LSO Live LSO 0030

Critical regard for Shostakovich's cinematic evocation of the first Russian Revolution of 1905 has been rising of late. Not that our ability to "decode" a subtext has led inevitably to readings of superior insight. When, in 2002, Mstislav Rostropovich addressed the audience after conducting the work in New York, he had something other than the 1956 Hungarian Uprising in mind when he said, "This music is like a ghost coming from people who were killed a hundred years ago—and at this moment, I think of September 11 for you." For whatever reason, this symphony has long inspired Shostakovich's friends and acolytes to explore diverse interpretative options, and Rostropovich's may well be the most spacious ever.

The frisson of a special event is felt from the start in the eerie, almost inaudible breath of sound with which the strings conjure up the frozen hush and epic breadth of Mother Russia. While there are few notes on the page, the atmosphere is potent. For the buildup to the "Bloody Sunday" massacre, the trombones supply astonishing, leering glissandos. And, for good or ill, the conductor's highly personalized nuancing at the height of the clamor is typical of his brand of music making. The finale's opening paragraph, articulated with tremendous cut and thrust by the strings, is another high point. So too, in a different way, is the evocative cor anglais solo taken by Christine Pendrill.

This searing performance was captured live in London's Barbican Hall. Applause is excluded, which sits well with Rostropovich's unilateral resolve to keep Shostakovich's final bell and tam-tam strokes ringing on and on. The message is universal. My advice: play loud or not at all. **DG**

> *"[His songs] spring up close by, sometimes float by . . . [or] flare up like lightning."*
>
> Anna Akhmatova, in Laurel Fay's *Shostakovich: A Life*

Other Recommended Recordings

Leningrad Philharmonic Orchestra • Yevgeny Mravinsky
Melodiya MEL CD 10 00772 (6 CDs)
Scorching intensity from the team long considered the composer's preferred interpreters

Houston Symphony Orchestra • Leopold Stokowski
EMI 7243 5 65206 2 2
Disdaining textual verisimilitude, Stokowski engenders unparalleled warmth in sound

Moscow Philharmonic Orchestra • Kirill Kondrashin
Melodiya MEL CD 10 01065 (11 CDs)
A hard-pressed assault on the score, cutting its duration to less than fifty-four minutes

Michael Tippett | Symphony no. 2 (1957)

Genre | Orchestral
Conductor | Colin Davis
Performers | London Symphony Orchestra
Year recorded | 1967
Label | Decca 475 6750 (6 CDs)

"Turn on to Tippett," said the T-shirts when the composer visited the United States in the 1970s. You may achieve that through the lithe rhythms of the Concerto for Double String Orchestra, or the spirituals of *A Child of Our Time*, or the rich textures of the *Corelli Fantasia*, or the different moods of each of the operas. But if you find yourself turning on to the Second Symphony, you will have reached somewhere close to the heart of Tippett's music. There may even be a particular moment that does the trick: perhaps when the pounding rhythms and athletic violin descant of the opening give way to a tangle of woodwind lines, as if you have suddenly come across a sunlit glade in a tropical forest; or when the dazzling light at the start of the slow movement fades and the strings sing a simple, soulful melody; or when the clarinet takes off in a series of rocketlike arcs at the end of the dancing scherzo; or when, after the patchwork finale has found its way back to the pounding rhythms of the opening, the last chord is left glittering in the air.

Much of the symphony sends the violins in particular hurtling through high, fast-moving, irregular figuration in tricky rhythms, making it notoriously difficult to play. On Richard Hickox's recording—and even more so on the one conducted late in his life by Tippett himself—the faster tempi are notched down in the interests of safety. But in the work's first recording—which is currently available, well remastered, only in a six-disc "Tippett Collection" of the major orchestral and instrumental works—the London Symphony Orchestra bowls through all the difficulties with astonishing collective virtuosity, fired by conductor Colin Davis to provide a masterpiece with the virtuoso performance it deserves. **AB**

"Four broadly conceived emotional states . . . reflected in four movements . . . joy; tenderness; gaiety; fantasy."

Michael Tippett

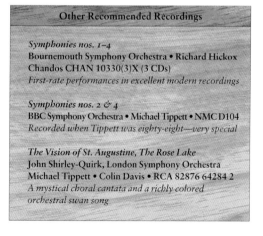

Other Recommended Recordings

Symphonies nos. 1–4
Bournemouth Symphony Orchestra • Richard Hickox
Chandos CHAN 10330(3)X (3 CDs)
First-rate performances in excellent modern recordings

Symphonies nos. 2 & 4
BBC Symphony Orchestra • Michael Tippett • NMC D104
Recorded when Tippett was eighty-eight—very special

The Vision of St. Augustine, The Rose Lake
John Shirley-Quirk, London Symphony Orchestra
Michael Tippett • Colin Davis • RCA 82876 64284 2
A mystical choral cantata and a richly colored orchestral swan song

Olivier Messiaen | Catalogue d'oiseaux (1958)

Genre | Instrumental
Instrument | Piano
Performer | Peter Hill
Years recorded | 1986–89
Label | Regis RRC 7001 (7 CDs)

It has to be admitted that *Catalogue d'oiseaux* (*Catalogue of Birds*) is hardly the most enticing title for a set of piano pieces lasting at least two and a half hours. In fact, this spectacularly misnamed cycle of dramatic aural portraits stands as one of Messiaen's greatest achievements. Far from being a list of birdcalls, *Catalogue d'oiseaux* is a series of paintings in sound, the thirteen pieces depicting natural scenes from around France. In posing a gargantuan challenge of virtuosity and interpretation to the pianist, Messiaen knew that complete performances of *Catalogue d'oiseaux* would be a rarity. Nonetheless, from the symmetrical arrangement of the thirteen pieces within seven books, the interrelationships between pieces or books, and the progression of the means of expression, it is clear that *Catalogue d'oiseaux* is more than just a collection of disparate nature portraits: it is a cycle.

As with any great masterpiece, *Catalogue d'oiseaux* works on many levels. Messiaen reinvents his parameters with each of these nature portraits, so that each has its own form, its own way of presenting the musical material, its own way of telling its story. It is Peter Hill's ability to conjure up Messiaen's images that puts his classic recording in a class of its own. He has the essential virtuosity, but he also draws on an exceptional palette of color and takes extraordinary care with the voicing within individual chords, such as during the magical opening of "L'alouette lulu." In Hill's hands each piece has its own character; from the craggy mountain landscape of the opening "Le chocard des alpes," via the soporific stillness of Provence in July for "L'alouette calandrelle," and exuberance of "Le traquet rieur," to the final desolation of "Le courlis cendré," the pacing and mood are spellbinding. **CD**

> *"Nature is the supreme resource."*
>
> Olivier Messiaen

Other Recommended Recordings

Yvonne Loriod
Warner 2564 62162-2 (18 CDs)
This is the jewel-in-the-crown recording of Warner's Messiaen Edition

Roger Muraro
Accord 461 907-2 (7 CDs)
Muraro combines dazzling virtuosity with an exceptional range of pianistic color

Carl-Axel Dominique
BIS CD-594/596 (3 CDs)
Dominique is especially fine in the long central piece, "La rousserolle effarvatte"

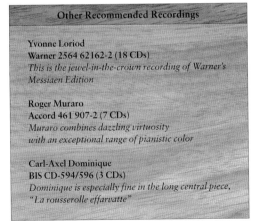

Luciano Berio | Sequenzas (1958–2002)

Genre | Instrumental
Performers | Various, including Nora Shulman (flute),
Alain Trudel (trombone), Jasper Wood (violin)
Years recorded | 1998–2004
Label | Naxos 8.557661–63 (3 CDs)

Luciano
BERIO

**Sequenzas
I-XIV**
for Solo Instruments

Flute • Harp
Soprano • Piano
Trombone • Viola
Oboe • Violin
Clarinet • Trumpet
Guitar • Bassoon
Accordion • Cello
Saxophones

3 CDs

Luciano Berio (1925–2003) was born in northern Italy, near the French border. He taught piano at home, and entered the Milan Conservatoire after World War II, but a hand injury directed his energies into composition, where his ever-enquiring nature led him to break musical boundaries at every turn. Starting with Serialism, he then worked with electronic music in the 1950s, creating one of the masterpieces of the genre, *Visage*, based on the voice of the singer Cathy Berberian. He had a continuing interest in expanding or arranging his own and other composers' music: Monteverdi, Schubert, Mahler, and Lennon/McCartney were all subjected to his gaze, as were the folksongs he arranged for Berberian. He taught in the United States in the 1960s, and during this time composed the successful Sinfonia for Leonard Bernstein and the Swingle Singers. By the time of his return to Italy in 1972, he was that country's leading composer, and in demand worldwide. Pieces for every combination, usually with a strong theatrical content, flowed right up to his death.

The series of fourteen *Sequenzas*, which came at intervals throughout his creative life, were all written for specific musicians, and all have the drama that is inevitable with a single player stretched to the limits of virtuosity. They also encompass a wide variety of moods, from the humor of the trombone *Sequenza*, inspired by the clown, Grock, through the claustrophobic mutterings of the soprano, to the flamenco-flavored guitar *Sequenza*. The Naxos recording was, however, the first to include the final cello *Sequenza*, and each of the musicians brings intense concentration and imagination to this music—which all adds up to a portrait of the most user-friendly composer of the avant-garde. **MC**

"I've every respect for virtuosity, even if that word can give rise to scornful sniggers."

Luciano Berio

Other Recommended Recordings

String Quartets
Arditti Quartet • Montaigne MO 782155
Early and late works, played by the premier new-music quartet

Rendering
London Symphony Orchestra • Luciano Berio
RCA 09026 68894 2
Berio's take on Schubert's unfinished final symphony

Folksongs
Cathy Berberian, Juilliard Ensemble • Luciano Berio
RCA 09026 62540 2
Delightful arrangements, with the best interpreter

Berio, arguably the most important Italian composer since Puccini. ➔

Hanns Eisler | Deutsche Sinfonie (1959)

Genre | Choral
Conductor/Performers | Lothar Zagrosek; Hendrikje
Wangemann, Annette Markert, Matthias Goerne, Peter Lika
Year recorded | 1995
Label | Decca 448 389-2

Hanns Eisler (1898–1962) was born in Leipzig, the son of
the distinguished philosopher Rudolf Eisler. At the turn of
the century the family moved to Vienna, and the young
Eisler served in the Austro-Hungarian army during the
final years of World War I, an experience that sharpened
his political awareness in the coming years. In 1919, Eisler
studied composition privately with Schoenberg, following
his teacher to Berlin in 1925. The relationship between the
two composers became strained, however, as a result of
Eisler's increasing commitment to left-wing politics and
his decision to apply himself almost exclusively to the
composition of agitprop music for the theater and films.
In 1930, Eisler began a lifelong partnership with Bertolt
Brecht, following the poet and playwright into forced exile
first in Europe and then in the United States after the Nazis
came to power in 1933. Both artists returned to the new
German Democratic Republic after being deported from
the United States during the McCarthy trials of 1948.

Conceived over an unusually long period of time, the
eleven-movement *Deutsche Sinfonie* was one of the major
products of Eisler's exile years. As a powerful document
of anti-Fascist resistance, the work features compelling
settings of Brecht's poems "To the fighters in the
concentration camps," "At Potsdam Unter den Eichen," and
"Sonnenburg," and culminates in two extended cantatas
and a highly charged twelve-note Allegro for orchestra.

The impact of the *Deutsche Sinfonie* is enhanced in
this studio recording featuring the outstanding Matthias
Goerne, with superb orchestral playing from the Leipzig
Gewandhaus Orchestra under the committed direction of
Lothar Zagrosek. All in all, one of the undoubted highlights
of Decca's invaluable "Entartete Musik" series. **EL**

> *"I wanted to convey grief
> without sentimentality,
> and struggle without the
> use of militaristic music."*

Hanns Eisler on the *Deutsche Sinfonie*

Other Recommended Recordings

*Kleine Sinfonie op. 29, 5 Orchesterstücke,
Sturm-Suite, Kammersinfonie, op. 69*
Deutsche Symphony Orchestra Berlin • Hans E. Zimmer
Capriccio 10500
Useful conspectus of Eisler's orchestral output

Hollywood Liederbuch
Matthias Goerne, Eric Schneider • Decca 475 053-2
A moving artistic testament to Eisler's years of exile

Complete piano & chamber music
Christoph Keller (piano), Zürich Chamber Ensemble
Accord 476 239-8 (4 CDs)
Excellent performances of some fascinating repertoire

Hanns Eisler, whose art was inseparable from his political beliefs. ➡

Francis Poulenc | La voix humaine (1959)

Genre | Opera
Conductor | Georges Prêtre
Performers | Julia Migenes, French National Orchestra
Year recorded | 1990
Label | Warner 2564 60680-2

Poulenc
La Voix humaine

Julia Migenes
Orchestre National de France
Georges Prêtre

elātus

It was Poulenc's publisher in the late 1950s who suggested that the composer might consider turning Jean Cocteau's monologue *La voix humaine* into an opera. Poulenc was intrigued. He and Cocteau went back nearly forty years, when the poet had been adopted as artistic advisor and general cultural gadfly by the group of composers Les Six. It was Cocteau who had provided the scenario for their collaborative ballet *Les mariés de la Tour Eiffel* and the words for some of Poulenc's early *mélodies*.

"A man of song in all its forms" was how Poulenc described himself to a friend; he was an emotional man too, his own love affairs with men brought misery and despair more often than contentment. As he began to write *La voix humaine*, Poulenc was enduring an enforced separation from his lover, Lucien, and it is clear that he identified completely with his heroine, humiliated by her unseen and unheard lover at the end of a telephone line that keeps being interrupted.

It is the orchestra that is given the melodies, sometimes too sweet for comfort and therefore an ironic comment on the disintegrating love affair. The vocal part is set as arioso with only the briefest of melodic flights. By now Poulenc was a master of prosody, and every word is crystal clear with the orchestra at a discreet distance leaving the stage free for a tortured soul.

Julia Migenes charts a heartfelt course through the one-sided conversation. She is by turns passionate, angry, self-deprecating, ironic, and overwhelmed by despair. This is a performance by a great singing actress. Naturally, it helps to have Georges Prêtre in charge. As the conductor of the first performance in February 1959, he understands this music for the "human voice" like few others. **CC**

> *"Having brought this beautiful, sad child into the world, all that we went through . . . [is] worthwhile."*
>
> **Poulenc to Denise Duval, who sang the first Elle**

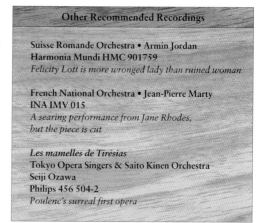

Other Recommended Recordings

Suisse Romande Orchestra • Armin Jordan
Harmonia Mundi HMC 901759
Felicity Lott is more wronged lady than ruined woman

French National Orchestra • Jean-Pierre Marty
INA IMV 015
A searing performance from Jane Rhodes,
but the piece is cut

Les mamelles de Tirésias
Tokyo Opera Singers & Saito Kinen Orchestra
Seiji Ozawa
Philips 456 504-2
Poulenc's surreal first opera

Dmitri Shostakovich | Cello Concerto no. 1 (1959)

Genre | Concerto
Performers/Conductor | Mstislav Rostropovich, Leningrad Philharmonic Orchestra; Gennady Rozhdestvensky
Year recorded | 1961
Label | BBC Legends BBCL 4143-2

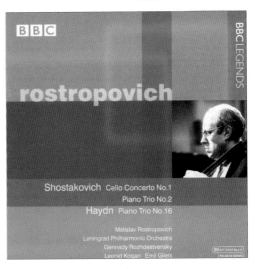

Shostakovich's concerto was inspired by the cellist Mstislav Rostropovich—specifically his performance of Prokofiev's Symphony-Concerto. Terse and rhythmically vital, it is powered by sardonic humor. With its mischievous quote from Stalin's favorite folksong, the protest is palpable.

The irresistible, motoric rhythms of the biting first movement give way to a ghostly, keening song in the chilling Moderato, a small voice in a wilderness that intensifies into passionate outcry. In the extended cadenza, the cello embarks on a long, lonely musical journey in search of a way back home. Shostakovich achieves this homecoming with a long meditation on themes past and future, gradually building in speed, virtuosity, and range until angry orchestral interjections herald a rambunctious finale. The solo horn acts as partner and echo at key moments. Like the cello, it is no mellow tenor but a rasping, assertive character, while clarinets scream out in grotesque chorus. In the hands of a virtuoso team, this concerto is a thrilling, rollercoaster ride, plunging into the depths of despair and dancing on hot coals.

The recording of Rostropovich's live performance in 1961 may not be technically polished, but it feels as if the music is exploding from the white-hot crucible of its creation; it reeks of the sharp, sour scent of fear that epitomized Soviet Russia. The winds and brass of the Leningrad Philharmonic have that inimitable stinging quality; their chords stab and whine. In time, the technical challenges would melt away, but here it feels as if the composer had succeeded in pushing the virtuoso to his limits. It is that edge-of-the-seat quality that gives this recording the power to transport us back into the heart of darkness out of which this concerto emerged. **HW**

> *"One of the great predators in the zoological garden of cello repertoire—wild and dangerous."*
>
> Pieter Wispelwey

Other Recommended Recordings

Truls Mørk, London Symphony Orchestra
Mariss Jansons • Virgin 7243 45145 2 4
Masterly, impassioned reading from the burnished-toned Mørk

Pieter Wiseplwey, Australian Chamber Orchestra
Richard Tognetti • Channel CCS 15398
Piquant, articulate reading fueled by nervous energy

Mstislav Rostropovich, Philadelphia Orchestra
Eugene Ormandy
Sony MHK 63327
The original first recording supervised by the composer

Benjamin Britten | A Midsummer Night's Dream (1960)

Genre | Opera
Conductor/Performers | Richard Hickox; James Bowman,
Lillian Watson, Donald Maxwell, Trinity Boys Choir
Year recorded | 1990
Label | Virgin 0946 3 81832 2 8 (2 CDs)

With comparatively little time to spare before the 1960 Aldeburgh Festival, Britten turned to a ready-made libretto for his chamber opera *A Midsummer Night's Dream*. He and Peter Pears, who was to play Flute, adapted Shakespeare's popular comedy to make it a feasible length for the opera house—they cut almost half of the original text—and moved the emphasis away from the human court in Athens to the magical world of the wood. Here the King and Queen of the Fairies, Oberon and Titania, are arguing about a charming Indian Prince that she took from him. Furious, Oberon summons Puck—played by an acrobat— to fetch a potent juice that causes the recipient to love the next living thing encountered. Comic situations arise as Titania becomes enamored of a human transformed into an ass. Similarly, four human lovers are thrown into confusion by the effects of this juice, though all is resolved happily by the end. A further comic subplot is introduced by the "rude mechanicals" who are planning to perform a play at the Athenian court. The structure conceived for this opera coincided well with Britten's compositional approach at that time, creating specific instrumental timbres and harmonic colors suited to each set of characters. So the fairies are introduced with bright, percussive scales, supported by harps, and the "rude mechanicals" occupy a more hearty world, inaugurated with trombone blasts.

Richard Hickox's recording is distinguished by its superb lineup of singers who throw themselves into the absurdities of the action. Chief among these is James Bowman, who delivers Oberon's twisted and magical lines beautifully. The well-trained boys of Trinity School are also in fine form, spitting out their words with great clarity. **SW**

> *"I always feel* A Midsummer Night's Dream *to be by a very young man, whatever Shakespeare's actual age . . ."*
>
> Benjamin Britten

Other Recommended Recordings

Alfred Deller, Elizabeth Harwood, London Symphony Orchestra • Benjamin Britten
Decca 425 663-2 (2 CDs)
Britten weaves delightful orchestral magic

Gloriana
Welsh National Opera Chorus & Orchestra
Charles Mackerras • Argo 440 213-2
Dramatic account of Britten's still underrated work

Nocturne
Peter Pears, English Chamber Orchestra
Benjamin Britten • Decca 436 395-2
Recording of Britten's orchestral cycle sung with clarity

Dmitri Shostakovich | String Quartet no. 8 (1960)

Genre | Chamber
Performers | Borodin Quartet: Mikhail Kopelman,
Andrei Abramenkov, Dmitri Shebalin, Valentin Berlinsky
Year recorded | 1978
Label | Melodiya MEL CD 10 01077 (6 CDs)

The Eighth is the most celebrated of Shostakovich's quartets, both in its original guise and in the string orchestra transcription by Rudolf Barshai—a founding member of the Borodin Quartet. This is music that communicates so directly to present-day audiences that sniffier critics have questioned its efficacy as a finished work of art. For Soviet officialdom, the work was a memorial to "victims of fascism and war," the creative upshot of a visit to the city of Dresden. It is obvious, though, that the traumas of personal loss and self-betrayal are as important.

Emotionally at sea, with a young family to support, Shostakovich had at last been persuaded to join the Communist Party. The timing suggests that he was flattered into believing that such a move would assist the halting process of liberalization. Or perhaps he merely wanted to guarantee the rehabilitation of his own out-of-favor works. Since many close and valued colleagues had been members for years, the wilder stories about Shostakovich's subsequent soul-searching need not detain us. That said, the score tells its own story of thwarted individualism, making allusions to earlier works, and deploying his musical cryptogram as a key building block.

With five recordings by the Borodin Quartet in circulation, one or other must be self-recommending, even allowing for the fact that the work was premiered, as usual, by Shostakovich's friends in the Beethoven Quartet. Behind the facade, Borodin members were often ideologically at war, yet they bring their trademark unanimity, warmth, and depth of tone to a work they have championed. The relative astringency of the sound of the Melodiya version, set down after the defection of two key members to the West, keeps expressivity within bounds. **DG**

> *"I started thinking . . . nobody is likely to write a work in memory of me, so I had better write one myself."*
>
> **Dmitri Shostakovich in a letter to Isaak Glikman**

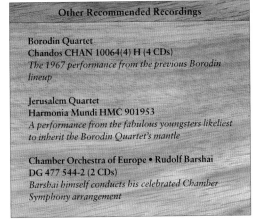

Other Recommended Recordings

Borodin Quartet
Chandos CHAN 10064(4) H (4 CDs)
The 1967 performance from the previous Borodin lineup

Jerusalem Quartet
Harmonia Mundi HMC 901953
A performance from the fabulous youngsters likeliest to inherit the Borodin Quartet's mantle

Chamber Orchestra of Europe • Rudolf Barshai
DG 477 544-2 (2 CDs)
Barshai himself conducts his celebrated Chamber Symphony arrangement

Krzysztof Penderecki
Threnody to the Victims of Hiroshima (1960)

Genre | Orchestral
Conductor | Krzysztof Penderecki
Performers | London Symphony Orchestra
Year recorded | 1972
Label | EMI 7243 5 65077 2 2

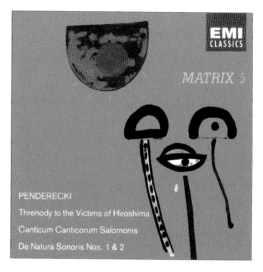

PENDERECKI
Threnody to the Victims of Hiroshima
Canticum Canticorum Salomonis
De Natura Sonoris Nos. 1 & 2

Threnody is significant musically and politically, being a product of the liberalization of the Polish regime during the mid-1950s, when the Soviet-controlled government relaxed its control over Polish society and culture. While the works of Penderecki's tutor Wiechowitz demonstrated the constraints imposed by the old order, he was sufficiently aware of new developments to pass this knowledge on to his pupil. With formal experimentation, banned under the tenets of Communism, being once more permitted, Penderecki (born in 1933) embraced a ferociously avant-garde approach with this short but uncompromising piece, scored for fifty-two stringed instruments. Much of the work is made up of dense clusters of notes that evolve into one vast swath of quarter-tones, providing a queasy sense of resolution at the climax of less than ten minutes of deeply uneasy listening. One source of inspiration was the composer's experience in writing electronic music, which had led him to re-evaluate the relationship between music and "noise." Comparisons with the seminal glissando-driven Xenakis composition *Metastaseis* are often made, but Penderecki's is essentially a work of microcosmic detail, demanding repeated listening. It is worth noting, without detracting from the work's power in any way, that its origins were exploratory.

Penderecki's recording is profoundly captivating, arguably definitive, and usefully comes as part of a collection featuring seven other orchestral pieces. Other versions may be better at revealing the piece's structural minutiae, which is as much a consequence of recording technology as of differences in artistic interpretation. **RT**

"I address my music to . . . 'a feeling, thinking, breathing, suffering man.'"

Krzysztof Penderecki

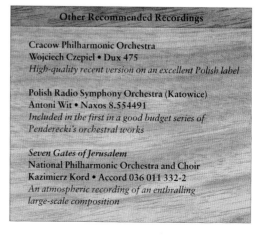

Other Recommended Recordings

Cracow Philharmonic Orchestra
Wojciech Czepiel • Dux 475
High-quality recent version on an excellent Polish label

Polish Radio Symphony Orchestra (Katowice)
Antoni Wit • Naxos 8.554491
Included in the first in a good budget series of Penderecki's orchestral works

Seven Gates of Jerusalem
National Philharmonic Orchestra and Choir
Kazimierz Kord • Accord 036 011 332-2
An atmospheric recording of an enthralling large-scale composition

Penderecki was figurehead of the Polish avant-garde in the 1960s. ➔

Karlheinz Stockhausen
Kontakte (1960)

Genre | Chamber
Performers | Jonny Axelsson
(percussion), Fredrik Ullén (piano)
Year recorded | 2000
Label | Caprice CAP 21642

Electronic instruments and music had been around since the 1920s, but it was only in the studios of Cologne Radio in the 1950s that their potential started to be realized. The nature of Stockhausen's discovery (first heard in *Gesang der Jünglinge* of 1956) was to make audible what the Greeks had intuited millennia before: that sound is made up of pulses—the faster the pulses, the higher the pitch.

Kontakte takes the discovery a step further by using live musicians: a percussionist and a pianist. Given the primitive nature of the technology—it meant hundreds of hours of taping sounds, splicing them together by hand, then trying to notate them—it is a testament to Stockhausen's imagination and his immense care in realizing his ideas that not only is *Kontakte* the first masterpiece of the electronic genre, but one of the most lasting.

In a live performance, the loudspeakers are placed at the corners of the hall. Just as a xylophone riffs on stage, a super-xylophone appears to spin around one's ears, not just from side to side, but over the top, too. The variety of sounds is tremendous. All that is required of the listener is to stay alert to the continual switches of moment within the sixteen sections of the work.

Stockhausen made two versions, one with live performers and one without. The subtle shifts in emphasis in the tape part are clearer without the "distraction" of pianist and percussionist, but a significant element of "Contact" is lost. The vagaries of sound and availability rule out the Stockhausen-supervised recordings; not a fatal blow thanks to the up-to-date engineering of this Swedish disc and the virtuosity of its young performers. **PQ**

Bernd Alois Zimmermann
Die Soldaten (1960, *rev.* 1964)

Genre | Opera
Conductor/Performers | Bernhard
Kontarsky; Stuttgart Opera Chorus
Year recorded | 1989
Label | Teldec 9031 72775-2

In the depressed and angry culture of postwar Germany, where rejection of the past seemed the only way forward for many artists, Zimmermann (1918–70) showed how many options were still open to a modern composer. He himself took nearly all of them. Notwithstanding his own description of his language as "collage" and his unselfconscious appropriation of Baroque, Romantic, and Modernist styles as well as jazz and electronics, it would be easy but wrong to see him as an imitator, a pluralist. *Die Soldaten* (*The Soldiers*) welds all of the above elements into the most important German opera composed after *Wozzeck*, and the most painfully affecting.

Wozzeck is the source of its structure, which pieces together Baroque musical forms into a puzzle of four acts, united by a tone row. Behind both the *Woyzeck* of Buchner (1813–37) and Berg, and *Die Soldaten* of Jakob Lenz (1751–92) and Zimmermann lies a revulsion for military brutality and pessimism that spans the ages. Even their heroines share the name of Marie, but in the later opera she is the main character, starting out as the well-to-do fiancée of a draper turned conscript, Stolzius, then becoming the raped plaything of officers, and finally reduced to a street beggar. Her downfall is plotted in a staging so ambitious that the Cologne Opera House, having commissioned the opera, rejected it: it lay unheard for five years.

The Stuttgart production conducted by Bernhard Kontarsky is the only recording—it is also available on DVD on Arthaus Musik 100 270. So vast are the demands upon a large cast, huge orchestra, and the best-equipped opera house, that there is unlikely to be another for years. **PQ**

Elliott Carter
Double Concerto (1961)

Genre | Concerto
Performers | Sara Laimon,
Steven Beck, Sequitur
Year recorded | 2003
Label | Albany TROY 607

Benjamin Britten
War Requiem (1962)

Genre | Choral
Performers | Peter Pears, Dietrich Fischer-
Dieskau, Galina Vishnevskaya
Year recorded | 1963
Label | Decca 414 383-2 (2 CDs)

Born in New York in 1908, Elliott Carter says his Double Concerto "gives the impression of being continuous, of evolving constantly from beginning to end." The division of forces superficially evokes the concerto grosso genre—harpsichord and piano are each surrounded by a nine-piece "orchestra"—but the imitation crucial to the older model is replaced by a prevailing dynamic of Aristotelian antitheses, lending the hope (hardly fulfilled here) of eventual synthesis. In fact, there is a Classical basis for the work in Carter's study of the Roman philosopher Lucretius, who noted the fluxy nature of the world; a view expanded by Alexander Pope: "Lo! Thy dread empire, Chaos! is restored / Light dies before thy uncreating word."

With a sure and even Classical sense of proportion, the central Adagio pursues other, more complementary modes of interaction, led by the winds of each group (perhaps suggested to Carter by the slow movements of Mozart piano concertos), inspiring a balletic delicacy of motion from their colleagues. There is even a climactic duet for the soloists and a moment of complete quiet that recalls the Neo-Classical Stravinsky, poised between regret and revival, before the contest is resumed and the harpsichord's earlier cadenza is balanced by inevitably more dominant solo spots for the piano.

There were two superb recordings of the Double Concerto on LP, with the harpsichordist Paul Jacobs (some prefer the CBS account conducted by Frederick Prausnitz). Albany's recording on CD of the New York–based group Sequitur has the intimacy that contributes toward accuracy and balance in this ferocious score. **PQ**

The consecration of Coventry Cathedral in 1962 called for a large-scale musical work affirming the reconciliation of formerly warring nations—this new building replaced the cathedral destroyed by German bombing in November 1940. Britten's pacifist credentials and his facility with grand musical structures made him the ideal composer for this task. By setting the war poetry of Wilfred Owen alongside portions of the Latin Requiem Mass text, he created a work that summons a Christian response yet also questions the certitude enshrined in the ancient words. He brought together soloists from the three main countries that had fought in Western Europe, creating a foreground where two soldiers (tenor and baritone) reflect on the grim realities of twentieth-century combat. At a distance, the ethereal and angelic soprano offers words of comfort supported by the invocations of a treble choir and chamber organ. Regarded by many as Britten's greatest masterpiece, the War Requiem's message has as vital an impact today as it did at the first performance.

It is difficult to imagine a more convincing recording than Britten's. All three soloists (Vishnevskaya had been prevented from taking part in the premiere by the Soviet authorities) convey subtle understanding of their roles. The Melos Ensemble and London Symphony Orchestra bring the battlefields vividly to life. The choirs (the London Symphony Chorus and the Bach Choir) sing with colossal power, at times impassioned, then calm and imploring. Part of the recording's success is down to John Culshaw, the Decca producer, whose brilliant direction of the sound engineers came from his subtle understanding of the work. **SW**

György Ligeti
Aventures & Nouvelles aventures (1962, *rev.* 1966)

Genre | Music Theater
Conductor/Performers | Pierre Boulez; Jane Manning,
Mary Thomas, William Pearson, Ensemble InterContemporain
Year recorded | 1981
Label | DG 477 6443 (4 CDs)

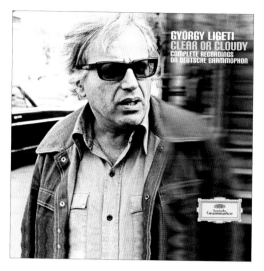

A village in Transylvania, 1928. A young Ligeti (1923–2006) reads fantastical stories by day and dreams of spiders by night, slowly devising an invented world, *Kylwiria*, with its own language. Thirty years later and the man was reading Edward Lear and Lewis Carroll, a bright new light on the avant-garde scene after the triumph of his orchestral piece, *Atmosphères,* and the *succès de scandale* occasioned by his *Poème symphonique for a Hundred Metronomes*. Even then he was putting clear water between the strictures and systems of Stockhausen and others by reinventing the past. In this he was greatly aided by Bruno Maderna, another oblique adherent to Darmstadt tenets, who gave the first truly successful performances of *Aventures*.

Ligeti envisaged a scenario encompassing six areas of human emotion: "humorous, ghostly, horrific, mystical, sentimental, and erotic." The three singers embody these in a psychological caricature, switching roles in an instant. The band of players helps out, especially in the set pieces that come close to the sadness-beyond-words of a Chaplin or a Harold Lloyd. Deprived of visual context, however, the pieces lose much of the slapstick humor, and the psychotic mood changes remain. Boulez and his team had the essential experience of performing it live, but in the studio they focused on total fidelity to the crazy leaps and grunts, swoonings, and groanings that pepper the manipulation of the International Phonetic Alphabet. They do not play it for laughs. On disc at least, *Aventures & Nouvelles aventures* makes a greater impact as a work that would be the first of many attempts to rejuvenate sound in what Ligeti called "an exchange between order and chaos." **PQ**

> *"Composition consists . . . of injecting a system of links into naive musical ideas."*
>
> Joshua Bell

Other Recommended Recordings

Kagel: 1898, Musik für Renaissance-Instrumenten
Cologne Children's Choir • Kagel, etc. • DG 459 570-2
More modern and sometimes savage theatrical engagements with the past

La Monte Young: Response to Henry Flynt, Nam June Paik: One for Violin Solo, etc.
Various artists • RCA 74321 73652-2
A provocative survey of the "Fluxus" culture

Olga Neuwirth: Bählamms Fest
Klangforum Wien • Johannes Kalitzke
Kairos KAI 0012342
Another surrealist madhouse-opera

Dmitri Shostakovich
Symphony no. 13, "Babi Yar" (1962)

Genre | Orchestral
Conductor/Performers | Kirill Kondrashin; Artur Eisen,
Moscow Philharmonic Orchestra, RSFSR Academic Choir
Year recorded | c.1967
Label | Melodiya MEL CD 10 01065 (11 CDs)

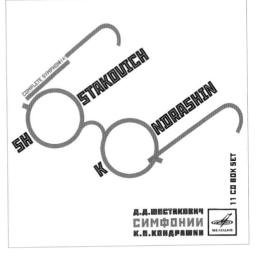

Shostakovich here confounds expectations not merely by selecting the poet Yevgeny Yevtushenko's vivid, dissenting verses, but presenting them in an idiom of Mussorgskian simplicity, unimpeachably "correct" from the official Soviet point of view. It is no accident that the composer follows the Twelfth Symphony's revolutionary *Dawn of Humanity* with a consecutive opus focusing on anti-Semitism and the enduring legacy of Stalinism. Plainly, every word is meant to come through. This might be thought to necessitate urgent tempi, a Russian choir, and a real bass.

Following Yevgeny Mravinsky's much-discussed refusal to undertake the premiere, Shostakovich found in Kirill Kondrashin a stalwart interpreter, unfazed by the political machinations surrounding the concert. One or other Kondrashin recording is an essential purchase in a work where authenticity of experience really counts.

Though undoubtedly the finest studio recording it has yet received, Kondrashin's Melodiya version is not without its problems. Artur Eisen, the magnificent soloist, has to cope with a sanitized text for "Babi Yar" that weakens the author's personal identification with the fate of the Jewish people: the indictment of anti-Semitism becomes less specific to Mother Russia and we are reminded of her "heroic deed in blocking the way to Fascism." You will need to acquire the necessary texts to find out precisely what is going on as they are not included. Rival Western accounts make a different impact. More concerned with the symphonic than the dramatic, they bring subtlety and refinement to the settings, but remain slightly removed from the emotional immediacy. **DG**

> *"[He] never interfered with my work . . . he noted down [what] he wanted to tell me."*
>
> **Kirill Kondrashin**

Other Recommended Recordings

Sergei Leiferkus, New York Philharmonic
Kurt Masur • Teldec 4509 90848-2
Light-textured with Yevtushenko reciting "Babi Yar"

Sergei Aleksashkin, Choral Academy Moscow, West
German Radio Symphony Orchestra • Rudolf Barshai
Regis RRC 1102
Bargain account from one of the composer's colleagues

Jan-Hendrik Rootering, Netherlands Radio
Philharmonic Orchestra • Mark Wigglesworth
BIS SACD 1543
Typically attentive and serious-minded music making in unbeatable sonics

Olivier Messiaen
Et exspecto resurrectionem mortuorum (1964)

Genre | Orchestral
Conductor/Performers | Pierre Boulez;
Percussions de Strasbourg, Domaine Musical Orchestra
Year recorded | 1966
Label | Warner 2564 62162-2 (18 CDs)

In the autumn of 1963, Messiaen received his most prestigious commission to date: a request from the French minister of culture for a work to commemorate the dead of the two World Wars. Typically, Messiaen produced a work concentrating upon resurrection, taking its title from the end of the Nicene Creed: *Et exspecto resurrectionem mortuorum* (*And I await the resurrection of the dead*). Written for an ensemble of winds and percussion, with the lower brass dominating, *Et exspecto* begins with a "De profundis," the cry from the depths of Psalm 130, but rapidly turns to the afterlife. It was composed with the acoustics of cathedrals in mind and sounds like it was hewn from rock. It was first heard in the Sainte-Chapelle in Paris, then in Chartres Cathedral, but Messiaen also wanted to hear *Et exspecto* "in the high mountains at La Grave, facing the Meije glacier, in those powerful and solemn landscapes that are my true homeland."

In the score, Messiaen lavishes praise on a performance given in the "concerts of the Domaine Musical created by Pierre Boulez, where one hears the most beautiful performances of contemporary music." With its concentration upon the qualities of individual chords, notes, and sounds, and an organist's ear for the musical space needed, *Et exspecto* could be tailor-made for Boulez. This first recording is unsurpassed for pacing, drama, and weight of expression. From the first cavernous notes of the contrabassoon and saxhorn, via the dramatic eruptions of gongs and tam-tams, to the relentless strides of the great multitude of the resurrected, the gestures are devastatingly effective. **CD**

> "*I wanted . . . the sun shining . . . [with] reflections on the instruments.*"

Olivier Messiaen

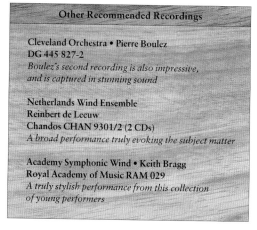

Other Recommended Recordings

Cleveland Orchestra • Pierre Boulez
DG 445 827-2
Boulez's second recording is also impressive, and is captured in stunning sound

Netherlands Wind Ensemble
Reinbert de Leeuw
Chandos CHAN 9301/2 (2 CDs)
A broad performance truly evoking the subject matter

Academy Symphonic Wind • Keith Bragg
Royal Academy of Music RAM 029
A truly stylish performance from this collection of young performers

French composer Olivier Messiaen, pictured in 1967. ●

Giacinto Scelsi
String Quartet no. 4 (1964)

Genre | Chamber
Performers | Quartet of Klangforum Wien
Ensemble
Year recorded | 1996
Label | Kairos 0012162 KAI

Like a beach washed smooth by the tide, the music of Giacinto Scelsi (1905–88) betrays little trace of foreign influence or even human intervention: it just is. The man himself retreated from view, and he literally blocked any attempt to take his photograph. Such nuggets of fact we have prove irrelevant: an aristocratic background, Parisian surrealist contacts, and Schoenberg disciples, an "improvisational" style of composing, partially dependent on a collaborator, that has attracted the charge of fraud.

In his aspiration toward an all-embracing mysticism, Scelsi might appear to be an Italian Stockhausen, except that he took a contrarian attitude toward his music and his audience, maintaining a disdain as to whether it was listened to at all. What mattered was pure sound, and the unexplored area between consonance and dissonance: an obsession shared by composers like Claude Vivier and Romanian musicians such as the conductor Sergiu Celibidache or composer Stefan Niculescu. Like Iannis Xenakis, he was indifferent to the vocal origin of music and the need of music and musicians to breathe. The Fourth Quartet is the most searing example of this desire to open sound, moving toward a single point of light, the note E.

The quartet members of Klangforum Wien pursue their journey toward E with exquisite tuning, while lacking the direction that marked out a deleted recording by the Arditti Quartet, which is matchless. However, Klangforum's Kairos disc also contains a string orchestra version that Scelsi made three years later. Renamed *Natura renovatur* and here performed by the Klangforum Wien Ensemble, it reveals another, more serene side to the work. **PQ**

"All my music and my poetry have come about almost without any thinking."

Giacinto Scelsi

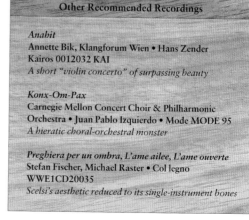

Other Recommended Recordings

Anahit
Annette Bik, Klangforum Wien • Hans Zender
Kairos 0012032 KAI
A short "violin concerto" of surpassing beauty

Konx-Om-Pax
Carnegie Mellon Concert Choir & Philharmonic
Orchestra • Juan Pablo Izquierdo • Mode MODE 95
A hieratic choral-orchestral monster

Preghiera per un ombra, L'ame ailee, L'ame ouverte
Stefan Fischer, Michael Raster • Col legno
WWE1CD20035
Scelsi's aesthetic reduced to its single-instrument bones

Benjamin Britten
Curlew River (1964)

Genre | Opera
Conductor/Performers | Benjamin Britten; Peter Pears, John Shirley-Quirk, Bruce Webb, English Opera Group
Year recorded | 1965
Label | Decca 421 858-2

During his 1955–56 tour of East Asia, Britten encountered a range of cultural stimuli that were to have a huge impact on the rest of his creative life. These led to the creation of his series of three "Church parables," of which *Curlew River* was the first. This combines Japanese medieval Noh play techniques with Gagaku court music. The story begins with a belligerent Ferryman, a more sanguine Traveler, and the intense Madwoman. Various people are traveling on a pilgrimage across the river to a shrine built in memory of a boy who died exactly a year ago; he had been enslaved by a foreigner and forced to journey on until he died of exhaustion. The Madwoman reveals that this is her son and mourns his loss with intense pain. While praying at his grave she experiences his presence in a vision.

Britten's librettist, William Plomer, devised a series of frames through which the drama could be viewed and gave it a context reflecting the world of medieval England, setting it by a "Fenland river." The whole story is told by monks who process in singing the plainchant hymn "Te lucis ante terminum." The introspective shape of this musical genesis provides the material for everything that follows, including the Abbot's introductory homily and robing music; accompaniment is provided by a group of only seven instrumentalists in a sparse musical language that reveals its austere Japanese heritage.

This recording captures the intimacy of the piece; it is as though the listener is in church hearing the monks process past and reliving the story with them. Peter Pears is remarkably moving in the difficult role of the Madwoman, ably supported by singers and instrumentalists alike. **SW**

> *"Was there not something— many things—to be learned from it?"*
>
> Britten's first response to Noh theater

Other Recommended Recordings

Academy of St. Martin in the Fields • Neville Marriner
Philips 454 469-2
Brilliant interpretation by Philip Langridge

The Burning Fiery Furnace
Peter Pears, English Opera Group • Benjamin Britten
Decca 414 663-2
Thrilling and colorful performance in this second Church Parable

The Prodigal Son
Peter Pears, English Opera Group • Benjamin Britten
Decca 425 713-2
A darker work, with Robert Tear and John Shirley-Quirk

Peter Maxwell Davies
Second Fantasia on John Taverner's *In Nomine* (1964)

Genre | Orchestral
Conductor | Peter Maxwell Davies
Performers | SW German Radio Orchestra
Year recorded | 1998
Label | www.maxopus.com

In common with many postwar European composers, Peter Maxwell Davies (b. 1934) looked for the seeds of renewal in music of the Renaissance. He had studied a great deal of it by himself as a teenager and then as a student; by the time he was thirty, he had completed the first act of a huge opera inspired by the life and works of John Taverner. The Fantasia reworks much of that music with even keener focus on its seed, the "In nomine" from Taverner's Mass *Gloria tibi trinitatis*. On one level, this Fantasia aligns its composer with Tye, Tallis, Ferrabosco, and countless others who wrote around the plainsong fragment with Taverner's five-part harmony. On another, it gains from the longterm fulfillment and subsequent subversion of ideas in a way familiar to anyone who knows Mahler's work: there are harmonic suggestions of the Adagio from the Tenth Symphony, but Maxwell Davies has said that the Third Symphony was important to him while composing it. The thirteen sections run together as three "movements," which could be read as a symphony: the first six sections even transmute sonata form, though what holds the ear are the slowly shifting sands of melody, reforming from sonata form to scherzo to a slow threnody for strings in the genre spawned by Taverner's original.

The first recording, by Charles Groves, is widely available and decently engineered, but a more modern recording with the composer conducting the SW German Radio Orchestra is available from Davies's own website and more successfully makes music from the notes. **PQ**

Henri Dutilleux
Métaboles (1964)

Genre | Orchestral
Conductor | Mstislav Rostropovich
Performers | French National Orchestra
Year recorded | 1982
Label | Warner 0927 49830-2

Henri Dutilleux was born in 1916. Having studied at the Paris Conservatoire, he won the Prix de Rome, then worked at French Radio before becoming a teacher, first at the École Normale, then back at the Paris Conservatoire. The first work that he acknowledges is the Piano Sonata of 1948, and his fastidious nature means that he writes slowly and with care, so the catalog of his works is relatively small. He never embraced the avant-garde, and his style is a continuation of the French mainstream, full of sounds that are at the same time precise and sensual. Whether the forces are large or small, he is expert at using them to maximum effect. His works have been championed by major figures: Charles Münch, Isaac Stern, Mstislav Rostropovich, and Seiji Ozawa among them.

Métaboles—the title gives a hint of metamorphosis—was commissioned for the fortieth anniversary of the Cleveland Orchestra, and first conducted by George Szell, who thought highly enough of the piece to repeat it in future seasons. It was an ideal piece for him, a short concerto for orchestra that showed off all the sections of his superbly trained band in its five brief movements.

It is an ideal way into the world of Dutilleux, especially in the performance led by Rostropovich, with the orchestra on tip-top form. There is excitement in the wind-dominated opening, a veiled lushness in the strings, brass with a real French sound, and vitally rhythmic percussion—all coming together to make one of the most gripping scores from this ever-fascinating composer. **MC**

Dmitri Shostakovich
String Quartet
no. 10 (1964)

Genre | Chamber
Performers | Borodin Quartet: Rostislav Dubinsky
Yaroslav Alexandrov, Dmitri Shebalin, Valentin Berlinsky
Year recorded | 1967
Label | Chandos CHAN 10064(4) H (4 CDs)

Cognoscenti out of sympathy with the "socialist realist" mode of address adopted by Shostakovich in his big concert works have often expressed a high regard for the Tenth Quartet. It is one of his more thoughtful middle-period pieces, looking forward as well as back with a serenity and repose rare in the composer's output. That said, the elusive, pared-down lines of its first movement are succeeded by an Allegretto furioso as fierce as any of Shostakovich's scherzos. The Adagio is at once heartfelt and tightly controlled, another of his strict passacaglia forms, while the hurdy-gurdy finale pulls together threads in deft, classically satisfying fashion before melting away.

Many Westerners became acquainted with the Shostakovich quartets through the Borodin Quartet. Their earlier recorded series includes this persuasive account of the Tenth. The music's passages never simply bludgeon the listener into submission and the sound remains warm. It is as if every phrase is given its own life and character without threatening the remarkable cohesiveness of the whole. The performance was taped a decade after Rudolf Barshai had left the ensemble, but before Rostislav Dubinsky and Yaroslav Alexandrov departed for the West.

The score bears a dedication to Shostakovich's friend and protégé Moise Weinberg, a half-serious attempt to trump Weinberg's own burgeoning quartet sequence. It was then transcribed by Barshai for his Moscow Chamber Orchestra, a version that has not gripped the imagination to the same extent as his treatment of the Eighth. **DG**

Leonard Bernstein
Chichester Psalms
(1965)

Genre | Choral
Conductor/Performers | Leonard Bernstein;
Vienna Jeunesse Choir, Israel Philharmonic Orchestra
Year recorded | 1977
Label | DG 447 954-2

It is the most improbable title in the catalog of Leonard Bernstein's compositions. New York, Vienna, Salzburg, Milan, Tokyo, even London, yes: but Chichester, a modest cathedral city near the English south coast? It is there because of an inspired commission from the dean of Chichester Cathedral, Walter Hussey, for a choral work for the 1965 Southern Cathedrals Festival. Bernstein responded to it with a setting of three psalms, each juxtaposed with part of another, all in Hebrew. Psalm 100 is set with tremendous panache in fast septuple time; Psalm 131 to a shapely melody in a gently undulating ten-in-a-bar. In between comes a movement that is unforgettable: a simple, tranquil setting for solo treble (or countertenor) and high voices of Psalm 23, "The Lord is my Shepherd," interrupted and counterpointed by the lower voices singing the angry "Why do the Nations Rage?" This interruption was adapted from a discarded chorus in *West Side Story*, and other ideas were salvaged from an abandoned Broadway project.

Bernstein was an inspiring conductor of his own music, and in his second recording of the *Chichester Psalms*, he conveys the energy and the tenderness of the score to perfection. It is in the spirit of both the commission and the work that the 1977 Berlin Festival, and this recording, have brought together the young Viennese choir and the Israel Philharmonic Orchestra. As the closing passage, on words from Psalm 133, says: "Behold how good and how pleasant it is for brethren to dwell together in unity." **AB**

Rodion Shchedrin | Carmen Suite (1967)

Genre | Ballet
Conductor | Mikhail Pletnev
Performers | Russian National Orchestra
Year recorded | 1998
Label | DG 471 136-2

Rodion Shchedrin (*b.* 1932) occupies a difficult middle ground between the established Russian-Soviet masters, Prokofiev and Shostakovich, and the more overtly rebellious, agonized younger generation of Schnittke and Gubaidulina. He has perhaps remained at heart a theatrical entertainer, though his celebrated *Carmen* ballet, the centerpiece of Mikhail Pletnev's Shchedrin collection, is not wholly typical. Shostakovich chose to work within the Soviet establishment's "liberal" wing. So, too, did Shchedrin. He is not the only composer of our time who might be described as an eclectic.

A gifted pianist and a superb orchestrator, Shchedrin has toyed with just about every contemporary technique of composition. His output includes six piano concertos and several stage works based on Russian literary classics. While many of his earlier works clatter away amiably enough, the Second Symphony, premiered in 1965, is made of sterner stuff, the frequent recourse to radical musical languages validated by the themes of peace and war, life and death. There are earnest emotings and there are novelties, like the fantasy on the sound of an orchestra tuning up and the very 1960s deployment of "House of Horror" harpsichord. Recent works like the Cello Concerto, "Sotto voce," come closer to the ecstatic, contemplative Tavener of *The Protecting Veil*.

What Pletnev provides is a hi-fi testimonial for the composer as prankster. Shchedrin's deliberately tacky and provocative reworking of Bizet continues to hold the stage and is popular in the concert hall, too. Echt-Soviet options notwithstanding, this is the crispest recording it is likely to receive, faithfully reproducing both supercharged string tone and percussive intrusions. **DG**

> *". . . I have always believed that real music has the power to overcome the régime and all its ideological taboos."*

Rodion Shchedrin in a letter to *Gramophone*

Other Recommended Recordings

Bolshoi Theater Orchestra • Gennady Rozhdestvensky
DVD: Video Artists International VAI 4294
Audio-visual record with Maya Plisetskaya and Nikolai Fadeyechev dancing the lead roles

Symphony no. 2
BBC Philharmonic • Vassily Sinaisky
Chandos CHAN 9552
Sinaisky demonstrates his prowess in a key 1960s work

Cello Concerto, "Sotto voce"
Marko Ylönen, Helsinki Philharmonic Orchestra
Olli Mustonen • Ondine ODE 955-2
A fine example of Shchedrin's eloquent late manner

Dmitri Shostakovich | Seven Blok Romances (1967)

Genre | Vocal
Performers | Galina Vishnevskaya (soprano), Ulf Hoelscher (violin), Mstislav Rostropovich (cello), Vasso Devetzi (piano)
Year recorded | 1974
Label | EMI 7243 5 62830 2 2

Galina Vishnevskaya and her husband, Mstislav Rostropovich, close friends with Shostakovich, inspired some of his most memorable works. These settings of verses by Alexander Blok were written for Vishnevskaya shortly after she had starred in Mikhail Shapiro's official 1966 film of *Katerina Izmailova*, the revised version of *Lady Macbeth of Mtsensk*. Between shooting sessions, she performed with Shostakovich at the piano for the only time in their lives, but it was not until he had endured a further period of hospitalization that he invited her to his dacha to play her the new cycle. Vishnevskaya describes it as a "work of agonizing beauty. . . . He seems to survey his life journey as if from the vault of the heavens, and he addresses himself to those spiritual values for whose sake alone life is worth living." The first public performance, sporadically available on disc, was the event of the season, featuring Vishnevskaya and Rostropovich, as well as David Oistrakh. Moisey Weinberg substituted for Shostakovich as the composer was too unwell to take the piano part.

Unusually, Shostakovich deploys his resources in a somewhat piecemeal fashion, with different instrumental combinations from the piano trio underpinning each song. The mood deepens as the composition proceeds, moving through childlike vulnerability to anger and lamentation yet retaining a confessional intimacy and warmth. Vishnevskaya's visceral recording is currently presented in a vocal program that yokes together the other Shostakovich pieces dedicated to her: five blackly humorous *Satires* by Sasha Chorny (1960) and the orchestral arrangement of Mussorgsky's *Songs and Dances of Death* (1962). The bonus is a selection from *Lady Macbeth of Mtsensk*, always one of her finest characterizations. **DG**

> *"I'm dedicating this to you, Galya, if you don't object . . ."*
>
> Shostakovich on Galina Vishnevskaya's *Galina*

Other Recommended Recordings

Joan Rodgers, Beaux Arts Trio
Warner 2564 62514-2
The one Western soprano with truly idiomatic Russian

Songs, vols. 1–5
Various artists • Yuri Serov
Delos DE 3304; DE 3307; DE 3309; DE 3313; DE 3317 (5 separate CDs)
A series taking in all Shostakovich's songs with piano

Suite on Verses of Michelangelo
Ildar Abdrazakov, BBC Philharmonic
Gianandrea Noseda • Chandos CHAN 10358
Orchestral version of his final vocal meditations

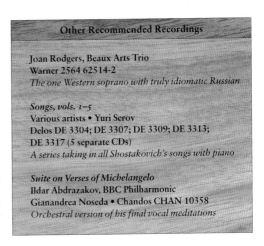

György Ligeti | String Quartet no. 2 (1968)

Genre | Chamber
Performers | LaSalle Quartet: Walter Levin,
Henry Meyer, Peter Kamnitzer, Jack Kirstein
Year recorded | 1969
Label | DG 477 6443 (4 CDs)

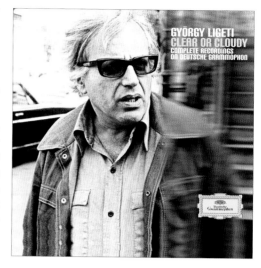

In a stream of works through the 1960s and early 1970s, Ligeti created an utterly new and consistent sound-world while each time reinventing the form that world took. The Second Quartet crystallizes many of those innovations in one five-movement structure. If it is a pocketbook of Ligetian style as the world came to know it until the 1980s—and Ligeti acknowledged this in 1978 by declaring it his most important work up to that point—it also makes an appeal to our primal senses every bit as frank as the composer's models in Bartók and Beethoven, with a coherence rooted in what he referred to as "deep-frozen expressionism." The wild striving and appeal to the outermost reaches of Strauss and Schoenberg are there, but so exaggerated as to be either too close or too distant for comfort: like Bluebeard's wives, living creatures of flesh and blood, but transformed into painful memories.

Discursive outer movements enclose three studies in what the composer referred to self-consciously as the "Ligeti sound"—slowly shifting harmonies, pizzicato clockwork going awry, and violent gestures "to be played as if possessed." The meticulously notated score is full of such instructions, and it took the members of the LaSalle Quartet, who had commissioned it, more than a year of rehearsals before they felt confident enough to present the piece in public. Once they had done so, in December 1969, they set down a recording that benefits from total immersion in the polyrhythmic interplay that is Ligeti's trademark, but also from their own collective identity, nourished by the Viennese classics. Where more modern recordings sign off with gnomic, glassy confidence, the LaSalle Quartet allows you to believe in the possibility of some more tender assurance. **PQ**

> "... without being torn out of their traditional character, the instruments speak a new language."
>
> **Rolf Gaska,** *Neue Zeitschrift für Musik*

Other Recommended Recordings

San Francisco Polyphony • Berlin Philharmonic Orchestra • Jonathan Nott • Warner 8573 88261-2
A romping climax to Ligeti's investigations in the field of orchestral "micropolyphony"

Requiem, Clocks and Clouds etc.
London Voices, Berlin Philharmonic Orchestra
Jonathan Nott • Warner 8573 87631-2
Ligeti both stark and sensuous

Marie Luise Neunecker, Saschko Gawriloff,
Pierre-Laurent Aimard • Sony SK 62309
Ligeti's later, more consonant style is presaged in the Horn Trio, his take on a Brahmsian genre

György Ligeti, one of the great originals in twentieth-century music. ➲

Dmitri Shostakovich
Violin Sonata (1968)

Genre | Chamber
Performers | Oleg Kagan (violin),
Sviatoslav Richter (piano)
Year recorded | 1985
Label | Regis RRC 1128

The story goes that when Shostakovich composed his Second Violin Concerto for David Oistrakh, he intended it as a sixtieth birthday present, but confused the dates. And so, after completing his Twelfth Quartet, he embarked on a Violin Sonata, only to deliver the score late.

Though the work contains none of his legendary warmth, Oistrakh's musical personality may have had some influence on the high seriousness of a piece that is stark, implacable, and "difficult." It has been suggested that the stalking, accompanimental unisons heard at the outset of the first movement, and the violin's tentative response, may be a deliberate echo of Prokofiev's wartime First Violin Sonata, with which Oistrakh was closely associated. More plausible is the notion that its bleak nihilism and lack of resolution relate to a preoccupation with mortality that permeates much of Shostakovich's later music. As was now his wont, the composer deployed twelve-note rows as thematic material within a broadly tonal context.

In 1969, with Sviatoslav Richter, Oistrakh performed the Violin Sonata in public concerts in Moscow and Leningrad and their Melodiya recording carries unimpeachable authority. Given its absence from the catalog, the performance with the greatest intensity is this close-miked live relay in which Richter's partner is Oleg Kagan, a violinist who enjoyed a twenty-year association with the great pianist but disliked studio work and died young. If the results are white-hot rather than squeaky-clean, the coupling is an added attraction—Richter with Yuri Bashmet on peak form in a daringly spacious account of the Viola Sonata, Shostakovich's last completed work. **DG**

Karlheinz Stockhausen
Stimmung (1968)

Genre | Choral
Director | Gregory Rose
Performers | Singcircle
Year recorded | 1983
Label | Hyperion CDA 66115

In 1968, at the height of flower power, Stockhausen was living in Connecticut with the painter Mary Bauermeister and their two small children. A trip to New Mexico had filled him with awe for Aztec and Mayan civilizations. In the space of a decade, he had moved a long way from the devoted Roman Catholic who, during the composition of *Gruppen*, attended Mass every Sunday. The previous year, he had composed *Hymnen* from forty national anthems; the "found object" for his focus in *Stimmung* was more basic still, a sustained B flat major chord with the added partials from the overtone series that one does not exactly hear in a chord but that give it richness.

There is a serene peace to *Stimmung* that resonates with its beachside origins; you can even hear the Pacific swell in the whistling from which the work emerges and to which it returns. The compositional processes combine arcane formulae and improvisational brilliance in a typical Stockhausen mix, but the result is a mesmerizing one-off.

The Stockhausen foundation offers a luxuriously packaged CD of the old DG recording, but Hyperion's recording is much more widely available. In fact, I find the voices in the modern recording much easier on the ear and, though he directs a relatively quick performance, Gregory Rose captures the mellow, blissed-out mood—and wit—that gained it notoriety among the more dessicated divisions of the avant-garde. You might even count it a blessing that he retains the original German for the composer's erotic poetry, though for many, lines like "Your breasts are like your breasts, only yours" and "My phallus is my soul" are part of *Stimmung's* charm. **PQ**

Luciano Berio
Sinfonia (1969)

Genre | Vocal/Orchestral
Conductor | Peter Eötvös
Performers | London Voices
Year recorded | 2004
Label | DG 477 5380

By 1968, Luciano Berio had been living in the United States for some time, and his standing was higher with each new composition. He must have seemed a natural choice to be commissioned for the 125th anniversary of the New York Philharmonic, but whether Leonard Bernstein or the audience expected what they got is a moot point. *Sinfonia* is one of the most memorable and original works in Berio's output and of the twentieth century as a whole. Berio was only too aware of the rising tide of voices against the Vietnam War and against racial segregation, and these feelings are filtered into a mix that also includes fragments of text by Claude Lévi-Strauss and Samuel Beckett.

The eight virtuoso vocal parts were originally written for the Swingle Singers—famous for their jazz versions of Bach—and they had to speak, sing, declaim, and mutter: One of the movements is a meditation on the death of Martin Luther King, with the words "O King" split into their component sounds. The central part of the work is built around the scherzo of Mahler's "Resurrection" Symphony, with quotes from pieces by Beethoven, Debussy, Stravinsky, Ravel, Berg, and many others, which surface in the intricate melee, triggered by association with the text.

Such a multilayered work needs a performance that balances all the elements, not least the amplified voices. London Voices has an impressive track record in the work, and Peter Eötvös is a past master at clarifying complex textures, while the Gothenburg Symphony Orchestra sounds as if it has been playing the music all its life. The recording is equally stunning, with a perspective and depth that match the extraordinary music. **MC**

Dmitri Shostakovich
Symphony no. 14 (1969)

Genre | Vocal
Conductor/Performers | Mstislav
Rostropovich; Galina Vishnevskaya
Year recorded | 1973
Label | Elatus 2564 61374-2

Shostakovich was in a quandary about whether to admit this eleven-movement song-symphony to his official symphonic canon. Dedicating the score to Benjamin Britten implied not only a Western unveiling at Aldeburgh but a shift away from the public rhetoric of his recent orchestral work. The music needed to be purer and tighter to appeal to his much-admired colleague and friend. The result is a post-Mahlerian symphony that wrests a sort of affirmation from its unflinching contemplation of death. The political dimension is there, too, as Shostakovich rails against a world that has failed.

Having completed the work in record time, Shostakovich worried that he would not live to hear it, so a private run-through under Rudolf Barshai was arranged for June 1969 with soloists Margarita Miroshnikova and Evgeny Vladimirov. Subsequent premieres were given by Galina Vishnevskaya and Mark Reshetin.

Confusingly for those who read the piece as deliberately subversive in intent, several Soviet LP versions had made it to the West by the early 1970s. Mstislav Rostropovich's, though less taut than Barshai's with the Moscow Chamber Orchestra, is certainly maximally expressive. Shostakovich was present at the sessions and Rostropovich has spoken of the recording as his "calling-card" as a conductor. Above all, the extraordinary Galina Vishnevskaya (Rostropovich's wife) demands to be heard. This is doubtless why her husband insisted that their collaboration be resurrected when he tackled the rest of the symphonies in exile. Understatement was not on the agenda in 1973 and the sound stands up well. **DG**

Elliott Carter | Concerto for Orchestra (1969)

Genre | Orchestral
Conductor | Michael Gielen
Performers | SW German Radio Orchestra
Year recorded | 1992
Label | Arte Nova 74321 27773 2

The Concerto for Orchestra might be Elliott Carter's most complex work, but it reflects a life spent in New York and the social and cultural winds of change that have blown so furiously during his lifetime. He used a poem by St. John Perse, "Vents" ("Winds"), to fulfill a commission from the New York Philharmonic and Leonard Bernstein. Carter saw in the poem "expansive descriptions of a United States constantly swept by forces like winds, forces that are always transforming, remolding or obliterating the past and introducing the fresh and the new." In that sense, the concerto follows in a tradition of exuberant celebrations of national character by Bartók, Enescu, and Elgar, but the poem shapes the structure in a way that an Alpine landscape does *Gruppen*; the notes pursue quite other, nonillustrative goals.

The orchestra is divided into four groups, each group dominating a movement in turn. Following Perse, a programmatic account of the concerto would move from dry winds (summer) to clouds of insects (autumn), human contemplation (winter), and finally human action (spring). From the very opening, marked "misterioso," the throbbing of harp and tuba suggest some huge force is on the move. This accelerates through the first movement and slows through the second to what Carter calls the "recitative-like character" of the third, where phrases begin progressively slower and end progressively faster, bursting into the whirlwind of the finale.

The three recordings the work has received each have their merits, though the finest, conducted by Oliver Knussen, is currently absent from the catalogue. Nonetheless, Michael Gielen can handle such textures with rare clarity, and his German orchestra follows him with a will. **PQ**

ELLIOTT CARTER

Piano Concerto
Concerto for Orchestra
Three Occasions for Orchestra

SWR Symphony Orchestra
Michael Gielen

"The . . . force with which the work explodes its . . . structural scaffolding is astonishingly persuasive."

Arnold Whittall

Other Recommended Recordings

Holidays Overture, Symphony no. 1, Piano Concerto
Nashville Symphony Orchestra
Kenneth Schermerhorn • Naxos 8.559151
Carter unbuttoned, traditional, and challenging

Symphonia • **BBC Symphony Orchestra**
Oliver Knussen • DG 459 660-2
The climax of Carter's later output

Cello Concerto, ASKO Concerto, Boston Concerto
Nicolas Hodges, Fred Sherry • Oliver Knussen
Bridge 9184
Variously scintillating takes on a genre that has increasingly preoccupied Carter

Elliott Carter, the father figure of modernist American music. ➔

Morton Feldman | Cello and Orchestra (1972)

Genre | Concerto
Performers/Conductor| Siegfried Palm, Saarbrucken Radio Symphony Orchestra; Hans Zender
Year recorded | 1973
Label | CPO 999 483-2

The score of *Cello and Orchestra* specifies its length as eighteen minutes and twenty-six seconds. Can this represent the work of a man who wrote a six-hour-long string quartet? Composers do talk about needing time to express ideas and solve problems, but in much of Feldman's work, the chosen sounds seem to shape the overall construction, rather than the more conventional reverse. *Cello and Orchestra* has moved past the aphoristic blocks of notation of his earliest pieces and comes before the extended repetition of his late period. What you hear is an almost unbroken high cantilena for the soloist, punctuated by richly dissonant orchestral chords. The cellist's part is marked piano or pianissimo almost throughout, and the accompaniment is commensurately hushed, thinning gradually to two-part chords or just quiet timpani rolls. The end is poised, focused, alert, waiting....

This is not an invitation to relax—look to Webern for the tension Feldman derives from the cello's melody and the weightless, apparently static chords below it. He is too deeply in love with the sounds to let them go, testing every note and chord for weight, timbre, and shimmering beauty. He plays with memory, apparently promising revelation or resolution. Only afterward is it plain that the journey was the thing, not the destination. The friendship and work of visual artists whom he met in mid-twentieth-century New York were important influences on Feldman.

This authoritative performance was recorded by the performers who had given the work's premiere only a few weeks beforehand. The set also includes other concertante works—all crucially recorded with the careful balance that should make listening to Morton Feldman such a sensuous experience. **PQ**

> *"I never feel that my music is sparse or minimalist; the way fat people never really think they're fat."*

Morton Feldman

Other Recommended Recordings

Rothko Chapel (1971)
South West German Vocal Ensemble • Rupert Huber
Hänssler 93023
His most famous work, a coolly ecstatic homage in memory of his painter friend

String Quartet II • FLUX Quartet • Mode MODE 112
More varied and engaging than its reputation as a monstre sacré might suggest

Film scores including *Jackson Pollock*, *The Sin of Jesus*, and *Something Wild*
Ensemble recherche • Kairos 0012292 KAI
Another side of Feldman, spanning three decades

Morton Feldman was John Cage's most devoted disciple. ➡

Elliott Carter
String Quartet no. 3
(1971)

Genre | Chamber
Performers | Arditti Quartet: Irvine Arditti, Ashot Sarkissjan, Ralf Ehlers, Lucas Fels
Year recorded | 1987
Label | Etcetera KTC 2507

From the First Quartet toward an apogee of development in the Third, Carter united abstract concepts with their dramatic realization—in this case, the bestowing of individual character upon each member of the ensemble. All his chamber music aspires toward a conversational flexibility, even if at points in the Third you cannot make out what anyone is saying. Tellingly, Carter calls his pitch-and-rhythm synopsis for this quartet a rhyme scheme.

Aiming for "a form that is simultaneously organic and fragmented," Carter divided the quartet in two: the second violin and cello are Duo II, playing strictly in time; the first violin and viola are Duo I, asked to play with rubato, across the measure line. Each duo plays unrelated sections, with its own set of intervals and related rhythms: Duo I opens furioso, while Duo II imposes longer notes, marked maestoso. Briefly, the sections coincide at about five minutes in, as both duos play "pizzicato giusto," but they are mostly rotated; the music of each duo returns, but never in the same combination. After a while, the effect is of contemplating the same object from many angles.

All four recordings (two with its first performers, the Juilliard Quartet, two with the Arditti Quartet) have sensibly used the stereo spread to place the two duos as far apart from each other as possible. The Arditti's first version is worth tracking down for its obstreperous exuberance, but their more recent recording currently has the field to itself and—as part of a package of the first four quartets—it is indispensable. **PQ**

Dmitri Shostakovich
Symphony no. 15
(1971)

Genre | Orchestral
Conductor | Kurt Sanderling
Performers | Berlin Philharmonic
Year recorded | 1999
Label | Berliner Philharmoniker BPH 0611

This is one of Shostakovich's most accomplished orchestral works, translucent in scoring and surprisingly melodic. Its meaning, however, remains elusive. The composer quotes, without explanation, from Wagner, Rossini, and a host of his own works but, as he told Isaak Glikman, "I don't myself quite know why the quotations are there, but I could not, could not, not include them."

Small wonder that relatives, friends, and disciples seem to have quite different ideas about the music's character. For some this is a brilliant concerto for orchestra, for others a coming to terms with death. During the Soviet era it was thought politic to liken its first movement to a toy shop but, in any half-decent performance, the superficial sense of childlike innocence is rapidly corrupted.

For those listeners who admire his relatively sober interpretative manner, Sanderling belongs with the dwindling line of conducting greats, and his Shostakovich always had particular authority. He first encountered the composer in wartime Siberia, having fled Hitler's Germany for Stalin's Utopia, and they remained close until Sanderling's departure for East Germany in 1960. Toward the end of his career, he became especially identified with the Fifteenth, making two commercial recordings and introducing the work to the players of the Berlin Philharmonic in 1988.

While other interpreters offer greater incisiveness, none demonstrate such care over the articulation of phrases nor suggest the same burden of experience. **DG**

Morton Feldman | Cello and Orchestra (1972)

Genre | Concerto
Performers/Conductor| Siegfried Palm, Saarbrucken Radio
Symphony Orchestra; Hans Zender
Year recorded | 1973
Label | CPO 999 483-2

The score of *Cello and Orchestra* specifies its length as eighteen minutes and twenty-six seconds. Can this represent the work of a man who wrote a six-hour-long string quartet? Composers do talk about needing time to express ideas and solve problems, but in much of Feldman's work, the chosen sounds seem to shape the overall construction, rather than the more conventional reverse. *Cello and Orchestra* has moved past the aphoristic blocks of notation of his earliest pieces and comes before the extended repetition of his late period. What you hear is an almost unbroken high cantilena for the soloist, punctuated by richly dissonant orchestral chords. The cellist's part is marked piano or pianissimo almost throughout, and the accompaniment is commensurately hushed, thinning gradually to two-part chords or just quiet timpani rolls. The end is poised, focused, alert, waiting. . . .

This is not an invitation to relax—look to Webern for the tension Feldman derives from the cello's melody and the weightless, apparently static chords below it. He is too deeply in love with the sounds to let them go, testing every note and chord for weight, timbre, and shimmering beauty. He plays with memory, apparently promising revelation or resolution. Only afterward is it plain that the journey was the thing, not the destination. The friendship and work of visual artists whom he met in mid-twentieth-century New York were important influences on Feldman.

This authoritative performance was recorded by the performers who had given the work's premiere only a few weeks beforehand. The set also includes other concertante works—all crucially recorded with the careful balance that should make listening to Morton Feldman such a sensuous experience. **PQ**

> *"I never feel that my music is sparse or minimalist; the way fat people never really think they're fat."*
>
> Morton Feldman

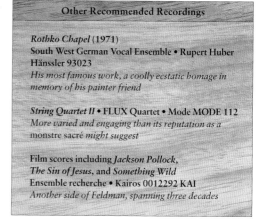

Other Recommended Recordings

Rothko Chapel (1971)
South West German Vocal Ensemble • Rupert Huber
Hänssler 93023
His most famous work, a coolly ecstatic homage in memory of his painter friend

String Quartet II • FLUX Quartet • Mode MODE 112
More varied and engaging than its reputation as a monstre sacré might suggest

Film scores including *Jackson Pollock*,
The Sin of Jesus, and *Something Wild*
Ensemble recherche • Kairos 0012292 KAI
Another side of Feldman, spanning three decades

Morton Feldman was John Cage's most devoted disciple. ➲

Harrison Birtwistle
The Triumph of Time (1972)

Genre | Orchestral
Conductor | Elgar Howarth
Performers | Philharmonia Orchestra
Year recorded | 1993
Label | NMC Ancora NMC D088

A student encounter with Satie's *Gymnopédies* is one of the lesser-known influences on the artist hailed by Lord Gowrie (then Chairman of the Arts Council) as today's leading living British artist in any medium. Satie's piano studies cast sideways glances at the same object (visual and musical); over the course of the last fifty years, Birtwistle has expanded and contracted the nature of that glance into original and utterly compelling treatments of the passage of time. The same, often mythic, story is told from different perspectives, involving us in its complexities and yet distancing us from its details; a motif is viewed under different harmonic lights to see not how it changes but how our perception of it does.

Birtwistle deals in the monumental and the timeless, and what his musical biographer, Jonathan Cross, calls the "uncompromisingly modernist surface" of his music need blind no one to the thread of melody that runs through a work like *The Triumph of Time*. The subject comes from an engraving by Pieter Brueghel, a funereal procession that carries echoes of Ligeti's *Le grand macabre*, but Birtwistle is devoid of the Hungarian composer's zaniness. Reiterations of a saxophone motif and a long melody for cor anglais accumulate dense eruptions of energy, moving forward, yet without a goal in sight.

In the continued absence of the recording made by Pierre Boulez for Argo, NMC's reissue of a Collins disc is invaluable, not least for its engineering. Birtwistle's idiosyncratically weighted orchestra may stem both from his experience as a clarinettist and a disdain for the metropolitan sophistication of orchestral culture. **PQ**

Bruno Maderna
Aura (1972)

Genre | Orchestral
Conductor | Zoltán Peskó
Performers | BBC Symphony Orchestra
Year recorded | 1979
Label | Fonit 0927 43406-2

Among the composers who gave Darmstadt its identity as an experimental laboratory of musical discovery in the 1950s, Bruno Maderna was the least doctrinaire. His work as a scholar and conductor of the broadest range of Western music enriched a basic commitment to the Serial cause most famously spearheaded at the time by Stockhausen. In his late orchestral works, of which *Aura* is the finest, Maderna follows Stockhausen in dividing the orchestra into groups, without Stockhausen's conversational or organic intent: According to the composer, "the title refers to the radiations of all possible consequences which emanate from a central musical object." Maderna mixed precise notation and controlled improvisation with a playfulness that the German composer would not have countenanced. His division of the orchestra is clear and fairly consistent—the strings paint the backdrop to the melodic traceries of the winds, which are occasionally punctuated by brassy exclamations.

A second section advances a model of continuity, led by the oboe. The model is threatened and then scattered to the four winds by a percussion sunburst. The energy from this dissipates through fanfare fragments, yielding finally to an unaffected flute statement that is, as Arnold Whittall writes, "the perfect response to the sustained, aspiring intensity that has gone before."

Of the two recordings available, Giuseppe Sinopoli's is more forthright and probably better rehearsed, but Zoltan Pesko captures more of *Aura's* continuity. Fonit's disc also offers two works for solo violin that further reveal the composer's ability to make Serialism sing. **PQ**

Einojuhani Rautavaara
Cantus arcticus (1972)

Genre | Orchestral
Conductor/Performers | Leif Segerstam; Helsinki Philharmonic Orchestra
Year recorded | 2005
Label | Ondine ODE 1041-2

As the leading Finnish composer of the post-Sibelius generation, Rautavaara has long been celebrated in his own country. During the 1990s, however, he achieved worldwide renown and created something of a sensation in terms of record sales. After studies at the Sibelius Academy and University in Helsinki, he was exposed to the expressionistic Neo-Romanticism of Berg during a short spell in Vienna. He then took up a scholarship at the Juilliard School in New York, studying there with Persichetti and at Tanglewood with Copland and Sessions. All those influences can be discerned at different times in his music, which nevertheless remains utterly individual.

The Rautavaara bandwagon began to roll in 1994, set in motion by the release on BMG's Catalyst label of material mostly licensed from Rautavaara's faithful record label, the Helsinki-based Ondine. That disc included the haunting *Cantus arcticus* (*Concerto for Birds and Orchestra*), in which the cries of real birds are combined with evocative scoring for a symphony orchestra. It was followed by releases of works from Rautavaara's "Angel" Series, which between them sold tens of thousands of units worldwide.

The birdsong, as heard on this performance under Leif Segerstam, was recorded near the Arctic Circle and on the bogs of Liminka in northern Finland. The sounds of spring birds in bogland are gradually blended with woodwind sonorities in the first movement, while the second, "Melancholy," features the warbling of the shore lark, considerably slowed down. The final movement, "Swans migrating," builds to a powerful climax before bringing this uniquely atmospheric work to a quiet close. **BM**

Benjamin Britten
Death in Venice (1973)

Genre | Opera
Conductor/Performers | Steuart Bedford; Peter Pears, John Shirley-Quirk
Year recorded | 1974
Label | Decca 425 669-2 (2 CDs)

Britten's final opera contemplates many of his artistic concerns in a masterpiece that explores fresh sound-worlds and establishes a more fluid, cinematic approach to music drama. He had contemplated an opera based on Thomas Mann's novella for many years, choosing Myfanwy Piper to be the librettist.

The distinguished writer Gustav von Aschenbach is drawn to Venice to refresh his waning creative powers. There, he is beguiled by the beauty and potential of a young Polish boy, Tadzio, who is staying at the same hotel. Increasingly, Aschenbach becomes infatuated with the youth and falls in love with him. He becomes aware of the danger of cholera in the city but cannot leave because of his obsession and he succumbs to the fatal disease. Beyond this surface, the story is deeply concerned with the trials of artistic creation, the confrontation of chaos and order, Apollo and Dionysus, and beauty and wisdom.

Death in Venice contains some of Britten's most sublime and inspired music: the limpid waves that are his evocation of the watery city, the glorious view of Venice shown to Aschenbach from his hotel, the tuned percussion music that signifies the otherworldly beauty of Tadzio, the highly charged erotic dream, and the final bars as the music of boy and man combine in death. Steuart Bedford's 1974 recording, supervised by the composer, is an inspiring account. Peter Pears, for whom the role of Aschenbach was written, brilliantly portrays the wide-ranging thoughts and feelings of the eminent creator and John Shirley-Quirk's varied appearances as the characters who seal Aschenbach's fate are evoked with subtle artistry. **SW**

Dmitri Shostakovich | String Quartet no. 15 (1974)

Genre | Chamber
Performers | Borodin Quartet: Rostislav Dubinsky,
Yaroslav Alexandrov, Dmitri Shebalin, Valentin Berlinsky
Year recorded | 1979
Label | Melodiya MEL CD 10 01077 (6 CDs)

Shostakovich wrote his last quartet when he was terminally ill and beset by challenges both personal and political. His psychological makeup was very different from that of his friends, Mstislav Rostropovich and Galina Vishnevskaya, who were about to go into exile rather than compromise their firm moral support for the likes of Aleksandr Solzhenitsyn and Andrei Sakharov. Shostakovich, however, continued to perform his official functions when he was well enough to do so, reserving his palpable distress for his art. The Fifteenth is one of only three of the quartets not to carry a dedication, and its chain of six, bleak Adagio movements implies that, for the composer, this is very much a personal requiem .

The work was intended to be unveiled by the Beethoven Quartet, but the death of its cellist, Sergey Shirinsky, after a morning rehearsal led Shostakovich to look elsewhere. A reconstituted Beethoven Quartet did, however, give the Moscow premiere on January 11, 1975, but the younger Taneyev Quartet had been entrusted with the first performance in Leningrad on November 15, 1974. Mindful of his own mortality, the composer had not wanted to delay.

In the West, the quartet most closely identified with the piece is inevitably the Borodin, whose richer, subtler playing style has been accompanied by a touch of theater in live concert, the music given in sepulchral gloom, with no applause permitted until after the players have left the platform. On disc, Shostakovich's dark visions seem to inhabit their own special purgatory. The spareness and desolation, from which not even the lyrical nocturne of the fourth movement offers much respite, has a hypnotic effect reminiscent of the world of Alfred Schnittke. **DG**

"Play it so that flies drop dead in mid-air, and the audience start leaving the hall from sheer boredom."

Dmitri Shostakovich, quoted by Fyodor Druzhinin

Other Recommended Recordings

Beethoven Quartet
Melodiya MEL CD 10 00863
*Stark reading by the ensemble closest to the composer,
though only one original quartet member remained*

Fitzwilliam Quartet
Decca 455 776-2 (6 CDs)
*Another great recording by the group that premiered
the work in the United Kingdom*

Keller Quartet
ECM 461 815-2
*Hushed tones, maximum finesse, perfect sonics; plus
a Schnittke coupling to carry forward stylistic threads*

Pierre Boulez | Rituel: in memorium Bruno Maderna (1975)

Genre | Orchestral
Conductor | Pierre Boulez
Performers | BBC Symphony Orchestra
Year recorded | 1976
Label | Sony SK 45839

Rituel is a rarity among Boulez's works. It was composed quickly and has never been subjected to the extensive revisions that are so characteristic of his music. He wrote it after his friend Bruno Maderna died from cancer at the age of fifty-three. Like Boulez, Maderna was a composer of the avant-garde, and a conductor—though his sympathies were much wider. As well as the moderns, and the inevitable Mahler, Maderna performed music as early as Josquin's, and through the Baroque, Classical, and Romantic periods—a range that mirrored that of his teacher, Hermann Scherchen.

Boulez's response to Maderna's death was a piece that makes a devastating effect, less by complexity, than by an accumulation of simplicities. It is a series of verses and choruses, with the orchestra divided into eight groups of increasing size, from a single oboe to fourteen brass instruments. Each group also includes a percussionist who sets up a regular rhythm in the verses, where the overall feeling is of several overlapping funeral processions moving at different, uncoordinated speeds, the conductor deciding precisely when to bring each group in. It is one of Boulez's freest scores in this respect, and its limited harmonic palette and pulsing rhythms have led some to describe it as his most minimal.

Its flexibility of form means that no two recordings of *Rituel* will be exactly the same, but this is the most involving. It was made not long after the first performance, when the death of Maderna was fresh in the minds of Boulez, and the BBC Symphony Orchestra, with whom he had often worked, and conducted in his last concert. The air of tragedy is palpable, and the sense of a communal act of mourning deeply moving. **MC**

> "*Rituel* is different.
> It is based on just
> one chord, that's all."
>
> Pierre Boulez

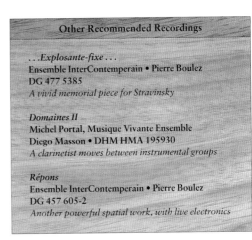

Other Recommended Recordings

. . .Explosante-fixe . . .
Ensemble InterContemperain • Pierre Boulez
DG 477 5385
A vivid memorial piece for Stravinsky

Domaines II
Michel Portal, Musique Vivante Ensemble
Diego Masson • DHM HMA 195930
A clarinetist moves between instrumental groups

Répons
Ensemble InterContemperain • Pierre Boulez
DG 457 605-2
Another powerful spatial work, with live electronics

Steve Reich | Music for 18 Musicians (1976)

Genre | Chamber
Performers | Steve Reich and Musicians: voices, violin, cello, pianos, clarinets, bass clarinets, xylophones, marimbas, maracas
Year recorded | 1978
Label | ECM 821 417-2

STEVE REICH
Music for 18 Musicians

ECM NEW SERIES

Given that Steve Reich once declared that classical music had no relevance to his work, it is ironic to observe how pieces such as *Music for 18 Musicians* are now passing into the repertoire. It is fair to say that this fascinating composition marked a significant turning point in Reich's career. His earliest works were firmly experimental, created by a process of pattern superimposition that was partly inspired by his interest in African and Balinese music. Rather like the change-ringing of church bells, pieces like *Drumming* and *It's Gonna Rain* were driven by these overlaid patterns that would gradually shift out of phase, thus producing endless subtle variations on themselves.

Composed for a large ensemble consisting mainly of tuned percussion, pianos, woodwinds, and voices, *Music for 18 Musicians* had a two-year gestation period that culminated in a performance in New York Town Hall in 1976. The piece demonstrated that Reich's ideas could be translated into a compelling, captivating musical language, readily appreciable by a wide and diverse audience.

It has been noted by commentators that Steve Reich was the first non-pop composer to have been associated with high-profile record labels from the very beginning of his career. However, the original recording of *Music for 18 Musicians* remains a landmark, bringing with it the sense of nervous excitement and the awareness of fresh ideas that was, and remains, as much a feature of the music as its distinctive structure and instrumentation. Interestingly, this recording was originally intended for release on DG, but, despite the label's enthusiasm for the music, it was deemed that a mainstream classical label would be unable to market such a release, so DG altruistically handed it over to the esoterica-friendly ECM. **RT**

"He didn't reinvent the wheel so much as he showed us a new way to ride."

John Adams on Steve Reich

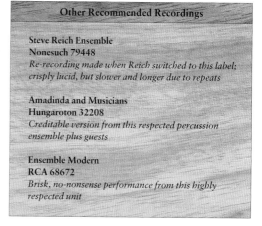

Other Recommended Recordings

Steve Reich Ensemble
Nonesuch 79448
Re-recording made when Reich switched to this label; crisply lucid, but slower and longer due to repeats

Amadinda and Musicians
Hungaroton 32208
Creditable version from this respected percussion ensemble plus guests

Ensemble Modern
RCA 68672
Brisk, no-nonsense performance from this highly respected unit

Steve Reich, pictured in 1982. ➔

Philip Glass
Einstein on the Beach (1976)

Genre | Opera
Conductor | Philip Glass
Performers | Philip Glass Ensemble
Year recorded | 1979
Label | Sony SM4K 87970 (4 CDs)

Einstein on the Beach is arguably one of the most revolutionary works in the history of music theater. Comprising a resolutely nonlinear narrative, accompanied by a sectional score that evolves slowly even when the tempo is blisteringly fast, the work has been described by Glass's collaborator, Robert Wilson, as an "opera" in the literal sense of a "work." In reality, it has little in common with conventional opera and perhaps less in common with Glass's subsequent operas than might be imagined. The disparate narrative elements include a train, a spaceship, a courtroom, an account of the attractions of Paris, and some extraordinary prose by Christopher Knowles, a (then) young autistic man whose unique approach to language invests the phrase "differently abled" with a whole new meaning. The music, written primarily for Glass's Ensemble of keyboards, woodwinds, and voice, is perhaps some of the finest to come from this period of his work.

Attempting to convey such a piece via any audio-only medium is problematic, but in the absence of a full DVD release, the only video material available is a mainly documentary VHS issue from Direct Cinema. In the meantime, opinion as to the relative merit of the two recorded *Einsteins* is polarized. This is the original version, first released on LP by the independent Tomato label and subsequently issued on CBS, which in turn was acquired by Sony. The attractions of this version are the predigital instrumental timbres and the general absence of slickness, but also such details as the spoken text contributed by Samuel M. Johnson, who sadly had died by the time the rival Nonesuch version was recorded. **RT**

Henryk Górecki
Symphony no. 3 (1976)

Genre | Orchestral
Conductor/Performers | David Zinman;
Dawn Upshaw, London Sinfonietta
Year recorded | 1992
Label | Nonesuch 7559 79282-2

It is perhaps surprising to think that this powerfully devotional composition caused controversy when it first attracted critical attention via this CD. With undisguised glee, the record company subsequently took two pages of advertising in *Gramophone* magazine. The first page quoted the various reviewers who had condemned the work as inconsequential and simplistic. The second simply listed the statistics relating to the disc's exceptionally high sales figures and chart success. The point may have been unsubtly made, but it did at least demonstrate that listeners were perfectly capable of taking new music on board if it spoke to them in the right way. That said, many who extended their exploration of Górecki's music in the hope of finding more of the same were brought to a juddering halt by the realization that he was, for the most part, a committed avant-gardist.

The composition's bleak origins actually provide a pointer to the nature of the music, revolving as it does around a prayer scratched by a teenaged girl onto the wall of a Gestapo jail. The piece, subtitled "Symphony of Sorrowful Songs," was written to mark the fiftieth anniversary of the Nazi naval bombardment of Danzig (Gdansk) on September 1, 1939. From the point of view of performance, the symphony is robust but strangely inflexible, but Zinman draws a passionate account from the London Sinfonietta with apparent ease. Above all, though, it is Dawn Upshaw's voice, conveying seemingly contradictory qualities of vulnerability and resilience that forms the emotional core of the work, that carries this recording to extraordinary heights. **RT**

György Ligeti | Le grand macabre (1977, *rev.* 1996)

Genre | Opera
Conductor/Performers | Esa-Pekka Salonen; Graham Clark, Laura Claycomb
Year recorded | 1998
Label | Sony S2K 62312

In his magnum opus, György Ligeti set out to bring the paintings of Bosch and Brueghel to life as a surreal apocalyptic comedy. The plot is set in "Brueghelland," where the Great Macabre, Nekrotzar, announces he will destroy the world at midnight. We are introduced to a cast of bizarre characters: the drunken Piet the Pot, who becomes Nekrotzar's steed as he rides forth on his mission; the constantly copulating lovers Amanda and Amando, who are oblivious to the fate awaiting them; the ineffectual ruler, Prince Go-Go, and his henpecked court astrologer Astradamors; and the chief-of-police Gepopo. The moral of the story? Since we are all going to die anyway, we might as well eat and drink as much as we can while we wait.

The music is more mercurial than in his earlier *Aventures and Nouvelles aventures*, the closest Ligeti had previously come to operatic writing. There is wit and profundity in equal measure: The opera opens with a prelude for car horns, there are apocalyptic sounds from brass and percussion, while the entwining music for the lovers has ravishing echoes of Monteverdi.

The work underwent various changes following its Stockholm premiere in 1978, but after much musical rewriting it reached what Ligeti felt was a definitive form for a staging at the Salzburg Festival in 1997, the performance from which this recording derives. It has a wonderful sense of theatricality, as well as some superb singing—from Graham Clark (Piet the Pot), Laura Claycomb (Amanda), Charlotte Hellekant (Amando)—and playing by the Philharmonia Orchestra under the direction of Esa-Pekka Salonen. **MR**

John Corigliano Clarinet Concerto (1977)

Genre | Concerto
Performer/Conductor | Richard Stoltzman; Lawrence Leighton Smith
Year recorded | 1987
Label | RCA 09026 61360 2

John Corigliano was born in New York, where his father was concertmaster of the Philharmonic. Soon after graduating from Columbia University, the young composer worked with Leonard Bernstein on the now-legendary Young People's Concerts. And it was Bernstein who commissioned Corigliano's Clarinet Concerto as one of a series of commissions designed to showcase the New York Philharmonic's first chair players. Movie director Ken Russell heard one of the first performances of the concerto and was so impressed that he hired Corigliano to compose the music for his film *Altered States*; the score was later nominated for an Academy Award.

Corigliano's style is as eclectic as the New York music scene itself, as the Clarinet Concerto amply demonstrates. The first movement, entitled "Cadenzas," is unabashedly modernist. In its opening section, the clarinet scurries frantically about as the orchestra growls and twitters; in the second part, the music grows wilder, as if the soloist were dancing on hot coals. The second movement, by contrast, is a lyrical, deeply expressive elegy in memory of Corigliano's father, while the finale (in another twist) makes use of a theme from a 1597 Sonata by Giovanni Gabrieli. Corigliano also adopts Gabrieli's antiphonal technique, creating a fast-paced dialogue between instrumental groups placed strategically throughout the concert hall. It is a boldly theatrical touch and makes for a thrilling 3-D sonic effect when heard in performance. Stanley Drucker recorded the concerto with the New York Philharmonic in 1980, but Richard Stoltzman's recording from London is even more viscerally exciting. **AFC**

Toru Takemitsu
A Flock Descends into the Pentagonal Garden (1977)

Genre | Orchestral
Conductor | Tadaaki Otaka
Performers | BBC National Orchestra of Wales
Year recorded | 1995
Label | BIS CD-760

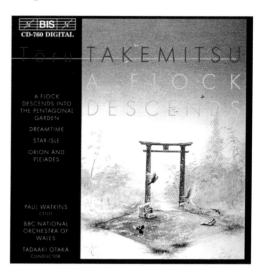

Not only are the titles of Toru Takemitsu's work some of the most poetic in all music, they are nearly always visually inspired, especially within the natural world. Though he composed no opera, he saw much of what he wrote in visual terms. His vivid and witty film music is only now being appreciated outside Japan.

A Flock Descends into the Pentagonal Garden may not be Takemitsu's most sophisticated work, but it is surely his best known, and entirely typical of his talent for harmonizing Eastern and Western music into a personal landscape or dreamscape. The work was inspired by a dream involving a photograph of Marcel Duchamp, who had cut his hair in the form of a star-shaped garden. The chords near the opening represent the garden—softly contoured, owing more to Debussy's faun than Messiaen's "Eastern" vocabulary, yet more dissonant than either of them and organized around a kind of pentatonic Serialism. The oboe motif is the bird, which insinuates itself into the textures of the garden in variation-like episodes that owe little to Western notions of continuity. Tremolo for the beating wings is a rare naturalistic touch; otherwise we are in the realm of the garden as a metaphor for ordered growth. The closing chord evokes both the sound of the *sho*, a Japanese mouth organ, and the dissipated resolution of Alban Berg's *Lulu* and Violin Concerto.

Both available recordings have an idiomatic, sensuous allure thanks to their conductors' wide experience with Eastern and Western music. If I prefer Tadaaki Otaka on BIS to Seiji Ozawa on DG, it is because Otaka's coupling includes the fine cello concerto, *Orion and Pleiades*. **PQ**

> "As long as I live I shall choose sound as something to confront silence."

Toru Takemitsu

Other Recommended Recordings

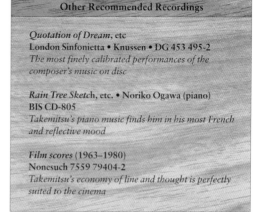

Quotation of Dream, etc
London Sinfonietta • Knussen • DG 453 495-2
The most finely calibrated performances of the composer's music on disc

Rain Tree Sketch, etc. • Noriko Ogawa (piano)
BIS CD-805
Takemitsu's piano music finds him in his most French and reflective mood

Film scores (1963–1980)
Nonesuch 7559 79404-2
Takemitsu's economy of line and thought is perfectly suited to the cinema

Toru Takemitsu, a Japanese composer with a French musical accent. ➔

Arvo Pärt | Fratres (1977)

Genre | Chamber
Performers | Gidon Kremer, Keith Jarrett, cellists of the
Berlin Philharmonic Orchestra
Year recorded | 1983
Label | ECM 817 764-2

The "holy minimalist" epithet is arguably a tasteless one, but it has at least served to convey the gist of Estonian composer Arvo Pärt's philosophy. In musical terms, however, his "tintinnabulist" approach is actually as rigorous as any academic compositional formula, even if the rules for its application are more flexible. Derived from the composer's experience of chant and its mystical connotations, its central structure is the triad, a simple chord that Pärt perceived as having a bell-like sound ("tintinnabuli" is a wonderfully onomatopoeic Latin word for bells). The music that results combines this back-to-basics perception of the European tradition with the music of the Orthodox Church, a vital source of inspiration for the composer. However, *Fratres* is as liberal in other ways as Pärt's thinking is specific, in that it exists in several versions for varied combinations of instruments. The version for violin and piano has been recorded for Catalyst by Maria Bachmann and by Tasmin Little for EMI, the string orchestra version by numerous groups, and so on. Nevertheless, it is the composer's extensive discography for the German ECM label that began and, to a large extent, continues the process of making his music widely known.

This particular issue is typical of the pellucid, expansive ECM production style that is entirely appropriate to Pärt's music. There is a more pragmatic reason for choosing this particular disc, too, as it contains two versions of the piece. One is the violin and piano version alluded to above (from 1980), while the other is scored for twelve cellos (1983). The varied voices of these instruments reveal subtle shifts in intensity and emphasis and between them provide a captivating insight into this particular piece and Pärt's work as a whole. **RT**

"If there were no continual effort to start from the beginning there would be no art."

Arvo Pärt

Other Recommended Recordings

Estonian Philharmonic Chamber Choir, Theatre of Voices, Pro Arte Singers • Paul Hillier
Harmonia Mundi HMC 907407
A superb collection of Pärt's choral music

Tabula rasa, etc.
Gil Shaham (violin), Gothenburg Symphony Orchestra
Neeme Järvi • DG 457 647-2
Järvi controls the orchestra with impressive judgment

Simon Haram, members of Michael Nyman Band
Black Box BBM 54603
A lively mixed program of music by Pärt, Nyman, Adams, and others

Einojuhani Rautavaara | Angels and Visitations (1978)

Genre | Orchestral
Conductor | Leif Segerstam
Performers | Helsinki Philharmonic Orchestra
Year recorded | 1996
Label | Ondine ODE 881-2

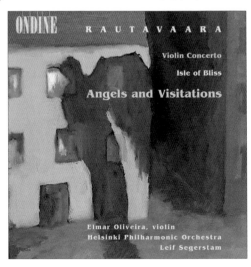

Angels and Visitations, composed in 1978, is the first and arguably the finest work in Rautavaara's "Angel" Series, a sequence that also includes *Angel of Dusk*, *Playgrounds for Angels*, and the *Seventh Symphony*, subtitled "Angel of Light." The composer is eager to point out, however, that the creatures that figure in these works are not traditional angels—or as Rautavaara himself put it, not "the angel of the Christian kitsch, which looks like a pretty blonde girl in a nightgown with swan wings." Rather they are manifestations of "other realities [that] exist beyond those we are normally aware of." Such manifestations are related to the visions of William Blake and the awesome figures of Rilke's poetry, whose angels have a terrible aspect.

Angels and Visitations was, in fact, initially inspired by a reading of verses by Rilke: ". . . should one suddenly press me to his heart: I would perish by his more powerful presence." These lines caused a memory to resurface in Rautavaara's mind of a vision that had troubled his dreams at the age of seven or eight: a vision of an enormous, gray, silent creature that would approach the boy and try to suffocate him by clasping him in its arms.

Leif Segerstam's excellent recording for Ondine with the Helsinki Philharmonic Orchestra superbly captures the terrible, demonic aspects of these visitations, as well as the calmer moments inspired by more benevolent angel presences. At the height of the struggle with the sinister apparition, a terrifying "lion's roar" is heard—a part taken with aplomb by Leif Segerstam himself on this recording. Also memorable is the grandiloquent hymnlike theme that wells up from the depths on brass instruments—its return toward the end signifying a victory of some sort over the powers of darkness. **BM**

> *"I feel self-conscious about the fact that angels have become popular . . . with the New Age phenomenon."*
>
> Einojuhani Rautavaara

Other Recommended Recordings

Symphony no. 7, "Angel of Light," Annunciations
Helsinki Philharmonic Orchestra • Leif Segerstam
Ondine ODE 869-2
Rautavaara's other great "Angel" work

On the Last Frontier, Anadyomene, Flute Concerto
Helsinki Philharmonic Orchestra • Leif Segerstam
Ondine ODE 921-2
More Romantic mysticism from Rautavaara

Piano Concerto no. 3 "Gift of Dreams," Autumn Gardens • Helsinki Philharmonic Orchestra
Vladimir Ashkenazy • Ondine ODE 950-2
Concerto commissioned and played by Ashkenazy

Pierre Boulez | Notations (1978 ongoing)

Genre | Orchestral
Conductor | David Robertson
Performers | Lyons National Orchestra
Year recorded | 2002
Label | Naïve MO 782163

The list of Boulez's works is relatively small, not only because a great deal of his life has been taken up with conducting and organizing, but also because of his tendency to revise and rewrite pieces. Sometimes they remain as works in progress—most famously the Third Piano Sonata, begun in 1955 and still not completed. At the other end of the spectrum is *Sur incises*, an expansion for three pianos, three harps, and three percussionists, lasting well over half an hour, of the three-and-a-half-minute solo piano *Incises*. Somewhere in between comes the fate of *Notations*.

These began life as a series of piano pieces in 1945 during Boulez's early serial phase: There were twelve of them, each twelve measures long, and they lasted ten minutes. Thirty years later, as an experienced conductor, and with an ear second to none for sonority, he began to transcribe the pieces for orchestra, but he quickly realized that they needed to be expanded to justify the large forces he intended to use. So far he has completed five: The first four came fairly quickly, and were premiered in 1980. Since then, various deadlines have come and gone for the second group of four, commissioned by the Chicago Symphony Orchestra. The only one of that group to have appeared is the seventh, which lasts about eight minutes and is slow, in contrast to the others, which are either fleet and mercurial or are driven forward with a motoric pulse.

Together the pieces add up to one of the great modern orchestral showpieces, which David Robertson conducts with absolute conviction—not surprising for someone who has worked extensively with Boulez. And his Lyons National Orchestra responds to the considerable challenges with sensitivity and virtuosity. **MC**

> *"The seeds were there, far away, and then I began to conceive these as seeds for new thinking . . ."*
>
> Pierre Boulez

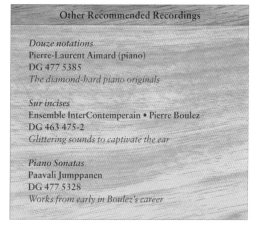

Other Recommended Recordings

Douze notations
Pierre-Laurent Aimard (piano)
DG 477 5385
The diamond-hard piano originals

Sur incises
Ensemble InterContemporain • Pierre Boulez
DG 463 475-2
Glittering sounds to captivate the ear

Piano Sonatas
Paavali Jumppanen
DG 477 5328
Works from early in Boulez's career

Michael Tippett | String Quartet no. 4 (1978)

Genre | Chamber
Performers | The Lindsays: Peter Cropper, Ronald Birks, Robin Ireland, Bernard Gregor-Smith
Year recorded | 1988
Label | ASV CD DCA 608

It might come as a surprise, but the most important influence on Tippett's music was always Beethoven. He once described Beethoven's dramatic sonata form, with its inbuilt oppositions, as his "first and deepest musical experience," one that "remains essential to me." Beethoven's fugues were also significant models. And look at the instrumental genres in which Tippett composed multiple works: symphony, piano sonata, string quartet—all forms in which Beethoven excelled.

Admittedly the quartets, in particular, are hardly as evenly spaced in Tippett's output as in Beethoven's. He wrote his first three in the 1930s and 1940s, but then came a thirty-year gap. At first, opera largely took over; and then the homogeneous quartet medium was unsuited to the hard-edged new style he developed in the 1960s, with different-colored fragments arranged in mosaic patterns. But by the late 1970s, he was looking for a reconciliation between that and his earlier lyricism; and one of the works in which he achieved it was the Fourth Quartet. Here the Beethoven influence comes specifically from his late quartets, in the sharply contrasting ideas brought together in each movement, the linking of all four movements into a continuous whole, as in op. 131, and the recurring use in the strenuous finale of a motif from the *Grosse Fuge*.

The Fourth Quartet makes heavy demands both on the players—magnificently surmounted by The Lindsays—and on the listener. You might get on better at first with the more friendly Fifth, which is all song and dance. But it is worth persevering with this example of Tippett still wrestling with new ideas in his seventies. In the words of T. S. Eliot—another significant influence on Tippett—"Old men ought to be explorers." **AB**

> *"A density of harmony and richness of texture . . . that almost burst the bounds of the medium."*
>
> **Meirion Bowen**

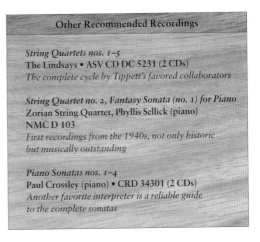

Other Recommended Recordings

String Quartets nos. 1–5
The Lindsays • ASV CD DC 5231 (2 CDs)
The complete cycle by Tippett's favored collaborators

String Quartet no. 2, Fantasy Sonata (no. 1) for Piano
Zorian String Quartet, Phyllis Sellick (piano)
NMC D 103
First recordings from the 1940s, not only historic but musically outstanding

Piano Sonatas nos. 1–4
Paul Crossley (piano) • CRD 34301 (2 CDs)
Another favorite interpreter is a reliable guide to the complete sonatas

John Cage | Roaratorio (1979)

Genre | Chamber/Tape
Performers | John Cage, Joe Heaney, Seamus Ennis,
Paddy Glackin, Matt Malloy, Peadher Mercier, Mell Mercier
Year recorded | 2002
Label | Mode 28–29 (2 CDs)

"It reminds me of being in Dublin. Well . . . almost. Maybe paralytic drunk in Dublin, with a head full of poisonous mushrooms that some Scotsman just off the boat from Amsterdam passed off as genuine fairy toadstools guaranteed to make you see Queen Maeve, Cuchulainn and the ghost of Molly what's-her-name and her cartload of leprechauns." So what's not to like?

Subtitled "An Irish Circus on Finnegans Wake," this piece is perhaps analogous to Derek Jarman's film adaptation of *The Tempest*, greeted with indifference by some film critics but endorsed by many Shakespeare scholars as being true to the spirit of the original play. The above description of *Roaratorio* is from literary commentator Allen B. Ruch, who clearly has no problem conceiving of this work as an auditory counterpart to James Joyce's linguistic firework display of a novel. The piece is made up of readings from the text delivered in a variety of vocal styles, traditional Irish music, and a scattergun collage of other sounds that are determined aleatorically. The apparently simultaneous discharge of all these elements, none of which makes specific sonic reference to the others, is, of course, not only everything Ruch says it is but also, paradoxically, far closer to our real experience of sound and music than any conventional composition.

Attempting to convey such a capricious yet all-enveloping sonic experience via a polycarbonate disc almost seems like a foolhardy undertaking—so it is all the more commendable that this recording works as well as it does, given the seemingly contradictory need to convey both the detail and, for want of a better word, the atmosphere of—as Joyce put it—"this long-awaited Messiah of Roaratorios." **RT**

JOHN CAGE ROARATORIO

riverrun, past Eve and Adam's, from swerve of shore to bend of bay, brings us by a commodius vicus of recirculation back to Howth Castle and Environs.

Sir Tristram, violer d'amores, fr'over the short sea, had passencore rearrived from North Armorica on this side the scraggy isthmus of Europe Minor to wielderfight his penisolate war: nor had topsawyer's rocks by the stream Oconee exaggerated themselse to Laurens County's gorgios while they went doublin their mumper all the time: nor avoice from afire bellowsed mishe mishe to tauftauf thuartpeatrick: not yet, though venissoon after, had a kidscad buttended a bland old isaac: not yet, though all's fair in vanessy, were sosie sesthers wroth with twone nathandjoe. Rot a peck of pa's malt had Jhem or Shen brewed by arclight and rory end to the regginbrow was to be seen ringsome on the aquaface.

The fall (bababadalgharaghtakamminarronnkonnbronntonnerronntuonnthunntrovarrhounawnskawntoohoohoordenenthurnuk!) of a once wallstrait oldparr is retaled early in bed and later on life down through all christian minstrelsy. The great fall of the offwall entailed at such short notice the pftjschute of Finnegan, erse solid man, that the humptyhillhead of humself prumptly sends an unquiring one well to the west in quest of his tumptytumtoes: and their upturnpikepointandplace is at the knock out in the park where oranges have been laid to rust upon the green since devlinsfirst loved livvy.

"I think the artists . . . who resist our understanding are the ones to whom we will continue to be grateful."

John Cage on James Joyce

Other Recommended Recordings

10+2: 12 American Text Sound Pieces
John Cage, Charles Dodge, Robert Ashley, John Giorno, etc. • Other Minds 1006
More text-based pieces from Cage and others

Empty Words III
John Cage (voice) • Ampersand 6
Remarkable example of the speaking voice as instrument

Voice and Piano
Anna Clementi (voice), Steffen Schleiermacher (piano) Dabringhaus und Grimm MDG 6131076
Includes another setting of Joyce

John Cage, who attempted to redefine what we think of as music. ●

George Benjamin | **Ringed by the Flat Horizon** (1980)

Genre | Orchestral
Conductor | Mark Elder
Performers | BBC Symphony Orchestra
Year recorded | 1985
Label | Nimbus NI 5643

Sofia Gubaidulina **Offertorium** (1980)

Genre | Concerto
Performer | Gidon Kremer (violin)
Conductor | Charles Dutoit
Year recorded | 1988
Label | DG 471 625-2

Born in 1960, George Benjamin started composing when he was seven. He became a pupil of Messiaen at the age of sixteen, and, as a sideline, also studied the piano with Yvonne Loriod. His name first hit the wider public when *Ringed by the Flat Horizon*, which he had written for the University Orchestra in Cambridge, was played at the popular BBC Proms concert series, and taken up worldwide. Benjamin has since built up a busy international career as a conductor, pianist, and teacher. But his new works are eagerly awaited, and all show a fastidious sense of form, color, and invention, whether for full orchestra: *Sudden Time*, *Palimpsest*; small ensemble: *Three Inventions*, *Octet*; piano: *Sortilèges*, *Three Studies*; or opera: *Into the Little Hill*.

Ringed by the Flat Horizon was, according to the composer, inspired by "a dramatic photograph of a thunderstorm over the New Mexico desert and an extract from T. S. Eliot's 'The Waste Land.'" In its twenty minutes, it paints a picture of a storm engulfing the landscape, and so follows in the footsteps of other great musical storms—Beethoven's in the "Pastoral" Symphony, or Rossini's in the *William Tell Overture*. What is so impressive is the precision of the depiction of the storm, with an infallible command of instrumental timbre, and a sense of pacing as organic as nature itself, and a form that contains two climaxes—one for the lightning, and, after a looming delay, another for the answering thunder.

Mark Elder conducted the premiere and the Proms performance of the piece, and this white-hot recording still holds the field after more than twenty years. **MC**

Emerging from the long shadow of the former Soviet Union, Sofia Gubaidulina claims to have been influenced by Schoenberg and Webern—not so much in terms of adhering to strict Serialist principles, as being aware that self-determination should be central to the work of any composer. This is certainly true in her case. Having studied in Kazan and Moscow, she made a friend of Shostakovich but fell foul of the Soviet regime's suspicion of progressive composition and was denounced in 1979 for allowing her music to be promoted outside the Soviet Union. The U.S.S.R. had harassed Shostakovich in the same way some thirty years previously.

Offertorium is perhaps Gubaidulina's most successful work. It is a violin concerto in the sense that Messiaen's *Turangalîla* is a symphony; it qualifies in scale but certainly not in structure, nor in how it presents itself to the listener. Instead, phrases and responses are thrown back and forth between orchestra and soloist like pieces of incriminating evidence that neither wants to be caught with. The violin uses many of its exposed passages to explore its own world, often at the extremes of its musical capacity. Sudden surges from the orchestra are offset by improbable instrumental combinations (a Gubaidulina trademark) playing in isolation. All in all, this is a demanding work requiring repeated listening, but is nonetheless rewarding for those willing to engage with it on its own terms.

Gidon Kremer is largely responsible for bringing the piece to a wider audience. His conviction and obvious appreciation of the music's severe aesthetic is communicated perfectly. **RT**

Brian Ferneyhough
Funérailles (1980)

Genre | Chamber
Performers | Arditti Quartet, Ensemble Recherche
Year recorded | 2005
Label | Stradivarius STR 33739

Brian Ferneyhough was initially impelled to write his own music by the allure of high-modernist masterpieces such as Boulez's Second Piano Sonata. It lacks an ideology and in that sense makes an optimistic statement, echoing Tippett's desire to write music that says "yes," not "no." His move to Germany in the 1960s probably contributed to the absence of national identity in his music, but it also meant that he is now far better known in continental Europe than in the English-speaking world.

All kinds of works for large ensemble or solo instruments are more obviously virtuosic than *Funérailles*, but the appeal of this two-part work is that it comments on itself in ways that open doors on the composer's aesthetic world. He says that it represents "a ceremony taking place behind a curtain or far away." A muted and often homogeneous ensemble of seven strings and harp create a ritual between them—then parts of it respond to the ritual, or reject it altogether to find new paths. It is a multidimensional sort of composition that demands multidimensional listening. The cardinal principles of tension and relaxation still govern all the notes, but often the principles work against each other simultaneously in different parts; hence the sensation of continuous action even at a basic slow tempo. *Funérailles II* adds extra layers to the commentary—where a chord in *Funérailles I* acted as a gateway to a new direction, that chord is expanded into a passage of continuous action. The Arditti Quartet's recording effectively supersedes the Boulez-led account made at the time of the premiere by being considerably slower, better recorded, and thus easier to follow. **PQ**

Tristan Murail
Gondwana (1980)

Genre | Orchestral
Conductor | Yves Prin
Performers | French National Orchestra
Year recorded | 1980
Label | Naïve MO 782175

Tristan Murail may be better known as a player of the ondes-martenot—the electronic keyboard instrument brought to prominence by the scores of Messiaen—but his own music shows him to be one of the most original French composers in the post-Messiaen generation. He is one of the pioneers of "spectral music," a style of composition that uses electronic techniques to return to sound in its elemental state, deriving harmonies and structures from natural harmonic scales, rather than the well-tempered one that has dominated Western music since the time of Bach. So it is appropriate that the work that made his name should take its title from one of the two land masses that comprised the Earth's dry land millions of years ago.

Gondwana can be listened to poetically, as a sonic history of that vast mass as it remakes itself through eruptions, compressions, and expansions. More abstract ears will hear a series of huge waves that flow between extremes of "pure" consonant chorales and "dirty" explosions of noise. Beneath the turbulent surface of *Gondwana*, however, lies the feeling of monumental force that recalls the ancient Indian legend of a whole continent under the sea, where time moves much more slowly, if at all. Such a preoccupation with simultaneous and contrasting rates of musical change is one way in which Murail and his contemporaries have been inspired by Sibelius, and there is a Sibelian inevitability and intensity to the final explosion and its coda. The single recording currently available documents the work's atmospheric world premiere. **PQ**

Jonathan Harvey | Mortuos plango, vivos voco (1980)

Genre | Electro-acoustic tape
Commissioned by | Pierre Boulez, IRCAM
Performers | Not applicable
Year recorded | 1980, remixed 1999
Label | Sargasso SCD 28029

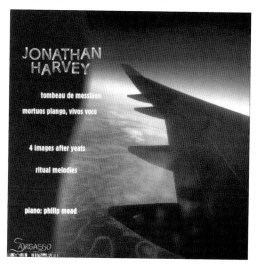

Peer acknowledgement among contemporary composers often seems comparable to that of the acting profession in Hollywood, albeit with rather more restraint and dignity. Polite mutual approval is the norm, all-out assaults on alternative aesthetics are rare (although a nonacademic pedigree is rarely taken seriously) and the occasional eulogizing of one composer by another will often be mysteriously reflected in, say, the commissioning of a work by one for a festival organized by the other. All this is worth saying if only because few pieces have attracted such unqualified admiration from within the Senior Common Room of new music as *Mortuos plango, vivos voco*, while at the same time speaking so directly to listeners.

The piece is constructed using the uncompromisingly avant-garde techniques of computer manipulation and is realized as a four-channel recording, but the sonic substance of the piece is as human—or as divine—as its means of production is not. The original sources are a church bell and the voice of Jonathan Harvey's chorister son, but as the piece develops these sounds are carefully and elegantly transformed in ways that see them merging into something far greater than the sum of their parts. The ethereal beauty of this process is a perfect expression of the composer's religious convictions, both musically and in the wider allegorical sense. *Mortuos plango, vivos voco* was commissioned by IRCAM, the new music research institute where Harvey had worked during the 1980s at the invitation of its founder, Pierre Boulez.

The recommended CD is in fact the third instance of the work being released on a commercial disc, following earlier issues on Erato and Wergo, and is a 1999 remix of the original recording. **RT**

> *"I've always felt one could get more out of music than just a simple instrumental line."*
>
> Jonathan Harvey

Other Recommended Recordings

Bhakti
Spectrum • Guy Protheroe • NMC CD 001
Another unmissable piece with tape

From Silence, Nataraja, Ritual Melodies
MIT Chamber Ensemble, Harrie Starreveld (flute), Rene Eckhardt (piano) • Bridge 9031
Duo, chamber, and electro-acoustic works, expertly done

Songs of Heaven and Earth
Choir of Queen's College, Cambridge
Guild GMCD 7265
Choral music featuring works by Harvey, Britten, Vaughan Williams, and others

William Bolcom | Songs of Innocence and Experience (1981)

Genre | Choral
Conductor/Performers | Leonard Slatkin; University of
Michigan Musical Society & Symphony Orchestra
Year recorded | 2004
Label | Naxos 8.559216-18 (3 CDs)

WILLIAM BOLCOM

Songs of Innocence and of Experience
(William Blake)

Soloists • Choirs

University of Michigan
School of Music
Symphony Orchestra

University Musical
Society

Leonard Slatkin

Born in Seattle, Washington, in 1938, William Bolcom is fascinated with popular music. He is a superb ragtime pianist and has performed and recorded with his wife, mezzo-soprano Joan Morris, wide swaths of the rich literature of American popular song. Bolcom's own compositions often incorporate vernacular elements, as one can hear in the composer's magnum opus, *Songs of Innocence and Experience*.

This vast song cycle, inspired by William Blake's visionary poetry, took a quarter-century to complete. Bolcom calls Blake "the most urgent of poets" and also identifies with the poet's stylistic range. The composer notes that in Blake, "exercises in elegant Drydenesque diction are placed cheek by jowl with ballads that could have come from one of the 'songsters' of his day. . . . The apparent disharmony of each clash and juxtaposition eventually produces a deeper and more universal harmony." In his music, Bolcom follows suit; twangy country and western tunes and funky rhythm and blues numbers rub shoulders with songs that are set in a contemporary (yet lyrical) classical vein. Always, though, the driving force behind the music is the character and message of Blake's verses. And, like Blake, Bolcom makes the teeming diversity of his style seem all of a piece.

Given its length and the size of the forces required, performing Bolcom's *Songs of Innocence and Experience* is, by necessity, a labor of love. On the work's premiere recording, the love is audible. Conducted by Leonard Slatkin, a veteran champion of Bolcom's music, and featuring musicians from the University of Michigan, where Bolcom has taught since 1973, the performance conveys a rare sense of occasion. **AFC**

> *"If any one work of mine has been the chief source and progenitor of the others, I would . . . say that this is it."*
>
> William Bolcom

Other Recommended Recordings

John Murphy (piano)
Albany TROY 325
Inventive, tuneful rags, comparable with Joplin's

Violin Concerto, Symphony no. 5, Fantasia concertante
Sergiu Luca, American Composers Orchestra
Dennis Russell Davies • Phoenix 164
Stunning sampler of Bolcom's orchestral music

A View from the Bridge
Lyric Opera of Chicago • Dennis Russell Davies
New World Records 80588-2
Bolcom's eclectic style complements Miller's classic American tragedy

John Tavener
Funeral Ikos (1981)

Genre | Choral
Performers | Choir of King's College, Cambridge
Year recorded | 2005
Label | EMI 7243 5 58088 2 0

John Tavener's fascination with plainchant and the music of the liturgy is widely documented, but this piece in particular gives an interesting insight into his unique approach to vocal harmony, which is to deploy it in such a way that it does not appear to be there. This is actually a very "composerly" idea and is in many ways far more interesting than the way in which Tavener's sincerely held but ultimately personal religious convictions have been inflated by commentators to the extent that it is almost impossible to perceive his music for what it actually is.

Blowing aside the fog of incense, we discern an astute and sophisticated compositional maverick. Tavener demonstrated as long ago as 1968, with his seminal composition *The Whale*, that he was eminently capable of marshaling the avant-garde techniques of the day, although his deployment of them indicated a healthy scepticism. Despite its Old Testament theme (the piece is based on the story of Jonah), his religious conversion came later, in 1977, since when it has become his main source of musical inspiration and spiritual guidance.

Funeral Ikos is a work for unaccompanied mixed choir. Its text is derived with meticulous scholarship from the Order for the Burial of Dead Priests of the Orthodox Church, yet—perhaps despite its implied profundity—it is in fact a highly workable piece of choral music that has been widely recorded. This is gracefully mobile music that flows from one development to the next, its harmonic adjustments subtle and internalized. All this is perfectly realized on this CD, *Voices of Praise*, where it rubs shoulders with the likes of Parry and Wesley. **RT**

Olivier Messiaen
Saint François d'Assise (1983)

Genre | Opera
Conductor/Performers | Kent Nagano; José van Dam, Dawn Upshaw
Year recorded | 1998
Label | DG 445 176-2 (4 CDs)

Messiaen's *Saint François d'Assise* differs from other operas. It is not just the Wagnerian length or that the extraordinary colors of this sublime masterpiece require an enormous orchestra and chorus: *Saint François* is unusual because the drama is of an interior, spiritual nature, with no hint of the affairs, intrigues, and murders that normally characterize the genre. Rather than biographical detail, Messiaen presents eight stylized episodes, each characteristic of an aspect of the saint's life. The exuberantly colorful richness of the music reflects St. Francis's spiritual wealth rather than his outward poverty.

It has been suggested that *Saint François* is not an opera at all, but this is an ill-founded notion that, despite occasional faults, Peter Sellars's 1992 Salzburg Festival production dispelled. Messiaen's greatest masterpiece is now entering the repertoire and coming to be recognized as one of the iconic operas of the twentieth century.

This mesmerizing performance was captured, thanks to the persistence of Kent Nagano, at the 1998 revival of Sellars's production. Featuring the incomparable José van Dam, who created the title role, Dawn Upshaw in stunning voice as the Angel, Chris Merritt (Lépreux), Urban Malmberg (Frère Léon), and the Hallé Orchestra performing at an unsuspected level of virtuosity and commitment, this is a worthy introduction to the piece for those not fortunate enough to have experienced this astonishing work in the opera house. The live recording does remarkable justice to the wealth of detail within this vast score, which contains elements of just about everything that Messiaen did. **CD**

Oliver Knussen | **Where the Wild Things Are** (1984)

Genre | Opera
Conductor/Performers | Oliver Knussen; Lisa Saffer, Mary King, London Sinfonietta
Year recorded | 1999
Label | DG 469 556-2 (2 CDs)

Oliver Knussen's stature on the British music scene during the past thirty years owes much to his tireless and generous promotion of others. Most of his own music comes from an assured early blooming that produced three symphonies and several song cycles. These already showed how a finely tuned ear could assimilate serial procedures within clear, luminous textures that sound much simpler than they look on the page. The two operas after Maurice Sendak that form the cornerstone of his career took up much of the 1980s and new works have since been scarce but always welcome: the Violin Concerto (2002) became an instant hit with soloists and audiences.

Wild Things stages in very short scenes the fantasy of a naughty child, Max, who has been sent to bed without any supper. Crucially, both narrative and music are memorable, one always walking hand in hand with the other; having noted the Mussorgskian Coronation of Max by his island-dwelling Wild Things, you find that the real climax comes with the subsequent "Wild Rumpus" of unbridled thrill, owing hardly more to Ravel and Stravinsky than to conventional counterpoint. Repeated A flats work as unconscious anchors for the ear, and we are back in Max's bedroom before we know it, with the nightmare banished and a hot dinner awaiting him: a gentle, subtle send-off that recalls both Ravel's *L'enfant et les sortilèges* and Debussy's *La boîte à joujoux*, which is quoted at the head of the score. The later DG recording scores over the original Glyndebourne cast production if only because it includes the companion piece, *Higgelty Piggelty Pop!*, which is more operatic in scale and character. **PQ**

Olivier Messiaen | **Livre du Saint Sacrement** (1984)

Genre | Instrumental
Instrument | Organ
Performer | Jennifer Bate
Year recorded | 1987
Label | Regis RRC 2052 (2 CDs)

Messiaen is a rarity among composers for having made a significant and influential contribution to the repertoire for both the organ and the concert hall. *Livre du Saint Sacrement* is the last and the largest of his organ cycles. Composed in the slipstream of his opera *Saint François d'Assise*, it stands as the summa for his own instrument, meditating on the Eucharist. The eighteen movements are divided into three broad sections, with four contemplations of Christ followed by two groups of seven movements respectively exploring pertinent episodes of Christ's life on Earth and the mysteries of the Eucharist.

The cycle ranges from moments of serene calm to the most dazzling toccatas, with textures from single plainchant lines to the thickest chords, and from the most consonant harmony to the harshest and most extraordinary dissonances in the representation of darkness following the crucifixion. Ultimately it conveys profound belief and an unshakable sense of hope.

Livre du Saint Sacrement was Messiaen's only major organ work that he never performed himself, but he invited Jennifer Bate to make her recording on his own instrument at the St. Trinité in Paris. Other performers can sound impatient, but Bate, fully equipped with the technical and emotional resources necessary for a successful performance, remains the only organist who has truly entered Messiaen's timescale, giving the music space to breathe. Then there is the huge benefit of having the exact palette of organ colors that the composer had in mind when writing the cycle, infusing this peerless performance with a mesmerizing atmosphere. **CD**

Hans Werner Henze | Symphony no. 7 (1984)

Genre | Orchestral
Conductor | Sylvain Cambreling
Performers | South West German Radio Orchestra
Year recorded | 2001
Label | Hänssler CD 93.047

No single work can sum up the protean nature of Hans Werner Henze's achievement, but this Hänssler disc neatly symbolizes the two physical and spiritual homes of a composer who self-consciously inherited the mantle of German symphonism while being drawn over the Alps toward the more gamesome Italianate vocal temperament. Henze had written his Sixth Symphony in Cuba in 1969, at the height of his political activism; surely it was a final rejection of German history, the Fascism he so reviled in the person of his father, the sacred cow of tradition? When the Berlin Philharmonic Orchestra commissioned a Seventh in 1983, Henze proved everyone wrong; it was a "German symphony that deals with German matters" and heralded a late period comparable to Richard Strauss's for its lush rapprochement with the past.

The four movements strive toward an apex of annihilating bleakness. The first movement's dance builds to one frenzied catastrophe after another—though the pure energy of Beethoven's Seventh may also lie in the background (given that Henze's Eighth is a puckish fantasy work and the Ninth a choral apotheosis). The second movement's "funeral ode" finally settles in Bluebeard's Lake of Tears; the Bartók that so energized early works like the First Symphony and Solo Cello Suite never disappeared altogether. A scherzo as black as any Mahler painted leads into the finale, an orchestral setting of a poem by Hölderlin, "a final apocalyptic vision of a cold and speechless world devoid of human life."

It is not Henze's finest work—such masterpieces from the 1960s as *Tristan*, *Elegy for Young Lovers*, and *The Raft of the Medusa* have fallen out of the catalog—but it can hardly fail to leave an impression. **PQ**

> "I can now see my music in a dialectic and inspirative . . . relation to music that is centuries old."

Hans Werner Henze

Other Recommended Recordings

Voices (1973)
Sarah Walker, Paul Sperry, London Sinfonietta
Hans Werner Henze • Explore EXP 007/8
Henze's homage to his beloved Monteverdi

The Bassarids
Vienna State Opera • Christoph von Dohnányi
Orfeo C 605032 I
A watershed opera-symphony on Euripides's tragedy

Ode to the West Wind, etc.
Gustav Rivinius, Saarbrucken RSOrchestra
Stanislaw Skrowaczewski • Arte Nova 74321 89404 2
An early "setting" of Shelley for cello and orchestra

An early picture of Hans Werner Henze, a truly European composer. ➔

Helmut Lachenmann
Mouvement (—vor der Erstarrung) (1984)

Genre | Orchestral
Conductor | Peter Eötvös
Performers | Ensemble Modern
Year recorded | 1994
Label | ECM 461 949-2

Helmut Lachenmann   Schwankungen am Rand

Peter Eötvös   Ensemble Modern   ECM NEW SERIES

Lachenmann is one of the most vital forces in German music of the last forty years. His eloquent writings and much that is said about him—including Henze's dismissal of "musica negativa"— tend to suggest a parody of Modernist music: what might be left, perhaps, once all music is destroyed. Not so. Fragmentation and dissolution shape his works; yet there is a predominating vitality about his determination to find new sounds in unfamiliar contexts, and even to rescue familiar sounds from staleness.

Mouvement (—vor der Erstarrung) (Movement—Before Paralysis) can suggest the final, spasmodic jerkings of a musical corpse; Lachenmann uses the image of a beetle "struggling on its back, continuing to work with empty learned mechanisms . . . seeking and trying new beginnings." Yet the structure and progress of the work acknowledge Romantic convention: There are three parts, each subdivided into three parts, played continuously. In the first, breathing and bowing sounds build to a kind of toccata with prominent parts for toy alarm bells (an anti-technological raspberry at IRCAM, who commissioned the piece); then there is an instrumental "setting" of the folksong "O du lieber Augustin" that Schoenberg quotes in his epoch-making Second String Quartet; then a finale that builds toward and dies away from a whirling tarantella, at the point where sonata form would place the central climax. It makes for thrilling instrumental theater, especially with the split-second timing of Ensemble Modern; and the more you know it, the more "natural" its discontinuities become. Lachenmann is a witty, friendly man and his music shares those attributes. **PQ**

> *"Good old music is in our hearts. . . . We know it is exhausted."*
> Helmut Lachenmann

Other Recommended Recordings

Ausklang
Massimiliano Damerini, Cologne Radio Symphony Orchestra • Peter Eötvös • Col legno WWE1CD 31862
The "piano concerto" succeeding Mouvement

Das Mädchen mit dem Schwefelhölzern
SW German Radio Symphony Orchestra
Sylvain Cambreling • ECM 476 128-3
A Modernist opera that refreshed the genre

Saarbrücken Radio Symphony Orchestra
Myung-Whun Chung • RCA 74321 73657 2
Staub—a "taking back" of Beethoven's Ninth, after Mann's Leverkühn

John Adams
Harmonielehre (1985)

Genre | Orchestral
Conductor | Edo de Waart
Performers | San Francisco Symphony
Year recorded | 1985
Label | Nonesuch 7559 79115-2

Although John Adams is closely associated with the music scene on the West Coast, he has a tough, independent streak that stems from his New England roots. Eschewing the Modernist techniques he was taught at Harvard University, Adams embraced the Minimalism of Philip Glass and Steve Reich. Minimalism in its pure forms, however, is limited in its potential, so Adams began pushing the boundaries. His first breakthrough was *Shaker Loops* for strings, a propulsive work that suggests travel and transformation. *Harmonielehre* is the great masterpiece of Adams's early period. The title means "book of harmony" and is taken from a 1911 treatise by Arnold Schoenberg. The composer described it as a marriage of "the developmental techniques of Minimalism with the harmonic and expressive world of fin de siècle late Romanticism." From its attention-grabbing opening—a series of huge, hammering chords—across the desolate, Sibelian landscape of the central movement, to the slow-burn grandeur of the finale, *Harmonielehre* stakes out its new musical territory with uncommon assurance.

John Adams has enjoyed a long association with the San Francisco Symphony. In 1978, he was appointed the orchestra's new music advisor, so by the time this recording was made in 1985—just three days after the premiere performance of *Harmonielehre*—the musicians were not only comfortable with Adams's style but fervent advocates. Edo de Waart confidently negotiates the music's complex rhythmic changes, and holds the work's various threads tautly together while retaining an atmosphere of epic adventure. **AFC**

> *"An instance when composer, conductor, and orchestra create an inexplicable bond."*
>
> **John Adams**

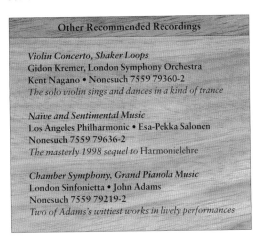

Other Recommended Recordings

Violin Concerto, Shaker Loops
Gidon Kremer, London Symphony Orchestra
Kent Nagano • Nonesuch 7559 79360-2
The solo violin sings and dances in a kind of trance

Naïve and Sentimental Music
Los Angeles Philharmonic • Esa-Pekka Salonen
Nonesuch 7559 79636-2
The masterly 1998 sequel to Harmonielehre

Chamber Symphony, Grand Pianola Music
London Sinfonietta • John Adams
Nonesuch 7559 79219-2
Two of Adams's wittiest works in lively performances

György Ligeti
Études (1985–2004)

Genre | Instrumental
Instrument | Piano
Performer | Pierre-Laurent Aimard
Year recorded | 1995
Label | Sony SK 62308

Piano studies—the French name *études* has obstinately stuck for some reason—often produce some of a composer's finest music. Ligeti is the latest in a line of *étude* composers that includes Chopin, Schumann, Liszt, and Debussy, though he was not a virtuoso pianist—he did not begin playing until he was fourteen. He described the *études* as the result of his own pianistic inability, saying that he wanted to achieve "the transformation of inadequacy into professionalism." He certainly managed that: No piano pieces of the late twentieth century have been taken up so enthusiastically by so many pianists, or been so popular with audiences.

The influences are wide, with hints of Bartók in some of the dance-rhythms, as well as the African music that so fascinated Ligeti. Then there is Debussy or Messiaen in the quieter sonorities and harmonies, the repetitive sounds of Minimalism, and jazz occasionally lurking in the background. It is a tribute to Ligeti's acute ear and skills as a composer that the music never sounds like pastiche, and that the pieces are completely pianistic.

Pierre-Laurent Aimard's CD includes fifteen out of the final tally of eighteen *études*, and despite other fine recordings, his is one that generates the most visceral excitement in the showstoppers such as "Automne à Varsovie" or "L'éscalier du diable" (which rivals Liszt at his most diabolical). He also finds crystalline delicacy in "Cordes vides," and the cool Bill Evans–like "Arc-en-ciel." "A well-formed piano work produces physical pleasure," said Ligeti, and that is the effect of Aimard's involved and totally involving playing. **MC**

Witold Lutosławski
Chain 2 (1985)

Genre | Concerto
Performer | Anne-Sophie Mutter
Conductor | Witold Lutosławski
Year recorded | 1988
Label | DG 471 588-2

In their lives and their music, Polish composers have been unusually preoccupied by the need and desire for personal freedom. Lutosławski himself denied that his music could be "read" in terms of political content or reaction, but it is hard not to see his long-standing creative drive to reconcile coherent structures and individual freedom of expression as profoundly antitotalitarian art. This violin concerto represents in all but name the most formal and one of the most elegant solutions he devised.

Lutosławski described his "chain" form as "two structurally independent strands." These experiments in chance operations are very different in character from those of John Cage. The first and third sections of the work may be titled "ad libitum," but these sections are more like slow movements, while the metrically explicit "a battuta" sections spring forward, recalling Beethoven's frequent use of the term in the quick movements of his string quartets. At the climax of the slow third section, the violins in the accompanying ensemble borrow the chain of melody from the violin and take it to ecstatic heights. The finale alternates metrically free and strict sections, with Mendelssohnian fleet-footedness confronted and annihilated by an orchestral catastrophe. The soloist reflects on this in rhapsodic vein, drawing almost to silence before rediscovering the scherzo music for a dashing but expressively ambivalent close.

Anne-Sophie Mutter's recording is preferable to its rivals for her fully projected sense of an individual personality and for the self-effacing elegance of the composer's conducting. **PQ**

Alfred Schnittke
String Trio (1985)

Genre | Chamber
Performers | Gidon Kremer,
Yuri Bashmet, Mstislav Rostropovich
Year recorded | 1995
Label | EMI 7243 5 55627 2 2

Alfred Schnittke had the grave misfortune to be born in the Soviet Volga Republic in 1934. A highly original, nonconformist artist, he devised a bittersweet, blackly comic expression for the oppressed human spirit. Those in the House of Composers censored his unsettling, polystylistic music, which veered between poking fun at the serious business of composition and music history, and howling in the dark with a raw, visceral power.

The String Trio was commissioned to commemorate Alban Berg's centenary, and Schnittke poured into it his love of Vienna, a city he had lived in for a decisive period in his adolescence. The String Trio resonates with memories of Schubert, Mahler, and the expressive language of Berg. The fluent first movement examines a simple descending figure, constantly reharmonizing and fragmenting it, recalling dances and laughter. In the slow movement that follows, the same figure becomes a distant memory, a specter now appearing in chilling, tragic guise, interspersed by bold sequential outbursts. The string trio is a notoriously difficult medium to write for, but Schnittke succeeds by creating more than one voice for each instrument. This is partly why the work translates so well to string orchestra—it has twice been orchestrated. There is also an illuminating version with piano replacing viola.

Schnittke's music has been accused of "kitsch," and he himself as representing "an attitude of cultural alienation." In the String Trio, we are drawn into a work of precious intimacy between the composer and his performers—in this recording his closest friends and advocates—and between the composer and his revered musical past. **HW**

Milton Babbitt
Transfigured Notes (1986)

Genre | Orchestral
Conductor | Gunther Schuller
Performers | Boston Orchestra
Year recorded | 1991
Label | GM 2060 CD

It has become a critical cliché to talk of Milton Babbitt in apologetic terms of his twinkly smile and scintillating conversation, as though bearing in mind the image of a kindly old grandfather will make listening to his music easier. Babbitt encourages a playful approach to his music with titles such as *The Joy of More Sextets*, written soon after *Transfigured Notes*, and the ultimate tease from 2003, *Swan Song no. 1*. In terms of what you hear, it would also be dangerous to focus on Babbitt's mathematical background and pioneering embrace of "total Serialism," where each element of a composition is generated with reference to a determined system.

Some listeners will find the piano music or music for solo instruments more accessible, and Babbitt's expertise in jazz and other popular musics feeds into his piano music more audibly than other genres. That is slightly missing the point. This work for string orchestra takes its cue from Schoenberg's *Verklärte Nacht*, and the story behind that work is set in a forest. Babbitt's work may have little else in common with Schoenberg's—though if you join the dots of the first half together in one way you may find a certain Romantic sensuality—but the forest is an ideal metaphor for Babbitt's music, where repetition is unknown and continual, proliferating growth is the natural law. Find a path, stick to it, get lost a few times, and enjoy the experience.

The composer-conductor Gunther Schuller apparently lost $42,000 putting together the performances that make up this recording after two conductors rejected the work as unplayable. It was worth every cent. **PQ**

Peter Sculthorpe | Earth Cry (1986)

Genre | Orchestral
Conductor | Stuart Challender
Performers | Sydney Symphony Orchestra
Year recorded | 1989
Label | ABC 426 481-2

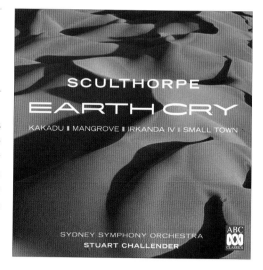

At a chance meeting in the Melbourne Botanical Gardens in the late 1930s, the schoolboy Peter Sculthorpe told Percy Grainger that he wanted to write music for a living. Grainger told him that if he was to become a truly Australian composer, he should look north to the islands for his inspiration. Thirty years later, Sculthorpe's groundbreaking *Sun Music* series of four orchestral showpieces did just that, using as their models the traditional music of Indonesia and Southeast Asia.

By the time *Earth Cry* arrived in 1986, Sculthorpe had not only become Australia's most successful composer, but his music was unmistakably "Australian" in its gestures, filled with didjeridu-like drones powering through the bass, and with string glissandos sounding like flocks of wild birds taking flight in the northern wetlands.

Earth Cry was explicit in its nationalist intentions, eschewing the European aesthetic by using a foot-stomping theme from the Arrernte people of Central Australia that grounded it firmly in the earth of the Australian outback. Dark and brooding, intensely dramatic, and moving with a primeval orchestral force (think Sibelius meets *The Rite of Spring* somewhere near a deep gorge in the Northern Territory), *Earth Cry* has become an Australian classic, simultaneously a showstopper and a work that speaks from the unique anthropological and geographical perspective of Australia.

This impassioned performance, recorded in 1989, captures the national pride of a confident Sydney Symphony Orchestra, fresh from triumphs on a U.S. tour the previous year. It also commemorates revered homegrown chief conductor Stuart Challender, who sadly died just two years later. **MB**

> *"For me, Australia is the center of the world."*
>
> Peter Sculthorpe

Other Recommended Recordings

Songs of Sea and Sky
Queensland Orchestra • Michael Christie
ABC 476 192-1
Sculthorpe's orchestral music with the didjeridu

Earth Cry, Piano Concerto
New Zealand Symphony Orchestra • James Judd
Naxos 8.557382
Spirited performances from across the Tasman

String Quartets, vols. 1–2
Goldner Quartet • Tall Poppies TP089, TP090 (2 CDs)
Definitive readings of some of Sculthorpe's characteristic chamber music

Philip Glass | Violin Concerto (1987)

Genre | Concerto
Performers | Adele Anthony, Ulster Orchestra
Conductor | Takuo Yuasa
Year recorded | 1999
Label | Naxos 8.554568

More than a few listeners who had admired the early works of Philip Glass were moved to voice their disapproval when he began to write for conventional musical forces rather than phalanxes of keyboards and woodwinds or highly constrained solo instruments. Not only that, his adoption of forms entirely associated with the most conventional concert music—the symphony, the concerto, the quartet—seemed like a further step backward. *Einstein on the Beach* had ensured that he would never be associated with mainstream opera, even if its successors *Akhnaten* and *Satyagraha* did constitute rather more of a compromise with tradition. Yet by the late 1980s, he had seemingly settled for filling the usual allotted slots in the kind of concert program that his audience's grandparents would have recognized.

Whether this was partly a pragmatic decision and partly an artistic one is perhaps debatable, but what is clear is that by the time Glass began producing works like the Violin Concerto, he had reached some sort of truce with the ideas of melody and conventional musical structure. Happily, this did not result in a descent into self-imitation, as this gorgeous whirlwind of a concerto testifies. The subtle polishing of near-repeated elements is still central to the music, as are the helter-skelter arpeggios (here augmented by a growling backdrop of percussion) and stabbing chordal punctuation. What has changed is the sense of scale, as this is a composer willing to work with large blocks of sound as much as with intricate shifts of interlocking detail. Despite its budget price, this recording is both intelligent and vibrant. Adele Anthony delivers a spirited, almost feline performance that Takuo Yuasa wisely does nothing to inhibit. **RT**

> *"I spent years subtracting things from my music. Now I'm deciding what to put back in."*
>
> Philip Glass

Other Recommended Recordings

Robert McDuffie, Houston Symphony Orchestra
Christoph Eschenbach • Telarc 80494
A substantial, elevating performance

Gidon Kremer, Vienna Philharmonic Orchestra
Christoph von Dohnányi • DG 4451585
Kremer excels particularly in the more lyrical passages

Symphony no. 3, "The Light," etc.
Stuttgart Chamber Orchestra, Vienna Radio
Symphony Orchestra • Dennis Russell Davies
Nonesuch 79581
A fine symphony and much else, including a sorely underrated orchestral short

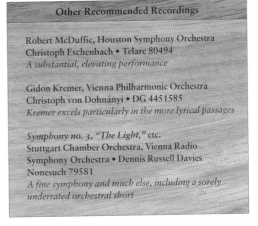

John Adams | Nixon in China (1987)

Genre | Opera
Conductor/Performers | Edo de Waart; James Maddalena,
Sanford Sylvan, Carolann Page, Orchestra of St. Luke's
Year recorded | 1987
Label | Nonesuch 7559 79177-2 (2 CDs)

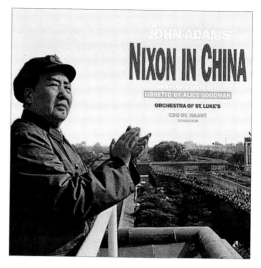

Few contemporary operas have generated so much buzz
as John Adams's *Nixon in China*. As the composer recalls, "an
unstaged sing-through with piano accompaniment . . . five
months before the actual premiere attracted critics from
twelve national newspapers and was even mentioned . . .
on the *NBC Nightly News*." Amazingly, given such intense
anticipation, the opera lived up to the hype. Together with
librettist Alice Goodman and director Peter Sellars, Adams
took a small slice of American history—Richard Nixon's
1972 visit to China—and created a very human drama, full
of wit and pathos. Adams's portrayal of Nixon is especially
sharp. In his first aria, "News has a kind of mystery," in which
the music conveys the former president's inner thoughts
as he greets the Chinese dignitaries, jittery syncopations
humorously capture his well-known nervous manner,
though there is an overarching lyricism, too—a yearning
for achievement and greatness that immediately makes
his character sympathetic. The other principal roles are
drawn with equal subtlety, and even the shrill Chiang
Ch'ing (Madame Mao) is shown to have a vulnerable side.

Musically, the score draws from a variety of sources,
mixing big band jazz with harmonies and textures that
suggest traditional Chinese music, all woven together into
a coherent yet colorful minimalist fabric.

This is the only recording of *Nixon in China*. Made after
the first series of performances, it features the original cast,
and the singers' intensive immersion in their roles reaps
enormous rewards. Carolann Page finds a girlish eagerness
and melancholy in Pat Nixon, James Maddalena gets
Nixon's awkwardness just right, and Sanford Sylvan gives
Chou En-lai an elegiac nobility that remains etched in the
memory long after the opera is over. **AFC**

> "*. . . theater is appropriate
> for the contemplation
> and discussion of the most
> urgent issues in our lives.*"
> Michael Steinberg

Other Recommended Recordings

The Death of Klinghoffer
Lyon Opera Orchestra • Kent Nagano
Nonesuch 7559 79281-2
*Part Passion play, part opera—a meditation
on brutality*

I Was Looking at the Ceiling and Then I Saw the Sky
Ensemble • John Adams • Nonesuch 7559 79473-2
This pop-opera reveals Adams as an expert tunesmith

El Niño
Deutsches Symphony Orchestra Berlin • Kent Nagano
Nonesuch 7559 79634-2
Adams's sublime answer to Handel's Messiah

Sellars's iconic production of *Nixon in China* revived in London in 2000.

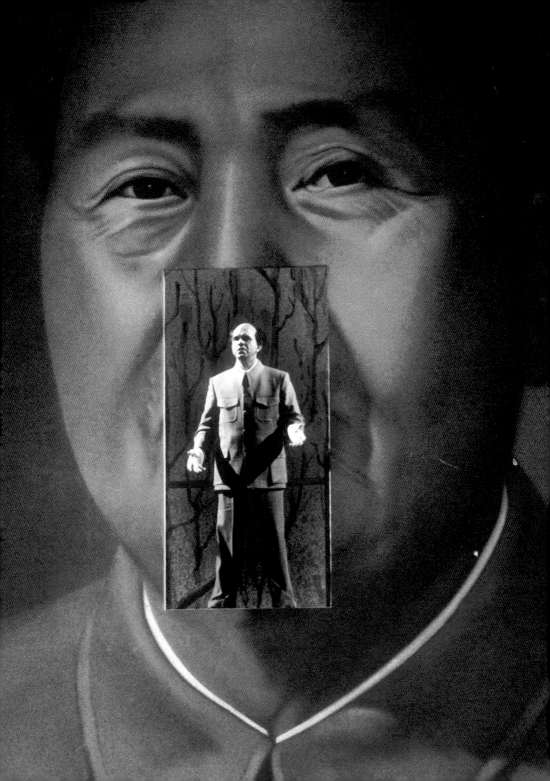

John Tavener
The Protecting Veil (1987)

Genre | Concerto
Performer/Conductor | Steven Isserlis;
Gennady Rozhdestvensky
Year recorded | 1991
Label | Virgin 0946 3 63293 2 1

If the idea of a work stretching to three quarters of an hour for just cello and strings, with little musical development in the traditional sense, and in fact relatively little change in mood, fills you with trepidation, fear not. John Tavener has described the work as an "ikon in sound" and this well captures its meditative, ecstatic spirit. The high keening of the solo cello opening is counterbalanced by low, growling strings, an effect that is immediately ear-catching, with the cello static while the harmonies gradually fill out in the orchestra. Tavener delights in bringing his soloist in and out of focus, swooping around a sequence of voluptuous string textures. The accompaniment is largely chordal, at least initially, with the composer teasing the ear with his harmonies, warm and euphonious, and yet often with an alien note or two, adding a degree of edginess. The work itself gets its name from the Russian Orthodox Feast of the Protecting Veil of the Mother of God, which arose from an incident in the tenth century when the Virgin Mary is said to have appeared at the Church of Vlacherni in Constantinople. The eight sections of the work, which play without a break, mark key incidents in her life. The end returns—appropriately—to the mood of the beginning, evoking the tears of the Mother of God.

The Protecting Veil was written for acclaimed British cellist Steven Isserlis, and his recording remains unrivaled, not only in terms of intensity but in the plangent sound he coaxes from the instrument. It remains one of the most original and influential works of so-called "mystic Minimalism," and its effectiveness seems more profound on every repeated hearing. **HS**

Louis Andriessen
De Materie (1988)

Genre | Music Theater
Conductor/Performers | Reinbert de
Leeuw; Netherlands Chamber Choir
Year recorded | 1994
Label | Nonesuch 79367-2

Born in Utrecht in 1939, Louis Andriessen grew up under the spell of Bach's organ music, French classics, Stravinsky, and the propulsive rhythms of bebop. In the 1970s, he was captivated by the Minimalist experiments of Glass, Riley, and Reich. All these influences fused in a mature style of great vigor, textural originality, and freshness. He decided early on not to write for traditional groups and formed a "democratic" ensemble, in which the relationship between composer and performers would be a two-way process.

Andriessen is a naturally dramatic composer and his operas *Rosa, a Horse Drama* and *Writing to Vermeer* are both significant. The music theater work *De Materie* (*Matter*) best encapsulates Andriessen's concerns: the relationship between the spiritual and the material. It begins by assaulting the ear with 144 identical fortissimo chords. We observe the formation of the Dutch Republic, and glimpse the craft of shipbuilding. Part 2 is an aria for soprano and orchestra on the "seventh vision" by the medieval mystic Hadewijch. As she weaves her erotically charged vision of union with God, metallophones, pianos, and strings beat regular chords that reconstruct Rheims Cathedral in sound. In Part 3, "De Stijl," we are thrown into the twentieth century with a powerful boogie-woogie bass, for a musical working-out of Mondrian's *Composition with Red, Yellow, and Blue*. Part 4 develops into a monumental pavanelike dance, culminating in a lamentation from Marie Curie on the death of her husband, Pierre. This absorbing work is performed with passionate commitment by two ensembles (Schoenberg and Asko) and a choir steeped in Andriessen's sound-world. **HW**

Ross Edwards
Maninyas (1988)

Genre | Concerto
Performers/Conductor | Dene Olding, Sydney Symphony; Stuart Challender
Year recorded | 1990
Label | ABC 438 610-2

While living at Pearl Beach, north of Sydney, in the late 1970s, Australian composer Ross Edwards underwent a crisis of musical confidence. Casting off his fascination with abstract music and inspired by the sounds of the natural environment around him, he reconstructed his entire musical language. This resulted in two distinct but related new styles within his music. One, more austere and formal in character, he labeled "sacred," while the other, more outgoing, buoyant, and dancelike, he gave the nonsense title "Maninyas."

During the 1980s, piece after piece by Edwards bore the latter title, and when the ABC commissioned a violin concerto for Dene Olding and the Sydney Symphony Orchestra to play in the bicentennial celebration year of 1988, Edwards reworked two of the Maninya pieces and separated them by a new modal cadenza and chorale.

The resultant *Maninyas* Violin Concerto became a cause célèbre in Australian music, immediately engaging in style, popular with audiences, and convincing a generation of young composers that it was okay to write a tune. While the concerto is traditional in conception, its musical substance is straight out of the contemporary Asia Pacific, reflecting Edwards's interest not just in the music of non-Western cultures but also in the kind of natural soundscapes that make the Australian environment unique.

This particular performance was made in the shadow of conductor Stuart Challender's terminal illness, the vibrant rhythms and life force of the music adding poignancy to the knowledge that this would be his last recording to be released. **MB**

Steve Reich
Different Trains (1988)

Genre | Chamber
Performers | Kronos Quartet, Dene Olding, Sydney Symphony Orchestra
Year recorded | 1989
Label | Nonesuch 7559 79176-2

One of the most popular pieces of newish music, Steve Reich's *Different Trains* is scored for a string quartet that performs to a recorded accompaniment, made up of further overdubbed quartet parts plus train sounds and fragments of spoken narrative. Reich appropriates the melodic structures that occur naturally within the spoken phrases and applies them to the instrumental lines, creating a kind of echo effect that is highly effective. But behind this welcoming exterior lies a chilling subtext. As a young child, Reich spent four years traveling by train across the United States between the homes of his divorced parents. The piece expresses the realization that as a Jew, his experience of trains would probably have entailed transportation to a Nazi death camp had his family resided in Europe at the time.

Different Trains was written for the Kronos Quartet and premiered in London in 1988. The group committed the work to disc almost immediately and it is this performance, balancing technical sophistication with an appropriately edgy urgency, that remains definitive. That said, the work is subtly flexible in surprising ways, such as in the balance between the recorded and live instruments and the prominence given to the spoken texts. This, together with developments in recording technology that at least allow a trade-off between the grittiness of the original and the lucidity of subsequent versions, allows new interpretations to have their own validity, as varied and as collectable as a selection of Beethoven quartets. All we are lacking is a brand new multichannel performance on SACD, a format ideally suited to music such as this. **RT**

Mark-Anthony Turnage | Three Screaming Popes (1989)

Genre | Orchestral
Conductor | Simon Rattle
Performers | City of Birmingham Symphony Orchestra
Year recorded | 1992
Label | EMI 7243 5 55091 2 3

Mark-Anthony Turnage came close to being tagged the bad boy of British composition—but Steve Martland had already gotten that gig, and Turnage was and remains rather too good at everything he does to be taken anything other than very seriously. Indeed, it seems almost unfair that a single composer should not just be capable of both jazz-influenced composition and imaginative classical orchestration, but also of handling them in ways that would surely have attracted the approval of Duke Ellington and Rimsky-Korsakov respectively.

All that said, Turnage's sources of inspiration are frequently unconventional. *Three Screaming Popes* is a musical response to the ferocious painting by Francis Bacon, who, no doubt coincidentally, might once have been cast as the bad boy of British art had he not similarly bogged down by genuine talent. Despite its scope, rollercoaster dynamics, harmonic bravado, and sheer pace, the piece is a tour de force of orchestral skill.

The additional works on this disc are excellent, too, notably *Kai*, featuring what Turnage has described as his "favorite string instrument," the cello, and *Momentum*, written without undue pomp to celebrate the opening of Birmingham's Symphony Hall. Simon Rattle, soloist Ulrich Heinen, ensemble, and orchestra all excel and, no doubt thanks to the composer's residency in Birmingham, are clearly conversant not just with the notes on the page but with Turnage's style in general—a luxury when recording new music. The disc has an open, spacious sonic quality that is ideally suited to its contents. It still seems odd to see this CD in EMI's British Composers series alongside fellows like Finzi and Holst, but it does at least indicate that Turnage is getting the respect he deserves. **RT**

"I struggle to move from darkness to light."

Mark-Anthony Turnage

Other Recommended Recordings

English National Opera • Paul Daniel • ENO Alive 1
The Silver Tassie *proves Turnage is also a talented opera composer*

Evelyn Glennie, BBC Symphony Orchestra
Leonard Slatkin • Chandos CHAN 10018
Fractured Lines *was a colorful Proms commission with a strong free-jazz element*

Scorched
John Scofield, John Pattituci, Peter Erskine,
HR Big Band • Hugh Wolff • DG 474 729-2
Turnage in jazz mode on a world-famous classical label

György Kurtág | Officium breve (1989)

Genre | Chamber
Performers | Keller Quartet: András Keller, János Pilz,
Zoltán Gál, Judit Szabó
Year recorded | 1995
Label | ECM 453 258-2

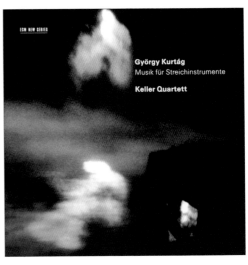

György Kurtág
Musik für Streichinstrumente

Keller Quartett

György Kurtág was thirty-three when he wrote the string quartet that he called his op. 1, after hearing Stockhausen's *Gruppen* and Ligeti's *Artikulation* in Cologne. The medium has remained at the center of his output ever since; only fifty minutes of it, but every gesture tells a story. The story of the first movement of op. 1 is entirely characteristic: "An insect seeks the light. The [final] flageolet chord symbolizes the ray of light and there is all this junk in between." That Kafka-esque sense of compressed tragedy runs through his work: stories of memory and often of grief.

This "Short Office" is a secular requiem in memory of Kurtág's fellow Hungarian composer Endre Szervánszky, but four of the fifteen tiny movements are also dedicated to other friends. The first note picks up the final note of op. 1 and tries it out, tuning it with the fifths of open strings—that is all. Open fifths run through the rest of the work, as do sighing gestures extracted from a canon by Webern, which is quoted complete in the tenth movement and inspires two little fantasy-canons along the way. Kurtág, however, never lets systems get in the way of expressive honesty—the notes are too carefully chosen for that. Their impact is more like that of Janáček, heightened by contrast. The sighs become a lullaby; then a whispered conversation; then an outburst of grief. Szervánszky himself finally appears, in the tender C major of his Serenade for Strings; and Kurtág discreetly closes his "mini-requiem" like a book of remembrance that contains different ways of grieving.

The Arditti Quartet is as sensitive as ever but too dryly recorded; every note needs space to make its point. The Keller Quartet's slightly more expansive approach therefore pays off, with a tonal richness that aptly recalls the Viennese masters of quartet writing. **PQ**

"My mother tongue is Bartók, and Bartók's mother tongue was Beethoven."

György Kurtág

Other Recommended Recordings

Kyrill Rybakov (clarinet), Alexander Trostiansky (violin), Alexei Lyubimov (piano)
ECM 476 310-8
The Webern stream in Russia: music permanently in the act of saying goodbye by Silvestrov and Ustvolskaya

Theodor Anzellotti (accordion), Arditti Quartet
Winter & Winter 910 097-2
The introverted side of Matthias Pintscher, a German contemporary of Adès

Concord Quartet • New World NW 80551
Webern's economy given an American, polystylistic twist in George Rochberg's String Quartets nos. 3–6

James MacMillan
Veni, veni, Emmanuel (1992)

Genre | Concerto
Performers | Colin Currie, Ulster Orchestra
Conductor | Takuo Yuasa
Year recorded | 1997
Label | Naxos 8.554167

James MacMillan's music is undeniably modern and possessed of the kind of academic sophistication that makes analytical listeners nod with approval, yet at the same time his work has the sort of straightforward audience-appeal normally associated with far lighter stuff. There can be no better example of this than *Veni, veni, Emmanuel*, a percussion concerto on a devotional theme, premiered by Evelyn Glennie and the Scottish Chamber Orchestra in 1992. The soloist plays a vast assortment of percussion, including tam-tams, two snare drums, congas, timbales, gongs, woodblocks, and marimba, which, as the composer specifically states, makes him or her an equal partner with the orchestra. The musical material is in fact derived from the Advent plainchant that gives the work its title, but intermingled with this are musical representations of the human heartbeat, dance motifs, and Advent texts.

While Glennie commands all the speed and dexterity necessary for such a piece, she is inclined not to give her instruments enough time to "speak" properly, while her oddly incremental dynamic sense is also not ideal in such a context. It falls to Colin Currie, less famous but perhaps more conventionally musical, to produce the most satisfying version of the work to date. The Ulster Orchestra under Takuo Yuasa has made several excellent recordings of contemporary music for Naxos, but this example is outstanding. Currie knows exactly how to juggle the varied responses of his instrumental array to produce a unified sound that nonetheless retains all of the natural textural contrasts the work demands, and the orchestra responds willingly and sensitively. **RT**

Olivier Messiaen
Éclairs sur l'Au-delà . . . (1992)

Genre | Orchestral
Conductor | Myung-Whun Chung
Performers | Bastille Opera Orchestra
Year recorded | 1994
Label | DG 439 929-2

When it emerged in the early 1990s that Messiaen was composing an eleven-movement work for the 150th anniversary of the New York Philharmonic, expectations were raised of another colossal monument in the manner of works such as *La transfiguration, Des canyons aux étoiles* or even *Saint François d'Assise*. In fact, when *Éclairs sur l'au-délà . . .* was performed, just over six months after the composer's death, the most striking characteristic was its restraint. By contrast with *Des canyons*, in which he had created an enormous aural portrait despite having just forty players at his disposal, *Éclairs* frequently sounds like chamber music that just happens to require an orchestra to perform it. The most successful purveyor of musical overstatement since Wagner became, in his final years, a master of delectable understatement.

Myung-Whun Chung, one of Messiaen's favored conductors, was able to bring an authority and experience to this final masterpiece, so that it sounds more like an interpretation of a work that is two decades rather than just two years old. The virtuosity is certainly there, notably when birdsong is flying round the orchestra at extreme velocity. Chung also brings the serenity that is essential to this series of meditations on the afterlife, especially in the three beautiful slow movements that provide the framework for *Éclairs*. Chung also finds plenty of sparkle in the music of stars and nebulae and the dazzling kaleidoscopes of color. It is not necessary to share Messiaen's theological outlook in order to be beguiled by his calm message of belief. Simply sit back and be charmed. **CD**

Simon Bainbridge
Ad ora incerta (1994)

Genre | Vocal
Conductor/Performers | Martyn
Brabbins; Susan Bickley, Kim Walker
Year recorded | 1997
Label | NMC D059

György Kurtág
Stele (1994)

Genre | Orchestral
Conductor/Performers | Claudio
Abbado; Berlin Philharmonic Orchestra
Year recorded | 1994
Label | DG 447 761-2

To write poetry after the Holocaust is barbaric, claimed Theodor Adorno, but the creative work of Paul Celan and Primo Levi, both survivors and poets, seemed to prove him wrong—until their suicides acquiesced in his negation. Yet at the end of the millennium, two British composers wrote works that, unusually, stand up to the fathomless pain of their subject matter: Harrison Birtwistle in *Pulse Shadows* and Simon Bainbridge, whose song cycle of four poems by Levi won the Grawemeyer Prize in 1997.

"The Crow's Song" opens with the twittering of birds over a neon-lit landscape, somehow artificial—what Michael Zev Gordon calls his "luminous textural tracery and sensuous melodic nuance"; the bassoon spirals up to meet the mezzo-soprano soloist, who then spirals down in lamentation. There is something of Berg, Mahler too, about that sense of melody always moving forward but toward remembrance. Instrumental and vocal soloists shadow each other and take greater prominence in the two more lightly scored inner movements before the huge and harrowing finale that remembers Auschwitz, "Buna." Here, too, the productive debt to Mahler's *Das Lied von der Erde* is most evident; Levi's "empty companion who no longer has a name" inevitably recalls Hans Bethge's unnamed friend in "*Der Abschied*": "I shall journey to my native land. . . . My heart is still and awaits its hour." Neither Levi nor Bainbridge follows Mahler, however, to his "distant horizons."

The recording is coupled with a further four settings of Levi by Bainbridge. Scored for chamber ensemble, they also move on from the abstract promise of Bainbridge's earlier work to an unremittingly direct eloquence. **PQ**

The only uncharacteristic feature of *Stele* is its relatively large scale, dictated by Kurtág's acceptance of a commission from the Berlin Philharmonic Orchestra and Claudio Abbado. Otherwise it is vintage Kurtág.

The opening part proceeds to pay homage to the giants of orchestral music in a series of vignettes moving through the sections of the orchestra. The opening unison G is that of Beethoven's Leonore Overture no. 3; over the final chorale for four tenor tubas, Kurtág has written "Feierlich: Hommage à Bruckner." He explicitly marks the second section "Lamentoso," but that is in the sense of women's ritual keening and tearing of hair: it is marked "wild, excited, impatient" and races off in a desperate fugato. This is twice interrupted—first by a memory of the first movement, then by another chorale, again presented in turn by different sections of the orchestra. It dies to the immense shuddering of the last section, which Kurtág orchestrated from a piano piece in memory of his teacher, András Mihaly—though you would never know it, so compelling is the tone palette: Thomas Adès has described it as "a procession of heavy, luminous chords, like great hieroglyphs spanned by a fine seam of melody." The melody seems to find voice in another chorale, aspiring this time, before the shuddering chords return, like stifled sobs. Like much of Kurtág's work, it speaks of a grief so deep that listening should feel like an intrusion; yet the voice speaking is always a little distant.

There are two recordings: Michael Gielen's on BMG is heavier and slightly slower than the Berlin dedicatees on DG, who are, in any case, much easier to find. **PQ**

Magnus Lindberg | Aura (1994)

Genre | Orchestral
Conductor | Oliver Knussen
Performers | BBC Symphony Orchestra
Year recorded | 1998
Label | DG 463 184-2

The Finnish composer Magnus Lindberg has written a four-movement work with superficial symphonic credentials—the second movement slow and stern, the third scurrying and preparatory to the finale, which culminates in a march described by the composer as acting "like a strong magnet, picking up all kinds of material presented earlier in the work." Yet Lindberg declines to name *Aura* a symphony. It does use recognizably symphonic processes of development that are sometimes obscured by the sheer energy expended in their generation. The thunderous pedal points and chorales that secure resolution at the climax of the first and last movements show how Lindberg is no longer rebelling against a national heritage. This may not be Sibelian music, but it is characteristically Finnish, exulting in the full panoply of orchestral resources to give dramatic voice to abstract goals.

What *Aura* distills from the boiling crucible of Lindberg's earlier work, exemplified by *Kraft*, is a readily appreciable continuity. The studies with Gérard Grisey and Stockhausen's collaborator Vinko Globokar, the work with computer-generated music, and the enthusiasm for Pink Floyd and the Berlin punk scene, have been absorbed into what Oliver Knussen identifies as "a rich and thrilling command of long-range harmonic thinking."

Oliver Knussen could hardly have championed Lindberg's cause more eloquently than with this recording of *Aura*. Players and conductor are made to work very hard indeed, and few if any orchestras have this idiom under their fingers as confidently as the BBC Symphony does. The coupling, *Engine*, is only smaller in terms of resources—the title says it all, and the London Sinfonietta builds up an exhilarating head of steam. **PQ**

> "*Music is much more complex [than language] and the semantics are not really about comprehension.*"

Magnus Lindberg

Other Recommended Recordings

Kraft, Piano Concerto
Magnus Lindberg, Finnish Radio Symphony Orchestra
Esa-Pekka Salonen • Ondine ODE 1017-2
The major work of Lindberg's early maturity

Clarinet Concerto, Gran Duo, Chorale
Kari Krikku, Finnish Radio Symphony Orchestra
Sakari Oramo • Ondine ODE 1038-2
Recordings of the later Lindberg in more lyrical vein

Per Nørgård: Symphonies nos. 4 and 5
Leif Segerstam, Danish Radio Symphony Orchestra
Chandos CHAN 9533
An even more individual voice in Nordic music

Carl Vine | Percussion Symphony (1995)

Genre | Orchestral
Conductor | Edo de Waart
Performers | Synergy, Sydney Symphony Orchestra
Year recorded | 1996
Label | ABC 476 7179 (2 CDs)

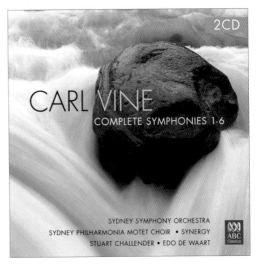

Carl Vine burst on to the Australian scene in 1978 with his dazzling score to the Sydney Dance Company's production *Poppy*, and immediately became a figurehead for the younger generation of composers who eschewed the slow rhythms that had characterized Australian compositions in the 1960s. More attuned to the sensibilities of the Parisian salon than the antipodean outback, he had an interest in electronic music and was also an outstanding pianist.

During the 1980s, Vine's Flederman contemporary music group was a leading ensemble in the Australian avant-garde, but the music that truly established his reputation and demonstrated his popular appeal came in the traditional forms of the sonata, string quartet, concerto, and, most of all, in his six symphonies.

When the four-member Australian percussion group Synergy suggested he write a new work for them in 1995, the project grew to include the ABC's Sydney Symphony Orchestra, who ended up commissioning his Fifth Symphony as the *Percussion Symphony*. For Australian audiences who had been alienated from contemporary music for a generation, it demonstrated that a return to traditional orchestral forms could be simultaneously popular and artistically significant.

Things go bang and crash within the work and there is a rip-roaring tarantella finale, but the overwhelming impression is intimate and reflective, the symphony's slow and powerful middle section making a profound impression. This performance dates from 1996—the year in which the Keating government's Creative Nation statement created the Sydney Symphony as a national flagship company—and finds the orchestra enjoying its golden years under conductor Edo de Waart. **MB**

"Vine is a major talent just waiting to be discovered here in the Old World."

Michael White, *Independent on Sunday*, March 1995

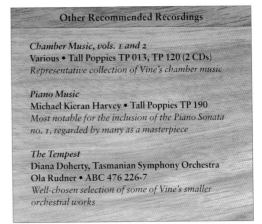

Other Recommended Recordings

Chamber Music, vols. 1 and 2
Various • Tall Poppies TP 013, TP 120 (2 CDs)
Representative collection of Vine's chamber music

Piano Music
Michael Kieran Harvey • Tall Poppies TP 190
Most notable for the inclusion of the Piano Sonata no. 1, regarded by many as a masterpiece

The Tempest
Diana Doherty, Tasmanian Symphony Orchestra
Ola Rudner • ABC 476 226-7
Well-chosen selection of some of Vine's smaller orchestral works

Mark-Anthony Turnage | Blood on the Floor (1996)

Genre | Chamber
Conductor | Peter Rundel
Performers | John Scofield, Peter Erskine, Ensemble Modern
Year recorded | 2001
Label | Decca 468 814-2

The avant-garde composer John White has suggested that the problem with classical music is that "most of what you hear is development noise." It is an interesting, if perverse, point of view, particularly when applied to a composer like Turnage who actually excels in this old-fashioned discipline yet decides to cause consternation by inserting improvised elements into what its detractors say would otherwise have been an excellent composition.

The mistaken presumption is, of course, that musicians who improvise are, by definition, unable to contribute to the development of a piece yet, as any jazz listener will tell you, they in fact do very little else. Turnage—as much influenced by the music of Miles Davis and Bill Evans as by their classical counterparts—is one of the few composers of concert music who actually realizes this, which is why he can take the contributions of jazz virtuosi and knit them into a contemporary ensemble composition such as this. However, *Blood on the Floor* is anything but a good-time roar-up. Rather, the work is an apocalyptic depiction of urban decay, paranoia, and drug addiction. Its title is derived from a painting by Francis Bacon, an artist whose work recreates internal psychological states as often uncomfortable shared experiences. The music is frequently disturbing, alternating between frenetic hyperactivity and more introspective passages shot through with a kind of queasy fatalism. There is quite a lot of cozy, friendly, modern music in the racks these days. This is not it. Turnage's younger brother died of a drug overdose and the sixth movement of the work is dedicated to him.

Here *Blood on the Floor* forms part of a two-disc set of Turnage's music that also includes other highly recommendable works such as *Your Rockaby*. **RT**

"Probably the nastiest thing I have written."

Mark-Anthony Turnage on *Blood on the Floor*

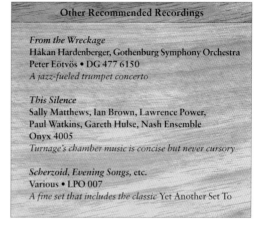

Other Recommended Recordings

From the Wreckage
Håkan Hardenberger, Gothenburg Symphony Orchestra
Peter Eötvös • DG 477 6150
A jazz-fueled trumpet concerto

This Silence
Sally Matthews, Ian Brown, Lawrence Power,
Paul Watkins, Gareth Hulse, Nash Ensemble
Onyx 4005
Turnage's chamber music is concise but never cursory

Scherzoid, Evening Songs, etc.
Various • LPO 007
A fine set that includes the classic Yet Another Set To

Thomas Adès | Asyla (1997)

Genre | Orchestral
Conductor | Simon Rattle
Performers | City of Birmingham Symphony Orchestra
Year recorded | 1998
Label | EMI 7243 5 56818 2 9

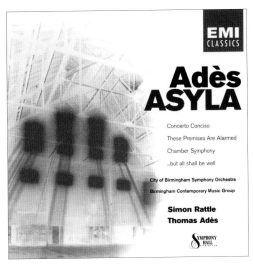

Thomas Adès's music can seem like a giant trick played against the ears—it should not work, but somehow it does. There is an airy, idyllic air about the Piano Quintet or Act 2 of his opera *The Tempest* that simply seems too good to be true—and it is, even when you feel yourself swooning in melodic bliss and wondering why all serious new music cannot have memorable tunes like this. The composer's facility is such that he seems perfectly comfortable working in any idiom and making it his own: you could call *Asyla* a symphony in E flat minor, but it would mean little. The key and the "asyla" of the title are perpetually threatened, on the verge of splintering into catastrophe. Suspense is constant. If the work is symphonic, it comes through most obviously in a Mahlerian use of a huge orchestra and in the fulfillment of Hans Keller's demand for a "large scale integration of contrasts," with themes from the first three movements meshing in uneasy peace in the finale. There is even the right number of movements, but Alex Ross's description of four "violently contrasted symphonic episodes" is nearer the mark. The third movement's thrash-scherzo has become notorious for recreating a dry-iced 1990s club in the concert hall with alarming verisimilitude, though again total involvement in the pounding rhythms is always subverted by harmonic restlessness and the sense of drug-induced fakery that is implied by its subtitle, "Ecstasio." You never know where you are with Adès's music, and perhaps that is the way the composer likes it.

Simon Rattle conducted the first performance of *Asyla* and programmed it for his final concerts as chief conductor of the Birmingham orchestra. This authoritative recording is taken from those concerts. **PQ**

> "*One can't compose slightly, much as one can't get slightly pregnant.*"
>
> Thomas Adès

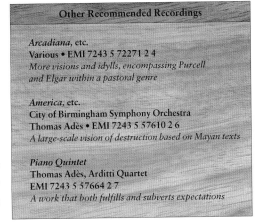

Other Recommended Recordings

Arcadiana, etc.
Various • EMI 7243 5 72271 2 4
More visions and idylls, encompassing Purcell and Elgar within a pastoral genre

America, etc.
City of Birmingham Symphony Orchestra
Thomas Adès • EMI 7243 5 57610 2 6
A large-scale vision of destruction based on Mayan texts

Piano Quintet
Thomas Adès, Arditti Quartet
EMI 7243 5 57664 2 7
A work that both fulfills and subverts expectations

Sofia Gubaidulina | Canticle of the Sun (1997)

Genre | Choral
Conductor | Stefan Parkman
Performers | David Geringas, Danish National Radio Choir
Year recorded | 1999
Label | Chandos CHAN 10106

If there is an afterlife, Christian or otherwise, it seems highly likely that Gubaidulina's *Canticle of the Sun* is being played there even now. This is not simply a matter of the work's devotional intent, but of the inevitable otherness of such a place. With religion repressed under the Soviet regime, it was hardly surprising that some sort of spiritual faith would be a significant factor in the aesthetic makeup of many of the composers who found themselves free to express themselves after the collapse of the old order. The *Canticle* both encompasses and transcends this process, but does so via Gubaidulina's unique musical vision.

The theme of the Sun as the bringer of both the light of inspiration and of guidance permeates the piece, the vocal component of which is a response to a text by St. Francis of Assisi. The piece is dedicated to Mstislav Rostropovich, perceived by the composer as embodying both aspects of the Sun's theme. At one level the music retains a simplicity of the kind associated with plainchant and other devotional music. That said, the arguably incompatible instrumental combination of cello, chamber choir, and percussion seemingly offers the potential for intrusiveness, but in the event the delicate phrasing and timbres in combination with the cello's skittering, ectoplasmic presence makes for a musical experience quite unlike any other.

Like much of Gubaidulina's work, the attractions of this piece require a certain perceptual shift in order properly to inhabit her unconventional sound world. Both choir and soloists are thoroughly engaged in this process on this disc, but David Geringas in particular is outstanding in his ability to integrate the contrasting sonority of his instrument into this striking soundscape that is both so alien and so human. **RT**

> "... *inner independence was simply ... unacceptable. Wherever it was detected in music, it was objected to.*"
>
> Sofia Gubaidulina on Soviet repression

Gubaidulina, one of the most significant Russians since Shostakovich. ➲

Peteris Vasks | Violin Concerto, "Distant Light" (1997)

Genre | Concerto
Performers | Katarina Andreasson (violin/director),
Swedish Chamber Orchestra,
Year recorded | 2004
Label | BIS CD-1150

The rise to international prominence of composers from the Baltic countries is one of the most significant recent developments in classical music. The essential optimism of this concerto seems to represent this music's newfound freedom, although paradoxically one of its main attractions for listeners from old Europe is its elusive but somehow undeniable familiarity. The animation of Bruch, the pastoral grace of Vaughan Williams, the traditionalism of Brahms, and the capriciousness, wistfulness, and triumphalism of Kreisler all seem to be implied in this powerful work, yet at the same time its identity is unique.

Peteris Vasks was born in Latvia in 1946 and studied in Riga and Vilnius in neighboring Lithuania, but his subsequent international reputation has resulted in his works being recorded by many labels worldwide. His earliest pieces showed an avant-garde influence, yet his style has also been shaped by folk music and Minimalism. "Distant Light" is a typically precise title for a piece that is, like much of his output, specifically programmatic and representative of nonmusical events or phenomena; other compositions have titles such as *Landscape with Birds* and *The Lime Tree*.

Selecting a single recommendation for this work is difficult, as there are also very fine versions available on Hyperion, Ondine, and Teldec, each with their own distinct virtues, and even by the standards of the most traditional violin concerto, this piece offers enormous scope for individual expression. However, the BIS recording was made in the presence of the composer, which argues for its definitive nature, while the additional works on the disc are equally compelling. The lucid and aerated recording quality of the BIS disc is a further point in its favor. **RT**

> *"I burn in my works. It is my fire that I give to you."*
>
> **Peteris Vasks**

Other Recommended Recordings

String Quartet no. 4
Kronos Quartet • Nonesuch 7559 79695-2
Grammy-nominated recording by the doyens of modern chamber music

Dona nobis pacem
Estonian Philharmonic Chamber Choir • Paul Hillier
Harmonia Mundi HMU 807311
A Vask choral piece

Symphony no. 3, Cello Concerto
Marko Ylonen, Tampere Philharmonic Orchestra
John Storgårds • Ondine ODE 1086-5
Impeccable recording of other Vasks orchestral works

Gérard Grisey | Quatre chants pour franchir le seuil (1998)

Genre | Vocal
Performers | Catherine Dubosc, Klangforum Wien
Conductor | Sylvain Cambreling
Year recorded | 2000
Label | Kairos 0012252 KAI

Gérard Grisey studied with two of the three towering figures in postwar French music, Messiaen and Dutilleux, and was promoted by the third, Boulez, despite their compositional differences (Grisey was one of the first to turn against the tide of total Serialism). What Grisey achieved with *Partiels* was a different kind of unified composition that owes more to the electronic experiments of Varèse and Stockhausen, deriving harmony, timbre, and dynamic from the properties of individual pitches. Grisey, however, felt no imperative to create a brave new world but rather to refresh consonance, which had been scorned by most musical innovators for the past sixty years.

So, against a backdrop of quiet, breathing noise, *Four Songs for Crossing the Threshold* opens with a sad, descending, nontempered melody, evocative of ancient culture, yet timeless. The four songs derive from four different cultures—Christian, Egyptian, Greek, and Mesopotamian—and their oblique poetry views death from afar, with serenity, as though death itself was a friend dimly perceived at the end of a long tunnel. This is all the more remarkable in the context of Grisey's sudden death from an aneurysm mere weeks after completing the score. The fifteen-strong accompaniment was selected from "a musical need, that of opposing the lightness of the soprano voice with something deeply massive, weighty yet sumptuous and colored." So the second movement thrums with low bells and harp and steel drums, while the soprano intones a slow litany of hieroglyphic fragments of serendipitous profundity: "903: destroyed; 1050: formula for being a god. . . ." Catherine Dubosc enhances the work's single recording with her limpid delivery: Mélisande straying into a yet more gnomic, timeless world. **PQ**

> *"I never think of music in terms of declamation and rhetoric and language."*
>
> Gérard Grisey

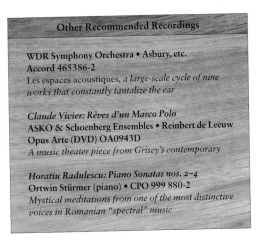

Other Recommended Recordings

WDR Symphony Orchestra • Asbury, etc.
Accord 465386-2
Les espaces acoustiques, a large-scale cycle of nine works that constantly tantalize the ear

Claude Vivier: Rêves d'un Marco Polo
ASKO & Schoenberg Ensembles • Reinbert de Leeuw
Opus Arte (DVD) OA0943D
A music theater piece from Grisey's contemporary

Horatiu Radulescu: Piano Sonatas nos. 2–4
Ortwin Stürmer (piano) • CPO 999 880-2
Mystical meditations from one of the most distinctive voices in Romanian "spectral" music

Wolfgang Rihm | Deus Passus (2000)

Genre | Choral
Conductor/Performers | Helmuth Rilling; Juliane Banse,
Christoph Prégardien, Andreas Schmidt, Gächinger Kantorei
Year recorded | 2000
Label | Hänssler CD 98.397 (2 CDs)

Born in Karlsruhe in 1952, Wolfgang Rihm was drawn to the arts from an early age. At first, he was interested in images and words, copying pictures and writing poems and stories before he discovered music. Precocious enough to want to compose a Mass when he was only eight or nine, he has become an amazingly prolific composer in an age where such things are perhaps distrusted. He studied with Stockhausen, among others, but his music never followed trends for the sake of it. In 1974, he was berated at that bastion of the avant-garde, the Donaueschingen Festival, for the expressive and subjective nature of his music. Since then, he has produced more than two hundred works in all genres: orchestral, including *Gesungene Zeit*—written for Anne-Sophie Mutter—vocal, chamber, choral, and opera: his *Jacob Lenz* is a much performed piece of music theater.

Deus Passus was one of four passion settings that were commissioned from four composers by the International Bachakademie Stuttgart for the 250th anniversary of Bach's death in 2000. Rihm subtitled the work "Fragments of a St. Luke Passion," and used only part of the traditional gospel text, together with words from other sources—most notably the *Tenebrae* by Paul Celan that brings the work to a close. It is a somber, concentrated work that puts Rihm firmly in the German tradition, a line extending through Berg, Mahler, and Brahms—right back to Bach himself.

This recording was made at the work's premiere, and the distinguished cast (which also includes Iris Vermillion and Cornelia Kallisch) sings with total dedication. Helmuth Rilling clarifies the orchestral textures (produced by the Bach-Collegium, Stuttgart), which could so easily be murky rather than darkly burnished, and paces the largely slow music to devastating cumulative effect. **MC**

> *"Wolfgang Rihm [reaches an audience] most effectively with the direct emotional access of his music."*
>
> Christoph Prégardien

Other Recommended Recordings

Die Hamletmaschine
Mannheim National Theater Chorus & Orchestra
Peter Schneider • Wergo WER 61952 (2 CDs)
Live recording of a multifaceted piece of music theater

Tutuguri—Poème dansé
Stuttgart Radio Symphony Orchestra • Fabrice Bollon
Hänssler CD 93.069 (2 CDs)
Viscerally powerful ballet score

Lieder
Clare Lesser, David Lesser
Metier MSV CD 92068
A good introduction to a vast area of Rihm's output

Helmuth Rilling is the artistic director of Stuttgart's *Festivalensemble*. ➔

Wolfgang Rihm | Jagden und Formen (2001)

Genre | Orchestral
Conductor | Dominique My
Performers | Ensemble Modern
Year recorded | 2001
Label | DG 471 558-2

Like Boulez, Rihm has a tendency to view his pieces as works in progress, rather than finished artifacts. So he is always revisiting old ground, taking the material off in new directions, or adding another layer of complexity, like an artist overpainting a preexisting canvas. In *Jagden und Formen*, three works from the mid-1990s have been reordered, cut, and pasted, with extra linking material, to create something new. Even *Jagden und Formen* itself has appeared in several different versions, although the one premiered around the time of this recording seems to be the last word, at least for the moment.

The title *Jagden und Formen* means "Hunts and Forms," and implies a search for a formal structure, and one of some urgency. In complete contrast to the slow unfolding of *Deus Passus*, *Jagden und Formen* explodes with a crack of the whip and two violins frantically chasing each other. For a quarter of an hour, there is hardly any let-up in the dynamic and energetic musical activity, which takes place in a strong six-eight pulse—the meter that has always been associated with hunting. Wind and brass dominate the writing: There is an especially telling part for the cor anglais, which often weaves a slow lyrical line through the surrounding maelstrom. But moments of repose are infrequent, and tend to serve as launchpads for the next display of fireworks, which keep exploding in various colorful ways.

This sort of exhilarating writing can be effective only with a performance to match, and the Frankfurt-based Ensemble Modern manages it with a precision and confidence that overflows with life. Stunningly recorded, with enormous attention to detail, this CD shows that Modernism still has much to offer. **MC**

"Dear Wolfgang Rihm, Please only heed your inner voice. With kindest regards. Yours,"

Karlheinz Stockhausen

Other Recommended Recordings

String Quartets nos. 7–9
Minguet Quartet
Col Legno WWE1CD 20213
A way into the quartets from this impressive survey

Gesungene Zeit
Anne-Sophie Mutter, Chicago Symphony Orchestra
James Levine • DG 437 093-2
Mutter spins a stratospheric, long melodic line of ethereal beauty

Chiffre-Zyklus • **MusikFabrik** • **Stefan Asbury**
CPO 777 169-2 (2 CDs)
A set of pieces burgeoning from one small original

Wolfgang Rihm, the most important contemporary German composer. ➔

Julian Anderson | Book of Hours (2004)

Genre | Chamber
Conductor | Oliver Knussen
Performers | Birmingham Contemporary Music Group
Year recorded | 2005
Label | NMC D121

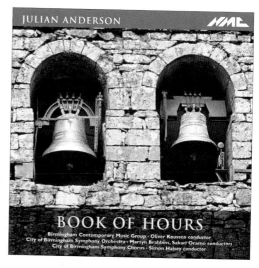

One of Seamus Heaney's recent poems talks about "Filling the stillness with life." That is what Julian Anderson does. In an oeuvre of chamber, vocal, and especially orchestral music, neither especially small nor large for a composer in his early forties, every note is a reason for sound and not silence. Studies and friendships with many of the major figures in British music from the last thirty years, and a deep familiarity with music from around the world, have in fact shaped a personal language that prizes beauty and continuity. He is in the vanguard of composers who are reasserting the importance of melody as a carrier of musical argument. The sources of those melodies often lie in folk materials and the pitch analysis of spectral music: the one apparently timeless and naive, the other technologically complex, but they are united in ensemble pieces such as *Khorovod* to timeless and weightless effect.

Book of Hours is the first piece Anderson has written where his work with electronic pitch spectra is explicitly revealed in a tape part with live ensemble. The book opens with a scale, which multiplies with counterpoint, repetition, and other tricks that turn the pages quickly, and sometimes abruptly. In Part 2, the scale and its development are revisited and remembered; sometimes they are misremembered but with the threads of memory drawn taut until, with emphatic restatement of the scale, they snap into an extended cadenza for electronics alone. This itself moves rapidly through bell-capped exaltation to thumping annihilation, at which point the live ensemble returns to pick up the pieces. This definitive recording was made by frequent musical partners during Anderson's period as composer-in-residence with the City of Birmingham Symphony Orchestra. **PQ**

> "Anderson's music is fundamentally about felicity—bright . . . impeccably made, happy."
>
> Robin Holloway

Conductor Oliver Knussen pictured in 1991. ⊙

Glossary

Adagio
Tempo marking: slow.

Allegretto
Tempo marking: fastish.

Allegro
Tempo marking: fast (**allegro non troppo** = not too fast).

Andante
Tempo marking: moderately.

Aria
Italian for "song," although generally used for vocal solos within operas, oratorios, and other large-scale works.

Baritone
Male voice between tenor and bass.

Baroque
Musical era that lasted roughly from the mid-seventeenth to the mid-eighteenth centuries (from late Monteverdi to the death of Handel), characterized by the establishment of tonalities and keys over modes as the foundation of musical structure. Key composers included Vivaldi, Bach, and Handel.

Baroque suite
A group of dances, often (by Bach's time) highly stylized in relation to the original forms; synonymous with "partita"; might include gavottes, gigues, and minuets.

Bass
The lowest male voice.

Basso continuo
The foundation for much Baroque music in which the bass line and main harmonies are played by keyboard and one or more string instruments.

Bel canto
Literally "good singing," a style of vocalizing that dominated Italian opera in the early nineteenth century, characterized by a smooth melodiousness.

Cabaletta
In Italian opera, the end section of a two-part aria, usually in fast tempo to create a sense of rising excitement.

Cantabile
"Songlike."

Cantata
A vocal form—often multi-movement although it can take many guises—usually on religious subjects; most characteristic are those of Bach, with their mixture of choruses and solo numbers.

Chromaticism
Music characterized by use of adjacent semitones in melodies or harmonies. Opposite of "diatonicism," which keeps to the basic chords and intervals of the scale.

Classical
The era of music from the mid-eighteenth century into the early nineteenth, characterized by Enlightenment ideas of order and proportion, and coinciding with similar ideals in European architecture looking back to Greek models. Key composers included Haydn, Mozart, and Beethoven.

Coloratura
A florid vocal style and voice type, often characterized by high notes, runs, and trills—the best-known coloratura parts in opera are the Queen of Night in Mozart's *Magic Flute* and Zerbinetta in Strauss's *Ariadne auf Naxos*.

Concertante
A group of solo instruments set against an orchestra.

Concerto
Form for a solo instrument (sometimes more than one) and orchestra. The original Italian term has elements of both "togetherness" and "conflict." It

usually has three movements—fast–slow–fast, although there are plenty of variants.

Concerto grosso/concerti grossi
A Baroque form of the concerto that pits two or more groups of instruments against each other, such as a trio of soloists and an orchestra.

Con moto
"With movement."

Continuo
See **basso continuo**

Contralto
The lowest female singing voice (sometimes abbreviated to "alto").

Countertenor
High, falsetto male voice.

Da capo
Literally, back to the beginning.

Da capo aria
Three-part aria that returns to the first section (da capo) after a contrasting middle one; characteristic of the operas of Handel and others.

Descant
A melodic line played or sung above the main melody.

Étude
French for "study"; a piece of music originally designed purely for instruction, but in the hands of Chopin and later composers taking on a higher role.

Fantasia/fantasy
Both an all-purpose term for a work a composer does not feel fits into a set form (e.g., a synonym for "rhapsody," as a free-flowing instrumental movement) and an elaboration of a musical idea or ideas.

Intermezzo
A piece dividing one piece from another (e.g., scenes of an opera).

Kapellmeister
Musician in charge of a court chapel, but will also see to secular music making. Often employed as multitasking composer, choirmaster, and instrumentalist.

Key
The tonal foundation of music; there are 24 keys, 12 major and 12 minor. A piece said to be in a given key will be centered around the tonality related to that fundamental note, however, it is the relationships between different keys that gives music its larger sense of direction.

Larghetto
Tempo marking: slowish.

Largo
Tempo marking: slow.

Legato
Smooth/smoothly.

Leitmotif
"Leading motive"—a melodic or harmonic idea used to characterize a person or concept, particularly in Wagner's operas, which helps build the musical flow of the drama.

Lied/Lieder
German for "song"/"songs."

Maestro di capella
See **Kapellmeister**

Mezzo-soprano
Female voice between soprano and contralto.

Minuet/menuetto/menuet
Stately dance in triple time established in the Baroque era as an instrumental form and in the Classical era as the favored dance movement in sonatas and symphonies; precursor to the waltz.

Motet
Multi-voice setting of a religious text, usually in Latin, for use in

church services. The English-language equivalent is the anthem.

Obbligato
A prominent solo part, e.g., for an instrument in an aria.

Opera buffa
Italian comic opera.

Opéra comique
French comic opera.

Opera seria
Italian opera on high-minded subjects, particularly of the Baroque and Classical eras.

Oratorio
Religious equivalent of opera (though unstaged), often on biblical subjects with solo singers representing characters.

Partita
See **Baroque suite**

Passacaglia/passacaille
A variation form in which the same melody, bass line, or harmonic sequence is repeated insistently while the rest of the music changes around it.

Polyphony
Music in three or more independent lines, often in Renaissance church music, where no one voice hogs the limelight.

Presto
Tempo marking: very fast.

Programmatic/program music
Music based on an underlying extra-musical subject, such as a work of literature or landscape.

Recitative
Singing style in which the vocal line takes on the rhythms and speed of speech. In Baroque and Classical opera and oratorio it often provides the narration between the more musically rich arias and ensembles.

Register
Part of the range of an instrument or voice.

Registration
The combination of organ stops for a passage of music, or the keyboard on a multi-keyboard harpsichord.

Ripieno
The largest group of musicians in a concerto grosso.
See also **concerto grosso**.

Ritornello
A section of music that keeps returning, as in the main orchestral interjections in a Baroque concerto.

Romantic
Musical period that dominated the nineteenth century and extended into the twentieth, characterized by music full of emotion and passion. Key composers included Schumann, Wagner, Tchaikovsky, and Brahms.

Rondo
A movement in which a particular central theme is repeated a number of times, each appearance separated by passages of contrasting music (e.g., it might take the form ABACADA).

Scherzo
Italian for "joke," a fast movement in a symphony or other multi-movement work that by the time of Beethoven had replaced the statelier minuet.

Semi-opera
An operatic work that perhaps has too much spoken material or dance to be deemed a true opera, such as the masquelike works of Purcell.

Sonata
The most important abstract instrumental form, either for one instrument or two. First established in the Baroque era, it is usually in three or four movements.

Sonata form

A major frame of musical construction established in the Classical era with the consolidation of tonality. While it can appear in many guises, it usually has an "exposition," which presents two contrasting themes often in different keys; a "development" that breaks up and explores further the musical ideas and in different keys; and a "recapitulation" that puts them all back together in the home key.

Song cycle

Collection of songs, occasionally telling a story but more often exploring a theme through a related set of poems.

Soprano

High female voice.

Sound-world

The particular character of a given composer's music, or the combination of elements that make one composer's music different from another's.

Symphonic poem

A (usually) single-movement work in symphonic form that expresses an extra-musical subject, be it a story (such as Strauss's *Don Juan*) or some other form of inspiration.

Symphony

The most important form of orchestral music, usually abstract, though it can be programmatic. More or less invented by Haydn in the mid-eighteenth century, it grew to have generally four movements—a sonata-form fast opening movement, a slow movement, a minuet or scherzo, and a fast finale. *See also* **programmatic**.

Tenor

High male voice.

Theorbo

Plucked bass instrument, related to the guitar.

Through-composed

Music, usually in opera, written in long, continuous spans rather than being broken up into sections such as arias, duets, etc.; or a song setting that does not simply repeat the same music for each stanza; or an instrumental work that shares material throughout its movements.

Tone poem

Symphonic poem.

Trio sonata

Baroque form for three instrumental parts, although the bass one of these may be played by more than one instrument as a continuo (hence not always three players in total).

Tutti

"Everyone." In a concerto often the sections for full orchestra between those where the soloist dominates.

Twelve-note

Musical system devised by Arnold Schoenberg in the early twentieth century in which all twelve notes of the chromatic scale have equal weight—in its crudest form no note should be sounded again until the other 11 have been heard.

Verismo

"Realism"—a trend in opera, with plots dealing with real, believable people and situations, rather than the nineteenth century's prevailing nobles and mythical figures.

Viola d'amore

Type of viola with a second set of strings behind the main ones that vibrate in sympathy, but are not played as such.

Viola da gamba/viol

Cellolike, bowed string instrument held between the knees (gamba).

Vivace

Tempo marking: lively.

Composer Index

Contributors

Colin Anderson (CA) has been an enthusiastic record collector for more than thirty years (having started as a teenager). As a freelance writer on music, he writes booklet notes and contributes to various publications, including *Fanfare*, *International Piano*, *International Record Review*, and *What's On in London*. He also edits The Classical Source, www.classicalsource.com.

Nicholas Anderson (NA) studied at New College, Oxford, and Durham University. For twenty years he worked for the BBC as a music producer, since when he has continued broadcasting and writing. He is the author of *Baroque Music from Monteverdi to Handel* (Thames & Hudson, 1994) and has contributed to various books, symposiums, and journals.

Edward Bhesania (EB) reviews for *The Strad*, *The Stage*, *The Tablet*, and *International Piano*. He has also contributed to *The Observer* and *BBC Music Magazine*, and written program notes for the London Symphony Orchestra and the BBC Proms.

David Breckbill (DB) (Ph.D. in Musicology, University of California, Berkeley) resides in Nebraska (USA). An educator and pianist, he writes extensively on the history of Wagner performance and reviews recordings for *BBC Music Magazine*, *ARSC Journal*, and other publications.

Anthony Burton (AB) is a former BBC Radio 3 music producer, now a freelance writer and broadcaster on a variety of musical topics. He reviews CDs for *BBC Music Magazine*, and is a frequent contributor to Radio 3's *CD Review* program.

Martin Buzacott (MB) is senior music critic for *The Courier-Mail* and an adjunct professor at the University of Queensland, Australia. He has written the forthcoming *The Rite of Spring: 75 Years of ABC Music-Making* (ABC Books), and (with Andrew Ford) *Speaking in Tongues: The Songs of Van Morrison* (ABC, 2005).

Deborah Calland (DC) studied at the Royal Academy of Music in London and has since pursued a multifaceted career as a trumpeter, teacher, and music editor. To date, she has produced ten books for student trumpeters.

Martin Cotton (MC) was a producer at BBC Radio 3 until 1994. He now divides his time working between producing radio programs and CDs, reviewing for *BBC Music Magazine* and BBC Radio 3's *CD Review*, and music examining.

Christopher Cook (CC) broadcasts on BBC Radios 3 and 4 and is a regular contributor to *Gramophone* and *International Record Review*. He has also written for *BBC Music Magazine*. He is obsessive about bel canto opera, the forgotten corners of verismo, and French *mélodie*. Pray for him.

Christopher Dingle (CD) is author of *The Life of Messiaen* (Cambridge University Press, 2007), and is coeditor with Nigel Simeone of *Olivier Messiaen: Music, Art and Literature* (Ashgate, 2007). He is assistant course director at Birmingham Conservatoire and writes for *BBC Music Magazine*.

Jessica Duchen (JD) is the author of biographies of Korngold and Fauré (published by Phaidon) and the novels *Rites of Spring* and *Alicia's Gift* (Hodder & Stoughton). Her music journalism appears frequently in the *Independent*.

Andrew Farach-Colton (AFC) is a regular contributor to *Gramophone*, *Opera News*, and *The Strad*. A pianist by training, he is a graduate of Dartmouth College and received a doctorate in music from the Peabody Conservatory.

Hilary Finch (HF) has been a music critic and feature writer for *The Times* since 1980. With a particular interest in song and in the music of the Nordic countries, she also contributes regularly to *Opera*, *BBC Music Magazine*, and BBC Radio 3.

David Gutman (DG) is a prolific writer of program notes who, since

1996, has provided advice on further listening and reading for the BBC Proms. He has written four books on subjects ranging from Prokofiev to John Lennon and is a contributor to *Gramophone*, *International Record Review*, and *The Stage*.

Stephen Johnson (SJ) studied music at Leeds and Manchester Universities. Since then he has written regularly for the *Independent* and the *Guardian*, and was chief music critic of the *Scotsman* (1968–89). He is the author of *Bruckner Remembered* (Faber, 1998) and studies of Mahler and Wagner (Naxos, 2006; 2007). He is also the presenter of BBC Radio 3's *Discovering Music*, and a regular contributor to *BBC Music Magazine*. In 2003 he was voted Amazon.com Classical Music Writer of the Year.

Graeme Kay (GK) read languages and law at Cambridge, before joining Scottish Opera. Switching from management to journalism, he edited *Classical Music*, *Opera Now*, and *BBC Music Magazine*. Now classical producer for BBC Radio 3 Interactive, and a network presenter, he continues to write and lecture widely on concert music and opera.

Erik Levi (EL) is reader in music at Royal Holloway University of London, reviews CDs regularly for *BBC Music Magazine* and works as a professional accompanist. He is

author of *Music in the Third Reich* (Palgrave Macmillan, 1994) and a forthcoming study entitled *Mozart and the Nazis*.

Max Loppert (ML) was chief critic of the London *Financial Times* (1980–96) and associate editor of *Opera* (1986–97). He now lives in Italy, from where he writes for *Opera* and other journals, while continuing work on his study of Gluck for Faber Music.

Malcolm MacDonald (MM) is editor of *Tempo*, the independent quarterly review of modern music. He has written books on Varèse, on the British composers Havergal Brian and John Foulds, and is the author of the "Master Musicians" volumes on Brahms and Schoenberg.

Naomi Matsumoto (NM) was awarded a Ph.D. from the University of London for her thesis on the seventeenth-century origins of the operatic mad scene. She is currently a visiting lecturer at Goldsmiths College, University of London, and is a member of the Society for Seventeenth-Century Music in the United States.

Barry Millington (BM) is chief music critic for the *London Evening Standard* and the author/editor of seven books on Wagner, including the "Master Musicians" volume and *The Wagner Compendium* (Thames & Hudson, 2001). He is coeditor,

with Stewart Spencer, of *The Wagner Journal*.

David Nice (DN) is the author of *Prokofiev: A Biography* (Yale University Press, 2003) and of short studies of Elgar, Richard Strauss, and Tchaikovsky. He broadcasts regularly on BBC Radio 3 and is a visiting lecturer on Goldsmiths College's Russian music degree course.

Tim Parry (TLP) works as an editor and writer, specializing in piano music and the nineteenth century. His interests include the music of Liszt, piano transcriptions, and—outside music—wine (which he ought to drink less) and cricket (which he ought to play more).

Stephen Pettitt (SP) has been music critic for *The Times*, the *Financial Times*, the *Sunday Express*, and the *Evening Standard* and contributes regularly to the *Sunday Times* and many music magazines. He also writes for the *Spectator*, gives talks, and broadcasts, and has written introductory studies to Handel and to opera.

Tully Potter (TP) edits *Classic Record Collector* and is historical consultant to *The Strad*. Trained as a singer, he became interested in string playing and has made a study of performance practice, as shown in recordings.

George Pratt (GP) emeritus professor of music at the University of Huddersfield, has spent his life sharing musical enthusiasm with university students, radio listeners, and others through the Incorporated Society of Musicians (president), the UK Schools National Curriculum, and reviewing recordings. He is one of the authors of *Aural Awareness* (OUP, 1998), designed to stretch listening skills.

Peter Quantrill (PQ) read Classics and was a choral scholar at Magdalene College, Cambridge, before joining the staff of *Gramophone*. He is now a member of the magazine's reviewing panel and the annotator for the London Chamber Orchestra. He also contributes regularly to *The Strad*, *Choir & Organ*, www.maxopus.com, as well as BBC Radio 3, and BBC Four television.

Graham Rogers (GR) works for BBC Radio 3. His writing includes digital radio text and interactive program notes for television broadcasts of the BBC Proms concerts. As a choral singer, he has performed with many of the world's greatest conductors and soloists.

Matthew Rye (MR) studied music at Oxford and Birmingham Universities, specializing in composition, and has been a music critic for the *Daily Telegraph*, reviewing concerts, opera,

and CDs, since 1995. He worked for many years on the staff of *BBC Music Magazine* and as reviews editor of *The Strad*, the specialist title for string players. As a writer he has also contributed to the *Independent*, *The Sunday Times*, and a wide variety of classical music journals, and he has written numerous concert program and CD booklet notes. His particular interests include twentieth-century British opera, upon which subject he contributed to the *Blackwell History of Music in Britain* (Blackwell, six volumes), and central European music of the early twentieth century.

Jan Smaczny (JS) was educated at the University of Oxford and the Charles University, Prague. A well-known authority on Czech music, he reviews frequently for *BBC Music Magazine*. Since 1996 he has been professor of music at Queen's University, Belfast.

Harriet Smith (HS) is a writer, editor, and broadcaster. She was founding editor of *International Piano Quarterly* and *International Record Review* before becoming editor of *BBC Music Magazine*. She now combines her twin passions for music and gardening from an idyllic hovel in Kent, southeast England.

Carlos María Solare (CMS) is a violist and musicologist based in Berlin. He contributes to

The Strad, *Opera*, *Classic Record Collector*, *MGG* (*Musik in Geschichte und Gegenwart*), and Grove Online. His primary research fields are the musical theater of the nineteenth and early twentieth centuries and the history of performance practice of string instruments.

Roger Thomas (RT) reviews for *BBC Music Magazine* and has also written for *Gramophone*, *Music Teacher*, and many other publications. He is the author of more than a dozen educational music books (published by Heinemann) and lectures on music at Brunel University.

Helen Wallace (HW) is consultant editor, formerly editor, of *BBC Music Magazine*. Her publications include *Spirit of the Orchestra* (Orchestra of the Age of Enlightenment, 2006) and *Boosey & Hawkes: The Publishing Story* (Boosey & Hawkes, 2007). She is a regular reviewer on BBC Radio 4's *Front Row*, and chairs the jury for the *BBC Music Magazine* Awards.

Simon Whalley (SW) is a composer, teacher, and conductor. His works have been performed across the globe from Washington, D.C. to Moscow. He is the fellow and director of chapel music at Keble College, Oxford, and also teaches at Abingdon School.

Picture Credits

Every effort has been made to credit the copyright holders of the images used in this book. We apologise for any unintentional omissions or errors and will insert the appropriate acknowledgement to any companies or individuals in any subsequent edition of the work.

Acknowledgments

645 Lebrecht Music & Arts
649 Erich Auerbach/Getty Images
651 G. MacDomnic/Lebrecht Music & Arts
655 John Loengard/Time Life Pictures/Getty Images
661 Bettmann/Corbis
663 Bettmann/Corbis
669 Lipnitzki/Roger Viollet/Getty Images
675 Ted Streshinsky/Corbis
677 Lebrecht Music & Arts
681 Ernst Haas/Getty Images
683 Lebrecht Music & Arts
687 Condé Nast Archive/Corbis
691 Evening Standard/Getty Images
697 Lebrecht Music & Arts
701 Keith Saunders/ArenaPAL
705 Erich Auerbach/Getty Images
711 Lipnitzki/Roger Viollet/Getty Images
715 Baron/Getty Images
723 Tina Tahiw/Shotview Photographers/DG
725 Erich Auerbach/Getty Images
737 Erich Auerbach/Getty Images
741 Marion Kalter/Lebrecht Music & Arts
743 Hulton-Deutsch Collection/Corbis
747 Lebrecht Music & Arts
751 Condé Nast Archive/Corbis
755 Condé Nast Archive/Corbis
759 Sipa Press/Rex Features
763 Hansel Mieth/Time Life Pictures/Getty Images
765 Fox Photos/Getty Images
775 Hulton Archive/Getty Images
777 Erich Auerbach/Getty Images
783 Time & Life Pictures/Getty Images
787 Tully Potter Collection
795 Lebrecht Music & Arts
797 Boosey & Hawkes Music Publishers Ltd/ArenaPAL
801 Bernard Gotfryd/Getty Images
803 Alex Bender/Picture Post/Getty Images
805 Klaus Hennch /ArenaPAL
807 Condé Nast Archive/Corbis
811 David E. Scherman/Time Life Pictures/Getty Images
819 Bernard Gotfryd/Getty Images
832-833 Schott Music GmbH & Co. KG, Mainz, Germany
845 Gordon Parks/Time Life Pictures/Getty Images
849 Stephan Danelian/Sony
853 Metropolitan Opera
855 Arnold Newman/Getty Images
861 Erich Auerbach/Getty Images
863 Ralph Crane/Time Life Pictures/Getty Images
869 Hulton Archive/Getty Images
875 Erich Auerbach/Getty Images
883 Marco Borggreve/ArenaPAL
887 Marion Kalter/Lebrecht Music & Arts
891 George Newson/Lebrecht Music & Arts
897 Deborah Feingold/Corbis
901 George Newson/Lebrecht Music & Arts
907 Betty Freeman/Lebrecht Music & Arts
915 Erich Auerbach/Getty Images
923 Clive Barda/ArenaPAL
935 Victor Bazhenov/Lebrecht Music & Arts
939 Michael Latz/Bachacademie
941 Betty Freeman/Lebrecht Music & Arts
943 Neil Libbert/Lebrecht Music & Arts

We would like to express our gratitude
to the following:

Editors:

Carol King
Lucinda Hawksley
Orla Thomas
Peter Somerford

Indexer:

Kay Ollerenshaw

Image Libraries

AKG Images

David Price-Hughes

ArenaPAL

Primrose Metcalf

Art Archive

Anna Barrett

Bridgeman Art Library

Jenny Page

Lebrecht Music & Arts

Elbie Lebrecht

Music Labels

Coda Distribution Ltd

Simon Ashurst

EMI Classics

Michael Gooding
Alexa Pentecost

Harmonia Mundi

Celia Ballantyne

Select Music

Libby Jones

Universal Classics

Louise Ringrose

Warner Music

Lucy Bright

White Label Productions

Anna Cohen

Music Stores

MDC Classic Music Ltd

Alan Goulden
Martin Halstead